REGIONAL PROTECTION OF HUMAN RIGHTS

REGIONAL PROTECTION OF HUMAN RIGHTS

Dinah Shelton

Library of Congress Cataloging-in-Publication Data

Shelton, Dinah

   Regional protection of human rights / by Dinah Shelton

     v. cm.

   Includes bibliographical references and index.

   Contents: Introduction — The normative instruments — State obligations — The regional human rights institutions — Protecting human rights through individual cases — Responding to widespread violations — Towards the future.

   ISBN 978-0-19-537165-9 ((2-volume set) : alk. paper)

   ISBN 978-0-19-533339-8 ((volume 1 : clothbound) : alk. paper)

   ISBN 978-0-19-533340-4 ((volume 2 : paperback) : alk. paper)

   1. Human rights.   I. Title.

   K3240.S526 2007

   341.4'8—dc22

                             2007028864

Note to Readers:

This publication is designed to provide accurate and authoritative information in regard to the subject matter covered. It is based upon sources believed to be accurate and reliable and is intended to be current as of the time it was written. It is sold with the understanding that the publisher is not engaged in rendering legal, accounting, or other professional services. If legal advice or other expert assistance is required, the services of a competent professional person should be sought. Also, to confirm that the information has not been affected or changed by recent developments, traditional legal research techniques should be used, including checking primary sources where appropriate.

(Based on the Declaration of Principles jointly adopted by a Committee of the American Bar Association and a Committee of Publishers and Associations.)

You may order this or any other Oxford University Press publication by visiting the Oxford University Press website at www.oup.com

What more is man to you than to behold
A flock of sheep that cower in the fold?
For men are slain as much as other cattle,
Arrested, thrust in prison, killed in battle,
In sickness often and mischance, and fall,
Alas, too, for no guilt at all.
Where is right rule in your foreknowledge, when
Such torments fall on innocent, helpless men?

> Geoffrey Chaucer, *The Canterbury Tale*s
> (Coghill trans. 1951), p. 51

Imagine that you see the wretched strangers,
Their babies at their backs, with their poor luggage
Plodding to th' ports and coasts for transportation,
And that you sit as kings in your desires,
Authority quite silenced by your brawl
And you in ruff of your opinions clothed:
What had you got? I'll tell you. You had taught
How insolence and strong hand should prevail,
How order should be quelled – and by this pattern
Not one of you should live an agèd man,
For other ruffians as their fancies wrought
With selfsame hand, self reasons, and self right
Would shark on you, and men like ravenous fishes
Would feed on one another.

> *Sir Thomas More*, "Hand D"
> (attributed to Shakespeare), reprinted in
> Stephen Greenblatt, *Will in the World*, 2004, pp. 263–64

CONTENTS

FOREWORD

The present book is the first devoted to comparing the European, Inter-American and African systems for the protection of human rights. It also discusses the prospects for regional systems in the Middle East and Asia. This text is intended for advanced courses in international human rights law as well as for practitioners working in the regional and global human rights systems.

The materials emphasize the jurisprudence of the European and Inter-American Courts and decisions of the Inter-American and African Commissions, including decisions on the interpretation and application of various human rights, complaint procedures and remedies. The relevant basic texts are reproduced in the documentary supplement. The contents have been selected in light of the author's experience with the regional institutions, shaped by several decades of teaching human rights, and the helpful comments and suggestions of reviewers and other scholars.

This book aims to expose readers to the primary texts of each system and their interrelationships, to enable them to apply those documents to ever-changing factual situations, and to alert them to the dynamic nature of regional human rights law and institutions. It also seeks to relate regional systems to national law and to the global system for the protection of human rights. In this context, it highlights regional similarities and divergences, comparing the systems to each other and to the global norms that have emerged in the past half century.

The text illustrates how international human rights law is interpreted and implemented by the growing number of regional institutions. The selections offer examples of political, economic and social problems as well as legal issues to show the impact of international human rights law and institutions on the constitutions, law, policies and societies of the regions discussed. In addition to serving as a text for courses on human rights law, this book may prove useful in courses on international law, international relations, regional studies and political science. It may also serve as a resource for lawyers and non-governmental organizations litigating cases in the regions and for all those concerned with the protection of human rights.

DINAH L. SHELTON

ACKNOWLEDGMENTS

The author wishes to acknowledge with appreciation the permission granted to reproduce extracts from the following articles and books quoted in this volume:

Blaustein & Flanz (eds.), CONSTITUTIONS OF THE COUNTRIES OF THE WORLD, Oceana Publ., Inc.

Thomas Buergenthal, *Self-Executing and Non-Self-Executing Treaties in National and International Law*, 235 RECUEIL DES COURS 303 (1992).

Thomas. Buergenthal, *The Inter-American System for the Protection of Human Rights*, ANUARIO JURIDICO INTERAMERICANO 1981 (OAS, 1982), pp. 85–87.

Thomas Buergenthal, *The Inter-American System for the Protection of Human Rights*, in T. Meron (ed.), HUMAN RIGHTS IN INTERNATIONAL LAW, pp. 454–455, Oxford University Press, 1984, Vol. II.

Elizabeth F. Defeis, *Human Rights and the European Union: Who Decides? Possible Conflicts between the European Court of Justice and the European Court of Human Rights*, 19 DICK. INT'L L. J. 301 (2001).

Martin Eaton and Jeroen Schokkenbroek, *Reforming the Human Rights Protection System Established by the European Convention on Human Rights*, 26 HRLJ 1 (2005)

Stephen Greenblatt, WILL IN THE WORLD (2004).

Jean-Marie Henckaerts, *The Protection of Human Rights in the European Union: Overview . . .* , 22 INT'L J. LEGAL INFO. pp. 228–239 (1994).

Christof Heyns, *The African Regional Human Rights System: The African Charter*, 108 PENN ST. L. REV. 679 (2004)

Peter Leuprecht, *Innovations in the European System of Human Rights Protection: Is Enlargement Compatible with Reinforcement?* 8 TRANSNAT'L L. & CONTEMP. PROBS. 313 (1998).

Janet Koven Levit, *The Constitutionalization of Human Rights in Argentina: Problem or Promise?* 37 COLUM. J. TRANSNAT'L L. 281 (1999).

Cecilia Medina, *The Role of Country Reports in the Inter-American System of Human Rights*, in D. Harris and S Livingstone, THE INTER-AMERICAN HUMAN RIGHTS SYSTEM (Oxford University Press, 1998).

Rachel Murray, HUMAN RIGHTS IN AFRICA: FROM THE OAU TO THE AFRICAN UNION (Cambridge University Press, 2006).

A.R. Mowbray, *The Development of Positive Obligations under the European Convention on Human Rights by the European Court of Human Rights* (Hart Publishing: Oxford/Portland, Ore., 2004).

Vitit Muntarbhorn, *Asia, Human Rights and the New Millennium: Time for a Regional Human Rights Charter?*, 8 TRANSNAT'L L. & CONTEMP. PROBS. 407 (1998).

Hans-Jürgen Papier, *Execution and Effects of the Judgments of the European Court of Human Rights from the Perspective of German National Courts*, 27 HRLJ 1 (2006).

Randall Peerenboom, *Beyond Universalism and Relativism: The Evolving Debates About 'Values in Asia'* 14 IND. INT'L & COMP. L. REV. 1 (2003).

Søren C. Prebensen, *Inter-State Complaints under Treaty Provisions – The Experience under the European Convention on Human Rights*, 20 HRLJ 446 (1999).

Mervat Rishmawi, The *Revised Arab Charter on Human Rights: A Step Forward?* 5 HUM. RTS. L. REV. 361 (2005).

Erika Schlager, *A Hard Look at Soft Law: The OSCE in* COMMITMENT AND COMPLIANCE: THE ROLE OF NON-BINDING NORMS IN THE INTERNATIONAL LEGAL SYSTEM (D. Shelton, ed. Oxford University Press, 2000).

Yuval Shany, *Toward a General Margin of Appreciation Doctrine in International Law?* 16 EJIL 907 (2006).

Dinah Shelton, *Private Violence, Public Wrongs, and the Responsibility of States*, 13 FORDHAM INT'L L.J. (1989–90) 1.

Dinah Shelton, *The Promise of Regional Human Rights Systems* in THE FUTURE OF HUMAN RIGHTS (B. Weston & S. Marks, eds., Transnational Press, 2000).

Dinah Shelton, REMEDIES IN INTERNATIONAL HUMAN RIGHTS LAW (Oxford University Press, 2005).

Dinah Shelton, *The Practice of the Inter-American Commission on Human Rights in Issuing Precautionary Measures*, in MESURES CONSERVATOIRES ET DRTOIS FONDAMENTAUX 165 (2005).

Louis B. Sohn, *The New International Law: Protection of the Rights of Individuals Rather than States*, 32 AM.U.L. REV. 1–10 (1982).

Li-ann Thio, *Implementing Human Rights in ASEAN Countries: 'Promises to Keep and Miles to Go Before I Sleep'* 2 YALE HUM. RTS. & DEV. L.J. 1 (1999).

A.P. van der Mei, *The Advisory Jurisdiction of the African Court on Human and Peoples' Rights*, 5 AFR. H.R.L.J. 27 (2005).

Frans Viljoen, *The African Charter on Human and Peoples' Rights: The Travaux Preparatoires in the Light of Subsequent Practice*, 25 HRLJ 313 (2004).

Frans Viljoen & Lirette Louw, *State Compliance with the Recommendations of the African Commission on Human and Peoples' Rights, 1994–2004*, 101 AJIL 1 (2007).

ABBREVIATIONS

ACHPR	African Convention on Human and Peoples' Rights
Afr. Comm. H.P.R.	African Commission on Human and Peoples' Rights
AJIL	American Journal of International Law
ASEAN	Association of South-East Asian Nations
CCPR	Committee on Civil and Political Rights (United Nations)
CDBI	Steering Committee on Bioethics
CEJIL	Center for Justice and International Law
COE	Council of Europe
CONFENIAE	Confederation of Indigenous Nationalities of the Ecuadorian Amazon
COM	Committee of Ministers of the Council of Europe
CPT	Committee for the Prevention of Torture (Europe)
ECHR	European Convention for the Protection of Human Rights
ECJ	European Court of Justice
EHRR	European Human Rights Reports
EJIL	European Journal of International Law
EPIL	Encyclopedia of Public International Law
ERRC	European Roma Rights Centre
ETUC	European Trade Union Confederation
EU	European Union
Eur. Ct.H.R.	European Court of Human Rights
FSIA	U.S. Foreign Sovereign Immunities Act
GAOR	General Assembly Official Records
HRA	Human Rights Act 1998 (England)
HRLJ	Human Rights Law Journal
IACHR	Inter-American Commission on Human Rights
ICESCR	International Covenant on Economic, Social, and Cultural Rights
ICJ	International Court of Justice
ICLQ	International and Comparative Law Quarterly
ICTY	International Criminal Tribunal for the Former Yugoslavia
ILC	International Law Commission
Inter-Am. Ct.H.R.	Inter-American Court of Human Rights
IOE	International Organization of Employers
NDDC	Niger Delta Development Commission
NGO	Non-governmental organization
OAS	Organization of American States
OAU	Organization of African Unity
OPIP	Organization of Indigenous Peoples of Pastaza
OSCE	Organization for Security and Cooperation in Europe
SERAC	Social and Economic Rights Action Center
TEU	Treaty of European Union
UDHR	Universal Declaration of Human Rights
UN	United Nations
UNDP	United Nations Development Programme
UNICE	Union of Industrial and Employers' Confederation of Europe

BIBLIOGRAPHICAL NOTE ON PRINT AND INTERNET RESOURCES

For information on the history of human rights, see, generally, L. SOHN & T. BUERGENTHAL, INTERNATIONAL PROTECTION OF HUMAN RIGHTS (1973). For an overview of current international human rights law, see, generally, T. BUERGENTHAL, D. SHELTON & D. STEWART, HUMAN RIGHTS IN A NUTSHELL (4th. ed. 2005); L. HENKIN, THE AGE OF RIGHTS (1990). Regarding the United Nations and human rights, see P. ALSTON (ed.) THE UNITED NATIONS AND HUMAN RIGHTS: A CRITICAL APPRAISAL (1992); I. COTLER & E. ELIADIS (eds.), INTERNATIONAL HUMAN RIGHTS LAW: THEORY AND PRACTICE (1992); J. HUMPHREY, HUMAN RIGHTS AND THE UNITED NATIONS: A GREAT ADVENTURE (1984); D. MCGOLDRICK, THE HUMAN RIGHTS COMMITTEE: ITS ROLE IN THE DEVELOPMENT OF THE INTERNATIONAL COVENANT ON CIVIL AND POLITICAL RIGHTS (1991); H. TOLLEY, THE UN COMMISSION ON HUMAN RIGHTS (1987); D. WEISSBRODT, THE UN COMMISSION ON HUMAN RIGHTS, ITS SUB-COMMISSION AND RELATED PROCEDURES (1993); UN Centre for Human Rights, *United Nations Action in the Field of Human Rights* (1994). UN human rights texts are reproduced in *Human Rights: A Compilation of International Instruments* (UN Pub. No. E.93.XIV.1, 2 vols. 1993).

For comparative analyses of regional and global systems, see A.A. Cançado Trindade, *Co-Existence and Co-Ordination of Mechanisms of International Protection of Human Rights (At Global and Regional Levels)*, 202 RECUEIL DES COURS 10 (1987); H. Gros Espiell, *La Convention americaine et la Convention européenne des droits de l'homme — analyse comparative*, 218 RECUEIL DES COURS 167 (1991); H. HANNUM (ed.), GUIDE TO INTERNATIONAL HUMAN RIGHTS PRACTICE (4th ed. 2004): P. Kunig, *Regional Protection of Human Rights: A Comparative Introduction*, in P. KUNIG, W. BENEDEK & C. MAHALU, REGIONAL PROTECTION OF HUMAN RIGHTS BY INTERNATIONAL LAW: THE EMERGING AFRICAN SYSTEM 31 (1985); A.G. MOWER, REGIONAL HUMAN RIGHTS: A COMPARATIVE STUDY OF THE WEST EUROPEAN AND THE EVOLUTION OF THE INTER-AMERICAN SYSTEM (1991); B. Weston et al., *Regional Human Rights Regimes: A Comparison and Appraisal*, 20 VAND.J.TRANSNAT'L L. 585(1987); R. Murray, *On-Site Visits by the African Commission on Human and Peoples' Rights: A Case Study and Comparison with the Inter-American Human Rights Commission*, 11 AFR. J. INT'L. & COMP. L. 960 (1999).

On the European human rights system, see, generally, J. FAWCETT, THE APPLICATION OF THE EUROPEAN CONVENTION ON HUMAN RIGHTS (2D ED. 1987); G. COHEN-JONATHAN, LA CONVENTION EUROPÉENNE DES DROITS DE L'HOMME (1989); P. VAN DIJK & G. VAN HOOF, THEORY AND PRACTICE OF THE EUROPEAN CONVENTION ON HUMAN RIGHTS (1990); M. JANIS, EUROPEAN HUMAN RIGHTS

Law (1990); R. MacDonald, E. Matscher & H. Petzold (eds.) The European System for the Protection of Human Rights (1993); A.H. Robertson & J.G. Merrills, Human Rights in Europe (3d ed. 1993); I. Cameron, An Introduction to the European Convention on Human Rights (1993); F. Jacobs and R.C.A. White, The European Convention on Human Rights (1996), ch. 1; H.C. Yorrow, The Margin of Appreciation Doctrine in the Dynamics of European Human Rights Jurisprudence (1996); R. Beddard, Human Rights and Europe (1993), ch. 3; A. Drzemczewki, *The Prevention of Human Rights Violations: Monitoring Mechanisms of the Council of Europe*, in L.-A. Sicilianos (ed.), The Prevention of Human Rights Violations 139 (2001); R. Blackburn and J. Polakiewicz (eds.), The European Convention on Human Rights 1950–2000 (2000). The drafting history of the ECHR can be found in Council of Europe, *Collected Edition of the 'Travaux Préparatoires' of the European Convention on Human Rights* (8 vols., 1975–85). Recent developments in the European system are discussed in R. Bernhardt, *Reform of the Control Machinery under the European Convention on Human Rights: Protocol No. 11*, 89 AJIL 145; N. Bratza and M. O'Boyle, *The Legacy of the Commission to the New Court under the Eleventh Protocol*, in M. de Salvia and M. Villiger (eds.), The Birth of European Human Rights Law: Essays in Honour of Carl Aage Nørgaard (1998), at 388; A. Drzemczewski, *The European Human Rights Convention: Protocol No. 11—Entry into Force and First Year of Application*, 21 Hum. Rts. L.J. 1 (2000);

For readings on domestic application of the European Convention, see A. Drzemczewski, European Human Rights Convention in Domestic Law: A Comparative Study (1983); J. Polakiewicz & Jacob-Foltzer, *The European Human Rights Convention in Domestic Law: The Impact of the Strasbourg Case-Law Where Direct Effect Is Given to the Convention*, 12 HRLJ 65 and 125 (1991); T. Barkhuysen, M. van Emmerijk, and P. van Kempen, The Execution of Strasbourg and Geneva Human Rights Decisions in the National Legal Order (1999); A. Loux and W. Finnie, Human Rights and Scots Law: Comparative Perspectives on the Incorporation of the ECHR (1999); J.P. Gardner (ed.), Aspects of Incorporation of the European Convention of Human Rights into Domestic Law (1993).

On the European Social Charter, see, generally, D. Harris, The European Social Charter (1984); *Waking 'Sleeping Beauty': The Revised European Social Charter*, 7 Human Rights Brief 24 (2000); Fuchs, *The European Social Charter: Its Role in Present–Day Europe and Its Reform*, in K. Drzewicki, C. Krause & A. Rosas, Social Rights as Human Rights: A European Challenge 151 (1994). See also R. Goebel, *Employee Rights in the European Community: A Panorama from the 1974 Social Action Program to the Social Charter of 1989*, 17 Hastings Int'l. & Comp. L. Rev. 1, 58 (1993); Lundberg, *The Protection of Social Rights in the European Community: Recent Developments*, in Drzewicki et al., *supra*, at 169, on the distinction between the European Community's Social Charter and the European Social Charter of the Council of Europe. On other Council of Europe human rights treaties, see M. Evans & R. Morgan, Preventing Torture:

A STUDY OF THE EUROPEAN CONVENTION FOR THE PREVENTION OF TORTURE AND INHUMAN OR DEGRADING TREATMENT OR PUNISHMENT (1998); E. Riedel, *Global Responsibilities and Bioethics: Reflections on the Council of Europe's Bioethics Convention*, 5 IND. J. GLOBAL LEG. STUD. 179 (1997).

On the European Union and human rights, see E. Stein, *Lawyers, Judges and the Making of a Transnational Constitution*, 75 AJIL1, 16 (1981). J. Weiler, *Protection of Fundamental Human Rights within the Legal Order of the Communities*, in R. BERNHARDT & J.A. JOLOWICZ (eds.), INTERNATIONAL ENFORCEMENT OF HUMAN RIGHTS 113 (1987); F.G. Jacobs, *Protection of Human Rights in the Member States of the European Community: Impact of the Case Law of the Court of Justice*, in J. O'REILLY, HUMAN RIGHTS AND CONSTITUTIONAL LAW (ESSAYS IN HONOR OF BRIAN WALSH) 243 (1992); L. BETTEN AND D. MACDEVITT (eds.), THE PROTECTION OF FUNDAMENTAL SOCIAL RIGHTS IN THE EUROPEAN UNION (1996); H. SCHERMERS & D. WAELBROECK, JUDICIAL PROTECTION IN THE EUROPEAN COMMUNITIES 37 (5TH ED. 1992); N. NEUWAHL & A. ROSAS (eds.), THE EUROPEAN UNION AND HUMAN RIGHTS (1995); P. ALSTON (ed.), THE EU AND HUMAN RIGHTS (1999); Flaherty & Lally-Green, *Fundamental Rights in the European Union*, 36 DUQUESNE L. REV. 249 (1998); Lenaerts, *Respect for Fundamental Rights as a Constitutional Principle of the European Union*, 6 COLUMBIA J. EUR. L. 1 (2000).

Works on the OSCE include: A. BLOED & P. VAN DIJK (eds.), ESSAYS ON HUMAN RIGHTS IN THE HELSINKI PROCESS (1985); T. Buergenthal, *The CSCE Rights System*, 25 GEO. WASH. J. INT'L. & ECON. L. 333 (1993); J. MARESCA, TO HELSINKI: THE CONFERENCE ON SECURITY AND COOPERATION IN EUROPE, 1973–1975 (1987); W. KOREY, THE PROMISE TO KEEP: HUMAN RIGHTS, THE HELSINKI PROCESS AND AMERICAN FOREIGN POLICY (1993); J. Helgesen, *Between Helsinkis— and Beyond? Human Rights in the CSCE Process*, in A. ROSAS & J. HELGESEN (eds.), HUMAN RIGHTS IN A CHANGING EAST/WEST PERSPECTIVE 241 (1987); E. Schlager, *The Procedural Framework of the CSCE: From the Helsinki Consultation to the Paris Charter, 1972–1990*, 12 HRLJ 221 (1991); P. Van Dijk, *The Implementation of the Helsinki Final Act: The Creation of New Structures or the Involvement of Existing Ones*, 10 MICH. J. INT'L. L. 10, 113–15 (1989); E. Schlager, *A Hard Look at Compliance with 'Soft' Law: The Case of the OSCE*, in D. SHELTON (ed.), COMMITMENT AND COMPLIANCE: THE ROLE OF NON-BINDING NORMS IN THE INTERNATIONAL LEGAL SYSTEM; T. Buergenthal, *The Copenhagen CSCE Meeting: A New Public Order for Europe*, 11 HRLJ 217 (1990); L. SOHN (ed.), THE CSCE AND THE TURBULENT NEW EUROPE (GWU–IRLI, l993).

On the evolution of the Inter-American system, see T. Buergenthal, *The Revised OAS Charter and the Protection of Human Rights*, 69 AJIL 828, at 829 (1975); A. Cançado Trindade, *The Evolution of the Organization of American States (OAS) System of Human Rights Protection: An Appraisal*, 26 GERM. Y.B. INT'L. L. (1982) 498–514; C. Garcia Bauer, *La Conferencia Interamericana de Rio de Janeiro y su importancia para la proteccion de los derechos humanos*, in HUMAN RIGHTS IN THE AMERICAS (OAS, 1984), 62–79; D. Shelton, *Implementation Procedures of the American Convention on Human Rights*, 26 GERM. Y.B. INT'L. L. 238 (1983);

R. Norris, *Observations In Loco: Practice and Procedure of the Inter–American Commission on Human Rights, 1979–1983*, 19 Tex. Int'l. L.J. 285 (1984); T. Buergenthal, *The Inter-American System for the Protection of Human Rights*, in T. Meron (ed), Human Rights in International Law: Legal and Political Issues (1984) 429–493; T. Buergenthal, *Implementation in the Inter–American Human Rights System*, in R. Bernhardt & J.A. Jolowicz (eds.), International Enforcement of Human Rights 57, 61 (1987); H. Caminos et al., *The OAS Charter after Forty Years*, 82 Am. Soc'y. Int'l. L. Proc. 101 (1988); C. Medina–Quiroga, The Battle of Human Rights: Gross, Systematic Violations and the Inter–American System 85 (1988); D. Shelton, *The Inter–American System for the Protection of Human Rights: Emergent Law*, in I. Cotler & F.P. Eliades (eds.), International Human Rights Law: Theory and Practice 369, 370 (1992); S. Davidson, The Inter–American Court of Human Rights (1992); T. Buergenthal, *Judicial Fact–Finding: The Inter–American Human Rights Court*, in R. Lillich (ed.), Fact-Finding before International Tribunals 261, 263–64 (1992); T. Buergenthal, *Interim Measures in the Inter-American Court of Human Rights*, in R. Bernhardt (ed.), Interim Measures Indicated by International Courts 69, 72 (1994); J. Pasqualucci, *Advisory Practice and Procedure: Contributing to the Evolution of International Human Rights Law*, 38 Stan. J. Int'l. L. (2002); D. Shelton, *The Inter–American Human Rights System*, in H. Hannum (ed.), Guide to International Human Rights Practice 121 (4th ed. 2005).

On the Inter-American Commission and its powers, see F.V. Garcia Amador, *Atribuciones de Ia Comision Interamericana de Derechos Humanos en relacion con los Estados Miembros de Ia OEA que son partes en Ia Convencion de 1969*, in Human Rights in the Americas (Washington D.C.: CIDH 1984), 177–187; F.V. Garcia Amador, La competencia de Ia Comision Interamericana de Derechos Humanos y las obligaciones internacionales de Cuba en Ia materia, Institute of Inter-American Studies, Monograph No. 1984–2 (Miami, 1984); A. Gomez Moreno, *La expulsion colectiva de extranjeros (La Comision Interamericana de Derechos Humanos y el case El Salvador-Honduras)*, in Human Rights in the Americas (Washington D.C.: CIDH 1984), 80–92; C. Medina, *The Inter-American Commission on Human Rights and the Inter-American Court of Human Rights: Reflections on a Joint Venture*, 12 Hum. Rts. Q. 429 (1990); *Organizacion y funcionamiento de Ia Comision Interamericana de Derechos Humanos*, Annuario juridico interamericano (1984), 164–191; D.J. Padilla, *The Inter-American Commission on Human Rights in the Organization of American States: A Case Study*, 9 Am. U.J. Int'l. L. & Pol'y 95 (1993); D. Shelton, *The Inter-American Human Rights System*, in H. Hannum (ed.) Guide to International Human Rights Practice (4d ed. 2004); *The Inter-American Commission on Human Rights: A Promise Unfulfilled* 48 The Record of the Bar of the City of New York 589 (1993).

For further reading on the Inter-American Court, see T. Buergenthal, *The Inter-American Court of Human Rights*, 76 AJIL 1 (1982); T. Buergenthal, *The Advisory Practice of the Inter–American Human Rights Court*, 79 AJIL 1 (1985); C. Cerna,

The Inter-American Court of Human Rights, in M. Janis (ed.) International Courts for the Twenty-first Century 117 (1992); C. Cerna, *The Structure and Functioning of the Inter-American Court of Human Rights: 1979–1992*, 62 Brit. Y.B. Int'l. L. 135 (1992); A. C. Chueca Sancho, *La jurisprudencia de la Corte Interamericana de Derechos Humanos*, 3 Annuario de derechos humanos 573 (1984–85); S. Davidson, *The Inter-American Court of Human Rights* (1992); F. V. Garcia, Instituto Interamericao de Derechos Humanos, La Corte Interamericana de Derechos Humanos: Estudios y Documentos (1986); J.-G. Mahinga, *La contribution de la Cour interamericaine des droits de l'homme: la protection de la personne humaine: premieres tendances*, 69 Revue de droit int'l. et de droit compare 44 (1992); A. H. Pereira, *La proteccion de los derechos humanos par La Corte Interamericana de Derechos Humanos*, 40 Revista de la Fac. de derecho de Mex. 231 (1990); D. Shelton, *Review of State Action by International Courts*, 12 Fordham Int'l. L.J. 361 (1989).

For analysis of the African system, see U.O. Umozurike, *The African Charter on Human and Peoples' Rights*, 77 AJIL 902, 911 (1983); N. Enugu, The African Charter on Human and Peoples' Rights: Rights and Duties (1990); N.S. Rembe, The System of Protection of Human Rights under the African Charter on Human and Peoples' Rights: Problems and Prospects (1991); U.O. Umozurike, Five Years of the African Commission on Human and People's Rights (1992); K. Mbaye, *The African Charter on Human and Peoples' Rights*, 1 EPIL 54 (1992); K. Mbaye, Les droits de l'homme en Afrique (1992); E. Ankumah, The African Commission on Human and Peoples' Rights Practice and Procedures (1996); C. Heyns, Human Rights Law in Africa (1997); O. Umozurike, The African Charter on Human and Peoples' Rights (1997); G. Naldi & K. Magliveras, *Reinforcing the African System of Human Rights: The Protocol on the Establishment of a Regional Court of Human and Peoples' Rights*, 16 Neth. Q. Hum. Rts. 431 (1998); C. Anyangwe, "Obligations of States Parties to the African Charter on Human and Peoples' Rights," 10 Afr. J. Int'l. & Comp. L. 625 (1998); A. Chidi, *The Individual Complaints Procedure of the African Commission on Human and Peoples' Rights: A Preliminary Assessment*, 8 Transnat'l. L. & Contemp. Probs. 359 (1998); O. Dingake, *Protection of Human Rights in Africa*, 10 Transnat'l. L. & Contemp. Probs. 371 (2000); U. Essien, *The African Commission on Human and Peoples' Rights: Eleven Years After*, 6 Buff. Hum. Rts. L. Rev. 93 (2000); V. Nmemielle, The African Human Rights System: Law, Practices and Institutions (2001); The African Charter on Human and Peoples' Rights: The System in Practice, 1986–2000 (M. Evans and R. Murray, eds. 2002); G. W. Mugwanya, Human Rights in Africa: Enhancing Human Rights through the African Regional Human Rights System (2003); C. Flinterman and E. Ankumah, *The African Charter on Human and Peoples' Rights*, in *Guide to International Human Rights Practice* (4th ed. H. Hannum ed. 2004); R. Murray, Human Rights in Africa: From the OAU to the African Union (2004); F. Ouguergouz, The African Charter on Human and Peoples' Rights: A Comprehensive Agenda for Human Dignity and Sustainable Democracy in Africa (2004).

For the drafting history of the African Charter and the work of the Commission, see K. Mbaye, *Introduction to the African Charter on Human and Peoples' Rights*, in International Commission of Jurists, HUMAN AND PEOPLES' RIGHTS IN AFRICA AND THE AFRICAN CHARTER 19 (1985); R. Gittleman, *The African Charter on Human and Peoples' Rights: A Legal Analysis*, 22 VA. J. INT'L. L. 667 (1982); B. Ramcharan, *The Travaux Préparatoires of the African Commission on Human and Peoples' Rights*, 13 HRLJ 307 (1992); E. Bello, *Article 22 of the African Charter on Human and People's Rights*, in E. BELLO & B. AJIBOLA (eds.), ESSAYS IN HONOR OF JUDGE TASLIM OLAWALE ELIAS, vol. I, at 447 (1991); U.O. Umozurike, *The African Charter on Human and Peoples' Rights*, 77 AJIL 902, 911 (1983); A. Aidoo, *Africa: Democracy without Human Rights?* 15 Hum. RTS. Q. 703 (1993); R. MURRAY, THE AFRICAN COMMISSION ON HUMAN AND PEOPLES' RIGHTS AND INTERNATIONAL LAW (2000); E.A. ANKUMAH, THE AFRICAN COMMISSION ON HUMAN AND PEOPLES' RIGHTS: PRACTICE AND PROCEDURE (1996);

For a discussion of the African Court, see A. Anthony, *Beyond the Paper Tiger: The Challenge of a Human Rights Court in Africa*, 32 TEXAS INT'L. L.J. 511 (1997); M. wa Matua, *The African Human Rights Court: A Two-Legged Stool?*, 21 HUM. RTS. Q. 342 (1999); J. Mubangizi and A. O'Shea, *An African Court of Human and Peoples' Rights*, 23 S. AFR. Y.B. INT'L. L. 256 (2000); E. de Wet, *The Protection Mechanism under the African Charter and the Protocol on the African Court of Human and Peoples' Rights*, in G. ALFREDSSEN ET AL. (eds.), INTERNATIONAL HUMAN RIGHTS MONITORING MECHANISMS 713 (2001); A.P. van der Mei, *The New African Court on Human and Peoples' Rights: Towards an Effective Human Rights Protection Mechanism for Africa?* 2005 LEIDEN J. INT'L. L.; A.P. van der Mei, *The Advisory Jurisdiction of the African Court on Human and Peoples' Rights*, 5 AFR. H.R.L.J. 27 (2005).

On the African Children's Convention, see D.M. Chirwa, *The Merits and Demerits of the African Charter on the Rights and Welfare of the Child*, 10 INT'L. J. CHILDREN'S RTS. 157 (2002).

The documentation and jurisprudence of the three regional systems are readily accessible through the Internet.

The Council of Europe's website is www.coe.int. The site links to all the Council's organs, including the Parliamentary Assembly, the Committee of Ministers and the European Court of Human Rights, as well as the treaty office. The latter will give access to the text of all agreements, signatures, ratifications and reservations. The Council's website also has a subject listing for human rights, which leads to all the various instruments, procedures and jurisprudence. The European Court and its jurisprudence can be reached directly at www.echr.coe.int. A search device (HUDOC) allows a search by specific rights, countries, name of applicant, or keywords.

The OAS website, www.oas.org, first requires the visitor to choose from one of the four official languages. Once this is done, a dropdown menu at the top of the screen lists OAS sectors and topics, including human rights. Selecting the topic "human rights" brings a choice of linking to the Inter-American Commission on Human Rights or the Inter-American Court of Human Rights. Basic texts, reports, decisions and judgments are available. The Court's direct address is www.corteidh. or.cr.

The African Commission on Human and Peoples Rights is directly accessible at www.achpr.org.

Other sites that have documentation and jurisprudence on the regional systems include:

The University of Minnesota's human rights library: www1.umn.edu/humanrts

The University of Witwatersrand, South Africa: www.law.wits.ac.za/humanrts

CHAPTER I

INTRODUCTION

The international protection of human rights developed as a distinct and fundamental branch of international law relatively recently, although a limited set of legal norms designed to protect individuals against mistreatment has been in existence since the beginnings of the Law of Nations. Even a cursory review of legal systems for the protection of human rights demonstrates the rapid expansion of this field since the end of World War II. During this period, nearly all global and regional organizations have adopted human rights standards and addressed human rights violations by member states. As a consequence, no state today can claim that its treatment of those within its jurisdiction is a matter solely of domestic concern.

This chapter takes a brief look at the history of human rights law, then examines the development of regional organizations and the role that promotion and protection of human rights play in them. It examines in particular the question of what human rights obligations states assume upon joining the regional bodies. To begin, the following reading outlines some key developments in human rights law at the global and regional levels.

1. The Evolution of International Concern with Human Rights

Louis B. Sohn, *The New International Law: Protection of the Rights of Individuals Rather than States,* 32 Am.U.L. Rev. 1–10 (1982) (extracts, some notes omitted).

. . . The human rights revolution did not appear suddenly full-grown, like Minerva springing from Jupiter's head. Its main substantive rules and its procedural safeguards can be traced back many centuries, to the origin of international law itself.

A. The Origins of the Human Rights Revolution

The oldest method of protecting the rights of individuals was self-help, not only by the victim, but also by his family, his clan, his nation, and ultimately his sovereign or state. The Bible documents numerous applications of the old adage 'an eye for an eye, a tooth for a tooth,' or, more often, a life for a life. This rule also was applied in medieval times, as illustrated in Shakespeare's Romeo and Juliet. . . .

A similar problem arose very early in the international field. Citizens travelling in a foreign country were robbed, enslaved, or killed, sometimes by bandits, sometimes by the feudal lords through whose domains they travelled, or by the soldiers of the country's ruler, for whom a foreigner was fair game, a source of combat booty even if the two countries were not at war. Similarly, mariners frequently looted foreign ships travelling on the high seas.

Two sets of rules quickly emerged. First, a state was responsible for what happened within its territory and for its citizens' conduct on the high seas, and, second, the foreigner's home state was entitled to demand reparations for any resulting injury to its citizens. A citizen, especially a merchant, was a valuable asset, and those who damaged that asset diminished the wealth of the foreign prince. Accordingly, the perpetrators were responsible to him as though they had injured a member of his family. If the persons responsible for the injury were not forced to pay for the damage, or if their ruler refused to take action, international responsibility did arise. The foreign ruler, his assets, and his citizens were deemed to be collectively responsible for the damage to the foreign citizen; as a first step, the victim's ruler was entitled to authorize the victim, his family, or his partners in the commercial venture to use self-help against the other country and its citizens. The ruler issued letters of marque and reprisal authorizing the capture of vessels or cargoes belonging to the state responsible for the wrong.

To mitigate the harshness of this rule, several procedural safeguards were soon devised. Prior to asking his sovereign for letters of reprisal, a citizen had to attempt to obtain justice from the government of the country in which the damage had occurred or whose citizens inflicted the injury. Only when justice was denied and further complaints by his sovereign were rejected did reprisals come into play. When capturing the foreign country's ships on the high seas, the victim was entitled to take only what was due to him. Some countries, especially France and Great Britain, required strict accounting to the government that issued the letters of marque and reprisal.

The mitigating procedure of international law developed as early as 450 B.C., in the Greek treaty between Oeantheia and Chalaeum, two cities on the Gulf of Corinth. This treaty permitted capture only on the high seas, not in or near a port. The idea of exhaustion of local remedies and denial of justice can be traced at least to the ninth century, for example, to the treaties between Naples and Benevent in 836 and between Emperor Lothar I and Venice in 840. Later treaties exempted certain categories of foreign citizens from reprisals, including scholars, students, and merchants attending fairs. This method of law enforcement lasted until the nineteenth century; as late as 1858, in the Aves Island case, the United States threatened to issue letters of reprisal against Venezuela if the latter continued to deny justice.

The next steps were removal of self-help from private hands and centralization of that power in the government. When injury was inflicted on citizens of a country, that country blockaded the wrongdoer's ports, and, if necessary, occupied a part of the country, in order to encourage settlement of the dispute. For example, in 1850 Great Britain blockaded Greece in order to obtain satisfaction for the claims of two men, M.M. Finley and Pacifico; in 1902 Germany, Great Britain, and Italy blockaded the coast of Venezuela and forced that country to accept an international arbitration of their citizens' claims arising from the Venezuelan civil war.

In some of these cases, settlement of the injured citizens' claims was imposed by force on the state held responsible for the injuries. In other cases, the matter was submitted for a binding decision to an international claims commission or an arbitral tribunal. Thus, the third stage, decision by an international court of disputes about violations of foreign citizens' rights, was reached. The Permanent Court of International Justice, established in 1920, as well as its successor, the International Court of Justice, established in 1945, heard a number of cases involving private rights. As the Permanent Court of International Justice stated, however, '[o]nce a State has taken up a case on behalf of one of its subjects before an international tribunal, in the eyes of the latter, the State is sole claimant.'[1] Thereafter, the state is said to be 'asserting its own rights—its right to ensure in the person of its subject, respect for the rules of international law.'[2]

Nevertheless, the burden of exhausting local remedies remained with the private claimant. Until he had exhausted the local remedies, his state was not entitled to bring an international claim. In the words of the International Court of Justice: '[T]he State where the violation has occurred should have an opportunity to redress it by its own means, within the framework of its own domestic legal system.'[3] As will become evident below, the principle of exhaustion of local remedies has been incorporated into the new law of human rights; a claimant must exhaust local remedies without being adequately satisfied before seeking redress on the international plane.

. . . In a few special situations . . . international protection has been given to citizens suffering from domestic persecution. Tyrannical conduct of a government towards its subjects and gross mistreatment of national or religious minorities have occasionally reached a level at which intervention in the name of humanity was considered permissible. The idea of humanitarian intervention was familiar even in ancient China, where Mencius supported the notion of liberation from tyrants.[4] In the era of enlightenment, Emerich de Vattel stated in his Le Droit des Gens that if 'persecution is carried out to an intolerable degree . . . all Nations may give help to an unfortunate people.'[5]

Humanitarian intervention has occurred in cases of persecution of minorities, especially in the Middle East. Thus, in 1860 the major European powers forced Turkey to accept intervention, 'in the name of Europe,' by French military forces to protect the Christian population in Lebanon against massacres by the Druses.[6] Atrocities in Bulgaria in the 1870s led to Russian intervention, and in the 1878 Treaty of Berlin, Turkey accepted special provisions for the protection of minorities.[7]

A recurring claim, which has been made with some justification, is that countries that engaged in 'humanitarian' intervention were motivated more by a desire to establish spheres of influence or to obtain commercial advantages than by an altru-

---

[1] *Mavrommatis Palestine Concessions (Greece v. Gr. Brit.)*, 1924 P.C.I.J., ser. A, No. 2, at 12 (Judgment of Aug. 30).

[2] *Id.*

[3] *Interhandel (Switz. v. U.S.)*, 1959 I.C.J. 6, 27 (Preliminary Objections Judgment of Mar. 21) (because of Swiss company's failure to exhaust U.S. judicial remedies, court dismissed claim brought by Swiss government on behalf of company).

[4] See L. GILES, THE BOOK OF MENCIUS 35 (1942); D. LAU, MENCIUS 69 (1970).

[5] E. VATTEL, THE LAW OF NATIONS, bk. II, § 56, at 62 (London 1758), reprinted in 3 THE CLASSICS OF INTERNATIONAL LAW 134 (J. Scott ed. 1916).

[6] A. TIBAWI, A MODERN HISTORY OF SYRIA 121–33 (1969). See also L. SOHN & T. BUERGENTHAL, THE INTERNATIONAL PROTECTION OF HUMAN RIGHTS 159 (1973); see generally *id.* at 143–78 (collection of correspondence concerning the massacres and subsequent intervention).

[7] *Id.* at 178–79.

istic motive to alleviate human suffering. In addition, a familiar argument is that humanitarian intervention, being available only to major powers, created a one-sided relationship, without possibility of reciprocal action by the smaller powers.[8]

Consequently, when the map of Eastern Europe was redrawn after the First World War, responsibility for the protection of minorities was taken out of the hands of major powers and transferred to the League of Nations. In his famous 1919 letter to the Polish Government, Georges Clemenceau explained that the Great Powers would no longer use the right to intervene for political purposes; henceforth, the League of Nations would guarantee certain essential rights of minorities in Eastern Europe.

The League of Nations' system of minority protection functioned well for fifteen years. Nevertheless, with the advent of the Nazi regime in Germany and its barbaric treatment of minorities, the neighboring countries objected that they alone were bound by minority-protection obligations, while the major powers had no similar responsibilities. After the Second World War, therefore, an attempt to revive the minority-protection treaties and to vest in the United Nations the authority to guarantee rights under these treaties did not succeed. Instead, a broader system of protection for human rights was established, with the expectation that it would be applied to all human beings, in large and small countries alike. . . .

The traditional systems of protecting foreigners and minorities have not disappeared completely. In recent years, the protection of foreigners and minorities has become a major concern of the international community. Many of the procedural rules that were developed for the protection of foreigners and minorities have found their way into the systems of protection of human rights established after 1945. In addition, a comparison of the rules of substantive law applied by international arbitral tribunals and claims commissions in the past two centuries with those embodied in recent instruments on human rights clearly demonstrates that the new rules owe their content not only to domestic constitutional provisions but also to international jurisprudence. This is especially true in such areas as arbitrary arrest, mistreatment of prisoners, access to courts, and adequacy of judicial proceedings. Of course, as will be seen, the new international law of human rights extends far beyond the areas traditionally considered proper for international claims.

Similarly, there has been some incorporation of the concept of humanitarian intervention into the United Nations' system. After some hesitation, the United Nations agreed that in cases of gross and persistent violations of human rights as a matter of national policy, as in the case of South African apartheid, the United Nations can deal with the matter regardless of the provision in the U.N. Charter that prohibits the United Nations from 'interven[ing] in matters which are essentially within the domestic jurisdiction of any state.' Gross violations of human rights are now considered to be matters of international rather than domestic concern, and to represent possible threats to the peace, thus allowing the United Nations to go beyond mere condemnation and to impose sanctions against a violator if necessary.

---

8 See W. HALL, A TREATISE ON INTERNATIONAL LAW 302–09 (4th ed. 1895); E. STOWELL, INTERVENTION IN INTERNATIONAL LAW 53–62 (1921).

Collective intervention by regional organizations also has been allowed on some occasions, most recently in Chad. . . .

B. The Human Rights Revolution: The Aftermath of the Second World War

1. Effect of the Second World War

Returning now to the position of individuals in international law in 1945, it is quite clear that apart from a few anomalous cases, in which individuals were allowed to vindicate their rights directly on the basis of a special international agreement, individuals were not subjects of rights and duties under international law. They merely benefited indirectly from the rule that a state could consider any injury to its citizen as an injury to itself and therefore could attempt to obtain reparation for it. Once a state received compensation from another state for the injury to its citizen, however, it had no duty under international law to transfer that compensation to the citizen; if, for economic or political reasons, the state relinquished the claim or settled it for some small percentage of its original amount, its citizen was deprived of further recourse against the offending state. Thus, a person's protection depended on the conduct of his state, and stateless persons were entitled to no protection whatsoever.

At the same time, a state's own citizens were almost completely at its mercy, and international law had little to say about mistreatment of persons by their own government. As noted above, humanitarian intervention by another state, if not completely illegal, was often attributable to political or economic interests rather than concern about human rights. In many instances, such interventions resulted in the imposition of colonial rule. Although perhaps more humane, colonial rule was seldom considered by the people concerned as an improvement over the prior government.

At the termination of the Second World War, two events completely changed the status of individuals under international law. Both were closely connected with Nazi actions and with other atrocities committed before and during the war. The first event was the punishment of war criminals at Nuremberg and Tokyo; the second was the desire to prevent the recurrence of such crimes against humanity through development of new standards for the protection of human rights.

. . . .

2. Codification of the newly recognized human rights

. . . [I]ndividuals gained rights under international law and, to some extent, means for vindication of those rights on the international plane. This development entailed four different law-building stages: assertion of international concern about human rights in the U.N. Charter; listing of those rights in the Universal Declaration of Human Rights; elaboration of the rights in the International Covenant on Civil and Political Rights and in the International Covenant on Economic, Social and Cultural Rights; and the adoption of some fifty additional declarations and conventions concerning issues of special importance, such as discrimination against women, racial discrimination and religious intolerance. The pyramid of documents, with the Charter at its apex, has become a veritable internationalization and codification of human rights law, an international bill of human rights much more detailed than its French and American counterparts.

    . . . .

i. The U.N. Charter

. . . Great ideas cannot be imprisoned; they must be able to move freely from one part of the earth to another. The U.N. Charter contains several such ideas, which revolutionized the world, although no one knew in 1945 how successful the drafters of the Charter would be in planting in that document the seeds from which many mighty trees would grow.

The most influential of these ideas are that human rights are of international concern, and that the United Nations has the duty to promote 'universal respect for, and observance of, human rights and fundamental freedoms for all without distinction as to race, sex, language and religion.' Although these two ideas were born out of the disasters of the Second World War, they are even more meaningful today than at the time they were first formulated. It is our common duty not only to respect human rights ourselves but also to promote their 'universal respect' and to ensure that they are observed throughout the globe. All members of the United Nations—not only the original 50, but the more than 150 members today—have pledged to 'take joint and separate action,' in cooperation with the United Nations for the achievement of these great purposes. In the Charter's preamble, the peoples of the United Nations as well as their governments, have reaffirmed their 'faith in fundamental human rights, in the dignity and worth of the human person, in the equal rights of men and women and of nations large and small.' In that statement the authors of the Charter anticipated not only the racial revolution, but also the feminist revolution and the need to provide for equality notwithstanding gender. They did not anticipate, however, that more than one hundred nations, most of them small, would clamor for equality with the fifty nations that dominated the world in 1945.

ii. The Universal Declaration of Human Rights

Although the U.N. Charter mentions human rights in many places, time constraints at the San Francisco conference made it impossible to prepare a more detailed document paralleling the national bills or declarations of the rights of man and of the citizen. It was promised at that time, however, that the United Nations would commence the drafting of an International Bill of Rights as one of the first items of business. The Commission on Human Rights was established in 1946, only a few months after the Charter came into force, and was asked to prepare such a document. It soon became obvious that the task could take a long time and, in view of the urgency of the matter, that the first step should be a declaration of general principles, to be followed later by a document containing more precise obligations.

Two years later the first document—the Universal Declaration of Human Rights—was ready. On December 10, 1948, the General Assembly, after some amendments, approved it unanimously, with eight abstentions: the Soviet bloc, Saudi Arabia, and the Union of South Africa. Although some delegations emphasized that the Universal Declaration of Human Rights was not a treaty imposing legal obligations, others more boldly argued that it was more than an ordinary General Assembly resolution, that it was a continuation of the Charter and shared the dignity of that basic document. It merely expressed more forcefully rules that already were recognized by customary international law. Under the latter view, the Declaration would possess a binding character . . . . The Declaration itself proclaims that it is 'a common standard of achievement for all peoples and all nations.' It exhorts every individual and every organ of society to strive, 'by progressive measures, national and international, to secure . . . universal and effective recognition and observance of the rights and freedoms therein.'

Even if governments and scholars were originally in disagreement regarding the importance, status, and effect of the Universal Declaration, practice in the United Nations soon confounded the doubters. Several of the governments that originally were skeptical about the value of the Declaration did not hesitate to invoke it against other countries. Thus, the United States invoked it in the so-called Russian Wives Case, and the General Assembly declared that Soviet measures preventing Russian wives from leaving the Soviet Union in order to join their foreign husbands were 'not in conformity with the Charter,' citing articles 13 and 16 of the Declaration in support of its conclusion. The Soviet Union, which originally claimed that the Declaration violated the Charter's prohibition against interference in a state's internal affairs, later voted for many resolutions charging South Africa with violations of the Universal Declaration.

. . . The Declaration thus is now considered to be an authoritative interpretation of the U.N. Charter, spelling out in considerable detail the meaning of the phrase 'human rights and fundamental freedoms,' which Member States agreed in the Charter to promote and observe. The Universal Declaration has joined the Charter of the United Nations as part of the constitutional structure of the world community. The Declaration, as an authoritative listing of human rights, has become a basic component of international customary law, binding on all states, not only on members of the United Nations. Another revolutionary step thus has been taken in protecting human rights on a worldwide scale. . . .

[C]. The International Covenants: Overview

When the Commission on Human Rights finished the Universal Declaration, it began preparing the other part of the International Bill of Rights, a convention containing precise obligations that would be binding on the States Parties. There were initial fears that the various rights would drown in a sea of limitations and exception, but this danger was avoided by careful delineation of the conditions under which rights could be limited, and identification of those rights that could not be limited under any circumstances. Another difficulty did, however, arise. It proved impossible to formulate in a parallel manner all the rights listed in the Universal Declaration; it became necessary to divide the materials into two categories: civil and political rights; and economic, social, and cultural rights. These two categories were embodied in two separate Covenants—a name that was preferred to the less solemn 'convention'—each differing from the other in several respects. The main difference was in their treatment after coming into force. States Parties were to give the Covenant on Civil and Political Rights immediate effect through appropriate legislative or other measures and by making available an effective remedy to any person whose rights have been violated. In contrast, each State Party to the Covenant on Economic, Social and Cultural Rights agreed only to take steps, to the maximum of its available resources, toward a progressive realization of the rights recognized in that Covenant. The Covenant thus contained a loophole: because a state's obligation was limited to the resources available to it, a poor state could proceed slowly, progressing only as fast as its resources permitted. If its resources should diminish, for example, during an economic crisis, its progress could wane. In contrast, the Covenant on Civil and Political Rights permits no such excuses; a state must guarantee civil and political rights fully on ratification, subject only to the limitations [permitted by the agreement].

. . . Another general point must be made. Although the rights protected by the Covenants are stated with greater precision than those listed in the Universal Declaration, the former are broad enough in scope to surmount differences among various political, economic, and social systems, as well as among widely differing cultures and stages of development. Consequently, only the last factor—differences in stages of development, especially economic development—need be taken into account in applying the Covenant on Economic, Social and Cultural Rights. In contrast, even that factor does not excuse nonimplementation of the Covenant on Civil and Political Rights.

The Covenants and national constitutions or laws are meant to coexist. The Covenants do not supersede any constitutions or laws that provide more protection to individuals. Where the Covenants go beyond a domestic law in protecting a particular right, the state concerned has the duty to adopt any additional legislative or other measures that may be necessary to give effect to the right recognized in the Covenants.

[1]. The International Covenant on Civil and Political Rights

. . . .

The Covenant on Civil and Political Rights is to be implemented through a combination of international and domestic law. Its enforcement relies in the first place on national institutions, as each State Party has the duty to ensure that any person whose rights under the Covenant have been violated has an effective remedy against the violator and the access for that purpose to appropriate judicial, administrative, or legislative authorities. . . .

At the same time, because individuals' rights are embodied in an international instrument, other States Parties are entitled to demand that it be implemented properly. No longer is an individual's international protection limited to the state of his nationality and subject to its whims. Now, for the first time, any among the more than [150] States Parties can complain that another state has violated the rights of one of its own citizens. Although similar opportunities had been available in the past, never before have they occurred on such a grand scale. Any state can now become an international ombudsman, protecting human rights anywhere for purely humanitarian reasons, without any ulterior motives. . . .

The Covenant on Civil and Political Rights is the least novel of human rights instruments. It reflects human rights values that have been developing in many countries of the world since the signing of the Magna Carta. Both old and new national constitutions contain similar principles. In addition, international arbitral tribunals have applied these principles extensively in cases of international responsibility for injuries to aliens. The Covenant and the European Convention, as well as the inter-American and African instruments, thus contain generally accepted principles that apply not only to the parties to these instruments, but also to other states. The law of human rights as embodied in the international instruments is not merely treaty law, but rather has become a part of international customary law of general application, except in areas in which important reservations have been made. These documents do not create new rights; they recognize them. Although the line between codification and development of international law is a thin one, the consensus on virtually all provisions of the Covenant on Civil and Political Rights is so widespread that they can be considered part of the law of mankind. . . . Thus, an important step has been taken in enlarging the scope of international law and in providing international protection to many important individual rights.

. . .

[2]. Development of the Concept of Economic, Social, and Cultural Rights

[Following World War I and] as a counterbalance to the [Communist] Third International . . . the Paris Peace Conference established the first international institution for social justice: the International Labour Organisation (ILO). The ILO proved to be particularly successful as an international social institution. Over the years it developed many international labor standards, in the form of conventions and recommendations, as well as an effective system of supervision through periodic reports and the investigation of complaints.

Nevertheless, it was in response to the Nazi tyranny rather than as a sequel to the ILO that President Roosevelt conceived the idea of an instrument dealing with economic and social rights. In his 'Four Freedoms' message to the U.S. Congress in 1941, President Roosevelt mentioned not only freedom of speech and expression, freedom of religion, and freedom from fear (including freedom from wars of aggression), but also 'freedom from want.' The latter requires 'economic understandings which will secure to every nation a healthy peacetime life for its inhabitants—everywhere in the world.' In his 1944 Message to Congress, President Roosevelt spelled out in more detail the rights that were embraced in his concept of 'freedom from want.' He pointed out that 'true individual freedom cannot exist without economic security and independence'; that 'people who are hungry and out of a job are the stuff of which dictatorships are made;' and that 'in our day these economic truths have become accepted as self-evident.' He knew well that in the United States in the 1930's it was the New Deal, with its economic, social, and labor reforms, that prevented economic and social chaos. He felt that, similarly, global chaos and totalitarianism could be stopped only by drastic economic and social reforms throughout the world. Although his two messages were directed primarily to a domestic audience, his words had a worldwide impact, and were not forgotten when the United Nations began to address human rights issues.

. . . In his 1944 message . . . President Roosevelt linked the demand for a just and durable system of peace with the need for 'a decent standard of living for all individual men and women and children in all nations.' He emphasized that 'freedom from fear is eternally linked with freedom from want.' When he said that a nation, no matter how high its general standard of living may be, 'cannot be content . . . if some fraction of its people—whether it be one-third or one-fifth or one-tenth—is ill-fed, ill-clothed, ill-housed and insecure,' he had Americans in mind. Nevertheless, that message was even more valid for other peoples, as was the rest of his statement in which he emphasized that 'true individual freedom cannot exist without economic security and independence.' Although the United States since its inception had been concerned with certain inalienable political rights designed to safeguard life and liberty, the time had come, the President believed, to accept some economic truths as self-evident and, accordingly, to accept a second Bill of Rights, providing 'a new basis of security and prosperity . . . for all—regardless of station, race, or creed.' He then presented a list, much longer than that in the 1941 message, of the rights to be included in the second Bill of Rights. . . .

[3] The International Covenant on Economic, Social and Cultural Rights

Although the provisions of the Universal Declaration relating to economic, social and cultural rights were quite detailed, the Human Rights Commission prepared an even more comprehensive document—the International Covenant on Economic, Social and Cultural Rights. This Covenant, completed in 1966, came into force in 1976. . . .

The drafters had to solve several other general problems in connection with the introductory clauses to the Covenant on Economic, Social and Cultural Rights. It was agreed first that each State Party should undertake 'to take steps, individually and through international assistance and co-operation, especially economic and technical, to the maximum of its available resources, with a view to achieving progressively the full realization of the rights recognized in the present Covenant by all appropriate means, including particularly the adoption of legislative measures.' This was an 'umbrella' provision covering all the rights in the Covenant, replacing an unsuccessful attempt to incorporate detailed restrictions and exceptions into each article. Traces of the abandoned approach to exceptions still may be found in some articles of the Covenant, especially in the fine print of articles 13 and 14, which deal with the right to education.

The main emphasis in the text of article 2 is on the 'progressive' nature of the obligation to achieve economic, social, and cultural rights. The drafters recognized in particular that many countries do not yet have the necessary resources, and that time would be needed to develop them. To speed up this development, the text included a gentle hint that states endowed with better resources and technological know how should help their less fortunate brethren. This should be accomplished 'through international assistance and co-operation, especially economic and technical.' Although the Covenant allows states some latitude regarding the 'appropriate means' required for the full realization of economic, social, and cultural rights, the drafters felt that 'legislative measures' should not be neglected, because such measures could help establish the policies to be pursued and could provide the necessary legal and administrative framework for the implementation of these policies.

. . . . It also was noted that in an interdependent world a state can never be sure what resources are at its disposal; international economic conditions and terms of trade change constantly and rapidly and are not subject to the control of any one state. Furthermore, the reference to 'available resources' and the use of the term 'progressively' apparently distinguished between developed and developing countries, yet at the same time imposed on all states a general obligation to achieve progressively higher levels of fulfillment of rights. The phrase 'available resources' contemplates not only the national resources of a county, but also the resources that it might be able to obtain from other countries or international institutions. To implement this idea, the Covenant imposes on the Economic and Social Council the duty to alert those international institutions concerned with the furnishing of technical assistance to any matters in the national reports that could assist such institutions in deciding on 'international measures likely to contribute to the effective progressive implementation' of the Economic, Social and Cultural Covenant. In addition, States Parties to the Covenant agreed that 'international action for the achievement of the rights recognized in the . . . Covenant includes . . . the furnishing of technical assistance.' Thus, the Covenant clearly recognizes a collective obligation to improve economic, social, and cultural standards, another important step toward an interdependent world community.

[D] . . . Collective Rights

One of the main characteristics of humanity is that human beings are social creatures. Consequently, most individuals belong to various units, groups, and communities; they are simultaneously members of such units as a family, religious community, social club, trade union, professional association, racial group, people, nation, and state. It is not surprising, therefore, that international law not only recognizes inalienable rights of individuals, but also recognizes certain collective rights that are exercised jointly by individuals grouped into larger communities, including peoples and nations. These rights are still human rights; the effective exercise of collective rights is a precondition to the exercise of other rights, political or economic or both. If a community is not free, most of its members are also deprived of many important rights.

1. The right of self-determination

International law has long been concerned with one of the most basic of collective rights: the right of self-determination. Many wars were fought in the name of the principle of self-determination, and the international community has often come to the assistance of those who have invoked that principle. . . . The Charter of the United Nations emphasizes that 'friendly relations among nations shall be based on respect for the principle of equal rights and self-determination of peoples.' The General Assembly itself decided that both Covenants should contain an article on self-determination. The final version of article 1(1) of both Covenants begins with this phrase: 'All peoples have the right to self-determination,' and concludes with this sentence: 'By virtue of that right they freely determine their political status and freely pursue their economic, social and cultural development.'

2. The right to development

One facet of the right of self-determination is the right of a people to 'freely pursue their economic, social and cultural development.' The most recent regional human rights instrument, the African Charter on Human and Peoples' Rights, rephrases this right slightly to read: 'All peoples shall have the right to their economic, social and cultural development with due regard to their freedom and identity and in the equal enjoyment of the common heritage of mankind.' In addition, the African Charter proclaims that states have the duty to ensure, individually or collectively, the exercise of the right to development.

The right to development can be traced to the 1944 Declaration of Philadelphia, which was incorporated into the ILO Constitution of 1946. That Declaration affirmed the following principle: 'All human beings, irrespective of race, creed or sex, have the right to pursue both their material well-being and their spiritual development in conditions of freedom and dignity, of economic security and equal opportunity.'

A U.N. working group of governmental experts, after studying the various documents on the subject, came to the conclusion that the right to development has both a collective and an individual dimension.[9] The holders of the collective right to development are peoples and states. Each group of states, especially the developed states, should act to make possible the enjoyment of the right by all states. The basic purpose of the development right in its individual dimension is 'integral development,' that is, satisfaction of a number of 'basic or fundamental needs' of the individual. According to another view, the right to development involves far more than the mere satisfaction of basic needs; its objective is to establish conditions of equality of opportunity among all peoples, with a view to the fulfillment of the human person. Consistent with that opinion, the individual right to development may be considered a multidimensional, composite right, covering all civil, political, economic, social, and cultural rights necessary for the 'full development of the individual and the protection of his dignity.'

... Development should not be considered in purely economic terms.... The right to development thus requires careful balancing of the interests of the community and of individuals. A healthy regard for the rights of the individual is indispensable for a state's success in pursuing its right to development. At the same time it has been said that the 'right to development is for a people what human rights are for an individual. It represents the transposition of human rights to the level of the international community.' ...

3. The right of peace

Analogously, one can say that without peace there can be no human rights. Wars not only result in great loss of human life; they are also inimical to human rights. Even preparation for war often results in the curtailment of human rights. The converse is also true: a country that grossly violates human rights is more likely to start a war than a country in which freedom flourishes. Alternately, gross violations of human rights in a country can lead to military intervention by another country; such intervention can easily escalate into a larger war.

... In 1976, the U.N. Commission on Human Rights pointed out that 'everyone has the right to live in conditions of international peace and security and fully to

---

[9] Report of the Working Group to the Commission on Human Rights, U.N. Doc. E/CN.4/1489, at 5 (1982).

enjoy economic, social and cultural rights and civil and political rights.'[10] The Commission added that 'unqualified respect for and the promotion of human rights and fundamental freedoms require the existence of international peace and security.' It also noted that 'flagrant and massive violations of human rights, including economic, social and cultural rights, may lead the world into armed conflicts.' According to its recommendation, all states should make an effort to create the most favorable conditions for the maintenance of international peace and security 'through respect for and the promotion of human rights and fundamental freedoms, including the right to life, liberty and security of person.'

. . .The right to peace has been primarily discussed as an individual right, but there is general agreement that any such right necessarily has both individual and collective aspects; as in the case of the right to development, these aspects reinforce one another and are not mutually exclusive. . . .

Undoubtedly, if mankind wants to promote human rights and social and economic progress, it must secure peace on earth. Recognition of a right to peace—or, preferably, a right to live in peace, both individual and collective—is a step in the right direction.

4. Other . . . rights

The African Charter proclaims: 'All peoples shall have the right to a general satisfactory environment favourable to their development.' Similarly, a UNESCO colloquium on new human rights, held in Mexico City in 1980, discussed 'the right to a healthy and ecologically balanced environment.' This idea may be traced to the following basic principle of the 1972 Stockholm Declaration on the Human Environment: 'Man has the fundamental right to freedom, equality and adequate conditions of life, in an environment of a quality that permits a life of dignity and well-being, and he bears a solemn responsibility to protect and improve the environment for present and future generations. . . .' This principle can be traced to an even more explicit proposal by the United States: 'Every human being has a right to a healthful and safe environment, including air, water and earth, and to food and other material necessities, all of which should be sufficiently free from contamination and other elements which detract from the health or well-being of man.'

Issues Raised by the Recognition of Collective Rights

. . . The new group of human rights has been given a variety of names: the third generation of human rights; rights of solidarity; collective rights, or rights of every human being and of all human beings taken collectively; synthetic rights; consolidated rights; communal rights; rights of the peoples, or populist or popular rights; joint rights of individuals and other groups, or rights exercised by individuals separately and jointly; and new rights or new dimensions of existing rights. Without delving into semantics, it is obvious that each phrase has, or could have, different connotations and consequences. For example, the author of the phrase 'third generation of human rights,' Karel Vasak of UNESCO, views these rights as 'infusing the human dimension into areas where it has all too often been missing having been left to the

---

10 U.N. Commission on Human Rights, Res. 5 (XXXII), 60 U.N. ESCOR Supp. (No. 3), at 62, U.N. Doc. E/5768 (E/CN.4/1213 (1976).

State or States.'[11] Such rights can be realized only 'through the concerted efforts of all the actors on the social scene: the individual, the State, public and private bodies, and the international community.' Vasak also has pointed out that the first two generations of human rights were designed to achieve the first two of the three guiding principles of the French Revolution—*liberté* and *égalité*—while the third generation is predicated on brotherhood—*fraternité*. According to Vasak, the new rights, even more than the rights belonging to the first two categories, are based on the sense of solidarity, without which the chief concerns of the world community, such as peace, development and environment, cannot be realized.The very terminology used, especially the word 'generation,' has created some problems. To many persons, the word connotes a succeeding generation replacing on older one, rather than generations existing convivially vivially together. Some of the hostility to the economic, social, and cultural rights can be traced to insistence by several proponents that these new rights should have precedence over the old ones, that they were more important than the old rights they supposedly replaced, and that the old rights would have to wait in line until the basic needs represented by the new rights had been satisfied properly. Much time passed before the two categories—civil and political rights on the one hand, and economic, social, and cultural rights on the other hand—were considered to be interdependent and complementary: achievement of the rights in either category can be accomplished only with the help of the rights in the other category, and, similarly, failure in one area is likely to bring deterioration in the other. The same problem arises now regarding the third category of rights. Proponents claim that if the new rights are not soon achieved, our planet will become uninhabitable; there will be no human rights or even human beings about which to worry. Opponents argue that humanity has survived for many centuries without the new rights, that these rights are not likely to be implemented in any reasonable way in the foreseeable future, and that these new rights merely cause confusion because they are vague and exaggerated in scope.

It has also been said that claims for new rights distort the meaning of human rights 'by pretending that all objects of human desire are 'rights' which can be had, if not for the asking then at least for the demanding,' especially if one talks of such 'rights' as rights 'to a happy childhood, to self-fulfillment, to development.' Finally, some dissenters argue that as long as the law of human rights is in turmoil, states cannot be expected to agree on implementation measures and, furthermore, that those states that want to avoid the strengthening of implementation measures might be inclined, as a diversion to press for drastic changes in and additions to the law.

Conclusion

... By 1968, the Teheran International Conference on Human Rights had already stated in its Declaration that

> [s]ince human rights and fundamental freedoms are indivisible, the full realization of civil and political rights without the enjoyment of economic, social and cultural rights, is impossible. The achievement of lasting progress in the implementation of

---

11 Lecture by Karel Vasak, Tenth Study Session of the International Institute of Human Rights (July 1979), quoted by S. Marks, Emerging Human Rights: A New Generation for the 1980s? 33 RUTGERS L. REV. 435 (1981), at 441. [The concept of 'generations of human rights' has continued to prove controversial. Ed.]

human rights is dependent on sound and effective national and international policies of economic development.

In a similar spirit the crucial 1977 General Assembly Resolution 32/130 on alternative approaches to the improvement of United Nations effectiveness in promoting human rights noted, *inter alia*:

> (a) All human rights and fundamental freedoms are indivisible and interdependent; equal attention and urgent consideration should be given to the implementation, promotion and protection of both civil and political, and economic, social and cultural rights; . . .

> (d) Consequently, human rights questions should be examined globally, taking into account both the overall context of the various societies in which they present themselves, as well as the need for the promotion of the full dignity of the human person and the development and well-being of the society. . . .

. . . Like the economic, social, and cultural rights, the new rights, even if not immediately attainable, establish new goals that can be achieved progressively, by one laborious step after another. They are vast and overwhelming, but so are our problems. The damage to humanity that might be inflicted by a nuclear war or an environmental catastrophe is almost beyond comprehension; we need to grasp any tool that is available to stem an engulfing tide that is of horrifying proportions. . . . We are in a desperate situation; we need to be brave. As Virgil said, *audentes fortuna juvat*: fortune helps the daring.

---

2. The History and Place of Human Rights in Regional Organizations

The United Nations Charter and the Universal Declaration of Human Rights established a basic framework of human rights law at the global level. Subsequently, states in various geopolitical regions of the world, sharing a common history and values, found it useful to go further and develop regional norms and institutions to guarantee human rights.

A human rights system can be said to consist of (1) a list or lists of internationally-guaranteed human rights and corresponding state duties, (2) permanent institutions, and (3) compliance or enforcement procedures. So defined, regional human rights systems exist in Europe, the Americas and Africa. The Arab League has a nascent system based on the 1994 Arab Charter for Human Rights, which the League revised in 2004. In recent years, NGOs supported by the United Nations have sought to create a regional system or systems within the Asia-Pacific region, as discussed in Chapter VII.

The existing systems have experienced important changes in membership and confronted new issues in the past decade; in response they have adopted new normative instruments and procedures. In this section we look at the creation and evolution of regional organizations and the role that concern for human rights plays within them.

**Dinah Shelton, *The Promise of Regional Human Rights Systems in* THE FU-
TURE OF HUMAN RIGHTS** (B. Weston & S. Marks, eds., Transnational Press, 2000)
(revised and updated, some footnotes omitted).

. . . [R]egional systems are a product of the global concern with human rights that
emerged at the end of the Second World War. Given the widespread movement for
human rights, it should not be surprising that regional organizations being created
or reformed after the War should have added human rights to their agendas. All
of them drew inspiration from the human rights provisions of the United Nations
Charter and the Universal Declaration of Human Rights.

. . . [Different] historical and political factors encouraged each region to focus
on human rights issues. The Americas had a tradition of regional approaches to
international issues, including human rights, growing out of regional solidarity developed during the movements for independence. Pan American Conferences had
taken action on several human rights matters well before the creation of the United
Nations. In addition, as early as 1907 some states in the region created the Central
American Court of Justice. The court had jurisdiction over cases of "denial of justice" between a government and a national of another state, if the cases were of an
international character or concerned alleged violations of a treaty or convention.
This history of concern led the Organization of American States to refer to human
rights in its Charter and to adopt the Inter-American Declaration on the Rights and
Duties of Man about seven months before the United Nations approved the Universal Declaration of Human Rights.

Europe had been the theater of the greatest atrocities of the Second World War
and felt compelled to press for international human rights guarantees as part of
European reconstruction. Faith in western European traditions of democracy, the
rule of law and individual rights inspired belief that a regional system could be successful in avoiding future conflict and in stemming post-war revolutionary impulses
supported by the Soviet Union.

Somewhat later, African states emerged from colonization as self-determination
became a recognized part of the human rights agenda; continued struggles for national cohesion as well as human rights abuses in South Africa encouraged regional
action in Africa. The United Nations had also abandoned its earlier opposition to
the creation of regional human rights system and actively supported the creation of
a system in Africa. . . .

A[nother] impulse to regionalism came from frustration at the long-stalled efforts of the United Nations to conclude a human rights treaty to complete the international bill of rights. Indeed, it took nearly two decades to finalize and adopt
the two UN Covenants. During the process, it became clear that the compliance
mechanisms at the global level would not be strong and any judicial procedures to
enforce human rights would have to be on the regional level. As a result, beginning
with Europe, regional systems focused on the creation of procedures of redress,
establishing control machinery to supervise the implementation and enforcement
of the guaranteed rights. The functioning European and Inter-American courts are
one of the great contributions to human rights by regional systems. The June 8, 1998

protocol to the African Charter, creating a court in the African system, . . . add[s] to the regional protections.

Thus, regional systems have elements of uniformity and diversity in their origins. All of them began as the global human rights system was developing and they were inspired by the agreed universal norms. At the same time, each region had its own issues and concerns. As the systems have evolved, the universal framework within which they began and their own interactions have exercised a strong influence. . . . Each uses the jurisprudence of the other systems and amends or strengthens its procedures in reference to the experience of the others.

───────────────

The following materials examine the place of human rights within each regional system and the consequent obligations of the member states and those associated with each organization. Compare the provisions of each organization's founding statute: How much similarity or diversity is there in the origins and purposes of the regional organizations? How strong is their concern for human rights as reflected in their constituting instrument? What does the European Court of Human Rights mean when it calls the European Convention on Human Rights the "constitutional order" of Europe?

A. The Council of Europe

The European system began when ten Western European states signed the Statute of the Council of Europe (COE) on May 5, 1949.[12] The COE has since expanded to include Central and Eastern European countries, bringing the total membership to forty-six. The COE Statute articulates the values, principles and aims of the organization, including the importance of respect for human rights.

Statute of the Council of Europe

Preamble

. . .

Convinced that the pursuit of peace based upon justice and international cooperation is vital for the preservation of human society and civilization;

Reaffirming their devotion to the spiritual and moral values which are the common heritage of their peoples and the true source of individual freedom, political liberty and the rule of law, principles which form the basis of all genuine democracy;

Believing that, for the maintenance and further realization of these ideals and in the interests of economic and social progress, there is a need of a closer unity between all like-minded countries of Europe;

───────────────

[12] The original members were Belgium, Denmark, France, Ireland, Italy, Luxembourg, Netherlands, Norway, Sweden and the United Kingdom.

Considering that, to respond to this need and to the expressed aspirations of their peoples in this regard, it is necessary forthwith to create an organization which will bring European States into closer association, . . .

Article 1

a The aim of the Council of Europe is to achieve a greater unity between its members for the purpose of safeguarding and realizing the ideals and principles which are their common heritage and facilitating their economic and social progress.

b This aim shall be pursued through the organs of the Council by discussion of questions of common concern and by agreements and common action in economic, social, cultural, scientific, legal and administrative matters and in the maintenance and further realization of human rights and fundamental freedoms. . . .

Article 3

Every member of the Council of Europe must accept the principles of the rule of law and of the enjoyment by all persons within its jurisdiction of human rights and fundamental freedoms, and collaborate sincerely and effectively in the realisation of the aim of the Council as specified in Chapter I.

Given the limited number of original parties and the context in which the treaty was adopted, there was a common vision about the organization deriving from the constitutional and cultural traditions of the founding states. This original vision is described in the following extract.

Peter Leuprecht, *Innovations in the European System of Human Rights Protection: Is Enlargement Compatible with Reinforcement?* 8 TRANSNAT'L L. & CONTEMP. PROBS. 313–317 (1998).

The Council, founded in 1949, was the first European organization to be established after World War II. Its philosophical and political roots go back to the fight and resistance against Nazism and Fascism; the horrors and crimes they had brought about should not be allowed to recur. "Never again" was the motto of the pioneers of post-war European unification and of the founding fathers of the Council of Europe. They were determined to build a new, united Europe on solid foundations, on a set of strong shared values and principles, those of pluralist democracy, the rule of law, and human rights, and the Council of Europe was to be the incarnation and the guardian of these fundamental and interconnected values and principles. Under its founding treaty, signed in London on May 5, 1949, respect for, and compliance with, these values and principles was to be both the chief condition for admission of a country to the Council and the main and lasting obligation of all its members.

Over the years, the Council of Europe has set up a system of human rights protection which, in spite of certain weaknesses and shortcomings, can be regarded as the most advanced international human rights structure in the world today. Post-war Europe has gone particularly far in the internationalization of human rights. This worldwide phenomenon, inaugurated by the 1948 Universal Declaration of Human Rights, owes a great deal to Europe—not to Europe's virtue, but to its past failure and responsibility, to the monstrous crimes of which it was the theater under totalitarian, Nazi and Fascist regimes, to this explosion of barbarism at the very heart of the European continent, which believed itself so civilized. Bitter experience impressed upon Europeans that the state can fail in its role as the custodian of human rights and become an instrument of oppression, that it can be not only the protector, but also the gravedigger of human rights. In the interest of the defense of these rights, it was felt necessary to give independent international bodies a watching brief over state behavior.

The first expression of the new Europe's commitment to the international protection of human rights was the European Convention on Human Rights (ECHR), signed in Rome on November 4, 1950. For the then twelve signatory governments, it represented "the first steps for the collective enforcement of certain of the rights stated in the Universal Declaration." The ECHR was indeed the first international treaty to translate principles proclaimed in the Universal Declaration into legally binding obligations.

The ECHR, though a regional treaty, is firmly based on the principle of the universality of human rights; it does not guarantee the rights of Europeans, but sets up a European regional system for the protection of universal human rights. In accordance with Article 1, "the High Contracting Parties shall secure to everyone within their jurisdiction the rights and freedoms" enshrined in the Convention. It is significant that a considerable number of individual complaints emanate from persons who are not nationals of the contracting states and who seek, often successfully, the protection of the ECHR and its control machinery.

The wording of the Preamble to the ECHR shows, however, that the ECHR was not seen by its authors to be the last word in the field of human rights protection; a kind of final codification of those rights. The ECHR's catalogue of rights is an open one which, over the years, has been enriched by several additional protocols. In this area, the Council of Europe's approach has been, and must remain, dynamic, in line with Article 1 of its Statute, which refers to the "maintenance and further realization of human rights and fundamental freedoms."

. . . .

The importance of the ECHR lies not only in the breadth of the rights it covers, but also, and particularly, in the supranational control machinery it has set up to investigate and remedy alleged violations and ensure compliance with the obligations it imposes. It has been kept under constant review, with the aim of enhancing the protection it affords, by improving the existing procedures.

The Convention and its machinery are, of course, not designed to take the place of national systems for the protection of human rights. Their purpose is, rather, to provide a subsidiary international guarantee, supplementing the right of redress in individual states. Since the ECHR has been incorporated in the domestic law of nearly all of its contracting states, any person can, in principle, invoke its provisions directly in applying or appealing to a national court or authority in any of those states.

. . . .

The main criterion for measuring the success of a human rights system is whether it effectively helps the people. The ECHR system has certainly done so. It has made it possible not only to put a great number of individual situations straight, but to remedy general situations, laws, and practices which were not in line with the requirements of the Convention. It prevents and remedies human rights violations. It is also revealing to see who turns to the Strasbourg institutions; many of the applicants are poor, destitute, exposed, and vulnerable, and therefore in greatest need of protection of their fundamental rights. The ECHR system is not a luxury for rich people. There are no economic or financial obstacles to access to the Strasbourg bodies; a system of legal aid is provided by the budget of the Council of Europe.

As the European Commission and Court of Human Rights have stated in no uncertain terms, the ECHR has become a constitutional instrument of European public order. In the words of its late President, Rolv Ryssdall, the Court has become "a quasi-constitutional court for the whole of Europe." The Strasbourg case law has had far-reaching and highly positive effects on the legal systems and the social reality in the contracting states. Both the Court and the Commission command a high degree of authority. Although it is in the first place the duty of domestic courts and authorities to apply the ECHR, the Commission and Court have become "'masters' of their treaty" and are recognized as such. A fruitful dialogue has developed between the Strasbourg institutions and domestic courts whose respective case law mutually support and enrich each other.

The end of the Cold War enabled Central and Eastern European nations to join the Council of Europe after declaring their acceptance of the principles spelled out in Article 3 of the Council's Statute. Present membership in the Council is *de facto* conditioned upon adherence to the European Convention on Human Rights (ECHR, 1950) and its Protocols. As set forth in the Statute of the Council of Europe, the Committee of Ministers[13] has the authority to invite European States to become members of the Council of Europe (Statute, Articles 4, 5 and 6). The Committee may also suspend or terminate membership. When the Committee of Ministers receives an official application for membership, it consults the Parliamentary Assembly[14] pursuant to Statutory Resolution (51)30. The Parliamentary Assembly examines whether the candidate fulfils all the necessary requirements, in particular those spelled out in Article 3 of the Statute. This is done by an on-site visit by parliamentary committees and also by fact-finding missions by experts. The Assembly may seek specific commitments by the state to undertake reforms and improvements in its domestic laws and practices. If the state is admitted to membership, fulfillment of these commitments is monitored by the Assembly.

The opinion of the Assembly is published and transmitted to the Committee of Ministers. If the Committee, based on the Assembly's opinion, decides that a State can be admitted, it adopts a resolution inviting that State to become a member.

---

13   The Committee of Ministers (COM) is composed of the Foreign Affairs Ministers of all the member states, or their permanent diplomatic representatives.

14   The Parliamentary Assembly of the Council of Europe (PACE) is a grouping of 630 members (315 representatives and 315 substitutes) from the 46 national parliaments.

The invitation specifies the number of seats that the State will have in the Assembly as well as its contribution to the budget (Statute, Article 6). Once invited, a State becomes a member by depositing an instrument of accession with the Secretary General. From this point on, the Parliamentary Assembly monitors the commitments made as a condition of membership, while the Court hears cases asserting that a state has failed to live up to its legal obligations deriving from the ECHR. The Committee of Ministers enforces these judgments. See the note on the Greek Case, *infra* p. 30.

The legal criteria and some of the problems that have arisen with new applications for membership are discussed in the following materials. Before reading them, it will be useful to review the provisions of the Statute of the Council of Europe that govern membership, to understand the objections to admitting Belarus. Consider along with the reading: What makes a state seek membership in the Council of Europe? Are the reasons sufficiently strong to make the Council's voice effective in pressing for the rule of law and respect for human rights? Does the Parliamentary Assembly seek more pressure on Belarus than the Committee of Ministers is willing to exert? How far can the Council of Europe legally press Belarus for changes in its political and legal system? How do the views of the representatives of Poland and the Ukraine differ on the issue? Does a state seeking membership retain much exclusive domestic jurisdiction over its governance?

i. Applicants for Membership: The Case of Belarus

The question of membership for Belarus first came on the agenda of the COE Parliamentary Assembly in September 1992, when the Assembly decided to grant the Belarus Parliament special guest status. The Belarus authorities submitted an application for membership on March 12, 1993. In April 1993 the Committee of Ministers forwarded this application to the Parliamentary Assembly for its opinion.

On November 7, 1996, in response to Belarus President Lukashenko's proposals for constitutional change, the Parliamentary Assembly's Standing Committee adopted Resolution 1102 (1996) on Belarus. This resolution called for "the organization of a round table of all interested parties and institutions to provide an opportunity for productive political dialogue and a more consensual approach to constitutional reform."

After a November 24, 1996 referendum, the Bureau of the Assembly suspended the Belarus Parliament's special guest status on January 13, 1997. The President of the Assembly stated that the new Constitution was illegal and that the way in which the new Parliament had been set up deprived it of democratic legitimacy. The Assembly nonetheless decided to keep the channels of contact open and to closely follow developments in that country. In January 2000, in Recommendation 1441, the Assembly considered that the political evolution in Belarus continued to preclude a change in its relations with the Council of Europe. In November 2001, the Parliamentary Assembly decided to be present during the presidential elections, together with other international observers. The conclusions of the delegation stated that although the elections process "failed to meet the standards of the Council of Europe, some positive tendencies were observed such as the emergence of civil society." The delegation also agreed that the isolation policy of the prior ten years had "proved not to be effective."

In June 2002, an Ad Hoc Committee of the Assembly's Bureau traveled to Minsk to discuss political developments. In 2004, the Parliamentary Assembly adopted two recommendations to the Committee of Ministers. In 2006, the Parliamentary Assembly and other international observers monitored the presidential election in Belarus.

Parliamentary Assembly, *Situation in Belarus*, Doc. 9543, 13 September 2002 Report, Political Affairs Committee, Rapporteur: Mr. Wolfgang Behrendt, Germany, Socialist Group.

Despite some progress, Belarus shows severe democratic deficits and it does not yet meet the Council of Europe's relevant standards. The electoral process is imperfect, human rights violations continue, civil society remains embryonic, the independence of the judiciary is doubtful, local government is underdeveloped and Parliament has limited powers.

The Assembly is seriously concerned, in particular, about the lack of progress regarding the cases of missing people, as well as attacks on freedom of expression and of the media. It notes, however, that a new awareness seems to develop in Belarus, in particular in parliamentary circles, on the question of the abolition of the death penalty.

For the time being, a discussion neither on full membership of Belarus in the Council of Europe nor on the restoration of Special Guest Status in the Assembly can be put on the agenda. However, depending on future developments regarding the competences of the Belarussian Parliament and its commitment to fostering democratic development in Belarus, the Bureau may reconsider the restoration of Special Guest Status of the Parliament of Belarus.

Co-operation between the Council of Europe and Belarus should continue and develop, in particular at the parliamentary level, in order to promote democratic reforms in the country through political dialogue and by the means of the Organisation's specific instruments. . . .

IV. Main indicators for fulfillment of Council of Europe standards

Death penalty

15. The [Belarus] Parliament organized, on 30 May 2002 in Minsk, a hearing on 'Legal and political problems concerning the abolition of the death penalty in Belarus'. Mr. Stankevic (Lithuania, LDR) represented the Parliamentary Assembly at this hearing. . . .

18. The Ad Hoc Committee welcomed the efforts of the Parliament to open a public discussion on the abolition of the death penalty. It stressed that, on this issue, parliamentarians must lead, not follow, the public opinion and encouraged the Parliament to call for a moratorium on the death penalty. During the seminar in Minsk, jointly organized by the Parliament and the Ad Hoc Committee, several members of the Belarus Parliament had a rather positive approach to the question. The rep-

resentatives of the opposition, at the meeting with the Council of the Opposition parties, declared that they were against the death penalty.

Freedom of the media

19. The independent media is still subject to pressure and harassment from the authorities. The new draft media law has been transferred to the parliament but was not yet submitted to the expertise of the Council of Europe as requested by the Committee on Culture and Education of the Parliamentary Assembly, following a hearing on the situation of the media in Belarus on 24 January 2002. The main problems which the press would seem to be exposed to are: direct censorship (especially during the election campaign), seizure of equipment, massive inspections, interference with the editorial independence and, above all, criminal charges and reprimand (closure of the newspaper after two reprimands).

. . . .

24. In a Resolution adopted on 2 July 2002, on the 'Freedom of the Press in Belarus', the EP expressed "its deep concern at the persistent lack of freedom" and urged the Belarus authorities "to stop their harassment of independent newspapers" and called on the President and the government "to amend legislation on the mass media in the light of international standards".

Freedom of association

25. There are still good reasons for concern about restrictions of the freedom of assembly and association. On Sunday, 24 March 2002, approximately 600 people gathered in Minsk to celebrate the 84th anniversary of the establishment of the Belarus National Republic in 1918. This Freedom Day demonstration was organized by some opposition parties (BPF, United Civil Party, Charter 97) and some other groups. Police carried out 59 arrests. On 19 April, 3000 people in Minsk participated in a protest march called "You cannot live like this" in reaction to current human rights violations. It was violently dispersed by special police units and more than 100 people were arrested. Most of them face fines and up to 15-day prison sentences. People arrested during the above-mentioned and other pro-democracy rallies included opposition leaders such as Mrs. Lyudmila Graznova and Mr. Nikolai Statkevitch.

Missing people

26. The lack of progress regarding the cases of the politicians and a journalist, Mr. Zavadski, who have disappeared is disappointing. Despite assurances by the authorities about the smooth running of investigations, there is, at present, no reliable information. The impunity of the perpetrators may lead to new disappearances. The disappearance, on 19 January 2002, of Mr. Yuras Korban, 24 years old, Deputy Chairman of the Belarus Popular Front Adrazhenne and Head of the Centre for Civic Initiatives, is the most recent example.

27. The Ad Hoc Committee and myself, as Rapporteur, give our full support to the initiative for an independent committee to be set up by the Parliamentary Assembly in order to help clarify the circumstances of these disappearances. The Committee on Legal Affairs and Human Rights has now decided to move forward with this proposal and set up an Ad Hoc Committee. It would be most appropriate

if the parliamentarians were helped in this undertaking by high level professional expertise.

Repression of opponents—Bandazhevski case

28. In comparison to a few years ago, when I first drew the attention of the Parliamentary Assembly to the persecution of the opponents of the regime in my first report, the situation has improved slightly. International pressure combined with the eagerness of the regime to improve its image have led to the release of some known figures or to the review of their cases on rare occasions, as for instance Mr. Vladimir Koudinov and Mr. Andrei Klimov. At the same time, other critical minds are being arrested and given disproportionate prison sentences, such as Professor Iury Bandazhevski, founder and director of the Gomel medical institute and a scientist of international renown (specialist in medical research on nuclear radioactivity). . . .

V. Conclusions

. . . .

33. Under these circumstances, and having scrupulously examined past Parliamentary Assembly texts and decisions, I am unfortunately not in a position to recommend the restoration of special guest status of the Belarus Parliament in the Parliamentary Assembly. The situation can, of course, change in the course of the autumn, when the National Assembly restarts its legislative activity and hopefully adopts a number of laws which can convince us.

Parliamentary Assembly, *Situation in Belarus*, Doc. 9543, Report of the Debate of 26 September 2002 at 10 A.M.

Mr. SHYBKO (Ukraine).—I am a member of the Ukrainian opposition—the opposition to the authoritarian regime of President Kuchma. So I, as an insider, know all too well how much international organizations, primarily the Council of Europe, can help in the development of democracy, the rule of law and human rights. I can say with gratitude that your assistance has been vital for us, and we feel its importance today, with all the events taking place in Ukraine.

Can we take this assistance away from the people of Belarus? At the latest presidential elections the authorities deceived the people, but can we deprive them of our help? I do not think so. It is a paradox that the country at the very centre of Europe feels isolated. It is another paradox that the European states, whether they want it or not, have reduced their influence in Belarus.

Membership in the Council of Europe could be beneficial for Belarus in several ways. First, representatives of the Council of Europe could be inside the country, which would make it much more difficult for the authorities to limit their presence or ban them. Second, one could distribute information on the principles of democracy. Today access to this information in Belarus is quite limited. Third, we could support Belarus citizens in their efforts to develop democracy.

After all, the Council of Europe can review the implementation of the country's commitments at any time, and this can also be a form of influence.

Mr. MARKOWSKI (Poland).—Belarus is Poland's nearest neighbour. We have a common history and our political situation in the twentieth century was similar. Now we are on our way towards the European Union and we are members of NATO. However, the political and economic situation in Belarus is not stable. The economic situation there is like it was fifty years ago in the Soviet Union. Belarus is not even on the way to being a real free market. In Belarus there is no economic growth, and we cannot see any signs of changes. People earn US$15 to US$20 a month. It is a real tragedy for the whole nation.

The opposition has no rights. Many politicians were captured and the Belarussian courts did nothing. Investigations are always closed, without any results. Victor Gancziar, vice-speaker of the Belarussian Parliament; Jurij Zacharenko, ex-Ministry; Krasucki, who sponsored opposition; Dymitri Zawadzki, a journalist; and a few weeks ago, Jkaras Korba, a young politician from the countryside—as you see, their names are very well known. We have no idea how many nameless people were captured. All those people were fighting with the Lukaszenko regime. In Belarus there can be only one politician. He is the president and a "father of the whole nation". In fact, he is parliament, government and a main court.

Belarussian courts cannot be real courts because they are not independent. All independent newspapers were closed. "Pagonia" journalists are without work, without the necessary conditions for life. Some of them are in prison. There is one policeman for every sixty-five people. Belarus should be one of the world safest countries, but police and the secret service are not used to serving the people and their country. They are only used to fighting any opposition.

We are talking today about human rights in Belarus. We can use one sentence: it is enough. There are no human rights in Belarus. So far, Belarus is not a democratic and independent country. So far, there are not any rights. Belarus is a large country, the future neighbour of the European Union, a country with traditions, with a big population. Those people do not need a dictator in the form of a person or another country that wants to achieve its political interests. That is why international authorities have to do their best to achieve real independence in Belarus.

———————

Parliamentary Assembly, Resolution 1306 (2002), *Situation in Belarus,* adopted 27 September 2002.

1. The Parliamentary Assembly recalls that the question of Belarus has been on its agenda since September 1992. The Special Guest status granted to the Parliament of Belarus was suspended in January 1997. The Assembly, however, decided at that time to keep the channels of contact open with all the political forces in Belarus and to follow developments closely in that country. In January 2000, in its Recommendation 1441 on the situation in Belarus, the Assembly considered that political progress in the country was not yet of a nature to allow a change in relations with the Council of Europe.

2. The Assembly has since continued to do its best to maintain dialogue with Belarus. Isolating the country was not considered a good policy and the Assembly has

carefully avoided applying double standards in its evaluation of the situation in Belarus. The Council of Europe standards on pluralist democracy and the protection of human rights and individual freedoms have constituted the principle yardstick in its evaluation.

3. Today, despite some progress in a number of areas, the democratisation process in Belarus appears to be stagnant. Moreover, relations between Belarus and the international community remain strained. A key example is the tension between Belarus and the Organisation for Security and Co-operation in Europe (OSCE) due to a crisis over the mandate of the OSCE Advisory and Monitoring Group (AMG), which culminated in the refusal by the Belarusian authorities to issue visas to and to accredit the AMG officials. The Ad hoc Committee on Belarus of the Bureau of the Assembly expressed its extreme concern about the situation after its visit to the country in June 2002.

4. The Assembly is seriously concerned about the lack of progress made in clarifying the cases of missing people. Despite assurances from the Belarusian authorities about ongoing investigations into their cases, no reliable information, let alone any concrete results, are available at present. The Assembly encourages the setting up by its Committee on Legal Affairs and Human Rights of an ad hoc sub-committee in order to help clarify the circumstances of these disappearances, and appeals to the Belarusian authorities to provide this ad hoc sub-committee with all necessary information.

5. Recent developments in Belarus have also given rise to growing concern regarding freedom of expression and of the media. The independent media continue to be subject to increasing pressure and harassment from the Belarusian authorities. The recent convictions of journalists for their opinions are unacceptable. As regards the audiovisual media, the creation of a second semi-independent television channel has not yet delivered the results expected by the public. The new draft law on the media has not yet been adopted by the Parliament, and the proposals made by the Assembly to the authorities to submit the draft law to the expertise of the Council of Europe has not been followed up.

6. The Assembly notes with satisfaction the release from prison of Mr. Andrei Klimov, prominent businessman and opposition politician, in March 2002, and urges the authorities to reconsider other cases of imprisonment on political grounds, including those relating to sentenced journalists.

7. Having welcomed the earlier release from custody of Mr. Mikhail Chigir, former Prime Minister of Belarus, in its Resolution 1441 (2000), the Assembly notes with concern that Mr. Chigir was sentenced in July 2002 by a district court in Minsk to a suspended prison sentence of three years with the confiscation of his property. The Assembly continues to be worried about the fairness of Mr. Chigir's trial, as well as the treatment of political opponents by state authorities in general. It also expresses its concern regarding the situation of independent trade unions.

8. The Assembly notes that a new awareness seems to be developing in Belarus, in particular in parliamentary circles, on the question of the abolition of the death penalty. It welcomes the hearing on this issue organized by the Parliament of Belarus in May 2002 and notes the recommendations addressed by the parliament to

the government on the possibility of a step-by-step approach from a moratorium regarding the death penalty to its eventual abolition, with the exception of some specific grave crimes.

9. At present, Belarus shows severe democratic deficits and it does not yet meet the Council of Europe's relevant standards. The electoral process is imperfect, human rights violations continue, civil society remains embryonic, the independence of the judiciary is doubtful, local government is underdeveloped and, last but not least, parliament has limited powers. Although there is now a new awareness among a group of parliamentarians as to an increase in parliamentary competences, relations between the regime and foreign powers, the European Union and other international organisations remain tense.

10. Against this background, the Assembly considers that for the time being a discussion on full membership of Belarus in the Council of Europe cannot be put on the agenda. However, depending on future developments regarding the competences of the Belarusian Parliament and its commitment to fostering democratic development in Belarus, the Bureau of the Assembly may reconsider the restoration of Special Guest status of the Parliament of Belarus with the Assembly.

11. In the meantime, co-operation between the Council of Europe and Belarus should continue and develop in specific areas such as parliamentary co-operation in the form of dialogue and the organisation of joint seminars on specific topics; co-operation programmes targeted at local elected representatives especially regarding policy issues on education, employment and social security; co-operation with the Venice Commission with a view to improving concepts of governance; co-operation projects for developing civil society; legislative assistance with the laws on the media, religion, the ombudsman and defamation, and also training programmes for journalists. In this regard the Assembly also draws the attention of member states to the importance of bilateral contacts at parliamentary level between member states and Belarus.

12. The Assembly also encourages the Council of Europe's Commissioner for Human Rights to pay particular attention to the situation in Belarus with a view to fostering respect for human rights in that country.

—————————

In 2004, the Parliamentary Assembly adopted two Recommendations, 1657 (2004), and 1658 (2004) concerning Belarus. The first recommendation related to disappeared persons and recommended that the Committee of Ministers consider suspending the participation of Belarus in various Council of Europe agreements and activities, as well as any contacts between the Council of Europe and the Belarusian government on a political level, until "sufficient progress" has been made in investigating, prosecuting and punishing those responsible for the involuntary disappearances of persons in the country. The second text recommended that the Committee of Ministers take into account persecution of the press in Belarus "when deciding on action" concerning the state. The Committee of Ministers sent the following official reply to the Parliamentary Assembly.

Reply from the Committee of Ministers to the Parliamentary Assembly, adopted at the 898th meeting of the Ministers' Deputies (30 September 2004)

1. The Committee of Ministers examined with great concern Parliamentary Assembly Recommendations 1657 (2004) on disappeared persons in Belarus and 1658 (2004) on the persecution of the press in the Republic of Belarus, which the Parliamentary Assembly adopted on 28 April 2004, and Resolutions 1371 (2004) and 1372 (2004) on the same subjects, adopted at the same time. The Committee of Ministers confirms that its goal is that Belarus, as an integral part of Europe and a country whose people contributed to the common European heritage, should become a fully-fledged member of the Council of Europe. In order to bring Belarus closer to the international community and to the Council of Europe, it is clear that the human rights situation must improve.

2. The Committee of Ministers agrees with the Parliamentary Assembly that there is a need for an independent inquiry into the disappearances mentioned in Resolution 1371 (2004). It considers that any allegations about involvement of senior politicians and high-ranking officials in these disappearances and in the dissimulation of the truth must be verified and perpetrators duly punished. The Chair of the Committee of Ministers will send a request in that sense to the competent Belarusian authorities. Such an inquiry should be totally independent.

3. The Committee of Ministers also endorses the emphasis which the Parliamentary Assembly places on freedom of the press and the independence of the media, as a prerequisite for the operation of any genuine democracy and one of the four criteria—along with a properly working parliament, abolition of the death penalty and respect for human rights in general—which the international community singled out as being necessary for Belarus' integration into the European family. In this connection, the Committee of Ministers encourages the measures recommended by the Parliamentary Assembly in paragraph 14 of Resolution 1372 (2004). It encourages the Belarusian authorities to take all appropriate action to implement them. The Council of Europe stands ready to provide necessary assistance in particular through the Venice Commission. It also encourages the provision of objective and impartial broadcasting programmes and print and Internet publications aimed specifically at the Belarusian public, as the Assembly suggests. In this respect, the assistance given for the last 10 years by the Council of Europe towards the development of independent media in Belarus, particularly on Internet, will be continued and, as far as possible, intensified.

4. Regarding the Assembly's proposal that the Committee of Ministers "considers suspending the participation of Belarus in various Council of Europe agreements and activities, as well as any contacts between the Council of Europe and the Belarusian Government on a political level," the Committee of Ministers recalls the following:

   – Belarus is a Party to a number of international conventions. Participation in these conventions is subject to the provisions of international law;
   – Belarus participates as an observer in certain intergovernmental activities of the Council of Europe. This participation could be considered as a useful com-

munication channel for the Belarusian authorities but should not be seen as a Council of Europe support of the present authorities' stand;
– the Council of Europe also provides assistance to civil society. This assistance should be enhanced with the perspective of a European future for the country.

5. The Committee of Ministers will continue a detailed examination of all the options available. It will bear in mind the need to persuade Belarusian society that the country can have a European future and that choosing the path of democratic and economic development followed by all the other countries in Europe is in the long term interest of the people of Belarus. In this context, the Committee of Ministers believes that contacts between the Parliamentary Assembly of the Council of Europe and the Parliament of Belarus could play an important positive role.

6. The Committee of Ministers believes that the international community—including the Council of Europe—should make every effort to bring about positive developments in Belarus. Activities planned for 2004 with NGO partners of the Council of Europe mainly concern awareness-raising of the standards of the European Convention on Human Rights. The Committee of Ministers will aim to convince the authorities to remove administrative and fiscal obstacles which threaten the proper functioning and the mere existence of the NGOs as well as at promoting cooperation between NGOs in Belarus and in neighbouring countries.

7. The Committee of Ministers stresses that the forthcoming parliamentary elections provide an opportunity for the Belarus authorities to demonstrate their willingness to move towards democracy and shared European values and to avoid repeating the shortcomings registered during the previous ballots. At the Committee of Ministers' request, the Secretary General has urged the Belarus authorities, by a letter of July 23, to conduct the elections in accordance with the Code of good practice in electoral matters adopted by the Venice Commission and endorsed by the Committee of Ministers at its 114th Ministerial Session. The Secretary General strongly encouraged them to invite representatives of the international community to observe the process of those elections. The Committee of Ministers believes that free and fair elections, including equal opportunities for all political forces during the campaign period, would indeed constitute an important first step towards reaching the benchmarks established by the international community and would help create a new climate between Belarus and the Council of Europe.

8. The Committee of Ministers remains however very concerned, following new developments that unfolded during the summer months, in particular mass arrests following street demonstrations. It urges that persons arrested while exercising their fundamental freedoms be speedily released.

Further the Committee learned that President Lukashenko has called for a referendum to be held together with the parliamentary elections on 17 October 2004 to change the constitution of Belarus to allow a president to run without limitations in future presidential elections. It recognises the right of Belarus to hold a referendum as a way to decide on its political and constitutional organisation but stresses the need to hold such a referendum in accordance with Council of Europe and OSCE standards and norms.

––––––––––––––––––

At the beginning of 2007, Belarus remained an applicant state, along with Montenegro, which applied for membership on June 6, 2006. In a speech given at the conclusion of a two-day visit to Belarus (January 18–19, 2007), the President of the Parliamentary Assembly, René van der Linden, called for fresh co-operation with Belarus in order to end its isolation. During his visit, the Assembly President met with the Speaker of the Belarus House of Representatives and the Foreign Affairs Minister. The President called for the release of all those imprisoned for allegedly political reasons, and offered dialogue with Belarus based on respect for and the implementation of Council of Europe values such as the freedom of expression, the organization of free and fair elections and the abolition of the death penalty. He also called for greater dialogue among all the political forces in the country and met with members of the opposition and representatives of civil society and NGOs. At the end of his visit, Mr. van der Linden addressed students at the Belarusian State University, and met leading religious figures.

The President proposed several steps to promote Council of Europe values in Belarus, facilitate dialogue and intensify contacts:

- To send international experts to make an independent assessment of whether alleged political prisoners in Belarus should be considered as such.
- To open a Council of Europe office in Minsk, as called for by the Parliamentary Assembly.
- To intensify exchanges between students in Belarus and other European countries, and simplify visa procedures to enable such exchanges.
- To make use of existing Council of Europe mechanisms, such as the Venice Commission, its body of independent experts in constitutional law, and the Committee for the Prevention of Torture.

Are these measures, alone or in connection with other actions, likely to have an impact on Belarus?

ii. Enforcing Obligations against Member States

Note on the Greek Case: Following a military coup d'etat in Greece in April 1967, Denmark, Norway, Sweden and the Netherlands filed two interstate applications against the Greek government, alleging violations of ECHR articles 3, 5, 6, 7, 9, 10, 11, 13 and 14. *Denmark, Norway, Sweden, Netherlands v. Greece* (App. Nos. 3321/23/67 & 3344/67), Jan 24, 1968, 11 YB EUR. CONV. HUM. RTS. (1968). The applications alleged widespread arbitrary detentions, torture, irregular trials before military courts, and press censorship. The report of the European Commission on Human Rights concluded that the Greek government had violated all of the cited rights with the exception of Article 7. The confidential report was transmitted to the Committee of Ministers, but also found its way into the press. On December 12, 1969, the same day the Committee of Ministers was to meet to decide the case and vote on a motion submitted by the Parliamentary Assembly to suspend or expel the government from the Council, Greece denounced the Convention. It later returned, following the restoration of democratic governance. Why did Greece withdraw from the Council of Europe? Does withdrawal have any consequences? For documents and materials on the case, see: 12 YB EUR. CONV. HUM. RTS. 126–

28, 130 (1969) and Committee of Ministers Res. DH(70)1, April 15, 1970; LOUIS SOHN & THOMAS BUERGENTHAL, INTERNATIONAL PROTECTION OF HUMAN RIGHTS 1059–1090 (1973).

Thus far, the Greek case is unique in the history of the Council of Europe. More common are problems that have arisen with rapid expansion of the Council's membership to include the formerly communist states of Central and Eastern Europe. In the following extract, Peter Leuprecht criticizes the rapid enlargement and suggests what must be done to ensure the continued viability of the European system. Mr. Leuprecht was an official of the Council of Europe between 1961 and 1997. From 1980 to 1993, he served as Director of Human Rights and was then elected Deputy Secretary General. He resigned from his post in 1997, after the admission of Russia, because he objected to what he viewed as a dilution of Council of Europe standards and values.

Peter Leuprecht, *Innovations in the European System of Human Rights Protection: Is Enlargement Compatible with Reinforcement?* 8 TRANSNAT'L L. & CONTEMP. PROBS. 313 at 325–333 (1998)(footnotes omitted).

Europe and the world have undergone dramatic changes in the last few years. . . . [I]t certainly is no exaggeration to say that, with the fall of communism and the ending of the cold war, 1989 marked an historical turning point. Vaclav Havel, whose personal itinerary from dissident to President of the Czech Republic symbolizes the magnitude of the change, has expressed the view that the collapse of the communist empire is an event comparable in scale to the fall of the Roman empire. However, this historic transformation is not, as some people have argued, the "end of history" or the "final victory" of the "Western system," liberalism, capitalism, or whatever. Talking about the end of history and final victories reveals an unhistorical or anti-historical way of looking at the world.

From a value-oriented perspective, the 1989 upheavals in Central and Eastern Europe seem to have signified a decisive comeback of the free and responsible human being, belonging to a democratic society and possessed of inalienable rights and dignity. . . . The aspiration to pluralist democracy, the rule of law, justice, freedom, and human rights made powerful, surging headway in Central and Eastern Europe and swept away old totalitarian regimes. But the situation of post-1989 Europe gives rise to fear as well as hope; this is a period not only of tremendous opportunity, but also of formidable threat and challenge. Europe now has a historic opportunity to overcome its anti-cultural and anti-historical division and to reconcile its geography with its history.

. . . .

Since 1989, the Council of Europe has undergone spectacular enlargement. A reunited Germany is part of the organization, whose membership has soared from twenty-three states in 1989 to forty[-six in 2007]. . . . One of the questions now is where Europe ends. This enlargement reflects, of course, a highly positive development and remarkable progress for the cause which is the Council's raison d'être. At the same time, it brings with it new challenges. The Council's role is no longer limited to the defense of pluralist democracy, the rule of law, and human rights. Its new task is to play an active role in "democracy-building" in the post-communist countries, and to this end important programs have been created and implemented, some of which are conducted jointly with the European Commission.

. . . .

B. Enlargement without Dilution?

The Council of Europe's Statute lays down precise and strict conditions for the admission of members. At the 1993 Vienna Summit, the Heads of State and Government, after having affirmed that the Council is "the preeminent European political institution capable of welcoming, on an equal footing and in permanent structures, the democracies of Europe freed from communist oppression," elaborated on the statutory requirements for accession to the Council:

> Such accession presupposes that the applicant country has brought its institutions and legal system into line with the basic principles of democracy, the rule of law and respect for human rights. The people's representatives must have been chosen by means of free and fair elections based on universal suffrage. Guaranteed freedom of expression and notably of the media, protection of national minorities and observance of the principles of international law must remain, in our view, decisive criteria for assessing any applications for membership. An undertaking to sign the European Convention on Human Rights and accept the Convention's supervisory machinery in its entirety within a short period is also fundamental. We are resolved to ensure full compliance with the commitments accepted by all member states within the Council of Europe.

The full acceptance of the ECHR has become a political condition for admission to the Council. The practice is that new members sign the ECHR on the day they formally join the organization and then proceed rapidly to ratify it. All . . . member states of the Council are now parties to the ECHR.

. . . .

Strictly speaking, admission to the Council implies that its supreme political bodies, the Parliamentary Assembly and the Committee of Ministers, consider the applicant country "willing and able" to comply with the Council's basic standards and the essential requirements of pluralist democracy, the rule of law, and respect for human rights. The idea implied in both Article 4 of the Council's Statute and in the passage of the Vienna Declaration quoted above is that a country must have put its house in order before being admitted to the Council. In reality, of course, transition from a totalitarian to a democratic regime is a long and arduous undertaking; pluralist democracy, the rule of law, and respect for human rights are not achieved overnight. It therefore may be difficult to judge whether the process of transition is sufficiently advanced and whether and when admission to the Council can be justified. This said, intellectual honesty requires acknowledging that some of the countries admitted in recent years clearly did not comply with the statutory requirements at the time of accession. This is demonstrated by the fact that, to be admitted, they had to undertake specific and, in certain cases, numerous and far-reaching commitments, referred to explicitly in the Assembly's Opinions on the accession of new members, and often referred to by the Committee of Ministers in its Resolutions inviting states to join the Council. It is not without significance that, in its Opinion on Russia's request for membership, the Parliamentary Assembly, while referring to Article 4 of the Statute, actually departs from its wording by using the future tense: "the Assembly believes that Russia—in the sense of Article 4 of the Statute—is clearly willing and will be able in the near future to fulfill the provisions for membership. . . ."

It thus is indisputable that the Council of Europe has lowered its standards for admission in recent years. This critical development probably began with the accession of Romania in October 1993, which at the time was far from fulfilling the statutory conditions (although it must be admitted that, since then, the situation in Romania has improved considerably). After the adhesion of Romania, there developed a kind of "domino effect:" following the admission of country X, it was argued that, although country Y did not comply with the statutory requirements, the situation in country Y was not really worse than in country X and that therefore, as a matter of fairness and justice, country Y should be admitted also. The two most recent admissions are telling examples of the opportunistic and unprincipled "Realpolitik" pursued by the political bodies of the Council of Europe

The Russian Federation formally applied for membership in the Council on May 7, 1992. The competent Committees of the Parliamentary Assembly gave serious consideration to the application. "Eminent lawyers" produced a detailed "Report on the conformity of the legal order of the Russian Federation with Council of Europe standards" with very clear conclusions. The report said that Russia was on the road to democracy, but that it still had a long way to go, that there was no rule of law there, and that, despite considerable progress, Russia did not (yet) comply with the principle "of the enjoyment by all persons within its jurisdiction of human rights and fundamental freedoms." The overall conclusion of the "eminent lawyers" was that Russia's legal order did not, for the time being, comply with the norms of the Council of Europe as provided for by the Statute and developed by the organs of the ECHR.

On February 2, 1995, the Parliamentary Assembly, referring to the conflict in Chechnya, condemned "the indiscriminate and disproportionate use of force by the Russian military, in particular against the civil population, which is in violation of the 1949 Geneva Conventions and their 1977 Second Protocol as well as of the OSCE Code of Conduct on Politico-Military Aspects of Security, accepted by Russia as recently as December 1994." The Assembly stated that "these actions also constitute a grave violation of the Council of Europe's most elementary human rights principles, which Russia, by requesting membership of the Organization, pledged to uphold." Considering these factors, the Assembly decided "to suspend the procedure concerning its statutory opinion on Russia's request for membership."

A year later, on January 15, 1996, notwithstanding that the war in Chechnya continued with increased intensity and atrocity, the Parliamentary Assembly recommended that the Committee of Ministers invite the Russian Federation to become a member of the Council of Europe. How does one explain this "U-turn?" The numerous "commitments and understandings" listed in the Assembly's Opinion certainly do not suffice to explain it. What factors led the Assembly to change its attitude? Before its vote, several governments, particularly of major West European countries, actively lobbied parliamentarians to obtain a favorable decision. Germany's Chancellor Kohl threw his whole weight in for the same purpose, and other West European leaders obviously did not want to be perceived as being less enthusiastic than him. One underlying motive certainly was to help President Yeltsin in his then forthcoming presidential election; and he did, of course, not fail to celebrate Russia's admission to the Council as a major success of his policies. The Russian leadership itself gave to understand that Russian accession would occur "now or never," a move of blackmail or poker that ultimately produced the desired effect.

The way in which Russia has honored its numerous commitments leaves much to be desired. One of these was "to sign within one year and ratify within three years from the time of accession Protocol No. 6 to the European Convention on Human Rights on the abolition of the death penalty . . . , and to put into place a moratorium on executions with effect from the day of accession." A year after Russia's accession, the Assembly was led to "condemn Russia for having violated her commitment to put into place a moratorium on executions" and to deplore the executions that had taken place. The Assembly had received reliable information that 53 executions had been carried out in Russia in the first half of 1996. It appears that, since then, a moratorium on executions has been put into place in the country.

. . . .

The politicians and diplomats responsible for this policy of enlargement (incoherent and unprincipled, in my judgment) are, of course, trying to justify it. One of the official arguments is that the Council pursues a policy of "enlargement without dilution, without any lowering of its standards"—an argument which clearly does not withstand scrutiny. According to another argument (in my view extremely simplistic), "it is better to include than to exclude." To include into what? Into an amorphous arrangement without principles and values? This is not what the Council of Europe was supposed to be, and it is not what Europe needs. It also is argued that by admitting countries, even if they are far from meeting the statutory requirements, one helps to promote the cause of democracy, the rule of law, and human rights in the countries concerned. With a certain irony, I have called this the policy of "therapeutic" admission. The idea of therapy cannot be lightly dismissed. Some of the countries concerned suffer from serious evils and will have to go through a long healing process, but success in therapy presupposes the consent of the "patient." Unfortunately, some of the leaders of the countries involved do not appear really willing to push through the necessary reforms and to honor their commitments.

The Council of Europe should by no means be indifferent or inactive with regard to the countries in transition; on the contrary, it has a moral duty to help them. The question is: how can it most effectively contribute to the building not of a façade or Potemkin village of democracy, but of a genuinely democratic regime and society? Much greater efforts should have been made before the accession of certain countries, when the Council could still hold out the "carrot," i.e., the certificate of democracy which membership in the organization used to confer and which the post-communist countries were so eager to obtain, not only and not principally because of its intrinsic value, but because it is regarded as a key that opens other doors, particularly those of the European Union. Unfortunately, this certificate has been devalued by its over-generous distribution.

In the new circumstances, the need for monitoring compliance with commitments undertaken has been increasingly felt—that is to say, political monitoring, in addition to the numerous supervisory mechanisms provided for by different Council of Europe conventions. Such monitoring is conducted by the two main political bodies of the Council, the Committee of Ministers and the Parliamentary Assembly. The former conducts its monitoring behind closed doors; as a rule, "offenders" do not run the risk of publicity. This is one of the major drawbacks of the system. Monitoring by the Assembly seems to have more "teeth," the system having developed over the years. In April 1997, the Assembly created a special Committee on the Honoring of Obligations and Commitments by Member States (Monitoring Committee), and its results seem relatively promising. In any event, serious monitoring is essential if the basic values and standards of the Council of Europe are not to be further diluted.

. . . .

The cause of human rights in Europe will not be helped if the ideological confrontation of the past is replaced by a hollow, deceptive consensus. It would be disastrous if the attention given the values and principles of pluralist democracy, the rule of law, and human rights were mere lip-service, an institutional ritual with no real significance.

Questions and Comments

1. Have Prof. Leuprecht's concerns and warnings been borne out in practice during the past decade? Consider the following indications:

- Russia is now the subject of more complaints to the European Court than any other member state.
- Russian politicians have criticized the Court, calling it anti-Russian and politicized.
- In December 2006, the Russian State Duma (the lower house of parliament) refused to ratify Protocol 14 to the European Convention, designed to improve operations at the Court.
- Commentators have noted that the Russian government has complied, sometimes grudgingly, with judgments issued against it by the Court for the payment of compensation and it has reformed some of its laws, although the European Parliament and Committee of Ministers complain that the pace of reform is too slow.
- Some authors are optimistic about the gradual improvement of human rights in Russia due to the influence of the European Convention, noting that Russia has effectively abolished the death penalty and that a growing body of European human rights case law is now part of Russia's own legislative framework, cited in Russian judicial opinions, and apparent in the new Criminal Procedure Code. *See*: J.D. Kahn, *Russia's 'Dictatorship of Law' and the European Court of Human Rights*, REVIEW OF CENTRAL AND EAST EUROPEAN LAW (Jan. 2004).
- An informed observer says that the ECHR "has emerged as a powerful check on the excesses of the Russian bureaucracy and failures by the country's own investigative organs and courts to follow Russia's laws." The European Court "has entered Russian popular

consciousness as a port of last resort for those seeking justice because the Russian state does bow to its judgments—albeit with some very public grumbling." Peter Finn, *Europe's Long Legal Tether on Russia*, WASHINGTON POST, Oct. 23, 2006, p. A01.

• From the institutional side, the former President of the Court has repeatedly insisted that the Court will not accept any weakening of the Convention standards or the creation of double standards for old and new member states. See: LUZIUS WILDHABER, THE EUROPEAN COURT OF HUMAN RIGHTS 1998–2006: HISTORY, ACHIEVEMENTS, REFORM 14, 64–65 (2007).

• In a dramatic incident, President Wildhaber fell critically ill of blood poisoning shortly after an October 2006 trip to Russia for a conference of constitutional lawyers and judges. After his retirement at the end of 2006 and after the poisoning of Russian agent Litvinenko by polonium in London, Wildhaber publicly speculated that the Russian government had poisoned him. The Swiss hospital that had treated him when he was "minutes from death" had destroyed his blood samples, making it impossible to determine the origin of the sudden illness. THE GUARDIAN, Jan. 31, 2007.

2. As you study the European system and its functioning in the remaining chapters, consider whether the problem is solely a Russian one or whether the European system lacks the procedures and institutions to confront gross and systematic violations? What legal options does the Council of Europe have in its relations with Russia? What options are politically feasible? Do the problems that have emerged regarding some of the former states in the Soviet Union, including Russia, shed further light on the case of Belarus?

iii. Human Rights in Observer States

The Council of Europe insists that non-member states seeking to participate in its work accept its commitment to human rights. On May 14, 1993, the Committee of Ministers, after consulting the Parliamentary Assembly, decided to grant observer status to any state wishing to co-operate with the organization and willing to accept the principles of democracy, the rule of law and respect for human rights and fundamental freedoms of all persons within its jurisdiction. Statutory Resolution (93)26. The states which are approved can appoint a permanent observer to the Council of Europe and send observers to various committees of experts and conferences of specialized ministers. Observer status gives no right to be represented on the Committee of Ministers or the Parliamentary Assembly. The Committee of Ministers may suspend or withdraw observer status, after consulting the Parliamentary Assembly.

Japan and the United States were granted observer status on January 10, 1996, pursuant to Committee of Ministers Resolution (95)37 of December 7, 1995. In recent years, the compliance of these states with European human rights norms has been raised by the Parliamentary Assembly. Consider the following resolution. Does it have legal or political significance? Compare the responses of the U.S. and Japan to the concerns expressed by the Parliamentary Assembly.

Parliamentary Assembly Res. 1349 (2003), Abolition of the Death Penalty in Council of Europe Observer States, adopted Oct. 1, 2003.

1. The Parliamentary Assembly of the Council of Europe refers to Resolution 1253 (2001) and Recommendation 1522 (2001) on the abolition of the death penalty in Council of Europe Observer states.

2. The Assembly once more reaffirms its complete opposition to capital punishment, which has no legitimate place in the penal systems of modern civilized societies. The Assembly considers that its application constitutes torture and inhuman and degrading punishment and is thus a severe violation of universally recognised human rights.

3. Under Statutory Resolution (93) 26 of the Committee of Ministers on Observer status, a state wishing to become a Council of Europe Observer has to be willing to accept the principles of democracy, the rule of law, and the enjoyment by all persons within its jurisdiction of human rights and fundamental freedoms. Japan and the United States of America (both granted Observer status in 1996) keep the death penalty on their statute books and carry out executions. For this reason, the Assembly found Japan and the United States in violation of their obligations under Statutory Resolution (93) 26 in Resolution 1253 (adopted on 25 June 2001).

4. In that resolution, the Assembly consequently required Japan and the United States to institute without delay a moratorium on executions and take the necessary steps to abolish the death penalty. At the same time, it resolved to take all necessary measures to assist Japan and the United States in their endeavours, in particular by promoting parliamentary dialogue in all forms. In Recommendation 1522, the Assembly recommended that the Committee of Ministers proceed in the same way at governmental level.

5. The Assembly has been successful in initiating a dialogue with Japanese parliamentarians, in particular with the Diet members' League for the Abolition of the Death Penalty. In May 2002, the Assembly's Committee on Legal Affairs and Human Rights, in co-operation with the league, organised a conference on Justice and Human Rights in Council of Europe Observer States, in Tokyo, which took the abolition debate to the highest levels of Japanese politics. Unfortunately, while the dialogue with Japanese parliamentarians is fruitful and ongoing, Japan has not yet abolished the death penalty and has carried out five executions since June 2001. An abolition bill, while gaining growing support, has not yet mustered the votes needed to pass the Diet.

6. In contrast, the Assembly has largely failed in its efforts to promote transatlantic parliamentary dialogue. A conference in the United States on Justice and Human Rights in Council of Europe Observer States organized by the Assembly's Committee on Legal Affairs and Human Rights in April 2003 attracted few Illinois state parliamentarians in Springfield (despite the valued support of the Illinois State Senate President and prominent abolitionist politicians), and none in Washington, D.C. The number of abolitionist American jurisdictions has remained low at thirteen, while Illinois remains the only jurisdiction applying a moratorium on executions. Since June 2001, 137 executions have been carried out in seventeen American jurisdictions, including at federal level.

7. The Assembly thus regrets having to find Japan and the United States, once more, in violation of their fundamental obligation to respect human rights under Statutory Resolution (93) 26, due to their continued application of the death penalty.

8. The Assembly thus requires Japan and the United States to make more of an effort to take the necessary steps to institute a moratorium on executions with a view to abolishing the death penalty.

9. The Assembly asks the Japanese Parliament and Government to continue and deepen its constructive dialogue with the Council of Europe on this issue. In the meantime, it reiterates its demands that the conditions on "death row" be immediately improved, that the secrecy surrounding executions be ended and that access to post-conviction and post-appeal judicial review be broadened for "death row" inmates, and supports the Japanese political and NGO movement working towards these aims and towards the establishment of a moratorium on executions.

10. The Assembly asks the United States Congress and Government, at federal and state level to enter into a more constructive dialogue with the Council of Europe on this issue. It encourages American politicians to create abolitionist "caucuses" in their respective parliamentary assemblies, and to continue to engage opponents of abolition in informed debate.

11. The Assembly supports the American political and NGO movement aimed at putting into place moratoria on executions and restricting the application of the death penalty (in particular, against juvenile defendants and foreign nationals), as well as efforts to reinforce legal guarantees and due process in these cases.

12. The Assembly thus decides to intensify its dialogue with parliamentarians from Japan with a view to encouraging rapid progress on the institution of a moratorium on executions and the abolition of the death penalty, and to continue its efforts to enter into a dialogue with parliamentarians from the United States (both state and federal) with a view to supporting them in their endeavors to institute moratoria on executions and abolish the death penalty. To this end, the Assembly will invite parliamentarians from both countries to a parliamentary conference to be held in 2004 on effective criminal justice in a human rights framework.

13. The Assembly resolves to debate the abolition of the death penalty in Council of Europe member and Observer states whenever the necessity arises, on the decision of the Bureau, and, in any case, at the latest in the year 2005.

See also Parliamentary Assembly, Rec. 1627 (2003), *Abolition of the death penalty in Council of Europe Observer States*, adopted Oct. 1, 2003, in which the Parliamentary Assembly asked the Committee of Ministers to ensure that, henceforth, Observer status with the Council of Europe be granted only to countries which have already abolished the death penalty, or which at least strictly respect a moratorium on executions. The Assembly recommended that the Committee of Ministers:

i. transmit Resolution 1349 (2003) to the governments of the countries concerned, stressing the importance that the Council of Europe attaches to the abolition of the death penalty;

ii. intensify its dialogue on the abolition of the death penalty with the governments of the countries concerned with a view to encouraging rapid progress on the issue, especially as it is becoming increasingly difficult for the Council of Europe to accept that Observer states make use of the death penalty;

iii. take effective measures to encourage compliance by Japan and the United States of America with Assembly Recommendation 1522 (2001) and Resolution 1349 (2003) on the abolition of the death penalty in Council of Europe Observer states;

iv. make it a minimum requirement for existing Council of Europe Observer states wishing to have their rights under Statutory Resolution (93) 26 extended to show their willingness to engage in a fruitful dialogue at parliamentary and governmental level with the Council of Europe on the abolition of the death penalty, if they have not yet abolished it, or put into place a moratorium on executions;

v. report to the Assembly by January 2004 on the progress, since June 2002, of their dialogue on this issue with the countries concerned.

Note on Council of Europe review of U.S. Detentions at Guantánamo Base, Secret Prisons, and Renditions. In addition to raising the issue of the death penalty, the Parliamentary Assembly has spoken out on the lawfulness of detentions by the United States at its naval base in Guantánamo, Cuba. In Resolution 1433 (2005), adopted April 26, 2005, the Assembly determined, "[o]n the basis of an extensive review of legal and factual material from . . . reliable sources, . . . that the circumstances surrounding detentions by the United States at Guantánamo Bay show unlawfulness and inconsistency with the rule of law." The resolution called on the United States Government "to ensure respect for the rule of law and human rights by remedying the situation and specifically:

i. to cease immediately all ill-treatment of Guantánamo Bay detainees;

ii. to investigate, prosecute and punish all instances of unlawful mistreatment of detainees, no matter what the status or office of the person responsible;

iii. to allow all detainees to challenge the lawfulness of their detention before a regularly constituted court competent to order their release if detention is not lawful;

iv. to release immediately all those detainees against whom there is not sufficient evidence to justify laying criminal charges;

v. to charge those suspected of criminal offences and bring them for trial before a competent, independent and impartial tribunal guaranteeing all the procedural safeguards required by international law, without delay, whilst excluding imposition of the death penalty against them;

vi. to respect its obligations under international law and the Constitution of the United States to exclude any statement established to have been made as a result of torture or other cruel, inhuman or degrading treatment or punishment from any proceedings, except against a person accused of such ill-treatment as evidence that the statement was made;

vii. to cease immediately the practice of secret detentions and to ensure full respect for the rights of any detainees currently held in secret, in particular the prohibition on torture and cruel, inhuman or degrading treatment and the right to have relatives informed of the fact of detention, to recognition as a person before the law, to judicial review of the lawfulness of detention and to release or trial without delay;

viii. to allow access to all detainees by family members, legal representatives, consular representatives and officials of international humanitarian and human rights organizations;

ix. to cease the practice of "rendition" in violation of the prohibition on *non-refoulement*;

x. not to return or transfer detainees in reliance on "diplomatic assurances" from countries known to engage in the systematic practice of torture and in all cases unless the absence of a risk of ill-treatment is firmly established;

xi. to comply fully and promptly with the recommendations of the ICRC and to avoid any actions that might have the effect of undermining its activities, reputation or standing.

The Assembly called on member states of the Council of Europe not to permit their authorities to participate or assist in the interrogation of Guantánamo Bay detainees; to refuse to comply with United States' requests for extradition of terrorist suspects liable to detention at Guantánamo Bay; to refuse to comply with United States' requests for mutual legal assistance in relation to Guantánamo Bay detainees, other than by providing exculpatory evidence, or unless in connection with legal proceedings before a regularly constituted court; and to ensure that their territory and facilities are not used in connection with practices of secret detention or rendition in possible violation of international human rights law. In Recommendation 1699 of the same day, the Assembly asked the Committee of Ministers to transmit the resolution to the United States.

The Council of Europe institutions also commissioned studies and adopted resolutions concerning secret detentions and renditions involving the United States and Council of Europe member states. In Recommendation 1754 (2006), *Alleged secret detentions and unlawful inter-state transfers of detainees involving Council of Europe member states*, the Parliamentary Assembly urged the Committee of Ministers to draft a recommendation containing "common measures to guarantee more effectively the human rights of persons suspected of terrorist offences who are captured from, detained in or transported through Council of Europe member states;" and "a set of minimum requirements for 'human rights protection clauses', for inclusion in bilateral and multilateral agreements with third parties, especially those concerning the use of military installations on the territory of Council of Europe member states." The Assembly also urgently requested the launching of an international initiative, expressly involving the United States as an observer state to the Council of Europe, to develop a common, global strategy to address terrorism. According to the Assembly, "the strategy should conform in all its elements with the fundamental principles of our common heritage in terms of democracy, human rights and respect for the rule of law." The Assembly envisaged that in instances where states are unable or unwilling to prosecute persons accused of terrorist acts, the states could bring these persons within the jurisdiction of an international court that is competent to try them: "One possibility worth considering would be to vest such a competence in the International Criminal Court, whilst renewing invitations to join this court to the United States and other countries that have not yet done so." *See also*: *Assembly debate* on 27 June 2006 (17th Sitting) and Assembly Doc. 10957, *Report of the Committee on Legal Affairs and Human Rights*, rapporteur: Mr. Dick Marty. The Committee of Ministers responded to the Assembly by stating that it would take the recommendations under advisement. Doc. 11040, *Reply from the Committee of Ministers adopted at the 974th meeting of the Ministers' Deputies* (27 September 2006).

On June 8, 2007, the rapporteur, Mr. Marty, issued his second report, which asserted that so-called "high-value" detainees were held in secret CIA detention centers in Poland and Romania between 2002 and 2005, based on a secret agreement between the US and NATO allies in October 2001 that provided the framework for the CIA to hold the detainees in Europe. The report was based in part on the cross-referenced testimonies of over 30 serving and former members of intelligence services in the US and Europe, and on a new analysis of computer "data strings" from the international flight planning system. The Parliamentary Assembly adopted Resolution 1562 (2007) in response to the report. The Resolution found that the detainees were subjected to sometimes-protracted inhuman and degrading treatment. Certain "enhanced" interrogation methods were found to fulfill the definition of torture and inhuman and degrading treatment in Article 3 of the European Convention on Human Rights and the United Nations Convention Against Torture. Furthermore, secret detention as such was said to be contrary to many international undertakings, both of the United States and of the Council of Europe member states concerned. The Resolution in paragraph 18 called upon:

18.1. the governments of all Council of Europe member states to:

18.1.1. make a full commitment that they will play no future part in allowing the transportation through their states, or the holding for any length of time, of any remaining detainees currently held at Guantánamo Bay;

18.1.2. make available to their national parliaments all relevant information held by them, including witness statements, relating to the role of their state in the practice of extraordinary rendition or the holding of prisoners in secret detention centres in their state, should they wish to conduct an inquiry;

18.2. the governments of all Council of Europe member states who did not respond to the request made by the rapporteur and the Parliamentary Assembly of the Council of Europe fully to explain their reasons for failing to co-operate;

18.3. the parliaments and judicial authorities of all Council of Europe member states to:

18.3.1. elucidate fully, by reducing to a reasonable minimum the restrictions of transparency founded on concepts of state secrecy and national security, the secret services' wrongful acts committed on their territory with regard to secret detentions and unlawful transfers of detainees; and

18.3.2. ensure that the victims of such unlawful acts are fittingly rehabilitated and compensated;

18.4. NATO to make public the additional components to the NATO authorisation of 4 October 2001 that have until now remained secret;

The U.S. continues to enjoy observer status despite its lack of response on the issue of the death penalty and its policies on detainees. The Committee of Ministers has shown no inclination to take any action. Is this further evidence supporting Peter Leuprecht's assertion that the Council of Europe is diluting its concern for human rights and the rule of law?

B. Other European Institutions

Following the creation of the Council of Europe and adoption of the European Convention on Human Rights in 1950, European states began founding and joining other regional organizations. The European Union (EU) and the Organization for Security and Cooperation in Europe (OSCE) are the two entities most directly involved with human rights. The EU is the smallest of the European regional groupings, with twenty-seven participating states, all of them also members of the Council of Europe and the OSCE. The OSCE is the largest organization and includes the United States and Canada among its fifty-six participating states, making it more of an Atlantic than a European body. In addition to their considerable difference in size, the EU and OSCE are quite unalike in structure and powers. The EU is a supranational body with legislative powers over its member states; the OSCE lacks a treaty basis and did not even become an "organization" until two decades after its participating states began meeting. These differences are explored below with a focus on the role of human rights law in each of the organizations.

i. The European Union

The original treaties[15] establishing what has become the European Union aimed at economic integration of member states through the elimination of internal barriers to the free movement of goods, services and people. The powers of the institutions created by the treaties gradually expanded in order to achieve the aim of the founders. As a consequence, EC legislative and administrative activities increasingly affected the rights of individuals and companies guaranteed under domestic law and the ECHR. Observers expressed concern that there might be no remedy against human rights violations because neither the ECHR nor member state constitutional guarantees applied to EC institutions. The following extract describes the evolution of EU law in response to this concern.

---

[15] Three separate communities were established: the European Coal and Steel Community (ECSC), the European Economic Community (EEC) and the European Atomic Energy Community (Euratom). The so-called Merger Treaty, which took effect on July 1, 1967, integrated these three communities into one organizational structure referred to as the European Community or Communities (EC). Recently, through the coming into force of the Treaty of Maastricht, the European Community has been transformed into the European Union.

Jean-Marie Henckaerts, *The Protection of Human Rights in the European Union: Overview . . . ,* 22 INT'L J. LEGAL INFO. 228–239 (1994) (bibliography and some footnotes omitted).

The treaties establishing the European Communities ("EC") are virtually silent on the protection of human rights. Some earlier, more ambitious plans for European integration . . . dealt with the issue to some extent. However, these plans had failed and the EC founding fathers wanted to confine the treaty to the bare necessities of an economic community. They probably also thought that as the scope of Community law was essentially limited to economic and technical issues, human rights problems would not occur. Judicial practice would prove the contrary.

. . . .

Early Case Law

The issue arose as early as 1959, when a German coal wholesale company invoked its (German) constitutional right to free establishment of trade against wholesaling restrictions authorized by the High Authority of the Coal and Steel Community.[16] The Court of Justice refused to entertain this claim because, as a Community institution, it had to observe Community law only and it was "not competent to apply the national law of the Member States."[17] A year later the Court refused in identical terms to have regard to Article 14 of the German Basic Law. A third early case is reported in which the Court adopted the same defensive position.[18] The Court of Justice adopted this defensive attitude in a first attempt to establish the principle of supremacy of Community law. It enunciated the supremacy postulate very clearly in the 1964 case of *Costa v. ENEL* in which it stated unequivocally that Community law was to take precedence over the domestic law of Member States.[19] Supremacy of Community law was the only avenue to assure a uniform application of Community law throughout the Community. Not to accept the supremacy principle was equal to calling the entire legal basis of the Community itself into question.

While this defensive attitude could be justified by the Court's concern for the autonomy and primacy of Community law, it was, nevertheless, bound to draw criticism because no provision was made in this structure for human rights concerns. The Court of Justice was asking national courts to recognize as its highest law a body of Community law that was not subject to any bill of rights. Inevitably some national courts were not willing to accept this kind of unchecked supremacy. In 1967, the German Constitutional Court held that because the Community legal order lacked any protection of human rights, it had no lawful democratic basis. Therefore, the transfer of powers from Germany to the Community could not deprive German citizens of the protection accorded to them by their constitution. Hence, Community law had to be examined at the national level to ensure that it was compatible with domestic constitutional provisions. This was a brutal blow to the concept of

---

[16] Case 1/58, *Friedrich Stork & Co. v. High Authority of the European Coal and Steel Community*, [1959] E.C.R. 17.

[17] Id. at 26.

[18] Case 40/64, *Sgarlata and others v. Commission of the European Economic Community*, [1965] E.C.R. 215, 227.

[19] Case 6/64, *Costa v. ENEL*, [1964] E.C.R. 585.

uniformity and supremacy, the very concepts the Court had tried to protect. But because it had done so without having regard to human rights, the Court in fact risked to reach the opposite result. The Court reacted swiftly to redress the situation. In 1969, in *Stauder v. City of Ulm*, the Court held in dicta that it must ensure the observance of the "the fundamental rights of the individual enshrined in the general principles of Community law and protected by the Court."[20] The Court's approach relied on the very general provision of Article 164 of the EEC Treaty which requires the Court to "ensure that in the interpretation and application of the Treaty the law is observed." *Stauder* made clear that "the law" includes "fundamental rights of the individual." *Stauder's* vague formula did not specify any rights nor did it point to any general principles of Community law from which those rights were to be distilled. Answers to these questions were provided in two subsequent cases. A year after *Stauder*, the *Internationale Handelsgesellschaft* case was referred to the Court by a German Administrative Court that wanted to override Community regulations because they were contrary to the German Basic Law.[21] The Court of Justice reiterated its strong emphasis on the supremacy of Community law but added that respect for basic rights forms an integral part of that law. According to the Court, the protection of basic rights is inspired by the common constitutional traditions of the Member States, but must, nevertheless, be ensured within the framework of the structure and objectives of the Community. Yet the German Constitutional Court, on the finding that the protection of fundamental rights in the Community still contained lacunae, decided that German constitutional guarantees had to prevail as long as the EC had not developed a similarly adequate system (so-called *Solange I* decision, "solange" being German for "as long as").[22]

In *Nold v. Commission*, the Court went one step further and, in addition to the common constitutional traditions, drew inspiration from "international treaties for the protection of human rights on which the Member States [had] collaborated or of which they [were] signatories."[23] The evolution after *Nold* is marked by an increasing reliance on international treaties, more specifically the European Convention on Human Rights ("ECHR").[24] Rather than to embark in each case on a comparative constitutional study, the Court made use of an existing catalogue of human rights that all Member States had already agreed upon, namely the ECHR.

---

[20]   Case 29/69, *Stauder v. City of Ulm*, [1969] E.C.R. 415, 9 C.M.L.R. 112, 119 (1970).

[21]   Case 11/70, *Internationale Handelsgesellschaft mbH v. Einfuhrund Vorratstelle fr Getreide und Futter-mittel*, [1970] E.C.R. 1125, 8 COMMON MKT. L. REV. 250 (1971).

[22]   Bundesverfassungsgerichtshof, Decision of May 19, 1974, Bverfge 37, 271, 2 C.M.L.R. 540, 551 (1974); see a similar decision by the Italian Constitutional Court in the case of *Frontini v. Ministero delle Finanze*, Dec. 27, 1973, no. 183, 18 GIURISPRUDENZA COSTITUZIONALE 2401 (1973), 2 C.M.L.R. 372, 383 (1974).

[23]   Case 4/73, *J. Nold, Kohlen-und BaustoffgroBhandlung v. Commission of the European Communities*, [1974] E.C.R. 491, 507. The Court had to use this formula because France had not yet ratified the European Convention on Human Rights. In fact, France ratified the Convention on May 3, 1974 which was less than 2 weeks before the *Nold* judgment was rendered (May 14, 1974).

[24]   *See especially* Case 260/89, *Elliniki Radiophonia Tileorassi-Anonimi Etairia v. Dimotiki Etairia Pliro-forissis*, [1991] E.C.R. 2925. On the legal basis for this evolution, see Mendelson, Maurice H., *The European Court of Justice and Human Rights*, 1 Y.B. EUR. L. 125, 152–162 (1981).

In *Rutili v. Minister for the Interior*, the ECHR is for the first time referred to explicitly.[25]. . . . *Rutili* set the precedent for reviewing Member States' public policy derogations from Community law under human rights standards.

In the case of *Hauer v. Land Rheinland-Pfalz*, the claimant alleged that a Community measure prohibiting her to plant new vines in her vineyard violated her right to property as guaranteed in the German Constitution.[26] The Court reaffirmed its refusal to review Community law under national constitutional law. Instead, the Court examined the Community measure under Article 1 of Protocol No. 1 to the ECHR which allows the regulation of property use "in accordance with the general interest." A similar provision was found in the German Basic Law and in the Irish and Italian Constitutions and was commonly applied in the administrative practice of all Member States. Therefore, the "general interest" exception to the right to property was clearly part of the common constitutional heritage of the Member States that informs the body of human rights the Court of Justice must uphold as part of Community law. In later decisions, several other ECHR provisions were taken into account.[27] In *Regina v. Kent Kirk*, the Court itself for the first time introduced a reference to the ECHR.[28]

The Court's efforts to build a Community human rights order based upon the common constitutional heritage of the Member States was well received by national courts. In 1986, in the so-called *Solange II* decision, the German Constitutional Court hesitantly yet effectively ceded to the Court of Justice and reversed its reasoning of *Solange I* in that it found no reason to review community measures under the German Constitution as long as the protection of human rights in the Community was as adequate as the German system. Similarly positive were the reactions of the Community's political institutions and the Member States. In fact, the Court's approach with regard to the ECHR was expressly ratified by the 1977 Joint Declaration on Fundamental Rights and by the 1987 Single European Act, amending the EEC Treaty, which expressly mention the ECHR as one of the sources of the fundamental rights recognized by the EC. Formal treaty status is given to the ECHR in Article F(2) of the Common Provisions of the Treaty on European Political Union, signed at the Maastricht Summit of December 1991 which provides that:

> The Union shall respect fundamental rights as guaranteed by the European Convention for the Protection of Human Rights and Fundamental Freedoms and as they result from the constitutional traditions common to the Member States as general principles of Community law.

. . . .

---

[25] Case 36/75, *Roland Rutili v. Minister for the Interior*, [1975] E.C.R. 1219, 1232.

[26] Case 44/79, *Liselotte Hauer v. Land Rheinland-Pfalz*, [1979] E.C.R. 3727.

[27] *See, e.g.*, Case 98/79, *Josette Pecastaing v. Belgian State*, [1980] E.C.R. 691 (Article 6); Case 209–215/78 and 218/78, *Heintz van Landewyck Srl and Others v. Commission of the European Communities*, [1980] E.C.R. 3125 (Article 6); Case 136/79, *National Panasonic (UK) Ltd. v. Commission of the European Communities*, [1980] E.C.R. 2033 (Article 8); Cases 100–103/80, *S.A. Musique Diffusion Française and Others v. Commission of the European Communities*, [1983] E.C.R. 1825 (Article 6); Case 222/84, *Johnston v. Chief Constable of the Royal Ulster Constabulary*, [1986] E.C.R. 1651, 3 C.M.L.R. 240 (1986) (Articles 6 and 13); *see also* Foster, Nigel, *The European Court of Justice and the European Convention for the Protection of Human Rights*, 8 HUM. RTS. L.J. 245, 264–266 (1987).

[28] Case 63/83, *Regina v. Kent Kirk*, [1984] E.C.R. 2689, 2718 where the Court refers to Article 7 ECHR.

In the cases discussed so far, with the exception of *Rutili*, the Court was asked to review Community measures under Community human rights standards. A completely different question arose when the Court was asked to review national legislation under these standards. In *Cinetheque SA v. Federation nationale des cinemas français*, the Court was asked whether a French law prohibiting the sale of videos the first year after the release of the film in theaters violated the freedom of expression as contained in Article 10 ECHR.[29] The Court, however, declined to review the French legislation under Article 10 ECHR. According to the Court: "Although it is true that it is the duty of this Court to ensure observance of fundamental rights in the field of Community law, it has no power to examine the compatibility with the European Convention of national legislation which concerns, as in this case, an area which falls within the jurisdiction of the national legislator." This "rather severe self-inflicted restriction" has not yet been reversed, but its scope has been substantially restricted in subsequent cases.

. . . . The rule that Member States' actions are reviewable when they are implementing Community legislation was enunciated in broader terms in the case of *Wachauf v. Germany*, a case dealing with the Community milk quota system.[30] In *Wachauf* the Court held that the requirements of the protection of fundamental rights in the Community legal order "are also binding on the Member States when they implement Community rules."

. . . .

Notwithstanding the absence of any mention or list of fundamental rights within the EC Treaties, the European Court of Justice, in what may be called its most striking contribution to the development of a constitution for Europe, has read an unwritten bill of rights into Community law. This development was prodded by some provocative, but nevertheless justifiable, decisions of the German, and later the Italian, Constitutional Court. It was not, initially, the expression of a higher aspiration to protect human rights, but a mere practical and defensive tactic of the Court to preserve the integrity of Community law as crystallized in the concept of supremacy. Inevitably, this has provoked some sarcasm on the side of scholars as to the Court's good intentions with the furtherance of fundamental human rights. It remains, nevertheless, a fortunate and indeed inevitable evolution, both for the Community legal order and for the human rights cause.

The relationship between EU law and institutions and the European Court of Human Rights has become a matter of considerable discussion as human rights law has gradually become a significant part of European Union law. The following case, which was brought before courts in Ireland and from there first to the European Court of Justice and thereafter to the European Court of Human Rights, explores the relationship between national law, EU law and the European Convention on Human Rights. It also serves to update the Henckaerts overview, by describing developments in EU human rights law after 1994. Note that the Court does not dis-

---

[29] Cases 60–61/84, *Cinetheque S.A. and Others v. Federation nationale des cinemas français*, [1985] E.C.R. 2605.
[30] Case 5/88, *Hubert Wachauf v. Federal Republic of Germany*, [1989] E.C.R. 2609.

cuss the legal effect of binding UN Security Council resolutions, which could have been an issue; the ECJ has addressed this matter in the context of human rights in the *Kadi* case, pp. 123–133.

Bosphorus Hava Yollari Turizm Ve Ticaret Anonim Şirketi v. Ireland [GC], (App. no. 45036/98), Judgment of 30 June 2005, Eur. Ct. H.R. (some footnotes omitted and paragraphs re-numbered).

[FACTS: the Irish government impounded an aircraft belonging to Yugoslav Airlines (JAT) but leased to a Turkish company for a 4 year period. The impoundment was pursuant to EU Regulation 990/93 which in turn implemented Security Council Resolution 890, imposing sanctions against Yugoslavia (FRY). A Grand Chamber of the European Court heard the Turkish company's argument that its property rights under the European Convention were violated by the Irish actions. The ECJ had already decided that Article 8 of EC Regulation 990/93 applied to the JAT aircraft, even though the owner had leased it to an undertaking with no links to the FRY.]

. . . .

1. Article 6 (formerly Article F) of the Treaty on European Union of 1992 ("the TEU")[31] reads as follows:

    1. The Union is founded on the principles of liberty, democracy, respect for human rights and fundamental freedoms, and the rule of law, principles which are common to the Member States.

    2. The Union shall respect fundamental rights, as guaranteed by the European Convention for the Protection of Human Rights and Fundamental Freedoms signed in Rome on 4 November 1950 and as they result from the constitutional traditions common to the Member States, as general principles of Community law.

    3. The Union shall respect the national identities of its Member States.

    4. The Union shall provide itself with the means necessary to attain its objectives and carry through its policies.

2. The Treaty of Amsterdam 1997 required the ECJ, in so far as it had jurisdiction, to apply human rights standards to acts of Community institutions and gave the European Union the power to act against a Member State that had seriously and persistently violated the principles of the Article 6(1) of the TEU cited directly above.[32]

3. The Charter of Fundamental Rights in the European Union, proclaimed in Nice on 7 December 2000 (not fully binding),[33] states in its preamble that it:

    reaffirms, with due regard for the powers and tasks of the Community and the Union and the principle of subsidiarity, the rights as they result, in particular, from

---

[31] [The TEU, also known as the Maastricht Treaty, transformed the European Community into the European Union. It is reprinted at 36 Int'l Legal Mat. 253, at 256 (1992). Ed.]

[32] [Article 7, a new provision in the Treaty, established a procedure that can be used to suspend certain membership rights if a "serious and persistent" breach of human rights occurs in a member state. Ed.]

[33] [In June 1999, the EU decided to draft a European Charter of Fundamental Rights to cover all rights that pertain to the Union's citizens, in effect combining the guarantees of the European Convention on Human Rights, the European Social Charter, and other human rights instruments. A working group of representatives of the member state governments, and representatives of the Commission, the Parliament and national parliaments drafted the Charter. The Charter was not concluded as a treaty, due to lack of agree-

the constitutional traditions and international obligations common to the Member States, the Treaty on European Union, the Community Treaties, the European Convention for the Protection of Human Rights and Fundamental Freedoms, the Social Charters adopted by the Community and by the Council of Europe and the case-law of the Court of Justice of the European Communities and of the European Court of Human Rights.

Article 52(3) of the Charter provides:

In so far as this Charter contains rights which correspond to rights guaranteed by the Convention for the Protection of Human Rights and Fundamental Freedoms, the meaning and scope of those rights shall be the same as those laid down by the said Convention. This provision shall not prevent Union law providing more extensive protection.

4. The Treaty establishing a Constitution for Europe, signed on 29 October 2004 (not in force), provides in its Article I-9 entitled "Fundamental Rights":

1. The Union shall recognise the rights, freedoms and principles set out in the Charter of Fundamental Rights which constitutes Part II.

2. The Union shall accede to the European Convention for the Protection of Human Rights and Fundamental Freedoms. Such accession shall not affect the Union's competences as defined in the Constitution.

3. Fundamental rights, as guaranteed by the European Convention for the Protection of Human Rights and Fundamental Freedoms and as they result from the constitutional traditions common to the Member States, shall constitute general principles of the Union's law.

The above-described Charter of Fundamental Rights has been incorporated as Part II of this constitutional treaty.

2. Other relevant provisions of the EC Treaty

5. Article 5 (now Article 10) provides:

Member States shall take all appropriate measures, whether general or particular, to ensure fulfilment of the obligations arising out of this Treaty or resulting from action taken by the institutions of the Community. They shall facilitate the achievement of the Community's tasks. They shall abstain from any measure which could jeopardise the attainment of the objectives of this Treaty.

6. Article 189 (now Article 249), in so far as relevant, reads as follows:

A regulation shall have general application. It shall be binding in its entirety and directly applicable in all Member States. . . .

The description of a Regulation as being "binding in its entirety" and "directly applicable" in all Member States means that it takes effect[34] in the internal legal orders of Member States without the need for domestic implementation.

7. Article 234 (now Article 307) reads as follows:

The rights and obligations arising from agreements concluded before 1 January 1958 or, for acceding States, before the date of their accession, between one or more

---

ment among the member states on this point, but was "proclaimed" at the meeting of the Council of the European Union in Nice on December 18, 2000. However, the European Commission's opinion is that the Charter may be regarded, including by the Court of Justice, as an important source of binding principles of fundamental rights. Ed.]

[34] Regulations enter into effect on the date specified therein or, where there is no such date specified, 20 days after publication in the Official Journal (Article 191(2), now 254(2)).

Member States on the one hand, and one or more third countries on the other, shall not be affected by the provisions of this Treaty.

To the extent that such agreements are not compatible with this Treaty, the Member State or States concerned shall take all appropriate steps to eliminate the incompatibilities established. Member States shall, where necessary, assist each other to this end and shall, where appropriate, adopt a common attitude.

In applying the agreements referred to in the first paragraph, Member States shall take into account the fact that the advantages accorded under this Treaty by each Member State form an integral part of the establishment of the Community and are thereby inseparably linked with the creation of common institutions, the conferring of powers upon them and the granting of the same advantages by all the other Member States.

. . . .

THE LAW

. . . .

Article 1 of Protocol no. 1 to the Convention

8. This Article reads as follows:

> Every natural or legal person is entitled to the peaceful enjoyment of his possessions. No one shall be deprived of his possessions except in the public interest and subject to the conditions provided for by law and by the general principles of international law.
>
> The preceding provisions shall not, however, in any way impair the right of a State to enforce such laws as it deems necessary to control the use of property in accordance with the general interest or to secure the payment of taxes or other contributions or penalties.

9. It was not disputed that there was an "interference" (the detention of the aircraft) with the applicant's "possessions" (the benefit of its lease of the aircraft) and the Court does not see any reason to conclude otherwise (*see*, for example, *Stretch v. the United Kingdom*, no. 44277/98, §§ 32–35, 24 June 2003). . . .

2. The legal basis for the impugned interference

10. The parties strongly disagreed as to whether the impoundment was at all times based on legal obligations on the Irish State flowing from Article 8 of EC Regulation 990/93.

For the purposes of its examination of this question, the Court recalls that it is primarily for the national authorities, notably the courts, to interpret and apply domestic law even when that law refers to international law or agreements. Equally, the Community judicial organs are better placed to interpret and apply EC law. In each instance, the Court's role is confined to ascertaining whether the effects of such adjudication are compatible with the Convention (see, *mutatis mutandis*, *Waite and Kennedy*, cited above, § 54, and *Streletz, Kessler and Krenz v. Germany* [GC], nos. 34044/96, 35532/97, 44801/98, § 49, ECHR 2001-II).

11. While the applicant alluded briefly to the Irish State's role in the EC Council, the Court notes that the applicant's essential standpoint was that it was not challenging the provisions of the Regulation itself but rather their implementation.

12. Once adopted, EC Regulation 990/93 was "generally applicable" and "binding in its entirety" (pursuant to Article 189, now Article 249, of the EC Treaty), so that it applied to all Member States none of whom could lawfully depart from any of its provisions. In addition, its "direct applicability" was not, and in the Court's view could not be, disputed. The Regulation became part of domestic law with effect from 28 April 1993 when it was published in the Official Journal, prior to the date of the impoundment and without the need for implementing legislation.

. . . .

Accordingly, the Irish authorities rightly considered themselves obliged to impound any departing aircraft to which they considered Article 8 of EC Regulation 990/93 applied. Their decision that it did so apply was later confirmed, *inter alia*, by the ECJ.

13. Thereafter, the Court finds persuasive the European Commission's submission that the State's duty of loyal co-operation (Article 5, now Article 10, of the EC Treaty) required it to appeal the High Court judgment of June 1994 to the Supreme Court in order to clarify the interpretation of EC Regulation 990/93. This was the first time that Regulation had been applied and the High Court's interpretation differed from that of the Sanctions Committee, a body appointed by the UN to interpret the UNSC Resolution implemented by the EC Regulation.

14. The Court would also agree with the Government and the European Commission that the Supreme Court had no real discretion to exercise, either before or after its preliminary reference to the ECJ, for the reasons set out below.

In the first place, there being no domestic judicial remedy against its decisions, the Supreme Court had to make the preliminary reference it did having regard to the terms of Article 177 (now Article 234) of the EC Treaty and the judgment of the ECJ in the *CILFIT* case:[35] the answer to the interpretative question put to the ECJ was not clear (the conclusions of the Sanctions Committee and the Minister for Transport conflicted with those of the High Court); the question was of central importance to the case; and there was no previous ruling by the ECJ on the point. . . .

Secondly, the ECJ ruling was binding on the Supreme Court.

Thirdly, the ruling of the ECJ effectively determined the domestic proceedings in the present case. . . .

15. For these reasons, the Court finds that the impugned interference was not the result of an exercise of discretion by the Irish authorities, either under EC or Irish law, but rather amounted to compliance by the Irish State with its legal obligations flowing from EC law and, in particular, Article 8 of EC Regulation 990/93.

3. Whether the impoundment was justified

(a) The general approach to be adopted

16. Since the second paragraph is to be construed in the light of the general principle enunciated in the opening sentence of Article 1, there must exist a reasonable

---

35 [*CILFIT Srl v. Ministro della Sanita*, Case 283/81 [1982] ECR 3415. The ECJ in *CILFIT* indicated that a court of final instance would not be obliged to make a reference to the ECJ if the question of EC law was not relevant (i.e. could not affect the outcome of the case); the provision had already been interpreted by the ECJ; and the correct application of EC law was so obvious as to leave no scope for reasonable doubt.]

relationship of proportionality between the means employed and the aim sought to be realised: the Court must determine whether a fair balance has been struck between the demands of the general interest in this respect and the interest of the individual company concerned. In so determining, the State enjoys a wide margin of appreciation with regard to the means chosen to be employed and to the question of whether the consequences are justified in the general interest for the purpose of achieving the objective pursued (the *AGOSI* case, § 52).

17. The Court considers it evident from its finding . . . that the general interest pursued by the impugned action was compliance with legal obligations flowing from the Irish State's membership of the EC.

It is, moreover, a legitimate interest of considerable weight. The Convention has to be interpreted in the light of any relevant rules and principles of international law applicable in relations between the Contracting Parties (Article 31 § 3 (c) of the Vienna Convention on the Law of Treaties of 23 May 1969 and *Al-Adsani v. the United Kingdom* [GC], no. 35763/97, § 55, ECHR 2001-XI), which principles include that of *pacta sunt servanda*. The Court has also long recognised the growing importance of international co-operation and of the consequent need to secure the proper functioning of international organisations (the above-cited cases of *Waite and Kennedy*, at §§ 63 and 72 and *Al-Adsani*, § 54. See also Article 234 (now Article 307) of the EC Treaty). Such considerations are critical for a supranational organisation such as the EC.[36] This Court has accordingly accepted that compliance with EC law by a Contracting Party constitutes a legitimate general interest objective within the meaning of Article 1 of Protocol No. 1 (*mutatis mutandis, S.A. Dangeville v. France*, cited above, at §§ 47 and 55).

18. The question is therefore whether, and if so to what extent, that important general interest of compliance with EC obligations can justify the impugned interference by the State with the applicant's property rights.

19. The Convention does not, on the one hand, prohibit Contracting Parties from transferring sovereign power to an international (including a supranational) organisation in order to pursue co-operation in certain fields of activity. . . . Moreover, even as the holder of such transferred sovereign power, that organisation is not itself held responsible under the Convention for proceedings before, or decisions of, its organs as long as it is not a Contracting Party. . . .

20. On the other hand, it has also been accepted that a Contracting Party is responsible under Article 1 of the Convention for all acts and omissions of its organs regardless of whether the act or omission in question was a consequence of domestic law or of the necessity to comply with international legal obligations. Article 1 makes no distinction as to the type of rule or measure concerned and does not exclude any part of a Contracting Party's "jurisdiction" from scrutiny under the Convention (*United Communist Party of Turkey and Others v. Turkey* judgment of 30 January 1998, Reports, 1998-I, § 29).

21. In reconciling both these positions and thereby establishing the extent to which State action can be justified by its compliance with obligations flowing from its membership of an international organisation to which it has transferred part of

---

36 *Costa v. Ente Nazionale per l'Energia Electtrica* (ENEL), Case 6/64, [1964] ECR 585.

its sovereignty, the Court has recognised that absolving Contracting States completely from their Convention responsibility in the areas covered by such a transfer would be incompatible with the purpose and object of the Convention: the guarantees of the Convention could be limited or excluded at will thereby depriving it of its peremptory character and undermining the practical and effective nature of its safeguards. . . . The State is considered to retain Convention liability in respect of treaty commitments subsequent to the entry into force of the Convention (*mutatis mutandis*, . . . *Prince Hans-Adam II of Liechtenstein v. Germany* [GC], no. 42527/98, § 47, ECHR 2001-VIII).

22. In the Court's view, State action taken in compliance with such legal obligations is justified as long as the relevant organisation is considered to protect fundamental rights, as regards both the substantive guarantees offered and the mechanisms controlling their observance, in a manner which can be considered at least equivalent to that for which the Convention provides (. . . an approach with which the parties and the European Commission agreed). By "equivalent" the Court means "comparable": any requirement that the organisation's protection be "identical" could run counter to the interest of international co-operation pursued. However, any such finding of equivalence could not be final and would be susceptible to review in the light of any relevant change in fundamental rights' protection.

23. If such equivalent protection is considered to be provided by the organisation, the presumption will be that a State has not departed from the requirements of the Convention when it does no more than implement legal obligations flowing from its membership of the organisation.

However, any such presumption can be rebutted if, in the circumstances of a particular case, it is considered that the protection of Convention rights was manifestly deficient. In such cases, the interest of international co-operation would be outweighed by the Convention's role as a "constitutional instrument of European public order" in the field of human rights (*Loizidou v. Turkey (preliminary objections)*, judgment of 23 March 1995, Series A no. 310, § 75).

24. It remains the case that a State would be fully responsible under the Convention for all acts falling outside its strict international legal obligations. The numerous Convention cases cited by the applicant . . . confirm this. Each case . . . concerned a review by this Court of the exercise of State discretion for which EC law provided. . . .

25. Since the impugned act constituted solely compliance by Ireland with its legal obligations flowing from membership of the EC, the Court will now examine whether a presumption arises that Ireland complied with its Convention requirements in fulfilling such obligations and whether any such presumption has been rebutted in the circumstances of the present case.

(b) Was there a presumption of Convention compliance at the relevant time?

26. The Court has described the fundamental rights guarantees of the EC which govern Member States, Community institutions together with natural and legal persons ("individuals").

While the constituent EC treaty did not initially contain express provisions for the protection of fundamental rights, the ECJ subsequently recognised that such rights were enshrined in the general principles of Community law protected by it and that the Convention had a "special significance" as a source of such rights. Respect for fundamental rights has become "a condition of the legality of Community acts" and in carrying out this assessment the ECJ refers extensively to Convention provisions and to this Court's jurisprudence. At the relevant time, these jurisprudential developments had been reflected in certain treaty amendments (notably those aspects of the Single European Act 1986 and of the TEU).

This evolution has continued thereafter. The Treaty of Amsterdam 1997 is referred to . . . above. Although not fully binding, the provisions of the Charter of Fundamental Rights of the European Union were substantially inspired by those of the Convention and the Charter recognises the Convention as establishing the minimum human rights standards. Article I-9 of the later Treaty establishing a Constitution for Europe (not in force) provides for the Charter to become primary law of the European Union and for the Union to accede to the Convention.

27. However, the effectiveness of such substantive guarantees of fundamental rights depends on the mechanisms of control in place to ensure observance of such rights.

28. The Court has referred to the jurisdiction of the ECJ in, *inter alia*, annulment actions (Article 173, now Article 230), in actions against Community institutions for failure to perform Treaty obligations (Article 175, now Article 232), to hear related pleas of illegality under Article 184 (now Article 241) and in cases against Member States for failure to fulfil Treaty obligations (Articles 169, 170 and 171, now Articles 226, 227 and 228).

29. It is true that access of individuals to the ECJ under these provisions is limited: they have no *locus standi* under Articles 169 and 170; their right to initiate actions under Articles 173 and 175 is restricted as is, consequently, their right under Article 184; and they have no right to take an action against another individual.

30. It nevertheless remains the case that actions initiated before the ECJ by the Community institutions or a Member State constitute important control of compliance with Community norms to the indirect benefit of individuals. Individuals can also bring an action for damages before the ECJ in respect of the non-contractual liability of the institutions.

31. Moreover, it is essentially through the national courts that the Community system provides a remedy to individuals against a Member State or another individual for a breach of EC law. Certain EC Treaty provisions envisaged a complementary role for the national courts in the Community control mechanisms from the outset, notably Article 189 (the notion of direct applicability, now Article 249) and Article 177 (the preliminary reference procedure, now Article 234). It was the development by the ECJ of important notions such as the supremacy of EC law, direct effect, indirect effect and State liability which greatly enlarged the role of the domestic courts in the enforcement of Community law and its fundamental rights' guarantees.

The ECJ maintains its control on the application by national courts of EC law, including its fundamental rights guarantees, through the procedure for which Article 177 of the EC Treaty provides. . . . While the ECJ's role is limited to responding to the interpretative or validity question referred by the domestic court, the response will often be determinative of the domestic proceedings and detailed guidelines on the timing and content of a preliminary reference have been laid down by the EC treaty provision and developed by the ECJ in its case-law. The parties to the domestic proceedings have the right to put their case to the ECJ during the Article 177 process. It is further recalled that national courts operate in legal systems into which the Convention has been incorporated, albeit to differing degrees.

32. In such circumstances, the Court finds that the protection of fundamental rights by EC law can be considered to be, and to have been at the relevant time, "equivalent" to that of the Convention system. Consequently, the presumption arises that Ireland did not depart from the requirements of the Convention when it implemented legal obligations flowing from its membership of the EC.

(c) Has that presumption been rebutted in the present case?

33. The Court has had regard to the nature of the interference, to the general interest pursued by the impoundment and by the sanctions regime and to the ruling of the ECJ (. . .), a ruling with which the Supreme Court was obliged to and did comply. It considers it clear that there was no dysfunction of the mechanisms of control of the observance of Convention rights.

In the Court's view, therefore, it cannot be said that the protection of the applicant's Convention rights was manifestly deficient with the consequence that the relevant presumption of Convention compliance by the respondent State has not been rebutted.

4. Conclusion under Article 1 of Protocol No. 1

34. It follows that the impoundment of the aircraft did not give rise to a violation of Article 1 of Protocol No. 1 to the Convention.

The European Court here gives deference to the regulation adopted by the EU and implemented by Ireland. For a similar case, in which the Court declined to hear applicants' claim that their property rights were infringed by French incorporation and enforcement of EU law, see *Coopérative des agriculteurs de Mayenne and Coopérative laitiére Maine-Anjou v. France*, App. No. 16931/04, admissibility decision of Oct. 10, 2006. In turn, the European Court of Justice has deferred to the jurisprudence of the European Court when the meaning or scope of a right contained in the European Convention is before it. This has not answered all issues of potential conflict or concern. Some commentators have seen the two systems as competing and have proposed radical solutions. Clemens Rieder, for example, expresses concern about the fragility of the ECHR due to its new member states and its traditional deference to national decision-making. He also points to the considerable length of proceedings as a reason to avoid having the EU accede to the ECHR. His conclusion:

> Taking the arguments above seriously, the best-case scenario would clearly be the
> EU adopting its own independent human rights system. Toth[37] even suggests a

---

[37] A.G. Toth, *The European Union and Human Rights: The Way Forward*, 34 COMMON MKT L. REV. 491, 499 (1997).

complete withdrawal by the EU Member States from the European Convention. As a consequence, the ECJ would have to jump in and take over human rights protection completely. The idea that the ECJ would deal with human rights issues, irrespective of whether there is a linkage to EU law or not, is less revolutionary than it seems at first sight, if one shares the opinion . . . that today there are hardly any fields where the ECJ is excluded from scrutiny. . . . In any case, whether one follows the idea of an absolutely encompassing ECJ with respect to human rights, or if one is of the opinion that the ECJ's authority should be tied to EU competences, the EU Charter can offer valuable help in both scenarios . . . [T]he strings of 'classical' human rights (as vested by the European Convention) and market rights would, with the EU Charter, come together in the hands of the ECJ. This Court, as the final authority, would then be in a position to decide about these rights and could balance them accordingly. These adaptations are crucial in order to prevent the Union from becoming a paradise for lawyers but a nightmare for its citizens.

Clemens Rieder, *Protecting Human Rights within the European Union: Who is Better Qualified to do the Job—The European Court of Justice or the European Court of Human Rights?*, 20 Tul. Eur. Civ. L.R. 73, 106 (2005). The potential for conflicting interpretations of rights and possible solutions to the problem are further discussed in the following extract.

Elizabeth F. Defeis, *Human Rights and the European Union: Who Decides? Possible Conflicts between the European Court of Justice and the European Court of Human Rights,* 19 Dick. Int'l L. J. 301, at 309, 313, 315–22, 325–30 (2001) (some footnotes omitted).

A noted scholar of the European Union, Phillip Alston has stated "the ECJ deserves immense credit for pioneering the protection of fundamental human rights within the legal order of the Community when the Treaties themselves were silent on this matter."[38] Indeed this observation is well founded.

. . . .

The aspect of human rights that the court has dealt with most exhaustively is the general principle of equal treatment (or nondiscrimination). This principle was firmly established in Article 141 (ex Article 119) of the EEC, which guarantees equal pay for equal work based on gender and the court has developed a fairly extensive jurisprudence with respect to gender equality in the workplace. Perhaps because of its explicit treaty foundation and the frequent requests for preliminary rulings and subsequent council directives the principle of equal treatment based on gender appears to be the most frequent human rights issue addressed by the court. The court has also ruled on provisions in secondary legislation dealing with civil, social, and economic rights, discrimination based on nationality, groups in the agricultural sector, and affirmative action.

Initially, the ECJ's emphasis on human rights was implemented through "negative integration" in which Community institutions were prohibited from acting in any way that could lead to a violation of the fundamental principles of human rights

---

[38] Philip Alston & J.H.H. Weiler, *An "Ever Closer Union" in Need of a Human Rights Policy*, 9 E.J.I.L. 658 at 709.

much in the same way that the court developed its protection of the Community's four freedoms—goods, workers, service, and capital. However, the European Court of Justice has been instrumental in developing an evolving jurisprudence with respect to human rights and has recognized the numerous rights that must be respected.

. . . .

Although the court has taken a strong position with respect to ensuring that Community actions adhere to human rights standards, it is much more deferential when national legislation is in issue. The court is reluctant to address claims of human rights violations in national legislation that implicate Community law.

Thus, in *Cinetheque*, the Court declined to review French legislation under Article 10 of the ECHR to determine whether a French law that prohibited the sale of videotapes during their first year of release violated one's freedom of expression.[39] The Court stated: "Although it is true that it is the duty of this Court to ensure observance of fundamental rights in the field of Community law, it has no power to examine the compatibility with the European Convention of national legislation which concerns, as in this case, an area which falls within the jurisdiction of the national legislator."[40]

Similarly, in *Kremzow v. Austria*,[41] the ECJ was asked for a preliminary ruling on the question of whether the Austrian court's failure to implement a decision of the ECHR concerning a violation of a defendant's right to defend himself in a criminal proceeding violated his rights under Community law. The defendant argued that the Austrian court violated his right to freedom of movement under community law by unlawful detention.

The court rejected Kremzow's interpretation of the freedom of movement provision of the EC Treaty. Although the deprivation of liberty prevents a person from exercising freedom of movement, the court did not find a sufficient connection with Community law to justify the application of Community provisions. The court said: "where national legislation is concerned with a situation which, as in the case at issue in the main proceedings, does not fall within the field of application of Community law, the court cannot, in a reference for a preliminary ruling, give the interpretive guidance necessary for the national court to determine whether that national legislation is in conformity with the fundamental rights whose observance the court ensures, such as those deriving in particular from the Convention." Similarly, in *SPUC v. Grogan*, the court refused to offer an opinion on whether the dissemination of information about abortion services abroad violated the Article 10 guarantee of freedom of expression contained in the ECHR.[42]

. . . .

---

[39] Cases 60–61/84, *Cinetheque S.A. and Others v. Federation nationale des cinemas français*, 1985 E.C.R. 2605.

[40] Id. at 2627.

[41] Case C/29919, *Kremzow v. Republiek Osterrich*, [1997] 3 S.M.L.R. 1289.

[42] *SPUC v. Grogan*, (Case C-159/90.

Potential Clash between ECJ and ECHR Jurisdiction

Until now, the European Court of Justice derived its human rights standards primarily from the constitutions of member states and Community law, but it also referred to the Convention on Human Rights and other international treaties. Although it has referred to decisions of the ECJ, it has not specifically ruled that the decisions of the ECHR are controlling on matters of interpretation of human rights but looks to their cases for guidance. The European Court of Justice and the European Court of Human Rights have sometimes interpreted the rights outlined in the Convention on Human Rights differently. Now that the Amsterdam Treaty defines fundamental rights as those in the European Convention on Human Rights and grants the European Court of Justice the explicit task of expounding upon these rights, there exists a possible conflict between the European Court of Justice's interpretation and that of the European Court of Human Rights.

In the past, the ECJ has taken several approaches when faced with deciding human rights issues that were to come before the ECHR or which had already been decided by that court. Some cases involve actual conflict based upon differing interpretation of the relevant provisions of the Convention, other cases appear inconsistent in result, but where the court based its decision on an analysis of a different fundamental right and those cases that recognized that a fundamental right guaranteed by the ECHR was involved but in which the court avoided ruling on the content of that right.

An example of the first category is in the area of privacy rights. At the center of the possible conflict lies the differing interpretation of Article 8 of the Convention on Human Rights guarantee of the right to "privacy in the home and in correspondence."

The European Court of Justice has interpreted the right to privacy of Article 8 as not encompassing business activities.[43] In *Hoechst*, the defendant challenged the decision of the EC Commission that required various businesses to submit to investigations into their possible participation in agreements or concerted practices that fixed prices and quotas or sales objectives of goods in the European Community.[44] Hoechst refused to submit to the investigation and only permitted the investigation after a search warrant was issued. Hoechst argued that the actions of the Commission were void in that they infringed on the fundamental right to the inviolability of the home. The court held that "[a]rticle 8(1) of the European Convention on Human Rights is concerned primarily with the development of individual's personal freedom and may not therefore be extended to business premises."

---

[43] In *Hoechst*, the EC Commission adopted a series of decisions requiring various businesses to submit to investigations into their possible participation in agreements or concerted practices that fixed prices and quotas or sales objectives of PVC and polyethylene in the European Community. Hoechst (Case 46/87) refused to submit to the investigation and only permitted the investigation after a search warrant was issued. Hoechst applied to the court for a declaration that the series of decisions were void for infringement of the fundamental right to the inviolability of the home. The court held, that Article 8(1) of the European Convention on Human Rights is concerned primarily with the development of individual's personal freedom and may not therefore be extended to business premises. *Hoechst*, 4 C.M.L.R. 410 (1991).

[44] *Hoechst*, 4 C.M.L.R. 410 at I. A (1991).

Two years later, the European Court of Human Rights held that a "search of professional activities and premises" constitutes a violation of the right to privacy.[45] The applicant was a lawyer whose offices were searched by the German police pursuant to a search warrant issued by the Munich District Court. The applicant complained that the search had violated his right to respect for his home and correspondence as guaranteed by Article 8. The court held that: interpreting the terms 'private life' and 'home' as encompassing certain professional or business activities or premise is consonant with the object and purpose of Article 8 and such an interpretation would not unduly hamper the ability of the states to conduct a search.

A similar conflict is presented in the interpretations of the right against self-incrimination as found in Article 6. The European Court of Justice held that Article 6 only applies to criminal investigations, not to administrative procedures.[46] In *Orkem*, the applicant was requested to produce documents in connection with an E.C. commission's request for information in connection with an investigation of the applicant for infringements of competition law. The court held that: "the right not to give evidence against oneself only applied to a person charged with an offense in criminal proceedings." The court further held that individuals might not rely on this right against self-incrimination when questioned with infringements in the economic sphere.

Yet, in a subsequent case, the European Court of Human Rights reached a different result.[47] In *Funke*, after a search by French customs officials failed to produce sufficient evidence to lead to criminal proceedings for currency and capital transfer offenses, the applicant was asked to produce certain specific documents. When he refused, he was prosecuted and ordered to pay a fine and also a daily penalty until he complied. The European Court of Human Rights held that a person is entitled under Article 6 to remain silent and not incriminate himself, and any attempt to use pecuniary sanction to force him to produce self-incriminating documents was a breach of Article 6.

The second category, namely, where the respective courts focus on different rights to resolve the issue before it, can be illustrated by the treatment of homosexuals by the courts. In *Grant v. South-West Trains*, the European Court of Justice held that prohibition of discrimination based on sex, a fundamental principal of Community Law, did not cover discrimination on the grounds of sexual orientation.[48] In that case, an employer granted concessionary travel tickets to members of its staff for one legal spouse or for one "common law opposite sex spouse" subject to a statutory declaration being made that a "meaningful relationship" had existed for a period of two years or more. Ms. Grant applied for travel concessions for her female partner with whom she declared she had a "meaningful relationship" for over two years. South-West Trains refused the application, stating that the non-married concession only applied to partners of the opposite sex. The court held that this denial of benefits does not constitute discrimination prohibited by Article 141 (ex Article 119) or Council Directive 75/117.

---

45 *Niemietz v. Germany*, 16 E.H.R.R. 97 P 33 (1993).
46 *Orkem SA v. EC Commissions*, E.C.R. 3283, 4 C.M.L.R. 502 (1989).
47 *Funke v. France*, 1 C.M.L.R. 897 (1993).
48 Case 249/96, *Grant v. South-West Trains*, 1 C.M.L.R. 993 (1998).

In so ruling, the court disregarded the opinion of the Advocate General who suggested that the policy of SWT regarding travel concessions for same-sex couples violated Article 141 (ex Article 119) of the EC Treaty. Rather, the court focused on "the present state of the law within the Community" and noted that although the European Parliament declared that it deplores all forms of discrimination based on an individual's sexual orientation, the Community itself had not adopted "rules providing for such equivalence." It also looked at decisions of the European Court on Human Rights and the Commission on Human Rights to determine the present state of the law within the Community and deferred to national legislators to address discrimination based on sexual orientation.

In its more recent opinions, the European Court of Human Rights has taken a different approach and issued two separate opinions in which it struck down the investigation and discharge for homosexuality of individuals in the English Armed Forces.[49] In *Smith and Grady v. United Kingdom* and *Lustig-Prean & Beckett v. United Kingdom*, the applicants complained that the investigation into their homosexuality and their discharge from the military on the sole ground that they are homosexual constituted violations of Article 8 of the Convention, right to respect for private and family life, taken alone and in conjunction with Article 14, non-discrimination rights.... The court held that such investigation and discharge constitutes a violation of the right to privacy as contained in Article 8 of the Convention on Human Rights....

Although the issue of a violation of the non-discrimination guarantee was raised in both cases, the court grounded its decision on a violation of privacy rights. Thus, although not directly conflicting with the ECJ decision in *South-West*, it clearly exemplifies a different sensitivity to issues of homosexual discrimination....

In the third category of potential conflicts, the ECJ has avoided ruling on a fundamental rights question that arose in a sensitive context and in which the sensibilities of a member state was involved. This category is best illustrated by *SPUC v. Grogan* in which a violation of freedom of expression was alleged in addition to violation of Community law.

In *Grogan*, an injunction was sought by the Society for the Protection of Unborn Children against the activities of various students' organizations who provided information on abortion clinics in the UK without charging a fee.[50] The question referred to the ECJ was whether abortion clinics constitute services within the meaning of Article 60 of the EEC Treaty and, if so, whether the Treaty provisions on the freedom to supply services precluded a national law that prohibited the provision of information concerning abortion services legally carried on in another Member state. It was also alleged that the ban on the provision of such information violated Article 10 of the ECHR.

.... [T]he European Court of Justice was faced with a dilemma. A similar case, *Open Door Counseling and Dublin Well Woman v. Ireland*, would soon be decided by the ECHR in which the Article 10 question was squarely presented. If the decision rendered by the ECJ was inconsistent with the subsequent ruling of the ECHR,

---

49 *Smith and Grady v. United Kingdom*, 33985/96 & 33986/96 Sept. 27, 1999.
50 *SPUC v. Grogan*, (Case C-159/90).

the doctrine of supremacy of Community law would be cast into doubt. Moreover, a ruling that the injunction violated Article 10 of the Convention would further exacerbate relations with Ireland.

The ECJ thus . . . held consistent with its prior opinions, that medical termination of pregnancy performed in accordance with the law of the state in which it is carried out constitutes a service within the meaning of Article 60 of the EEC Treaty. However, the court found that the link between the activities of the students and the medical services performed in another state was "too tenuous" to be regarded as a restriction within the meaning of Article 59 of the Treaty pertaining to restrictions on the prohibition of services. The court based its holding on the fact that the students were not acting on behalf of the out of state medical providers or as the court termed it "on behalf of an economic operator established in a member state." Because the challenged rule fell outside the scope of Community law, the court reasoned that it was not appropriate for the court to assess the compatibility of the national rule with fundamental rights, in particular, those specified in the European Convention on Human Rights. Thus, the court declined to rule on the issue of whether the prohibition on the dissemination of information on medical services in another country violated Article 10 of the ECHR. The ruling was widely criticized both by legal scholars and commentators.

Just one year later, the European Court of Human Rights was squarely presented with the precise issue presented in the *Grogan* case, namely whether an injunction prohibiting the furnishing information by a non-profit organization concerning the availability of out of state abortion services violated Article 10 of the ECHR, and the court in Strasbourg ruled that it did. In *Open Door Counseling and Dublin Well Women*, the court held that an injunction imposed by the Irish court restricting clinical staff from imparting information to pregnant women concerning abortion facilities outside Ireland by way of non-directive counseling constituted a restraint on freedom to impart information and violated Article 10 of the ECHR. The court considered whether the injunction was necessary in a democratic society as permitted by Article 10(2) of the Convention and acknowledged that the aim of the national rule was legitimate, that is, the protection of morals as reflected in Irish law. At the outset, it noted that freedom of expression also applies to ideas or information that might offend or shock the government or a segment of any population. Without this pluralism, tolerance and broad-mindedness there would not exist a democratic society.

The court emphasized that the absolute nature of the injunction, which imposed perpetual restraint regardless of age, health, or reason for seeking canceling or terminating pregnancy, was disproportionate. Thus, the court invalidated the injunction in a situation similar to the one avoided by the ECJ earlier. The strong dissenting opinion in the case underscores the controversial nature of the issue that both courts were faced with deciding.

One might speculate as to how the ECJ would rule if faced with the issue again, albeit in a slightly different factual setting. Clearly, to follow the ruling of the ECHR would exacerbate the already tenuous relation with a member state. The larger question remains however, would it consider itself bound to follow the decision of the ECHR.

D. Expanded Jurisdiction of the ECJ and Human Rights.

. . . . Several proposals have been put forth with respect both to strengthening human rights protections within the European Union and with developing a more comprehensive and integrated system for the protection of human rights.

Early on it was argued that the EU should join the ECHR as a member in its own right. However, the decision of the ECJ *in Re: Accession of the Community to the European Human Rights Convention* makes clear that absent treaty modification, the EU could not accede to the ECHR because it would result in a fundamental change in the community system. While the opinion itself was widely criticized there appears to be little momentum with respect acceding to the Convention at the present time.

It has also been suggested the Union itself enact a catalogue of rights that would be uniform throughout the Union. . . . [However, o]ne commentator has called the adoption of a Charter of Fundamental Freedoms the worst possible scenario, since it would establish a dual system of human rights protection in Europe and a splitting up of rights which would undermine the authority of the Convention and the Convention system.[51]

Another option proposed is to incorporate all substantive provisions of the European Convention as a separate title to the EEC Treaty, as an amendment to the Charter and to include the protection of human rights and fundamental freedoms as an objective of the Community and the Union. The jurisdiction of the ECJ would be enlarged to encompass human rights issues not only as they pertain to community action, but also to actions of member states. All member states of the EU would then withdraw from the Convention leaving the ECJ as ultimate guarantors of human rights in the European Union. This approach would drastically alter the nature of the EU and appears to have gained little support.

Others have suggested that when an issue pertains to human rights, the matter should be referred to the ECHR for a preliminary ruling by the ECHR that would be binding on the ECJ. For the same reasons advanced in the accession case, it seems unlikely that the ECJ would allow the ECJ to be subjected to the decisions of another international institution. . . .

Clearly, what is needed is a more holistic approach to the protection of fundamental rights in the European Union. However, the ECJ in the past has shown leadership in the area of protecting human rights, even without specific textual authorization in the EEC Charter. It has taken positions on human rights that are in some instances broader than the position taken by the ECHR. In addition, increasingly, both courts look to decisions and jurisprudence of the other for guidance. While neither will consider itself bound by the other court's decision, there is clearly deference and one can expect closer cooperation between the two courts as the jurisdiction of the ECJ expands with respect to human rights. It is a basic principle of

---

[51] A. G. Toth, *The European Union and Human Rights: The Way Forward*, 34 Common Mkt. L. Rev. 491–92 (1997).

European Union Law that a community national who travels to a member state and exercises Treaty rights, such as to work, enjoys the right to be treated to the same living and working conditions as nationals of the host state. Community nationals should also be entitled to assume that throughout the European Union, they will enjoy fundamental human rights, in particular those set forth in the ECHR, that are interpreted and administered uniformly throughout the Union. In other words, as Advocate General Jacobs has said, the new European citizen should be able to say *'civic Europeus sum'* and to invoke that status in order to oppose any violation of his fundamental rights. As the jurisprudence of both the ECJ and the ECHR continue to develop, this should be the case.

Questions and Comments

1. Are protections in the EU "comparable" or "equivalent" to the ECHR? What is the significance of treating them as such?
2. What difference would it make if the EU ratified the ECHR? Would the ECJ then be required to conform its jurisprudence to that of the European Court of Human Rights?
3. Read the EU Charter of Fundamental Rights. How do its guarantees differ from those contained in the ECHR?
4. What does the European Court mean when it says that "a State would be fully responsible under the Convention for all acts falling outside its strict international legal obligations?"
5. How serious is the potential for conflict between EU and ECHR law? What options does a state have when faced with divergent interpretations of rights by the two European Courts?
6. Would a dual system of human rights guarantees solve the problem of potential conflict or create even more difficulties for member states?

ii. Organization for Security and Cooperation in Europe (OSCE)

In 1975, thirty-three European nations, the United States and Canada signed the Helsinki Final Act (HFA) to conclude the Conference on Security and Cooperation in Europe (CSCE). Albania was the only European country that refused to join. With the end of the Cold War, the membership of the CSCE expanded to more than fifty nations, including Albania and the former Soviet Republics in Europe and Central Asia. The HFA creatively linked human rights and security concerns, giving human rights an important place on the political agenda of East-West relations. In 1994 the CSCE became the Organization for Security and Cooperation in Europe (OSCE).

The OSCE's human rights system consists of a catalog of human rights and duties and various supervisory institutions that have evolved over time. This evolution was possible because of the manner in which the HFA was drafted and the follow-up mechanism it established.

The HFA is not a treaty and it was not intended by the participating states to create binding legal obligations. A state's failure to comply with any of the HFA commitments thus will have political but not legal consequences. The history of the HFA suggests that its political character has not proved detrimental to its normative content nor to objectives it was designed to achieve. The HFA and other texts that built upon it have set useful standards which have been invoked in an international arena and in national contexts to improve human rights.

The HFA consists of four chapters or so-called "baskets." Basket I, entitled "Questions Relating to Security in Europe," consists of two sections ("Principles Guiding Relations Between Participating States," and "Confidence-Building Measures and Certain Aspects of Security and Disarmament"). Basket II deals with "Cooperation in the Field of Economics, of Science and Technology and of the Environment." The subject of Basket III is "Cooperation in Humanitarian and Other Fields." Basket IV, the final chapter, spells out the so-called "follow-up" process.

Human rights issues are addressed primarily in the Guiding Principles proclaimed in Basket I and to some extent in Basket III. Two of the ten Guiding Principles deal with human rights. Principle VII concerns "Respect for human rights and fundamental freedoms, including the freedom of thought, conscience, religion or belief," while Principle VIII addresses "Equal rights and self-determination of peoples." Other paragraphs address sovereignty, the use of force, inviolability of frontiers, territorial integrity, peaceful settlement of disputes, non-intervention in internal affairs, cooperation of states, and fulfillment in good faith of international legal obligations.

Principle VII consists of eight unnumbered paragraphs. In the first two paragraphs the participating States undertake to "respect human rights and fundamental freedoms" and to "promote and encourage the effective exercise of civil, political, economic, social, cultural and other rights and freedoms...." This principle also deals with freedom of religion, rights of individuals belonging to national minorities, and the "right of the individual to know and act upon his rights and duties in this field." The last paragraph of Principle VII committed the participating States to act in conformity with the purposes and principles of the Charter of the United Nations and with the Universal Declaration of Human Rights and to fulfill their obligations as states parties to other international human rights agreements.

This paragraph appears to have been the first time the Soviet Union acknowledged the normative character of the Universal Declaration of Human Rights, which it had abstained from voting on in the United Nations.

Basket IV established a follow-up process which has been instrumental in the long-term success of the OSCE. Participating States periodically convene intergovernmental conferences to undertake "a thorough exchange of views... on the implementation of the provisions of the Final Act...." These follow-up conferences provide a forum to review compliance with human rights commitments and to expand the human rights catalog through amplifying, reinterpreting and extensively revising the HFA. The meetings also have been used to focus public attention on the failure of certain states to live up to their human rights commitments. By the latter part of the 1980's, the discussion of specific human rights violations was routine during CSCE follow-up meetings.

The normative evolution referred to has been accomplished by the consensus adoption at each conference of a "concluding document" in which the participants proclaim new OSCE commitments or expand, modify or interpret the scope and meaning of existing ones. These documents include discussion of the rights of minorities, the rule of law and democratic governance, as well as the traditional list of individual rights. In this respect, the OSCE pioneered a holistic approach to human rights that has emerged in other human rights settings more recently. *See OSCE Handbook* (3rd ed. 1999).

Human Dimension Mechanism

The Vienna Concluding Document (1989) consolidated the subject of human rights, previously dealt with as a Basket I item, with the human contact and related humanitarian topics set out in Basket III, and it subsumed both topics under the heading of the "Human Dimension of the CSCE." It also established the Human Dimension Mechanism for dealing with the non-observance by states of with their human dimension commitments. Subsequent OSCE conferences, among them the Copenhagen (1990), Moscow (1991) and Helsinki (1992), expanded the scope of the Mechanism in order to make it more effective.

The Mechanism consists of a multi-stage process of negotiations, mediation, and fact-finding, involving bilateral and multilateral negotiations, and OSCE missions of experts and rapporteurs assisted by the OSCE Office for Democratic Institutions and Human Rights (ODIHR). The process usually begins when one or more states claim that another state is not living up to its OSCE human dimension commitments. The states concerned conduct a diplomatic exchange, for which specific time-limits are provided. If the matter is not resolved, the states may bring it to the attention of all OSCE states and place the matter on the agenda of OSCE follow-up or human dimension conferences. If this process does not produce results, the OSCE may appoint expert missions or rapporteur missions to investigate the charges as third-party fact-finders and mediators. As a rule, the missions are established by mutual consent of the states concerned, although such consent is not necessary in serious situations. In such cases a mission may be convoked whenever a group of states or the OSCE Senior Council considers it necessary.

High Commissioner on National Minorities

With the end of the Cold War, real and potential conflicts posed by minority issues, including the armed conflict in the former Yugoslavia, began to threaten the peaceful transition to democracy in Eastern and Central Europe and in the former Soviet Republics. The Copenhagen Concluding Document in 1990 proclaimed a series of important OSCE commitments on minority rights. These commitments were expanded in the Report of the Geneva Meeting of Experts on National Minorities (1991). That report, in turn, was incorporated by reference into the Moscow Concluding Document (1991). In 1992 the OSCE established the office of the High Commissioner on National Minorities (HCNM) to "provide 'early warning' and, as appropriate, 'early action' at the earliest possible stage in regard to tensions involving national minority issues which have not yet developed beyond an early warning stage, but, in the judgment of the High Commissioner, have the potential to develop into a conflict within the CSCE area, affecting peace, stability or relations between participating States, requiring the attention of and action by the Council [of Ministers of Foreign Affairs] or the CSE [Committee of Senior Officials]."

As this mandate indicates, the principal function of the HCNM is to address minority problems before they degenerate into serious conflicts. In all activities, the High Commissioner is to be guided by "CSCE principles and commitments." The HCNM is to "work in confidence and . . . act independently of all parties involved in the tensions." The first highly effective High Commissioner, Mr. Van der Stoel rendered extremely useful mediating and advisory services to governments and national minorities in a number of countries, resolving potentially explosive conflicts or, at least, getting different groups together in the hope of finding solutions.

Representative on Freedom of the Media

The useful work of the High Commissioner on National Minorities led the OSCE to confront another problem and establish the post of Representative on Freedom of the Media. Created in November 1997, the Representative "address[es] serious problems caused by, *inter alia*, obstruction of media activities and unfavorable working conditions for journalists." *Mandate of the OSCE Representative on Freedom of the Media* (November 5, 1997), PC JOURNAL No. 137, Decision No. 193, para. 2. The Media Representative acts as an advocate, observing relevant media developments in OSCE participating States and promoting compliance with OSCE principles and commitments regarding freedom of expression and free media. The Representative also aims to provide early warning on violations of freedom of expression, concentrating on rapid response to serious non-compliance with OSCE principles and commitments by participating States. Where problems arise, the Representative seeks direct contacts with the participating State and other parties involved, assesses the facts and seeks to resolve the issue. The Representative collects and receives information on the situation of the media, including information about hate speech, from participating States, organizations or institutions, media and their representatives, and relevant NGOs. The Representative reports to the Permanent Council, recommending further action where appropriate.

The European Court of Human Rights has relied on OSCE documents in several cases. *See*: *Russian Conservative Party of Entrepreneurs and Others v. Russia*, judgment of Jan. 11, 2007, in which the European Court of Human Rights quoted from the OSCE Final Report on parliamentary elections in the Russian Federation, using it in part to hold that the elections "acclaimed as competitive and pluralistic by international observers" did not unduly restrict the individual applicant's right to take part in free elections. Id., para. 80. The Court also referred to OSCE findings in *Chapman v. the United Kingdom*, Rep. 2001-I (Jan 18, 2001)(concerning the situation of Roma and Sinti minorities in Europe generally and the UK specifically) and in the *Case of Sukhovetskyy v. Ukraine*, app. 13716/02, judgment of March 28, 2006 (holding that there was no violation in requiring electoral candidates to pay a financial deposit).

While these judgments indicate the utility of OSCE investigations of human rights issues, some commentators have questioned the relevance and effectiveness of the OSCE in the post-Cold War era. Erika Schlager noted that the OSCE's "dynamic, multilateral diplomatic process" is perceived to have played a role in ending the Cold War, in large part by fostering compliance by Communist countries with international human rights norms, but she also observed that the OSCE of today is fundamentally different from the original CSCE. The factors that previously made the Helsinki process successful in promoting compliance with its human rights norms have changed and new factors arguably have made the OSCE more limited in this regard. The developments she notes are contained in the following extract.

Erika Schlager, *A Hard Look at Soft Law: The OSCE in* COMMITMENT AND COMPLIANCE: THE ROLE OF NON-BINDING NORMS IN THE INTERNATIONAL LEGAL SYSTEM (D. Shelton, ed. 2000).

[In the HFA] human rights are explicitly linked to consideration of other issues. The HFA states that, "[a]ll the principles set forth above are of primary significance and, accordingly, they will be equally and unreservedly applied, each of them being interpreted taking into account the others." Human rights were thus linked to security issues and to economic and environmental issues, to process and substance. In practice, the integration of and balance of all the "baskets" of the Helsinki Accords was a cornerstone of the process and helped ensure that human rights were not subordinated to other issues.

The linkage was an especially important feature during the early phase of the Helsinki process. If the Soviets wanted to talk about arms reductions, they also had to talk about human rights; if they wanted a follow-up meeting on economic cooperation, they had to agree to a meeting on human contacts and freedom of movement. In short, linkage between issues of interest to Eastern countries (arms negotiations and, to a lesser degree, economic cooperation) and issues of interest to Western countries (human rights and humanitarian concerns) kept both sides engaged in these issues in the face of strong centrifugal forces that could have easily pulled one or the other away from the negotiating table. Today, without the linkages of the Cold War period, the incentives for states to comply are much weaker. The "newly admitted participating States," principally the Central Asian States that joined the CSCE when the Soviet Union collapsed, come to hear their respective human rights records criticized at OSCE meetings today because their attendance is paid for by the Western states which seek to reform them. . . .

During the CSCE meetings, new agreements were negotiated and adopted because of shortcomings in the implementation of existing agreements. Western countries formulated proposals for new agreements to strengthen compliance with existing agreements in areas where they felt non-compliance was the most egregious. For the most part, the new commitments resulted in relatively modest expansions of existing language on human rights, with the most dramatic progress achieved in 1989–91.[52] Nevertheless, many observers believed that each successive CSCE meeting helped increase the pressure on Communist regimes to undertake more sweeping reforms in human rights and other areas.

. . .

To be successful, the Helsinki process needed to coincide with three other elements. First, it needed the human rights groups, east and west, to serve as its engine. They were the ones who turned it into a catalyst for change and kept it from merely validating the status quo. They examined every agreement and compared it to the reality they saw; when reality was found wanting, they sought to change reality to make it more closely mirror the rights and freedoms pronounced in Helsinki agreements. Second, the Helsinki process required the political will of a community of states to articulate a common view of right and wrong, to interpret Helsinki agreements in a way that advanced human rights and deprived human rights violators of a cloak of legitimacy. U.S. leadership was necessary in this but not sufficient. Had the United States spoken alone, its voice probably would not have carried. The perception of the Warsaw Pact as inherently threatening fostered alliance solidarity among Western countries and contributed to their willingness to raise human rights issues. Third, the Helsinki process required leaderships that were capable of being shamed.[53] The emergence of reformist leaders in Central and Eastern Europe in the late 1980's made it possible for compliance with the Helsinki process to become a measure of their progress.

Today, the OSCE participating States that were traditional champions of human rights are relatively reluctant to raise cases and situations of non-compliance. Several factors have contributed to this. First, many human rights violations of the past, such as political imprisonment, have dramatically decreased and there are fewer complaints to be made. Second, human rights problems in the post-Cold War context may be harder to identify specifically as human rights problems as opposed to, for instance, intra or inter-state political conflict. A marked degree of confusion has characterized governmental responses to many post-1990 human rights problems relating to claims of self-determination, minority rights, and citizenship in the context of state succession. In earlier years, many OSCE participating states strongly agreed on the key human rights norms and what constituted an actual human rights violation. Thus, there was wide agreement that Natan Sharansky, Lech Walesa, and Vaclav Havel were political prisoners.

Third, there is a widespread perception among OSCE participating states that governments now generally possess the political will to comply with human rights obligations. Non-complying countries need technical expertise, time, patience and support to make the transition to democracy. Many governments also appear reluctant to criticize countries where human rights problems defy an easy answer or immediate solution. Post-Communist countries, for instance, almost universally lack

---

[52] For the evolution of various commitments, see HUMAN RIGHTS COMMITMENTS WITHIN THE CSCE PROCESS: NATURE, CONTENTS AND APPLICATION IN FINLAND, a publication of the Advisory Board for International Human Rights Affairs (2nd ed., 1994). The book includes a chart of human rights commitments compiled from CSCE documents.

[53] Mikhail Gorbachev, Wojciech Jaruzelski, and Imre Poszgay were capable of being shamed; Nicolae Ceausescu and Milos Jakes were not.

qualified judges which, in turn, has a negative impact on those countries' abilities to fulfill OSCE standards relating to the rule of law. The OSCE "answer" to ameliorating this problem has been to support democracy training programs through the ODIHR.

Fourth, many countries view the practice of criticizing other countries, even at closed-door OSCE meetings, as a vestige of the confrontational Cold War period. This view is especially widespread among European Union member states, a club with an ever increasing membership. Finally, there appears to have been an unwritten assumption that with the advent of democracy, evidenced by free and fair elections, human rights problems automatically diminish. Those participating in the OSCE only now may be coming to grips with the idea that free and fair elections can install anti-democratic dictators in office.

In sum, while implementation review was the principle means through which the Helsinki process fostered human rights compliance during the period running from roughly 1975 to 1990, the political dynamic in the OSCE has changed in the post-Cold War period. There is vastly diminished willingness on the part of the participating States to utilize the OSCE as a forum to engage in public review of non-compliance.

———————————

For other analysis of the recent work of the OSCE, see: M. BOTHE, N. RONZIITE AND A. ROSAS, THE OSCE IN THE MAINTENANCE OF PEACE AND SECURITY (1997); P. CUMPER AND S. WHEATLEY (EDS) MAJORING IN MINORITIES: MINORITY RIGHTS IN THE 'NEW' EUROPE (1999); W. ZELLNER, ON THE EFFECTIVENESS OF THE OSCE MINORITY REGIME (1999).

C. The Americas

The inter-American system for the protection of human rights is characterized by its dual institutional structure—one having evolved from the Charter of the Organization of American States and the other created by the entry into force of the American Convention on Human Rights. While the present human rights system functions within the Organization of American States, the inter-American system as such predates the 1948 Charter that created the OAS.

i. Human Rights in the Americas 1826–1948

The origins of the present system can be traced to the 1826 Congress of Panama, urged by Simon Bolivar to consider a confederation of Latin American States. The Treaty of Perpetual Union, League, and Confederation adopted at that meeting would have joined Colombia (which included Ecuador, Panama and Venezuela), Mexico, Central America and Peru, but only Colombia ratified the treaty. Nevertheless, this Congress set a precedent for a series of regional meetings to discuss mutual defense and other forms of cooperation.

Prior to 1890 the regional meetings, or Congresses, were convoked in response to specific problems or needs. They were institutionalized with the holding of the First International American Conference (Washington, D. C., 1889–1890), which established "The International Union of American Republics" to promote the collection and distribution of commercial information. Its purposes were to be carried out by "The Commercial Bureau of the American Republics" which was created at the same time.

The International Conferences of American States met regularly until 1938, with a hiatus produced by World War II.[54] At the Fourth Conference (Buenos Aires, 1910), the "International Union" and the "Commercial Bureau" were renamed the "Union of American Republics" and the "Pan American Union," respectively. In subsequent years, the functions of the Pan American Union were broadened; under the Charter of the OAS it became the General Secretariat of the Organization.

In addition to the regularly scheduled international conferences, the American States met on six occasions in the period 1936–1947 to consider problems of war, peace and security. The Inter-American Conference for the Maintenance of Peace (Buenos Aires, 1936) created a new mechanism or procedure, called "consultation" as a response to unforeseen and urgent situations. The outbreak of World War II led to three meetings of consultation.[55] As the end of the war drew near, a special Inter-American Conference on Problems of War and Peace (Mexico, 1945) studied ways to strengthen the inter-American system. Within the next few years, the Inter-American Treaty of Reciprocal Assistance (1947), known also as the Rio Pact, and the Charter of the Organization of American States (Bogota, 1948) were signed.

The American States manifested their concern with the protection of human rights from the very origin of the inter-American system. The Treaty of Perpetual Union, League and Confederation (Panama, 1826), Arts. 23 and 27, recognized the principle of juridical equality of nationals of a state and foreigners; in addition, the Contracting Parties pledged themselves to cooperate in the abolition of the slave trade.

In the Twentieth Century prior to World War II, specific treaties reflected hemispheric concerns. The initial focus was upon the rights of aliens,[56] followed by an emphasis on questions of nationality and asylum,[57] and finally, conventions related to peace and the rights of women.[58] In addition, conference resolutions re-

---

[54] Second International Conference of American States (Mexico City, 1901–1902); Third ICAS (Rio de Janeiro, 1906); Fourth ICAS (Buenos Aires, 1910); Fifth ICAS (Santiago, 1923); Sixth ICAS (Havana, 1928); Seventh ICAS (Montevideo, 1933); Eighth ICAS (Lima, 1938); Ninth ICAS (Bogota, 1948).

[55] Meetings of Consultation: 1st (Panama, 1939); 2nd (Havana, 1940); 3rd (Rio de Janeiro, 1942); 4th (Washington, D. C., 1951); 5th (Santiago, 1959); 6th (San Jose, 1960); 7th (San Jose, 1960); 8th (Punta del Este, 1962); 9th (Washington, D. C., 1964); 10th (Washington, D. C., 1965); 11th (Washington, D. C., Buenos Aires and Punta del Este, 1966); 12th (Washington. D. C., 1967); 13th (Washington, D. C., 1969–1981); 14th (Washington, D.C., 1971); 15th (Quito, 1974); 16th (San Jose, 1975); 17th (Washington, D. C., 1978); 18th (Washington, D. C., 1982).

[56] Treaty for the Extradition of Criminals and for Protection against Anarchism (1902); Convention relative to the Rights of Aliens (1902); Convention on Private International Law (1928); Convention on the Status of Aliens (1928).

[57] Convention establishing the Status of Naturalized Citizens who again take up Residence in the Country of Origin (1906); Convention on Asylum (1928); Convention on the Nationality of Women (1933); Convention on Nationality (1933); Convention on Extradition (1933); Convention on Political Asylum (1933).

[58] Convention on the Rights and Duties of States (1933); Convention for the Maintenance, Preservation and Reestablishment of Peace (1936); Convention concerning Peaceful Orientation of Public Instruction (1936); Inter-American Convention on the Granting of Political Rights to Women (1948); Inter-American Convention on the Granting of Civil Rights to Women (1948).

lated to human rights became common in the immediate pre-War period; many of the early ones referred to labor conditions. Concern for labor, women and children continued through the war years, but other resolutions reflected wartime preoccupations: 1936: "Humanization of War;" 1938: "Defense of Human Rights" and "Persecution for Racial or Religious Motives;" 1942: "Humanization of War;" 1945: "War Crimes," "Free Access to Information," "International Protection of the Essential Rights of Man," "Racial Discrimination," and "Persecution of the Jews."

ii. The OAS and Human Rights

The Inter-American system as it exists today began with the transformation of the Pan American Union into the Organization of American States. The OAS Charter, a multilateral treaty that is the constitution of the OAS, was opened for signature in Bogotá, Colombia, in 1948 and entered into force in 1951. The Charter has been amended by the Protocol of Buenos Aires, which came into effect in 1970, and by the Protocols of Cartagena de Indias, Managua, and Washington, in force since 1988, 1996 and 1997, respectively. The thirty-five OAS member states are all the sovereign states of the Americas: Antigua and Barbuda, Argentina, The Bahamas, Barbados, Belize, Bolivia, Brazil, Canada, Chile, Colombia, Costa Rica, Cuba, Dominica, Dominican Republic, Ecuador, El Salvador, Grenada, Guatemala, Guyana, Haiti, Honduras, Jamaica, Mexico, Nicaragua, Panama, Paraguay, Peru, St. Kitts and Nevis, St. Lucia, St. Vincent and the Grenadines, Suriname, Trinidad and Tobago, United States, Uruguay, and Venezuela. Although the Castro government was expelled from the Organization in 1962, Cuba remains a Member State.

The 1948 Charter made few references to human rights, but one important provision was Article 3(j), now Article 3(l), wherein "the American States proclaim the fundamental rights of the individual without distinction as to race, nationality, creed, or sex" to be among the principles to which they are committed. Human rights also appeared in Article 13, now Article 17, which declared that "each State has the right to develop its cultural, political and economic life freely and naturally," but that "in this free development, the State shall respect the rights of the individual and the principles of universal morality."

The 1948 Charter did not define "the fundamental rights of the individual" to which Articles 3 and 17 referred, nor did it create any institution to promote their observance. However, the same diplomatic conference which concluded the OAS Charter also proclaimed the American Declaration of the Rights and Duties of Man, some seven months prior to the UN's adoption of the Universal Declaration of Human Rights. Promulgated in the form of a simple conference resolution, the Declaration provides an extensive catalog of human rights and serves to give definition to the Charter's general commitment to human rights.

The OAS discharges its functions through various organs foreseen in the Charter, including the General Assembly and Permanent Council. The General Assembly meets once a year in regular session and in as many special ones as necessary. It is the supreme policy-setting organ of the Organization. Each Member State has one vote in the Assembly. The Permanent Council is composed of the permanent representatives of each Member State to the OAS. The Council serves as the Organization's decision-making organ between Assembly sessions and performs various other functions bearing on the resolution of disputes and peacekeeping. Both organs have jurisdiction to deal with human rights matters.

Thomas Buergenthal, *The Inter-American System for the Protection of Human Rights*, ANUARIO JURIDICO INTERAMERICANO 1981 (OAS, 1982) pp. 105–109, 80–81.

Until 1970, the human rights system of the OAS was based on a very weak constitutional foundation. The Commission [on Human Rights approved in 1959] lacked an express treaty basis and derived its existence from OAS conference resolutions of uncertain legal force. This situation changed dramatically with the entry into force of the Protocol of Buenos Aires, which effected extensive amendments of the OAS Charter. The newly revised Charter changed the status of the Commission from an "autonomous entity of the OAS' into one of the principal organs of the OAS. Its functions were defined as follows in Article 112 of the amended Charter:

> There shall be an Inter-American Commission on Human Rights, whose principal function shall be to promote the observance and protection of human rights and to serve as a consultative organ of the Organization in these matters.
>
> An Inter-American Convention on human rights shall determine the structure, competence, and procedure of this Commission, as well as those of other organs responsible for these matters.

Although the Protocol of Buenos Aires entered into force in 1970—one year after the American Convention on Human Rights was adopted—it was drafted in 1967. At that time the Convention was not yet in existence.

The drafters of the Protocol consequently attached a transitory provision to the revised OAS Charter, in which they provided that "until the Inter-American convention on human rights, referred to in [Article 112], enters into force, the present Inter-American Commission on Human Rights shall keep vigilance over the observance of human rights."

These provisions of the revised OAS Charter gave institutional legitimacy to the Commission by recognizing it as a treaty-based OAS organ. Moreover, through the transitory provision, the Commission's Statute became an inherent part of the Charter itself. The revised Charter thus effectively legitimated the powers that the Commission exercised under Articles 9 and 9 (bis) of its Statute and it recognized the normative character of the American Declaration of the Rights and Duties of Man as a standard by which to judge the human rights activities of all OAS Member States.(. . .)

——————————

Interpretation of the American Declaration of the Rights and Duties of Man
within the Framework of Article 64 of the American Convention on Human
Rights, Advisory Opinion OC-10/89 of July 14, 1989, 10 Inter-Am. Ct. H.R. (Ser.
A) (1989), reprinted in *Annual Report* 1989, at 109, O.A.S. Doc. OEA/Ser.L/V/III,
doc. 14 (1989) (some references omitted).

1. By note of February 17, 1988, the Government of the Republic of Colombia . . . submitted to the Inter-American Court of Human Rights a request for an
advisory opinion on the interpretation of Article 64 of the American Convention on
Human Rights . . . in relation to the American Declaration of the Rights and Duties
of Man. . . .

2. The Government requests a reply to the following question:

Does Article 64 authorize the Inter-American Court of Human Rights to render
advisory opinions at the request of a member state or one of the organs of the OAS,
regarding the interpretation of the American Declaration of the Rights and Duties of
Man, adopted by the Ninth International Conference of American States in Bogota in
1948?

The Government adds:

The Government of Colombia understands, of course, that the Declaration is not a
treaty. But this conclusion does not automatically answer the question. It is perfectly
reasonable to assume that the interpretation of the human rights provisions contained
in the Charter of the OAS, as revised by the Protocol of Buenos Aires, involves, in principle, an analysis of the rights and duties of man proclaimed by the Declaration, and
thus requires the determination of the normative status of the Declaration within the
legal framework of the inter-American system for the protection of human rights.

The applicant Government points out that

[F]or the appropriate functioning of the inter-American system for the protection
of human rights, it is of great importance to know what the juridical status of the
Declaration is, whether the Court has jurisdiction to interpret the Declaration, and
if so, what the scope of its jurisdiction is within the framework of Article 64 of the
Convention.

. . . .

4. By note of March 2, 1988, pursuant to Article 52 of the Court's Rules of Procedure, the Secretariat requested written observations on the question from all the
member states of the Organization of American States . . . , and through the Secretary General, from the organs listed in Article 51 of the Charter of the OAS, or
Article 52 of the Charter as revised by the Protocol of Cartagena de Indias, after its
entry into force for the ratifying states.

. . . .

11. In its written observations, the Government of Costa Rica "believes that notwithstanding its great success and nobility, the American Declaration of the Rights
and Duties of Man is not a treaty as defined by international law, so Article 64 of the
American Convention does not authorize the Inter-American Court to interpret
the Declaration. Nevertheless, that could not in any way limit the Court's possible
use of the Declaration and its precepts to interpret other, related juridical instruments or a finding that many of the rights recognized therein have become international customary law."

12. The Government of the United States of America believes:

The American Declaration of the Rights and Duties of Man represents a noble statement of the human rights aspirations of the American States. Unlike the American Convention, however, it was not drafted as a legal instrument and lacks the precision necessary to resolve complex legal questions. Its normative value lies as a declaration of basic moral principles and broad political commitments and as a basis to review the general human rights performance of member states, not as a binding set of obligations.

The United States recognizes the good intentions of those who would transform the American Declaration from a statement of principles into a binding legal instrument. But good intentions do not make law. It would seriously undermine the process of international lawmaking—by which sovereign states voluntarily undertake specified legal obligations—to impose legal obligations on states through a process of "re-interpretation" or "inference" from a non-binding statement of principles.

13. For its part, the Government of Peru said that

[A]lthough the Declaration could have been considered an instrument without legal effect before the American Convention on Human Rights entered into force, the Convention has recognized its special nature by virtue of Article 29, which prohibits any interpretation excluding or limiting the effect that the American Declaration of the Rights and Duties of Man and other international acts of the same nature may have and has thus given the Declaration a hierarchy similar to that of the Convention with regard to the States Parties, thereby contributing to the promotion of human rights in our continent.

14. The Government of Uruguay affirmed that

i) The Inter-American Court of Human Rights is competent to render advisory opinions on any aspect of the American Declaration of the Rights and Duties of Man in relation to the revised Charter of the Organization of American States and the American Convention on Human Rights, within the scope of Article 64 of the latter.

ii) The juridical nature of the Declaration is that of a binding, multilateral instrument that enunciates, defines and specifies fundamental principles recognized by the American States and which crystallizes norms of customary law generally accepted by those States.

15. The Government of Venezuela asserted that

[A]s a general principle recognized by international law, a declaration is not a treaty in the true sense because it does not create juridical norms, and it is limited to a statement of desires or exhortations. A declaration creates political or moral obligations for the subjects of international law, and its enforceability is thus limited in contrast to a treaty, whose legal obligations are enforceable before a jurisdictional body.

The Government recognizes that the Declaration is not a treaty in the strict sense. The Court will surely ratify this position, and it should also decide that it is not competent to interpret the American Declaration of the Rights and Duties of Man adopted in Bogota in 1948, given that the Declaration is not a treaty "concerning the protection of human rights in the American states," as required by Article 64 of the American Convention on Human Rights.

. . . .

29. The Court will now address the merits of the question before it.

30. Article 64(1) of the Convention authorizes the Court to render advisory opinions regarding the interpretation of this Convention or of other treaties concerning

the protection of human rights in the American states. That is, the object of the advisory opinions of the Court is treaties.

. . . .

31. According to the Vienna Convention on the Law of Treaties of 1969

'treaty' means an international agreement concluded between States in written form and governed by international law, whether embodied in a single instrument or in two or more related instruments and whatever its particular designation (Art. 2(1) (a)).

32. The Vienna Convention of 1986 on the Law of Treaties among States and International Organizations or among International Organizations provides as follows in Article 2(1)(a):

'treaty' means an international agreement governed by international law and concluded in written form:

(i) between one or more States and one or more international organizations; or

(ii) between international organizations, whether that agreement is embodied in a single instrument or in two or more related instruments and whatever its particular designation.

33. In attempting to define the word "treaty" as the term is employed in Article 64(1), it is sufficient for now to say that a "treaty" is, at the very least, an international instrument of the type that is governed by the two Vienna Conventions. Whether the term includes other international instruments of a conventional nature whose existence is also recognized by those Conventions (Art. 3, Vienna Convention of 1969; Art. 3, Vienna Convention of 1986), need not be decided at this time. What is clear, however, is that the Declaration is not a treaty as defined by the Vienna Conventions because it was not approved as such, and that, consequently, it is also not a treaty within the meaning of Article 64(1).

. . . .

37. The American Declaration has its basis in the idea that "the international protection of the rights of man should be the principal guide of an evolving American law." This American law has evolved from 1948 to the present; international protective measures, subsidiary and complementary to national ones, have been shaped by new instruments. As the International Court of Justice said: "an international instrument must be interpreted and applied within the overall framework of the juridical system in force at the time of the interpretation " (*Legal Consequences for States of the Continued Presence of South Africa in Namibia (South West Africa) notwithstanding Security Council Resolution 276* (1970), Advisory Opinion, I.C.J. Reports 1971, p. 16 ad 31). That is why the Court finds it necessary to point out that to determine the legal status of the American Declaration it is appropriate to look to the inter-American system of today in the light of the evolution it has undergone since the adoption of the Declaration, rather than to examine the normative value and significance which that instrument was believed to have had in 1948.

38. The evolution of the here relevant "inter-American law" mirrors on the regional level the developments in contemporary international law and especially in human rights law, which distinguished that law from classical international law to a significant extent. That is the case, for example, with the duty to respect certain essential human rights, which is today considered to be an *erga omnes* obligation

(*Barcelona Traction, Light and Power Company, Limited, Second Phase*, Judgment, I.C.J. Reports 1970, p. 3. For an analysis following the same line of thought see also *Legal Consequences for States of the Continued Presence of South Africa in Namibia (South West Africa) notwithstanding Security Council Resolution 276* (1970) supra 37, p. 16 ad 57; cfr. *United States Diplomatic and Consular Staff in Tehran*, I.C.J. Reports 1980, p. 3 ad 42).

39. The Charter of the Organization refers to the fundamental rights of man in its Preamble (paragraph three) and in Arts. 3(j), 16, 43, 47, 51, 112 and 150; Preamble (paragraph four), Arts. 3(k), 16, 44, 48, 52, 111 and 150 of the Charter revised by the Protocol of Cartagena de Indias, but it does not list or define them. The member states of the Organization have, through its diverse organs, given specificity to the human rights mentioned in the Charter and to which the Declaration refers.

40. This is the case of Article 112 of the Charter (Art. 111 of the Charter as amended by the Protocol of Cartagena de Indias) which reads as follows:

> There shall be an Inter-American Commission on Human Rights, whose principal function shall be to promote the observance and protection of human rights and to serve as a consultative organ of the Organization in these matters. An inter-American convention on human rights shall determine the structure, competence, and procedure of this Commission, as well as those of other organs responsible for these matters.

Article 150 of the Charter provides as follows:

> Until the inter-American convention on human rights, referred to in Chapter XVIII (Chapter XVI of the Charter as amended by the Protocol of Cartagena de Indias), enters into force, the present Inter-American Commission on Human Rights shall keep vigilance over the observance of human rights.

41. These norms authorize the Inter-American Commission to protect human rights. These rights are none other than those enunciated and defined in the American Declaration. That conclusion results from Article 1 of the Commission's Statute, which was approved by Resolution No. 447, adopted by the General Assembly of the OAS at its Ninth Regular Period of Sessions, held in La Paz, Bolivia, in October, 1979. That Article reads as follows:

> 1. The Inter-American Commission on Human Rights is an organ of the Organization of the American States, created to promote the observance and defense of human rights and to serve as consultative organ of the Organization in this matter.
> 2. For the purposes of the present Statute, human rights are understood to be:
>   a. The rights set forth in the American Convention on Human Rights, in relation to the States Parties thereto;
>   b. The rights set forth in the American Declaration of the Rights and Duties of Man, in relation to the other member states.

Articles 18, 19 and 20 of the Statute enumerate these functions.

42. The General Assembly of the Organization has also repeatedly recognized that the American Declaration is a source of international obligations for the member states of the OAS. For example, in Resolution 314 (VII-O/77) of June 22, 1977, it charged the Inter-American Commission with the preparation of a study to "set forth their obligation to carry out the commitments assumed in the American Declaration of the Rights and Duties of Man." In Resolution 371 (VIII-O/78) of July 1, 1978, the General Assembly reaffirmed "its commitment to promote the obser-

vance of the American Declaration of the Rights and Duties of Man," and in Resolution 370 (VIII-O/78) of July 1, 1978, it referred to the "international commitments" of a member state of the Organization to respect the rights of man "recognized in the American Declaration of the Rights and Duties of Man." The Preamble of the American Convention to Prevent and Punish Torture, adopted and signed at the Fifteenth Regular Session of the General Assembly in Cartagena de Indias (December, 1985), reads as follows:

> Reaffirming that all acts of torture or any other cruel, inhuman, or degrading treatment or punishment constitute an offense against human dignity and a denial of the principles set forth in the Charter of the Organization of American States and in the Charter of the United Nations and are violations of the fundamental human rights and freedoms proclaimed in the American Declaration of the Rights and Duties of Man and the Universal Declaration of Human Rights.

43. Hence it may be said that by means of an authoritative interpretation, the member states of the Organization have signaled their agreement that the Declaration contains and defines the fundamental human rights referred to in the Charter. Thus the Charter of the Organization cannot be interpreted and applied as far as human rights are concerned without relating its norms, consistent with the practice of the organs of the OAS, to the corresponding provisions of the Declaration.

44. In view of the fact that the Charter of the Organization and the American Convention are treaties with respect to which the Court has advisory jurisdiction by virtue of Article 64(1), it follows that the Court is authorized, within the framework and limits of its competence, to interpret the American Declaration and to render an advisory opinion relating to it whenever it is necessary to do so in interpreting those instruments.

45. For the member states of the Organization, the Declaration is the text that defines the human rights referred to in the Charter. Moreover, Articles 1(2)(b) and 20 of the Commission's Statute define the competence of that body with respect to the human rights enunciated in the Declaration, with the result that to this extent the American Declaration is for these States a source of international obligations related to the Charter of the Organization.

46. For the States Parties to the Convention, the specific source of their obligations with respect to the protection of human rights is, in principle, the Convention itself. It must be remembered, however, that, given the provisions of Article 29(d), these States cannot escape the obligations they have as members of the OAS under the Declaration, notwithstanding the fact that the Convention is the governing instrument for the States Parties thereto.

47. That the Declaration is not a treaty does not, then, lead to the conclusion that it does not have legal effect, nor that the Court lacks the power to interpret it within the framework of the principles set out above.

Questions and Comments

1. What was the legal effect of the OAS Charter amendments effectuated by the Protocol of Buenos Aires, especially the references to the Inter-American Commission on Human

Rights? Is Judge Buergenthal's thesis that the Protocol established the normative status of the American Declaration affirmed in the Court's advisory opinion?

2. Contrast the place and importance of human rights in the OAS in 1948 and today. Note that in the late 1980s, widespread and rapid democratization swept the hemisphere, leading to calls for strengthening of the system. In 1992, the OAS Permanent Council convened the Sixteenth Special Session of the General Assembly to examine proposed OAS Charter amendments concerning suspension of governments in case of anti-democratic coups and the issue of extreme poverty in the region. The OAS adopted the Protocol of Washington in the District of Columbia on December 14, 1992. It provides for the suspension of any member whose democratically constituted government has been overthrown by force. On the other topic of concern, the Protocol added to the organization's purposes and principles the topic of eradication of extreme poverty, called "an obstacle to the full democratic development of the peoples of the hemisphere." Article 33 was amended to detail the program for addressing the problem of poverty. The Permanent Council asked for further amendments to address extreme poverty and to enable it to function more effectively in its delivery of technical cooperation services and the OAS adopted the Protocol of Managua on June 10, 1993 in which it created a new Inter-American Council for Integral Development to replace several former bodies.

3. What specific human rights obligations bind OAS member states pursuant to the Charter?

4. Is the American Declaration legally binding on all OAS member states? Is it a treaty? Is it customary international law? By what process did it come to be "a source of international obligation?" How do the views of the member states that intervened in the advisory proceedings differ on this point? If the Declaration is not a treaty, how should it be interpreted and applied?

5. The Protocol of Cartagena de Indias added paragraph (e) to Article 3. It provides:

> Every State has the right to choose, without external interference, its political, economic, and social system and to organize itself in the way best suited to it, and has the duty to abstain from intervening in the affairs of another State. Subject to the foregoing, the American States shall cooperate fully among themselves, independently of the nature of their political, economic, and social systems.

The United States declared at the time of signing the Protocol: "Article 3 of the Charter, as amended by the Protocol, paragraph (e), must be interpreted consistent with, and does not derogate from, the democratic principles embodied in paragraph (d) of this same article. Accordingly, it neither bars the promotion under the Charter and Rio Treaty of democracy and security by the Organization and its member states, nor requires the OAS or its member states to accept regimes that are undemocratic or otherwise hostile to inter-American values, nor is it intended in any way to change the fundamental character of the OAS as an organization of democratic states." Does this statement have any legal significance?

iii. Member State Obligations: The Case of Cuba

According to the OAS Statute, Article 6, any independent American State desiring to become a member of the Organization should address the Secretary General and declare that it is willing to sign and ratify the Charter of the Organization and "to accept all the obligations inherent in membership," which include human rights obligations. No state has been denied membership or expelled based on human rights violations since the Organization was established, but other actions have been taken, including suspending the right of a government to participate while maintaining the state's legal obligations.

The region has long expressed its concern with the interrelated topics of democratic governance, human rights, and the rule of law. At the Tenth Inter-American Conference in 1954, Resolution XXVII, *Strengthening of the System for the Protection of Human Rights* declared that the strengthening of democracy and its effective exercise require measures to ensure the full operation of democratic institutions, among them systems for the protection of the rights and freedoms of man through international or collective action. The Conference concluded that fundamental human rights can be achieved only under a system of representative democracy. Resolution XXX addressed the right to vote and to participate in government, paying tribute to those countries which had taken measures to extend the right of suffrage and eliminate discrimination, as well as lauding their efforts to broaden and strengthen institutions of representative democracy. The subsequent Declaration of Caracas expressed the conviction of the American States that "one of the most effective means of strengthening their democratic institutions is to increase respect for the individual and social rights of man, without any discrimination. . . ."

The Fifth Meeting of Consultation of the Ministers of Foreign Affairs in 1959 adopted another important text on political rights. The two main agenda items of the conference were international tension in the Caribbean region and the effective exercise of representative democracy and human rights. The text adopted, known as the Declaration of Santiago, Chile, affirms that effective exercise of representative democracy is the best vehicle for the promotion of social and political progress. *Fifth Meeting of Consultation of Ministers of Foreign Affairs, Final Act,* OEA/Ser.C/II.5, pp. 4–6. Moreover, an improved standard of living throughout the hemisphere is said to be the best and firmest foundation on which to base the practical exercise of democracy and to stabilize its institutions. Human rights and fundamental freedoms and the exercise of representative democracy were affirmed as essential to harmony among the American republics. The resolution made it explicit that "the existence of antidemocratic regimes constitutes a violation of the principles on which the Organization of American States is founded, and a danger to united and peaceful relationships in the hemisphere."

In the light of the relevant OAS Charter provisions and cited resolutions, consider the following actions taken by the OAS institutions. In particular, consider how to reconcile the demands imposed by the Charter's two obligations of respect for human rights and non-intervention in domestic affairs. In respect to the action taken, note that concern with human rights in Cuba accompanied the Cuban revolution of the late 1950s, but it was only with the Cuban missile crisis of 1962 that the OAS took a decision concerning the Cuban government.

Exclusion of the Present Government of Cuba from Participation in the Inter-American System, Resolution VI, Eighth Meeting of Consultation of Ministers of Foreign Affairs, Jan-22–31, 1962.

WHEREAS:

The inter-American system is based on consistent adherence by its constituent states to certain objectives and principles of solidarity, set forth in the instruments that govern it;

Among these objectives and principles are those of respect for the freedom of man and preservation of his rights, the full exercise of representative democracy, nonintervention of one state in the internal or external affairs of another, and rejection of alliances and agreements that may lead to intervention in America by extracontinental powers;

The Seventh Meeting of Consultation of Ministers of Foreign Affairs, held in San Jose, Costa Rica, condemned the intervention or the threat of intervention of extracontinental communist powers in the hemisphere and reiterated the obligation of the American states to observe faithfully the principles of the regional organization;

The present Government of Cuba has identified itself with the principles of Marxist-Leninist ideology, has established a political, economic, and social system based on that doctrine, and accepts military assistance from extracontinental communist powers, including even the threat of military intervention in America on the part of the Soviet Union;

The abovementioned Report of the Inter-American Peace Committee also states that:

It is evident that the ties of the Cuban Government with the Sino-Soviet bloc will prevent the said government from fulfilling the obligations stipulated in the Charter of the Organization and the Treaty of Reciprocal Assistance;

Such a situation in an American state violates the obligations inherent in membership in the regional system and is incompatible with that system;

The attitude adopted by the present Government of Cuba and its acceptance of military assistance offered by extracontinental communist powers breaks down the effective defense of the inter-American system; and

No member state of the inter-American system can claim the rights and privileges pertaining thereto if it denies or fails to recognize the corresponding obligations,

The Eighth Meeting of Consultation of Ministers of Foreign Affairs, Serving as Organ of Consultation in Application of the Inter-American Treaty of Reciprocal Assistance

DECLARES:

1. That, as a consequence of repeated acts, the present Government of Cuba has voluntarily placed itself outside the inter-American system.

2. That this situation demands unceasing vigilance on the part of the member states of the Organization of American States, which shall report to the Council any fact or situation that could endanger the peace and security of the hemisphere.

3. That the American states have a collective interest in strengthening the inter-American system and reuniting it on the basis of respect for human rights and the

principles and objectives relative to the exercise of democracy set forth in the Charter of the Organization;

and, therefore

RESOLVES:

1. That adherence by any member of the Organization of American States to Marxism-Leninism is incompatible with the inter-American system and the alignment of such a government with the communist bloc breaks the unity and solidarity of the hemisphere.

2. That the present Government of Cuba, which has officially identified itself as a Marxist-Leninist government, is incompatible with the principles and objectives of the inter-American system.

3. That this incompatibility excludes the present Government of Cuba from participation in the inter-American system.

4. That the Council of the Organization of American States and the other organs and organizations of the inter-American system adopt without delay the measures necessary to comply with this resolution.

_____

Questions and Comments

1. Does the OAS Charter provide a legal basis for the decision to exclude Cuba's government from its rights of participation?

2. The resolution remains in force; has the breakup of the Soviet Union and end of communist rule in Russia taken away the rationale for excluding the Cuban government?

3. What, if anything, does this resolution have to do with human rights? Would human rights violations without "extra-continental" participation provide grounds for suspending a government's participation in the OAS?

iv. Responses to Extra-Legal Assumptions of Power

In 1991, the OAS adopted Resolution 1080, or the "Santiago Commitment," instructing the Secretary General to convene the Permanent Council or the General Assembly in the event of "a sudden or irregular interruption" of the democratic process in a member state, and to act to resolve that conflict. *See:* OAS General Assembly Resolution 1080, *Representative Democracy*, Resolution AG/RES. 1080 (XXI-O/91), adopted at the fifth plenary session, held on June 5, 1991. A year later, on December 14, 1992, the OAS adopted the Washington Protocol to the OAS Charter, becoming the first regional organization to allow suspension of a member state in the event that its democratically elected government is overthrown by force. Before Resolution 1080 was superseded by the Washington Protocol, the OAS used it in four instances in which either a military coup, self-coup by an elected President, or severe civil-military crisis occurred. Two of the resolutions adopted are reproduced below.

Some observers have criticized the OAS's failure to invoke Resolution 1080 more frequently or more effectively. Only in the case of the *coup d'etat* in Haiti in 1991, which overthrew a president elected under an internationally-monitored election, did the OAS decide to use Resolution 1080 to deny recognition to coup leaders and demand immediate reinstatement of the former government. The resolution urged member states to "isolate" those holding power by taking diplomatic and economic sanctions. See MRE/RES/1/91 *Support for the Democratic Government of Haiti*. Subsequently, a Meeting of Foreign Ministers urged OAS Member States to freeze the bank accounts of the coup members and to embargo the country except for humanitarian aid. The United Nations also took action after the OAS referred the problem of Haiti to the Security Council. In July 1993, the Haitian military leaders agreed to negotiations which led to the Governors Island Agreement; failure of the military to implement the agreement led to further UN and OAS action strengthening the sanctions. On September 23, 1993, the UN Security Council approved a mission to Haiti to supervise the police and military and a month later re-imposed an oil and arms embargo. By the end of 1992, the OAS could invoke Article 9 of the Protocol of Washington, although it had not been widely ratified. The OAS efforts were not limited to restoration of the former government; between the coup of September 29, 1991 and February 1994, the Inter-American Commission made four on-site visits to Haiti and reported on "an alarming number of human rights violations."

Does Article 9 provide a stronger legal basis for action than Resolution 1080? Does the Charter amendment explain the sanctions imposed on Haiti or are they more likely a result of international commitment to President Aristide because of UN and OAS certification of his election as free and fair? Could or should the OAS take more forceful measures against those overthrowing a legitimate government? If so, why has it refrained from doing so? For an overview of OAS resolutions on democracy and human rights, see D. Shelton, *Representative Democracy and Human rights in the Western Hemisphere*, 12 H.R.L.J. 353 (1991).

Article 9, OAS Charter, as Amended by the Protocol of Washington

A Member of the Organization whose democratically constituted government has been overthrown by force may be suspended from the exercise of the right to participate in the sessions of the General Assembly, the Meeting of Consultation, the Councils of the Organization and the Specialized Conferences as well as in the commissions, working groups and any other bodies established.

   a) The power to suspend shall be exercised only when such diplomatic initiatives undertaken by the Organization for the purpose of promoting the restoration of representative democracy in the affected Member State have been unsuccessful;

   b) The decision to suspend shall be adopted at a special session of the General Assembly by an affirmative vote of two-thirds of the Member States;

   c) The suspension shall take effect immediately following its approval by the General Assembly;

   d) The suspension notwithstanding, the Organization shall endeavor to undertake additional diplomatic initiatives to contribute to the re-establishment of representative democracy in the affected Member State;

   e) The Member which has been subject to suspension shall continue to fulfill its obligations to the Organization;

f) The General Assembly may lift the suspension by a decision adopted with the approval of two-thirds of the Member States;

g) The powers referred to in this article shall be exercised in accordance with this Charter.

OAS Permanent Council, *The Situation in Peru,* CP/RES. 579 (897/92).

THE PERMANENT COUNCIL OF THE ORGANIZATION OF AMERICAN STATES,

BEARING IN MIND that the Preamble to the Charter of the Organization of American States establishes that representative democracy is an indispensable condition for the stability, peace and development of the region;

BEARING IN MIND that one of the fundamental purposes of the OAS is to promote and consolidate representative democracy, with due respect for the principle of nonintervention;

REAFFIRMING the Santiago Commitment to Democracy and the Renewal of the Inter-American System;

MINDFUL that the grave events in Peru constitute an interruption of the democratic institutional political process in that country in the terms of resolution AG/RES. 1080 (XXI-O/91) "Representative Democracy," and

HAVING HEARD the Report of the Secretary General of the Organization on the situation in Peru and the statements by delegations,

RESOLVES:

1. To deplore the events that have taken place in Peru and express its deepest concern about their effects on the validity of the institutional mechanisms of representative democracy in the region.

2. To urge the authorities in that country to immediately reinstate democratic institutions and full respect for human rights under the rule of law.

3. In view of the gravity of those events in Peru, to convoke an ad hoc meeting of Ministers of Foreign Affairs in accordance with resolution AG/RES. 1080 (XXI-O/91) "Representative Democracy," and to instruct the Secretary General to that effect.

OAS Permanent Council, *Support for the Democratic Government of Venezuela,* CP/RES. 599 (925/92).

THE PERMANENT COUNCIL OF THE ORGANIZATION OF AMERICAN STATES,

BEARING IN MIND that the Preamble of the Charter of the OAS establishes that "representative democracy is an indispensable condition for the stability, peace and development of the region", and that one of the essential purposes of the Organization is "to promote and consolidate representative democracy, with due respect for the principle of nonintervention;"

RECALLING the Santiago Commitment to Democracy and the Renewal of the Inter-American System, adopted by the General Assembly at its twenty-first regular session in Santiago, Chile; CP/RES. 576 (887/92) "Support for the Democratic Government of Venezuela", adopted by the Permanent Council on February 4, 1992; and AG/RES. 1189 (XXII-O/92) "Support for the Democratic Government of Venezuela," adopted by the General Assembly at its twenty-second regular session in Nassau, The Bahamas;

CONSIDERING today's events, which constitute an attempted coup d'etat to overthrow the legitimate Government of the Republic of Venezuela;

RESOLVES:

1. To protest and condemn in the strongest terms the armed uprising against the democratic Government of Venezuela.

2. To express its resolute and unconditional support to the constitutional Government of Venezuela and its solidarity with President Carlos Andres Perez and the Venezuelan people.

3. To repudiate all those who, through the use of force, attempt to usurp popular sovereignty and interrupt the functioning of any democratically elected government in the hemisphere.

4. To reiterate the decision of the governments of the member states to abide by and strengthen the principles of democratic solidarity, in keeping with the OAS Charter, and to reaffirm that there is no more room in the hemisphere for regimes established by dint of force.

5. To instruct the Chairman of the Permanent Council to transmit this resolution to the Government of the Republic of Venezuela.

6. To instruct the Secretary General of the Organization to transmit this resolution to the United Nations and to circulate it immediately as widely as possible.

---

v. Sanctioning a Government for Human Rights Violations: The Somoza Case

In November 1978, the Inter-American Commission on Human Rights published its *Report on the Situation of Human Rights in Nicaragua*, the result of an on-site visit to the country. OAS Doc. OEA/Ser.L/V/II.45, doc. 18 rev. 1. The Commission decided to undertake the report because of a large body of complaints, communications and other data alleging widespread violations of human rights in the country. One of the most serious complaints concerned 338 peasants captured by the National Guard between 1975 and 1977. Credible sources declared that out of this group of *campesinos*, seventeen were released after having been imprisoned without trial for eighteen months; the remaining 321 were never seen again and were presumed dead. The report noted that the lack of respect for human rights in Nicaragua was neither recent nor sporadic, but rather constituted a system practiced for many years. The report dealt, however, exclusively with the state of emergency then in effect in Nicaragua, which had existed during the greater part of the administration of President Somoza which began on December 1, 1974. Due to the declared State of Siege applicable when constitutional rights were suspended,

Martial Law applied throughout the country, a regime the Commission described as "lending itself to a systematic and generalized violation of human rights established in the American Declaration of the Rights and Duties of Man." The Commission concluded that the government was responsible for serious and widespread violations of human rights and humanitarian law, involving large numbers of deaths, torture, arbitrary detention, and denial of the freedoms of expression, religion and assembly. While the violations affected all sectors of the Nicaraguan population, the victims were mostly poor and young people between the ages of 14 and 21. The report was delivered to the Ministers of Foreign Affairs, who adopted the following resolution.

Resolution II, XVII Meeting of Consultation of Ministers of Foreign Affairs, Washington DC, Sept. 21, 1978, OAS Doc. OEA/Ser.F/II.17, Doc. 40/79, rev. 2, June 23, 1979, pp. 1–2.

WHEREAS:
- The people of Nicaragua are suffering the horrors of a fierce armed conflict that is causing grave hardships and loss of life, and has thrown the country into a serious political, social, and economic upheaval;
- The inhumane conduct of the dictatorial regime governing the country, as evidence by the report of the Inter-American Commission on Human Rights, is the fundamental cause of the dramatic situation faced by the Nicaraguan peoples and;
- The spirit of solidarity that guides Hemisphere relations places an unavoidable obligation on the American countries to exert every effort within their power, to put an end to the bloodshed and to avoid the prolongation of this conflict which is disrupting the peace of the Hemisphere;

The Seventeenth Meeting of Consultation of Ministers of Foreign Affairs,

DECLARES:
    That the solution of the serious problem is exclusively within the jurisdiction of the people of Nicaragua.
    That in the view of the Seventeenth Meeting of Consultation of Ministers of Foreign Affairs this solution should be arrived at on the basis of the following:
    1. Immediate and definitive replacement of the Somoza regime.
    2. Installation in Nicaraguan territory of a democratic government, the composition of which should include the principal representative groups which oppose the Somoza regime and which reflects the free will of the people of Nicaragua.
    3. Guarantee of the respect for human rights of all Nicaraguans without exception.
    4. The holding of free elections as soon as possible, that will lead to the establishment of a truly democratic government that guarantees peace, freedom and justice.

RESOLVES:

1. To urge the member states to take steps that are within their reach to facilitate an enduring and peaceful solution of the Nicaraguan problem on the bases set forth above, scrupulously respecting the principle of nonintervention and abstaining from any action that might be in conflict with the above basis or be incompatible with a peaceful and enduring solution to the problem.

2. To commit their efforts to promote humanitarian assistance to the people of Nicaragua and to contribute to the social and economic recovery of the country.

3. To keep the Seventeenth Meeting of Consultation of Ministers of Foreign Affairs open while the present situation continues.

——————

Questions and Comments

1. In 1981, Anastasio Somoza wrote his memoirs, entitled *Nicaragua Betrayed* (Boston: Western Islands Publishers, 1981). In the book, he noted that the draft resolution against him had fourteen co-sponsors and required only three additional members to reach the two-thirds majority needed to pass. It easily achieved this number. According to Somoza, the resolution was legally binding on the entire membership of the OAS and it consequently "banished my government in the family of nations." He announced his resignation, stating "our government cannot continue with the OAS resolution which was passed." He wanted "all of my people to know that I was not leaving because of fear, I was leaving because I had seventeen nations against me in the OAS and they were demanding my resignation." *Id* at 264, 266–67.

2. Was the OAS resolution concerning Somoza a good precedent? Was he correct that it was legally binding? In any event, what action does it allow or require other OAS member states to take in respect to Nicaragua?

3. Could the OAS have suspended the Nicaraguan government from participation in the organization in lieu of the resolution it adopted? Do you think the action would have been as effective?

D. Africa

The African Charter on Human and Peoples Rights, which entered into force October 21, 1986, established a system for the protection and promotion of human rights that was designed to function within the institutional framework of the Organization of African Unity (OAU), a regional intergovernmental organization founded in 1963. The main objectives of the OAU were, *inter alia*, to rid the continent of the remaining vestiges of colonization and apartheid; to promote unity and solidarity among African States; to coordinate and intensify cooperation for development; to safeguard the sovereignty and territorial integrity of Member States; and to promote international cooperation within the framework of the United Nations. As a continental organization the OAU provided a forum for Member States to adopt coordinated positions on matters of common concern to the continent in international fora and defend the interests of Africa. The OAU Coordinating Committee for the Liberation of Africa worked to forge an international consensus in support of the liberation struggle and the fight against apartheid.

In July 1999, the OAU Assembly decided to convene an extraordinary session to expedite the process of economic and political integration in the continent. On September 9, 1999, the Heads of State and Government of the Organization of African Unity issued a Declaration (the Sirte Declaration) calling for the establishment of an African Union, with a view to accelerating the process of integration in the continent to enable it to play a stronger role in the global economy while addressing social, economic and political problems of the continent. The evolution of African concern with human rights is described in the following extract.

Rachel Murray, *Human Rights in Africa: From the OAU to the African Union* *(2006),* pp. 2, 7, 21–22, 33, 77–80, 81, 97, 103–04, 113 (references omitted).

A number of All-African Peoples' Conferences were held in the late 1950s and early 1960s with the aim of encouraging those who were not yet liberated to liberate themselves and to organize non-violent revolution in Africa. Even at this stage the seeds of some human rights issues that would find their way into the OAU can be discerned with condemnation of racism in South Africa, the call for the need for universal vote and concerns about religious separatism, among others. . . .

The provisions of the OAU Charter make little express mention of human rights. Instead they reflect the dominating concerns of Africa at that time, namely to ensure the independence of those African Peoples who were still colonized, condemnation of apartheid regimes in southern Africa, and protecting the newly acquired statehood. . . .

It is also worth mentioning a number of other smaller issues which had some impact on the OAU choosing to consider human rights as part of its remit. Firstly, the work of the International Labour Organization (ILO) and other international organizations prompted the OAU organs to consider issues like workers' rights from an early stage in its history. Events and conferences held at the international level (some of which were held in Africa) in which African states were involved also prompted the OAU to consider some aspects of human rights . . . Secondly, the decision of the OAU organs during the 1980s to grant observer status to NGOs may also have had some (much lesser) role to play when those, albeit a very limited number, were admitted on the basis of their role in human rights. . . .

From the late 1970s onwards a number of important events define the OAU/AU move to increased attention to human rights. Encouragement at the UN level for regional human rights mechanisms, NGO lobbying and a recognition by some African leaders themselves that human rights in another state were also their concern fed into the adoption by the OAU of the African Charter on Human and Peoples' Rights in 1981. With its coming into force in 1986, human rights were thus official recognized in the OAU, albeit still in a rather limited fashion given the independent focus of the Charter and its weak enforcement mechanisms. . . .

The provisions of the [African Union's] Constitutive Act suggest that human rights will indeed play a greater role in the work of the Union than they did in the OAU. . . .Human Rights are mentioned specifically with states being "determined to promote and protect human and peoples' rights, consolidate democratic institutions and culture and to ensure good governance and the rule of law." The central

Objectives, in Article 3, and Principles, in Article 4, of the Union noted that the Union's aims include not only achieving "greater unity and solidarity between the African countries and the peoples of Africa" and accelerating development but also the need to "promote peace, security and stability on the continent." It is recognized that there is a need to "encourage international co-operation, taking due account of the Charter of the United Nations and the Universal Declaration of Human Rights" and "promote and protect human and peoples' rights in accordance with the African Charter on Human and Peoples' Rights and other relevant human rights instruments." Thus state should . . . promote gender equality, have "respect for democratic principles, human rights, the rule of law and good governance," respect the sanctity of life and condemn unconstitutional changes of government. . . .

On the face of it, therefore, the Constitutive Act of the AU appears to give an important place to human rights and an indication that they will play a significant role in the AU. . . .

Much of the OAU's attention has been focused on unconstitutional changes of government. Since African states began to attain their independence there has been a proliferation of dictatorships across the continent as well as ongoing conflicts. This issue has received an increasing amount of the OAU's attention, as reflected in the adoption by the Assembly of Heads of State and Government in June 1997 of a Decision on the Unconstitutional Changes of Government in Africa [AHG/ Dec.150 (XXXVI)]. Changes to "constitutional" government have been deemed to be unlawful by the OAU and are listed in its Declaration on the Framework for an OAU Response to Unconstitutional Changes in Government as:

1. a military coup d'etat against a democratically elected Government;

2. intervention by mercenaries to replace a democratically elected government;

3. replacement of democratically elected Governments by armed dissident groupsand rebel movements;

4. the refusal by an incumbent government to relinquish power to the winning party after free, fair and regular elections.

. . . [T]here have been various attempts by states to prevent the attendance at OAU summits of heads of state who have acquired power as a result of a coup. Yet, as Akinyemi notes, "no hard and definite conclusions can be drawn from these episodes. . . .

Other documents indicate, however, that the OAU has condemned on numerous occasions the taking of power through "violent" or "unconstitutional" means. Thus, where "legitimate" governments have been overthrown, and where there has been assassination of political leaders, this has been deemed to be unconstitutional by the OAU.

The OAU has condemned coups and military takeovers which have taken place in many states such as Sierra Leone, DRC, Niger, Guinea Bissau, the Comoros and Central African Republic. Coups have been seen as resulting in "flagrant violations of the basic principles of our continental Organization and of the United Nations . . . [and are] unacceptable and anachronistic, which is in contradiction of our commitment to promote democratic principles and conditions." . . .

There is some suggestion that . . . it is therefore lawful to overthrow a military regime. Thus, the Council of Ministers, for example, in respect of Sierra Leone, "welcomed the overthrow of the military junta which has opened the way for the re-instatement of the democratically elected government . . . through the early resto-ration of constitutional order and the reinstatement of the legitimate government." The OAU has called on other states not to recognize unconstitutional regimes and has argued there is a duty on other states not to cooperate with such a regime and also to support the people towards restoring democracy. In addition, the OAU has also suggested there may be a duty to intervene.

. . . [T]he OAU/AU organs have considered human rights to be an important ele-ment of a state's obligation. One of the ways in which they have done this is through developing and expanding on th[e] concept of what constitutes a democratic state.

. . . [T]he OAU has consolidated this closer link between democracy and human rights, stressing that the protection of human rights is essential for a democracy, namely "constitutional recognition of fundamental rights and freedoms in confor-mity with the Universal Declaration of Human Rights of 1948 and the African Char-ter on Human and Peoples' Rights of 1981" as well as the "guarantee and promotion of human rights.". . . .

. . . With recent changes in respect of the AU and its Constitutive Act, . . . the potential to maintain the link between democracy and human rights is large. A Commissioner on Political Affairs has been created, whose portfolio will cover hu-man rights, democracy, good governance and electoral institutions, among other things, and there are explicit references in the Constitutive Act to democracy and human rights as well as "condemnation and rejection of unconstitutional changes in governments" in its Principles and the power to suspend states from the Union who come to power through unconstitutional means. . . .

Yet this rhetoric has so far not been accompanied by enforcement. . . . There needs to be greater attention to the mechanisms and machinery under the AU to do so.

Today, the AU is Africa's principal organization for the promotion of socio- eco-nomic integration of the continent. It focuses on issues of peace, security and sta-bility as a prerequisite for the implementation of the Union's development and in-tegration agenda. The AU's stated objectives, as follows, include human rights:

- To achieve greater unity and solidarity between the African countries and the peoples of Africa;
- To defend the sovereignty, territorial integrity and independence of its Mem-ber States;
- To accelerate the political and socio-economic integration of the continent;
- To promote and defend African common positions on issues of interest to the continent and its peoples;
- To encourage international cooperation, taking due account of the Charter of the United Nations and the Universal Declaration of Human Rights;
- To promote peace, security, and stability on the continent;

- To promote democratic principles and institutions, popular participation and good governance;
- To promote and protect human and peoples' rights in accordance with the African Charter on Human and Peoples' Rights and other relevant human rights instruments;
- To establish the necessary conditions which enable the continent to play its rightful role in the global economy and in international negotiations;
- To promote sustainable development at the economic, social and cultural levels as well as the integration of African economies;
- To promote co-operation in all fields of human activity to raise the living standards of African peoples;
- To coordinate and harmonize the policies between the existing and future Regional Economic Communities for the gradual attainment of the objectives of the Union;
- To advance the development of the continent by promoting research in all fields, in particular in science and technology;
- To work with relevant international partners in the eradication of preventable diseases and the promotion of good health on the continent.

The AU organs include the following bodies that have competence over human rights matters:

The Assembly of Heads of State and Government or their duly accredited representatives, the supreme organ of the Union.

The Executive Council, composed of Ministers or Authorities designated by the Governments of Members States. The Executive Council reports to the Assembly.

The Commission, composed of the Chairperson, the Deputy Chairperson, eight Commissioners and Staff members. Each Commissioner is responsible for one portfolio. The political affairs portfolio contains the issues of human rights, democracy, good governance, electoral institutions, civil society organizations, humanitarian affairs, refugees, and returnees and internally displaced persons. The Commission is involved in the day-to-day management of the African Union: it represents the Union; elaborates draft common positions of the Union; prepares strategic plans and studies for the consideration of the Executive Council; elaborates, promotes, coordinates and harmonizes the programs and policies of the Union; and ensures the mainstreaming of gender in all programs and activities of the Union.

The Permanent Representatives' Committee, composed of Permanent Representatives of Member States accredited to the Union. The Permanent Representatives Committee is charged with the responsibility of preparing the work of the Executive Council.

The AU Charter provided for a Court of Justice. This would have been in addition to the African Court on Human and Peoples Rights created by a 1998 Protocol to the African Charter on Human and Peoples Rights. In July 2004, the AU decided to merge the two Courts. The Statute of Merger was approved by the Assembly of Heads of State in July, 2006.

Conclusions

This chapter has illustrated the commonalities and differences in the role of human rights in the main organizations of three regions. It is clear that each region had a particular historical, political and cultural context in which human rights became a matter of regional concern and this context led the member states to give varying prominence to human rights within each of the regional organizations. The chapter has also demonstrated the evolutionary character of the regional organizations; each of them has undergone reform since its creation and has strengthened the human rights obligations of member states. Amendment or replacement of basic instruments has generally been accompanied by additional focus on human rights. This is not to say that actual respect for human rights by member states has always kept pace with the regional standards; compliance remains an issue in all the systems. New member states and new issues have brought new challenges to each system, in some respects minimizing their historical differences and making them more alike. In response, the systems have increasingly converged by developing similar norms, institutions and procedures to promote and protect human rights. The next chapter will examine the specific human rights instruments that apply in each of the regions, how they are interpreted and implemented and how they interact with each other and with global norms.

CHAPTER II
THE NORMATIVE INSTRUMENTS

1. Introduction

The human rights guarantees of the regional systems have a juridical foundation in legally binding treaties. Non-binding normative texts also play a significant role in the protection of human rights in each region. This chapter examines the human rights instruments adopted by each of the regional systems, comparing their texts and some of the main rules governing their interpretation. The chapter also addresses the important issue of how the instruments relate to each other and to global human rights standards. The last section considers the role of regional human rights law in the domestic legal systems of the member states.

Regional human rights instruments should be understood in the context of international relations at the relevant period. During the Cold War, debate over human rights was often framed in ideological terms, with the West commonly insisting on the centrality of civil and political rights, while the Soviet Union and its allies asserted the primacy of economic, social and cultural rights. At the global level, this debate resulted in the initially unified list of human rights set forth in the Universal Declaration of Human Rights giving way to separate United Nations Covenants, one on Civil and Political Rights and the other on Economic, Social and Cultural Rights. Two years after adopting the Covenants in 1966, the international community attempted a reconciliation of rights at the first United Nations Conference on Human Rights, held in Teheran. The Teheran Final Act pronounced that all human rights are indivisible. Elaborating on this text, the 1993 Vienna Second World Conference on Human Rights proclaimed in paragraph 5 of its Declaration and Program of Action that all human rights are universal, indivisible, interdependent and interrelated. The international community must treat human rights globally in a fair and equal manner, on the same footing and with the same emphasis.

Despite insistence and official agreement on the interdependence and indivisibility of rights, efforts are still often made to classify rights based on their content, their perceived importance, or their scope. *See generally* A. Rosas & M. Scheinin, *Categories and Beneficiaries of Human Rights*, in An Introduction to the International Protection of Human Rights 49 (R. Hanski & M. Suksi, eds., 1998). The distinction made by the two UN Covenants between civil and political rights, on the one hand, and economic, social and cultural rights, on the other hand, lingers, but is debated. The rights to education and to property, and rights of workers, sometimes appear in both sets of rights, as does the right to be free from discrimination in the exercise of guaranteed rights. Nonetheless, the European system followed the United Nations in adopting separate instruments for civil and political rights and for economic, social and cultural rights; the Inter-American system added the latter set to the American Convention by means of a protocol. In contrast, the African system integrated all categories of rights, including group rights, into a single African Charter on Human and Peoples' Rights.

Some measure of classification or prioritization may be useful or even necessary. National and local governments must balance specific rights with the common interest and values of society in considering whether to adopt proposed legislation or executive measures, almost inevitably giving some rights priority over others. Governments and national and international tribunals also must make decisions between rights that conflict or are in tension. Authorities may be called upon to choose, for example, between upholding respect for property rights or ensuring the right to a safe and healthy environment, or between the exercise of freedom of expression and the right of minorities to be free from disparaging speech.

The relative priority of rights may be established within the texts or by interpreting them. Some rights are explicitly designated non-derogable, others have limitations or clawback clauses, and a few are called "fundamental." Violations of some rights have broad consequences, either because standing to complain of their violation is extended to all states (*erga omnes* obligations) or because international criminal responsibility attaches to those who commit violations. Some rights may fall into the category of *jus cogens* or peremptory norms.

In examining the normative instruments in the regional systems, consider the juridical weight afforded to each text. Are all the instruments equally binding in law? Compare the rights protected and the language that is used. How much similarity is there? What are the major differences? Do the differences reflect particular concerns within the region? For further discussion of categories of human rights, *see* CLASSER LES DROITS DE L'HOMME (E. Bribosia and L. Hennebel, eds., 2004).

2. An Overview of the Regional Human Rights Instruments

A. Europe

i. The European Convention for the Protection of Human Rights and Fundamental Freedoms

The Council of Europe's human rights system began with the adoption of the Convention for the Protection of Human Rights and Fundamental Freedoms on November 4, 1950 (entry into force Sept. 3, 1953), which guarantees core civil and political rights. The Convention is only open to adherence by member states of the Council of Europe. In the preamble to the European Convention on Human Rights, the contracting parties declared that they were "reaffirming their devotion to the spiritual and moral values which are the common heritage of their peoples and the true source of individual freedom, political liberty and the rule of law, the principles which form the basis of all genuine democracy." See J.G. Merrills, *The Council of Europe (1): The European Convention on Human Rights*, in AN INTRODUCTION TO THE INTERNATIONAL PROTECTION OF HUMAN RIGHTS 221 (R. Hanski & M. Suksi, eds., 1997). According to Merrills, "[m]any statesmen of the

immediate post-war epoch had been in resistance movements or in prison during the Second World War and were acutely conscious of the need to prevent any
recrudescence of dictatorship in Western Europe." Merrills also saw the emergence
of the East-West conflict as a stimulus to closer ties in Western Europe.

In the *Message to Europeans,* adopted by the Congress of Europe 8–10 May
1948, those proposing the European Convention made clear their intent:

> We desire a Charter of Human Rights guaranteeing liberty of thought, assembly
> and expression as well as the right to form a political opposition;
>
> We desire a Court of Justice with adequate sanctions for the implementation of this
> Charter.

Message to Europeans, quoted in Council of Europe, Report of the Control System of the European Convention on Human Rights 4, (H(92)14)(Dec. 1992).

A Resolution adopted by the same Congress stated its conviction "that in the interest of human values and human liberty, the (proposed) Assembly should make
proposals for the establishment of a Court of Justice with adequate sanctions for
the implementation of this Charter, and to this end any citizen of the associated
countries shall have redress before the Court, at any time and with the least possible delay, of any violation of his rights as formulated in the Charter." *Id.*

The decision to draft the European Convention was made after the UN General Assembly adopted the Universal Declaration of Human Rights when it became
clear that it would take the UN years to reach agreement on transforming the
Declaration into binding treaty obligations. The original European Convention included a short list of rights: right to life; right not to be subjected to torture, inhuman or degrading treatment or punishment; freedom from slavery; right to liberty,
security of person, and due process of law; freedom from ex post facto laws and
punishment; right to private and family life; freedom of thought, conscience and
religion; freedom of expression and of peaceful assembly; and the right to marry
and found a family. Article 14 proclaimed non-discrimination in the "enjoyment of
the rights and freedoms" guaranteed by the Convention. The Convention required
the Contracting Parties to provide an "effective remedy before a national authority" to anyone whose rights have been violated (Art. 13) and to secure the rights to
"everyone" within their jurisdiction (Art. 1) without regard to nationality.

The original rights and obligations have been expanded by Additional Protocols, binding on the states that have ratified them. The first Protocol added a right
to property, a right to education and the undertaking by the Contracting Parties
to hold free and secret elections at reasonable intervals. Protocol No. 4 enlarged
the list further by proscribing deprivation of liberty for failure to comply with contractual obligations, by guaranteeing the right to liberty of movement, and by prohibiting forced exile of nationals and the collective expulsion of aliens. Protocol
No. 7 expanded the rights of aliens, by requiring states to accord them various due
process safeguards in deportation proceedings. Protocol No. 6 abolished the death
penalty during peacetime, while Protocol No. 13 prohibited the death penalty under all circumstances.

Protocol No. 7 added rights of appeal in criminal proceedings and compensation in cases of miscarriage of justice, prohibited double jeopardy, and called for

guarantees of equality of rights and responsibilities between spouses. Protocol No. 12 augmented the non-discrimination guarantee in Convention Art. 14 by providing that "the enjoyment of any right set forth by law shall be secured without discrimination on any ground . . .," adding that no one shall be discriminated against by any public authority. The other Protocols introduced institutional changes relating to the Convention organs and procedures; these procedural protocols have been ratified by all 46 contracting parties to the Convention. In contrast, none of the Protocols adding additional rights has been accepted by all the Convention parties. Only Russia has failed to adhere to Protocol 6, on abolition of the death penalty during peacetime.

ii. Other Council of Europe Conventions

The human rights work of the Council of Europe has included adoption of other human rights instruments, including treaties specifically designed to prevent violations rather than remedy them after they occur. The following section presents an overview of the key texts.

The European Social Charter

The European Social Charter complements the ECHR by establishing a regional European system for the protection of economic and social rights. Like the ECHR, the Charter has evolved over time. The original Charter was opened for signature on October 18, 1961 and entered into force on February 26, 1965. All but six of the forty-six Member States of the Member States of the Council of Europe are parties to the original Charter or the Charter as it has been revised; nearly all of the states that have yet to ratify are new member states. An Additional Protocol to the Charter, expanding its catalog of rights, was concluded on May 5, 1988 and entered into force on September 4, 1992. On October 21, 1991 the Turin Protocol Amending the European Social Charter was signed. This instrument reformed the supervisory mechanism of the Charter and most of its provisions were implemented quickly through actions taken by the supervisory organs pending its entry into force.

Two further instruments continued the evolution of the Social Charter. On November 9, 1995, an Additional Protocol provided for a system of collective complaints; it entered into force on July 1, 1998. Finally, in 1996, a revised Social Charter, bringing up to date the earlier documents and adding some new rights, was opened for signature. It entered into force on July 1, 1999 and it will progressively replace the original Charter as each state becomes a party to it. As the consolidated text, it is the basic instrument described in the following sections.

The rights in the Social Charter

The Revised Charter proclaims a list of 31 categories of "rights and principles," including the right to work, to just conditions of work, to safe working conditions, to fair remuneration, to organize, and to bargain collectively. The right of workers to equal treatment and non-discrimination on the grounds of sex, the right to be informed and consulted, and the right to take part in the determination and improvement of the working conditions and environment in places of employment, are included. The Revised Charter also establishes the right of disabled persons to training and rehabilitation, and the equal right to engage in gainful occupations in the territory of other Contracting Parties.

The Revised Charter proclaims the right of children, of young people, and of employed women to protection. Also recognized are the right of the family to social, legal and economic protection, the right of mothers and children to social and economic protection, and the right of migrant workers and their families to protection and assistance. Additional rights listed in the Charter are the right to vocational guidance and training, to protection of health, to social security, to social and medical assistance, and the right to benefit from social welfare services. The Charter provides that "every elderly person has the right to social protection" and contains guarantees in case of termination of employment or employer insolvency. Protections also are afforded for dignity at work, against discrimination due to family responsibilities, and against poverty. Finally, it contains the right of everyone to housing, a matter considered in detail below.

These rights are proclaimed in general terms in Part I of the Revised Charter, where the High Contracting Parties declare that they "... accept as the aim of their policy, to be pursued by all appropriate means both national and international in character, the attainment of conditions in which ... [these] rights and principles may be effectively realized." These "rights and principles," or policy objectives are to be transformed into enforceable rights. Part II of the Revised Charter defines the meaning and elaborates on the "rights and principles" proclaimed in general terms in Part I.

State obligations

Article A (Part III) of the Revised Charter specifies the obligations the States Parties assume by ratifying the Charter. The instrument gives the states a set of options. First, by becoming a party to the Charter, a state undertakes "to consider Part I of this Charter as a declaration of the aims which it will pursue by all appropriate means...." Charter, Art. A(1)(a). Second, the state must accept as binding upon it the undertakings contained in at least six out of nine articles found in Part II. The nine provisions are Article 1 (right to work), Article 5 (right to organize), Article 6 (right to bargain collectively), Article 7 (the right of children and young persons to protection), Article 12 (right to social security), Article 13 (right to social and medical assistance), Article 16 (right of the family to social, legal and economic protection), Article 19 (right of migrant workers and their families to protection and assistance) and Article 20 (right to equal opportunities and equal treatment in matters of employment and occupation without discrimination on the grounds of sex). Third, each State Party must select another specified number of rights or sub-categories of rights with which it agrees to comply. *See* Revised Charter, Art. A(1)(c).

This flexible system encourages states to ratify the Charter without forcing them either to accept all the rights it proclaims or to make complex reservations. It is also drafted so as to ensure that all States Parties will at the very least be bound to guarantee some of the most basic rights. Very few states have accepted all the rights the Charter proclaims.

The European Committee of Social Rights ascertains whether countries have honored their undertakings set out in the Charter. Its fifteen independent, impartial members are elected by the Council of Europe's Committee of Ministers for a period of six years, renewable once. The Committee determines whether or not national law and practice in the States Parties are in conformity with Article 24 of the Charter, as amended by the 1991 Turin Protocol.

The reporting system

The Charter establishes a reporting system to monitor state compliance with the treaty obligations. Every year the States Parties submit a report indicating how they implement the Charter in law and in practice. Each report concerns some of the accepted provisions of the Charter. In odd years the report addresses the core provisions (Articles 1, 5, 6, 7, 12, 13, 16, 19 and 20; States must have accepted at least 6 of these 9 Articles). In even years, states report on half of the other provisions.

The Social Rights Committee examines the reports and decides whether or not the situations in the countries concerned are in conformity with the Charter. Its decisions, known as "conclusions", are published every year. If a state takes no action on a Committee conclusion to the effect that it does not comply with the Charter, the Committee of Ministers may address a recommendation to that state, asking it to change the situation in law and/or in practice. The Committee of Ministers' work is prepared by a Governmental Committee comprising representatives of the governments of the States Parties to the Charter, assisted by observers representing European employers' organizations and trade unions. The Parliamentary Assembly of the Council of Europe also receives the reports of the ECSR and the Governmental Committee.

The Collective Complaints Procedure

The 1995 Additional Protocol providing for a system of collective complaints allows complaints of "unsatisfactory application of the Charter" (Art. 1) to be filed with the Committee. Complaints may originate with one of several types of groups:

- international organizations of employers and trade unions which participate in the work of the Governmental Committee according to Article 27(2), i.e. European Trade Union Confederation (ETUC), Union of Industrial and Employers' Confederations of Europe (UNICE) and International Organization of Employers (IOE);
- other international non-governmental organizations having consultative status with the Council of Europe and appearing on a special list drawn up by the Governmental Committee; and
- national organizations of employers and trade unions from the Contracting Party concerned.

Each state also may declare that it accepts the right of its national non-governmental organizations to lodge complaints against it. Organizations may submit complaints only in respect of those matters regarding which they have been recognized as having particular competence.

The complaint file must contain the following information:

a. the name and contact details of the organization submitting the complaint;

b. proof that the person submitting and signing the complaint is entitled to represent the organization lodging the complaint;

c. the state against which the complaint is directed;

d. an indication of the provisions of the Charter that have allegedly been violated;

e. the subject matter of the complaint, i.e. the point(s) in respect of which the state in question has allegedly failed to comply with the Charter, along with the relevant arguments, with supporting documents.

The Committee examines the complaint and, if the formal requirements have been met, declares it admissible. Once the complaint has been declared admissible, a written procedure is set in motion, with an exchange of memorials between the parties. The Committee may decide to hold a public hearing. The Committee then takes a decision on the merits of the complaint, which it forwards to the parties concerned and the Committee of Ministers in a report, which is made public within four months of its being forwarded. On the basis of the report, the Committee of Ministers adopts a resolution on the matter, which may contain recommendations to the State concerned. At the time the resolution is adopted, or four months after the Committee of Ministers receives the report, the Parliamentary Assembly also receives the report, which is then made public. The State must submit information on its measures to comply with the recommendations made. Art. 10.

After the Protocol entered into force, the first application received, *International Commission of Jurists v. Portugal*, Application No. 1/1998, complained of child labor in violation of Charter art. 7(1). The ECSR transmitted the report containing its decision on the merits of the complaint to the Committee of Ministers on September 10, 1999. The Committee of Ministers adopted Resolution ChS (99)4 on December 15, 1999 agreeing that a violation had been shown. Several consecutive complaints were then lodged against France, Italy, Greece and Portugal concerning the right of armed forces to organize and bargain collectively. The complaint in *International Federation of Human Rights Leagues v. Greece*, Application No. 7/2000, alleged that a number of legislative provisions and regulations violate Charter Article 1 (para. 2) (prohibition of forced labor). The ECSR transmitted the report finding violations to the Committee of Ministers on December 12, 2000 which made recommendations to the government. As of the end of 2006, an additional 26 complaints had been registered, raising not only issues of labor relations but also issues of poverty and the right to housing.

The European Convention against Torture

On November 26, 1987, the Council of Europe adopted the European Convention for the Prevention of Torture and Inhuman or Degrading Treatment or Punishment. Protocol No. I to the Torture Convention permits states from outside the region to join upon invitation. A Second Protocol amends the election process for members to the Committee for the Prevention of Torture. The aim of the Convention against Torture is to enhance protection of persons deprived of their liberty by establishing non-judicial machinery to prevent torture. The Convention neither defines torture nor contains substantive provisions concerning it or inhuman or degrading treatment or punishment. Those aspects, as well as the consideration of individual complaints, are left to the ECHR and its Court. The Court has adopted the definition of torture contained in the U.N. Convention against Torture.

The Committee for the Prevention of Torture (CPT) is composed of independent and impartial experts equal in number to the states parties. The members are elected by the Committee of Ministers. The CPT's mandate is "to examine the treatment of persons deprived of their liberty with a view to strengthening, if necessary, the protection of such persons from torture and from inhuman or degrading treatment or punishment." (Art. 1) The CPT thus has the power to visit places of detention of any kind, such as prisons, police cells, military barracks, and mental hospitals, to examine the treatment of detainees and, if appropriate, to make recommendations to the State concerned. The Committee, based on a principle of "cooperation" between the Committee and the competent national authorities, exercises its functions in strict confidentiality.

The Committee carries out periodic visits to all Contracting Parties and may organize such *ad hoc* visits "as appear to it to be required in the circumstances." The Committee is obliged to notify the State concerned of its intention to carry out such a visit, but no specific period of notice is required. A visit could take place immediately after the notification. Government objections to the time or place of a visit can be justified only on grounds of national defense, public safety, serious disorder, the medical condition of a person or that an urgent interrogation relating to a serious crime is in progress. In such cases the state must immediately take steps to allow the Committee to visit as soon as possible.

Between its creation and 2006, the CPT made 135 periodic visits and 82 *ad hoc* visits, but the number of *ad hoc* visits continually increased and in 2006 exceeded that of periodic visits. Between 2000 and 2006, for example, the CPS made nine visits to the Northern Caucasus region of Russia. After each visit the CPT draws up a report setting out its findings and making recommendations. The Committee publicizes its findings only if a state fails to cooperate with it or refuses to make improvements following the Committee's recommendations, or with the state's consent. More than 200 reports have been published. In addition, the Committee's annual report to the Committee of Ministers is available as a public document. In its 2006 report, the CPT stressed cooperation with the United Nations and proposed that the results of its visits to the 14 states bound by both the European Convention for the Prevention of Torture and the UN's Optional Protocol to the Convention against Torture be forwarded immediately and systematically to the UN Committee on a confidential basis. The CPT also issued a general statement condemning mechanical restraints such as handcuffs, metal chains and cage beds in psychiatric facilities.

Protection of National Minorities

The issue of national minorities became increasingly important in the Council of Europe in the 1980s as ethnic conflicts re-emerged in the region. The *European Charter for Regional or Minority Languages*, adopted November 5, 1992 (entry into force March 1, 1998) was a first effort by the organization to afford protection to indigenous linguistic groups. The aims of the agreement are to protect and promote regional or minority languages of Europe and to respect the right of individuals to use a regional or minority language in private and public life.

The Languages Charter, like the European Social Charter, first enunciates the objectives and principles that Parties undertake to apply in taking stated specific measures to promote the use of regional or minority languages in public life. Each Party commits to apply a minimum of thirty-five paragraphs or sub-paragraphs chosen from among the measures and must select three paragraphs or sub-paragraphs from each of the Articles 8 (education) and 12 (cultural activities and facilities) and one from each of the Articles 9 (judicial authorities), 10 (administrative authorities and public services), 11(media) and 13 (economic and social life).

Upon ratification, acceptance or approval of the treaty, each party must specify the language or languages to which the selected paragraphs shall apply. Compliance is monitored through state periodic reports that are examined by a committee of experts. Groups or associations within a state may submit information or comments to the committee relating to the state's compliance with its undertakings. On the basis of the state report and the information received, the committee prepares a report for the Committee of Ministers which may make recommendations to the state party. The Committee of Ministers also appoints from each member state a person to sit on the committee of experts.

On November 10, 1994 the Council of Europe adopted another treaty related to this topic, the *Framework Convention for the Protection of National Minorities*. Council of Europe, Doc. H (94) 10. The Convention entered into force on February 1, 1998. The title of the Framework Convention indicates its programmatic, non-constraining nature, a consequence of the political controversy surrounding the issue. Although the instrument is legally binding, the principles contained in it require the adoption of national laws and policies by states parties to give them effect.

Section I of the Framework Convention sets out general principles on the protection of national minorities, a term not defined in the text. Section II lays down more specific principles: non-discrimination; promotion of effective equality; promotion of conditions to preserve and develop culture and religion, language, and traditions; freedom of assembly, association, expression, thought, conscience and religion; access to and use of media; language rights; education; transfrontier contacts; international and transfrontier cooperation; participation in economic, cultural and social life; participation in public life; and prohibition of forced assimilation. Section IV concerns monitoring of state compliance and confers supervisory authority on the Committee of Ministers, assisted by an Advisory Committee, a body of between twelve and eighteen persons appointed by the Committee of Ministers. States parties are to file periodic reports on the legislative and other measures they take to give effect to the principles of the Framework Convention. The reports are examined by the Advisory Committee, which prepares an opinion on the measures taken. The Committee of Ministers then issues its conclusions concerning the adequacy of the measures taken by the State Party and may make recommendations to the state. The opinion of the Advisory Committee, any comments on it by the State Party, and the conclusions and recommendations of the Committee of Ministers are made public.

Human Rights and Biomedicine

The Convention on Human Rights and Biomedicine (April 4, 1997, in force December 1, 1999) was the first legally-binding international text designed to preserve human rights through a series of principles and prohibitions concerning bioethics, medical research, prior informed consent, rights to private life and information, organ transplantation, and public debate.

The Convention declares that "the interests and welfare of the human being shall prevail over the sole interest of society or science" (Art. 2). It bans all forms of discrimination based on a person's genetic make-up (Art. 11) and allows predictive genetic tests only for medical purposes (Art. 12). Genetic engineering is also permitted, but only for preventive, diagnostic or therapeutic reasons and where it does not aim to change the genetic make-up of a person's descendants (Art. 13). It prohibits the use of techniques of medically assisted procreation to help choose the sex of a child, except where it would avoid a serious hereditary condition (Art. 14). The Convention sets out detailed and precise rules related to medical research, especially for people who cannot give their consent. It prohibits the creation of human embryos for research purposes and requires an adequate protection of embryos where countries allow using them in research.

The Convention stipulates that all patients have a right to be informed about their health, including the results of predictive genetic tests, but also recognizes the patient's right not to know (Art. 11). The Convention prohibits the removal from persons unable to give consent of organs and other tissues which cannot be regenerated (Art. 19). Under certain conditions regenerative tissue (especially marrow) may be transferred between siblings (Art. 20).

The human body and body parts may not be utilized for financial gain (Art. 21). States Parties to the Convention are to provide judicial protection with respect to the rights contained in the Convention. The Steering Committee on Bioethics (CDBI), or any other committee designated by the Committee of Ministers or the States Parties may request the European Court of Human Rights to give advisory opinions on legal questions concerning the interpretation of the Convention.

The Council of Europe adopted an Additional Protocol on the Prohibition of Cloning Human Beings (January 12, 1998, entry into force March 1, 2001), which prohibits "any intervention seeking to create a human being genetically identical to another human being, whether living or dead" (Art. 1). It rules out any exception to this ban, even in the case of a completely sterile couple and bars States Parties from derogating to the provisions of the Protocol (Art. 2).

Questions and Comments

What is the value added of the additional Council of Europe treaties? Why not simply add further additional protocols to the ECHR? Consider whether the non-judicial supervisory procedures adopted for the new treaties provide an explanation and reflect a shift from post-hoc remedies to prevention of violations.

B. The Americas

Unlike other regional systems, but similar to the United Nations, the inter-American human rights system has two distinct legal sources. One set of rights and obligations has evolved from the Charter of the Organization of American States, the other set is based on the American Convention on Human Rights. The Charter-based obligations apply to all thirty-five Member States of the OAS. The Convention is legally binding only on the States Parties to it.[1] The two sets of rights, duties, institutions and procedures overlap and interact in a variety of ways. In some cases, the legal mechanisms and norms from both sources apply to different aspects of the same human rights situation.

i. American Declaration of the Rights and Duties of Man

The OAS Charter mentions human rights, but does not define or list such rights. To give meaning to the term, the Ninth International Conference of American States proclaimed the American Declaration of the Rights and Duties of Man on May 2, 1948. The preamble of the American Declaration emphasizes that "the international protection of the rights of man should be the principal guide of an evolving American law." The body of the American Declaration proclaims civil and political as well as economic, social and cultural rights and contains a list of duties.

The legal status of the American Declaration, which was adopted as a non-binding conference resolution, has changed over time with the institutional evolution of the OAS. In 1959, the Fifth Meeting of Consultation of Ministers of Foreign Affairs approved the establishment of the Inter-American Commission on Human Rights and a year later, the OAS Council adopted the Statute of the Commission. The 1960 Statute, Art. 1, designated the Commission as an "autonomous entity" of the OAS, created "to promote respect for human rights." Article 2 of the Statute defined the term human rights: "for the purpose of this Statute, human rights are understood to be those set forth in the American Declaration of the Rights and Duties of Man." The adoption of the Statute began the process of transforming the Declaration into an important normative instrument. Today, as Advisory Opinion OC-10, reprinted in Chapter I, reflects, it is deemed to be the single text that em-

---

[1] The following states are parties to the Convention: Argentina, Barbados, Bolivia, Brazil, Chile, Colombia, Costa Rica, Dominica, Dominican Republic, Ecuador, El Salvador, Grenada, Guatemala, Haiti, Honduras, Jamaica, Mexico, Nicaragua, Panama, Paraguay, Peru, Suriname, Uruguay and Venezuela. Canada, the United States, and some of the smaller English-speaking Caribbean nations have not ratified the Convention. Trinidad and Tobago denounced the Convention effective in 1999. The United States signed the Convention and President Carter referred it to the Senate for its advice and consent to ratification. It remains pending in the Senate.

bodies an authoritative interpretation of "the fundamental rights of the individual," which Article 3(l) of the OAS Charter proclaims.

The 1967 Protocol of Buenos Aires, which amended the OAS Charter, entered into force in 1970. The Protocol changed the status of the Commission, transforming it into a formal organ of the OAS, whose "principal function shall be to promote the observance and protection of human rights and to serve as a consultative organ of the Organization in these matters." OAS Charter, as amended, Arts. 51 and 112(1), now Arts. 53 and 106(1). The Protocol added two other provisions concerning human rights. The first, Article 112(2), now 106(2), provides that "an inter-American convention on human rights shall determine the structure, competence and procedures of this Commission. . . ." The other addition was Article 150, now 145, which reads as follows: "Until the inter-American convention on human rights, . . . enters into force, the present Inter-American Commission on Human Rights shall keep vigilance over the observance of human rights."

ii. The Conventions

On November 20, 1969, the OAS adopted the American Convention on Human Rights to which the amended OAS Charter referred. The Convention was patterned on the European Convention on Human Rights, adopting its original institutional framework in particular. The drafters of the American Convention also drew heavily on the American Declaration of the Rights and Duties of Man and on the International Covenant on Civil and Political Rights, especially in formulating its catalogue of some two dozen civil and political rights. Beyond these rights, the Convention contains an undertaking by the states parties to take progressive measures for "the full realization of the rights implicit in the economic, social, educational, scientific, and cultural standards set forth in the Charter of the Organization of American States as amended by the Protocol of Buenos Aires." (Art. 26.)

The Convention's Protocol of San Salvador on economic, social and cultural rights details the rights to work, unionize and strike, the right to social security and to health, the right to a healthy environment, and the rights to food and to education. The Protocol adds a right to the benefits of culture, as well as to the protection of the family, the rights of children, the elderly and the handicapped. Another Protocol, on abolition of the death penalty, entered into force in 1993.

Like the European system, the Inter-American system has expanded its protections over time through the adoption of additional human rights instruments:

Inter-American Convention to Prevent and Punish Torture, Dec. 9, 1985 in force Feb. 28, 1987

Despite the exclusive reference to torture in the name of the Convention, the text addresses cruel, inhuman and degrading treatment as well as torture. The Convention reaffirms that all acts of torture or any other cruel, inhuman, or degrading treatment or punishment constitute an offense against human dignity and a denial of the principles set forth in the Charter of the Organization of American States and in the Charter of the United Nations and are violations of the fundamental human rights and freedoms proclaimed in the American Declaration of the Rights and Duties of Man and the Universal Declaration of Human Rights. The purpose of the convention is to ensure that the global and regional instruments against torture are made effective. The State Parties undertake to prevent and punish torture in accordance with the terms of the Convention (Art. 1). The emphasis is on prevention and punishment (Art. 6), training of police officers and other public officials responsible for detainees (Art. 7) and remedies for torture victims (Arts. 8–10). States parties have an obligation to extradite or prosecute offenders found in the jurisdiction and to report to the Inter-American Human Rights Commission on implementing measures they have adopted.

Inter-American Convention on the Prevention, Punishment, and Eradication of Violence against Women, June 9, 1994, in force March 5, 1995

The women's convention is most widely ratified of all the Inter-American treaties, with 32 states parties as of the beginning of 2007. It was the first human rights agreement addressing violence against women to be adopted anywhere in the world. The scope of the Convention is broad, in defining violence against women as "any act or conduct, based on gender, which causes death or physical, sexual or psychological harm or suffering to women, whether in the public or the private sphere." (Art. 1) The Convention reaffirms that "every woman has the right to the recognition, enjoyment, exercise and protection of all human rights and freedoms embodied in regional and international human rights instruments," explicitly restating many of the rights. State parties are obliged to pursue, by all appropriate means and without delay, policies to prevent, punish and eradicate violence against women, including specific measures listed in Arts. 7–9.

Implementation is monitored by reports and petitions. The States Parties are to include in their national reports to the Inter-American Commission of Women information on measures adopted to prevent and prohibit violence against women, and to assist women affected by violence, as well as on any difficulties they observe in applying those measures, and the factors that contribute to violence against women. The right of individual petition to the Inter-American Commission is extended to breaches of the state obligations listed in Article 7. The Commission is to consider such claims in accordance with the norms and procedures governing petitions established by the American Convention on Human Rights and the Commission's Statutes and Regulations. Article 11 provides that the States Parties to this Convention and the Inter-American Commission of Women may request of the Inter-American Court of Human Rights advisory opinions on the interpretation of this Convention, but there is no reference to the Court's contentious jurisdiction.

States may file reservations that are compatible with the object and purpose of the Convention and not of a general nature, but in contrast to the UN's Convention on the Elimination of All Forms of Discrimination against Women, no state has filed a reservation to the OAS Convention.

Inter-American Convention on Forced Disappearance of Persons, June 9, 1994, in force March 28, 1996

The first Convention to address forced disappearances, this treaty calls the practice a grave and abominable offense against the inherent dignity of the human being, and one that contradicts the principles and purposes enshrined in the Charter of the Organization of American States. It also labels the systematic practice of forced disappearance a crime against humanity. The aim of the Convention is to prevent, punish, and eliminate the forced disappearance of persons in the Hemisphere. No new rights are enshrined; rather the emphasis is on state obligations to enact and enforce laws criminalizing disappearances. Various provisions call for cooperation and mutual assistance between states to investigate, prosecute and punish those responsible for forced disappearances. Article 14 calls on the Inter-American Commission to take urgent measures in respect to petitions alleging forced disappearances, without prejudice to a later decision on admissibility.

Inter-American Convention on the Elimination of All Forms of Discrimination against Persons with Disabilities, June 7, 1999, in force Sept. 14, 2001.

The most recent of the Inter-American Conventions is also ground-breaking, as reflected in the preambular paragraph that cites to numerous soft law texts adopted by the United Nations and the OAS, and to a single ILO Convention on vocational rehabilitation and employment of disabled persons. The objectives of the Convention are to prevent and eliminate all forms of discrimination against persons with disabilities and to promote their full integration into society. Articles 3 through 5 detail the obligations of states parties. Unlike all the other human rights conventions adopted by the OAS, this one creates a new supervisory body, a Committee for the Elimination of All Forms of Discrimination against Persons with Disabilities, composed of one representative appointed by each state party. The Committee is to review state reports on implementation; no mention is made of individual petitions to the Inter-American Commission.

As can be seen from the above materials, the Inter-American system started with a longer list of human rights than that contained in the European Convention on Human Rights, but it also had more serious human rights problems to confront. Over time, standard-setting in the Inter-American system has been particularly innovative, as the OAS became the first regional or global institution to adopt instruments on violence against women, disappearances and disabilities. It also adopted a protocol on economic, social and cultural rights, something left to a separate convention in Europe. Unlike the European system, however, Inter-American institutional reform has been far less important, especially regarding the Charter-based procedures. These issues will be taken up in Chapter III, but already it may be debated whether or not a system that has a shorter list of rights with strong enforcement is preferable to an ambitious list of rights accompanied by weaker international supervision. One factor to consider is that international institutions and procedures exist as "subsidiary" to national implementation of rights and any international system is thus largely dependent for its success on national incorporation and enforcement. A third model of regional human rights protection exists in Africa, discussed next.

C. Africa

F. Viljoen, *The African Charter on Human and Peoples' Rights: The Travaux Preparatoires in the Light of Subsequent Practice,* 25 HRLJ 313–315 (2004) (footnotes omitted).

Although efforts to establish an African regional human rights system predate 1979, the process within the OAU officially started in July 1979 at the OAU Assembly of Heads of State and Government, held in Monrovia, Liberia. On the initiative of President Senghor of Senegal, Senegal and Mauritius, supported by Nigeria and Uganda, proposed that the OAU Assembly adopt a resolution to set in motion the process towards adopting an African human rights instrument. This resolution called on the Secretary General to "(a) draw the attention of Member States to certain international conventions whose ratification would help to strengthen Africa's struggle against certain scourges, especially apartheid and racial discrimination, trade imbalance and mercenarism; (b) organize as soon as possible, in an African capitol, a restricted meeting of highly qualified experts to prepare a preliminary draft of an "African Charter on Human and Peoples' Rights" providing inter alia for the establishment of bodies to promote and protect human and peoples' rights."

However, before this meeting could take place (but after the adoption of the Assembly's resolution), the United Nations organized a regional seminar to discuss the establishment of an African Commission on Human Rights. The seminar was hosted by the Liberian government, and took place in Monrovia, Liberia from 10 to 21 September 1979. By then, the UN had for a number of years been advocating for the establishment of a regional human rights institution in Africa. The Monrovia seminar should be seen as a culmination of these efforts. The Secretariat of the UN Division of Human Rights prepared a draft, intended to serve as a basis for discussion (the UN proposal). . . . The seminar then adopted the "Monrovia Proposal for the setting-up of an African Commission on Human Rights" (Monrovia proposal) and submitted it to the OAU for its consideration. It is important to note that this process focused primarily on a human rights mechanism and not on the elaboration of a substantive rights framework.

From 28 November to 8 December the same year, a group of African experts met in Dakar, constituting a meeting of "highly qualified experts" mandated by the OAU Assembly resolution. . . . The meeting adopted the guiding principle that "the African Charter on Human and Peoples' Rights should reflect the African conception of human rights. . . . The African Charter should take as a pattern the African philosophy of law and meet the needs of Africa."

The basis of their deliberations was a working document prepared by Keba M'Baye, then President of the International Court of Justice. Ibrahima Fall, dean of the Faculty of Law in Dakar and Mohamadou M'Backe, judge of the Senegalese

Supreme Court, assisted him in the drafting process. This proposal (the M'Baye proposal) drew largely from the provisions of the UN Covenant on Economic, Social and Cultural Rights (ICESCR) and the American Convention on Human Rights. The M'Baye proposal used the Monrovia draft as the basis for its provisions on an institutional mechanism. . . .The 10-day meeting of the group [of experts] culminated in the adoption of a vastly different proposal (the Dakar draft).

The Dakar draft had to be submitted to a group of governmental experts. . . .This meeting was scheduled for 24 March 1980, but never took place for want of a quorum. According to some, this was due to deliberate attempts to derail the process by some states that were not prepared to openly oppose the creation of a Charter. After this failure, the Secretary-General changed tactics. Rather than referring the issue to an *ad hoc* meeting of governmental experts, he initiated a ministerial conference. At his initiative, the President of one of the very few consistently democratic African countries at the time, The Gambia, invited the ministers to meet in Banjul.

The Dakar draft was then submitted for discussion to a meeting of ministers of justice of OAU member states. This meeting took place from 9 to 16 June 1980 in Banjul and was also only partially successful, as the participants managed to finalize deliberating on the Preamble and only 11 of the more than 60 articles. "Drafting" time was lost as delegations used the opportunity to make "general statements" about the realization of human rights in their own countries, and asked questions about the "small Committee of Experts requested to prepare the Preliminary Draft . . . ". After some prodding by the OAU Council of Ministers and the Assembly, the ministerial group managed to finalize the draft (the Banjul draft) at a further meeting, held in Banjul from 7 to 19 January 1981. Two factors caused the second meeting to accelerate the process. The first was the fact that some members of the delegation of Upper Volta (now Burkina Faso) were politically victimized after the Banjul meeting of June 1980. This put "the necessity not only to insist on human rights but also on the importance of their effectiveness" in a new light. The second factor was the result of political pressure of a different nature: At the Seventeenth Ordinary Session of the Assembly of Heads of State and Government, the ministerial meeting was urged to "exert efforts to complete its work." . . .

On 10 June 1981 Edem Kodjo, the then Secretary-General of the OAU presented the Banjul draft to the OAU Council of Ministers. The Council considered the draft Charter. Several of the Ministers raised points of criticism about the draft, amongst others that it could be "misinterpreted" to give rise to a conflict with the constitutions or laws of member states, and that it does not make clear that the Commission cannot interfere in the "internal affairs of states" or that the OAU Assembly is the sole interpreter of the Charter. Nevertheless, the Council "took note of the draft", and submitted it without amendment to the Assembly for its consideration, and recommending that the Assembly adopts it.

During its Eighteenth Session, on 17 June 1981 in Nairobi, the Assembly adopted the African Charter. This date, now celebrated as a decisive moment for human rights promotion in Africa, passed almost unnoticed at the Assembly session. . . . The proposal for the Charter's adoption was postponed until midnight of the last day of the meeting. At that stage, President Jawara of The Gambia urged for the adoption of the Charter. Perhaps motivated by the late hour and fatigue after days of deliberations, the heads of states present adopted it without debate. No formal vote was even taken on the matter. The unamended Banjul draft (but for a name change suggested by the Assembly) thus became the final version of the African Charter (or "Banjul Charter") despite misgivings expressed by the Council of Ministers.

––––––––––––

Christof Heyns, *The African Regional Human Rights System: The African Charter,* 108 PENN ST. L. REV. 679, 680, 681–82, 700–701 (2004) (footnotes omitted)

. . . The central document of the African regional system, the African Charter on Human and Peoples' Rights ("African Charter"), was opened for signature in 1981 and entered into force in 1986. It has been ratified by all fifty-three member states of the OAU/AU. . . .

In addition to the African Charter, the African regional human rights system is comprised of the OAU Convention Governing the Specific Aspects of Refugee Problems in Africa ("African Refugee Convention") of 1969, which entered into force in 1974 (44 ratifications); . . . the African Charter on the Rights and Welfare of the Child ("African Children's Charter") of 1990, which came into force in 1999 (32 ratifications) [and the Protocol to the African Charter on the Rights of Women in Africa of July 11, 2003]. A special monitoring body for the African Children's Charter has been created. The African Committee on the Rights and Welfare of the Child had its first meeting in 2002 in Addis Ababa, Ethiopia.

The relatively unknown Cultural Charter for Africa of 1976 came into force in 1990 (33 state parties). There are also two African treaties dealing with the environment, although not from a human rights perspective. . . .

. . . . Several reasons have been advanced for why only a Commission, and not a Court, was provided for in the African Charter in 1981 as the body responsible for monitoring compliance of state parties with the Charter. On the one hand there is the more idealistic explanation that the traditional way of solving disputes in Africa is through mediation and conciliation, not through the adversarial, "win or lose" mechanism of a court. On the other hand there is the view that the member states of the OAU were protective of their newly found sovereignty, and did not wish to limit it by means of a supra-national court. . . .

It should be noted . . . that the Charter has a very expansive approach in respect to interpretation. In terms of articles 60 and 61, the Commission has to draw inspiration from international human rights law in interpreting the provisions of the Charter. The Commission has used these provisions very liberally in a number of instances to bring the Charter in line with international practices, and the claw-back clauses are no exception.

. . . .

V. Conclusion

Much remains to be done to make the African human rights system effective. I would venture to say there are a number of determinants for the effectiveness of any regional human rights systems, which include the following.

An adequate level of compliance with human rights norms on the domestic level must occur in a significant number of the state parties. Working national human rights systems are the building blocks of an effective regional system. If the level of respect for human rights norms on the domestic level is low, and domestic courts are not effective in implementing these norms, there can be little hope for supra-national enforcement.

The necessary political will must be present in the regional organization of which the system forms part, to ensure that the system really works and is not an empty facade. The regional organization is the primary body through which peer pressure must be channeled. The all-important selection process of Commissioners and Judges must be taken seriously by the regional body. The budgets allocated to human rights organizations also often have an important influence on how effective they are. The system must be properly serviced and able administrators appointed.

Publicity for the work of the monitoring body or bodies of the system is essential. The decisions and resolutions of these bodies must be available, and disseminated on the national and regional level, to have an impact. Publicity is needed so that those who want to comply voluntarily know what is expected of them, but it is also necessary to ensure that shame or peer pressure can be mobilized against recalcitrant states. Peer pressure can change behaviour by inducing shame, or if that does not work, by mobilizing stronger forms of sanctions against states. All of this is possible only when there is sufficient publicity. The responsibility to see to it that there is publicity lies on the regional system, the states, and civil society alike.

Trade and other links must exist between the state parties before a regional human rights system can be enforced effectively. Without trade, diplomatic communication, travel, and other links between state parties, the conditions to impose sanctions to affect the behavior of states do not exist.

The independence, creativity, and wisdom of those who run the system are absolutely crucial. This includes the Commissioners (and judges) and the staff of the Commission (and Court), as well as the officials of the regional organization.

Resources are important, but the proper management of whatever resources are available is more important.

The African regional human rights system is faced with almost insurmountable challenges: massive violations on a continent of immense diversity, where a tradition of domestic compliance with human rights norms is still to be established. The trade and communication links that are necessary to exercise influence over member states in many cases do not exist.

Moreover, the system itself is also not currently well equipped to face these challenges. The African Charter has severe shortcomings and is in need of reform. The shortcomings in the African Charter relate to the norms recognized (the omission of important civil and political as well as socio-economic rights, the inclusion of concepts that are not easy to translate into legal terms, and the absence of adequate rules in respect to restrictions on rights) as well as the monitoring mechanism itself (none of the main monitoring procedures allowed by the Commission—individual communications, state reports, and special rapporteurs—are provided for explicitly in the Charter, and the provisions concerning secrecy and massive violations should be scrapped). The African Charter should be reformed to keep abreast of the times.

The continuous creation of new mechanisms for the protection of human rights in Africa is not necessarily helping the situation. Instead of focusing on getting the mechanism created by the African Charter, the African Commission, to function properly, new mechanisms are created, such as the African Human Rights Court. Even before the African Human Rights Court is established, the NEPAD African Peer Review Mechanism is developed, and so forth. In themselves all of these mechanisms could be a viable starting point, but the current proliferation of mechanisms means that there is a lack of focus of resources and effort, with the result that none of them might be in a position to make any difference.

The question should be asked which mechanism is mostly likely to make a significant impact on human rights in Africa, and that particular mechanism should be supported and developed until it is functioning properly before other mechanisms are created.

If all the effort that goes into developing new mechanisms goes into the Charter and the Commission, and thereafter the African Human Rights Court, we would be able to point to a specific mechanism that makes a real difference towards consolidating the gains of the struggles of the people of Africa.

Questions and Comments:

1. It is notable that each of the regional systems built upon the prior experience of those created earlier. Thus, the American Convention was drafted taking into account the European Convention and the UN Covenants. In turn, the African Charter used the American Convention and the Covenants. Yet, the African Charter omits mention of several rights which have assumed importance in the European and Inter-American systems, including the right to privacy, to vote, to be elected to public office in periodic elections (although the Commission has found these rights to be implicit in the Charter's guarantee of the "right to political participation"), and the prohibition against forced or compulsory labor. How significant are these omissions in the light of African Charter Articles 60 and 61?

2. Is it legally significant that no formal vote was taken to adopt the African Charter?

3. Christof Heyns lists a number of criteria for ensuring the effectiveness of a regional human rights system. Do the materials thus far allow you to judge whether or not some of these criteria are met in the three regional systems? In addition to the criteria he lists, would you include the necessity of a well-drafted set of rights and duties? How well do the three systems meet this standard?

3. Universality and Regional Diversity

The debate over universality and diversity in human rights law is inescapable when evaluating regional systems. Some critics assert that all law is culturally relative and assert that human rights law emerged from and reflects exclusively western legal, cultural and political traditions. This relativistic claim challenges the very foundation of the international human rights system, which is based on recognition of transcendent, universal rights which individuals are entitled to enjoy solely by virtue of their status as human beings. Comparing the regional systems allows for partial testing of the competing theses of universality and cultural relativism; it is important in this respect to consider regional priorities and problems of implementation and compliance as well as the legal instruments. Nonetheless, as the extracts reprinted below illustrate, the legal instruments creating the various regional systems refer to and make use of the Universal Declaration of Human Rights (UDHR) and the Charter of the United Nations, providing a measure of uniformity in the fundamental guarantees and a reinforcement of the universal character of the UDHR.

The influence of universal norms on regional systems has a counterpart in the impact of regional values on global human rights guarantees. Indeed, Inter-American regional meetings played a key role in the development of the UN's Universal Declaration of Human Rights. At the International American Conference of War and Peace, held at Chapultepec, Mexico in March 1943, twenty-one American states asked for a bill of human rights to be included in the Charter of the United Nations. Three of these countries (Chile, Cuba, and Panama) were the first ones to submit a draft for such a bill. At the San Francisco Conference they lobbied for inclusion of a bill of rights in the Charter. Other Latin American countries prepared other drafts that became part of the background to the drafting of the Universal Declaration. The text submitted by the Inter-American Juridical Committee was particularly influential. The Chilean draft and the work of the Chilean delegate, Hernan Santa Cruz, were also important.

The rights contained in the regional treaties also reflect the human rights norms set forth in other global human rights declarations and conventions, in particular the United Nations Covenants on Civil and Political Rights (CCPR) and Economic, Social and Cultural Rights (CESCR). In addition, each successive system has looked to normative instruments and the jurisprudence of those systems founded earlier. Yet, there are clear differences in the regional instruments within the framework of the universal norms. The differences may be less pronounced than appears at first reading, however, because of treaty provisions regarding choice of law and canons of interpretation developed by the commissions and courts. The resulting cross-referencing and mutual influence in jurisprudence is producing some convergence in fundamental human rights principles.

The materials throughout this book will further examine the convergences and divergences in regional human rights law. Note that in recent years, many of the arguments asserting that specific regional or cultural values differ from human rights norms have come from Asia, which lacks a regional human rights system. *Compare, e.g.*, Bilahari Kausikan, *Asia's Different Standard*, 92 Foreign Pol'y 24 (Fall 1993), with Aryeh Neier, *Asia's Unacceptable Standard*, 92 *id.* 42 (Fall 1993) and Amartya Sen, *Human Rights and Asian Values*, The New Republic, July 14–July 21, 1997. Do "Asian values" explain why there is no Asian regional human rights system? The issue is examined further in Chapter VII. For African views, see, e.g., Josiah A.M. Cobbah, *African Values and the Human Rights Debate: An African Perspective*, 9 HUM. RTS. Q. 309 (1987); Makau Mutua, *Savages, Victims, and Saviors: The Metaphor of Human Rights*, 42 HARV. INT'L L.J. 201 (2001).

A. The Universal Declaration and Regional Human Rights Instruments

The United Nations was initially skeptical of regional protection of human rights, despite references in regional texts to the United Nations Charter and the Universal Declaration of Human Rights. According to two of the leading experts, "[f]or a long time, regionalism in the matter of human rights was not popular at the United Nations: There was often a tendency to regard it as the expression of a breakaway movement, calling the universality of human rights into question. However, the continual postponements of work on the International Human Rights Covenants led the UN to rehabilitate, and to be less suspicious (less jealous, some would say) towards, regionalism in human rights, especially after the adoption of the Covenants in 1966." 2 THE INTERNATIONAL DIMENSIONS OF HUMAN RIGHTS 451 (Karel Vasak & Philip Alston, eds., 1982).

There has been considerable discussion of the issue of universal human rights and the challenge of cultural relativism. The topic was debated thoroughly at the UN's 1993 World Conference on Human Rights, held in Vienna. The conference, in which all UN member states participated, adopted the following statement by consensus:

> All human rights are universal, indivisible and interdependent and interrelated. The international community must treat human rights globally in a fair and equal manner, on the same footing, and with the same emphasis. While the significance of national and regional particularities and various historical, cultural and religious backgrounds must be borne in mind, it is the duty of States, regardless of their political, economic and cultural systems, to promote and protect all human rights and fundamental freedoms.

World Conference on Human Rights, *Final Declaration and Programme of Action*, UN Doc. A/CONF.157/23 (July 12, 1993), sec. I, para. 5, reprinted in 32 ILM 1661 (1993).

The Vienna Declaration and Programme of Action recognized a need to consider the possibility of establishing regional and subregional arrangements for the promotion and protection of human rights where they do not already exist. The World Conference also recommended that more resources should be made available for the strengthening of regional arrangements under the program of technical cooperation in the field of human rights of the Office of the United Nations High Commissioner for Human Rights. Following the Vienna Conference the UN Human Rights Commission began adopting annual resolutions in support of regional human rights systems. In 2005, for example, the Commission reaffirmed that regional arrangements play an important role in promoting and protecting human rights and should reinforce universal human rights standards, as contained in international human rights instruments. It welcomed the progress achieved in the establishment of regional and subregional arrangements for the promotion and

protection of human rights and invited States in areas in which regional arrangements in the field of human rights do not yet exist to consider concluding agreements with a view to establishing suitable regional machinery for the promotion
and protection of human rights. UN Commission on Human Rights, Res. 2005/73,
Regional arrangements for the promotion and protection of human rights, April 20,
2005.

Contrast this with article 4 of the Universal Declaration on Cultural Diversity,
proclaimed by the UN Educational, Scientific, and Cultural Organization on Nov.
2, 2001:

> The defense of cultural diversity is an ethical imperative, inseparable from respect
> for human dignity. It implies a commitment to human rights and fundamental free-
> doms, in particular the rights of persons belonging to minorities and those of indig-
> enous peoples. No one may invoke cultural diversity to infringe upon human rights
> guaranteed by international law, nor to limit their scope.

Are the two declarations consistent? To what extent can respect for cultural diversity coexist with the application of universal human rights?

Despite UN support for regional systems, debate over their value remains alive
among some commentators. Those who focus on the textual divergences, without
considering the converging jurisprudence discussed below, remain convinced that
regional efforts "are a step in the wrong direction" because "[b]y decentralizing human rights enforcement away from the United Nations system, human rights, once
heralded as universal values that cannot vary from nation to nation or from region
to region, are now becoming increasingly region-specific." Melissa Robbins, *Comment: Powerful States, Customary Law and the Erosion of Human Rights through
Regional Enforcement*, 35 CAL. W. INT'L L.J. 275 (2005). In contrast, other analysts
point to the profound diversity that in fact exists in the international community
and note that regional systems are not the problem, because the international system is already structured to allow for diverse interpretations of the system's generally abstract rights, due to the UN's reliance upon the primacy of state implementation and weak mechanisms for international supervision. "Standing alone, generally stated abstract norms such as equal protection, privacy, free speech, or family life are even more indeterminate internationally than they are within domestic
legal orders." Douglas Lee Donoho, *Autonomy, Self-Governance, and the Margin
of Appreciation: Developing a Jurisprudence of Diversity within Universal Human
Rights*, 15 EMORY INT'L L. REV. 391, 429 (2001). As Donoho points out, claims of
diversity are often disingenuous, used by repressive governments to serve their political purposes under the guise of the "tired debate" over cultural relativism. This
relativism debate is different from a legitimate concern with diversity, autonomy
and the value of self-governance, reflected in the principles of subsidiarity and
federalism, which infuse regional human rights protection. The tension between
universality and diversity is encapsulated at the global level in the Vienna Declaration provision quoted above, which appears to suggest a balance between universal
values and local traditions. In the end, the quality of international institutions may
determine whether or not rights become uniformly meaningful and effective. In
this context, "the tension between universal rights, self-governance, autonomy and

diversity may perhaps best be played out in the context of concrete dispute resolution. The critical question is how international institutions cast in this role may effectively accommodate diversity and yet preserve, promote, and develop universal human rights values." *Id.* at 440.

The following extracts contain references to global legal instruments as well as to regional traditions. Are they in keeping with the consensus statement of the Vienna Conference? How similar are they? How much emphasis is there on universality and how much on the values of the region? Are the references to the global instruments legally significant?

European Convention on Human Rights and Fundamental Freedoms

Preamble

The governments signatory hereto, being members of the Council of Europe,

Considering the Universal Declaration of Human Rights proclaimed by the General Assembly of the United Nations on 10th December 1948;

Considering that this Declaration aims at securing the universal and effective recognition and observance of the Rights therein declared;

Considering that the aim of the Council of Europe is the achievement of greater unity between its members and that one of the methods by which that aim is to be pursued is the maintenance and further realisation of human rights and fundamental freedoms;

Reaffirming their profound belief in those fundamental freedoms which are the foundation of justice and peace in the world and are best maintained on the one hand by an effective political democracy and on the other by a common understanding and observance of the human rights upon which they depend;

Being resolved, as the governments of European countries which are like-minded and have a common heritage of political traditions, ideals, freedom and the rule of law, to take the first steps for the collective enforcement of certain of the rights stated in the Universal Declaration,

Have agreed as follows . . .

American Convention on Human Rights

Preamble

The American states signatory to the present Convention,

Reaffirming their intention to consolidate in this hemisphere, within the framework of democratic institutions, a system of personal liberty and social justice based on respect for the essential rights of man;

Recognizing that the essential rights of man are not derived from one's being a national of a certain state, but are based upon attributes of the human personality, and that they therefore justify international protection in the form of a convention reinforcing or complementing the protection provided by the domestic law of the American states;

Considering that these principles have been set forth in the Charter of the Organization of American States, in the American Declaration of the Rights and Duties of Man, and in the Universal Declaration of Human Rights, and that they have been reaffirmed and refined in other international instruments, worldwide as well as regional in scope;

Reiterating that, in accordance with the Universal Declaration of Human Rights, the ideal of free men enjoying freedom from fear and want can be achieved only if conditions are created whereby everyone may enjoy his economic, social, and cultural rights, as well as his civil and political rights; and

Considering that the Third Special Inter-American Conference (Buenos Aires, 1967) approved the incorporation into the Charter of the Organization itself of broader standards with respect to economic, social, and educational rights and resolved that an inter-American convention on human rights should determine the structure, competence, and procedure of the organs responsible for these matters,

Have agreed upon the following . . .

Article 29. Restrictions Regarding Interpretation

No provision of this Convention shall be interpreted as:

> a. permitting any State Party, group, or person to suppress the enjoyment or exercise of the rights and freedoms recognized in this Convention or to restrict them to a greater extent than is provided for herein;
> b. restricting the enjoyment or exercise of any right or freedom recognized by virtue of the laws of any State Party or by virtue of another convention to which one of the said states is a party;
> c. precluding other rights or guarantees that are inherent in the human personality or derived from representative democracy as a form of government; or
> d. excluding or limiting the effect that the American Declaration of the Rights and Duties of Man and other international acts of the same nature may have.

The Constitutive Act of the African Union

Article 3 Objectives

The objectives of the Union shall be to:

> (a) achieve greater unity and solidarity between the African countries and the peoples of Africa;
> (b) defend the sovereignty, territorial integrity and independence of its Member States;
> (c) accelerate the political and socio-economic integration of the continent;
> (d) promote and defend African common positions on issues of interest to the continent and its peoples;
> (e) encourage international cooperation, taking due account of the Charter of the United Nations and the Universal Declaration of Human Rights. . . .

African Charter on Human and Peoples Rights

Preamble

The African States members of the Organization of African Unity, parties to the present convention entitled "African Charter on Human and Peoples' Rights", . . .

Reaffirming the pledge they solemnly made in Article 2 of the said Charter [of the Organization of African Unity] to eradicate all forms of colonialism from Africa, to coordinate and intensify their cooperation and efforts to achieve a better life for the

peoples of Africa and to promote international cooperation having due regard to the Charter of the United Nations and the Universal Declaration of Human Rights;
. . .

Reaffirming their adherence to the principles of human and peoples' rights and freedoms contained in the declarations, conventions and other instrument adopted by the Organization of African Unity, the Movement of Non-Aligned Countries and the United Nations;

Firmly convinced of their duty to promote and protect human and people' rights and freedoms taking into account the importance traditionally attached to these rights and freedoms in Africa;

Have agreed as follows: . . .

Article 60

The Commission shall draw inspiration from international law on human and peoples' rights, particularly from the provisions of various African instruments on human and peoples' rights, the Charter of the United Nations, the Charter of the Organization of African Unity, the Universal Declaration of Human Rights, other instruments adopted by the United Nations and by African countries in the field of human and peoples' rights as well as from the provisions of various instruments adopted within the Specialized Agencies of the United Nations of which the parties to the present Charter are members.

The Arab Charter on Human Rights (2004), Preamble

Rejecting all forms of racism and Zionism, which constitute a violation of human rights and a threat to international peace and security, recognizing the close link between human rights and international peace and security, reaffirming the principles of the Charter of the United Nations, the Universal Declaration of Human Rights and the provisions of the two International Covenants on civil and political rights and on economic, social and cultural rights, and having regard to the Cairo Declaration on Human Rights in Islam. . . .

B. Invoking Universal Norms in Regional Systems

Human rights instruments, like constitutional bills of rights, are often written in general terms that must be interpreted and applied by national authorities and international monitoring bodies. The regional commissions and courts often cite to global norms, as well as to other regional human rights law, when applying their own instruments; the extent to which they are obliged to follow UN law is a matter of considerable discussion. The cases below illustrate the use of UN materials by regional bodies and the potential problems that may arise in practice. The first and third cases are from the European Court of Human Rights and the second from the Court of First Instance of the European Union. The final matter arose in the African Commission on Human and Peoples Rights. Consider, in reading each of the cases, the use of international standards. Do the various decision-making bodies use them as binding, authoritative, or relevant to the case before them? How should they treat them?

Nachova and Others v. Bulgaria [GC], (App. nos. 43577/98 and 43579/98), Judgment of 6 July 2005, Eur. Ct. H.R.

> [FACTS: The case concerned the death of two unarmed 21 year old Bulgarians of Romani or gypsy origin who were shot by military police during an attempted arrest. The two men had escaped from detention where they were being held for being absent without leave from their compulsory military service. The circumstances of the killings were in dispute.]

. . .

34. Mr. Angelov's grandmother, Ms Tonkova, gave the following account of the events: Her grandson and Mr. Petkov had been in her house when they had noticed a jeep approaching. She had gone outside and seen four men in uniform. They had all entered the yard. One of them had gone round the house and started shooting with an automatic rifle for a very long time. The other three men were also armed but had not fired any shots. She had been in the yard, pleading with the man who had been shooting to stop. However, he had walked towards the back of the house. Then she had heard shooting in the backyard. She had followed and then seen her grandson and Mr. Petkov lying in the neighbors' yard with bullet wounds.

35. According to another neighbor, Mr. M.M., all three policemen were shooting. Two of them had fired shots in the air and the third officer—who had been on the west side of the house (Major G.)—had been aiming at someone. Mr. M.M. had heard some fifteen to twenty shots, perhaps more. Then he had seen the military policemen go to the neighboring yard, where Mr. Angelov and Mr. Petkov had fallen. That yard belonged to Mr. M.M. and his daughter. On seeing his grandson—a young boy—standing there, Mr. M.M. had asked Major G. for permission to approach and to take him away. Major G. had pointed his gun at him in a brutal manner and had insulted him, saying: "You damn Gypsies!"

B. The investigation into the deaths

36. On 19 July 1996 all the officers involved made separate reports on the incident to the Vratsa Military-Police Unit. None of them was tested for alcohol.

37. A criminal investigation into the deaths was opened the same day and between 4 p.m. and 4.30 p.m. a military investigator inspected the scene. . . .

41. On 21 July 1996, a pathologist carried out an autopsy. . . .

43. The report concluded that the injuries had been caused by an automatic rifle fired from a distance. . . .

50. On 31 March 1997 the investigator completed the preliminary investigation and drew up a final report. He noted that Mr. Angelov and Mr. Petkov had escaped from detention while serving a prison sentence, and had thus committed an offence. Major G. had done everything within his power to save their lives: he had instructed them to stop and surrender and had fired warning shots. He had aimed at them only after seeing that they were continuing to run away and might escape. He had not sought to injure any vital organs. The investigator therefore concluded that Major G. had acted in accordance with Regulation 45 of the Military-Police Regulations

and made a recommendation to the Pleven Regional Prosecution Office that the investigation should be closed as Major G. had not committed an offence.

51. On 8 April 1997 the Pleven Military Prosecutor accepted the investigator's recommendation and closed the preliminary investigation into the deaths. He concluded that Major G. had proceeded in accordance with Regulation 45 of the Military-Police Regulations. He had warned the two men several times and fired shots in the air. He had shot them only because they had not surrendered, as there had been a danger that they might escape. He had sought to avoid inflicting fatal injuries. No one else had been hurt.

52. When describing the victims' personal circumstances, including details of their family, education and previous convictions, the prosecutor stated in the order that both men originated from "minority families", an expression mainly used to designate people from the Roma minority.

53. By an order of 11 June 1997 the prosecutor of the Armed Forces Prosecutor's Offices dismissed the applicants' subsequent appeal on the grounds that Mr. Angelov and Mr. Petkov had provoked the shooting by trying to escape and that Major G. had taken the steps required by law in such situations. Therefore, the use of arms had been lawful under Regulation 45 of the Military-Police Regulations.

54. On 19 November 1997 the prosecutor from the Investigation Review Department of the Armed Forces Prosecutor's Office dismissed a further appeal on grounds similar to those that had been relied on by the other public prosecutors. . . .

IV. RELEVANT INTERNATIONAL AND COMPARATIVE LAW

A. United Nations principles on the use of force

71. The United Nations Basic Principles on the Use of Force and Firearms by Law Enforcement Officials were adopted on 7 September 1990 by the Eighth United Nations Congress on the Prevention of Crime and the Treatment of Offenders.[2]

72. Paragraph 9 provides:

> Law enforcement officials shall not use firearms against persons except in self-defense or defense of others against the imminent threat of death or serious injury, to prevent the perpetration of a particularly serious crime involving grave threat to life, to arrest a person presenting such a danger and resisting their authority, or to prevent his or her escape, and only when less extreme means are insufficient to achieve these objectives. In any event, intentional lethal use of firearms may only be made when strictly unavoidable in order to protect life.

73. According to other provisions of the Principles, law enforcement officials shall "act in proportion to the seriousness of the offence and the legitimate objective to be achieved" (paragraph 5). Also, "Governments shall ensure that arbitrary or abusive use of force and firearms by law enforcement officials is punished as a criminal offence under their law" (paragraph 7). National rules and regulations on the use of

---

[2] [UN Congresses on Crime have been held every five years since 1955. They are a global forum of government delegations, non-governmental organizations and experts in the field of crime prevention and criminal justice. They exchange information about best practices and draft normative guidelines for states. They have had considerable impact on the laws and policies of states around the world. The 11th Congress was held in Bangkok in 2005. Ed.]

firearms should "ensure that firearms are used only in appropriate circumstances and in a manner likely to decrease the risk of unnecessary harm".

74. Paragraph 23 of the Principles states that victims or their family should have access to an independent process, "including a judicial process." Further, paragraph 24 provides:

> Governments and law enforcement agencies shall ensure that superior officers are held responsible if they know, or should have known, that law enforcement officials under their command are resorting, or have resorted, to the unlawful use of force and firearms, and they did not take all measures in their power to prevent, suppress or report such use.

75. The United Nations Principles on the Effective Prevention and Investigation of Extra-Legal, Arbitrary and Summary Executions, adopted on 24 May 1989 by the Economic and Social Council Resolution 1989/65, provide, *inter alia*, that there shall be a thorough, prompt and impartial investigation of all suspected cases of extra-legal, arbitrary and summary executions and that the investigation should aim at, *inter alia*, determining "any pattern or practice which may have brought about" the death. Paragraph 11 states:

> In cases in which the established investigative procedures are inadequate because of a lack of expertise or impartiality, because of the importance of the matter or because of the apparent existence of a pattern of abuse, and in cases where there are complaints from the family of the victim about these inadequacies or other substantial reasons, Governments shall pursue investigations through an independent commission of inquiry or similar procedure. Members of such a commission shall be chosen for their recognized impartiality, competence and independence as individuals. In particular, they shall be independent of any institution, agency or person that may be the subject of the inquiry. The commission shall have the authority to obtain all information necessary to the inquiry and shall conduct the inquiry as provided in these Principles.

Paragraph 17 states:

> A written report shall be made within a reasonable time on the methods and findings of such investigations. The report shall be made public immediately and shall include the scope of the inquiry, procedures, methods used to evaluate evidence as well as conclusions and recommendations based on findings of fact and on applicable law. . . .

B. International instruments and comparative law on racist violence

76. Article 4 of the International Convention on the Elimination of all forms of Racial Discrimination, ratified by Bulgaria in 1966, in force since 1969 and published in the State Gazette in 1992, provides, in so far as relevant:

> States Parties . . . undertake to adopt immediate and positive measures designed to eradicate all incitement to, or acts of, [racial] discrimination and, to this end. . . .
>
> (a) Shall declare an offence punishable by law . . . all acts of violence or incitement to such acts against any race or group of persons of another color or ethnic origin. . . .

77. In its views of 16 March 1993 in communication no. 4/91, *L.K. v. the Netherlands*, which concerned racist threats uttered by private individuals against Mr. L.K. and the inadequate reaction by the authorities to the victim's complaint, the Committee on the Elimination of All Forms of Racial Discrimination stated, *inter alia*,

that it was incumbent on the State to investigate with due diligence and expedition cases of incitement to racist discrimination and violence.

78. Article 6 of the Council of Europe's Framework Convention for the Protection of National Minorities, in force in Bulgaria since 1999, provides, in so far as relevant:

> The Parties undertake to take appropriate measures to protect persons who may be subject to threats or acts of discrimination, hostility or violence as a result of their ethnic, cultural, linguistic or religious identity.

79. In its decision of 21 November 2002, the United Nations Committee Against Torture ("CAT"), examining Complaint No. 161/2000 submitted by Hajrizi Dzemajl and others against Yugoslavia, found that a mob action by non-Roma residents of Danilovgrad, Montenegro, who destroyed a Roma settlement on 14 April 1995 in the presence of police officers, was "committed with a significant level of racial motivation". That fact aggravated the violation of Article 16 § 1 of the UN Convention against Torture and Other Cruel, Inhuman or Degrading Treatment or Punishment found in the case. In assessing the evidence, the CAT noted that it had not received a written explanation from the State party concerned and decided to rely on "the detailed submissions made by the complainants".

80. European Union Council Directive 2000/43/CE of 29 June 2000 implementing the principle of equal treatment between persons irrespective of racial or ethnic origin and Council Directive 2000/78/CE of 27 November 2000 establishing a general framework for equal treatment in employment and occupation, provide, in Article 8 and Article 10 respectively:

> 1. Member States shall take such measures as are necessary, in accordance with their national judicial systems, to ensure that, when persons who consider themselves wronged because the principle of equal treatment has not been applied to them establish, before a court or other competent authority, facts from which it may be presumed that there has been direct or indirect discrimination, it shall be for the respondent to prove that there has been no breach of the principle of equal treatment.
>
> 2. Paragraph 1 shall not prevent Member States from introducing rules of evidence which are more favorable to plaintiffs.
>
> 3. Paragraph 1 shall not apply to criminal procedures.
>
> . . . .
>
> 5. Member States need not apply paragraph 1 to proceedings in which it is for the court or competent body to investigate the facts of the case.

81. In 2002 the EC Commission published a Proposal for a Council Framework Decision on Combating Racism and Xenophobia Article 8 of which includes, among measures to be implemented by member States in that area, action to ensure that in criminal law racial motivation is taken into consideration as an aggravating circumstance.

82. In April 2005 the European Monitoring Centre on Racism and Xenophobia published a comparative overview of racist violence and responses to it in fifteen of the member States of the European Union. It noted, *inter alia*, that, traditionally, the criminal law in most of the jurisdictions surveyed did not specifically refer to "racist violence", the focus not being on the motivation behind acts of violence. However, that tradition was slowly changing as laws began to recognize crime as "racially

motivated". In particular, racist motivation was increasingly being considered as an aggravating factor for sentencing purposes under the legislation of some member States. The relevant legislation in the following countries specifically provided for that possibility: Austria, Belgium, Denmark, Finland, France, Italy, Portugal, Spain, Sweden and the United Kingdom. In particular, Article 132–76 of the French Penal Code, which was introduced in February 2003, provides in its second paragraph for an "objective" definition of racism as an aggravating circumstance leading to an increase in sentence:

> The penalties incurred for a crime or major offence shall be increased where the offence is committed on account of the victim's actual or supposed membership or non-membership of a particular ethnic group, nation, race or religion.

The aggravating circumstance defined in the first paragraph is constituted where the offence is preceded, accompanied or followed by written or spoken comments, images, objects or acts of any kind which damage the honor or consideration of the victim or of a group of persons to which the victim belongs on account of their actual or supposed membership or non-membership of a particular ethnic group, nation, race or religion.

THE LAW

. . . .

93. Article 2, which safeguards the right to life, ranks as one of the most fundamental provisions in the Convention and enshrines one of the basic values of the democratic societies making up the Council of Europe. The Court must subject allegations of breach of this provision to the most careful scrutiny. In cases concerning the use of force by State agents, it must take into consideration not only the actions of the agents of the State who actually administered the force but also all the surrounding circumstances including such matters as the relevant legal or regulatory framework in place and the planning and control of the actions under examination (see *McCann and Others v. the United Kingdom*, judgment of 27 September 1995, Series A no. 324, p. 46, § 150 and *Makaratzis v. Greece* [GC], no. 50385/99, §§ 57–59, 20 December 2004).

94. As the text of Article 2 § 2 itself shows, the use of lethal force by police officers may be justified in certain circumstances. However, any use of force must be no more than "absolutely necessary", that is to say be strictly proportionate in the circumstances. In view of the fundamental nature of the right to life, the circumstances in which deprivation of life may be justified must be strictly construed (see *Andronicou and Constantinou v. Cyprus*, judgment of 9 October 1997, *Reports of Judgments and Decisions* 1997-VI, pp. 2097–98, § 171, p. 2102, § 181, p. 2104, § 186, p. 2107, § 192 and p. 2108, § 193; and *McKerr v. the United Kingdom*, no. 28883/95, §§ 108 et seq., ECHR 2001-III).

95. Accordingly, and with reference to Article 2 § 2(b) of the Convention, the legitimate aim of effecting a lawful arrest can only justify putting human life at risk in circumstances of absolute necessity. The Court considers that in principle there can be no such necessity where it is known that the person to be arrested poses no threat to life or limb and is not suspected of having committed a violent offence, even if a failure to use lethal force may result in the opportunity to arrest the fugitive

being lost (see the Court's approach in *McCann and Others*, cited above, pp. 45–46, §§ 146–50 and pp. 56–62, §§ 192–214 and, more recently, in *Makaratzis*, cited above, §§ 64–66; see also the Court's condemnation of the use of firearms against unarmed and non-violent persons trying to leave the former German Democratic Republic in *Streletz, Kessler and Krenz v. Germany* [GC], nos. 34044/96, 35532/97 and 44801/98, §§ 87, 96 and 97, ECHR 2001-II).

96. In addition to setting out the circumstances when deprivation of life may be justified, Article 2 implies a primary duty on the State to secure the right to life by putting in place an appropriate legal and administrative framework defining the limited circumstances in which law-enforcement officials may use force and firearms, in the light of the relevant international standards (see *Makaratzis*, cited above, §§ 57–59, and the relevant provisions of the United Nations Basic Principles on the Use of Force and Firearms by Law Enforcement Officials in paragraphs 71–74 above). In line with the above-mentioned principle of strict proportionality inherent in Article 2 (see *McCann and Others*, cited above, p. 46, § 149), the national legal framework regulating arrest operations must make recourse to firearms dependent on a careful assessment of the surrounding circumstances, and, in particular, on an evaluation of the nature of the offence committed by the fugitive and of the threat he or she posed.

97. Furthermore, the national law regulating policing operations must secure a system of adequate and effective safeguards against arbitrariness and abuse of force and even against avoidable accident (see *Makaratzis*, cited above, § 58). In particular, law-enforcement agents must be trained to assess whether or not there is an absolute necessity to use firearms not only on the basis of the letter of the relevant regulations but also with due regard to the pre-eminence of respect for human life as a fundamental value (see the Court's criticism of the "shoot to kill" instructions given to soldiers in *McCann and Others*, cited above, pp. 61–62, §§ 211–214).

. . . .

99. The Court notes as a matter of grave concern that the relevant regulations on the use of firearms by the military police effectively permitted lethal force to be used when arresting a member of the armed forces for even the most minor offence. Not only were the regulations not published, they contained no clear safeguards to prevent the arbitrary deprivation of life. Under the regulations it was lawful to shoot any fugitive who did not surrender immediately in response to an oral warning and the firing of a warning shot in the air. The laxity of the regulations on the use of firearms and the manner in which they tolerated the use of lethal force were clearly exposed by the events that led to the fatal shooting of Mr. Angelov and Mr. Petkov and by the investigating authorities' response to those events. The Court will revert to these matters later.

100. Such a legal framework is fundamentally deficient and falls well short of the level of protection "by law" of the right to life that is required by the Convention in present-day democratic societies in Europe.

. . . .

105. In the event, the regulations in place permitted a team of heavily armed officers to be dispatched to arrest the two men in the absence of any prior discussion

of the threat, if any, they posed or of clearing warnings on the need to minimize any risk to life. In short, the manner in which the operation was planned and controlled betrayed a deplorable disregard for the pre-eminence of the right to life.

(iii) The actions of the arresting officers

106. It was undisputed that Mr. Angelov and Mr. Petkov had served in the Construction Force, a special army institution in which conscripts discharged their duties as construction workers on non-military sites. They had been sentenced to short terms of imprisonment for non-violent offences. They had escaped without using violence, simply by leaving their place of work, which was outside the detention facility. While they had previous convictions for theft and had repeatedly been absent without leave, they had no record of violence. Neither man was armed or represented a danger to the arresting officers or third parties, a fact of which the arresting officers must have been aware on the basis of the information available to them. In any event, upon encountering the men in the village of Lesura, the officers, or at least Major G., observed that they were unarmed and not showing any signs of threatening behavior.

107. Having regard to the above, the Court considers that in the circumstances that obtained in the present case any resort to potentially lethal force was prohibited by Article 2 of the Convention, regardless of any risk that Mr. Angelov and Mr. Petkov might escape. As stated above, recourse to potentially deadly force cannot be considered as "absolutely necessary" where it is known that the person to be arrested poses no threat to life or limb and is not suspected of having committed a violent offence.

108. In addition, the conduct of Major G., the military police officer who shot the victims, calls for serious criticism in that he used grossly excessive force. . . .

109. The Court finds that the respondent State failed to comply with its obligations under Article 2 of the Convention in that the relevant legal framework on the use of force was fundamentally flawed and Mr. Angelov and Mr. Petkov were killed in circumstances in which any use of firearms to effect their arrest was incompatible with Article 2 of the Convention. Furthermore, grossly excessive force was used. There has therefore been a violation of Article 2 of the Convention as regards the deaths of Mr. Angelov and Mr. Petkov.

2. Whether the investigation into the deaths of Mr. Angelov and Mr. Petkov was effective, as required by Article 2 of the Convention

. . . .

119. In the present case there has been a violation of the respondent State's obligation under Article 2 § 1 of the Convention to investigate the deprivation of life effectively. . . .

166. . . . [T]he investigator and the prosecutors involved in the present case had before them plausible information which was sufficient to alert them to the need to carry out an initial verification and, depending on the outcome, an investigation into possible racist overtones in the events that led to the death of the two men.

167. However, the authorities did nothing to verify Mr. M.M.'s statement. They omitted to question witnesses about it. Major G. was not asked to explain why he

had considered it necessary to use such a degree of force. No attempt was made to verify Major G.'s record and to ascertain, for example, whether he had previously been involved in similar incidents or whether he had ever been accused in the past of displaying anti-Roma sentiment. Those failings were compounded by the behavior of the investigator and the prosecutors, who, as the Court has found above, disregarded relevant facts and terminated the investigation, thereby shielding Major G. from prosecution.

168. The Court thus finds that the authorities failed in their duty under Article 14 of the Convention taken together with Article 2 to take all possible steps to investigate whether or not discrimination may have played a role in the events. It follows that there has been a violation of Article 14 of the Convention taken together with Article 2 in its procedural aspect. . . .

Questions and Comments

1. In paragraph 96, does the Court incorporate UN standards on the use of force into Article 2 as a basis for finding a violation of the right to life? Does this case suggest that a litigator in the European system would be wise to refer to universal treaties and declarations relevant to the case?

2. Many of the cited documents are non-binding recommendations or codes of conduct. Does this fact appear significant to the Court?

3. *Nachova* was the first case in which the European Court coupled a finding that Article 14 was violated with a violation of Article 2. In all prior cases where the issue arose, the Court had found that its determination of the "substantive" claim made it unnecessary to consider the question of discrimination in the violation. What might have motivated the Court's decisions in the past and what influence did the international materials referred to have on the outcome of this case?

4. The next case confronts the issue of hierarchy of legal norms. Beyond the specific questions addressed in the decision, consider whether or not human rights have or should have a preferred status in international law.

Yassin Abdullah Kadi v. Council of the European Union and Commission of the European Communities, Case T-315–01, Judgment of the Court of First Instance (Second Chamber, extended composition) of 21 September 2005, [2005] ECR II-3649.

> [The applicant, a citizen of Saudi Arabia, sought annulment of Council and Commission measures which, inter alia, froze his assets in Europe on the basis that the UN listed him as a person associated with Usama bin Laden, the Al-Qaeda network and the Taliban. The relationship between mandatory decisions of the UN Security Council, EU law and the European Convention on Human Rights was a focus of the case].

. . . .

10. On 15 October 1999 the Security Council of the United Nations (the Security Council) adopted Resolution 1267 (1999). . . . In the second paragraph of the resolution the Security Council demanded that the Taliban should without further delay turn Usama bin Laden over to the appropriate authorities. In order to ensure

compliance with that demand, paragraph 4(b) of Resolution 1267 (1999) provides that all the States must, in particular, "freeze funds and other financial resources, including funds derived or generated from property owned or controlled directly or indirectly by the Taliban, or by any undertaking owned or controlled by the Taliban, as designated by the [Sanctions] Committee [it] established . . . , and ensure that neither they nor any other funds or financial resources so designated are made available, by their nationals or by any persons within their territory, to or for the benefit of the Taliban or any undertaking owned or controlled, directly or indirectly, by the Taliban, except as may be authorised by the Committee on a case-by-case basis on the grounds of humanitarian need."

11. . . . [A] committee of the Security Council composed of all its members (the "Sanctions Committee"), [was] responsible in particular for ensuring that the States implement the measures imposed . . . , designating the funds or other financial resources referred to . . . and considering requests for exemptions from the measures imposed. . . .

13. On 14 February 2000, on the basis of Articles 60 EC and 301 EC, the Council adopted Reg. (EC) No 337/2000 concerning a flight ban and a freeze of funds and other financial resources in respect of the Taliban of Afghanistan (OJ 2000 L 43, p. 1).

14. On 19 December 2000 the Security Council adopted Resolution 1333 (2000), demanding, inter alia, that the Taliban should comply with Resolution 1267 (1999), and, in particular, that they should cease to provide sanctuary and training for international terrorists and their organisations and turn Usama bin Laden over to appropriate authorities to be brought to justice. The Security Council decided in particular to strengthen the flight ban and freezing of funds imposed under Resolution 1267 (1999). Accordingly paragraph 8(c) of Resolution 1333 (2000) provides that the States are, inter alia, "[t]o freeze without delay funds and other financial assets of Usama bin Laden and individuals and entities associated with him as designated by the [Sanctions Committee], including those in the Al-Qaeda organisation, and including funds derived or generated from property owned or controlled directly or indirectly by Usama bin Laden and individuals and entities associated with him, and to ensure that neither they nor any other funds or financial resources are made available, by their nationals or by any persons within their territory, directly or indirectly for the benefit of Usama bin Laden, his associates or any entities owned or controlled, directly or indirectly, by Usama bin Laden or individuals and entities associated with him including the Al-Qaeda organisation".

15. In the same provision, the Security Council instructed the Sanctions Committee to maintain an updated list, based on information provided by the States and regional organisations, of the individuals and entities designated as associated with Usama bin Laden, including those in the Al-Qaeda organisation.

16. In paragraph 23 of Resolution 1333 (2000), the Security Council decided that the measures imposed inter alia by paragraph 8 were to be established for 12 months and that, at the end of that period, it would decide whether to extend them for a further period on the same conditions. . . .

18. On 6 March 2001, on the basis of Articles 60 EC and 301 EC, the Council adopted Regulation (EC) No 467/2001 prohibiting the export of certain goods and services to Afghanistan, strengthening the flight ban and extending the freeze of funds and other financial resources in respect of the Taliban of Afghanistan, and repealing Regulation No 337/2000 (OJ 2001 L 67, p. 1).

. . . .

22. On 8 March 2001 the Sanctions Committee published a first consolidated list of the entities which and the persons who must be subjected to the freezing of funds pursuant to Security Council Resolutions 1267 (1999) and 1333 (2000). That list has since been amended and supplemented several times.

23. On 19 October 2001 the Sanctions Committee published a new addition to its list of 8 March 2001, including in particular the name of the following person:

– Al-Qadi, Yasin (a.k.a. Kadi, Shaykh Yassin Abdullah; a.k.a. Kahdi, Yasin), Jeddah, Saudi Arabia.'

24. By Commission Regulation (EC) No 2062/2001 of 19 October 2001 amending, for the third time, Regulation No 467/2001 (OJ 2001 L 277, p. 25), the name of the person in question was added, with others, to Annex I to that regulation.

25. [In 2002 and 2003, the Security Council extended the freeze and the EU adopted regulations to comply. SC Res. 1390 (2002), and EC Reg. 881/2002).] . . .

32. On 20 December 2002 the Security Council adopted Resolution 1452 (2002), intended to facilitate the implementation of counter-terrorism obligations. Paragraph 1 of that resolution provides for a number of derogations from and exceptions to the freezing of funds and economic resources imposed by Resolutions 1267 (1999), 1333 (2000) and 1390 (2002) which may be granted by the Member States on humanitarian grounds, on condition that the Sanctions Committee gives its consent.

. . . .

Findings of the Court

. . . .

Concerning the relationship between the international legal order under the United Nations and the domestic or Community legal order

181. From the standpoint of international law, the obligations of the Member States of the United Nations under the Charter of the United Nations clearly prevail over every other obligation of domestic law or of international treaty law including, for those of them that are members of the Council of Europe, their obligations under the European Convention on Human Rights and, for those that are also members of the Community, their obligations under the EC Treaty.

182. As regards, first, the relationship between the Charter of the United Nations and the domestic law of the Member States of the United Nations, that rule of primacy is derived from the principles of customary international law. Under Article 27 of the Vienna Convention on the Law of Treaties of 23 May 1969, which consolidates those principles (and Article 5 of which provides that it is to apply to any treaty which is the constituent instrument of an international organisation and

to any treaty adopted within an international organisation), a party may not invoke the provisions of its internal law as justification for its failure to perform a treaty.

183. As regards, second, the relationship between the Charter of the United Nations and international treaty law, that rule of primacy is expressly laid down in Article 103 of the Charter which provides that, "[i]n the event of a conflict between the obligations of the Members of the United Nations under the present Charter and their obligations under any other international agreement, their obligations under the present Charter shall prevail." In accordance with Article 30 of the Vienna Convention on the Law of Treaties, and contrary to the rules usually applicable to successive treaties, that rule holds good in respect of Treaties made earlier as well as later than the Charter of the United Nations. According to the International Court of Justice, all regional, bilateral, and even multilateral, arrangements that the parties may have made must be made always subject to the provisions of Article 103 of the Charter of the United Nations (judgment of 26 November 1984, delivered in the *Case concerning Military and Paramilitary Activities in and against Nicaragua (Nicaragua v. United States of America)*, ICJ Reports, 1984, p. 392, paragraph 107).

184. That primacy extends to decisions contained in a resolution of the Security Council, in accordance with Article 25 of the Charter of the United Nations, under which the Members of the United Nations agree to accept and carry out the decisions of the Security Council. According to the International Court of Justice, in accordance with Article 103 of the Charter, the obligations of the Parties in that respect prevail over their obligations under any other international agreement (Order of 14 April 1992 (provisional measures), *Questions of Interpretation and Application of the 1971 Montreal Convention arising from the Aerial Incident at Lockerbie (Libyan Arab Jamahiriya v United States of America)*, ICJ Reports, 1992, p. 16, paragraph 42, and Order of 14 April 1992 (provisional measures), *Questions of Interpretation and Application of the 1971 Montreal Convention arising from the Aerial Incident at Lockerbie (Libyan Arab Jamahiriya v United Kingdom)*, ICJ Reports, 1992, p. 113, paragraph 39).

185. With more particular regard to the relations between the obligations of the Member States of the Community by virtue of the Charter of the United Nations and their obligations under Community law, it may be added that, in accordance with the first paragraph of Article 307 EC, The rights and obligations arising from agreements concluded before 1 January 1958 or, for acceding States, before the date of their accession, between one or more Member States on the one hand, and one or more third countries on the other, shall not be affected by the provisions of this Treaty.

. . . .

193. . . . . [T]he Community must be considered to be bound by the obligations under the Charter of the United Nations in the same way as its Member States, by virtue of the Treaty establishing it.

194. In that regard, it is not in dispute that at the time when they concluded the Treaty establishing the European Economic Community the Member States were bound by their obligations under the Charter of the United Nations.

195. By concluding a treaty between them they could not transfer to the Community more powers than they possessed or withdraw from their obligations to third countries under that Charter (see, by analogy, Joined Cases 21/72 to 24/72 *International Fruit Company and Others* [1972] ECR 1219, paragraph 11).

196. On the contrary, their desire to fulfil their obligations under that Charter follows from the very provisions of the Treaty establishing the European Economic Community and is made clear in particular by Article 224 and the first paragraph of Article 234 (see, by analogy, *International Fruit*, paragraphs 12 and 13, and the Opinion of Advocate General Mayras in those cases, ECR 1231, at page 1237).

. . . .

Concerning the scope of the review of legality that the Court must carry out

209. As a preliminary point, it is to be borne in mind that the European Community is based on the rule of law, inasmuch as neither its Member States nor its institutions can avoid review of the question whether their acts are in conformity with the basic constitutional charter, the Treaty, which established a complete system of legal remedies and procedures designed to enable the Court of Justice to review the legality of acts of the institutions.

. . . .

212. The question that arises in this instance is, however, whether there exist any structural limits, imposed by general international law or by the EC Treaty itself, on the judicial review which it falls to the Court of First Instance to carry out with regard to that regulation.

213. It must be recalled that the contested regulation, adopted in the light of Common Position 2002/402, constitutes the implementation at Community level of the obligation placed on the Member States of the Community, as Members of the United Nations, to give effect, if appropriate by means of a Community act, to the sanctions against Usama bin Laden, members of the Al-Qaeda network and the Taliban and other associated individuals, groups, undertakings and entities, which have been decided and later strengthened by several resolutions of the Security Council adopted under Chapter VII of the Charter of the United Nations. The recitals of the preamble to that regulation refer expressly to Resolutions 1267 (1999), 1333 (2000) and 1390 (2002).

214. In that situation, as the institutions have rightly claimed, they acted under circumscribed powers, with the result that they had no autonomous discretion. In particular, they could neither directly alter the content of the resolutions at issue nor set up any mechanism capable of giving rise to such alteration.

215. Any review of the internal lawfulness of the contested regulation, especially having regard to the provisions or general principles of Community law relating to the protection of fundamental rights, would therefore imply that the Court is to consider, indirectly, the lawfulness of those resolutions. In that hypothetical situation, in fact, the origin of the illegality alleged by the applicant would have to be sought, not in the adoption of the contested regulation but in the resolutions of the Security Council which imposed the sanctions. . . .

216. In particular, if the Court were to annul the contested regulation, as the applicant claims it should, although that regulation seems to be imposed by inter-

national law, on the ground that that act infringes his fundamental rights which are protected by the Community legal order, such annulment would indirectly mean that the resolutions of the Security Council concerned themselves infringe those fundamental rights. In other words, the applicant asks the Court to declare by implication that the provision of international law at issue infringes the fundamental rights of individuals, as protected by the Community legal order.

. . . .

221. In light of the considerations set out . . . above, the claim that the Court of First Instance has jurisdiction to review indirectly the lawfulness of such a decision according to the standard of protection of fundamental rights as recognised by the Community legal order, cannot be justified either on the basis of international law or on the basis of Community law.

222. First, such jurisdiction would be incompatible with the undertakings of the Member States under the Charter of the United Nations, especially Articles 25, 48 and 103 thereof, and also with Article 27 of the Vienna Convention on the Law of Treaties.

223. Second, such jurisdiction would be contrary to provisions both of the EC Treaty, especially Articles 5 EC, 10 EC, 297 EC and the first paragraph of Article 307 EC, and of the Treaty on European Union, in particular Article 5 EU, in accordance with which the Community judicature is to exercise its powers on the conditions and for the purposes provided for by the provisions of the EC Treaty and the Treaty on European Union. It would, what is more, be incompatible with the principle that the Community's powers and, therefore, those of the Court of First Instance, must be exercised in compliance with international law. . . .

224. It has to be added that, with particular regard to Article 307 EC and to Article 103 of the Charter of the United Nations, reference to infringements either of fundamental rights as protected by the Community legal order or of the principles of that legal order cannot affect the validity of a Security Council measure or its effect in the territory of the Community (see, by analogy, Case 11/70 *Internationale Handelsgesellschaft* [1970] ECR 1125, paragraph 3; Case 234/85 Keller [1986] ECR 2897, paragraph 7, and Joined Cases 97/87 to 99/87 *Dow Chemical Ibérica and Others v Commission* [1989] ECR 3165, paragraph 38).

225. It must therefore be considered that the resolutions of the Security Council at issue fall, in principle, outside the ambit of the Court's judicial review and that the Court has no authority to call in question, even indirectly, their lawfulness in the light of Community law. On the contrary, the Court is bound, so far as possible, to interpret and apply that law in a manner compatible with the obligations of the Member States under the Charter of the United Nations.

226. None the less, the Court is empowered to check, indirectly, the lawfulness of the resolutions of the Security Council in question with regard to *jus cogens*, understood as a body of higher rules of public international law binding on all subjects of international law, including the bodies of the United Nations, and from which no derogation is possible.

227. In this connection, it must be noted that the Vienna Convention on the Law of Treaties, which consolidates the customary international law and Article 5 of

which provides that it is to apply to any treaty which is the constituent instrument of an international organisation and to any treaty adopted within an international organisation, provides in Article 53 for a treaty to be void if it conflicts with a peremptory norm of general international law (*jus cogens*), defined as a norm accepted and recognised by the international community of States as a whole as a norm from which no derogation is permitted and which can be modified only by a subsequent norm of general international law having the same character. Similarly, Article 64 of the Vienna Convention provides that: If a new peremptory norm of general international law emerges, any existing treaty which is in conflict with that norm becomes void and terminates.

228. Furthermore, the Charter of the United Nations itself presupposes the existence of mandatory principles of international law, in particular, the protection of the fundamental rights of the human person. In the preamble to the Charter, the peoples of the United Nations declared themselves 'determined to reaffirm faith in fundamental human rights, in the dignity and worth of the human person'. In addition, it is apparent from Chapter I of the Charter, headed Purposes and Principles, that one of the purposes of the United Nations is to encourage respect for human rights and for fundamental freedoms.

229. Those principles are binding on the Members of the United Nations as well as on its bodies. Thus, under Article 24(2) of the Charter of the United Nations, the Security Council, in discharging its duties under its primary responsibility for the maintenance of international peace and security, is to act 'in accordance with the Purposes and Principles of the United Nations'. The Security Council's powers of sanction in the exercise of that responsibility must therefore be wielded in compliance with international law, particularly with the purposes and principles of the United Nations.

230. International law thus permits the inference that there exists one limit to the principle that resolutions of the Security Council have binding effect: namely, that they must observe the fundamental peremptory provisions of *jus cogens*. If they fail to do so, however improbable that may be, they would bind neither the Member States of the United Nations nor, in consequence, the Community.

231. The indirect judicial review carried out by the Court in connection with an action for annulment of a Community act adopted, where no discretion whatsoever may be exercised, with a view to putting into effect a resolution of the Security Council may therefore, highly exceptionally, extend to determining whether the superior rules of international law falling within the ambit of *jus cogens* have been observed, in particular, the mandatory provisions concerning the universal protection of human rights, from which neither the Member States nor the bodies of the United Nations may derogate because they constitute intransgressible principles of international customary law (Advisory Opinion of the International Court of Justice of 8 July 1996, *The Legality of the Threat or Use of Nuclear Weapons*, Reports 1996, p. 226, paragraph 79; see also, to that effect, Advocate General Jacobs's Opinion in *Bosphorus*, paragraph 189 above, paragraph 65).

232. It is in the light of those considerations that the pleas alleging breach of the applicants' fundamental rights must be examined.

Concerning the alleged breaches of the applicant's fundamental rights

. . . .

234. The applicant alleges a breach of his right to respect for property, as guaranteed by Article 1 of the First Additional Protocol to the ECHR, and also a breach of the principle of proportionality as a general principle of Community law. . . .

241. [I]t must be noted that while Article 17(1) of the Universal Declaration of Human Rights, adopted by the General Assembly of the United Nations on 10 December 1948, provides that '[e]veryone has the right to own property alone as well as in association with others,' Article 17(2) of that Universal Declaration specifies that '[n]o one shall be arbitrarily deprived of his property.'

242. Thus, in so far as respect for the right to property must be regarded as forming part of the mandatory rules of general international law, it is only an arbitrary deprivation of that right that might, in any case, be regarded as contrary to *jus cogens*.

243. Here, however, it is clear that the applicant has not been arbitrarily deprived of that right.

244. In fact, in the first place, the freezing of his funds constitutes an aspect of the sanctions decided by the Security Council against Usama bin Laden, members of the Al-Qaeda network and the Taliban and other associated individuals, groups, undertakings and entities.

245. In that regard, it is appropriate to stress the importance of the campaign against international terrorism and the legitimacy of the protection of the United Nations against the actions of terrorist organisations. . . .

247. . . . The measures in question pursue therefore an objective of fundamental public interest for the international community.

248. In the second place, freezing of funds is a temporary precautionary measure which, unlike confiscation, does not affect the very substance of the right of the persons concerned to property in their financial assets but only the use thereof.

249. In the third place, the resolutions of the Security Council at issue provide for a means of reviewing, after certain periods, the overall system of sanctions.

250. In the fourth place, as will be explained below, the legislation at issue settles a procedure enabling the persons concerned to present their case at any time to the Sanctions Committee for review, through the Member State of their nationality or that of their residence.

251. Having regard to those facts, the freezing of the funds of persons and entities suspected, on the basis of information communicated by the Member States of the United Nations and checked by the Security Council, of being linked to Usama bin Laden, the Al-Qaeda network or the Taliban and of having participated in the financing, planning, preparation or perpetration of terrorist acts cannot be held to constitute an arbitrary, inappropriate or disproportionate interference with the fundamental rights of the persons concerned.

252. It follows from the foregoing that the applicant's arguments alleging breach of the right to respect for property and of the general principle of proportionality must be rejected.

. . . .

255. With regard . . . to the applicant's alleged right to be heard by the Council in connection with the adoption of the contested regulation, it must be borne in mind that, according to settled case-law, observance of the right to a fair hearing is, in all proceedings initiated against a person which are liable to culminate in a measure adversely affecting that person, a fundamental principle of Community law which must be guaranteed even in the absence of any rules governing the proceedings at issue. That principle requires that any person on whom a penalty may be imposed must be placed in a position in which he can effectively make known his views on the evidence on the basis of which the sanction is imposed. . . .

256. The Council and the Commission were, however, right in observing that this case-law was developed in areas such as competition law, anti-dumping action and State aid, but also disciplinary law and the reduction of financial assistance, in which the Community institutions enjoy extensive powers of investigation and inquiry and wide discretion . . . [Here, the institutions had no powers of investigation or discretion.]

260. The applicant's arguments based on the alleged infringement of his right to be heard by the Council in connection with the adoption of the contested regulation must therefore be rejected.

261. As regards, second, the applicant's alleged right to be heard by the Sanctions Committee in connection with his inclusion in the list of persons whose funds must be frozen pursuant to the Security Council's resolutions at issue, it is clear that no such right is provided for by the resolutions in question.

262. Nevertheless, although the resolutions of the Security Council concerned and the subsequent regulations that put them into effect in the Community do not provide for any right of audience for individual persons, they set up a mechanism for the re-examination of individual cases, by providing that the persons concerned may address a request to the Sanctions Committee, through their national authorities, in order either to be removed from the list of persons affected by the sanctions or to obtain exemption from the freezing of funds. . . .

264. With particular regard to an application for re-examination of an individual case, for the purpose of having the person concerned removed from the list of persons affected by the sanctions, section 7 of the Guidelines of the [Sanctions] Committee for the conduct of its work, adopted on 7 November 2002 and amended on 10 April 2003, provides [a procedure for individuals to petition their government to request review of the case. The government then may approach the government that recommended the listing and the Sanctions Committee].

265. The Court finds that, by adopting those Guidelines, the Security Council intended to take account, so far as possible, of the fundamental rights of the persons entered in the Sanctions Committee's list, and in particular their right to be heard. . . .

267. Admittedly, the procedure described above confers no right directly on the persons concerned themselves to be heard by the Sanctions Committee, the only authority competent to give a decision, on a State's petition, on the re-examination of their case. Those persons are thus dependent, essentially, on the diplomatic protection afforded by the States to their nationals.

268. Such a restriction of the right to be heard, directly and in person, by the competent authority is not, however, to be deemed improper in the light of the mandatory prescriptions of the public international order. On the contrary, with regard to the challenge to the validity of decisions ordering the freezing of funds belonging to individuals or entities suspected of contributing to the financing of international terrorism, adopted by the Security Council through its Sanctions Committee under Chapter VII of the Charter of the United Nations on the basis of information communicated by the States and regional organisations, it is normal that the right of the persons involved to be heard should be adapted to an administrative procedure on several levels, in which the national authorities referred to in Annex II of the contested regulation play an indispensable part. . . .

273. In any case, the fact remains that any opportunity for the applicant effectively to make known his views on the correctness and relevance of the facts in consideration of which his funds have been frozen and on the evidence adduced against him appears to be definitively excluded. Those facts and that evidence, once classified as confidential or secret by the State which made the Sanctions Committee aware of them, are not, obviously, communicated to him, any more than they are to the Member States of the United Nations to which the Security Council's resolutions are addressed.

274. None the less, in circumstances such as those of this case, in which what is at issue is a temporary precautionary measure restricting the availability of the applicant's property, the Court of First Instance considers that observance of the fundamental rights of the person concerned does not require the facts and evidence adduced against him to be communicated to him, once the Security Council or its Sanctions Committee is of the view that that there are grounds concerning the international community's security that militate against it.

275. It follows that the applicant's arguments alleging breach of his right to be heard by the Sanctions Committee in connection with his inclusion in the list of persons whose funds must be frozen pursuant to the resolutions of the Security Council in question must be rejected.

Concerning the alleged breach of the right to effective judicial review. . . .

285. . . . [T]here is no judicial remedy available to the applicant, the Security Council not having thought it advisable to establish an independent international court responsible for ruling, in law and on the facts, in actions brought against individual decisions taken by the Sanctions Committee.

286. However, it is also to be acknowledged that any such lacuna in the judicial protection available to the applicant is not in itself contrary to *jus cogens*.

287. Here the Court would point out that the right of access to the courts, a principle recognised by both Article 8 of the Universal Declaration of Human Rights and Article 14 of the International Covenant on Civil and Political Rights, adopted by the United Nations General Assembly on 16 December 1966, is not absolute. On the one hand, at a time of public emergency which threatens the life of the nation, measures may be taken derogating from that right, as provided for on certain conditions by Article 4(1) of that Covenant. On the other hand, even where those exceptional circumstances do not obtain, certain restrictions must be held to be inherent

in that right, such as the limitations generally recognised by the community of nations to fall within the doctrine of State immunity (see, to that effect, the judgments of the European Court of Human Rights in *Prince Hans-Adam II of Liechtenstein v Germany* of 12 July 2001, Reports of Judgments and Decisions 2001-VIII, paragraphs 52, 55, 59 and 68, and in *McElhinney v Ireland* of 21 November 2001, Reports of Judgments and Decisions 2001-XI, in particular paragraphs 34 to 37) and of the immunity of international organisations (see, to that effect, the judgment of the European Court of Human Rights in *Waite and Kennedy v Germany* of 18 February 1999, Reports of Judgments and Decisions, 1999I, paragraphs 63 and 68 to 73).

288. In this instance, the Court considers that the limitation of the applicant's right of access to a court, as a result of the immunity from jurisdiction enjoyed as a rule, in the domestic legal order of the Member States of the United Nations, by resolutions of the Security Council adopted under Chapter VII of the Charter of the United Nations, in accordance with the relevant principles of international law (in particular Articles 25 and 103 of the Charter), is inherent in that right as it is guaranteed by *jus cogens.*

289. Such a limitation is justified both by the nature of the decisions that the Security Council is led to take under Chapter VII of the Charter of the United Nations and by the legitimate objective pursued. In the circumstances of this case, the applicant's interest in having a court hear his case on its merits is not enough to outweigh the essential public interest in the maintenance of international peace and security in the face of a threat clearly identified by the Security Council in accordance with the Charter of the United Nations. In this regard, special significance must attach to the fact that, far from providing for measures for an unlimited period of application, the resolutions successively adopted by the Security Council have always provided a mechanism for re-examining whether it is appropriate to maintain those measures after 12 or 18 months at most have elapsed. . . .

290. Last, the Court considers that, in the absence of an international court having jurisdiction to ascertain whether acts of the Security Council are lawful, the setting-up of a body such as the Sanctions Committee and the opportunity, provided for by the legislation, of applying at any time to that committee in order to have any individual case re-examined, by means of a procedure involving both the petitioned government' and the designating government' (see paragraphs 263 and 264 above), constitute another reasonable method of affording adequate protection of the applicant's fundamental rights as recognised by *jus cogens.*

291. It follows that the applicant's arguments alleging breach of his right to effective judicial review must be rejected.

292. None of the applicant's pleas in law or arguments having been successful, the action must be dismissed.

———————

Al-Adsani v. The United Kingdom [GC], (App. no. 35763/97), Judgment of 21 November 2001, Eur. Ct. H.R., 34 EHRR 11 (2002)

[This well-known case addresses the role of general international law in interpreting and applying the ECHR. The applicant sued the government of Kuwait in the UK courts for alleged acts of torture in Kuwait, including burns covering 25% of his total body surface area. Once in England, he was diagnosed as suffering from severe post-traumatic stress disorder, aggravated by the fact that he received threats warning him not to take action or give publicity to his plight. He nonetheless brought a civil action, which was dismissed based on the law granting sovereign immunity to foreign governments. At the European Court, the applicant contended that the United Kingdom had failed to secure his right not to be tortured, contrary to Article 3 of the Convention read in conjunction with Articles 1 and 13. The Court rejected this argument because "[t]he applicant does not contend that the alleged torture took place within the jurisdiction of the United Kingdom or that the United Kingdom authorities had any causal connection with its occurrence. In these circumstances, it cannot be said that the High Contracting Party was under a duty to provide a civil remedy to the applicant in respect of torture allegedly carried out by the Kuwaiti authorities." *Id.* para. 40. The applicant also alleged that he was denied access to a court in the determination of his claim against the State of Kuwait and that this constituted a violation of Article 6 § 1 of the Convention. On this point, the Court held that Article 6 applied, but was not violated despite the *jus cogens* nature of the prohibition of torture. The relevant paragraphs follow.]

52. In *Golder v. the United Kingdom* (judgment of 21 February 1975, Series A no. 18, pp. 13–18, §§ 28–36) the Court held that the procedural guarantees laid down in Article 6 concerning fairness, publicity and promptness would be meaningless in the absence of any protection for the pre-condition for the enjoyment of those guarantees, namely, access to a court. It established this as an inherent aspect of the safeguards enshrined in Article 6, referring to the principles of the rule of law and the avoidance of arbitrary power which underlie much of the Convention. Thus, Article 6 § 1 secures to everyone the right to have any claim relating to his civil rights and obligations brought before a court.

53. The right of access to a court is not, however, absolute, but may be subject to limitations; these are permitted by implication since the right of access by its very nature calls for regulation by the State. In this respect, the Contracting States enjoy a certain margin of appreciation, although the final decision as to the observance of the Convention's requirements rests with the Court. It must be satisfied that the limitations applied do not restrict or reduce the access left to the individual in such a way or to such an extent that the very essence of the right is impaired. Furthermore, a limitation will not be compatible with Article 6 § 1 if it does not pursue a legitimate aim and if there is no reasonable relationship of proportionality between the means employed and the aim sought to be achieved (see *Waite and Kennedy v. Germany* [GC], no. 26083/94, § 59, ECHR 1999-I).

54. The Court must first examine whether the limitation pursued a legitimate aim. It notes in this connection that sovereign immunity is a concept of international law, developed out of the principle *par in parem non habet imperium*, by virtue of which one State shall not be subject to the jurisdiction of another State. The Court considers that the grant of sovereign immunity to a State in civil proceedings pur-

sues the legitimate aim of complying with international law to promote comity and good relations between States through the respect of another State's sovereignty.

55. The Court must next assess whether the restriction was proportionate to the aim pursued. It reiterates that the Convention has to be interpreted in the light of the rules set out in the Vienna Convention on the Law of Treaties of 23 May 1969, and that Article 31 § 3 (c) of that treaty indicates that account is to be taken of "any relevant rules of international law applicable in the relations between the parties". The Convention, including Article 6, cannot be interpreted in a vacuum. The Court must be mindful of the Convention's special character as a human rights treaty, and it must also take the relevant rules of international law into account (see, *mutatis mutandis, Loizidou v. Turkey* (merits), judgment of 18 December 1996, *Reports* 1996-VI, p. 2231, § 43). The Convention should so far as possible be interpreted in harmony with other rules of international law of which it forms part, including those relating to the grant of State immunity.

56. It follows that measures taken by a High Contracting Party which reflect generally recognised rules of public international law on State immunity cannot in principle be regarded as imposing a disproportionate restriction on the right of access to a court as embodied in Article 6 § 1. Just as the right of access to a court is an inherent part of the fair trial guarantee in that Article, so some restrictions on access must likewise be regarded as inherent, an example being those limitations generally accepted by the community of nations as part of the doctrine of State immunity.

57. The Court notes that the 1978 Act, applied by the English courts so as to afford immunity to Kuwait, complies with the relevant provisions of the 1972 Basle Convention, which, while placing a number of limitations on the scope of State immunity as it was traditionally understood, preserves it in respect of civil proceedings for damages for personal injury unless the injury was caused in the territory of the forum State. Except insofar as it affects claims for damages for torture, the applicant does not deny that the above provision reflects a generally accepted rule of international law. He asserts, however, that his claim related to torture, and contends that the prohibition of torture has acquired the status of a *jus cogens* norm in international law, taking precedence over treaty law and other rules of international law.

58. Following the decision to uphold Kuwait's claim to immunity, the domestic courts were never required to examine evidence relating to the applicant's allegations, which have, therefore, never been proved. However, for the purposes of the present judgment, the Court accepts that the ill-treatment alleged by the applicant against Kuwait in his pleadings in the domestic courts, namely, repeated beatings by prison guards over a period of several days with the aim of extracting a confession (. . .), can properly be categorised as torture within the meaning of Article 3 of the Convention (see *Selmouni v. France* [GC], no. 25803/94, ECHR 1999-V, . . .).

59. Within the Convention system it has long been recognised that the right under Article 3 not to be subjected to torture or to inhuman or degrading treatment or punishment enshrines one of the fundamental values of democratic society. It is an absolute right, permitting of no exception in any circumstances (. . .). Of all the

categories of ill-treatment prohibited by Article 3, "torture" has a special stigma, attaching only to deliberate inhuman treatment causing very serious and cruel suffering (. . .).

60. Other areas of public international law bear witness to a growing recognition of the overriding importance of the prohibition of torture. Thus, torture is forbidden by Article 5 of the Universal Declaration of Human Rights and Article 7 of the International Covenant on Civil and Political Rights. The United Nations Convention against Torture and Other Cruel, Inhuman and Degrading Treatment or Punishment requires, by Article 2, that each State Party should take effective legislative, administrative, judicial or other measures to prevent torture in any territory under its jurisdiction, and, by Article 4, that all acts of torture should be made offences under the State Party's criminal law. In addition, there have been a number of judicial statements to the effect that the prohibition of torture has attained the status of a peremptory norm or *jus cogens*. For example, in its judgment of 10 December 1998 in *Furundzija*, the International Criminal Tribunal for the Former Yugoslavia referred, *inter alia*, to the foregoing body of treaty rules and held that "[b]ecause of the importance of the values it protects, this principle [proscribing torture] has evolved into a peremptory norm or *jus cogens*, that is, a norm that enjoys a higher rank in the international hierarchy than treaty law and even 'ordinary' customary rules". Similar statements have been made in other cases before that tribunal and in national courts, including the House of Lords in the case of *ex parte Pinochet* (No. 3).

61. While the Court accepts, on the basis of these authorities, that the prohibition of torture has achieved the status of a peremptory norm in international law, it observes that the present case concerns not, as in *Furundzija* and *Pinochet*, the criminal liability of an individual for alleged acts of torture, but the immunity of a State in a civil suit for damages in respect of acts of torture within the territory of that State. Notwithstanding the special character of the prohibition of torture in international law, the Court is unable to discern in the international instruments, judicial authorities or other materials before it any firm basis for concluding that, as a matter of international law, a State no longer enjoys immunity from civil suit in the courts of another State where acts of torture are alleged. In particular, the Court observes that none of the primary international instruments referred to (Article 5 of the Universal Declaration of Human Rights, Article 7 of the International Covenant on Civil and Political Rights and Articles 2 and 4 of the UN Convention) relates to civil proceedings or to State immunity.

62. It is true that in its Report on Jurisdictional Immunities of States and their Property (. . .) the working group of the International Law Commission noted, as a recent development in State practice and legislation on the subject of immunities of States, the argument increasingly put forward that immunity should be denied in the case of death or personal injury resulting from acts of a State in violation of human rights norms having the character of *jus cogens*, particularly the prohibition on torture. However, as the working group itself acknowledged, while national courts had in some cases shown some sympathy for the argument that States were not entitled to plead immunity where there had been a violation of human rights

norms with the character of *jus cogens*, in most cases (including those cited by the applicant in the domestic proceedings and before the Court) the plea of sovereign immunity had succeeded.

63. The ILC working group went on to note developments, since those decisions, in support of the argument that a State may not plead immunity in respect of human rights violations: first, the exception to immunity adopted by the United States in the amendment to the Foreign Sovereign Immunities Act (FSIA) which had been applied by the United States courts in two cases; secondly, the *ex parte Pinochet (No. 3)* judgment in which the House of Lords "emphasised the limits of immunity in respect of gross human rights violations by State officials". The Court does not, however, find that either of these developments provides it with a firm basis on which to conclude that the immunity of States *ratione personae* is no longer enjoyed in respect of civil liability for claims of acts of torture, let alone that it was not enjoyed in 1996 at the time of the Court of Appeal's judgment in the present case.

64. As to the amendment to the FSIA, the very fact that the amendment was needed would seem to confirm that the general rule of international law remained that immunity attached even in respect of claims of acts of official torture. Moreover, the amendment is circumscribed in its scope: the offending State must be designated as a State sponsor of acts of terrorism, and the claimant must be a national of the United States. The effect of the FSIA is further limited in that after judgment has been obtained, the property of a foreign State is immune from attachment or execution unless one of the statutory exceptions applies.

65. As to the *ex parte Pinochet (No. 3)* judgment (. . .), the Court notes that the majority of the House of Lords held that, after the UN Convention and even before, the international prohibition against official torture had the character of *jus cogens* or a peremptory norm and that no immunity was enjoyed by a torturer from one Torture Convention State from the criminal jurisdiction of another. But, as the working group of the ILC itself acknowledged, that case concerned the immunity *ratione materiae* from criminal jurisdiction of a former head of State, who was at the material time physically within the United Kingdom. As the judgments in the case made clear, the conclusion of the House of Lords did not in any way affect the immunity *ratione personae* of foreign sovereign States from the civil jurisdiction in respect of such acts (see in particular, the judgment of Lord Millett, . . .). In so holding, the House of Lords cited with approval the judgments of the Court of Appeal in *Al-Adsani* itself.

66. The Court, while noting the growing recognition of the overriding importance of the prohibition of torture, does not accordingly find it established that there is yet acceptance in international law of the proposition that States are not entitled to immunity in respect of civil claims for damages for alleged torture committed outside the forum State. The 1978 Act, which grants immunity to States in respect of personal injury claims unless the damage was caused within the United Kingdom, is not inconsistent with those limitations generally accepted by the community of nations as part of the doctrine of State immunity.

67. In these circumstances, the application by the English courts of the provisions of the 1978 Act to uphold Kuwait's claim to immunity cannot be said to have amounted to an unjustified restriction on the applicant's access to a court.

It follows that there has been no violation of Article 6 § 1 of the Convention in this case.

———————————

Questions and Comments

1. The *Kadi* and *Al-Adsani* cases distinguish between human rights that are considered peremptory norms or *jus cogens* and those which are not. Why is this important? Does either Court explain how it determines that some rights are peremptory norms and others are not? Which, if any, rights asserted by Mr. Kadi are found to be peremptory norms? Do you agree that the powers of the U.N. Security Council are limited by peremptory human rights norms? If so, who may judge when the Security Council has violated such norms?

2. The *Kadi* case is on appeal. In the meantime, other individuals and groups have mounted similar and equally unsuccessful challenges to the EC regulations taken to implement sanctions mandated by Security Council Resolutions 1267 (1999), 1333 (2000), 1390 (2002), 1526 (2004) and 1617 (2005). See Case T-306/01 *Yusef and Al Barakaat International Foundation v. Council and Commission* [2005] ECR II-3533, appeal pending. In Case T-253/02, *Chafiq Ayadi v. Council* (July 12, 2006), the Second Chamber of the Court of First Instance reaffirmed the court's limited and indirect power to review Security Council decisions for conformity to *jus cogens* human rights norms. It also reaffirmed that the Court has no power to determine whether or not there was an error in assessing the facts and evidence relied on by the Security Council in support of the measures it has taken or to check the appropriateness and proportionality of those measures. In Case T-228/02, *Organisation des Modjahedines du peuple d'Iran v. Council*, judgment of 12 December 2006, the Court distinguished the above cases wherein the EU institutions and member states were mandated to take the actions they did by the Security Council. In this case, in contrast, the relevant Security Council resolution left it to each UN member state to identify the persons, groups and entities whose funds were to be frozen, in accordance with the rules in their own legal order. The EU Council thus had discretion to adopt its own measures, but was in principle bound to observe the right to a fair hearing and effective judicial protection. Nonetheless, the Court recognized that the effectiveness of a freeze on funds would be jeopardized by prior notification of the targeted individual or group and therefore "an initial measure freezing funds must, by its very nature, be able to benefit from a surprise effect and to be applied with immediate effect." Para. 128. After the fact, however, individuals must be notified of the evidence adduced against them, in so far as reasonably possible, and the parties must have the opportunity to request an immediate re-examination of the initial measure freezing their funds. Once the funds have been frozen, the element of surprise disappears and any subsequent decision to maintain a freeze on funds must be preceded by the possibility of a further hearing and, where appropriate, notification of any new evidence, subject to the legitimate requirements of security that might preclude revealing all evidence. The Court noted that such restrictions are consistent with the case law of the European Court of Human Rights, even under the more stringent standards of criminal proceedings.

3. On the issue of human rights as peremptory norms (*jus cogens*) see also: Inter-Am. Ct.H.R., *Juridical Condition and Rights of the Undocumented Migrants*, Advisory Opinion

OC-18/03, Sept. 17, 2003. In this opinion, the Court addressed the issue of *jus cogens* in general and as concerns the right to be free from discrimination:

98. Originally, the concept of *jus cogens* was linked specifically to the law of treaties. As *jus cogens* is formulated in Article 53 of the Vienna Convention on the Law of Treaties, "[a] treaty is void if, at the time of its conclusion, it conflicts with a peremptory norm of general international law." Likewise, Article 64 of the Convention refers to *jus cogens superviniente*, when it indicates that "[i]f a new peremptory norm of general international law emerges, any existing treaty which is in conflict with that norm becomes void and terminates." *Jus cogens* has been developed by international case law and legal writings.[3]

99. In its development and by its definition, *jus cogens* is not limited to treaty law. The sphere of *jus cogens* has expanded to encompass general international law, including all legal acts. *Jus cogens* has also emerged in the law of the international responsibility of States and, finally, has had an influence on the basic principles of the international legal order.

100. In particular, when referring to the obligation to respect and ensure human rights, regardless of which of those rights are recognized by each State in domestic or international norms, the Court considers it clear that all States, as members of the international community, must comply with these obligations without any discrimination; this is intrinsically related to the right to equal protection before the law, which, in turn, derives "directly from the oneness of the human family and is linked to the essential dignity of the individual."[4] The principle of equality before the law and non-discrimination permeates every act of the powers of the State, in all their manifestations, related to respecting and ensuring human rights. Indeed, this principle may be considered peremptory under general international law, inasmuch as it applies to all States, whether or not they are party to a specific international treaty, and gives rise to effects with regard to third parties, including individuals. This implies that the State, both internationally and in its domestic legal system, and by means of the acts of any of its powers or of third parties who act under its tolerance, acquiescence or negligence, cannot behave in a way that is contrary to the principle of equality and non-discrimination, to the detriment of a determined group of persons.

101. Accordingly, this Court considers that the principle of equality before the law, equal protection before the law and non-discrimination belongs to *jus cogens*, because the whole legal structure of national and international public order rests on it and it is a fundamental principle that permeates all laws. Nowadays, no legal act that is in conflict with this fundamental principle is acceptable, and discriminatory treatment of any person, owing to gender, race, color, language, religion or belief, political or other opinion, national, ethnic or social origin, nationality, age, economic situation, property, civil status, birth or any other status is unacceptable. This principle (equality and non-discrimination) forms part of general international law. At the existing stage of the development of international law, the fundamental principle of equality and non-discrimination has entered the realm of *jus cogens*.

The Inter-American Court has been the most assertive of international tribunals in declaring norms to be *jus cogens*. In addition to the opinion just cited, *see also* the case of *Almonacid-Arellano et al v. Chile*, 154 Inter-Am.Ct.H.R.(ser. C) (Sept. 26, 2006), para. 153, in which the Court announced its belief that the non-applicability of statutes of limitations to crimes against humanity is a norm *jus cogens*. In *La Cantuta v. Peru*, judgment of Nov. 29, 2006, 162 Inter-Am.Ct.H.R. (Ser. C), para. 160, the Court held that access to justice constitutes a peremptory norm of international law. No evidence was cited in either of these cases for the peremptory nature of the norm.

---

3 Cf. *I.C.T.Y., Trial Chamber II: Prosecutor v. Anto Furundzija, Judgment of 10 December 1998, Case No. IT-95–17/1-T, paras. 137–146, 153–157; Application of the Convention on the Prevention and Punishment of the Crime of Genocide, Preliminary Objections, Judgment, I.C.J. Reports 1996, p. 595; Barcelona Traction, Light and Power Company, Limited, Judgment, I.C.J. Reports 1970, p. 3, and Reservations to the Convention on Genocide, Advisory Opinion: I.C.J. Reports 1951, p. 15.*

4 *Legal Status and Human Rights of the Child, supra note 1, para. 45; Proposed Amendments to the Naturalization Provisions of the Constitution of Costa Rica, supra note 32, para. 55.* [Internal cross-references here are to the Advisory Opinion Ed.]

4. Does the Court imply in the *Al-Adsani* case that any state law or conduct that conforms to international law will be acceptable as a proportionate limitation on the enjoyment of rights guaranteed by the European Convention? Should this be the rule? If *jus cogens* signifies a norm from which no derogation is permitted, how can a limitation on remedies for acts of torture be acceptable?

5. For an analysis of the concept and application of *jus cogens* in international law, see D. Shelton, *Hierarchy of Sources of International Law*, 100 AJIL 290 (2006).

Note on the Right of Peoples to Self-Determination. Article 1 of the two United Nations Covenants on human rights sets forth in identical terms the right of peoples to self-determination. The UN Committee on Civil and Political Rights (CCPR) has determined that it lacks jurisdiction over alleged violations of the right of self-determination, however, because it is a "peoples' right" and not an individual right. The Committee pointed to the language of the Optional Protocol to the Covenant on Civil and Political Rights, which creates a petition procedure for the submission of "communications from individuals." See *Bernard Ominayak, Chief of the Lubicon Lake Band v. Canada*, UN Doc. A/45/40, vol. II 27 (1990); see also CCPR, General Comment 12, *The right to self-determination of peoples* (Article 1), 13 April 1984. Regionally, the African Charter is the only instrument in force to include self-determination among the guaranteed rights, but the as-yet-unratified 2004 Revised Arab Charter also enshrines it in Article 2. Notably, during the period the African Charter was being drafted, several African states remained European colonies or were governed by white minority regimes. See R. Murray, HUMAN RIGHTS IN AFRICA (2004), pp. 9–17; F. Viljoen, *The African Charter on Human and Peoples Rights: The Travaux Preparatoires in the Light of Subsequent Practice*, 25 HRLJ 314 at 317–318 (2004). Now that all African states are independent, the continued application of the right of self-determination has been doubted, but petitions invoking the right have been submitted to the African Commission. For a comparison of the right to self-determination in UN and African law see F. Ouguergouz, op. cit. pp. 227–269.

In thinking about this issue and considering the case that follows, how relevant is it that the African system has insisted on the sanctity of the national boundaries existing at independence? See OAU, *Resolution on the Intangibility of Frontiers*, AHG/Res. 16(1), 21 July 1964. See also the Dec. 22, 1986 judgment of the International Court of Justice in *Frontier Dispute (Burkina Faso v. Rep. of Mali)*, 1986 I.C.J. Rep. 554.

Katangese Peoples' Congress v. Zaire, (Comm. 75/92), *8th Annual Activity Report of the Afr. Comm. H.P.R. 1994–1995*, Annex VI.

The Facts

1. The communication was submitted in 1992 by Mr. Gerard Moke, President of the Katangese Peoples' Congress requesting the African Commission on Human and Peoples' Rights to: recognize the Katangese Peoples' Congress as a liberation movement entitled to support in the achievement of independence for Katanga; recognize the independence of Katanga; help secure the evacuation of Zaire from Katanga.

The Law

2. The claim is brought under Article 20(1) of the African Charter on Human Rights. There are no allegations of specific breaches of other human rights apart from the claim of the denial of self-determination.

3. All peoples have a right to self-determination. There may however be controversy as to the definition of peoples and the content of the right. The issue in the case is not self-determination for all Zaireoise as a people but specifically for the Katangese. Whether The Katangese consist of one or more ethnic groups is, for this purpose immaterial and no evidence has been adduced to that effect.

4. The Commission believes that self-determination may be exercised in any of the following ways independence, selfgovernment, local government, federalism, confederalism, unitarism or any other form of relations that accords with the wishes of the people but fully cognisant of other recognised principles such as sovereignty and territorial integrity.

5. The Commission is obligated to uphold the sovereignty and territorial integrity of Zaire, member of the OAU and a party to the African Charter on Human and Peoples' Rights

6. In the absence of concrete evidence of violations of human rights to the point that the territorial integrity of Zaire should be called to question and in the absence of evidence that the people of Katanga are denied the right to participate in Government as guaranteed by Article 13(1) of the African Charter, the Commission holds the view that Katanga is obliged to exercise a variant of self-determination that is compatible with the sovereignty and territorial integrity of Zaire.

FOR THE ABOVE REASONS, THE COMMISSION

Declares that the case holds no evidence of violations of any rights under the African Charter. There quest for independence for Katanga therefore has no merit under the African Charter on Human and Peoples' Rights.

Questions and Comments

1. On what grounds did the African Commission decide the case against the Katangese Peoples' Congress? Does the fact that it was a decision on the merits imply that the Kantagese are a people and the Peoples' Congress represents them? Does the case mean that the right to self-determination is justiciable in the African system? If so, who has standing to assert it? Under what circumstances would the Commission find a violation of the right? See: Comm. 102/93, *Constitutional Rights Project and Civil Liberties Organization v. Nigeria*, 12th Ann. Rep. ACHPR 1998/1999; Comm. 147/95 and 149/96, *Sir Dawda K. Jawara v. The Gambia*, 13th Ann. Rep. ACHPR; *Resolution on the Military*, adopted 3 Nov. 1993, 16th Sess., AHG/201 (XXXI), annex VII.

2. Considerable literature exists on the right to self-determination in international law. Prominent works include: K. KNOP, DIVERSITY AND SELF-DETERMINATION IN INTERNATIONAL LAW (2002); P. ALSTON, PEOPLES' RIGHTS (2001); R. McCORQUODALE, SELF-DETERMINATION IN INTERNATIONAL LAW (2000); T.D. MUSGRAVE, SELF-DETERMINATION AND NATIONAL MINORITIES (1997); A. CASSESE, SELF-DETERMINATION OF PEOPLES—A LEGAL REAPPRAISAL (1995); C. TOMUSCHAT, MODERN LAW OF SELF-DETERMINATION

(1993); M. POMERANCE, SELF-DETERMINATION IN LAW AND PRACTICE (1982); Y. AL-
EXANDER & R. FRIEDLANDER (EDS.), SELF-DETERMINATION: NATIONAL, REGIONAL AND
GLOBAL DIMENSIONS (1980). In the African context, see R.N. Kiwanuka, *The Meaning of
'People' in the African Charter on Human and Peoples' Rights*, 82 AJIL 80 (1988).
3. To what extent is uniformity in the interpretation or application of rights important?
Should the regional systems always follow the United Nations in developing human rights
law? How much regional diversity is appropriate?
4. When different norms might apply, what choice of law principle(s) could assist in decision-making? Note the approach of the Inter-American Court of Human Rights, set forth
in Inter-Am. Ct. H.R., *Compulsory Membership in an Association Prescribed by Law for the
Practice of Journalism (Arts. 13 and 29 American Convention on Human Rights)*, Advisory
Opinion OC-5/85 of November 13, 1985, Ser. A, No. 5, below.

C. Convergence of Regional Norms?

Choice of law principles contained in the regional treaties or implied from their
provisions generally call for application of the rule most favorable to the individual, making it important to compare the texts of all applicable instruments. Specifically, the European Convention Article 60 provides that nothing in the convention
"shall be construed as limiting or derogating from any of the human rights and
fundamental freedoms which may be ensured under the laws of any High Contracting Party or under any other agreement to which it is a Party." The American
Convention more broadly provides that no provision of the Convention can be interpreted to restrict a right recognized in the national or international law applicable to a state party, allowing reference to customary international law as well as
treaties and domestic law. The Convention further allows reference to or application of the American Declaration and "other international acts of the same nature"
as well as "other rights or guarantees that are inherent in the human personality or
derived from representative democracy as a form of government." Art. 29 (c),(d).

The African Charter, Article 60, is particularly broad in referencing or incorporating other legal guarantees. It mandates the African Commission to "draw inspiration from international law on human and peoples' rights," explicitly mentioning
the UN Charter, the UDHR, and other instruments adopted by the UN, including
the UN specialized agencies. Article 61 adds a list of "subsidiary measures to determine principles of law": other general or special international conventions, African practices "consistent with international norms on human and peoples' rights,"
customs generally accepted as law, general principles of law recognized by African
States as well as legal precedents and doctrine. The future African court is similarly directed in Protocol Article 7 to apply the provisions of the African Charter
and "other human rights instruments."

The formulation of a few provisions explicitly includes reference to international law as a measure to determine the scope of protection afforded. The European
Convention affirms in Article 15 that measures taken by a state in derogation of
the Convention cannot be "inconsistent with [that state's] other obligations under
international law." The first article of Protocol I to the European Convention also
invokes international law in providing that "Every natural or legal person is entitled to the peaceful enjoyment of his possessions. No one shall be deprived of his

possessions except in the public interest and subject to conditions provided for by law and by the general principles of international law." The European Court of Human Rights has viewed the reference to international law as a reference to the customary international law of state responsibility. *The Case of James*, 98 Eur. Ct. H.R. (ser. A) at 9 (1985); *Case of Lithgow*, 102 Eur. Ct. H.R. (ser. A) at 4 (1984).

Given the mention of other human rights texts and general international law, it is not surprising that decisions by regional institutions often refer to the law of other regions or to human rights guarantees in United Nations instruments and jurisprudence. The European Court of Human Rights has utilized article 19(2) of the CCPR to extend the application of Article 10 of the European Convention to cover freedom of artistic expression. See: *Muller et al v. Switzerland*, 133 Eur. Ct.H.R. (Ser. A)(1988) para. 27. It has referred to the UN Convention on the Rights of the Child in regard to education and both the CCPR and American Convention in regard to the right to a name. See: *Costello-Roberts v. UK.*, 247C Eur.Ct.H.R. (Ser.A)(1993) para. 27; *Burghartz v. Switzerland*, 280B Eur.Ct.H.R. (Ser.A)(1994) para. 24. In the *Soering* case the Court found implicit in Article 3 of the European Convention the obligation contained in Article 3 of the UN Torture Convention not to extradite someone who might face torture. *Soering v. UK*, 161 Eur.Ct.H.R. (Ser.A)(1989) para. 88. Referring to the UN Torture Convention the Court said, "The fact that a specialized treaty should spell out in detail a specific obligation attaching to the prohibition of torture does not mean that an essentially similar obligation is not already inherent in the general terms of Article 3 of the European Convention." The former European Commission also found it useful to interpret the provisions of the Convention by referring to provisions contained in other international legal instruments for the protection of human rights, especially those which contain broader guarantees. See Case no 210/92, *Gestra v. Italy*, 80A Dec.& Rep. 93 (1995).

The decisions of the African Commission also show the influence of the other regional systems. The Commission has adopted several doctrines established in European and Inter-American case law: presumption of the truth of the allegations from the silence of government,[5] the notion of continuing violations,[6] continuity of obligations despite a change of government,[7] state responsibility for failure to act,[8] and a presumption that the state is responsible for custodial injuries. In its first country report, which concerned Nigeria, the African Commission made use of regional precedents. After Nigeria complained of the lack of a hearing, the Commission noted that Nigeria had never responded to communications and that for the Commission to postpone decisions indefinitely while waiting for the gov-

---

[5] "The African Commission . . . has set out the principle that where allegations of human rights abuse go uncontested by the government concerned, even after repeated notifications, the Commission must decide on the facts provided by the complainant and treat those facts as given. This principle conforms with the practice of other human rights adjudicatory bodies and the Commission's duty to protect human rights." Comms Nos. 25/89/47/90, 56/91, 100/93, *Free Legal Assistance Group, Lawyers' Committee for Human Rights, Union Interafricaine des Droits de l'Homme, Les Temoins de Jehovah v. Zaire*, Annex VIII, at 7.

[6] See e.g. Comm. 142/94 *Muthuthurin Njoka v. Kenya*, at 13 and Comm. 64/92 reprinted in 18 HRLJ 29 (1997).

[7] Joined cases 83/92, 88/93, 91/93 *Jean Yaovi Degli, Union Interafricaine des Droits de l'Homme, Commission International de Juristes v. Togo*.

[8] Comm. 74/92, *Commission Nationale des Droits de l'homme et des Libertes v. Chad*.

ernment to send a representative would make the communications procedure hostage to governments, and effectively place in the government's hands the ability to prevent any decisions. The Commission noted that these consequences have been recognized by other international human rights bodies such as the Inter-American Commission on Human Rights, and the African Commission was inspired by their example. *Human Rights Report on the Situation in Nigeria*, Doc.II/ES/ACHPR/3 Add.1 (1995).

The Inter-American Court also uses other international court decisions and international human rights instruments to interpret and apply Inter-American norms. The Court has referred to decisions of the European Human Rights Commission and Court in its judgments and advisory opinions, e.g., *The Effect of Reservations on the Entry into Force of the American Convention*, 2 Inter-Am.Ct.H.R. (Ser.A)(1983) para. 29; *The Word "Laws" in Article 30 of the American Convention on Human Rights*, 6 Inter-Am.Ct.H.R. (Ser.A)(1986) para 20; *Compusory Membership in an Association Prescribed by Law for the Practice of Journalism*, Advisory Opinion OC-5/85 of November 13, 1985, 5 Inter-Am.Ct.H.R. (Ser. A)(1985), paras. 43–46, 69; *In the Matter of Viviana Gallardo et al v. Government of Costa Rica*, Decision of Nov. 13, 1981, Inter-Am.Ct.H.R. 12, OEA/Ser.L/V/III.7 doc 13, Ser. A and B. No G/101/81 (1982), paras. 26–27; *Gangaram Panday v. Suriname*, 16 Inter-Am.Ct.H.R. (Ser.C)(1994) para. 39; *Caballero Delgado and Santana Case* (Preliminary Objections), 17 Inter-Am.Ct.H.R. (Ser.C)(1994). The Court has indicated that it will use cases decided by the European Court and the UN Human Rights Committee when their value is to augment rights protection but not to restrict rights, as the following extract explains.

Compulsory Membership in an Association Prescribed by Law for the Practice of Journalism, Advisory Opinion OC-5/85 of November 13, 1985, 5 Inter-Am. Ct.H.R. (Ser. A)(1985).

... The Court must also take account of the Preamble of the Convention in which the signatory states reaffirm "their intention to consolidate in this hemisphere, within the framework of democratic institutions, a system of personal liberty and social justice based on respect for the essential rights of man."

42. These articles define the context within which the restrictions permitted under Article 13(2) must be interpreted. It follows from the repeated reference to "democratic institutions, representative democracy" and "democratic society" that the question whether a restriction on freedom of expression imposed by a state is "necessary to ensure" one of the objectives listed in subparagraphs (a) or (b) must be judged by reference to the legitimate needs of democratic societies and institutions.

43. In relation to this point, the Court believes that it is useful to compare Article 13 of the Convention with Article 10 of the (European) Convention for the Protection of Human Rights and Fundamental Freedoms ... and with Article 19 of the International Covenant on Civil and Political Rights. ...

44. It is true that the European Convention uses the expression "necessary in a democratic society", while Article 13 of the American Convention omits that phrase.

This difference in wording loses its significance, however, once it is recognized that the European Convention contains no clause comparable to Article 29 of the American Convention, which lays down guidelines for the interpretation of the Convention and prohibits the interpretation of any provision of the treaty "precluding other rights and guarantees . . . derived from representative democracy as a form of government." The Court wishes to emphasize, furthermore, that Article 29(d) bars interpretations of the Convention "excluding or limiting the effect that the American Declaration of the Rights and Duties of Man may have," which instrument is recognized as forming part of the normative system for the OAS Member States in Article 1(2) of the Commission's Statute. Article XXVIII of the American Declaration of the Rights and Duties of Man reads as follows:

> The rights of man are limited by the rights of others, by the security of all, and by the just demands of the general welfare and the advancement of democracy. The just demands of democracy must consequently guide the interpretation of the Convention and, in particular, the interpretation of those provisions that bear a critical relationship to the preservation and functioning of democratic institutions.

45. The form in which Article 13 of the American Convention is drafted differs very significantly from Article 10 of the European Convention, which is formulated in very general terms. Without the specific reference in the latter to "necessary in a democratic society," it would have been extremely difficult to delimit the long list of permissible restrictions. As a matter of fact, Article 19 of the Covenant, which served, in part at least, as a model for Article 13 of the American Convention, contains a much shorter list of restrictions than does the European Convention. The Covenant, in turn, is more restrictive than the American Convention, if only because it does not expressly prohibit prior censorship.

46. It is important to note that the European Court of Human Rights, in interpreting Article 10 of the European Convention, concluded that "necessary", while not synonymous with "indispensable", implied "the existence of a 'pressing social need'" and that for a restriction to be "necessary" it is not enough to show that it is "useful", "reasonable" or "desirable". (Eur. Court H. R., *The Sunday Times Case*, judgment of 26 April 1979, Series A no. 30, para. 59, pp. 35–36.) This conclusion, which is equally applicable to the American Convention, suggests that the "necessity" and, hence, the legality of restrictions imposed under Article 13(2) on freedom of expression, depend upon a showing that the restrictions are required by a compelling governmental interest. Hence if there are various options to achieve this objective, that which least restricts the right protected must be selected. Given this standard, it is not enough to demonstrate, for example, that a law performs a useful or desirable purpose; to be compatible with the Convention, the restrictions must be justified by reference to governmental objectives which, because of their importance, clearly outweigh the social need for the full enjoyment of the right Article 13 guarantees. Implicit in this standard, furthermore, is the notion that the restriction, even if justified by compelling governmental interests, must be so framed as not to limit the right protected by Article 13 more than is necessary. That is, the restriction must be proportionate and closely tailored to the accomplishment of the legitimate governmental objective necessitating it. (*The Sunday Times Case, supra*, para.

62, p. 38. See also Eur. Court H. R., *Barthold* judgment of 25 March 1985, Series A no. 90, para. 59, p. 2.)

47. Article 13(2) must also be interpreted by reference to the provisions of Article 13(3), which is most explicit in prohibiting restrictions on freedom of expression by "indirect methods and means . . . tending to impede the communication and circulation of ideas and opinions." Neither the European Convention nor the Covenant contains a comparable clause.

It is significant that Article 13(3) was placed immediately after a provision Article 13(2)—which deals with permissible restrictions on the exercise of freedom of expression. This circumstance suggests a desire to ensure that the language of Article 13(2) not be misinterpreted in a way that would limit, except to the extent strictly necessary, the full scope of the right to freedom of expression.

48. Article 13(3) does not only deal with indirect governmental restrictions, it also expressly prohibits "private controls" producing the same result. This provision must be read together with the language of Article 1 of the Convention wherein the States Parties "undertake to respect the rights and freedoms recognized (in the Convention) . . . and to ensure to all persons subject to their jurisdiction the full exercise of those rights and freedoms. . . ." Hence, a violation of the Convention in this area can be the product not only of the fact that the State itself imposes restrictions of an indirect character which tend to impede "the communication and circulation of ideas and opinions", but the State also has an obligation to ensure that the violation does not result from the "private controls" referred to in paragraph 3 of Article 13.

49. The provisions of Article 13(4) and 13(5) have no direct bearing on the questions before the Court in the instant application and, consequently, do not need to be analyzed at this time.

50. The foregoing analysis of Article 13 shows the extremely high value that the Convention places on freedom of expression. A comparison of Article 13 with the relevant provisions of the European Convention (Article 10) and the Covenant (Article 19) indicates clearly that the guarantees contained in the American Convention regarding freedom of expression were designed to be more generous and to reduce to a bare minimum restrictions impeding the free circulation of ideas.

51. With respect to the comparison between the American Convention and the other treaties already mentioned, the Court cannot avoid a comment concerning an interpretation suggested by Costa Rica in the hearing of November 8, 1985. According to this argument, if a right recognized by the American Convention was regulated in a more restrictive way in another international human rights instrument, the interpretation of the American Convention would have to take those additional restrictions into account for the following reasons:

> If it were not so, we would have to accept that what is legal and permissible on the universal plane would constitute a violation in this hemisphere, which cannot obviously be correct. We think rather that with respect to the interpretation of treaties, the criterion can be established that the rules of a treaty or a convention must be interpreted in relation with the provisions that appear in other treaties that cover the same subject. It can also be contended that the provisions of a regional treaty must be

interpreted in the light of the concepts and provisions of instruments of a universal character.

It is true, of course, that it is frequently useful—and the Court has just done it—to compare the American Convention with the provisions of other international instruments in order to stress certain aspects concerning the manner in which a certain right has been formulated, but that approach should never be used to read into the Convention restrictions that are not grounded in its text. This is true even if these restrictions exist in another international treaty.

52. The foregoing conclusion clearly follows from the language of Article 29 which sets out the relevant rules for the interpretation of the Convention. Subparagraph (b) of Article 29 indicates that no provision of the Convention may be interpreted as restricting the enjoyment or exercise of any right or freedom recognized by virtue of the laws of any State Party or by virtue of another convention to which one of the said states is a party.

Hence, if in the same situation both the American Convention and another international treaty are applicable, the rule most favorable to the individual must prevail. Considering that the Convention itself establishes that its provisions should not have a restrictive effect on the enjoyment of the rights guaranteed in other international instruments, it makes even less sense to invoke restrictions contained in those other international instruments, but which are not found in the Convention, to limit the exercise of the rights and freedoms that the latter recognizes.

In sum, many areas of jurisprudence show convergence, but there is also evidence of divergence in the application of some norms. The most evident differences lie in the areas of derogation from enunciated rights in international treaties and the protection of non-derogable rights, a topic discussed in Chapter III. Some authors point to a relative conservatism of the European Court of Human Rights, which has appeared concerned that where national interests are at stake, a state condemned for wrongfully suspending rights might withdraw from the Convention. See: Fionnuala Ni Aolain, *The Emergence of Diversity: Differences in Human Rights Jurisprudence*, 19 FORDHAM INT'L L. J. 101 (1995); for an earlier study of the subject see Joan F. Hartman, *Derogation from Human Rights Treaties in Public Emergencies*, 22 HARV. INT'L L. J. 1 (1981).

To the extent there is a convergence of human rights norms, it is in large part stimulated by litigators who draw attention to the relevant case law of other systems and help to expand human rights protections by obtaining a favorable ruling in one system, then invoking it in another. This tendency is enhanced by the liberal standing rules of the Inter-American and African systems. Many complaints are filed by non-governmental organizations familiar with and operating in more than one system. Most of the communications submitted to the African system thus far, for example, have come from groups such as Amnesty International, the International Commission of Jurists, and the Lawyers Committee for Human Rights. In the European system, briefs submitted *amicus curiae* by NGOs similarly draw attention to regional and global norms and jurisprudence.

4. Comparing the Contents

All of the regional institutions have interpreted the scope and meaning of the rights guaranteed by the relevant normative instruments. Many cases across the three systems raise similar issues and the opinions and judgments concerning them often seek inspiration or guidance in the decisions of other regional and global bodies. This jurisprudential cross-referencing or cross-fertilization could help develop consistent human rights law among the various tribunals. At the same time, each system's caseload is different and reflects the particular problems of the region and the guarantees of the normative instruments. In Europe, a majority of cases have concerned Articles 5 and 6, which guaranteed access to justice and due process. Only in relatively recent periods have issues of the right to life and torture arisen with any frequency within Europe. In contrast, nearly all of the early cases at the Inter-American Court involved extra-judicial killing, torture, and forced disappearance. The African system has dealt with all of these issues, as it has challenged dictatorial regimes engaged in widespread violations, but the African system has also addressed economic, social and cultural rights that are largely outside the jurisdiction of the other regional bodies.

The normative instruments contain numerous provisions that affect the scope and effective implementation of protected rights. Various clauses allow restrictions on particular rights for reasons of national security or general welfare. Others permit some rights to be suspended temporarily during periods of emergency. As will be seen below, states may further restrict certain rights by reservations made at the time of ratification.

A. Introduction to Treaty Interpretation

Human rights instruments, like many national bills of rights, are written in general terms, leaving ample scope for judges and commissioners to interpret their provisions and for national authorities to take different views about their meaning. The Vienna Convention on the Law of Treaties (in force January 27, 1980) is the primary source of rules for treaty interpretation. Although the Vienna Convention was not in force when the ECHR was concluded, the European Court of Human Rights, in *Golder v. U.K.*, established that the terms of the Vienna Convention concerning interpretation are applicable to the ECHR because they enunciate "generally accepted principles of international law." *Golder v. United Kingdom*, 1 Eur. H.R. Rep. 524, para. 29 (1975); *see also Luedicke, Belkacem and Koç v. Germany*, 2 Eur. H.R. Rep. 149, para. 46. (1978). As will be seen below, the other regional bodies have also applied the Vienna Convention while noting the uniqueness of human rights treaties.

i. Vienna Convention on the Law of Treaties

The relevant provisions of the Vienna Convention on the Law of Treaties read as follows:

Article 31 General Rule of Interpretation

1. A treaty shall be interpreted in good faith in accordance with the ordinary meaning to be given to the terms of the treaty in their context and in the light of its object and purpose.

2. The context for the purpose of the interpretation of a treaty shall comprise, in addition to the text, including its preamble and annexes:

   a) any agreement relating to the treaty which was made between all the parties in connection with the conclusion of the treaty;

   b) any instrument which was made by one or more parties in connection with the conclusion of the treaty and accepted by the other parties as an instrument related to the treaty.

3. There shall be taken into account together with the context:

   a) any subsequent agreement between the parties regarding the interpretation of the treaty or the applications of its provisions;

   b) any subsequent practice in the application of the treaty which establishes the agreement of the parties regarding its interpretation;

   c) any relevant rules of international law applicable in the relations between the parties.

4. A special meaning shall be given to a term if it is established that the parties so intended.

Article 32 Supplementary Means of Interpretation

Recourse may be had to supplementary means of interpretation, including the preparatory work of the treaty and the circumstances of its conclusion in order to confirm the meaning resulting from the application of article 31, or to determine the meaning when the interpretation according to article 31:

   a) leaves the meaning ambiguous or obscure; or

   b) leads to a result which is manifestly absurd or unreasonable.

———————————

While making use of the Vienna Convention rules, regional institutions have given a dynamic reading to the human rights guarantees contained in their normative instruments, rather than relying on a static interpretation of terms. This approach has allowed the texts to evolve as circumstances change and new problems arise. The European Court of Human Rights has confirmed that "the Convention is a living instrument which . . . must be interpreted in the light of the present-day conditions." *Tyrer v. United Kingdom*, 26 Eur. Ct. H.R. (ser. A) (1978)at 10. The Inter-American Court has similarly emphasized the notion of evolving American law.

See *Interpretation of the American Declaration of the Rights and Duties of Man within the Framework of Article 64 of the American Convention*, at paras. 37–38.

The commissions and courts also must pay attention to the delicate matter of deference to national authorities in the application of guaranteed rights. The European Court, in particular, has been reluctant to impose uniform interpretation of every aspect of the Convention's rights. The degree to which the Court allows national differences to affect the Convention's guarantees is expressed in the doctrine of "margin of appreciation" which in turn reflects the Court's view of its role as a subsidiary one.

ii. Deference to National Authorities

Y. Shany, "**Toward a General Margin of Appreciation Doctrine in International Law?**" 16 *EJIL* 907 (2006), pp. 909–14, 927, 929 (footnotes renumbered, some footnotes omitted)

The margin of appreciation doctrine, most renowned for its application in the case law of the European Court of Human Rights (ECtHR), establishes a methodology for scrutiny by international courts of the decisions of national authorities—i.e., national governments, national courts and other national actors. While the case law of the ECtHR and other international tribunals on the contours of the doctrine is somewhat inconsistent, two principal elements may be identified: (i) *Judicial deference*—international courts should grant national authorities a certain degree of deference and respect their discretion on the manner of executing their international law obligations. Thus, international courts ought not to replace the discretion and independent evaluation exercised by national authorities—i.e., refrain from reviewing national decisions *de novo*. Rather, international judicial bodies should exercise judicial restraint;[9] (ii) *Normative flexibility*—international norms subject to the doctrine have been characterized as open-ended or unsettled.[10] Such norms provide limited conduct-guidance and preserve a significant 'zone of legality' within which states are free to operate.[11] Consequently, different national authorities, in distinct states, could conceivably reach different, yet lawful decisions regarding the application of the same international norm.[12] Although these two elements are analytically separable—the first element primarily relates to norm-application, while

---

[9] *James v UK*, 8 EHRR (1986) 123, at 1142–143 ('[T]he Court cannot substitute its own assessment for that of the national authorities'); *Karatas v Turkey* [1999] IV ECtHR 81, at 120 (Joint Partly Dissenting Opinion of Judges Wildhaber, Pastor Ridruejo, Costa and Baka)('In the assessment of whether restrictive measures are necessary in a democratic society, due deference will be accorded to the State's margin of appreciation; the democratic legitimacy of measures taken by democratically elected governments commands a degree of judicial self-restraint'). . . .

[10] *See, e.g., Sheffield v UK*, 27 EHRR (1998) 163, at 179 and 192; *Odiévre v France*, judgment of 13 Feb. 2003, at para. 40.

[11] *See, e.g., VO v France*, ECtHR judgment of 8 July 2004, at para. 82.

[12] *See, e.g., Final Report to the Prosecutor by the Committee Established to Review the NATO Bombing Campaign Against the Federal Republic of Yugoslavia* (2000), *available at* http://www.un.org/icty/pressreal/nato061300.htm, at para. 50. See also Donoho, *Autonomy, Self-Government, and the Margin of Appreciation: Developing a Jurisprudence of Diversity within Universal Human Rights*, 15 EMORY INT'L L REV (2001) 391, at 457; Greer, *Constitutionalising Adjudication under the European Convention on Human Rights*, 23 OXFORD J LEGAL STUDIES (2003) 405, at 409.

the second to norm-interpretation—international courts have not always distinguished between the two. Furthermore, the two elements intertwine: the construction of international norms in an ambiguous manner might facilitate the exercise of judicial deference and *vice versa*. Hence, the policy rationales that support granting national actors some deference and those which sustain judicial acknowledgement of normative ambiguity reinforce one another.

However, it must be stressed that the margin of appreciation afforded to states is never unlimited—i.e., there is no total deference to the national decision-making process. First, states must always exercise their discretion in good faith. Second, international courts are ultimately authorized to review whether national decisions are reasonable—namely, whether the course of action selected by the state conforms with the object and purpose of the governing norm. This might include *inter alia* assessment of the national decision-making process (for instance, whether all pertinent considerations were taken into account) and the substantive outcome (for instance, whether the decision promotes the attainment of the overarching norms).[13] Hence, the margin of appreciation doctrine does not preclude judicial review, but rather works to limit its scope of operation. The authority of international courts and tribunals to grant states a margin of appreciation is rarely grounded in explicit treaty norms. Instead, the capacity to employ the doctrine seems to derive from the inherent power of international judicial bodies to determine their own procedures and to effectively exercise their jurisdiction (these authorities are sometimes couched in explicit 'general powers' rules of procedure). Such broad powers arguably include the ability of courts to set applicable standards of review. Alternatively, the margin of appreciation could be linked to the inherent judicial authority to settle 'the method of handling the evidence' or 'make an objective assessment of the matter'. . . .

It is not surprising that much of the criticism directed against possible recourse to the margin of appreciation doctrine has focused on its normative guidance-eroding implications. For example, it was argued that the doctrine encourages non-uniform, subjective or relativist applications of international law, detracting thereby from the conduct-regulating quality of legal rules and undermining their authority and perceived fairness (for instance, the expectation that like cases will be treated alike).[14] The doctrine arguably contributes to obliteration of the boundaries of legality, and might reinforce perceptions of international law as non-law—i.e., a loose system of non-enforceable principles, containing little, if any real constraints on state power. In short, the doctrine has been described as an insidious method to enable powerful

---

13 *See Rekvényi v Hungary,* 30 EHRR (2000) 518, at 549 ('[T]he court has to satisfy itself that the national authorities applied standards which were in conformity with the principles embodied in art 10 and, moreover, that they based their decisions on an acceptable assessment of the relevant facts'). . . .

14 See, e.g., *Certain Aspects of the Laws on the Use of Languages in Education in Belgium (No 2)* (Merits), 1 EHRR 252, at 353 (1967), Partly Dissenting Opinion of Judge Wold; Lord Lester of Herne Hill, *Universality Versus Subsidiarity: A Reply* [1998] EUR HUM. RTS L. REV. 73, at 75; E. Benvenisti, *Margin of Appreciation, Consensus and Universal Values,* 31 NYU J. INT'L L. & POL'Y (1999) 843, at 844; Besselink, *Entrapped by the Maximum Standard: On Fundamental Rights, Pluralism and Subsidiarity in the European Union,* 35 COM-MON MKT. L. REV. 629, at 639–640 (1998); P VAN DIJK AND G VAN HOOF, THEORY AND PRACTICE OF THE EUROPEAN CONVENTION ON HUMAN RIGHTS (3rd edn, 1998), at 93. . . .

states to evade the objective rule of international law,[15] and as a sophisticated way to reintroduce the 'S word' into international life.[16]

. . . .

[I]t would be deplorable if application of the margin of appreciation doctrine were to result in a significant dilution of the degree of objective legal certainty which appertains to important international law norms—for instance, in promoting divergent interpretations as to whether certain interrogation techniques constitute prohibited torture.[17] . . . Perpetuating normative ambiguity . . . might encourage states to evade inconvenient legal obligations and render such obligations meaningless.

However, different international law norms are endowed with different levels of inherent legal certainty. Furthermore, some law-application exercises, i.e., interactions between facts and law, are by their very nature less certain than others and hinge upon intrinsically indeterminate circumstances. I submit that in cases where the application of law is inherently or inevitably uncertain there are strong policy reasons which support recourse to the margin of appreciation doctrine. Since the ideal of legal certainty remains largely unattainable in such cases, regardless of whether the doctrine is applied or not, the guidance-eroding disadvantages that attach to the application of the doctrine are greatly reduced.[18] Furthermore, . . . national authorities enjoy comparative institutional advantages over international courts with regard to fact-finding and fact-assessing exercises, but not in relation to norm-interpretation projects. As a result, a general margin of appreciation doctrine should mainly govern fact-intensive law-application decisions and not norm-intensive law-interpretation processes, whose ultimate elaboration should remain the exclusive province of the international judiciary. While distinctions between certain and uncertain norms and between law-interpretation and law-application exercises are never clear-cut, some distinctive indicators exist. Ultimately, it would be for international courts to determine whether deference to national authorities is warranted, and to what extent. This judicial 'gatekeeper' role is vital in order to prevent misuse of the doctrine in a manner which might undermine the rule of international law.

. . . .

The . . . case law of the ECtHR indicates that the manner of application of the doctrine depends on a variety of factors, which determine the scope of margin afforded to the national authorities. Three factors are particularly pertinent:[19] (i) *comparative advantage of local authorities*—subjective norms (i.e., circumstance-dependent), which domestic institutions are better situated to assess, should entail a broader margin than objective norms, whose manner of application the ECtHR can

---

[15] See, e.g., Feingold, *The Doctrine of Margin of Appreciation and the European Convention on Human Rights*, 53 NOTRE DAME L REV (1977) 90, at 95.

[16] L. Henkin, *That "S" Word: Sovereignty, and Globalization, and Human Rights, et cetera*, 68 FORDHAM L REV (1999) 1, at 7.

[17] See, e.g., Department of Defense Working Group Report on Detainee Interrogations in the Global War Against Terrorism: Assessment of Legal, Historical, Policy and Operational Considerations, 6 Mar. 2003, available at http://stopimperialism.be/military_0604.pdf, at 10–16.

[18] On the link between legal certainty and the margin of appreciation doctrine, see, e.g., *Rees v UK*, 9 EHRR (1987) 56, at 67.

[19] See Brems, *The Margin of Appreciation Doctrine in the Case Law of the European Court of Human Rights*, 56 HEIDELBERG J. INT'L L. (1996) 240, at 256. . . .

independently assess;[20] (ii) *indeterminacy of the applicable standard*—the greater is the degree of European consensus on the application of the standard, the narrower is the margin that should be accorded to state parties;[21] (iii) *nature of the contested interests*—the importance of the national interest at stake ought to be balanced against the nature of the individual rights compromised by the reviewed limitation. The width of the margin to be granted to states should reflect this balancing formula.[22]

. . .

Questions and Comments

A former judge of the European Court of Human Rights summed up the Court's approach to interpretation:

> The general rules of treaty interpretation are in principle also applicable to human rights treaties, but the object and purpose of these treaties are different and, therefore, the traditional rules need some adjustment. The notions contained in human rights conventions have an autonomous international meaning; however, such meaning must be determined by a comparative analysis of the legal situation in the participating states. To the extent that this analysis shows considerable differences and disparities among the states, a national 'margin of appreciation' is and must be recognized. Human rights treaties must be interpreted in an objective and dynamic manner, by taking into account social conditions and developments; the ideas and conditions prevailing at the time when the treaties were drafted retain hardly any continuing validity. Nevertheless, treaty interpretation must not amount to treaty revision. Interpretation must therefore respect the text of the treaty concerned.

Judge R. Bernhardt, *Thoughts on the Interpretation of Human Rights Treaties*, in F. MATSCHER AND H. PETZOLD, PROTECTING HUMAN RIGHTS: THE EUROPEAN DIMENSION (Koln, 1988) 70–71. See also Paolo Carozza, *Subsidiarity as a Structural Principle of International Human Rights Law*, 97 AJIL 38 (2003); Paul Mahoney, *Universality versus Subsidiarity in the Strasbourg Case Law on Free Speech: Explaining Some Recent Judgments*, 1997 EUR.HUM.RTS.L.REV. 364.

---

20 See *Sunday Times v UK* (1980) 2 EHRR 245, at para. 59.
21 For criticism of the Court's emphasis on consensus, see . . . Helfer, *Consensus, Coherence and the European Convention on Human Rights*, 26 CORNELL INT'L L.J. (1993) 133, at 141–142 . . . ; Carozza, *Uses and Misuses of Comparative Law in International Human Rights: Some Reflections on the Jurisprudence of the European Court of Justice*, 73 NOTRE DAME L.REV. (1998) 1217. . . .
22 For example, see *Leander v Sweden*, 9 EHRR (1987) 433, at para. 59 ('[T]he national authorities enjoy a margin of appreciation, the scope of which will depend not only on the nature of the legitimate aim pursued but also on the particular nature of the interference involved. In the instant case, the interest of the respondent State in protecting its national security must be balanced against the seriousness of the interference with the applicant's right to respect for his private life'). See also *Rekvényi, supra* note 9, at 534; *Çakici v Turkey*, 31 EHRR (2001) 135, at 191–192; *The Observer v UK*, 14 EHRR (1992) 153, at 218 (Partly Dissenting Opinion of Judge Morneilla) ('It is true that the State's margin of appreciation is wider when it is a question of protecting national security than when it is a question of maintaining the authority of the judiciary by safeguarding the rights of the litigants'). The first case litigated by the Court, the *Lawless* case, also comports with this trend: *Lawless v Ireland, supra* note 82. But see *Rotaru v Romania* [2000] V ECtHR 61, at 134–135; *Smith v UK*, 29 EHRR (2000) 493, at 530; *Tinnelly & Sons v UK*, 27 EHRR (1999) 249, at 288. Note also that the Court held that no margin of appreciation exists at all in cases alleging torture or inhuman or degrading treatment or punishment: *Chahal v UK*, 23 EHRR (1997) 413, at 457. For discussion of the application of the margin of appreciation doctrine to security-related ECtHR cases, see Greer, *supra* note [8], at 427. . . .

iii. Evolving Standards

The question of the degree of deference that should be afforded to national authorities frequently arises when novel issues are presented to the Court as a result of scientific and technological innovations. The human rights implications of the medical procedure of "gender reassignment" are among these issues. The following case demonstrates the Court's evolutionary approach to interpreting the Convention. Is it appropriate for the Court to set European-wide standards on these matters, including marriage, or is this a subject better left to the individual states to determine?

Christine Goodwin v. the United Kingdom [GC], (App. no. 28957/95), Judgment of 11 July 2002, Eur. Ct. H.R., 35 EHRR 18 (2002).

. . . .

71. This case raises the issue whether or not the respondent State has failed to comply with a positive obligation to ensure the right of the applicant, a post-operative male to female transsexual, to respect for her private life, in particular through the lack of legal recognition given to her gender re-assignment.

72. The Court recalls that the notion of "respect" as understood in Article 8 is not clear cut, especially as far as the positive obligations inherent in that concept are concerned: having regard to the diversity of practices followed and the situations obtaining in the Contracting States, the notion's requirements will vary considerably from case to case and the margin of appreciation to be accorded to the authorities may be wider than that applied in other areas under the Convention. In determining whether or not a positive obligation exists, regard must also be had to the fair balance that has to be struck between the general interest of the community and the interests of the individual, the search for which balance is inherent in the whole of the Convention (*Cossey v. the United Kingdom* judgment of 27 September 1990, Series A no. 184, p. 15, § 37).

73. The Court recalls that it has already examined complaints about the position of transsexuals in the United Kingdom (see the *Rees v. the United Kingdom* judgment of 17 October 1986, Series A no. 106, the *Cossey v. the United Kingdom* judgment, cited above; the *X., Y. and Z. v. the United Kingdom* judgment of 22 April 1997, Reports of Judgments and Decisions 1997-II, and the *Sheffield and Horsham v. the United Kingdom* judgment of 30 July 1998, Reports 1998-V, p. 2011). In those cases, it held that the refusal of the United Kingdom Government to alter the register of births or to issue birth certificates whose contents and nature differed from those of the original entries concerning the recorded gender of the individual could not be considered as an interference with the right to respect for private life (the above-mentioned *Rees* judgment, p. 14, § 35, and *Cossey* judgment, p. 15, § 36). It also held that there was no positive obligation on the Government to alter their existing system for the registration of births by establishing a new system or type of documentation to provide proof of current civil status. Similarly, there was no duty on the Government to permit annotations to the existing register of births, or to keep any such annotation secret from third parties (the above-mentioned *Rees*

judgment, p. 17, § 42, and *Cossey* judgment, p. 15, §§ 38–39). It was found in those cases that the authorities had taken steps to minimize intrusive enquiries (for example, by allowing transsexuals to be issued with driving licenses, passports and other types of documents in their new name and gender). Nor had it been shown that the failure to accord general legal recognition of the change of gender had given rise in the applicants' own case histories to detriment of sufficient seriousness to override the respondent State's margin of appreciation in this area (the *Sheffield and Horsham* judgment cited above, p. 2028–29, § 59).

74. While the Court is not formally bound to follow its previous judgments, it is in the interests of legal certainty, foreseeability and equality before the law that it should not depart, without good reason, from precedents laid down in previous cases (see, for example, *Chapman v. the United Kingdom* [GC], no. 27238/95, ECHR 2001-I, § 70). However, since the Convention is first and foremost a system for the protection of human rights, the Court must have regard to the changing conditions within the respondent State and within Contracting States generally and respond, for example, to any evolving convergence as to the standards to be achieved (see, amongst other authorities, the *Cossey* judgment, p. 14, § 35, and *Stafford v. the United Kingdom* [GC], no. 46295/99, judgment of 28 May 2002, to be published in ECHR 2002-, §§ 67–68). It is of crucial importance that the Convention is interpreted and applied in a manner which renders its rights practical and effective, not theoretical and illusory. A failure by the Court to maintain a dynamic and evolutive approach would indeed risk rendering it a bar to reform or improvement (see the above-cited *Stafford v. the United Kingdom* judgment, § 68). In the present context the Court has, on several occasions since 1986, signaled its consciousness of the serious problems facing transsexuals and stressed the importance of keeping the need for appropriate legal measures in this area under review (see the *Rees* judgment, § 47; the *Cossey* judgment, § 42; the *Sheffield and Horsham* judgment, § 60).

75. The Court proposes therefore to look at the situation within and outside the Contracting State to assess "in the light of present-day conditions" what is now the appropriate interpretation and application of the Convention (see the *Tyrer v. the United Kingdom* judgment of 25 April 1978, Series A no. 26, § 31, and subsequent case-law).

2. The applicant's situation as a transsexual

76. The Court observes that the applicant, registered at birth as male, has undergone gender re-assignment surgery and lives in society as a female. Nonetheless, the applicant remains, for legal purposes, a male. This has had, and continues to have, effects on the applicant's life where sex is of legal relevance and distinctions are made between men and women, as, *inter alia*, in the area of pensions and retirement age. For example, the applicant must continue to pay national insurance contributions until the age of 65 due to her legal status as male. However as she is employed in her gender identity as a female, she has had to obtain an exemption certificate which allows the payments from her employer to stop while she continues to make such payments herself. Though the Government submitted that this made due allowance for the difficulties of her position, the Court would note that

she nonetheless has to make use of a special procedure that might in itself call attention to her status.

77. It must also be recognized that serious interference with private life can arise where the state of domestic law conflicts with an important aspect of personal identity (see, *mutatis mutandis*, *Dudgeon v. the United Kingdom* judgment of 22 October 1981, Series A no. 45, § 41). The stress and alienation arising from a discordance between the position in society assumed by a post-operative transsexual and the status imposed by law which refuses to recognize the change of gender cannot, in the Court's view, be regarded as a minor inconvenience arising from a formality. A conflict between social reality and law arises which places the transsexual in an anomalous position, in which he or she may experience feelings of vulnerability, humiliation and anxiety.

78. In this case, as in many others, the applicant's gender re-assignment was carried out by the national health service, which recognizes the condition of gender dysphoria and provides, *inter alia*, re-assignment by surgery, with a view to achieving as one of its principal purposes as close an assimilation as possible to the gender in which the transsexual perceives that he or she properly belongs. The Court is struck by the fact that nonetheless the gender re-assignment which is lawfully provided is not met with full recognition in law, which might be regarded as the final and culminating step in the long and difficult process of transformation which the transsexual has undergone. The coherence of the administrative and legal practices within the domestic system must be regarded as an important factor in the assessment carried out under Article 8 of the Convention. Where a State has authorized the treatment and surgery alleviating the condition of a transsexual, financed or assisted in financing the operations and indeed permits the artificial insemination of a woman living with a female-to-male transsexual (as demonstrated in the case of *X., Y. and Z. v. the United Kingdom* . . .), it appears illogical to refuse to recognize the legal implications of the result to which the treatment leads.

79. The Court notes that the unsatisfactory nature of the current position and plight of transsexuals in the United Kingdom has been acknowledged in the domestic courts (see *Bellinger v. Bellinger*, paragraph 52) and by the Interdepartmental Working Group which surveyed the situation in the United Kingdom and concluded that, notwithstanding the accommodations reached in practice, transsexual people were conscious of certain problems which did not have to be faced by the majority of the population.

80. Against these considerations, the Court has examined the countervailing arguments of a public interest nature put forward as justifying the continuation of the present situation. It observes that in the previous United Kingdom cases weight was given to medical and scientific considerations, the state of any European and international consensus and the impact of any changes to the current birth register system.

3. Medical and scientific considerations

81. It remains the case that there are no conclusive findings as to the cause of transsexualism and, in particular, whether it is wholly psychological or associated with physical differentiation in the brain. The expert evidence in the domestic case

of *Bellinger v. Bellinger* was found to indicate a growing acceptance of findings of sexual differences in the brain that are determined pre-natally, though scientific proof for the theory was far from complete. The Court considers it more significant however that transsexualism has wide international recognition as a medical condition for which treatment is provided in order to afford relief (for example, the Diagnostic and Statistical Manual fourth edition (DSM-IV) replaced the diagnosis of transsexualism with "gender identity disorder"; see also the International Classification of Diseases, tenth edition (ICD-10)). The United Kingdom national health service, in common with the vast majority of Contracting States, acknowledges the existence of the condition and provides or permits treatment, including irreversible surgery. The medical and surgical acts which in this case rendered the gender re-assignment possible were indeed carried out under the supervision of the national health authorities. Nor, given the numerous and painful interventions involved in such surgery and the level of commitment and conviction required to achieve a change in social gender role, can it be suggested that there is anything arbitrary or capricious in the decision taken by a person to undergo gender re-assignment. In those circumstances, the ongoing scientific and medical debate as to the exact causes of the condition is of diminished relevance.

82. While it also remains the case that a transsexual cannot acquire all the biological characteristics of the assigned sex (*Sheffield and Horsham*, p. 2028, § 56), the Court notes that with increasingly sophisticated surgery and types of hormonal treatments, the principal unchanging biological aspect of gender identity is the chromosomal element. It is known however that chromosomal anomalies may arise naturally (for example, in cases of intersex conditions where the biological criteria at birth are not congruent) and in those cases, some persons have to be assigned to one sex or the other as seems most appropriate in the circumstances of the individual case. It is not apparent to the Court that the chromosomal element, amongst all the others, must inevitably take on decisive significance for the purposes of legal attribution of gender identity for transsexuals (see the dissenting opinion of Thorpe LJ in *Bellinger v. Bellinger*; and the judgment of Chisholm J in the Australian case, *Re Kevin*).

83. The Court is not persuaded therefore that the state of medical science or scientific knowledge provides any determining argument as regards the legal recognition of transsexuals.

4. The state of any European and international consensus

84. Already at the time of the *Sheffield and Horsham* case, there was an emerging consensus within Contracting States in the Council of Europe on providing legal recognition following gender re-assignment (see § 35 of that judgment). The latest survey submitted by Liberty in the present case shows a continuing international trend towards legal recognition. . . . In Australia and New Zealand, it appears that the courts are moving away from the biological birth view of sex (as set out in the United Kingdom case of *Corbett v. Corbett*) and taking the view that sex, in the context of a transsexual wishing to marry, should depend on a multitude of factors to be assessed at the time of the marriage.

85. The Court observes that in the case of Rees in 1986 it had noted that little common ground existed between States, some of which did permit change of gender and some of which did not and that generally speaking the law seemed to be in a state of transition (see § 37). In the later case of *Sheffield and Horsham*, the Court's judgment laid emphasis on the lack of a common European approach as to how to address the repercussions which the legal recognition of a change of sex may entail for other areas of law such as marriage, filiation, privacy or data protection. While this would appear to remain the case, the lack of such a common approach among forty-three Contracting States with widely diverse legal systems and traditions is hardly surprising. In accordance with the principle of subsidiarity, it is indeed primarily for the Contracting States to decide on the measures necessary to secure Convention rights within their jurisdiction and, in resolving within their domestic legal systems the practical problems created by the legal recognition of post-operative gender status, the Contracting States must enjoy a wide margin of appreciation. The Court accordingly attaches less importance to the lack of evidence of a common European approach to the resolution of the legal and practical problems posed, than to the clear and uncontested evidence of a continuing international trend in favour not only of increased social acceptance of transsexuals but of legal recognition of the new sexual identity of post-operative transsexuals.

5. Impact on the birth register system

86. In the *Rees* case, the Court allowed that great importance could be placed by the Government on the historical nature of the birth record system. The argument that allowing exceptions to this system would undermine its function weighed heavily in the assessment.

87. It may be noted however that exceptions are already made to the historic basis of the birth register system, namely, in the case of legitimization or adoptions, where there is a possibility of issuing updated certificates to reflect a change in status after birth. To make a further exception in the case of transsexuals (a category estimated as including some 2,000–5,000 persons in the United Kingdom according to the Interdepartmental Working Group Report, p. 26) would not, in the Court's view, pose the threat of overturning the entire system. Though previous reference has been made to detriment suffered by third parties who might be unable to obtain access to the original entries and to complications occurring in the field of family and succession law (see the *Rees* judgment, p. 18, § 43), these assertions are framed in general terms and the Court does not find, on the basis of the material before it at this time, that any real prospect of prejudice has been identified as likely to arise if changes were made to the current system.

88. Furthermore, the Court notes that the Government have recently issued proposals for reform which would allow ongoing amendment to civil status data. It is not convinced therefore that the need to uphold rigidly the integrity of the historic basis of the birth registration system takes on the same importance in the current climate as it did in 1986.

6. Striking a balance in the present case

89. The Court has noted above the difficulties and anomalies of the applicant's situation as a post-operative transsexual. It must be acknowledged that the level of daily interference suffered by the applicant in *B. v. France* (judgment of 25 March 1992, Series A no. 232) has not been attained in this case and that on certain points the risk of difficulties or embarrassment faced by the present applicant may be avoided or minimized by the practices adopted by the authorities.

90. Nonetheless, the very essence of the Convention is respect for human dignity and human freedom. Under Article 8 of the Convention in particular, where the notion of personal autonomy is an important principle underlying the interpretation of its guarantees, protection is given to the personal sphere of each individual, including the right to establish details of their identity as individual human beings (see, *inter alia, Pretty v. the United Kingdom*, no. 2346/02, judgment of 29 April 2002, § 62, and *Mikulić v. Croatia*, no. 53176/99, judgment of 7 February 2002, § 53, both to be published in ECHR 2002- . . .). In the twenty first century the right of transsexuals to personal development and to physical and moral security in the full sense enjoyed by others in society cannot be regarded as a matter of controversy requiring the lapse of time to cast clearer light on the issues involved. In short, the unsatisfactory situation in which post-operative transsexuals live in an intermediate zone as not quite one gender or the other is no longer sustainable. Domestic recognition of this evaluation may be found in the report of the Interdepartmental Working Group and the Court of Appeal's judgment of *Bellinger v. Bellinger*.

91. The Court does not underestimate the difficulties posed or the important repercussions which any major change in the system will inevitably have, not only in the field of birth registration, but also in the areas of access to records, family law, affiliation, inheritance, criminal justice, employment, social security and insurance. However, as is made clear by the report of the Interdepartmental Working Group, these problems are far from insuperable, to the extent that the Working Group felt able to propose as one of the options full legal recognition of the new gender, subject to certain criteria and procedures. As Lord Justice Thorpe observed in the *Bellinger* case, any "spectral difficulties", particularly in the field of family law, are both manageable and acceptable if confined to the case of fully achieved and post-operative transsexuals. Nor is the Court convinced by arguments that allowing the applicant to fall under the rules applicable to women, which would also change the date of eligibility for her state pension, would cause any injustice to others in the national insurance and state pension systems as alleged by the Government. No concrete or substantial hardship or detriment to the public interest has indeed been demonstrated as likely to flow from any change to the status of transsexuals and, as regards other possible consequences, the Court considers that society may reasonably be expected to tolerate a certain inconvenience to enable individuals to live in dignity and worth in accordance with the sexual identity chosen by them at great personal cost.

92. In the previous cases from the United Kingdom, this Court has since 1986 emphasised the importance of keeping the need for appropriate legal measures under review having regard to scientific and societal developments. Most recently in

the *Sheffield and Horsham* case in 1998, it observed that the respondent State had not yet taken any steps to do so despite an increase in the social acceptance of the phenomenon of transsexualism and a growing recognition of the problems with which transsexuals are confronted (cited above). Even though it found no violation in that case, the need to keep this area under review was expressly re-iterated. Since then, a report has been issued in April 2000 by the Interdepartmental Working Group which set out a survey of the current position of transsexuals in *inter alia* criminal law, family and employment matters and identified various options for reform. Nothing has effectively been done to further these proposals and in July 2001 the Court of Appeal noted that there were no plans to do so. It may be observed that the only legislative reform of note, applying certain non-discrimination provisions to transsexuals, flowed from a decision of the European Court of Justice of 30 April 1996 which held that discrimination based on a change of gender was equivalent to discrimination on grounds of sex.

93. Having regard to the above considerations, the Court finds that the respondent Government can no longer claim that the matter falls within their margin of appreciation, save as regards the appropriate means of achieving recognition of the right protected under the Convention. Since there are no significant factors of public interest to weigh against the interest of this individual applicant in obtaining legal recognition of her gender re-assignment, it reaches the conclusion that the fair balance that is inherent in the Convention now tilts decisively in favor of the applicant. There has, accordingly, been a failure to respect her right to private life in breach of Article 8 of the Convention.

II. ALLEGED VIOLATION OF ARTICLE 12 OF THE CONVENTION

94. The applicant also claimed a violation of Article 12 of the Convention, which provides as follows:

Men and women of marriageable age have the right to marry and to found a family, according to the national laws governing the exercise of this right.

. . . .

B. The Court's assessment

97. The Court recalls that in the cases of *Rees, Cossey* and *Sheffield and Horsham* the inability of the transsexuals in those cases to marry a person of the sex opposite to their re-assigned gender was not found in breach of Article 12 of the Convention. These findings were based variously on the reasoning that the right to marry referred to traditional marriage between persons of opposite biological sex (the *Rees* judgment, p. 19, § 49), the view that continued adoption of biological criteria in domestic law for determining a person's sex for the purpose of marriage was encompassed within the power of Contracting States to regulate by national law the exercise of the right to marry and the conclusion that national laws in that respect could not be regarded as restricting or reducing the right of a transsexual to marry in such a way or to such an extent that the very essence of the right was impaired (the *Cossey* judgment, p. 18, §§ 44–46, the *Sheffield and Horsham* judgment, p. 2030, §§ 66–67). Reference was also made to the wording of Article 12 as protecting marriage as the basis of the family (*Rees, loc. cit.*).

98. Reviewing the situation in 2002, the Court observes that Article 12 secures the fundamental right of a man and woman to marry and to found a family. The second aspect is not however a condition of the first and the inability of any couple to conceive or parent a child cannot be regarded as *per se* removing their right to enjoy the first limb of this provision.

99. The exercise of the right to marry gives rise to social, personal and legal consequences. It is subject to the national laws of the Contracting States but the limitations thereby introduced must not restrict or reduce the right in such a way or to such an extent that the very essence of the right is impaired (see the *Rees* judgment, p. 19, § 50; the *F. v. Switzerland* judgment of 18 December 1987, Series A no. 128, § 32).

100. It is true that the first sentence refers in express terms to the right of a man and woman to marry. The Court is not persuaded that at the date of this case it can still be assumed that these terms must refer to a determination of gender by purely biological criteria (as held by Ormrod J. in the case of *Corbett v. Corbett*). There have been major social changes in the institution of marriage since the adoption of the Convention as well as dramatic changes brought about by developments in medicine and science in the field of transsexuality. The Court has found above, under Article 8 of the Convention, that a test of congruent biological factors can no longer be decisive in denying legal recognition to the change of gender of a post-operative transsexual. There are other important factors—the acceptance of the condition of gender identity disorder by the medical professions and health authorities within Contracting States, the provision of treatment including surgery to assimilate the individual as closely as possible to the gender in which they perceive that they properly belong and the assumption by the transsexual of the social role of the assigned gender. The Court would also note that Article 9 of the recently adopted Charter of Fundamental Rights of the European Union departs, no doubt deliberately, from the wording of Article 12 of the Convention in removing the reference to men and women. . . .

101. The right under Article 8 to respect for private life does not however subsume all the issues under Article 12, where conditions imposed by national laws are accorded a specific mention. The Court has therefore considered whether the allocation of sex in national law to that registered at birth is a limitation impairing the very essence of the right to marry in this case. In that regard, it finds that it is artificial to assert that post-operative transsexuals have not been deprived of the right to marry as, according to law, they remain able to marry a person of their former opposite sex. The applicant in this case lives as a woman, is in a relationship with a man and would only wish to marry a man. She has no possibility of doing so. In the Court's view, she may therefore claim that the very essence of her right to marry has been infringed.

102. The Court has not identified any other reason which would prevent it from reaching this conclusion. The Government have argued that in this sensitive area eligibility for marriage under national law should be left to the domestic courts within the State's margin of appreciation, adverting to the potential impact on already existing marriages in which a transsexual is a partner. It appears however

from the opinions of the majority of the Court of Appeal judgment in *Bellinger v. Bellinger* that the domestic courts tend to the view that the matter is best handled by the legislature, while the Government have no present intention to introduce legislation (see paragraphs 52–53).

103. It may be noted from the materials submitted by Liberty that though there is widespread acceptance of the marriage of transsexuals, fewer countries permit the marriage of transsexuals in their assigned gender than recognise the change of gender itself. The Court is not persuaded however that this supports an argument for leaving the matter entirely to the Contracting States as being within their margin of appreciation. This would be tantamount to finding that the range of options open to a Contracting State included an effective bar on any exercise of the right to marry. The margin of appreciation cannot extend so far. While it is for the Contracting State to determine *inter alia* the conditions under which a person claiming legal recognition as a transsexual establishes that gender re-assignment has been properly effected or under which past marriages cease to be valid and the formalities applicable to future marriages (including, for example, the information to be furnished to intended spouses), the Court finds no justification for barring the transsexual from enjoying the right to marry under any circumstances.

104. The Court concludes that there has been a breach of Article 12 of the Convention in the present case.

. . . [The Court found no breaches of Articles 13 and 14 of the Convention]

Questions and Comments

1. Article 12 has a "clawback" clause, a reference to defining the scope of the right by national law. How does the Court interpret this expressly deferential provision? On clawback clauses, *see infra* p. 250–254.

2. Are human rights instruments different from other treaties in the emphasis given to evolutionary interpretation in contrast to original intent? What does it mean to call a human rights treaty a "living instrument?" What weight should be given to the fact, noted by the Inter-American Commission in Case 2141, para. 19, that the majority of American states permitted abortion at the time the Declaration was drafted?

3. Consider the following extract from the case of *Selmouni v. France*, 1999-V E.H.R.R. (GC) (July 28, 1999) alleging torture of a detainee. Does the Court go too far in interpreting the treaty, to the point where it is imposing new obligations on states parties to which they have not consented?

> 96. In order to determine whether a particular form of ill-treatment should be qualified as torture, the Court must have regard to the distinction, embodied in Article 3, between this notion and that of inhuman or degrading treatment. As the European Court has previously found, it appears that it was the intention that the Convention should, by means of this distinction, attach a special stigma to deliberate inhuman treatment causing very serious and cruel suffering.

> 97. The United Nations Convention against Torture and Other Cruel, Inhuman or Degrading Treatment or Punishment, which came into force on 26 June 1987, also makes such a distinction, as can be seen from Articles 1 and 16. . . .

> 99. The acts complained of were such as to arouse in the applicant feelings of fear, anguish and inferiority capable of humiliating and debasing him and possibly breaking his physical and

moral resistance. The Court therefore finds elements which are sufficiently serious to render such treatment inhuman and degrading. . . . In any event, the Court reiterates that, in respect of a person deprived of his liberty, recourse to physical force which has not been made strictly necessary by his own conduct diminishes human dignity and is in principle an infringement of the right set forth in Article 3. . . .

100. In other words, it remains to be established in the instant case whether the "pain or suffering inflicted on Mr. Selmouni can be defined as "severe" within the meaning of Article 1 of the United Nations Convention. The Court considers that this "severity" is, like the "minimum severity" required for the application of Article 3, in the nature of things, relative; it depends on all the circumstances of the case, such as the duration of the treatment, its physical or mental effects and, in some cases, the sex, age and state of health of the victim, etc.

101. The Court has previously examined cases in which it concluded that there had been treatment which could only be described as torture. . . . However, having regard to the fact that the Convention is a "living instrument which must be interpreted in the light of present-day conditions," the Court considers that certain acts which were classified in the past as "inhuman and degrading treatment" as opposed to "torture" could be classified differently in future. It takes the view that the increasingly high standard being required in the area of the protection of human rights and fundamental liberties correspondingly and inevitably requires greater firmness in assessing breaches of the fundamental values of democratic societies.

4. What distinguishes torture from cruel, inhuman or degrading treatment, factually and legally?

5. The European and Inter-American systems have recently received a growing number of cases on poor prison conditions, a topic that also dominates federal habeas corpus litigation in the United States. See: Peers v. Greece, (App. no. 28524/95), Judgment of 19 April 2001; Eur.Ct.H.R. (violations of Articles 3, 8), McGlinchey v. United Kingdom, (App. no. 50390/99),29 April 2003 (violations of Article 3, 13); Valašinas v. Lithuania, (App. no. 44558/98), Judgment of 24 July 2001 (violation of Article 8). Unlike the U.S. cases, however, the applicants in the European system are represented and many receive legal aid. In Peers v. Greece, para. 74, the Court stated that "in the present case there is no evidence that there was a positive intention of humiliating or debasing the applicant. However, the Court notes that, although the question whether the purpose of the treatment was to humiliate or debase the victim is a factor to be taken into account, the absence of any such purpose cannot conclusively rule out a finding of violation of Article 3." (Citing V. v. the United Kingdom [GC], no. 24888/94, § 71, ECHR 1999-IX). Is the standard thus an objective one, or is it based on the subjective feelings of humiliation of the prisoner? In Valašinas v. Lithuania, para. 103, the Court noted that "the absence of an adequate supply of toilet paper in a prison may raise an issue under Article 3 of the Convention." Do you agree?

6. The European system has also faced cases concerning the detention of individuals who are in poor health, elderly or frail. The Court often approaches these cases by evaluating whether or not the treatment afforded in detention is similar to that available outside prison. See, e.g. Mouisel v. France, No. 67263/01, ECHR 2002-IX; Henaf v. France, No. 65436/01, ECHR 2002-IX; Farbtuhs v. Latvia, No. 4672/02, judgment of 2 Dec. 2004; and Gelfman v. France, No. 25875/03, judgment of 14 Dec. 2004. Other applicants under threat of deportation have alleged that they will be at risk of ill-treatment or even death if returned to their country of origin. It is insufficient to show that the general situation in the country is dangerous; an applicant must establish a direct and personal risk of ill-treatment. There has also been an increase in the number of cases in which applicants have submitted that they will not receive sufficient medical care in the country of destination. See e.g. D. v. the United Kingdom, Judgment of 2 May 1997, Rep. 1997-III; Kalishnikov v. Russia, (App. no. 47095/99), Judgment of 15 July 2002, Eur. Ct. H.R., 36 EHRR 34 (2003).

iv. Implied Rights

The *Christine Goodwin* judgment could be read as simply interpreting the rights in the European Convention or it could be read to imply rights that states parties never intended to be included among the guarantees. Compare the following case, in which the Court denies the claimed implied right to divorce. Does it go further than the preceding case? What is the practical result of the judgment, given that the Court finds a violation with respect to the third applicant?

Johnston and Others v. Ireland, (App. no. 9697/82), Judgment of 18 December 1986, 112 Eur. Ct. H.R. (Ser. A), 9 EHRR 203 (1987).

. . . .

38. The application of Roy Johnston, Janice Williams-Johnston and Nessa Williams-Johnston was lodged with the Commission on 16 February 1982. The applicants complained of the absence of provision in Ireland for divorce and for recognition of the family life of persons who, after the breakdown of the marriage of one of them, are living in a family relationship outside marriage. They alleged that on this account they had been victims of violations of Articles 8, 9, 12 and 13 of the Convention and also of Article 14 (taken in conjunction with Articles 8 and 12).

39. The Commission declared the application admissible on 7 October 1983.

AS TO THE LAW

. . . .

II. SITUATION OF THE FIRST AND SECOND APPLICANTS

A. Inability to divorce and re-marry

1. Articles 12 and 8

. . . .

50. The applicants stated that, as regards this part of the case, the central issue was not whether the Convention guaranteed the right to divorce but rather whether the fact that they were unable to marry each other was compatible with the right to marry or re-marry and with the right to respect for family life, enshrined in Articles 12 and 8.

The Court does not consider that the issues arising can be separated into watertight compartments in this way. In any society espousing the principle of monogamy, it is inconceivable that Roy Johnston should be able to marry as long as his marriage to Mrs. Johnston has not been dissolved. The second applicant, for her part, is not complaining of a general inability to marry but rather of her inability to marry the first applicant, a situation that stems precisely from the fact that he cannot obtain a divorce. Consequently, their case cannot be examined in isolation from the problem of the non-availability of divorce.

(a) Article 12

51. In order to determine whether the applicants can derive a right to divorce from Article 12, the Court will seek to ascertain the ordinary meaning to be given to the terms of this provision in their context and in the light of its object and pur-

pose (see the *Golder* judgment of 21 February 1975, Series A no. 18, p. 14, § 29, and Article 31 § 1 of the Vienna Convention of 23 May 1969 on the Law of Treaties).

52. The Court agrees with the Commission that the ordinary meaning of the words "right to marry" is clear, in the sense that they cover the formation of marital relationships but not their dissolution. Furthermore, these words are found in a context that includes an express reference to "national laws"; even if, as the applicants would have it, the prohibition on divorce is to be seen as a restriction on capacity to marry, the Court does not consider that, in a society adhering to the principle of monogamy, such a restriction can be regarded as injuring the substance of the right guaranteed by Article 12.

Moreover, the foregoing interpretation of Article 12 is consistent with its object and purpose as revealed by the *travaux préparatoires*. The text of Article 12 was based on that of Article 16 of the Universal Declaration of Human Rights, paragraph 1 of which reads:

> Men and women of full age, without any limitation due to race, nationality or religion, have the right to marry and to found a family. They are entitled to equal rights as to marriage, during marriage and at its dissolution.

In explaining to the Consultative Assembly why the draft of the future Article 12 did not include the words found in the last sentence of the above-cited paragraph, Mr. Teitgen, Rapporteur of the Committee on Legal and Administrative Questions, said:

> In mentioning the particular Article of the Universal Declaration, we have used only that part of the paragraph of the Article which affirms the right to marry and to found a family, but not the subsequent provisions of the Article concerning equal rights after marriage, since we only guarantee the right to marry. (Collected Edition of the *Travaux préparatoires*, vol. 1, p. 268)

In the Court's view, the *travaux préparatoires* disclose no intention to include in Article 12 any guarantee of a right to have the ties of marriage dissolved by divorce.

53. The applicants set considerable store on the social developments that have occurred since the Convention was drafted, notably an alleged substantial increase in marriage breakdown.

It is true that the Convention and its Protocols must be interpreted in the light of present-day conditions (see, amongst several authorities, the above-mentioned *Marckx* judgment, Series A no. 31, p. 26, § 58). However, the Court cannot, by means of an evolutive interpretation, derive from these instruments a right that was not included therein at the outset. This is particularly so here, where the omission was deliberate.

It should also be mentioned that the right to divorce is not included in Protocol No. 7 to the Convention, which was opened to signature on 22 November 1984. The opportunity was not taken to deal with this question in Article 5 of the Protocol, which guarantees certain additional rights to spouses, notably in the event of dissolution of marriage. Indeed, paragraph 39 of the explanatory report to the Protocol states that the words "in the event of its dissolution" found in Article 5 "do not imply any obligation on a State to provide for dissolution of marriage or to provide any special forms of dissolution."

54. The Court thus concludes that the applicants cannot derive a right to divorce from Article 12. That provision is therefore inapplicable in the present case, either on its own or in conjunction with Article 14.

(b) Article 8

55. The principles which emerge from the Court's case-law on Article 8 include the following.

> (a) By guaranteeing the right to respect for family life, Article 8 presupposes the existence of a family (see the above-mentioned *Marckx* judgment, Series A no. 31, p. 14, § 31).
> (b) Article 8 applies to the "family life" of the "illegitimate" family as well as to that of the "legitimate" family (ibid.).
> (c) Although the essential object of Article 8 is to protect the individual against arbitrary interference by the public authorities, there may in addition be positive obligations inherent in an effective "respect" for family life. However, especially as far as those positive obligations are concerned, the notion of "respect" is not clear-cut: having regard to the diversity of the practices followed and the situations obtaining in the Contracting States, the notion's requirements will vary considerably from case to case.

Accordingly, this is an area in which the Contracting Parties enjoy a wide margin of appreciation in determining the steps to be taken to ensure compliance with the Convention with due regard to the needs and resources of the community and of individuals (see the *Abdulaziz, Cabales and Balkandali* judgment of 28 May 1985, Series A no. 94, pp. 33–34, § 67).

56. In the present case, it is clear that the applicants, the first and second of whom have lived together for some fifteen years, constitute a "family" for the purposes of Article 8. They are thus entitled to its protection, notwithstanding the fact that their relationship exists outside marriage.

The question that arises, as regards this part of the case, is whether an effective "respect" for the applicants' family life imposes on Ireland a positive obligation to introduce measures that would permit divorce.

57. It is true that, on this question, Article 8, with its reference to the somewhat vague notion of "respect" for family life, might appear to lend itself more readily to an evolutive interpretation than does Article 12. Nevertheless, the Convention must be read as a whole and the Court does not consider that a right to divorce, which it has found to be excluded from Article 12, can, with consistency, be derived from Article 8 a provision of more general purpose and scope. The Court is not oblivious to the plight of the first and second applicants. However, it is of the opinion that, although the protection of private or family life may sometimes necessitate means whereby spouses can be relieved from the duty to live together (see the above-mentioned *Airey* judgment, Series A no. 32, p. 17, § 33), the engagements undertaken by Ireland under Article 8 cannot be regarded as extending to an obli-

gation on its part to introduce measures permitting the divorce and the re-marriage which the applicants seek.

58. On this point, there is therefore no failure to respect the family life of the first and second applicants.

2. Article 14, taken in conjunction with Article 8

59. The first and second applicants complained of the fact that whereas Roy Johnston was unable to obtain a divorce in order subsequently to marry Janice Williams-Johnston, other persons resident in Ireland and having the necessary means could obtain abroad a divorce which would be recognised de jure or de facto in Ireland. They alleged that on this account they had been victims of discrimination, on the ground of financial means, in the enjoyment of the rights set forth in Article 8, contrary to Article 14. . . .

This allegation, contested by the Government, was rejected by the Commission.

60. Article 14 safeguards persons who are "placed in analogous situations" against discriminatory differences of treatment in the exercise of the rights and freedoms recognised by the Convention (see, as the most recent authority, the *Lithgow and Others* judgment of 8 July 1986, Series A no. 102, p. 66, § 177).

The Court notes that under the general Irish rules of private international law foreign divorces will be recognised in Ireland only if they have been obtained by persons domiciled abroad. It does not find it to have been established that these rules are departed from in practice. In its view, the situations of such persons and of the first and second applicants cannot be regarded as analogous.

61. There is, accordingly, no discrimination, within the meaning of Article 14.

3. Article 9

62. The first applicant also alleged that his inability to live with the second applicant other than in an extra-marital relationship was contrary to his conscience and that on that account he was the victim of a violation of Article 9 of the Convention, which guarantees to everyone the "right to freedom of thought, conscience and religion".

The applicant supplemented this allegation, which was contested by the Government and rejected by the Commission, by a claim of discrimination in relation to conscience and religion, contrary to Article 14 taken in conjunction with Article 9.

63. It is clear that Roy Johnston's freedom to have and manifest his convictions is not in issue. His complaint derives, in essence, from the non-availability of divorce under Irish law, a matter to which, in the Court's view, Article 9 cannot, in its ordinary meaning, be taken to extend.

Accordingly, that provision, and hence Article 14 also, are not applicable.

4. Conclusion

64. The Court thus concludes that the complaints related to the inability to divorce and re-marry are not well-founded.

. . . .

III. SITUATION OF THE THIRD APPLICANT

A. Article 8

70. The applicants alleged that, in violation of Article 8, there had been an interference with, or lack of respect for, their family life on account of the third applicant's situation under Irish law. . . .

71. Roy Johnston and Janice Williams-Johnston have been able to take a number of steps to integrate their daughter in the family. However, the question arises as to whether an effective "respect" for family life imposes on Ireland a positive obligation to improve her legal situation.

. . . .

74. As is recorded in the Preamble to the European Convention of 15 October 1975 on the Legal Status of Children born out of Wedlock, "in a great number of member States of the Council of Europe efforts have been, or are being, made to improve the legal status of children born out of wedlock by reducing the differences between their legal status and that of children born in wedlock which are to the legal or social disadvantage of the former". Furthermore, in Ireland itself this trend is reflected in the Status of Children Bill recently laid before Parliament.

In its consideration of this part of the present case, the Court cannot but be influenced by these developments. As it observed in . . . *Marckx [v. Belgium]* . . . , "respect" for family life, understood as including the ties between near relatives, implies an obligation for the State to act in a manner calculated to allow these ties to develop normally (Series A no. 31, p. 21, § 45). And in the present case the normal development of the natural family ties between the first and second applicants and their daughter requires, in the Court's opinion, that she should be placed, legally and socially, in a position akin to that of a legitimate child.

75. Examination of the third applicant's present legal situation, seen as a whole, reveals, however, that it differs considerably from that of a legitimate child; in addition, it has not been shown that there are any means available to her or her parents to eliminate or reduce the differences. Having regard to the particular circumstances of this case and notwithstanding the wide margin of appreciation enjoyed by Ireland in this area, the absence of an appropriate legal regime reflecting the third applicant's natural family ties amounts to a failure to respect her family life.

Moreover, the close and intimate relationship between the third applicant and her parents is such that there is of necessity also a resultant failure to respect the family life of each of the latter. Contrary to the Government's suggestion, this finding does not amount, in an indirect way, to a conclusion that the first applicant should be entitled to divorce and re-marry; this is demonstrated by the fact that in Ireland itself it is proposed to improve the legal situation of illegitimate children, whilst maintaining the constitutional prohibition on divorce.

76. There is accordingly, as regards all three applicants, a breach of Article 8 under this head.

77. It is not the Court's function to indicate which measures Ireland should take in this connection; it is for the State concerned to choose the means to be utilised in its domestic law for performance of its obligation under Article 53 (see the above-mentioned *Airey* judgment, Series A no. 32, p. 15, § 26, and the above-mentioned

Marckx judgment, Series A no. 31, p. 25, § 58). In making its choice, Ireland must ensure that the requisite fair balance is struck between the demands of the general interest of the community and the interests of the individual. . . .

———————

Note on *Pretty v. United Kingdom*, (App. no. 2346/02), Judgment of April 29, 2002, Eur. Ct. H.R., 35 EHRR 1 (2002). The applicant, a 43-year-old woman suffering from a progressive neuro-degenerative disease of motor cells within the central nervous system, challenged the British law that makes it a crime to assist another to commit suicide (section 2(1) of the Suicide Act 1961). The Court reviewed its jurisprudence on the interpretation of Article 2 and rejected the applicant's assertion that the right to life should be interpreted to include the right to die:

1. The consistent emphasis in all the cases before the Court has been the obligation of the State to protect life. The Court is not persuaded that "the right to life" guaranteed in Article 2 can be interpreted as involving a negative aspect. While, for example, in the context of Article 11 of the Convention, the freedom of association was found to involve not only a right to join an association but a corresponding right not to be forced to join an association, the Court observes that the notion of a freedom implies some measure of choice as to its exercise (see the *Young, James and Webster v. the United Kingdom* judgment of 13 August 1981, Series A no. 44, § 52, and *Sigurdur A. Sigurjónsson v. Iceland* judgment of 30 June 1993, Series A no. 264, pp. 15–16, § 35). Article 2 of the Convention is phrased in different terms. It is unconcerned with issues to do with the quality of living or what a person chooses to do with his or her life. To the extent that these aspects are recognised as so fundamental to the human condition that they require protection from State interference, they may be reflected in the rights guaranteed by other Articles of the Convention, or in other international human rights instruments. Article 2 cannot, without a distortion of language, be interpreted as conferring the diametrically opposite right, namely a right to die; nor can it create a right to self-determination in the sense of conferring on an individual the entitlement to choose death rather than life.

2. The Court accordingly finds that no right to die, whether at the hands of a third person or with the assistance of a public authority, can be derived from Article 2 of the Convention. It is confirmed in this view by the recent Recommendation 1418 (1999) of the Parliamentary Assembly of the Council of Europe (. . .).

3. . . .

4. The Court finds that there has been no violation of Article 2 of the Convention.

The Court also found no violation of Article 3 or 8. Is the Court correct that the right to life provision is unconcerned with the quality of life? Should it be concerned? How should a human rights court or commission distinguish between its function to apply rights in an evolutionary manner and its lack of mandate to draft new rights?

B. Comparing the Contents: Selected Issues

While there are similarities and even identical language with respect to some of the rights contained in the regional instruments, other rights vary in the scope of protection afforded. The following section examines one such right, the right to life, as it is found in the three regional systems and as it has been interpreted. It then compares the place of economic, social and cultural rights in the three systems.

i. The Right to Life

The language of the provisions on the right to life varies, as the texts below indicate. In comparing them, consider whether the instruments concluded later in time appear to draw on those written earlier. Recall that representatives from the Council of Europe and the United Nations were present during the drafting of the American Convention. Note that the European and American Conventions originally restricted, but did not prohibit states from imposing capital punishment, while more recently the clear trend has been in favor of abolition of the death penalty. On April 28, 1983, the Council of Europe adopted Protocol No. 6 concerning the peacetime abolition of the death penalty, which has been accepted by every member state except Russia. In 1989, the United Nations General Assembly adopted a Protocol to the United Nations Covenant on Civil and Political Rights, also aimed at the abolition of the death penalty. A year later, on July 8, 1990, the OAS adopted a similar protocol to the American Convention. Finally, on May 3, 2002, the Council of Europe adopted Protocol No. 13 to the European Convention, eliminating the death penalty under all circumstances. The African Charter does not mention the issue.

Not all states have adhered to the instruments that would bind them to eliminate capital punishment. This raises questions about whether or under what conditions the death penalty remains permissible. All the instruments require states not to deprive a person of life "arbitrarily." In the case of *International Pen, Constitutional Rights Project, Interights on behalf of Ken Saro-Wiwa Jr. and Civil Liberties Organisation v. Nigeria*, (Comms. 137/94, 139/94, 154/96, and 161/97), 12th Annual Activity Report of the Afr. Comm. H.P.R.1998–1999, Annex V, pp. 62–73, the African Commission did not condemn the application of the death penalty *per se*, or discuss its place in the African system, but held that the implementation of such a sentence following a trial that lacked fundamental due process guarantees renders the resulting deprivation of life arbitrary, in violation of Article 4. In 1999, the African Commission adopted a "Resolution urging the States to envisage a Moratorium on the Death Penalty" in which the Commission not only proposed the moratorium, but asked that states "reflect on the possibility of abolishing the death penalty." 15 Nov. 1999, *13th Annual Report of the Commission 1999/2000*. At the time, at least nineteen states parties to the African Charter had legally abolished the death penalty or no longer applied it in practice. *Id.* Is it possible that the evolution in the other systems influenced the African Commission? For further discussion of the right to life, see Chapter III (3).

ECHR, Article 2 – Right to Life

1 Everyone's right to life shall be protected by law. No one shall be deprived of his life intentionally save in the execution of a sentence of a court following his conviction of a crime for which this penalty is provided by law.

2 Deprivation of life shall not be regarded as inflicted in contravention of this article when it results from the use of force which is no more than absolutely necessary:

a. in defence of any person from unlawful violence;

b. in order to effect a lawful arrest or to prevent the escape of a person lawfully detained;

c. in action lawfully taken for the purpose of quelling a riot or insurrection.

American Declaration on the Rights and Duties of Man, Article I

Every human being has the right to life, liberty and the security of his person.

American Convention on Human Rights, Article 4. Right to Life

1. Every person has the right to have his life respected. This right shall be protected by law and, in general, from the moment of conception. No one shall be arbitrarily deprived of his life.

2. In countries that have not abolished the death penalty, it may be imposed only for the most serious crimes and pursuant to a final judgment rendered by a competent court and in accordance with a law establishing such punishment, enacted prior to the commission of the crime. The application of such punishment shall not be extended to crimes to which it does not presently apply.

3. The death penalty shall not be reestablished in states that have abolished it.

4. In no case shall capital punishment be inflicted for political offenses or related common crimes.

5. Capital punishment shall not be imposed upon persons who, at the time the crime was committed, were under 18 years of age or over 70 years of age; nor shall it be applied to pregnant women.

6. Every person condemned to death shall have the right to apply for amnesty, pardon, or commutation of sentence, which may be granted in all cases. Capital punishment shall not be imposed while such a petition is pending decision by the competent authority.

African Charter on Human and Peoples Rights, Article 4

Human beings are inviolable. Every human being shall be entitled to respect for his life and the integrity of his person. No one may be arbitrarily deprived of this right.

On another aspect of the right to life, the American Convention is the only instrument to call for life to be respected from the moment of conception. As the first case below indicates, there have been attempts to invoke this provision to interpret the earlier American Declaration. Is this appropriate? Consider also whether the reference to the moment of conception in the American Convention has led to an interpretation that makes the scope of the right to life considerably different in the Americas than in Europe. Would the European cases have come out differently in the Inter-American system?

Res. 23/81, Case 2141 (United States), March 6, 1981, *Annual Report of the Inter-American Commission on Human Rights 1980–1981*, OEA/Ser.L/V/II.54, doc. 9 rev. 1, 16 October 1981.

1. On January 19, 1977, Christian B. White and Gary K. Potter, filed with the Inter-American Commission on Human Rights a petition against the United States of America and the Commonwealth of Massachusetts for the purposes established in the Statute and Regulations of the Commission. The petition is accompanied by a cover letter of the Catholics for Christian Political Action, signed by Gary Potter, President. [The petition was filed in the name of "Baby Boy," alleging: *Victim was killed by abortion process (hysterectomy), by Dr. Kenneth Edelin, M.D., in violation of the right to life granted by the American Declaration of the Rights and Duties of Man, as clarified by the definition and description of the American Convention on Human Rights. The violations of the following rights granted by the American Declaration of the Rights and Duties of Man, Chapter 1, Article I (". . . right to life . . .", Article II ("All persons are equal before the law . . . without distinction as to race, sex, language, creed, or any other factor," here, age), Article VII ("All children have the right to special protection, care, and aid") and Article XI ("Every person has the right to the preservation of his health . . . ") began on January 22, 1973, when the Supreme Court of the United States handed down its decisions in the cases of Roe vs. Wade, 410 U.S. 113 and Doe vs. Bolton, 410 U.S. 179.]* . . .

1. The basic facts described in the petition as alleged violations of articles I, II, VII and IX of the American Declaration occurred on January 22, 1973 (date of the decisions of cases *Roe v. Wade* and *Doe v. Bolton* by U.S. Supreme Court), October 3, 1973 (date of abortion of Baby Boy performed at the Boston City Hospital) and December 17, 1976 (date of final decision of the Supreme Judicial Court of Massachusetts that acquitted Dr. Edelin, the performer of the abortion.) The defendant, the U.S. Government is not a state party to the American Convention on Human Rights. The petition was filed on January 19, 1977, before the Convention entered into force on July 18, 1978. . . .

7. The facts of the case are not in controversy. The text of the decision of the Supreme Judicial Court of Massachusetts, produced by petitioners, was accepted as authentic. Only the merits are under scrutiny. The consideration of those facts and the terms of such decision and the analysis of rules and precedents of U.S. Supreme Court, applicable to this case, indicate that there was no internal remedy to be exhausted by the petitioners before applying to the international jurisdiction. . . .

15. The international obligation of the United States of America, as a member of the Organization of American States (OAS), under the jurisdiction of the Inter-American Commission on Human Rights (IACHR) is governed by the Charter of OAS (Bogotá, 1948) as amended by the Protocol of Buenos Aires on February 27, 1967, ratified by United States on April 23, 1968.

16. As a consequence of articles 3 i, 16, 51 e, 112 and 150 of this Treaty, the provisions of other instruments and resolutions of the OAS on human rights acquired binding force. Those instruments and resolutions approved with the vote of U.S. Government, are the following:

– American Declaration of the Rights and Duties of Man (Bogotá, 1948)
– Statute and Regulations of the IACHR 1960, as amended by resolution XXII of the Second Special Inter-American Conference (Rio de Janeiro, 1965)
– Statute and Regulations of IACHR of 1979–1980.

17. Both Statutes provide that, for the purpose of such instruments, the IACHR is the organ of the OAS entrusted with the competence to promote the observance and respect of human rights. For the purpose of the Statutes, human rights are understood to be the rights set forth in the American Declaration in relation to States not parties to the American Convention on Human Rights (San José, 1969). (Articles 1 and 2 of 1960 Statute and article 1 of 1979 Statute).

18. The first violation denounced in the petition concerns article I of the American Declaration of Rights and Duties of Man: "Every human being has the right to life . . . ". The petitioners admitted that the Declaration does not respond "when life begins," "when a pregnancy product becomes a human being" or other such questions. However, they try to answer these fundamental questions with two different arguments:

a) The *travaux preparatoires*, the discussion of the draft Declaration during the IX International Conference of American States at Bogotá in 1948 and the final vote, demonstrate that the intention of the Conference was to protect the right to life "from the moment of conception."

b) The American Convention on Human Rights, promulgated to advance the Declaration's high purposes and to be read as a corollary document, gives a definition of the right to life in article 4.1: "This right shall be protected by law from the moment of conception."

A brief legislative history of the Declaration does not support the petitioner's argument, as may be concluded from the following information and documents:

a) Pursuant to Resolution XL of the Inter-American Conference on Problems of War and Peace (Mexico, 1945), the Inter-American Juridical Committee of Río de Janeiro, formulated a preliminary draft of an International Declaration of the Rights and Duties of Man to be considered by the Ninth International Conference of American States (Bogotá, 1948). This preliminary draft was used by the Conference as a basis of discussion in conjuction with the draft of a similar Declaration prepared by the United Nations in December, 1947.

b) Article 1—Right to Life—of the draft submitted by the Juridical Committee reads: "Every person has the right to life. This right extends to the right to life from the moment of conception; to the right to life of incurables, imbeciles and the insane. Capital punishment may only be applied in cases in which it has been prescribed by pre-existing law for crimes of exceptional gravity." (Novena Conferencia International Americana—*Actas y Documentos* Vol. V Pág. 449).

c) A Working Group was organized to consider the observations and amendments introduced by the Delegates and to prepare an acceptable document. As a result of its work, the Group submitted to the Sixth Committee a new draft entitled *American Declaration of the Fundamental Rights and Duties of Man*, article I of which reads: "Every human being has the right to life, liberty, security and integrity of the person."

d) This completely new article I and some substantial changes introduced by the Working Group in other articles has been explained, in its Report of the Working Group to the Committee, as a compromise to resolve the problems raised by the Delegations of Argentina, Brazil, Cuba, United States of America, Mexico, Peru, Uruguay and Venezuela, mainly as consequence of the conflict existing between the laws of those States and the draft of the Juridical Committee. (*Actas y Documentos* Vol. 5, pp. 474–484, 495–504, 513–515).

e) In connection with the right to life, the definition given in the Juridical Committee's draft was incompatible with the laws governing the death penalty and abortion in the majority of the American States. In effect, the acceptance of this absolute concept—the right to life from the moment of conception—would imply the obligation to derogate the articles of the Penal Codes in force in 1948 in many countries because such articles excluded the penal sanction for the crime of abortion if performed in one or more of the following cases: A-when necessary to save the life of the mother; B-to interrupt the pregnancy of the victim of a rape; C-to protect the honor of an honest woman; D-to prevent the transmission to the fetus of a hereditary or contagious disease; E-for economic reasons (angustia económica).

f) In 1948, the American States that permitted abortion in one of such cases and, consequently, would be affected by the adoption of article I of the Juridical Committee, were; Argentina—article 86 n.1, 2 (cases A and B); Brasil—article n. I, II (A and B); Costa Rica—article 199 (A); Cuba—article 443 (A, B and D); Ecuador—article 423 n.l, 2 (A and B); Mexico (Distrito y Territorios Federales)—articles 333e, 334 (A and B); Nicaragua—article 399 (frustrated attempt) (C); Paraguay—article 352 (A); Peru—article 163 (A-to save the life or health of the mother); Uruguay—article 328 n. 1–5 (A, B, C. and F—the abortion must be performed in the three first months from conception); Venezuela—article 435 (A); United States of America—see the State laws and precedents; Puerto Rico SS 266, 267 (A) (*Códigos Penales Iberoamericanos*—Luis Jiménez de Asua—Editorial Andrés Bello—Caracas, 1946—volúmenes I y II).

g) On April 22, 1948, the new article I of the Declaration prepared by the Working Group was approved by the Sixth Committee with a slight change in the wording of the Spanish text (there was no official English text at that stage) (*Actas y Documentos*) vol. V pages 510–516 and 578). Finally, the definitive text of the Declaration in Spanish, English, Portuguese and French was approved by the 7th plenary Session of the Conference on April 30, 1948, and the Final Act was signed May 2nd. The only difference in the final text is the elimination of the word "integrity" (*Actas y Documentos* vol. VI pages 297–298; vol. I pages 231, 234, 236, 260, 261).

h) Consequently, the defendant is correct in challenging the petitioners' assumption that article 1 of the Declaration has incorporated the notion that the right of life exists from the moment of conception. Indeed, the conference faced this question but chose not to adopt language which would clearly have stated that principle.

20. The second argument of the petitioners, related to the possible use of the Convention as an element for the interpretation of the Declaration requires also a study of the motives that prevailed at the San José Diplomatic Conference with the adoption of the definition of the right to life.

21. The Fifth Meeting of Consultation of Ministers of Foreign Affairs of the OAS, held at Santiago, Chile in 1959, entrusted the Inter-American Council of Jurists with the preparation of a draft of the Convention on Human Rights contemplated by the American States since the Mexico Conference in 1945.

22. The draft, concluded by the Commission in about two weeks, developed the American Declaration of Bogotá, but has been influenced also by other sources, including the work in course at the United Nations. It consists of 88 articles, beginning with a definition of the right to life (Article 2), which reintroduced the concept that "This right shall be protected by law from the moment of conception." (*Inter-American Yearbook*, 1968—Organization of American States, Washington, 1973—pages 67, 237.)

23. The Second Special Conference of Inter-American States (Rio de Janeiro, 1965) considered the draft of the Council with two other drafts presented by the Governments of Chile and Uruguay, respectively, and asked the Council of the OAS, in cooperation with the IACHR, to prepare the draft of the Convention to be submitted to the diplomatic conference to be called for this purpose.

24. The Council of the OAS, considering the Opinion enacted by the IACHR on the draft convention prepared by the Council of Jurists, give a mandate to Convention to be submitted as working document to the San José conference (Yearbook, 1968, pages 73–93.)

25. To accommodate the views that insisted on the concept "from the moment of conception," with the objection raised, since the Bogota Conference, based on the legislation of American States that permitted abortion, *inter alia*, to save the mother's life, and in case of rape, the IACHR, redrafting article 2 (Right to life), decided, by majority vote, to introduce the words "in general." This compromise was the origin of the new text of article 2:1. Every person has the right to have his

life respected. This right shall be protected by law, *in general*, from the moment of conception." (*Yearbook*, 1968, page 321.)

26. The rapporteur of the *Opinion* proposed, at this second opportunity for discussion of the definition of the right of life, to delete the entire final phrase " . . . in general, from the moment of conception." He repeated the reasoning of his dissenting opinion in the Commission based on the abortion laws in force in the majority of the American States, with an addition: "to avoid any possibility of conflict with article 6, paragraph 1, of the United Nations Covenant on Civil and Political Rights, which states this right in a general way only." (*Yearbook*, 1968—page 97).

27. However, the majority of the Commission believed that, for reasons of principle, it was fundamental to state the provision on the protection of the right to life in the form recommended to the Council of the OAS in its Opinion (Part One). It was accordingly decided to keep the text of paragraph 1 without change. (*Yearbook*, 1968, page 97).

28. In the Diplomatic Conference that approved the American Convention, the Delegations of Brazil and the Dominican Republic introduced separate amendments to delete the final phrase of paragraph 1 of article 3 (Right to life) "in general, from the moment of conception". The United States delegation supported the Brazilian position. (*Conferencia Especializada Interamericana sobre Derechos Humanos—Actas Documentos*—Washington 1978 (reprinted)—pages 57, 121 y 160.)

29. Conversely, the Delegation of Ecuador supported the deletion of the words "and in general". Finally, by majority vote, the Conference adopted the text of the draft submitted by the IACHR and approved by the Council of the OAS, which became the present text of article 4, paragraph 1, of the American Convention (ACTAS Y DOCUMENTOS—pages 160 and 481.)

30. In the light of this history, it is clear that the petitioners' interpretation of the definition given by the American Convention on the right to life is incorrect. The addition of the phrase "in general, from the moment of conception" does not mean that the drafters of the Convention intended to modify the concept of the right to life that prevailed in Bogota, when they approved the American Declaration. The legal implications of the clause "in general, from the moment of conception" are substantially different from the shorter clause "from the moment of conception" as appears repeatedly in the petitioners' briefs.

31. However, accepting *gratia argumentandi*, that the American Convention had established the absolute concept of the right to life from the moment of conception—it would be impossible to impose upon the United States Government or that of any other State Member of the OAS, by means of "interpretation," an international obligation based upon a treaty that such State has not duly accepted or ratified.

32. The question of what reservation to article I of the Convention should be admissible, as suggested by President Jimmy Carter in his Letter of Transmittal to the Senate on February 23, 1978, has no direct link with the objective of the petition. This is not the appropriate place or opportunity for the consideration of this matter.

33. The other rights which the petitioners contend were violated—Articles II, VII and XI of the American Declaration—have no direct relation to the facts set forth

in the petition, including the decision of the U.S. Supreme Court and the Supreme Judicial Court of Massachusetts which were challenged in this case.

Boso v. Italy, (App. 50490/99), Eur. Ct.H.R. Rep. 2002-VII, Admissibility Decision of Sept. 5, 2002.

[The applicant challenged Italian Law no. 194 of 1978, by virtue of which his wife had been able to terminate her pregnancy, as a violation of Article 2 of the European Convention.]

. . . .

The Court considers that it is not required to determine whether the foetus may qualify for protection under the first sentence of Article 2. . . . Even supposing that, in certain circumstances, the foetus might be considered to have rights protected by Article 2 of the Convention, the Court notes that in the instant case, although the applicant did not state the number of weeks that had elapsed before the abortion or the precise grounds on which it had been carried out, it appears from the evidence that his wife's pregnancy was terminated in conformity with section 5 of Law no. 194 of 1978.

In this connection, the Court notes that the relevant Italian legislation authorises abortion within the first twelve weeks of a pregnancy if there is a risk to the woman's physical or mental health. Beyond that point, an abortion may be carried out only where continuation of the pregnancy or childbirth would put the woman's life at risk, or where it has been established that the child will be born with a condition of such gravity as to endanger the woman's physical or mental health. It follows that an abortion may be carried out to protect the woman's health.

In the Court's opinion, such provisions strike a fair balance between, on the one hand, the need to ensure protection of the foetus and, on the other, the woman's interests. Having regard to the conditions required for the termination of pregnancy and to the particular circumstances of the case, the Court does not find that the respondent State has gone beyond its discretion in such a sensitive area (see *H. v. Norway*, no. 17004/90, Commission decision of 19 May 1992, DR 73, p. 155).

It follows that this complaint must be dismissed as being manifestly ill-founded, pursuant to Article 35 §§ 3 and 4 of the Convention.

. . .

VO v. France [GC], (App. no. 53924/00), Judgment of 8 July 2004, Eur. Ct. H.R.

[The applicant complained that the French authorities breached Article 2 by refusing to classify as unintentional homicide the negligent taking of her unborn child's life.]

5. Unlike Article 4 of the American Convention on Human Rights, which provides that the right to life must be protected "in general, from the moment of conception", Article 2 of the Convention is silent as to the temporal limitations of the right to life and, in particular, does not define "everyone" ("*toute personne*") whose

"life" is protected by the Convention. The Court has yet to determine the issue of the "beginning" of "everyone's right to life" within the meaning of this provision and whether the unborn child has such a right.

To date it has been raised solely in connection with laws on abortion. Abortion does not constitute one of the exceptions expressly listed in paragraph 2 of Article 2, but the Commission has expressed the opinion that it is compatible with the first sentence of Article 2 § 1 in the interests of protecting the mother's life and health because "if one assumes that this provision applies at the initial stage of the pregnancy, the abortion is covered by an implied limitation, protecting the life and health of the woman at that stage, of the 'right to life' of the foetus" (see *X v. the United Kingdom*, Commission decision cited above, p. 253).

6. Having initially refused to examine *in abstracto* the compatibility of abortion laws with Article 2 of the Convention (see *X v. Norway*, no. 867/60, Commission decision of 29 May 1961, Collection of Decisions, vol. 6, p. 34, and *X v. Austria*, no. 7045/75, Commission decision of 10 December 1976, DR 7, p. 87), the Commission acknowledged in *Brüggemann and Scheuten* (cited above) that women complaining under Article 8 of the Convention about the Constitutional Court's decision restricting the availability of abortions had standing as victims. It stated on that occasion: " . . . pregnancy cannot be said to pertain uniquely to the sphere of private life. Whenever a woman is pregnant her private life becomes closely connected with the developing foetus" (ibid., p. 116, § 59). However, the Commission did not find it "necessary to decide, in this context, whether the unborn child is to be considered as 'life' in the sense of Article 2 of the Convention, or whether it could be regarded as an entity which under Article 8 § 2 could justify an interference 'for the protection of others' " (ibid., p. 116, § 60). It expressed the opinion that there had been no violation of Article 8 of the Convention because "not every regulation of the termination of unwanted pregnancies constitutes an interference with the right to respect for the private life of the mother" (ibid., pp. 116–17, § 61), while emphasising: "There is no evidence that it was the intention of the Parties to the Convention to bind themselves in favour of any particular solution" (ibid., pp. 117–18, § 64).

7. In *X v. the United Kingdom* (cited above), the Commission considered an application by a man complaining that his wife had been allowed to have an abortion on health grounds. While it accepted that the potential father could be regarded as the "victim" of a violation of the right to life, it considered that the term "everyone" in several Articles of the Convention could not apply prenatally, but observed that "such application in a rare case—e.g. under Article 6, paragraph 1—cannot be excluded" (p. 249, § 7; for such an application in connection with access to a court, see *Reeve v. the United Kingdom*, no. 24844/94, Commission decision of 30 November 1994, DR 79-A, p. 146). The Commission added that the general usage of the term "everyone" ("*toute personne*") and the context in which it was used in Article 2 of the Convention did not include the unborn. As to the term "life" and, in particular, the beginning of life, the Commission noted a "divergence of thinking on the question of where life begins" and added: "While some believe that it starts already with conception, others tend to focus upon the moment of nidation, upon the point that the foetus becomes 'viable', or upon live birth" (*X v. the United Kingdom*, p. 250, § 12).

The Commission went on to examine whether Article 2 was "to be interpreted: as not covering the foetus at all; as recognising a 'right to life' of the foetus with certain implied limitations; or as recognising an absolute 'right to life' of the foetus" (ibid. p. 251, § 17). Although it did not express an opinion on the first two options, it categorically ruled out the third interpretation, having regard to the need to protect the mother's life, which was indissociable from that of the unborn child: "The 'life' of the foetus is intimately connected with, and it cannot be regarded in isolation of, the life of the pregnant woman. If Article 2 were held to cover the foetus and its protection under this Article were, in the absence of any express limitation, seen as absolute, an abortion would have to be considered as prohibited even where the continuance of the pregnancy would involve a serious risk to the life of the pregnant woman. This would mean that the 'unborn life' of the foetus would be regarded as being of a higher value than the life of the pregnant woman" (ibid., p. 252, § 19). The Commission adopted that solution, noting that by 1950 practically all the Contracting Parties had "permitted abortion when necessary to save the life of the mother" and that in the meantime the national law on termination of pregnancy had "shown a tendency towards further liberalisation" (ibid., p. 252, § 20).

8. In *H. v. Norway* (cited above), concerning an abortion carried out on non-medical grounds against the father's wishes, the Commission added that Article 2 required the State not only to refrain from taking a person's life intentionally but also to take appropriate steps to safeguard life (p. 167). It considered that it did not have to decide "whether the foetus may enjoy a certain protection under Article 2, first sentence", but did not exclude the possibility that "in certain circumstances this may be the case notwithstanding that there is in the Contracting States a considerable divergence of views on whether or to what extent Article 2 protects the unborn life" (ibid.). It further noted that in such a delicate area the Contracting States had to have a certain discretion, and concluded that the mother's decision, taken in accordance with Norwegian legislation, had not exceeded that discretion (p. 168).

9. . . . .

10. It follows from this recapitulation of the case-law that in the circumstances examined to date by the Convention institutions—that is, in the various laws on abortion—the unborn child is not regarded as a "person" directly protected by Article 2 of the Convention and that if the unborn do have a "right" to "life", it is implicitly limited by the mother's rights and interests. The Convention institutions have not, however, ruled out the possibility that in certain circumstances safeguards may be extended to the unborn child. That is what appears to have been contemplated by the Commission in considering that "Article 8 § 1 cannot be interpreted as meaning that pregnancy and its termination are, as a principle, solely a matter of the private life of the mother" (see *Brüggemann and Scheuten*, cited above, pp. 116–17, § 61) and by the Court in the above-mentioned *Boso* decision. It is also clear from an examination of these cases that the issue has always been determined by weighing up various, and sometimes conflicting, rights or freedoms claimed by a woman, a mother or a father in relation to one another or *vis-à-vis* an unborn child.

2. Approach in the instant case

11. The special nature of the instant case raises a new issue. The Court is faced with a woman who intended to carry her pregnancy to term and whose unborn child was expected to be viable, at the very least in good health. Her pregnancy had to be terminated as a result of an error by a doctor and she therefore had to have a therapeutic abortion on account of negligence by a third party. The issue is consequently whether, apart from cases where the mother has requested an abortion, harming a foetus should be treated as a criminal offence in the light of Article 2 of the Convention, with a view to protecting the foetus under that Article. This requires a preliminary examination of whether it is advisable for the Court to intervene in the debate as to who is a person and when life begins, in so far as Article 2 provides that the law must protect "everyone's right to life".

12. As is apparent from the above recapitulation of the case-law, the interpretation of Article 2 in this connection has been informed by a clear desire to strike a balance, and the Convention institutions' position in relation to the legal, medical, philosophical, ethical or religious dimensions of defining the human being has taken into account the various approaches to the matter at national level. This has been reflected in the consideration given to the diversity of views on the point at which life begins, of legal cultures and of national standards of protection, and the State has been left with considerable discretion in the matter, as the opinion of the European Group on Ethics in Science and New Technologies at the European Commission appositely puts it: "the . . . Community authorities have to address these ethical questions taking into account the moral and philosophical differences, reflected by the extreme diversity of legal rules applicable to human embryo research . . . It is not only legally difficult to seek harmonisation of national laws at Community level, but because of lack of consensus, it would be inappropriate to impose one exclusive moral code".

It follows that the issue of when the right to life begins comes within the margin of appreciation which the Court generally considers that States should enjoy in this sphere, notwithstanding an evolutive interpretation of the Convention, a "living instrument which must be interpreted in the light of present-day conditions" (see *Tyrer v. the United Kingdom*, judgment of 25 April 1978, Series A no. 26, pp. 15–16, § 31, and subsequent case-law). The reasons for that conclusion are, firstly, that the issue of such protection has not been resolved within the majority of the Contracting States themselves, in France in particular, where it is the subject of debate and, secondly, that there is no European consensus on the scientific and legal definition of the beginning of life.

. . . .

13. At European level, the Court observes that there is no consensus on the nature and status of the embryo and/or foetus, although they are beginning to receive some protection in the light of scientific progress and the potential consequences of research into genetic engineering, medically assisted procreation or embryo experimentation. At best, it may be regarded as common ground between States that the embryo/foetus belongs to the human race. The potentiality of that being and its capacity to become a person—enjoying protection under the civil law, moreover,

in many States, such as France, in the context of inheritance and gifts, and also in the United Kingdom—require protection in the name of human dignity, without making it a "person" with the "right to life" for the purposes of Article 2. The Oviedo Convention on Human Rights and Biomedicine, indeed, is careful not to give a definition of the term "everyone", and its explanatory report indicates that, in the absence of a unanimous agreement on the definition, the member States decided to allow domestic law to provide clarification for the purposes of the application of that Convention. The same is true of the Additional Protocol on the Prohibition of Cloning Human Beings and the Additional Protocol on Biomedical Research, which do not define the concept of "human being". It is worth noting that the Court may be requested under Article 29 of the Oviedo Convention to give advisory opinions on the interpretation of that instrument.

14. Having regard to the foregoing, the Court is convinced that it is neither desirable, nor even possible as matters stand, to answer in the abstract the question whether the unborn child is a person for the purposes of Article 2 of the Convention ("*personne*" in the French text). As to the instant case, it considers it unnecessary to examine whether the abrupt end to the applicant's pregnancy falls within the scope of Article 2, seeing that, even assuming that that provision was applicable, there was no failure on the part of the respondent State to comply with the requirements relating to the preservation of life in the public-health sphere. With regard to that issue, the Court has considered whether the legal protection afforded the applicant by France in respect of the loss of the unborn child she was carrying satisfied the procedural requirements inherent in Article 2 of the Convention.

15. In that connection, it observes that the unborn child's lack of a clear legal status does not necessarily deprive it of all protection under French law. However, in the circumstances of the present case, the life of the foetus was intimately connected with that of the mother and could be protected through her, especially as there was no conflict between the rights of the mother and the father or of the unborn child and the parents, the loss of the foetus having been caused by the unintentional negligence of a third party.

16. In *Boso*, cited above, the Court said that even supposing that the foetus might be considered to have rights protected by Article 2 of the Convention, Italian law on the voluntary termination of pregnancy struck a fair balance between the woman's interests and the need to ensure protection of the unborn child. In the present case, the dispute concerns the involuntary killing of an unborn child against the mother's wishes, causing her particular suffering. The interests of the mother and the child clearly coincided. The Court must therefore examine, from the standpoint of the effectiveness of existing remedies, the protection which the applicant was afforded in seeking to establish the liability of the doctor concerned for the loss of her child *in utero* and to obtain compensation for the abortion she had to undergo. The applicant argued that only a criminal remedy would have been capable of satisfying the requirements of Article 2 of the Convention. The Court does not share that view, for the following reasons.

17. The Court reiterates that the first sentence of Article 2, which ranks as one of the most fundamental provisions in the Convention and also enshrines one of

the basic values of the democratic societies making up the Council of Europe (see *McCann and Others v. the United Kingdom*, judgment of 27 September 1995, Series A no. 324, pp. 45–46, § 147), requires the State not only to refrain from the "intentional" taking of life, but also to take appropriate steps to safeguard the lives of those within its jurisdiction (see, for example, *L.C.B. v. the United Kingdom*, judgment of 9 June 1998, *Reports of Judgments and Decisions* 1998-III, p. 1403, § 36).

18. Those principles apply in the public-health sphere too. The positive obligations require States to make regulations compelling hospitals, whether private or public, to adopt appropriate measures for the protection of patients' lives. They also require an effective independent judicial system to be set up so that the cause of death of patients in the care of the medical profession, whether in the public or the private sector, can be determined and those responsible made accountable (see *Powell v. the United Kingdom* (dec.), no. 45305/99, ECHR 2000-V, and *Calvelli and Ciglio*, cited above, § 49).

19. Although the right to have third parties prosecuted or sentenced for a criminal offence cannot be asserted independently (see *Perez v. France* [GC], no. 47287/99, § 70, ECHR 2004-I), the Court has stated on a number of occasions that an effective judicial system, as required by Article 2, may, and under certain circumstances must, include recourse to the criminal law. However, if the infringement of the right to life or to physical integrity is not caused intentionally, the positive obligation imposed by Article 2 to set up an effective judicial system does not necessarily require the provision of a criminal-law remedy in every case. In the specific sphere of medical negligence, "the obligation may for instance also be satisfied if the legal system affords victims a remedy in the civil courts, either alone or in conjunction with a remedy in the criminal courts, enabling any liability of the doctors concerned to be established and any appropriate civil redress, such as an order for damages and for the publication of the decision, to be obtained. Disciplinary measures may also be envisaged" (see *Calvelli and Ciglio*, cited above, § 51; *Lazzarini and Ghiacci v. Italy* (dec.), no. 53749/00, 7 November 2002; and *Mastromatteo v. Italy* [GC], no. 37703/97, § 90, ECHR 2002-VIII).

. . . .

20. The Court accordingly concludes that, even assuming that Article 2 was applicable in the instant case, there has been no violation of Article 2 of the Convention.

Questions and Comments

1. To what extent do the decisions in the above cases follow the canons of interpretation set out in the Vienna Convention? To what extent should they?

2. How should one interpret an omission? Does the rejection of the second sentence of the original draft of Article 1 of the American Declaration ("This right extends to the right to life from the moment of conception; to the right to life of incurables, imbeciles and the insane.") necessarily lead to the conclusion reached by the Commission? What does the omission mean for incurables and others mentioned in the same sentence?

3. Is the fetus a human being under the Inter-American Commission decision? A person? Are the two different? Could the fetus be seen as both and still not have a protectable right to life? Is Article XXVIII of the American Declaration relevant to the interpretation of Article I?

4. May the American Convention be used to interpret the rights contained in the American Declaration? What about the reverse situation? Once a state has ratified the American Convention, what happens to the rights in the Declaration that are not guaranteed by the Convention? Convention Articles 26 and 29 as well as the Protocol of San Salvador are implicated in the treatment of economic, social and cultural rights contained in the Declaration. This issue is discussed further in the next section of the Chapter.

5. If the Foreign Minister's office in Canada sought your advice on the question of whether or not its law allowing broad access to abortions violates the American Convention, what would you reply? What options does Canada have if it seeks to maintain its law as it is and ratify the American Convention?

6. What does the Inter-American Court mean in saying that developments in human rights law distinguish it from classical international law to a significant extent? What is an *erga omnes* obligation? Are all human rights protections *erga omnes* obligations? If not, what criteria distinguish *erga omnes* obligations?

7. Does the American Declaration prohibit capital punishment? In *Roach and Pinkerton v. the U.S.*, the Inter-American Commission found that the U.S. had violated the right to life guaranteed by the American Declaration by executing two juveniles. Res. 3/87, *Annual Rep. I-A Comm. H.R. 1985–87*, OEA/Ser.L/V/II.71, doc. 9, rev. 1, at 148. How much of an impact do such decisions have on U.S. law and practice? See *Thompson v. Oklahoma*, 108 S.Ct. 2687 (1988); *Sanford v. Kentucky*, 109 S.Ct. 2969 (1989) and, most recently, *Roper v. Simmons*, 543 U.S. 551 (2005). See also Carly Baetz-Stangel, *The Role of International Law in the Abolition of the Juvenile Death Penalty*, 16 FLA. J. INT'L L. 955 (2005) and *Soering v. United Kingdom*, European Court of Human Rights, Judgment of July 7, 1989, 11 HRLJ 335 (1990), finding that the "death row phenomenon" in the United States constitutes cruel, inhuman or degrading treatment.

8. Other cases at the Inter-American Commission challenging U.S. death penalty practices include: *Domingues v. United States*, Case 12.285, Inter-Am. C.H.R., Report No. 62/02 (merits), OEA/Ser.L/V/II.116, Doc. 33 (Oct. 22, 2002); *Napoleon Beazley v. United States*, Case 12.412, Inter-Am. C.H.R., Report No. 101/03 (merits), OEA/Ser./L/V/II.114 Doc. 70 rev. 1 (Dec. 29, 2003); *Gary Graham v. United States*, Case No. 11.193, Inter-Am. C.H.R., Report No. 97/03 (merits), OEA/Ser./L/V/II.114 Doc. 70 rev. 1 (Dec. 29, 2003); *Douglas Christopher Thomas v. United States*, Case No. 12.240, Inter-Am. C.H.R. Report No. 100/03 (merits), OEA/Ser./L/V/II.114 Doc. 70 rev. 1, (Dec. 29, 2003).

9. The African Commission has stated: "The right to life is the fulcrum of all other rights. It is the fountain through which other rights flow, and any violation of this right without due process amounts to arbitrary deprivation of life." Comm. 223/98, *Forum of Conscience v. Sierra Leone*, 14th Ann.Rep.Afr.Comm.H.P.R. 2000–2001, para. 19 of the decision. Is this as far as the African Commission can go on the issue of the death penalty? Could it be argued today that capital punishment is prohibited by customary international law?

ii. Economic, Social and Cultural Rights

The regional systems began with quite different approaches to economic, social and cultural rights. The European system enshrined them in a separate treaty system, the European Social Charter, adopted in 1961. The American Convention contains a single article on the topic, Art. 26. In contrast, the African Charter, like the American and Universal Declarations fully includes economic, social and cultural rights, as well as civil and political rights. The different approaches are accompanied by differences in the compliance mechanisms. Even where the rights are justiciable, human rights tribunals sometimes consider it appropriate to afford a wide margin of appreciation to states parties in respect to such rights, where issues of economic policy and availability of resources come into play.

The differences in the regional systems on this issue reflect the considerable academic and political debate over the content and proper procedures to implement economic and social rights, but they also reflect the different conditions within each region. The following cases from each of the systems indicate how litigants and the regional bodies approach matters of economic and social rights. It is notable that the underlying problems are not all that different in the cases included, but the characterization given them differs considerably. Could the *SERAC* case have been brought in the European system by reformulating it and asserting civil and political rights were violated? Could the *Taskin* case be litigated as a case of economic and social rights in the African system? If the cases are interchangeable, but only the specific rights invoked change, can civil and political rights and economic, social and cultural rights be separated or are they truly indivisible and interdependent?

For further reading see: D. Beetham, *What Future for Economic and Social Rights?* 43 POLITICAL STUDIES 41 (1995); Amartya Sen, *Freedom and Needs*, THE NEW REPUBLIC (Jan. 10 and 17, 1994) 31; P. HUNT, RECLAIMING SOCIAL RIGHTS: INTERNATIONAL AND COMPARATIVE Perspectives (1996); A. EIDE, C. KRAUSE & A. ROSAS (EDS) ECONOMIC, SOCIAL AND CULTURAL RIGHTS: A TEXTBOOK (1994).

Africa

The Social and Economic Rights Action Center and the Center for Economic and Social Rights (SERAC) v. Nigeria, (Comm. 155/96), *15th Annual Activity Report of the Afr. Comm. H.P.R. 2001–2002*, Annex V, pp. 31–44, decision of October 27, 2001.

. . . .

1. The present Communication alleges a concerted violation of a wide range of rights guaranteed under the African Charter for Human and Peoples' Rights. Before we venture into the inquiry whether the Government of Nigeria has violated the said rights as alleged in the Complaint, it would be proper to establish what is generally expected of governments under the Charter and more specifically vis-à-vis the rights themselves.

2. Internationally accepted ideas of the various obligations engendered by human rights indicate that all rights—both civil and political rights and social and economic—generate at least four levels of duties for a State that undertakes to adhere to a rights regime, namely the duty to respect, protect, promote, and fulfil these rights. These obligations universally apply to all rights and entail a combination of negative and positive duties. As a human rights instrument, the African Charter is not alien to these concepts and the order in which they are dealt with here is chosen as a

matter of convenience and in no way should it imply the priority accorded to them. Each layer of obligation is equally relevant to the rights in question.[23]

3. At a primary level, the obligation to **respect** entails that the State should refrain from interfering in the enjoyment of all fundamental rights; it should respect right-holders, their freedoms, autonomy, resources, and liberty of their action.[24] With respect to socio economic rights, this means that the State is obliged to respect the free use of resources owned or at the disposal of the individual alone or in any form of association with others, including the household or the family, for the purpose of rights-related needs. And with regard to a collective group, the resources belonging to it should be respected, as it has to use the same resources to satisfy its needs.

4. At a secondary level, the State is obliged to **protect** right-holders against other subjects by legislation and provision of effective remedies.[25] This obligation requires the State to take measures to protect beneficiaries of the protected rights against political, economic and social interferences. Protection generally entails the creation and maintenance of an atmosphere or framework by an effective interplay of laws and regulations so that individuals will be able to freely realize their rights and freedoms. This is very much intertwined with the tertiary obligation of the State to **promote** the enjoyment of all human rights. The State should make sure that individuals are able to exercise their rights and freedoms, for example, by promoting tolerance, raising awareness, and even building infrastructures.

5. The last layer of obligation requires the State to **fulfill** the rights and freedoms it freely undertook under the various human rights regimes. It is more of a positive expectation on the part of the State to move its machinery towards the actual realization of the rights. This is also very much intertwined with the duty to promote mentioned in the preceding paragraph. It could consist in the direct provision of basic needs such as food or resources that can be used for food (direct food aid or social security).[26]

6. Thus States are generally burdened with the above set of duties when they commit themselves under human rights instruments. Emphasizing the all embracing nature of their obligations, the International Covenant on Economic, Social, and Cultural Rights, for instance, under Article 2(1), stipulates exemplarily that States *"undertake to take steps . . . by all appropriate means, including particularly the adoption of legislative measures."* Depending on the type of rights under consideration, the level of emphasis in the application of these duties varies. But sometimes, the need to meaningfully enjoy some of the rights demands a concerted action from the State in terms of more than one of the said duties. Whether the government of Nigeria has, by its conduct, violated the provisions of the African Charter as claimed by the Complainants is examined here below.

---

[23] See generally, Asbjørn Eide, *Economic, Social and Cultural Rights As Human Rights* in Asbjørn Eide, Catarina Krause and Allan Rosas (eds.) ECONOMIC, SOCIAL, AND CULTURAL RIGHT: A TEXTBOOK (1995) PP. 21–40.

[24] Krzysztof Drzewicki, *Internationalization of Human Rights and Their Juridization* in Raija Hanski and Markku Suksi (Eds.), Second Revised Edition, AN INTRODUCTION TO THE INTERNATIONAL PROTECTION OF HUMAN RIGHTS: A TEXTBOOK (1999), p. 31.

[25] Drzewicki, *ibid.*

[26] *See* Eide, in Eide, Krause and Rosas, *op cit.*, p. 38.

7. In accordance with Articles 60 and 61 of the African Charter, this communication is examined in the light of the provisions of the African Charter and the relevant international and regional human rights instruments and principles. The Commission thanks the two human rights NGOs who brought the matter under its purview: the Social and Economic Rights Action Center (Nigeria) and the Center for Economic and Social Rights (USA). Such is a demonstration of the usefulness to the Commission and individuals of *actio popularis*, which is wisely allowed under the African Charter. It is a matter of regret that the only written response from the government of Nigeria is an admission of the gravamen of the complaints which is contained in a *note verbale. . . .* In the circumstances, the Commission is compelled to proceed with the examination of the matter on the basis of the uncontested allegations of the Complainants, which are consequently accepted by the Commission.

8. The Complainants allege that the Nigerian government violated the right to health and the right to clean environment as recognized under Articles 16 and 24 of the African Charter by failing to fulfill the minimum duties required by these rights. This, the Complainants allege, the government has done by:

- Directly participating in the contamination of air, water and soil and thereby harming the health of the Ogoni population,
- Failing to protect the Ogoni population from the harm caused by the NNPC Shell Consortium but instead using its security forces to facilitate the damage
- Failing to provide or permit studies of potential or actual environmental and health risks caused by the oil operations. . . .

9. These rights recognise the importance of a clean and safe environment that is closely linked to economic and social rights in so far as the environment affects the quality of life and safety of the individual.[27] As has been rightly observed by Alexander Kiss, "an environment degraded by pollution and defaced by the destruction of all beauty and variety is as contrary to satisfactory living conditions and the development as the breakdown of the fundamental ecologic equilibria is harmful to physical and moral health."[28]

10. The right to a general satisfactory environment, as guaranteed under Article 24 of the African Charter or the right to a healthy environment, as it is widely known, therefore imposes clear obligations upon a government. It requires the State to take reasonable and other measures to prevent pollution and ecological degradation, to promote conservation, and to secure an ecologically sustainable development and use of natural resources. Article 12 of the International Covenant on Economic, Social and Cultural Rights (ICESCR), to which Nigeria is a party, requires governments to take necessary steps for the improvement of all aspects of environmental and industrial hygiene. The right to enjoy the best attainable state of physical and mental health enunciated in Article 16(1) of the African Charter and the right to a general satisfactory environment favourable to development (Article 16(3)) already noted obligate governments to desist from directly threatening

---

[27] See also General Comment No. 14 (2000) of the Committee on Economic, Social and Cultural rights.
[28] HUMAN RIGHTS IN THE TWENTY FIRST CENTURY: A Global Challenge, edited by Kathleen E. Mahoney and Paul Mahoney; article by Alexander Kiss, *Concept and Possible Implications of the Right to Environment* at 553.

the health and environment of their citizens. The State is under an obligation to re-spect the just noted rights and this entails largely non-interventionist conduct from the State for example, not from carrying out, sponsoring or tolerating any practice, policy or legal measures violating the integrity of the individual.[29]

11. Government compliance with the spirit of Articles 16 and 24 of the African Charter must also include ordering or at least permitting independent scientific monitoring of threatened environments, requiring and publicizing environmental and social impact studies prior to any major industrial development, undertaking appropriate monitoring and providing information to those communities exposed to hazardous materials and activities and providing meaningful opportunities for individuals to be heard and to participate in the development decisions affecting their communities.

12. We now examine the conduct of the government of Nigeria in relation to Articles 16 and 24 of the African Charter. Undoubtedly and admittedly, the gov-ernment of Nigeria, through NNPC has the right to produce oil, the income from which will be used to fulfill the economic and social rights of Nigerians. But the care that should have been taken as outlined in the preceding paragraph and which would have protected the rights of the victims of the violations complained of was not taken. To exacerbate the situation, the security forces of the government en-gaged in conduct in violation of the rights of the Ogonis by attacking, burning and destroying several Ogoni villages and homes.

13. The Complainants also allege a violation of Article 21 of the African Charter by the government of Nigeria. The Complainants allege that the Military govern-ment of Nigeria was involved in oil production and thus did not monitor or regulate the operations of the oil companies and in so doing paved a way for the Oil Consor-tiums to exploit oil reserves in Ogoniland. Furthermore, in all their dealings with the Oil Consortiums, the government did not involve the Ogoni Communities in the decisions that affected the development of Ogoniland. The destructive and self-ish role played by oil development in Ogoniland, closely tied with repressive tactics of the Nigerian Government, and the lack of material benefits accruing to the local population,[30] may well be said to constitute a violation of Article 21. . . .

14. The origin of this provision may be traced to colonialism, during which the human and material resources of Africa were largely exploited for the benefit of outside powers, creating tragedy for Africans themselves, depriving them of their birthright and alienating them from the land. The aftermath of colonial exploitation has left Africa's precious resources and people still vulnerable to foreign misappro-priation. The drafters of the Charter obviously wanted to remind African govern-ments of the continent's painful legacy and restore co-operative economic develop-ment to its traditional place at the heart of African Society.

15. Governments have a duty to protect their citizens, not only through appro-priate legislation and effective enforcement but also by protecting them from dam-

---

[29] See Scott Leckie, *The Right to Housing, in* ECONOMIC, Social and Cultural Rights (eds) Eide, Krause and Rosas, (Martinus Nijhoff Publishers 1995).

[30] See a report by the Industry and Energy Operations Division West Central Africa Department "De-fining an Environmental Development Strategy for the Niger Delta" Volume 1—Paragraph B(1.6–1.7) at Page 2–3.

aging acts that may be perpetrated by private parties *(See Union des Jeunes Avocats /Chad*[31]). This duty calls for positive action on part of governments in fulfilling their obligation under human rights instruments. The practice before other tribunals also enhances this requirement as is evidenced in the case *Velàsquez Rodríguez v. Honduras.*[32] In this landmark judgment, the Inter-American Court of Human Rights held that when a State allows private persons or groups to act freely and with impunity to the detriment of the rights recognized, it would be in clear violation of its obligations to protect the human rights of its citizens. Similarly, this obligation of the State is further emphasized in the practice of the European Court of Human Rights, in *X and Y v. Netherlands.*[33] In that case, the Court pronounced that there was an obligation on authorities to take steps to make sure that the enjoyment of the rights is not interfered with by any other private person.

16. The Commission notes that in the present case, despite its obligation to protect persons against interferences in the enjoyment of their rights, the Government of Nigeria facilitated the destruction of the Ogoniland. Contrary to its Charter obligations and despite such internationally established principles, the Nigerian Government has given the green light to private actors, and the oil Companies in particular, to devastatingly affect the well-being of the Ogonis. By any measure of standards, its practice falls short of the minimum conduct expected of governments, and therefore, is in violation of Article 21 of the African Charter.

17. The Complainants also assert that the Military government of Nigeria massively and systematically violated the right to adequate housing of members of the Ogoni community under Article 14 and implicitly recognized by Articles 16 and 18(1) of the African Charter. . . .

18. Although the right to housing or shelter is not explicitly provided for under the African Charter, the corollary of the combination of the provisions protecting the right to enjoy the best attainable state of mental and physical health, cited under Article 16 above, the right to property, and the protection accorded to the family forbids the wanton destruction of shelter because when housing is destroyed, property, health, and family life are adversely affected. It is thus noted that the combined effect of Articles 14, 16 and 18(1) reads into the Charter a right to shelter or housing which the Nigerian Government has apparently violated.

19. At a very minimum, the right to shelter obliges the Nigerian government not to destroy the housing of its citizens and not to obstruct efforts by individuals or communities to rebuild lost homes. The State's obligation to respect housing rights requires it, and thereby all of its organs and agents, to abstain from carrying out, sponsoring or tolerating any practice, policy or legal measure violating the integrity of the individual or infringing upon his or her freedom to use those material or other resources available to them in a way they find most appropriate to satisfy individual, family, household or community housing needs.[34] Its obligations to protect obliges it to prevent the violation of any individual's right to housing by any other individual or non-state actors like landlords, property developers, and land owners,

---

[31] Communication 74/92.

[32] *See*, Inter-Am. Ct Hum. Rts, *Velàsquez Rodrígeuz* Case, Judgment of July 19, 1988, Series C, No. 4.

[33] 91 ECHR (1985) (Ser. A) at 32.

[34] Scott Leckie, *The Right to Housing in* Eide, Krause and Rosas, *op cit.*, 107–123, at p. 113.

and where such infringements occur, it should act to preclude further deprivations as well as guaranteeing access to legal remedies.[35] The right to shelter even goes further than a roof over ones head. It extends to embody the individual's right to be let alone and to live in peace—whether under a roof or not.

20. The protection of the rights guaranteed in Articles 14, 16 and 18 (1) leads to the same conclusion. As regards the earlier right, and in the case of the Ogoni People, the Government of Nigeria has failed to fulfill these two minimum obligations. The government has destroyed Ogoni houses and villages and then, through its security forces, obstructed, harassed, beaten and, in some cases, shot and killed innocent citizens who have attempted to return to rebuild their ruined homes. These actions constitute massive violations of the right to shelter, in violation of Articles 14, 16, and 18(1) of the African Charter.

21. The particular violation by the Nigerian Government of the right to adequate housing as implicitly protected in the Charter also encompasses the right to protection against forced evictions. The African Commission draws inspiration from the definition of the term "forced evictions" by the Committee on Economic Social and Cultural Rights which defines this term as "the permanent removal against their will of individuals, families and/or communities from the homes and/or which they occupy, without the provision of, and access to, appropriate forms of legal or other protection."[36] Wherever and whenever they occur, forced evictions are extremely traumatic. They cause physical, psychological and emotional distress; they entail losses of means of economic sustenance and increase impoverishment. They can also cause physical injury and in some cases sporadic deaths. . . . Evictions break up families and increase existing levels of homelessness.[37] In this regard, General Comment No. 4 (1991) of the Committee on Economic, Social and Cultural Rights on the right to adequate housing states that "all persons should possess a degree of security of tenure which guarantees legal protection against forced eviction, harassment and other threats" (E/1992/23, annex III. Paragraph 8(a)). The conduct of the Nigerian government clearly demonstrates a violation of this right enjoyed by the Ogonis as a collective right.

22. The Communication argues that the right to food is implicit in the African Charter, in such provisions as the right to life (Art. 4), the right to health (Art. 16) and the right to economic, social and cultural development (Art. 22). By its violation of these rights, the Nigerian Government trampled upon not only the explicitly protected rights but also upon the right to food implicitly guaranteed.

23. The right to food is inseparably linked to the dignity of human beings and is therefore essential for the enjoyment and fulfillment of such other rights as health, education, work and political participation. The African Charter and international law require and bind Nigeria to protect and improve existing food sources and to ensure access to adequate food for all citizens. Without touching on the duty to improve food production and to guarantee access, the minimum core of the right to food requires that the Nigerian Government should not destroy or contaminate

---

35 *Ibid.* pp. 113–114.
36 *See* General Comment No.7 (1997) on the right to adequate housing (Article 11.1): Forced Evictions.
37 *Ibid.* p. 113.

food sources. It should not allow private parties to destroy or contaminate food sources, and prevent peoples' efforts to feed themselves.

24. The government's treatment of the Ogonis has violated all three minimum duties of the right to food. The government has destroyed food sources through its security forces and State Oil Company; has allowed private oil companies to destroy food sources; and, through terror, has created significant obstacles to Ogoni communities trying to feed themselves. The Nigerian government has again fallen short of what is expected of it as under the provisions of the African Charter and international human rights standards, and hence, is in violation of the right to food of the Ogonis.

25. The Complainants also allege that the Nigerian Government has violated Article 4 of the Charter which guarantees the inviolability of human beings and everyone's right to life and integrity of the person respected. Given the wide spread violations perpetrated by the Government of Nigeria and by private actors (be it following its clear blessing or not), the most fundamental of all human rights, the right to life has been violated. The Security forces were given the green light to decisively deal with the Ogonis, which was illustrated by the widespread terrorizations and killings. The pollution and environmental degradation to a level humanly unacceptable has made it living in the Ogoni land a nightmare. The survival of the Ogonis depended on their land and farms that were destroyed by the direct involvement of the Government. These and similar brutalities not only persecuted individuals in Ogoniland but also the whole of the Ogoni Community as a whole. They affected the life of the Ogoni Society as a whole. The Commission conducted a mission to Nigeria from the 7th–14th March 1997 and witnessed first hand the deplorable situation in Ogoni land including the environmental degradation.

26. The uniqueness of the African situation and the special qualities of the African Charter on Human and Peoples' Rights imposes upon the African Commission an important task. International law and human rights must be responsive to African circumstances. Clearly, collective rights, environmental rights, and economic and social rights are essential elements of human rights in Africa. The African Commission will apply any of the diverse rights contained in the African Charter. It welcomes this opportunity to make clear that there is no right in the African Charter that cannot be made effective. As indicated in the preceding paragraphs, however, the Nigerian Government did not live up to the minimum expectations of the African Charter.

27. The Commission does not wish to fault governments that are laboring under difficult circumstances to improve the lives of their people. The situation of the people of Ogoniland, however, requires, in the view of the Commission, a reconsideration of the Government's attitude to the allegations contained in the instant communication. The intervention of multinational corporations may be a potentially positive force for development if the State and the people concerned are ever mindful of the common good and the sacred rights of individuals and communities. The Commission however takes note of the efforts of the present civilian administration to redress the atrocities that were committed by the previous military

administration as illustrated in the Note Verbale referred to in paragraph 30 of this decision.

For the above reasons, the Commission,

Finds the Federal Republic of Nigeria in violation of Articles 2, 4, 14, 16, 18(1), 21 and 24 of the African Charter on Human and Peoples' Rights;

Appeals to the government of the Federal Republic of Nigeria to ensure protection of the environment, health and livelihood of the people of Ogoniland by:

- Stopping all attacks on Ogoni communities and leaders by the Rivers State Internal Securities Task Force and permitting citizens and independent investigators free access to the territory;
- Conducting an investigation into the human rights violations described above and prosecuting officials of the security forces, NNPC and relevant agencies involved in human rights violations;
- Ensuring adequate compensation to victims of the human rights violations, including relief and resettlement assistance to victims of government sponsored raids, and undertaking a comprehensive cleanup of lands and rivers damaged by oil operations;
- Ensuring that appropriate environmental and social impact assessments are prepared for any future oil development and that the safe operation of any further oil development is guaranteed through effective and independent oversight bodies for the petroleum industry; and
- Providing information on health and environmental risks and meaningful access to regulatory and decision-making bodies to communities likely to be affected by oil operations.

Urges the government of the Federal Republic of Nigeria to keep the African Commission informed of the outcome of the work of:

- The Federal Ministry of Environment which was established to address environmental and environment related issues prevalent in Nigeria, and as a matter of priority, in the Niger Delta area including the Ogoni land;
- The Niger Delta Development Commission (NDDC) enacted into law to address the environmental and other social related problems in the Niger Delta area and other oil producing areas of Nigeria; and
- The Judicial Commission of Inquiry inaugurated to investigate the issues of human rights violations.

Questions and Comments

1. Do you agree that all rights in the African Charter may be made effective? Is this the same as saying that they are justiciable? Should they be? What are the corresponding state obligations? Are economic and social rights interpreted and applied differently from civil and political rights? Should they be? Note that few of the Commission's decisions to date have addressed substantive issues concerning economic, social and cultural rights. In addition to *SERAC*, above, see *Free Legal Assistance Group et al. v. Zaire*, where the Commission noted simply that the "failure of the Government to provide basic services such as

safe drinking water and electricity and the shortage of medicines" constitutes a violation of Article 16, which guarantees every individual the best attainable states of physical and mental health. The same decision concluded that the government's closure of secondary schools and universities violated the right to education under Article 17. Decision of April, 1996, 9th Ann. Activities Rep., reprinted at 4 *Int'l Hum. Rts. Rep.* 89 (1997) and 18 *HRLJ* 32 (1997).

2. Property rights were briefly addressed in *Constitutional Rights Project et al. v. Nigeria*, Comm. 105/93 *et al.*, Decision of October 31, 1998, 12th Ann. Activities Rep. ("The right to property necessarily includes a right to have access to property of one's own and the right that one's property not be removed."). On the linkages between civil and political rights with economic, social and cultural rights, *see* Chidi Odinkalu, *Analysis of Paralysis or Paralysis of Analysis? Implementing Economic, Social, and Cultural Rights Under the African Charter on Human and Peoples' Rights*, 23 Hum. Rts. Q. 327 (2001). Generally, *see* Chidi Odinkalu and Camilla Christensen, *The African Commission on Human and Peoples' Rights: The Development of Its Non-State Communications Procedures*, 20 Human Rts Q. 235 (1998).

3. In the *SERAC* case, one of the issues concerned alleged violations of the right to housing. Is there such a right in the African Charter? If it is not explicitly found in the text, is the Commission exceeding its mandate by implying the right to housing, or is it simply making use of its powers under Charter Articles 60 and 61? What is the government obligated to do? Contrast the following materials from the European system.

Europe

The next extracts examine aspects of the right to housing in the European system, beginning with the European Social Charter. For an overview of the Charter, see Chapter II (2)(A)(ii). The Charter has been referred to as "the counterpart, in the field of economic and social rights, of the much better known European Convention on Human Rights." Robin Churchill & Urfan Khaliq, *The Collective Complaints System of the European Social Charter: An Effective Mechanism for Ensuring Compliance with Economic and Social Rights?*, 15 Eur. J. Int'l L. 417 (2004). As Churchill & Khaliq note, the collective complaints mechanism was intended to enhance the effectiveness of the Charter, which previously relied on self-reporting by the states parties to supervise compliance. However, not all Council of Europe member states have accepted the system and it has not been widely used to date, making it difficult to judge its ability to induce changes in state performance on economic and social rights. The following materials provide a comparative example, using one case from the collective complaints procedure of the ESC and the other from the European Court of Human Rights. Consider the venues and types of cases that may be brought pursuant to the two treaties. Assuming the states in question are parties to both agreements, did the applicants have a choice of forum? If so, what would be the advantages and disadvantages of one procedure over the other? How do these cases compare to the African Commission's decision in *SERAC*?

European Roma Rights Centre v. Italy (Merits), European Committee of Social Rights, Complaint No. 27/2004, Dec. 7, 2005 (citations omitted)

. . . .

5. The ERRC alleges that the housing situation of Roma in Italy amounts to a violation of Article 31 of the Revised European Social Charter. In particular the ERRC alleges that Roma are denied an effective right to housing because of the shortage of and inadequate living conditions in camping sites, the forced evictions Roma are often subject to, and the fact that Roma have no access to accommodation other than camping sites. In addition, it alleges that segregationist policies and practices in the field of housing constitute racial discrimination contrary to Article 31 read alone or in conjunction with Article E. . . .

THE LAW

11. Articles 31 and E of the Revised European Social Charter and the first paragraph of the Appendix read as follows:

Article 31–The right to housing
With a view to ensuring the effective exercise of the right to housing, the Parties undertake to take measures designed:

    1. to promote access to housing of an adequate standard;

    2. to prevent and reduce homelessness with a view to its gradual elimination;

    3. to make the price of housing accessible to those without adequate resources.

Article E—Non-discrimination
The enjoyment of the rights set forth in this Charter shall be secured without discrimination on any ground such as race, colour, sex, language, religion, political or other opinion, national extraction or social origin, health, association with a national minority, birth or other status.

Paragraph 1 of the Appendix—Scope of the Revised European Social Charter in terms of persons protected

1. Without prejudice to Article 12, paragraph 4, and Article 13, paragraph 4, the persons covered by Articles 1 to 17 and 20 to 31 include foreigners only in so far as they are nationals of other Parties lawfully resident or working regularly within the territory of the Party concerned, subject to the understanding that these articles are to be interpreted in the light of the provisions of Articles 1 and 19. This interpretation would not prejudice the extension of similar facilities to other persons by any of the Parties.

ON THE ALLEGED VIOLATION OF ARTICLE 31 TAKEN TOGETHER WITH ARTICLE E

12. The Committee considers that the complaint raises three specific issues:

– the insufficient capacity of and inadequate living conditions in camping sites for Roma who choose to follow an itinerant lifestyle or who are forced to do so;

– the systematic eviction of Roma from sites or dwellings unlawfully occupied by them;

– the lack of permanent dwellings of an acceptable quality to meet the needs of Roma wishing to settle.

13. The Committee observes that in connection with each of these three issues the ERRC relies on both Article 31 as such and Article 31 taken together with Article E. The Committee considers that the discrimination Roma endure as regards housing on the Italian territory applies to all three aspects above. It follows that the Committee understands the arguments of the complainant as implying that the situation violates Article 31 taken together with Article E.

i) The Government's objection based on the scope of the Charter

14. Repeating the arguments presented at the admissibility stage, the Government considers that the complaint falls outside the personal and material scope of the Charter, and must therefore be declared inadmissible.

15. Firstly, the Government contends that the majority of Roma people in Italy do not fall within the personal scope of the Revised Charter because they do not meet the conditions laid down in Article 1 of the Appendix, namely that they are nationals of other parties lawfully resident or working regularly within the territory of the party concerned. It argues that the majority of Roma are either nationals of third countries or illegal migrants. Moreover, for the purposes of Article 31 the Government considers it impossible to distinguish Roma who are Italian citizens or nationals of other parties to the Charter or the Revised Charter, lawfully residing in Italian territory, within the total Roma population.

16. . . . .

17. The Government denies that Article E can be relied on to broaden the personal scope of the Revised Charter. It also rejects the comparison with other international conventions. Firstly, there is as yet no international customary rule granting a right to housing to all persons present in the territory of a state. Secondly, the explicit definition of personal scope in the Appendix to the Charter clearly indicates the intention of the Parties.

18. The Committee . . . notes that the parties do not question the fact that the groups covered by the complaint in fact include Italian citizens and nationals of parties to the Charter or the Revised Charter lawfully resident in Italy. It follows that the Italian Government's contention that it would be impossible "to separate the behaviours contested in a manner to apply the principle of Article 31 of the Charter only to those persons covered by the Charter itself" cannot prevent the Committee from exercising its authority to review the application of Article 31 of the Charter. Even assuming that, as the Government contends, it is impossible to distinguish among Roma to whom the protection afforded by Article 31 shall be compulsorily guaranteed and those Roma to whom, according to the Appendix (paragraph 1), the guarantee of such protection remains within the remit of States parties, the Committee does not see how such a circumstance would exempt the State from the obligation of ensuring that protection.

ii) Preliminary issues

Scope of Article 31

The Committee recalls that Article 31 is directed to the prevention of homelessness with its adverse consequences on individuals' personal security and well being. The right to housing secures social inclusion and integration of individuals into society and contributes to the abolishment of socio-economic inequalities.

Scope of Article E

19. The Committee recalls that in its decision on the right to housing of Roma in Greece it emphasised that "one of the underlying purposes of the social rights protected by the Charter is to express solidarity and promote social inclusion. It follows that States must respect difference and ensure that social arrangements are not such as would effectively lead to or reinforce social exclusion."

20. Similarly, equal treatment requires a ban on all forms of indirect discrimination, which can arise "by failing to take due and positive account of all relevant differences or by failing to take adequate steps to ensure that the rights and collective advantages that are open to all are genuinely accessible by and to all."

21. In this case, equal treatment implies that Italy should take measures appropriate to Roma's particular circumstances to safeguard their right to housing and prevent them, as a vulnerable group, from becoming homeless.

Data collection

22. The Government states that it does not possess precise data on the Roma population, not even the number of Roma who hold Italian citizenship.

23. The Committee recalls that when it is generally acknowledged that a particular group is or could be discriminated against, the state authorities have a responsibility for collecting data on the extent of the problem. The gathering and analysis of such data (with due safeguards for privacy and against other abuses) is indispensable to the formulation of rational policy. Similarly, if homelessness is to be progressively reduced as required by Article 31§2 of the Revised Charter, states will need the necessary factual information to deal with the problem. The regular collection of detailed information and statistics is a first step towards achieving this objective.

24. Finally, the Committee notes that when credible evidence is adduced alleging discrimination it becomes incumbent on the State party concerned to answer to the allegations by pointing to, for example, legislative or other measures introduced, statistics and examples of relevant case-law. More precise allegations call for more detailed response.

Responsibility of the state

25. In support of its claims, the Government states that local authorities are responsible for the management and upkeep of camping sites and that many regions (Calabria, Emilia-Romagna, Friuli-Venezia-Giulia, Lazio, Liguria, Piedmont, Sardinia, Tuscany, Veneto, and the Autonomous Province of Trento) and certain municipalities (Bologna and Rome) have adopted specific measures on behalf of their Roma and Sinti populations since 1984.

26. The Committee recalls that "even if under domestic law local or regional authorities, trade unions or professional organisations are responsible for exercising a particular function, states parties to the Charter are still responsible, under their international obligations to ensure that such responsibilities are properly exercised." Thus, ultimate responsibility for policy implementation, involving at a minimum

oversight and regulation of local action, lies with the Italian state. Moreover, as a signatory to the Revised Charter and the party against which complaints are lodged, the Government must be able to show that both local authorities and itself have taken practical steps to ensure that local action is effective.

iii) As to the alleged insufficiency and inadequacy of camping sites

27. The ERRC maintains that Roma camping sites fail to meet minimum living standards and amount to deliberate segregation by the Italian authorities in violation of Article 31 in combination with Article E.

28. Italy is accused of actively pursuing a policy of racial segregation and boasting of a network of ghettos aimed at preventing Roma from integrating into mainstream Italian society. Such a policy is based on the assumption that Roma and Sinti are "nomads" who can only live on the edges of society.

29. According to the ERRC, camping site facilities are inadequate, with limited or no access to basic amenities such as water, electricity and sewage and solid waste removal. Although three-quarters of the camps have running water and electricity, such services are not sufficient to meet the needs, while very few camps are provided with sewage facilities and even fewer with waste collection. Moreover, the majority of camps are infested with insects and rats and only one-third are surfaced with asphalt.

30. The ERRC states that when places have been allocated in camping sites, the normal size of Roma families has never been taken into account, as in the case of the Arrivore Camp in Turin.

31. The ERRC cites in support of its submissions the results of field studies carried out between 1999 and 2004 and interviews with representatives of NGOs active in the Roma field. The complaint provides detailed descriptions of the situation in many Roma camps throughout Italy. Additional factual information appears in the ERRC publication *Campland: Racial segregation of Roma in Italy* (appended to the complaint).

32. The Government contests all the allegations and affirms that national and local authorities have taken the appropriate legislative and regulatory measures, and that administrative and judicial protection is available. Furthermore, it adds that no evidence is provided by the complainant to support its allegations other than the statements of those concerned. According to the Government, appropriate action has been taken in circumstances where credible and concrete evidence has come to light.

33. The Government contends that "authorised" camps are meant for a specific number of persons and provided accordingly with basic amenities. Subsequent inadequacies result from the misbehaviour of the Roma community, who set up unauthorised camps or introduce into authorised camps new residents who were not originally catered for, actions for which the authorities are not responsible.

34. The Committee observes that other than referring to local authority regulations (which were only provided as an appendix to the last written submission by Italy), the Government has adduced no evidence to refute the complainant's allegations. Instead, on the one hand it claims to have taken all the necessary legal measures to safeguard Roma living conditions, while on the other it places responsibility

for such an inadequate situation on the Roma themselves, who would be responsible for having seriously damaged the facilities placed at their disposal. Similarly, the Government has not produced any evidence to show that the number of camps is sufficient, but has confined itself to recognising the existence of unauthorised camps, whose establishment is attributed to Roma misbehaviour.

35. Article 31§1 guarantees access to adequate housing, which means a dwelling which is structurally secure; safe from a sanitary and health point, i.e. it possesses all basic amenities, such as water, heating, waste disposal, sanitation facilities, electricity; not overcrowded and with secure tenure supported by law. The temporary supply of shelter cannot be considered as adequate and individuals should be provided with adequate housing within a reasonable period.

36. The Committee recalls that Article 31§1 E enshrines the prohibition of discrimination and establishes an obligation to ensure that, in absence of objective and reasonable justifications (see paragraph 1 of the Appendix), any group with particular characteristics, including Roma, benefit in practice from the rights in the Charter. On the contrary, by persisting with the practice of placing Roma in camps the Government has failed to take due and positive account of all relevant differences, or adequate steps to ensure their access to rights and collective benefits that must be open to all.

37. The Committee therefore finds that Italy failed to show that:

– it has taken adequate steps to ensure that Roma are offered housing of a sufficient quantity and quality to meet their particular needs;
– it has ensured or has taken steps to ensure that local authorities are fulfilling their responsibilities in this area.

The Committee therefore finds that the situation constitutes a violation of Article 31§1 taken together with Article E.

iv) As to forced evictions and other sanctions

38. The ERRC alleges that the practice of forced evictions, threats of forced eviction, systemic destruction of property and invasion of Roma dwellings by the Italian authorities is in violation of Article 31§1 in combination with Article E.

39. According to the ERRC, the Italian authorities frequently evict Roma from sites they have occupied for some time and provide no alternative housing or resettle them in at least substandard housing. It provides several examples of cases where Roma, both settled and itinerant, have been prosecuted for occupying unauthorised sites and following their eviction have been sent to other already overcrowded camps or left with no alternative solution (the 2004 eviction from the Via Adda 14 building in Milan for example). Evictions from unauthorised camping sites are allegedly often carried out without procedural safeguards, such as formal warrants, and are accompanied by the destruction of personal belongings (Camp Barzaghi, Camp Casilino 700). It is also claimed that when such evictions take place, Roma are regularly taken to a police station for identity checks, and if they are in the country unlawfully they are taken into custody and eventually deported. The ERRC asserts that these operations are often carried out at night or at dawn by police of-

ficers in riot gear who sometimes act violently (Camp Barzaghi, Casilino 700, Tor de' Cenci).

40. The Government challenges the allegations and states that the authorities try to secure the transfer of persons lawfully present in Italian territory to more appropriate accommodation. It also states that during the evictions reported by the complainant, at least in Rome and Milan (Via Adda 14 building and Camp Barzaghi), there were no acts of violence or misconduct recorded and all the actions were carried out on the basis of orders issued by the competent authorities and under the supervision of immigrants' or Roma organisations. In the Via Adda eviction, the 60 persons out of 263 who were lawfully present in Italy were transferred to a reception centre and the rest were taken to a police station for identity checks.

41. The Committee notes with regard to Article 31§2 that States Parties must make sure that evictions are justified and are carried out in conditions that respect the dignity of the persons concerned, and that alternative accommodation is available. The law must also establish eviction procedures, specifying when they may not be carried out (for example, at night or during winter), provide legal remedies and offer legal aid to those who need it to seek redress from the courts. Compensation for illegal evictions must also be provided.

42. The Committee finds that Italy has failed to establish that the relevant evictions it carried out satisfy these conditions, and has not provided credible evidence to refute the claims that Roma have suffered unjustified violence during such evictions. The Committee therefore considers that the situation constitutes a violation of Article 31§2 in combination with Article E.

v) As to the lack of permanent dwellings

43. The ERRC argues that the Italian authorities' policy of dismantling inadequate and overcrowded camping sites is not accompanied by any measures to offer the displaced Roma alternative accommodation. Eviction generally leads to the further establishment of substandard and inevitably racially segregated housing in camps or elsewhere. On the other hand, Roma are largely denied access to social housing. Access is regulated by a points system the criteria of which, such as the nature and length of the residence permit or the type of previous dwelling, are hard for Roma to meet. Similarly, it is not much easier for Roma who have been granted refugee status to obtain housing.

44. The Government denies that Roma are discriminated against in the allocation of social housing since anyone fulfilling the objective criteria is entitled to such accommodation. The Government does not specify what form these criteria take.

45. The Committee recalls that Article 31§1 guarantees access to adequate housing. Under Article 31§3 it is incumbent on States Parties to adopt appropriate measures for the construction of housing, in particular social housing. Furthermore, they must ensure access to social housing for disadvantaged groups, including equal access for nationals of other Parties to the Charter lawfully residents or regularly working on their territory.

46. The Committee acknowledges that the State Party is committed to the principle of equal treatment for Roma as regards access to social housing, but has failed to provide any information to show that this right of access is effective in practice

or that the criteria regulating access to social housing are not discriminatory. The Committee recalls that the principle of non-discrimination in Article E includes also indirect discrimination. Its failure to take into consideration the different situation of Roma or to introduce measures specifically aimed at improving their housing conditions, including the possibility for an effective access to social housing, means that Italy is in violation of Article 31§§1 and 3 taken together with Article E.

CONCLUSION

For these reasons, the Committee concludes

- – Unanimously that the insufficiency and inadequacy of camping sites constitute a violation of Article 31§1 of the European Social Charter taken together with Article E;
- – Unanimously that forced eviction and other sanctions constitute a violation of Article 31§2 of the European Social Charter taken together with Article E;
- – Unanimously that the lack of permanent dwellings constitutes a violation of Articles 31§1 and 31§3 of the European Social Charter taken together with Article E.

The Committee of Ministers subsequently adopted Resolution ResChS(2006)4, *Collective complaint No. 27/2004 by the European Roma Rights Centre against Italy, May 3, 2006*, in which it noted the measures already taken by the Italian authorities at the local and national levels and the government's undertaking to bring the situation into conformity with the Revised Charter by increasing such measures, including the adoption of a legislative framework. The Committee said it was looking forward to Italy reporting that the situation had improved in its next report concerning the relevant provisions of the Revised European Social Charter.

Taskin and Others v. Turkey, App. No. 46117/99 Eur.Ct.H.R. (Nov. 10, 2004)

. . . .

11. The case concerns the granting of permits to operate a gold mine in Ovacýk, in the district of Bergama (Izmir). The applicants live in Bergama and the surrounding villages. . . .

13. The applicants alleged that, as a result of the Ovacýk gold mine's development and operations, they had suffered and continued to suffer the effects of environmental damage; specifically, these include the movement of people and noise pollution caused by the use of machinery and explosives.

. . . .

THE LAW

II. ON THE ALLEGED VIOLATION OF ARTICLE 8 OF THE CONVENTION

103. The applicants alleged that both the national authorities' decision to issue a permit to use a cyanidation operating process in a gold mine and the related decision-making process had given rise to a violation of their rights guaranteed by Article 8 of the Convention. . . .

1. Applicability of Article 8

111. The Court notes, firstly, that the applicants live in Dikili and in the villages of Çamköy and Süleymaniye, localities situated near the Ovacýk gold mine, where gold is extracted by sodium cyanide leaching.

112. Several reports have highlighted the risks posed by the gold mine. On the basis of those reports, the Supreme Administrative Court concluded on 13 May 1997 that the decision to issue a permit had not been compatible with the public interest. It found that, given the gold mine's geographical location and the geological features of the region, the use of sodium cyanide in the mine represented a threat to the environment and the right to life of the neighbouring population, and that the safety measures which the company had undertaken to implement did not suffice to eliminate the risks involved in such an activity.

113. The Court points out that Article 8 applies to severe environmental pollution which may affect individuals' well-being and prevent them from enjoying their homes in such a way as to affect their private and family life adversely, without, however, seriously endangering their health (see *López Ostra v. Spain*, judgment of 9 December 1994, Series A no. 303-C, § 51).

The same is true where the dangerous effects of an activity to which the individuals concerned are likely to be exposed have been determined as part of an environmental impact assessment procedure in such a way as to establish a sufficiently close link with private and family life for the purposes of Article 8 of the Convention. If this were not the case, the positive obligation on the State to take reasonable and appropriate measures to secure the applicant's rights under paragraph 1 of Article 8 would be set at nought.

114. In view of the Supreme Administrative Court's finding in its judgment of 13 May 1997, the Court concludes that Article 8 is applicable.

Compliance with Article 8

115. The Court points out that in a case involving State decisions affecting environmental issues there are two aspects to the inquiry which it may carry out. First, the Court may assess the substantive merits of the national authorities' decision to ensure that it is compatible with Article 8. Secondly, it may scrutinise the decision-making process to ensure that due weight has been accorded to the interests of the individual (see, *mutatis mutandis, Hatton and Others v. the United Kingdom* [GC], No. 36022/97, § 99, ECHR 2003-VIII).

a) The substantive aspect

116. The Court has repeatedly stated that in cases raising environmental issues the State must be allowed a wide margin of appreciation (see *Hatton and Others*, cited above, § 100, and *Buckley v. the United Kingdom*, judgment of 25 September 1996, *Reports of Judgments and Decisions* 1996-IV, §§ 74-77).

117. In the instant case, the Court notes that the authorities' decision to issue a permit to the Ovacýk gold mine was annulled by the Supreme Administrative Court. After weighing the competing interests in the present case against each other, the latter based its decision on the applicants' effective enjoyment of the right to life and the right to a healthy environment and concluded that the permit did not serve the

public interest (*ibid*). In view of that conclusion, no other examination of the material aspect of the case with regard to the margin of appreciation generally allowed to the national authorities in this area is necessary. Consequently, it remains for the Court to verify whether, taken as a whole, the decision-making process was conducted in a manner which complied with the procedural guarantees in Article 8.

b) The procedural aspect

118. The Court reiterates that, according to its settled case-law, whilst Article 8 contains no explicit procedural requirements, the decision-making process leading to measures of interference must be fair and such as to afford due respect to the interests of the individual as safeguarded by Article 8 (see, *mutatis mutandis*, *McMichael v. the United Kingdom*, judgment of 24 February 1995, Series A No. 307-B, p. 55, § 87). It is therefore necessary to consider all the procedural aspects, including the type of policy or decision involved, the extent to which the views of individuals were taken into account throughout the decision-making process, and the procedural safeguards available (see *Hatton and Others*, cited above, § 104). However, this does not mean that decisions can only be taken if comprehensive and measurable data are available in relation to each and every aspect of the matter to be decided.

119. Where a State must determine complex issues of environmental and economic policy, the decision-making process must firstly involve appropriate investigations and studies in order to allow them to predict and evaluate in advance the effects of those activities which might damage the environment and infringe individuals' rights and to enable them to strike a fair balance between the various conflicting interests at stake (see *Hatton and Others*, cited above, § 128). The importance of public access to the conclusions of such studies and to information which would enable members of the public to assess the danger to which they are exposed is beyond question (see, *mutatis mutandis*, *Guerra and Others v. Italy*, judgment of 19 February 1998, *Reports* 1998-I, p. 223, § 60, and *McGinley and Egan v. the United Kingdom*, judgment of 9 June 1998, *Reports* 1998-III, p. 1362, § 97). Lastly, the individuals concerned must also be able to appeal to the courts against any decision, act or omission where they consider that their interests or their comments have not been given sufficient weight in the decision-making process (see, *mutatis mutandis*, *Hatton and Others*, cited above, § 127).

120. In the instant case, the decision to issue a permit to the Ovacýk gold mine, taken on 19 October 1994 by the Ministry of the Environment, was preceded by a series of investigations and studies carried out over a long period. An impact report was drawn up in accordance with section 10 of the Environment Act. On 26 October 1992 a public information meeting was held for the region's inhabitants. During that meeting, the impact study was brought to the public's attention and participants had an opportunity to present their comments. The applicants and the inhabitants of the region had access to all the relevant documents, including the report in question.

121. When, on 13 May 1997, the Supreme Administrative Court, acting on an application for judicial review, annulled the decision of 19 October 1994, it cited the State's positive obligation concerning the right to life and the right to a healthy en-

vironment. Referring to the conclusions of the impact study and the other reports, it held that, due to the gold mine's geographical location and the geological features of the region, the operating permit did not serve the general interest; those studies had outlined the danger of the use of sodium cyanide for the local ecosystem, and human health and safety.

122. The judgment of 13 May 1997 became enforceable at the latest after being served on 20 October 1997; however, the Ovacýk gold mine was not ordered to close until 27 February 1998, i.e. ten months after the delivery of that judgment and four months after it had been served on the authorities.

123. As to the Government's argument that the authorities had complied fully with judicial decisions after 1 April 1998, it does not stand up to scrutiny. Firstly, the long dispute concerning the lawfulness of the permits issued by various ministries following the Prime Minister's intervention on 1 April 2000 was caused solely by the authorities' refusal to comply with the courts' decisions and with the domestic legislation. In fact, in the light of Paragraph 6 of the regulations on impact reports, those permits could have no legal basis in the absence of a decision, based on an impact report, to issue authorisation. Furthermore, no mention is made of any new decision that would replace the decision set aside by the courts.

Moreover, this argument by the Government has never been accepted by those domestic courts which have been called upon to rule on the lawfulness of subsequent decisions.

124. The Court would emphasise that the administrative authorities form one element of a State subject to the rule of law, and that their interests coincide with the need for the proper administration of justice. Where administrative authorities refuse or fail to comply, or even delay doing so, the guarantees enjoyed by a litigant during the judicial phase of the proceedings are rendered devoid of purpose (see, *mutatis mutandis*, *Hornsby v. Greece*, judgment of 19 March 1997, *Reports* 1997-II, pp. 510–511, § 41).

125. This finding appears all the more necessary in that the circumstances of the case clearly demonstrate that, notwithstanding the procedural guarantees afforded by Turkish legislation and the implementation of those guarantees by judicial decisions, the Council of Ministers, by a decision of 29 March 2002 which was not made public, authorised the continuation of production at the gold mine, which had already begun to operate in April 2001. In so doing, the authorities deprived the procedural guarantees available to the applicants of any useful effect.

c) Conclusion

126. The Court finds, therefore, that the respondent State did not fulfil its obligation to secure the applicants' right to respect for their private and family life, in breach of Article 8 of the Convention.

There has consequently been a violation of that provision.

[The Court also found a violation of Article 6(1) resulting from the Turkish authorities' refusal to comply with the judgments of the administrative courts, but found it unnecessary to address the complaints based on Articles 2 and 13. The Court awarded the applicants EUR 3,000 each in moral damages.]

Note on Environment and Health Cases in the ECHR: As the *Taskin* case indicates, despite the fact that the European Convention contains neither a right to health nor a right to environment, cases have been brought for injury due to pollution, invoking the right to life (Art. 2) and the right to information (Art. 10), as well as the right to privacy and family life (Art. 8). Decisions of the former Commission and the Court indicate that environmental harm attributable to state action or inaction that has significant injurious effect on a person's home or private and family life constitutes a breach of Article 8(1). The harm may be excused under Article 8(2) if it results from an authorized activity of economic benefit to the community in general, as long as there is no disproportionate burden on any particular individual; *i.e.* the measures must have a legitimate aim, be lawfully enacted, and be proportional. States enjoy a margin of appreciation in determining the legitimacy of the aim pursued.

The first major decision of the Court on environmental harm as a breach of the right to respect for privacy and the home was *Lopez-Ostra v. Spain*, 303-C Eur. Ct. H.R. (1994). The applicant and her daughter suffered serious health problems from the fumes of a tannery waste treatment plant which operated alongside the apartment building where they lived. The plant opened without a required license and without having followed the procedure for obtaining one. The applicant was eventually forced to move due to the pollution levels. The Court noted that severe environmental pollution may affect individuals' well-being and prevent them from enjoying their homes in such a way as to affect their private and family life. It found that the determination of whether this violation had occurred should be tested by striking a fair balance between the interest of the town's economic well-being and the applicant's effective enjoyment of her right to respect for her home and her private and family life. The Court found that the state exceeded its margin of appreciation and awarded compensation. See also *Anna Maria Guerra and 39 others against Italy*, 1998–1 ECHR, judgment of 19 February 1998.

Many of the European environmental cases invoking the protection of privacy and home life involve noise pollution. See *Arrondelle v. United Kingdom*, (1980)19 DR 186; (1982) 26 DR 5, in which the applicant complained of noise from Gatwick Airport and a nearby motorway; *Powell & Raynor v. United Kingdom*, 172 Eur.Ct. H.R. (1990), in which the Court found that aircraft noise from Heathrow Airport constituted a violation of Article 8, but was justified under Article 8(2) as "necessary in a democratic society" for the economic well-being of the country and was proportional if it did not "create an unreasonable burden for the person concerned," a test that could be met by the State if the individual had "the possibility of moving elsewhere without substantial difficulties and losses;" and *Hatton and Others v. The United Kingdom* (GC, 2003, 37 EHRR 28) applying a "fair balance" test and finding no violation due to aircraft noise from Heathrow Airport.

In *Oneryildiz v. Turkey* (GC, Nov. 30, 2004), the first environmental case involving loss of life, the Court held national authorities responsible for the deaths of the applicants' close relatives and for the destruction of their property due to a methane explosion at a municipal waste dump known to be in danger of such an explosion. See Chapter III (2). The Court held that Article 2 includes a positive obligation on states to take appropriate steps to safeguard the lives of those within their jurisdiction. This obligation extends to any activity, whether public or not, "in which the right to life may be at stake, and a fortiori in the case of industrial activities which by their very nature are dangerous, such as the operation of waste-collection sites." *Oneryildiz*, para. 71. The primary duty on the state is to put into place a legislative and administrative framework governing the licensing, setting up, operation, security and supervision of dangerous activities and must make it compulsory for all those concerned to take practical measures to ensure the effective protection of citizens whose lives might be endangered by the inherent risks. In this respect, the Court echoes some of the duties identified by the African Commission in *SERAC*. The Court included the public's right to information among the preventive measure that the state must take to protect the right to life, and found that the right to information "is supported by current developments in European standards," citing Parliamentary Assembly Resolution 587 (1975) on problems connected with the disposal of urban and industrial waste, Resolution 1087 (1996) on the consequences of the Chernobyl disaster, and Recommendation 1225 (1993) on the management, treatment, recycling and marketing of waste, as well as Committee of Ministers Recommendation R (96) 12 on the distribution of powers and responsibilities between central authorities and local and regional authorities with regard to the environment. The Court also mentioned the Convention on Civil Liability for Damage resulting from Activities Dangerous to the Environment (Lugano, 21 June 1993, ETS No. 150) and the Convention on the Protection of the Environment through Criminal Law (Strasbourg, 4 November 1998, ETS No. 172). These environmental measures together with Resolution 1087 (1996) made it obvious to the Court that public access to clear and full information about dangerous activities is a basic human right.

In the case of *Fadeyeva v. Russia*, App no. 55723/00, judgment of 9 June 2005, involving industrial pollution from a steel plant, the Court summarized its earlier jurisprudence, noting that Article 8 is not violated every time that environmental deterioration occurs: e.g., no right to nature preservation is as such included among the rights and freedoms guaranteed by the Convention. Thus, in order to raise an issue under Article 8 the interference must directly affect the applicant's home, family or private life. Moreover, the adverse effects of environmental pollution must attain a certain minimum level if they are to fall within the scope of Article 8. The assessment of that minimum is relative and depends on all the circumstances of the case, such as the intensity and duration of the nuisance, its physical or mental effects. The general environmental context should be also taken into account. There would be no arguable claim under Article 8 if the detriment complained of was negligible in comparison to the environmental hazards inherent to life in every modern city.

In applying its balancing test, the Court noted that in recent decades environmental pollution has become a matter of growing public concern. The Court reaffirmed that it will not substitute its judgment for those of national authorities as to the best policy to adopt in this respect, but it will continue to evaluate the domestic measures under a highly deferential standard of "manifest error of appreciation" by the national authorities in striking a fair balance between the competing interests of different private actors in this sphere. The Court will first examine the decision-making process for fairness and due respect for the interests of the individual guaranteed by Article 8, and only in exceptional circumstances will it go beyond this evaluation to revise the material conclusions of the domestic authorities. In this instance, the Court assessed the conduct of the parties, noting that the government had failed to comply with its domestic laws and that the individual lacked the information or ability to take action to protect herself. She had no realistic hope of being removed from the source of pollution. In contrast, the State had at its disposal a number of tools capable of preventing or minimizing the pollution. The Court recalled that its task was not to determine what exactly should have been done to reduce pollution in a more efficient way, but to assess whether the Government approached the problem with due diligence and gave consideration to all the competing interests. The Court reiterated that the State has the burden to justify, using detailed and rigorous data, a situation in which certain individuals bear a heavy burden on behalf of the rest of the community. In view of the materials before it, the Court could not conclude that, in regulating the steel-plant's industrial activities, the authorities gave due weight to the interests of persons living in close proximity to its premises.

Finally, the case of *Okyay and Others v. Turkey* (App. no. 36220/97, judgment of 12 July 2005) concerned the failure of Turkish authorities to enforce their own constitutional and statutory environmental laws. The applicants complained under Article 6 of the Convention that their right to a fair hearing had been breached on account of the administrative authorities' failure to enforce the judicial orders to halt the operations of the Yataðan, Gökova (Kemerköy) and Yeniköy thermal-power plants in the Muðla province of south-west Turkey. Relying on Article 56 of the Turkish Constitution[38] and section 3 (a) of the Environment Act, the applicants argued that it was their constitutional right to live in a healthy and balanced environment, and their duty to ensure the protection of the environment and to prevent environmental pollution. In examining this case, the European Court not only referred to the domestic law of Turkey, but also to Principle 10 of the 1992 Rio Declaration on Environment and Development and to Parliamentary Assembly Recommendation 1614 (2003) on Environment and Human Rights. Given the applicant's constitutional rights and the international law on point, the Court was satisfied that the applicants could arguably claim that they were entitled under Turkish law to protection against damage to the environment caused by the power plants' hazardous activities. It followed that there existed a genuine and serious "dispute" concerning a "civil right," thus Article 6 applied and had been violated.

In sum, environmental rights have found a place in the European system, despite the lack of reference to them in the Convention.

---

[38] Article 56 of the Constitution provides:
Everyone has the right to live in a healthy, balanced environment. It shall be the duty of the State and the citizens to improve and preserve the environment and to prevent environmental pollution. . . . The State shall perform this task by utilising and supervising health and social welfare institutions in both the public and private sectors. . . .

The Inter-American System:

The Inter-American region, like Africa, faces serious economic and social challenges that impact the enjoyment of all human rights. The legal protection of economic, social and cultural rights is complex. The Declaration includes the full range of rights: civil, political, economic, social and cultural. The Convention contains a single article on the topic, Article 26, entitled "Economic, Social and Cultural Rights." In 1988, the OAS adopted the Protocol of San Salvador, adding Economic and Social Rights, but specified that only the trade union rights of Article 8 and the right to education in Article 13 may be subject to the Convention's individual petition process. For the remaining rights, the Commission is given a mandate to formulate observations and recommendations to states, taking into account the progressive nature of the obligations. Protocol of San Salvador, Art. 19. The interaction of the various legal texts is the subject of debate. States not party to the Convention may be the object of petitions with respect to all the rights contained in the Declaration; is it possible that they may escape this procedure with respect to economic and social rights by ratifying the Convention? The following materials indicate the Commission's approach thus far and the debate among human rights scholars and activists on the justiciability of economic and social rights in the Inter-American system.

In its 1979–1980 annual report, the Commission first addressed the issue of economic and social rights, positing a relationship between neglect of them on the one hand "and suppression of political participation, on the other. That relationship, as has been shown, is in large measure one of cause and effect. In other words, neglect of economic and social rights, especially when political participation has been suppressed, produces the kind of social polarization that then leads to acts of terrorism by and against the government." The Commission made clear its view that failure to respect economic and social rights is a cause of violence and social conflicts, but noted that it had been

> extremely cautious in this sensitive area, because it recognized the difficulty of establishing criteria that would enable it to measure the states' fulfillment of their obligations. It has also seen the very difficult options that the governments face when allocating resources between consumption and investment, and, hence, between current and future generations. Economic policy and national defense policy are closely related to national sovereignty.

Annual Report of the Inter-American Commission on Human Rights, OAS Doc. OEA/Ser.L/V/II.50, Doc. 13 rev. 12 October 1980, Ch. VI.

Nonetheless, the Commission found a legal obligation and basis for its own supervision of compliance with that obligation:

> The essence of the legal obligation incurred by any government in this area is to strive to attain the economic and social aspirations of its people, by following an order that assigns priority to the basic needs of health, nutrition and education. The priority of the "rights of survival" and "basic needs" is a natural consequence of the right to personal security.
>
> According to development experts, life expectancy, infant mortality and illiteracy are the best indicators to measure the well-being of the population of a country,

and to evaluate the progress being made towards higher levels of economic and social well-being for the general populace.

. . . .

To date, there is no political or economic system or individual development model
that has demonstrated a clearly superior capability to promote economic and social
rights; but whatever the system or model may be, it must assign priority to attaining
those fundamental rights that make it possible to eliminate extreme poverty.

The Organization of American States and, in particular, the Inter-American Commission on Human Rights as the organ specifically charged with promoting and
defending human rights, is duty-bound to take a more active role in protecting
economic, social and cultural rights, just as it is with respect to civil and political
rights.

In this delicate and difficult question of the promotion of economic, social and cultural rights, the Commission cannot help but recognize that just as each government has an obligation to work to increase the national wealth and ensure its equitable distribution so that each and every one of the inhabitants of the respective
country may benefit thereby, the more developed countries have an obligation vis-
à-vis the less developed countries. Without solid support from the wealthy countries within the area, development of the poorer countries is almost impossible.

Id.

The Commission urged OAS member states to provide information concerning health, nutrition and literacy levels and the measures they were adopting to
improve those levels so that the Commission could expand its efforts to make economic and social rights effective. The following year, the Commission reported on
the reaction to its comments: "These considerations . . . were shared by the General Assembly, which reaffirmed in its resolutive paragraph 8 of Resolution 510
(X-0/80) the conviction of the IACHR that effective protection of human rights
should also extend to economic, social and cultural rights, and, in that regard, emphasized to the governments of economically more developed member states the
responsibility to make every possible effort to participate fully in cooperation for
hemispheric development, since it is a fundamental means of helping alleviate extreme poverty in the Americas, especially in the most needy countries and regions.
The Commission considers that the next General Assembly should reinforce this
commitment by adopting specific measures for the effective fulfillment of the
above-mentioned resolution." Annual Report of the Commission 1980–1981,
OEA/Ser.L/V/II.54, Doc. 9 rev. 116 October 1981, Ch. V. Beginning with country
reports on El Salvador (1978), Nicaragua (1981) and Guatemala (1981), the Commission started to examine economic, social and cultural rights as well as civil and
political rights in the hemisphere. Over a decade later, with support from the General Assembly, the Commission issued a broad statement on economic, social and
cultural rights:

Annual Report of the Inter-American Commission on Human Rights 1993,
OAS Doc OEA/Ser.L/V.85 Doc. 9 rev., 11 Feb. 1994, Ch. V.

I. The Realization of Economic, Social and Cultural Rights in the Region

. . . .

The Commission has prepared the following report on economic, social and cultural rights in response to the General Assembly's resolution AG/RES. 1213 (XXIII-0/93) which urges the Inter-American Commission on Human Rights ("Commission") to continue "its work in support of economic, social and cultural rights in order to contribute to the development of the member states."

The underlying premise of this report is the principle set forth in the General Assembly's resolution AG/RES. 1213 (XXIII-093):

> That the ideal of a free human being, *unfettered by fear or poverty*, can only be realized if conditions are established which permit individuals to enjoy their economic, social, and cultural rights, as well as their civil and political rights (emphasis supplied).

This resolution is itself inspired by the member states' commitment to the principles established in the OAS Charter. Article 33 of the Charter stipulates:

> that equality of opportunity, equitable distribution of wealth and income and the full participation of their peoples in decisions relating to their own development are, among others, basic objectives of integral development.

Moreover, in article 44(f) of the Charter, the member states agree to encourage:

> The incorporation and increasing participation of the marginal sectors of the population, in both rural and urban areas, in the economic, social, civic, cultural and political life of the nation, in order to achieve the full integration of the national community, acceleration of the process of social mobility, and the consolidation of the democratic system.

These principles are reaffirmed in the American Convention on Human Rights ("American Convention"), which, in Article 1, obliges the signatory states:

> to respect the rights and freedoms recognized herein and to ensure to all persons subject to their jurisdiction the *free and full exercise* of those rights and freedoms, *without any discrimination* for reasons of race, color, sex, language, religion, political or other opinion, national or social origin, *economic status*, birth, or any other social condition (emphasis supplied).

Article 26 of the American Convention articulates the principle of progressive development. It states:

> State Parties undertake to adopt measures, both internally and through international cooperation, especially those of an economic and technical nature, with a view to achieving progressively, by legislation or other appropriate means, the full realization of the rights implicit in the economic, social, educational, scientific, and cultural standards set forth in the Charter of the Organization of American States as amended by the Protocol of Buenos Aires.

The American Declaration of the Rights and Duties of Man ("Declaration") sets forth in its Preamble that the American peoples "have as their principal aim the protection of the essential rights of man and the creation of circumstances that will permit him to achieve spiritual and material progress . . ." The Declaration acknowledges that the initial system of protection it established was one suited to "the present social and juridical conditions, not without recognition (on the part of the American States) that they should increasingly strengthen that system in the international field as conditions become more favorable." The Declaration enumerates a list of civil and political rights as well as economic, social and cultural ones.

In light of the need to increasingly strengthen the system, the Additional Protocol to the American Convention on Human Rights Concerning Economic, Social and Cultural Rights ("Protocol of San Salvador") adopted by the General Assembly in 1988 signals a further commitment within the Inter-American human rights system to enforce these rights. The Protocol compiles in treaty form principles of social equality and individual rights set forth in earlier human rights instruments, including the OAS Charter and General Assembly Resolutions. Article 1 of the Protocol of San Salvador establishes that:

> The States Parties to this Additional Protocol to the American Convention on Human Rights undertake to adopt the necessary measures, both domestically and through international cooperation, especially economic and technical, to the extent allowed by their available resources, and taking into account their degree of development, for the purpose of achieving progressively and pursuant to their internal legislations, the full observance of the rights recognized in this Protocol.

Articles 10, 11, 12 and 13 of the Protocol of San Salvador guarantee the rights to health, a healthy environment, to food, and to education respectively. The respect for these rights guarantees basic needs for survival, which in combination with the other rights set forth in the Protocol, such as the right to work (Article 6), to just, equitable, and satisfactory conditions of work (Article 7), to trade union rights (Article 8), to social security (Article 9), to the benefits of culture (14), to the protection and formation of families (Article 15) etc., create the conditions "whereby everyone may enjoy his economic, social and cultural rights as well as his civil and political rights" (Preamble to Protocol).

I. The Indivisibility Of Civil And Political Rights, And Economic, Social And Cultural Rights

The Commission has always recognized "the organic relationship between the violation of the rights to physical safety on the one hand, and neglect of economic and social rights and the suppression of political participation. Any distinctions drawn between civil and political rights and economic, social and cultural rights are categorical formulations that detract from the promotion and guarantees of human rights.

Freedom from fear and want necessarily entails the guarantee of civil and political rights. Through popular participation those who are affected by the neglect of their economic and social rights are able to participate in the decisions that concern the allocation of national resources and the establishment of social, educational, and health care programs. Popular participation, which is the aim of a representative democracy, guarantees that all sectors of society have an input during the formulation, application and review of national policies. While, on one hand, it may be asserted that political participation enforces the protection of economic, social and cultural rights, at the same time, the implementation of these rights creates the condition in which the general population is able, i.e. is healthy and educated, to participate actively and productively in the political decision-making process.

The formalities of a democracy through the election of presidents and parliamentarians is not a strong enough foundation to ensure stable and enduring political and economic systems. This is demonstrated by the fact that despite the region's transition to democratic rule over the past decade, there has been a marked increase in the incidence of poverty which, in effect, endangers political stability in many of the region's states. For example, in 1980, 41% of the total population in Latin America were living below the poverty level. By the end of the decade, this number had risen to more than 45%.

Poverty is, in part, a result of a state's inadequate commitment and organization to protect and promote economic, social and cultural rights. As discussed above, the state's failure to guarantee economic, social and cultural rights, also signals a lack of civil and political guarantees. The ability to participate in society comprises civil and political rights, together with economic, social and cultural rights. It therefore follows that without progress in the area of economic and social rights, the pursuit of civil and political rights (which have been attained with great hardship and human sacrifice) will remain merely aspirations for particularly those sectors with the least resources and lowest levels of education. In the final analysis, the consolidation of representative democracy—a major goal of the member states—entails the exercise of full membership for *all* in society.

In this respect, the Commission cites Article 33 of the Charter which stipulates "that equality of opportunity, equitable distribution of wealth and income and the full participation of their peoples in decisions related to their own development are, among others, basic objectives of integral development."

When the most vulnerable members of society are denied access to the basic needs for survival which would enable them to break out of their condition, it results in the right to be free from discrimination; the right to the consequent principles of equality of access, equity and distribution; and the general commitment to protect the vulnerable elements in society being willingly or complicitly contravened. Moreover, without satisfaction of these basic needs, an individual's survival is directly threatened. This obviously diminishes the individual's rights to life, personal security, and as discussed above, the right to participate in the political and economic processes.

The Commission notes that poverty has its greatest impact on children. According to the Inter-American Children's Institute, 45% of Latin America's population are children, and around 50% of these live in conditions of extreme poverty. Extreme poverty is described as a condition of life so limited by malnutrition, disease, illiteracy, low life expectancy and high infant mortality as to be beneath any rational definition of human decency and dignity. Without food and access to basic health services, and with little or no education or no time to become educated, as they must either fend for themselves or help their families, these children remain trapped in a daily struggle for survival.

II. The Principle of Progressive Achievement

The principle that economic, social and cultural rights are to be achieved progressively does not mean that governments do not have the immediate obligation to make efforts to attain the full realization of these rights. The rationale behind the principle of progressive rights is that governments are under the obligation to ensure conditions that, according to the state's material resources, will advance gradually and consistently toward the fullest achievement of these rights.

Moreover, the progressive development of rights is not limited to economic, social and cultural rights but is applicable to and inherent in all human rights instruments as they are elaborated and expanded. Human rights treaties frequently include provisions which either implicitly or explicitly envision expansion of the rights contained therein. The method by which they are expanded may depend on the direct application of provisions set forth in the treaty itself, or through amendments or additional protocols that complement, elaborate or perfect rights already established in the treaty. An example is the evolution and expansion of the Inter-American human rights instruments. The principles articulated in the American Declaration of the Rights and Duties of Man were elaborated and expanded into the American Convention on Human Rights. Similarly, the Protocol of San Salvador is an extension of norms and principles set forth in the previous two texts as well as in the Charter.

It therefore follows that the obligation of member states to observe and defend the human rights of individuals within their jurisdictions, as set forth in both the American Declaration and the American Convention, obligates them, regardless of the level of economic development, to guarantee a minimum threshold of these rights. A state's level of development may be a factor that is calculated into the analysis of its implementation of these rights, but this is not a factor that precludes the state's obligation to implement, to the best of its abilities, these rights. Rather the principle of progressivity demands that as the level of development in a state improves, so must its level of commitment to guaranteeing economic, social and cultural rights. This follows because the guarantee of economic, social and cultural rights requires, in most instances, public expenditure for social programs.

In theory, the more resources a state has, the greater its ability to provide services that guarantee economic, social and cultural rights. This idea is affirmed in article 32 of the OAS Charter which describes development as the "primary responsibility of each country and should constitute an integral and *continuous process* for the establishment of a *more just* economic and social order . . ." (emphasis supplied). The Commission notes, however, that in view of the unequal distribution of wealth within the states in the region, coupled with other structural inadequacies (as will be discussed below), an increase in national revenues does not automatically translate into an improvement in the general welfare of the entire population. The commitment of states to take steps with the aim to achieving progressively the full realization of economic, social and cultural rights requires an effective use of resources available to guarantee a minimum standard of living for all.

III. Factors That Contribute To the Neglect of Economic, Social and Cultural Rights

In a joint 1993 Report published by the World Bank and the International Monetary Fund ("IMF"), Latin America is singled out as the region of the world with the most unequal distribution of wealth, a situation which has been worsening since the 1950s. The report explains that the poorest 20% of the population in Latin America and the Caribbean receives 4% of their national revenues whereas the richest 10% of the population in this region receives between 42–43% of the revenues. Similarly, the 1992 Human Development Report of the UNDP notes that while Latin America has some of the most advanced economies of the developing world, these countries at the same time, also have some of the sharpest contrasts between their social classes, with millions of people living below poverty levels.

Some examples set forth in the UNDP report are: Brazil which has one of the most unequal distributions of income in the world with the richest 20% of the population receiving 26 times the income of the poorest 20%; in Chile, between 1970 and 1988, the real income of the poorest 20% fell by 3% while that of the richest 20% increased by 10%. Similarly in the United States, the UNDP Report indicates that by desegregating the white, black and hispanic communities in terms of their purchasing power, education and health, there is a marked distinction that reflects the unequal access to education and basic health services. The white population in the United States, taken by itself, would rank number one in the world in terms of human development, whereas the black population would rank 31 and the hispanic population 35.

The 1991 UNDP Report indicates that Costa Rica has a good record for guaranteeing the basic needs of its people. Social reforms began in the 1940s following the abolishment of the Army and the subsequent creation of health, education, and social insurance institutions. Primary health care was emphasized beginning in the 1970s with rural and community health programs.

It is argued that the world economic recession during the 1980s, compounded by the foreign debt crisis that afflicts most member states, accounts for the incidence in poverty. On the other hand, however, the structural economic adjustments that many states in the region have implemented to make them eligible for international financial loans, have required drastic reductions precisely in the area of public expenditures at a time when the vulnerable groups in these societies are most in need of social programs. Thus, an unintentional result of these economic adjustment programs has in fact been a deepening of poverty. It is the poor who bear the majority of economic and social burdens wrought by restrictions in public expenditures.

Economic adjustments should not entail a decreased observance of human rights. Instead, they can be used to redress social imbalances and correct the structural violations that are built into the economic and social structures of countries in the region. In fact, the prevailing view on adjustment has recently altered. The World Bank and, to some extent, the International Monetary Fund have begun incorporating the need for poverty alleviation and social safety nets into their adjustment policies and programs.

IV. Country Reports

At the behest of the General Assembly, in June 1993, the Commission asked all member states to provide information on measures implemented to enhance economic, social and cultural rights. The Commission is appreciative of the efforts of member states that submitted reports regarding the status of these rights in their jurisdiction as well as reports that address that status of the rights of children, women, and the handicapped in their countries. In 1993, Canada, Chile, the Dominican Republic, El Salvador, Mexico, Nicaragua, Panama, Paraguay, and Venezuela submitted reports. These reports set forth the applicable laws that cover specific rights and also include, in many cases, programs of action that the respective governments have already implemented or intend to implement. Many of the reports also point out the failures and inequities within their systems.

. . . .

V. Analysis of the Effective Use and Allocation of Resources

In determining whether adequate measures have been taken to implement and secure economic, social and cultural rights, the Commission shall pay close attention to the equitable and effective use of available resources and the allocation of public expenditures to social programs that address the living conditions of the more vulnerable sectors of society which have been historically excluded from the political and economic processes.

. . . .

In general, throughout the region, there are unacceptable numbers of people who live in conditions that deny them a minimum level of material well-being which is able to guarantee respect of their rights to personal security, dignity, equality of opportunity and freedom from discrimination.

VI. Recommendations

In light of the above, the Commission recommends the following:

1. Member states should guarantee conditions that enable people to gain access to food, health services and education, and should fully enforce minimum wage laws. To this end, member states should reform basic economic and political structures that inhibit the development of such conditions.

2. When formulating domestic economic policies, member states should guarantee an economic environment that will enable the poor to participate in the political and economic decision-making processes. As an example, member states should promote respect for labor unions, including their rights to organize, bargain collectively and conduct strikes with the state playing a neutral role.

3. Member states should ensure that socially disadvantaged groups, particularly minorities, do not suffer disproportionately from economic adjustment measures.

4. When formulating the initial study for economic structural adjustment programs and the development and financial institutions with which they work, member states should avoid programs that exacerbate the conditions of the poor.

5. The Secretary General should appoint a Special Rapporteur to study and devise methods to monitor and supervise economic adjustment measures that affect the enjoyment of economic, social, and cultural rights. The Rapporteur's assignment should include the establishment of institutional arrangements between economic agencies, human rights agencies, and the states concerned.

6. States which have not yet done so should ratify the Additional Protocol to the American Convention on Human Rights in the Area of Economic, Social and Cultural Rights, "Protocol of San Salvador," and other relevant international instruments. States should establish legislation that makes those rights meaningful and effective.

7. Social data is critical to the development of plans for improving economic, social and cultural rights. Hence, member states should institute methods for social and economic data collection and report this information annually to the Executive Committees of the Inter-American Economic and Social Council and the Inter-American Council for Education, Science and Culture as stipulated in article 42 of the American Convention. In the process of preparing the reports, wide participation by citizens and nongovernmental organizations should be encouraged.

In the extract above, the Commission fails to discuss whether or not it has jurisdiction to accept petitions alleging violations of economic and social rights, but advocates have used a combination of the Declaration and Convention Article 26 to file such claims in recent years. The Commission has admitted at least one such petition, below, but some lawyers within the Commission's staff express the view that the Convention fully supercedes the Declaration and that Article 26 does not provide a basis for complaints to be filed on economic, social or cultural rights.

The Kichwa Peoples of the Sarayaku Community and Its Members v. Ecuador,
Report No. 64/04, Petition 167/03 (Admissibility), (Oct. 13, 2004)

1. On December 19, 2003, the Inter-American Commission on Human Rights received a petition lodged by the Association of Kichwa Peoples of Sarayaku, the Center for Justice and International Law (CEJIL), and the Center for Economic and Social Rights, alleging the responsibility of the Republic of Ecuador to the detriment of the Kichwa indigenous people of the Sarayaku community and its members.

2. The petitioners allege that the State is responsible for a series of acts and omissions harming the Kichwa peoples of Sarayaku because it has allowed an oil company to carry out activities on the ancestral lands of the Sarayaku community without its consent, it has persecuted community leaders, and has denied judicial protection and legal due process to the Sarayaku community. In addition, the State has allowed third parties to systematically violate the rights of the Sarayaku community. In light of the foregoing, they claim that the State is responsible for violating the fundamental individual and collective rights of the Sarayaku community and its members, specifically the right to property (Article 21), judicial protection (Article 25), due process (Article 8), freedom of movement (Article 22), personal integrity (Article 5),

personal liberty and security (Article 7), life (Article 4), freedom of association (Article 16), political participation (Article 23), freedom of expression (Article 13), juridical personality (Article 3), freedom of conscience and religion (Article 12), the rights of the child (Article 19), equality (Article 24), health and culture (Article 26, in accordance with Articles XI and XIII of the American Declaration of the Rights and Duties of Man) under the American Convention on Human Rights (hereinafter the "American Convention" or the "Convention"). They also allege that the State has failed to comply with its general obligations to respect and guarantee the aforementioned rights (Article 1(1)) and to adopt domestic legal provisions to make them effective (Article 2), both under the American Convention.

. . . .

4. The Commission concludes in this report, without prejudging the merits of the case, that the petition is admissible in accordance with Articles 46 and 47 of the Convention and that it will continue to analyze the alleged violations of Articles 4, 5, 7, 8, 12, 13, 16, 19, 21, 22, 23, 24, 25, 26 relative to Articles 1(1) and 2 of this instrument. It further decides to advise the parties of its decision and publish it in its Annual Report.

III. POSITIONS OF THE PARTIES

. . . .

22. In 1996, the Ecuadorian State signed a partnership contract with the Argentine company called the Compañía General de Combustible (hereinafter the "CGC" or the "oil company"), for oil exploration and exploitation on 200,000 hectares in the Pastaza province located in an area known as "Block 23" [*Bloque 23*]. Sixty-five percent of this block consists of the legal ancestral lands of the Sarayaku indigenous community. The petitioners claim that the participation contract between the State and the oil company was entered into without respect for the regulatory, constitutional, and conventional procedures set forth in domestic and international law. Moreover, this was done without consultation of the Sarayaku indigenous community and did not fulfill the requirement of obtaining the community's free and informed consent in order to carry out extractive activities on its territory.

23. The petitioners assert that, although the exploration phase was supposed to start in 1997 according to the contract, the CGC did not launch this phase of seismic prospecting until November 2002, four years after the new Ecuadorian Political Constitution took effect, and three years after Convention 169 on Indigenous and Tribal Peoples in Independent Countries of the International Labor Organization (hereinafter "ILO Convention 169") entered into force. The petitioners assert that, under the new Political Constitution and ILO Convention 169, it was incumbent upon the State to take all necessary measures to respect and ensure the rights of the Kichwa people of Sarayaku to their land, including the obligation to consult with them, to facilitate their participation in all decisions, and to seek their free and informed consent prior to commencing exploration activities.

24. The petitioners say that, beginning in 2002, when the oil company launched the seismic prospecting phase in Sarayaku territory, violations against the fundamental human rights of the Sarayaku people intensified to the extent that on November 25, 2002, the Governor of Pastaza province, the army headquarters of

Pastaza province, the Association of Sarayaku, the Confederation of Indigenous Nationalities of the Ecuadorian Amazon (CONFENIAE), and the Organization of Indigenous Peoples of Pastaza (OPIP) signed an agreement in which the CGC company pledged to respect the rights of the Sarayaku community.

25. On November 27, 2002, the Sarayaku people were declared to be under the protection of the Ecuadorian Ombudsman in a resolution stating that "all authorities, public officials, and natural and juridical persons shall observe, respect, attend to, and ensure the rights of the aforementioned Sarayaku community and all its members and, in particular, the right to maintain, develop, and strengthen its cultural identity and other aspects of its nationality, as well as to preserve its inalienable ownership of Sarayaku communal lands and the permanent use, usufruct, administration, and conservation of natural resources." The resolution further states that:

> No person, authority or official may impede the free transit, movement, navigation, and intercommunication of Sarayaku community members throughout the lands and rivers as they require and need in the exercise of their legitimate rights. Anyone who should obstruct, oppose, impede, or limit the right to free transit and movement of members of this community shall be subject to the penalties and sanctions established under Ecuadorian law.

26. Notwithstanding the Ombudsman's resolution, the petitioners claim that between November 2002 and February 2003, oil company employees and guards, with the acquiescence of members of the Armed Forces, made incursions into Sarayaku territory and destroyed woodlands, sources of food, medicines, and cultural heritage. In addition, during this period, there were a series of threats, assaults, illegal detentions, and abuses against members of the Sarayaku people which constituted systematic violations of the fundamental rights of the Sarayaku indigenous community and its members.

. . . .

29. According to the petitioners, a policy of harassment and threats that has existed since 1996 against the Sarayaku community and those helping to defend their rights intensified after November 2002, because of the community's position concerning oil exploration and exploitation within the ancestral territory of the Kichwa people of Sarayaku. They say that the incursions into Sarayaku territory have caused serious harm to the life of the community. The detonations of explosives have destroyed significant areas of woodlands, water sources, caves, subterranean rivers, and sacred sites, and have caused animals to migrate to more remote areas. Explosives planted in traditional hunting areas have endangered the life of the inhabitants, and made it impossible to search for food; they have altered life cycles and deprived families of food sources. They also state that the indigenous people of Sarayaku have been harmed in their right to use and enjoy their land, and in the special relationship they have with the land. Specifically, their subsistence as a people has been jeopardized as they are prevented from obtaining basic food, traditional medicine, and healthcare, and from transmitting their cultural heritage to future generations.

30. The petitioners add that the traditional political structures of the Sarayaku community have been harmed directly through threats, persecution, and the physi-

cal, psychological and moral torture of its members and especially its leaders, for expressing their opposition to the State's oil policy.

. . . .

34. In a note received by the Inter-American Commission on June 2, 2004, the State outlined its position regarding the procedural aspects of the petition seeking an exception to the failure to exhaust domestic remedies. It asserted that the Ecuadorian State has no obligations under ILO Convention 169 [which it had not ratified at the time it signed the oil concession contract], and requested, finally, that the petition be declared inadmissible and the case closed.

. . . .

[The state also argued that domestic remedies remained to be exhausted.]

46. In light of the foregoing, the State does not believe it is necessary to examine the merits of the petition, since it cannot be accepted by the Commission, and requests that the petition be declared inadmissible and immediately closed.

IV. ANALYSIS OF ADMISSIBILITY

A. The Commission's Competence ratione personae, *ratione materiae, ratione temporis* and *ratione loci*

47. The petitioners are entitled, in principle, under Article 44 of the American Convention, to lodge petitions before the IACHR. The petition names as the alleged victims the Kichwa indigenous people of the Sarayaku community and its members, on whose behalf the State undertook to respect and ensure the rights recognized in the American Convention. Insofar as the State is concerned, the Commission points out that Ecuador has been a State Party to the American Convention since December 28, 1977, when it deposited its respective instrument of ratification. Therefore, the Commission has *ratione personae* competence to examine the petition.

48. The Commission has *ratione loci* competence to hear the petition as it alleges violations of rights protected by the American Convention that occurred in the territory of a State Party to that treaty. The IACHR has *ratione temporis* competence because the obligation to respect and ensure the rights protected by the American Convention already were in effect for the State on the date on which the alleged violations occurred. Finally, the Commission has *ratione materiae* competence because the petition claims violations of human rights protected by the American Convention.

49. The Commission lacks competence with respect to the petitioner's claim that the Ecuadorian State should be found to have failed to comply with ILO Convention 169. Nonetheless, it can and must use Convention 169 as a guideline for interpreting conventional obligations, in light of the provisions of Article 29 of the American Convention.

. . . .

C. Colorable claim

74. The Commission believes that the acts denounced by the petitioners regarding irregularities in the consultation process conducted by the State with respect to the oil exploration and exploitation concession granted to a company to be carried out in the ancestral territory of the Kichwa indigenous people of Sarayaku, as well

as the threats, attacks, persecution, and harassment directed against members and leaders of that nationality and its respective traditional organization, and the threats and harassment suffered by the girls of the community, and the restrictions placed on movement using the Community's access routes, if proved, could constitute violations of the rights guaranteed in Articles 4 (life), 5 (personal integrity), 7 (personal liberty and security), 8 (due process), 12 (freedom of religion and conscience), 13 (freedom of thought and expression), 16 (association), 19 (rights of the child), 21 (property), 22 (freedom of movement), 23 (political participation), 24 (equality before the law), 25 (judicial protection), and 26 (progressive development), all of the American Convention, in relation to Articles 1(1) and 2 of the same instrument. Moreover, there is no evidence of a lack of merits or inadmissibility of the petition lodged. Therefore, the Commission believes that the requirements established in Article 47(b) and (c) of the American Convention have been satisfied.

75. Likewise, the Commission believes that the acts denounced in the petition do not contain sufficient elements to claim a violation of Articles 3 and 4 of the American Convention.

V. CONCLUSIONS

76. The Commission rejects the objection regarding the exhaustion of domestic remedies lodged by the Ecuadorian State and concludes that it is competent to examine the claims submitted by the petitioners concerning the alleged violation of Articles 4, 5, 7, 8, 12, 13, 16, 19, 21, 22, 23, 24, 25, 26 relative to Articles 1(1) and 2 of the American Convention and that the petition meets the admissibility requirements set forth in Articles 46 and 47 of the American Convention.

Questions and Comments

1. The effort to litigate economic and social rights in the Inter-American system has given rise to considerable debate. *See*: James L. Cavallaro & Emily J. Schaffer, *Less as More: Rethinking Supranational Litigation of Economic and Social Rights in the Americas*, 56 HASTINGS L.J. 217 (2005); Tara Melish, *Rethinking the "Less as More" Thesis: Supranational Litigation of Economic, Social and Cultural Rights in the America*, 39 NYY J. INT'L L. & POL. 171 (2006); James L. Cavallaro & Emily Schaffer, Rejoinder: *Justice before Justiciability: Inter-American Litigation and Social Change*, 39 NYU J. INT'L L.& POL. 345 (2006); Tara Melish, Counter-Rejoinder: *Justiced vs. Justiciability? Normative Neutrality and Technical Precision, the Role of the Lawyer in Supranational Social Rights Litigation*, 39 NYU J. INT'L L. & POL. 385 (2006). In this debate, consider how the Declaration, Convention and Protocol of San Salvador inter-relate: does it make sense that states not party to the Convention would be subject to petitions alleging violations of economic and social rights, while states parties to the Convention and Protocol would have to answer only with respect to the two rights expressly made justiciable by the Protocol? Does Article 26 imply that the Commission and Court have jurisdiction to accept cases invoking economic and social rights?

2. The *Kitchwa* case invokes a wide range of civil, political, economic, social and cultural rights. Among them is the right to property, normally listed among civil and political rights, but one equally at home as an economic right. What is property? Does it include indigenous rights in ancestral lands never demarcated or registered? See *Mayagna (Sumo) Awas Tingni Community v. Nicaragua*, 79 Inter-Am.Ct.H.R.(Ser.C)(2001); *Case of Moiwa-*

na Village v. Suriname, Judgment of June 15, 2005, 124 Inter-Am. Ct. H.R. (Ser. C) (2005). The European Convention, Protocol I guaranteed peaceful enjoyment of "possessions." Does this term include malpractice or other civil claims for damages? Is it equivalent to "asset?" See *Draon v. France* [GC], (App. no. 1513/03), Judgment of 6 October 2005 (holding that "for a claim to be capable of being considered an "asset" falling within the scope of Article 1 of Protocol No. 1, the claimant must establish that it has a sufficient basis in national law, for example where there is settled case-law of the domestic courts confirming it. Where that has been done, the concept of "legitimate expectation" can come into play." Para. 208). Note that in *Oneryildiz v. Turkey*, infra pp. 413-423, the European Court rejected the government's argument that slum dwellers had no property interest because the land had been illegally occupied. The Court noted that the government had provided public services and collected taxes and therefore was estopped to deny a property interest in the applicants.

3. How much deference should be afforded a government's claims of necessity or redress of past injustices as a rationale for restrictive economic measures? One of the most difficult issues in a number of African countries is land reform; actions by the government of Zimbabwe have been harshly criticized as human rights violations. See *Executive Summary of the Report of the Fact-finding Mission to Zimbabwe*, 24th to 28th June 2002, *17th Annual Activity Report of the Afr. Comm. H.P.R. 2003–2004*, Annex II, pp. 13–17, which made the following findings:

> The Mission observed that Zimbabwean society is highly polarised. It is a divided society with deeply entrenched positions. The land question is not in itself the cause of division. It appears that at heart is a society in search of the means for change and divided about how best to achieve change after two decades of dominance by a political party that carried the hopes and aspirations of the people of Zimbabwe through the liberation struggle into independence.
>
> There is no doubt that from the perspective of the fact-finding team, the land question is critical and that Zimbabweans, sooner or later, needed to address it. The team has consistently maintained that from a human rights perspective, land reform has to be the prerogative of the government of Zimbabwe. The Mission noted that Article 14 of the African Charter states "The right to property shall be guaranteed. *It may only be encroached upon in the interest of public need or in the general interest of the community and in accordance with the provisions of appropriate laws*". It appears to the Mission that the Government of Zimbabwe has managed to bring this policy matter under the legal and constitutional system of the country. It now means that land reform and land distribution can now take place in a lawful and orderly fashion.
>
> There was enough evidence placed before the Mission to suggest that, at the very least during the period under review, human rights violations occurred in Zimbabwe.

The Government replied:

6.3 The land and the land reform programme in Zimbabwe is a socioeconomic and political imperative. It is an undisputed fact that the land issue was actually one of the primary reasons for the protracted war of liberation and that up to 1999, the unequal distribution of land had remained a serious concern, whose implications had a potential to destabilize the post colonial Zimbabwe. Zimbabwe's economy is agriculturally based and, out of a total land area of 39 million hectares, 33.3 million is suitable for agriculture. Half of this land was, up to 1999 occupied by 6 000 white commercial farmers while 840 000 communal farmers (blacks) occupied the other half. The uneven distribution of land between the large scale commercial sector and the communal areas also extended to the suitability of land for agricultural purposes. The commercial farms were largely located in the high rainfall areas, found in regions I, II and III while the communal lands are concentrated in regions IV and V which are characterized by very poor soils and low rainfall patterns. Out of the land in the fertile regions, I, II and III, some belonged to absentee landlords and was either not being put to use at all or was being managed from abroad, some was under-utilised, and other prime agricultural land had been converted to safari hunting while the majority of the black people either had no land or were overcrowded on over-utilised and often barren rural land.

6.4 As is the case in all matters which are covered in this Report, it is unfortunate that the Fact Finding Mission did not find time to see for themselves the conditions under which the rural black persons live, nor did the Mission see the cramped, pathetic and squalid conditions of the black farm workers compared to the grandiose lifestyle in which their white masters lived and, in some cases, still live some 23 years after independence. Up until the implementation of the land reform programme, none of the non governmental organizations and human rights defenders saw the need to put the issue of the living conditions of farm workers on the agenda of the African Commission on Human and Peoples' Rights and this is a question the Commission still did not consider in its Report. Even the trade unionists did not regard the farm worker befitting their representation until the emergence of the agrarian reform.

6.5 As all parties in Zimbabwe now concede (the opposition doing so reluctantly), land reform was necessary in order to address the imbalances in land, which were created by the colonial Governments, thereby achieving equitable land distribution and decongesting over populated rural areas. Land reform was also necessary to meet the land needs of indigenous citizens and successful smallholder farmers who wanted to enter into commercial agriculture for the economic development of the country. In fact, Article 22 of the Charter recognizes the right of all peoples to economic, social and cultural development. It is in the spirit of that article and other economic considerations that Zimbabwe embarked upon the land reform programme.

Further discussions and investigations led the African Commission to adopt the following resolution:

Resolution on the Situation of Human Rights in Zimbabwe, 5 December 2005, *20th Annual Activity Report of the Afr. Comm. H.P.R. 2006*, Annex III, pp. 85–86.

The African Commission on Human and Peoples' Rights meeting at its 38th Ordinary Session in Banjul, The Gambia from 21 November to 5 December 2005;

Considering that Zimbabwe is a Party to the *African Charter on Human and Peoples' Rights* and other international human rights instruments;

Recalling the recommendations to the government of Zimbabwe contained in the African Commission Report of the Fact-Finding Mission to Zimbabwe in June 2002;

Further recalling the recommendations to the government of Zimbabwe by the United Nations Special Envoy on Human Settlement Issues in Zimbabwe contained in her Report published on 22 July 2005;

Deeply concerned by the continued undermining of the independence of the judiciary through defiance of court orders, harassment and intimidation of independent judges and the executive ouster of the jurisdiction of the courts;

Further concerned by the continuing human rights violations and the deterioration of the human rights situation in Zimbabwe, the lack of respect for the rule of law and the growing culture of impunity;

Alarmed by the number of internally displaced persons and the violations of fundamental individual and collective rights resulting from the forced evictions being carried out by the government of Zimbabwe;

1. **Condemns** the human rights violations currently being perpetrated in Zimbabwe;

2. **Urges** the government of Zimbabwe to cease the practice of forced evictions throughout the country, and to adhere to its obligations under the *African Charter on Human and Peoples' Rights* and other international human rights instruments to which Zimbabwe is a party;

3. **Urges** the government of Zimbabwe to implement without further delay the recommendations contained in the African Commission Report of the 2002 Fact-Finding Mission to Zimbabwe and the recommendations in the July 2005 Report of the UN Special Envoy on Human Settlement Issues, in particular to ensure full and unimpeded access for the provision of aid and protection to the victims of the forced evictions and demolitions by impartial national and international humanitarian agencies and human rights monitors, and to ensure that those responsible for the violations are brought to justice without delay;

4. **Calls** on the government of Zimbabwe to respect the fundamental rights and freedoms of expression, association and assembly by repealing or amending repressive legislation, such as the *Access to Information and Protection of Privacy Act*, the *Broadcasting Services Act* and the *Public Order and Security Act*;

5. **Calls** on the government of Zimbabwe to uphold the principle of separation of powers and the independence of the judiciary and urges the government of Zimbabwe to repeal or amend Constitutional Amendment (No.17) and provide an environment conducive to constitutional reform based on fundamental rights;

6. **Calls** on the government of Zimbabwe to cooperate with the African Commission Special Rapporteur on Refugees, Asylum Seekers and Internally Displaced Persons in Africa and other African Commission Special Mechanisms, including allowing a Fact-Finding Mission to investigate the current situation of internally displaced persons in Zimbabwe;

7. **Urges** the African Union to renew the mandate of the African Union Envoy to Zimbabwe to investigate the human rights implications and humanitarian consequences of the mass evictions and demolitions.

<hr/>

The government of Zimbabwe called the resolution "a resolution of Western sponsored NGOs, either resident in the West, or who though on Zimbabwean soil, are set up and are being solely funded by the West in order to demonize Zimbabwe and further their not so hidden agenda of regime change." Is the government pursuing a legitimate aim of land reform or is it repressing political opponents under the guise of economic reform? Are these issues of civil and political or economic and social rights? According to an authoritative commentary on the African Charter, "the right to property was probably the most controversial of all rights discussed in the negotiations relating to the African Charter . . ." F. Ouguergouz, The African Charter on Human and Peoples' Rights: A Comprehensive Agenda for Human Dignity and Sustainable Development in Africa (2005), 152. An early version of Article 14 provided guarantees only "where the right to property is guaranteed by state legislation" (id.), but ultimately a right to property, with limitations, was included in the Charter. The Zimbabwe case is the first in which the Commission has fully considered the scope of this right. It has also alluded to the right to property in the case of mass expulsions. See e.g., Comm. 159/96, *Union Interafricaine des Droits de l'Homme et al v. Angola*, 11th Annual Report of the Commission 1997–1998. Is this a topic on which regional divergence exists on the scope of the right or is the same right being applied in widely different circumstances?

C. Limitations and Clawback Clauses

Each right in the regional treaties has a defined scope that limits its application; sometimes the limits are established by interpretation and in other cases the text itself sets forth definitions or exclusions. See, for example, the prohibition of forced labor in the European Convention on Human Rights, Art. 4. It excludes from its scope, inter alia, civic duties such as serving on a jury or military service. In addition to definitions or interpretations that circumscribe rights, some provisions in the regional texts have "limitations clauses" which set forth the modalities and scope of state discretion to restrict the exercise of the rights to which such clauses are attached. See, for example, Articles 8–11 of the European Convention on Human Rights. The African Charter also contains provisions that permit rights to be limited or circumscribed by reference and deference to national law. These are known as "clawback" clauses. Interpretation of these provisions is essential to avoid their being used to extinguish the enjoyment of guaranteed rights.

i. Application of Limitation Clauses

Like several other rights in the European Convention, Article 10 is drafted in two paragraphs, the first paragraph setting forth the right and the second one establishing the scope of permissible state limitations on the right, which is not an absolute one. According to Article 10(2), any limitation must be prescribed by law and be necessary "in a democratic society," as well as aimed at one of the permissible objectives set forth in the article. Applications alleging violations of Article 10 of the European Convention began arriving soon after the European Court began to function and continue to be major source of important jurisprudence. The Court has described freedom of expression as "one of the basic conditions for the progress of democratic societies and for the development of each individual." *Handyside v. the United Kingdom*, 24 Eur. Ct.H.R. (ser. A) (7 Dec. 1976). The first reported Article 10 case, *De Beker v. Belgium*, 4 Eur. Ct.H.R. (Ser. B), was brought by a journalist subject to a lifelong prohibition on exercising the functions of author or journalist. It was struck off the list after Belgium changed its law, favorable to the applicant, while the case was under consideration. Other early cases, including *Handyside, supra*, challenged prior censorship or punishment after the fact for publications contrary to state law or policy. The first judgment to find a violation was *Sunday Times v. the United Kingdom (No. 1)* 30 Eur.Ct.H.R. (ser.A)(26 April 1979), wherein the applicant challenged an injunction restraining publication of articles about the drug thalidomide. By the 1980s, appeals from defamation convictions began appearing. The *Lingens* judgment was the first to find a violation based on defamation law. *Lingens v. Austria*, (App. no. 9815/82), Judgment of 8 July 1986, 103 Eur. Ct. H.R. (Ser. A), 8 EHRR 407 (1986). A few cases have challenged state licensing of radio and television programs and stations. See e.g. *Groppera Radio AG and others v. Switzerland*, 173 Eur.Ct.H.R. (ser.A) (28 March 1990); *Autronic AG v. Switzerland*, 178 Eur.Ct.H.R. (ser. A)(22 May 1990); *Informationsverein Lentia and Others v. Austria*, 276 Eur.Ct.H.R. (ser. A) (24 Nov. 1993). In *Open Door Counselling Ltd. and Dublin Well Woman*, 246 Eur.Ct.H.R. (ser. A)(Oct. 29 1992), the Court found a violation of Article 10 when the Irish Supreme Court restrained the applicant counseling agencies from providing pregnant women with information concerning abortion facilities abroad. Particularly difficult issues have arisen in respect to restrictions on hate speech, broadly considered to include blasphemy laws. See, e.g. *Jersild v. Denmark*, (App. no. 15890/8), Judgment of 22 August 1994, 298 Eur. Ct. H.R (Ser. A), 19 EHRR 1 (1995); *Wingrove v. the United Kingdom*, (App. no. 17419/90), Judgment of 25 November 1996, Eur. Ct. H.R., 24 EHRR 1 (1997), and *Otto-Preminger-Institut v. Austria*, (App. no. 13470/87), Judgment of 23 August 1994, 295-A Eur. Ct. H.R. (Ser. A), 19 EHRR 34 (1995). The following cases illustrate the scope of state discretion to regulate artistic expression in Europe and the very different approach of the Inter-American system:

Müller and Others v. Switzerland, (App. no. 10737/84), 133 Eur. Ct. H.R. (Ser. A), 13 EHRR 212 (1991).

. . . .

9. Josef Felix Müller has exhibited on his own and with other artists on many occasions, particularly since 1981, both in private galleries and in museums, in Switzerland and elsewhere.

With the assistance of the Federal Office of Culture, he took part in the Sydney Biennial in Australia in 1984, as Switzerland's representative. He has been awarded several prizes and has sold works to museums such as the Kunsthalle in Zürich.

10. In 1981, the nine [other] applicants mounted an exhibition of contemporary art in Fribourg at the former Grand Seminary, a building due to be demolished. The exhibition, entitled "Fri-Art 81", was held as part of the celebrations of the 500th anniversary of the Canton of Fribourg's entry into the Swiss Confederation. The organisers invited several artists to take part, each of whom was allowed to invite another artist of his own choosing. The artists were meant to make free use of the space allocated to them. Their works, which they created on the spot from early August 1981 onwards, were to have been removed when the exhibition ended on 18 October 1981.

11. In the space of three nights Josef Felix Müller, who had been invited by one of the other artists, produced three large paintings (measuring 3.11m x 2.24m, 2.97m

x 1.98m and 3.74m x 2.20m) entitled "Drei Nächte, drei Bilder" ("Three Nights, Three Pictures"). They were on show when the exhibition began on 21 August 1981. The exhibition had been advertised in the press and on posters and was open to all, without any charge being made for admission. The catalogue, specially printed for the preview, contained a photographic reproduction of the paintings.

12. On 4 September 1981, the day of the official opening, the principal public prosecutor of the Canton of Fribourg reported to the investigating judge that the paintings in question appeared to come within the provisions of Article 204 of the Criminal Code, which prohibited obscene publications and required that they be destroyed. . . .

14. On 24 February 1982, the court sentenced each of them to a fine of 300 Swiss francs (SF) for publishing obscene material (Article 204 § 1 of the Criminal Code)—the convictions to be deleted from the criminal records after one year—but acquitted them on the charge of infringing freedom of religious belief and worship (Article 261). It also ordered that the confiscated paintings should be deposited in the Art and History Museum of the Canton of Fribourg for safekeeping. . . .

15. All the applicants appealed on points of law on 24 February 1982; in particular, they challenged the trial court's interpretation as regards the obscenity of the relevant paintings. . . .

16. The Fribourg Cantonal Court, sitting as a court of cassation, dismissed the appeals on 26 April 1982. . . .

17. On 18 June 1982, the applicants lodged an application for a declaration of nullity (Nichtigkeitsbeschwerde) with the Federal Court. They sought to have the judgment of 26 April set aside and the case remitted with a view to their acquittal and the return of the confiscated paintings or, in the alternative, merely the return of the paintings. . . .

18. The Criminal Cassation Division of the Federal Court dismissed the appeal on 26 January 1983. . . .

Finally, the Criminal Cassation Division of the Federal Court declared the alternative application for return of the paintings to be inadmissible as it had not first been made before the cantonal courts.

19. On 20 January 1988, the Sarine District Criminal Court granted an application made by Josef Felix Müller on 29 June 1987 and ordered the return of the paintings.

Josef Felix Müller recovered his paintings in March 1988.

. . . .

AS TO THE LAW

26. The applicants complained that their conviction and the confiscation of the paintings in issue violated Article 10 of the Convention. . . . The Government rejected this contention. The Commission too rejected it with regard to the first of the measures complained of but accepted it with regard to the second.

27. The applicants indisputably exercised their right to freedom of expression—the first applicant by painting and then exhibiting the works in question, and the nine others by giving him the opportunity to show them in public at the "Fri-Art 81" exhibition they had mounted.

Admittedly, Article 10 does not specify that freedom of artistic expression, in issue here, comes within its ambit; but neither, on the other hand, does it distinguish between the various forms of expression. As those appearing before the Court all acknowledged, it includes freedom of artistic expression—notably within freedom to receive and impart information and ideas—which affords the opportunity to take part in the public exchange of cultural, political and social information and ideas of all kinds. Confirmation, if any were needed, that this interpretation is correct, is provided by the second sentence of paragraph 1 of Article 10, which refers to "broadcasting, television or cinema enterprises", media whose activities extend to the field of art. Confirmation that the concept of freedom of expression is such as to include artistic expression is also to be found in Article 19 § 2 of the International Covenant on Civil and Political Rights, which specifically includes within the right of freedom of expression information and ideas "in the form of art".

28. The applicants clearly suffered "interference by public authority" with the exercise of their freedom of expression—firstly, by reason of their conviction by the Sarine District Criminal Court on 24 February 1982, which was confirmed by the Fribourg Cantonal Court on 26 April 1982 and then by the Federal Court on 26 January 1983, and secondly on account of the confiscation of the paintings, which was ordered at the same time but subsequently lifted.

Such measures, which constitute "penalties" or "restrictions", are not contrary to the Convention solely by virtue of the fact that they interfere with freedom of expression, as the exercise of this right may be curtailed under the conditions provided for in paragraph 2. Consequently, the two measures complained of did not infringe Article 10 if they were "prescribed by law", had one or more of the legitimate aims under paragraph 2 of that Article and were "necessary in a democratic society" for achieving the aim or aims concerned.

Like the Commission, the Court will look in turn at the applicants' conviction and at the confiscation of the pictures from this point of view.

I. The applicants' conviction

1. "Prescribed by law"

29. In the applicants' view, the terms of Article 204 § 1 of the Swiss Criminal Code, in particular the word "obscene", were too vague to enable the individual to regulate his conduct and consequently neither the artist nor the organisers of the exhibition could foresee that they would be committing an offence. This view was not shared by the Government and the Commission.

According to the Court's case-law, "foreseeability" is one of the requirements inherent in the phrase "prescribed by law" in Article 10 § 2 of the Convention. A norm cannot be regarded as a "law" unless it is formulated with sufficient precision to enable the citizen—if need be, with appropriate advice—to foresee, to a degree that is reasonable in the circumstances, the consequences which a given action may entail (see the *Olsson* judgment of 24 March 1988, Series A no. 130, p. 30, § 61 (a)). The Court has, however, already emphasised the impossibility of attaining absolute precision in the framing of laws, particularly in fields in which the situation changes according to the prevailing views of society (see the *Barthold* judgment of 25 March

1985, Series A no. 90, p. 22, § 47). The need to avoid excessive rigidity and to keep pace with changing circumstances means that many laws are inevitably couched in terms which, to a greater or lesser extent, are vague (see, for example, the *Olsson* judgment previously cited, ibid.). Criminal-law provisions on obscenity fall within this category.

In the present instance, it is also relevant to note that there were a number of consistent decisions by the Federal Court on the "publication" of "obscene" items. These decisions, which were accessible because they had been published and which were followed by the lower courts, supplemented the letter of Article 204 § 1 of the Criminal Code. The applicants' conviction was therefore "prescribed by law" within the meaning of Article 10 § 2 of the Convention.

2. The legitimacy of the aim pursued

30. The Government contended that the aim of the interference complained of was to protect morals and the rights of others. On the latter point, they relied above all on the reaction of a man and his daughter who visited the "Fri-Art 81" exhibition.

The Court accepts that Article 204 of the Swiss Criminal Code is designed to protect public morals, and there is no reason to suppose that in applying it in the instant case the Swiss courts had any other objectives that would have been incompatible with the Convention. Moreover, as the Commission pointed out, there is a natural link between protection of morals and protection of the rights of others.

The applicants' conviction consequently had a legitimate aim under Article 10 § 2.

3. "Necessary in a democratic society"

31. The submissions of those appearing before the Court focused on the question whether the disputed interference was "necessary in a democratic society" for achieving the aforementioned aim.

In the applicants' view, freedom of artistic expression was of such fundamental importance that banning a work or convicting the artist of an offence struck at the very essence of the right guaranteed in Article 10 and had damaging consequences for a democratic society. No doubt the impugned paintings reflected a conception of sexuality that was at odds with the currently prevailing social morality, but, the applicants argued, their symbolical meaning had to be considered, since these were works of art. Freedom of artistic expression would become devoid of substance if paintings like those of Josef Felix Müller could not be shown to people interested in the arts as part of an exhibition of experimental contemporary art.

In the Government's submission, on the other hand, the interference was necessary, having regard in particular to the subject-matter of the paintings and to the particular circumstances in which they were exhibited.

For similar reasons and irrespective of any assessment of artistic or symbolical merit, the Commission considered that the Swiss courts could reasonably hold that the paintings were obscene and were entitled to find the applicants guilty of an offence under Article 204 of the Criminal Code.

32. The Court has consistently held that in Article 10 § 2 the adjective "necessary" implies the existence of a "pressing social need" (see, as the most recent authority, the *Lingens* judgment of 8 July 1986, Series A no. 103, p. 25, § 39). The Contracting States have a certain margin of appreciation in assessing whether such a need exists, but this goes hand in hand with a European supervision, embracing both the legislation and the decisions applying it, even those given by an independent court (ibid.). The Court is therefore empowered to give the final ruling on whether a "restriction" or "penalty" is reconcilable with freedom of expression as protected by Article 10 (ibid.).

In exercising its supervisory jurisdiction, the Court cannot confine itself to considering the impugned court decisions in isolation; it must look at them in the light of the case as a whole, including the paintings in question and the context in which they were exhibited. The Court must determine whether the interference at issue was "proportionate to the legitimate aim pursued" and whether the reasons adduced by the Swiss courts to justify it are "relevant and sufficient" (see the same judgment, p. 26, § 40).

33. In this connection, the Court must reiterate that freedom of expression, as secured in paragraph 1 of Article 10, constitutes one of the essential foundations of a democratic society, indeed one of the basic conditions for its progress and for the self-fulfilment of the individual. Subject to paragraph 2, it is applicable not only to "information" or "ideas" that are favourably received or regarded as inoffensive or as a matter of indifference, but also to those that offend, shock or disturb the State or any section of the population. Such are the demands of that pluralism, tolerance and broadmindedness without which there is no "democratic society" (see the *Handyside* judgment of 7 December 1976, Series A no. 24, p. 23, § 49). Those who create, perform, distribute or exhibit works of art contribute to the exchange of ideas and opinions which is essential for a democratic society. Hence the obligation on the State not to encroach unduly on their freedom of expression.

34. Artists and those who promote their work are certainly not immune from the possibility of limitations as provided for in paragraph 2 of Article 10. Whoever exercises his freedom of expression undertakes, in accordance with the express terms of that paragraph, "duties and responsibilities"; their scope will depend on his situation and the means he uses (see, mutatis mutandis, the *Handyside* judgment previously cited, p. 23, § 49). In considering whether the penalty was "necessary in a democratic society", the Court cannot overlook this aspect of the matter.

35. The applicants' conviction on the basis of Article 204 of the Swiss Criminal Code was intended to protect morals. Today, as at the time of the *Handyside* judgment (previously cited, p. 22, § 48), it is not possible to find in the legal and social orders of the Contracting States a uniform European conception of morals. The view taken of the requirements of morals varies from time to time and from place to place, especially in our era, characterised as it is by a far-reaching evolution of opinions on the subject. By reason of their direct and continuous contact with the vital forces of their countries, State authorities are in principle in a better position than the international judge to give an opinion on the exact content of these re-

quirements as well as on the "necessity" of a "restriction" or "penalty" intended to meet them.

36. In the instant case, it must be emphasised that—as the Swiss courts found both at the cantonal level at first instance and on appeal and at the federal level— the paintings in question depict in a crude manner sexual relations, particularly between men and animals. They were painted on the spot—in accordance with the aims of the exhibition, which was meant to be spontaneous—and the general public had free access to them, as the organisers had not imposed any admission charge or any age-limit. Indeed, the paintings were displayed in an exhibition which was unrestrictedly open to—and sought to attract—the public at large.

The Court recognises, as did the Swiss courts, that conceptions of sexual morality have changed in recent years. Nevertheless, having inspected the original paintings, the Court does not find unreasonable the view taken by the Swiss courts that those paintings, with their emphasis on sexuality in some of its crudest forms, were "liable grossly to offend the sense of sexual propriety of persons of ordinary sensitivity" (see paragraph 18 above). In the circumstances, having regard to the margin of appreciation left to them under Article 10 § 2, the Swiss courts were entitled to consider it "necessary" for the protection of morals to impose a fine on the applicants for publishing obscene material.

The applicants claimed that the exhibition of the pictures had not given rise to any public outcry and indeed that the press on the whole was on their side. It may also be true that Josef Felix Müller has been able to exhibit works in a similar vein in other parts of Switzerland and abroad, both before and after the "Fri-Art 81" exhibition (see paragraph 9 above). It does not, however, follow that the applicants' conviction in Fribourg did not, in all the circumstances of the case, respond to a genuine social need, as was affirmed in substance by all three of the Swiss courts which dealt with the case.

37. In conclusion, the disputed measure did not infringe Article 10 of the Convention.

II. The confiscation of the paintings

1. "Prescribed by law"

38. In the applicants' submission, the confiscation of the paintings was not "prescribed by law" for it was contrary to the clear and unambiguous terms of Article 204 § 3 of the Swiss Criminal Code, which lays down that items held to be obscene must be destroyed.

The Government and the Commission rightly referred to the development of Swiss case-law with regard to this provision, beginning with the Federal Court's judgment of 10 May 1963 in the Rey case; since then, where an obscene item is of cultural interest and difficult or impossible to replace, such as a painting, it has been sufficient, in order to satisfy the requirements of Article 204 § 3 of the Criminal Code, to take whatever measures the court considers essential to withhold it from the general public. In 1982, confiscation was the measure envisaged under the relevant case-law and was as a rule employed for this purpose. Accessible to the public and followed by the lower courts, this case-law has alleviated the harshness of Article 204 § 3. The impugned measure was consequently "prescribed by law" within the meaning of Article 10 § 2 (Art. 10–2) of the Convention.

2. *The legitimacy of the aim pursued*

39. The confiscation of the paintings—the persons appearing before the Court were in agreement on this point—was designed to protect public morals by preventing any repetition of the offence with which the applicants were charged. It accordingly had a legitimate aim under Article 10 § 2.

3. *"Necessary in a democratic society"*

40. Here again, those appearing before the Court concentrated their submissions on the "necessity" of the interference.

The applicants considered the confiscation to be disproportionate in relation to the aim pursued. In their view, the relevant courts could have chosen a less Draconian measure or, in the interests of protecting human rights, could have decided to take no action at all. They claimed that by confiscating the paintings the Fribourg authorities in reality imposed their view of morals on the country as a whole and that this was unacceptable, contradictory and contrary to the Convention, having regard to the well-known diversity of opinions on the subject.

The Government rejected these contentions. In declining to take the drastic measure of destroying the paintings, the Swiss courts took the minimum action necessary. The discharge of the confiscation order on 20 January 1988, which the first applicant could have applied for earlier, clearly showed that the confiscation had not offended the proportionality principle; indeed, it represented an application of it.

The Commission considered the confiscation of the paintings to be disproportionate to the legitimate aim pursued. In its view, the judicial authorities had no power to weigh the conflicting interests involved and order measures less severe than confiscation for an indefinite period.

41. It is clear that notwithstanding the apparently rigid terms of paragraph 3 of Article 204 of the Criminal Code, the case-law of the Federal Court allowed a court which had found certain items to be obscene to order their confiscation as an alternative to destruction. In the present case, it is the former measure which has to be considered under Article 10 § 2 of the Convention.

42. A principle of law which is common to the Contracting States allows confiscation of "items whose use has been lawfully adjudged illicit and dangerous to the general interest" (see, mutatis mutandis, the *Handyside* judgment previously cited, Series A no. 24, p. 30, § 63). In the instant case, the purpose was to protect the public from any repetition of the offence.

43. The applicants' conviction responded to a genuine social need under Article 10 § 2 of the Convention. The same reasons which justified that measure also apply in the view of the Court to the confiscation order made at the same time.

Undoubtedly, as the applicants and the Commission rightly emphasised, a special problem arises where, as in the instant case, the item confiscated is an original painting: on account of the measure taken, the artist can no longer make use of his work in whatever way he might wish. Thus Josef Felix Müller lost, in particular, the opportunity of showing his paintings in places where the demands made by the protection of morals are considered to be less strict than in Fribourg.

It must be pointed out, however, that under case-law going back to the Fahrner case in 1980 and which was subsequently applied in the instant case, it is open to the owner of a confiscated work to apply to the relevant cantonal court to have the confiscation order discharged or varied if the item in question no longer presents any danger or if some other, more lenient, measure would suffice to protect the interests of public morals. In its decision of 20 January 1988, the Sarine District Criminal Court stated that the original confiscation "was not absolute but merely of indeterminate duration, which left room to apply for a reconsideration". It granted Mr. Müller's application because "the preventive measure [had] fulfilled its function, namely to ensure that such paintings [were] not exhibited in public again without any precautions" (ibid.).

Admittedly, the first applicant was deprived of his works for nearly eight years, but there was nothing to prevent him from applying earlier to have them returned; the relevant case-law of the Basle Court of Appeal was public and accessible, and, what is more, the Agent of the Government himself drew his attention to it during the Commission's hearing on 6 December 1985; there is no evidence before the Court to show that such an application would have failed.

That being so, and having regard to their margin of appreciation, the Swiss courts were entitled to hold that confiscation of the paintings in issue was "necessary" for the protection of morals.

44. In conclusion, the disputed measure did not infringe Article 10 of the Convention.

"The Last Temptation of Christ" Case, Judgment of February 5, 2001, 73 Inter-Am. Ct. H.R. (Ser. C) (2001).

1. On January 15, 1999, the Inter-American Commission on Human Rights . . . submitted to the Court an application against the Republic of Chile . . . , arising from a petition (No. 11,803), received by the Secretariat of the Commission on September 3, 1997. The Commission invoked Articles 50 and 51 of the American Convention on Human Rights . . . and Articles 32 ff. of the Rules of Procedure in its application. The Commission filed this case for the Court to decide whether Chile had violated Articles 13 (Freedom of Thought and Expression) and 12 (Freedom of Conscience and Religion) of the Convention. The Commission also requested the Court to declare that, as a result of the alleged violations of the said articles, Chile had failed to fulfill Articles 1(1) (Obligation to Respect Rights) and 2 (Domestic Legal Effects) of the Convention.

2. According to the petition, the said violations were committed to the detriment of Chilean society and, in particular, Juan Pablo Olmedo Bustos, Ciro Colombara López, Claudio Márquez Vidal, Alex Muñoz Wilson, Matías Insunza Tagle and Hernán Aguirre Fuentes, as a result of the "judicial censorship of the cinematographic exhibition of the film "The Last Temptation of Christ", confirmed by the Supreme Court of Chile [. . .] on June 17, 1997."

3. The Commission also requested the Court to order the State:

1. To authorize the normal cinematographic exhibition and publicity of the film "The Last Temptation of Christ."

2. To adapt its constitutional and legal norms to the standards of freedom of expression embodied in the American Convention, [in order] to eliminate prior censorship of cinematographic productions and their publicity.

3. To ensure that, in the exercise of their different powers, public bodies [,] their authorities and officials [effectively] exercise the rights and freedoms of expression, conscience and religion recognized in the American Convention and [. . .] abstain from imposing prior censorship on cinematographic productions.

4. To make reparations to the victims in this case for the damage suffered.

5. To pay the costs and reimburse the expenses incurred by the victims when litigating this case in both [the] domestic sphere and before the Commission and the Court, as well as reasonable fees for their representatives.

. . . .

VII. PROVEN FACTS

60. After examining the documents, the statements of the witnesses and expert witnesses and the declarations of the State and the Commission during the proceeding, the Court considers that the following facts have been proved:

a. Article 19(12) of the 1980 Constitution of Chile establishes a "system of censorship for the exhibition and publicity of cinematographic productions."

b. Decree Law No. 679 of October 1, 1974, authorizes the Cinematographic Classification Council to supervise cinematographic exhibition in Chile and classify films. The Regulation to this law is contained in the Supreme Decree on Education No. 376 of April 30, 1975. The Cinematographic Classification Council is part of the Ministry of Education.

c. On November 29, 1988, the Cinematographic Classification Council refused to allow the exhibition of the film "The Last Temptation of Christ", following a petition submitted by United International Pictures Ltd. The company appealed the Council's decision, but it was confirmed by a court of appeal, in a judgment of March 14, 1989.

d. On November 11, 1996, following a further petition by United International Pictures Ltd., the Cinematographic Classification Council reviewed the prohibition to exhibit the film "The Last Temptation of Christ" and, in session No. 244, by a majority of votes authorized its exhibition for an audience of 18 years of age or more.

e. Following a remedy for protection filed by Sergio García Valdés, Vicente Torres Irarrázabal, Francisco Javier Donoso Barriga, Matías Pérez Cruz, Jorge Reyes Zapata, Cristian Heerwagen Guzmán and Joel González Castillo, for and in the name of Jesus Christ, the Catholic Church and themselves, on January 20, 1997, the Court of Appeal of Santiago admitted the remedy for protection and annulled the administrative decision adopted by the Cinematographic Classification Council in session No. 244, on November 11, 1996.

f. After an appeal of the judgment of the Court of Appeal of Santiago, of January 20, 1997, filed by Claudio Márquez Vidal, Alex Muñoz Wilson, Matías Insunza Tagle and Hernán Aguirre Fuentes, the Supreme Court of Justice of Chile confirmed the decision appealed against on June 17, 1997.

g. On April 14, 1997, the President of the Republic, Eduardo Frei Ruiz-Tagle, addressed a message to the Chamber of Deputies in which he submitted a draft constitutional reform to article 19(12) of the Constitution that intended to eliminate cinematographic censorship and substitute it by a system of classification that embodied the right to free artistic creation.

h. On November 17, 1999, the Chamber of Deputies adopted the draft constitutional reform that intended to eliminate prior censorship of the exhibition and publicity of cinematographic production by 86 votes in favor, no votes against and six abstentions.

i. Up until February 5, 2001, the date on which this judgment was delivered, the steps for the adoption of the draft constitutional reform had not been completed.

j. As a result of the facts of this case, the victims and their representatives submitted elements to justify the expenses incurred while processing the different domestic and international procedures, and the Court reserves the authority to evaluate these.

VIII. ARTICLE 13 FREEDOM OF THOUGHT AND EXPRESSION

. . . .

Considerations of the Court

. . . .

64. With regard to the content of the right to freedom of thought and expression, those who are protected by the Convention not only have the right and the freedom to express their own thoughts, but also the right and freedom to seek, receive and impart information and ideas of all kinds. Consequently, freedom of expression has an individual and a social dimension:

> It requires, on the one hand, that no one be arbitrarily limited or impeded in expressing his own thoughts. In that sense, it is a right that belongs to each individual. Its second aspect, on the other hand, implies a collective right to receive any information whatsoever and to have access to the thoughts expressed by others.[39]

65. With regard to the first dimension of the right embodied in the said article, the individual one, freedom of expression is not exhausted in the theoretical recognition of the right to speak or write, but also includes, inseparably, the right to use any appropriate method to disseminate thought and allow it to reach the greatest number of persons. In this respect, the expression and dissemination of thought and information are indivisible, so that a restriction of the possibilities of dissemination represents directly, and to the same extent, a limit to the right to free expression.

66. Regarding the second dimension of the right embodied in Article 13 of the Convention, the social element, it is necessary to indicate that freedom of expres-

---

[39] *Compulsory membership in an Association Prescribed by Law for the Practice of Journalism* (Articles 13 and 29 American Convention on Human Rights). Advisory Opinion OC-5/85 of November 13, 1985. Series A No.5, para. 30.

sion is a way of exchanging ideas and information between persons; it includes the right to try and communicate one's point of view to others, but it also implies everyone's right to know opinions, reports and news. For the ordinary citizen, the knowledge of other people's opinions and information is as important as the right to impart their own.

67. The Court considers that both dimensions are of equal importance and should be guaranteed simultaneously in order to give total effect to the right to freedom of thought and expression in the terms of Article 13 of the Convention.

68. As the cornerstone of a democratic society, freedom of expression is an essential condition for society to be sufficiently informed.

69. The European Court of Human Rights has indicated that:

[The] supervisory function [of the Court] signifies that [it] must pay great attention to the principles inherent in a 'democratic society'. Freedom of expression constitutes one of the essential bases of such a society, one of the primordial conditions for its progress and for the development of man. Article 10(2) [of the European Convention on Human Rights][40] is valid not only for the information or ideas that are favorably received or considered inoffensive or indifferent, but also for those that shock, concern or offend the State or any sector of the population. Such are the requirements of pluralism, tolerance and the spirit of openness, without which no 'democratic society' can exist. This means that any formality, condition, restriction or sanction imposed in that respect, should be proportionate to the legitimate end sought.

Also, those who exercise their freedom of expression assume 'obligations and responsibilities', the scope of which depends on the context and the technical procedure used.[41]

70. It is important to mention that Article 13(4) of the Convention establishes an exception to prior censorship, since it allows it in the case of public entertainment, but only in order to regulate access for the moral protection of children and adolescents. In all other cases, any preventive measure implies the impairment of freedom of thought and expression.

71. In the instant case, it has been proved that, in Chile, there is a system of prior censorship for the exhibition and publicity of cinematographic films and that, in principle, the Cinematographic Classification Council prohibited exhibition of the film "The Last Temptation of Christ" and, reclassifying it, permitted it to be exhibited to persons over 18 years of age (*supra* para. 60 a, c and d). Subsequently, the Court of Appeal of Santiago decided to annul the November 1996 decision of the Cinematographic Classification Council, owing to a remedy for protection

---

[40] This article establishes that: 2. The exercise of these freedoms, which entail rights and responsibilities, may be subject to certain formalities, conditions, restrictions or sanctions, established by law, which constitute necessary measures, in a democratic society, for national security, territorial integrity or public security, defense of order and prevention of crime, protection of health or morals, protection of the reputation or the rights of third parties, in order to prevent the dissemination of confidential information or to guarantee the authority and impartiality of the Judiciary.

[41] *cf. Eur. Court H.R., Handyside case, judgment of 7 December 1976, Series A No. 24,* para. 49; *Eur. Court H.R., The Sunday Times case, judgment of 26 April 1979, Series A no. 30,* paras. 59 and 65; *Eur. Court H.R., Barthold judgment of 25 March 1985, Series A no. 90,* para. 55; *Eur. Court H.R., Lingens judgment of 8 July 1986, Series A no. 103,* para. 41; *Eur. Court H.R Müller and Others judgment of 24 May 1988, Series A no. 133,* para. 33; and *Eur. Court HR, Otto-Preminger-Institut v. Austria judgment of 20 September 1994, Series A no. 295-A,* para. 49.

filed by Sergio García Valdés, Vicente Torres Irarrázabal, Francisco Javier Donoso Barriga, Matías Pérez Cruz, Jorge Reyes Zapata, Cristian Heerwagen Guzmán and Joel González Castillo, "for and in the name of Jesus Christ, the Catholic Church and themselves"; a decision that was confirmed by the Supreme Court of Justice of Chile. Therefore, this Court considers that the prohibition of the exhibition of the film "The Last Temptation of Christ" constitutes prior censorship in violation of Article 13 of the Convention.

72. This Court understands that the international responsibility of the State may be engaged by acts or omissions of any power or organ of the State, whatsoever its rank, that violate the American Convention. That is, any act or omission that may be attributed to the State, in violation of the norms of international human rights law engages the international responsibility of the State. In this case, it was engaged because article 19(12) of the Constitution establishes prior censorship of cinematographic films and, therefore, determines the acts of the Executive, the Legislature and the Judiciary.

73. In the light of the foregoing considerations, the Court declares that the State violated the right to freedom of thought and expression embodied in Article 13 of the American Convention, to the detriment of Juan Pablo Olmedo Bustos, Ciro Colombara López, Claudio Márquez Vidal, Alex Muñoz Wilson, Matías Insunza Tagle and Hernán Aguirre Fuentes.

IX. ARTICLE 12 FREEDOM OF CONSCIENCE AND RELIGION
Considerations of the Court

. . . .

77. In the instant case, the Commission believes that prohibiting the exhibition of the film "The Last Temptation of Christ", which, in their opinion, is a work of art with religious content, violated Article 12 of the Convention. This prohibition was based on a series of considerations that interfere improperly with freedom of conscience and religion. The State believes that the right embodied in this article was not affected, since it considers that the right of individuals to maintain, change, profess and disseminate their religions or beliefs was not violated by prohibiting the exhibition of the film. The Court must determine whether Article 12 of the Convention was violated by prohibiting the exhibition of this film.

78. The judgment of the Court of Appeal of Santiago of January 20, 1997, confirmed by the Supreme Court of Justice of Chile on June 17, 1997, indicated that:

> In the film, the image of Christ is deformed and diminished, to the utmost. In this way, the problem is posed of whether it is possible, in the name of freedom of expression, to destroy the sincere beliefs of a great many people. The Constitution seeks to protect the individual, his institutions and his beliefs, because these are the most central elements for the individual to participate and coexist harmoniously in a pluralist world. Pluralism does not mean denigrating and destroying the beliefs of others, whether they are a majority or a minority, but assuming them as a contribution to the interaction of society, which is based on respect for the essence and context of the ideas of others.
>
> No one doubts that the greatness of a nation can be measured by the attention it gives to the values that allowed it to exist and grow. If these are neglected [or] abused, as the image of Christ is deformed and abused, the nation is endangered, because the

values on which it is based are disregarded. Attending to the need for information or expression is closely related to the truth of the facts and, consequently, the historical distortion of a fact or a person ceases to be information or expression. Accordingly, the judges believe that the right to emit an opinion is the right to describe a reality but never to deform it, reinventing it.

It was based on these considerations that this Court of Appeal, in a judgment confirmed by the Supreme Court of Justice, prohibited the exhibition of the film "The Last Temptation of Christ".

79. According to Article 12 of the Convention, the right to freedom of conscience and religion allows everyone to maintain, change, profess and disseminate his religion or beliefs. This right is one of the foundations of democratic society. In its religious dimension, it constitutes a far-reaching element in the protection of the convictions of those who profess a religion and in their way of life. In this case, however, there is no evidence to prove that any of the freedoms embodied in Article 12 of the Convention have been violated. Indeed, the Court understands that the prohibition of the exhibition of the film "The Last Temptation of Christ" did not impair or deprive anyone of their right to maintain, change, profess or disseminate their religion or beliefs with total freedom.

80. In view of the foregoing, the Court concludes that the State did not violate the right to freedom of conscience and religion embodied in Article 12 of the American Convention.

. . . .

Questions and Comments

1. In this, the first opinion of the Inter-American Court on the subject, does the Court elevate freedom of expression to a "preferred freedom"?

2. How does the Inter-American Convention differ from the European Convention on the scope of freedom of expression? Are there historical reasons for the differences? Does the European Court defer too much to local sensibilities in the *Müller* case? How would it have decided the issue of banning the film Last Temptation of Christ? See *Otto Preminger Institut v. Austria, supra*.

3. Do different kinds of speech (commercial, political, artistic) have different levels of protection? Should they?

4. How do the guarantees of European Convention Article 8 and Article 10 interrelate? Does Article 8 permit restrictions on the exercise of freedom of expression to protect the privacy or reputation of individuals? Are the rights similarly protected in the Inter-American system? Compare the provisions of the respective treaties and the following cases: *Van Hannover v. Germany*, App. no. 59320/00, Judgment of 24 June 2004, 40 EHRR 1 (2005) and *Enforceability of the Right to Reply or Correction (Arts. 14(1) and 2 American Convention on Human Rights*, Advisory Opinion OC-7/86 of August 29, 1986, 7 Inter-Am. Ct. H.R. (Ser. A) (1986).

5. The African Charter provision on the right to information and freedom of expression, Article 9, is drafted in very general terms and contains a broad limitation clause. The Commission has nonetheless stated that "freedom of expression is a fundamental human right, essential to an individual's personal development, political consciousness and participation in the public affairs of his country." Comm. 212/98, *Amnesty International v. Zambia*, 12th

Annual Report of the Commission 1998–1999. The Commission has been critical of restrictions on the press. See e.g, Comm. 102/93, *Constitutional Rights Project and Civil Liberties Organization v. Nigeria,*12th Annual Activity Report of the Commission, 1998–1999; Comms. 105/93, 128/94, 130/94, 152/96, *Media Rights Agenda, Constitutional Rights Project v. Nigeria,* id. *See generally* C.E. Welch Jr., *The African Charter and Freedom of Expression in Africa,* 4 BUFFALO H.R.L.REV. 103 (1998).

6. Most limitations clauses only permit a right to be restricted based on law, raising the question of defining what constitutes a law for this purpose. The following case explores the issue:

The Word "Laws" in Article 30 of the American Convention on Human Rights,
Advisory Opinion OC-6/86 of May 9, 1986, 6 Inter-Am. Ct. H.R. (Ser. A) (1986).

. . . .

9. This request for an advisory opinion has been presented to the Court by the Government of Uruguay, a State Party to the American Convention and a Member State of the OAS. Under Article 64(1) of the Convention, "the member states of the Organization may consult the Court regarding the interpretation of this Convention or of other treaties concerning the protection of human rights in the American states." The request of the Government seeks an interpretation of Article 30 of the Convention and therefore comes under the terms of Article 64. . . .

12. The Convention establishes:

> Article 30. Scope of Restrictions
> The restrictions that, pursuant to this Convention, may be placed on the enjoyment or exercise of the rights or freedoms recognized herein may not be applied except in accordance with laws enacted for reasons of general interest and in accordance with the purpose for which such restrictions have been established.

13. This article must be "interpreted in good faith in accordance with the ordinary meaning to be given to the terms of this treaty in their context and in the light of its object and purpose" (Art. 31, Vienna Convention on the Law of Treaties (hereinafter "the Vienna Convention")). The terms used limit the restrictions that may be placed on the rights or freedoms recognized in the Convention to those cases where such restrictions derive from laws that meet the requirements imposed by the article itself.

14. Article 30 refers to the restrictions that the Convention itself authorizes with respect to the different rights and freedoms recognized therein. It must be emphasized that, under the Convention (Art. 29(a)), all acts directed toward the supression of any one of the rights set forth therein are illicit. In exceptional circumstances and under conditions precisely spelled out, the Convention allows the temporary suspension of some of the obligations assumed by the states (Art. 27). Under normal circumstances, there can only be "restrictions" to the enjoyment and exercise of such rights. The distinction between restriction and supression of the enjoyment or exercise of rights and freedoms derives from the Convention itself (Arts. 16(3), 29(a) and 30). We are here dealing with an important distinction and the amendment introduced on the matter during the last stage of the drafting of the Convention, at the Specialized Conference of San José, to include the words "to the enjoyment or exercise," clarified this point conceptually (Conferencia Especializada

Interamericana sobre Derechos Humanos, San José, Costa Rica, 7–22 de noviembre de 1969, *Actas y Documentos*, OEA/Ser.K/XVI/1.2, Washington, D.C. 1973 (hereinafter "*Actas y Documentos*") repr. 1978, esp. at 274).

15. The Court will now analyze the question of whether "the word 'laws' used (in Article 30) refers to laws in the formal sense—a legal norm passed by the Legislature and promulgated by the Executive Branch in the manner prescribed by the Constitution"—or whether, on the other hand, it is used "in the material sense, as a synonym for the entire body of law (*ordenamiento jurídico*), without regard to the procedure followed in creating such norms and the normative rank assigned to it within the hierarchical order of the particular legal system."

16. The question before us does not go beyond inquiring as to the meaning that the word "laws" has in Article 30 of the Convention. It is, therefore, not a question of giving an answer that can be applied to each case where the Convention uses such terms as "laws", "law", "legislative provisions", "provisions of the law", "legislative measures", "legal restrictions", or "domestic laws." On each occasion that such expressions are used, their meaning must be specifically determined.

17. Notwithstanding the above, the criteria of Article 30 are applicable to all those situations where the word "laws" or comparable expressions are used in the Convention in referring to the restrictions that the Convention itself authorizes with respect to each of the protected rights. In effect, the Convention does not limit itself to setting forth a group of rights and freedoms whose inviolability is assured to each individual, but also refers to the special circumstances in which it is possible to restrict the enjoyment or exercise of such rights or freedoms without violating them. Article 30 cannot be regarded as a kind of general authorization to establish new restrictions to the rights protected by the Convention, additional to those permitted under the rules governing each one of these. The purpose of the article, on the contrary, is to impose an additional requirement to legitimize individually authorized restrictions.

18. In reading Article 30 in conjunction with other articles in which the Convention authorizes the application of limitations or restrictions to specific rights or freedoms, it is evident that the following conditions must be concurrently met if such limitations or restrictions are to be implemented:

a) that the restriction in question be expressly authorized by the Convention and meet the special conditions for such authorization;

b) that the ends for which the restriction has been established be legitimate, that is, that they pursue "reasons of general interest" and do not stray from the "purpose for which (they) have been established." This teleological criterion, the analysis of which has not here been requested, establishes control through the deviation of power;

c) that such restrictions be established by laws and applied pursuant to them.

19. The meaning of the word "laws" must be sought as a term used in an international treaty. It is not, consequently, a question of determining the meaning of the word "laws" within the context of the domestic law of a State Party.

20. In this regard, the Court takes into account the fact that the legal regimes of the States Parties to the Convention each have their source in a different tradition.

Some States Parties can be said to form part of the Common Law system while others follow the Civil Law system. Their constitutional systems evince peculiarities which can be traced to their individual juridical and political developments. The concept of "laws" employed can not be interpreted in the abstract and, consequently, must not be divorced from the context of the legal system which gives meaning to the term "laws" and affects its application (cf. Eur. Court H. R., *The Sunday Times* case, judgment of 26 April, 1979. Series A no. 30, para. 47).

21. The meaning of the word "laws" in the context of a system for the protection of human rights cannot be disassociated from the nature and origin of that system. The protection of human rights, particularly the civil and political rights set forth in the Convention, is in effect based on the affirmation of the existence of certain inviolable attributes of the individual that cannot be legitimately restricted through the exercise of governmental power. These are individual domains that are beyond the reach of the State or to which the State has but limited access. Thus, the protection of human rights must necessarily comprise the concept of the restriction of the exercise of state power.

22. In order to guarantee human rights, it is therefore essential that state actions affecting basic rights not be left to the discretion of the government but, rather, that they be surrounded by a set of guarantees designed to ensure that the inviolable attributes of the individual not be impaired. Perhaps the most important of these guarantees is that restrictions to basic rights only be established by a law passed by the Legislature in accordance with the Constitution. Such a procedure not only clothes these acts with the assent of the people through its representatives, but also allows minority groups to express their disagreement, propose different initiatives, participate in the shaping of the political will, or influence public opinion so as to prevent the majority from acting arbitrarily. Although it is true that this procedure does not always prevent a law passed by the Legislature from being in violation of human rights—a possibility that underlines the need for some system of subsequent control—there can be no doubt that it is an important obstacle to the arbitrary exercise of power.

23. The above may be inferred from the "principle"—a term used by the Permanent Court of International Justice (*Consistency of Certain Danzig Legislative Decrees with the Constitution of the Free City*, Advisory Opinion, 1935, P.C.I.J., Series A/B, No. 65, p. 56)—of legality. This principle, which is found in almost all the constitutions of the Americas drafted since the end of the 18th century, is one and the same as the idea and the development of law in the democratic world and results in the acceptance of the existence of the so-called requirement of law (*reserva de ley*), by which fundamental rights can only be restricted by law, the legitimate expression of the will of the people.

24. Under democratic constitutionalism, the requirement of law (*reserva de ley*) in cases of interference in the realm of freedom is essential to the legal protection and full existence of human rights. For the principles of legality and requirement of law (*reserva de ley*) to be an effective guarantee of the rights and freedoms of the individual, not only must the latter be formally proclaimed but there must also be

a system that will effectively ensure their application and an effective control of the manner in which the organs exercise their powers.

25. As far back as 1789, the Declaration of the Rights of Man and the Citizen stated in its Article 4 that

Liberty consists in the power to do anything that does not injure others; accordingly, the exercise of the natural rights of each man has for its only limits those that secure to the other members of society the enjoyment of these same rights. These limits can be determined only by law.

Since that time, this concept has been a fundamental principle of democratic constitutional development.

26. From that perspective, one cannot interpret the word "laws," used in Article 30, as a synonym for just any legal norm, since that would be tantamount to admitting that fundamental rights can be restricted at the sole discretion of governmental authorities with no other formal limitation than that such restrictions be set out in provisions of a general nature. Such an interpretation would lead to disregarding the limits that democratic constitutional law has established from the time that the guarantee of basic human rights was proclaimed under domestic law. Nor would it be consistent with the Preamble to the American Convention, according to which "the essential rights of man are ... based upon attributes of the human personality and ... they therefore justify international protection in the form of a convention reinforcing or complementing the protection provided by the domestic law of the American states."

27. Within the framework of the protection of human rights, the word "laws" would not make sense without reference to the concept that such rights cannot be restricted at the sole discretion of governmental authorities. To affirm otherwise would be to recognize in those who govern virtually absolute power over their subjects. On the other hand, the word "laws" acquires all of its logical and historical meaning if it is regarded as a requirement of the necessary restriction of governmental interference in the area of individual rights and freedoms. The Court concludes that the word "laws," used in Article 30, can have no other meaning than that of formal law, that is, a legal norm passed by the legislature and promulgated by the Executive Branch, pursuant to the procedure set out in the domestic law of each State.

28. The Convention not only requires a law in order to legitimate restrictions to the enjoyment or exercise of rights or freedoms, but also demands that such laws be enacted "for reasons of general interest and in accordance with the purpose for which such restrictions have been established." The concept that those restrictions which are permitted must be applied "with the purpose for which such restrictions have been established" was already recognized in the Draft Convention on Human Rights drawn up by the Inter-American Council of Jurists (1959). That Draft stated that such restrictions "shall not be applied with any other purpose or design than that for which they have been established" (*Inter-American Yearbook on Human Rights*, 1968, Washington, D.C.: General Secretariat, OAS, 1973, at 248). On the other hand, the requirement that the application of the restrictions be in accordance with "laws enacted for reasons of general interest" is the result of an amend-

ment introduced in the final draft at the Specialized Conference of San Jose in 1969 (*Actas y Documentos, supra* 14 at 274).

29. The requirement that the laws be enacted for reasons of general interest means they must have been adopted for the "general welfare" (Art. 32(2)), a concept that must be interpreted as an integral element of public order (ordre public) in democratic states, the main purpose of which is "the protection of the essential rights of man and the creation of circumstances that will permit him to achieve spiritual and material progress and attain happiness" (American Declaration of the Rights and Duties of Man (hereinafter American Declaration), First Introductory Clause).

30. "General welfare" and "public order" are terms of the Convention that must be interpreted with reference to the treaty, which has its own philosophy under which the American States "require the political organization of these States on the basis of the effective exercise of representative democracy" (Charter of the OAS, Art. 3(d)); and the rights of man, which "are based upon attributes of his human personality," must be afforded international protection (American Declaration, Second Introductory Clause; American Convention, Preamble, para. 2).

31. In this connection, the Court has already stated that

> Within the framework of the Convention, it is possible to understand the concept of general welfare as referring to the conditions of social life that allow members of society to reach the highest level of personal development and the optimum achievement of democratic values. In that sense, it is possible to conceive of the organization of society in a manner that strengthens the functioning of democratic institutions and preserves and promotes the full realization of the rights of the individual. . . . The Court must recognize, nevertheless, the difficulty inherent in the attempt of defining with precision the concepts of "public order" and "general welfare." It also recognizes that both concepts can be used as much as to affirm the rights of the individual against the exercise of governmental power as to justify the limitations on the exercise of those rights in the name of collective interests. In this respect, the Court wishes to emphasize that "public order" or "general welfare" may under no circumstances be invoked as a means of denying a right guaranteed by the Convention or to impair or deprive it of its true content (See Art. 29(a) of the Convention). Those concepts, when they are invoked as a ground for limiting human rights, must be subjected to an interpretation that is strictly limited to the "just demands" of "a democratic society," which takes account of the need to balance the competing interests involved and the need to preserve the object and purpose of the Convention (*Compulsory Membership in an Association Prescribed by Law for the Practice of Journalism* (Arts. 13 and 29 American Convention on Human Rights), Advisory Opinion OC-5/85 of November 13, 1985. Series A No. 5, paras. 66 and 67).

32. Law in a democratic state is not merely a mandate of authority cloaked with certain necessary formal elements. It denotes a content and is directed towards a specific goal. The concept of "laws" referred to in Article 30, interpreted in the context of the Convention and in the light of its object and purpose, cannot be examined solely in terms of the principle of legality (see supra 23). In the spirit of the Convention, this principle must be understood as one in which general legal norms must be created by the relevant organs pursuant to the procedures established in the constitutions of each State Party, and one to which all public authorities must strictly adhere. In a democratic society, the principle of legality is inseparably linked to that of

legitimacy by virtue of the international system that is the basis of the Convention as it relates to the "effective exercise of representative democracy," which results in the popular election of legally created organs, the respect of minority participation and the furtherance of the general welfare, inter alia (see supra 22).

33. The Declaration of Mexico affirmed that the "purpose of the State is the happiness of man in society. The interests of the community should be harmonized with the rights of the individual. The American man cannot conceive of living without justice, just as he cannot conceive of living without liberty" ("Declaration of Mexico" of March 6, 1945, para. 12. *The International Conferences of American States, Second Supplement, 1942–1954.* Washington, D.C.: Pan American Union, Department of Legal Affairs, 1958 at 75).

34. The meaning of the word "laws" in Article 30 cannot be disassociated from the intention of all the American States, as expressed in the Preamble to the Convention, "to consolidate in the hemisphere within the framework of democratic institutions a system of personal liberty and social justice based on respect for the essential rights of man" (Preamble of the Convention, para. 1). Representative democracy is the determining factor throughout the system of which the Convention is a part. It is a "principle" reaffirmed by the American States in the OAS Charter, the basic instrument of the inter-American system. The Convention itself expressly recognizes political rights (Art. 23), which are included among those rights that cannot be suspended under Article 27. This is indicative of their importance in the system.

35. The "laws" referred to in Article 30 are, therefore, normative acts directed towards the general welfare, passed by a democratically elected legislature and promulgated by the Executive Branch. This meaning is fully consistent with the general context of the Convention, in line with the philosophy of the inter-American system. Only formal law, as the Court understands that term, can restrict the enjoyment and exercise of the rights recognized by the Convention.

36. The above does not necessarily negate the possibility of delegations of authority in this area, provided that such delegations are authorized by the Constitution, are exercised within the limits imposed by the Constitution and the delegating law, and that the exercise of the power delegated is subject to effective controls, so that it does not impair nor can it be used to impair the fundamental nature of the rights and freedoms protected by the Convention.

37. The necessary existence of the elements inherent in the concept of law in Article 30 of the Convention leads to the conclusion that, for purposes of the interpretation of this Article, the concepts of legality and legitimacy coincide, inasmuch as only a law that has been passed by democratically elected and constitutionally legitimate bodies and is tied to the general welfare may restrict the enjoyment or exercise of the rights or freedoms of the individual.

38. Consequently, in reply to the question presented by the Government of Uruguay on the interpretation of the word "laws" in Article 30 of the Convention,

THE COURT IS OF THE OPINION, Unanimously,

That the word "laws" in Article 30 of the Convention means a general legal norm tied to the general welfare, passed by democratically elected legislative bodies established by the Constitution, and formulated according to the procedures set forth by the constitutions of the States Parties for that purpose.

Questions and Comments

Is the definition of "law" only concerned with process or is it also attentive to the content of the measure?

ii. Implied Limitations

Hirst v. the United Kingdom (No. 2) [GC], (App. no. 74025/01), Judgment of 6 October 2005, Eur. Ct. H.R. (footnotes omitted).

THE FACTS

I. THE CIRCUMSTANCES OF THE CASE

11. The applicant was born in 1950.

12. On 11 February 1980, the applicant pleaded guilty to manslaughter on ground of diminished responsibility. His plea of guilty was accepted on the basis of medical evidence that the applicant was a man with a gross personality disorder to such a degree that he was amoral. He was sentenced to a term of discretionary life imprisonment.

13 . . . .

14. The applicant . . . is barred by section 3 of the Representation of the People Act 1983 from voting in parliamentary or local elections. . . .

II. RELEVANT DOMESTIC LAW AND PRACTICE

21. Section 3 of the Representation of the People Act 1983 provides:

(1) A convicted person during the time that he is detained in a penal institution in pursuance of his sentence . . . is legally incapable of voting at any parliamentary or local election.

22. This section re-enacted without debate the provisions of section 4 of the Representation of the People Act 1969, the substance of which dated back to the Forfeiture Act 1870 of the previous century, which in turn reflected earlier rules of law relating to the forfeiture of certain rights by a convicted "felon" (the so-called "civic death" of the times of King Edward III).

23. The disqualification does not apply to persons imprisoned for contempt of court (section 3(2)a) or to those imprisoned only for default in, for example, paying a fine (section 3(2)c).

24. During the passage through Parliament of the Representation of the People Act 2000, which permitted remand prisoners and unconvicted mental patients to vote, Mr. Howarth MP, speaking for the Government, maintained the view that "it should be part of a convicted prisoner's punishment that he loses rights and one of them is the right to vote". The Act was accompanied by a statement of compatibility under section 19 of the Human Rights Act 1998, namely, a statement that in intro-

ducing the measure in Parliament the Secretary of State considered its provisions to be compatible with the Convention.

III. RELEVANT INTERNATIONAL MATERIALS

. . . .

E. Law and practice in Contracting States

33. According to the Government's survey based on information obtained from its diplomatic representation, eighteen countries allowed prisoners to vote without restriction (Albania, Azerbaijan, Croatia, the Czech Republic, Denmark, Finland, the Former Yugoslav Republic of Macedonia, Germany, Iceland, Lithuania, Moldova, Montenegro, the Netherlands, Portugal, Slovenia, Sweden, Switzerland, Ukraine), in thirteen states all prisoners were barred from or unable to vote (Armenia, Belgium, Bulgaria, Cyprus, Estonia, Georgia, Hungary, Ireland, Russia, Serbia, Slovakia, Turkey, the United Kingdom), while in 12 states the right to vote of prisoners could be limited in some other way (Austria, Bosnia and Herzegovina, France, Greece, Italy, Luxembourg, Malta, Norway, Poland, Romania, Spain).

34. Other material before the Court indicates that in Romania prisoners may be debarred from voting if the principal sentence exceeds two years, while in Latvia prisoners serving a sentence of imprisonment in penitentiaries are not entitled to vote, as are prisoners in Liechtenstein.

. . . .

THE LAW

I. ALLEGED VIOLATION OF ARTICLE 3 OF PROTOCOL NO. 1 TO THE CONVENTION

40. The applicant complains that he has been disenfranchised, invoking Article 3 of Protocol No. 1 which provides:

> The High Contracting Parties undertake to hold free elections at reasonable intervals by secret ballot, under conditions which will ensure the free expression of the opinion of the people in the choice of the legislature.

. . . .

B. The Court's assessment

1. General principles

56. Article 3 of Protocol No. 1 appears at first sight to differ from the other rights guaranteed in the Convention and protocols as it is phrased in terms of the obligation of the High Contracting Party to hold elections which ensure the free expression of the opinion of the people rather than in terms of a particular right or freedom.

57. However, having regard to the preparatory work to Article 3 of the Protocol and the interpretation of the provision in the context of the Convention as a whole, the Court has established that it guarantees individual rights, including the right to vote and to stand for election (see *Mathieu-Mohin and Clerfayt v. Belgium*, judgment of 2 March 1987, Series A no. 113, pp. 22–23, §§ 46–51). Indeed, it was considered that the unique phrasing was intended to give greater solemnity to the

Contracting States' commitment and to emphasise that this was an area where they were required to take positive measures as opposed to merely refraining from interference (*Mathieu-Mohin*, § 50).

58. The Court has had frequent occasion to underline the importance of democratic principles underlying the interpretation and application of the Convention (see, among other authorities, *United Communist Party of Turkey and Others v. Turkey*, judgment of 30 January 1998, *Reports of Judgments and Decisions* 1998-I, § 45) and it would use this occasion to emphasise that the rights guaranteed under Article 3 of Protocol No. 1 are crucial to establishing and maintaining the foundations of an effective and meaningful democracy governed by the rule of law (see also the importance of these rights as recognised internationally, Relevant International Materials, paragraphs 26–39 above).

59. As pointed out by the applicant, the right to vote is not a privilege. In the twenty-first century, the presumption in a democratic State must be in favour of inclusion, as may be illustrated, for example, by the parliamentary history of the United Kingdom and other countries where the franchise was gradually extended over the centuries from select individuals, elite groupings or sections of the population approved of by those in power. Universal suffrage has become the basic principle (*Mathieu-Mohin*, § 51, citing *X. v. Germany*, no. 2728/66, Commission decision of 6 October 1967, Collection 25, pp. 38–41).

60. Nonetheless, the rights bestowed by Article 3 of Protocol No. 1 are not absolute. There is room for implied limitations and Contracting States must be given a margin of appreciation in this sphere.

61. There has been much discussion of the width of this margin in the present case. The Court would re-affirm that the margin in this area is wide (*Mathieu-Mohin*, § 52, and more recently, *Matthews v. United Kingdom* [GC], no. 24833/94, § 63, ECHR 1999-I; *Labita v. Italy* [GC], no. 26772/95, § 201, ECHR 2000-IV, and *Podkolzina v. Latvia*, no. 46726/99, § 33, ECHR 2002-II). There are numerous ways of organising and running electoral systems and a wealth of differences, *inter alia*, in historical development, cultural diversity and political thought within Europe which it is for each Contracting State to mould into their own democratic vision.

62. It is, however, for the Court to determine in the last resort whether the requirements of Article 3 of Protocol No. 1 have been complied with; it has to satisfy itself that the conditions do not curtail the rights in question to such an extent as to impair their very essence and deprive them of their effectiveness; that they are imposed in pursuit of a legitimate aim; and that the means employed are not disproportionate (see *Mathieu-Mohin*, § 52). In particular, any conditions imposed must not thwart the free expression of the people in the choice of the legislature—in other words, they must reflect, or not run counter to, the concern to maintain the integrity and effectiveness of an electoral procedure aimed at identifying the will of people through universal suffrage. For example, the imposition of a minimum age may be envisaged with a view to ensuring the maturity of those participating in the electoral process or, in some circumstances, eligibility may be geared to criteria, such as residence, to identify those with sufficiently continuous or close links to, or a stake in, the country concerned (*Hilbe v. Liechtenstein* (dec.) no. 31981/96, ECHR

1999-VI, *Melnychenko v. Ukraine*, no. 17707/02, § 56, ECHR 2004-X). Any departure from the principle of universal suffrage risks undermining the democratic validity of the legislature thus elected and the laws which it promulgates. Exclusion of any groups or categories of the general population must accordingly be reconcilable with the underlying purposes of Article 3 of Protocol No. 1 (see, *mutatis mutandis, Aziz v. Cyprus*, no. 669949/01, § 28, ECHR 2004-V).

2. Prisoners

63. The present case highlights the status of the right to vote of convicted prisoners who are detained.

64. The case-law of the Convention organs has, in the past, accepted various restrictions on certain convicted persons.

65. In some early cases, the Commission considered that it was open to the legislature to remove political rights from persons convicted of "uncitizenlike conduct" (gross abuse in their exercise of public life during the Second World War) and from a person sentenced to eight months' imprisonment for refusing to report for military service, where reference was made to the notion of dishonour that certain convictions carried with them for a specific period and which might be taken into account by the legislature in respect of the exercise of political rights (no. 6573/74, Commission decision of 19 December 1974, Decisions and Reports (DR) 1, p. 87, and no. 9914/82, Commission decision of 4 July 1983, DR 33, p. 245). In *Patrick Holland v. Ireland* (no. 24827/94, Commission decision of 14 April 1998, DR 93, p. 15), where, since there was no provision permitting a serving prisoner to vote in prison, the applicant, who was sentenced to seven years for possessing explosives, was *de facto* deprived of the vote, the Commission found that the suspension of the right to vote did not thwart the free expression of the opinion of the people in the choice of the legislature and could not be considered arbitrary in the circumstances of the case.

66. The Court itself rejected complaints about a judge-imposed bar on voting on a Member of Parliament, convicted of fiscal fraud offences and sentenced to three years' imprisonment with the additional penalty of being barred from exercising public functions for two years (*M.D.U. v. Italy*, no. 58540/00, decision of 28 January 2003).

67. The Government argued that the *Chamber* judgment finding a violation in respect of the bar on this applicant, a prisoner sentenced to life imprisonment, was an unexpected reversal of the tenor of the above cases.

68. This is however the first time that the Court has had occasion to consider a general and automatic disenfranchisement of convicted prisoners. It would note that in *Patrick Holland*, the case closest to the facts of the present application, the Commission confined itself to the question of whether the bar was arbitrary and omitted to give attention to other elements of the test laid down by the Court in *Mathieu-Mohin*, namely, the legitimacy of the aim and the proportionality of the measure. In consequence, the Court cannot attach decisive weight to the decision. The Chamber's finding of a violation was therefore not in contradiction of a previous judgment of the Court; on the contrary, the Chamber sought to apply the precedent of *Mathieu-Mohin* to the facts before it.

69. In this case, the Court would begin by underlining that prisoners in general continue to enjoy all the fundamental rights and freedoms guaranteed under the Convention save for the right to liberty, where lawfully imposed detention expressly falls within the scope of Article 5 of the Convention. For example, prisoners may not be ill-treated, subjected to inhuman or degrading punishment or conditions contrary to Article 3 of the Convention (see, among many authorities, *Kalashnikov v. Russia*, no. 47095/99, ECHR 2002-VI; *Van der Ven v. the Netherlands*, no. 50901/99, ECHR 2003-II); they continue to enjoy the right to respect for family life (*Ploski v. Poland*, no. 26761/95, judgment of 12 November 2002; *X. v. the United Kingdom*, no. 9054/80, Commission decision of 8 October 1982, DR 30, p. 113), the right to freedom of expression (*Yankov v. Bulgaria*, no. 39084/97, §§ 126–145, ECHR 2003-XII, *T. v. the United Kingdom*, no. 8231/78, Commission report of 12 October 1983, DR 49, p. 5, §§ 44–84), the right to practise their religion (*Poltoratskiy v. Ukraine*, no. 38812/97, §§ 167–171, ECHR 2003-V), the right of effective access to a lawyer or to court for the purposes of Article 6 (*Campbell and Fell v. the United Kingdom*, judgment of 28 June 1984, Series A, no. 80; *Golder v. the United Kingdom*, judgment of 21 February 1975, Series A, no. 18), the right to respect for correspondence (*Silver and Others v. the United Kingdom*, judgment of 25 March 1983, Series A no. 61) and the right to marry (*Hamer v. the United Kingdom*, no. 7114/75, Commission report of 13 December 1979, DR 24, p. 5; *Draper v. the United Kingdom*, no. 8186/78, Commission report of 10 July 1980, DR 24, p. 72). Any restrictions on these other rights require to be justified, although such justification may well be found in the considerations of security, in particular the prevention of crime and disorder, which inevitably flow from the circumstances of imprisonment (see, for example, *Silver*, cited above, §§ 99–105, where broad restrictions on the right of prisoners to correspond fell foul of Article 8 but stopping of specific letters, containing threats or other objectionable references were justifiable in the interests of the prevention of disorder or crime).

70. There is, therefore, no question that a prisoner forfeits his Convention rights merely because of his status as a person detained following conviction. Nor is there any place under the Convention system, where tolerance and broadmindedness are the acknowledged hallmarks of democratic society, for automatic disenfranchisement based purely on what might offend public opinion.

71. This standard of tolerance does not prevent a democratic society from taking steps to protect itself against activities intended to destroy the rights or freedoms set forth in the Convention. Article 3 of Protocol No. 1, which enshrines the individual's capacity to influence the composition of the law-making power, does not therefore exclude that restrictions on electoral rights are imposed on an individual who has, for example, seriously abused a public position or whose conduct threatened to undermine the rule of law or democratic foundations (see, for example, no. 6573/74, cited above; and, *mutatis mutandis, Glimmerveen and Hagenbeek v. the Netherlands,* applications nos. 8348/78 and 8406/78, Commission decision of 11 October 1979, DR 18, p. 187, where the Commission declared inadmissible two applications concerning the refusal to allow the applicants, who were the leaders of a proscribed organisation with racist and xenophobic traits, to stand for election).

The severe measure of disenfranchisement must, however, not be undertaken lightly and the principle of proportionality requires a discernible and sufficient link between the sanction and the conduct and circumstances of the individual concerned. The Court notes in this regard the recommendation of the Venice Commission that the withdrawal of political rights should only be carried out by express judicial decision. As in other contexts, an independent court, applying an adversarial procedure, provides a strong safeguard against arbitrariness.

3. Application in the present case

72. Turning to this application, the Court recalls that the applicant, sentenced to life imprisonment for manslaughter, was disenfranchised during his period of detention by section 3 of the 1983 Act which applied to persons convicted and serving a custodial sentence. The Government argued that the Chamber erred in its approach, claiming that it had assessed the compatibility of the legislation with the Convention in the abstract without consideration of whether removal of the vote from the applicant as a person convicted of a serious offence and sentenced to life imprisonment disclosed a violation. The Court does not accept this criticism. The applicant's complaint was in no sense an *actio popularis*. He was directly and immediately affected by the legislative provision of which complaint is made and in these circumstances the Chamber was justified in examining the compatibility with the Convention of such a measure, without regard to the question whether if the measure had been framed otherwise and in a way which was compatible with the Convention, the applicant might still have been deprived of the vote. The Divisional Court similarly examined the compatibility with the Convention of the measure in question. It would not in any event be right for the Court to assume that, if Parliament were to amend the current law, restrictions on the right to vote would necessarily still apply to post-tariff life prisoners or to conclude that such an amendment would necessarily be compatible with Article 3 of Protocol No. 1.

73. The Court will therefore determine whether the measure in question pursued a legitimate aim in a proportionate manner having regard to the principles identified above.

a. Legitimate aim

74. The Court would recall that Article 3 of Protocol No.1 does not, as other provisions of the Convention, specify or limit the aims which a measure must pursue. A wider range of purposes may therefore be compatible with Article 3 (see, for example, *Podkolzina*, cited above, § 34). The Government have submitted that the measure pursues the aim of preventing crime by sanctioning the conduct of convicted prisoners and also the aim of enhancing civic responsibility and respect for the rule of law. The Court would note that at the time of the passage of the latest legislation the Government stated that the aim of the bar on convicted prisoners was to confer an additional punishment. This was also the position espoused by the Secretary of State in the domestic proceedings brought by the applicant. While the primary emphasis at the domestic level may perhaps have been the idea of punishment, it may nevertheless be considered as implied in the references to the forfeiting of rights that the measure is meant to give an incentive to citizen-like conduct.

75. Although rejecting the notion that imprisonment after conviction involves the forfeiture of rights beyond the right to liberty, and especially the assertion that voting is a privilege not a right, the Court accepts that section 3 may be regarded as pursuing the aims identified by the Government. It recalls that the Chamber in its judgment expressed reservations as to the validity of these aims, citing the majority opinion of the Canadian Supreme Court in *Sauvé No. 2* (see paragraphs 44–47 of the *Chamber* judgment). However, whatever doubt there may be as to the efficacy of achieving these aims through a bar on voting, the Court finds no reason in the circumstances of this application to exclude these aims as untenable or *per se* incompatible with the right guaranteed under Article 3 of Protocol No. 1.

b. Proportionality

76. The Court recalls that the Chamber found that the measure lacked proportionality, essentially as it was an automatic blanket ban imposed on all convicted prisoners which was arbitrary in its effects and could no longer be said to serve the aim of punishing the applicant once his tariff (that period representing retribution and deterrence) had expired.

77. The Government have argued that the measure was proportionate, pointing out *inter alia* that it only affected some 48,000 prisoners (not the 70,000 stated in the *Chamber* judgment which omitted to take into account prisoners on remand who were no longer under any ban) and submitting that the ban was in fact restricted in its application as it affected only those convicted of crimes serious enough to warrant a custodial sentence and not including those detained on remand, for contempt of court or default in payment of fines. On the latter point, the Latvian Government have also placed emphasis on the fact that in Contracting States imprisonment was the last resort of criminal justice. The Court, firstly, does not regard the difference in numbers identified above to be decisive. The fact remains that it is a significant figure and it cannot be claimed that the bar is negligible in its effects. Secondly, while it is true that there are categories of detained persons unaffected by the bar, it nonetheless includes a wide range of offenders and sentences, from one day to life and from relatively minor offences to offences of the utmost gravity. Further, the Court observes that, even in the case of offenders whose offences are sufficiently serious to attract an immediate custodial sentence, whether the offender is in fact deprived of the right to vote will depend on whether the sentencing judge imposes such a sentence or elects for some other form of disposal, such as a community sentence. In this regard, it may be noted that in sentencing the criminal courts in England and Wales make no reference to disenfranchisement and it is not apparent, beyond the fact that a court considered it appropriate to impose a sentence of imprisonment, that there is any direct link between the facts of any individual case and the removal of the right to vote.

78. The width of the margin of appreciation has been emphasised by the Government which argued that where the legislature and domestic courts have considered the matter and there is no clear consensus in Contracting States, it must be within the range of possible approaches to remove the vote from any person whose conduct was so serious as to merit imprisonment.

79. As to the weight to be attached to the position adopted by the legislature and judiciary in the United Kingdom, there is no evidence that Parliament has ever sought to weigh the competing interests or to assess the proportionality of a blanket ban on the right of a convicted prisoner to vote. It is true that the question was considered by the multi-party Speaker's Conference on Electoral Law in 1968 which unanimously recommended that a convicted prisoner should not be entitled to vote. It is also true that the Working Party, which recommended the amendment to the law to allow unconvicted prisoners to vote, recorded that successive Governments had taken the view that convicted prisoners had lost the moral authority to vote and did not therefore argue for a change in the legislation. It may perhaps be said that, by voting the way they did to exempt unconvicted prisoners from the restriction on voting, Parliament implicitly affirmed the need for continued restrictions on the voting rights of convicted prisoners. Nonetheless it cannot be said that there was any substantive debate by members of the legislature on the continued justification in light of modern day penal policy and of current human rights standards for maintaining such a general restriction on the right of prisoners to vote.

80. It is also evident from the judgment of the Divisional Court that the nature of the restrictions, if any, to be imposed on the right of a convicted prisoner to vote was in general seen as a matter for Parliament and not for the national courts. The court did not therefore undertake any assessment of proportionality of the measure itself. It may also be noted that the court found support in the decision of the Federal Court of Appeal in *Sauvé No. 2*, which was later overturned by the Canadian Supreme Court.

81. As regards the existence or not of any consensus among Contracting States, the Court would note that, although there is some disagreement about the state of the law in certain States, it is undisputed that the United Kingdom is not alone among Convention countries in depriving all convicted prisoners of the right to vote. It may also be said that the law in the United Kingdom is less far-reaching than in certain other States. Not only are exceptions made for persons committed to prison for contempt of court or for default in paying fines, but unlike the position in some countries, the legal incapacity to vote is removed as soon as the person ceases to be detained. However the fact remains that it is a minority of Contracting States in which a blanket restriction on the right of convicted prisoners to vote is imposed or in which there is no provision allowing prisoners to vote. Even on the Government's own figures the number of such States does not exceed 13. Moreover, and even if no common European approach to the problem can be discerned, this cannot of itself be determinative of the issue.

82. Therefore, while the Court reiterates that the margin of appreciation is wide, it is not all-embracing. Further, although the situation was somewhat improved by the Act of 2000 which for the first time granted the vote to persons detained on remand, section 3 of the 1983 Act remains a blunt instrument. It strips of their Convention right to vote a significant category of persons and it does so in a way which is indiscriminate. The provision imposes a blanket restriction on all convicted prisoners in prison. It applies automatically to such prisoners, irrespective of the length of their sentence and irrespective of the nature or gravity of their offence

and their individual circumstances. Such a general, automatic and indiscriminate restriction on a vitally important Convention right must be seen as falling outside any acceptable margin of appreciation, however wide that margin might be, and as being incompatible with Article 3 of Protocol No. 1.

83. Turning to the Government's comments concerning the lack of guidance from the Chamber as to what, if any, restrictions on the right of convicted prisoners to vote would be compatible with the Convention, the Court notes that its function is in principle to rule on the compatibility with the Convention of the existing measures. It is primarily for the State concerned to choose, subject to supervision by the Committee of Ministers, the means to be used in its domestic legal order in order to discharge its obligation under Article 46 of the Convention (see, among other authorities, *Assanidze v. Georgia* [GC], no. 71503/01, § 202, ECHR 2004-II; *Öcalan v. Turkey* [GC], no. 46221/99, § 210, 2005- . . .). In cases where a systemic violation has been found the Court has, with a view to assisting the respondent State to fulfil its obligations under Article 46, indicated the type of measure that might be taken to put an end to the situation found to exist (see, for example, *Broniowski v. Poland* [GC], no. 31443/96, §§ 193–194, ECHR 2004- . . .). In other exceptional cases, the nature of the violation found may be such as to leave no real choice as to the measures required to remedy it and the Court may decide to indicate only one such measure (see *Assanidze*, cited above, § 202).

84. In a case such as the present, where Contracting States have adopted a number of different ways of addressing the question of the right of convicted prisoners to vote, the Court must confine itself to determining whether the restriction affecting all convicted prisoners in custody exceeds any acceptable margin of appreciation, leaving it to the legislature to decide on the choice of means for securing the rights guaranteed by Article 3 of Protocol No. 1 (see, for example, the cases concerning procedures governing the continued detention of life prisoners, where Court case-law and domestic legislation have evolved progressively: *Thynne, Wilson and Gunnell v. the United Kingdom*, judgment of 25 October 1990, Series A no. 190-A, *Singh v. the United Kingdom*, judgment of 21 February 1996, *Reports* 1996-I, *Stafford v. the United Kingdom* [GC], no. 46295/99, ECHR 2002-IV).

85. The Court concludes that there has been a violation of Art. 3 of Protocol No. 1.

Questions and Comments

What is the legal basis for implied limitations? Are such limitations consistent with the general approach to interpreting human rights treaties?

iii. Clawback Clauses

Some of the provisions in the African Charter refer to the exercise of the guaranteed rights "according to" or "under" domestic law. In the eyes of the Commission, the provisions must be narrowly interpreted:

> International human rights standards must always prevail over contradictory national law. Any limitation on the rights of the Charter must be in conformity with the provisions of the Charter. In contrast to other international human rights instruments, the African Charter does not contain a derogation clause. Therefore limitations on the rights and freedoms enshrined in the Charter cannot be justified by emergencies or special circumstances. The only legitimate reasons for limitations to the rights and freedoms of the African Charter are found in Article 27.2, that is that the rights of the Charter 'shall be exercised with due regard to the rights of others, collective security, morality and common interest.' The reasons for possible limitations must be founded in a legitimate state interest and the evils of limitations of rights must be strictly proportionate with and absolutely necessary for the advantages which are to be obtained. Even more important, a limitation may never have as a consequence that the right itself becomes illusory.

Media Rights Agenda, Constitutional Rights Project, et al. v. Nigeria, Comm. 105/93 *et al.*, Decision of Oct. 31, 1998, 12th Ann. Activities Rep., reprinted at 7 Int'l Human Rts. Rep. at 271. at paras. 66–70. The Commission further elaborated its views on clawback clauses in the following decision:

Amnesty International v. Zambia, (Comm. 212/98), *12th Annual Activity Report of the Afr. Comm. H.P.R. 1998–1999*, Annex V, pp. 76–81.

1. The communication is submitted by Amnesty International on behalf of William Steven Banda and John Lyson Chinula.

2. Complainant alleges that Zambia has violated the provisions of African Charter in that:

3. Mr. William Steven Banda was served with a deportation order on 10 November 1991. The reason given was that "in my opinion by his presence he (is) likely to be a danger to peace and good order in Zambia". He contested the order through the courts of Zambia.

4. On 25 October 1994, William Steven Banda was deported to Malawi unlawfully, wrongfully and out of political malice. He alleges that he was blindfolded and drugged, driven by Zambian immigration service and para-military police officers. He entered Malawi through Mchinji border post and later dumped at Lilongwe Police station. . . .

12. Mr. Mulonda, for the government, stated that the government did not act with political malice. It acted within the law. The investigations against Banda began in 1976 and against Chinula in 1974 long before the present regime came into power. He denied that the deportees were drugged and dumped across the border. He stated that the Malawi authorities received them. The government of Zambia was acting within its sovereign rights in ordering its internal affairs, regulating im-

migration and was within the provision or limitation of the right stipulated in Article12: "This right may only be subject to restriction as provided for by law for the protection of nation security, law and order, public health and morality". . . .

49. The Government of Zambia has relied on the "draw-back" clause of Article 12(2):

> This right may only be subject to restrictions, provided for by law for the protection of national security, law or order, public health or morality . . .

50. The deportation order also stated that the deportees were considered "a danger to peace and good order to Zambia". The Commission is of the view that the "claw-back" clauses must not be interpreted against the principles of the Charter. Recourse to these should not be used as a means of giving credence to violations of the express provisions of the Charter. Secondly, the rules of natural justice must apply. Among these are in the *audi alterm partem* rule, the right to be heard, the right of access to the Court. The Court in Zambia, in Banda's case failed to examine the basis of administrative action and as such, it has not been proved that the deportees were indeed a danger to law and order. In any event the suggestion that they were "likely" to be a danger was vague and not proved. It is important for the Commission to caution against a too easy resort to the limitation clauses in the African Charter. The onus is on the state to prove that it is justified to resort to the limitation clause. The Commission should act bearing in mind the provisions of Articles 61 and 62 of the Charter.

[The Commission found that the government had violated Articles Article 2, 7(1) (a), 8, 9(2),10 and 18(1) and (2)]

Questions and Comments

1. What are the "rules of natural justice" to which the African Commission refers?

2. Who has the burden of proof on the permissibility of national laws restricting the exercise of rights? See Comm. 224/98, *Media Rights Agenda v. Nigeria*: "For a State to [invoke a clawback clause], it must show that such a law is consistent with its obligations under the Charter. It is therefore not enough for a State to plead the existence of a law, it has to go further to show that such a law falls within the permissible restrictions under the Charter and therefore in conformity with its Charter obligation," para. 75 of the decision, 14th Ann. Report of the Commission 2000–2001.

3. In addition to clawback clauses, the African Charter is notable for its inclusion of duties. A distinguished African jurist and former vice president of the International Court of Justice, who played an important role in drafting the African Charter, has said that "in Africa, laws and duties are regarded as being two facets of the same reality: two inseparable realities." Keba Mbaye, "Introduction to the African Charter on Human and Peoples' Rights," *in* International Commission of Jurists, *Human and Peoples' Rights in Africa and the African Charter* 19, at 27 (1985). See also: Makau wa Mutua, "The Banjul Charter and the African Cultural Fingerprint: An Evaluation of the Language of Duties," 35 Va. J. Int'l L. 339 (1995). Mbaye suggests that it should therefore come as no surprise to anyone that the African Charter proclaims duties as well as rights. Does it make a difference whether an individual's rights are limited by the rights of others or by considerations of collective security? Note that Article 29 imposes on the individual the duty "to respect his parents at

all times, to maintain them in case of need" and "to preserve and strengthen social and national solidarity, particularly when the latter is threatened." Arts. 29(1) and 29(4). How do the first two duties differ from the third?

4. To what extent do regional instruments outside Africa contain clawback clauses? See, e.g. European Convention on Human Rights, Art. 12 and its application in the case of *B. and L. v. The United Kingdom*, judgment of 13 September 2005. The European Court of Human Rights addressed a national law that prohibited marriage between a father-in-law and daughter-in-law, following their respective divorces. The prohibition was based on the Marriage Act 1949 as amended by the Marriage (Prohibited Degrees of Relationship) Act 1986. The Government conceded that the prohibition on parents-in-law marrying children-in-law constituted a limitation on the "capacity" to marry, but submitted that a marriage was possible provided both respective former spouses were dead or permission was granted by way of a personal Act of Parliament. According to the government, these requirements were proportionate having regard to the complexity of relationships, the harm to others that was potentially involved in such marriages and the requirements of the protection of morals. The government noted that in this case the marriage would have the effect of making the first applicant step-father of his grandson, a situation which in its view "could well be deeply confusing and disturbing for a child." The government also contended that the limitation constituted a "national law governing the exercise of this right" and was thereby permissible, since it did not impair the very essence of the right and could be justified in the public interest.

The Court agreed with applicants that Article 12 secures the fundamental right of a man and woman to marry and to found a family, but noted that the exercise of the right to marry gives rise to social, personal and legal consequences. It is therefore subject to the national laws of the Contracting States, provided that the limitations introduced do not restrict or reduce the right in such a way or to such an extent that the very essence of the right is impaired.

As the Court pointed out, Article 12 expressly provides for regulation of marriage by national law, given the sensitive moral choices concerned and the importance to be attached to the protection of children and the fostering of secure family environments. As a consequence, the Court stated that it would not rush to substitute its own judgment in place of the authorities who are best placed to assess and respond to the needs of society. It noted that there are a large number of Contracting States which have a similar bar in their law, reflecting apparently similar concerns about allowing marriages of this degree of affinity.

Examining the facts of the case in the context pertaining in the United Kingdom, the Court observed that the bar on marriage was aimed at legitimate purposes: protecting the integrity of the family (preventing sexual rivalry between parents and children) and preventing harm to children who may be affected by the changing relationships of the adults around them. However, it found that the bar on marriage did not prevent the relationships occurring. No incest or other criminal law provisions prohibited extra-marital relationships between parents-in-law and children-in-law being established, notwithstanding that children may live in these homes. It could not therefore be said that the ban on the applicants' marriage prevented any alleged confusion or emotional insecurity to the second applicant's son.

Finally, the Court noted that the law was subject to exceptions. Marriages could take place, pursuant to a personal Act of Parliament, which had been granted. In the *Monk* case, where there were also children in the household, it was declared that the impediment placed on the marriage served no useful purpose of public policy. The inconsistency between the stated aims of the incapacity and the waiver applied in some cases was found to undermine the rationality and logic of the measure. The Government argued that the Parliamentary procedure provided a means of ensuring that exceptions were only made where no harm would ensue. The Court commented that there was no indication of any detailed investigation into family circumstances in the Parliamentary procedure. In any event, this was deemed to be a cumbersome and expensive vetting process not appearing to offer a practically accessible or effective mechanism for individuals to vindicate their rights. The Court said it also would "view with reservation" a system that would require a person of full age in possession of his or her mental faculties to submit to a potentially intrusive investigation to ascertain whether it was suitable to marry another. The Court therefore concluded that there had been, in the circumstances of the case, a violation of Article 12 of the Convention. *See also Johnston and Others v. The United Kingdom, infra* at pp. 164–169.

5. In the African system, is it clear that Article 27.2 applies to all the clawback clauses, including those that provide for the exercise of rights "according to the law"?

6. Do the European, Inter-American and African institutions apply the same tests for the permissibility of limitations and clawback clauses? Does the European Court treat the Art. 12 clawback clause like the limitations provision contained in Article 10(2)? Should there be any difference in approach?

7. Is it appropriate to grant a "margin of appreciation" on limitations when the text of the Convention establishes a standard of "necessity" for restrictions? Should a state's determination of "necessity" be subject to strict scrutiny by the European Court?

5. Domestic Application of Regional Instruments

None of the regional human rights treaties specifies how the guaranteed rights are to be ensured in domestic law. That is a matter left to each state party. The status and effect of treaties vary considerably among states, as the following constitutional provisions indicate. Some constitutions make treaties in force for the state directly applicable by courts as domestic law; other constitutions require implementing legislation. Yet a third group of states applies the doctrine of self-executing treaties, which looks to the language of the instrument, the intent of the parties, and constitutional allocation of competence to determine which treaty provisions may be enforceable without legislative action. The existence of supervisory commissions and courts which may issue decisions or judgments against the state raises yet another problem of domestic enforcement and compliance, discussed in the following Chapter.

A. The Use of Reservations

When a state adheres to a multilateral treaty, it may seek to create its own exceptions to the treaty and limit its obligations through attaching reservations which are filed with its instrument of ratification or accession. According to the provisions of the Vienna Convention on the Law of Treaties, quoted in the Inter-American Court's advisory opinion below, a reservation is permitted unless the treaty bars reservations in general or the type filed in particular, or the reservation is "incompatible with the object and purpose of the treaty." Vienna Convention, Art. 19. The European and American Conventions each contain a provision governing the permissibility of reservations; the African Charter does not, leaving the matter to be governed by general international law. As you read the following materials, consider whether the "minimum standards" set forth in human rights treaties should be subject to reservations at all? If so, who determines whether or not a particular reservation is compatible with the object and purpose of the treaty? How should that be determined? How have the regional tribunals addressed this question?

i. Europe

Article 64, European Convention on Human Rights

    1. Any State may, when signing the Convention or when depositing its instrument of ratification, make a reservation in respect of any particular provision of the Convention to the extent that any law then in force in its territory is not in conformity with the provision. Reservations of a general character shall not be permitted under this Article.

    2. Any reservation made under this Article shall contain a brief statement of the law concerned.

Note on *Belilos v. Switzerland*: In the *Belilos Case*, the European Court of Human Rights assessed the compatibility with Article 64 of an "interpretative declaration" of Switzerland to Article 6 of the European Convention. Switzerland did not contest the jurisdiction of the Court to decide this issue. The Court looked behind the title given to the Swiss declaration to establish its legal character as a reservation. It then inquired whether the declaration amounted to an impermissible general reservation. In this regard the Court said: "By 'reservation of a general character' in Article 64 is meant in particular a reservation couched in terms that are too vague or broad for it to be possible to determine their exact meaning and scope."

The Swiss declaration said:

> The Swiss Federal Council considers that the guarantee of fair trial in Article 6, paragraph 1, of the Convention, in the determination of civil rights and obligations or any criminal charge against the person in question is intended solely to ensure ultimate control by the judiciary over the acts or decisions of the public authorities relating to such rights or obligations or the determination of such a charge.

The Court held this declaration contravened the prohibition on general reservations. The Court also held the Swiss failed to submit a statement of the law concerned, as required in Article 64, para. 2. The Court then turned to the merits, finding it "beyond doubt" that Switzerland is bound by the Convention irrespective of the validity of the declaration. The Court unanimously held there had been a breach of Article 6, para. 1, of the Convention. See Eur. Ct.H.R., *Belilos Case*, Judgment of 29 April 1988, Ser. A No. 132. For another case in which the European Court examined and upheld the validity of a reservation, see *Helle v. Finland*, Rep. 1997-VIII, judgment of Dec. 19.

ii. The Americas

The Effect of Reservations on the Entry into Force of the American Convention (Arts. 74 and 75), Advisory Opinion OC-2/82 of September 24, 1982, 2 Inter-Am. Ct. H.R. (Ser. A) (1982).

1. STATEMENT OF THE ISSUES

. . . .

8. The Commission submitted the following question to the Court:

From what moment is a state deemed to have become a party to the American Convention on Human Rights when it ratifies or adheres to the Convention with one or more reservations: from the date of the deposit of instrument of ratification or adherence or upon the termination of the period specified in Article 20 of the Vienna Convention on the Law of Treaties?

18. In answering this question, the Court notes that two provisions of the Convention provide a starting point for its inquiry. The first is Article 74 (2). . . . The second provision is Article 75. . . .

19. The language of Article 74 (2) is silent on the issue whether it applies exclusively to ratifications and adherences which contain no reservations or whether it also applies to those with reservations. Furthermore, whether and to what extent Article 75 helps to resolve the question before the Court can be answered only following an analysis of that stipulation as well as of other relevant provisions of the Convention in their context and in the light of the object and purpose of the Convention (Vienna Convention on the Law of Treaties, hereinafter cited as "Vienna Convention", Art. 31) and, where necessary, by reference to its drafting history (Vienna Convention, Art. 32). Moreover, given the reference in Article 75 to the Vienna Convention, the Court must also examine the relevant provisions of that instrument.

20. The reference in Article 75 to the Vienna Convention raises almost as many questions as it answers. The provisions of that instrument dealing with reservations provide for the application of different rules to different categories of treaties. It must be determined, therefore, how the Convention is to be classified for purposes of the here relevant provisions of the Vienna Convention, keeping in mind the language of Article 75 and the purpose it was designed to serve.

21. The provisions of the Vienna Convention that bear on the question presented by the Commission read as follows:

Article 19 Formulation of reservations

A State may, when signing, ratifying, accepting, approving or acceding to a treaty, formulate a reservation unless:

    (a) the reservation is prohibited by the treaty;

    (b) the treaty provides that only specified reservations, which do not include the reservation in question, may be made; or

    (c) in cases not falling under subparagraphs (a) and (b), the reservation is incompatible with the object and purpose of the treaty.

Article 20 Acceptance of and objection to reservations

1. A reservation expressly authorized by a treaty does not require any subsequent acceptance by the other contracting States unless the treaty so provides.

2. When it appears from the limited number of the negotiating States and the object and purpose of a treaty that the application of the treaty in its entirety between all the parties is an essential condition of the consent of each one to be bound by the treaty, a reservation requires acceptance by all the parties.

3. When a treaty is a constituent instrument of an international organization and unless it otherwise provides, a reservation requires the acceptance of the competent organ of that organization.

4. In cases not falling under the preceding paragraphs and unless the treaty otherwise provides:

(a) acceptance of another contracting State of a reservation constitutes the reserving State a party to the treaty in relation to that other State if or when the treaty is in force for those States;

(b) an objection of another contracting State to a reservation does not preclude the entry into force of the treaty as between the objecting and reserving States unless a contrary intention is definitely expressed by the objecting State;

(c) an act expressing a State's consent to be bound by the treaty and containing a reservation is effective as soon as at least one other contracting State has accepted the reservation.

5. For the purposes of paragraphs 2 and 4 and unless the treaty otherwise provides, a reservation is considered to have been accepted by a State if it shall have raised no objection to the reservation by the end of a period of twelve months after it was notified of the reservation or by the date on which it expressed its consent to be bound by the treaty, whichever is later. (. . .)

22. Turning first to Article 19, the Court concludes that the reference in Article 75 to the Vienna Convention was intended to be a reference to paragraph (c) of Article 19 of the Vienna Convention. Paragraphs (a) and (b) are inapplicable on their face since the Convention does not prohibit reservations and since it does not specify the permissible reservations. It follows that Article 75 must be deemed to permit States to ratify or adhere to the Convention with whatever reservations they wish to make, provided only that such reservations are not "incompatible with the object and purpose" of the Convention. (. . .)

26. Having concluded that States ratifying or adhering to the Convention may do so with any reservations that are not incompatible with its object and purpose, the Court must now determine which provisions of Article 20 of the Vienna Convention apply to reservations made to the Convention. The result of this inquiry will of necessity also provide the answer to the question posed by the Commission. This is so because, if under the Vienna Convention reservations to the Convention are not deemed to require acceptance by the other States Parties, then for the here relevant purposes Article 74 of the Convention applies and a State ratifying or adhering to it with or without a reservation is deemed to be a State Party as of the date of the deposit of the instrument of ratification or adherence. (Vienna Convention, Art. 20 (1).) On the other hand, if acceptance of the reservation is required under the Vienna Convention, a reserving State would be deemed to become a State Party only on the date when at least one other State Party has accepted the reservation either expressly or by implication. (Vienna Convention, Arts. 20 (4) (c) and 20 (5).)

27. In the opinion of the Court, only paragraph 1 or paragraph 4 of Article 20 of the Vienna Convention can be deemed to be relevant in applying Articles 74 and 75 of the Convention. Paragraph 2 of Article 20 is inapplicable, inter alia, because the object and purpose of the Convention is not the exchange of reciprocal rights between a limited number of States, but the protection of the human rights of all individual human beings within the Americas, irrespective of their nationality. Moreover, the Convention is not the constituent instrument of an international organization. Therefore, Article 20 (3) is inapplicable.

28. In deciding whether the Convention envisages the application of paragraph 1 or paragraph 4 of Article 20 of the Vienna Convention, the Court notes that the principles enunciated in Article 20 (4) reflect the needs of traditional multilateral international agreements which have as their object the reciprocal exchange, for the mutual benefit of the States Parties, of bargained for rights and obligations. In this context, and given the vastly increased number of States comprising the international community today, the system established by Article 20 (4) makes considerable sense. It permits States to ratify many multilateral treaties and to do so with the reservations they deem necessary; it enables the other contracting States to accept or reject the reservations and to determine whether they wish to enter into treaty relations with the reserving State; and it provides that as soon as at least one other State Party has accepted the reservation, the treaty enters into force with respect to the reserving State.

29. The Court must emphasize, however, that modern human rights treaties in general, and the American Convention in particular, are not multilateral treaties of the traditional type concluded to accomplish the reciprocal exchange of rights for the mutual benefit of the contracting States. Their object and purpose is the protection of the basic rights of individual human beings, irrespective of their nationality, both against the State of their nationality and all other contracting States. In concluding these human rights treaties, the States can be deemed to submit themselves to a legal order within which they, for the common good, assume various obligations, not in relation to other States, but towards all individuals within their jurisdiction.

34. In this context, it would be manifestly unreasonable to conclude that the reference in Article 75 to the Vienna Convention compels the application of the legal regime established by Article 20 (4), which makes the entry into force of a ratification with a reservation dependent upon its acceptance by another State. A treaty which attaches such great importance to the protection of the individual that it makes the right of individual petition mandatory as of the moment of ratification, can hardly be deemed to have intended to delay the treaty's entry into force until at least one other State is prepared to accept the reserving State as a party. Given the institutional and normative framework of the Convention, no useful purpose would be served by such a delay.

35. Accordingly, for the purpose of the present analysis, the reference in Article 75 to the Vienna Convention makes sense only if it is understood as an express authorization designed to enable States to make whatever reservations they deem appropriate, provided the reservations are not incompatible with the object and

purpose of the treaty. As such, they can be said to be governed by Article 20 (1) of the Vienna Convention and, consequently, do not require acceptance by any other State Party.

36. The Court notes, in this connection, that Article 20 (1), in speaking of "a reservation expressly authorized by a treaty," is not by its terms limited to specific reservations. A treaty may expressly authorize one or more specific reservations or reservations in general. If it does the latter, which is what the Court has concluded to be true of the Convention, the resultant reservations, having been thus expressly authorized, need not be treated differently from expressly authorized specific reservations. The Court wishes to emphasize, in this connection, that unlike Article 19 (b), which refers to "specified reservations," Article 20 (1) contains no such restrictive language, and therefore permits the interpretation of Article 75 of the Convention adopted in this opinion.

37. Having concluded that reservations expressly authorized by Article 75, that is, all reservations compatible with the object and purpose of the Convention, do not require acceptance by the States Parties, the Court is of the opinion that the instruments of ratification or adherence containing them enter into force, pursuant to Article 74, as of the moment of their deposit.

38. The States Parties have a legitimate interest, of course, in barring reservations incompatible with the object and purpose of the Convention. They are free to assert that interest through the adjudicatory and advisory machinery established by the Convention. They have no interest in delaying the entry into force of the Convention and with it the protection that treaty is designed to offer individuals in relation to States ratifying or adhering to the Convention with reservations.

40. For these reasons, (. . .)

THE COURT IS OF THE OPINION

By unanimous vote, that the Convention enters into force for a State which ratifies or adheres to it with or without a reservation on the date of the deposit of its instrument of ratification or adherence.

Restrictions to the Death Penalty (Arts. 4(2) and 4(4) American Convention on Human Rights), Advisory Opinion OC-3/83 of September 8, 1983, 3 Inter-Am. Ct. H.R. (Ser. A) (1983).

STATEMENT OF THE ISSUES

8. Invoking Article 64 (1) of the Convention, the Commission requested the Court, in communications of April 15 and 25, 1983, to render an advisory opinion on the following questions relating to the interpretation of Article 4 of the Convention: (. . .)

2. May a government, on the basis of a reservation to Article 4 (4) of the Convention made at the time of ratification, adopt subsequent to the entry into force of the Convention a law imposing the death penalty for crimes not subject to this sanction at the moment of ratification?

10. In its explanation of the considerations giving rise to the request, the Commission informed the Court of the existence of certain differences of opinion between it and the Government of Guatemala concerning the interpretation of the last sentence of Article 4 (2) of the Convention as well as on the effect and scope of Guatemala's reservation to the fourth paragraph of that article. That reservation reads as follows:

> The Government of the Republic of Guatemala, ratifies the American Convention on Human Rights, signed in San José, Costa Rica, on the 22nd of November of 1969, making a reservation with regard to Article 4, paragraph 4 of the same, inasmuch as the Constitution of the Republic of Guatemala, in its Article 54, only excludes from the application of the death penalty, political crimes, but not common crimes related to political crimes.

The specific legal problem presented by the Commission is whether a reservation drafted in the aforementioned terms can be invoked by a State Party to permit it to impose the death penalty for crimes to which such penalty did not apply at the time of its ratification of the Convention. That is, in particular, whether this reservation can be invoked, as the Government of Guatemala did before the Commission in order to justify the application of the death penalty to common crimes connected with political crimes to which that penalty did not previously apply. During the public hearing, the Delegates of the Commission stated that the problem that had arisen with respect to Guatemala's reservation had been referred to the Court as an example in order to highlight the underlying legal problem. (. . .)

IV. MEANING AND INTERPRETATION OF THE TEXTS

47. The questions formulated by the Commission present a number of more general issues which need to be explored. In the first place, in order to interpret Article 4 (2) of the Convention, it is necessary to determine within what context that treaty envisages the application of the death penalty, which in turn calls for the interpretation of Article 4 as a whole. In the second place, it is also necessary to determine what general principles apply to the interpretation of a reservation which, although authorized by the Convention, nevertheless restricts or weakens the system of protection established by that instrument. Finally, it is necessary to resolve the specific hypothetical question that has been submitted to the Court.

48. The manner in which the request for the advisory opinion has been framed reveals the need to ascertain the meaning and scope of Article 4 of the Convention, especially paragraphs 2 and 4, and to determine whether these provisions might be interrelated. To this end, the Court will apply the rules of interpretation set out in the Vienna Convention, which may be deemed to state the relevant international law principles applicable to this subject.

49. These rules specify that treaties must be interpreted "in good faith in accordance with the ordinary meaning to be given to the terms of the treaty in their context and in the light of its object and purpose". [Article 31 (1), Vienna Convention.] Supplementary means of interpretation, especially the preparatory work of the treaty, may be used to confirm the meaning resulting from the application of the foregoing provisions, or when it leaves the meaning ambiguous or obscure or leads to a result which is manifestly absurd or unreasonable. [Ibid., Article 32.]

50. This method of interpretation respects the principle of the primacy of the text, that is, the application of objective criteria of interpretation. In the case of human rights treaties, moreover, objective criteria of interpretation that look to the texts themselves are more appropriate than subjective criteria that seek to ascertain only the intent of the Parties. This is so because human rights treaties, as the Court has already noted, "are not multilateral treaties of the traditional type concluded to accomplish the reciprocal exchange of rights for the mutual benefit of the contracting States"; rather "their object and purpose is the protection of the basic rights of individual human beings, irrespective of their nationality, both against the State of their nationality and all other contracting States". (*The Effect of Reservations*, para. 29).

51. An analysis of the system of death penalties permitted within certain limits by Article 4, raises questions about the extent to which the enjoyment and the exercise of the rights and liberties guaranteed by the Convention may be restricted. It also raises questions about the scope and meaning of the application of such restrictions. Here the principles derived from Articles 29 (a) and 30 of the Convention are of particular relevance. Those articles read:

Article 29 Restrictions Regarding Interpretation
No provision of this Convention shall be interpreted as:

a) permitting any State Party, group, or person to suppress the enjoyment or exercise of the rights and freedoms recognized in this Convention or to restrict them to a greater extent than is provided for herein,

b) restricting the enjoyment or exercise of any right or freedom recognized by virtue of the laws of any State Party or by virtue of another convention to which one of the said states is a party,

c) precluding other rights or guarantees that are inherent in the human personality or derived from representative democracy as a form of government, or

d) excluding or limiting the effect that the American Declaration of the Rights and Duties of Man and other international acts of the same nature may have.

Article 30 Scope of Restrictions
The restrictions that, pursuant to this Convention, may be placed on the enjoyment or exercise of the rights or freedoms recognized herein may not be applied except in accordance with laws enacted for reasons of general interest and in accordance with the purpose for which such restrictions have been established.

52. The purpose of Article 4 of the Convention is to protect the right to life. But this article, after proclaiming the objective in general terms in its first paragraph, devotes the next five paragraphs to the application of the death penalty. The text of the article as a whole reveals a clear tendency to restrict the scope of this penalty both as far as its imposition and its application are concerned. (. . .)

59. It follows that, in interpreting the last sentence of Article 4 (2) "in good faith in accordance with the ordinary meaning to be given to the terms of the treaty in their context and in the light of its object and purpose," (Vienna Convention, Art. 31(1)) there cannot be the slightest doubt that Article 4 (2) contains an absolute prohibition that no State Party may apply the death penalty to crimes for which it was not provided previously under the domestic law of that State. No provision of the Convention can be relied upon to give a different meaning to the very clear text of Article 4 (2), in fine. The only way to achieve a different result would be by means of a timely reservation designed to exclude in some fashion the application of the

aforementioned provision in relation to the State making the reservation. Such a reservation, of course, would have to be compatible with the object and purpose of the treaty.

V. RESERVATIONS TO THE AMERICAN CONVENTION ON HUMAN RIGHTS

60. Article 75 of the Convention declares that it is subject to reservations only in conformity with the provisions of the Vienna Convention. As this Court has already stated, the reference to Article 75 makes sense only if it is understood as an express authorization designed to enable States to make whatever reservations they deem appropriate, provided the reservations are not incompatible with the object and purpose of the treaty. As such, they can be said to be governed by Article 20 (1) of the Vienna Convention and, consequently, do not require acceptance by any other State Party. (*The Effect of Reservations*, para. 35).

61. Consequently, the first question which arises when interpreting a reservation is whether it is compatible with the object and purpose of the treaty. Article 27 of the Convention allows the States Parties to suspend, in time of war, public danger, or other emergency that threatens their independence or security, the obligations they assumed by ratifying the Convention, provided that in doing so they do not suspend or derogate from certain basic or essential rights, among them the right to life guaranteed by Article 4. It would follow therefrom that a reservation which was designed to enable a State to suspend any of the non-derogable fundamental rights must be deemed to be incompatible with the object and purpose of the Convention and, consequently, not permitted by it. The situation would be different if the reservation sought merely to restrict certain aspects of a non-derogable right without depriving the right as a whole of its basic purpose. Since the reservation referred to by the Commission in its submission does not appear to be of a type that is designed to deny the right to life as such, the Court concludes that to that extent it can be considered, in principle, as not being incompatible with the object and purpose of the Convention.

62. Reservations have the effect of excluding or modifying the provisions of a treaty and they become an integral part thereof as between the reserving State and any other States for whom they are in force. Therefore, without dealing anew with the question of reciprocity as it relates to reservations which, moreover, is not fully applicable as far as human rights treaties are concerned, it must be concluded that any meaningful interpretation of a treaty also calls for an interpretation of any reservation made thereto. Reservations must of necessity therefore also be interpreted by reference to relevant principles of general international law and the special rules set out in the Convention itself.

63. It follows that a reservation must be interpreted by examining its text in accordance with the ordinary meaning which must be attributed to the terms in which it has been formulated within the general context of the treaty of which the reservation forms an integral part. This approach must be followed except when the resultant interpretation would leave the meaning ambiguous or obscure or would lead to a result which is manifestly absurd or unreasonable. A contrary approach might ultimately lead to the conclusion that the State is the sole arbiter of the extent of its international obligations on all matters to which its reservation relates, including

even all such matters which the State might subsequently declare that it intended the reservation to cover.

64. The latter result cannot be squared with the Vienna Convention which provides that a reservation can be made only when signing, ratifying, accepting, approving or acceding to a treaty. [Vienna Convention, Article 19.] Thus, without excluding the possibility that supplementary means of interpretation might, in exceptional circumstances, be resorted to, the interpretation of reservations must be guided by the primacy of the text. A different approach would make it extremely difficult for other States Parties to understand the precise meaning of the reservation.

65. In interpreting reservations, account must be taken of the object and purpose of the relevant treaty which, in the case of the Convention involves the "protection of the basic rights of individual human beings, irrespective of their nationality, both against the State of their nationality and all other contracting States". [Supra, para. 29.] The purpose of the Convention imposes real limits on the effect that reservations attached to it can have. If reservations to the Convention, to be permissible, must be compatible with the object and purpose of the treaty, it follows that these reservations will have to be interpreted in a manner that is most consistent with that object and purpose.

66. The Court concludes, furthermore, that since a reservation becomes an integral part of the treaty, the reservation must also be interpreted by reference to the principles set out in Article 29 of the Convention. Thus, consistent with the considerations that have been noted above, the Court is of the view that the application of paragraph a) of Article 29 compels the conclusion that a reservation may not be interpreted so as to limit the enjoyment and exercise of the rights and liberties recognized in the Convention to a greater extent than is provided for in the reservation itself.

INTERPRETATION OF A RESERVATION TO ARTICLE 4(4)

67. Keeping the preceding considerations in mind and in view of the fact that a clear answer to the first question submitted by the Commission is provided by the text of Article 4 (2) of the Convention, the Court can now proceed to an examination of the second question. . . . In other words, may a State that has made a reservation to Article 4 (4) of the Convention, which article prohibits the application of the death penalty to common crimes related to political offenses, validly assert that the reservation extends by implication to Article 4 (2) and invoke the reservation for the purpose of applying the death penalty to crimes to which that penalty did not previously apply notwithstanding the prohibition contained in Article 4 (2)? The difficulties that might have arisen if one sought to answer this question in the abstract disappeared once the Commission called the Court's attention to the text of Guatemala's reservation. The Court will therefore analyze the question by reference to that reservation, which it will have to examine in some detail.

68. In relating Article 4 (4) to Article 4 (2), the Court finds that each provision, in its context, is perfectly clear and that each has a different meaning. Thus, while Article 4 (2) imposes a definite prohibition on the death penalty for all categories of offenses as far as the future is concerned, Article 4 (4) bans it for political offenses and related common crimes. The latter provision obviously refers to those offenses

which prior thereto were subject to capital punishment, since for the future the prohibition set forth in paragraph 2 would have been sufficient. The Court is here therefore dealing with two rules having clearly different purposes: while Article 4 (4) is designed to abolish the penalty for certain offenses, Article 4 (2) seeks to bar any extension of its use in the future. In other words, above and beyond the prohibition contained in Article 4 (2), which deals with the extension of the application of capital punishment, Article 4 (4) adds a further prohibition that bars the application of the death penalty to political offenses related to common crimes even if such offenses were previously punished by that penalty.

69. Accordingly, given the context of the Commission's request, what is the effect of a reservation to Article 4 (4) of the Convention? In answering this question, it must be remembered above all, that a State reserves no more than what is contained in the text of the reservation itself. Since the reservation may go no further than to exempt the reserving State from the prohibition of applying the death penalty to political offenses or related crimes, it is apparent that all other provisions of the article remain applicable and in full force for the reserving State.

70. Furthermore, if Article 4, whose second paragraph clearly establishes an absolute prohibition on the extension of the death penalty in the future, is examined as a whole, it becomes clear that the only subject reserved is the right to continue the application of the death penalty to political offenses or related common crimes to which that penalty applied previously. It follows that a State which has not made a reservation to paragraph 2 is bound by the prohibition not to apply the death penalty to new offenses, be they political offenses, related common crimes or mere common crimes. On the other hand, a reservation made to paragraph 2, but not to paragraph 4, would permit the reserving State to punish new offenses with the death penalty in the future provided, however, that the offenses in question are mere common crimes not related to political offenses. This is so because the prohibition contained in paragraph 4, with regard to which no reservation was made, would continue to apply to political offenses and related common crimes.

71. The Court does not believe, moreover, that it can be reasonably argued that a reservation to Article 4 (4) can be extended to encompass Article 4 (2) on the grounds that the reservation relating to the prohibition of the death penalty for political offenses and related common crimes would make no sense if it were inapplicable to new offenses not previously punished with that penalty. Such a reservation does in fact have a purpose and meaning standing alone; it permits the reserving State to avoid violating the Convention if it desires to continue to apply the death penalty to common crimes related to political offenses, which penalty existed at the time the Convention entered into force for that State. The Court having established, moreover, that the aforementioned provisions of Article 4 apply to different issues, [see paragraph 68, supra] there is no reason for assuming either as a matter of logic or law that a State which when ratifying the Convention, made a reservation to one provision, was in reality attaching a reservation to both provisions.

72. The foregoing conclusions apply, in general, to the reservation made by Guatemala when it ratified the Convention. The reservation is based solely on the fact that "the Constitution of the Republic of Guatemala, in its Article 54, only excludes

from the application of the death penalty, political crimes, but not common crimes related to political crimes". This explanation merely refers to a reality of domestic law. The reservation does not suggest that the Constitution of Guatemala requires the application of the death penalty to common crimes related to political offenses, but rather that it does not prohibit the application of the death penalty to such crimes. Guatemala was, therefore, not debarred from making a more extensive commitment on the international plane.

73. Since the reservation modifies or excludes the legal effects of the provision to which it is made, the best way to demonstrate the effect of the modification is to read the provision as it has been modified. The substantive part of the reservation "only excludes political crimes from the application of the death penalty, but not common crimes related to political crimes." It is clear and neither ambiguous nor obscure, and it does not lead to a result that is absurd or unreasonable, applying the ordinary meaning to the terms to read the article as modified by the reservation as follows: "4 (4) In no case shall the capital punishment be inflicted for political offenses", thus excluding the related common crimes from the political offenses that were reserved. No other modification of the Convention can be derived from this reservation, nor can a State claim that the reservation permits it to extend the death penalty to new crimes or that it is a reservation also to Article 4 (2).

74. It follows that if the Guatemalan reservation is interpreted in accordance with the ordinary meaning to be given to its terms, within the general context of the Convention and taking into account its object and purpose, one has to conclude that in making the reservation, what Guatemala did was to indicate that it was unwilling to assume any commitment other than the one already provided for by its Constitution. The Court finds that in its reservation Guatemala failed to manifest its unequivocal rejection of the provision to which it attached a reservation. Although this fact does not transfer the reservation into one that is unique in character, it does at the very least reinforce the view that the reservation should be narrowly interpreted.

Questions and Comments: The Debate over Reservations to Human Rights Treaties

1. Commentators familiar with the matter noted the impact the above proceeding had on the government: " . . . shortly before the Court began its deliberations, the State Party announced that it had suspended the executions of those tried by the Courts of Special Jurisdiction. The fact that the announcement was made by the State Party at the public hearing of the Court held in conjunction with the Commission's request for an advisory opinion is not without significance." See C. Moyer & D. Padilla, *Executions in Guatemala as Decreed by the Courts of Special Jurisdiction in 1982–83: A Case Study*, in HUMAN RIGHTS IN THE AMERICAS (1984), at 280.

2. How are reservations regulated under the American and European Conventions?

3. How are reservations restricted by international law?

4. What is the object and purpose of the regional human rights treaties? Was the Guatemalan reservation compatible with the object and purpose of the Convention? Was the Swiss "declaration?" Who decides?

5. Must reservations be accepted by other States Parties before the convention enters into force for the reserving state? Must reservations be accepted by other States Parties in order to become effective?

6. What guidelines does the Inter-American Court establish for the interpretation of reservations to the American Convention?

7. Explain the Court's ruling that a reservation to art. 4 (4) could not be interpreted as encompassing art. 4 (2).

8. What is the consequence of a determination that a reservation is incompatible with the object and purpose of one of the regional human rights treaties?

9. Consider the following reservation by El Salvador in relation to Article 19 of the Vienna Convention and the provisions of the American Convention. Is it compatible with the American Convention?

> Art. 1
>
> The American Convention on Human Rights, known as the "Pact of San Jose, Costa Rica," signed at San Jose, Costa Rica, on 22 November 1969, composed of a preamble and eighty-two articles, approved by the Executive Branch in the Field of Foreign Affairs by Agreement 405, dated June 14 of the current year, is hereby ratified, with the reservation that such ratification is understood without prejudice to those provisions of the Convention that might conflict with express precepts of the Political Constitution of the Republic.
>
> El Salvador's Reservation to the American Convention, IACHR, *Basic Documents Pertaining to Human Rights in the Inter-American System* (2001).

10. Compare the previous reservation to that submitted by Moldova to the European Convention on Human Rights; does this reservation comply with the requirements for reservations set forth in the European Convention?:

> *Declaration contained in the instrument of ratification, deposited on 12 September 1997-Or. Mol./Fr.*
>
> The Republic of Moldova declares that it will be unable to guarantee compliance with the provisions of the Convention in respect of omissions and acts committed by the organs of the self-proclaimed Trans-Dniester republic within the territory actually controlled by such organs, until the conflict in the region is finally settled."

11. While the African Charter does not contain a provision on reservations, several states have filed them, among them South Africa and Egypt. Consider the following two texts. The Republic of South Africa attached "Declarations and reservations" when acceding to the African Charter on Human and Peoples' Rights. Its statement said:

> [I]t is the view of the Republic of South Africa that there should be consultation between States parties to the Charter, inter alia, to:
>
>> (i) consider possible measures to strengthen the enforcement mechanisms of the Charter;
>>
>> (ii) clarify the criteria for the restrictions of rights and freedoms recognised and guaranteed in the Charter; and
>>
>> (iii) bring the Charter into line with the United Nations' resolutions regarding the characterisation of Zionism.

Egypt filed this statement:

> *Declarations and reservations by EGYPT made upon ratification, accession or succession of the ACHPR*
>
> Having considered the African Charter on Human and Peoples' Rights, the Arab Republic of Egypt signed the said Charter on 16 November 1981 and attached hereto is the following instrument of ratification:

Having accepted all the provisions of the African Charter on Human and Peoples' Rights with the approval of the People's Assembly and with the reservation that article 8 and paragraph 3 of article 8 and paragraph 3 of article 18 be implemented in accordance with the Islamic Law and that, as far as the Arab Republic of Egypt is concerned, the provision of the first paragraph of article 9 should be [confined] to such information as could be obtained within the limits of the Egyptian laws and regulations;

We hereby declare acceptance and ratification of the said Charter.

What law governs the acceptability of these statements? Are both of them reservations?

12. The International Covenant on Civil and Political Rights neither prohibits reservations nor discusses what reservations are permitted. In 1994, the Human Rights Committee issued an important General Comment on this topic (General Comment No. 24 (52) of 2 Nov. 1994, CCPR/C/21/Rev.1/Add.6, 15 HRLJ 464 (1994)). Like the European Court, the Committee indicated in the General Comment that any statement, whatever name or title a state attaches to it, which purports to exclude or modify the legal effect of a treaty, constitutes a reservation. Applying the object and purpose test of the Vienna Convention, the Committee said:

> Reservations that offend peremptory norms would not be compatible with the object and purpose of the Covenant. Although treaties that are mere exchanges of obligations between States allow them to reserve inter se application of rules of general international law, it is otherwise in human rights treaties, which are for the benefit of persons within their jurisdiction. Accordingly, provisions in the Covenant that represent customary international law (and a fortiori when they have the character of peremptory norms) may not be the subject of reservations. Accordingly, a State may not reserve the right to engage in slavery, to torture, to subject persons to cruel, inhuman or degrading treatment or punishment, to arbitrarily deny freedom of thought, conscience and religion, to presume a person guilty unless he proves his innocence, to execute pregnant women or children, to permit the advocacy of national, racial or religious hatred, to deny to persons of marriageable age the right to marry, or to deny to minorities the right to enjoy their own culture, profess their own religion, or use their own language. And while reservations to particular clauses of article 14 may be acceptable, a general reservation to the right to a fair trial would not be.
>
> (...) While there is no automatic correlation between reservations to nonderogable provisions, and reservations which offend against the object and purpose of the Covenant, a State has a heavy onus to justify such a reservation. The Committee also said that reservations would not be acceptable that removed the right to a remedy for human rights violations or other "important supportive guarantees." In addition, reservations that attempt to evade international supervisory machinery would be incompatible with the object and purpose of the treaty. States should not attach so many reservations that in effect they do not accept the Covenant.

Although the Committee looked to the Vienna Convention for the definition of reservations and the object and purpose test, it rejected the Vienna Convention provisions on the role of State objections to nonconforming reservations, finding those rules inappropriate in regard to human rights treaties. "The absence of protest by States cannot imply that a reservation is either compatible or incompatible with the object and purpose of the Covenant. Instead, it necessarily falls to the Committee to determine whether a specific reservation is compatible with the object and purpose of the Covenant. The normal consequence of an unacceptable reservation is not that the Covenant will not be in effect at all for a reserving party. Rather, such a reservation will generally be severable, in the sense that the Covenant will be operative for the reserving party without benefit of the reservation." For further reading, see LIESBETH LIJNSZAAD, RESERVATIONS TO UN HUMAN RIGHTS TREATIES: RATIFY AND RUIN? (1995).

Following the judgments reprinted above and the CCPR's General Comment, the International Law Commission (ILC) decided to study the question of reservations to treaties, with a clear focus on the practice of human rights bodies. The General Assembly approved the ILC's proposal, following which the ILC appointed one of its members as rapporteur on the topic. Between 1994 and 2005, ten reports examined the practice on reservations. In 1997, the ILC adopted preliminary conclusions on reservations to normative multilateral treaties, including human rights treaties. The report expressly rejected the notion of a special regime of reservations for human rights treaties. It noted that the role of monitoring bodies in regard to the permissibility of reservation was the most controversial question under consideration and that there were two entirely opposed positions. Both extreme positions were found unsatisfactory. Instead, it was agreed that "human rights bodies could and should assess whether reservations were permissible when that was necessary for the exercise of their functions. They could not, however, have more competence in that regard than was necessary for them to discharge their main responsibility." In particular, they could not draw any consequences from such an assessment. The one exception noted was for regional bodies vested with powers to make binding decisions; i.e. the European and Inter-American Courts. "While he still had doubts about the merits of some decisions by those bodies, he recognized that the stronger solidarity at the regional level than at the universal level could warrant the establishment under regional treaties of machinery with broader powers which reflected precisely those community ties." ILC, Annual Report, UN Doc. A/CN.4/Ser.A/1997, Add.1 (Part 2), Ch. V, para 82–84. Do you agree?

B. National Constitutions and Laws

i. Constitutional Provisions

The Constitution of Austria

Article 9. International Law, Transfer of Powers

1. The generally recognized rules of international law are regarded as integral parts of federal law.

2. Legislation or a treaty requiring sanction in accordance with Article 50 (1) can transfer specific federal competencies to intergovernmental organizations and their authorities and can within the framework of international law regulate the activity of foreign states' agents inside Austria as well as the activity of Austrian agents abroad.

Article 50. Treaties

1. Political treaties, and others in so far as their contents modify or complement existent laws, may only be concluded with the sanction of the House of Representatives.

2. At the time of giving its sanction to a treaty which falls under Paragraph (1), the House of Representatives can decide that the treaty in question shall be implemented by the issue of laws.

3. The provisions of Article 42 (1) to (4)[on procedure] and, should constitutional law be modified or complemented by the treaty, the provisions of Article 44 (1) [on procedure] apply analogously to resolutions of the House of Representatives in accordance with Paragraphs (1) and (2). In a vote of sanction adopted pursuant to Paragraph (1), such treaties or such provisions as are contained in treaties shall be explicitly specified as "constitutionally modifying".

Article 145. International Law

The Constitutional Court pronounces judgment on contraventions of international law in accordance with the provisions of a special Federal law.

Basic Law of the Federal Republic of Germany

Article 24 [International organizations]

(1) The Federation may by a law transfer sovereign powers to international organizations.

(1a) Insofar as the Länder are competent to exercise state powers and to perform state functions, they may, with the consent of the Federal Government, transfer sovereign powers to transfrontier institutions in neighboring regions.

(2) With a view to maintaining peace, the Federation may enter into a system of mutual collective security; in doing so it shall consent to such limitations upon its sovereign powers as will bring about and secure a lasting peace in Europe and among the nations of the world.

(3) For the settlement of disputes between states, the Federation shall accede to agreements providing for general, comprehensive, and compulsory international arbitration.

Article 25 [International law and federal law]

The general rules of international law shall be an integral part of federal law. They shall take precedence over the laws and directly create rights and duties for the inhabitants of the federal territory.

Article 100 [Compatibility of laws with the Basic Law]

(1) If a court concludes that a law on whose validity its decision depends is unconstitutional, the proceedings shall be stayed, and a decision shall be obtained from the Land court with jurisdiction over constitutional disputes where the constitution of a Land is held to be violated, or from the Federal Constitutional Court where this Basic Law is held to be violated. This provision shall also apply where the Basic Law is held to be violated by Land law and where a Land law is held to be incompatible with a federal law.

(2) If, in the course of litigation, doubt exists whether a rule of international law is an integral part of federal law and whether it directly creates rights and duties for

the individual (Article 25), the court shall obtain a decision from the Federal Constitutional Court.

_____

The Constitution of Argentina

Article 75 Congress is empowered:

22. To approve or reject treaties concluded with other nations and international organizations, and concordats with the Holy See. Treaties and concordats have a higher hierarchy than laws. The American Declaration of the Rights and Duties of Man; the Universal Declaration of Human Rights; the American Convention on Human Rights; the International Pact on Economic, Social and Cultural Rights; the International Pact on Civil and Political Rights and its empowering Protocol; the Convention on the Prevention and Punishment of Genocide; the International Convention on the Elimination of all Forms of Racial Discrimination; the Convention on the Elimination of all Forms of Discrimination against Woman; the Convention against Torture and other Cruel, Inhuman or Degrading Treatments or Punishments; the Convention on the Rights of the Child; in the full force of their provisions, they have constitutional hierarchy, do not repeal any section of the First Part of this Constitution [containing the Bill of Rights] and are to be understood as complementing the rights and guarantees recognized herein. They shall only be denounced, in such event, by the National Executive Power after the approval of two-thirds of all the members of each House. In order to attain constitutional hierarchy, the other treaties and conventions on human rights shall require the vote of two-thirds of all the members of each House, after their approval by Congress.

23. To legislate and promote positive measures guaranteeing true equal opportunities and treatment, the full benefit and exercise of the rights recognized by this Constitution and by the international treaties on human rights in force, particularly referring to children, women, the aged, and disabled persons. To issue a special and integral social security system to protect children from abandonment, since pregnancy up to the end of elementary education, and to protect the mother during pregnancy and the period of lactation.

24. To approve treaties of integration which delegate powers and jurisdiction to supranational organizations under reciprocal and equal conditions, and which respect the democratic order and human rights. The rules derived therefrom have a higher hierarchy than laws. The approval of these treaties with Latin American States shall require the absolute majority of all the members of each House. In the case of treaties with other States, the National Congress, with the absolute majority of the members present of each House, shall declare the advisability of the approval of the treaty which shall only be approved with the vote of the absolute majority of all the members of each House, one hundred and twenty days after said declaration of advisability.

The denouncement of the treaties referred to in this subsection shall require the prior approval of the absolute majority of all the members of each House.

_____

Constitution of Venezuela (1999)

Article 19: The State shall guarantee to every individual, in accordance with the progressive principle and without discrimination of any kind, unrenounceable, indivisible and interdependent enjoyment and exercise of human rights. Respect for and the guaranteeing of these rights is obligatory for the organs of Public Power, in accordance with the Constitution, the human rights treaties signed and ratified by the Republic and any laws developing the same. . . .

Article 22: The recitation of rights and guarantees contained in this Constitution and in international instruments concerning human rights are not to be understood as negating others inherent to individuals, not expressly mentioned in such recitation. The absence of a law regulating these rights shall not adversely affect the exercise thereof.

Article 23: The treaties, pacts and conventions relating human rights which have been executed and ratified by Venezuela have a constitutional rank, and prevail over internal legislation, insofar as they contain provisions concerning the enjoyment and exercise of such rights that are more favorable than those established by this Constitution and the laws of the Republic, and shall be immediately and directly applied by the courts and other organs of the Public Power. . . .

Article 29: The State is obliged to investigate and legally punish offenses against human rights committed by its authorities. Actions to punish the offense of violating humanity rights, serious violations of human rights and war crimes shall not be subject to statute of limitation. Human rights violations and the offense of violating humanity rights shall be investigated and adjudicated by the courts of ordinary competence. These offenses are excluded from any benefit that might render the offenders immune from punishment, including pardons and amnesty.

Article 30: The State has the obligation to make full reparations to the victims of human rights violations for which it may be held responsible, and to the legal successors to such victims, including payment of damages. The State shall adopt the necessary legislative measures and measures of other nature to implement the reparations and damage compensation provided for under this article. The State shall protect the victims of ordinary crimes and endeavor to make the guilty parties provide reparations for the inflicted damages.

Article 31: Everyone has the right, on the terms established by the human rights treaties, pacts and conventions ratified by the Republic, to address petitions and complaints to the intentional organs created for such purpose, in order to ask for protection of his or her human rights. The State shall adopt, in accordance with the procedures established under this Constitution and by the law, such measures as may be necessary to enforce the decisions emanating from international organs as provided for under this article.

Constitution of South Africa (1996)

39. (1) When interpreting the Bill of Rights, a court, tribunal or forum

a. must promote the values that underlie an open and democratic society based on human dignity, equality and freedom;
b. must consider international law; and
c. may consider foreign law.

(2) When interpreting any legislation, and when developing the common law or customary law, every court, tribunal or forum must promote the spirit, purport and objects of the Bill of Rights.

(3) The Bill of Rights does not deny the existence of any other rights or freedoms that are recognised or conferred by common law, customary law or legislation, to the extent that they are consistent with the Bill.

International agreements

231. (1) The negotiating and signing of all international agreements is the responsibility of the national executive.

(2) An international agreement binds the Republic only after it has been approved by resolution in both the National Assembly and the National Council of Provinces, unless it is an agreement referred to in subsection (3).

(3) An international agreement of a technical, administrative or executive nature, or an agreement which does not require either ratification or accession, entered into by the national executive, binds the Republic without approval by the National Assembly and the National Council of Provinces, but must be tabled in the Assembly and the Council within a reasonable time.

(4) Any international agreement becomes law in the Republic when it is enacted into law by national legislation; but a self-executing provision of an agreement that has been approved by Parliament is law in the Republic unless it is inconsistent with the Constitution or an Act of Parliament.

(5) The Republic is bound by international agreements which were binding on the Republic when this Constitution took effect.

Customary international law

232. Customary international law is law in the Republic unless it is inconsistent with the Constitution or an Act of Parliament.

Application of international law

233. When interpreting any legislation, every court must prefer any reasonable interpretation of the legislation that is consistent with international law over any alternative interpretation that is inconsistent with international law.

Constitution of Mozambique

Art. 62(2): The Republic of Mozambique shall accept, observe and apply the principles of the United Nations Charter and of the Charter of the Organization of African Unity.

---

ii. Case Study: Argentina

Janet Koven Levit, *The Constitutionalization of Human Rights in Argentina: Problem or Promise?* 37 COLUM. J. TRANSNAT'L L. 281, 293–301, 304–12, 324–26, 329–30, 335–37, 343–44 (1999)(some footnotes omitted, renumbered)

Many modern constitutions incorporate human rights norms, borrowing from international and regional human rights treaties. . . . South American constitutions fall into one of two broad groups. The first group includes constitutions that incorporate the "spirit" of human rights treaties.[42] In general, these constitutions are skeletal reflections of international human rights treaties, incorporating many core rights—core ideas—but lacking the flesh to make these rights as robust as their treaty-based counterparts. The second group, on the other hand, incorporates the texture and nuances of international treaty-based rights.

Constitutions in the first group frequently are "missing" several rights found in the international treaties, leaving conspicuous gaps in the constitutional treatment of human rights. None of the constitutions in this group contain the following rights: the right to self-determination; an explicit gender equality provision; a provision for the minimum due process rights for aliens facing expulsion; a prohibition on traffic in women; or the right to recognition as a person before the law. Most constitutions in this group lack a provision promising prisoners "humane" treatment, including segregation of convicted criminals from those criminal defendants awaiting trial and segregation of juveniles from adults; granting ethnic or religious minorities the right to enjoy their culture and group identity; prohibiting war propaganda and advocacy of racial, national or religious hate; and prohibiting imprisonment for contractual debt. A few of the constitutions have some dramatic omissions. The Venezuelan and Uruguayan Constitutions contain no clause prohibiting slavery and slave trade. Chile's Constitution contains no prohibition on torture or other cruel, inhumane or degrading treatment. Uruguay's Constitution does not proscribe the use of ex post facto laws and does not grant citizens freedom of thought, conscience or religion. While the American Convention also excludes some of these rights, the aforementioned constitutions are striking in their omission of several rights in addition to those that the American Convention chose not to codify.

Those rights that the constitutions include tend to be skeletal replicas of the rather developed rights found in the International Covenant and the American Convention. Other rights are significantly less expansive in scope. For example, criminal defense rights are generally sparse, granting many fewer protections than

---

[42]   See Const. Bol. (1967, amended 1995); Const. Chile (1980, amended 1989); Const. Peru (1993); Const. Uru. (1967, reinstated 1985); Const. Venez. (1961, amended 1983).

those granted in the International Covenant and American Convention. The freedom of conscience and religion clauses in some constitutions are rather narrow. As opposed to the approach in the international treaties, many constitutions' "right to life" provisions do not evince discomfort with the death penalty. Constitutional clauses regarding torture appear thin when juxtaposed with international analogs.

Some constitutional provisions in this group ostensibly mimic international treaties but carve elastic exceptions that envelop the substantive right. Some constitutions exclude entire groups of people from constitutional protections.[43] Frequently, "state of emergency" provisions, which allow the executive (usually with some type of nodding acquiescence from the legislature) to suspend certain rights in the face of an extreme crisis, are artfully drafted to create gaping loopholes that detract from the potency of many rights. Sometimes the triggering event—the emergency—is defined in such broad, catch-all terms that the executive could "legitimately" invoke the "state of emergency" clause in a wide range of situations.[44] The International Covenant and American Convention do not allow derogation of certain rights, even when a "state of emergency" is in effect. Most constitutions, like the International Covenant and the American Convention, limit the number of rights/prohibitions that the executive and/or legislature may curtail. This list, however, is frequently shorter than the International Covenant and the American Convention, meaning that the number of suspendable rights is somewhat greater.[45] In providing for basic core rights, these constitutions are true to the "spirit" of the international human rights treaties but do not mirror their nuances, depth, or texture.

The second group of constitutions[46] integrates not merely the spirit, but also the letter, of international human rights treaties. These constitutions emulate, or even surpass, international treaties in scope and breadth. In this group, international treaties conspicuously infiltrate national constitutions, serving as models for the content and scope of constitutional rights.

In general, the constitutions in the second group contain most of the rights enumerated in the International Covenant and the American Convention. Constitutional provisions tend to mirror international rights; other provisions, most notably constitutional protection of criminal defendants, are significantly more robust than those developed in the international instruments. Some constitutions expand the

---

[43] For instance, Peru's constitutional provision regarding "personal freedom and security" contains many of the same protections found in Article 9 of the International Covenant and in Article 7 of the American Convention—no arbitrary arrest, right to be informed about the reasons for the arrest, prompt recourse to judicial scrutiny of legality of custody—but suspends these very protections when suspected drug traffickers, terrorists, or spies are under scrutiny. See Const. Peru art. 2(24)(f).

[44] .... Peru's Constitution sanctions usage of the "state of emergency" clause "in case of a disturbance of the peace or of the internal order, catastrophe, or grave circumstances affecting the life of the nation." Const. Peru art. 137(1). Venezuela's "state of emergency" clause covers internal or external conflicts, "disorder that may disturb the peace," or "grave circumstances that affect economic or social life." Const. Venez. arts. 240–41. Under Chile's state of emergency provision, enumerated rights may be suspended during "foreign or internal war, internal disturbances, emergency, and public calamity." Const. Chile art. 39.

[45] For example, Venezuela apparently permits the suspension of most rights. See Const. Venez. arts. 240–42, 244. Similarly, Uruguay allows the derogation of all rights related to individual security in order to apprehend "guilty parties," presumably including the right to life, the prohibition on torture, and the prohibition on punishment for contractual liability. See Const. Uru. art. 31.

[46] See Const. Braz. (1988); Const. Colom. (1991); Const. Ecuador (1979, amended 1992); Const. Para. (1992).

scope of various rights. Other constitutional rights are more potent because they are affirmative, creating state obligations. Some constitutional rights are stronger because they eliminate encroaching exceptions.

. . . .

2. Constitutional Status of Human Rights Norms

Many modern constitutions address the status of international human rights norms or, more generally, international law.[47] . . . [A] focus on South American constitutions . . . suggests the following broad groupings: 1) constitutions which place international treaties on a par with domestic law; 2) constitutions that deem international treaties superior to domestic law but inferior to the constitution; and 3) constitutions that do not explicitly (or implicitly) address the status of international law.

The constitutions which place international law on a par with domestic law expose international norms to subsequent statutory invalidation. International treaty norms thus become vulnerable and manipulable, depending on the sentiments and mood of transient legislatures. The Peruvian Constitution clearly states that treaties are a part of "national law."[48] The Venezuelan Constitution requires the legislature to pass laws validating all international treaties or conventions, relegating these international norms to the status of a domestic law.[49] Other constitutions do not explicitly address the status of international law, but divide power over international treaties among the executive, who concludes treaties, and the legislative branch, which ratifies treaties. Domestic constitutional law interpreting these provisions frequently relegates international treaties to the status of a domestic statute.[50]

On the other hand, some constitutions explicitly elevate international norms, or a specific group of international norms. Paraguay's Constitution ranks sources of law, with international treaties and conventions falling below its Constitution but above "laws dictated by Congress."[51] Colombia's Constitution elevates international

---

[47] . . . [T]he constitutional status of human rights treaties, principally the European Convention on Human Rights, has been a significant aspect of constitutional reform efforts in Central and Eastern Europe. See European Convention for the Protection of Human Rights and Fundamental Freedoms, opened for signature Nov. 4, 1950, Europ. T.S. No. 5, 213 U.N.T.S. 222 (entered into force Sept. 5, 1953). See also . . .; Eric Stein, *International Law in Internal Law: Toward Internationalization of Central-Eastern European Constitutions?*, 88 AJIL 427 (1994); Wiktor Osiatynski, *Rights in New Constitutions of East Central Europe*, 26 COLUM. HUM. RTS. L. REV. 111, 161 (1994); Dalibor Jilek, *Human Rights Treaties and the New Constitutions*, 8 CONN. J. INT'L L. 407 (1993).

[48] Const. Peru art. 55.

[49] See Const. Venez. art. 128. Venezuela has determined, via its Constitution, that, for the most part, treaties will be non-self-executing, requiring domestic facilitating legislation prior to having legal effect. See Restatement (Third) of the Foreign Relations Law of the United States § 111(3), 111(4) (1986). Most commentators believe that non-self-executing treaties, once executed, are tantamount to domestic statutes. See id. § 111, cmts. (h), (i), reporter's notes 5, 6. See also Héctor Gros Espiell, *Los Tratados sobre Derechos Humanos y el Derecho Interno* in TEMAS DE DERECHO INTERNACIONAL: EN HOMENAJE A FRIDA M. PFIERTER DE ARMAS BAREA 61, 63 (R.E. Vineusa ed., 1989); Mónica Pinto, TEMAS DE DERECHOS HUMANOS 66 (1997) (stating that Venezuela's Constitution places international norms on a par with domestic law).

[50] See Const. Uru. arts. 85(7), 85(20). Héctor Gros Espiell, LA CONSTITUCIÓN Y LOS TRATADOS INTERNACIONALES (Ministerio de Relaciones Exteriores, Montevideo, 1997) (discussing Uruguayan constitutional jurisprudence interpreting these provisions and concluding that international law and domestic law share the same legal status); Pinto, supra note 50, at 66 (stating that Uruguay's Constitution places international norms on a par with domestic law). See also Const. Bol. arts. 59(12); 96(2); 228; Pinto, supra note 50, at 66 (arguing that Bolivia's Constitution places international norms on a par with domestic law).

[51] Const. Para. art. 137.

treaties that "recognize human rights and that prohibit their limitation in states of emergency." Const. Colom. art. 93. Ecuador's Constitution is not explicit in its treatment of international human rights norms; it sanctifies "fundamental human rights" and guarantees "free and effective exercise and enjoyment of the civil, political, economic, social and cultural rights enunciated in declarations, pacts, agreements and other international instruments in force," while it relegates international treaties or agreements to the status of a "secondary" or non-constitutional norm. Juxtaposing these constitutional provisions, one can logically conclude that international treaty norms float somewhere between the Constitution and domestic law in Ecuador's domestic legal hierarchy.

Other constitutions leave the status of international norms ambiguous. Chile's Constitution, for example, mimics the constitutional division of power among the executive and the legislative branches found in the Uruguayan and Bolivian Constitutions, suggesting that international norms would be on a par with domestic norms. Yet, a relatively recent amendment to Chile's Constitution charges state agencies with the duty "to respect and promote the rights guaranteed" in international treaties,[52] suggesting that such norms are cloaked with special domestic standing. Thus, Chile's Constitution is rather ambiguous regarding the precise status of international norms.

The legal status of international treaties and conventions provides an additional axis for comparison of South American constitutions. Whether constitutions place international norms on a par with domestic law, above domestic law, or leave the issue unresolved, none of these constitutions explicitly or implicitly place international law on par with the constitution itself.[53]

C. Argentina's Constitution In Context: Pre-1994

Prior to 1994, Argentina's Constitution did not explicitly address the status of international treaties. Similar to the Uruguayan, Brazilian and Bolivian Constitutions, Argentina's Constitution divided power over international treaties among the three branches. The Constitution also stated in Article 31 that the Constitution, the laws that are passed by Congress pursuant to the Constitution, and treaties with foreign powers are the supreme law of the land; and that provincial authorities are obliged to conform to this law—suggesting some type of parity between the Constitution and international treaties. On the other hand, the Constitution provided in Article 27

---

[52] Const. Chile art. 5.

[53] While none of the South American constitutions place international norms on par with constitutional norms, some European constitutions arguably elevate international norms to a constitutional status. Id. at 64–65. See also supra notes 93–97 and accompanying text; Const. Czech Rep. art. 10 (Dec. 21, 1992) ("Ratified and promulgated international treaties on human rights and fundamental freedoms to which the Czech Republic is a party are directly binding and take precedence over the law"); Const. Slovk. art. 1 (Sept. 8, 1992) ("International treaties on human rights and basic liberties that were ratified by the Slovakia and promulgated in a manner determined by law take precedence over its own laws, providing that they secure a greater extent of constitutional rights and liberties"); Const. Hung. art. 7 (Dec. 31, 1990) ("The legal system of the Republic of Hungary accepts the universally recognized rules and regulations of international law, and harmonizes the internal laws and statutes of the country with the obligations assumed under international law."). Constitutional jurisprudence in some Central American countries, namely Nicaragua, Panama, and Costa Rica, suggests that some international norms may have constitutional standing. See Instituto Interamericano de Derechos Humanos, Guía sobre Aplicación del Derecho Internacional en la Jurisdicción Interna 42 (1996).

that "[t]he federal government will be charged with relations with foreign powers, through treaties that are in conformity with the public principles that are set forth in this Constitution," implying that international norms stand inferior to the Constitution. While many commentators interpreted Article 31 through a federalist lens, focusing on what it stated about province/federal government relations rather than what it stated about the status of international treaties vis-à-vis the Constitution, the juxtaposition of these various provisions created some ambiguity regarding the precise status of international norms.

Argentine constitutional jurisprudence resolved some of this ambiguity prior to the 1994 constitutional reform. The most significant case was *Ekmekdjián v. Sofovich*.[54] In this case, the petitioner sought to respond to some religiously "inflammatory" statements that the respondent read on television. In support, the petitioner relied on the "right to reply" found in the American Convention. Yet, domestic law also governed the "right to reply." In ultimately relying on the American Convention, the Court decided that an international treaty, properly ratified pursuant to the Constitution, stands superior to domestic law. Thus, as opposed to the practice in the United States, a subsequent domestic law could not trump an international treaty provision, and Argentine domestic law could not constrict the scope or efficacy of international treaty provisions. Furthermore, the Court concluded that an international treaty provision, properly ratified, is presumptively self-executing as long as it is capable of "immediate operation, without additional institutions." Thus, *Ekmekdjián* placed international treaties on a supra-statutory level and, by holding that they were presumptively self-executing documents, transformed them into a potent source of law which the Court itself harnessed to decide the case.

However, two subsequent Supreme Court opinions limited the reach of *Ekmekdjián*. In *Fibraca*, the Court examined a potential conflict between a treaty with the Holy See and the Constitution.[55] The Court refused to extend the holding of *Ekmekdjián* to the Constitution, stating that international treaties' supra-statutory status did not place them on a par with the Constitution. The Court thereby underscored that the Constitution reigned supreme in the legal hierarchy. In *Hagelin*,[56] the lower court relied on the American Convention in granting the plaintiff indemnification for his daughter's illegal detention and subsequent disappearance, rather than a domestic indemnification law designed primarily as a remedy in light of Argentina's economic problems in the late 1980s. While the Court reaffirmed the supremacy of international law over domestic law, it held that the former trumps the latter only in the face of a real legal conflict, such that the conflicting laws must be significantly, if not completely, congruent and the underlying purposes behind the laws must be similar. Thus, if a domestic law is designed to deal with a specific problem, as the indemnification law in question, and an international norm deals more generically with a similar issue, the international norm is not deemed to be in conflict and may not trump the domestic norm. On the eve of the constitutional reform, Argentina's

---

[54] "Ekmekdjián," CSJN (1992), reprinted in Juan Antonio Travieso, JURISPRUDENCIA DE LOS TRIBUNALES ARGENTINOS SOBRE DERECHOS HUMANOS Y GARANTIAS 11 (1996) (concerning right to reply and freedom of speech).

[55] See "Fibraca Constructora, S.C.A.," CSJN 154 E.D. 164, 165 (1993).

[56] "Hagelin, Ragnar," CSJN (1993), reprinted in Travieso, supra note 55, at 37.

Constitution could be aligned with those constitutions that place international law somewhere between domestic law and constitutional norms.

D. Argentina's 1994 Constitution

Argentina's 1994 constitutional reform altered the Constitution's standing in terms of status and substance. Article 75(22) endowed nine international human rights treaties with constitutional standing, and otherwise reaffirmed the Supreme Court's decisions by providing all other international treaties with supra-statutory standing. Thus, domestic law cannot trump an international norm, and certain international human rights norms, to be interpreted in harmony with the rest of the 1994 Constitution, stand on par with the Constitution itself.

In terms of substance, it is important first to examine Argentina's new Constitution independent of Article 75(22). . . . Without Article 75(22), Argentina's Constitution remains highly reminiscent of its predecessor and similar to those constitutions that reflect the spirit, rather than the scope, of human rights treaties. Significantly, in reforming the Constitution in 1994, Argentina left Chapter 1, "Declaration, Rights, Guarantees," almost untouched. Chapter 2, "New Rights and Guarantees," a fresh addition to the 1994 Constitution, presented Argentina with the opportunity to "update" many rights, adding nuances to make its constitutional rights as robust as those in the international documents. Chapter 2, however, only nominally improved Argentina's substantive inclusion of human rights as set forth in the American Convention and International Covenant. The Constitution now provides explicitly for "equality of opportunity and treatment and the full exercise of rights recognized in this Constitution"; "real equality of opportunity between men and women in accessing elected and party office"; habeas corpus; ethnic and religious minority rights; and somewhat veiled allusions to children's rights. In addition, Chapter 2 begins with a reaffirmation of the Constitution and the democratic system. Otherwise, Chapter 2 differs from the type of fundamental rights included in the International Covenant and the American Convention, addressing instead political corruption, political parties, environmental rights, and consumer protection. While these aforementioned rights, if implemented, will significantly improve the human rights situation in Argentina, Argentina's Constitution still lacks explicit reference to many rights, most notably, the right to peaceful assembly and protection from imprisonment for debts.

The Argentine Constitutional Assembly also failed to embrace the constitutional reform process as an opportunity to fortify those bare-bones rights which the 1853 Constitution listed. Protections for criminal defendants remain scant; with the exception of the added habeas corpus rights, the provisions for liberty and security of the person are thin; and freedom of expression and religion clauses are generally narrower in scope than international counterparts. In sum, of the nineteen rights that Argentina's Constitution now shares with the international instruments, eleven are significantly less "muscular" than the international norms, without the nuances, subtleties, and refinements included in the international instruments. The "state of emergency" clause, which, despite being the target of constitutional reform, does not circumscribe the number or types of rights that may be suspended, potentially undermines the potency and scope of all constitutional protections. Thus, Argentina's Constitution would have remained in first group of constitutions in terms of substance.

Now consider the effect of Article 75(22). The Argentine Constitution is no longer a succinct document containing 110 constitutional provisions but rather a compendium of the constitutional text and the nine human rights treaties which, by virtue of their constitutional status, are effectively incorporated into the constitutional text. Therefore, every right, every privilege, every guarantee, that the anointed human rights treaties grant are part of Argentina's Constitution. Whereas some constitutions merely incorporate the spirit of human rights treaties and others more accurately reflect their scope and breadth, Argentina's Constitution takes a further step: wholesale incorporation of the treaties themselves. The Constitution now mirrors these select human rights treaties, identical in scope, form, and substance. In this sense, Argentina's actions are unique in South America and, arguably, the world. The 1994 constitutional reforms thus forced a shift along both comparative axes, substance and status, leaving the Argentine Constitution unparalleled in South America.

· · · ·

While the Argentine courts are not currently meeting their potential, they are the key domestic transnational actors and should serve as the crucial link between written, constitutional guarantees and the vindication of individual rights. They may invigorate human rights treaties and interpret international norms. They are, for all intents and purposes, the domestic "transmission belt," carrying international human rights norms to an individual level and thus transporting international law to the most fundamental unit in domestic society.

The Inter-American human rights system is also an important transnational actor. When Argentina incorporated the American Convention into its Constitution, it imported not only the rights contained therein but also the system which the Convention consecrates. Argentina thus internalized and constitutionalized the entire regional system, comprised of an investigative/executive prong, the Inter-American Commission on Human Rights, and a judicial prong, the Inter-American Court of Human Rights. One of these now-constitutionalized provisions requires that individuals seeking to vindicate rights before the Commission, and later the Court, exhaust domestic legal remedies, including the domestic court system. Thus, Argentina's Constitution, albeit through the appendage of the American Convention, contains a provision which requires petitioners to utilize the domestic court system completely before tapping the Inter-American system. Argentina's Constitution recasts the Inter-American Commission and Court as appellate-like tribunals, creating, in the words of one delegate, "a fourth and fifth" level of judicial review.

· · · ·

Argentina's human rights internalization strategy may have some unexpected, yet largely untapped allies. Apparently, the impetus for constitutionalization of human rights treaties was not a magnanimous desire to sanctify human rights or a desire to repent for a dark past; it was instead an outgrowth of regional integration and regional trading blocks—namely Mercosur—and Argentina's desire to be a welcome and powerful member of such blocs. In debate and public statements regarding Article 75(22), delegates incessantly referenced economic integration, and virtually all the delegates that spoke about the provision underscored its importance in terms of Mercosur and/or economic integration. For some delegates, sovereignty was the link: if sovereignty concerns had created resistance to human rights treaties and systems in the past, then Argentina's entrance into Mercosur, and its concomitant abdication of power to a supranational entity, neutralized these concerns. Other delegates believed that if Argentina was going to make an honest attempt to join the international community, its joining a regional trade bloc was insufficient—Argentina also needed to participate in a multitude of international organizations, including those that promoted human rights. As proof, many delegates referenced other countries who had constitutionally elevated the status of international human rights norms as part of a concerted effort to enhance the states' standing and prominence in the international community.

The ultimate structure of Article 75 further illustrates the marriage between human rights and trading interests. Article 75 also provides the following: 1) Congress has the power to approve and disapprove of treaties regarding international/regional integration even if it involves delegating power to supranational entities; 2) these treaties enjoy a status superior to domestic law; and 3) approval of integration treaties with Latin American states only requires an absolute majority vote of both houses of the legislature. In fact, most members of the Constitutional Assembly that proposed language concerning incorporation of international human rights norms concurrently proposed language concerning the approval and status of treaties regarding integration. Human rights, international trade, and regional integration became a tightly knit package, and the Constitution reflects this interwoven relationship.

Those affiliated with trading interests and successful regional integration thus maintain a stake in the effective internalization of human right norms. As several delegates stated, Argentina's human rights record is a potent indicator of its ability to cooperate in regional economic relationships. Among the Argentine business community, therefore, Article 75(22) may find engaged members of its epistemic community.

. . . .

The glimmer—the incipient promise—in Argentina's internalization experiment may also be traced to the identity and enthusiasm of various transnational actors. By publicizing international human rights, Article 75(22) may transform the bearers of those rights—individuals—into transnational actors. While linking Article 75(22) to the creation of a fertile legal climate for regional economic integration effectively removed human rights from debate and discussion, it also created potential allies among the trade and business communities. Finally, the energy and enthusiasm of NGOs, who themselves are members of Article 75(22)'s epistemic community, are helping transform passive transnational actors—the courts—into active, energetic transnational actors. Both the problems and the promises in Argentina's internalization strategy suggest that a large coterie of energetic and cooperative transnational actors create the "transmission belt" necessary to propel nations not only toward compliance, but also toward obedience of international norms.

Furthermore, the nature of the internalization strategy may determine its ulti-mate effectiveness. In describing transnational legal process, Professor Koh notes that internalization may take place via legal, political or social means.[57] Argentina's experience suggests that in countries where the rule of law and the judiciary have historically been weak, internalization must be multifaceted, including legal, politi-cal, and social strategies. On its face, Article 75(22), a constitutional amendment, is a prototypical example of legal internalization. It strives to harness law to drive internalization of international norms. Law, however, is one of the weaker Argen-tine institutions and, within law, the Constitution is perhaps the weakest. While a naked law, especially in a country like Argentina, will not significantly further obe-dience, it may animate political and social actors who, in turn, may further obedi-ence. In antiseptically removing "human rights" from debate and effectively treating Article 75(22) as an afterthought—an appendage necessary to facilitate economic integration efforts—the members of the Constitutional Assembly missed an op-portunity to transform much of the human rights community into effective social and political actors with a stake in successful internalization of human rights law. Legal internalization did not trigger concomitant social and political internalization processes. And law alone is rather hollow in Argentina. Argentina now faces a chal-lenge: it must transform a legal gesture into concrete, programmatic change.

---

iii. Self-executing and Non-self-executing Treaties

T. Buergenthal, "Self-Executing and Non-Self-Executing Treaties in National and International Law," 235 *Recueil des Cours* 303 (1992).[Footnotes omitted.]

As a general proposition, there are two distinct methods or approaches that char-acterize the manner in which States give domestic legal effect to treaties. First there are the countries where a treaty acquires, in principle at least, the status of domestic law upon its ratification and promulgation in the State concerned. This is true in much of Latin America, in the United States, in various countries in Western Eu-rope (for example Germany, France, Italy and Spain), and in some African States. In these countries the legislature or one branch of the legislature participates in the process that authorizes the executive branch to ratify the treaty. Here legisla-tive consent to ratification can be equated to some extent to the role the legislature performs when it adopts a piece of legislation that becomes law with the approval of the executive branch: the legislature authorizes the ratification of the treaty and, once the executive branch has ratified it, the treaty is deemed to have acquired the status of domestic law.

In the second group of countries a duly ratified treaty does not *ipso facto* enjoy the status of domestic law. This is true in the United Kingdom, in Ireland, and in some present and former British Commonwealth countries, whether in Africa, Asia, the Caribbean or the Middle East. Here, although the treaty binds the State inter-

---

57   Harold Hongju Koh, *Why Do Nations Obey International Law?*, 106 Yale L.J. 2599, 2634 (1997) (review-ing Abram Chayes & Antonia Handler Chayes, THE NEW SOVEREIGNTY: COMPLIANCE WITH INTERNA-TIONAL REGULATORY AGREEMENTS (1995)

nationally upon its ratification, that act alone does not have the legal consequence of transforming the provisions of the treaty into domestic law. In these countries, as a rule, the executive branch alone decides whether to ratify the treaty; it has the power to take this action without requiring the approval of the legislature. That is to say, the executive branch in these countries is authorized to bind the country internationally by ratifying the treaty. Legislative involvement is necessary, however, before the provisions of the treaty can acquire the status of domestic law. This approach ensures that the treaty-making power, being vested in the executive branch, does not deprive the legislative branch of its domestic law-making functions. By contrast, in the group of countries first mentioned, where the legislative branch discharges a legislative role in the ratification process, there is usually no need for a two-stage process consisting of ratification followed by domestic implementing legislation.

A much smaller group of States, among them the Scandinavian countries, have a mixed system. Here the legislature must approve the ratification of the treaty before the executive branch may bind the country internationally, but this legislative action does not have the effect of transforming the treaty into domestic law. Specific action by the legislative branch is required after the treaty has been ratified, however, to give it domestic law status.

Self-Executing Treaties in Domestic Law

The mere fact, however, that in a given State treaties acquire the status of domestic law upon their ratification does not necessarily mean that a specific treaty or treaty provision will there be deemed capable of creating legal rights or obligations directly enforceable in the courts. Whether they do or not depends upon many factors. These tend to be lumped together by characterizing or labeling the treaty as "self-executing" or "non-self-executing." If the treaty is said to be self-executing, it will be directly enforceable in the courts. Treaties or treaty provisions that are determined to be non-self-executing do not without some further legislative or executive measure (in addition to the measures that approved the ratification of the treaty) give rise to legal rights or obligations enforceable in the domestic courts. Whether a treaty is or is not self-executing is a domestic law question in that domestic law determines whether the treaty created rights that domestic courts are empowered to enforce in a State. The courts may and often do answer this question differently in different countries, depending upon their national constitutions, legal traditions, historical precedents and political institutions. Although certain types of treaties, usually those that call expressly for further domestic legislative measures or those that contain only very general or so-called programmatic commitments, will in most States be deemed non-self-executing, that is not always the case. It is therefore not unusual to find that one and the same treaty or treaty provision may be self-executing in one State and non-self-executing in another. Hence, the specific language of the treaty is not necessarily determinative. It is also not unusual for some provisions of a treaty to be self-executing and for others not. . . .

International law recognizes that States may conclude a treaty which requires the contracting parties to ensure that all or some of its provisions have the status of directly applicable domestic law and be enforced as such by their national courts.

But treaties seldom impose such a requirement because, in general, the parties to a treaty are interested in ensuring only that its substantive obligations be complied with, leaving it to each State to decide how that obligation will be executed on the domestic plane. One reason why most treaties adopt this approach is that, as we have seen, States are governed by different constitutional rules or employ different legal techniques to implement treaties on the domestic plane. Moreover, most of the time it does not really matter to the States parties to a treaty how each of them complies with its provisions, whether they do so by statute, administrative regulation or judicial decrees; what matters is that they comply with the substantive obligations.

Suppose that the States parties decide that all or some provisions of a treaty should be accorded the force of directly applicable domestic law and that they so provide expressly in the treaty. Does this fact make the treaty self-executing on the domestic plane? As soon as the question is put in this fashion, it becomes clear that two very distinct issues are being confused: the international law obligation to make the treaty directly applicable and the domestic law power or competence of national courts to comply with the international law obligation. The question whether a provision of a treaty is directly enforceable domestic law or self-executing in a given State can ultimately only be answered by reference to the law of the particular country. In a dualist State the mere ratification of the treaty would not transform its provision into domestic law even if the States parties specified that status in the treaty. Here, additional domestic legislation would be required to comply with that treaty obligation. In some monist States, as we shall see, an express undertaking in the treaty to make it directly applicable will enable, but not necessarily compel, the domestic courts to characterize the treaty as self-executing; but there are other monist States where that result will not always be possible, notwithstanding the clear intention of the parties. In short, a treaty that, as a matter of international law, is deemed to be directly applicable is not self-executing ipso facto under the domestic law of the States parties to it. All that can be said about such a treaty is that the States parties thereto have an international law obligation to take whatever measures are necessary under their domestic law to ensure that the specific provisions of the treaty, not only its substantive obligations, are accorded the status of domestic law.

Questions and Comments

Does the OAS Charter contain self-executing rights? Consider the following case:

In re Alien Children Education Litigation, 501 F. Supp. 544 (S.D.Tx. 1980).

I. INTRODUCTION

. . .

At issue is a statute which prohibits the use of a state fund to educate persons who are not citizens of the United States or "legally admitted aliens." Tex. Educ. Code Ann. tit. 2, § 21.031 (Vernon 1980). That statute by negative implication also permits local school officials to exclude undocumented children from the public schools. Plaintiffs assert that the statute denies them equal protection of the laws, is preempted by federal legislation, and conflicts with federal treaties and foreign policy.

C. The Challenged Statute

Prior to September 1, 1975, the Texas Education Code provided that all children between six and twenty-one years of age were entitled to attend the public schools of the district where they resided. Funds were provided to the school districts by the State in proportion to the school district's average daily attendance. All children were counted in the calculation of average daily attendance provided they satisfied the age and residency requirements.

In April, 1975, the Attorney General of Texas, upon a request made by the Commissioner of Education, issued an opinion holding that all children within the State were entitled to attend public schools in the district of their residence regardless of whether they were legally or illegally within the United States. Prior to the Attorney General's Opinion there had been no established policy regarding the admission of undocumented children to the public schools. A small number of school districts excluded undocumented children at that time.

In May, 1975, the Texas Legislature amended the Texas Education Code. The amended statute, Tex.Educ.Code Ann. tit. 2, § 21.031, provides in pertinent part:

(a) All children who are citizens of the United States or legally admitted aliens and who are over the age of five years and under the age of 21 years on the first day of September of any scholastic year shall be entitled to the benefits of the Available School Fund for that year.

(b) Every child in this state who is a citizen of the United States or a legally admitted alien and who is over the age of five years and not over the age of 21 years on the first day of September of the year in which admission is sought shall be permitted to attend the public free schools of the district in which he resides or in which his parent, guardian, or the person having lawful control of him resides at the time he applies for admission.

(c) The board of trustees of any public free school district of this state shall admit into the public free schools of the district free of tuition all persons who are either citizens of the United States or legally admitted aliens and who are over five and not over 21 years of age at the beginning of the scholastic year if such person or his parent, guardian or person having lawful control resides within the school district.

Accordingly, undocumented children are not entitled to attend public school and they may not be counted when calculating the average daily attendance which determines the school district's share of the Available School Fund. Local school districts are given the discretion to deny admission or to permit attendance upon payment of tuition.

Needless to say, the effect of the new statute is to exclude undocumented children from the Texas public schools. Although some school districts continue to educate all children, the majority exclude them or require tuition. There was no evidence that any undocumented children are presently attending school upon payment of tuition. . . .

IV. INTERNATIONAL LAW AND FOREIGN POLICY

A. Section 21.031 and United States Treaty Obligations

The United States is a member of the Organization of American States, having ratified that organization's Charter on June 19, 1951. 2 UST. 2394, T.I.A.S. No. 2361 (entered into force December 13, 1951). The Charter was amended by the 1967 Protocol of Buenos Aires, which was ratified by the United States on April 26, 1968. T.I.A.S. No. 6847, O.A.S.T.S. No. 1-A, O.A.S.O.R., O.E.A./Ser. A/2, add 2 (entered into force February 27, 1970). Among the provisions of the amended Charter are several articles dealing with education. Article 31 provides:

> To accelerate their economic and social development, in accordance with their own methods and procedures and within the framework of the democratic principles in the institutions of the inter-American system, the member states agree to dedicate every effort to achieve the following basic goals: . . .
>
> h) Rapid eradication of illiteracy and expansion of educational opportunities for all;

Article 47 provides:

> The Member States will exert the greatest efforts, in accordance with their constitutional processes, to insure the effective exercise of the right to education on the following bases:
>
> a) Elementary education, compulsory for children of school age, shall also be offered to all others who can benefit from it. When provided by the State it shall be without charge;
>
> b) Middle-level education shall be extended progressively to as much of the population as possible, with a view to social improvement. It shall be diversified in such a way that it meets the development needs of each country without prejudice to providing a general education; and
>
> c) Higher education shall be available to all, provided that, in order to maintain its high level, the corresponding regulatory or academic standards are met.

The plaintiffs assert that Article 47 of the amended Charter is a self-executing treaty provision which invalidates section 21.031 under the supremacy clause, U.S. Const. art. VI, cl. 2.

A treaty is an international agreement of a contractual nature between two or more independent nations. Treaties made under the authority of the United States are the supreme law of the land. Nonetheless, a treaty becomes the internal law of the United States and has the effect of domestic law only when that treaty is given effect by congressional legislation or is, by its nature, self-executing. *Whitney v. Robertson*, 124 U.S. 190, 194, 8. S.Ct. 456, 458, 31 L.Ed. 386 (1888); *Foster v. Neilson*, 27 U.S. (2 Pet.) 253, 311, 7 L.Ed. 415 (1829); *United States v. Postal*, 589 F.2d 862, 875 (5th Circ. 1979); *Sei Fujii v. State*, 38 Cal.2d 718, 242 P.2d 617 (1952); Restatement (Second) of Foreign Relations Law of the United States, § 141 (1965) (hereinafter Restatement). According to the Restatement, "[n]ot all treaties made by the United States have immediate effect as domestic law in the United States upon becoming binding between the United States and the other parties. Restatement § 141, comment a at 432. A treaty becomes effective as domestic law of the United States at the time it becomes binding on the United States if it is self-executing, or, if it is non-self-executing, only when it is implemented by act of Congress.

Whether a treaty is self-executing is a matter of interpretation to be determined by the courts. *United States v. Postal*, 589 F.2d 862, 876 (5th Cir. 1979); *Diggs v. Richardson*, 555 F.2d 848, 851 (D.C. Cir. 1976). There are two principal elements to the question whether a treaty is self-executing. First, the language of the treaty must manifest that the parties intend to confer rights or obligations on the citizenry of the compacting nations. See *People of Saipan v. United States Dep't of Interior*, 502 F.2d 90, 101 (9th Cir. 1974) (Trask, J., concurring). Second, "if the instrument is uncertain, recourse may be had to the circumstances surrounding its execution . . . " *Sei Fujii v. State*, 38 Cal.2d 718, 721–22, 242 P.2d 617, 620 (1952). Applying those principles, the court concludes that Article 47 of the amended Charter of the Organization of American States was not intended to be self-executing; it was not addressed to the judicial branch of our government. *Diggs v. Richardson*, 555 F.2d 848, 851 (D.C. Cir. 1976).

Article 47 (a) is no doubt sufficiently direct to imply the intention to create affirmative and judicially enforceable rights. The article read as a whole, however, belies that construction. Article 47 begins with the statement that "The Member States will exert the greatest efforts, in accordance with their constitutional processes, to insure the effective exercise of the right to education . . . " This is not the kind of promissory language which confers rights in the absence of implementing legislation. The parties have engaged to perform a particular act, that is, to exert the greatest efforts to advance the cause of education. They have not contracted to provide free public education to all children of school age within the country. The court concludes that Article 47 of the amended Charter of the Organization of American States is a non self-executing treaty and that it does not invalidate inconsistent state laws.

B. Section 21.031 and the Conduct of Foreign Affairs

The Constitution entrusts the conduct of foreign affairs to the President and the Congress. A state statute that intrudes into or interferes with the conduct of foreign policy cannot stand. The plaintiffs assert that section 21.031 must be invalidated under the supremacy clause, U.S. Const. art. VI, cl. 2, because it impermissibly interferes with federal foreign policy. They maintain that the eradication of illiteracy and the expansion of educational opportunities are elements of our foreign policy, and they contend that these elements are evidenced by treaties, international agreements, and active support for the international recognition of human rights. . . .

A treaty, even if non self-executing, evidences federal activities and policy in the field of foreign affairs. Accordingly, even though Article 47 of the amended Charter of the Organization of American States is not a self-executing treaty provision, it demonstrates a federal commitment to education which we have affirmed to the international community. Before deciding whether the right to education is a component of foreign policy which ousts inconsistent state law, other rights or provisions found in the amended Charter should be considered. This is necessary because the executive and legislative intent to make these provisions a part of foreign policy, thereby overriding state and federal laws, must be considered. The "shifting winds at the State Department" cannot control whether a particular state statute is in conflict with the United States conduct of foreign relations. See *Zschernig v. Miller*,

389 U.S. 429, 443, 88 S.Ct. 664, 672, 19 L.Ed.2d 683 (1968) (Stewart, J., concurring). Nonetheless, whether the signing and ratification of a treaty was such an exercise of foreign policy that the states thereafter are prevented from enacting inconsistent laws regarding activities traditionally within their sphere is an issue which may be resolved by construing the intent of those who signed or ratified.

Article 31 is a sufficient example of the breadth of the rights recognized by the amended Charter. Without in any way disparaging the admirable goals represented by Article 31, the court concludes that the President and the Congress did not enter into this treaty as an act of foreign relations which displaces inconsistent state law. Article 31 also should not be used by the judicial branch as a test for all state and federal statutes which touch on the subjects embraced by the Article. If signing a treaty necessarily had the effect of displacing inconsistent state and federal laws, the question of whether a treaty was self-executing and thus had the effect of domestic law would be unnecessary.

The reservation made by the Senate when ratifying the Charter supports the conclusion that it was not an act of foreign policy ousting the states' ability to interfere with the achievement of the goals established in the Charter:

> [T]he Senate gives its advice and consent to ratification of the Charter with the reservation that none of its provisions shall be considered as enlarging the powers of the Federal Government of the United States or limiting the powers of the several states of the Federal Union with respect to any matters recognized under the Constitution as being within the reserved powers of the several states.

The Charter of the Organization of American States is not a superior federal policy to which state law must yield when it impairs the policy represented by that Charter.

The plaintiffs also point to other international instruments which support their position that the right to education is universally recognized. The American Declaration of the Rights and Duties of Man, O.A.S.O.R., O.E.A./Ser. L/V/II, 23, Doc. 21, Rev. 2 (English 1975); the International Covenant on Economic, Social, and Cultural Rights, G.A.Res. 2200 A (XXI) (1966); the [American Convetion] on Human Rights, O.A.S.T.S. No. 36, at 1, O.A.S.O.R., O.E.A./Ser.L/V/II, 23, Doc. 21 Rev. 2 (English 1977); the Declaration on the Rights of the Child, G.A.Res. 1386 (1959). These human rights instruments recognize the right of all persons to literacy or to a free primary education. The plaintiffs also point to the emphasis by the current administration on the international recognition of all human rights. That the State denies undocumented children the right to education may be hypocritical; it is not an impermissible interference with the power to conduct foreign relations.

There is no recorded decision which holds that the federal recognition of human rights, by itself, prevents the states from interfering with the enjoyment of those rights. The cases on which the plaintiffs rely were resolved on a much narrower basis. . . .

Durand and Ugarte v. Peru, Judgment of August 16, 2000, 68 Inter-Am. Ct. H.R. (Ser. C) (2000).

1. . . . The Commission started this case to entitle the Court to decide whether the State of Peru had violated the following Articles of the Convention: 1(1) (Obligation to Respect Rights), 2 (Duty to Adopt the Clauses of National Law), 4 (Right to Life), 7(6) (Right to Personal Freedom), 8(1) (Judicial Guarantees), 25(1) (Judicial Protection) and 27(2) (Suspension of Guarantees), to the detriment of Mr. Nolberto Durand Ugarte and Mr. Gabriel Pablo Ugarte Rivera. . . .

4.1.2 VIOLATION OF ARTICLE 4(1) RIGHT TO LIFE

. . . .

Based on the circumstances that surrounded the riots' subduing at El Frontón [prison], mainly regarding the disproportionate use of force by Peruvian Navy and the fact that for 14 years the whereabouts of Nolberto Ugarte and Gabriel Pablo Ugarte Rivera has been unknown, it is possible to conclude that their lives were arbitrarily deprived by Peruvian authorities in violation of Article 4 of the Convention.

36. As a consequence, the Court concludes that the State violated, to the detriment of Nolberto Durand Ugarte and Gabriel Ugarte Rivera, Article 4(1) of the Convention.

. . . .

XII VIOLATION OF ARTICLES 7(1) AND 7(5) RIGHT TO PERSONAL FREEDOM

37. Regarding the violation of Articles 7(1) and 7(5) of the Convention, the Commission stated that on February 14 and 15, 1986, Nolberto Durand Ugarte and Gabriel Pablo Ugarte Rivera, respectively, were detained by some members of the Directorship against Terrorism, without a warrant or having found them guilty of a flagrant felony, under suspicion of having participated in terrorists acts. . . .

38. The Court considers that even though the facts stated in the application regarding the fact that Nolberto Durand and Gabriel Pablo Ugarte Rivera were detained without a warrant or having been found guilty of flagrant felony, or lessened by the State also, the Peruvian Constitution itself exempted cases of terrorism from this rule. On the other hand, and regarding the accused detention term, it is convenient to observe that the quoted constitutional notion only authorized detention by a term not over 15 days with the obligation to render an account to the State Attorney's Office and the corresponding jurisdictional agency. As has been previously stated, Mr. Durand Ugarte was presented before the competent jurisdictional agency on March 4, 1986, that is, 17 days after his detention. Mr. Ugarte Rivera on that same day, that is, 18 days after his detention, both cases after elapsed the 15 days term allowed by the Political Constitution of Peru and, as a result, violating Article 7(5) of the Convention.

39. As a consequence, the Court states that the State violated, to the detriment of Nolberto Durand Ugarte and Gabriel Pablo Ugarte Rivera, Articles 7(1) and 7(5) of the American Convention.

XV NON-COMPLIANCE OF ARTICLES 1(1) AND 2 OBLIGATION TO RESPECT RIGHTS AND DUTY TO ADOPT DOMESTIC LEGAL EFFECTS

. . . .

42. Article 1(1) of the Convention stipulates that

[t]he States Parties to this Convention undertake to respect the rights and freedoms recognized herein and to ensure to all persons subject to their jurisdiction the free and full exercise of those rights and freedoms, without any discrimination for reasons of race, color, sex, language, religion, political or other opinion, national or social origin, economic status, birth, or any other social condition.

43. Article 2 of the Convention determines that

Where the exercise of any of the rights or freedoms referred to in Article 1 is not already ensured by legislative or other provisions, the States Parties undertake to adopt, in accordance with their constitutional processes and the provisions of this Convention, such legislative or other measures as may be necessary to give effect to those rights or freedoms.

44. In the same sense, in [an]other case the [PCIJ] has stated that:

[r]egarding people's law, a customary rule prescribes that a State, which has entered into an international agreement, must introduce in its national law the necessary assumed modifications to ensure the execution of obligations assumed. This rule is universally valid and has been considered by the jurisprudence as an evident principle ("principe allant de soi"; *Echange des populations grecques et turques, avis consultatif*, 1925, C.P.J.I., Series B. No. 10, p. 20). In this sequence of ideas, the American Convention states the obligation of every State Party to adapt its national law to dispositions of said Convention, to guarantee the rights recognized therein.[58]

45. In this sense, in another case the Court stated that

[t]he general duty of Article 2 of the American Convention implies the adoption of measures in two ways. On the one hand, derogation of rules and practices of any kind that imply the violation of guarantees in the Convention. On the other hand, the issuance of rules and the development of practices leading to an effective enforcement of said guarantees.[59]

46. The Court warns that, based on this judgment, the State violated Articles 4(1), 7(1), 7(5), 7(6), 8(1) and 25(1) of the American Convention, to the detriment of Nolberto Durand Ugarte and Gabriel Pablo Ugarte Rivera; therefore, it has not fulfilled its general duty of respecting the rights and freedoms recognized therein and of ensuring its free and full exercise, as stipulated in Article 1(1) of the Convention. Also, in the present case Article 2 of the Convention was violated, because the State had not taken appropriate measures of its internal law which allow making effective the rights established on the said Convention.

47. As a consequence, the Court concludes that the State has failed to comply with the general obligations of Articles 1(1) and 2 of the American Convention on Human Rights.

---

[58] Garrido and Baigorria Case. Reparations. Judgment of August 27, 1998. Series C No. 39, para. 68.
[59] Castillo Petruzzi *et al* Case, para. 207.

Civil Liberties Organization v. Nigeria, (Comm. 129/94), *9th Annual Activity Report of the Afr. Comm. H.P.R. 1995–1996,* Annex on Communications, OAU Doc. AGH/Res.207 (XXXII).

The Facts

1. The communication is filed by the Civil Liberties Organization, a Nigerian NGO. The communication alleges that the military government of Nigeria has enacted various decrees in violation of the African Charter, specifically the Constitution (Suspension and Modification) Decree No. 107 of 1993, which not only suspends the Constitution but also specifies that no decree promulgated after December 1983 can be examined in any Nigerian Court; and the Political Parties (Dissolution) Decree No. 114 of 1993, which in addition to dissolving political parties, ousts the jurisdiction of the courts and specifically nullifies any domestic effect of the African Charter.

2. The communication complains that the ousting of the jurisdiction of the courts in Nigeria to adjudicate the legality of any decree threatens the independence of the judiciary and violates Article 26 of the African Charter.

3. The communication also complains that this ouster of the jurisdiction of the courts deprives Nigerians of their right to seek redress in the courts for government acts that violate their fundamental rights, in violation of Articles 7 (1) (a) of the African Charter.

. . . .

The Law

The Merits

10. Article 7 of the African Charter provides:

   1. Every individual shall have the right to have his cause heard. This comprises:
      a) The right to an appeal to competent national organs against acts violating his fundamental rights as guaranteed by conventions, law, regulations and customs in force.

11. The Constitution (Suspension and Modification) Decree 1993, (5) reads:

   No question as to the validity of this Decree or any other Decree made during the period 31st December 1983 to 26th August 1993 or made after the commencement of this Decree or of an Edict shall be entertained by a court of law in Nigeria.

12. The Political Parties (Dissolution) Decree 12993, 13 (1) reads:

   Notwithstanding anything contained in the Constitution of the Federal Republic of Nigeria 1979, as amended, the African Charter on Human and Peoples' Rights (Ratification and Enforcement) Act or any other enactment, no proceeding shall lie or be instituted in any court for or on account of any act, matter or thing done or purported to be done in respect of this Decree.

13. The reference in Article 7(1) (a) to "fundamental rights as guaranteed by conventions . . . in force" signifies the rights in the Charter itself, among others. Given that Nigeria ratified the African Charter in 1983, it is presently a convention in enforce in Nigeria. If Nigeria wished to withdraw its ratification, it would have to undertake an international process involving notice, which it has not done. Nigeria

cannot negate the effects of its ratification of the Charter through domestic action. Nigeria remains under the obligation to guarantee the rights of Article 7 to all of its citizens.

14. The ousting of jurisdiction of the courts of Nigeria over any decree enacted in the past ten years, and those to be subsequently enacted, constitutes an attack of incalculable proportions on Article 7. The complaint refers to a few examples of decrees which violate human rights but which are now beyond review by the courts. An attack of this sort on the jurisdiction of the courts is especially invidious, because while it is a violation of human rights in itself, it permits other violations of rights to go unredressed.

16. Article 26 of the African Charter reiterates the right enshrined in Article 7 but is even more explicit about States Parties' obligations to "guarantee the independence of the Courts and allow the establishment and improvement of appropriate national institutions entrusted with the promotion and protection of the rights and freedoms guaranteed by the present Charter." While Article 7 focuses on the individual's right to be heard, Article 26 speaks of the institutions which are essential to give meaning and content to that right. This Article clearly envisions the protection of the courts which have traditionally been the bastion of protection of the individual's rights against the abuses of State power.

16. The communication notes that Nigeria fully incorporated the African Charter upon ratification in 1983. The African Charter upon ratification in 1983. The African Charter (Ratification and Enforcement Act) specified:

> 1. As from the commencement of this Act, the provisions of the African Charter on Human and Peoples' Rights . . . shall, subject as thereunder provided, have force of law in Nigeria and shall be given full recognition and effect and be applied by all authorities and persons exercising legislative, executive or judicial powers in Nigeria.

It is this Act that is repealed by clause 13 (1) of the Political Parties Dissolution Decree.

17. Any doubt that may exist as to Nigeria's obligations under the African Charter is dispelled by reference to Article 1 of the Charter, which reads:

> The Member States . . . Parties to the present Charter shall recognize the rights, duties and freedoms enshrined in this Charter and shall undertake to adopt legislative or other measures to give effect to them.

18. The African Commission has to express its approval of Nigeria's original incorporation of the Charter, an incorporation that should set a standard for all Africa, and its sadness at the subsequent nullification of this incorporation. The Commission must emphasize, however, that the obligation of the Nigerian government to guarantee the right to be heard to its citizens still remains, unaffected by the purported revocation of domestic effect of the Charter. The Charter remains in force in Nigeria, and notwithstanding the Political Parties Dissolution Decree, the Nigerian government has the same obligations under the Charter as if it had never revoked. These obligations include guaranteeing the right to be heard.

Questions and Comments

1. In the law of treaties, what does "self-executing" mean?

2. In the constitutional provisions reprinted above, which of them indicate that some or all treaties are self-executing and which designate them as non-self executing?

3. Does the language of Article 2 of the American Convention mark it as a self-executing treaty?

4. Who decides whether a treaty is self-executing? What factors are considered?

5. Note the State Department's recommendation to the Senate of the United States regarding ratification of the American Convention:

> The Convention begins with a general provision on nondiscrimination (Article 1), and follows with an obligation to adopt legislative or other measures as may be necessary to give effect to the rights and freedoms protected by the Convention (Article 2). While the latter provision thus indicates that the substantive provisions of the Convention are not self-executing, in order to avoid possible discrepancies in wording and to leave the implementation of all substantive provisions to the domestic legislative and judicial process, the following declaration is recommended:
>
> > "The United States declares that the provisions of Articles 1 through 32 of this Convention are not self-executing."

Are U.S. courts bound by this declaration?

iv. Legislative Incorporation: The UK Human Rights Act 1998

Al-Skeini and Others (Respondents) v. Secretary of State for Defense (Appellant) and Others, *on appeal from:* [2005] EWCA Civ 1609, judgment of June 13, 2007, [2007] UKHL 26 (Consolidated Appeals)

LORD BINGHAM OF CORNHILL

1. These proceedings arise from the deaths of six Iraqi civilians, and the brutal maltreatment of one of them causing his death, in Basra. Each of the deceased was killed (or, in one case, is said to have been killed) and the maltreatment was inflicted by a member or members of the British armed forces. In each case a close relative of the deceased has applied in the High Court in London for an order of judicial review against the Secretary of State for Defence, seeking to challenge his refusal (by a letter of 26 March 2004) to order an independent enquiry into the circumstances of this maltreatment and these deaths, and his rejection of liability to afford the claimants redress for causing them. These six cases have been selected as test cases from a much larger number of claims in order, at this stage, to resolve certain important and far-reaching issues of legal principle.

2. The claimants found their claims in the English court on the Human Rights Act 1998 ("the HRA" or "the Act"). To succeed each claimant must show that a public authority has acted unlawfully, that is, incompatibly with a Convention right of the claimant or the deceased (section 6(1) of the Act). A Convention right means a right set out in one of the articles of the European Convention on Human Rights reproduced in Schedule 1 to the Act (sections 1(1), 1(3) and 21(1))....

   . . . .

A. Does the HRA apply to acts done outside the territory of the UK?

8. The HRA is a statute enacted by Parliament. Where an issue arises as to its meaning, it must be construed. This is a task which only a UK court can perform. The court in Strasbourg is the ultimate authority on interpretation of the European Convention, but it cannot rule on the interpretation of a domestic statute. That is the task which the House is now called upon to perform.

9. In carrying out that task the House must employ the familiar tools of statutory interpretation. The starting point is the language of the Act, from which the court seeks to derive the meaning of what Parliament has enacted. . . . It is of course very relevant that the HRA is directed to the protection of human rights, with particular reference to the European Convention, which the UK ratified on 8 March 1951 and which came into force on 3 September 1953 when Luxembourg became the tenth contracting state to ratify.

10. Since 3 September 1953 the UK has been bound in international law to comply with the obligations undertaken in the Convention, and in later protocols to the Convention which it has formally ratified. But for upwards of 40 years the UK took no step to give domestic legal effect to these international obligations. The object of the HRA was to do so. This object could have been achieved by a simple incorporation of the Convention (or some or all of its articles) into domestic law. But this is not what was done. . . . The technique adopted . . . was to provide in section 6(1) that "It is unlawful for a public authority to act in a way which is incompatible with a Convention right". A "Convention right", by section 1, meant a right or fundamental freedom set out in articles 2 to 12 and 14 of the Convention, articles 1 to 3 of the First Protocol and articles 1 and 2 of the Sixth Protocol, as read with articles 16 to 18 of the Convention, subject to any designated derogation or reservation. The listed articles were set out in Schedule 1 to the Act. "The Convention" was defined in section 21(1) of the Act to mean the Convention agreed by the Council of Europe at Rome on 4 November 1950 "as it has effect for the time being in relation to the United Kingdom". Thus, . . . there is a distinction between (1) rights arising under the Convention and (2) rights created by the 1998 Act by reference to the Convention: These two sets of rights now exist side by side. But there are significant differences between them. The former existed before the enactment of the 1998 Act and they continue to exist. They are not as such part of this country's law because the Convention does not form part of this country's law. That is still the position. These rights, arising under the Convention, are to be contrasted with rights created by the 1998 Act. The latter came into existence for the first time on 2 October 2000. They are part of this country's law. The extent of these rights, created as they were by the 1998 Act, depends upon the proper interpretation of that Act . . . " The focus of this opinion, at this stage of the enquiry, is on the extent of the rights arising under the Act, not those arising under the Convention. Hence the need for careful consideration, in the first instance, of the Act.

11. In resisting the interpretation, upheld by the courts below, that the HRA has extra-territorial application, the Secretary of State places heavy reliance on what he describes as "a general and well established principle of statutory construction". This is (see Bennion, *Statutory Interpretation*, 4th ed (2002), p 282, section 106)

that "Unless the contrary intention appears, Parliament is taken to intend an Act to extend to each territory of the United Kingdom but not to any territory outside the United Kingdom." . . .

12. In argument before the courts below, the claimants relied on another presumption of statutory interpretation: that, as put by the Divisional Court in paragraph 301 of its judgment, "a domestic statute enacting international treaty obligations will be compatible with those obligations". The Divisional Court appears to have given some weight to this presumption, and in the Court of Appeal Sedley LJ appears to have accepted (paragraph 186) that "absent some clear indication to the contrary, domestic legislation is to be taken to have been intended to cohere with the state's international obligations". . . .

13. The Secretary of State points, in support of his submission, to the absence from the HRA of any of the forms of words used where Parliament intends a provision to have extra-territorial application. Examples were given in argument: "who commits, in a foreign country" (Criminal Justice Act 1948, s 31(1)); "whether in the United Kingdom or elsewhere" (Army Act 1955, s 70(1)); "whether in or outside the United Kingdom" (Geneva Conventions Act 1957, s 1(1)); "acts committed . . . outside the United Kingdom by a United Kingdom national, a United Kingdom resident or a person subject to UK service jurisdiction" (International Criminal Court Act 2001, s 51(2)). There is, I think, force in this point, unless a clear inference of extra-territorial application can otherwise be drawn from the terms of the Act. It cannot be doubted that, if Parliament had intended the Act to have extraterritorial application, words could very readily have been found to express that intention.

14. The Convention provides in article 1 that "The High Contracting Parties shall secure to everyone within their jurisdiction the rights and freedoms defined in Section 1 of this Convention". The Secretary of State points out that article 1 is not one of the articles to which domestic effect is given by section 1 of and Schedule 1 to the HRA. Therefore, he argues, the scope of the Act is to be found in construction of the Act and not construction of article 1 of the Convention. The claimants reject this argument, pointing out that article 1 confers and defines no right, like the other articles specified in section 1 of the Act and the Schedule. Article 1 of the Convention is omitted because, like article 13 (also omitted), it is provided for in the Act. I would for my part accept that Parliament intended the effect of the Act to be governed by its terms and not, save by reference, the Convention, consistently with the scheme described in paragraph 10 above. Thus there was no need to include article 1 in section 1 of the Act and the Schedule, nor article 13 since the Act contains its own provisions as to remedies in sections 4 and 8. But it is not strictly correct that only articles defining or conferring rights are included in section 1 and the Schedule, since articles 16 to 18 are referred to and included, and they define and confer no right. Had article 1 been included in section 1 and the Schedule, this would have assisted the claimants, since by 1997–1998 the Strasbourg jurisprudence had recognised some limited exceptions to the territorial focus of the Convention, and it could have been said that Parliament intended the territorial scope of the Act to be subject to the same limited exceptions. As it is, the omission of any reference to article 1 is of some negative assistance to the Secretary of State.

. . . .

24. In the course of its careful consideration of this question the Divisional Court observed (in paragraph 304 of its judgment): "It is intuitively difficult to think that Parliament intended to legislate for foreign lands". In similar vein, Brooke LJ in the Court of Appeal said (para 3): "It may seem surprising that an Act of the UK Parliament and a European Convention on Human Rights can arguably be said to confer rights upon citizens of Iraq which are enforceable against a UK governmental authority in the courts of England and Wales". I do not think this sense of surprise, which I share, is irrelevant to the court's task of interpretation. It cannot of course be supposed that in 1997–1998 Parliament foresaw the prospect of British forces being engaged in peacekeeping duties in Iraq. But there can be relatively few, if any, years between 1953 and 1997 in which British forces were not engaged in hostilities or peacekeeping activities in some part of the world, and it must have been appreciated that such involvement would recur. This makes it the more unlikely, in my opinion, that Parliament could, without any express provision to that effect, have intended to rebut the presumption of territorial application so as to authorise the bringing of claims, under the Act, based on the conduct of British forces outside the UK and outside any other contracting state. Differing from the courts below, I regard the statutory presumption of territorial application as a strong one, which has not been rebutted. . . .

26. I would accordingly hold that the HRA has no extra-territorial application. A claim under the Act will not lie against the Secretary of State based on acts or omissions of British forces outside the United Kingdom. This does not mean that members of the British armed forces serving abroad are free to murder, rape and pillage with impunity. They are triable and punishable for any crimes they commit under the three service discipline Acts already mentioned, no matter where the crime is committed or who the victim may be. They are triable for genocide, crimes against humanity and war crimes under the International Criminal Court Act 2001. The UK itself is bound, in a situation such as prevailed in Iraq, to comply with The Hague Convention of 1907 and the Regulations made under it. The Convention provides (in article 3) that a belligerent state is responsible for all acts committed by members of its armed forces, being obliged to pay compensation if it violates the provisions of the Regulations and if the case demands it. By article 1 of the Geneva IV Convention the UK is bound to ensure respect for that convention in all circumstances and (Article 3) to prohibit (among other things) murder and cruel treatment of persons taking no active part in hostilities. Additional obligations are placed on contracting states by protocol 1 to Geneva IV. An action in tort may, on appropriate facts, be brought in this country against the Secretary of State: see *Bici v Ministry of Defence* [2004] EWHC 786 (QB). What cannot, it would seem, be obtained by persons such as the present claimants is the remedy they primarily seek: a full, open, independent enquiry into the facts giving rise to their complaints, such as articles 2 and 3 of the Convention have been held by the Strasbourg court to require. But there are real practical difficulties in mounting such an enquiry.

B. The extra-territorial scope of the Convention

27. Consistently with their conclusion that the extra-territorial scope of the HRA matched that of the Convention, it was necessary for the courts below to rule (following the Strasbourg jurisprudence) what the extra-territorial scope of the Convention was, in order to decide whether the six claims now in issue fall within it. Had I concluded that the extraterritorial scope of the Act and the Convention were co-extensive, I should similarly have felt constrained to follow that course. But I have reached a different conclusion. I think it not only unnecessary but unwise to express an opinion whether cases 1–5 fall within the jurisdiction of the UK under article 1 of the Convention, or on what precise basis case 6 should be held to do so. I reach this conclusion with regret and a sense of ingratitude having regard to the extensive, erudite and interesting argument directed to the question, but for what I regard as important reasons.

. . . .

Conclusion

33. Since I conclude that no claim by any of the claimants will lie in this country under the Act, I do not think it useful to discuss the violation issue. For all these reasons I would dismiss the claimants' appeal, allow the Secretary of State's cross-appeal against the Court of Appeal's ruling on the applicability of the HRA to Mr. Mousa's case and set aside the order for remission of Colonel Mousa's claim, which must be dismissed. I would invite the parties to make written submissions on costs within 14 days.

LORD RODGER OF EARLSFERRY

. . . .

36. As was explained in *In re McKerr* [2004] 1 WLR 807, the Convention right of a relative under article 2 to insist on an inquiry being held where a death has been caused by agents of the state is procedural or adjectival. In domestic law it arises only where the killing itself could be unlawful under section 6 of the 1998 Act by reason of being incompatible with article 2 as set out in the Schedule. For that reason, the key question in these appeals is whether the killing of these individuals by British forces in Iraq could be unlawful under section 6 of the Act.

37. Section 6(1) provides: "It is unlawful for a public authority to act in a way which is incompatible with a Convention right." The words are quite general and, on its face, the provision contains no geographical limitation—hence the issue between the parties about its proper scope. The Secretary of State points out that Parliament has not chosen to use the kind of specific wording that would show that it was intended to apply outside the United Kingdom. That comment is, of course, correct, but it does not really go anywhere since the Secretary of State is merely drawing attention to a defining feature of any case where the issue is whether a statute is to be construed as applying, by implication, to conduct outside the United Kingdom.

. . . .

43. In turning to that question, I am, of course, aware that, before the 1998 Act was passed, Government rhetoric referred to "bringing rights home" and to the advantages that would result for "the British people". In reality, the Act also applies

to anyone who lives here and, indeed, to anyone who is within the territory of the United Kingdom. Immigrants and asylum-seekers, for whom the United Kingdom has never been "home", can invoke the provisions of the 1998 Act. The Government rhetoric was not an accurate guide to the application of the Act within the United Kingdom. In these circumstances, in deciding the geographical reach of section 6, I attach no importance to the language of the White Paper ("Rights Brought Home: The Human Rights Bill", (October 1997, Cm 3782)). The passages from Hansard to which we were referred also contained nothing on which it would be safe to rely. Nor did I find anything in the minutiae of the language of the Act which told in favour of any particular view of its geographical reach.

44. So far as the application of statutes is concerned, there is a general rule that legislation does not apply to persons and matters outside the territory to which it extends: Bennion, *Statutory Interpretation*, p 306. But the cases show that the concept of the territoriality of legislation is quite subtle—"slippery" is how Lord Nicholls of Birkenhead described it in *R (Quark Fishing Ltd) v Secretary of State for Foreign and Commonwealth Affairs* [2006] 1 AC 529, 545, para 32.

45. Behind the various rules of construction, a number of different policies can be seen at work. For example, every statute is interpreted, "so far as its language permits, so as not to be inconsistent with the comity of nations or the established rules of international law":

Maxwell on The Interpretation of Statutes (12th edition, 1969), p 183. It would usually be both objectionable in terms of international comity and futile in practice for Parliament to assert its authority over the subjects of another sovereign who are not within the United Kingdom. So, in the absence of any indication to the contrary, a court will interpret legislation as not being intended to affect such people. They do not fall within "the legislative grasp, or intendment," of Parliament's legislation, to use Lord Wilberforce's expression in *Clark v Oceanic Contractors Inc* [1983] 2 AC 130, 152C-D. In *Ex p Blain* (1879) 12 Ch D 522 the question was whether the court had jurisdiction, by virtue of the Bankruptcy Act 1869, to make an adjudication of bankruptcy against a foreigner, domiciled and resident abroad, who had never been in England. James LJ said, at p 526:

"But, if a foreigner remains abroad, if he has never come into this country at all, it seems to me impossible to imagine that the English legislature could have ever intended to make such a man subject to particular English legislation." On this general approach, for instance, there can be no doubt that, despite the lack of any qualifying words, section 6(1) of the 1998 applies only to United Kingdom public authorities and not to the public authorities of any other state.

46. Subjects of the Crown, British citizens, are in a different boat. International law does not prevent a state from exercising jurisdiction over its nationals travelling or residing abroad, since they remain under its personal authority: *Oppenheim's International Law* (ninth edition, 1992), vol 1, para 138. So there can be no objection in principle to Parliament legislating for British citizens outside the United Kingdom, provided that the particular legislation does not offend against the sovereignty of other states. . . .

47. The cases indicate . . . that British individuals or firms or companies or other organisations readily fall within the legislative grasp of statutes passed by Parliament. So far as they are concerned, the question is whether, on a fair interpretation, the statute in question is intended to apply to them only in the United Kingdom or also, to some extent at least, beyond the territorial limits of the United Kingdom. Here, there is no doubt that section 6 applies to public authorities such as the armed forces within the United Kingdom: the only question is whether, on a fair interpretation, it is confined to the United Kingdom.

. . .

49. Again, this rule of construction has to be seen against the background of international law. One state is bound to respect the territorial sovereignty of another state. So, usually, Parliament will not mean to interfere by legislating to regulate the conduct of its citizens in another state. Such legislation would usually be unnecessary and would often be, in any event, ineffective. But sometimes Parliament has a legitimate interest in regulating their conduct and so does indeed intend its legislation to affect the position of British citizens in other states. For example, section 72 of the Sexual Offences Act 2003 makes certain nasty sexual conduct in other countries an offence under English law. So, if the words of a statute are open to more than one interpretation, whether or not it binds British citizens abroad "seems to depend . . . entirely on the nature of the statute": *Maxwell on The Interpretation of Statutes*, p 169.

. . .

52. In the same way, when considering the application of the 1998 Act, it is necessary to have regard to its overall nature and purpose.

53. In the first place, the burden of the legislation falls on public authorities, rather than on private individuals or companies. Most of the functions of United Kingdom public authorities relate to this country and will therefore be carried out here. Moreover, exercising their functions abroad would often mean that the public authorities were encroaching on the sovereignty of another state. Nevertheless, where a public authority has power to operate outside of the United Kingdom and does so legitimately—for example, with the consent of the other state—in the absence of any indication to the contrary, when construing any relevant legislation, it would only be sensible to treat the public authority, so far as possible, in the same way as when it operates at home.

54. The purpose of the 1998 Act is to provide remedies in our domestic law to those whose human rights are violated by a United Kingdom public authority. Making such remedies available for acts of a United Kingdom authority on the territory of another state would not be offensive to the sovereignty of the other state. There is therefore nothing in the wider context of international law which points to the need to confine sections 6 and 7 of the 1998 Act to the territory of the United Kingdom.

55. One possible reason for confining their application in that way would, however, be if their scope would otherwise be unlimited and they would, potentially at least, confer rights on people all over the world with little or no real connexion with the United Kingdom. There is, however, no such danger in this case since the 1998 Act has a built-in limitation. By section 7(1) and (7), only those who would

be victims for the purposes of article 34 of the Convention in proceedings in the Strasbourg Court can take proceedings under the 1998 Act. Before they could sue, claimants would therefore have to be "within the jurisdiction" of the United Kingdom in terms of article 1 of the Convention. Whatever the precise boundaries of that limitation, it blunts the objection that a narrow construction of the territorial application of the Act is the only way to prevent it having extravagant effects which could never have been intended. The requirement for a claimant to be within the jurisdiction of the United Kingdom is a further assurance that, if the Act were interpreted and applied in that way, the courts in this country would not be interfering with the sovereignty or integrity of another state.

56. By this somewhat circuitous route, I arrive at what is surely the crucial argument in favour of the wider interpretation of section 6. The Secretary of State accepts that "the central purpose" of Parliament in enacting sections 6 and 7 was "to provide a remedial structure in domestic law for the rights guaranteed by the Convention": *Aston Cantlow and Wilmcote with Billesley Parochial Church Council v Wallbank* [2004] 1 AC 546, 564, para 44, per Lord Hope of Craighead. In other words, claimants were to be able to obtain remedies in United Kingdom courts, rather than having to go to Strasbourg. The Secretary of State also accepts that, while the jurisdiction of states for the purposes of article 1 of the Convention is essentially territorial, in exceptional cases, "acts of the contracting states performed, or producing effects, outside their territories can constitute an exercise of jurisdiction by them within the meaning of article 1 of the convention": *Bankovic v Belgium* (2001) 11 BHRC 435, 450, para 67. Nevertheless, the Secretary of State says that sections 6 and 7 are to be interpreted in such a way that, in these exceptional cases, a victim is left remediless in the British courts. Contrary to the central policy of the Act, the victim must resort to Strasbourg.

57. My Lords, I am unable to accept that submission. It involves reading into sections 6 and 7 a qualification which the words do not contain and which runs counter to the central purpose of the Act. That would be to offend against the most elementary canons of statutory construction which indicate that, in case of doubt, the Act should be read so as to promote, not so as to defeat or impair, its central purpose. If anything, this approach is even more desirable in interpreting human rights legislation. As Lord Brown of Eaton-under-Heywood points out, this interpretation also ensures that, in these exceptional cases, the United Kingdom is not in breach of its article 13 obligation to afford an effective remedy before its courts to anyone whose human rights have been violated within its jurisdiction.

58. The speech of Lord Nicholls of Birkenhead in *R (Quark Fishing Ltd) v Secretary of State for Foreign and Commonwealth Affairs* [2006] 1 AC 529, 546, para 34, provides powerful support for that approach: "To this end the obligations of public authorities under sections 6 and 7 mirror in domestic law the treaty obligations of the United Kingdom in respect of corresponding articles of the Convention and its protocols. That was the object of these sections. As my noble and learned friend, Lord Hope of Craighead, has said, the 'purpose of these sections is to provide a remedial structure in domestic law for the rights guaranteed by the Convention': *Aston Cantlow and Wilmcote with Billesley Parochial Church Council v Wallbank*

[2004] 1 AC 546, 564, para 44. Thus, and this is the important point for present purposes, the territorial scope of the obligations and rights created by sections 6 and 7 of the Act was intended to be co-extensive with the territorial scope of the obligations of the United Kingdom and the rights of victims under the Convention. The Act was intended to provide a domestic remedy where a remedy would have been available in Strasbourg. Conversely, the Act was not intended to provide a domestic remedy where a remedy would not have been available in Strasbourg. Accordingly, in order to identify the territorial scope of a 'Convention right' in sections 6 and 7 it is necessary to turn to Strasbourg and consider what, under the Convention, is the territorial scope of the relevant Convention right." . . .

59. For these reasons, section 6 should be interpreted as applying not only when a public authority acts within the United Kingdom but also when it acts within the jurisdiction of the United Kingdom for purposes of article 1 of the Convention, but outside the territory of the United Kingdom.

. . . .

61. In the case of the sixth appellant, the deceased, Mr. Baha Mousa, was taken to a detention unit in a British military base in Basra where, it is said, he was so brutally beaten by British troops that he died of his injuries. The Secretary of State accepts that, since the events occurred in the British detention unit, Mr. Mousa met his death "within the jurisdiction" of the United Kingdom for purposes of article 1 of the Convention. In these circumstances the parties are agreed that, because of certain factual developments since the decision of the Court of Appeal, the sixth appellant's case should be remitted to the Divisional Court.

62. So far as the other appellants are concerned, the relevant facts are carefully described in the judgment of the Divisional Court, [2007] QB 140, 160–165, paras 55–80. I gratefully adopt that account. I have also had the privilege of considering what Lord Brown is going to say about the question of jurisdiction under the Convention. In all essentials I agree with him. In these circumstances, especially where the issues have also been exhaustively analysed in the Divisional Court and Court of Appeal, nothing would be gained by me going over all of the same ground. I therefore add only some additional observations on the issues raised.

63. The European Convention is a treaty under international law. Somewhat unusually, it confers rights on individuals against the contracting parties. While the Geneva Conventions on the Protection of War Victims 1949 apply "in all circumstances", the geographical scope of the rights under the European Convention is more limited: under article 1, the States Parties are bound to "secure to everyone within their jurisdiction the rights and freedoms defined in Section 1" of the Convention.

64. It is important therefore to recognise that, when considering the question of jurisdiction under the Convention, the focus has shifted to the victim or, more precisely, to the link between the victim and the contracting state. For the purposes of the extra-territorial effects of section 6 of the 1998 Act, the key question was whether a public authority—in this case the Army in Iraq—was within Parliament's legislative grasp when acting outside the United Kingdom. By contrast, for the purposes of deciding whether the Convention applies outside the territory of

the United Kingdom, the key question is whether the deceased were linked to the United Kingdom when they were killed. However reprehensible, however contrary to any common understanding of respect for "human rights", the alleged conduct of the British forces might have been, it had no legal consequences under the Convention, unless there was that link and the deceased were within the jurisdiction of the United Kingdom at the time. For, only then would the United Kingdom have owed them any obligation in international law to secure their rights under article 2 of the Convention and only then would their relatives have had any rights under the 1998 Act.

65. What is meant by "within their jurisdiction" in article 1 is a question of law and the body whose function it is to answer that question definitively is the European Court of Human Rights. . . .

. . . .

67. The problem which the House has to face, quite squarely, is that the judgments and decisions of the European Court do not speak with one voice. If the differences were merely in emphasis, they could be shrugged off as being of no great significance. In reality, however, some of them appear much more serious and so present considerable difficulties for national courts which have to try to follow the jurisprudence of the European Court.

68. Faced with these conflicting elements in the case law, national courts are justified in giving pre-eminence to the decision of the Grand Chamber in *Bankovic v Belgium* (2001) 11 BHRC 435. . . .

. . . .

84. In all the circumstances I would dismiss the Secretary of State's cross-appeal, dismiss the appeals of the first five appellants and remit the sixth appellant's case to the Divisional Court.

BARONESS HALE OF RICHMOND

. . . .

87. The Human Rights Act extends to England and Wales, Scotland and Northern Ireland: see s 22(6). But by itself this tells us nothing about the public authorities to which section 6(1) applies, or about the acts to which it applies, or about the people for whose benefit it applies.

88. . . . In common with Lord Rodger, I can find nothing in the Act which indicates that section 6 should not apply to Mr. Mousa's case and several good reasons why it should. In particular, it has many times been said that the object of the Human Rights Act was to give people who would be entitled to a remedy against the United Kingdom in the European Court of Human Rights in Strasbourg a remedy against the relevant public authority in the courts of this country. The United Kingdom now accepts that it would be answerable in Strasbourg for the conduct of the British army while Mr. Mousa was detained in a British detention unit in Basra. It would be consistent with the purpose of the Act to give his father a remedy against the army in the courts of this country.

89. But that of course would depend upon establishing a breach of section 6. . . . But inherent in the text of the Convention itself is another limitation: article 1 only requires that "the High Contracting Parties shall secure to everyone within

their jurisdiction the rights and freedoms defined in Section 1 of this Convention". The second question, therefore, is whether any of the individuals involved were "within the jurisdiction" of the United Kingdom at the time of their deaths.

90. . . . While it is our task to interpret the Human Rights Act 1998, it is Strasbourg's task to interpret the Convention. It has often been said that our role in interpreting the Convention is to keep in step with Strasbourg, neither lagging behind nor leaping ahead: no more, as Lord Bingham said in *R (Ullah) v Special Adjudicator* [2004] UKHL 26; [2004] 2 AC 323, para 20, but certainly no less: no less, as Lord Brown says at para 106, but certainly no more. If Parliament wishes to go further, or if the courts find it appropriate to develop the common law further, of course they may. But that is because they choose to do so, not because the Convention requires it of them.

91. The Strasbourg case law is quite plain that liability for acts taking effect or taking place outside the territory of a member state is exceptional and requires special justification. This court should not extend the liability of one member state, thus necessarily expecting that other member states would do the same, unless it is quite clear that Strasbourg would require this of us. I agree with my noble and learned friends that there is more to be learned from the decision of the Grand Chamber in *Bankovic v Belgium* (2001) 11 BHRC 435 than there is from the observations of the Chamber in *Issa v Turkey* (2004) 41 EHRR 567. *Bankovic* does not lead me to the conclusion that Strasbourg would inevitably hold that the deceased, other than Mr. Mousa, were within the jurisdiction of the United Kingdom when they met their deaths. . . .

LORD CARSWELL

93. Mr. Baha Mousa died as a result of appalling maltreatment in a prison occupied and run by British military personnel. His treatment cannot for a moment be defended, but due to a regrettable paucity of evidence it has not proved possible to bring to justice those responsible for his death.

94. The families of the deceased persons understandably want a full and effective investigation carried out into each death. Certain investigations were done by the Army authorities, but the relatives claim that they were insufficiently thorough and seek to have the government put in train more extensive inquiries at which evidence and opinions on all sides can be advanced.

95. The government has been unwilling to commit itself to conduct further inquiries, but the appellants, who are relatives of the deceased persons, claim that it is bound to do so by the terms of the European Convention for the Protection of Human Rights and Fundamental Freedoms ("the Convention") as applied in domestic law by the Human Rights Act 1998. It is not in dispute that under article 2, as interpreted by Strasbourg jurisprudence, an obligation to conduct a proper investigation into a death caused by agents of the state is imposed upon a contracting state (though it is not admitted by the Secretary of State that the investigations carried out were insufficient to discharge such an obligation). The anterior question before the House, however, is whether the Convention obligation applied at all in respect of deaths caused in Iraq. That involves two issues (a) whether the Human Rights Act 1998 applies to acts or omissions of the state agencies of the United Kingdom

outside the territorial boundaries of the UK (b) if so, whether the deceased persons were within the jurisdiction of the United Kingdom, within the meaning of article 1 of the Convention, when they were killed in Iraq.

96. These two issues are closely interlinked, for the conclusion which one reaches on the extent of the UK's jurisdiction within article 1 has a considerable bearing on the intention which one imputes to Parliament in respect of the territorial extent of the Human Rights Act. . . . For the reasons set out by Lord Rodger, I respectfully agree that section 6 of the Human Rights Act 1998 is to be interpreted as applying both when a public authority acts within the boundaries of the United Kingdom and when it acts outside those boundaries but within the jurisdiction of the United Kingdom for the purposes of article 1 of the Convention.

. . . .

98. The stringency of the test for establishing jurisdiction makes it the more likely that Parliament intended the Human Rights Act to operate extra-territorially within the jurisdiction of the United Kingdom, as Lord Brown points out in paragraph 150 of his opinion. This assists one to accommodate the intention of Parliament, as it has to be ascertained by the courts, with the statements made inside and outside Parliament at the time when it was passed. Although those statements may be to some extent rhetorical rather than definitive, they point very clearly to a general intention to equate the scope of the Act with the scope of the Convention.

99. In the result I would dismiss the appeals of the first five appellants, dismiss the Secretary of State's cross-appeal and make the order proposed by Lord Rodger to remit the sixth appellant's case to the Divisional Court.

LORD BROWN OF EATON-UNDER-HEYWOOD

. . . .

102. Your Lordships are here called on to decide two very important questions which arise by way of preliminary issue. One concerns the reach of the European Convention on Human Rights: Who, within the meaning of article 1 of the Convention, is to be regarded as "within [a contracting party's] jurisdiction" so as to require that state to "secure to [them] the rights and freedoms" defined in the Convention? The other concerns the reach of the Human Rights Act 1998 (the Act), the only basis on which the domestic courts have jurisdiction to hear human rights claims: Does the Act apply extra-territorially and, if so, in what way?

Article 1—the reach of the Convention

105. The ultimate decision upon this question, of course, must necessarily be for the European Court of Human Rights. As Lord Bingham of Cornhill observed in *R (Ullah) v Special Adjudicator* [2004] 2 AC 323, 350 (para 20), "the Convention is an international instrument, the correct interpretation of which can be authoritatively expounded only by the Strasbourg court." In the same paragraph Lord Bingham made two further points: first, that a national court "should not without strong reason dilute or weaken the effect of the Strasbourg case law"; secondly that, whilst member States can of course legislate so as to provide for rights more generous than those guaranteed by the Convention, national courts should not interpret the Convention to achieve this: the Convention must bear the same meaning for all

states party to it. Para 20 ends: "The duty of national courts is to keep pace with the Strasbourg jurisprudence as it evolves over time: no more, but certainly no less."

106. I would respectfully suggest that last sentence could as well have ended: "no less, but certainly no more." There seems to me, indeed, a greater danger in the national court construing the Convention too generously in favour of an applicant than in construing it too narrowly. In the former event the mistake will necessarily stand: the member state cannot itself go to Strasbourg to have it corrected; in the latter event, however, where Convention rights have been denied by too narrow a construction, the aggrieved individual *can* have the decision corrected in Strasbourg. *Ullah,* of course, was concerned with the particular scope of individual Convention rights, there article 9, in the context of removing non-nationals from a member state. Lord Bingham's cautionary words must surely apply with greater force still to a case like the present. As the Grand Chamber observed in *Bankovic v Belgium* (2001) 11 BHRC 435, 449 (para 65): "the scope of article 1 . . . is determinative of the very scope of the contracting parties' positive obligations and, as such, of the scope and reach of the entire Convention system of human rights' protection."

107. Your Lordships accordingly ought not to construe article 1 as reaching any further than the existing Strasbourg jurisprudence clearly shows it to reach.

. . . .

132. Taken as a whole, . . . whatever else may be said of the Strasbourg jurisprudence, it cannot be said to establish clearly that any of the first five appellants come within the UK's article 1 jurisdiction. As for the sixth case, I for my part would recognise the UK's jurisdiction over Mr. Mousa only on the narrow basis found established by the Divisional Court, essentially by analogy with the extra-territorial exception made for embassies (an analogy recognised too in *Hess v United Kingdom* (1975) 2 DR 72, a Commission decision in the context of a foreign prison which had itself referred to the embassy case of *X v Federal Republic of Germany*). In the light of those conclusions as to the reach of the Convention I come now to the Human Rights Act 1998.

The reach of the Human Rights Act

. . . .

137. How, then, should the presumption against extra-territoriality—the presumption that, unless the contrary intention appears from the "language", "object", "subject-matter" or "history" of the enactment (see *Maxwell on The Interpretation of Statutes* quoted by Lord Bingham at para 11 of his opinion), Parliament does not intend a statute to operate beyond the territorial limits of the UK—apply in the case of the Human Rights Act?

138. The object, subject-matter and history of this Act all seem to me highly relevant to this question. It cannot simply be treated as just another domestic statute. Rather it is focused upon the Convention (although not, of course, incorporating it), its very purpose being to ensure that, from the date it took effect, it would no longer be necessary for victims to complain about alleged violations of the Convention internationally in Strasbourg instead of domestically in the UK. It is less than obvious that Parliament would have wanted to confine its effect rigidly within the borders of

the UK rather than allow it to extend also to the handful of cases where Strasbourg recognises an extraterritorial reach for the Convention itself.

139. Section 6 of the Human Rights Act makes it unlawful for a "public authority" to "act" in a way incompatible with "a Convention right". There can be no doubt that a "public authority" means a public authority of Great Britain and Northern Ireland, just as the "legislation" referred to in sections 3 and 6 of the Act means legislation enacted in Great Britain and Northern Ireland. It is not, however, suggested that the claimant (the alleged victim) need be present in the UK (let alone a British citizen) nor that the decision complained of need have been taken in the United Kingdom (consider, for example, a decision taken by a minister travelling abroad).

140. What object would be served by construing and applying the Act so that Convention rights only take effect within the territory of the UK i.e. only where the result of the violation is actually felt within the UK? Suppose British police were responsible for a forcible extradition (as in the *Öcalan* line of cases), or that British Embassy officials were wrongly to refuse diplomatic asylum (as was asserted but not substantiated in *R (B) v Secretary of State for Foreign and Commonwealth Affairs* [2005] QB 643), or that British judges were to sit as such overseas (as asserted in respect of French judges in *Drozd* and as Scottish judges in fact did sit in Holland on the *Lockerbie* case). Or suppose that Corporal Payne, who pleaded guilty to ill-treating Mr. Mousa and has recently been sentenced to a year's imprisonment, had instead been court-martialled in Iraq. What good reason could there be for requiring any human rights complaints arising in any of these situations (Article 6 complaints, for example, in the last two cases) to be taken to Strasbourg rather than brought under the Act? Similarly, surely, in the case of the sixth appellant.

141. The essential rationale underlying the presumption against extraterritoriality is that ordinarily it is inappropriate for one sovereign legislature to intrude upon the preserve of another. . . . Lord Hoffmann said that in principle the question is always one of construction. As to this he cited Lord Wilberforce's speech in *Clark v Oceanic Contractors Inc* [1983] 2 AC 130, 152, saying that the question "requires an inquiry to be made as to the person with respect to whom Parliament is presumed, in the particular case, to be legislating. Who, it is to be asked, is within the legislative grasp, or intendment, of the statute under consideration?"

. . . .

143. I have already acknowledged that the House's decision in *Quark* cannot be regarded as reliable authority on the present question given that it was not directly in issue there. It is nonetheless noteworthy that in Lord Nicholls' view (at para 34) "the territorial scope of the obligations and rights created by sections 6 and 7 of the Act was intended to be co-extensive with the territorial scope of the obligations of the United Kingdom and the rights of victims under the Convention." . . .

144. As to *B*, the decision of a strong Court of Appeal which *is* directly in point, again it seems to me noteworthy that the Court "reached the conclusion that the Human Rights Act 1998 requires public authorities of the United Kingdom to secure those Convention rights defined in section 1 of the Act within the jurisdiction of the United Kingdom as that jurisdiction has been identified by the Strasbourg Court." (para 79).

. . . .

147. . . . I respectfully take a different view as to the application here of the presumption considered by Lord Bingham at para 12. Diplock LJ in *Salomon v Commissioners of Customs and Excise* [1967] 2 QB 116, 144 referred to this as "a *prima facie* presumption that Parliament does not intend to act in breach of international law, including therein specific treaty obligations". Certainly the UK undertook no *specific treaty obligation* to incorporate the Convention into domestic law; the Strasbourg Court has said that many times. Article 13 does, however, impose upon the UK an international law obligation to afford "everyone whose rights and freedoms as set forth in [the] Convention are violated . . . an effective remedy before a national authority". As the Court explained in *James v United Kingdom* (1986) 8 EHRR 123, 158–159: "Although there is thus no obligation to incorporate the Convention into domestic law, by virtue of article 1 of the Convention the substance of the rights and freedoms set forth must be secured under the domestic legal order, in some form or another, to everyone within the jurisdiction of the contracting states. Subject to the qualification explained in the following paragraph [the qualification that article 13 does not go so far as to guarantee a remedy allowing a contracting state's laws as such to be challenged before a national authority on the ground of being contrary to the Convention, the qualification which defeated the applicant in the *James* case itself], article 13 guarantees the availability within the national legal order of an effective remedy to enforce the Convention rights and freedoms in whatever form they may happen to be secured."

148. . . . In the *Observer* case domestic common law, and in *McCann* the Gibraltar Constitution, enabled the respective complaints to be considered on their merits. The position, however, was different in *Smith and Grady v United Kingdom* (1999) 29 EHRR 493. There article 13 *was* held to be violated: "the threshold at which [the domestic courts] could find the Ministry of Defence policy irrational was placed so high that it effectively excluded any consideration by the domestic courts of the question of whether the interference with the applicants' rights answered a pressing social need or was proportionate to the national security and public order aims pursued . . . " So too article 13 would be found violated here if the Act were held not to apply to Mr. Mousa's case: his complaints could not then be considered on their merits under domestic law.

149. If, therefore, it were necessary to resort to a countervailing presumption to justify construing the Act so as to apply extraterritorially to the limited extent necessary to correspond with the Strasbourg case law on the reach of article 1, I would conclude that the *Salomon* presumption is indeed available to the appellants here.

150. Not only, of course, did he conclude that the Act has extraterritorial application but so too, in fully and carefully reasoned judgments, did both courts below. In para 301 of its judgment, cited by Lord Bingham at para 25, the Divisional Court found it "counterintuitive [where article 1 has been given an essentially territorial effect] to expect to find a parliamentary intention that there should be gaps between the scope of the Convention and an Act which was designed to bring rights home". True, at para 304, the Divisional Court also found it "intuitively difficult to think that Parliament intended to legislate in foreign lands". But that was in the context

of the "effective control of an area" exception. As foreshadowed in para 103 above, I, like the Divisional Court, am readier to conclude that Parliament intended the Act to operate extra-territorially in a case where article 1 jurisdiction falls within one of the narrow categories of exception established under the Strasbourg case law (as in the sixth appellant's case), than I might be were Strasbourg to construe the reach of the Convention substantially more widely. Even then I would probably still feel bound to conclude that Parliament intended the Act to have the same extra-territorial effect as the Convention. Indeed, having now had the advantage of reading in draft the speech prepared by my noble and learned friend Lord Rodger of Earlsferry, I think that likely. But I would certainly feel less surprised by a suggestion to the contrary. I do not, however, expect to be faced with this difficulty. Rather I am confident . . . that the Strasbourg court will continue to maintain the *Bankovic* approach which seems to me only logical.

151. In the final result I would dismiss the appeals of each of the first five appellants and dismiss too the cross-appeal by the respondent as to the applicability of the Human Rights Act to the sixth appellant's case. That being so it is agreed between the parties that, in the light of factual developments since the Court of Appeal's order, the sixth appellant's case should be remitted to the Divisional Court to join the other cases which have been stayed for the substantive issues to be decided in the light of up to date evidence and amended pleadings.

Questions and Comments

1. What was the purpose of the Human Rights Act 1998? Are the judges agreed on this question?

2. How much deference do the Law Lords indicate is due the judgments of the European Court of Human Rights? Absent the Human Rights Act would the judgments have any significance for British judges?

3. Why did Parliament omit Convention articles 1 and 13 from the Human Rights Act?

4. On the European Court's jurisprudence concerning extraterritorial application of the Convention, see Chapter V(2)(D).

Final Questions and Comments

1. Judge Antonio Augusto Cançado Trindade has asserted that there are both approximations and convergence in the case law of the three regional human rights systems and this has generated "a common understanding . . . that human rights treaties are endowed with a special nature . . . ; that human rights treaties have a normative character, of *ordre public*; that their terms are to be autonomously interpreted; that in their application one ought to ensure an effective protection (*effet utile*) of the guaranteed rights; that the obligations enshrined therein to have an objective character, and are to be duly complied with by the States Parties, which have the additional common duty of exercise of the collective guarantee of the protected rights; and that permissible restrictions (limitations and derogations) to the exercise of the guaranteed rights are to be restrictively interpreted." A.A. Cancado Trindade, *The Development of International Human Rights Law by the Operation and the Case-Law of the European and the Inter-American Courts of Human Rights*, 25 HRLJ 157 (2004). Do you agree with the principles he enunciates? Does the case law support them?

2. Is there an underlying and agreed conceptual framework or rationale for the protection of human rights in the regions? See Case C-36/02, *Omega Spielhallen und Automatenaufstellungs-GMBH v. Oberburgermeisterin der Bundesstadt Bonn* (Reference for a preliminary ruling), European Court of Justice, judgment of 14 Oct. 2004 (First Chamber), reprinted in 25 HRLJ 255 (2004), in which the Court upheld a ban on laser games simulating acts of homicide, despite the EU's principle of freedom to provide services, on the basis that such games could be deemed to violate public policy because they offend human dignity. The Court agreed with the Advocate General that respect for human dignity is a general principle of law contained in the Community legal order. The Advocate General had further comments on human dignity—itself a right protected by the German Constitution—and respect for human rights:

> 74. There is hardly any legal principle more difficult to fathom in law than that of human dignity. . . .
>
> 75. Human dignity is an expression of the respect and value to be attributed to each human being on account of his or her humanity. It concerns the protection of and respect for the essence or nature of the human being per se—that is to say, the 'substance' of mankind. Mankind itself is therefore reflected in the concept of human dignity; it is what distinguishes him from other creatures. . . .
>
> 76. Human dignity, as a fundamental expression of an element of mankind founded simply on humanity, forms the underlying basis and starting point for al human rights distinguishable from it; at the same time it is the point of convergence of individual human rights in the light of which they are to be understood and interpreted. Mention is therefore made by German theorists, for instance, of human dignity as the 'fundamental principle' of human rights.
>
> 77. . . . It reflects the idea that every individual human being is considered to be endowed with inherent and inalienable rights.
>
> 78. A variety of religious, philosophical and ideological reasoning could be given as the basis for this analysis. All in all, human dignity has its roots deep in the origins of a conception of mankind in European culture that regards man as an entity capable of spontaneity and self-determination. Because of his ability to forge his own free will, he is a person (subject) and must not be downgraded to a thing or object.
>
> 79. That link between the concept of dignity and those of the self-determination and freedom of mankind clearly shows why the idea of the dignity of man also often finds expression in other concepts and principles that have to be safeguarded, such as personality and identity.
>
> 80. Furthermore, the concept of the legal equality of all is also inherent in the idea of human rights in general and human dignity in particular, so that reference is also often made of the phrase 'égale dignité', which embraces both concepts.
>
> 81. As an emanation and as specific expressions of human dignity, however, all (particular) human rights ultimately serve to achieve human dignity. . . .

Is this conception one of "European culture", as the Advocate General states, or one that would resonate in the other regional systems as well?

5. For further reading on the interpretation and domestic application of human rights norms, see: R. Blackburn & J. Polakiewicz, Fundamental Rights in Europe: The European Convention on Human Rights and its Member States, 1950–2000 (OUP, 2001); K.L. Bodnick, *Comment: Bringing Ireland Up to Par: Incorporating the European Convention for the Protection of Human Rights and Fundamental Freedoms*, 26 Fordham Int'l L.J. 397 (2003); T. Buergenthal, *Modern Constitutions and Human Rights Treaties*, 36 Colum. J. Transnatl L. 211 (1997); A. Cassese, *Modern Constitutions and International Law*, 192 Recueil des Cours 331 (1985); B. Conforti and F. Francioni (eds.), Enforcing Human Rights in Domestic Courts (The Hague: Nijhoff, 1997); H.F. Panhuys, *The Netherlands Constitution and International Law: A Decade of Experi-*

ence, 58 AJIL 88 (1964); I. Seiderman, HIERARCHY IN INTERNATIONAL LAW: THE HUMAN RIGHTS DIMENSION (Antwerp: Intersentia, 2001); I. Seidl-Hohenveldern, *Transformation or Adoption of International Law into Municipal Law*, 12 ICLQ 88 (1963); D. Sloss, *The Domestication of International Human Rights: Non-Self-Executing Declarations and Human Rights Treaties*, 24 YALE J. INT'L L. 129 (1998); C.M. Vasquez, *The Four Doctrines of Self-Executing Treaties*, 89 AJIL 695 (1995); V.S. Vereshchetin, *New Constitutions and the Old Problem of the Relationship between International Law and National Law*, 7 EJIL 29 (1996); Jane Jensen, *The Impact of the European Convention for the Protection of Human Rights on National Law*, 52 U. CINN. L. REV. 760 (1983).

CHAPTER III
STATE OBLIGATIONS

1. Introduction

The obligations of states parties to the regional human rights instruments are similar and include duties of abstention ("negative" obligations) and of action ("positive" obligations). The European Convention requires States Parties to "secure" to everyone within their jurisdiction the guaranteed rights (Art. 1). The States Parties to the American Convention have an obligation not only "to respect" the rights guaranteed in the Convention, but also "to ensure" the free and full exercise of these rights (Art. 1). In addition, there is an explicit obligation in the American Convention to adopt legislative or other measures to give effect to the rights where domestic law does not already ensure them (Art. 2). The African Charter calls on states parties to recognize the rights in the Charter and, like the American Convention, provides that states parties undertake to adopt legislative or other measures to give effect to Charter-guaranteed rights (Art. 1). See, generally, C. Anyangwe, *Obligations of States Parties to the African Charter on Human and Peoples' Rights*, 10 AFR. J. INT'L & COMP. L. 625 (1998). While the scope of obligation is broad, it is not unlimited. An act or omission in breach of an international obligation cannot always be attributed to the state.

This chapter examines the jurisprudence of the regional systems on the scope of state duties, including the amount of discretion afforded governments to limit the exercise of rights during periods of emergency. It also reviews efforts to assess state compliance with the decisions and judgments of regional bodies.

2. Identifying the State and the Obligations

In an era when privatization and de-regulation has been common, regional tribunals have had to ascertain what conduct (act or omission) can be attributed to a state, to which state it should be attributed, and whether or not that conduct breaches a right guaranteed by the relevant regional instrument. The law of state responsibility holds a state responsible only for its acts or omissions in breach of an international obligation. See ILC, Draft Articles on Responsibility of States for Internationally Wrongful Acts, *in Report of the International Law Commission on the Work of Its Fifty-third Session*, UN GAOR, 56th Sess., Supp. No. 10, at 43, UN Doc. A/56/10 (2001), *reprinted in* JAMES CRAWFORD, THE INTERNATIONAL LAW COMMISSION'S ARTICLES ON STATE RESPONSIBILITY: INTRODUCTION, TEXT AND COMMENTARIES (2002). States thus are not responsible for the wrongful conduct of private parties as such, but acts will be attributed to the state if it is complicit in or condones private wrongdoing. See *United States Diplomatic and Consular Staff in Tehran* (U.S. v. Iran), 1980 ICJ Rep. 3 (May 24). The existence of death squads, militias and other organized violent groups has given rise to numerous cases exploring the scope of state obligations to prevent, investigate, prosecute and punish their acts. Para-military groups have long been a problem in the Inter-American system, but they have now surfaced in Europe and Africa as well. The *Velasquez Rodriguez* and *Jehovah's Witnesses* cases below illustrate the approach of the regional bodies to defining the scope of state responsibility in this respect.

The problems of attribution are even more difficult when the conduct relates to historical injustices and efforts to remedy them. Within Europe, lingering issues related to World War II continue to arise, as well as a raft of cases emerging from the reunification of Germany and democratization in former Communist countries. These cases not only raise questions of identifying who is responsible for the asserted human rights violations, but also concern the legality of state measures to punish or forgive past wrongs. Materials later in the chapter turn specifically to questions of amnesties and lustration laws.

Velasquez Rodriguez Case, **Merits**, Judgment of July 29, 1988, 4 Inter.-Am. Ct. H.R. (Ser. C) (1988).

1. The Inter-American Commission on Human Rights submitted the instant case to the Inter-American Court of Human Rights . . . on April 24, 1986. It originated in a petition (No. 7920) against the State of Honduras . . ., which the Secretariat of the Commission received on October 7, 1981. . . .

3. According to the petition filed with the Commission, and the supplementary information received subsequently, Manfredo Velásquez, a student at the National Autonomous University of Honduras, "was violently detained without a warrant for his arrest by members of the National Office of Investigations (DNI) and G-2 of the Armed Forces of Honduras." The detention took place in Tegucigalpa on the afternoon of September 12, 1981. According to the petitioners, several eyewitnesses reported that Manfredo Velásquez and others were detained and taken to the cells of Public Security Forces Station No. 2 located in the Barrio El Manchén of Tegucigalpa, where he was "accused of alleged political crimes and subjected to harsh interrogation and cruel torture." The petition added that on September 17, 1981, Manfredo Velásquez was moved to the First Infantry Battalion, where the interrogation continued, but that the police and security forces denied that he had been detained. . . .

. . . .

159. The Commission has asked the Court to find that Honduras has violated the rights guaranteed to Manfredo Velasquez by Articles 4, 5 and 7 of the Convention. The Government has denied the charges and seeks to be absolved.

160. This requires the Court to examine the conditions under which a particular act, which violates one of the rights recognized by the Convention, can be imputed to a State Party thereby establishing its international responsibility.

161. Article 1(1) of the Convention provides:

Article 1. Obligation to Respect Rights

1. The States Parties to this Convention undertake to respect the rights and free-doms recognized herein and to ensure to all persons subject to their jurisdiction the free and full exercise of those rights and freedoms, without any discrimination for reasons of race, color, sex, language, religion, political or other opinion, national or social origin, economic status, birth, or any other social condition.

162. This article specifies the obligation assumed by the States Parties in rela-tion to each of the rights protected. Each claim alleging that one of those rights has been infringed necessarily implies that Article 1(1) of the Convention has also been violated.

163. The Commission did not specifically allege the violation of Article 1(1) of the Convention, but that does not preclude the Court from applying it. The precept contained therein constitutes the generic basis of the protection of the rights recog-nized by the Convention and would be applicable, in any case, by virtue of a general principle of law, *iura novit curia*, on which international jurisprudence has repeat-edly relied and under which a court has the power and the duty to apply the juridical provisions relevant to a proceeding, even when the parties do not expressly invoke them (*"Lotus", Judgment* No. 9, 1927, P.C.I.J., Series A No. 10, p. 31 and Eur. Court HR., *Handyside Case*, Judgment of 7 December 1976, Series A No. 24, para. 41).

164. Article 1(1) is essential in determining whether a violation of the human rights recognized by the Convention can be imputed to a State Party. In effect, that article charges the States Parties with the fundamental duty to respect and guaran-tee the rights recognized in the Convention. Any impairment of those rights which can be attributed under the rules of international law to the action or omission of any public authority constitutes an act imputable to the State, which assumes re-sponsibility in the terms provided by the Convention.

165. The first obligation assumed by the States Parties under Article 1(1) is "to respect the rights and freedoms" recognized by the Convention. The exercise of public authority has certain limits which derive from the fact that human rights are inherent attributes of human dignity and are, therefore, superior to the power of the State. On another occasion, this Court stated:

> The protection of human rights, particularly the civil and political rights set forth in the Convention, is in effect based on the affirmation of the existence of certain in-violable attributes of the individual that cannot be legitimately restricted through the exercise of governmental power. These are individual domains that are beyond the reach of the State or to which the State has but limited access. Thus, the protection of human rights must necessarily comprise the concept of the restriction of the exercice of state power (*The Word "Laws" in Article 30 of the American Convention on Human Rights*, Advisory Opinion OC-6/86 of May 9, 1986. Series A No. 6, para. 21.)

166. The second obligation of the States Parties is to "ensure" the free and full exercise of the rights recognized by the Convention to every person subject to its jurisdiction. This obligation implies the duty of the States Parties to organize the governmental apparatus and, in general, all the structures through which public power is exercised, so that they are capable of juridically ensuring the free and full enjoyment of human rights. As a consequence of this obligation, the States must

prevent, investigate and punish any violation of the rights recognized by the Convention and, moreover, if possible attempt to restore the right violated and provide compensation as warranted for damages resulting from the violation.

167. The obligation to ensure the free and full exercise of human rights is not fulfilled by the existence of a legal system designed to make it possible to comply with this obligation—it also requires the government to conduct itself so as to effectively ensure the free and full exercise of human rights.

168. The obligation of the States is, thus, much more direct than that contained in Article 2, which reads:

> Article 2. Domestic Legal Effects
> Where the exercise of any of the rights or freedoms referred to in Article 1 is not already ensured by legislative or other provisions, the States Parties undertake to adopt, in accordance with their constitutional processes and the provisions of this Convention, such legislative or other measures as may be necessary to give effect to those rights or freedoms.

169. According to Article 1(l), any exercise of public power that violates the rights recognized by the Convention is illegal. Whenever a State organ, official or public entity violates one of those rights, this constitutes a failure of the duty to respect the rights and freedoms set forth in the Convention.

170. This conclusion is independent of whether the organ or official has contravened provisions of internal law or overstepped the limits of his authority: under international law a State is responsible for the acts of its agents undertaken in their official capacity and for their omissions, even when those agents act outside the sphere of their authority or violate internal law.

171. This principle suits perfectly the nature of the Convention, which is violated whenever public power is used to infringe the rights recognized therein. If acts of public power that exceed the State's authority or are illegal under its own laws were not considered to compromise that State's obligations under the treaty, the system of protection provided for in the Convention would be illusory.

172. Thus, in principle, any violation of rights recognized by the Convention carried out by an act of public authority or by persons who use their position of authority is imputable to the State. However, this does not define all the circumstances in which a State is obligated to prevent, investigate and punish human rights violations, nor all the cases in which the State might be found responsible for an infringement of those rights. An illegal act which violates human rights and which is initially not directly imputable to a State (for example, because it is the act of a private person or because the person responsible has not been identified) can lead to international responsibility of the State, not because of the act itself, but because of the lack of due diligence to prevent the violation or to respond to it as required by the Convention.

173. Violations of the Convention cannot be founded upon rules that take psychological factors into account in establishing individual culpability. For the purposes of analysis, the intent or motivation of the agent who has violated the rights recognized by the Convention is irrelevant—the violation can be established even if the identity of the individual perpetrator is unknown. What is decisive is whether a violation of the rights recognized by the Convention has occurred with the support

or the acquiescence of the government, or whether the State has allowed the act to take place without taking measures to prevent it or to punish those responsible. Thus, the Court's task is to determine whether the violation is the result of a State's failure to fulfill its duty to respect and guarantee those rights, as required by Article 1(1) of the Convention.

174. The State has a legal duty to take reasonable steps to prevent human rights violations and to use the means at its disposal to carry out a serious investigation of violations committed within its jurisdiction, to identify those responsible, to impose the appropriate punishment and to ensure the victim adequate compensation.

175. This duty to prevent includes all those means of a legal, political, administrative and cultural nature that promote the protection of human rights and ensure that any violations are considered and treated as illegal acts, which, as such, may lead to the punishment of those responsible and the obligation to indemnify the victims for damages. It is not possible to make a detailed list of all such measures, since they vary with the law and the conditions of each State Party. Of course, while the State is obligated to prevent human rights abuses, the existence of a particular violation does not, in itself, prove the failure to take preventive measures. On the other hand, subjecting a person to official, repressive bodies that practice torture and assassination with impunity is itself a breach of the duty to prevent violations of the rights to life and physical integrity of the person, even if that particular person is not tortured or assassinated, or if those facts cannot be proven in a concrete case.

176. The State is obligated to investigate every situation involving a violation of the rights protected by the Convention. If the State apparatus acts in such a way that the violation goes unpunished and the victim's full enjoyment of such rights is not restored as soon as possible, the State has failed to comply with its duty to ensure the free and full exercise of those rights to the persons within its jurisdiction. The same is true when the State allows private persons or groups to act freely and with impunity to the detriment of the rights recognized by the Convention.

177. In certain circumstances, it may be difficult to investigate acts that violate an individual's rights. The duty to investigate, like the duty to prevent, is not breached merely because the investigation does not produce a satisfactory result. Nevertheless, it must be undertaken in a serious manner and not as a mere formality preordained to be ineffective. An investigation must have an objective and be assumed by the State as its own legal duty, not as a step taken by private interests that depends upon the initiative of the victim or his family or upon their offer of proof, without an effective search for the truth by the government. This is true regardless of what agent is eventually found responsible for the violation. Where the acts of private parties that violate the Convention are not seriously investigated, those parties are aided in a sense by the government, thereby making the State responsible on the international plane.

178. In the instant case, the evidence shows a complete inability of the procedures of the State of Honduras, which were theoretically adequate, to carry out an investigation into the disappearance of Manfredo Velásquez, and of the fulfillment of its duties to pay compensation and punish those responsible, as set out in Article 1 (1) of the Convention.

179. As the Court has verified above, the failure of the judicial system to act upon the writs brought before various tribunals in the instant case has been proven. Not one writ of habeas corpus was processed. No judge has access to the places where Manfredo Velásquez might have been detained. The criminal complaint was dismissed.

180. Nor did the organs of the Executive Branch carry out a serious investigation to establish the fate of Manfredo Velásquez. There was no investigation of public allegations of a practice of disappearances nor a determination of whether Manfredo Velásquez had been a victim of that practice. The Commission's requests for information were ignored to the point that the Commission had to presume, under Article 42 of its Regulations, that the allegations were true. The offer of an investigation in accord with Resolution 30/83 of the Commission resulted in an investigation by the Armed Forces, the same body accused of direct responsibility for the disappearances. This raises grave questions regarding the seriousness of the investigation. The Government often resorted to asking relatives of the victims to present conclusive proof of their allegations even though those allegations, because they involved crimes against the person, should have been investigated on the Government's own initiative in fulfillment of the State's duty to ensure public order. This is especially true when the allegations refer to a practice carried out within the Armed Forces, which, because of its nature, is not subject to private investigations. No proceeding was initiated to establish responsibility for the disappearance of Manfredo Velásquez and apply punishment under internal law. All of the above leads to the conclusion that the Honduran authorities did not take effective action to ensure respect for human rights within the jurisdiction of that State as required by Article 1 (1) of the Convention.

181. The duty to investigate facts of this type continues as long as there is uncertainty about the fate of the person who has disappeared. Even in the hypothetical case that those individually responsible for crimes of this type cannot be legally punished under certain circumstances, the State is obligated to use the means at its disposal to inform the relatives of the fate of the victims and, if they have been killed, the location of their remains.

182. The Court is convinced, and has so found, that the disappearance of Manfredo Velásquez was carried out by agents who acted under cover of public authority. However, even had that fact not been proven, the failure of the State apparatus to act, which is clearly proven, is a failure on the part of Honduras to fulfill the duties it assumed under Article 1 (1) of the Convention, which obligated it to ensure Manfredo Velásquez the free and full exercise of his human rights.

183. The Court notes that the legal order of Honduras does not authorize such acts and that internal law defines them as crimes. The Court also recognizes that not all levels of the Government of Honduras were necessarily aware of those acts, nor is there any evidence that such acts were the result of official orders. Nevertheless, those circumstances are irrelevant for the purposes of establishing whether Honduras is responsible under international law for the violations of human rights perpetrated within the practice of disappearances.

184. According to the principle of the continuity of the State in international law, responsibility exists both independently of changes of government over a period of time and continuously from the time of the act that creates responsibility to the time when the act is declared illegal. The foregoing is also valid in the area of human rights although, from an ethical or political point of view, the attitude of the new government may be much more respectful of those rights than that of the government in power when the violations occurred.

185. The Court, therefore, concludes that the facts found in this proceeding show that the State of Honduras is responsible for the involuntary disappearance of Angel Manfredo Velásquez Rodríguez. Thus, Honduras has violated Articles 7, 5 and 4 of the Convention. . . .

Case of 97 Members of the Gldani Congregation of Jehovah's Witnesses and 4 Others v. Georgia, Application no. 71156/01, Eur.Ct.H.R., 3 May 2007.

. . . .

9. The applicants are 97 members of the Gldani Congregation of Jehovah's Witnesses. . . .

10. The facts of the case, as submitted by the parties, may be summarised as follows.

11. During a religious meeting on 17 October 1999, the Congregation, composed of 120 persons, was attacked by a group of Orthodox believers led by Mr. Basil Mkalavishvili ("Father Basil"). Father Basil had been a priest in the autocephalous Orthodox Church of Georgia prior to being defrocked by that denomination on 31 July 1995 following his adhesion to the League of Separatist Priests of Greece. The Synod also accused him of various acts of physical aggression against members of the Orthodox Church, and of insulting the Catholicos-Patriarch of All Georgia.

12. Towards noon on 17 October 1999 one of the applicants, Mr. Mirian Arabidze, saw Father Basil's group, made up of several dozen individuals, arriving at the service entrance of the theatre in which the Congregation was holding its meeting.

13. Ms Nunu Gviniashvili, an applicant, has described the fear experienced by members of the Congregation who had previously seen television broadcasts showing acts of aggression by Father Basil and his supporters against Jehovah's Witnesses.

14. The attackers, some of whom wore cassocks, were shouting and advancing with large iron crosses and sticks in their hands. One of the attackers (Ms Lia Akhalkatsi, according to the applicants) was filming their progress. When the attackers reached the back door of the meeting room, several Jehovah's Witnesses, including Mr. M. Arabidze, tried to hold the door closed until the other participants could leave the room by the main entrance. In the meantime, however, some of Father Basil's supporters had also arrived at the building's main entrance, and the Jehovah's Witnesses found themselves trapped between two groups of attackers. Only a few were able to take refuge in the cellar and called the police from their mobile telephones.

15. In the meeting room, about 60 Jehovah's Witnesses were beaten and struck with crosses, sticks and belts.

16. Mr. Mirian Arabidze was also beaten and, when he fell to the ground, his attacker (Mr Mikheil Nikolozishvili, according to the applicants) told him that he was "going to die for Jehovah!". The recording of the attack shows that several stick-wielding men surrounded the applicant, who immediately covered his head with his hands but fell to the ground under their blows. He was subsequently kicked in the head and back.

17. Ms Roza Kinkladze, applicant, was struck on the face, head and back. Ms Natela Kobaidze, applicant, was struck on the face and her lips started bleeding. She also sustained a sprained thumb. Ms Nino Dzhanashvili, applicant, was struck and pushed in the stairs. Having fallen to the ground, she saw Ms Nino Gnolidze, Ms Nino Lelashvili and Ms Nora Lelashvili, applicants, lying on the ground unconscious. Ms Lia Bakhutashvili, applicant, was attacked by three women and a young priest, who kicked her, tore her clothing and pulled her by the hair. The same priest used a cross and a stick to beat applicant Ms Nora Lelashvili, who fainted. Her daughter, Nino Lelashvili, was dragged along the ground, kicked in the face and flogged with a belt until she lost consciousness. Mr. Merab Zhizhilashvili, applicant, was hit with sticks and punched. Having fallen to the ground, he was kicked and his clothing was torn. Ms Ia Chamauri, applicant, was struck on the head with a belt. Mr. Vladimer Kokosadze, applicant, was also beaten ruthlessly by six men. Nonetheless, he successfully negotiated with Father Basil and his right-hand man, Mr. P. Ivanidze, to obtain permission for thirty women and children, who were locked inside the theatre director's office, to leave the building. They were allowed to leave but were followed and attacked in the street.

18. Mr. Alexi Khitarishvili, applicant, was beaten, then trampled on when he fell to the ground. His glasses were broken. The recording of the attack shows that several men held this applicant upright and shaved his head while pronouncing "in the name of the Father and of the Son and of the Holy Ghost!" Having been unable to shave him completely, the exasperated attackers continued to insult and strike him. The applicant, who could hear his mother screaming in the distance as she was attacked by a group of women, lost consciousness.

19. The blood-spattered men, women and children ran from the building. 16 victims were immediately admitted to hospital. . . .

21. Extracts from the medical records of certain applicants, updated during their hospitalisation, were submitted to the Court. . . .

. . . .

28. Mr. Amiran Arabidze claimed that, when the attack began, he managed to leave the building and went to the police. Ms Eka Kerdzevadze stated that, after escaping from the attack, she and her husband went to the police in Gldani micro-district III and informed the police officers that the Jehovah's Witnesses were being subjected to a violent attack in the theatre building. The police merely recorded this statement but chose not to intervene. Ms Lia Sidamonidze also claimed that she had gone to the same police station with several other Jehovah's Witnesses. The head of the police station replied that "in the attackers' place, he would have given

the Jehovah's Witnesses an even worse time!" While escaping from the site of the attack, Mr. Vladimer Kokosadze met three police officers on the road; after listening to his request to take action, they replied that they "didn't get involved in that type of incident".

29. However, according to Ms Leila Mchedlishvili, Ms Dodo Kakhishvili, Ms Makvala Mamukadze and Ms Shakhina Sharipov, it was only when the police arrived on the scene that the Jehovah's Witnesses who were still trapped in the theatre were able to escape. According to Ms Shakhina Sharipova, one of the victims rushed up to a police officer, showing him the hand which Father Basil had wounded with a blow from a cross, and said: "Look what Basil has just done to me!"

30. All the applicants testified that when the victims managed to escape from the building they were confronted by a cordon of Father Basil's supporters, gathered in front of the exit. These women had been instructed to restrain the victims and push them back inside the building, where the attacks were continuing. In addition, they carried out body-searches of the victims, emptying their pockets and bags. Bibles, religious literature and tracts were then confiscated and thrown into a nearby fire. The victims were forced to remain in front of the fire and watch it. During the search, handbags were torn and thrown on the ground. Ms Makvala Mamukadze, applicant, had her handbag taken from her: it contained money, the keys of her flat, a Bible and her watch. These objects were never returned to her. The attackers allegedly also stole other personal effects belonging to the victims, such as jewellery and cameras.

31. Without exception, all 58 applicants complained that they were mocked, insulted, called every name imaginable—including "traitors"—and accused of "selling out the motherland for a bag of rice". The majority of applicants claimed that the attackers smelled of alcohol.

32. The above-mentioned applicants confirmed the acts of aggression against the 15 of their companions who had been attacked with the greatest violence. . . .

33. The police who arrived at the scene decided to take Mr. Mirian Arabidze to the police station, where he was insulted by police officers. Father Basil and his supporter Mikheil Nikolozishvili, who were also at the police station, attempted to attack the victim again.

34. The recording of the Gldani attack was broadcast on the national television channels Rustavi-2 and Kavkasia on 17, 18 and 19 October 1999. Father Basil, Mr. P. Ivanidze and other members of their group were clearly identifiable from these recordings. Their names were also submitted to the relevant authorities by the victims.

35. The recording of the news broadcast of 18 October 1999 on the Rustavi-2 channel, submitted to the Court by the applicants, illustrated the facts of the attack as set out above. It does not appear that the applicants responded to the acts of violence to which they were subjected. The recording shows a fire containing burning books, and Father Basil and his supporters praying and singing. It also includes an extract from an interview with Father Basil who, standing with the fire in the background, explains the validity of his actions and expresses satisfaction at their outcome.

36. In several subsequent interviews Father Basil claimed that, before going to a particular place, he would alert the police and the State security services, so that the latter would not intervene. This complicity was also noted by the non-governmental organisations which issued a joint statement on 13 March 2001.

37. Interviewed after the attack on the applicants, the Georgian President stated that he condemned any form of pogrom and that an investigation should be conducted to ensure that the perpetrators of the attacks were prosecuted in criminal proceedings.

38. Between 17 and 29 October 1999, about 70 victims of the Gldani attack . . . lodged a complaint with the Tbilisi Public Prosecutor and asked that their attackers be punished.

39. Criminal proceedings were instituted by the investigation unit of the Gldani District of the Ministry of the Interior, but the proceedings were suspended, initially on 13 September and again on 3 December 2000, on the ground that the perpetrators of the attack had not been identified. When the proceedings resumed for the last time in March-April 2001 . . . , the investigating officer, Mr. K., indicated to the victims that they should not expect an outcome anytime in 2001. In spite of five reminders addressed to the Georgian Procurator General, the last of which was dated 8 March 2001, no action was taken on these complaints.

. . .

52. In the meantime, having been placed under investigation, Mr. Mirian Arabidze was accused of having committed acts endangering public order during the attack in question. In particular, he was charged with having "used an object as a weapon" against another person.

53. On 16 August 2000 the criminal trial of Mr. Mirian Arabidze and two of Father Basil's supporters began at the Gldani-Nadzaladevi Court of First Instance in Tbilisi. One of the defendants confirmed that she had burned books, as her faith and Father Basil had directed her to. She asserted that she was prepared to kill on behalf of the Orthodox faith.

54. In the afternoon a group of believers led by Father Basil burst into the courtroom. They assaulted the Jehovah's Witnesses, journalists and the foreign observers who were present in the courtroom. The attackers were equipped with iron crosses and used them as weapons. They took control of the courtroom. The court imposed no penalties on the believers who had occupied the courtroom by force.

55. This attack was filmed and the recording was broadcast on the Rustavi-2 and Kavkasia channels. The recording of a television news programme, broadcast on 16 and 17 August 2000 (and submitted by the applicants to the Court) shows that, on the first day, the attacks took place within the courtroom. Father Basil can be seen entering the court during the hearing with several dozen of his supporters (80, according to the reporter), who are carrying a large white cross, icons and a bell which one of the attackers (Mr Z. Lomthathidze, according to the applicants) is pealing, while the others attack the Jehovah's Witnesses, their lawyers and the foreign observers. The victims are punched out of the courtroom. On the following day Mr. D.P. and Mr. G.B., two human rights activists, were kicked outside the courtroom and Mr. Mirian Arabidze's lawyers were attacked.

56. At the close of this trial on 28 September 2000, Mr. Mirian Arabidze was found guilty of having committed acts endangering public order during the attack against the Congregation on 17 October 1999 and given a suspended sentence of three years' imprisonment for having caused minor injuries to Mr. M. Nikolozishvili and to another member of Father Basil's group.

57. On the same date, the judge decided not to determine the guilt of Father Basil's two supporters and to return the part of the case which concerned them for further investigation, particularly with a view to determining the ownership and value of the literature which was destroyed, and the legal status of the entity which had assembled the Jehovah's Witnesses for the meeting on 17 October 1999.

58. On 14 May 2001 the Tbilisi Court of Appeal overturned the judgment convicting Mr. Mirian Arabidze and sent the case back for further investigation.

59. On 11 October 2001 the Georgian Supreme Court quashed the appeal court's judgment and acquitted Mr. Mirian Arabidze. In its judgment, the Supreme Court considered it "established" that, on 17 October 1999, Father Basil's group had gone to the Gldani premises on its own initiative and that a confrontation had taken place between "persons of differing religious convictions. During that confrontation, several individuals had been injured and religious literature belonging to the Jehovah's Witnesses had been burnt". The Supreme Court found that the Gldani meeting had not represented any danger to public order. It established that the authorities had not imposed any restrictive measure in that connection and that, consequently, Father Basil had had no grounds for interfering with Mr. Mirian Arabidze's exercise of his right as guaranteed by Article 9 of the Convention and Article 19 of the Constitution.

60. In the meantime, on 13 February 2001, 14 volumes of petitions demanding protection for Jehovah's Witnesses were delivered to the administration of the Georgian President. The attack against the applicants and other acts of religiously-motivated violence were brought to the attention of the Head of State. By an order of 22 March 2001, the President ordered the Procurator-General, the Ministry of the Interior and the Ministry of State Security to take special measures to put an end to religiously-motivated crimes, identify their perpetrators and punish those responsible.

61. On 15 March 2001, after examining the complaints concerning acts of violence perpetrated "for years" by Father Basil and Mr. P. Ivanidze, the Procurator-General's Office decided to join them and ordered that the case file (no. 0100118) be investigated. On 30 March 2001 Father Basil was placed under investigation on a charge of organising collective actions which endangered public order and of participating in such actions (Article 226 of the Criminal Code), and on a charge of illegally preventing the conduct of religious rites (Article 155 § 1 of the Criminal Code).

62. On 2 April 2001 the investigator responsible for the case applied to the Vake-Saburtalo Court of First Instance seeking to have Father Basil placed in pre-trial detention. The court did not allow this application and imposed a less onerous preventative measure, namely judicial supervision.

63. Following a letter of 8 March 2001 in which the applicants' lawyer requested information as to which department held the case file and what progress had been made with the case, the applicants' lawyer was informed on 26 April 2001 that the proceedings had again been resumed. He learned at this point that they had been suspended on 3 December 2000. On the same date, Ms Patman Tabagari and Mr. Vladimer Kokosadze, applicants, were also informed in writing that the proceedings had been resumed.

64. On 8 May 2001 the investigator informed the victims' lawyer that he would not have time to examine the case before December 2001. . . .

68. In addition to the Gldani attack at the centre of these proceedings, the applicants described several other attacks carried out by Father Basil and his group, with a view to illustrating the general context in which the Jehovah's Witnesses were obliged to live. In particular, they referred to the attacks of 8 and 16 September 2000 in Zugdidi and Marneuli in which, according to the applicants, representatives of the State played a direct role (see *Begeluri and 98 Others v. Georgia*, no. 28490/02, application pending); the attack in the office of the Ombudsperson of the Republic on 22 January 2001; the attack on a meeting of Jehovah's Witnesses, held on 22 January 2001 in a private individual's home on the Verkhana alley, Tbilisi; the attack on Jehovah's Witnesses on 27 February 2001 during their meeting in a private home in the Mount Elia district of Tbilisi; the attack on Jehovah's Witnesses meeting on 5 and 6 March 2001 in a private residence in Sachkhere; the attack on 30 April 2001 against the Jehovah's Witnesses' new site on Verkhana alley, Tbilisi; the setting alight, in the early morning of 31 May 2001, of a house belonging to a family of Jehovah's Witnesses, of which there remained only a large pile of ashes and rubble, etc. . . .

70. In total, the Jehovah's Witnesses alleged that they had been subjected to 138 attacks between October and November 2002 and that 784 complaints had been lodged with the relevant authorities. No careful and serious investigation had been carried out into any of those complaints.

. . .

76. On 13 March 2001 several non-governmental organisations—the Association Law and Freedom, the Atlantic Council of Georgia, the Black Sea Media Institute, Caucasian House, the Forensic Examination Foundation, Former Political Prisoners for Human Rights, the Georgian Young Lawyers Association, the Human Rights Centre, the Human Rights Group of the Caucasian Institute for Peace, Democracy and Development, the Independent Journalists' Club, the International Society for Fair Elections and Democracy, the Landowners Rights Protection Association, Liberty Institute, Tbilisi Press Club and Transparency International—Georgia issued a joint declaration stating:

> "During last two years we are evidencing massive infringement of freedom of religion and persecution of religious minorities. The Government of Georgia is completely unable to protect human rights and minorities. Moreover, violation of human rights take place with the silent consent of the State, very often with its inspiration and sometimes with active participation of State officials, especially those of law enforcement agencies. On the basis of the aforesaid, it should be noted without exaggeration that religious minorities in Georgia face permanent danger, intimidation and

terror . . . , Jehovah's Witnesses . . . have suffered attacks, persecution, bodily insult and harassment. Frequent pogroms take place in their offices and churches. Their literature, holy objects of worship and other belongings were destroyed . . . The most significant pogroms took place in Tbilisi, Marneuli and Zugdidi. Police were aware of these actions without any reaction or were participating in them, while prosecutors and judges convicted the victims. Vasil Mkalavishvili has openly confirmed on TV that he notifies police and security in advance of carrying out his pogroms. Deputy Minister of State Security declared at a Parliamentary hearing that the State should restrict the activities of non-traditional religious sects. Similar declarations have been made by other senior government officials—for example, the Tbilisi police chief . . . "

THE LAW

I. ALLEGED VIOLATION OF ARTICLE 3 OF THE CONVENTION

80. The applicants considered that they had been victims of violations of Article 3 of the Convention . . .

(a) General principles

95. The Court reiterates that Article 3 of the Convention must be regarded as one of the most fundamental provisions of the Convention and as enshrining core values of the democratic societies making up the Council of Europe (see *Pretty v. the United Kingdom*, no. 2346/02, § 49, ECHR 2002-III). In contrast to the other provisions in the Convention, it is cast in absolute terms, without exception or proviso, or the possibility of derogation under Article 15 of the Convention (see, *inter alia, Chahal v. the United Kingdom*, judgment of 15 November 1996, *Reports of Judgments and Decisions* 1996-V, p. 1855, § 79). The Court also points out that ill-treatment must attain a minimum level of severity if it is to fall within the scope of Article 3. The assessment of this minimum is, in the nature of things, relative and depends on all the circumstances of the case (see *Labita v. Italy*, judgment of 6 April 2000, *Reports* 2000-IV, § 120).

96. In general, actions incompatible with Article 3 of the Convention incur the liability of a contracting State only if they were inflicted by persons holding an official position. However, the obligation on the High Contracting Parties under Article 1 of the Convention to secure to everyone within their jurisdiction the rights and freedoms defined in the Convention, taken in conjunction with Article 3, requires States to take measures designed to ensure that individuals within their jurisdiction are not subjected to torture or inhuman and degrading treatment or punishment, including such treatment administered by private individuals (see *Pretty*, cited above, §§ 50 and 51). A positive obligation on the State to provide protection against inhuman or degrading treatment has been found to arise in a number of cases (see *A. v. the United Kingdom*, judgment of 23 September 1998, *Reports* 1998-VI, p. 2699, § 22; *Z and Others v. the United Kingdom* [GC], no. 29392/95, § 73, ECHR 2001-V; and *M.C. v. Bulgaria*, no. 39272/98, § 149, ECHR 2003-XII).

This protection calls for reasonable and effective measures, including with regard to children and other vulnerable individuals (see *Okkalý v. Turkey*, no. 52067/99, § 70, ECHR 2006- . . . (extracts), in order to prevent ill-treatment of which the authorities were or ought to have been aware (see *Mubilanzila Mayeka and Kaniki Mitunga v. Belgium*, no. 13178/03, § 53, 12 October 2006).

97. Furthermore, Article 3 of the Convention gives rise to a positive obligation to conduct an official investigation (see *Assenov and Others v. Bulgaria*, judgment of 28 October 1998, Reports 1998-VIII, p. 3290, § 102). Such a positive obligation cannot be considered in principle to be limited solely to cases of ill-treatment by State agents (see *M.C. v. Bulgaria*, cited above, § 151).

Thus, the authorities have an obligation to take action as soon as an official complaint has been lodged. Even in the absence of an express complaint, an investigation should be undertaken if there are other sufficiently clear indications that torture or ill-treatment might have occurred. A requirement of promptness and reasonable expedition is implicit in this context. A prompt response by the authorities in investigating allegations of ill-treatment may generally be regarded as essential in maintaining public confidence in their maintenance of the rule of law and in preventing any appearance of collusion in or tolerance of unlawful acts. Tolerance by the authorities towards such acts cannot but undermine public confidence in the principle of lawfulness and the State's maintenance of the rule of law (see *Batý and Others v. Turkey*, nos. 33097/96 and 57834/00, § 136, ECHR 2004-IV (extracts); *Abdülsamet Yaman v. Turkey*, no. 32446/96, § 60, 2 November 2004; and, *mutatis mutandis, Paul and Audrey Edwards v. the United Kingdom*, no. 46477/99, § 72, ECHR 2002-II).

(b) Application of those principles to the present case

(i) As to the treatment inflicted

98. In the light of the information before it, the Court notes that the acts of violence complained of by the applicants in the instant case were committed on 17 October 1999 by a group of Orthodox individuals lead by Father Basil. The Government did not dispute that fact.

99. The Court notes that the attack of 17 October 1999 was directed against all of the members of the Congregation (120, according to the applicants), who were meeting in a theatre for religious purposes. However, the applicants, of whom there are 101, themselves acknowledge that only about sixty members of the Congregation were beaten and 16 hospitalised. The Court notes that, of the applicants who were subjected to acts of physical aggression, only some submitted appropriate evidence to prove that they had experienced treatment alleged to be contrary to Article 3 of the Convention (see *Davtian v. Georgia*, no. 73241/01, § 37, 27 July 2006, and *Berktay v. Turkey*, no. 22493/93, § 165, 1 March 2001). . . .

102. Given the nature of the treatment inflicted on the 25 applicants [whose medical records were submitted], the Court considers that that treatment reached the threshold of inhuman treatment within the meaning of Article 3 of the Convention. . . .

103. The same applies to the severe beating inflicted on the children. . . .

104. With regard to 14 [other] applicants . . . , the Court notes that, in their statements, they also claimed to have been subjected to acts of violence, without however specifying the nature and gravity of the treatment inflicted, which makes it

impossible to assess whether the latter reached the level required to be classified as inhuman within the meaning of Article 3 of the Convention.

105. In any event, having regard to the evidence adduced, including the video recording of the attack in question and the applicants' statements, the Court considers that the treatment inflicted on those 14 individuals and the applicants mentioned . . . above falls within the scope of Article 3 of the Convention and amounts to degrading treatment. . . .

It appears from the case file, and the Government do not dispute this, that the attackers' aim was to humiliate and publicly debase the applicants in such a way as to arouse a feeling of terror and inferiority, so that, morally broken by this physical and verbal abuse (see *Ireland v. the United Kingdom*, judgment of 18 January 1978, Series A no. 25, p. 66, § 167), they would act against their wills and conscience (see *mutatis mutandis, Raninen v. Finland*, judgment of 16 December 1997, *Reports* 1997-VIII, pp. 2821-2822, § 55, and *Keenan v. the United Kingdom*, no. 27229/95, § 110, ECHR 2001-III) and desist from holding religious meetings in line with their faith, considered unacceptable by Father Basil and his supporters. . . . In this connection, the Court attaches weight to the fact that the attack in question was filmed by a member of the group of attackers, and probably intended to be shown to third parties. . . . Indeed, a video recording of the attack was broadcast on two national television channels over several days . . . , which enabled a wide audience to see the violent scenes to which the applicants were subjected, including the religiously-inspired humiliation inflicted on Mr. Alexi Khitarishvili. . . .

[The Court concludes that these acts cannot be attributed to the Government.]

(ii) As to the authorities' reaction and the follow-up given to the complaints by the 42 applicants concerned (paragraphs 102–105 above)

110. The Court notes at the outset that, contrary to the applicants' claims, it has not been shown that the police had been warned by Father Basil in advance of the attack at issue in the instant case. In addition, the video recording of the disputed events, submitted by the applicants, does not show that police officers took part in the acts of aggression against them. As no other evidence has been submitted to that effect, the Court does not find it established that, during the attack in question, representatives of the State were present on the scene.

111. On the other hand, the case file contains sufficiently concordant evidence, to which the Government have not advanced any valid submissions, concerning the refusal by police officers, having been alerted by the applicants by different means and at a sufficiently early stage, to take action promptly to end the violence and to protect the victims. When the police did eventually arrive on the scene, some applicants who were still trapped inside the building were able to escape, but it does not appear that the police intervention was targeted. Indeed, by the time the police officers arrived, numerous acts of aggression, including the most violent, had already taken place, the victims had been bullied and insulted, their personal effects had been confiscated and their religious literature burnt.

112. As to subsequent events, the Court notes, and the Government does not contest this, that those violent and humiliating acts were more than sufficiently brought to the attention of the relevant authorities.

113. In particular, from the day after the attack the 42 applicants . . . contacted the Tbilisi city prosecutor to complain of the acts to which they had been subjected. A prosecution was set in motion, but only 11 applicants, namely Mr. Mirian Arabidze, Mr. Ilia Mantskava, Mr. Vladimer Kokosadze, Mr. Shota Maisuradze, Ms Nora Lelashvili, Ms Natela Kobaidze, Ms Patman Tabagari, Ms Nino Lelashvili, Ms Zaira Dzhikurashvili, Ms Ia Chamauri and Ms Makvala Mamukadze, were recognised as civil parties in the case.

114. It is to be noted that the authorities responsible for the investigation had a duty to act promptly to verify the information, which was also brought to their attention by the 31 other applicants, to institute a prosecution in the event of evidence of an offence and to take the necessary measures to elucidate the truth (Articles 24 § 4, 261 § 1 and 265 § 4 of the CCP). However, the authorities gave no follow-up to the complaints of these 31 applicants, who had submitted specific details of the physical abuse sustained by them and by their children, an offence under Article 125 of the Criminal Code, and of the unlawful prevention, using force, of their religious gathering, an offence under Articles 155 and 166 of the same Code.

115. The Government submitted no explanation as to this total failure to react on the part of the authorities.

116. As to the complaints submitted by the 11 applicants who were recognised as civil parties to the proceedings, between 9 December 1999, when their case file was sent to the Tbilisi municipal police, and 31 January 2000, the case was sent back and forth between the various departments of the prosecution service and the police before being submitted once again to the Tbilisi municipal police. The Government have provided no explanation as to the grounds and usefulness of these transfers.

117. The police investigator responsible for the case on the last-mentioned date carried out, more than three months later, an identification parade and cross-examination of four persons with Mr. Mirian Arabidze, a civil party. The latter identified Mr. M. Nikolozishvili and another person as his attackers. Having initially stated that, on account of his Orthodox faith, he could not be impartial in the case, the police investigator decided to place Mr. Mirian Arabidze under examination, while leaving unresolved the responsibility of Mr. M. Nikolozishvili and the second presumed attacker. No action was ever taken subsequent to Mr. Mirian Arabidze's identification of those two individuals as the persons responsible for his ill-treatment. Committed for trial with two of Father Basil's supporters who were suspected of burning religious literature, Mr. Mirian Arabidze was convicted of having endangered public order, while the question of the guilt of Father Basil's two supporters was sent back for additional investigation, an investigation which has resulted in no decision to date.

118. The Court regrets that, in those circumstances, the domestic authorities and the Government in its pleadings before the Court have continued to assert that that the impossibility of conducting an investigation in the present case was to be explained by the failure to identify the perpetrators of the violence. Such a justification of the relevant authorities' inactivity is all the more shocking in that the police officers who attended the scene did not arrest any of the attackers; that, on the day of the attack, Father Basil and Mr. M. Nikolozishvili were present in the

police station beside Mr. Mirian Arabidze, who was the only person to be arrested; that on 17, 18 and 19 October 1999 the national television channels broadcast material showing the violence inflicted on the applicants; that the recording of one of those broadcasts, in the Court's possession, not only enables the identify of Father Basil and Mr. P. Ivanidze to be ascertained, but, on account of its precision, shows the identity of the majority of the attackers; that, in the interview broadcast on the national channel Rustavi-2 on 18 October 1999, Father Basil speaking against the background of a fire burning the applicants' religious literature, expressed satisfaction about his actions and explained in what way they were justified.

119. Regard being had to all the circumstances described above, the Court concludes that the relevant authorities, having had at their disposal sufficient tangible evidence in good time in order to fulfil the task incumbent on them under the law, were clearly negligent in identifying the suspects (see *Indelicato v. Italy*, no. 31143/96, § 37, 18 October 2001). They thus allowed the limitation period to elapse without good reason.

120. The fact that, following a decree by the Georgian President, dated 22 March 2001, and pressure from the international community, Father Basil and Mr. P. Ivanidze were charged on 4 October 2001 in other cases of religiously-motivated violence, and that those proceedings resulted in their conviction and that of four other attackers on 31 January 2005 does not alter the fact that the question of those individuals' responsibility, and that of several dozen other attackers, for the violence inflicted on the applicants on 17 October 1999 was never the subject of a serious investigation. The mere fact of beginning an investigation which, as in the instant case, is interrupted several times for no reason that could be described as valid and which never results in any decision cannot satisfy the requirements of Article 3 of the Convention (see Davtian v. Georgia, no. 73241/01, § 46, 27 July 2006, and, mutatis mutandis, Selmouni v. France [GC], no. 25803/94, §§ 78–79, ECHR 1999-V).

121. The Government's argument that it is currently no longer possible "for procedural reasons" to conduct an investigation into those events and that, furthermore, the Jehovah's Witnesses have been living in peace since the revolution of November 2003 cannot affect this position. On this latter point, the Court would reiterate that the only responsibility that was engaged under the Convention was that of the Georgian State as a continuous entity, and not that of a specific government or political authority. The Court cannot have regard to domestic institutional or political disagreements (see, *mutatis mutandis, Assanidze v. Georgia* [GC], no. 71503/01, § 149, ECHR 2004-II).

122. Finally, the Court notes that the 31 applicants about whose complaints no action was taken were never informed of the reasons for such failure to act. The 11 applicants who were recognised as civil parties were not kept informed of the progress of the proceedings and the repeated transfers of their case between the various departments. The decision to suspend the investigation on 13 September 2000 was not served on them. After being resumed on 24 October 2000, the investigation was again suspended on 3 December 2000. This decision was also not brought to the applicants' attention. The lawyer for certain of their number only learnt of it by chance on 26 April 2001.

123. Thus, having alerted the relevant authorities of the ill-treatment sustained by them (Articles 235 § 1 and 265 § 1 of the CCP), the applicants were deprived of any possibility of relying on the hierarchical and judicial means of appeal available to them under Articles 235 § 2 and 242 § 2 of the CCP in order to challenge the repeated suspension of the investigation in their case, which they considered unjustified.

124. In sum, the Court notes that the police refused to intervene promptly at the scene of the incident to protect the applicants concerned, and the children of certain of their number, from ill-treatment and that the applicants were subsequently faced with total indifference on the part of the relevant authorities who, for no valid reason, refused to apply the law in their case. In the Court's opinion, such an attitude on the part of authorities under a duty to investigate criminal offences was tantamount to undermining the effectiveness of any other remedies that may have existed.

125. The Court thus concludes that the Georgian State has failed to comply with its positive obligations under Article 3 of the Convention with regard to the 42 applicants concerned.

II. ALLEGED VIOLATION OF ARTICLE 9 OF THE CONVENTION

126. Relying on Article 9 of the Convention, the applicants complained that their right to manifest their religion through prayer, meetings and the collective performance of rites had been violated. . . .

130. . . . [T]the Court reiterates that the freedom of religion protected by Article 9 is one of the foundations of a "democratic society" within the meaning of the Convention. It is one of the most vital elements that go to make up the identity of believers and their conception of life. Religious freedom is primarily a matter of individual conscience, but it also "implies", *inter alia*, freedom to "manifest [one's] religion" (see *Kokkinakis v. Greece*, judgment of 25 May 1995, Series A no. 260, § 31). Participation in the life of a religious community is a manifestation of one's religion, protected by Article 9 of the Convention (see *Hassan and Chaush v. Bulgaria* [GC], no. 30985/96, § 62, ECHR 2000-XI).

131. On several occasions, the Court has held that in exercising its regulatory power in this sphere and in its relations with the various religions, denominations and beliefs, the State has a duty to remain neutral and impartial (see *Hassan and Chaush*, cited above, § 78; *Manoussakis and Others v. Greece*, judgment of 26 September 1996, *Reports* 1996-IV, § 47; and *Metropolitan Church of Bessarabia and Others v. Moldova*, no. 45701/99, § 123, ECHR 2001-XII), which is incompatible with any power on the State's part to assess the legitimacy of religious beliefs (see, *mutatis mutandis*, *Cha'are Shalom Ve Tsedek v. France* [GC], no. 27417/95, § 84, ECHR 2000-VII).

132. The Court wishes to emphasise that, in the name of freedom of religion, it is not authorised to apply improper pressure on others from a wish to promote one's religious convictions (see *Larissis and Others v. Greece*, judgment of 24 February 1998, *Reports* 1998-I, §§ 54 and 59). However, the role of the authorities in such circumstances is not to remove the cause of tension by eliminating pluralism, but to ensure that the competing groups tolerate each other (see *Serif v. Greece*, no.

38178/97, § 53, ECHR 1999-IX). This State role is conducive to public order, religious harmony and tolerance in a democratic society (see *Refah Partisi (the Welfare Party) and Others v. Turkey* [GC], nos. 41340/98, 41342/98, 41343/98 and 41344/98, § 91, ECHR 2003-II) and can hardly be conceived as being likely to diminish the role of a faith or a Church with which the population of a specific country has historically and culturally been associated.

133. In the instant case, on account of their religious beliefs, which were considered unacceptable, the 96 applicants were attacked, humiliated and severely beaten during their congregation's meeting on 17 October 1999. Their religious literature was confiscated and burnt, and the applicants themselves were forced to look at the fire. One of the applicants, Mr. A. Khitarishvili, had his head shaved to the sound of prayers, by way of religious punishment. Having been treated in this way, the applicants were subsequently confronted with total indifference and a failure to act on the part of the authorities, who, on account of the applicants' adherence to a religious community perceived as a threat to Christian orthodoxy, took no action in respect of their complaints. Deprived of any remedy, the applicants could not enforce their rights to freedom of religion before the domestic courts. As the attack against the applicants on 17 October 1999 constituted the first act of large-scale aggression against the Jehovah's Witnesses, the authorities' negligence opened the doors to a generalisation of religious violence throughout Georgia by the same group of attackers (see paragraphs 43, 61, 65 and 68 above). The applicants were thus led to fear that they would be subjected to renewed violence on each fresh manifestation of their faith.

134. Having regard to those circumstances, the Court considers that, through their inactivity, the relevant authorities failed in their duty to take the necessary measures to ensure that the group of Orthodox extremists led by Father Basil tolerated the existence of the applicants' religious community and enabled them to exercise freely their rights to freedom of religion.

135. There has accordingly been a violation of Article 9 of the Convention in respect of all 96 applicants.

. . .

IV. ALLEGED VIOLATION OF ARTICLE 14 IN CONJUNCTION WITH ARTICLES 3 AND 9 OF THE CONVENTION

138. According to the applicants, the acts of religiously-motivated violence committed against them had been tolerated by the authorities because they had been committed against a religious minority in the name of the Orthodox faith. The authorities had simply refused to apply the law in their case on account of their faith.

139. The Court reiterates that the difference in treatment described in Article 14 of the Convention is discriminatory if it "lacks an objective and reasonable justification", that is, if it does not pursue "a legitimate aim" or if there is "not a reasonable relationship of proportionality between the means employed and the aim pursued". Moreover the Contracting States enjoy a certain margin of appreciation in assessing whether and to what extent differences in otherwise similar situations justify a different treatment (see *Camp and Bourimi v. the Netherlands*, no. 28369/95,

§ 37, ECHR 2000-X, and *Thlimmenos v. Greece* [GC], no. 34369/97, § 44, ECHR 2000-IV).

140. Having examined all the evidence in its possession, the Court observes that, in the instant case, the refusal by the police to intervene promptly at the scene of the incident in order to protect the applicants, and the children of some of their number, from acts of religiously-motivated violence, and the subsequent indifference shown towards the applicants by the relevant authorities, was to a large extent the corollary of the applicants' religious convictions. The Government have not adduced any counter-arguments. In the Court's opinion, the comments and attitude of the State employees who were alerted about the attack or subsequently instructed to conduct the relevant investigation cannot be considered compatible with the principle of equality of every person before the law. No justification for this discriminatory treatment in respect of the applicants has been put forward by the Government.

141. The Court considers that the negligent attitude towards extremely serious unlawful acts, shown by the police and the investigation authorities by the police on account of the applicants' faith, enabled Father Basil to continue to advocate hatred through the media and to pursue acts of religiously-motivated violence, accompanied by his supporters, while alleging that the latter enjoyed the unofficial support of the authorities. This would suggest to civil society a reasonable doubt as to the criminals' complicity with the State representatives.

142. The Court therefore concludes that the applicants concerned were victims of a violation of Article 14 in conjunction with Articles 3 and 9 of the Convention.

. . .

[The Court awarded non-pecuniary reparations in amounts ranging from EUR 120 to 700 per applicant for the violation of Article 3, EUR 150 each for the violation of Article 9, and a total of EUR 12,103 for attorneys fees.]

Questions and Comments

1. In each of the above cases, who was primarily responsible for the injury to the applicant? On what basis was the conduct attributed to the defendant state?

2. What duty of care is imposed on the governments in each of these cases? Is the state an insurer of individuals against wrongful private conduct?

3. The government of Georgia referred to the "Rose Revolution" that occurred in the state, arguing in effect that it should not be held responsible for the failing of the prior Communist government—is this a legitimate defense?

4. State responsibility for human rights violations during periods of armed conflict raise particular problems. Evidence may be difficult to obtain and conflicting. The state may lack control over parts of its territory or may attempt to shift responsibility to insurgents. Many such cases have arisen out of periods of conflict in South-East Turkey and other areas where separatist movements exist. See *Ilaşcu and others v. Russia and Moldova*, App. No. 48787/99, judgment of 8 July 2004, concerning violations in the "Moldavian Republic of Transdniestria," a region which declared independence from Moldova in 1991. The claim of independence has not been recognized by the international community but the separatist movement enjoys considerable support from the Russian government. The Court found violations of the Convention by both Moldova and Russia. Moldova's "declaration" when

it ratified the Convention that it lacked control over Transdneistrian territory was not accepted as a reservation because it did not refer to any specific provision of the Convention or to domestic law. In addition to these cases, the issue of responsibility for civilian deaths during counter-insurgency activities has been central to the rising number of cases arising out of the conflict in Chechnya. See e.g., *Case of Khashiyev and Akayeva v. Russia*, judgment of 24 February 2005 (holding Russia responsible for violations of Article 2, 3 and 13); *Case of Bazorkina v. Russia, (App. No. 69481/01)*, judgment of 27 July 2006 (finding state responsibility for the disappearance of applicant's son in Chechnya, violations of Articles 2, 3, 5 and 13); and *Chitayev and Chitayev v. Russia*, App. No. 59334/00, judgment of 18 January 2007 (unanimously finding Russia responsible for torture and wrongful detention in Chechnya).

5. The African Commission has determined that the Sudanese government is complicit in atrocities committed by the *janjaweed* militia in the Darfur region. *See: Resolution on the Situation of Human Rights in the Darfur Region in Sudan*, 20th Activity Report (Dec. 5, 2005), in which the African Commission expresses its deep concern about the continuing grave violations of human rights and international humanitarian law in Darfur committed by parties to the conflict, in particular the continued depopulation of vast areas in the region of their indigenous owners, threats of violence, intimidation and assault against UN agencies and humanitarian organizations, the targeting and killing of AU troops in Darfur, and the killing and abduction of staff members of national and international humanitarian organisation, and calls upon the Sudanese government to comply with its obligations under the *African Charter on Human and Peoples' Rights*, the *AU Constitutive Act*, the *UN Charter* and other relevant instruments to which the Sudan is a State Party, and comply with the following:

> **a. Cease**, with immediate effect, all attacks against civilians in Darfur and end the grave violations of human and peoples' rights, in particular the forced de-population of entire areas in the region, rape and sexual violence against women and girls, abduction of women and children, and to cease all support to the *Janjaweed* militiamen, including the provision of supplies.

6. The following cases, while not involving an armed separatist movement, also concern the responsibility of a state for the governmental acts of "autonomous" regions.

Case of Assanidze v. Georgia, Application no. 71503/01, Eur. Ct. H.R. (GC), ECHR 2004-II, 8 April 2004

. . . .

21. The applicant was formerly the mayor of Batumi, the capital of the Ajarian Autonomous Republic, and a member of the Ajarian Supreme Council. He was arrested on 4 October 1993 on suspicion of illegal financial dealings in the Batumi Tobacco Manufacturing Company, a private company, and the unlawful possession and handling of firearms. He was convicted on 28 November 1994 and given an immediate custodial sentence of eight years; orders were made for the confiscation of his assets and requiring him to make good the pecuniary losses sustained by the company. . . .

22. By Decree no. 1200 of 1 October 1999, the Georgian President granted the applicant a pardon suspending the remaining two years of his sentence. . . .

23. Despite the presidential pardon, the applicant remained in custody in the short-term remand prison of the Ajarian Ministry of Security.

24. The Batumi Tobacco Manufacturing Company immediately challenged Presidential Decree no. 1200 of 1 October 1999 in the High Court of the Ajarian Autonomous Republic on the ground that it had been granted unlawfully. . . .

28. In a decision of 24 March 2000, the Tbilisi Court of Appeal dismissed the Batumi Tobacco Manufacturing Company's complaints as unfounded. It ruled that the procedural defects pleaded (the failure to obtain the opinion of the Pardons Board and the applicant's lack of remorse) did not render the President's order unlawful, as the right of pardon was an absolute constitutional right vested in the President of Georgia. . . . The Court of Appeal also noted that the company was not entitled in law to call for the reopening of the criminal proceedings against the applicant. It stated that it considered the applicant's detention to be in violation of Article 5 § 1 of the European Convention on Human Rights.

29. On 11 July 2000 the Supreme Court of Georgia dismissed an appeal on points of law by the Batumi Tobacco Manufacturing Company as unfounded. . . .

30. Even after 11 July 2000 the local authorities in the Ajarian Autonomous Republic continued to hold the applicant in the short-term remand prison of the Ajarian Ministry of Security in Batumi. . . .

B. The applicant's second conviction and subsequent acquittal

1. On 12 November 1999 Mr. David Assanidze, a close relative of the applicant who had been sentenced to twenty years' imprisonment by the Supreme Court of Georgia on 20 September 1996, gave an interview on a television channel broadcasting in the Ajarian Autonomous Republic in which he affirmed that the applicant had been one of his accomplices.

2. Following that interview the applicant, who had remained in custody after being pardoned by the President on 1 October 1999, was charged on 11 December 1999 with being a member of a criminal association in 1993 and with the attempted kidnapping of V.G., the head of the regional department of the Ministry of the Interior for Khelvachauri (Ajarian Autonomous Republic). . . .

3. Consequently, on 2 October 2000 the applicant was convicted and sentenced to twelve years' imprisonment to be served in a strict-regime prison. . . .

4. The applicant appealed on points of law to the Supreme Court of Georgia. The central authorities made various attempts to secure his transfer from Batumi to Tbilisi for the day of the hearing. The Georgian Minister of Justice requested the Ajarian authorities through the intermediary of the Georgian Minister of State Security and the Public Defender (Ombudsperson) to arrange for the applicant's transfer to the capital, but in vain.

5. On 29 January 2001 the Criminal Affairs Chamber of the Supreme Court of Georgia heard the appeal in the applicant's absence; it quashed the judgment of 2 October 2000 and acquitted the applicant. . . .

6. It held that the applicant could not be found guilty on the sole basis of affirmations made by Mr. David Assanidze six years after the events in issue. . . .

7. In addition, the Supreme Court found serious procedural defects in the criminal proceedings against the applicant. . . .

8. On 29 January 2001 the President of the Chamber of the Supreme Court forwarded the short version of the judgment acquitting the applicant to the Minister

of Justice, the director of the department responsible for the execution of sentences at the Ministry of Justice and the governor of the short-term remand prison of the Ajarian Ministry of Security for execution. He informed them that they would receive the reasoned version of the judgment subsequently.

9. On 5 February 2001 the President of the Chamber sent them the reasoned version of the judgment acquitting the applicant for execution.

10. That judgment was never executed and the applicant remains in custody in the short-term remand prison of the Ajarian Ministry of Security.

11. The applicant's unlawful detention was denounced on a number of occasions by the General Prosecutor's Office of Georgia, the Public Defender, the Georgian Ministry of Justice and the Legal Affairs Committee of the Georgian Parliament. They contacted the local authorities concerned in the Ajarian Autonomous Republic, seeking his immediate release. . . .

12. The central authority's efforts to secure the applicant's release were unsuccessful. . . .

THE LAW

II. THE RESPONDENT STATE'S JURISDICTION AND RESPONSIBILITY UNDER ARTICLE 1 OF THE CONVENTION

1. The Government's submissions

13. The Government accepted that the Ajarian Autonomous Republic was an integral part of Georgia and that the matters complained of were within the jurisdiction of the Georgian State. However, they did not touch upon the difficulties encountered by the central State authorities in exercising their jurisdiction in the Ajarian Autonomous Republic.

14. As a preliminary point, counsel for the Government drew the Court's attention to the fact that the Georgian central government had not informed the Ajarian authorities of the proceedings before the Court in the present case. Consequently, although directly implicated by the application, the Ajarian authorities had had no opportunity to explain to the Court why the applicant remained in custody.

Noting that the Ajarian Autonomous Republic was subject to Georgian law, counsel for the Government stressed that the Georgian Supreme Court had the power to overturn decisions of the Ajarian High Court on an appeal on points of law. He said that Georgian law was duly applied in the Republic and that, apart from the present case, with its strong political overtones, there was no problem of judicial cooperation between the central authorities and the local Ajarian authorities.

Counsel for the Government added that, unlike the other two autonomous entities (the Autonomous Republic of Abkhazia and the Tskhinvali region), the Ajarian Autonomous Republic had never had separatist aspirations and that any suggestion that it would refuse to cooperate with the central judicial authorities was unfounded. He also said that the Ajarian Autonomous Republic was not a source of conflict between different States and that the central State authorities exercised full jurisdiction over it.

2. The applicant's submissions

15. Like the Government, the applicant stated that there was no doubt that the Ajarian Autonomous Republic was part of Georgia, both under domestic and international law. He noted that the Ajarian Autonomous Republic was not a separatist region, that the Georgian State exercised its jurisdiction there and was answerable to the international courts for matters arising in all parts of Georgia, including Ajaria. He added that the central authority had no difficulty in exercising its jurisdiction in the Ajarian Autonomous Republic. In his view, the Supreme Court of Georgia was generally successful in supervising the functioning of the Ajarian courts, the instant case proving the sole exception to that rule.

16. The applicant considered that his inability to secure compliance with the judgment acquitting him was attributable domestically to the local Ajarian authorities, but also to the central authorities, whose actions had not been sufficiently effective, and to the President of Georgia, who had not played his role as guarantor of the State. In his submission, his application did not concern questions of jurisdiction or responsibility, but only the respondent State's failure to secure, by all available means, execution of a judicial decision.

3. The Court's assessment

(a) The question of "jurisdiction"

17. Article 1 of the Convention requires the States Parties to "secure to everyone within their jurisdiction the rights and freedoms defined in Section I of [the] Convention". It follows from this provision that the States Parties are answerable for any violation of the protected rights and freedoms of anyone within their "jurisdiction"—or competence—at the time of the violation.

In certain exceptional cases, jurisdiction is assumed on the basis of non-territorial factors, such as: acts of public authority performed abroad by diplomatic and consular representatives of the State; the criminal activities of individuals overseas against the interests of the State or its nationals; acts performed on board vessels flying the State flag or on aircraft or spacecraft registered there; and particularly serious international crimes (universal jurisdiction).

However, as a general rule, the notion of "jurisdiction" within the meaning of Article 1 of the Convention must be considered as reflecting the position under public international law (see *Gentilhomme and Others v. France*, nos. 48205/99, 48207/99 and 48209/99, § 20, 14 May 2002, and *Banković and Others v. Belgium and Others* (dec.) [GC], no. 52207/99, §§ 59–61, ECHR 2001-XII). That notion is "primarily" or "essentially" territorial (see *Banković and Others*, ibid.).

18. In addition to the State territory proper, territorial jurisdiction extends to any area which, at the time of the alleged violation, is under the "overall control" of the State concerned (see *Loizidou v. Turkey* (preliminary objections), judgment of 23 March 1995, Series A no. 310), notably occupied territories (see *Cyprus v. Turkey* [GC], no. 25781/94, ECHR 2001-IV), to the exclusion of areas outside such control (see *Banković and Others*, cited above).

19. The Ajarian Autonomous Republic is indisputably an integral part of the territory of Georgia and subject to its competence and control. In other words, there

is a presumption of competence. The Court must now determine whether there is valid evidence to rebut that presumption.

20. In that connection, the Court notes, firstly, that Georgia has ratified the Convention for the whole of its territory. Furthermore, it is common ground that the Ajarian Autonomous Republic has no separatist aspirations and that no other State exercises effective overall control there (see, by converse implication, *Ilaşcu and Others v. Moldova and Russia* (dec.) [GC], no. 48787/99, 4 July 2001, and *Loizidou*, cited above). On ratifying the Convention, Georgia did not make any specific reservation under Article 57 of the Convention with regard to the Ajarian Autonomous Republic or to difficulties in exercising its jurisdiction over that territory. Such a reservation would in any event have been ineffective, as the case-law precludes territorial exclusions (see *Matthews v. the United Kingdom* [GC], no. 24833/94, § 29, ECHR 1999-I) other than in the instance referred to in Article 56 § 1 of the Convention (dependent territories).

21. Unlike the American Convention on Human Rights of 22 November 1969 (Article 28), the European Convention does not contain a "federal clause" limiting the obligations of the federal State for events occurring on the territory of the states forming part of the federation. Moreover, since Georgia is not a federal State, the Ajarian Autonomous Republic is not part of a federation. It forms an entity which, like others (the Autonomous Republic of Abkhazia and, before 1991, the Autonomous District of South Ossetia), must have an autonomous status, which is a different matter. Besides, even if an implied federal clause similar in content to that of Article 28 of the American Convention were found to exist in the European Convention (which is impossible in practice), it could not be construed as releasing the federal State from all responsibility, since it requires the federal State to "immediately take suitable measures, in accordance with its constitution ... , to the end that the [states forming part of the federation] may adopt appropriate provisions for the fulfillment of [the] Convention".

22. Thus, the presumption referred to in paragraph [19] above is seen to be correct. Indeed, for reasons of legal policy—the need to maintain equality between the States Parties and to ensure the effectiveness of the Convention—it could not be otherwise. But for the presumption, the applicability of the Convention could be selectively restricted to only parts of the territory of certain States Parties, thus rendering the notion of effective human rights protection underpinning the entire Convention meaningless while, at the same time, allowing discrimination between the States Parties, that is to say between those which accepted the application of the Convention over the whole of their territory and those which did not.

23. The Court therefore finds that the actual facts out of which the allegations of violations arose were within the "jurisdiction" of the Georgian State (see *Bertrand Russell Peace Foundation Ltd v. the United Kingdom*, no. 7597/76, Commission decision of 2 May 1978, Decisions and Reports (DR) 14, pp. 117 and 124) within the meaning of Article 1 of the Convention.

(b) Issues of imputability and responsibility

24. The present application is distinguishable from the cases which the Court has been called upon to examine under Article 1 of the Convention. In those cases, the

notions of imputability and responsibility were considered as going together, the State only engaging its responsibility under the Convention if the alleged violation could be imputed to it (see *Loizidou*, cited above, pp. 20–22, §§ 52–56, and *Cyprus v. Turkey*, cited above, pp. 260–62, §§ 75–81).

In the aforementioned cases, the Court held, in particular, that the alleged violations of the Convention committed on part of the territory of the Contracting Party to the Convention could not engage that State's responsibility when the zone concerned was under the effective control of another State (see *Loizidou*, pp. 23–24, § 62). The position in the present case is quite different: no State apart from Georgia exercised control—and therefore had jurisdiction—over the Ajarian Autonomous Republic and indeed it has not been suggested otherwise before the Court, quite the opposite. The present application also differs from that in *Banković and Others*, which was distinguishable from the two preceding cases, in that the respondent States—which were parties to the Convention and members of NATO—did not exercise "overall control" over the territory concerned. In addition, the State which did have such control, the Federal Republic of Yugoslavia, was not a party to the Convention.

25. The applicant in the instant case is a person who, despite being acquitted by the Supreme Court of Georgia, nonetheless remains in the custody of the local Ajarian authorities. While attributing his continued detention to arbitrariness on the part of the local authorities, the applicant also complains that the measures taken by the central authority to secure his release have been ineffective.

As the case file shows, the central authorities have taken all the procedural steps possible under domestic law to secure compliance with the judgment acquitting the applicant, have sought to resolve the dispute by various political means and have repeatedly urged the Ajarian authorities to release him. However, no response has been received to any of their requests.

Thus, the Court is led to the conclusion that, under the domestic system, the matters complained of by the applicant were directly imputable to the local Ajarian authorities.

26. However, it must be reiterated that, for the purposes of the Convention, the sole issue of relevance is the State's international responsibility, irrespective of the national authority to which the breach of the Convention in the domestic system is imputable (see, *mutatis mutandis*, *Foti and Others v. Italy*, judgment of 10 December 1982, Series A no. 56, p. 21, § 63; *Zimmermann and Steiner v. Switzerland*, judgment of 13 July 1983, Series A no. 66, p. 13, § 32; and *Lingens v. Austria*, judgment of 8 July 1986, Series A no. 103, p. 28, § 46).

Even though it is not inconceivable that States will encounter difficulties in securing compliance with the rights guaranteed by the Convention in all parts of their territory, each State Party to the Convention nonetheless remains responsible for events occurring anywhere within its national territory.

Further, the Convention does not merely oblige the higher authorities of the Contracting States themselves to respect the rights and freedoms it embodies; it also has the consequence that, in order to secure the enjoyment of those rights and freedoms, those authorities must prevent or remedy any breach at subordinate levels (see *Ireland v. the United Kingdom*, judgment of 18 January 1978, Series A no. 25, pp. 90–91, § 239). The higher authorities of the State are under a duty to require their subordinates to comply with the Convention and cannot shelter behind their inability to ensure that it is respected (ibid., p. 64, § 159).

27. Despite the malfunctioning of parts of the State machinery in Georgia and the existence of territories with special status, the Ajarian Autonomous Republic is in law subject to the control of the Georgian State. The relationship existing between the local Ajarian authorities and the central government is such that only a failing on the part of the latter could make the continued breach of the provisions of the Convention at the local level possible. The general duty imposed on the State by Article 1 of the Convention entails and requires the implementation of a national system capable of securing compliance with the Convention throughout the territory of the State for everyone. That is confirmed by the fact that, firstly, Article 1 does not exclude any part of the member States' "jurisdiction" from the scope of the Convention and, secondly, it is with respect to their "jurisdiction" as a whole—which is often exercised in the first place through the Constitution—that member States are called on to show compliance with the Convention (see *United Communist Party of Turkey and Others v. Turkey*, judgment of 30 January 1998, *Reports* 1998-I, pp. 17-18, § 29).

28. The authorities of a territorial entity of the State are public-law institutions which perform the functions assigned to them by the Constitution and the law. In that connection, the Court reiterates that in international law the expression "governmental organisation" cannot be held to refer only to the government or the central organs of the State. Where powers are distributed along decentralised lines, it refers to any national authority exercising public functions. Consequently, such authorities have no standing to make an application to the Court under Article 34 of the Convention (see *Municipal Section of Antilly v. France* (dec.), no. 45129/98, ECHR 1999-VIII, and *Ayuntamiento de Mula v. Spain* (dec.), no. 55346/00, ECHR 2001-I).

These principles show that, in the present case, the Ajarian regional authorities cannot be described as a non-governmental organisation or group of individuals with a common interest, for the purposes of Article 34 of the Convention. Accordingly, they have no right to make an application to the Court or to lodge a complaint with it against the central authorities of the Georgian State.

29. The Court thus emphasises that the higher authorities of the Georgian State are strictly liable under the Convention for the conduct of their subordinates (see *Ireland v. the United Kingdom*, cited above, p. 64, § 159). It is only the responsibility of the Georgian State itself—not that of a domestic authority or organ—that is in issue before the Court. It is not the Court's role to deal with a multiplicity of national authorities or courts or to examine disputes between institutions or over internal politics.

30. The Court therefore finds that the actual facts out of which the allegations of violations arose were within the "jurisdiction" of Georgia within the meaning of Article 1 of the Convention and that, even though within the domestic system those matters are directly imputable to the local authorities of the Ajarian Autonomous

Republic, it is solely the responsibility of the Georgian State that is engaged under the Convention.

[Having held unanimously that the matters complained of were within the "jurisdiction" of Georgia within the meaning of Article 1 of the Convention and that only the responsibility of the Georgian State was engaged under the Convention, the Court unanimously found Article 5 §1 to have been violated due to the applicant's detention after 29 January 2001. The Court also held by fourteen votes to three that there had been a violation of Article 6 §1 on account of the failure to comply with the Georgian Supreme Court judgment of 29 January 2001. Other complaints were dismissed as untimely. The respondent state was directed to secure the applicant's release at the earliest possible date. The court also awarded damages, costs and attorneys fees.]

Questions and Comments

1. Would the Court have decided the case differently if Mr. Assanidze's detention was at the hands of Chechnyan separatists and the applicant was brought against Russia?

2. Note that the Committee of Ministers, in Resolution ResDH (2006)53, closed the file after finding that Georgia had complied with the Court's judgment and paid the damages awarded. The government reported to the COM that the applicant was released on September 4, 2004, the day after the Court's judgment. Furthermore, it reported that the former leader of the Autonomous Republic of Ajaria, who had been responsible for the failure to comply with the release order of Mr. Assanidze, had resigned and that elections on June 20, 2004 in the Autonomous Republic of Ajaria had resolved the difficulties encountered in exercising jurisdiction in the region. Finally, the government reported that the judgment of the European Court had received wide media coverage and had been transmitted to relevant authorities, particularly the national courts, to draw their attention to the requirements of the Convention. Given these events, how important do you think the European Court's judgment was in securing the release of the applicant?

3. In the following two cases, the question of state responsibility for the applicant's injuries extends further in time and distance. In addition, the first case addresses the state's "privatization" of reparations from World War II. Who is or should be held responsible in each instance?

Woś v. Poland, (App. no. 22860/02), Admissibility, Eur. Ct. H.R. Decision of March 1, 2005 Judgment of 8 June 2006, Eur. Ct. H.R., (internal cross-references and Polish terms omitted).

. . . .

I. THE CIRCUMSTANCES OF THE CASE

A. Historical background

9. The realities of the international situation following the end of the Second World War prevented the Republic of Poland from asserting any claims arising out of persecution of its citizens by Nazi Germany, including as forced labourers.

10. In the period immediately following the Second World War Poland did not conclude a specific agreement with Germany regarding the issue of reparations. It relied on the Potsdam Agreement of 1 August 1945, concluded by the Governments of the United States of America, the United Kingdom of Great Britain and Northern Ireland and the Union of Soviet Socialist Republics.

11. On 27 February 1953 the London Agreement on Germany's External Debts (London Debt Agreement) was concluded by the United States of America, Great Britain, France and the Soviet Union. Under this Agreement, consideration of claims arising out of the Second World War by countries which were at war with or were occupied by Germany during that war, and by nationals of such countries, against the Reich or agencies of the Reich was deferred until final settlement of the issue of reparations.

12. On 23 August 1953, a day after a similar declaration by the Government of the Soviet Union, the Government of Poland declared that it renounced any claims against Germany in respect of war reparations as of 1 January 1954. In a declaration of 27 September 1969, made at the United Nations, the Government of Poland clarified that the renouncement of 1953 did not affect individual claims arising out of unlawful acts.

13. It was only after the conclusion of the Treaty on the Final Settlement with respect to Germany of 12 September 1990 (the so-called Two-Plus-Four Treaty) and the conclusion of two treaties between the Federal Republic of Germany and the Republic of Poland in 1990[1] and 1991[2] that the issue of persons persecuted by the Nazi regime was addressed in the bilateral Agreement of 16 October 1991.

B. The circumstances of the case

14. The applicant was subjected to forced labour during the Second World War on the territory of occupied Poland. In February and March 1941 he worked on a German farm near Cielcza. Subsequently, from April 1941 to April/May 1944, the applicant worked as a forest labourer in Cielcza. He was finally relocated to an area situated 200 kilometres from his habitual place of residence, where he was required to reinforce German defences from May/June 1944 to 26 January 1945. In February 1944 the applicant reached the age of 16.

1. Proceedings concerning the first compensation scheme

15. On 20 October 1993 the applicant applied to the "Polish-German Reconciliation Foundation" for compensation payment on account of his forced labour from the funds contributed by the Government of the Federal Republic of Germany under the Agreement of 16 October 1991. On 2 February 1994 the Foundation's Verification Commission, having regard to a document issued by the social-security authority, established that the applicant had performed forced labour from February 1941 to January 1945 and awarded him PLN 1,050 in compensation. This payment was granted within the framework of the so-called primary payments. The issue of deportation was apparently not addressed in the decision. The applicant's appeal

---

[1] Treaty of 14 November 1990 on Confirmation of the Existing Border between the Federal Republic of Germany and the Republic of Poland.
[2] Treaty of 17 June 1991 on Good Neighbourliness and Friendly Cooperation.

against this decision was dismissed by the Appeal Verification Commission on an unspecified later date. The Appeal Verification Commission found that the amount of payment granted to the applicant had been calculated correctly.

16. On an unspecified date in 1999 the Foundation's Management Board adopted Resolution no. 29/99, which introduced a deportation requirement for claimants who had been forced labourers. The Resolution also provided that that those claimants who had performed forced labour as children under 16 years of age could be granted compensation payment regardless of whether the deportation condition was met.

17. On 2 March 2000, following the adoption of Resolution no. 29/99, the Foundation's Verification Commission granted the applicant a supplementary payment of PLN 365. The decision on supplementary payment was related to the applicant's forced labour while a child aged under 16 years (April 1941—February 1944). Thus, the period of forced labour from March 1944 to January 1945 was not taken into account because the deportation condition as defined in Resolution no. 29/99 had not been met for the relevant period. In the absence of appropriate evidence, the period of forced labour from February to March 1941 was not acknowledged.

18. On 12 March 2000 the applicant appealed to the Appeal Verification Commission against that decision, challenging the amount of compensation granted. It appears that the applicant complained that the period of his forced labour between May/June 1944 and 26 January 1945, in the particularly harsh conditions connected with his relocation, had not been taken into account by the Verification Commission. Having received no reply to his appeal, the applicant made further inquiries with the Foundation on 31 October 2000 and 3 January 2001.

19. In the meantime, the applicant had lodged a complaint with the Ombudsman about the Foundation's inactivity. On 4 April 2001 the Ombudsman informed the applicant that, regrettably, he was not in a position to question the lawfulness of resolutions adopted by the Polish-German Reconciliation Foundation or any other foundation. The Polish-German Reconciliation Foundation had been established pursuant to the Foundations Act of 6 April 1984. In this particular case, the Foundation operated under the supervision of the Minister of the State Treasury. Even so, the Ombudsman could not interfere with the Foundation's actions so long as they were in compliance with its Statute and other legal regulations. The Ombudsman also referred to the Supreme Court's Resolution of 31 March 1998, refusing to recognise the Polish-German Reconciliation Foundation as a public authority.

20. In a letter of 24 April 2001, the President of the Foundation's Appeal Verification Commission informed the applicant that, under the Foundation's by-laws in force at the material time (Resolution no. 29/99), only forced labourers who had been deported to the Third Reich or to an area occupied by the German Reich (with the exception of the territory of occupied Poland) were eligible for compensation. Finally, the applicant was informed that no further appeal lay against this decision by the Appeal Verification Commission.

21. Nevertheless, on an unspecified later date, the applicant lodged a complaint against the Appeal Verification Commission's decision of 24 April 2001 with the

Supreme Administrative Court. It appears that the applicant also challenged Resolution no. 29/99 in his complaint.

22. On 14 December 2001 the Supreme Administrative Court rejected the applicant's complaint, considering it inadmissible in law. It relied on Resolution no. OPS 3/01, adopted by the Supreme Administrative Court on 3 December 2001.

23. In a letter dated 23 September 2002 the Ministry of the State Treasury informed the applicant that, in order for a forced labourer to be granted compensation, it was necessary to him or her to comply with the deportation requirement as specified in Resolution no. 29/99 of the Foundation's Management Board.

2. Proceedings concerning the second compensation scheme

24. On 21 November 2000 the applicant applied to the Polish Foundation for compensation payment under the scheme for slave and forced labourers (the second compensation scheme), established under the Joint Statement of 17 July 2000, the German Law of 2 August 2000 on the Creation of the "Remembrance, Responsibility and Future" Foundation ("the German Foundation Act") and the subsequent Agreement of 16 February 2001 between the German Foundation and the Polish Foundation. On 17 April 2001 the Foundation's Verification Commission rejected his request on the ground that he did not satisfy the deportation requirement set out in section 11 § 1.2 of the German Foundation Act. It appears that the applicant did not appeal against the Verification Commission's decision of 17 April 2001. The applicant's subsequent complaints to the Minister of the State Treasury were to no avail. . . .

THE LAW

52. The applicant complained about the Polish-German Reconciliation Foundation's decisions partly refusing to grant him compensation. He further alleged, in substance, that he did not have access to a court in respect of the Foundation's decisions in his case. The Court considers that the applicant's complaints fall to be examined under Article 6 § 1 of the Convention.

A. Responsibility of the Polish State

53. As a preliminary issue, the Court has to determine whether Poland's responsibility under the Convention is engaged in respect of the acts of the Polish-German Reconciliation Foundation.

1. The parties' submissions

54. The Government argued that the Foundation was not a governmental agency. It was a fully independent entity operating under private law, and the Government could not be held responsible for its actions or decisions concerning individual applications for financial assistance. The Government submitted that supervisory functions exercised by the public authorities were limited to the examination of whether the Foundation's activities complied with its aims, its Statute and the applicable legislative provisions. According to the Government, it could not be overlooked that State supervision of foundations was limited only to their organs, whereas neither the founder nor the recipients of financial assistance were subject to any supervision by the State authorities.

55. The Government further submitted that two separate periods should be distinguished in the Foundation's activities. The first period began in 1991 with the establishment of the Foundation and ended in 2000, when the international agreement regarding compensation scheme for slave and forced labourers was concluded.

56. Having regard to the Agreement of 16 October 1991, the Government contended that in the first period of its activities the Foundation was fully authorised to define its own rules for awarding financial assistance to the victims of Nazi persecution. The rules adopted by the Foundation were exclusively a matter for its internal regulations, and any possibility of reviewing those rules was reserved solely for the Foundation's supervisory authority, which could apply to the courts to have a resolution adopted by the Foundation quashed. The Government further submitted that the Verification Commission and the Appeal Verification Commission were entirely independent from the Foundation's Management Board and the Supervisory Board. In addition to the right to file an appeal against the Verification Commission's decision, every person concerned had a right to lodge a complaint with the Minister responsible for supervising the Foundation.

57. The second period in the Foundation's activities started in 2001, when the Polish-German Reconciliation Foundation began to operate as the so-called Partner Organisation of the German Remembrance, Responsibility and Future Foundation. The Government contended that the legal and financial framework for voluntary payments by the German Government and German industry had been established on the basis of the Joint Statement of 17 July 2000 and the German Foundation Act. The German Foundation Act contained specific rules on eligibility for compensation payments and the division of funds among partner organisations.

58. The Government argued that both the Joint Statement and the German Foundation Act, which had been negotiated over a period of two years, constituted an integral whole. Further, they contended that Poland, like all the other signatories to the Joint Statement, could not apply its own regulations departing from the scheme, which was binding on all the parties to the agreement. The parties to this agreement, when making compensation payments to eligible persons, undertook to follow the criteria set out in the Foundation Act. The Government underlined that, consequently, the Polish-German Reconciliation Foundation, as one of the partner organisations, could not introduce its own rules for compensation payments.

59. The applicant argued that the Polish State was responsible for the acts of the Polish-German Reconciliation Foundation. He maintained that the Government had established the Foundation and entrusted it with its tasks. The applicant also submitted that members of the Foundation's Management Board were appointed and dismissed by the Government and that the Minister of the State Treasury supervised the Foundation's operations.

2. The Court's assessment

(a) Principles deriving from the Court's case-law

60. The Court has consistently held that the responsibility of a State is engaged if a violation of one of the rights and freedoms defined in the Convention is the result of non-observance by that State of its obligation under Article 1 to secure those rights

and freedoms in its domestic law to everyone within its jurisdiction (see, *mutatis mutandis, Young, James and Webster v. the United Kingdom*, judgment of 13 August 1981, Series A no. 44, p. 20, § 49). Article 1 makes no distinction as to the type of rule or measure concerned and does not exclude any part of the member States' "jurisdiction" from scrutiny under the Convention (see *the United Communist Party of Turkey and Others v. Turkey*, judgment of 30 January 1998, *Reports of Judgments and Decisions* 1998-I, pp. 17–18, § 29). Furthermore, the State cannot absolve itself from responsibility *ratione personae* by delegating its obligations to private bodies or individuals (see, *mutatis mutandis, Costello-Roberts v. the United Kingdom*, judgment of 25 March 1993, Series A no. 247-C, p. 58, § 27). The undertakings given by a Contracting State under Article 1 of the Convention include, in addition to the duty to refrain from interfering with enjoyment of the rights and freedoms guaranteed, positive obligations to take appropriate steps to ensure respect for those rights and freedoms within its territory (see, among other authorities, *Z. v. the United Kingdom* [GC], no. 29392/95, § 73, ECHR 2001-V).

(b) Application of the above principles to the present case

(i) General considerations

61. The Court accepts the argument advanced by the Government that two separate periods should be distinguished in the Foundation's operations. However, it finds that, for the purposes of State responsibility for the Foundation's acts under the Convention, the distinction proposed by the Government, although not without relevance, is not conclusive.

(α) As regards the first compensation scheme

62. The Court observes that the Polish-German Reconciliation Foundation was established in 1991 in implementation of the Agreement of 16 October 1991 concluded between the Governments of the Republic of Poland and the Federal Republic of Germany. The Foundation was established by the Minister-Head of the Cabinet Office (the Founder), acting on the initiative of the Government of Poland and on behalf of the Polish State Treasury. It is true that, in a formal sense, the Foundation is a private-law entity operating under the Foundations Act of 6 April 1984. However, it cannot be overlooked that the very existence of the Foundation was brought about by the action of a Government Minister in implementation of a bilateral agreement negotiated and co-shaped by the representatives of the Polish Government. Furthermore, the Foundation's Statute was drawn up by the Government Minister who acted as a Founder. The Court also notes that the Founder could decide whether the Foundation went into liquidation.

63. The Court notes that the tasks with which the Foundation was originally entrusted stemmed from the bilateral Agreement of 16 October 1991, which had been freely entered into by Poland. The Court recognises the specific character of the obligations undertaken by the Polish State under that agreement, namely to establish a body which would assess compensation claims by Polish citizens who had been persecuted under the Nazi regime and to distribute compensation payments provided for that purpose by the other party to the agreement. In the Court's view, the respondent Government had consented under the Agreement of 16 October

1991 to delegate these obligations to a body operating under private law. Thus, it established the Polish-German Reconciliation Foundation, a body exercising *quasi-public* functions, and entrusted it with the obligations arising out of the international agreement.

64. It is of significance that the Agreement of 16 October 1991 contained only a general clause to the effect that the Foundation's capital fund would be distributed among those victims of Nazi persecution who had been particularly wronged. The Court notes that, under the said Agreement, the Foundation was to define the necessary conditions for awarding compensation, i.e. grave harm to a claimant's health and his or her current difficult financial situation. These conditions were subsequently transposed into the Foundation's Statute and reflected in the by-laws adopted by the Foundation. It is apparent that the Agreement of 16 October 1991 specified only general requirements for the awarding of compensation by the Foundation, while leaving a substantial degree of regulatory powers to the Foundation in respect of the specific eligibility criteria and procedural rules to be applied. The Court notes that the power to regulate granted to the Foundation was considerable and has been extensively used, as evidenced, *inter alia*, by Resolution no. 29/99 introducing the deportation requirement.

(b) As regards the second compensation scheme

65. The Court observes that the respondent Government was a party to international negotiations which led to the adoption of the legal acts governing the operation of the second compensation scheme. The Court cannot but note that during these negotiations the Government of Poland entered into commitments which were subsequently made binding on the Polish-German Reconciliation Foundation. Thus, the Government recognised, at least implicitly, that it was able to exercise a measure of control over the Foundation. The Court also notes the grounds of the governmental bill on exemption of payments received in connection with the Nazi persecution from tax and duties, and the content of Annex no. 3 to the Agreement of 16 February 2001, in which the Government of Poland stated that it would oversee the process of disbursal of compensation payments by the Polish-German Reconciliation Foundation.

66. The Court also notes that, according to section 10 of the German Foundation Act, the Polish-German Reconciliation Foundation, as one of the partner organisations, was entrusted with evaluation of the compensation claims and disbursal of compensation payments to eligible claimants. In addition, this provision stipulated that the Remembrance, Responsibility and Future Foundation was neither authorised nor obligated in respect of approval and disbursal of compensation payments by the partner organisations. Thus, for all practical purposes, decisions to grant compensation payments were taken by the Polish-German Reconciliation Foundation. Admittedly, the basic eligibility criteria were determined in the German Foundation Act and as such they fell outside the jurisdiction of the respondent State. However, they were agreed upon by the Government of Poland in the course of the international negotiations which preceded the enactment of the German Foundation Act. In any event, the proximate cause of the Foundation's operation was, for both periods, an international agreement to which Poland was a party.

67. Furthermore, with regard to Resolution no. 15/2001 of 16 March 2001 by the Foundation's Management Board, the Court notes that certain funds received by the Government of Poland from the Government of the United States of America under the framework of the Victims of the Nazi Persecution Fund were subsequently allocated directly by the former to the Polish-German Reconciliation Foundation.

(c) As regards both compensation schemes

68. The Court attaches importance to the manner in which the governing and adjudicating bodies of the Foundation were created. It notes in particular that the Founder (a Government Minister) was empowered under the Statute to appoint and dismiss at his discretion all members of the Foundation's Supervisory Board and Management Board, which in turn were given responsibility for adopting the Foundation's by-laws. The Management Board was responsible for the appointment and dismissal of the Verification Commission, while the Supervisory Board had parallel powers in respect of the Appeal Verification Commission. Furthermore, a certain degree of control and supervision over the Foundation was exercised by the Minister of the State Treasury. The Court considers that by way of the above arrangements, the Government had at its disposal substantial means of influencing the Foundation's operations.

69. The Court notes that, according to the interpretation adopted by the domestic courts, the Foundation is not an organ of public administration and does not perform functions in the area of public administration (see paragraph 50 above). Furthermore, the domestic courts ruled that administrative functions could be delegated only by a statute, which was not the case with regard to the Foundation (see paragraph 46 above). Consequently, the Foundation's decisions in individual cases could not be reviewed by the Supreme Administrative Court. In this respect the Court would recall that it is not its task to substitute itself for the domestic jurisdictions. It is primarily for the national authorities, notably the courts, to resolve problems of interpretation of domestic legislation. The Court's role is confined to ascertaining whether the effects of such an interpretation are compatible with the Convention (see, *inter alia*, *Waite and Kennedy v. Germany* [GC], no. 26083/94, § 54, *Reports of Judgments and Decisions* 1999-I).

70. Having regard to the above-mentioned case-law of the domestic courts, the Court observes that their findings excluded the jurisdiction of the Polish courts in respect of reviewing individual decisions by the Foundation's bodies on compensation payments. It is not for the Court to call into question that such was a correct interpretation of Polish law applicable to foundations in general. At the same time, however, the respondent State, which had established the Foundation and entrusted it with the administration of both compensation funds, decided to exclude access to the courts in these matters. Against this background, the reasoning of the domestic courts in their decisions concerning the domestic status of the Foundation are not capable of ruling out entirely State responsibility under the Convention. It follows that the application cannot be rejected as incompatible *ratione personae* with the provisions of the Convention within the meaning of Article 35 § 3 of the Convention.

Conclusion

71. Having regard to the above general considerations, the Court is of the view that it cannot be said that the State exercised a pervasive influence in the daily operations of the Polish-German Reconciliation Foundation. It did not have direct influence over the decisions taken by the Foundation in respect of individual claimants; however, the State's role was crucial in establishing the overall framework in which the Foundation operated.

72. The Court considers that the fact that a State chooses a form of delegation in which some of its powers are exercised by another body cannot be decisive for the question of State responsibility *ratione personae*. In the Court's view, the exercise of State powers which affects Convention rights and freedoms raises an issue of State responsibility regardless of the form in which these powers happen to be exercised, be it for instance by a body whose activities are regulated by private law. The Convention does not exclude the transfer of competences under an international agreement to a body operating under private law provided that Convention rights continue to be secured (see, *mutatis mutandis, Matthews v. the United Kingdom* [GC], no. 24833/94, §32, *Reports of Judgments and Decisions 1999-I*). The responsibility of the respondent State thus continues even after such a transfer.

73. The Court observes that the respondent State has decided to delegate its obligations arising out of the international agreements to a body operating under private law. In the Court's view, such an arrangement cannot relieve the Polish State of the responsibilities it would have incurred had it chosen to discharge these obligations itself, as it could well have (see, *mutatis mutandis, Van der Mussele v. Belgium*, judgment of 23 November 1983, Series A no. 70, pp. 14–15, §§ 28–30; and *Costello-Roberts*, cited above, § 27). It should be recalled in this respect that the Convention is intended to guarantee rights that are not theoretical or illusory, but rights that are practical and effective (*Matthews v. the United Kingdom* [GC], cited above, § 34).

74. In conclusion, having regard to all the above considerations, the Court considers that the specific circumstances of the present case give rise to the conclusion that the actions of the Foundation "Polish-German Reconciliation" in respect of both compensation schemes are capable of engaging the responsibility of the State.

[On the merits, in a judgment of June 8, 2006, the Court refused to reconsider the issue of state responsibility and held that there had been a breach of Article 6(1), finding that the absolute exclusion of judicial review in respect of the decisions issued by the Foundation under the first compensation scheme was disproportionate to the legitimate aim pursued and impaired the very essence of the applicant's "right of access to a court" within the meaning of Article 6 § 1 of the Convention.]

Chahal v. the United Kingdom, (App. no. 23414/93), Judgment of 15 November 1996, Eur. Ct. H.R., 23 EHHR 413 (1997).

. . . .

12. The four applicants are members of the same family and are Sikhs. The first applicant, Karamjit Singh Chahal, is an Indian citizen who was born in 1948. He

entered the United Kingdom illegally in 1971 in search of employment. In 1974 he applied to the Home Office to regularise his stay and on 10 December 1974 was granted indefinite leave to remain under the terms of an amnesty for illegal entrants who arrived before 1 January 1973. Since 16 August 1990 he has been detained for the purposes of deportation in Bedford Prison.

The second applicant, Darshan Kaur Chahal, is also an Indian citizen who was born in 1956. She came to England on 12 September 1975 following her marriage to the first applicant in India, and currently lives in Luton with the two children of the family, Kiranpreet Kaur Chahal (born in 1977) and Bikaramjit Singh Chahal (born in 1978), who are the third and fourth applicants. By virtue of their birth in the United Kingdom the two children have British nationality.

13. The first and second applicants applied for British citizenship in December 1987. Mr. Chahal's request was refused on 4 April 1989 but that of Mrs Chahal is yet to be determined.

B. Background: the conflict in Punjab

14. Since the partition of India in 1947 many Sikhs have been engaged in a political campaign for an independent homeland, Khalistan, which would approximate to the Indian province of Punjab. In the late 1970s, a prominent group emerged under the leadership of Sant Jarnail Singh Bhindranwale, based at the Golden Temple in Amritsar, the holiest Sikh shrine. The Government submit that Sant Bhindranwale, as well as preaching the tenets of orthodox Sikhism, used the Golden Temple for the accumulation of arms and advocated the use of violence for the establishment of an independent Khalistan.

15. The situation in Punjab deteriorated following the killing of a senior police officer in the Golden Temple in 1983. On 6 June 1984 the Indian army stormed the temple during a religious festival, killing Sant Bhindranwale and approximately 1,000 other Sikhs. Four months later the Indian Prime Minister, Mrs Indira Gandhi, was shot dead by two Sikh members of her bodyguard. The ensuing Hindu backlash included the killing of over 2,000 Sikhs in riots in Delhi.

16. Since 1984, the conflict in Punjab has reportedly claimed over 20,000 lives, peaking in 1992 when, according to Indian press reports collated by the United Kingdom Foreign and Commonwealth Office, approximately 4,000 people were killed in related incidents in Punjab and elsewhere. There is evidence of violence and human rights abuses perpetrated by both Sikh separatists and the security forces.

C. Mr. Chahal's visit to India in 1984

17. On 1 January 1984 Mr. Chahal travelled to Punjab with his wife and children to visit relatives. He submits that during this visit he attended at the Golden Temple on many occasions, and saw Sant Bhindranwale preach there approximately ten times. On one occasion he, his wife and son were afforded a personal audience with him. At around this time Mr. Chahal was baptised and began to adhere to the tenets of orthodox Sikhism. He also became involved in organising passive resistance in support of autonomy for Punjab.

18. On 30 March 1984 he was arrested by the Punjab police. He was taken into detention and held for twenty-one days, during which time he was, he contended,

kept handcuffed in insanitary conditions, beaten to unconsciousness, electrocuted on various parts of his body and subjected to a mock execution. He was subsequently released without charge.

He was able to return to the United Kingdom on 27 May 1984, and has not visited India since.

D. Mr. Chahal's political and religious activities in the United Kingdom

19. On his return to the United Kingdom, Mr. Chahal became a leading figure in the Sikh community, which reacted with horror to the storming of the Golden Temple. He helped organise a demonstration in London to protest at the Indian Government's actions, became a full-time member of the committee of the "gurdwara" (temple) in Belvedere (Erith, Kent) and travelled around London persuading young Sikhs to be baptised.

20. In August 1984 Mr. Jasbir Singh Rode entered the United Kingdom. He was Sant Bhindranwale's nephew, and recognised by Sikhs as his successor as spiritual leader. Mr. Chahal contacted him on his arrival and toured the United Kingdom with him, assisting at baptisms performed by him. Mr. Rode was instrumental in setting up branches of the International Sikh Youth Federation ("ISYF") in the United Kingdom, and the applicant played an important organisational role in this endeavour. The ISYF was established to be the overseas branch of the All India Sikh Students' Federation. This latter organisation was proscribed by the Indian Government until mid-1985, and is reportedly still perceived as militant by the Indian authorities.

21. In December 1984 Mr. Rode was excluded from the United Kingdom on the ground that he publicly advocated violent methods in pursuance of the separatist campaign. On his return to India he was imprisoned without trial until late 1988. Shortly after his release it became apparent that he had changed his political views; he now argued that Sikhs should pursue their cause using constitutional methods, a view which, according to the applicants, was unacceptable to many Sikhs. The former followers of Mr. Rode therefore became divided.

22. In the United Kingdom, according to the Government, this led to a split in the ISYF along broadly north/south lines. In the north of England most branches followed Mr. Rode, whereas in the south the ISYF became linked with another Punjab political activist, Dr Sohan Singh, who continued to support the campaign for an independent homeland. Mr. Chahal and, according to him, all major figures of spiritual and intellectual standing within the United Kingdom Sikh community were in the southern faction.

E. Mr. Chahal's alleged criminal activities

23. In October 1985 Mr. Chahal was detained under the Prevention of Terrorism (Temporary Provisions) Act 1984 ("PTA") on suspicion of involvement in a conspiracy to assassinate the Indian Prime Minister, Mr. Rajiv Gandhi, during an official visit to the United Kingdom. He was released for lack of evidence. In 1986 he was arrested and questioned twice (once under the PTA), because he was believed to be involved in an ISYF conspiracy to murder moderate Sikhs in the United Kingdom. On both occasions he was released without charge. Mr. Chahal denied involvement in any of these conspiracies.

24. In March 1986 he was charged with assault and affray following disturbances at the East Ham gurdwara in London. During the course of his trial on these charges in May 1987 there was a disturbance at the Belvedere gurdwara, which was widely reported in the national press. Mr. Chahal was arrested in connection with this incident, and was brought to court in handcuffs on the final day of his trial. He was convicted on both charges arising out of the East Ham incident, and served concurrent sentences of six and nine months.

He was subsequently acquitted of charges arising out of the Belvedere disturbance. On 27 July 1992 the Court of Appeal quashed the two convictions on the grounds that Mr. Chahal's appearance in court in handcuffs had been seriously prejudicial to him.

F. The deportation and asylum proceedings

1. The notice of intention to deport

25. On 14 August 1990 the Home Secretary (Mr Hurd) decided that Mr. Chahal ought to be deported because his continued presence in the United Kingdom was unconducive to the public good for reasons of national security and other reasons of a political nature, namely the international fight against terrorism.

A notice of intention to deport was served on the latter on 16 August 1990. He was then detained for deportation purposes pursuant to paragraph 2 (2) of Schedule III of the Immigration Act 1971 and has remained in custody ever since.

2. Mr. Chahal's application for asylum

26. Mr. Chahal claimed that if returned to India he had a well-founded fear of persecution within the terms of the United Nations 1951 Convention on the Status of Refugees and applied for political asylum on 16 August 1990. He was interviewed by officials from the Asylum Division of the Home Office on 11 September 1990 and his solicitors submitted written representations on his behalf. He claimed that he would be subjected to torture and persecution if returned to India. . . .

27. On 27 March 1991 the Home Secretary refused the request for asylum. In a letter to the applicant, he expressed the view that the latter's known support of Sikh separatism would be unlikely to attract the interest of the Indian authorities unless that support were to include acts of violence against India. . . .

3. The advisory panel

29. Because of the national security elements of the case, there was no right of appeal against the deportation order. However, on 10 June 1991, the matter was considered by an advisory panel, chaired by a Court of Appeal judge, Lord Justice Lloyd, and including a former president of the Immigration Appeal Tribunal. . . .

32. He appeared before the panel in person, and was allowed to call witnesses on his behalf, but was not allowed to be represented by a lawyer or to be informed of the advice which the panel gave to the Home Secretary.

33. On 25 July 1991 the Home Secretary (Mr Baker) signed an order for Mr. Chahal's deportation, which was served on 29 July.

4. Judicial review

34. On 9 August 1991 Mr. Chahal applied for judicial review of the Home Sec-retaries' decisions to refuse asylum and to make the deportation order. Leave was granted by the High Court on 2 September 1991.

The asylum refusal was quashed on 2 December 1991 and referred back to the Home Secretary. The court found that the reasoning behind it was inadequate, prin-cipally because the Home Secretary had neglected to explain whether he believed the evidence of Amnesty International relating to the situation in Punjab and, if not, the reasons for such disbelief. The court did not decide on the validity of the depor-tation order. Mr. Justice Popplewell expressed "enormous anxiety" about the case.

35. After further consideration, on 1 June 1992 the Home Secretary (Mr Clarke) took a fresh decision to refuse asylum. He considered that the breakdown of law and order in Punjab was due to the activities of Sikh terrorists and was not evidence of persecution within the terms of the 1951 Convention. Furthermore, relying upon Articles 32 and 33 of that Convention, he expressed the view that, even if Mr. Cha-hal were at risk of persecution, he would not be entitled to the protection of the 1951 Convention because of the threat he posed to national security.

36. Mr. Chahal applied for judicial review of this decision, but then requested a postponement on 4 June 1992, which was granted.

37. In a letter dated 2 July 1992, the Home Secretary informed the applicant that he declined to withdraw the deportation proceedings, that Mr. Chahal could be deported to any international airport of his choice within India and that the Home Secretary had sought and received an assurance from the Indian Government (which was subsequently repeated in December 1995) in the following terms:

> We have noted your request to have a formal assurance to the effect that, if Mr. Karamjit Singh Chahal were to be deported to India, he would enjoy the same legal protection as any other Indian citizen, and that he would have no reason to expect to suffer mistreatment of any kind at the hands of the Indian authorities. I have the hon-our to confirm the above.

38. On 16 July 1992 the High Court granted leave to apply for judicial review of the decisions of 1 June 1992 to maintain the refusal of asylum and of 2 July 1992 to proceed with the deportation. . . .

39. The Court of Appeal (Criminal Division) quashed Mr. Chahal's 1987 convic-tions on 27 July 1992. The Home Secretary reviewed the case in the light of this development, but concluded that it was right to proceed with the deportation.

[Further appeals were denied.]

G. Current conditions in India and in Punjab

44. The current position with regard to the protection of human rights in India generally and in Punjab more specifically was a matter of dispute between the par-ties. A substantial amount of evidence was presented to the Court on this issue. . . .

3. Reports to the United Nations

51. The reports to the United Nations in 1994 and 1995 of the Special Rapporteur on torture and other cruel, inhuman and degrading treatment or punishment and in 1994 of the Special Rapporteur on extrajudicial, summary or arbitrary executions

and the Working Group on enforced and involuntary disappearances recounted that human rights violations on the part of the security forces were widespread in India. . . .

4. The United States' Department of State reports

52. The 1995 United States' Department of State report on India told of human rights abuses perpetrated by the Punjab police acting outside their home State. . . .

53. In contrast, the most recent Department of State report (March 1996) declared that insurgent violence had largely disappeared in Punjab and that there was visible progress in correcting patterns of abuse by the police.

. . . .

AS TO THE LAW

I. ALLEGED VIOLATION OF ARTICLE 3 OF THE CONVENTION

72. The first applicant complained that his deportation to India would constitute a violation of Article 3 of the Convention.

A. Applicability of Article 3 in expulsion cases

73. As the Court has observed in the past, Contracting States have the right, as a matter of well-established international law and subject to their treaty obligations including the Convention, to control the entry, residence and expulsion of aliens. Moreover, it must be noted that the right to political asylum is not contained in either the Convention or its Protocols (see the *Vilvarajah and Others v. the United Kingdom* judgment of 30 October 1991, Series A no. 215, p. 34, para. 102).

74. However, it is well established in the case-law of the Court that expulsion by a Contracting State may give rise to an issue under Article 3, and hence engage the responsibility of that State under the Convention, where substantial grounds have been shown for believing that the person in question, if expelled, would face a real risk of being subjected to treatment contrary to Article 3 in the receiving country. In these circumstances, Article 3 implies the obligation not to expel the person in question to that country (see the *Soering v. the United Kingdom* judgment of 7 July 1989, Series A no. 161, p. 35, paras. 90–91, the *Cruz Varas and Others v. Sweden* judgment of 20 March 1991, Series A no. 201, p. 28, paras. 69–70, and the above-mentioned *Vilvarajah and Others* judgment, p. 34, para. 103). . . .

B. Expulsion cases involving an alleged danger to national security

. . . .

79. Article 3 enshrines one of the most fundamental values of democratic society (see the *Soering* judgment, p. 34, para. 88). The Court is well aware of the immense difficulties faced by States in modern times in protecting their communities from terrorist violence. However, even in these circumstances, the Convention prohibits in absolute terms torture or inhuman or degrading treatment or punishment, irrespective of the victim's conduct. Unlike most of the substantive clauses of the Convention and of Protocols Nos. 1 and 4 (P1, P4), Article 3 makes no provision for exceptions and no derogation from it is permissible under Article 15 even in the event of a public emergency threatening the life of the nation (see the *Ireland v. the*

United Kingdom judgment of 18 January 1978, Series A no. 25, p. 65, para. 163, and also the *Tomasi v. France* judgment of 27 August 1992, Series A no. 241-A, p. 42, para. 115).

80. The prohibition provided by Article 3 against ill-treatment is equally absolute in expulsion cases. Thus, whenever substantial grounds have been shown for believing that an individual would face a real risk of being subjected to treatment contrary to Article 3 if removed to another State, the responsibility of the Contracting State to safeguard him or her against such treatment is engaged in the event of expulsion (see the *Vilvarajah and Others* judgment, p. 34, para. 103). In these circumstances, the activities of the individual in question, however undesirable or dangerous, cannot be a material consideration. The protection afforded by Article 3 is thus wider than that provided by Articles 32 and 33 of the United Nations 1951 Convention on the Status of Refugees.

81. Paragraph 88 of the Court's above-mentioned Soering judgment, which concerned extradition to the United States, clearly and forcefully expresses the above view. It should not be inferred from the Court's remarks concerning the risk of undermining the foundations of extradition, as set out in paragraph 89 of the same judgment, that there is any room for balancing the risk of ill-treatment against the reasons for expulsion in determining whether a State's responsibility under Article 3 is engaged.

82. It follows from the above that it is not necessary for the Court to enter into a consideration of the Government's untested, but no doubt bona fide, allegations about the first applicant's terrorist activities and the threat posed by him to national security.

C. Application of Article 3 in the circumstances of the case

. . . .

97. In determining whether it has been substantiated that there is a real risk that the applicant, if expelled to India, would be subjected to treatment contrary to Article 3, the Court will assess all the material placed before it and, if necessary, material obtained of its own motion (see the *Vilvarajah and Others* judgment, p. 36, para. 107). Furthermore, since the material point in time for the assessment of risk is the date of the Court's consideration of the case, it will be necessary to take account of evidence which has come to light since the Commission's review.

98. In view of the Government's proposal to return Mr. Chahal to the airport of his choice in India, it is necessary for the Court to evaluate the risk of his being ill-treated with reference to conditions throughout India rather than in Punjab alone. However, it must be borne in mind that the first applicant is a well-known supporter of Sikh separatism. It follows from these observations that evidence relating to the fate of Sikh militants at the hands of the security forces outside the State of Punjab is of particular relevance.

99. The Court has taken note of the Government's comments relating to the material contained in the reports of Amnesty International. Nonetheless, it attaches weight to some of the most striking allegations contained in those reports, particularly with regard to extrajudicial killings allegedly perpetrated by the Punjab police outside their home State and the action taken by the Indian Supreme Court, the

West Bengal State Government and the Union Home Secretary in response. Moreover, similar assertions were accepted by the United Kingdom Immigration Appeal Tribunal in *Charan Singh Gill v. Secretary of State for the Home Department* and were included in the 1995 United States' State Department report on India. The 1994 National Human Rights Commission's report on Punjab substantiated the impression of a police force completely beyond the control of lawful authority.

100. The Court is persuaded by this evidence, which has been corroborated by material from a number of different objective sources, that, until mid-1994 at least, elements in the Punjab police were accustomed to act without regard to the human rights of suspected Sikh militants and were fully capable of pursuing their targets into areas of India far away from Punjab.

101. The Commission found in paragraph 111 of its report that there had in recent years been an improvement in the protection of human rights in India, especially in Punjab, and evidence produced subsequent to the Commission's consideration of the case indicates that matters continue to advance.

In particular, it would appear that the insurgent violence in Punjab has abated; the Court notes the very substantial reduction in terrorist-related deaths in the region as indicated by the respondent Government. Furthermore, other encouraging events have reportedly taken place in Punjab in recent years, such as the return of democratic elections, a number of court judgments against police officers, the appointment of an ombudsman to investigate abuses of power and the promise of the new Chief Minister to "ensure transparency and accountability". In addition, the 1996 United States' State Department report asserts that during 1995 "there was visible progress in correcting patterns of abuse by the [Punjab] police".

102. Nonetheless, the evidence demonstrates that problems still persist in connection with the observance of human rights by the security forces in Punjab. As the respondent Government themselves recounted, the United Kingdom High Commission in India continues to receive complaints about the Punjab police, although in recent months these have related mainly to extortion rather than to politically motivated abuses. Amnesty International alleged that "disappearances" of notable Sikhs at the hands of the Punjab police continued sporadically throughout 1995 and the 1996 State Department report referred to the killing of two Sikh militants that year.

103. Moreover, the Court finds it most significant that no concrete evidence has been produced of any fundamental reform or reorganization of the Punjab police in recent years. The evidence referred to above would indicate that such a process was urgently required, and indeed this was the recommendation of the NHRC. Although there was a change in the leadership of the Punjab police in 1995, the director general who presided over some of the worst abuses this decade has only been replaced by his former deputy and intelligence chief.

Less than two years ago this same police force was carrying out well-documented raids into other Indian States and the Court cannot entirely discount the applicant's claims that any recent reduction in activity stems from the fact that key figures in the campaign for Sikh separatism have all either been killed, forced abroad or rendered inactive by torture or the fear of torture. Furthermore, it would appear from press reports that evidence of the full extent of past abuses is only now coming to light.

104. Although the Court is of the opinion that Mr. Chahal, if returned to India, would be most at risk from the Punjab security forces acting either within or outside State boundaries, it also attaches significance to the fact that attested allegations of serious human rights violations have been levelled at the police elsewhere in India. In this respect, the Court notes that the United Nations' Special Rapporteur on torture has described the practice of torture upon those in police custody as "endemic" and has complained that inadequate measures are taken to bring those responsible to justice. The NHRC has also drawn attention to the problems of widespread, often fatal, mistreatment of prisoners and has called for a systematic reform of the police throughout India.

105. Although the Court does not doubt the good faith of the Indian Government in providing the assurances mentioned above, it would appear that, despite the efforts of that Government, the NHRC and the Indian courts to bring about reform, the violation of human rights by certain members of the security forces in Punjab and elsewhere in India is a recalcitrant and enduring problem.

Against this background, the Court is not persuaded that the above assurances would provide Mr. Chahal with an adequate guarantee of safety.

106. The Court further considers that the applicant's high profile would be more likely to increase the risk to him of harm than otherwise. It is not disputed that Mr. Chahal is well known in India to support the cause of Sikh separatism and to have had close links with other leading figures in that struggle. The respondent Government have made serious, albeit untested, allegations of his involvement in terrorism which are undoubtedly known to the Indian authorities. The Court is of the view that these factors would be likely to make him a target of interest for hard-line elements in the security forces who have relentlessly pursued suspected Sikh militants in the past.

107. For all the reasons outlined above, in particular the attested involvement of the Punjab police in killings and abductions outside their State and the allegations of serious human rights violations which continue to be levelled at members of the Indian security forces elsewhere, the Court finds it substantiated that there is a real risk of Mr. Chahal being subjected to treatment contrary to Article 3 if he is returned to India.

Accordingly, the order for his deportation to India would, if executed, give rise to a violation of Article 3.

   . . . .

FOR THESE REASONS, THE COURT

1. Holds by twelve votes to seven that, in the event of the Secretary of State's decision to deport the first applicant to India being implemented, there would be a violation of Article 3 of the Convention;. . . .

5. Holds unanimously that there has been a violation of Article 13 in conjunction with Article 3 of the Convention;

6. Holds unanimously that the above findings of violation constitute sufficient just satisfaction as regards the claim for compensation for non-pecuniary damage. . . .

Questions and Comments

1. In the *Wos* case, the European Court of Human Rights makes the following statement: "there is no general obligation under the Convention for States to compensate wrongs inflicted in the past under the general cover of State authority." Why not?

2. Do you agree with the European Court's judgment in the Chahal case? Is it appropriate to hold a state party to the European Convention responsible for conduct undertaken by a state outside the system? Does the Court give any deference to the assurances of the Indian government? Should it? Should the Inter-American Commission refer or defer to this judgment in any case brought to challenge the United States rendition policy that allegedly sends suspected terrorists to countries that have been found to practice torture? Is the European Court correct that matters of national security cannot be balanced against the guarantees of Article 3? Why?

3. As some of the prior cases illustrate, regional tribunals have been clear that a state has an obligation not only to refrain from violating guaranteed rights, but also to prevent such violations being committed by private actors. The following section considers this question with a more general look at the nature and scope of state obligations.

3. The Nature of State Obligations

D. Shelton, "Private Violence, Public Wrongs, and the Responsibility of States" 13 Fordham Int'l L.J. (1989–90) 1. [Footnotes renumbered.]

International practice has long made clear that both acts and omissions may give rise to international liability, depending on the duty imposed under international law. In fact, one United Nations report noted that "the cases in which the international responsibility of a State has been invoked on the basis of an omission are perhaps more numerous than those based on action taken by a State." For example, in the *Russian Indemnity* case, the Permanent Court of Arbitration defined fault to include "an unlawful act or omission." Similarly, in the *Corfu Channel* case, Albania was held responsible for its failure to act because it knew or should have known of the illegal conduct involved. The International Court of Justice (the "ICJ") held that "it cannot be concluded from the mere fact of the control exercised by a State over its territory and waters that that State necessarily knew, or ought to have known, of any unlawful act perpetrated therein, nor yet that it necessarily knew, or should have known, the authors." However, once the evidence established that Albania knew or should have known of the illegal minelaying, its failure to act made the conduct imputable to it.

More recently, U.S. actions or inactions in regard to the contras gave rise to a Nicaraguan claim "attributing responsibility to the United States for activities of the contras," including the killing, wounding, or kidnapping of citizens of Nicaragua.[3] The International Court of Justice had to decide

> whether or not the relationship of the contras to the United States Government was so much one of dependence on the one side and control on the other that it would

---

[3] *Military and Paramilitary Activities in and Against Nicaragua (Nicar. v. U.S.)*, 1986, ICJ 4,63–64, para. 113 (Judgment of June 27).

be right to equate the contras, for legal purposes, with an organ of the United States Government, or as acting on behalf of that Government.[4]

The ICJ found that "there is no clear evidence of the United States having actually exercised such a degree of control in all fields as to justify treating the contras as acting on its behalf."[5] The Court took the following view:

> United States participation, even if preponderant or decisive, in the financing, orga-
> nizing, training, supplying and equipping of the contras, the selection of its military or
> paramilitary targets, and the planning of the whole of its operation, is still insufficient
> in itself, on the basis of the evidence in the possession of the Court, for the purpose
> of attributing to the United States the acts committed by the contras in the course of
> their military or paramilitary operations in Nicaragua. All the forms of United States
> participation mentioned above, and even the general control by the respondent State
> over a force with a high degree of dependency on it, would not in themselves mean,
> without further evidence, that the United States directed or enforced the perpetration
> of the acts contrary to human rights and humanitarian law alleged by the applicant
> States. Such acts could well be committed by members of the contras without the
> control of the United States. For this conduct to give rise to legal responsibility of
> the United States, it would in principle have to be proved that that State had effective
> control of the military or paramilitary operations in the course of which the alleged
> violations were committed.[6]

The ICJ therefore found that acts of the contras could not be imputed to the United States. The only question left for the court was whether any acts of the United States directly engaged its responsibility.[7] In this regard, it was relevant whether the United States "was, or must have been, aware at the relevant time that allegations of breaches of humanitarian law were being made against the contras."[8] In this context, the ICJ found the United States responsible for the publication of the manual on "Psychological Operations in Guerrilla Warfare," which could be seen to encourage violations of international humanitarian law.[9]

Section 207 of the *Restatement (Third) of the Foreign Relations Law of the United States* (the "Restatement") also provides that a state is responsible for any violation of its obligations under international law whether these violations result from action or inaction. The official comment to section 207 notes that "a state is responsible for injuries caused by . . . official failures, such as the failure to provide aliens reasonable police protection;" however, "the state is not responsible for injuries caused by private persons that result despite such police protection."

Similarly, the draft code of the law of state responsibility under consideration by the International Law Commission since 1963, declares that the conduct of private individuals shall not be considered acts of state. The Draft Code notes, however, that the state is responsible for inaction when it fails to carry out an international obligation to act.

---

4 Id. at 62, para. 109.
5 Id.
6 Id. at 64–65, para. 115.
7 Id. at 65, para. 116.
8 Id.
9 Id. at 129–30, paras. 254–56.

Fault

The issue of standard of care necessarily arose when a state's liability for the safety of foreign nationals was considered. It similarly arises in the context of human rights protections. Neither doctrine nor case law has arrived at a definitive determination of the limits of state responsibility, especially where the acts of private individuals are concerned. It has been questioned whether the state is strictly liable for human rights violations or whether there must be a basis in fault for attributing the violation to the state. . . .

With regard to aliens, a state was and is not held to guarantee the safety of an alien, but is responsible for injury when police protection falls below a minimum standard of reasonableness.[10] What constitutes reasonable police protection depends on all the circumstances. Of course, the state is also responsible for injuries resulting from private violence encouraged by government officials. The Honduran cases make clear that these same obligations of states are assured to all with regard to human rights guaranteed under the American Convention.

In order for the state to be liable, however, there must be a harmful act committed by an individual or group. In addition, it must also be possible to attribute to the state some conduct with respect to the act that implies the non-performance of an international duty. . . .

The duty of states has traditionally been formulated in terms of the concept of due diligence with regard to the protection of aliens. The Harvard Law School Draft on State Responsibility (the "Harvard Draft") provides that, where criminal conduct is concerned, "failure to exercise due diligence to afford protection to an alien, by way of preventive or deterrent measures, against any act wrongfully committed by any person" gives rise to state responsibility, as does failure to exercise due diligence to apprehend and to hold any person committing such an act.

The due diligence standard established that a state is not responsible for purely private harm. Tribunals also have made this clear, as, for example, in the Noyes case.'[11] This claim was brought after Noyes, a U.S. citizen driving through a village in Panama, was assaulted by participants in a political gathering that became violent. Noyes was assisted by a policeman who tried to prevent further violence. In rejecting Noyes' claim that Panama was responsible for his injuries, the Commission stated that

> [t]he mere fact that an alien has suffered at the hands of private persons an aggression, which could have been averted by the presence of a sufficient police force on the spot, does not make a government liable for damages under international law. There must be shown special circumstances from which the responsibility of the authorities arises: either their behavior in connection with the particular occurrence, or a general failure to comply with their duty to maintain order, to prevent crimes or to . . . punish criminals.[12]

Liability for lack of due diligence results from more than mere negligence on the part of state officials and, of course, from wilful conduct. Due diligence consists of

---

[10]   See Restatement (Third) of Foreign Relations (1987), para. 207 comment c.
[11]   *WA. Noyes Case* (Pan-U.S.), General Claims Commission, 6 R.Int'l Arb. Awards 308 (1933).
[12]   *Id.*

the reasonable measures of prevention that a well-administered government could be expected to exercise under similar circumstances. In U.S. tort law terms, "the [danger] reasonably to be perceived defines the duty to be obeyed."[13]

It is not lightly assumed that a state is responsible. "In other words, a State is not responsible unless it displayed, in the conduct of its organs or officials, patent or manifest negligence in taking the measures which are normally taken in the particular circumstances to prevent or punish the injurious acts."[14] Thus, a state's responsibility is not engaged by the private injurious act, but as a consequence of the response of its authorities to the act. . . .

In the *Iranian Hostage* case, the International Court of Justice held Iran responsible for the acts of the militants who seized the U.S. Embassy. While the acts were not initially "directly imputable to the Iranian State," the Iranian Government's subsequent approval of the militants' actions made them so. Moreover, Iran's failure "to take appropriate steps" to protect the Embassy "by itself constituted a clear and serious violation" of international law. . . .

In the *Neer* case, the Claims Commissioners held that international standards obligated governmental authorities to take affirmative actions to investigate and apprehend a wrongdoer and that failure to do so would be a breach of a legal duty, giving rise to international responsibility.

Rationale

It may prove difficult to draw the line between direct responsibility for complicity in wrongful acts and failure to exercise due diligence to protect against private violence. It is sometimes stated that the rationale for imposing liability on a state for failure to act to prevent or to remedy wrongful private conduct derives from a sense of the state's complicity in the wrongful acts.

In the *Janes* arbitration,[15] the Commissioners cautioned against too great a reliance on this factor in explaining why the Mexican government should be held liable for failing to apprehend and punish the killers of a United States national:

> At times international awards have held that, if a State shows serious lack of diligence in apprehending and/or punishing culprits, its liability is a derivative liability, assuming the character of some kind of complicity with the perpetrator himself and rendering the State responsible for the very consequences of the individual's misdemeanor. . . . The reasons upon which such a finding of complicity is usually based in cases in which a Government could not possibly have prevented the crime, is that the nonpunishment must be deemed to disclose some kind of approval of what has occurred, especially so if the Government has permitted the guilty parties to escape or has remitted the punishment by granting either pardon or amnesty. A reasoning based on presumed complicity may have some sound foundation in cases of nonprevention where a Government knows of an *intended* injurious crime, might have averted it, but for some reason constituting its liability did not do so. The present case is different; it is one of nonrepression. . . . [T]he Government is liable for not having measured

---

13 *Palsgraf v. Long Island R.R.*, 248 N.Y. 339, 344, 162 N.E. 99, 100 (1928).

14 F.V. GARCIA-AMADOR, L. SOHN & R. BAXTER, RECENT CODIFICATION OF THE LAW OF STATE RESPONSIBILITY FOR INJURIES TO ALIENS (1974) at 27.

15 *Laura MB. Janes (U.S. v. Mex.)* United States and United Mexican States Claims Commission, Op. of Comm'rs 108 (1927).

up to its duty of diligently prosecuting and properly punishing the offender . . . Even if the nonpunishment were conceived as some kind of approval—which in the Commission's view is doubtful—still approving of a crime has never been deemed identical with being an accomplice to that crime; and even if nonpunishment of a murdered really amounted to complicity in the murder, still it is not permissible to treat this derivative and remote liability not as an attenuate form of responsibility, but as just as serious as if the Government had perpetrated the killing with its own hands.'[16]

Although certain governmental actions will give rise to a sense of complicity in the private violations that occur, the *Janes* Commissioners and the Inter-American Court properly note that the state's responsibility actually derives from the breach of independent legal obligations. (. . .)

The following case is the first in the regional systems to address government obligations to reduce the risks to persons within its jurisdiction posed by hazardous economic activities. Central to the case is the question of the standard of care the government must exercise to avoid being held responsible for violating human rights. What standard is imposed by the European Court and is it appropriate?

Öneryildiz v. Turkey [GC], (App. no. 48938/99), Judgment of 30 November 2004, Eur. Ct. H.R. (references omitted).

. . . .

9. The applicant was born in 1955 and is now living in the district of Şirvan . . . , the area where he was born. At the material time he was living with twelve close relatives in the slum quarter (*gecekondu mahallesi*) of Kazem Karabekir in Ümraniye, a district of Istanbul, where he had moved after resigning from his post as a village guard in south-eastern Turkey.

10. Since the early 1970s a household-refuse tip had been in operation in Hekimbaşi a slum area adjoining Kazem Karabekir. On 22 January 1960 Istanbul City Council . . . had been granted use of the land, which belonged to the Forestry Commission (and therefore to the Treasury), for a term of ninety-nine years. Situated on a slope overlooking a valley, the site spread out over a surface area of approximately 350,000 sq. m and from 1972 onwards was used as a rubbish tip by the districts of Beykoz, Üsküdar, Kadeköy and Ümraniye under the authority and responsibility of the city council and, ultimately, the ministerial authorities. When the rubbish tip started being used, the area was uninhabited and the closest built-up area was approximately 3.5 km away. However, as the years passed, rudimentary dwellings were built without any authorisation in the area surrounding the rubbish tip, which eventually developed into the slums of Ümraniye. . . .

13. On 9 April 1991 Ümraniye District Council applied to the Third Division of the Üsküdar District Court for experts to be appointed to determine whether the rubbish tip complied with the relevant regulations, in particular the Regulations of 14 March 1991 on Solid-Waste Control. The district council also applied for an assessment of the damage it had sustained, as evidence in support of an action for

---

16 Id. at 114–15, paras. 19–20 (emphasis in original).

damages it was preparing to bring against the city council and the councils of the three other districts that used the tip. . . .

According to the experts' report, drawn up on 7 May 1991, the rubbish tip in question did not conform to the technical requirements set forth, inter alia, in regulations 24–27, 30 and 38 of the Regulations of 14 March 1991 and, accordingly, presented a number of dangers liable to give rise to a major health risk for the inhabitants of the valley, particularly those living in the slum areas: no walls or fencing separated the tip from the dwellings fifty metres away from the mountain of refuse; the tip was not equipped with collection, composting, recycling or combustion systems; and no drainage or drainage-water purification systems had been installed. The experts concluded that the Ümraniye tip "exposed humans, animals and the environment to all kinds of risks." In that connection the report, drawing attention first to the fact that some twenty contagious diseases might spread, underlined the following:

> . . . In any waste-collection site gases such as methane, carbon dioxide and hydrogen sulphide form. These substances must be collected and . . . burnt under supervision. However, the tip in question is not equipped with such a system. If methane is mixed with air in a particular proportion, it can explode. This installation contains no means of preventing an explosion of the methane produced as a result of the decomposition [of the waste]. May God preserve us, as the damage could be very substantial given the neighboring dwellings. . . .

On 27 May 1991 the report was brought to the attention of the four councils in question, and on 7 June 1991 the governor was informed of it and asked to brief the Ministry of Health and the Prime Minister's Environment Office.

14. Kadeköy and Üsküdar District Councils and the city council applied on 3, 5 and 9 June 1991 respectively to have the expert report set aside. In their notice of application the councils' lawyers simply stated that the report, which had been ordered and drawn up without their knowledge, contravened the Code of Civil Procedure. The three lawyers reserved the right to file supplementary pleadings in support of their objections once they had obtained all the necessary information and documents from their authorities. As none of the parties filed supplementary pleadings to that end, the proceedings were discontinued.

15. However, the Environment Office, which had been advised of the report on 18 June 1991, made a recommendation (no. 09513) urging the Istanbul Governor's Office, the city council and Ümraniye District Council to remedy the problems identified in the present case. . . .

16. On 27 August 1992 Şinasi Öktem, the mayor of Ümraniye, applied to the First Division of the Üsküdar District Court for the implementation of temporary measures to prevent the city council and the neighbouring district councils from using the waste-collection site. He requested, in particular, that no further waste be dumped, that the tip be closed and that redress be provided in respect of the damage sustained by his district.

On 3 November 1992 Istanbul City Council's representative opposed that request. Emphasizing the city council's efforts to maintain the roads leading to the rubbish tip and to prevent the spread of diseases, the emission of odors and the destruction of stray dogs, the representative submitted, in particular, that a plan to redevelop the site of the tip had been put out to tender. As regards the request for the temporary closure of the tip, the representative asserted that Ümraniye District Council was acting in bad faith in that, since it had been set up in 1987, it had done nothing to decontaminate the site.

The City Council had indeed issued a call for tenders for the development of new sites conforming to modern standards. The first planning contract was awarded to the American firm CVH2M Hill International Ltd, and on 21 December 1992 and 17 February 1993 new sites were designed for the European and Anatolian sides of Istanbul respectively. The project was due for completion in the course of 1993.

17. While those proceedings were still pending, Ümraniye District Council informed the mayor of Istanbul that from 15 May 1993 the dumping of waste would no longer be authorised.

18. On 28 April 1993 at about 11 a.m. a methane explosion occurred at the site. Following a landslide caused by mounting pressure, the refuse erupted from the mountain of waste and engulfed some ten slum dwellings situated below it, including the one belonging to the applicant. Thirty-nine people died in the accident. . . .

I. ALLEGED VIOLATION OF ARTICLE 2 OF THE CONVENTION

69. Taking the parties' arguments as a whole, the Court reiterates, firstly, that its approach to the interpretation of Article 2 is guided by the idea that the object and purpose of the Convention as an instrument for the protection of individual human beings requires its provisions to be interpreted and applied in such a way as to make its safeguards practical and effective.

70. In the instant case the complaint before the Court is that the national authorities did not do all that could have been expected of them to prevent the deaths of the applicant's close relatives in the accident of 28 April 1993 at the Ümraniye municipal rubbish tip, which was operated under the authorities' control.

71. In this connection, the Court reiterates that Article 2 does not solely concern deaths resulting from the use of force by agents of the State but also, in the first sentence of its first paragraph, lays down a positive obligation on States to take appropriate steps to safeguard the lives of those within their jurisdiction.

The Court considers that this obligation must be construed as applying in the context of any activity, whether public or not, in which the right to life may be at stake, and a fortiori in the case of industrial activities, which by their very nature are dangerous, such as the operation of waste-collection sites. . . .

74. To sum up, it considers that the applicant's complaint undoubtedly falls within the ambit of the first sentence of Article 2, which is therefore applicable in the instant case.

B. Compliance

(a) General principles applicable in the present case

(i) Principles relating to the prevention of infringements of the right to life as a result of dangerous activities: the substantive aspect of Article 2 of the Convention

89. The positive obligation to take all appropriate steps to safeguard life for the purposes of Article 2 entails above all a primary duty on the State to put in place a

legislative and administrative framework designed to provide effective deterrence against threats to the right to life.

90. This obligation indisputably applies in the particular context of dangerous activities, where, in addition, special emphasis must be placed on regulations geared to the special features of the activity in question, particularly with regard to the level of the potential risk to human lives. They must govern the licensing, setting up, operation, security and supervision of the activity and must make it compulsory for all those concerned to take practical measures to ensure the effective protection of citizens whose lives might be endangered by the inherent risks. . . .

(ii) Principles relating to the judicial response required in the event of alleged infringements of the right to life: the procedural aspect of Article 2 of the Convention

91. The obligations deriving from Article 2 do not end there. Where lives have been lost in circumstances potentially engaging the responsibility of the State, that provision entails a duty for the State to ensure, by all means at its disposal, an adequate response—judicial or otherwise—so that the legislative and administrative framework set up to protect the right to life is properly implemented and any breaches of that right are repressed and punished.

92. In this connection, the Court has held that if the infringement of the right to life or to physical integrity is not caused intentionally, the positive obligation to set up an "effective judicial system" does not necessarily require criminal proceedings to be brought in every case and may be satisfied if civil, administrative or even disciplinary remedies were available to the victims.

93. However, in areas such as that in issue in the instant case, the applicable principles are rather to be found in those which the Court has already had occasion to develop in relation notably to the use of lethal force, principles which lend themselves to application in other categories of cases. In this connection, it should be pointed out that in cases of homicide the interpretation of Article 2 as entailing an obligation to conduct an official investigation is justified not only because any allegations of such an offence normally give rise to criminal liability, but also because often, in practice, the true circumstances of the death are, or may be, largely confined within the knowledge of State officials or authorities.

In the Court's view, such considerations are indisputably valid in the context of dangerous activities, when lives have been lost as a result of events occurring under the responsibility of the public authorities, which are often the only entities to have sufficient relevant knowledge to identify and establish the complex phenomena that might have caused such incidents.

Where it is established that the negligence attributable to State officials or bodies on that account goes beyond an error of judgment or carelessness, in that the authorities in question, fully realizing the likely consequences and disregarding the powers vested in them, failed to take measures that were necessary and sufficient to avert the risks inherent in a dangerous activity, the fact that those responsible for endangering life have not been charged with a criminal offence or prosecuted may amount to a violation of Article 2, irrespective of any other types of remedy which individuals may exercise on their own initiative; this is amply evidenced by developments in the relevant European standards.

94. To sum up, the judicial system required by Article 2 must make provision for an independent and impartial official investigation procedure that satisfies certain minimum standards as to effectiveness and is capable of ensuring that criminal penalties are applied where lives are lost as a result of a dangerous activity if and to the extent that this is justified by the findings of the investigation. In such cases, the competent authorities must act with exemplary diligence and promptness and must of their own motion initiate investigations capable of, firstly, ascertaining the circumstances in which the incident took place and any shortcomings in the operation of the regulatory system and, secondly, identifying the State officials or authorities involved in whatever capacity in the chain of events in issue.

95. That said, the requirements of Article 2 go beyond the stage of the official investigation, where this has led to the institution of proceedings in the national courts; the proceedings as a whole, including the trial stage, must satisfy the requirements of the positive obligation to protect lives through the law.

96. It should in no way be inferred from the foregoing that Article 2 may entail the right for an applicant to have third parties prosecuted or sentenced for a criminal offence or an absolute obligation for all prosecutions to result in conviction, or indeed in a particular sentence.

On the other hand, the national courts should not under any circumstances be prepared to allow life-endangering offences to go unpunished. This is essential for maintaining public confidence and ensuring adherence to the rule of law and for preventing any appearance of tolerance of or collusion in unlawful acts. The Court's task therefore consists in reviewing whether and to what extent the courts, in reaching their conclusion, may be deemed to have submitted the case to the careful scrutiny required by Article 2 of the Convention, so that the deterrent effect of the judicial system in place and the significance of the role it is required to play in preventing violations of the right to life are not undermined.

(b) Assessment of the facts of the case in the light of these principles

(i) Responsibility borne by the State for the deaths in the instant case, in the light of the substantive aspect of Article 2 of the Convention

97. In the instant case the Court notes at the outset that in both of the fields of activity central to the present case—the operation of household-refuse tips . . . and the rehabilitation and clearance of slum areas . . .—there are safety regulations in force in Turkey.

It must therefore determine whether the legal measures applicable to the situation in issue in the instant case call for criticism and whether the national authorities actually complied with the relevant regulations.

98. To that end, the Court considers that it should begin by noting a decisive factor for the assessment of the circumstances of the case, namely that there was practical information available to the effect that the inhabitants of certain slum areas of Ümraniye were faced with a threat to their physical integrity on account of the technical shortcomings of the municipal rubbish tip. . . .

100. The Court considers that neither the reality nor the immediacy of the danger in question is in dispute, seeing that the risk of an explosion had clearly come

into being long before it was highlighted in the report of 7 May 1991 and that, as the site continued to operate in the same conditions, that risk could only have increased during the period until it materialized on 28 April 1993.

101. The Grand Chamber accordingly agrees with the Chamber that it was impossible for the administrative and municipal departments responsible for supervising and managing the tip not to have known of the risks inherent in methanogenesis or of the necessary preventive measures, particularly as there were specific regulations on the matter. Furthermore, the Court likewise regards it as established that various authorities were also aware of those risks, at least by 27 May 1991, when they were notified of the report of 7 May 1991.

It follows that the Turkish authorities at several levels knew or ought to have known that there was a real and immediate risk to a number of persons living near the Ümraniye municipal rubbish tip. They consequently had a positive obligation under Article 2 of the Convention to take such preventive operational measures as were necessary and sufficient to protect those individuals, especially as they themselves had set up the site and authorised its operation, which gave rise to the risk in question.

102. However, it appears from the evidence before the Court that the city council in particular not only failed to take the necessary urgent measures, either before or after 14 March 1991, but also—as the Chamber observed—opposed the recommendation to that effect by the Prime Minister's Environment Office. The Environment Office had called for the tip to be brought into line with the standards laid down in regulations 24 to 27 of the Regulations on Solid-Waste Control, the last-mentioned of which explicitly required the installation of a "vertical and horizontal drainage system" allowing the controlled release into the atmosphere of the gas accumulated.

103. The city council also opposed the final attempt by the mayor of Ümraniye to apply to the courts, on 27 August 1992, for the temporary closure of the waste-collection site. It based its opposition on the ground that the district council in question was not entitled to seek the closure of the site because it had hitherto made no effort to decontaminate it. Besides that ground, the Government also relied on the conclusions of the Chapman v. the United Kingdom judgment and criticised the applicant for having knowingly chosen to break the law and live in the vicinity of the rubbish tip.

However, those arguments do not stand up to scrutiny for the following reasons.

104. In the instant case, the Court has examined the provisions of domestic law regarding the transfer to third parties of public property, whether inside or outside the "slum rehabilitation and clearance zones." It has also studied the impact of various legislative initiatives designed to extend in practice the scope ratione temporis of Law no. 775 of 20 July 1966.

The Court concludes from these legal considerations that in spite of the statutory prohibitions in the field of town planning, the State's consistent policy on slum areas encouraged the integration of such areas into the urban environment and hence acknowledged their existence and the way of life of the citizens who had gradually caused them to build up since 1960, whether of their own free will or simply as a result of that policy. Seeing that this policy effectively established an amnesty for breaches of town-planning regulations, including the unlawful occupation of public property, it must have created uncertainty as to the extent of the discretion enjoyed by the administrative authorities responsible for applying the measures prescribed by law, which could not therefore have been regarded as foreseeable by the public.

105. This interpretation is, moreover, borne out in the instant case by the administrative authorities' attitude towards the applicant.

The Court observes that between the unauthorized construction of the house in issue in 1988 and the accident of 28 April 1993, the applicant remained in possession of his dwelling, despite the fact that during that time his position remained subject to the rules laid down in Law no. 775, in particular section 18, by which the municipal authorities could have destroyed the dwelling at any time. Indeed, this was what the Government suggested, although they were unable to show that in the instant case the relevant authorities had even envisaged taking any such measure against the applicant.

The authorities let the applicant and his close relatives live entirely undisturbed in their house, in the social and family environment they had created. Furthermore, regard being had to the concrete evidence adduced before the Court and not rebutted by the Government, there is no cause to call into question the applicant's assertion that the authorities also levied council tax on him and on the other inhabitants of the Ümraniye slums and provided them with public services, for which they were charged.

106. In those circumstances, it would be hard for the Government to maintain legitimately that any negligence or lack of foresight should be attributed to the victims of the accident of 28 April 1993, or to rely on the Court's conclusions in the case of Chapman v. the United Kingdom, in which the British authorities were not found to have remained passive in the face of Mrs Chapman's unlawful actions.

It remains for the Court to address the Government's other arguments relating, in general, to: the scale of the rehabilitation projects carried out by the city council at the time in order to alleviate the problems caused by the Ümraniye waste-collection site; the amount invested, which was said to have influenced the way in which the national authorities chose to deal with the situation at the site; and, lastly, the humanitarian considerations which at the time allegedly precluded any measure entailing the immediate and wholesale destruction of the slum areas.

107. The Court acknowledges that it is not its task to substitute for the views of the local authorities its own view of the best policy to adopt in dealing with the social, economic and urban problems in this part of Istanbul. It therefore accepts the Government's argument that in this respect, an impossible or disproportionate burden must not be imposed on the authorities without consideration being given, in particular, to the operational choices which they must make in terms of priorities and resources; this results from the wide margin of appreciation which States enjoy, as the Court has previously held, in difficult social and technical spheres such as the one in issue in the instant case.

However, even when seen from this perspective, the Court does not find the Government's arguments convincing. The preventive measures required by the positive obligation in question fall precisely within the powers conferred on the authorities and may reasonably be regarded as a suitable means of averting the risk brought to their attention. The Court considers that the timely installation of a gas-extraction system at the Ümraniye tip before the situation became fatal could have been an effective measure without diverting the State's resources to an excessive degree in breach of Article 65 of the Turkish Constitution or giving rise to policy problems to the extent alleged by the Government. Such a measure would not only have complied with Turkish regulations and general practice in the area, but would also have been a much better reflection of the humanitarian considerations which the Government relied on before the Court. . . .

109. In the light of the foregoing, the Court cannot see any reason to cast doubt on the domestic investigating authorities' findings of fact and considers that the circumstances examined above show that in the instant case the State's responsibility was engaged under Article 2 in several respects.

Firstly, the regulatory framework proved defective in that the Ümraniye municipal waste-collection site was opened and operated despite not conforming to the relevant technical standards and there was no coherent supervisory system to encourage those responsible to take steps to ensure adequate protection of the public and coordination and cooperation between the various administrative authorities so that the risks brought to their attention did not become so serious as to endanger human lives.

That situation, exacerbated by a general policy which proved powerless in dealing with general town-planning issues and created uncertainty as to the application of statutory measures, undoubtedly played a part in the sequence of events leading to the tragic accident of 28 April 1993, which ultimately claimed the lives of inhabitants of the Ümraniye slums, because the State officials and authorities did not do everything within their power to protect them from the immediate and known risks to which they were exposed.

110. Such circumstances give rise to a violation of Article 2 of the Convention in its substantive aspect; the Government's submission relating to the favourable outcome of the administrative action brought in the instant case . . . is of no consequence here, for the reasons set . . . out . . . below.

(ii) Responsibility borne by the State as regards the judicial response required on account of the deaths, in the light of the procedural aspect of Article 2 of the Convention. . . .

112. . . . It remains to be determined whether the measures taken in the framework of the Turkish criminal-law system following the accident at the Ümraniye municipal rubbish tip were satisfactory in practice, regard being had to the requirements of the Convention in this respect. . . .

38. In this connection, the Court notes that immediately after the accident had occurred on 28 April 1993 at about 11 a.m., the police arrived on the scene and interviewed the victims' families. In addition, the Istanbul Governor's Office set up a crisis unit, whose members went to the site on the same day. On the following day,

29 April 1993, the Ministry of the Interior ordered, of its own motion, the opening of an administrative investigation to determine the extent to which the authorities had been responsible for the accident. On 30 April 1993 the Üsküdar public prosecutor began a criminal investigation. Lastly, the official inquiries ended on 15 July 1993, when the two mayors, Mr. Sözen and Mr. Öktem, were committed for trial in the criminal courts.

Accordingly, the investigating authorities may be regarded as having acted with exemplary promptness and as having shown diligence in seeking to establish the circumstances that led both to the accident of 28 April 1993 and to the ensuing deaths. . . .

116. In the instant case, in a judgment of 4 April 1996 the Istanbul Criminal Court sentenced the two mayors in question to fines of TRL 610,000 (an amount equivalent at the time to approximately EUR 9.70), suspended, for negligent omissions in the performance of their duties within the meaning of Article 230 sec.1 of the Criminal Code. Before the Court, the Government attempted to explain why that provision alone had been applied in respect of the two mayors and why they had been sentenced to the minimum penalty applicable. However, it is not for the Court to address such issues of domestic law concerning individual criminal responsibility, that being a matter for assessment by the national courts, or to deliver guilty or not-guilty verdicts in that regard.

Having regard to its task, the Court would simply observe that in the instant case the sole purpose of the criminal proceedings in issue was to establish whether the authorities could be held liable for "negligence in the performance of their duties" under Article 230 of the Criminal Code, which provision does not in any way relate to life-endangering acts or to the protection of the right to life within the meaning of Article 2.

Indeed, it appears from the judgment of 4 April 1996 that the trial court did not see any reason to depart from the reasoning set out in the committal order issued by the Administrative Council and left in abeyance any question of the authorities' possible responsibility for the death of the applicant's nine relatives. The judgment of 4 April 1996 does, admittedly, contain passages referring to the deaths that occurred on 28 April 1993 as a factual element. However, that cannot be taken to mean that there was an acknowledgment of any responsibility for failing to protect the right to life. The operative provisions of the judgment are silent on this point and, furthermore, do not give any precise indication that the trial court had sufficient regard to the extremely serious consequences of the accident; the persons held responsible were ultimately sentenced to derisory fines, which were, moreover, suspended.

117. Accordingly, it cannot be said that the manner in which the Turkish criminal-justice system operated in response to the tragedy secured the full accountability of State officials or authorities for their role in it and the effective implementation of provisions of domestic law guaranteeing respect for the right to life, in particular the deterrent function of the criminal law.

41. In short, it must be concluded in the instant case that there has been a violation of Article 2 of the Convention in its procedural aspect also, on account of the

lack, in connection with a fatal accident provoked by the operation of a dangerous activity, of adequate protection "by law" safeguarding the right to life and deterring similar life-endangering conduct in future. . . .

[The Court also held by a vote of 15–2 that there had been a violation of the right to property, contained in Art. 1 of Protocol 1 and of the right to a remedy found in Art. 13 of the Convention.]

Note on the Duty of Care to Protect Life

1. Regional institutions have heard numerous cases where applicants have sought to impose responsibility on a government for the death of a family member. The cases raise difficult issues of attribution, evidence and standard of care. The controversial Grand Chamber decision in *McCann*, the first judgment in the European system finding a violation of Article 2, was decided by a vote of 10–9. *McCann v. The United Kingdom*, App. no. 18984/91, Judgment of 27 September 1995, 324 Eur. Ct. H.R. (Ser. A), 21 EHRR 97 (1996). The Court held that the UK government failed to adequately plan and prepare for an operation to arrest suspected IRA terrorists in Gibraltar, and as a result the suspects were shot to death by British soldiers. The Court said it must "subject deprivations of life to the most careful scrutiny, particularly where deliberate lethal force is used, taking into consideration not only the actions of the agents of the State who actually administer the force but also all the surrounding circumstances including such matters as the planning and control of the actions under examination." Id. para. 150. The Court found no premeditated plot to kill the suspects, but accepted "that the soldiers honestly believed, in the light of the information that they had been given . . . that it was necessary to shoot the suspects in order to prevent them from detonating a bomb and causing serious loss of life. The actions which they took, in obedience to superior orders, were thus perceived by them as absolutely necessary in order to safeguard innocent lives." Id. para 200. The Court added:

> . . . It considers that the use of force by agents of the State in pursuit of one of the aims delineated in paragraph 2 of Article 2 of the Convention may be justified under this provision where it is based on an honest belief which is perceived, for good reasons, to be valid at the time but which subsequently turns out to be mistaken. To hold otherwise would be to impose an unrealistic burden on the State and its law-enforcement personnel in the execution of their duty, perhaps to the detriment of their lives and those of others.
>
> It follows that, having regard to the dilemma confronting the authorities in the circumstances of the case, the actions of the soldiers do not, in themselves, give rise to a violation of this provision.
>
> 201. The question arises, however, whether the anti-terrorist operation as a whole was controlled and organized in a manner which respected the requirements of Article 2 and whether the information and instructions given to the soldiers which, in effect, rendered inevitable the use of lethal force, took adequately into consideration the right to life of the three suspects.

In response to this question, the Court held that

> 213. In sum, having regard to the decision not to prevent the suspects from travelling into Gibraltar, to the failure of the authorities to make sufficient allowances

for the possibility that their intelligence assessments might, in some respects at least, be erroneous and to the automatic recourse to lethal force when the soldiers opened fire, the Court is not persuaded that the killing of the three terrorists constituted the use of force which was no more than absolutely necessary in defense of persons from unlawful violence within the meaning of Article 2 para. 2 (a) of the Convention.

2. In *Makaratzis v. Greece*, No. 53924/00, judgment of July 8, 2004, 2004-VII ECHR, a Grand Chamber held the government responsible for violating Article 2 even though the applicant had not died. The Court found that a car chase through the streets of Athens and other police actions made the applicant the victim of conduct that put his life at risk and it had only been by good fortune that he had not been killed. According to the Court, the operation had involved a large number of police officers in a chaotic and largely uncontrolled chase in which there had been an absence of clear chains of command. There was no appropriate structure in domestic law and practice setting out clear guidelines and criteria governing the use of force. In addition to the substantive violation of Article 2, there was a procedural violation due to the conduct of an incomplete and inadequate investigation. Like the *Oneryildiz Case*, state responsibility was based on gross negligence of government officials. Is the Court placing too high a burden on the government?

3. In *Anguelova v. Bulgaria*, (Application no. 38361/97), Judgment of 13 June 2002, the European Court held the government responsible for an unexplained custodial death. Investigations conducted by the Bulgarian authorities ended with the conclusion that the death must have been caused by an accidental injury which pre-dated the young man's arrest. The applicant alleged that her son had been ill-treated and had died as a result of injuries inflicted by police officers, that he had not been provided with timely medical treatment while in custody and that the State authorities had failed to undertake a thorough and effective investigation. The Court recalled that persons in custody are in a vulnerable position and the authorities are under an obligation to account for their treatment. Consequently, where an individual is taken into police custody in good health but later dies, it is incumbent on the State to provide a plausible explanation of the events leading to his death (citing *Selmouni v. France* [GC], no. 25803/94, § 87, ECHR 1999-V, *Salman v. Turkey* [GC], no. 21986/93, § 97, ECHR 2000-VII; and *Velikova v. Bulgaria*, no. 41488/98, ECHR 2000-VI). Indeed, the burden of proof may be regarded as resting on the authorities to provide a satisfactory and convincing explanation. The Court found the Government's proposed conclusion that Mr. Zabchekov might have injured himself by falling "improbable" when examined in the light of all the surrounding facts. In assessing the evidence, the Court, attached significant weight to the information that the police officers behaved in a suspect manner and to the fact that the authorities accepted the credibility of their evidence despite serious indications calling for caution. The Court also held that Article 2 was violated due to the government's failure to provide medical treatment for the detainee and that the investigation lacked the requisite objectivity and thoroughness, a fact which decisively undermined the government's ability to establish the cause of death and the identity of the persons responsible. In addition, the Court held that injuries were indicative of inhuman treatment beyond the threshold of severity required

by Article 3 of the Convention and thus that article was also violated. In contrast to its judgment in *Nachova*, it did not find sufficient proof of racial motivation in the ill-treatment to constitute a violation of Article 14. Similar issues have arisen in the Inter-American system, although without the same presumptions being applied. *See, Gangarem Panday v. Suriname*, 16 Inter-Am.Ct.H.R. (ser. C)(1994).

A.R. Mowbray, *The Development of Positive Obligations under the European Convention on Human Rights by the European Court of Human Rights* (Hart Publishing: Oxford/Portland, Ore., 2004), pp. 2–3, 13, 15, 20, 28–30, 34, 38, 40, 43, 64, 68–69, 95–98, 100–101, 125, 129, 170–71, 213, 219–20, 224.

The Court has not provided an authoritative definition of positive obligations. However, Judge Martens defined them as 'requiring member states to . . . take action.' This simple definition captures the essence of the varied obligations . . . as it emphasizes that their key characteristic is the duty upon states to undertake specific affirmative tasks: examples include to investigate a killing, to protect vulnerable persons from serious ill-treatment inflicted by others, to provide arrested persons with a prompt explanation of the reasons for their arrest, to provide free legal assistance for impecunious criminal defendants, to provide legal recognition of the new gender acquired by transsexuals who have successfully completed gender reassignment treatment and to deploy reasonable police resources to protect medial organizations from unlawful violence directed at curbing the legitimate exercise of free expression. . . .

Are they derived from express textual requirements of the Convention or implied judicial creations? Where they are of the latter type what justifications have been articulated by the Court to explain their recognition and imposition on member states? Also, what methodology has been adopted by the Court to determine the existence, scope and breach of implied positive obligations?

. . . The Convention is mainly concerned not with what a State must do, but with what it must not do; that is, with its obligation to refrain from interfering with the individual's rights. Nevertheless, utilizing the principle of effectiveness, the Court has held that even in respect of provisions which do not expressly create a positive obligation, there may sometimes be a duty to act in a particular way. . . .

The analysis of the Court in *Ergi* [*v. Turkey*] is of great importance in the evolution of the positive obligation on states to exercise appropriate care in the planning and control of operations by their security forces. The judgment clearly elaborates the need for domestic authorities, when planning these operations, to have regard to the dangers posed to innocent bystanders from both security personnel and the suspected terrorists/criminals against whom the operation is directed. The authorities must develop and implement plans which 'take all feasible precautions . . . with a view to avoiding and, in any event, to minimizing, incidental loss of civilian life.' These are stringent requirements but given the importance of the right to life and the professionalism which can rightly be expected of security forces operating in democratic European states they are essential attributes of this positive obligation. . . .

The jurisprudential justifications for the imposition of this obligation are twofold. First, under Article 2(1) states are required to 'protect' everyone's right to life. This requirement is not satisfied merely by enacting laws seeking to protect the right to life, it also demands affirmative action by officials. Secondly, the circumstances where the deprivation of life are permitted under Article 2(2) have been, rightly, narrowly construed by the Court. Consequently, states have to ensure that the use of force by their security personnel (regular and civilian) meets the standard of being 'no more than absolutely necessary' for dealing with the three categories of situations where deadly force may be justified. In other words security force operations must involve a proportionate response to the threat they are aimed at combating. This is not, however, always a straightforward assessment for either the domestic authorities or the Court (e.g. the development of the heavily armed MMAD unit in response to a domestic hostage crisis in *Andronicou*). . . .

Outside of the extra-ordinary security situation in southeast Turkey the Court has been reluctant to determine that member states have failed to provide adequate police protection to vulnerable individuals living in the community. This is because the Court appreciates the difficult operational challenges facing domestic police forces and has been careful not to second-guess their *bona fide* practical actions. Even in a normal policing context successful applicants will need to be able to establish that the authorities knew, or ought to have known, of the immediate risk to the life of an identified individual (e.g. by potential victims and/or their families informing the police of the threats) and that the police (or other state agents) failed to take reasonable protective measures. These are clearly difficult burdens to satisfy.

. . .

. . . [W]here public authorities of member states are aware that a person has been killed, either by a public official or another private person, or they are confronted with an arguable claim that a detainee has disappeared in life-threatening circumstances they are now under a Convention positive obligation to diligently investigate the causes and circumstances of the death/disappearance.

In *McCann* the judgment stated that:

> 161. The Court confines itself to noting, like the Commission, that a general legal prohibition of arbitrary killing by the agents of the State would be ineffective, in practice, if there existed no procedure for reviewing the lawfulness of the use of lethal force by State authorities. The obligation to protect the right to life under this provision (art. 2), read in conjunction with the State's general duty under Article 1 (art. 2+1) of the Convention to 'secure everyone within their jurisdiction the rights and freedoms defined in [the] Convention', requires by implication that there should be some form of effective official investigation when individuals have been killed as a result of the use of force by, *inter alios*, agents of the State.

The latter part of the above explanation also highlights the practical factor that such killings may frequently occur in circumstances, such as during purported arrests of suspected criminals or whilst such person are being detained for questioning, where there are few, if any, independent witnesses to testify as to what occurred. Therefore, the Court was trying to ensure that state officials do not abuse their powers in these types of situations by obligating states to conduce effective investigations into all killings by their agents.

The case load crisis facing the Court in recent years appears to be another element in the creation of [a] positive obligation [of investigation]. In the report of the Evaluation Group, composed of Ambassador Harman, President Wildhaber and Deputy Secretary-General Kruger, examining the origins and solutions to the growing backlog of cases at Strasbourg, the Group identified one source of time-consuming and expensive activity of the Court as being fact-finding missions which had to be undertaken when national institutions failed to effectively investigate alleged breaches of Convention rights. The report noted that, "[t]o some extent, the Court has itself avoided the need to embark on fact-finding missions with their attendant problems by holding in its case-law that procedural deficiencies, such as lack of investigation or of a remedy, may of themselves constitute a violation of the Convention." This observation suggests that the imperative to maximize the use of the Court's limited financial and personnel resources has . . . played a part in the jurisprudential development of investigation obligations.

There is not a precise standard form of inquiry mandated by Article 2; instead it depends upon the circumstances of the particular killing, the processes of the relevant domestic legal system and the Court's evaluation of the effectiveness of the specific investigation. . . .

There are a number of cases where the Court has determined that state officials have failed to undertake effective investigations due to the omission of rudimentary forensic tests. . . . [I]t is clear that the Court expects states to ensure that investigators use well recognized forensic science methodology, such as the precise recording/photographing of the scene of the killing combined with subsequent laboratory tests on items found that the scene (including fingerprint, gunpowder and ballistic/metallurgic analyses), in order to discover the facts of the killings. Obviously, which precise forensic tests should be undertaken depends upon the circumstances of the killing and the types of evidence found at the scene. Investigators must, however, take reasonable steps to record and recover all relevant items at the scene so that later laboratory tests can be conducted. As forensic science technology evolves, *e.g.* the use of DNA profiling, so the Court ought, where appropriate, to require Article 2 investigations to sue the expanding techniques available. . . .

The Court's rejection of the prosecutor's plea of overwork as an excuse for tardiness in the conduct of the investigation echoes the Court's refusal to countenance the progressive growth in caseload as an excuse for domestic judges failing to determine criminal or civil cases within a reasonable time as required by Article 6(1).

We can conclude that in a relatively short period of time since the mid 1990s the Court has created a wide ranging and relatively well defined positive obligation requiring states to undertake effective investigations into killings. This obligation encompasses institutional elements (e.g. investigators must be independent of those state agents involved in the killing) and procedural duties (e.g. investigators should utilize appropriate forensic tests, such as ballistic examinations of bullets found at the scene of the killing, to determine the facts of the killing). Furthermore, it applies, depending upon the context of the killing, to a number of agencies within the law enforcement and criminal justice matrix including, civilian police and military investigators, public prosecutors, coroners and criminal courts. As the previous analysis of the Strasbourg case law reveals most of the breaches of this duty have occurred in the context of anti-terrorist campaigns in Turkey and Northern Ireland.

One of the values of this obligation is that the Court's judgments make clear that even in such dangerous situations all killings must be subject to thorough inquiries. Thereby, hopefully, restraining state agents from abusing their powers through the deterrent effect of knowing that any killings in which they are involved will be subject to rigorous investigations and prosecutions in the criminal courts.

Article 3: Prohibition of torture

The original Court held that under this Article states are obligated to take action to protect individuals from serious maltreatment which infringes the substantive prohibitions of the Article. In *A. v. United Kingdom*, when the applicant was six years old, his mother's partner (subsequently her husband) was given a police caution after he admitted hitting A. with a cane. Three years later a medical examination revealed that A. had a number of bruises on his legs and bottom consistent with blows from a garden cane. A.'s stepfather was charged with assault occasioning actual bodily harm. The trial judge directed the jury that it was for the prosecution to prove that the defendant's conduct was not a reasonable punishment of a child by his stepfather. By a majority verdict the jury found the stepfather not guilty. A. complained to the Commission alleging that, *inter alia*, the UK had violated Article 3 by failing to protect him from ill-treatment at the hands of this stepfather. The commission was unanimous in finding a breach of Article 3. Before the Court, the British government accepted that there had been a breach of that Article in this case. The Court unanimously, determined that the beating of A. fell within the scope of Article 3, though the Court did not specify which particular element was infringed (*i.e.* did the beating constitute 'inhuman' or 'degrading' treatment/punishment). It was then necessary to consider if the state was liable under the Convention for the stepfather's conduct. . . .

[W]hilst the Court has recognized an implied positive obligation upon states to conduct effective investigations into arguable claims of serious ill-treatment by state agents violating Article 3's substantive prohibitions, the application of this duty by different Chambers has been problematic. In particular, the circumstances when the Court will scrutinize domestic investigations under this Article, in contrast to utilizing Article 13, remain obscure. Additionally, the willingness of the Court to reach decisions on complaints relating to allegations of breaches of both the substantive prohibitions and effective investigation duties enshrined in Article 3 does not follow a consistent pattern. Consequently, the effective investigation obligation under Article 3 is less well developed and more uncertain in its application at Strasbourg that the corresponding obligation created via Article 2.

Article 5: Right to liberty and security

The . . . *Kurt* [*v. Turkey* judgment] was a significant development of the Court's jurisprudence which sought to enhance the protection of detainees by defining the types of custody records that authorities must maintain in respect of every person detained by state agents. Of course, the purpose of this duty is not that of simple record keeping but of providing accurate accounts of the location (and related information) of detainees. These records should be available to both senior officials who have responsibility for supervising the detention of persons (*e.g.* prison governors) and relevant non-state persons (*e.g.* the detainee's lawyer). Such forms of access will help to ensure the whereabouts and treatment of detainees can be monitored to facilitate compliance with their Convention rights. Conversely, the failure to maintain efficient custody records can exacerbate the potential danger of detainees disappearing without trace (possibly being murdered) as the facts of *Kurt* graphically illustrated.

Overall, the case law of the original and full-time Courts reveals that the positive obligation embodied in Article 5(4) has been invoked by an ever widening range of detainees, including vagrants, mentally ill patients, aliens facing deportation or extradition and criminals sentenced to life imprisonment. A major extension of this obligation was the original Court's development of the requirement for regular reviews by a 'court' of the need for the continuing detention of those detainees whose personal circumstances are liable to change over time, such as mentally ill patients, recidivists and British discretionary life prisoners. The current Court is continuing to reinforce the obligation (*e.g.* in *Stafford*).

Article 6: Right to a fair trial

Article 6 is the source of the largest number of complaints made to the Court. This can be explained, in part, by the scope of the provision which seeks to guarantee fair trials for both civil and criminal cases. As we examine the positive obligations derived from Article 6 we shall have to bear in mind the extent to which criminal proceedings are subject to more positive obligations due to the greater number of express rights conferred in respect of this type of proceedings. . . .

In regard to civil proceedings the Court has held that a person's right of access to a court for the determination of his/her civil rights and obligations is inherent in the right to a fair trial under Article 6(1). . . .

The full-time Court has endorsed the interpretation of its predecessor that there is no general right to civil legal aid under Article 6(1). Hence, states have considerable latitude under the Convention to choose whether to create general civil legal aid system and where these are established to fix the criteria of financial eligibility.

. . .The Court has also found several implied positive obligations within the text of Article 6. This aspect of the development of positive obligations under the Convention began quite early in the Court's jurisprudence in *Airey*, regarding the requirement to provide legal aid to civil claimants in complex proceedings as an element of the right to a fair hearing (Article 6(1)). Another example of an implied obligation is the duty upon criminal courts to adopt 'counterbalancing' procedures where they permit the use of anonymous witnesses (Article 6(3)(d) in *Doorson*). . . .

The full-time Court has generally been deepening and widening the scope of positive obligations under this Article. An illustration of the former phenomenon is the greater protection of prisoners' right to public hearings of criminal proceedings conducted in prisons exhibited in *Riepan*. The contemporary Court has also broadened the ambit of the implied obligation to provide civil legal assistance to encompass defendants in *McVicar* and the express obligation to provide criminal legal aid to cover significant pre-trial proceedings in *Berlinski*. These trends should be seen as an acknowledgement of the significance of positive obligations under this crucial Article.

Article 8: Right To Respect For Private And Family Life

The . . . [*Y v. U.K.*] judgment is very significant for the Court's willingness to require states to take positive measures to regulate the relationships between individuals. What is required of states clearly depends upon the type of relationship at issue. In Y.'s case there was an abuse of power by an adult over a disabled young person who was not capable of safeguarding her own interests. Hence the Court demanded state intervention through the enactment of criminal law protection for such vulnerable persons. Interestingly, the judgment did not contain an express justification for the recognition of positive obligations under Article 8, other than a reference to the earlier case of *Airey*.

In the subsequent case *of Johnston and Others v. Ireland*, the applicants sought to argue that the judgment in *Airey* should be extended to impose a positive obligation upon states to enable couples to obtain a divorce when their marriages have collapsed. However, an overwhelming majority of the Court, sixteen votes to one, was unwilling to expand the obligation that far. Taking account of the *travaux preparatories* revelation that the drafters deliberately limited Article 12 to include only the right to marry, the Court held that:

> 57. It is true that, on this question, Article 8, with its reference to the somewhat vague notion of 'respect' for family life, might appear to lend itself more readily to an evolutive [*sic.*] interpretation than does Article 12. Nevertheless, the Convention must be read as a while and the Court does not consider that a right to divorce, which it has found to be excluded from Article 12 can, with consistency, be derived from Article 8, provision of more general purpose and scope . . . although the protection of private or family life may sometimes necessitate means whereby spouses can be relived from the duty to live together (see the *Airey* judgment, para. 33), the engagements undertaken by Ireland under Article 9 cannot be regarded as extending to an obligation on its part to introduce measures permitting the divorce and the re-marriage which the applicants seek.

This is a vivid example of the Court's inability to use the concept of a positive obligation to create a right under the Convention which states excluded when drafting the Convention. The continuing sensitivity of some states to the recognition of a right to divorce was reflected in its further exclusion from Protocol 7 (guaranteeing *inter alia*, equality between spouses), which was opened for signature in 1984. The Irish electorate in 1995, by a 0.6% majority of the vote, decided to remove the constitution ban on divorce. . . .

Article 13: Right to an effective remedy

. . .[T]he Court has developed an expanding range of investigation obligations under Article 13. The justifications for recognizing these duties are the importance of the substantive rights involved (e.g. the right to life in *Kaya* and the prohibition of torture in *Askoy*), together with the vulnerability of the alleged victims *vis-à-vis* state agents. However, the Court has been opaque in referring, in *Yasa*, to the 'stricter' investigation duty under this Article compared with the inquiry obligation under Article 2. The Court did not explain in what ways the former duty was more demanding of states. Indeed, . . . the institutional and procedural requirements for inquires under Article 2 are stringent. Also, the Court has on a number of occasions (e.g. in *Velikova* and *Yasa*,) referred back to its earlier findings of breaches of the investigation duty under Article 2 to support its determinations that the similar duty under Article 13 has been violated in the same case. Another ambiguity in Article 13 cases relates to the circumstances where the Court is willing to examine whether there has been an effective investigation under both substantive Articles (i.e. Articles 2, 3, or 5) and Article 13. Judge Golcuklu has regularly dissented on the ground that once the Court has found a breach of the investigation obligation under the former Articles that excludes the need to reconsider the issue under Article 13. Furthermore, the Chamber determining the Northern Irish cases (*Kelly et al.*) ruled that no separate issue arose under Article 13. What appears to be decisive for the Court, although is not always clearly stated, is whether the lack of an effective investigation undermined the possibility of the complainant invoking any other domestic remedy (*e.g.* to claim compensation for the killing or serious maltreatment of his/her relative by state personnel). Where an effective investigation is the crucial foundation for other remedies then the Court is likely to examine the issue under Article 13, in addition to applying the analogous inquiry obligations under the substantive Articles, (as in *Akdeniz*).

Conclusions

. . . [W]hile some duties are at the negative end of the spectrum and others are at the positive (and many are in between), no right can, if one looks at social reality, be secured by the fulfillment of only one duty, or only one kind of duty. If one looks concretely at specific rights and the particular arrangements that it takes to defend or fulfill them, it always turns out in concrete cases to involve a mixed bag of actions and omissions . . . what one cannot find in practice is a right that is fully honored, or merely even adequately protected, only by negative duties or by positive duties. It is impossible, therefore, meaningfully and exhaustively to split all rights into two kinds based upon the nature of their implementing duties, because the duties are always a mixture of positive and negative ones.

Questions and Comments

1. Does a state have an obligation to investigate violations of all rights or only those involving personal security? Which violations require criminal prosecution? See: A. Mowbray, *Duties of Investigation under the European Convention on Human Rights*, 51 ICLQ 437 (2002); A.M. Latcham, *Duty to Punish: International Law and the Human Rights Policy of Argentina*, 7 B.U. INT'L L.J. 355 (1989).

2. If a state does not fully investigate or take other effective action when a violation occurs, does that always constitute a separate violation of the right to a remedy?

3. The African Commission has also held that the failure of a State Party to ensure respect for the rights contained in the Charter constitutes a violation even if neither the State nor its agents were the perpetrators of the violation. *Mouvement Burkinabé des Droits de L'Homme v. Burkina Faso*, Comm. 204/97, Decision of May 7, 2001.

4. What redress is appropriate for the compound violations involved in deprivations of the right to life and failure to investigate afterwards? What effect does or should it have if the individuals were targeted because they belong to an ethnic or racial minority?

5. For further reading on positive obligations in the European system, see: A. CLAPHAM, HUMAN RIGHTS IN THE PRIVATE SPHERE (Oxford, Clarendon Press, 1993); J. McBride, *Protecting Life: a Positive Obligation to Help*, 24 EUROPEAN LAW REVIEW HUMAN RIGHTS SURVEY 54 (1999); K. STARMER, EUROPEAN HUMAN RIGHTS LAW (London, Legal Action Group, 1999) ch 5; K. Starmer, *Positive Obligations Under the Convention*, in J. JOWELL & J. COOPER (EDS) UNDERSTANDING HUMAN RIGHTS PRINCIPLES (Oxford, Hart Publishing, 2001) 159.

4. The Obligations of Federal States

While all regional systems include federal states among their members, federalism has been a particular issue in the Inter-American context, as the following materials indicate.

T. Buergenthal, *The Inter-American System for the Protection of Human Rights*, ANUARIO JURIDICO INTERAMERICANO 1981 (OAS, 1982), pp- 85–87.

(...) Article 28 affects the domestic application of the American Convention in those states that have a federal system of government. Labeled the "federal clause," Article 28 reads in part as follows:

> 1. Where a State Party is constituted as a federal state, the national government of such state Party shall implement all the provisions of the Convention over whose subject matter it exercises legislative and judicial jurisdiction.
> 2. With respect to the provisions over whose subject matter the constituent units of the federal state have jurisdiction, the national government shall immediately take suitable measures, in accordance with its constitution and its laws, to the end that the competent authorities of the constituent units may adopt appropriate provisions for the fulfillment of this Convention.

Article 28 is an anachronism which harks back to the days of the League of Nations. Few modern international human rights instruments contain comparable clauses. The International Covenant on Civil and Political Rights adopts precisely the opposite principle by declaring in Article 50 that "the provisions of the present covenant shall extend to all parts of the federal states without any limitations or exceptions." The European Convention of Human Rights, the Genocide Convention, and the U.N. Racial Convention contain no federal clause; they apply with equal force in unitary as in federal states. Moreover, many states which have a strong federal tradition, including Canada and the Federal Republic of Germany, have been able to adhere to these instruments without federal-state reservations.

Article 28 of the American Convention found its way into the treaty because of U.S. insistence.[17] In explaining the meaning of this provision, the U.S. delegation to the San Jose conference reported to the Secretary of State that

> The present Convention ... does not obligate the U.S. Government to exercise jurisdiction over subject matter over which it would not exercise authority in the absence of the Convention. The U.S. is merely obligated to take suitable measures to the end that state and local authorities may adopt provisions for the fulfillment of this

---

[17] See Report of the United States Delegation to the Inter-American Conference on Protection of Human Rights, San Jose, Costa Rica, November 9–22, 1969, p. 37 (Dept. of State, 1970).

Convention. Suitable measures could consist of recommendations to the states, for example. The determination of what measures are suitable is a matter of internal decision. The Convention does not require enactment of legislation bringing new subject matter within the federal ambit.[18]

The U.S. delegation proposed Article 28 in order to ensure that a federal state not be deemed to have assumed any international obligation to prevent violations of the Convention involving rights or acts within the jurisdiction of any governmental entities other than the federal government. Moreover, by limiting the international obligations of the federal state to subject matter over which it exercises jurisdiction, the U.S. sought to indicate that such a state has no obligation under the Convention in situations where the federal government, although having jurisdiction, has not previously exercised it.

The ostensible simplicity of article 28 hides the legal complexities inherent in it. It raises difficult international and domestic law issues not fully perceived by its drafters. Whether a federal state, for example, 'exercises legislative and judicial jurisdiction' over a specific subject matter is an international law issue to the extent that it involves an interpretation of a treaty. But it can be decided in a given case only by reference to the domestic law of a particular country. This conclusion suggests the question whether and to what extent the Inter-American Court of Human Rights, which has jurisdiction to interpret and apply the American Convention, is empowered to verify a defense of a state party based on article 28. Suppose, for example, that a state defends its failure to enforce the American Convention on the ground that under its domestic law it lacks jurisdiction over a specific subject matter at issue. Is the Inter-American Court in such a case bound by the ipse dixit of the federal authority or is it free to examine the relevant domestic law and practice and determine for itself what the domestic law provides on the subject? To illustrate the problem, let us assume that in a case involving State X, counsel for X asserts that the subject matter of the claim is one over which the federal government exercises neither legislative nor judicial jurisdiction. Assume further that the complainant points to a decision of the Supreme Court of X, rendered in another case a year earlier, that plainly contradicts the view of counsel for X. Is the Inter-American Court free to consider the effect of the Supreme Court decision and, if so, may it receive expert evidence on the subject, or is it bound by X's statement as to what the law is?

The issues might be even more troublesome in a country which, in addition to being a federal state, determines that the Convention is non-self-executing. Here a domestic court might never get the opportunity to interpret Article 28 or to apply it by reference to other provisions of the American Convention, making it more difficult for the international tribunal to ascertain what the relevant domestic law is. Sight must also not be lost of the fact that in some federal systems it is by no means easy, even as a matter of domestic law, to determine what constitutes an 'exercise of jurisdiction' or what is meant by 'subject matter' as that term is used in Article 28.

---

[18]   Report of the U.S. Delegation, supra, at 37.

Questions and Comments

1. In a death penalty case involving the United States, the Inter-American Commission found the U.S. execution of minors to violate the American Declaration on the Rights and Duties of Man. In the U.S., criminal law is a matter largely left to the fifty states to regulate. What obligations does the U.S. have to address the laws and practices of its component states? Does the federal government acquire subject matter jurisdiction over this issue by ratifying the Convention?

2. What is the meaning of the phrase "suitable measures" in Convention Article 28(2)? Canada is another OAS Member State with a federal system. If it ratifies the Convention, would it comply with Article 28 by making recommendations to its provincial governments? Is Article 2 relevant?

3. Who decides whether a matter falls within the jurisdiction of the federal government or its constituent units? If the executive branch of a federal government makes that determination, are the organs of the OAS obligated to accept its determination?

4. Suppose that in a case pending before the Inter-American Court, counsel for State A asserts that the federal government of her country exercises neither legislative nor judicial jurisdiction over the matter. Counsel for the Commission introduces a recent Supreme Court decision which contradicts the assertion of counsel for State A. May the Inter-American Court inquire into the effect of the Supreme Court decision or is it bound by State A's assertion as to its domestic law?

The Commission's views on the obligations of federal states are indicated in the following case.

The Mexican Elections Case, Rep. No 14/93, Case 10.956, Annual Report of the Inter-American Commission on Human Rights 1993, OEA/Ser.L/V/II.85, doc. 9 rev., 11 February 1993, p. 259.

On May 6, 1991, the Inter-American Commission on Human Rights received a communication wherein Mr. Luis Felipe Bravo Mena of the Partido Acciòn Nacional (National Action Party—PAN) denounced numerous irregularities in the elections held in the State of Mexico between March and November 1990, which violated the political rights of the citizens of the State in general and of the Municipality of Naucalpan de Juarez in particular. This petition was forwarded to the Government of Mexico on October 17, 1991.

On February 14, 1992, the Government of Mexico replied to the Commission stating, in brief, that the IACHR did not have competence to take cognizance of the complaint, requesting that the Commission find it inadmissible on the grounds that internal remedies had not been exhausted and pointing out that the facts in the case did not constitute violations of the Inter-American Convention on Human Rights. The pertinent parts of this reply were forwarded to the petitioner on March 2, 1992.

On March 12, 1993, during its 83rd session, the Inter-American Commission on Human Rights carefully examined this case and decided to adopt Report No. 7/93 on a provisional basis. Said report was sent to the Government of Mexico, which was given 90 days in which to respond.

On June 3, 1993, the Government of Mexico sent its observations on the Report adopted by the Commission and asked that the IACHR:

- Order that the case be closed, since the grounds for the petition no longer obtain. Declare the petition inadmissible based on the evidence cited and the information subsequently reported; or
- Consider the matter settled, in light of the measures taken within the framework of domestic law (. . .).

In its reply, the Government of Mexico commented on the contents of the Commission's report, stating that "the Commission has a number of observations that can be easily acted upon; in fact, Mexico had introduced them into its laws even before the confidential report in question was approved (. . .). Other suggestions will require gradual measures that will be viable to the extent that the legal system is applied (. . .). But other observations go further than the petition and overstep the legal framework of the system agreed upon in San Jose (. . .)"

2.1 Background to the communications:

In the State of Mexico, a State Party constituted as a Federal State of the United Mexican States, elections were held in 1990 to elect new members to the local congress and officials of the 121 local governments in the state.

2.2 Summary of the arguments of the petitioner (communications of May 6, 1991, and April 27, 1992)

The petitioner describes a variety of irregularities that occurred during the election days and that, in his judgment, create a reasonable doubt as to the validity, authenticity and legality of the voting; his chief arguments are that there was no clear distinction between election officials, government officials and members of the Partido Revolucionario Institucional (Institutional Revolutionary Party—PRI); official election-related documents, such as ballots and the records of poll openings, ballot counting, and poll closings were distributed and delivered in vehicles bearing PRI campaign advertising; public funds were used for electioneering purposes, building public works and providing services with political strings attached.

The petitioner stated, in particular, that there were serious anomalies in the elections held on November 11, 1990: 80% of the individuals selected to serve as poll officials were deliberately replaced; at the last minute, over 20% of the polls were relocated away from their officially designated sites; the guarantees that enable voters to cast their votes freely and in private were lacking; the proper furnishings for voting were lacking; the political parties' poll watchers were prevented from overseeing and monitoring activities there by being required to stand five or six meters away; in "Operation Carousel", hundreds of repeat voters were mobilized and transported from one polling place to another, via collective means of transportation, to vote as many times as possible, and were supplied with the voter credentials needed to do so; finally, ballot boxes were stolen once the polls closed.

2.3 Arguments made by the Government of Mexico (notes of February 14, and August 4, 1992):

For its part, the Government of Mexico replied at length to each point alleged by the petitioner, using three main arguments: the Commission's alleged lack of competence; the failure to exhaust internal remedies, and the assertion that the facts denounced were not violations of the American Convention on Human Rights. The Government of Mexico described the structure of the electoral bodies, how their members are appointed and what their functions are; it also cited from all existing laws on the subject.

Observations

Under the American Convention, the political rights are those recognized in articles 1, 23 and 28 thereof.

The Commission's practice

Article 23 of the American Convention on Human Rights recognizes the following political rights:[19]

> 1. Every citizen shall enjoy the following rights and opportunities:
>   a. to take part in the conduct of public affairs, directly or through freely chosen representatives;
>   b. to vote and to be elected in genuine periodic elections, which shall be by universal and equal suffrage and by secret ballot that guarantees the free expression of the will of the voters; and
>   c. to have access, under general conditions of equality, to the public service of his country.
>   2. The law may regulate the exercise of the rights and opportunities referred to in the preceding paragraph only on the basis of age, nationality, residence, language, education, civil and mental capacity, or sentencing by a competent court in criminal proceedings.

The Government of Mexico contends that the facts denounced do not constitute violations of the American Convention on Human Rights, and cites Article 23 of the Convention, which it believes the petitioner has misinterpreted. It states that "while this article enumerates the three basic prerogatives that citizens enjoy where participation in government is concerned—namely, the right to take part in the conduct of public affairs, the right to vote and be elected in free and periodic elections, and the right to have access to public service—, it does not prescribe a prototype or model for either the election process, how the election is to be set up or who the election authorities are to be. This is the sovereign right of each country to decide." The Government added that "neither the Constitution nor the Election Law of the State of Mexico infringes those rights, as it will now be shown that the creation and structure of the election authorities and tribunals are neither subject to any political party's authority nor biased in its favor." The Government's analysis of the facts alleged by the petitioner begins with this statement and ends by stating that "a careful review of everything this Government has reported above is unmis-

---

[19] These same political rights are contained in Article XX of the American Declaration of the Rights and Duties of Man; Article 21 of the Universal Declaration of Human Rights, and Article 25 of the International Covenant on Civil and Political Rights.

takable proof that the election process and the elections themselves were conducted in accordance with the law."

In light of the provisions of Articles 1 and 2 of the American Convention on Human Rights which concern the obligations to investigate, safeguard and take domestic measures to ensure full exercise of human rights and in order to avoid any narrow interpretations of the Commission's competence, it will cite the finding of the Inter-American Court of Human Rights when examining these articles:

> The obligation to ensure the free and full exercise of human rights is not fulfilled by the existence of a legal system designed to make it possible to comply with this obligation—it also requires the government to conduct itself so as to effectively ensure the free and full exercise of human rights.[20]

When the scope of Article 23 was examined in the past,[21] the Commission explained, in detail, that if Article 23 was to be fully respected elections had to be authentic, universal, periodic, and by secret ballot or some other means that enabled voters to express their will freely. Laws alone will not suffice; the attitude must be one that encourages proper implementation, and must be consistent with generally recognized principles that govern a representative democracy. The IACHR is being asked to examine whether citizens who participated in a political process did so as equals, whether those political processes guaranteed the free and authentic will of the electorate and, therefore, whether the facts alleged constitute violations of political rights.

The Commission is competent to examine the instant case because it concerns the right to participate in government (Article 23) and the right to judicial protection (Article 25) protected under the American Convention on Human Rights, and the generic obligations contained in articles 1 and 2. Mexico is a State Party to the Convention, having ratified it on April 3, 1982.

The Government of Mexico argues that while the Commission is competent to defend the political rights protected under Article 23 of the Convention, no article of the Convention gives it the competence to rule on the States Parties' internal political processes, as the latter are conducted in the exercise of the people's right to self-determination and their sovereign right to decide for the political system that best suits them; declaring elections valid or invalid is the exclusive competence of the internal organs lawfully established under a given State's constitutional system.

In its arguments alleging that the Commission does not have jurisdiction, the Government acknowledges that the Commission may receive petitions or communications on alleged human rights violations which concern that Government; at the same time, however, it contends that the American Convention does not give the Commission the authority to decide whether elections are valid or to rule on the conduct of the authorities where elections are concerned.

As for the Government's allegations concerning sovereignty and nonintervention in a State's internal affairs as arguments for denying or limiting the Commission's

---

[20] Inter-American Court of Human Rights. Velasquez Rodriguez Case, Judgment of July 29,1988, paragraph 167.

[21] Report 01/90 on cases 9768, 9780 and 9828 (Mexico); Annual Report of the IACHR 1990–1991, Chapter V, Section III, "Human rights, political rights, and representative democracy in the Inter-American system".

competence, it might be well to recall what the Commission has said in this regard on previous occasions.[22]

Indeed, the premise must be that the principle of nonintervention is a rule of conduct governing the actions of States or groups of States, as stipulated in the Charter of the Organization (Article 18); this principle has been linked to the peoples' right to self-determination and independence, "with absolute respect for human rights and fundamental freedoms."[23]

The most fundamental level at which these basic principles have taken on the force of law is Article 16 of the Charter of the Organization, where the counterpart of a State's right to develop itself freely is its obligation to respect the rights of the individual. In the Inter-American system, it is the American Convention on Human Rights that recognizes these rights and contains provisions on the mechanisms and organs that are their means of protection.

The Commission—one of those organs of protection—is, according to its governing instruments: empowered to examine and evaluate the degree to which the internal legislation of the State party guarantees or protects the rights stipulated in the Convention and their adequate exercise and, obviously, among these, political rights. The IACHR is also empowered to verify, with respect to these rights, if the holding of periodic, authentic elections, with universal, equal, and secret suffrage takes place, within the framework of the necessary guarantees so that the results represent the popular will, including the possibility that the voters could, if necessary, effectively appeal against an electoral process that they consider fraudulent, defective, and irregular or that ignores the "right to have access, under general conditions of equality, to the public service of his country".[24]

As noted earlier, in Article 23 the American Convention speaks of "genuine periodic elections, which shall be by universal and equal suffrage and by secret ballot that guarantees the free expression of the will of the voters." The exercise of these rights is so essential if societies are to function normally that Article 27 of the Convention prohibits their suspension, regardless of the circumstance.

The close relationship between representative democracy as a form of government and the exercise of the political rights so defined, also presupposes the exercise of other fundamental rights: " . . . the concept of representative democracy is based on the principle that it is the people who are the nominal holders of political sovereignty and that, in the exercise of that sovereignty, elects its representatives—in indirect democracies—so that they may exercise political power. These representatives, moreover, are elected by the citizens to apply certain political measures, which at the same time implies the prior existence of an ample political debate on the nature of policies to be applied—freedom of expression—between organized political groups—freedom of association—that have had the opportunity to express themselves and meet publicly—freedom of assembly. At the same time, if these rights and freedoms are to be exercised, there must be a juridical and institutional

---

[22] Annual Report of the Inter-American Commission on Human Rights 1990–1991, Chapter V, Section III, "Human rights, political rights and representative democracy in the Inter-American system."

[23] Resolution adopted by the General Assembly at its second regular session, titled "Strengthening of the principles of nonintervention."

[24] Report 01/90, op. cit., paragraph 95.

system in which laws outweigh the will of leaders and in which some institutions exercise control over others for the sake of guaranteeing the integrity of the expression of the people's will—the rule of law.[25]

In the Commission's view, ratification of the American Convention creates more than an obligation to respect the exercise of the rights recognized therein; it also creates an obligation to guarantee the existence and exercise of all those rights, without distinction, because they constitute a whole and are mutually interdependent. It would therefore be senseless and even a breach of Article 29 of the Convention[26] to draw some distinctions or establish categories where there are none, or to give them the kind of literal interpretation that narrows their scope. As the Commission stated in Report 01/90, "Indeed, any mention of the right to vote and to be elected would be mere rhetoric if unaccompanied by a precisely described set of characteristics that the elections are required to meet." (Report 01/90, paragraph 88).

From the foregoing it follows that States are, as Article 2 of the Convention states, to adopt the legislative and other measures necessary to give effect to the rights and freedoms recognized in the Convention.

Finally, the Government contends that the electoral process being challenged was conducted in the exercise of the sovereign powers of the local executive and legislative branches of the State of Mexico. Under Mexico's federal system, these powers are reserved to the federated units of the United Mexican States and they alone have exclusive power to legislate, organize and regulate the exercise of the political rights of their citizenry. The Government ends by stating that the authorities charged with organizing, conducting and monitoring the election process being challenged, enjoy sovereign and exclusive governmental powers, because as their function is to see to it that the political rights, privileges and opportunities to which Article 41 of the Constitution refers materialize and are exercised.

The Commission must point out that under the 1969 Vienna Convention on the Law of Treaties, the American Convention is self-executing throughout the territory of the United Mexican States, because "Unless a different intention appears from the treaty or is otherwise established, a treaty is binding upon each party in respect of its entire territory." At the time it ratified the Convention, Mexico stipulated no reservations or amendments, which means that the provisions of Article 28, subparagraphs 1 and 2, are fully self-executing:

> Article 28. Federal Clause.
>
> 1. Where a State Party is constituted as a federal state, the national government of such State Party shall implement all the provisions of the Convention over whose subject matter it exercises legislative and judicial jurisdiction.

---

[25] Report 01/91 on cases 9768, 9780 and 9828 (Mexico), paragraphs 41 and 42; Annual Report of the Inter-American Commission 1989–1990, p. 107.

[26] Article 29. Restrictions Regarding Interpretation.
No provision of this Convention shall be interpreted as:
   a. permitting any State Party, group, or person to suppress the enjoyment or exercise of the rights and freedoms recognized in this Convention or to restrict them to a greater extent than is provided for herein;
   b. restricting the enjoyment or exercise of any right or freedom recognized by virtue of the laws of any State Party or by virtue of another convention to which one of the said states is a party;
   c. precluding other rights or guarantees that are inherent in the human personality or derived from representative democracy as a form of government; or d. excluding or limiting the effect that the American Declaration of the Rights and Duties of Man and other international acts of the same nature may have.

2. With respect to the provisions over whose subject matter the constituent units of the federal state have jurisdiction, the national government shall immediately take suitable measures, in accordance with its constitution and its laws, to the end that the competent authorities of the constituent units may adopt appropriate provisions for the fulfillment of this Convention.

Summing up the points made by the Commission thus far, one can conclude that Mexico, upon ratifying the American Convention on Human Rights, not only recognized the competence of the Inter-American Commission on Human Rights to state its opinion and conclusions, but also undertook to respect and guarantee the exercise of the political rights contemplated in Article 23 of the Convention. The latter includes the right to vote in elections, which shall have the minimum requirements needed to ensure that these rights are exercised fully. Under Article 2 of the Convention, Mexico also undertook to adopt the legislative measures needed to give effect to those rights. . . .

4. The configuration of the electoral bodies

4.1 Membership of the electoral bodies in case 10,956

The petitioner asserted that there was no clear separation between election officials, government officials (regardless of their level) and members of the Institutional Revolutionary Party; even the most elementary dividing line between the various levels of the government and parties collapsed, which automatically converted them into judge of and party to the case; the petitioner cited the case of Mr. Humberto Lira Mora who is Secretary General of Government of the State of Mexico, Chairman of the State Election Commission and Chief of the "Naucalpan Headquarters" in a work program implemented by the State Government to focus new government-funded public works in areas that the PRI lost in the 1988 federal elections and thereby win votes. He is also a prominent member of the PRI.

The petitioner further asserted that the Constitution of the State of Mexico and the Law on Political Organizations and Elections of the State of Mexico (LOPPEEM) made it possible to establish a system of election officials and tribunals that was totally accountable to and biased in favor of the PRI. The "L" Legislature of the Congress that voted in the amendments to the local state constitution and to the LOPPEEM was almost entirely composed of PRI deputies, who voted as a block and without giving even the most perfunctory consideration to the recommendations from the opposition deputies. All the appointments of election officials, from the Chairman of the State Electoral Commission to the last poll chairman and secretary and the magistrates on the Tribunal for Election Disputes, went to persons selected according to a one-sided standard. The system wiped out any semblance of impartiality on the part of the election authorities and bodies and their independence from the government and its party, while ensuring that the PRI's interests would be served, making the PRI both judge of and party to the entire election process.

On this point, the Government of Mexico replied that "it is strange that the petitioner is unaware that in any democracy it is the practice for members of the political parties that win the elections to hold the highest positions in government." This principle would apply in the case of Mr. Humberto Lira Mora, according to the Government. The fact that the majority in the Congress of the State of Mexico should be members of the PRI, it added, was decided by the will of the Mexican people exercising their right to vote, and was not something for which the Government could be held accountable. It concluded its comments on this point by stating that the petitioner's other value judgments about this issue prove nothing and are meaningless precisely because they are value judgments. It cited local constitutional provisions to show that legislative and election officials are elected and appointed democratically.

The Government's final observation on this point was that it was obvious that the election authorities of the State of Mexico gave the various social groups in the State and its political parties the opportunity to participate. It added that "there is no way that the method used to put together the electoral bodies and tribunal—which the petitioner alleges, without any basis or logical argument, is biased—could be construed as being in violation of the Convention."

When the petitioner made observations on the Government's reply to this point, the petitioner noted that "while it is indeed true that the Government has the authority and the responsibility to take charge of election matters and while it is also true that every government is represented in the membership of the electoral bodies, its representation must not upset the balance within those bodies and thereby make them biased, as is happening with the mechanisms that the law of the State of Mexico establishes. For example, under Article 58 of the LOPPEEM nine of the members of the State Election Commission are part of the formal structure of government (except for the notary public, who is appointed by the Commission, which is chaired by the Government Secretary who, inter alia, is empowered to give the "fiat" to serve as notary public); the others are representatives of the political parties. In the 1990 elections, there were eight that had the right to vote, which shows that even if all eight political parties (among them the Institutional Revolutionary Party) voted in favor of a given course of action, the Government could not be forced to act on that decision, since it has nine of the 17 votes on the State Commission."

As for the State Tribunal for Election Disputes, its members are also nominated by the State's Chief Executive and approved by the State Legislature. The petitioner stated that while it is the Government's authority and duty to take charge of election-related matters and that every government is represented in the electoral bodies, that representation must not upset the balance that such bodies must have and thereby make them biased, which is what is happening with the mechanisms established by the laws of the State of Mexico.

In its reply, the Government reiterated that all the political parties have the same rights to voice and vote in the various electoral bodies; that all are represented equally, and that the respective state powers coordinate their participation. It reasserted the legitimacy of the electoral bodies, duly constituted in accordance with the laws in effect in the State of Mexico, thanks to which its members are impartial.

4.2 The Commission's comments

The Commission must reassert that the State's authority to decide what the electoral bodies will be and how they will be structured implies that the genuine independence and impartiality that these electoral bodies exercise both within themselves and in relation to the system in which they discharge their functions, will guarantee the exercise of political rights. This will only be possible if all sectors of Mexican political life are guaranteed fair, participation, which means they must enjoy real, balanced representation on an equal footing with the government representatives serving on those bodies.

The Commission must point out that obviously the method used to select the members of the electoral bodies is not in itself a violation of the American Convention. Nevertheless, if the representation on such bodies is not balanced in a way that ensures their independence and impartiality, one can hardly say that the laws are being properly enforced or that the various situations put to them for consideration are being examined objectively. This is the kind of adjustments that have to be made to electoral bodies; while each State's preferences as to form or the models that it wants to use are its prerogative, certain guidelines of fairness—based on principles of representative democracy—have to be observed to enable all sectors involved in the political life of nations to participate. . . .

The Commission has analyzed the nature of political rights and the remedies provided under Mexican law. Its conclusions will not be changed by arguments that treat political rights as individual rights when they are not, or that resort to interesting discourses in comparative law to demonstrate the similarities between the Mexican system and those of other countries in this hemisphere. In fact some of the points raised by the Government are not even at issue, precisely because they have no direct bearing on the purpose of this report.

. . . .

The Government states that the IACHR report "overlooks the fact that Mexico's amparo is the simple, brief and effective remedy expressly provided for in the respective provisions of the American Declaration and the American Convention on Human Rights, as can be established from the travaux preparatoires, from inter-American jurisprudence and from the legal doctrine and constitutional philosophy of the hemisphere." . . .

No one is questioning either the validity or the value of the assertions that the Government of Mexico has made in this respect. However, the Government seems to forget that what is at issue here is not the nature of amparo or of any other remedy in respect of individual claims seeking restitution, suspension of acts and so on. The issue here is the need for Mexico's legal system to provide some effective remedy in the face of a violation of political rights, which are collective in nature. These are a people's rights and are recognized in both the American Declaration and the Convention. . . .

To avoid needless repetition, one need only cite the opinion of the Inter-American Court, which found that "In the international sphere what needs to be established is whether a law violates a State's international obligations under some treaty. The Commission can and must do this when examining the communications and petitions presented to it in which violations of human rights and freedoms protected by the Convention are alleged".[27]

---

27 Inter-American Court of Human Rights, Advisory Opinion OC 13/93, paragraph 30; see also paragraph 34.

Conclusions

On the basis of the foregoing considerations, the Inter-American Commission on Human Rights issues its final conclusions, bearing in mind preliminary report 7/93 and the reply provided by the Government of Mexico with respect to its recommendations.

In adopting its Report 7/93, the Commission examined in detail and drew up recommendations on the suitability of domestic remedies in terms of elections; the need for an evidentiary system that will allow citizens to enjoy simple, expeditious, and effective remedies in connection with political rights; and the composition of electoral bodies.

According to the Government of Mexico's statement to the Inter-American Commission on Human Rights, progress has been made at the legislative level, a fact which is important to note, and which is reflected in the amendments made to the Ley de Organizaciones Poiliticas y Procesos Electorales del Estado de Mexico[28] (law on political organizations and electoral processes of the Mexican state); some of the new provisions are in response to the recommendations issued by the Commission, and some others, independently of those recommendations, further the aim of ensuring free and genuine elections.

The amendments mentioned by the Government of Mexico have to do with the following topics: electoral organizations, financing of elections, voter rolls, ballot boxes, stages of the electoral process, election days, and remedy proceedings. Specifically, the legislative changes which the IACHR feels it is important to emphasize, because they represent progress, refer, where appropriate, to establishment of the concept of "citizen commissioners" as members of the State Electoral Commission and of the District and Municipal Electoral Commissions; to publicity concerning the actions of electoral authorities in the mass media; and to the adoption of measures to improve logistics on election days, such as the placement of ballot boxes, mainly. Additionally, the Government states, in response to the IACHR recommendations, that the responsibility to officially investigate situations that violate human rights "has been fully established, in terms of both criminal process and the electoral area". In this connection, it cites important jurisprudence of the Federal Electoral Tribunal[29] according to which "a local council has the authority to obtain all the admissible evidence it needs in order to issue its decisions objectively and impartially in strict adherence to law (. . .)".The Commission understands that this legal opinion shall be applied uniformly in electoral matters in the cases submitted to the pertinent bodies for consideration, to further the effectiveness of the challenge procedures themselves.

The Committee recognizes this progress with satisfaction and trusts that all of its recommendations to the authorities in that country shall be implemented through continuation of this legislative development process aimed at fully and effectively guaranteeing the political rights of Mexican citizens as recognized in the American Convention.

---

28 Published in Government Gazette No. 24, section four, February 4, 1993. In force on February 5, 1993.
29 Unanimous opinion SX-III-RA-003/91 Institutional Revolutionary Party (PRI),7/31/91; and unanimous opinion SX-III-002/91 Institutional Revolutionary Party (PRI), ibid, p.241.

The Inter-American Commission on Human Rights hopes that, as it was told by the authorities of that country, these amendments will effectively allow greater "authenticity, equality, and transparency" in current and future electoral processes, and trusts that the recommendations this Commission has been making for some time to the Mexican authorities will be carried out in legislatively and operationally by the competent authorities.

Questions and Comments

1. In the 1990s, the Commission received several petitions concerning elections in Mexico. See Resolution No. 01/90, Cases 9756, 9780 and 9828 (Mexico) of May 17, 1990 and Report No. 8/91, Cases 10.180 (Mexico) of 22 February 1991. In response to all the petitions, the government asserted the lack of Commission competence to examine electoral processes in a state. How convincing are the following government arguments:

   a. Electoral problems are matters of national sovereignty, controlled by Article 60 of the Federal Constitution. Decisions of electoral bodies thus "cannot be subject to international jurisdiction" or it would amount to an intervention into domestic matters in violation of Article 18 of the OAS Charter;

   b. The issues are related to "the exercise of the right of free self-determination of the Mexican people (. . .) which would be infringed if an international authority sought to invoke (. . .) considerations of any nature" (quoted from the Government's submission);

   c. Electoral matters are reserved to the internal jurisdiction of the individual states in the Mexican federal system;

   d. Any pronouncement of the Commission would be "political" in nature and not a legal interpretation of the Convention because the organization of elections is not governed by the treaty;

   e. Although the right to vote and to be elected is an individual right of immediate enforceability, the conduct of elections concerns a collective right that the State is obliged to develop progressively for its inhabitants, according to circumstances and conditions in each country; therefore the Commission cannot judge the actions of Mexico.

2. Does the Commission have the competence to send election observers into a component state in a federal system when there have been repeated allegations of violations of political rights?

3. What are the minimum requirements for a free and fair election?

4. Should the Commission investigate the criteria for registration of political parties?

5. State Obligations during Periods of Emergency

A. Introduction

Most treaties for the protection of human rights allow States Parties to derogate from their obligations in response to national emergencies. The derogation clauses of the European Convention, the International Covenant on Civil and Political Rights, and the American Convention are similar. All demand a serious threat to the nation as a condition precedent to derogation and limit the measures which may be taken to those strictly required by the exigencies of the situation, with the proviso that such measures not be inconsistent with other international obligations of the state concerned. There are nonetheless, differences in the specific language of the provisions, which are reprinted below. All three treaties list the rights which are considered non-derogable (those under the American Convention being more numerous), and all obligate the derogating party to notify the international organization concerned. The European Court must await for the question of derogation to arise as an issue of an individual petition or an inter-state application, but the Inter-American Commission is empowered to review suspected derogations *sua sponte*, giving it a theoretical ability—not yet utilized—to respond with greater efficacy to widespread violations of human rights. The African Charter contains no derogation provision, something the African Commission commented on in the case concerning *Chad*, reprinted below.

European Convention on Human Rights, Article 15

1. In time of war or other public emergency threatening the life of the nation any High Contracting Party may take measures derogating from its obligations under this Convention to the extent strictly required by the exigencies of the situation, provided that such measures are not inconsistent with its other obligations under international law.

2. No derogation from Article 2, except in respect of deaths resulting from lawful acts of war, or from Articles 3, 4 (paragraph 1) and 7 shall be made under this provision.

3. Any High Contracting Party availing itself of this right of derogation shall keep the Secretary General of the Council of Europe fully informed of the measure which it has taken and the reasons therefor. It shall also inform the Secretary General of the Council of Europe when such measures have ceased to operate and the provisions of the Convention are again being fully executed.

American Convention on Human Rights, Article 27

1. In time of war, public danger, or other emergency that threatens the independence or security of a State Party, it may take measures derogating from its obligations under the present Convention to the extent and for the period of time strictly required by the exigencies of the situation, provided that such measures are not inconsistent with its other obligations under international law and do not involve discrimination on the ground of race, color, sex, language, religion or social origin.

2. The foregoing provision does not authorize any suspension of the following articles: Article 3 (Right to Juridical Personality), Article 4 (Right to Life), Article 5 (Right to Humane Treatment), Article 6 (Freedom from Slavery), Article 9 (Freedom from Ex Post Facto Laws), Article 12 (Freedom of Conscience and Religion), Article 17 (Rights of the Family), Article 18 (Right to a Name), Article 19 (Rights of the Child), Article 20 (Right to Nationality), and Article 23 (Right to Participate in Government), or to the judicial guarantees essential for the protection of such rights.

3. Any State Party availing itself of the right of suspension shall immediately inform the other States Parties, through the Secretary General of the Organization of American States, of the provisions the application of which it has suspended, the reasons that gave rise to the suspension, and the date set for the termination of such suspension.

International Covenant on Civil and Political Rights, Article 4

1. In time of public emergency which threatens the life of the nation and the existence of which is officially proclaimed the States Parties to the present Covenant may take measures derogating from their obligations under the present Covenant to the extent strictly required by the exigencies of the situation, provided that such measures are not inconsistent with their obligations under international law and do not involve discrimination solely on the ground of race, colour, sex, language, religion or social origin.

2. No derogation from articles 6, 7, 8 (paragraphs I and 2), 11, 15, 16 and 18 may be made under this provision.

3. Any State Party to the present Covenant availing itself of the right of derogation shall immediately inform the other States Parties to the present Covenant, through the intermediary of the Secretary-General of the United Nations, of the provisions from which it has derogated and of the reasons by which it was actuated. A further communication shall be made, through the same intermediary, on the date on which it terminates such derogation.

Questions and Comments

1. Assuming a state is a party to one of the regional conventions and also to the ICCPR—would it make a difference in the State's obligations during a period of emergency?

2. Which system is more protective of human rights during emergencies?

B. Examples of Derogations and Suspensions

i. Europe

Declaration Contained in a Note Verbale from the Permanent Representation of the United Kingdom, dated 18 December 2001, registered by the Secretariat General on 18 December 2001—and withdrawn by a Note verbale from the Permanent Representation of the United Kingdom dated 16 March 2005, registered at the Secretariat General on 16 March 2005.

The United Kingdom Permanent Representative to the Council of Europe presents his compliments to the Secretary General of the Council, and has the honour to convey the following information in order to ensure compliance with the obligations of Her Majesty's Government in the United Kingdom under Article 15(3) of the Convention for the Protection of Human Rights and Fundamental Freedoms signed at Rome on 5 November 1950.

Public Emergency in the United Kingdom

The terrorist attacks in New York, Washington, D.C. and Pennsylvania on 11th September 2001 resulted in several thousand deaths, including many British victims and others from 70 different countries. In its resolutions 1368 (2001) and 1373 (2001), the United Nations Council recognised the attacks as a threat to international peace and security.

The threat from international terrorism is a continuing one. In its resolution 1373 (2001), the Security Council, acting under Chapter VII of the United Nations Charter, required all States to take measures to prevent the commission of terrorist attacks, including by denying safe haven to those who finance, plan, support or commit terrorist attacks.

There exists a terrorist threat to the United Kingdom from persons suspected of involvement in international terrorism. In particular, there are foreign nationals present in the United Kingdom who are suspected of being concerned in the commission, preparation or instigation of acts of international terrorism, of being members of organisations or groups which are so concerned or of having links with members of such organisations or groups, and who are a threat to the national security of the United Kingdom.

As a result, a public emergency, within the meaning of Article 15 (1) of the Convention, exists in the United Kingdom.

The Anti-terrorism, Crime and Security Act 2001

As a result of the public emergency, provision is made in the Anti-terrorism, Crime and Security Act 2001, *inter alia*, for an extended power to arrest and detain a foreign national which will apply where it is intended to remove or deport the person from the United Kingdom but where removal or deportation is not for the time being possible, with the consequence that the detention would be unlawful under existing domestic law powers. The extended power to arrest and detain will apply where the Secretary of State issues a certificate indicating his belief that the person's presence in the United Kingdom is a risk to national security and that he suspects the person of being an international terrorist. That certificate will be subject to an appeal to the Special Immigration Appeals Commission ("SIAC"), established under the Special Immigration Appeals Commission Act 1997, which will have power to cancel it if it considers that the certificate should not have been issued. There will be an appeal on a point of law from a ruling by SIAC. In addition, the certificate will be reviewed by SIAC at regular intervals. SIAC will also be able to grant bail, where appropriate, subject to conditions. It will be open to a detainee to end his detention at any time by agreeing to leave the United Kingdom.

The extended power of arrest and detention in the Anti-terrorism, Crime and Security Act 2001 is a measure which is strictly required by the exigencies of the situation. It is a temporary provision which comes into force for an initial period of 15 months and then expires unless renewed by the Parliament. Thereafter, it is subject to annual renewal by Parliament. If, at any time, in the Governments' assessment, the public emergency no longer exists or the extended power is no longer strictly required by the exigencies of the situation, then the Secretary of State will, by Order, repeal the provision.

Domestic law powers of detention (other than under the Anti-terrorism, Crime and Security Act 2001)

The Government has powers under the Immigration Act 1971 ("the 1971 Act") to remove or deport persons on the ground that their presence in the United Kingdom is not conducive to the public good on national security grounds. Persons can also be arrested and detained under Schedules 2 and 3 to the 1971 Act pending their removal or deportation. The courts in the United Kingdom have ruled that this power of detention can only be exercised during the period necessary, in all the circumstances of the particular case, to effect removal and that, if it becomes clear that removal is not going to be possible within a reasonable time, detention will be unlawful (R. v Governor of Durham Prison, ex parte Singh [1984] All ER 983).

Article 5(1)(f) of the Convention

It is well established that Article 5(1)(f) permits the detention of a person with a view to deportation only in circumstances where "action is being taken with a view to deportation" (Chahal v United Kingdom (1996) 23 EHRR 413 at paragraph 112). In that case the European Court of Human Rights indicated that detention will cease to be permissible under Article 5(1)(f) if deportation proceedings are not prosecuted with due diligence and that it was necessary in such cases to determine whether the duration of the deportation proceedings was excessive (paragraph 113).

In some cases, where the intention remains to remove or deport a person on national security grounds, continued detention may not be consistent with Article 5(1)(f) as interpreted by the Court in the *Chahal* case. This may be the case, for example, if the person has established that removal to their own country might result in treatment contrary to Article 3 of the Convention. In such circumstances, irrespective of the gravity of the threat to national security posed by the person concerned, it is well established that Article 3 prevents removal or deportation to a place where there is a real risk that the person will suffer treatment contrary to that article. If no alternative destination is immediately available then removal or deportation may not, for the time being, be possible even though the ultimate intention remains to remove or deport the person once satisfactory arrangements can be made. In addition, it may not be possible to prosecute the person for a criminal offence given the strict rules on the admissibility of evidence in the criminal justice system of the United Kingdom and the high standard of proof required.

Derogation under Article 15 of the Convention

The Government has considered whether the exercise of the extended power to detain contained in the Anti-terrorism, Crime and Security Act 2001 may be inconsistent with the obligations under Article 5(1) of the Convention. As indicated above, there may be cases where, notwithstanding a continuing intention to remove or deport a person who is being detained, it is not possible to say that "action is being taken with a view to deportation" within the meaning of Article 5(1)(f) as interpreted by the Court in the *Chahal case*. To the extent, therefore, that the exercise of the extended power may be inconsistent with the United Kingdom's obligations under Article 5(1), the Government has decided to avail itself of the right of derogation conferred by Article 15(1) of the Convention and will continue to do so until further notice. **Period covered: 18/12/2001–14/3/2005**

Withdrawal of Derogation Contained in a Note Verbale from the Permanent Representation of the United Kingdom **dated 16 March 2005, registered at the Secretariat General on 16 March 2005.**

The United Kingdom Permanent Representative to the Council of Europe presents his compliments to the Secretary General of the Council of Europe, and has the honour to refer to Article 15, paragraph 3, of the Convention for the Protection of Human Rights and Fundamental Freedoms, signed at Rome on 5 November 1950, as well as to the notification made by the then United Kingdom Permanent Representative to the then Secretary General under Article 15, paragraph 3, dated 18 December 2001.

The provisions referred to in the 18 December 2001 notification, namely the extended power of arrest and detention in the Anti-terrorism, Crime and Security Act 2001, ceased to operate on 14 March 2005. Accordingly, the notification is withdrawn as from that date, and the Government of the United Kingdom confirm that the relevant provisions of the Convention will again be executed as from then.

Declaration Contained in a Letter from the Minister of Foreign Affairs of Georgia, **dated 2 March 2006, transmitted by the Permanent Representation of Georgia and registered at the Secretariat General on 3 March 2006 and withdrawn by a letter from the Minister of Foreign Affairs of Georgia, dated 23 March 2006, registered at the Secretariat General on 28 March 2006.**

In conformity with Article 15 of the European Convention for the Protection of Human Rights and Fundamental Freedoms, I have to inform you that the President of Georgia on 26 February 2006 has issued the Decree No. 173 on "State of Emergency in the Khelvachauri district" which has been approved by the Parliament of Georgia on 28 February 2006.

The Decree is aimed at preventing further spread throughout Georgia of H5N1 virus (bird flu) that has been recently detected in the district in question.

Due to the state of emergency, in accordance with Article 15 of the European Convention for the Protection of Human Rights and Fundamental Freedoms, Georgia avails itself of the right of derogation from Article 1 (Protection of Property) of Protocol to the Convention and Article 2 (Freedom of Movement) of Protocol No. 4.

The restrictions imposed upon by the Decree are fully in line with provisions of Article 21, paragraphs 2 and 3 (on the restrictions related to property rights) and Article 22, paragraph 3 (on the restrictions related to the freedom of movement) and Article 46 (on the restrictions related to constitutional rights and freedoms) of the Constitution of Georgia and respective provisions of the Law on the State of Emergency of Georgia.

You will be informed in due course when the above Decree is abolished.

[**Note by the Secretariat**: The letter from the Minister of Foreign Affairs of Georgia, dated 23 March 2006, reads as follows:" *I have to inform you that the President of Georgia on 15 March 2006 has issued the Decree No. 199 on the "Abolishment of the State of Emergency in the Khelvachauri district" which has been approved by* *the Parliament of Georgia on 16 March 2006. According to the above Decree, the Presidential Decree No. 173 of 26 February 2006 "On State of Emergency in the Khelvachauri district" has been declared null and void."*]

ii. The Americas

Colombia:

By Decree No. 1900 of 2 November 1995, declaration of a State of internal disturbance throughout the national territory for a period of ninety (90) days. The state of internal disturbance by the National Government is justified by the fact that acts of violence attributed to criminal and terrorist organizations have occurred in difference regions of the country and are seriously and manifestly disturbing public order.

Ecuador:

17 July 2002

Sir,

In accordance with article 4 of the International Covenant on Civil and Political Rights, of which Ecuador is a State Party, and on behalf of the national Government, I am writing to notify you of the declarations of a state of national emergency this year declared by Dr. Gustavo Noboa Bejarano, President of the Republic, in accordance with the provisions of articles 180 and 181 of the Ecuadorian Constitution in force, and when they were lifted. The details of these declarations follow:

Executive Decree No. 2404 of 26 February 2002 (Official Register No. 525): A state of emergency is declared in Sucumbios and Orellana provinces. The reason for this measure is the serious situation arising out of problems of the Colombian conflict on the frontiers;

Executive Decree No. 2421 of 4 March 2002: The state of emergency in Sucumbios and Orellana provinces is declared over, and accordingly Executive Decree 2404 of 22 February 2002 is abrogated;

Executive Decree No. 2492 of 22 March 2002: State of emergency in Esmeraldas, Guayas Los Ríos, Manabí and El Oro provinces. The reason for this measure is the severe storm on the Ecuadorian coast. The state of emergency was lifted on 22 May pursuant to the legal provision embodied in article 182, paragraph 2, of the Ecuadorian Constitution to the effect that "a decree of a state of emergency shall remain in force for up to a maximum of 60 days";

Executive Decree No. 2625 of 7 May 2002 (Official Register No. 575 of 14 May 2002): State of national emergency in respect of land transport. (This state of emergency has not been lifted but, will last until 7 July, unless the President declares that it is lifted in advance.)

Accept, Sir, the renewed assurances of my highest consideration.

(Signed) Dr. Heinz Moeller Freile

C. Jurisprudence

i. Europe

Case of Ireland v. the United Kingdom, (App. no. 5310/71), Judgment of 18 January 1978 (plenary), 25 Eur. Ct. H.R. (Ser. A), 2 EHRR 25 (1979–1980).

PROCEDURE

1. This case was referred to the Court by the Government of Ireland. It originated in an application against the Government of the United Kingdom of Great Britain and Northern Ireland lodged by the applicant Government with the European Commission of Human Rights on 16 December 1971 under Article 24 of the Convention for the Protection of Human Rights and Fundamental Freedoms. The report drawn up by the Commission concerning the said application was transmitted to the Committee of Ministers of the Council of Europe on 9 February 1976. . . .

AS TO THE FACTS

I. THE EMERGENCY SITUATION AND ITS BACKGROUND

11. The tragic and lasting crisis in Northern Ireland lies at the root of the present case. In order to combat what the respondent Government describe as "the longest and most violent terrorist campaign witnessed in either part of the island of Ireland", the authorities in Northern Ireland exercised from August 1971 until December 1975 a series of extrajudicial powers of arrest, detention and internment. The proceedings in this case concern the scope and the operation in practice of those measures as well as the alleged ill-treatment of persons thereby deprived of their liberty.

12. Up to March 1975, on the figures cited before the Commission by the respondent Government, over 1,100 people had been killed, over 11,500 injured and more than £140,000,000 worth of property destroyed during the recent troubles in Northern Ireland. This violence found its expression in part in civil disorders, in part in terrorism, that is organised violence for political ends. . . .

II. EXTRAJUDICIAL DEPRIVATION OF LIBERTY

78. During the period under consideration, in addition to the ordinary criminal law which remained in force and in use, the authorities had various special powers to combat terrorism in Northern Ireland. These were all discretionary and underwent modification from time to time, as is described below; they enabled the authorities to effect extrajudicial deprivation of liberty falling into the following three basic categories:

- initial arrest for interrogation;
- detention for further interrogation (originally called "detention" and subsequently "interim custody");
- preventive detention (originally called "internment" and subsequently "detention").

79. In accordance with Article 15 para. 3 of the Convention, the United Kingdom Government sent to the Secretary-General of the Council of Europe, both before

and after the original application to the Commission, six notices of derogation in respect of these powers. Such notices, of which the first two are not pertinent in the present case, were dated 27 June 1957, 25 September 1969, 20 August 1971, 23 January 1973, 16 August 1973 and 19 September 1975 and drew attention to the relevant legislation and modifications thereof.

A. The special powers act and regulations there under

80. The Special Powers Act empowered the Minister of Home Affairs for Northern Ireland, until 30 March 1972, or, thereafter and until 8 August 1973, the Secretary of State for Northern Ireland to take all such steps and issue all such orders as might be necessary for preserving peace and maintaining order. It was an enabling Act whose substantive provisions were contained in Regulations made there under. Before direct rule, either House of Parliament of Northern Ireland could, at the time Regulations were made, request the Governor to annul them; subsequently, new Regulations were subject to approval by the United Kingdom Parliament.

The number and scope of the Regulations in force varied over the years; they could be brought into use without any legislative act or proclamation. Those relevant to the present case were made in 1956 (Regulations 11 and 12) and 1957 (Regulation 10). They were utilised to implement the policy of internment introduced on 9 August 1971 and advice of their use was given to the Secretary-General by the United Kingdom Government's notice of derogation of 20 August 1971 (Yearbook of the Convention, volume 14, page 32). . . .

The position concerning the review of internment orders by the courts was the same as under Regulations 10, 11 (1) and 11 (2) (see the *Kelly* case).

796 orders were made under Regulation 12 (1), all before the introduction of direct rule. Nearly 170 orders were still in force on 7 November 1972 when the Regulation was revoked by the Terrorists Order.

By 30 March 1972, 588 of the 796 cases had been reviewed by the advisory committee (although 451 internees refused to appear) and 69 releases recommended. Of the 69 individuals all were released except 6 who refused to give an undertaking as to future good behaviour. . . .

B. The terrorists order

85. The Terrorists Order, a temporary measure made under the Temporary Provisions Act, introduced an independent review of decisions on detention for further interrogation and on preventive detention whereas, previously, such decisions had been taken by the administrative authority alone. The Order revoked with effect from 7 November 1972 Special Powers Regulations 11 (2) and (4) and 12 (1)—but not 10 and 11 (1)—and converted existing detention or internment orders into interim custody orders. The Order defined "terrorism" as "the use of violence for political ends [including] any use of violence for the purpose of putting the public or any section of the public in fear".

The Secretary-General of the Council of Europe was advised of the making of this Order by the United Kingdom Government's notice of derogation of 23 January 1973 (Yearbook of the Convention, volume 16, pages 24 and 26). The Order . . . was repealed by the Emergency Provisions Act on 8 August. . . .

C. The emergency provisions act

88. The Emergency Provisions Act, based on the recommendations of the Diplock Commission, repealed with effect from 8 August 1973 the Special Powers Act, Regulations 10 and 11 (1) and the Terrorists Order but maintained in effect—under its own provisions—the existing interim custody and detention orders. The emergency powers contained in the new Act were to remain in force for one year unless renewed for a period not exceeding one year by an Order of the Secretary of State approved by both United Kingdom Houses of Parliament; they were in fact renewed for six-monthly periods commencing on 25 July 1974, 25 January 1975 and 25 July 1975 and then amended on 21 August 1975 by the Emergency Provisions Amendment Act. The Secretary-General of the Council of Europe was advised of the new legislation, and of the subsequent renewal and amendment of the emergency powers, by the United Kingdom Government's notices of derogation of 16 August 1973 (*Yearbook of the Convention*, volume 16, pages 26 and 28) and 19 September 1975 (document DH (75) 5, page 5).

The new Act (section 10 (5) and Schedule 1) re-enacted, in substance, the powers contained in the Terrorists Order, retaining its definition of terrorism. Accordingly, the powers to make interim custody and detention orders, and the review thereof by a commissioner and the appeal tribunal, continued . . . , with the significant differences that:

- the individual had to receive a written statement concerning the terrorist activities to be investigated by the commissioner at least seven (rather than three) days before the hearing;
- in addition to his optional power to refer, the Secretary of State had to refer to a commissioner the case of anyone held under a detention order for one year since the making of the order or for six months since the last review.

Section 10 of the Act also provided that any constable might arrest without warrant a person whom he suspected of being a terrorist; detention after arrest was limited to seventy-two hours. The Act conferred certain other powers of arrest (sections 11 and 12) which are not in issue in the present case.

. . . .

THE LAW

. . . .

II. ON ARTICLE 5

188. The substance of the Irish Government's allegations is that

- the various powers relating to extrajudicial deprivation of liberty which were used in the six counties from 9 August 1971 to March 1975 did not satisfy the conditions prescribed by Article 5;
- those powers violated Article 5 since they failed to meet in full the requirements of Article 15;
- those powers were furthermore exercised with discrimination and consequently also violated Article 14 taken together with Article 5.

189. The applicant Government are not asking the Court to give a ruling on the legislation subsequent to March 1975, the date of the final hearings of the Parties before the Commission. However, the Emergency Provisions Amendment Act, certain of whose provisions reintroduced the principle of detention by order of the Secretary of State for Northern Ireland, did not enter into force until 21 August 1975. An ex officio examination of those provisions is not called for: the information made available to the Court suggests that they have not been used since 5 December 1975 and, besides, does not indicate that resort was ever had to them before that date.

190. The legislation prior to March 1975 is criticised by the Irish Government as regards both its terms and its application. However, the first aspect is a matter for, and must be dealt with under, Articles 1 and 24. Only the second aspect is relevant under Article 5, taken alone or together with Articles 15 and 14. In addition, the scope of the Court's review extends to the application of that legislation between 9 August 1971 and March 1975 only as a practice and not in a given individual case; this is clear from the documents before the Court read as a whole and, in particular, from the decision of 1 October 1972 on the admissibility of the original application of 16 December 1971.

191. It will, of course, be necessary to have regard to Article 15 in deciding whether any derogation from Article 5 were, in the circumstances of the case, compatible with the Convention, but the Court considers that it should ascertain in what respects the measures complained of derogated from Article 5 before assessing them under Article 15.

. . .

193. In the Commission's opinion, the powers at issue—as exercised by the competent authorities—did not comply with paragraphs 1 to 4 of Article 5 on a number of points.

. . . .

201. On paragraphs 1 to 4 of Article 5, taken alone, the Court . . . arrives at conclusions in line with those of the Commission.

B. On Article 5 taken together with Article 15

202. The applicant Government maintain that the powers relating to extrajudicial deprivation of liberty which were applied in Northern Ireland from 9 August 1971 to March 1975 were not in complete conformity with Article 15 and, accordingly, violated Article 5.

The Commission is unanimous in not accepting this claim and it is disputed by the respondent Government.

203. Article 15 provides:

> 1. In time of war or other public emergency threatening the life of the nation any High Contracting Party may take measures derogating from its obligations under this Convention to the extent strictly required by the exigencies of the situation, provided that such measures are not inconsistent with its other obligations under international law.

2. No derogation from Article 2 (art. 2), except in respect of deaths resulting from lawful acts of war, or from Articles 3, 4 (paragraph 1) and 7 (art. 3, art. 4–1, art. 7) shall be made under this provision.

3. Any High Contracting Party availing itself of this right of derogation shall keep the Secretary-General of the Council of Europe fully informed of the measures which it has taken and the reasons therefore. It shall also inform the Secretary-General of the Council of Europe when such measures have ceased to operate and the provisions of the Convention are again being fully executed.

204. Article 5 does not appear amongst the entrenched provisions listed in paragraph 2 of Article 15 and is therefore one of the Articles subject to the "right of derogation" reserved by the Contracting States, the exercise of which is regulated by paragraphs 1 and 3.

1. On the "public emergency threatening the life of the nation"

205. Article 15 comes into play only "in time of war or other public emergency threatening the life of the nation". The existence of such an emergency is perfectly clear from the facts summarised above and was not questioned by anyone before either the Commission or the Court. The crisis experienced at the time by the six counties therefore comes within the ambit of Article 15.

2. On the "extent strictly required"

206. The Contracting States may make use of their right of derogation only "to the extent strictly required by the exigencies of the situation". The Irish Government consider the "extent strictly required" to have been exceeded, whereas the British Government and the Commission assert the contrary.

(a) The role of the Court

207. The limits on the Court's powers of review (see judgment of 23 July 1968 on the merits of the *"Belgian Linguistic"* case, Series A no. 6, p. 35, para. 10 in fine; *Handyside* judgment of 7 December 1976, Series A no. 24, p. 22, para. 48) are particularly apparent where Article 15 is concerned.

It falls in the first place to each Contracting State, with its responsibility for "the life of [its] nation", to determine whether that life is threatened by a "public emergency" and, if so, how far it is necessary to go in attempting to overcome the emergency. By reason of their direct and continuous contact with the pressing needs of the moment, the national authorities are in principle in a better position than the international judge to decide both on the presence of such an emergency and on the nature and scope of derogations necessary to avert it. In this matter Article 15 para. 1 leaves those authorities a wide margin of appreciation.

Nevertheless, the States do not enjoy an unlimited power in this respect. The Court, which, with the Commission, is responsible for ensuring the observance of the States' engagements (Article 19), is empowered to rule on whether the States have gone beyond the "extent strictly required by the exigencies" of the crisis (*Lawless* judgment of 1 July 1961, Series A no. 3, p. 55, para. 22, and pp. 57–59, paras. 36–38). The domestic margin of appreciation is thus accompanied by a European supervision.

(b) Questions of evidence

208. The Irish Government ask the Court to exclude from its examination the following material:

- by reason of their origin, the Diplock report, statements made before the Commission by the representatives of the United Kingdom and the memorandum by the Northern Ireland Office, annexed to the British memorial to the Court;
- for the reasons given in paragraph 210 below, the oral evidence obtained by the Commission under Article 14, including that of the witnesses G 1, G 2 and G 3, who were heard in London on 20 February 1975.

209. The Court is not bound, under the Convention or under the general principles applicable to international tribunals, by strict rules of evidence. In order to satisfy itself, the Court is entitled to rely on evidence of every kind, including, insofar as it deems them relevant, documents or statements emanating from governments, be they respondent or applicant, or from their institutions or officials. Here, there can scarcely be any question as to the relevance of the evidence which the Irish Government challenge. In particular, the fact that some of it was given in connection with Article 14 rather than Article 15 is of little moment.

210. The hearing of the evidence of G 1, G 2 and G 3 gives rise to rather complex questions. The applicant Government invite the Court not to take account of that evidence because it was heard in the absence of the Parties and without cross-examination, as a result of the wishes of the respondent Government who thereby allegedly failed in their obligation to cooperate in establishing the truth (Article 28, sub-paragraph (a) in fine, of the Convention).

The Court finds in the first place that it does not have jurisdiction to rule on the correctness of the procedure followed at that hearing. The Commission, with its independence from the Court when carrying out its fact-finding role (*Lawless* judgment of 14 November 1960, Series A no. 1, p. 11, second sub-paragraph), is master of its procedure and of the interpretation of its Rules of Procedure—in this case Rule 34 para. 2—which it draws up under Article 36 of the Convention.

On the other hand, the Court, being master of its own procedure and of its own rules (Article 55 of the Convention), has complete freedom in assessing not only the admissibility and the relevance but also the probative value of each item of evidence before it. It cannot attach to the evidence of G 1, G 2 and G 3 as much weight as to the evidence of witnesses who have been cross-examined. The Court looks upon the evidence of G 1, G 2 and G 3 as no more than one source of information amongst others and one which, being evidence coming from senior British officials, falls into a similar category to the respective statements made by the representatives of the two Governments to the Commission and the Court. Although that evidence was given on oath, it was obtained under conditions which reduce its weight. Besides, its importance was not over-estimated by the Commission which bore the absence of cross-examination in mind; the delegates took care to emphasise this.

(c) Questions concerning the merits

211. The Court has to decide whether the United Kingdom went beyond the "extent strictly required". For this purpose the Court must, as in the *Lawless* case

(judgment of 1 July 1961, Series A no. 3, pp. 57–59, paras. 36–37), enquire into the necessity for, on the one hand, deprivation of liberty contrary to paragraph 1 of Article 5 and, on the other hand, the failure of guarantees to attain the level fixed by paragraphs 2 to 4.

(i) On the necessity for derogation from paragraph 1 of Article 5 by extrajudicial deprivation of liberty

212. Unquestionably, the exercise of the special powers was mainly, and before 5 February 1973 even exclusively, directed against the IRA as an underground military force. The intention was to combat an organisation which had played a considerable subversive role throughout the recent history of Ireland and which was creating, in August 1971 and thereafter, a particularly far-reaching and acute danger for the territorial integrity of the United Kingdom, the institutions of the six counties and the lives of the province's inhabitants. Being confronted with a massive wave of violence and intimidation, the Northern Ireland Government and then, after the introduction of direct rule (30 March 1972), the British Government were reasonably entitled to consider that normal legislation offered insufficient resources for the campaign against terrorism and that recourse to measures outside the scope of the ordinary law, in the shape of extrajudicial deprivation of liberty, was called for. When the Irish Republic was faced with a serious crisis in 1957, it adopted the same approach and the Court did not conclude that the "extent strictly required" had been exceeded (*Lawless* judgment of 1 July 1961, Series A no. 3, pp. 35–36, para. 14, and pp. 57–58, para. 36).

However, under one of the provisions complained of, namely Regulation 10, a person who was in no way suspected of a crime or offence or of activities prejudicial to peace and order could be arrested for the sole purpose of obtaining from him information about others—and this sometimes occurred. This sort of arrest can be justifiable only in a very exceptional situation, but the circumstances prevailing in Northern Ireland did fall into such a category. Many witnesses could not give evidence freely without running the greatest risks; the competent authorities were entitled to take the view, without exceeding their margin of appreciation, that it was indispensable to arrest such witnesses so that they could be questioned in conditions of relative security and not be exposed to reprisals. Moreover and above all, Regulation 10 authorised deprivation of liberty only for a maximum of forty-eight hours.

213. From 9 August 1971 to 5 February 1973, the measures involving deprivation of liberty taken by the respondent State were used only against Republican terrorism even though as early as this period outrages, at first sporadic but later constantly more numerous, were attributable to Loyalist terrorism; even after 5 February 1973, the measures were applied against Republican terrorism to a much greater extent than against Loyalist terrorism despite the latter's organisation and extensive development shortly after 30 March 1972.

The Court will examine below whether the difference of treatment between the two types of terrorism was such as to violate Article 14 of the Convention.

This issue apart, it appears to the Court that the extrajudicial measures brought into operation could, in the situation described above, reasonably have been considered strictly required for the protection of public security and that, in the context of Article 15, their intrinsic necessity, once recognised, could not be affected by the restriction of their field of application.

214. The Irish Government submit that experience shows extrajudicial deprivation of liberty to have been ineffectual. They contend that the policy introduced on 9 August 1971 not only failed to put a brake on terrorism but also had the result of increasing it. Consequently, the British Government, after attenuating the policy in varying degrees following the introduction of direct rule, abandoned it on 5 December 1975: since then, it appears that no one has been detained in the six counties under the emergency legislation, despite the persistence of an intense campaign of violence and even though the Emergency Provisions Amendment Act has remained in force. This, claim the applicant Government, confirms that extrajudicial deprivation of liberty was not an absolute necessity.

The Court cannot accept this argument.

It is certainly not the Court's function to substitute for the British Government's assessment any other assessment of what might be the most prudent or most expedient policy to combat terrorism. The Court must do no more than review the lawfulness, under the Convention, of the measures adopted by that Government from 9 August 1971 onwards. For this purpose the Court must arrive at its decision in the light, not of a purely retrospective examination of the efficacy of those measures, but of the conditions and circumstances reigning when they were originally taken and subsequently applied.

Adopting, as it must, this approach, the Court accepts that the limits of the margin of appreciation left to the Contracting States by Article 15 para. 1 were not overstepped by the United Kingdom when it formed the opinion that extrajudicial deprivation of liberty was necessary from August 1971 to March 1975.

(ii) On the necessity for derogation from the guarantees under paragraphs 2 to 4 of Article 5

215. The Court must now examine under Article 15 para. 1 the necessity for the far-reaching derogations found by it to have been made from paragraphs 2 to 4 of Article 5.

216. Neither Regulations 10 and 11 (1) nor section 10 of the Emergency Provisions Act afforded any remedy, judicial or administrative, against arrests effected there under. Although persons arrested under Regulation 11 (1) could, before 7 November 1972, apply to the Civil Authority for release on bail, the Terrorists Order deprived them of this right by revoking Regulation 11 (4) under which it arose. However, the duration of such arrests never exceeded forty-eight hours as regards Regulation 10, seventy-two hours as regards section 10 of the Emergency Provisions Act and, in practice, seventy-two hours as regards Regulation 11 (1).

217. Similarly, Regulation 11 (2), Article 4 of the Terrorists Order and paragraph 11 of Schedule 1 to the Emergency Provisions Act did not provide for any remedy. Detention under Regulation 11 (2) sometimes continued for longer than twenty-eight days, but it was never to be for an indefinite period and the detainee could, if the administrative authority agreed, apply to the courts for release on bail (Regulation 11 (4) and the *McElduff* case, judgment of 12 October 1971). On the other hand,

interim custody imposed under Article 4 of the Terrorists Order, or subsequently under paragraph 11 of Schedule 1 to the Emergency Provisions Act, continued until adjudication by the commissioner; the Chief Constable invariably referred the case to him within the initial twenty-eight day time-limit but the commissioner gave his decision after several weeks or even after six months.

218. Individuals deprived of their liberty under Regulation 12 (1), Article 5 of the Terrorists Order or paragraph 24 of Schedule 1 to the Emergency Provisions Act were in many cases interned or detained for some years. Nevertheless, the advisory committee set up by Regulation 12 (1) afforded, notwithstanding its non-judicial character, a certain measure of protection that cannot be discounted. By establishing commissioners and an appeal tribunal, the Terrorists Order brought further safeguards which were somewhat strengthened by the Emergency Provisions Act.

219. There was in addition the valuable, if limited, review effected by the courts, when the opportunity arose, by virtue of the common law (see, for example, the *McElduff* case, judgment of 12 October 1971 on Regulations 11 (1) and 11 (2), the *Moore* case, judgment of 18 February 1972 on Regulation 10 and the *Kelly* case, judgment of 11 January 1973 on Regulations 11 (1), 11 (2) and 12 (1)).

220. An overall examination of the legislation and practice at issue reveals that they evolved in the direction of increasing respect for individual liberty. The incorporation right from the start of more satisfactory judicial, or at least administrative, guarantees would certainly have been desirable, especially as Regulations 10 to 12 (1) dated back to 1956–1957 and were made under an Act of 1922, but it would be unrealistic to isolate the first from the later phases. When a State is struggling against a public emergency threatening the life of the nation, it would be rendered defenceless if it were required to accomplish everything at once, to furnish from the outset each of its chosen means of action with each of the safeguards reconcilable with the priority requirements for the proper functioning of the authorities and for restoring peace within the community. The interpretation of Article 15 must leave a place for progressive adaptations.

The Northern Ireland Government sought in the first place—unsuccessfully—to meet the most pressing problem, to stem the wave of violence that was sweeping the region. After assuming direct responsibility for the future of the province, the British Government and Parliament lost little time in moderating in certain respects the severity of the laws applied in the early days. The Court asked itself whether those laws should not have been attenuated even more, especially as regards interim custody, but does not consider that it can give an affirmative answer. It must not be forgotten that the crisis experienced at the time by the six counties was serious and, hence, of a kind that justified far-reaching derogations from paragraphs 2 to 4 of Article 5. In view of the Contracting States' margin of appreciation, the Court does not find it established that the United Kingdom exceeded in this respect the "extent strictly required" referred to in Article 15 para. 1.

221. According to the applicant Government, the non-contested violations of Article 3 are relevant under Articles 5 and 15 taken together. They claim that deprivation of liberty was sometimes imposed on the strength of information extracted in conditions contrary to Article 3 and was thereby rendered unlawful under Ar-

ticle 15. The Irish argument is also said to be confirmed by the existence of those violations since they would probably have been prevented by the impugned legislation if it had afforded genuine guarantees to the persons concerned.

The Court emphasises, as do the respondent Government and the Commission that Articles 3 and 5 embody quite separate obligations. Moreover, the violations of Article 3 found in the present judgment fail to show that it was not necessary to apply the extrajudicial powers in force.

3. On the "other obligations under international law"

222. Article 15 para. 1 in fine prohibits any derogation inconsistent "with other obligations under international law". There is nothing in the data before the Court to suggest that the United Kingdom disregarded such obligations in this case; in particular, the Irish Government never supplied to the Commission or the Court precise details on the claim formulated or outlined on this point in their application of 16 December 1971.

4. On the observance of paragraph 3 of Article 15

223. The Court finds proprio motu, in the light of its *Lawless* judgment of 1 July 1961 (Series A no. 3, pp. 61–62, para. 47), that the British notices of derogation dated 20 August 1971, 23 January 1973 and 16 August 1973 fulfilled the requirements of Article 15 para. 3.

5. Conclusion

224. The Court has accordingly come to the conclusion that, since the requirements of Article 15 (art. 15) were met, the derogations from Article 5 (art. 5) were not, in the circumstances of the case, in breach of the Convention.

. . . .

SEPARATE OPINION OF JUDGE O'DONOGHUE

. . . .

I agree that the events justified derogation by the respondent Government under Article 15 but would point out the limitation imposed by that Article in requiring such departure from the Conventional obligations to be to the extent strictly required by the exigencies of the situation. I hope it will not be considered presumptuous to call special attention to the use of the word "strictly" and to suggest that some meaning be found for its insertion in the Article.

It is erroneous to seek to establish a parallel with the *Lawless* case where the threat was to a small unitary State, not long recovered from a civil war situation, whereas in this case the threat must relate to the existence of the United Kingdom and not to the Six Counties only. It is necessary to examine the extent to which Articles 5 and 6 were breached and to ascertain if the exigencies of the situation required those steps.

. . . Once again, it seems to me that the Court has strained beyond breaking point their conception of the margin of appreciation in Respondent's favour. . . .

SEPARATE OPINION OF JUDGE SIR GERALD FITZMAURICE

. . . .

ARTICLES 5 AND 15

38. Article 5 is the provision of the European Convention that safeguards freedom of the person by, in effect, prohibiting arrest or detention except for certain indicated purposes or in a number of listed cases. When, in circumstances of public emergency, a government wants to carry out arrests or detentions which it believes will not—or may not—fall within the permitted exceptions, Article 15 allows it (within stated limits and under specified conditions) to do so by taking measures derogating from what would otherwise be its obligations in this respect.

39. It is obvious that once a government has invoked Article 15—(it has to give what amounts to a notice of derogation to the Secretary-General of the Council of Europe)—the only relevant, or at least the principal issue will be whether the circumstances required by Article 15 in order to validate the derogations are present, and whether the derogations themselves fall within the limits laid down. Briefly, there must be "war or other public emergency threatening the life of the nation", and the derogations must not exceed what is "strictly required by the exigencies of the situation". Accordingly when, as in the present case, acts contrary to Article 5 are alleged by the plaintiff Government to have occurred, but the defendant Government has invoked Article 15, while the plaintiff Government denies that the conditions required by that provision are fulfilled, the enquiry ought to start with this Article since, if it was properly invoked, and if the acts or conduct complained of are validated under it, it will become unnecessary to consider whether, had this not been the case, they would have involved derogations from—i.e. infractions of—Article 5. Only if it appeared that Article 15 could not operate in favour of the defendant Government, either because there was not real public emergency or because the acts or conduct in issue went beyond what was required in order to deal with it, would it become essential to investigate the acts or courses of conduct themselves, so as to establish whether they did or did not amount to breaches of Article 5.

40. It may be asked what advantage this method of proceeding would have over that hitherto followed by the Court, namely of first enquiring whether there has, or but for Article 15 would have been, a breach of Article 5, and, if the answer is in the affirmative, only then going on to consider the applicability of Article 15. It seems to me not only that there are clear advantages in the method I suggest, but also that not adopting it is liable often to place the defendant Government in a false position.

41. If of course the defendant Government has not invoked Article 15 at all, and simply takes its stand on a denial that Article 5 has been infringed (e.g. because the arrest or detention involved came within one of the cases permitted by that provision), then clearly an enquiry into the Article 5 position is all that is necessary or possible. But where Article 15 was invoked, this either implies a tacit recognition that Article 5 has, or very possibly has been infringed, or renders that issue irrelevant except upon the assumption that, in all the circumstances of the case, Article 15 would not in any event validate the infraction. This last matter therefore becomes the primary issue and should be gone into first. Had the Court followed this method in the present case, some fourteen paragraphs and five pages of the Judgment could virtually have been omitted.

42. But the point has a substantive as well as a merely procedural aspect:

(a) Where it is the fact (as the Court has found in the present case) that although there would have been a breach of the Convention under Article 5, if that provision had stood alone,—but that, by reason of the operation of Article 15, the putative or potential breach resting on Article 5 is so to speak redeemed, discharged or re-habilitated,—then what really results, when the ultimate situation is reached, is simply that there is no breach of the Convention at all, as such. In these circumstances, it seems to me wrong, or at least inappropriate, to give the impression, as there will be a tendency to do, at least initially, that there is a breach of the Convention because the acts complained of, taken by themselves, would have derogated from Article 5. The whole point is that once the respondent Government has pleaded justification under Article 15, the situation as it might exist under Article 5 alone cannot properly be taken by itself. The Court's present method of dealing with the matter is to hold that there has been a breach of the Convention because of derogations from it under a certain Article,—but then to hold that, by reason of the provisions of another Article, these derogations are excusable. But this is clearly incorrect. Article 15, where applicable to the facts of the case, does not merely excuse acts otherwise inconsistent with Article 5: it nullifies them qua breaches of the Convention as a whole,—or at least justifies them, so that no breach results.

(b) This being so, it seems to me that the present system puts the emphasis in the wrong place. It involves coming to the consequences of the respondent Party having pleaded Article 15, only after establishing that there has been a breach of Article 5, thus putting that Party in the posture of being, in principle, a Convention-breaker, although it has taken all the steps necessary to invoke and bring into play Article 15 which specifically provides that, in certain circumstances "any High Contracting Party may take measures derogating from . . . this Convention". Moreover, there being in consequence no breach of the Convention as such, there cannot have been any breach of Article 5 either,—for Article 15 has acted retrospectively to prevent that. The respondent Party is therefore left in the invidious and false position of having prima facie violated the Convention, and having merely as it were subsequently atoned for that violation by bringing itself under Article 15,—whereas the true situation is that such a Party should be deemed never to have breached Article 5 at all as regards any acts for which Article 15 was invoked and found to be applicable. . . .

SEPARATE OPINION OF JUDGE MATSCHER

. . . .

In the present case we are dealing with the application of the extrajudicial powers of detention and internment which the Court has rightly—in view of the circumstances prevailing in Northern Ireland at the relevant time—considered to be compatible with the system for protecting fundamental rights set up by the Convention (Articles 5 and 6 taken together with Article 15.

It may be regarded as established that in the period up to 5 February 1973 these measures were applied only against Republican terrorists and not against Loyalist terrorists and that likewise in the subsequent period the measures in question affected the latter only to a far lesser extent. The crucial point is whether this different treatment was justified by objective and reasonable motives. If so, the difference is legitimate; if not, it constitutes discrimination within the meaning of Article 14.

There is no doubt that the extrajudicial measures were introduced at a time when terrorism of Republican origin had reached a high level. It has also been proved, however, that terrorism from Loyalist sources existed at the same time and on an increasing scale. That, from the quantitative point of view, a larger number of serious outrages were attributable to the Republican terrorists does nothing to alter the fact that in this same period two brands of terrorism were simultaneously rife in Northern Ireland. Moreover, at least from 1972 onwards, the two varieties of terrorism represented a comparable menace to law and order in the country. Nonetheless, up to 5 February 1973 the British authorities continued to apply the emergency measures to the Republican terrorists alone.

The reasons put forward by the respondent Government to justify such a difference hardly convince me, and it must also be remembered that, on this particular point, the respondent Government were very unforthcoming during the enquiry, so that an unfettered assessment of the evidence does not operate in their favour. Examination of the material before the Court would seem to me rather to permit the conclusion that, besides the bias on the part of the authorities which characterises the general situation in Northern Ireland not only in the course of history but also at the time in question, there was hesitation over talking equally energetic action against the Loyalist terrorists and over using emergency powers against them because of fear of the political repercussions of such a step. In my view, this is not a justification based on objective and reasonable motives. For want of such justification, the different treatment, which has been proved objectively, constitutes discrimination within the meaning of Article 14 of the Convention.

There is also another point of view to be taken into account. If the authorities deemed it necessary in order to combat terrorism to take emergency measures which weighed heavily on the population concerned, and if these measures were applied to only one section of the population whereas, in order to combat a comparable terrorist campaign originating from the other side—insofar as it was seriously combated -, they thought that they could confine themselves to the ordinary means of prevention and punishment, the question also arises whether the emergency measures were really indispensable within the meaning of Article 15 of the Convention.

Questions and Comments

1. Does this case suggest that a government may declare an emergency for only part of a state?
2. Why does Judge Fitzmaurice consider it important to decide issues of Article 15 before those concerning Article 5? Did the Court get it wrong?
3. Why wasn't selective prosecution sufficient to challenge these measures as discriminatory and therefore illegal?

4. Does the existence of non-derogable rights set up a de facto hierarchy among human rights guarantees?

Aksoy v. Turkey, (App. no. 21987/93), Judgment of 18 December 1996, Eur. Ct. H.R., 23 EHRR 553 (1997).

AS TO THE FACTS

I. Circumstances of the case

A. The applicant

7. The applicant, Mr. Zeki Aksoy, was a Turkish citizen who, at the time of the events in question, lived in Mardin, Kiziltepe, in South-East Turkey, where he was a metal worker. He was born in 1963 and was shot and killed on 16 April 1994. Since then, his father has indicated that he wishes to pursue the case.

B. The situation in the South-East of Turkey

8. Since approximately 1985, serious disturbances have raged in the South-East of Turkey between the security forces and the members of the PKK (Workers' Party of Kurdistan). This confrontation has so far, according to the Government, claimed the lives of 4,036 civilians and 3,884 members of the security forces.

9. At the time of the Court's consideration of the case, ten of the eleven provinces of south-eastern Turkey had since 1987 been subjected to emergency rule.

C. The detention of the applicant

10. The facts in the case are in dispute.

11. According to the applicant, he was taken into custody on 24 November 1992, between 11 p.m. and midnight. Approximately twenty policemen had come to his home, accompanied by a detainee called Metin who, allegedly, had identified the applicant as a member of the PKK, although Mr. Aksoy told the police that he did not know Metin.

12. The Government submitted that the applicant was arrested and taken into custody on 26 November 1992 at around 8.30 a.m., together with thirteen others, on suspicion of aiding and abetting PKK terrorists, being a member of the Kiziltepe branch of the PKK and distributing PKK tracts.

13. The applicant stated that he was taken to Kiziltepe Security Headquarters. After one night, he was transferred to Mardin Antiterrorist Headquarters.
He was allegedly detained, with two others, in a cell measuring approximately 1.5 x 3 metres, with one bed and a blanket, but no pillow. He was provided with two meals a day.

14. He was interrogated about whether he knew Metin (the man who had identified him). He claimed to have been told: "If you don't know him now, you will know him under torture."

According to the applicant, on the second day of his detention he was stripped naked, his hands were tied behind his back and he was strung up by his arms in the form of torture known as "Palestinian hanging". While he was hanging, the police connected electrodes to his genitals and threw water over him while they electrocuted him. He was kept blindfolded during this torture, which continued for approximately thirty-five minutes.

During the next two days, he was allegedly beaten repeatedly at intervals of two hours or half an hour, without being suspended. The torture continued for four days, the first two being very intensive.

15. He claimed that, as a result of the torture, he lost the movement of his arms and hands. His interrogators ordered him to make movements to restore the control of his hands. He asked to see a doctor, but was refused permission.

16. On 8 December 1992 the applicant was seen by a doctor in the medical service of the sub-prefecture. A medical report was prepared, stating in a single sentence that the applicant bore no traces of blows or violence. According to Mr. Aksoy, the doctor asked how his arms had been injured and was told by a police officer that he had had an accident. The doctor then commented, mockingly, that everyone who came there seemed to have an accident.

17. The Government submitted that there were fundamental doubts as to whether the applicant had been ill-treated while in police custody.

18. On 10 December 1992, immediately before his release, Mr. Aksoy was brought before the Mardin public prosecutor.

According to the Government, he was able to sign a statement denying any involvement with the PKK and made no complaint about having been tortured.

The applicant, however, submitted that he was shown a statement for signature, but said that its contents were untrue. The prosecutor insisted he sign it but Mr. Aksoy told him that he could not because he could not move his hands.

D. Events on the applicant's release

19. Mr. Aksoy was released on 10 December 1992. He was admitted to Dicle University Medical Faculty Hospital on 15 December 1992, where he was diagnosed as suffering from bilateral radial paralysis (that is, paralysis of both arms caused by nerve damage in the upper arms). He told the doctor who treated him that he had been in custody and strung up with his arms tied behind his back.

He remained at the hospital until 31 December 1992 when, according to the Government, he left without having been properly discharged, taking his medical file with him.

20. On 21 December 1992, the public prosecutor decided that there were no grounds to institute criminal proceedings against the applicant, although eleven of the others detained with him were charged.

21. No criminal or civil proceedings have been brought in the Turkish courts in relation to the alleged ill-treatment of the applicant.

E. The death of the applicant

22. Mr. Aksoy was shot dead on 16 April 1994. According to his representatives, he had been threatened with death in order to make him withdraw his application to the Commission, the last threat being made by telephone on 14 April 1994, and his murder was a direct result of his persisting with the application. The Government, however, submitted that his killing was a settling of scores between quarrel-

ling PKK factions. A suspect, allegedly a member of the PKK, has been charged with the murder. . . .

E. The Turkish derogation from Article 5 of the Convention

31. In a letter dated 6 August 1990, the Permanent Representative of Turkey to the Council of Europe informed the Secretary General of the Council of Europe that:

> The Republic of Turkey is exposed to threats to its national security in South East Anatolia which have steadily grown in scope and intensity over the last months so as to amount to a threat to the life of the nation in the meaning of Article 15 of the Convention.
>
> During 1989, 136 civilians and 153 members of the security forces have been killed by acts of terrorists, acting partly out of foreign bases. Since the beginning of 1990 only, the numbers are 125 civilians and 96 members of the security forces.
>
> The threat to national security is predominantly occurring in provinces . . . of South East Anatolia and partly also in adjacent provinces. Because of the intensity and variety of terrorist actions and in order to cope with such actions, the Government has not only to use its security forces but also take steps appropriate to cope with a campaign of harmful disinformation of the public, partly emerging from other parts of the Republic of Turkey or even from abroad and with abuses of trade-union rights.
>
> To this end, the Government of Turkey, acting in conformity with Article 121 of the Turkish Constitution, has promulgated on May 10, 1990 the decrees with force of law nos. 424 and 425. These decrees may in part result in derogating from rights enshrined in the following provisions of the European Convention for Human Rights and Fundamental Freedoms: Articles 5, 6, 8, 10, 11 and 13. A descriptive summary of the new measures is attached hereto. The issue of their compatibility with the Turkish Constitution is currently pending before the Constitutional Court of Turkey.
>
> The Government of Turkey will inform the Secretary General of the Council of Europe when the measures referred to above have ceased to operate.
>
> This notification is given pursuant to Article 15 of the European Convention of Human Rights.

Attached to this letter was a "descriptive summary of the content of the Decrees which have the force of law nos. 424 and 425". The only measure therein described relating to Article 5 of the Convention was as follows: "The Governor of the state of emergency region can order persons who continuously violate the general security and public order, to settle at a place to be specified by the Minister of the Interior outside the state of emergency region for a period which shall not exceed the duration of the state of emergency . . . "

32. By a letter of 3 January 1991 the Permanent Representative of Turkey informed the Secretary General that Decree no. 430 had been enacted, which limited the powers previously afforded to the Governor of the state of emergency region under Decrees nos. 424 and 425.

33. On 5 May 1992 the Permanent Representative wrote to the Secretary General that:

> As most of the measures described in the decrees which have the force of Law nos. 425 and 430 that might result in derogating from rights guaranteed by Articles 5, 6, 8, 10, 11 and 13 of the Convention are no longer being implemented, I hereby inform you that the Republic of Turkey limits henceforward the scope of its Notice of Dero-

gation with respect to Article 5 of the Convention only. The Derogation with respect to Articles 6, 8, 10, 11 and 13 of the Convention is no longer in effect; consequently, the corresponding reference to these Articles is hereby deleted from the said Notice of Derogation.

. . . .

AS TO THE LAW

II. THE GOVERNMENT'S PRELIMINARY OBJECTION

A. The arguments of those appearing before the Court

41. The Government asked the Court to reject the applicant's complaint under Article 3 of the Convention on the ground that, contrary to Article 26 of the Convention, he had failed to exhaust the domestic remedies available to him.

B. The Court's assessment

. . . .

54. The Court notes the provision under Turkish law of criminal, civil and administrative remedies against the ill-treatment of detainees by the agents of the State and it has studied with interest the summaries of judgments dealing with similar matters provided by the Government. However, as previously mentioned, it is not here solely concerned with the question whether the domestic remedies were in general effective or adequate; it must also examine whether, in all the circumstances of the case, the applicant did everything that could reasonably be expected of him to exhaust the national channels of redress.

55. For the purposes of this examination, the Court reiterates that it has decided to accept the Commission's findings of fact in the present case. The Commission . . . was of the view that the applicant was suffering from bilateral radial paralysis at the time of his interview with the public prosecutor.

56. The Court considers that, even if it were accepted that the applicant made no complaint to the public prosecutor of ill-treatment in police custody, the injuries he had sustained must have been clearly visible during their meeting. However, the prosecutor chose to make no enquiry as to the nature, extent and cause of these injuries, despite the fact that in Turkish law he was under a duty to investigate.

It must be recalled that this omission on the part of the prosecutor took place after Mr. Aksoy had been detained in police custody for at least fourteen days without access to legal or medical assistance or support. During this time he had sustained severe injuries requiring hospital treatment. These circumstances alone would have given him cause to feel vulnerable, powerless and apprehensive of the representatives of the State. Having seen that the public prosecutor was aware of his injuries but had taken no action, it is understandable if the applicant formed the belief that he could not hope to secure concern and satisfaction through national legal channels.

57. The Court therefore concludes that there existed special circumstances which absolved the applicant from his obligation to exhaust domestic remedies. Having reached this conclusion it does not consider it necessary to examine the applicant's

claim that there exists an administrative practice of withholding remedies in breach of the Convention.

III. THE MERITS

A. Alleged violation of Article 3 of the Convention

58. The applicant alleged that he was subjected to treatment contrary to Article 3 of the Convention. . . .

The Government considered the allegations of ill-treatment to be unfounded. The Commission, however, found that the applicant had been tortured.

59. The Government raised various objections to the way in which the Commission had evaluated the evidence. They pointed to a number of factors which, in their view, should have given rise to serious doubt as to whether Mr. Aksoy had been ill-treated as he claimed.

For example, they questioned why the applicant had made no complaint to the public prosecutor about having been tortured and found it difficult to understand why, if he had indeed been subjected to torture, he had not made any inculpatory confession. They also found it suspicious that he had waited for five days between being released from police custody and contacting the hospital and observed that it could not be assumed that nothing untoward had occurred in the meantime. Finally, they raised a number of points relating to the medical evidence, including the facts that the applicant took his medical records with him when he left hospital and that there was no medical evidence of burns or other marks left by the application of electric shocks.

60. The applicant complained of having been ill-treated in different ways. He claimed to have been kept blindfolded during interrogation, which caused disorientation; to have been suspended from his arms, which were tied together behind his back ("Palestinian hanging"); to have been given electric shocks, which were exacerbated by throwing water over him; and to have been subjected to beatings, slapping and verbal abuse. He referred to medical evidence from Dicle University Medical Faculty which showed that he was suffering from a bilateral brachial plexus injury at the time of his admission to hospital. This injury was consistent with Palestinian hanging.

He submitted that the treatment complained of was sufficiently severe as to amount to torture; it was inflicted with the purpose of inducing him to admit that he knew the man who had identified him.

In addition, he contended that the conditions in which he was detained and the constant fear of torture which he suffered while in custody amounted to inhuman treatment.

61. The Court, having decided to accept the Commission's findings of fact, considers that where an individual is taken into police custody in good health but is found to be injured at the time of release, it is incumbent on the State to provide a plausible explanation as to the causing of the injury, failing which a clear issue arises under Article 3 of the Convention (see the *Tomasi v. France* judgment of 27 August 1992, Series A no. 241-A, pp. 40–41, paras. 108–111 and the *Ribitsch v. Austria* judgment of 4 December 1995, Series A no. 336, p. 26, para. 34).

62. Article 3 (art. 3), as the Court has observed on many occasions, enshrines one of the fundamental values of democratic society. Even in the most difficult of circumstances, such as the fight against organised terrorism and crime, the Convention prohibits in absolute terms torture or inhuman or degrading treatment or punishment. Unlike most of the substantive clauses of the Convention and of Protocols Nos. 1 and 4 (P1, P4), Article 3 makes no provision for exceptions and no derogation from it is permissible under Article 15 even in the event of a public emergency threatening the life of the nation (see the *Ireland v. the United Kingdom* judgment of 18 January 1978, Series A no. 25,p. 65, para. 163, the *Soering v. the United Kingdom* judgment of 7 July 1989, Series A no. 161, p. 34, para. 88, and the *Chahal v. the United Kingdom* judgment of 15 November 1996, Reports 1996-V, p. 1855, para. 79).

63. In order to determine whether any particular form of ill-treatment should be qualified as torture, the Court must have regard to the distinction drawn in Article 3 between this notion and that of inhuman or degrading treatment. As it has remarked before, this distinction would appear to have been embodied in the Convention to allow the special stigma of "torture" to attach only to deliberate inhuman treatment causing very serious and cruel suffering (see the *Ireland v. the United Kingdom* judgment previously cited, p. 66, para. 167).

64. The Court recalls that the Commission found, inter alia, that the applicant was subjected to "Palestinian hanging", in other words, that he was stripped naked, with his arms tied together behind his back, and suspended by his arms.

In the view of the Court this treatment could only have been deliberately inflicted; indeed, a certain amount of preparation and exertion would have been required to carry it out. It would appear to have been administered with the aim of obtaining admissions or information from the applicant. In addition to the severe pain which it must have caused at the time, the medical evidence shows that it led to a paralysis of both arms which lasted for some time. The Court considers that this treatment was of such a serious and cruel nature that it can only be described as torture.

In view of the gravity of this conclusion, it is not necessary for the Court to examine the applicant's complaints of other forms of ill-treatment.

In conclusion, there has been a violation of Article 3 of the Convention.

B. Alleged violation of Article 5 para. 3 of the Convention

65. The applicant, with whom the Commission agreed, claimed that his detention violated Article 5 para. 3 of the Convention. . . .

66. The Court recalls its decision in the case of *Brogan and Others v. the United Kingdom* (judgment of 29 November 1988, Series A no. 145-B, p. 33, para. 62), that a period of detention without judicial control of four days and six hours fell outside the strict constraints as to time permitted by Article 5 para. 3. It clearly follows that the period of fourteen or more days during which Mr. Aksoy was detained without being brought before a judge or other judicial officer did not satisfy the requirement of "promptness".

67. However, the Government submitted that, despite these considerations, there had been no violation of Article 5 para. 3, in view of Turkey's derogation under Article 15 of the Convention. . . .

The Government reminded the Court that Turkey had derogated from its obligations under Article 5 of the Convention on 5 May 1992.

1. The Court's approach

68. The Court recalls that it falls to each Contracting State, with its responsibility for "the life of [its] nation", to determine whether that life is threatened by a "public emergency" and, if so, how far it is necessary to go in attempting to overcome the emergency. By reason of their direct and continuous contact with the pressing needs of the moment, the national authorities are in principle better placed than the international judge to decide both on the presence of such an emergency and on the nature and scope of the derogations necessary to avert it. Accordingly, in this matter a wide margin of appreciation should be left to the national authorities.

Nonetheless, Contracting Parties do not enjoy an unlimited discretion. It is for the Court to rule whether, inter alia, the States have gone beyond the "extent strictly required by the exigencies" of the crisis. The domestic margin of appreciation is thus accompanied by a European supervision. In exercising this supervision, the Court must give appropriate weight to such relevant factors as the nature of the rights affected by the derogation and the circumstances leading to, and the duration of, the emergency situation (see the *Brannigan and McBride v. the United Kingdom* judgment of 26 May 1993, Series A no. 258-B, pp. 49–50, para. 43).

2. Existence of a public emergency threatening the life of the nation

69. The Government, with whom the Commission agreed on this point, maintained that there was a public emergency "threatening the life of the nation" in South-East Turkey. The applicant did not contest the issue, although he submitted that, essentially, it was a matter for the Convention organs to decide.

70. The Court considers, in the light of all the material before it, that the particular extent and impact of PKK terrorist activity in South-East Turkey has undoubtedly created, in the region concerned, a "public emergency threatening the life of the nation" (see, mutatis mutandis, the *Lawless v. Ireland* judgment of 1 July 1961, Series A no. 3, p. 56, para. 28, the above-mentioned *Ireland v. the United Kingdom* judgment, p. 78, para. 205, and the above-mentioned *Brannigan and McBride* judgment, p. 50, para. 47).

3. Whether the measures were strictly required by the exigencies of the situation

(a) The length of the unsupervised detention

71. The Government asserted that the applicant had been arrested on 26 November 1992 along with thirteen others on suspicion of aiding and abetting PKK terrorists, being a member of the Kiziltepe branch of the PKK and distributing PKK tracts. He was held in custody for fourteen days, in accordance with Turkish law, which allows a person detained in connection with a collective offence to be held for up to thirty days in the state of emergency region.

72. They explained that the place in which the applicant was arrested and detained fell within the area covered by the Turkish derogation. This derogation was necessary and justified, in view of the extent and gravity of PKK terrorism in Turkey, particularly in the South East. The investigation of terrorist offences presented the

authorities with special problems, as the Court had recognised in the past, because the members of terrorist organisations were expert in withstanding interrogation, had secret support networks and access to substantial resources. A great deal of time and effort was required to secure and verify evidence in a large region confronted with a terrorist organisation that had strategic and technical support from neighbouring countries. These difficulties meant that it was impossible to provide judicial supervision during a suspect's detention in police custody.

73. The applicant submitted that he was detained on 24 November 1992 and released on 10 December 1992. He alleged that the post-dating of arrests was a common practice in the state of emergency region.

74. While he did not present detailed arguments against the validity of the Turkish derogation as a whole, he questioned whether the situation in South-East Turkey necessitated the holding of suspects for fourteen days or more without judicial supervision. He submitted that judges in South-East Turkey would not be put at risk if they were permitted and required to review the legality of detention at shorter intervals.

75. The Commission could not establish with any certainty whether the applicant was first detained on 24 November 1992, as he claimed, or on 26 November 1992, as alleged by the Government, and it therefore proceeded on the basis that he was held for at least fourteen days without being brought before a judge or other officer authorised by law to exercise judicial power.

76. The Court would stress the importance of Article 5 in the Convention system: it enshrines a fundamental human right, namely the protection of the individual against arbitrary interference by the State with his or her right to liberty. Judicial control of interferences by the executive with the individual's right to liberty is an essential feature of the guarantee embodied in Article 5 para. 3, which is intended to minimise the risk of arbitrariness and to ensure the rule of law (see the above-mentioned *Brogan and Others* judgment, p. 32, para. 58). Furthermore, prompt judicial intervention may lead to the detection and prevention of serious ill-treatment, which, as stated above, is prohibited by the Convention in absolute and non-derogable terms.

77. In the *Brannigan and McBride* judgment (cited above), the Court held that the United Kingdom Government had not exceeded their margin of appreciation by derogating from their obligations under Article 5 of the Convention to the extent that individuals suspected of terrorist offences were allowed to be held for up to seven days without judicial control.

In the instant case, the applicant was detained for at least fourteen days without being brought before a judge or other officer. The Government have sought to justify this measure by reference to the particular demands of police investigations in a geographically vast area faced with a terrorist organisation receiving outside support.

78. Although the Court is of the view—which it has expressed on several occasions in the past (see, for example, the above-mentioned Brogan and Others judgment)—that the investigation of terrorist offences undoubtedly presents the authorities with special problems, it cannot accept that it is necessary to hold a

suspect for fourteen days without judicial intervention. This period is exceptionally long, and left the applicant vulnerable not only to arbitrary interference with his right to liberty but also to torture. Moreover, the Government have not adduced any detailed reasons before the Court as to why the fight against terrorism in South-East Turkey rendered judicial intervention impracticable.

(b) Safeguards

79. The Government emphasised that both the derogation and the national legal system provided sufficient safeguards to protect human rights. Thus, the derogation itself was limited to the strict minimum required for the fight against terrorism; the permissible length of detention was prescribed by law and the consent of a public prosecutor was necessary if the police wished to remand a suspect in custody beyond these periods. Torture was prohibited by Article 243 of the Criminal Code and Article 135 (a) stipulated that any statement made in consequence of the administration of torture or any other form of ill-treatment would have no evidential weight.

80. The applicant pointed out that long periods of unsupervised detention, together with the lack of safeguards provided for the protection of prisoners, facilitated the practice of torture. Thus, he was tortured with particular intensity on his third and fourth days in detention, and was held thereafter to allow his injuries to heal; throughout this time he was denied access to either a lawyer or a doctor. Moreover, he was kept blindfolded during interrogation, which meant that he could not identify those who mistreated him. The reports of Amnesty International ("Turkey: a Policy of Denial", February 1995), the European Committee for the Prevention of Torture and the United Nations Committee against Torture (cited at paragraph 46 above) showed that the safeguards contained in the Turkish Criminal Code, which were in any case inadequate, were routinely ignored in the state of emergency region.

81. The Commission considered that the Turkish system offered insufficient safeguards to detainees, for example there appeared to be no speedy remedy of habeas corpus and no legally enforceable rights of access to a lawyer, doctor, friend or relative. In these circumstances, despite the serious terrorist threat in South-East Turkey, the measure which allowed the applicant to be detained for at least fourteen days without being brought before a judge or other officer exercising judicial functions exceeded the Government's margin of appreciation and could not be said to be strictly required by the exigencies of the situation.

82. In its above-mentioned *Brannigan and McBride* judgment, the Court was satisfied that there were effective safeguards in operation in Northern Ireland which provided an important measure of protection against arbitrary behaviour and incommunicado detention. For example, the remedy of habeas corpus was available to test the lawfulness of the original arrest and detention, there was an absolute and legally enforceable right to consult a solicitor forty-eight hours after the time of arrest and detainees were entitled to inform a relative or friend about their detention and to have access to a doctor (op. cit., pp. 55–56, paras. 62–63).

83. In contrast, however, the Court considers that in this case insufficient safeguards were available to the applicant, who was detained over a long period of time.

In particular, the denial of access to a lawyer, doctor, relative or friend and the absence of any realistic possibility of being brought before a court to test the legality of the detention meant that he was left completely at the mercy of those holding him.

84. The Court has taken account of the unquestionably serious problem of terrorism in South-East Turkey and the difficulties faced by the State in taking effective measures against it. However, it is not persuaded that the exigencies of the situation necessitated the holding of the applicant on suspicion of involvement in terrorist offences for fourteen days or more in incommunicado detention without access to a judge or other judicial officer.

4. Whether the Turkish derogation met the formal requirements of Article 15 para. 3

85. None of those appearing before the Court contested that the Turkish Republic's notice of derogation complied with the formal requirements of Article 15 para. 3, namely to keep the Secretary General of the Council of Europe fully informed of the measures which were taken in derogation from the Convention and the reasons therefor.

86. The Court is competent to examine this issue of its own motion (see the above-mentioned *Lawless* judgment, p. 55, para. 22, and the above-mentioned *Ireland v. the United Kingdom* judgment, p. 84, para. 223), and in particular whether the Turkish notice of derogation contained sufficient information about the measure in question, which allowed the applicant to be detained for at least fourteen days without judicial control, to satisfy the requirements of Article 15 para. 3. However, in view of its finding that the impugned measure was not strictly required by the exigencies of the situation, the Court finds it unnecessary to rule on this matter.

5. Conclusion

87. In conclusion, the Court finds that there has been a violation of Article 5 para. 3 of the Convention.

. . . .

D. Alleged violation of Article 25 para. 1 of the Convention

101. The applicant alleged that there had been an interference with his right of individual petition, in breach of Article 25 para. 1 of the Convention. . . .

102. It is to be recalled that Mr. Aksoy was killed on 16 April 1994; according to his representatives, this was a direct result of his persisting with his application to the Commission. It was alleged that he had been threatened with death in order to make him withdraw his application to the Commission, the last threat being made by telephone on 14 April 1994.

103. The Government, however, denied that there had been any interference with the right of individual petition. They submitted that Mr. Aksoy had been killed in a settling of scores between quarrelling PKK factions and told the Court that a suspect had been charged with his murder.

104. The Commission was deeply concerned by Mr. Aksoy's death and the allegation that it was connected to his application to Strasbourg. Nonetheless, it did not have any evidence on which to form a conclusion as to the truth of this claim or the responsibility for the killing.

105. The Court reiterates that it is of the utmost importance for the effective operation of the system of individual petition instituted by Article 25 of the Convention that applicants or potential applicants are able to communicate freely with the Commission without being subjected to any form of pressure from the authorities to withdraw or modify their complaints (see the *Akdivar and Others* judgment cited at paragraph 38 above, p. 1219, para. 105).

106. That being so, in the present case the Commission was unable to find any evidence to show that Mr. Aksoy's death was connected with his application, or that the State authorities had been responsible for any interference, in the form of threats or intimidation, with his rights under Article 25 para. 1, and no new evidence in this connection was presented to the Court.

The Court cannot therefore find that there has been a violation of Article 25 para. 1 of the Convention.

Questions and Comments

1. To what extent should the regional bodies evaluate the reasons that a state gives as the basis for suspending rights?
2. Would the failure to give the necessary notification render invalid any measures taken to suspend rights during a state of emergency?

ii. The Inter-American System

Report on the Situation of Human Rights in the Republic of Guatemala, I.-A. Comm. H.R., OAS Document, OEA/Ser. L/V/II.53, doc. 21 rev. 2, 13 October1981.

. . . .

9. In recent months, political and social violence has become more acute in Guatemala, to the obvious detriment of the right to life and other basic human rights.

This situation is made worse by the fact that the perpetrators of the acts of human rights violations enjoy complete impunity, and the Commission has not received indications from the Government of Guatemala that those responsible are being brought to trial or that measures have been taken for such purpose.[30]

10. This violence, springing from armed terrorist groups on both the right and the left, leads the Commission to once again emphasize its well-known doctrine on the matter. The Commission has repeatedly stressed the obligation the governments have of maintaining public order and the personal safety of the country's inhabitants. For that purpose, the governments must prevent and suppress acts of violence, even forcefully, whether committed by public officials or private individuals, whether their motives are political or otherwise.

In the life of any nation, threats to the public order or to the personal safety of its inhabitants coming from persons or groups making use of violence can reach such

---

[30] A pathetic example of this is made evident by the accusations and counteraccusations related to crimes that were made publicly in June 1981 by Col. Jesus Valiente Thilez, former Chief of Detectives, and the current Chief, Col. Pedro Garcia Arredondo, each accusing the other of committing common crimes. This, despite its having been extensively reported by the press, has not been subjected to any clarification by either the government or the judicial branch.

proportions that they require temporary suspension of the exercise of certain human rights.

Most of the constitutions of the American countries accept such limitations and even provide for certain institutions, such as the state of emergency or the state of siege, for such circumstances. Of course, in order for them to adopt such measures, there must be extremely serious reasons, since their establishment must be precisely in keeping with the need to preserve those rights and freedoms which have been threatened by disturbance of public order and personal safety.

Nevertheless, it is equally clear that certain basic rights must never be suspended, such as, among others, the right to life, the right to personal integrity, or the right to due process. In other words, the governments may not make use, under any circumstance, of summary execution, torture, or inhuman conditions of detention; nor may it deny certain minimum conditions of justice as a means for restoring public order. These means are proscribed in the constitutions and in the international instruments, both regional and universal.

Each government which faces a subversive threat must, consequently, choose between respect for the rule of law on the one hand, or fall into state terrorism on the other hand. When a government enjoys broad popular support, the choice of the first method will always be successful, as several countries have shown in the distant as well as the most recent past.

Habeas Corpus in Emergency Situations (Arts. 27(2), 25(1) and 7(6) American Convention on Human Rights), Advisory Opinion OC-8/87 of January 30, 1987, 8 Inter-Am. Ct. H.R, (Ser. A) (1987).

. . . .

11. The Commission submitted the following question to the Court:

Is the writ of habeas corpus, the legal basis of which is found in Articles 7 (6) and 25 (1) of the American Convention on Human Rights, one of the judicial guarantees that, pursuant to the last clause of Article 27 (2) of that Convention, may not be suspended by a State Party to the aforementioned American Convention?

. . .

14. The interpretation of Articles 25 (1) and 7 (6) of the Convention seeking to determine whether the suspension of habeas corpus is permissible during states of emergency, given the provisions of Article 27 (2), must take account of the rules of interpretation set out in the Vienna Convention on the Law of Treaties, which may be deemed to state the relevant international law principles applicable to this subject (cf. *Restrictions to the Death Penalty* (Arts. 4 (2) and 4 (4) American Convention on Human Rights), Advisory Opinion OC-3/83 of September 8, 1983. Series A No. 3, para. 48 [see supra p. 473] and other advisory opinions of the Court), and which read as follows:

A treaty shall be interpreted in good faith in accordance with the ordinary meaning to be given to the terms of the treaty in their context and in the light of its object and purpose (Art. 31(1)).

15. Note should also be taken of the provisions of Article 29 of the Convention.

16. Article 27 (2) must, therefore, be interpreted "in good faith" and keeping in mind the "object and purpose" (cf. *The Effect of Reservations*, para. 29) of the American Convention and the need to prevent a conclusion that could give rise to the suppression of "the enjoyment or exercise of the rights and freedoms recognized in this Convention or to restrict them to a greater extent than is provided for (t)herein" (Art. 29 (a)).

17. The Court will begin by examining some of the general problems involved in the interpretation of Article 27 of the Convention and then determine whether the proceedings to which Articles 25 (1) and 7 (6) apply are included among the essential judicial guarantees referred to in Article 27 (2).

18. Article 27 contains certain phrases that should be emphasized for purposes of this advisory opinion request. Thus, the title of this Article is "Suspension of Guarantees;" its first paragraph speaks of "derogating from obligations under the present Convention;" the second paragraph deals with the "suspension of . . . articles (rights)" guaranteeing certain rights; and the third paragraph refers to the "right of suspension." When the word "guarantees" is used in the second paragraph, it is precisely in order to prohibit suspension of essential judicial guarantees. An analysis of the terms of the Convention in their context leads to the conclusion that we are not here dealing with a "suspension of guarantees" in an absolute sense, nor with the "suspension of . . . (rights)," for the rights protected by these provisions are inherent to man. It follows therefrom that what may only be suspended or limited is their full and effective exercise. It is useful to note these differences in the terminology being used in order to clarify the conceptual basis of the instant advisory opinion. Nevertheless, the Court will use the phrase "suspension of guarantees" that is found in the Convention.

19. The starting point for any legally sound analysis of Article 27 and the function it performs is the fact that it is a provision for exceptional situations only. It applies solely "in time of war, public danger, or other emergency that threatens the independence or security of a State Party." And even then, it permits the suspension of certain rights and freedoms only "to the extent and for the period of time strictly required by the exigencies of the situation." Such measures must also not violate the State Party's other international legal obligations, nor may they involve "discrimination on the ground of race, color, sex, language, religion or social origin."

20. It cannot be denied that under certain circumstances the suspension of guarantees may be the only way to deal with emergency situations and, thereby, to preserve the highest values of a democratic society. The Court cannot, however, ignore the fact that abuses may result from the application of emergency measures not objectively justified in the light of the requirements prescribed in Article 27 and the principles contained in other here relevant international instruments. This has, in fact, been the experience of our hemisphere. Therefore, given the principles upon which the inter-American system is founded, the Court must emphasize that the suspension of guarantees cannot be disassociated from the "effective exercise of representative democracy" referred to in Article 3 of the OAS Charter. The soundness of this conclusion gains special validity given the context of the Convention,

whose Preamble reaffirms the intention (of the American States) "to consolidate in this hemisphere, within the framework of democratic institutions, a system of personal liberty and social justice based on respect for the essential rights of man." The suspension of guarantees lacks all legitimacy whenever it is resorted to for the purpose of undermining the democratic system. That system establishes limits that may not be transgressed, thus ensuring that certain fundamental human rights remain permanently protected.

21. It is clear that no right guaranteed in the Convention may be suspended unless very strict conditions—those laid down in Article 27 (1)—are met. Moreover, even when these conditions are satisfied, Article 27 (2) provides that certain categories of rights may not be suspended under any circumstances. Hence, rather than adopting a philosophy that favors the suspension of rights, the Convention establishes the contrary principle, namely, that all rights are to be guaranteed and enforced unless very special circumstances justify the suspension of some, and that some rights may never be suspended, however serious the emergency.

22. Since Article 27 (1) envisages different situations and since, moreover, the measures that may be taken in any of these emergencies must be tailored to "the exigencies of the situation," it is clear that what might be permissible in one type of emergency would not be lawful in another. The lawfulness of the measures taken to deal with each of the special situations referred to in Article 27 (1) will depend, moreover, upon the character, intensity, pervasiveness, and particular context of the emergency and upon the corresponding proportionality and reasonableness of the measures.

23. Article 27 (2), as has been stated, limits the powers of the State Party to suspend rights and freedoms. It establishes a certain category of specific rights and freedoms from which no derogation is permitted under any circumstances and it includes in that category "the judicial guarantees essential for the protection of such rights." (. . .)

24. The suspension of guarantees also constitutes an emergency situation in which it is lawful for a government to subject rights and freedoms to certain restrictive measures that, under normal circumstances, would be prohibited or more strictly controlled. This does not mean, however, that the suspension of guarantees implies a temporary suspension of the rule of law, nor does it authorize those in power to act in disregard of the principle of legality by which they are bound at all times. When guarantees are suspended, some legal restraints applicable to the acts of public authorities may differ from those in effect under normal conditions. These restraints may not be considered to be non-existent, however, nor can the government be deemed thereby lo have acquired absolute powers that go beyond the circumstances justifying the grant of such exceptional legal measures. The Court has already noted, in this connection, that there exists an inseparable bond between the principle of legality, democratic institutions and the rule of law (*The Word "Laws" in Article 30 of the American Convention on Human Rights*, Advisory Opinion OC-6/86 of May 9, 1986. Series A No. 6, para. 32.

26. The concept of rights and freedoms as well as that of their guarantees cannot be divorced from the system of values and principles that inspire it. In a democratic

society, the rights and freedoms inherent in the human person, the guarantees applicable to them and the rule of law form a triad. Each component thereof defines itself, complements and depends on the others for its meaning.

27. As the Court has already noted, in serious emergency situations it is lawful to temporarily suspend certain rights and freedoms whose free exercise must, under normal circumstances, be respected and guaranteed by the State. However, since not all of these rights and freedoms may be suspended even temporarily, it is imperative that "the judicial guarantees essential for (their) protection" remain in force. Article 27 (2) does not link these judicial guarantees to any specific provision of the Convention, which indicates that what is important is that these judicial remedies have the character of being essential to ensure the protection of those rights.

28. The determination as to what judicial remedies are "essential" for the protection of the rights which may not be suspended will differ depending upon the rights that are at stake. The "essential" judicial guarantees necessary to guarantee the rights that deal with the physical integrity of the human person must of necessity differ from those that seek to protect the right to a name, for example, which is also non-derogable.

29. It follows from what has been said above that the judicial remedies that must be considered to be essential within the meaning of Article 27 (2) are those that ordinarily will effectively guarantee the full exercise of the rights and freedoms protected by that provision and whose denial or restriction would endanger their full enjoyment.

30. The guarantees must be not only essential but also judicial. The expression "judicial" can only refer to those judicial remedies that are truly capable of protecting these rights. Implicit in this conception is the active involvement of an independent and impartial judicial body having the power to pass on the lawfulness of measures adopted in a state of emergency.

31. The Court must now determine whether, despite the fact that Articles 25 and 7 are not mentioned in Article 27 (2), the guarantees contained in Articles 25 (1) and 7 (6), which are referred to in the instant advisory opinion request, must be deemed to be among those "judicial guarantees" that are "essential" for the protection of the non-derogable rights.

32. Article 25 (1) of the Convention provides that:

> Everyone has the right to simple and prompt recourse, or any other effective recourse, to a competent court or tribunal for protection against acts that violate his fundamental rights recognized by the constitution or laws of the state concerned or by this Convention, even though such violation may have been committed by persons acting in the course of their official duties.

The above text is a general provision that gives expression to the procedural institution known as "amparo," which is a simple and prompt remedy designed for the protection of all of the rights recognized by the constitutions and laws of the States Parties and by the Convention. Since "amparo" can be applied to all rights, it is clear that it can also be applied to those that are expressly mentioned in Article 27 (2) as rights that are non-derogable in emergency situations.

33. In its classical form, the writ of habeas corpus, as it is incorporated in various legal systems of the Americas, is a judicial remedy designed to protect personal freedom or physical integrity against arbitrary detentions by means of a judicial decree ordering the appropriate authorities to bring the detained person before a judge so that the lawfulness of the detention may be determined and, if appropriate, the release of the detainee be ordered. The Convention proclaims this remedy in Article 7 (6) (. . .)

34. If the two remedies are examined together, it is possible to conclude that "amparo" comprises a whole series of remedies and that habeas corpus is but one of its components. An examination of the essential aspects of both guarantees, as embodied in the Convention and, in their different forms, in the legal systems of the States Parties, indicates that in some instances habeas corpus functions as an independent remedy. Here its primary purpose is to protect the personal freedom of those who are being detained or who have been threatened with detention. In other circumstances, however, habeas corpus is viewed either as the "amparo of freedom" or as an integral part of "amparo."

35. In order for habeas corpus to achieve its purpose, which is to obtain a judicial determination of the lawfulness of a detention, it is necessary that the detained person be brought before a competent judge or tribunal with jurisdiction over him. Here habeas corpus performs a vital role in ensuring that a person's life and physical integrity are respected, in preventing his disappearance or the keeping of his whereabouts secret and in protecting him against torture or other cruel, inhumane, or degrading punishment or treatment.

36. This conclusion is buttressed by the realities that have been the experience of some of the peoples of this hemisphere in recent decades, particularly disappearances, torture and murder committed or tolerated by some governments. This experience has demonstrated over and over again that the right to life and to humane treatment are threatened whenever the right to habeas corpus is partially or wholly suspended. (. . .)

37. A further question that needs to be asked, and which goes beyond the consideration of habeas corpus as a judicial remedy designed to safeguard the non-derogable rights set out in Article 27 (2), is whether the writ may remain in effect as a means of ensuring individual liberty even during states of emergency, despite the fact that Article 7 is not listed among the provisions that may not be suspended in exceptional circumstances.

38. If, as the Court has already emphasized, the suspension of guarantees may not exceed the limits of that strictly required to deal with the emergency, any action on the part of the public authorities that goes beyond those limits, which must be specified with precision in the decree promulgating the state of emergency, would also be unlawful notwithstanding the existence of the emergency situation.

39. The Court should also point out that since it is improper to suspend guarantees without complying with the conditions referred to in the preceding paragraph, it follows that the specific measures applicable to the rights or freedoms that have been suspended may also not violate these general principles. Such violation would occur, for example, if the measures taken infringed the legal regime of the state of

emergency, if they lasted longer than the time limit specified, if they were manifestly irrational, unnecessary or disproportionate, or if, in adopting them, there was a misuse or abuse of power.

40. If this is so, it follows that in a system governed by the rule of law it is entirely in order for an autonomous and independent judicial order to exercise control over the lawfulness of such measures by verifying, for example, whether a detention based on the suspension of personal freedom complies with the legislation authorized by the state of emergency. In this context, habeas corpus acquires a new dimension of fundamental importance.

41. . . .

42. From what has been said before, it follows that writs of habeas corpus and of "amparo" are among those judicial remedies that are essential for the protection of various rights whose derogation is prohibited by Article 27 (2) and that serve, moreover, to preserve legality in a democratic society.

43. The Court must also observe that the Constitutions and legal systems of the States Parties that authorize, expressly or by implication, the suspension of the legal remedies of habeas corpus or of "amparo" in emergency situations cannot be deemed to be compatible with the international obligations imposed on these States by the Convention.

44. Therefore, in response to the question posed by the Inter-American Commission relating to the interpretation of Articles 27 (2), 25 (1) and 7 (6) of the Convention,

THE COURT IS OF THE OPINION

Unanimously,

That, given the provisions of Article 27 (2) of the American Convention on Human Rights, the legal remedies guaranteed in Articles 7 (6) and 25 (1) of the Convention may not be suspended because they are judicial guarantees essential for the protection of the rights and freedoms whose suspension Article 27 (2) prohibits.

———————————

Judicial Guarantees in States of Emergency (Arts. 27(2), 25 and 8 American Convention on Human Rights), Advisory Opinion OC-9/87 of October 6, 1987, 9 Inter-Am. Ct. H.R, (Ser. A) (1987).

(. . .)

2. The Government asked the Court "to interpret the scope of the Convention's prohibition of the suspension of 'the judicial guarantees essential for the protection of such rights'. Because even 'in time of war, public danger, or other emergency that threatens the independence or security of a State Party' (Art. 27 (1)) it is not possible to suspend 'the judicial guarantees essential for the protection of such rights', the Government of Uruguay requests the Court's opinion, in particular, regarding: (a) which of these judicial guarantees are 'essential' and (b) the relationship between Article 27 (2), in that regard, and Articles 25 and 8 of the American Convention."

(. . .)

20. The Court shall first examine what are, according to the Convention, the "essential" judicial guarantees alluded to in Article 27 (2). In this regard, the Court has previously defined in general terms that such guarantees are understood to be "those that ordinarily will effectively guarantee the full exercise of the rights and freedoms protected by that provision and whose denial or restriction would endanger their full enjoyment" (*Habeas Corpus in Emergency Situations*, para. 29). Likewise, it has emphasized that the judicial nature of those guarantees implies "the active involvement of an independent and impartial judicial body having the power to pass on the lawfulness of measures adopted in a state of emergency" (*Ibid.*, para. 30).

21. From Article 27 (1), moreover, comes the general requirement that in any state of emergency there be appropriate means to control the measures taken, so that they are proportionate to the needs and do not exceed the strict limits imposed by the Convention or derived from it.

22. The Convention provides other criteria for determining the basic characteristics of judicial guarantees. The starting point of the analysis must be the obligation of every State Party to "respect the rights and freedoms recognized (in the Convention) and to ensure to all persons subject to their jurisdiction the free and full exercise of those rights and freedoms" (Art. 1(l)). From that general obligation is derived the right of every person, set out in Article 25 (1), "to simple and prompt recourse, or any other effective recourse, to a competent court or tribunal for protection against acts that violate his fundamental rights recognized by the constitution or laws of the state c6ncerned or by this Convention".

23. As the Court has already pointed out, Article 25 (1) of the Convention is a general provision that gives expression to the procedural institution known as amparo, which is a simple and prompt remedy designed for the protection of all the fundamental rights (*Habeas Corpus in Emergency Situations*, para. 32). This article also establishes in broad terms the obligation of the States to provide to all persons within their jurisdiction an effective judicial remedy to violations of their fundamental rights. It provides, moreover, for the application of the guarantee recognized therein not only to the rights contained in the Convention, but also to those recognized by the Constitution or laws. It follows, a fortiori, that the judicial protection provided by Article 25 of the Convention applies to the rights not subject to derogation in a state of emergency.

24. Article 25 (1) incorporates the principle recognized in the international law of human rights of the effectiveness of the procedural instruments or means designed to guarantee such rights. As the Court has already pointed out, according to the Convention:

> (...) States Parties have an obligation to provide effective judicial remedies to victims of human rights violations (Art. 25), remedies that must be substantiated in accordance with the rules of due process of law (Art. 8 (1)), all in keeping with the general obligation of such States to guarantee the free and full exercise of the rights recognized by the Convention to all persons subject to their jurisdictions (Art. 1) (*Velásquez Rodriguez, Fairen Garbi and Solis Corrales* and *Godinez Cruz* Cases, Preliminary Objections, Judgments of June 26, 1987, paras. 90, 91 and 92 respectively).

According to this principle, the absence of an effective remedy to violations of the rights recognized by the Convention is itself a violation of the Convention by the State Party in which the remedy is lacking. In that sense, it should be emphasized that, for such a remedy to exist, it is not sufficient that it be provided for by the Constitution or by law or that it be formally recognized, but rather it must be truly effective in establishing whether there has been a violation of human rights and in providing redress. A remedy which proves illusory because of the general conditions prevailing in the country, or even in the particular circumstances of a given case, cannot be considered effective. That could be the case, for example, when practice has shown its ineffectiveness: when the Judicial Power lacks the necessary independence to render impartial decisions or the means to carry out its judgments; or in any other situation that constitutes a denial of justice, as when there is an unjustified delay in the decision; or when, for any reason, the alleged victim is denied access to a judicial remedy.

25. In normal circumstances, the above conclusions are generally valid with respect to all the rights recognized by the Convention. But it must also be understood that the declaration of a state of emergency—whatever its breadth or denomination in internal law—cannot entail the suppression or ineffectiveness of the judicial guarantees that the Convention requires the States Parties to establish for the protection of the rights not subject to derogation or suspension by the state of emergency.

26. Therefore, any provision adopted by virtue of a state of emergency which results in the suspension of those guarantees is a violation of the Convention.

27. Article 8 (1) of the Convention points out that:

> Every person has the right to a hearing, with due guarantees and within a reasonable time, by a competent, independent, and impartial tribunal, previously established by law, in the substantiation of any accusation of a criminal nature made against him or for the determination of his rights and obligations of a civil, labor, fiscal, or any other nature.

In the Spanish text of the Convention, the title of this provision, whose interpretation has been specifically requested, is "Judicial Guarantees".[31] This title may lead to confusion because the provision does not recognize any judicial guarantees, strictly speaking. Article 8 does not contain a specific judicial remedy, but rather the procedural requirements that should be observed in order to be able to speak of effective and appropriate judicial guarantees under the Convention.

28. Article 8 recognizes the concept of "due process of law", which includes the prerequisites necessary to ensure the adequate protection of those persons whose rights or obligations are pending judicial determination. This conclusion is justifiable in that Article 46 (2) (a) uses the same expression in establishing that the duty to pursue and exhaust the remedies under domestic law is not applicable when the domestic legislation of the state concerned does not afford due process of law for the protection of the right or rights that have allegedly been violated.

29. The concept of due process of law expressed in Article 8 of the Convention should be understood as applicable, in the main, to all the judicial guarantees referred to in the American Convention, even during a suspension governed by Article 27 of the Convention.

---

[31] "Right to a Fair Trial" in the English text.

30. Reading Article 8 together with Articles 7 (6), 25 and 27 (2) of the Convention leads to the conclusion that the principles of due process of law cannot be suspended in states of exception insofar as they are necessary conditions for the procedural institutions regulated by the Convention to be considered judicial guarantees. This result is even more clear with respect to habeas corpus and amparo, which are indispensable for the protection of the human rights that are not subject to derogation and to which the Court will now refer.

31. Paragraph 6 of Article 7 (Right to Personal Liberty) recognizes and governs the remedy of habeas corpus. In another opinion, the Court has carefully studied habeas corpus as a guarantee not subject to derogation. It said in that regard:

> (H)abeas corpus performs a vital role in ensuring that a person's life and physical integrity are respected, in preventing his disappearance or the keeping of his whereabouts secret and in protecting him against torture or other cruel, inhumane, or degrading punishment or treatment (*Habeas Corpus in Emergency Situations*, supra 16, para. 35).

32. Regarding amparo, contained in Article 25 (1) of the Convention, the Court asserted the following in the advisory opinion just mentioned above:

> The above text (Art. 25 (1)) is a general provision that gives expression to the procedural institution known as "amparo", which is a simple and prompt remedy designed for the protection of all of the rights recognized by the constitutions and laws of the States Parties and by the Convention. Since "amparo" can be applied to all rights, it is clear that it can also be applied to those that are expressly mentioned in Article 27 (2) as rights that are non-derogable in emergency situations (*Ibid.*, para. 32)

33. Referring to these two judicial guarantees essential for the protection of the non-derogable rights, the Court held that the writs of habeas corpus and of "amparo" are among those judicial remedies that are essential for the protection of various rights whose derogation is prohibited by Article 27 (2) and that serve, moreover, to preserve legality in a democratic society (*Ibid.*, para. 42).

34. The Court adds that, moreover, there are other guarantees based upon Article 29 (c) of the Convention, which reads as follows:

> Article 29. Restrictions Regarding Interpretation
> No provision of this Convention shall be interpreted as:
>   c) precluding other rights or guarantees that are inherent in the human personality or derived from representative democracy as a form of government.

35. The Court has already referred to the rule of law, to representative democracy, and to personal liberty and has described in detail how essential they are to the inter-American system and in particular to the system for the protection of human rights contained in the Convention (see *Compulsory Membership in an Association Prescribed by Law for the Practice of Journalism* (Arts. 13 and 29 American Convention on Human Rights), Advisory Opinion OC-5/85 of November 13, 1985. Series A No. 5, para. 66; *The Word "Laws" in Article 30 of the American Convention on Human Rights*, Advisory Opinion OC-6/86 of May 9, 1986. Series A No 6, paras. 30 and 34 and *Habeas Corpus in States of Emergency*, supra 16, para 20). The Court considers it relevant to reiterate the following:

> In a democratic society, the rights and freedoms inherent in the human person, the guarantees applicable to them and the rule of law form a triad. Each component

thereof defines itself, complements and depends on the others for its meaning (*Habeas Corpus in Emergency Situations*, supra 16, para. 26).

When guarantees are suspended, some legal restraints applicable to the acts of public authorities may differ from those in effect under normal conditions. These restraints may not be considered to be non-existent, however, nor can the government be deemed thereby to have acquired absolute powers that go beyond the circumstances justifying the grant of such exceptional legal measures. The Court has already noted, in this connection, that there exists an inseparable bond between the principle of legality, democratic institutions and the rule of law (*Ibid.*, para. 24; see also *The Word "Laws"*, supra, para. 32).

36. The Court also said that the suspension of guarantees must not exceed that strictly required and that " any action on the part of the public authorities that goes beyond those limits, which must be specified with precision in the decree promulgating the state of emergency, would also be unlawful (. . .) (*Habeas Corpus in Emergency Situations*, supra 16, para. 38 p. 491]).

(I)t follows, that the specific measures applicable to the rights or freedoms that have been suspended may also not violate these general principles. Such violation would occur, for example, if the measures taken infringed the legal regime of the state of emergency, if they lasted longer than the time limit specified, if they were manifestly irrational, unnecessary or disproportionate, or if, in adopting them, there was a misuse or abuse of power (*Ibid.*, para. 39).

37. Thus understood, the "guarantees (. . .) derived from representative democracy as a form of government" referred to in Article 29 (c) imply not only a particular political system against which it is unlawful to rebel (*Ibid.*, para. 20), but the need that it be supported by the judicial guarantees essential to ensure the legality of the measures taken in a state of emergency, in order to preserve the rule of law (*Ibid.*, para. 40).

38. The Court holds that the judicial guarantees essential for the protection of the human rights not subject to derogation, according to Article 27 (2) of the Convention, are those to which the Convention expressly refers in Articles 7 (6) and 25 (1), considered within the framework and the principles of Article 8, and also those necessary to the preservation of the rule of law even during the state of exception that results from the suspension of guarantees.

39. When in a state of emergency the Government has not suspended some rights and freedoms subject to derogation, the judicial guarantees essential for the effectiveness of such rights and liberties must be preserved.

40. It is neither possible nor advisable to try to list all the possible "essential" judicial guarantees that cannot be suspended under Article 27 (2). Those will depend in each case upon an analysis of the juridical order and practice of each State Party, which rights are involved, and the facts which give rise to the question. For the same reasons, the Court has not considered the implications of other international instruments (Art. 27 (1)) that could be applicable in concrete cases.

41. Therefore,

THE COURT IS OF THE OPINION
Unanimously,

1. That the "essential" judicial guarantees which are not subject to derogation, according to Article 27 (2) of the Convention, include habeas corpus (Art. 7 (6)), amparo, and any other effective remedy before judges or competent tribunals (Art. 25 (1)), which is designed to guarantee the respect of the rights and freedoms whose suspension is not authorized by the Convention.
Unanimously,

2. That the "essential" judicial guarantees which are not subject to suspension include those judicial procedures, inherent to representative democracy as a form of government (Art. 29 (c)), provided for in the laws of the States Parties as suitable for guaranteeing the full exercise of the rights referred to in Article 27 (2) of the Convention and whose suppression or restriction entails the lack of protection of such rights.
Unanimously,

3. That the above judicial guarantees should be exercised within the framework and the principles of due process of law, expressed in Article 8 of the Convention.

Questions and Comments

1. The Inter-American Commission refers to the general obligation of a government to maintain public order and ensure the personal safety of the country's inhabitants. Does the American Convention clearly establish an international obligation on states parties to protect individuals from acts of private violence?

2. Does the Commission express or imply that under certain circumstances a state may have a duty to declare a state of emergency?

3. What is the meaning of the phrase "judicial guarantees essential for the protection" of the non-derogable rights listed in Article 27(2)? Could one argue that this phrase might refer to some of the guarantees contained in Article 7 (Right to Personal Liberty) and Article 8 (Right to a Fair Trial)? Is due process defined?

5. How would you ascertain whether the above measures were taken only to the extent and for the period of time strictly required by the exigencies of the situation?

6. What other international obligations might restrict the right of a state party to derogate under Article 27?

7. Suppose a petition alleging violation of a right suspended by Nicaragua was presented on November 3, 1979. The government of Nicaragua did not notify the Secretary General under Article 27 (3) until January 23, 1980. Is the government precluded from invoking derogation as a defense to the petition brought before the Commission?

8. The American Declaration contains no derogation provision; do states that are not party to the Convention have any obligations in this regard?

9. Is there a mechanism by which another state party to the Convention could challenge a state's failure to notify the Secretary General?

10. For further on the subject of derogations, see C. Grossman, *A Framework for the Examination of States of Emergency under the American Convention on Human Rights*, 1 AM. U. J. INT'L L. (1986); E. Jimenez de Arechaga, *La Convention Interamericana de Derechos Humanos como derecho interno* in NORMAS VIGENTES EN MATERIA DE DERECHOS HUMANOS

EN EL SISTEMA INTERAMERICANO 27–53(1988); F MELENDEZ, LA SUSPENSION DE LOS DERECHOS FUNDAMETALES EN EL DERECHO INTERNACIONAL CONVENCIONAL: ASPECTOS COMPARATIVOS (1987); M. Monroy Cabra, *Applicacion de la Convencion Americana sobre Derechos Humanos en el orden juridico interno*, in HUMAN RIGHTS IN THE AMERICAS 135–145 (OAS 1984).

iii. Africa

Commission Nationale des Droits de l'Homme et des Libertés/Chad, (Comm. 74/92), *9th Annual Activity Report of the Afr. Comm. H.P.R. 1995–1996*, Annex on Communications.

The Facts

1. The communication is brought by La Commission Nationale des Droits de l'Homme et des Libertés de la Fédération Nationale des Unions de Jeunes Avocats de France. The complaint alleges several massive and severe violations in Chad.

2. The complaint alleges that journalists are harassed, both directly and indirectly. These attacks are often by unidentified individuals who the complainants claim to be security service agents of the Government. The Government denies responsibility.

3. The complaint alleges the arbitrary arrest of several people, among those four members of the opposition party, R.D.P., by the security services. These people were never brought before a court, although they were eventually set free. 15 more people were illegally detained, but have now been liberated.

4. There are several accounts of killings, disappearances and torture. 15 people are reported killed, 200 wounded, and several persons tortured as a result of the civil war between the security services and other groups.

5. The communication alleges the assassination of Bisso Mamadou, who was attacked by armed individuals. The Minister responsible was warned of the danger to Mr. Bisso, but he refused to issue protection. Subsequently, the Minister did not initiate investigation into the killing.

6. The communication also alleges the assassination of Joseph Betudi, Vice-President of Ligue Tchadienne des Droits de l'Homme. It also contains allegations of inhuman treatment of prisoners.

. . . .

The Law

17. Article 1 of the African Charter reads:

The Member States of the Organization of African Unity parties to the present Charter shall recognize the rights, duties and freedoms enshrined in this Charter and shall undertake to adopt legislative or other measures to give effect to them.

18. In this case, the complainant claims that not only did Government agents commit violations of the African Charter, but that the state failed to protect the rights in the Charter from violation by other parties.

19. The Government claims that no violations were committed by its agents, and that it had no control over violations committed by other parties, as Chad is in a state of civil war.

20. The Charter specifies in Article 1 that the States Parties shall not only recognize the rights duties and freedoms adopted by the Charter, but they should also "undertake . . . . measures to give effect to them". In other words, if a state neglects to ensure the rights in the African Charter, this can constitute a violation, even if the State or its agents are not the immediate cause of the violation.

21. The African Charter, unlike other human rights instruments,[32] does not allow for states parties to derogate from their treaty obligations during emergency situations. Thus, even a civil war in Chad cannot be used as an excuse by the State violating or permitting violations of rights in the African Charter.

22. In the present case, Chad has failed to provide security and stability in the country, thereby allowing serious and massive violations of human rights. The national armed forces are participants in the civil war and there have been several instances in which the Government has failed to intervene to prevent the assassination and killing of specific individuals. Even where it cannot be proved that violations were committed by government agents, the government had a responsibility to secure the safety and the liberty of its citizens, and to conduct investigations into murders. Chad therefore is responsible for the violations of the African Charter.

23. The complainant claims that the events in Chad constitute violations of Articles 4 (right to life), (Prohibition of Torture, inhuman and degrading treatment), 6 (Right to Life and Security of Persons), 7 (Right to a Fair Trial), and 10 (Right to Freedom of Expression).

24. In the present case, there has been no substantive response from the Government of Chad, only a blanket denial of responsibility.

25. The African Commission, in several previous decisions, has set out the principle that where allegations of human rights abuse go uncontested by the Government concerned, Commission must decide on the facts provided by the complainant and treat those facts as given.[33] This principle conforms with the practice of other international human rights adjudicatory bodies and the Commission's duty to protect human rights. Since the Government of Chad does not wish to participate in a dialogue, that the Commission must, regrettably, continue its consideration of the case on the basis of facts and opinions submitted by the complaints alone.

26. Thus, in the absence of a substantive response by the Government, in keeping with its practice, the Commission will take its decisions based on the events alleged by the complainants.

FOR THESE REASONS, THE COMMISSION

Finds that there have been serious and massive violations of human rights in Chad.

Finds that there have been violations of Articles 4, 5, 6, 7.

Taken at the 18th Ordinary Session, Praia, Cape Verde, October, 1995.

---

[32] E.g. the European Convention on Human Rights, Article 15, the Inter-American Convention on Human Rights, and the International Covenant on Civil and Political Rights.

[33] See, e.g., the Commission's decisions in communications 59/91, 60/91, 64/91, 87/93 and 101/93.

Questions and Comments

Can the Commission be correct that there is no possibility to suspend rights in the African system? Or are derogations subsumed in the Charter's clawback clauses?

6. Amnesties, Lustration and Reconciliation

Like individual states, regional human rights bodies have grappled with the aftermath of human rights violations and struggled to determine the responsibility of governments towards perpetrators from a former regime, especially when violations have been widespread and sanctioned by domestic law. The Commissions and Courts have specifically considered whether or in what circumstances an amnesty for human rights violators should be respected following a change of government. In the late 1970's, a number of Latin American governments granted amnesty to the military, police and security forces for crimes such as kidnapping, assassination and torture. Military dictatorships were responsible for some of these laws. Others were promulgated by civilian governments in direct or indirect response to pressure from the military or security forces which benefited from the amnesty and succeeded in escaping responsibility for their actions.

Whatever the national legal bases for amnesties, their compatibility with regional human rights obligations is questionable, particularly when coupled with other domestic laws that preclude any civil redress for victims and survivors. The cases in section A reflect evolving views on the issue, from initial uncertainty to more critical evaluation. The first three cases are from the Inter-American system, the final one was decided in the African system. The nature of the violations and the political and legal contexts differ and raise the question of whether a uniform approach to the issue of amnesties is possible.

In contrast to amnesties for perpetrators, some states have enacted measures known as lustration laws that act in addition to or as a substitute for criminal prosecution and punishment. These measures bar those who have engaged in human rights violations from holding certain public offices or other positions. The permissibility of these measures is taken up in section B.

A. Amnesties

Chile, Annual Report of the Inter-American Commission on Human Rights 1989–1990, OEA/Ser.L/V/II/77, doc. 7 rev. 1, 17 May 1990, pp. 133–140.

On October 4, 1989, one year after the plebiscite in which the single candidacy of General Augusto Pinochet for a new eight-year presidential term was rejected, some 10 explosions were set off in the capital, which caused, among other damages, blackouts in several cities. Demonstrations against the military Government were also held, and barricades were set up to block automobile traffic in some popular neighborhoods. In addition, just two weeks before the elections, on the occasion of General Pinochet's birthday, some dynamite blasts were set off.

The period for registration of presidential and congressional candidates ended on August 11, 1989. After an electoral campaign that lasted almost five months, general elections were held on December 14, 1989, the first to be held in 19 years. Finally there were three candidates for the presidency and 530 for the 158 seats in the National Congress: 38 senate and 120 deputy seats. Of the total of 7,552,537 registered voters and 6,641,507 votes counted equivalent to 93% of the electorate, the official count of valid votes casts, excluding blank and invalid ballots, was as follows: Patricio Aylwin, 3,577,669 votes, or 55.2%; Hermin Buchi, 1,901,668 votes, or 29.4%; and Francisco Javier Ernizuriz, 998,783 votes, or 15.4%.

Notwithstanding Patricio Aylwin's victory, which gave him an electoral majority in both houses, he will not have a majority in the Senate since, in addition to the 38 senators elected, under the new Constitution there will be eight more senators appointed by President Pinochet, who will also be a senator-for-life. This might well make it possible for him to control the Senate, which has more powers in Chile than the Chamber of Deputies. The new democratic and constitutional Government will have to face the fact that General Augusto Pinochet is not retiring but will continue to serve as commander-in-chief of the Chilean Army.

Later, the Government Military Junta, which has exercised legislative power in Chile since 1973, passed a new constitutional organizational law on the Armed Forces and on the Carabineros as well as an unpublished law and approved the dissolution of the National Information Center (CNI) or political secret police. It appears that those laws were adopted after an agreement was reached between the military regime and the representatives of President-elect Patricio Aylwin.

On January 18, 1990, the Constitutional Tribunal, made up of seven members appointed by the military Government, established March 11 as the date for the new president to take office instead of March 14 as established by the Constitution, which stipulates that it is to be 90 days after the election; ratified the appointments of senators made by General Pinochet; and decided that they would join those elected by popular vote, contrary to the opposition position that the power set forth in the Constitution to appoint senators did not authorize General Pinochet's present regime to do so; moreover it decided that the power of the Chamber of Deputies to investigate the acts of public officials would be in effect only for those acts committed after March 11, which stripped the Chamber of Deputies of the power to investigate acts committed by the military regime. After these laws were passed, the elected civilian leaders who were about to take office criticized what was referred to as the "wave of laws and decrees" adopted in haste at the last minute by General Pinochet's regime.

Pursuant to the amnesty law decreed by the military regime, the military courts dismissed the actions instituted to clarify the situation of more than 130 missing detainees, without applying any sanctions.

Some of the measures adopted by the new Government to restore a democratic system in which human rights are safeguarded and fully observed and persons who violate them are duly punished were immediately announced by the President in the speech he made in the National Stadium.

Because of the situation caused by the political prisoners' hunger strike and of the overcrowding in Chile's prisons, the new Government studied and introduced a bill to be considered as a matter of the greatest urgency.

On April 25, the Chamber of Deputies passed the Government's bill on a general pardon, which could benefit almost 3,000 of the almost 24,000 prisoners in Chile's prisons. The pardon excludes those found guilty of abduction, armed robbery, murder, and drunk driving, as well as those convicted under the state security, antiterrorist and arms control laws. However, that bill, which passed by a majority, has been objected to by representatives of the National Renewal and Independent Democratic Union parties, who criticized that the pardon could be granted to those convicted of rape, incest, abortion and infanticide.

Accordingly, both the Chamber of Deputies and the Senate have set up human rights committees, which are now involved in clarifying their functions, discussing such issues as the power of Congress to grant the state the authority to work toward the objectives established by the international system in the area of human rights and also to examine the resolve of the Executive to meet these requirements. One of the documents drawn up in the upper chamber defines five specific functions of the congress in the defense of human rights: legislation, supervision, democratization, mediation, and the monitoring and promotion of human rights.

On April 24, President Aylwin's Government issued a decree on the establishment of the "National Committee for Truth and Reconciliation," which, because of its importance and its impact on this historic moment in the country, deserves to be duly underscored by citing, in part, the explanation given by the President himself on the Committee's purposes and objectives. In his inaugural address delivered on March 12 in the National Stadium of Santiago, he stated the following:

> At that time I said and I now repeat: The moral conscience of the nation is demanding that the truth be told on the disappearance of persons, the horrendous crimes and other serious human rights violations that took place under the dictatorship. We must address this sensitive matter by combining the virtues of justice and caution. Once responsibility for those acts has been determined, it will be time to forgive.
>
> On that occasion I went on to say: As part of this necessary pursuit of justice we must avoid the risk of wanting to relive other times, of recasting the quarrels of the past and of becoming indefinitely embroiled in investigations, recriminations and witch-hunts that detract us from our commitments to the future. I consider myself duty-bound not to allow time to slip away as we look toward the past. Chile's spiritual health obliges us to find ways to undertake these tasks of moral upgrading within a reasonable period so that, sooner rather than later, the time will come when, having been reconciled, we can all face the future with confidence and join forces in the efforts the country requires of us.
>
> To perform these tasks of moral upgrading, we must squarely address at least three issues, which, given their special importance, cannot be neglected:
>
>   a. The situation of detainees who have disappeared, been executed or been tortured to death, as well as abductions and cases of physical assault committed for political reasons;
>
>   b. The situation of persons in exile; and
>
>   c. The situation of the so-called "political prisoners".
>
> That leaves the pressing problem of violations of human rights and other acts of criminal violence that have taken such a high toll in victims and suffering in recent years. They remain an open wound on the national soul, which cannot be ignored. Nor will it heal as a result of efforts to forget it. These acts have seriously tarnished our historical image as a law-abiding country, which we must vindicate before the

international community. To turn a blind eye to what has happened or to ignore it as if nothing has occurred would be to perpetuate a constant source of pain, division, hatred and violence within our society. Only by clarifying the truth and seeking justice will we be able to establish the essential moral climate necessary for reconciliation and peace.

We are all well aware that bringing someone to trial for an alleged criminal act is the role of the courts of justice. My Government is firmly resolved to cooperate with the courts to the extent possible to enable them to fully play their role in determining individual responsibility in every case that has or will come before them. Given the features of judicial proceedings, which are necessarily defined in terms of each case and are often too lengthy, one cannot reasonably expect the whole truth about what happened to be learned within a reasonable period of time merely by following those procedures.

Moreover, it is obvious that delays in clarifying the truth disrupt community life and conspire against the desire of Chileans for peaceful reconciliation. Under these circumstances, a different course of action must be sought, which, without getting into the particulars of each case under the exclusive jurisdiction of the courts, will allow the Chilean people to establish a serious, well-founded collective idea of what actually took place in this important sphere.

It is the duty of every government body to respect and promote the natural rights embodied in the Constitution and in existing international treaties signed by Chile. That duty is especially incumbent on the President of the Republic, in his capacity as head of the Government and of the national administration and as the person responsible for promoting the nation's well-being.

Given these circumstances, after listening to the opinions of representatives of the most important human rights organizations and of eminent persons in the national legal and political spheres and after some serious soul-searching, I have decided to set up the "Committee for Truth and Reconciliation" on the topic of human rights, made up of individuals of the most impeccable moral character, to focus on the essential task of preparing a report that will in a brief period of time—six to nine months—establish the most complete picture possible of the most serious human rights violations committed between September 11, 1973 and March 11, 1990, whether in Chile or abroad, when the acts committed abroad have to do with the Chilean State or with Chilean political life.

With a view to defining the Committee's work and allowing it to perform its task within the aforementioned period, serious violations of human rights will be understood to be cases of detainees who have disappeared, been executed or been tortured to death, in which the State seems to bear some moral responsibility because of acts of its agents or people working for it, as well as abductions and acts of physical assault committed by individuals on political pretexts. It will be the function of the Committee:

    a. To establish the most complete picture possible of the serious acts in question, their background and the circumstances surrounding them;

    b. To identify their victims and establish their fate or their whereabouts;

    c. To recommend measures it considers just for relief or recovery;

    d. To recommend legal and administrative measures that, in its opinion, should be adopted to obstruct or prevent the commission of similar acts.

In no case will the Committee assume jurisdictional functions that are within the courts' purview or interfere in cases pending before the courts. It may therefore not determine whether individuals are responsible, under the law, for acts that it has learned about. If in the course of its work the Committee receives background information on acts that may be crimes, it will, confidentially and without delay, so inform the appropriate court.

In order to discharge its mission, the Committee will receive the background information provided to it by those involved, gather and evaluate all the information supplied to it by human rights organizations and conduct any investigations and take any steps necessary to ascertain the truth. Government officials and offices must provide it, within the sphere of their respective powers, with any assistance the Committee requests.

The proceedings of the Committee will be private. It is not meant to be a public forum to air charges and rekindle passions, but a serious and responsible body for shedding light on the truth and paving the way to reconciliation. When it completes its work, the Committee will submit to the President of the Republic a public report in which, on the basis of the background materials it collected, it expresses the conclusions it has reached based on the sound judgment and conscience of its members. (...) Having seen the report and taking into account the suggestions made by the Committee, the branches of Government may adopt, each within its sphere of competence, the measures they deem most prudent to achieve justice and reconciliation.

The Inter-American Commission on Human Rights wishes to indicate its decided support for the measures adopted by the Government of Chile and to express its backing of the important tasks assigned to the National Commission for Truth and Reconciliation that they should lead to a greater respect for human rights in Chile. The Inter-American Commission must also underscore its satisfaction on the re-establishment of representative democracy in Chile, the result of efforts and democratic convictions of its people, and offers its cooperation to the new Government, in any way it should deem useful, within the scope of the Commission's Rules of Procedure.

———————

Note on El Salvador's Amnesty Law. Four years after the favorable report on Chile, the Inter-American Commission reviewed El Salvador's amnesty law. Between the two reports, as the extract below indicates, the Commission decided individual cases challenging the legality of amnesties adopted in Argentina and Uruguay. The Salvadoran Congress passed Decree 486, a "General Amnesty Law for the Consolidation of Peace," following publication of a UN-sponsored Truth Commission report on human rights abuses in El Salvador. Article 1 of the Decree granted a "full, absolute and unconditional amnesty to all those who participated in any way in the commission, prior to January 1, 1992, of political crimes or common crimes linked to political crimes or common crimes in which the number of persons involved is no less than twenty." Article 2 of the General Amnesty Law broadened the definition of political crime to include "crimes against the public peace", "crimes against the activities of the courts," and crimes "committed on the occasion of or as a consequence of the armed conflict, without regard to political condition, militancy, affiliation or ideology." The final subparagraph of Article 4 provided: "The amnesty granted by this law extinguishes all civil liability."

The Inter-American Commission found the amnesty law deficient in several respects. The Commission first objected to the scope of immunity granted, especially in respect to crimes committed against the judicial process. It asserted "that a provision of this nature is very serious." The Commission's critique continued:

> It fails to see what justification there could be for including, in an amnesty law intended to 'promote and achieve national reconciliation',[34] crimes committed by officers of the court and by litigants in court proceedings, especially in a country where many criminal acts—including grave and systematic violations of basic human rights—went unpunished because that country had no trustworthy, independent and effective judiciary.
>
> On the matter of civil liability, the principle that the rights of victims should be safeguarded is generally recognized in laws and is one from which there can be no derogation except by virtue of an explicit provision.
>
> In the past, the Inter-American Commission on Human Rights has addressed the amnesty issue and has stated that independently of the problem of proving guilt, which in every case must be determined individually and with due process guarantees, by a pre-existing court which applies the law in force at the time the crime was committed, one of the first matters that the Commission feels obliged to give its opinion on in this regard is the need to investigate the human rights violations committed prior to the establishment of the democratic government (. . .) Every society has the inalienable right to know the truth about past events, as well as the motives and circumstances in which aberrant crimes came to be committed, in order to prevent repetition of such acts in the future. Moreover, the family members of the victims are entitled to information as to what happened to their relatives (. . .).[35]
>
> In reports 28/92 and 29/92, which concern individual cases involving Argentina and Uruguay, respectively, the premise used by the Inter-American Commission to make its legal arguments was the right of the claimants to some economic compensation "for damages and injuries caused by the State." It not only recommends to the States that they pay "just compensation for the violations" but also recommends the adoption of the measures necessary to clarify the facts and "identify those responsible for the human rights violations that occurred during the de facto period."[36]. . . .
>
> The competence of the Inter-American Commission on Human Rights to address the issue of whether domestic laws are compatible with the American Convention on Human Rights has been corroborated by the Inter-American Court, [which said] "the fact that these are domestic laws adopted in accordance with provisions of the Constitution means nothing if they are the means through which protected rights and freedoms are violated. The authority of the Commission is in no way constrained by the manner in which the Convention is violated."[OC-13/93]
>
> This last finding by the Court is particularly relevant to the analysis of the observations that the Government of El Salvador used to justify such a sweeping amnesty as the one approved. That amnesty extinguishes criminal and civil liability and thus disregards the legitimate rights of the victims' next-of-kin to reparation. Such a measure will do nothing to further reconciliation and is certainly not consistent with the provisions of Articles 1,2, 8 and 25 of the American Convention on Human Rights.

---

[34] Preambular paragraph No.4 of Decree 486 of 1993.

[35] Inter-American Commission on Human Rights, Annual Report 1985–1986, Chapter V "Areas in which steps need to be taken towards full observance of the human rights set forth in the American Declaration of the Rights and Duties of Man and the American Convention on Human Rights."

[36] Inter-American Commission on Human Rights, Annual Report 1992–1993, Reports 28/92 and 29/92.

Consequently, based on these considerations, the Inter-American Commission on Human Rights believes that regardless of any necessity that the peace negotiations might pose and irrespective of purely political considerations, the very sweeping General Amnesty Law passed by El Salvador's Legislative Assembly constitutes a violation of the international obligations it undertook when it ratified the American Convention on Human Rights, because it makes possible a "reciprocal amnesty" without first acknowledging responsibility (despite the recommendations of the Truth Commission); because it applies to crimes against humanity, and because it eliminates any possibility of obtaining adequate pecuniary compensation, primarily for victims.

Enactment of the Amnesty Law and El Salvador's International Commitments, Report on the Situation of Human Rights in El Salvador, Annual Report of the Inter-American Commission on Human Rights 1994, OEA/Ser.LIV/II.85, doc. 28 rev., 11 February 1994, pp. 69–79. It was another seven years before the Inter-American Court had its first opportunity to address the issue of amnesties. The two cases the Court has decided since 2001 reveal growing skepticism about the validity of domestic amnesty laws.

Chumbipuma Aguirre et al. v. Peru (Barrios Altos Case), judgment of March 14, 2001, 75 Inter-Am. Ct. H.R. (Ser. C) (2001).

. . . .

a) At approximately 11.30 p.m. on November 3, 1991, six heavily-armed individuals burst into the building located at No. 840 Jirón Huanta in the neighborhood known as Barrios Altos in Lima. When this irruption occurred, a "*pollada*" was being held, that is, a party to collect funds in order to repair the building. The assailants arrived in two vehicles, one a Jeep Cherokee and the other a Mitsubishi. These cars had police lights and sirens, which were turned off when they reached the place where the events took place;

b) The individuals, who ranged from 25 to 30 years of age, covered their faces with balaclava helmets and obliged the alleged victims to lie on the floor. Once they were on the floor, the assailants fired at them indiscriminately for about two minutes, killing 15 people and seriously injuring another four; one of the latter, Tomás Livias Ortega, is now permanently disabled. Subsequently, and with the same speed with which they had arrived, the assailants fled in the two vehicles, sounding their sirens once again;

c) The survivors stated that the detonations sounded "muffled", which appears to suggest that silencers were used. During the investigation, the police found 111 cartridges and 33 bullets of the same caliber at the scene of the crime; they corresponded to sub-machine guns;

d) The judicial investigations and newspaper reports revealed that those involved worked for military intelligence; they were members of the Peruvian Army who were acting on behalf of the "death squadron" known as the "Colina Group", who carried out their own anti-terrorist program. Information from different sources indicates that, in the instant case, the acts were executed in reprisal against alleged members of *Sendero Luminoso* (Shining Path);

e) A week after the attack, Congressman Javier Diez Canseco gave the press a copy of a document entitled *"Plan Ambulante"* (Door-to-door [salesmen] Plan), which described an intelligence operation implemented at the scene of the crime. According to this document, the "terrorists" had been meeting in the place where the events of the instant case took place since January 1989 and they concealed themselves by pretending that they were door-to-door salesmen. In June 1989, *Sendero Luminoso* had carried out an attack about 250 meters from the place where the Barrios Altos events occurred, in which several of the assailants were disguised as door-to-door salesmen.

f) On November 14, 1991, the senators of the Republic, Raúl Ferrero Costa, Javier Diez Canseco Cisneros, Enrique Bernales Ballesteros, Javier Alva Orlandini, Edmundo Murrugarra Florián and Gustavo Mohme Llona requested the full Senate of the Republic to clarify the facts of the Barrios Altos crime. On November 15 that year, the Senate adopted this *petitory* and appointed Senators Róger Cáceres Velásquez, Víctor Arroyo Cuyubamba, Javier Diez Canseco Cisneros, Francisco Guerra García Cueva and José Linares Gallo as members of an Investigation Committee, which was installed on November 27, 1991. On December 23, 1991, the Committee conducted an inspection of the building where the events took place, interviewed four people and executed other measures. The senatorial Committee did not complete its investigation, because the "Government of National Reconstruction and Emergency", which came to power on April 5, 1992, dissolved Congress and the Democratic Constituent Congress elected in November 1992 did not take up the investigation again or publish the senatorial Committee's preliminary findings;

g) Although the events occurred in 1991, the judicial authorities did not commence a serious investigation of the incident until April 1995, when the prosecutor of the Office of the Forty-first Provincial Criminal Prosecutor of Lima, Ana Cecilia Magallanes, accused five Army officials of being responsible for the events, including several who had already been convicted in the *La Cantuta* case. The five men accused were Division General Julio Salazar Monroe, at that time Head of the National Intelligence Service (SIN), Major Santiago Martín Rivas, and Sergeant Majors Nelson Carbajal García, Juan Sosa Saavedra and Hugo Coral Goycochea. On several occasions, the prosecutor tried unsuccessfully to compel the accused men to appear before the court to make a statement. Consequently, she filed charges before the Sixteenth Criminal Court of Lima. The military officers replied that the charges should be addressed to another authority and indicated that Major Rivas and the sergeant majors were under the jurisdiction of the Supreme Military Justice Council. As for General Julio Salazar Monroe, he refused to answer the summons, arguing that he had the rank of a Minister of State and therefore enjoyed the same privileges as the Ministers;

h) Judge Antonia Saquicuray of the Sixteenth Criminal Court of Lima initiated a formal investigation on April 19, 1995. Although this Judge tried to take statements from the alleged members of the "Colina Group" in prison, the Senior Military Command prevented this. The Supreme Military Justice Council issued a resolution establishing that the accused men and the Commander General of the Army and Head of the Joint Command, Nicolás de Bari Hermoza Ríos, were prevented from giving statements before any other judicial organ, because a case was being processed concurrently before military justice.

i) As soon as Judge Saquicuray's investigation began, the military courts filed a petition before the Supreme Court claiming jurisdiction in the case, alleging that it related to military officers on active service. However, before the Supreme Court could take a decision on this matter, the Congress of Peru adopted Amnesty Law No. 26479, which exonerated members of the army, police force and also civilians who had violated human rights or taken part in such violations from 1980 to 1995 from responsibility. The draft law was not publicly announced or discussed, but was adopted as soon as it was submitted, in the early hours of June 14, 1995. The President promulgated the law immediately and it entered into force on June 15, 1995. The effect of this law was to determine that the judicial investigations were definitively quashed and thus prevent the perpetrators of the massacre from being found criminally responsible;

j) Law No. 26479 granted an amnesty to all members of the security forces and civilians who had been accused, investigated, prosecuted or convicted, or who were carrying out prison sentences, for human rights violations. The few convictions of members of the security forces for human rights violations were immediately annulled. Consequently, eight men who had been imprisoned for the case known as "*La Cantuta*", some of whom were being prosecuted in the Barrios Altos case, were liberated;

k) On June 16, 1995, pursuant to the Constitution of Peru, which indicates that judges have the obligation not to apply those laws that they consider contrary to the provisions of the Constitution, Judge Antonia Saquicuray decided that article 1 of Law No. 26479 was not applicable to the criminal cases pending in her court against the five members of the National Intelligence Service (SIN), since the amnesty violated constitutional guarantees and the international obligations that the American Convention imposed on Peru. A few hours after this decision had been issued, the Prosecutor General, Blanca Nélida Colán, stated in a press conference that Judge Saquicuray's decision was an error; that the Barrios Altos case was closed; that the Amnesty Law had the status of a constitutional law; and that the prosecutors and judges who did not obey the law could be tried for malfeasance;

l) The lawyers of those accused in the Barrios Altos case appealed Judge Saquicuray's decision. The case was transferred to be heard by the Eleventh Criminal Chamber of the Lima Superior Court, whose three members would be responsible for revoking or confirming the decision. On June 27, 1995, Carlos Arturo Mansilla Gardella, Superior Prosecutor, defended all aspects of Judge Saquicuray's decision declaring Amnesty Law No. 26479 inapplicable in the Barrios Altos case. An audience on the applicability of the said law was arranged for July 3, 1995.

m) Judge Saquicuray's refusal to apply Amnesty Law No. 26479 led to another congressional investigation. Before the public hearing could be held, the Congress of Peru adopted a second amnesty law, Law No. 26492, which "was directed at interfering with legal actions in the Barrios Altos case". This law declared that the amnesty could not be "revised" by a judicial instance and that its application was obligatory. Moreover, it expanded the scope of Law No. 26479, granting a general amnesty to all military, police or civilian officials who might be the subject of indictments for human rights violations committed between 1980 and 1995, even though they had not been charged. The effect of this second law was to prevent the judges from determining the legality or applicability of the first amnesty law, invalidating Judge Saquicuray's decision and preventing similar decision in the future; and

n) On July 14, 1995, the Eleventh Criminal Chamber of the Lima Superior Court of Justice issued a decision on the appeal that was contrary to the decision by the Judge at the lower level; in other words, it decided that the proceeding in the Barrios Altos case should be quashed. In its judgment, this Chamber decided that the Amnesty Law was not contrary to the Constitution of the Republic or to international human rights treaties; that judges could not decide that laws adopted by Congress could not be applied, because that would go against the principle of the separation of powers; and ordered that Judge Saquicuray should be investigated by the Judiciary's internal control organ for having interpreted laws incorrectly.

The State's arguments

34. In its brief of February 19, 2001, and at the public hearing on March 14, 2001, Peru recognized its international responsibility in the instant case.

35. During the public hearing, the State's agent stated that:

The Government [of Peru] faces an extremely complex human rights agenda [; as part of this] re-establishing and normalizing its relations with the Honorable Inter-American Court of Human Rights has been and will be an essential priority. . . .

. . . [T]he State of Peru. . . . formulated an acquiescence in a communication of February 19, in which it recognized its international responsibility for the events that occurred on November 3, 1991 . . .

. . . [T]he Government's strategy in the area of human rights is based on recognizing responsibilities, but, above all, on proposing integrated procedures for attending to the victims based on three fundamental elements: the right to truth, the right to justice and the right to obtain fair reparation.

    . . .

[With regard to the] Barrios Altos case [, . . .] substantial measures have been taken to ensure that criminal justice will make a prompt decision on this case. However, we are faced with. . . . an obstacle, . . . we refer to the amnesty laws. The amnesty laws . . . directly entailed a violation of the right of all victims to obtain not only justice but also truth. . . . Consequently, the Government of Peru has suggested to the original petitioners, that is, the National Human Rights Coordinator, the possibility of advancing with friendly settlements, which entail effective solutions to this procedural obstacle . . .

    . . .

The State proposed to the petitioners the signature of a framework agreement on friendly settlement in the Barrios Altos case. The framework agreement proposed the explicit recognition of international responsibility concerning certain articles of the American Convention. In this respect, it was proposed to put in writing, in an agreement signed by the Commission, the State and the petitioners, that the State recognized its international responsibility for the violation of the right to life embodied in Article 4 of the American Convention on Human Rights, because of the deaths of [the above-mentioned persons]. The State also proposed to recognize its international responsibility for the violation of the right to humane treatment embodied in Article 5 of the American Convention on Human Rights in this framework agreement, because of the serious injuries to Natividad Condorcahuana Chicaña, Felipe León León, Tomás Livias Ortega and Alfonso Rodas Alvítez. Lastly, the State would recognize its international responsibility for the violation of the right to a fair trial and to judicial guarantees embodied in Articles 8 and 25 of the American Convention on Human Rights, because it had failed to conduct a thorough investigation of the facts and had not duly punished those responsible for the crimes against the above-mentioned persons. . . .

Based on this recognition of responsibilities . . . it suggested that the parties would inform the Court of their willingness to initiate a direct discussion in order to reach an agreement on a friendly settlement, which would seek to satisfy the claims for reparations. This agreement would evidently be submitted to the Honorable Court for official approval, as mandated in the Convention and the Court's Rules of Procedure. . . . Furthermore, the State proposed a preliminary agenda based on three points of substance: identification of mechanisms to fully clarify the facts on which the petition was based, including identification of the masterminds and perpetrators of the crime, the viability of criminal and administrative punishments for all those found responsible, and specific proposals and agreements on matters relating to reparations.

. . . To this end, the State proposed that the parties should request the Inter-American Court to deliver the judgment on merits immediately, establishing the international responsibility as determined by the Court and taking into account the brief on acquiescence that had been submitted. It also proposed that the parties should suggest to the Court that it suspend its decision on the start of the reparations procedure, for a period that the parties themselves would establish and that the Court considered acceptable. Once this period had expired, and if agreement had not been reached, the parties would commit themselves to request the corresponding judgment to be delivered, and also to comply with it and execute it in its entirety.

. . . [T]he State reiterated its willingness to enter into direct discussions in order to reach an effective solution . . . to attack the validity of the procedural obstacles that impede the investigation and punishment of those who are found responsible in the instant case; we refer, in particular, to the amnesty laws.

. . . The formula of annulling the measures adopted within the context of impunity in this case is, in our opinion, sufficient to promote a serious and responsible procedure to remove all the procedural obstacles linked to the facts; above all, it is the formula that permits, and this is our interest, recovering procedural and judicial options to respond to the mechanisms of impunity that were implemented in Peru in the recent past, in accordance with the law, and opening up the possibility . . . of bringing about a decision under domestic law, officially approved by the supreme court, that allows the efforts that . . . are being made to expedite . . . these cases, to be brought to a successful conclusion.

. . . .

The considerations of the Court

37. Article 52(2) of the Rules of Procedure establishes that:

If the respondent informs the Court of its acquiescence in the claims of the party that has brought the case, the Court shall decide, after hearing the opinions of the latter and the representatives of the victims or their next of kin, whether such acquiescence and its juridical effects are acceptable. In that event, the Court shall determine the appropriate reparations and indemnities.

38. Based on the statements of the parties at the public hearing of March 14, 2001, and in view of the acquiescence to the facts and the recognition of international responsibility by Peru, the Court considers that the dispute between the State and the Commission has ceased with regard to the facts that gave rise to the instant case.[37]

39. Consequently, the Court considers that the facts referred to in paragraph 2 of this judgment have been admitted. The Court also considers that, as the State has expressly recognized, it incurred international responsibility for violating Article 4 (Right to Life) of the American Convention . . . , and for violating Article 5 (Right to Humane Treatment). In addition, the State is responsible for violating Article 8 (Right to a Fair Trial) and Article 25 (Judicial Protection) of the American Convention as a result of the promulgation and application of Amnesty Laws No. 26479 and No. 26492. Finally, the State is responsible for failing to comply with Article 1(1) (Obligation to Respect Rights) and Article 2 (Domestic Legal Effects) of the American Convention on Human Rights as a result of the promulgation and application of Amnesty Laws No. 26479 and No. 26492 and the violation of the articles of the Convention mentioned above.

40. The Court recognizes that Peru's acquiescence makes a positive contribution to this proceeding and to the exercise of the principles that inspire the American Convention on Human Rights.

The Incompatibility of Amnesty Laws with the Convention

41. This Court considers that all amnesty provisions, provisions on prescription and the establishment of measures designed to eliminate responsibility are inadmissible, because they are intended to prevent the investigation and punishment of those responsible for serious human rights violations such as torture, extrajudicial, summary or arbitrary execution and forced disappearance, all of them prohibited because they violate non-derogable rights recognized by international human rights law.

42. The Court, in accordance with the arguments put forward by the Commission and not contested by the State, considers that the amnesty laws adopted by Peru prevented the victims' next of kin and the surviving victims in this case from being heard by a judge, as established in Article 8(1) of the Convention; they violated the right to judicial protection embodied in Article 25 of the Convention; they prevented the investigation, capture, prosecution and conviction of those responsible for the events that occurred in Barrios Altos, thus failing to comply with Article 1(1) of the Convention, and they obstructed clarification of the facts of this case. Finally, the adoption of self-amnesty laws that are incompatible with the Convention meant

---

[37] Cfr *Trujillo Oroza case*, Judgment of January 26, 2000, Series C No. 64, para. 40; *El Caracazo case*, Judgment of November 11, 1999, Series C No. 58, para. 41; *Benavides Cevallos case*, Judgment of June 19, 1998, Series C No. 38, para. 42; *Garrido and Baigorria case*, Judgment of February 2, 1996, Series C No. 26, para. 27; *El Amparo case*, Judgment of January 18, 1995, Series C No. 19, para. 20; and *Aloeboetoe et al. case*, Judgment of December 4, 1991, Series C No. 11, para. 23.

that Peru failed to comply with the obligation to adapt internal legislation that is embodied in Article 2 of the Convention.

43. The Court considers that it should be emphasized that, in the light of the general obligations established in Articles 1(1) and 2 of the American Convention, the States Parties are obliged to take all measures to ensure that no one is deprived of judicial protection and the exercise of the right to a simple and effective recourse, in the terms of Articles 8 and 25 of the Convention. Consequently, States Parties to the Convention which adopt laws that have the opposite effect, such as self-amnesty laws, violate Articles 8 and 25, in relation to Articles 1(1) and 2 of the Convention. Self-amnesty laws lead to the defenselessness of victims and perpetuate impunity; therefore, they are manifestly incompatible with the aims and spirit of the Convention. This type of law precludes the identification of the individuals who are responsible for human rights violations, because it obstructs the investigation and access to justice and prevents the victims and their next of kin from knowing the truth and receiving the corresponding reparation.

44. Owing to the manifest incompatibility of self-amnesty laws and the American Convention on Human Rights, the said laws lack legal effect and may not continue to obstruct the investigation of the grounds on which this case is based or the identification and punishment of those responsible, nor can they have the same or a similar impact with regard to other cases that have occurred in Peru, where the rights established in the American Convention have been violated.

. . . .

CONCURRING OPINION OF JUDGE SERGIO GARCÍA RAMÍREZ

. . . .

9. As regards Amnesty Laws No. 26.479 and No. 26.492, referred to in this case, I believe it is relevant to refer to what I have stated at some length in my concurring opinion to the judgment on reparations delivered by the Inter-American Court in the Castillo Páez (ICourtHR, *Castillo Páez case. Reparations (Article 63(1) of the American Convention on Human Rights*). Judgment of November 27, 1998. Series C No. 43, pp. 60 and ff.). In that concurring opinion, I expanded on the considerations that appear in the judgment itself, which clearly indicate the Court's opinion about these laws, an opinion that is fully applicable in the instant case.

10. In the said concurring opinion, I referred specifically to Amnesty Law No. 26.479, issued by Peru, corresponding to the category of so-called "self-amnesties", which are "promulgated by and for those in power", and differ from amnesties "that are the result of a peace process, have a democratic base and a reasonable scope, that preclude prosecution of acts or behaviors of members of rival factions, but leave open the possibility of punishment for the kind of very egregious acts that no faction either approves or views as appropriate" (para. 9)

11. I am very much aware of the advisability of encouraging civic harmony through amnesty laws that contribute to re-establishing peace and opening new constructive stages in the life of a nation. However, I stress—as does a growing sector of doctrine and also the Inter-American Court—that such forgive and forget provisions "cannot be permitted to cover up the most severe human rights violations, violations that

constitute an utter disregard for the dignity of the human being and are repugnant to the conscience of humanity" (Opinion cit., para. 7).

12. Therefore, the national system of laws that prevents the investigation of human rights violations and the application of the appropriate consequences does not satisfy the obligations assumed by a State Party to the Convention to respect the fundamental rights of all persons subject to its jurisdiction and provide the necessary means to this end (Article 1(1) and 2). The Court has maintained that the State may not invoke "difficulties of a domestic nature" to waive the obligation to investigate the facts that infringed the Convention and punish those who are found criminally responsible for them.

13. The principle, in international human rights law and in the most recent expressions of international criminal law, that the impunity of conduct that most gravely violates the essential legal rights protected by both forms of international law is inadmissible, is based on this reasoning. The codification of such conduct and the prosecution and punishment of the perpetrators—and other participants—is an obligation of the State, one that cannot be avoided by measures such as amnesty, prescription, admitting considerations that exclude incrimination, and others that could lead to the same results and establish the impunity of acts that gravely violate those primordial legal rights. Thus, extrajudicial executions, the forced disappearance of persons, genocide, torture, specific crimes against humanity and certain very serious human rights violations must be punished surely and effectively at the national and the international level.

14. The democratic system calls for a minimum punitive intervention of the State, which leads to the rational codification of unlawful conduct, but also requires that specific, extremely serious conduct should invariably be included in the punitive legislation, effectively investigated and duly punished. This requirement appears to be a natural counterpart of the principle of minimum punitive intervention. Together, they constitute two ways of putting the requirements of democracy into practice in the criminal system and ensuring that this system is exercised effectively.

15. The Court's judgment makes it clear that the self-amnesty laws referred to in this case are incompatible with the American Convention, which Peru signed and ratified, and which is therefore a source of the State's international obligations, entered into in the exercise of its sovereignty. In my opinion, this incompatibility signifies that those laws are null and void, because they are at odds with the State's international commitments. Therefore, they cannot produce the legal effects inherent in laws promulgated normally and which are compatible with the international and constitutional provisions that engage the State of Peru. The incompatibility determines the invalidity of the act, which signifies that the said act cannot produce legal effects.

16. The judgment establishes that the State, the Inter-American Commission and the victims, their next of kin or their authorized representatives must reach agreement on the corresponding reparations. Thus, the determination of the reparations is subject to an agreement between the parties—a concept that includes the victims, because it refers to acts relating to the procedural stage of reparations, in which they become a party to the proceeding; this is not in itself decisive, but must be re-

vised and approved by the Court. There is, therefore, a first limit to the dispositive possibilities of the parties, which is established having regard to the necessary fairness in procedures to protect human rights and which is even extended to friendly settlements before the Inter-American Commission.

17. Evidently, the above-mentioned agreement on reparations only extends to matters that, by their nature, may be stipulated by the parties—with the proviso indicated above—and not to matters that have been removed from this, owing to their social impact and importance. This implies another limit to the dispositive possibilities of the parties: they may agree on compensation, but they may not negotiate or decide on other types of reparation, such as the criminal prosecution of those responsible for the violations that have been recognized—unless it is a case of crimes whose prosecution is subject to a private proceeding, an infrequent occurrence in this sphere—or on the modification of the applicable legal framework in order to bring it into harmony with the provisions of the Convention. These are persisting State obligations, in the terms of the Convention and of the Court's judgment, whatever the settlement agreed between the parties.

Case of Almonacid-Arellano et al. v. Chile, judgment of Sept. 26, 2006, 154 Inter-Am.Ct.H.R.(ser. C).

[. . . .]

2. The Commission filed the application in the instant case before the Court so that it decide whether the State has violated the rights enshrined in Articles 8 (Judicial Guarantees) and 25 (Judicial Protection) of the American Convention, in relation to Article 1(1) (Obligation to Respect Rights) thereof, to the prejudice of Luis Alfredo Almonacid-Arellano's next of kin. Furthermore, the Commission requested the Court to declare that the State has violated the obligation arising from Article 2 (Obligation to Adopt Domestic Legal Remedies) of the Convention.

3. The facts set forth in the application filed by the Commission are related to the alleged failure to investigate and punish all those persons responsible for the extralegal execution of Mr. Almonacid-Arellano, based on the Amnesty Law enacted in Chile by Decree Law No. 2.191 of 1978, as well as to the alleged lack of reparation in favor of his next of kin.

[. . . .]

VII Proven Facts

82. After analyzing the evidence, the testimonies of witnesses and expert witnesses and the arguments of the Inter-American Commission, of the representatives and of the State, the Court finds the following facts to be proven. . . .

82(1) Luis Alfredo Almonacid-Arellano and Elvira del Rosario Gómez-Olivares got married and had three children: Alfredo, Alexis, and José Luis Almonacid-Gómez.

82(2) Mr. Almonacid-Arellano "was an elementary education teacher and activist in the Chilean Communist Party, party director candidate, provincial secretary of *Central Unitaria de Trabajadores—CUT* (Central Labor Union) and union leader of *Sindicato Unido de Trabajadores de Educación—SUTE* (Education Labor Union)."

a) Background: events occurred before August 21, 1990

. . . .

82(8) He [Mr. Almonacid-Arellano, 42 years old] was arrested at his home in the city of Rancagua by the police on September 16, 1973. As he was leaving his house to get into the police truck, his captors shot him. Police took him to Rancagua hospital, where he died the following day.

82(9) On October 3, 1973, the First Criminal Court of Rancagua initiated an investigation under case No. 40.184 for the death of Mr. Almonacid-Arellano, which was dismissed by the Court on November 7, 1973. The Appeals Court of Rancagua revoked said dismissal on December 7, 1973. After that date, the case was dismissed time and time again by the Criminal Court, while the Appeals Court continued revoking the dismissals ordered, until the temporary dismissal of the case was confirmed on September 4, 1974.

iii) Decree Law No. 2.191

82(10) On April 18, 1978, the *de facto* government ruling the country issued Decree Law No. 2.191, whereby it granted amnesty as follows:

Whereas:

1°- The country is now enjoying general peace, order and quietness, and the civil commotion stage has been overcome, thus leading to the conclusion of the state of siege and curfew in the entire national territory;

2°- Ethics demand the best efforts to strengthen the relations that join Chile as one nation, overcoming hostilities that are meaningless today and promoting initiatives to consolidate the reunification of the Chilean people;

3°- It is necessary to rely on strong national unity to support progress towards new institutions to rule the destiny of Chile.

The Government has decided to issue the following Decree Law:

Section 1—Amnesty shall be granted to all individuals who performed illegal acts, whether as perpetrators, accomplices or accessories after the fact, during the state of siege in force from September 11, 1973 to March 10, 1978, provided they are not currently subject to legal proceedings or have been already sentenced.

Section 2—Amnesty shall be further granted to those individuals who, to the date of this Decree Law, have been sentenced by military courts, after September 11, 1973.

Section 3—Amnesty, as specified in Section 1 above, shall not apply to any individuals against whom criminal actions are pending for parricide, infanticide, robbery aggravated by violence or intimidation, drug production or dealing, abduction of minors, corruption of minors, arson and other damage to property; rape, statutory rape, incest, driving under the influence of alcohol, embezzlement, swindling and illegal exaction, other fraudulent practices and deceit, indecent assault, crimes included in Decree Law No. 280 of 1974, as amended; bribery, fraud and smuggling, and crimes included in the Tax Code.

Section 4—The provisions of Section 1 shall not apply to any individuals allegedly responsible, whether as perpetrators, accomplices or accessories after the facts, for the events investigated under proceedings No. 192–78 before the Military Court of Santiago, *Ad Hoc* Prosecutor's Office.

Section 5—Any individual subject to this decree law who is not present in the territory of the Republic shall abide by the provisions of Section 3 of Decree Law No. 81 of 1973, to enter the country.

b) Events subsequent to August 21, 1990

i) Domestic judicial proceedings

82(11) On November 4, 1992 Mrs. Gómez-Olivares, through her representative, brought criminal charges before the First Criminal Court of Rancagua and requested the reopening of case No. 40.184. Based on the foregoing, the Court set aside the temporary dismissal of the case, and received the testimony of Manuel Segundo Castro-Osorio and Raúl Hernán Neveu-Cortesi, allegedly responsible for the death of Mr. Almonacid.

82(12) Through the resolutions of February 3 and June 3, 1993, and April 5, 1994, the First Criminal Court of Rancagua found it had no jurisdiction to decide on the case and ordered that the proceedings be transferred to the Military and Police Prosecutor's Office of San Fernando.

...[From 1994–1997 the case wound its way through civilian and military courts.]

82(19) On January 14, 1997, the Second Military and Police Prosecutor's Office of Santiago requested the Second Military Court of Santiago to "order the full and final dismissal of the proceedings [based] on the statute of limitations regarding the criminal liability" of Castro-Osorio and Neveu-Cortesi, pursuant to Decree Law No. 2.191.

82(20) On January 28, 1997, the Second Military Court of Santiago, without analyzing the evidence or deciding on the conclusion of the investigation, ordered the final dismissal of the case, pursuant to Decree Law No. 2.191. . . .

82(21) On February 26, 1997, Mrs. Gómez-Olivares, through her representative, filed a motion for appeal against the final dismissal ordered in the case. The motion was founded, among other things, on the fact that the dismissal ordered does not "precisely guarantee social peace or the stability of the Rule of Law" and the "copious international legislation approved by Chile [. . .] renders the enforcement of the amnesty law inadmissible." The case file was forwarded to the Court-Martial, which on March 25, 1998, confirmed the judgment of the Second Military Court of Santiago.

82(22) On April, 9, 1998, Mrs. Gómez-Olivares, through her representative, filed a motion for review regarding the judgment of the Court-Martial. . . .

82(23) The Supreme Court ruled on this motion on April 16, 1998, and "overruled it on the grounds that it was time-barred." On November 11, 1998, the Court ordered to close the case file. . . .

d) Reparation measures adopted in view of the gross human right violations committed during the de facto Government

82(26) On April 25, 1990, immediately after the end of the *de facto* Military Government, President Patricio Aylwin-Azocar, considering, among other things, "[t]hat the moral conscience of the Nation demands that the truth for the grave violations of human rights committed in our country between September 11, 1973 and

March 11, 1990 be brought to light," passed Supreme Decree No. 355, whereby the *Comisión Nacional de Verdad y Reconciliación* (National Truth and Reconciliation Commission) was established (hereinafter "the Truth Commission").

82(27) After performing the duties assigned thereto, the Truth Commission issued its report, unanimously agreed upon by its members, and submitted it to President Aylwin on February 8, 1991. For his part, President Aylwin disclosed the report to the public on March 4, 1991. At that opportunity, the President asked for forgiveness to the next of kin of the victims [. . .]

82(28) The report of the *Comisión Nacional de Verdad y Reconciliación* (Truth Commission) individually names the victims, including Mr. Almonacid-Arellano. Moreover, the Truth Commission made recommendations for symbolic reparation and restoration measures, both legal and administrative as well as related to social welfare.

82(29) On February 8, 1992, Law No. 19.123 was published in the Official Gazette, whereby the *Corporación Nacional de Reparación y Reconciliación* (National Reparation and Reconciliation Corporation) was established. The purpose of this Corporation was "to coordinate, perform, and promote any actions necessary to comply with the recommendations contained in the Report of the *Comisión Nacional de Verdad y Reconciliación* (National Truth and Reconciliation Commission)." To that effect, a monthly pension was granted to the next of kin of the victims of human rights violations or political violence, they were granted the right to receive certain free medical and educational benefits, and the children of the victims were exempted from military service, if summoned to do it.

82(30) On November 11, 2003, Supreme Decree No. 1.040 was published in the Official Gazette, whereby the *Comisión Nacional sobre Prisión Política y Tortura* (National Commission on Political Imprisonment and Torture) was created to find the truth regarding the individuals who were deprived of freedom and tortured for political reasons within the period of the *de facto* military Government. Moreover, in its final report the Commission proposed symbolic collective and individual reparation measures (embodied in Law No. 19.992).

82(31) On October 29, 2004, Law No. 19.980 was passed. Said Law amended Law No. 19.123 by broadening and adding new benefits for the next of kin of the victims, including a 50 percent increase in the amount of the monthly reparation pension; the empowerment of the President of the Republic to grant a maximum of 200 non-contributory pensions and the broadening of the scope of health benefits.

82(32) In addition to the foregoing, the State adopted the following reparation measures: i) *Programa de Apoyo a los Presos Políticos* (Political Prisoners Support Program) for individuals kept in custody as of March 11, 1990; ii) *Programa de Reparación y Atención Integral de Salud (PRAIS)* (Comprehensive Health Service and Reparation Program) for those affected by human rights violations; iii) *Programa de Derechos Humanos del Ministerio del Interior* (Human Rights Program of the Department of the Interior); iv) technological improvements for the Legal Medical Service; v) *Oficina Nacional del Retorno* (National Return Office); vi) *Programa para Exonerados Políticos* (Political Exoneration Program); vii) restitution of or compensation for property seized and acquired by the State; viii) the setting of the *Mesa de Diálogo sobre Derechos Humanos* (Human Rights Conversation Table), and ix) the presidential initiative *"No hay mañana sin ayer"* ("Yesterday for Tomorrow") of President Ricardo Lagos.

82(33) Lastly, the State has set up several memorials in honor of the victims of human rights violations.

e) Reparation measures granted to Mrs. Gómez-Olivares and her family

82(34) Mrs. Gómez-Olivares received a bonus in 1992, and was granted a monthly life pension. She is also the beneficiary of health benefits. Similarly, the children of Mrs. Gómez-Olivares and Mr. Almonacid-Arellano have received educational and economic reparations, including higher education grants. Furthermore, they also enjoy health benefits. All in all, Mrs. Gómez-Olivares and her children have received direct transfers in the amount of approximately US$ 98,000.00 (ninety-eight thousand United States Dollars), and scholarships in the amount of approximately US$ 12,180.00 (twelve thousand one hundred and eighty United States Dollars).

82(35) The State named a street "Luis Almonacid" and a residential area "Villa Professor Luis Almonacid," both in the city of Rancagua, and included the name of Mr. Almonacid-Arellano in the Memorial of Santiago's General Cemetery.

f) Regarding the damage inflicted on Mrs. Gómez-Olivares and her family

82(36) Mrs. Gómez-Olivares and her children endured pain and suffering as a result of the fact that those responsible for the death of Mr. Almonacid-Arellano had not been punished.

82(37) Mrs. Gómez-Olivares acted through representatives in the domestic proceedings of the instant case and the proceedings before the bodies of the Inter-American System of Human Rights, which resulted in costs and expenses.

VIII Failure to Comply with the General Duties Contained in Articles 1(1) and 2 of the American Convention (Obligation to Respect Rights and Obligation to adopt Domestic Legal remedies) and Violations of Articles 8 and 25 Thereof (Right to a Fair Trial and Right to Judicial Protection)

[. . .]

90. In the instant case, the Court has been requested to determine whether the State has complied with the general duties established in the aforementioned Articles 1(1) and 2 of the Convention upon keeping in force Decree Law No. 2.191 after the Chilean State ratified the Convention. On the other hand, the Court must determine whether the application of said decree law constitutes a violation of the rights embodied in Articles 8(1) and 25 of the Convention as regards Article 1(1) thereof, in detriment of the alleged victims in the instant case. For that purpose, the Court deems it appropriate to undertake the analysis of these questions as follows: a) first, it should be determined whether the murder of Mr. Almonacid-Arellano is a crime against humanity, b) second, if it is determined that such murder is a crime against humanity, the Court shall consider whether such crime may be susceptible of amnesty, c) third, in case it is determined that such crime may not be susceptible of amnesty, the Court shall analyze whether Decree Law No. 2.191 contemplates an amnesty for this crime and whether the State has violated the Convention in keeping such law in force, and d) finally, the Court shall analyze whether the enforce-

ment of such law by the judicial authorities in the instant case implies a violation of the rights embodied in Articles 8(1) and 25 of the Convention. [. . .]

91. Once the aforesaid has been determined, the Court shall address . . . the allegations made by the Inter-American Commission and the representative of the alleged victims as regards the fact that the military court did not have jurisdiction to hear the instant case, which fact they consider as a violation of Article 8(1) of the American Convention.

92. It should be pointed out that the State has merely objected to the admissibility of the case—issue which has already been determined by this Court in previous paragraphs—and has pointed out that the Chilean courts of justice no longer enforce Decree Law No. 2.191. The Court points out that the State has not affirmed at any time that the said decree law does not violate the American Convention. Indeed, the Agent for the State at the public hearing pointed out the following:

> I want to make it clear, and I will repeat here that the Chilean State is not defending the Decree Law of Amnesty. On the contrary, we do not consider that the Decree Law of Amnesty has any ethical or juridical value.

A) Validity and enforcement of Decree Law No. 2.191

a) Extra-legal execution of Mr. Almonacid-Arellano

93. In this section, the Court shall analyze whether the crime committed against Mr. Almonacid-Arellano may be considered as a crime against humanity. In this sense, the Court must analyze whether on September 17, 1973, date on which Mr. Almonacid-Arellano died, the murder constituted a crime against humanity, and it must also determine the circumstances surrounding such death.

94. The development of the concept of "crime against humanity" started at the beginning of the last century. In the preamble to The Hague Convention on Laws and Customs of War on Land, 1907 (Convention IV) the High Contracting Parties established that "the inhabitants and the belligerents remain under the protection and the rule of the principles of the law of nations, as they result from the usages established among civilized peoples, from the laws of humanity, and the dictates of the public conscience."[38] Likewise, the term "crimes against humanity and civilization" was used by the governments of France, the United Kingdom, and Russia on May 28, 1915 to denounce the massacre of Armenians in Turkey.[39]

95. Murder as a crime against humanity was included for the first time in Article 6(c) of the Charter of the International Military Tribunal of Nuremberg which was appendixed to the Agreement to establish an International Military Tribunal for the trial and punishment of the main war criminals of the European Axis countries, signed in London on August 8, 1945 (the "London Charter"). Shortly afterwards, on December 20, 1945, the Control Council Law No.10 also considered murder as a crime against humanity in its Article II(c). Similarly, the crime of murder was included in Article 5(c) of the Charter of the International Military Tribunal for the

---

[38] Cf. The Hague Convention of October 18, 1907 on Laws and Customs of War on Land (Hague IV.)

[39] Egon Schwelb, *Crimes Against Humanity*, British Yearbook of International Law. Vol 23, (1946), 178, page 181. "[C]rimes against humanity and civilization for which the members of the Turkish Government as well as the agents involved in the massacres are responsible."

trial of the main war criminals of the Far East (Tokyo Charter), adopted on January 19, 1946.

96. Furthermore, the Court acknowledges that the Nuremberg Charter played an important role in establishing the elements that characterize a crime as a "crime against humanity." This Charter provided the first articulation of the elements for such a crime.[40] The original conception of such elements remained basically unaltered as of the date of the death of Mr. Almonacid-Arellano, with the exception that crimes against humanity may be committed during both peaceful and war times.[41]

On that basis, the Court acknowledges that crimes against humanity include the commission of inhuman acts, such as murder, committed in a context of generalized or systematic attacks against civilians. A single illegal act as those mentioned above, committed within the described background, would suffice for a crime against humanity to arise. In the same sense, the International Tribunal for the Former Yugoslavia rendered judgment in the *Case of Prosecutor v. Dusko Tadic*, when considering that "a single act committed by a perpetrator within a context of a generalized or systematic attack against the civil population brings about individual criminal liability, and it is not necessary for the perpetrator to commit numerous offenses in order to be considered responsible."[42] All these elements were already legally defined when Mr. Almonacid-Arellano was executed.

97. On the other hand, the International Military Tribunal for the trial of the Major War Criminals (hereinafter the "Nuremberg Tribunal"), which had jurisdiction to hear the cases of crimes included in the London Charter, stated that the Nuremberg Charter "is the expression of International Law existing at the moment of its creation, and to such extent, is in itself a contribution to International Law."[43] In this way, it provided recognition to the existence of an international custom, as an expression of international law, which prohibited such crimes.

98. The prohibition of crimes against humanity, including murder, was further corroborated by the United Nations. On December 11, 1946, the General Assem-

---

[40] Article 6—The Tribunal established by the Agreement referred to in Article 1 hereof for the trial and punishment of the major war criminals of the European Axis countries shall have the power to try and punish persons who, acting in the interests of the European Axis countries, whether as individuals or as members of organizations, committed any of the following crimes:[. . .](c) CRIMES AGAINST HUMANITY: namely, murder, extermination, enslavement, deportation, and other inhumane acts committed against any civilian population, before or during the war; or persecutions on political, racial or religious grounds in execution of or in connection with any crime within the jurisdiction of the Tribunal, whether or not in violation of the domestic law of the country where perpetrated.

[41] *Cf.* United States Nuremberg Military Tribunal, *United States v. Ohlendort*, 15 I.L.R. 656 (1948); *United States v. Alstotter* (1948 Justice Case), in Trials of War Criminals Before the Nuremberg Military Tribunals Under Control Council Law No. 10 Vol. III 956 (U.S. Gov. Printing Office 1951); History of the UN War Crimes Commission and the Development of the Laws of War complied by the War Crimes Commission (1948); *Cf.* UN, Principles of International Law recognized in the Charter of the Nuremberg Tribunal. Adopted by the International Law Commission of the United Nations in 1950, UN Doc. A/1316 (1950), part III, para. 123; Article I(b) of the Convention on the non-Applicability of Statutory Limitations to War Crimes and Crimes against Humanity, adopted by the General Assembly of the United Nations in Resolution 2391 (XXIII) of November 25, 1968.

[42] *Cf.* International Criminal Tribunal for the Former Yugoslavia, *Case of Prosecutor v. Dusko Tadic*, IT-94-1-T, Opinion and Judgment, May 7, 1997, at para. 649. This was subsequently confirmed by the same court in the *Case of Prosecutor v. Kupreskic, et al*, IT-95-16-T, Judgment, January 14, 2000, at para. 550, and *Case of Prosecutor v. Kordic and Cerkez*, IT-95-14/2-T, Judgment, February 26, 2001, at para. 178.

[43] *Cf.* Trial of the Major War Criminals before the International Military Tribunal, Nuremberg, Germany, (1947) at 218.

bly confirmed "the principles of International Law recognized by the Charter of the Nuremberg Tribunal and the judgments of said Tribunal."[44] Furthermore, in 1947, the General Assembly entrusted the International Law Commission with "formulating the international law principles recognized by the Charter and by the judgments of the Nuremberg Tribunal."[45] These principles were adopted in 1950.[46] Among them, Principle VI(c) classifies murder as a crime against humanity. Likewise, the Court points out that Article 3 common to the Geneva Conventions of 1949, to which Chile has been a party since 1950, also prohibits "homicide in all its forms" of persons that do not directly take part in the hostilities.

99. Based on the preceding paragraphs, the Court finds that there is sufficient evidence to conclude that in 1973, year in which Mr. Almonacid-Arellano died, the commission of crimes against humanity, including murder committed in the course of a generalized or systematic attack against certain sectors of the civil population, was in violation of a binding rule of international law. Said prohibition to commit crimes against humanity is a *ius cogens* rule, and the punishment of such crimes is obligatory pursuant to the general principles of international law.

100. The European Court of Human Rights also rendered a judgment in that sense in the *Case of Kolk and Kislyiy v. Estonia*. In this case, Kolk and Kislyiy committed crimes against humanity in 1949 and were tried and convicted for such crimes by the Estonian courts in 2003. The European Court stated that even though the acts committed by those persons might have been legal pursuant to the domestic legislation then in force, the Estonian courts considered that they were crimes against humanity under international law at the moment of their commission, and that there was no reason to conclude otherwise.[47]

101. On the other hand, the Court points out that in 1998, when the application of Decree Law No. 2.191 was confirmed in the instant case, the Charters of the International Criminal Tribunals for the Former Yugoslavia (May 25, 1993) and Rwanda (November 9, 1994) had already been adopted, and articles 5 and 3 thereof reaffirm that murder is a serious international law crime. This criterion was confirmed by Article 7 of the Rome Statute (July 17, 1998) which created the International Criminal Court.

102. Now the Court must analyze whether the circumstances surrounding the death of Mr. Almonacid-Arellano could constitute a crime against humanity, as defined in the year 1973.

103. As it is evident from the chapter of Proven Facts, between September 11, 1973 and March 10, 1990 Chile was ruled by a military dictatorship which, by developing a state policy intended to create fear, attacked massively and systematically

---

[44] *Cf.* UN, Confirmation of the Principles of International Law recognized by the Charter of the Nuremberg Court adopted by the General Assembly of the United Nations in its Resolution 95(I), at its 55th plenary session on December 11, 1946.

[45] *Cf.* UN, Formulation of the Principles of International law recognized by the Charter and by the Judgments of the Nuremberg Tribunal, adopted by the General Assembly of the United Nations in Resolution 177 (II), at its 123rd plenary session on November 21, 1947.

[46] *Cf.* UN, Principles of International law recognized by the Charter of the Nuremberg Tribunal, adopted by the International Law Commission of the United Nations in 1950 (A/CN.4/34).

[47] *Cf. ECHR, Case of Kolk and Kislyiy v. Estonia*, Judgment of January 17, 2006. Apps No. 23052/04 and 24018/04.

the sectors of the civilian population that were considered as opponents to the regime. This was achieved by a series of gross violations of human rights and of international law, among which there are at least 3,197 victims of summary executions and forced disappearances, and 33,221 detainees, most of whom were tortured. Likewise, the Court considered proven that the most violent time of that repressive period was that of the first months of the *de facto* government. Approximately 57 percent of all deaths and disappearances occurred during the first months of the dictatorship. The execution of Mr. Almonacid-Arellano took place precisely during that time.

104. Considering the aforesaid, the Court determines that there is sufficient evidence to reasonably state that the extra-legal execution committed by State agents in detriment of Mr. Almonacid-Arellano, who was a member of the Communist Party and a candidate to preside the said party, as well as the Provincial Secretary of the *Central Unitaria de Trabajadores* (Labor Central Union) and *Magisterio* (SUTE) Union Leader -all of which was considered a threat to the dictatorship doctrine- was committed following a systematic and generalized pattern against the civilian population, and thus, it is a crime against humanity.

b) Impossibility to grant an amnesty for crimes against humanity

105. According to the International Law *corpus iuris*, a crime against humanity is in itself a serious violation of human rights and affects mankind as a whole. In the *Case of Prosecutor v. Erdemovic*, the International Tribunal for the Former Yugoslavia stated that:

> Crimes against humanity are serious acts of violence which harm human beings by striking what is most essential to them: their life, liberty, physical welfare, health, and or dignity. They are inhumane acts that by their extent and gravity go beyond the limits tolerable to the international community, which must perforce demand their punishment. But crimes against humanity also transcend the individual because when the individual is assaulted, humanity comes under attack and is negated. It is therefore the concept of humanity as victim which essentially characterizes crimes against humanity.[48]

106. Since the individual and the whole mankind are the victims of all crimes against humanity, the General Assembly of the United Nations has held since 1946[49] that those responsible for the commission of such crimes must be punished. In

---

[48] *Cf.* International Criminal Tribunal for the Former Yugoslavia, *Prosecutor v. Erdemovic*, Case No. IT-96-22-T, Sentencing Judgment, November 29, 1996, at para. 28. . . .

[49] *Cf.* UN, Extradition and punishment of war criminals, adopted by the General Assembly of the United Nations in Resolution 3 (I) of February 13, 1946; Confirmation of the Principles of International Law recognized by the Charter of the Nuremberg Tribunal, adopted by the General Assembly of the United Nations in Resolution 95 (I) of December 11, 1946; Extradition of war criminals and traitors, adopted by the General Assembly of the United Nations in Resolution 170 (II) of October 31, 1947; Question of the punishment of war criminals and of persons who have committed crimes against humanity, adopted by the General Assembly of the United Nations in Resolution 2338 (XXII) of December 18, 1967; Convention on the Non-Applicability of Statutory Limitations to War Crimes and Crimes against Humanity, adopted by the General Assembly of the United Nations in Resolution 2391 (XXIII) of November 25, 1968; Question of the punishment of war criminals and of persons who have committed crimes against humanity adopted by the General Assembly of the United Nations in Resolution 2712 (XXV) of December 14, 1970; Question of the punishment of war criminals and of persons who have committed crimes against humanity adopted by the General Assembly of the United Nations in Resolution 2840 (XXVI) of December 18, 1971, and Crime Prevention and Control, adopted by the General Assembly of the United Nations in Resolution 3021 (XXVII) of December 18, 1972.

that respect, they point out Resolutions 2583 (XXIV) of 1969 and 3074 (XXVIII) of 1973. In the former, the General Assembly held that the "thorough investigation" of war crimes and crimes against humanity, as well as the punishment of those responsible for them "constitute an important element in the prevention of such crimes, the protection of human rights and fundamental freedoms, the encouragement of confidence, the furtherance of cooperation among peoples and the promotion of international peace and security."[50] In the latter, the General Assembly stated the following:

> War crimes and crimes against humanity, wherever they are committed, shall be subject to investigation and the persons against whom there is evidence that they have committed such crimes shall be subject to tracing, arrest, trial and, if found guilty, to punishment.
>
> [...]
>
> States shall not take any legislative or other measures which may be prejudicial to the international obligations they have assumed in regard to the detection, arrest, extradition and punishment of persons guilty of war crimes and crimes against humanity.[51]

107. Likewise, Resolutions 827 and 955 of the Security Council of the United Nations,[52] together with the Charters of the Tribunals for the Former Yugoslavia (Article 29) and Rwanda (Article 28), impose on all Member States of the United Nations the obligation to fully cooperate with the Tribunals for the investigation and punishment of those persons accused of having committed serious International Law violations, including crimes against humanity. Likewise, the Secretary General of the United Nations has pointed out that in view of the rules and principles of the United Nations, all peace agreements approved by the United Nations can never promise amnesty for crimes against humanity.[53]

108. The adoption and enforcement of laws that grant amnesty for crimes against humanity prevents the compliance of the obligations stated above. The Secretary General of the United Nations, in his report about the establishment of the Special Tribunal for Sierra Leona stated the following:

> While recognizing that amnesty is an accepted legal concept and a gesture of peace and reconciliation at the end of a civil war or an internal armed conflict, the UN has consistently maintained the position that amnesty cannot be granted in respect of international crimes such as genocide, crimes against humanity, or violations of international humanitarian law.[54]

---

[50] *Cf.* UN, Question of the punishment of war criminals and of persons who have committed crimes against humanity, adopted by the General Assembly of the United Nations in Resolution 2583 (XXIV) of December 15, 1969.

[51] *Cf.* UN, Principles of International Cooperation in the Detection, Arrest, Extradition and Punishment of Persons Guilty of War Crimes and Crimes against Humanity, adopted by the General Assembly of the United Nations in Resolution 3074 (XXVIII) December 3, 1973.

[52] *Cf.* UN Resolution of the Security Council S/RES/827 for the establishment of the International Criminal Tribunal for the Former Yugoslavia of March 25, 1993; and Resolution of the Security Council S/RES/955 for the establishment of an International Criminal Case for Rwanda of November 8, 1994.

[53] *Cf.* UN Report of the Secretary General S/2004/616 on the Rule of Law and Transitional Justice in conflict and post-conflict societies of August 3, 2004, para. 10.

[54] *Cf.* UN Report of the Secretary General S/2000/915 on the establishment of a Tribunal for Sierra Leona, of October 4, 2000, para. 22.

109. The Secretary General also informed that the legal effects of the amnesty granted in Sierra Leona had not been taken into account "given their illegality pursuant to international law."[55] Indeed, the Charter for the Special Tribunal for Sierra Leona stated that the amnesty granted to persons accused of crimes against humanity, which are violations of Article 3 of the Geneva Conventions and Additional Protocol II, as well as of other serious violations of international humanitarian law, "shall not be an impediment to subject [them] to trial."

110. The obligation that arises pursuant to international law to try, and, if found guilty, to punish the perpetrators of certain international crimes, among which are crimes against humanity, is derived from the duty of protection embodied in Article 1(1) of the American Convention. [. . . .]

111. Crimes against humanity give rise to the violation of a series of undeniable rights that are recognized by the American Convention, which violation cannot remain unpunished. The Court has stated on several occasions that the State has the duty to prevent and combat impunity, which the Court has defined as "the lack of investigation, prosecution, arrest, trial, and conviction of those responsible for the violation of the rights protected by the American Convention."[56] Likewise, the Court has determined that the investigation must be conducted resorting to all legal means available and must be focused on the determination of the truth and the investigation, prosecution, arrest, trial, and conviction of those persons that are responsible for the facts, both as perpetrators and instigators, especially when State agents are or may be involved in such events.[57] In that respect, the Court has pointed out that those resources which, in view of the general conditions of the country or due to the circumstances of the case, turn to be deceptive, cannot be taken into account.[58]

[. . .]

113. It is worth mentioning that the State itself recognized in the instant case that "amnesty or self-amnesty laws are, in principle, contrary to the rules of international human rights law."

114. In view of the above considerations, the Court determines that the States cannot neglect their duty to investigate, identify, and punish those persons responsible for crimes against humanity by enforcing amnesty laws or any other similar domestic provisions. Consequently, crimes against humanity are crimes which cannot be susceptible of amnesty.

c) Enforcement of Decree Law No. 2.191 from August 21, 1990

115. Since it has already been established that the crime against Mr. Almonacid-Arellano is a crime against humanity, and that crimes against humanity cannot be

---

[55] *Cf.* UN Report of the Secretary General S/2000/915 on the establishment of a Tribunal for Sierra Leona, of October 4, 2000, para. 24.

[56] *Cf. Case of the Ituango Massacres*, para. 299; *Case of the "Mapiripán Massacre,"* Judgment of September 15, 2005. Series C No. 134, para. 237; *Case of the Moiwana Community*, Judgment of September 15, 2005. Series C No. 134, para. 203.

[57] *Cf. Case of Ximenes-Lopes*, para. 148; *Case of Baldeón-García*, para. 94; and *Case of the Pueblo Bello Massacre*, Judgment of January 31, 2006. Series C No. 140, para. 143.

[58] *Cf. Case of Baldeón-García*, para. 144; *Case of the 19 Merchants*, Judgment of July 5, 2004. Series C No. 109, para. 192; and *Case of Baena Ricardo et al. Jurisdiction.* Judgment of November 28, 2003. Series C No. 104, para. 77.

susceptible of amnesty, the Court must now determine if under Decree Law No. 2.191 amnesty is granted for such crime, and if such were the case, the Court must further determine whether the State has breached its obligation arising from Article 2 of the Convention upon keeping such law in force.

116. Article 1 of Decree Law No. 2.191 grants a general amnesty to all those responsible for "criminal acts" that were committed from September 11, 1973 to March 10, 1978. Furthermore, Article 3 of such Decree Law excludes a series of crimes from such amnesty. The Court notes that murder, being a crime against humanity, is not included on the list provided in Article 3 of the said Decree Law. This was also the determination made by the Chilean courts that heard the instant case upon its application. Likewise, this Court, though not requested to decide on other crimes against humanity in the instant case, draws the attention to the fact that other crimes against humanity such as forced disappearance, torture, and genocide, among others, are not excluded from such amnesty.

[. . . .]

119. Amnesty laws with the characteristics as those described above leave victims defenseless and perpetuate impunity for crimes against humanity. Therefore, they are overtly incompatible with the wording and the spirit of the American Convention, and undoubtedly affect rights embodied in such Convention. This constitutes in and of itself a violation of the Convention and generates international liability for the State.[59] Consequently, given its nature, Decree Law No. 2.191 does not have any legal effects and cannot remain as an obstacle for the investigation of the facts inherent to the instant case, or for the identification and punishment of those responsible therefor. Neither can it have a like or similar impact regarding other cases of violations of rights protected by the American Convention which occurred in Chile.[60]

120. On the other hand, even though the Court notes that Decree Law No. 2.191 basically grants a self-amnesty, since it was issued by the military regime to avoid judicial prosecution of its own crimes, it points out that a State violates the American Convention when issuing provisions which do not conform to the obligations contemplated in said Convention. The fact that such provisions have been adopted pursuant to the domestic legislation or against it, "is irrelevant for this purpose."[61] To conclude, the Court, rather than the process of adoption and the authority issuing Decree Law No. 2.191, addresses the *ratio legis*: granting an amnesty for the serious criminal acts contrary to international law that were committed by the military regime.

121. Since it ratified the American Convention on August 21, 1990, the State has kept Decree Law No. 2.191 in force for sixteen years, overtly violating the obligations set forth in said Convention. The fact that such Decree Law has not been applied by the Chilean courts in several cases since 1998 is a significant advance,

---

59 *Cf. Case of Barrios Altos. Interpretation of the Judgment on the Merits.* (art. 67 of the American Convention on Human Rights). Judgment of September 3, 2001. Series C No. 83, para. 18.

60 *Cf. Case of Barrios Altos, supra,* para. 44.

61 *Cf. Certain Powers of the Inter-American Commission of Human Rights* (arts. 41, 42, 44, 46, 47, 50 and 51 of the American Convention on Human Rights.). Advisory Opinion OC-13/93 of July 16, 1993. Series A No. 13, para. 26.

and the Court appreciates it, but it does not suffice to meet the requirements of Article 2 of the Convention in the instant case. Firstly because, as it has been stated in the preceding paragraphs, Article 2 imposes the legislative obligation to annul all legislation which is in violation of the Convention, and secondly, because the criterion of the domestic courts may change, and they may decide to reinstate the application of a provision which remains in force under the domestic legislation.

122. For such reasons, the Court determines that by formally keeping within its legislative *corpus* a Decree Law which is contrary to the wording and the spirit of the Convention, the State has not complied with the obligations imposed by Article 2 thereof.

d) Enforcement of Decree Law No. 2.191

123. The above mentioned legislative obligation established by Article 2 of the Convention is also aimed at facilitating the work of the Judiciary so that the law enforcement authority may have a clear option in order to solve a particular case. However, when the Legislative Power fails to set aside and/or adopts laws which are contrary to the American Convention, the Judiciary is bound to honor the obligation to respect rights as stated in Article 1(1) of the said Convention, and consequently, it must refrain from enforcing any laws contrary to such Convention. The observance by State agents or officials of a law which violates the Convention gives rise to the international liability of such State, as contemplated in International Human Rights Law, in the sense that every State is internationally responsible for the acts or omissions of any of its powers or bodies for the violation of internationally protected rights, pursuant to Article 1(1) of the American Convention.[62]

124. The Court is aware that domestic judges and courts are bound to respect the rule of law, and therefore, they are bound to apply the provisions in force within the legal system. But when a State has ratified an international treaty such as the American Convention, its judges, as part of the State, are also bound by such Convention. This forces them to see that all the effects of the provisions embodied in the Convention are not adversely affected by the enforcement of laws which are contrary to its purpose and that have not had any legal effects since their inception. In other words, the Judiciary must exercise a sort of "conventionality control" between the domestic legal provisions which are applied to specific cases and the American Convention on Human Rights. To perform this task, the Judiciary has to take into account not only the treaty, but also the interpretation thereof made by the Inter-American Court, which is the ultimate interpreter of the American Convention.

125. By the same token, the Court has established that "according to international law, the obligations that it imposes must be honored in good faith and domestic laws cannot be invoked to justify their violation."[63] This provision is embodied in Article 27 of the Vienna Convention on the Law of Treaties, 1969.

126. In the instant case, the Judiciary applied Decree Law No. 2.191, which had the immediate effect to discontinue the investigation and close the case file, thus

---

62 *Cf. Case of Ximenes-Lopes*, para. 172; and *Case of Baldeón-García*, para. 140.
63 *Cf. International Responsibility for the Issuance and Application of Laws in Violation of the Convention (Arts. 1 and 2 of the American Convention on Human Rights)*, Advisory Opinion OC-14/94 of December 9, 1994, Series A No. 14, para. 35.

granting impunity to those responsible for the death of Mr. Almonacid-Arellano. Pursuant to the aforesaid, his next of kin were prevented from exercising their right to a hearing by a competent, independent, and impartial court, and likewise, they were prevented from resorting to an effective and adequate remedy to redress the violations committed in detriment of their relative and to know the truth.

[...]

128. Therefore, the Court considers that the application of Decree Law No. 2.191 was contrary to the obligations embodied in Article 1(1) of the American Convention in violation of the rights of Elvira del Rosario Gómez-Olivares and of Alfredo, Alexis, and José Luis Almonacid-Gómez, embodied in Articles 8(1) and 25 of the Convention, for all of which the Chilean State is internationally responsible.

129. As a conclusion of all questions addressed in this section the Court A), considers that the murder of Mr. Almonacid-Arellano was part of a State policy to repress certain sectors of the civilian population, and that it constitutes an example of a number of other similar illegal acts that took place during that period. The crime committed against Mr. Almonacid-Arellano cannot be susceptible of amnesty pursuant to the basic rules of international law since it constitutes a crime against humanity. The State has violated its obligation to modify its domestic legislation in order to guarantee the rights embodied in the American Convention because it has enforced and still keeps in force Decree Law No. 2.191, which does not exclude crimes against humanity from the general amnesty it grants. Finally, the State has violated the right to a fair trial and the right to judicial protection and has not complied with its obligation to respect guarantees in detriment of the next of kin of Mr. Almonacid-Arellano, given the fact that it applied Decree Law No. 2.191 to the instant case.

B) Regarding the military jurisdiction

130. The American Convention in its Article 8(1) establishes that every person has the right to a hearing by a competent, independent, and impartial court. Thus, the Court has pointed out that "all persons subject to trial of any kind before a State body must have the guarantee that such body is impartial and acts in accordance with the procedure established by law to hear and decide the case submitted to it."[64]

131. The Court has established that in a democratic State, the military criminal jurisdiction must have a restrictive scope and must be exceptional and aimed at the protection of special legal interests related to the functions that the law assigns to the Military. Therefore, it must only try military men for the commission of crimes or offenses that due to their nature may affect military interests.[65] In that respect, the Court has held that "when the military courts assume jurisdiction over a matter that should be heard by the regular courts, the right to the competent judge is

---

[64] *Cf. Case of Herrera-Ulloa*, para. 169; and *Case of the Constitutional Court*. Judgment of January 31, 2001. Series C No. 71, para. 77.

[65] *Cf. Case of Palamara-Iribarne*. Judgment of November 22, 2005. Series C No. 135, para. 124; *Case of the "Mapiripán Massacre," supra*, para. 202; and *Case of 19 Tradesmen, supra*, para. 165.

violated, as is, *a fortiori*, due process of law, which, in turn, is closely linked to the right of access to justice."[66]

132. In the instant case, the Court has considered proven that on September 27, 1996 the Second Military Court of Santiago requested the First Criminal Court of Rancagua to decline jurisdiction to continue hearing the case on the grounds that on the date the events occurred the accused were under military jurisdiction. As a consequence of the aforesaid, the Supreme Court of Justice of Chile decided the issue of jurisdiction in favor of the Military Jurisdiction and closed the investigation in the instant case by the application of self-amnesty Decree Law.

133. Considering the aforesaid, the Court determines that the State has violated Article 8(1) of the American Convention, together with Article 1(1) thereof on the grounds that it granted jurisdiction to the military courts to hear the instant case, while said courts do not comply with the standards of competence, independence and impartiality mentioned above.

IX Reparations (Application of Article 63(1) of the American Convention)

. . . .

143. Pursuant to Article 63(1) of the American Convention, the Court considers Elvira del Rosario Gómez-Olivares and Alfredo, Alexis, and José Luis Almonacid-Gómez as "injured party," for being victims of the violations described in the previous chapter of this Judgment.

144. The Court shall now proceed to determine the reparation measures it deems appropriate for the instant case. In doing so, it shall first refer to those measures standing closer to *restitutio in integrum* among the violations stated in this Judgment, namely: the adaptation of domestic law to conform to the American Convention and the duty of the State to continue investigating this case, identify, prosecute, and punish those responsible, such measures being also part of the guarantees to prevent the repetition of acts in violation of human rights. Secondly, the Court shall refer to the financial compensation for pecuniary and non-pecuniary damage which the Commission and the representatives allege the beneficiaries have suffered as a consequence of the facts set forth in the instant case. Finally, the Court shall order that this Judgment be published as reparation for non-pecuniary damage.

B) Adaptation of domestic law . . .

145. As explained in paragraph 119 of this Judgment, the Court finds that, inasmuch as it seeks to grant amnesty to persons responsible for crimes against humanity, Decree Law No. 2.191 is inconsistent with the American Convention and, therefore, has no legal effects; consequently, the State must: i) ensure that it does not continue to hinder the investigation of Mr. Almonacid-Arellano's extra-legal execution and the identification and, as appropriate, punishment of those responsible, and ii) ensure that Decree Law No. 2.191 does not continue to hinder the investigation, prosecution and, as appropriate, punishment of those responsible for similar violations perpetrated in Chile.

---

66   *Cf. Case of Palamara-Iribarne, supra*, para. 143; *Case of 19 Tradesmen, supra*, para. 167; and *Case of Las Palmeras.* Judgment of December 6, 2001. Series C No. 90, para. 52.

146. The Court has found that the State has violated the rights established in Articles 8 and 25 of the American Convention in relation to Article 1(1) thereof, to the detriment of Elvira del Rosario Gómez-Olivares and Alfredo, Alexis, and José Luis Almonacid-Gómez. This violation occurred for two reasons: i) the granting of jurisdiction to the military courts to hear the case of Mr. Almonacid-Arellano's death, and ii) the application of Decree Law No. 2.191. The first violation resulted from Order of the Supreme Court of December 5, 1996 (*supra* para. 82(17)), whilst the second one was a consequence of the judgments of January 28, 1997 of the Second Military Court of Santiago (*supra* para. 82(20)) and of March 25, 1998 of the Court-Martial (*supra* para. 82(21)).

147. In view of the foregoing, the Court hereby orders that the State set aside the above mentioned domestic decisions and judgments, and refer the case file to a regular court, so that, by way of criminal proceedings, all those responsible for Mr. Almonacid-Arellano's death are identified and punished.

148. The Court has previously ruled that the right to know the truth is included in the right of victims or their next of kin to have the harmful acts and the corresponding responsibilities elucidated by competent State bodies, through the investigation and prosecution provided for in Articles 8 and 25 of the Convention.

149. Once more, the Court wishes to highlight the important role played by the different Chilean Commissions in trying to collectively build the truth of the events which occurred between 1973 and 1990. Likewise, the Court appreciates that the Report of the *Comisión Nacional de Verdad y Reconciliación* (National Truth and Reconciliation Commission) includes Mr. Almonacid-Arellano's name and a brief summary of the circumstances of his execution.

150. Notwithstanding the foregoing, the Court considers it relevant to remark that the "historical truth" included in the reports of the above mentioned Commissions is no substitute for the duty of the State to reach the truth through judicial proceedings. In this sense, Articles 1(1), 8 and 25 of the Convention protect truth as a whole, and hence, the Chilean State must carry out a judicial investigation of the facts related to Mr. Almonacid-Arellano's death, attribute responsibilities, and punish all those who turn out to be participants. Indeed, the Report of the *Comisión Nacional de Verdad y Reconciliación* (National Truth and Reconciliation Commission) concludes that:

> From the standpoint of prevention alone, this Commission believes that for the sake of achieving national reconciliation and preventing the recurrence of such events it is absolutely necessary that the government fully exercise its power to mete out punishment. Full protection of human rights is conceivable only within a state that is truly subject to the rule of law. The rule of law means that all citizens are subject to the law and to the courts, and hence that the sanctions contemplated in criminal law, which should be applied to all alike, should thereby be applied to those who infringe the laws which safeguard human rights.[67]

151. The State may not invoke any domestic law or provision to exonerate itself from the Court's order to have a criminal court investigate and punish those respon-

---

[67] *Cf.* Report of the *Comisión Nacional de Verdad y Reconciliación* (National Truth and Reconciliation Commission) (record of appendixes to the final written arguments of the State, Appendix 2, p. 2520).

sible for Mr. Almonacid-Arellano's death. The Chilean State may not apply Decree Law No. 2.191 again, on account of all the considerations presented in this Judgment, especially those included in paragraph 145. Additionally, the State may not invoke the statute of limitations, the non-retroactivity of criminal law or the *ne bis in idem* principle to decline its duty to investigate and punish those responsible.

152. Indeed, as a crime against humanity, the offense committed against Mr. Almonacid-Arellano is neither susceptible of amnesty nor extinguishable . . . .[C]rimes against humanity are intolerable in the eyes of the international community and offend humanity as a whole. The damage caused by these crimes still prevails in the national society and the international community, both of which demand that those responsible be investigated and punished. In this sense, the Convention on the Non-Applicability of Statutory Limitations to War Crimes and Crimes against Humanity[68] clearly states that "no statutory limitation shall apply to [said internationally wrongful acts], irrespective of the date of their commission."

153. Even though the Chilean State has not ratified said Convention, the Court believes that the non-applicability of statutes of limitations to crimes against humanity is a norm of General International Law (*ius cogens*), which is not created by said Convention, but it is acknowledged by it. Hence, the Chilean State must comply with this imperative rule.

154. With regard to the *ne bis in idem* principle, although it is acknowledged as a human right in Article 8(4) of the American Convention, it is not an absolute right, and therefore, is not applicable where: i) the intervention of the court that heard the case and decided to dismiss it or to acquit a person responsible for violating human rights or international law, was intended to shield the accused party from criminal responsibility; ii) the proceedings were not conducted independently or impartially in accordance with due procedural guarantees, or iii) there was no real intent to bring those responsible to justice.[69] A judgment rendered in the foregoing circumstances produces an "apparent" or "fraudulent" *res judicata* case.[70] On the other hand, the Court believes that if there appear new facts or evidence that make it possible to ascertain the identity of those responsible for human rights violations or for crimes against humanity, investigations can be reopened, even if the case ended in an acquittal with the authority of a final judgment, since the dictates of justice, the rights of the victims, and the spirit and the wording of the American Convention supersedes the protection of the *ne bis in idem* principle.

155. In the instant case, two of the foregoing conditions are met. Firstly, the case was heard by courts which did not uphold the guarantees of jurisdiction, independence and impartiality. Secondly, the application of Decree Law No. 2.191 did actually prevent those allegedly responsible from being brought before the courts and favored impunity for the crime committed against Mr. Almonacid-Arellano. The

---

[68]   Adopted by the General Assembly of the United Nations through Resolution 2391 (XXIII) of November 26, 1968, entered into force on November 11, 1970.

[69]   *Cf.* UN, Rome Statute of the International Criminal Court, adopted by the United Nations Diplomatic Conference of Plenipotentiaries on the Establishment of an International Criminal Court, UN Doc. A/CONF.183/9, July 17, 1998, Art. 20; Statute of the International Criminal Tribunal for the former Yugoslavia, S/Res/827, 1993, Art. 10, and Statute of the International Criminal Tribunal for Rwanda, S/Res/955, November 8, 1994, Art. 9.

[70]   *Cf. Case of Carpio-Nicolle et al.* Judgment of November 22, 2004. Series C No. 117, para. 131.

State cannot, therefore, rely on the *ne bis in idem* principle to avoid complying with the order of the Court. . . .

156. On the other hand, the State, in order to fulfill its duty to investigate, must guarantee that the necessary facilities shall be provided by all public institutions to the regular court trying Mr. Almonacid-Arellano's case. Hence, the former shall forward to said court any information or documents it may request, bring before it the persons it may subpoena, and perform the actions it may order.

157. Finally, the State must guarantee that Elvira del Rosario Gómez-Olivares and Alfredo, Alexis, and José Luis Almonacid-Gómez have full access to and capacity to act at all stages and instances of said investigation, pursuant to the domestic law and the provisions of the American Convention.[71] The results of the investigation shall be publicly disclosed by the State, so that the Chilean society may know the truth about the events of the instant case.[72]

C) Pecuniary and non-pecuniary damage

158. Pecuniary damage entails income loss or detriment, expenses incurred as a result of the events and pecuniary consequences causally linked to the violations.[73] Non-pecuniary damage may encompass both the suffering and distress caused to the victims of human rights violations and their next of kin and the impairment of highly significant values in connection with the individuals or their living conditions.[74]

[. . .]

160. . . . . Neither the representative nor the Commission have filed arguments or evidence to prove that the violations described in this Judgment caused pecuniary damage. Accordingly, the Court shall not award any compensation in this regard.

161. Regarding to non-pecuniary damage, the Court acknowledges that the victims of the instant case suffered as a result of the denial of justice arising from the facts analyzed in the foregoing chapters. Likewise, it takes cognizance of the representative's remark that the main interest of the victims of this case lies in achieving justice. On the other hand, the Court makes a positive assessment of the policy of reparation of human rights violations advanced by the State, pursuant to which Mrs. Gómez-Olivares and her children received an approximate amount of US$ 98,000.00, plus educational benefits in an approximate amount of US$ 12,180.00. In the light of the foregoing, the Court decides not to order the payment of economic compensation for non-pecuniary damage, for it believes, as in other cases, that this judgment is in and of itself a form of reparation,[75] and that the measures described in paragraphs 145 to 157 of this Judgment constitute due reparation under Article 63(1) of the American Convention.

---

[71] *Cf. Case of Montero-Aranguren et al., supra* para. 139; *Case of Baldeón-García, supra*, para. 199; and *Case of Blanco-Romero et al.* Judgment of November 28, 2005. Series C No. 138, para. 97.

[72] *Cf. Case of Montero-Aranguren et al., supra*, para. 139; *Case of Baldeón-García, supra*, para. 199; and *Case of the Pueblo Bello Massacre, supra*, para. 267.

[73] *Cf. Case of Ximenes-Lopes, supra*, para. 220; *Case of Baldeón-García, supra*, para. 183; and *Case of the Sawhoyamaxa Indigenous Community.* Judgment of March 29, 2006. Series C No. 146, para. 216.

[74] *Cf. Case of Montero-Aranguren et al., supra*, para. 130; *Case of the Ituango Massacres, supra*, para. 383; and *Case of Baldeón-García, supra*, para. 188.

[75] *Cf. Case of Montero-Aranguren et al., supra*, para. 131; *Case of Ximenes-Lopes, supra*, para. 236; and *Case of the Ituango Massacres, supra*, para. 387.

162. As it has ruled in other cases, the Court decides that, as satisfaction, the State shall publish the chapter on proven facts and the operative part of this Judgment, for a single time and without footnotes, in the Official Gazette and in another newspaper of wide national circulation. These publications shall be made within six months from the date of notification of this Judgment.

E) Costs and Expenses

163. Costs and expenses are included in the concept of reparation set forth in Article 63(1) of the American Convention, inasmuch as the steps taken by the victims in order to achieve justice, both at the domestic and international level, imply expenditures that must be compensated when the State is found to be internationally responsible by a condemnatory judgment. As regards reimbursement, it is for the Court to sensibly appraise its scope. Bearing in mind the nature of international jurisdiction for human rights protection, this appraisal may be made on the basis of the principle of equity and taking into account the expenses indicated by the parties, provided the *quantum* is reasonable.

164. In the instant case, the Court notes that the representative has not verified or proved any specific amount for costs and expenses, whereby it shall proceed to fix it on the grounds of equity. To this end, the Court considers that the costs and expenses arising from the domestic proceedings must be calculated as from December 5, 1996, the date on which the Supreme Court decided that the military courts had jurisdiction to continue hearing the case, since that date marked the beginning of the denial of justice analyzed in the instant case. Costs and expenses at the international level shall be calculated as from the filing of the application before the Inter-American Commission. Hence, the Court deems it fair to instruct the State to reimburse the amount of US$ 10,000.00 or an equivalent amount in Chilean currency, to Mrs. Elvira del Rosario Gómez-Olivares, who shall give her representative the amount due to him for costs and expenses.

X Method of Compliance

[. . . .]

170. In accordance with its constant practice, the Court retains the authority which derives from its jurisdiction and the provisions of Article 65 of the American Convention, to monitor full compliance with this judgment. The instant case shall be closed once the State has fully complied with the provisions herein set forth. Within one year from the date of notice of this judgment, the Chilean State shall submit to the Court a report on the measures adopted in compliance herewith.

Questions and Comments

What happens to an individual who was prosecuted and the case was dismissed because of an amnesty law? Does the individual benefit from the prohibition of double jeopardy if the amnesty is struck down? What if the amnesty is revoked years after the initial proceeding? Is there a time limit beyond which prosecutions should not take place? See *La Cantuta v. Peru*, judgment of Nov. 29, 2006, 162 Inter-Am. Ct. H.R. (ser. C).

Zimbabwe Human Rights NGO Forum v. Zimbabwe, Comm. 245/2002, 20th
Annual Activity Report, Annex, pp. 145–53.

Issue Four: The Clemency Order and the Respondent's State's human rights obligations under the African Charter

188. The complainant submits that by virtue of Clemency Order No 1 of 2000,
the victims of human rights abuses could not seek redress for the human rights
violations they suffered because they could not challenge the Clemency order. The
Clemency Order granted pardon *to every person liable to criminal prosecution for
any politically motivated crime* committed between January and July 2000. The Respondent State emphasised that the prerogative of clemency is recognised as an integral part of constitutional democracies. To ensure that those who had committed
more serious offences do not go unpunished, the Clemency Order excluded crimes
such as murder, rape, robbery, indecent assault, statutory rape, theft and possession
of arms. The Respondent State further noted that a decision by the African Commission that the Clemency Order is an abdication of Zimbabwe's obligations under
the African Charter would amount to undermining the whole notion of the clemency prerogative worldwide.

189. The African Commission would like to first of all address the assertion by
the Respondent State that *"a decision by the African Commission that the Clemency
Order is an abdication of Zimbabwe's obligations under the Charter would amount
to undermining the whole notion of the clemency prerogative worldwide"*. This assertion by the Respondent State seems to imply that the African Commission lacks the
competence to make a determination on this matter.

190. The African Commission was established to monitor and ensure the protection of all human rights enshrined in the African Charter. It does this through
among other things, making sure that policies and legislation adopted by States Parties to the African Charter do not contravene the provisions of the African Charter.
The fact that the doctrine of clemency is universally recognized does not preclude
the African Commission from making a determination on it, especially if it is believed that its use has been abused to the extent that human rights as contained in
the African Charter have been violated. The African Commission would also like
to emphasise the point that the African Charter is an International Treaty and it is
customary in international law that where domestic legislation, including a national
constitution is in conflict with international law, the latter prevails. The African
Commission is therefore competent to make a determination on any domestic legislation, including a domestic legislation in a constitutional democracy that grants
the Executive absolute discretion.

191. Having concluded that it has the competence to rule on the question of
the Clemency Order, the African Commission would now determine whether the
Clemency Order as issued by the Respondent State violated the latter's obligation
under the African Charter. The Clemency Order granted pardon to *every person liable to criminal prosecution for any politically motivated crime committed* between
January and July 2000.

192. The Order also granted a remission of the whole or remainder of the period of imprisonment to every person convicted of any politically motivated crime committed during the stated period. In terms of the Clemency Order, "a politically motivated crime" is defined as:

(a) Any offence motivated by the object of supporting or opposing any political purpose and committed in connection with

(i) The Constitutional referendum held on the 12th and 13th of February 2000; or

(ii) The general Parliamentary elections held on 24th and 25th June 2000;

whether committed before, during or after the said referendum or elections.

193. The only crimes exempted from the Clemency Order were murder, robbery, rape, indecent assault, statutory rape, theft, possession of arms and any offence involving fraud or dishonesty.

194. The Clemency Order under review in the present communication relates to a situation where non-state actors are alleged to have violated human rights, a situation of genaralised violence which according to the state was politically motivated, a situation which resulted in loss of life and property. In a bid to reconcile the population the Respondent State passed Decree No. 1 of 2000 adopting executive clemency to absolve perpetrators of violence if the latter related to "any offence motivated by the object of supporting or opposing any political purpose". The question for the African Commission is to determine whether the clemency order in question is a negation of the State's responsibility under Article 1 of the African Charter.

195. The term clemency is a general term for the power of an executive to intervene in the sentencing of a criminal defendant to prevent injustice from occurring.[76] The exercise of executive clemency is inherent in many, if not, all constitutional democracies of the world. National governments have chosen to implement clemency for a number of reasons. For instance, executive clemency exists to afford relief from undue harshness or evident mistake in the operation or enforcement of the criminal law. The administration of justice by the courts is not necessarily always just or certainly considerate of circumstances which may properly mitigate guilt. To afford remedy, it has always been thought essential to vest in some authority other that the courts, power to ameliorate or avoid particular criminal judgments.[77]

196. Clemency embraces the constitutional authority of the President to remit punishment using the distinct vehicles of pardons, amnesties, commutations, reprieves, and remissions of fines. An amnesty is granted to a group of people who commit political offences, e.g. during a civil war, during armed conflicts or during a domestic insurrection. A pardon may lessen a defendant's sentence or set it altogether. One may be pardoned even before being formally accused or convicted. While a pardon attempts to restore a person's reputation, a commutation of sentence is a more limited form of clemency. It does not remove the criminal stigma associated with the crime, it merely substitutes a milder sentence. A reprieve on its part postpones a scheduled execution.

---

76 Allison Madden, *Clemency for Battered Women who Kill their Abusers: Finding a Just Forum*, 4 HASTINGS WOMEN'S L.J 1, 50 (1993).

77 Linda Ammons, *Discretionary Justice: A Legal and Policy Analysis of a Governor's Use of the Clemency Power in the Cases of Incarcerated Battered Women*, 3 J.L & POLICY 1, 30 (1994).

197. Clemency orders are not peculiar to Zimbabwe. These are resorted to the world over generally in the interest of peace and security. In the history of Zimbabwe, it is a well known fact that Clemency orders have been resorted to as a process of easing tension and creating a new beginning. For instance, at Independence in 1979/80, amnesty was resorted to by former colonial regime in order to create an environment for the new independent dispensation and to reduce the tension between the nationalists and the former white rules. In the process, members of the former white regime who had been guilty of massive killings were beneficiaries of clemency. In another incident, following the civil war in the southern part of Zimbabwe involving two former nationalists movements, ZANU (PF) and the opposition (PF) ZAPU, an amnesty was resorted to in order to create an environment for a Peace Accord in 1987, which brought about permanent peace to Zimbabwe. The result was the release of several thousands of people including those who were guilty of massive human rights violations including murder, treason, and terrorism. Also generally, clemency is granted annually to serving prisoners for the purpose of giving them a new beginning, including those released on the humanitarian grounds.

198. Generally however, a Clemency power is used in a situation where the President believes that the public welfare will be better served by the pardon, or to people who have served part of their sentences and lived within the law, or a belief that a sentence was excessive or unjust or again for personal circumstances that warrant compassion. In all these situations, the President exercises a near absolute discretion.

199. The reason the framers of national constitutions vest this broad power in the executive branch is to ensure that the President would have the freedom to do what he/she deems to be the right thing. . . .

200. Over the years however, this strict interpretation of Clemency powers have been the subject of considerable scrutiny by international human rights bodies and legal scholars. It is generally believed that the single most important factor in the proliferation and continuation of human rights violations is the persistence of impunity, be it of a de *jure* or *de facto* nature. Clemency, it is believed, encourages *de jure* as well as *de facto* impunity and leaves the victims without just compensation and effective remedy. De jure impunity generally arises where legislation provides indemnity from legal process in respect of acts to be committed in a particular context or exemption from legal responsibility in respect of acts that have in the past been committed, for example, as in the present case, by way of clemency (amnesty or pardon). *De facto* impunity occurs where those committing the acts in question are in practice insulated from the normal operation of the legal system. That seems to be the situation with the present case.

201. There has been consistent international jurisprudence suggesting that the prohibition of amnesties leading to impunity for serious human rights has become a rule of customary international law. In a report entitled *"Question of the impunity of perpetrators of human rights violations (civil and political)"*, prepared by Mr. Louis Joinet for the Sub-commission on Prevention of Discrimination and Protection of Minorities, pursuant to Sub-commission decision 1996/119, it was noted that "amnesty cannot be accorded to perpetrators of violations before the victims have ob-

tained justice by means of an effective remedy" and that "the right to justice entails obligations for the State: to investigate violations, to prosecute the perpetrators and, if their guilt is established, to punish them".[78]

202. In his report, Mr. Joinet drafted a set of principles for the protection and promotion of human rights through action to combat impunity, in which he stated that "there can be no just and lasting reconciliation unless the need for justice is effectively justified" and that "national and international measures must be taken . . . with a view to securing jointly, in the interests of the victims of human rights violations, observance of the right to know and, by implication, the right to the truth, the right to justice and the right to reparation, without which there can be no effective remedy against the pernicious effects of impunity". The Report went on to state that "even when intended to establish conditions conducive to a peace agreement or to foster national reconciliation, amnesty and other measures of clemency shall be kept within certain bounds, namely: (a) the perpetrators of serious crimes under international law may not benefit from such measures until such time as the State has met their obligations to investigate violations, to take appropriate measures in respect of the perpetrators, particularly in the area of justice, by ensuring that they are prosecuted, tried and duly punished, to provide victims with effective remedies and reparation for the injuries suffered, and to take acts to prevent the recurrence of such atrocities.[79]

203. In its General Comment No. 20 on Article 7 of the ICCPR, the UN Human Rights Committee noted that "amnesties are generally incompatible with the duty of States to investigate such acts; to guarantee freedom from such acts within their jurisdiction; and to ensure that they do not occur in the future. States may not deprive individuals of the right to an effective remedy, including compensation and such full rehabilitation as may be possible".[80] In the case of *Hugo Rodríguez v. Uruguay*,[81] the Committee reaffirmed its position that amnesties for gross violations of human rights are incompatible with the obligations of the State party under the Covenant and expressed concern that in adopting the amnesty law in question, the State party contributed to an atmosphere of impunity which may undermine the democratic order and give rise to further human rights violations. The 1993 Vienna Declaration and Programme of Action supports this stand and stipulates that "States should abrogate legislation leading to impunity for those responsible for grave violations of human rights such as torture and prosecute such violations, thereby providing a firm basis for the rule of law".[82]

204. Importantly, the international obligation to bring to justice and punish serious violations of human rights has been recognized and established in all regional human rights mechanisms. The Inter-American Commission and Court of Human Rights have also decided on the question of amnesty legislation. The Inter-Ameri-

---

[78] See E/CN.4/Sub.2/1997/20/Rev.1, paras. 32 and 27.

[79] *Ibid.* Principles 18 and 25.

[80] See Human Rights Committee General Comment No. 20 (44) on Article 7, para. 15 at www.unhchr. ch/tbs/doc.nsf/view40?SearchView.

[81] *Rodríguez v. Uruguay*, Communication No. 322/1988, U.N. Doc. CCPR/C/51/D/322/1988 (1994).

[82] See The Vienna Declaration and Programme of Action, Section II, para. 60, at www.unhchr.ch/ huridocda/huridoca.nsf/Sym . . . /A..CONF.157.23.

can Commission on Human Rights has condemned amnesty laws issued by democratic successor Governments in the name of reconciliation, even if approved by a plebiscite, and has held them to be in breach of the 1969 American Convention on Human Rights, in particular the duty of the State to respect and ensure rights recognized in the Convention (article 1(1)), the right to due process of law (article 8) and the right to an effective judicial remedy (article 25). The Commission held further that amnesty laws extinguishing both criminal and civil liability disregarded the legitimate rights of the victims' next of kin to reparation and that such measures would do nothing to further reconciliation. Of particular interest are the findings by the Inter-American Commission on Human Rights that "amnesty" legislation enacted in Argentina and Uruguay violated basic provisions of the American Convention on Human Rights.[83] In these cases, the Inter-American Commission held that the legal consequences of the amnesty laws denied the victims the right to obtain a judicial remedy. The effect of the amnesty laws was that cases against those charged were thrown out, trials already in progress were closed, and no judicial avenue was left to present or continue cases. In consequence, the effects of the amnesty laws violated the right to judicial protection and to a fair trial, as recognized by the American Convention and in the present case, the African Charter.[84]

205. In Argentina, the national courts have found Argentina's *Full Stop Law*[85] and the *Due Obedience Law*[86] as incompatible with international law and in particular with Argentina's obligations to bring to justice and punish the perpetrators of gross human rights violations. This is because these two pieces of legislation had been enacted to prevent from prosecution low and high ranking military officials (government agents) who were involved in human rights violations and disappearances during the 1970s and 1980s.

206. The Inter-American Court stated in its first judgment that states must prevent, investigate and punish any violation of the rights recognized by the Convention.[87] This has been re-emphasized in subsequent cases. . . .

207. The European Court of Human Rights on its part has recognized that where the alleged violations include acts of torture or arbitrary killings, the state is under a duty to undertake an investigation capable of leading to the identification and punishment of those responsible.[88]

---

[83] Annual Report of the Inter-American Commission on Human Rights, 1992–1993.

[84] *Ibid.* See also Jayni Edelstein, *Rights, Reparations and Reconciliation: Some comparative notes*, Seminar No. 6, July 1994.

[85] Law No 23,429 of 12 December 1986.

[86] Law No. 23,521 of 4 June 1987. The Committee Against Torture took the view, in respect of these laws, that the passing of the "Full Stop" and "Due Obedience" Laws in Argentina by a "democratically elected" government for acts committed under a *de facto* government is "incompatible with the spirit and purpose of the Convention [against Torture and Other Cruel, Inhuman or Degrading Treatment or Punishment]" (Committee against Torture, Communications N° 1/1988, 2/1988 and 3/1988, Argentina, decision dated 23 November 1989, para. 9.)

[87] *Velasquez Rodriguez v Honduras*, Judgment of July 29, 1988, Inter-Am.Ct.H.R. (Ser. C) No. 4 (1988). para 166.

[88] European Court of Human Rights Case *Zeki Aksoy v. Turkey*, 18 December 1996, para 98. See also, *Aydin v. Turkey* App. No. 23178/94 Judgment of 25 September 1997, para 103; *Selçuk and Asker v. Turkey* App. Nos. 23184/94 and 23185/94 Judgment of 24 April 1998, para 96; *Kurt v. Turkey* App. No. 24276/94 Judgment of 25 May 1998, para 139; and *Keenan v. United Kingdom* App. No. 27229/95 Judgment of 3 April 2001, para 122.

208. The African Commission has also held amnesty laws to be incompatible with a State's human rights obligations.[89] Guideline No. 16 of the Robben Island Guidelines adopted by the African Commission during its 32nd session in October 2002 further states that 'in order to combat impunity States should: a) ensure that those responsible for acts of torture or ill-treatment are subject to legal process; and b) ensure that there is no immunity from prosecution for nationals suspected of torture, and that the scope of immunities for foreign nationals who are entitled to such immunities be as restrictive as is possible under international law'[90]

209. The UN Special Rapporteur on Torture has also expressed his opposition to the passing, application and non-revocation of amnesty laws (including laws in the name of national reconciliation, the consolidation of democracy and peace, and respect for human rights), which prevent torturers from being brought to justice and hence contribute to a culture of impunity. He called on States to refrain from granting or acquiescing in impunity at the national level, inter alia, by the granting of amnesties, such impunity itself constituting a violation of international law. As the International Criminal Tribunal for the former Yugoslavia Trial Chambers noted in the *Celibici* and *Furundzija* cases,[91] torture is prohibited by an absolute and non-derogable general rule of international law.

210. In the present communication, the African Commission has established that most of the atrocities, including human rights vioations, were pepetrated by non-state actors, that the State exercised due diligence in its response to the violence—investigated the allegations, amended some of its laws, and in some cases, paid compensation to victims. The fact that all the allegations could not be investigated does not make the State liable for the human rights violations alleged to have been committed by non-state actors. It suffices for the State to demonstrate that the measures taken were proportionate to deal with the situation, which in the present communication, the State seemed to have shown.

211. However, this Commission is of the opinion that by passing the Clemency Order No. 1 of 2000, prohibiting prosecution and setting free perpetrators of "politically motivated crimes", including alleged offences such as abductions, forced imprisonment, arson, destruction of property, kidnappings and other human rights violatins, the State did not only encourage impunity but effectively foreclosed any available avenue for the alleged abuses to be investigated, and prevented victims of crimes and alleged human rights violations from seeking effective remedy and compensation.

212. This act of the state constituted a violation of the victims' right to judicial protection and to have their cause heard under Article 7 (1) of the African Charter.

---

[89] See also: *Various communications v. Mauritania* Communications 54/91, 61/91, 96/93, 98/93, 164/97-196/97, 210/98 and *Jean Yokovi Degli on behalf of Corporal N. Bikagni, Union Interafricaine des Droits de l'Homme, Commission International de Juristes v Togo* Communications 83/92, 88/93, 91/93.

[90] Guidelines and Measures for the Prohibition and Prevention of Torture, Cruel, Inhuman or Degrading Treatment or Punishment in Africa (The Robben Island Guidelines), African Commission on Human and Peoples' Rights, 32nd Session, 17–23 October, 2002: Banjul, The Gambia. See also: *Various communications v. Mauritania* Communications 54/91, 61/91, 96/93, 98/93, 164/97–196/97, 210/98.

[91] IT-96-21-A, 20 February 2001, Appeals Chamber; *The Prosecutor v. Anto Furundzija* (IT-95-17/1-T), Trial Chamber II, Judgment, 10 Dec. 1998 (121 ILR 218) 45, 47, 48, 49, 61, 316, 333, 334, 337, 340, 342, 402, 469.

213. The protection afforded by Article 7 is not limited to the protection of the rights of arrested and detained persons but encompasses the right of every individual to access the relevant judicial bodies competent to have their causes heard and be granted adequate relief. If there appears to be any possibility of an alleged victim succeeding at a hearing, the applicant should be given the benefit of the doubt and allowed to have their matter heard. Adopting laws such as the Clemency Order No. 1 of 2000, that have the effect of eroding this opportunity, renders the victims helpless and deprives them of justice. To borrow from the Inter-American human rights system, the American Declaration of the Rights and Duties of Man[92] provides in Article XVIII that every person has the right to "resort to the courts to ensure respect for [their] legal rights," and to have access to a "simple, brief procedure whereby the courts" will protect him or her "from acts of authority that . . . violate any fundamental constitutional rights." The right of access is a necessary aspect of the right to "resort to the courts" set forth in Article XVIII.[93] The right of access to judicial protection to ensure respect for a legal right requires available and effective recourse for the violation of a right protected under the Charter or the Constitution of the country concerned.

214. In yet another jurisdiction, the Canadian Human Rights Charter[94] provides a similar guarantee in section 24(1), which establishes that: "[a]nyone whose rights or freedoms, as guaranteed by this Charter, have been infringed or denied may apply to a court of competent jurisdiction to obtain such remedy as the court considers appropriate and just in the circumstances". The effect of this right is to require the provision of a domestic remedy which enables the relevant judicial authority to deal with the substance of the complaint and grant appropriate relief where required. In addition to the explicit rights to judicial protection, implementation of the overarching objective of the Charter (ensuring the effectiveness of the fundamental rights and freedoms set forth), necessarily requires that judicial and other mechanisms are in place to provide recourse and remedies at the national level.

215. In light of the above, the African Commission holds that by enacting Decree No. 1 of 2000 which foreclosed access to any remedy that might be available to the victims to vindicate their rights, and without putting in place alternative adequate legislative or institutional mechanisms to ensure that perpetrators of the alleged

---

[92] American Declaration of the Rights and Duties of Man, O.A.S. Res. XXX, adopted by the Ninth International Conference of American States (1948), *reprinted in* Basic Documents Pertaining to Human Rights in the Inter-American System, OEA/Ser.L.V/II.82 doc.6 rev.1 at 17 (1992).

[93] *See generally*, IACHR, Resolutions N° 3/84, 4/84 and 5/85, Cases N° 4563, 7848 and 8027, Paraguay, published in *Annual Report of the IACHR 1983–84*, OEA/Ser.L/V/II.63, doc. 10, 24 Sept. 1984, at pp. 57, 62, 67 (addressing lack of access to judicial protection in proceedings involving expulsion of nationals; linking right to freely enter and remain in one's own country under Article VIII of the Declaration to the rights to a fair trial and due process under Articles XVIII and XXVI). *See also*, Report N° 47/96, Case 11.436, Cuba, in *Annual Report of the IACHR 1996*, OEA/Ser.L/V/ II.95, Doc. 7 rev., 14 March 1997, at para. 91, (citing *Annual Report of the IACHR 1994*, "Cuba," at p. 162, and addressing failure of State to observe freedom of movement of nationals under Article II via denial of exit permits from which no appeal is allowed). In the context of the American Convention, *see generally*, IACHR, Resolution N° 30/81, Case 7378, Guatemala, in *Annual Report of the IACHR 1980–81*, OEA/Ser.L/V/II.54, doc. 9 rev. 1, 16 Oct. 1981, p. 60, at 62 (addressing denial of right to judicial protection in expulsion of foreigner absent any form of due process), Report N° 49/99, Case 11.610, Mexico, *Annual Report of the IACHR 1998*, OEA/Ser.L/V/II.102, Doc. 6 rev., 16 April 1999, Vol. II; *see also*, Eur. Ct. H.R., Ashingdane Case, Ser. A No. 93 (1985) para. 55.

[94] THE CANADIAN CHARTER OF RIGHTS AND FREEDOMS, Ottawa, Canada, April 17, 1982.

atrocities were punished, and victims of the violations duly compensated or given other avenues to seek effective remedy, the Respondent State did not only prevent the victims from seeking redress, but also encouraged impunity, and thus reneged on its obligation in violation of Articles 1 and 7 (1) of the African Charter. The granting of amnesty to absolve perpetrators of human rights violations from accountability violates the right of victims to an effective remedy.[95]

For these reasons, the African Commission:

Holds that the Republic of Zimbabwe is in violation of Articles 1 and 7 (1) of the African Charter;

Calls on the Republic of Zimbabwe to establish a Commission of Inquiry to investigate the causes of the violence which took place from February—June 2000 and bring those responsible for the violence to justice, and identify victims of the violence in order to provide them with just and adequate compensation.

Request the Republic of Zimbabwe to report to the African Commission on the implementation of this recommendation during the presentation of its next periodic report.

Questions and Comments

1. The Inter-American Commission's reaction to Uruguay's amnesty, approved by referendum, can be found in IACHR, *Report 29192, Cases 10.029, 10.036, 10.145, 10.305, 10.372, 10.373, 10.374 and 10.375, Uruguay.* Annual Report of the Inter-American Commission on Human Rights 1992–1993, OEA/Ser.L/V/II.83, doc. 14 corr. 1, March 12, 1993, pp. 154–165.

2. Compare the measures adopted by El Salvador, Peru, Chile and Zimbabwe. Why did the Inter-American Commission support Chile's actions?

3. Do amnesty laws or pardons always violate the Convention? If civil remedies exist, can criminal sanctions be repealed? Is your answer the same if criminal penalties are provided, but no civil actions are permitted? What if only a Truth Commission is established? Does the nature of the violations affect the legality of an amnesty: are they banned for all violations, "gross" violations, or violations that constitute international crimes?

4. Does the Inter-American Convention for the Prevention and Punishment of Torture prohibit a State Party from granting amnesty to torturers? If amnesty is granted, could another state establish the civil responsibility of a torturer who comes within its jurisdiction?

5. Can or should the Commission comment on the length or nature of punishments imposed on perpetrators of human rights violations?

6. On amnesties, reconciliation, and the duty to prosecute, *see:* A.S. Brown, *Adios Amnesty: Prosecutorial Discretion and Military Trials in Argentina,* 37 TEXAS INT'L L.J. 203 (2002); C.M. Cerna, *Inter-American Court of Human Rights: Barrios Altos Case (Chumbipuma Aguirre et al. v Peru)—Introductory Note,* 41 ILM 91 (2002); J. S. Correa, *Dealing with Past Human Rights Violations: The Chilean Case after Dictatorship,* 67 NOTRE DAME L.REV. 1455 (1992); J. Dugard, *Dealing with Crimes of a Past Regime: Is Amnesty Still an Option?* 12 LEIDEN INT'L L.J. 1001 (1999); P. B. Hayner, *Fifteen Truth Commissions, 1974–1994: A Comparative Study,* HUM. RTS. Q. (1994); J. Kokott, *No Impunity for Human Rights Viola-*

---

[95] *See the African Commission's Principles and Guidelines on the Right to a Fair Trial and Legal Assistance in Africa, para C(d).*

tions in the Americas, 14 HRLJ 153 (1993); M. Koskenniemi, *Between Impunity and Show Trials,* 6 MAX PLANK YB U.N.L. 1 (2002); N.J. Kritz, *Coming to Terms with Atrocities: A Review of Accountability Mechanisms for Mass Violations of Human Rights,* 59 LAW & CONTEMP. PROBL. 127 (1996); A.J. Latcham, *Duty to Punish: International Law and the Human Rights Policy of Argentina,"* 7 B.U. INT'L L.J. 355 (1989); G. Meijide, *The Role of Historical Inquiry in Creating Accountability for Human Rights Abuses,* 12 B.C. THIRD WORLD L.J. 269 (1992); E. Mignone et al., *Dictatorship on Trial: Prosecution of Human Rights Violations in Argentina,* 10 YALE J. INT'L L. 118 (1984); J.J. Moore, *Note. Problems with Forgiveness: Granting Amnesty under the Arias Plan in Nicaragua and El Salvador,* 43 STAN.L.REV. (1991); D.F. Orentlicher, *Addressing Gross Human Rights Abuses: Punishment and Victim Compensation,* in L. HENKIN AND J.L. HARGROVE (EDS.), HUMAN RIGHTS: AN AGENDA FOR THE NEXT CENTURY (ASIL 1994);—*Settling Accounts: The Duty to Prosecute Human Rights Violations of a Prior Regime,* 100 YALE L.J. 2537 (1991); A. O'SHEA, AMNESTY FOR CRIME IN INTERNATIONAL LAW AND PRACTICE (2002); S. RATNER & J. ABRAMS, ACCOUNTABILITY FOR HUMAN RIGHTS ATROCITIES IN INTERNATIONAL LAW (2003); D. Robinson, *Serving the Interests of Justice: Amnesties, Truth Commission and the International Criminal Court,* 14 EJIL 481 (2003); N. Roht-Arriaza, *State Responsibility to Investigate and Prosecute Grave Human Rights Violations in International Law,* 78 CAL.L.REV. 449 (1990); SIM, SEMINAR ON THE RIGHT TO RESTITUTION, COMPENSATION AND REHABILITATION FOR VICTIMS OF GROSS VIOLATIONS OF HUMAN RIGHTS AND FUNDAMENTAL FREEDOMS (Neth. Inst. Human Rights, 1992); IACHR, Resolution 23/89, Case 10.031 (United States), *Annual Report of the Inter-American Commission on Human Rights* 1989–1990, OEA/Ser.LIV/II/77 rev. 1, doc. 7, 17 May 1990, pp. 62–73; United Nations, *Study Concerning the Rights to Restitution, Compensation and Rehabilitation for Victims of Gross Violations of Human Rights and Fundamental Freedoms,* Final Report submitted by Mr. Theo van Boven, Special Rapporteur, UN Doc. E/CN.4/Sub.2/1993/8.

B. Lustration

In sharp contrast to amnesties, some states have enacted lustration laws which prohibit those who have committed or threaten to commit human rights from holding public office or exercising other rights. In some instances, the individuals or groups in question have challenged the restrictions. The following cases are illustrative. Should individuals or groups that are dedicated to the violation of human rights—e.g. based on racism or religious intolerance—be barred from political office? Does it make a difference if those involved have been convicted of illegal conduct? What prior actions or offices should disqualify individuals from holding positions in human rights bodies? See D. W. Cassel, *Somoza's Revenge: A New Judge for the Inter-American Court of Human Rights,* 13 HRLJ 137 (1992).

Rios Montt v. Guatemala, **Rep. No. 30/93, Case 10.804** *Annual Report of the Inter-American Commission on Human Rights 1993,* OEA/Ser.L/V/II.85, doc. 9 rev., 11 February 1993, p. 206.

I. ORIGINAL PETITION OF THE COMPLAINANT

1. On March 4, 1991, the Commission received a petition transmitted to the Government on March 5, 1991, in which the petitioner, Jose Efraín Rios Montt, filed a complaint against the Guatemalan Government for alleged violations of the

American Convention on Human Rights because of the effects of the various resolutions and acts of the judicial, legislative and executive officials of the Government that declared his candidacy to the Presidency of Guatemala inadmissible.

2. The petition recounts the political background of Mr. Rios Montt from the year 1974, and states that on March 23, 1982, at the request of military officers, he was called upon to preside over the de facto government established by them, a call he accepted by assuming the position of chief of state. It states that during the period when the 1966 Constitution was in force, the penal code stipulated punishment for crimes of changing the constitutional order.

3. It states that the de facto government headed by him suspended the 1966 constitution and recounts how government posts and institutions were organized and describes the fight against subversion.

4. It notes that on August 8, 1983, the President of the Republic was deposed by another military coup, and the post was taken over by his Defense Minister, General Oscar Mejia Victores. Mr. Rios Montt then remained in Guatemala without being molested or accused or tried for the crimes provided for in the penal code on changing the constitutional order and other offenses arising from his exercise of the de facto presidency.

5. It states that the Chief of Government, General Mejia Victores, issued a decree of amnesty, a decree considered valid and in force by the 1985 Constituent Assembly. Mr. Rios Montt took advantage of that amnesty in running in the 1990 elections.

6. It says that the Constitutional Convention prepared and enacted the 1986 Constitution now in force, which contains limitations on access to the presidency of the republic, banning reelection to the presidency and providing in Article 186:

(. . .) the following may not hold this office:
   a) The leader and chiefs of any coup d'etat, armed revolution or similar movement that changes the constitutional order, nor those who become head of the government as a result of such actions.

7. The petition states that in 1990 various parties supported his candidacy for the presidency, and drew up a slate of candidates that included him and 70 other persons for the posts of Vice President, deputies and alternates to the National Congress and the Central American Parliament. It also states that the election officials, that is, the Registrar of Voters List and the Supreme Electoral Tribunal refused to register those candidates, and that he filed a complaint of constitutional rights violation (*recurso de amparo*) with the competent courts. It contends that at that time the National Congress tried to intimidate him by requesting an advisory opinion from the Constitutional Court on whether the Constitution prohibited him from serving as President or Vice President of the Republic. It also states that the Congress tried to file a political suit against the President of the Supreme Court, Dr. Edmundo Vazquez Martinez, to prevent that justice from granting the writ filed with it.

8. It states that the Constitutional Court handed down the decisions requested of it by ruling that such a ban is categorical and permanent (at any time).

9. It contends by way of background information that the Congress, in an effort to obstruct his right to defense, reduced from 30 to 5 days the period for appealing

the decisions of the Supreme Electoral Tribunal, thereby depriving him of his right of due process. It acknowledges that his right to file a complaint under the America Convention regarding those actions taken in 1989 is precluded because more than six months have elapsed.

15. Specific violations of the Convention

a. The petition contends that both in his personal capacity and as a candidate for President of the Republic, the provisions of the various organs of the Guatemalan Government violate in his case the right to a fair trial and guarantees of judicial protection (Article 8, subpar. 1 and 2; and 25 American Convention on Human Rights) and impartiality of the administration of justice (Article 31 of the American Convention on Human Rights).

b. The petition also alleges violation of the guarantee in Article 9 of the Convention because of application of an ex post facto law enacted, that is, Article 186.a of the Constitution, making it retroactive.

c. It also asserts that the Guatemalan law violates Article 23 subpar. 1 and 2 of the American Convention on Human Rights, by establishing for life the restriction on his political right to be elected to public office.

d. The petition also states that Article 186.a involves a dual penalty, because there are legal provisions in the Penal Code on changing the constitutional order that could have been applied before employing amnesty, and they were not applied, and they were released from doing so by the use of amnesty. It states further that application of the grounds of ineligibility of Article 186.a involves another penalty. . . .

e. The petitioner contends finally that the right of Guatemalan citizens who so desired to elect him as President of the Republic was being violated.

16. The petitioner accompanies his demand with documentation of the procedural acts and legislation indicated, and with press material regarding the facts set forth in his petition. This documentary material was completed by the petitioner on March 22 of this year, and that additional information was forwarded to the Government on March 26.

IV. CONSIDERATIONS REGARDING THE MERITS OF THE CASE

19. The right to be a candidate in a political election arises from Article 23 of the American Convention on Human Rights, which recognizes the rights of each individual: a) to take part in the conduct of public affairs, directly or through representatives; b) to be elected; and c) to have access, under general conditions of equality, to the public service.

This article also establishes limits on the regulations that the State can impose on these rights and opportunities; it may limit them only on the basis of age, nationality, residence, language, education, civil or mental capacity, or sentencing by a competent court in criminal proceedings.

20. The central issue the Commission must address is the following: Is the permanent ineligibility established in the Guatemalan Constitution in Article 186 regarding heads of political movements that breach the constitutional order or take

over the leadership of the State as a result of such breach consistent with this Article of the Convention and its supplementary articles?

21. The Commission should consider this question on three levels: one, the Convention as a whole and its relationship with the other principle instruments of the inter-American system; second, in the context of Guatemalan and international constitutional law; and finally, in light of the juridical circumstances that constitute and surround the decision of the Government in not accepting the candidacy of Mr. Rios Montt.

22. As to the first level, the Commission should take into consideration primarily the basis of the Supreme Court ruling in denying the petition of Mr. Rios Montt. The Supreme Court acknowledges the primacy the Guatemalan Constitution itself accords the American Convention on Human Rights in the domestic legal system. Based on this recognition the Court interprets Article 32 of the Convention as establishing a framework of interpretation applicable to the analysis when it says that: "The rights of each person are limited by the rights of others, by the security of all, and by the just demands of the general welfare, in a democratic society."

23. In this regard, the Commission considers the relevancy for the analysis of the other instruments of the inter-American system, first of all the Charter of the American States and the many pronouncements down through the Organization's one-hundred year history in reaffirming the constitutional democratic system as the bases and objectives of the action of the system and its component States.

24. Based on this premise, the Commission considers that the context of Guatemalan and international constitutional law in which this condition of ineligibility is placed is the appropriate dimension for analysis of the applicability of the Convention in general, and of the applicability of its Arts. 23 and 32 to the instant case, and from which the margin of appreciation allowed by inter-national law can emerge.

25. In this connection, the Commission takes into consideration that the ineligibility of those who lead movements of governments that breach the constitutional order appears in the successive Guatemalan constitutions since the beginning of this century and is maintained by the various reforms.'[96]

26. The Commission likewise considers that this ineligibility is not idiosyncratic to the Guatemalan constitutional tradition, but appears also—sometimes with virtually the same wording—in other constitutions of various Central American countries (Honduras, Nicaragua).[97]

27. Furthermore, the Commission takes into account that one of the common roots of this ineligibility is the General Treaty of Peace and Friendship concluded by the Governments of the Republics of Guatemala, El Salvador, Honduras, Nicaragua and Costa Rica in 1923, whereby the contracting parties undertake not to recognize the governments of any of the five republics if they are taken over by a coup d'etat or if any of high elected officials have been "head or one of the heads of a coup d'etat or revolution, . . . " their blood relatives, or anyone who has held high military com-

---

[96] Among others the Constitutions of 1927, art. 25; 1935, art. 65; 1941, art. 3; 1945, art. 131; 1956 art. 161, and 1986, art. 186.

[97] Nicaragua, 1950, art. 186; Honduras, 1982, art. 239 (referring to any head of the Executive Branch, whether he has been elected or has taken power through unconstitutional means).

mand immediately before or during such takeovers. The treaty also establishes the commitment to include the principle of non-reelection in their constitutions.

28. These principles rejecting the breach of the constitutional order, the disqualification of its leaders for high office, and non-reelection were adopted because they were considered as juridical principles of international relations and common defense of the democratic consolidation in the region.

These principles were adopted at the same time as Article XIV of the treaty, which establishes the most sweeping rejection of direct and indirect intervention in internal affairs. In other words, these principles were considered of such importance that they were placed outside and above any consideration of internal intervention.

29. It is accordingly established that this ineligibility set forth in Article 186 of the Guatemalan constitution is a customary constitutional rule with a strong tradition in Central America.

30. The Commission should also consider whether, in this same juridical context, this rule establishes an individual or general discriminatory principle that would be contrary not only to Article 23, Political Rights, of the American Convention on Human Rights, but also to the general principles in that Convention.

31. In this regard, the Commission recalls that this issue should be analyzed in light of the circumstances of the individual case and prevailing concepts in the historic period. Here again, the Commission should reaffirm the restrictive character that this margin of appreciation should utilize, which should always be conceived with a view to strengthening the system and its objectives.

32. The Commission finds that analysis of the condition of ineligibility applied to Mr. Rios Montt should be compared with other conditions of ineligibility in other constitutional law, to determine whether there is discrimination or whether conventional limits are exceeded. In this regard, the Commission recalls that various constitutional regimes establish as a condition of ineligibility, in some cases for a specified period, and in others as permanent ineligibility, the fact of having been the head of or exercised the power of the executive branch after being elected thereto.[98]

33. There would thus be constitutional conditions whereby high government officials elected in democratic elections cannot be reelected either for a certain period or for life. If the Commission considers that Article 86 establishes ineligibility that is inconsistent with the Convention, it would place in a privileged position those who breach the constitutional order compared to those who accede to high office in their countries constitutionally and democratically.

34. Furthermore, the Commission considers that comparative constitutional law stipulates different conditions of ineligibility seeking to avoid nepotism, conflict of interests (government contractors, etc.), membership in religious orders, other branches or services of the government (judges, those on active duty in the military, etc.). In other words, defense of the authenticity of political rights and of the authenticity of elections has led to various kinds of regulation on eligibility for serving

---

[98] The 1986 Constitution of Mexico, Art. 83 and the 1982 Constitution of Honduras, Art. 239, and the 1991 Constitution of Colombia, Art. 197 establish an absolute and permanent condition of ineligibility for heads of or appointees to the executive branch, and most of the constitutional provisions in the Americas that establish any restriction on reelection, whether on the number of terms or on consecutive terms.

as head of the executive branch, which must be considered in context for the Commission's assessment.

35. The same reasoning should be applied to the permanent ineligibility or ineligibility for life. If it is acceptable under constitutional law for a State to establish a constitutional term for democratically elected heads of state (Honduras, Mexico, Colombia, as cited), then it is perfectly conceivable that this same scope can be applied to those who lead a breach of constitution.

36. The Commission also considers the scope of the amnesty accorded to Mr. Rios Montt in 1986 and its ability to nullify the effects of the ineligibility clause in the Constitution. In this regard, the Supreme Court and the Constitutional Court have clearly established that such amnesty refers to possible crimes committed by those accorded amnesty but not to Mr. Rios Montt's becoming chief of state imposed by a military movement. Such Guatemalan jurisprudence falls within the same considerations indicated in the foregoing paragraphs and has antecedents in other countries. Thus, in the United States:

> It has been held that a statute which restored civil rights to convicted personssatisfying their sentence did not supersede the effect of a state constitutionalprovision prohibiting convicted felons from holding public office.

37. The Commission should also consider the admissibility of the petitioner's complaint regarding the inability to appear personally to defend the electoral rights established in the Guatemalan Voter Registration Law, which allows presentations only by parties (cf. paragraph 12).

In this regard, the Commission has kept in mind that provision and the parallel presentations made by the parties and by the petitioner before the various electoral and judicial administrative officials regarding the presidential candidacy of Mr. Rios Montt and his co-candidates. It is the Commission's understanding that while it is actually possible hypothetically that a restriction of this kind may prevent the full personal defense of a member of a slate of candidates and may curtail rights recognized in the Convention, that does not occur in the petitioner's case. This is due to the fact that many administrative and judicial complaints by the parties that nominated him for president, as well as the personal complaints of the candidate, set forth the same arguments and are based on the same facts.

It is therefore the Commission's understanding that in the case under review the candidate's ability to make an effective defense was not restricted nor was there any damage or impairment of his right.

38. The Commission should also consider the petitioner's complaint regarding the alleged violation of the right of Guatemalan citizens to be elected president, by applying of Article 186.a.

The Commission considers in this regard that the grounds for ineligibility emerge from an act of a Constitutional Convention elected by democratic vote in which the Guatemalan people decided through their representatives at that convention that it was necessary to maintain such grounds, which are already founded in Guatemala's constitutional history, and moreover to make them permanent.

Therefore as analyzed above, within those conditions any constitutional system of law possesses the right to make its operation more effective, and to defend the integrity of its citizens' rights.

IV. ACCORDINGLY, THE COMMISSION RESOLVES

1. That it is competent to decide on this case.

2. That the instant petition is inadmissible because the facts sub examine do not constitute a violation of the rights recognized by the Convention.

3. To publish this report in the Annual Report to the General Assembly.

Rainys and Gasparavičius v. Lithuania, (App. nos. 70665/01 and 74345/01), Judgment of 7 April 2005, Eur. Ct. H.R.

8. The first applicant, Mr. Raimundas Rainys, is a Lithuanian national who was born in 1949 and lives in Vilnius. The second applicant, Mr. Antanas Gasparavičius, is a Lithuanian national who was born in 1945 and lives in Kretinga. The facts of the case, as submitted by the parties, may be summarised as follows.

A. The first applicant

9. From 1975 to October 1991 the first applicant was an employee of the Lithuanian branch of the Soviet Security Service (hereinafter the "KGB"). Thereafter he found employment as a lawyer in a private telecommunications company.

10. On 17 February 2000 two authorities—the Lithuanian State Security Department and the Centre for Research into the Genocide and Resistance of the Lithuanian People—jointly concluded that the applicant was subject to the restrictions imposed under Article 2 of the Law on the Evaluation of the USSR State Security Committee (NKVD, NKGB, MGB, KGB) and the Present Activities of Permanent Employees of the Organisation (hereinafter "the Act", see paragraph 22 below). The conclusion confirmed that the applicant had the status of a "former KGB officer" as construed by the Act. As a result, on 23 February 2000 he was dismissed from his job at the telecommunications company.

11. The applicant brought an administrative action against the security intelligence authorities, arguing that his dismissal under Article 2 of the Act and the resultant inability to find employment were unlawful.

12. On 29 June 2000 the Higher Administrative Court found that the conclusion of 17 February 2000 had been substantiated, and that the applicant was subject to the restrictions imposed under Article 2 of the Act.

13. On 5 September 2000 the Court of Appeal rejected the applicant's appeal.

14. The applicant has been unemployed since 26 February 2002.

B. The second applicant

15. From 1971 until October 1991 the second applicant worked at the KGB. Thereafter he started practising as a barrister.

16. On an unspecified date in 2000, the Lithuanian State Security Department and the Centre for Research into the Genocide and Resistance of the Lithuanian

People jointly concluded that the applicant had the status of a "former KGB officer", and that he was thereby subject to the restrictions imposed under Article 2 of the Act. On 12 June 2000 the Bar informed him that he would be disbarred pursuant to that law.

17. The applicant brought an administrative action, claiming that his dismissal from the Bar would be unlawful. While the applicant did not contest the fact that he had worked for the KGB even following the declaration of Lithuanian independence on 11 March 1990, he submitted that thereafter he had worked as an informer for the authorities of independent Lithuania.

Furthermore, throughout his time at the KGB the applicant had allegedly only worked with cases concerning purely criminal investigations, not political persecutions. In the applicant's view, he had been entitled to be exempted from the employment restrictions, in accordance with Article 3 of the Act.

18. On 21 February 2001 the Vilnius Regional Administrative Court rejected the applicant's claim. The court found that he had indeed worked with criminal investigations while at the KGB, but that he had remained employed there until his retirement in October 1990. The court held that the exceptions in Article 3 of the Act were not applicable to the applicant, given that he did not end his employment with the KGB immediately after Lithuania's declaration of independence on 11 March 1990.

19. Upon the applicant's appeal, on 16 May 2001 the Supreme Administrative Court upheld this decision. The court reiterated that the applicant was not entitled to be exempted under Article 3 of the Act, as he had not ended his KGB employment immediately after 11 March 1990. Moreover, there was no plausible evidence attesting that thereafter the applicant had worked at the KGB as an agent of the authorities of independent Lithuania.

20. As a result of the proceedings on 29 May 2001 the applicant was disbarred.

21. He has now found employment in the business field.

II. RELEVANT DOMESTIC LAW AND PRACTICE

22. The Law on the Evaluation of the USSR State Security Committee (NKVD, NKGB, MGB, KGB) and the Present Activities of Former Permanent Employees of the Organisation was enacted on 16 July 1998 by the Seimas (Parliament) and promulgated by the President of the Republic. The Act reads as follows:

> *Article 1 Recognition of the USSR State Security Committee as a criminal organisation*
>
> The USSR State Security Committee (NKVD, NKGB, MGB, KGB—hereinafter SSC) is recognised as a criminal organisation which committed war crimes, genocide, repression, terror and political persecution in the territory of Lithuania when occupied by the USSR.
>
> *Article 2 Restrictions on the present activities of permanent employees of the SSC*
>
> For a period of 10 years from the date of entry into force of this Law, former employees of the SSC may not work as public officials or civil servants in government, local or defence authorities, the State Security department, the police, prosecution, courts or diplomatic service, customs, State supervisory bodies and other authorities monitoring public institutions, as lawyers and notaries, as employees of banks and other credit institutions, on strategic economic projects, in security companies

(structures), in other companies (structures) providing detective services, in communications systems, or in the educational system as teachers, educators or heads of institutions[;] nor may they perform a job requiring a weapon.

Article 3 Cases in which the restrictions shall not be applied

1. The restrictions provided for in Article 2 shall not be applied to former permanent employees of the SSC who, while working at the SSC, investigated only criminal cases and who discontinued their work at the SSC not later than 11 March 1990.

2. The Centre for Research into the Genocide and Resistance of the Lithuanian People and the State Security Department may [recommend by] a reasoned application that no restrictions under this law be applied to former permanent employees of the SSC who, within 3 months of the date of the entry into force of this Law, report to the State Security Department and disclose all information in their possession ... about their former work at the SSC and their current relations with former SSC employees and agents. A decision in this respect shall be taken by a commission of three persons set up by the President of the Republic. No employees of the Centre for Research into the Genocide and Resistance of the Lithuanian People or the State Security Department may be appointed to the commission. The commission's rules shall be confirmed by the President of the Republic."

Article 4 Procedure for implementation of the Act

The procedure for implementation of the Act shall be governed by [a special law]."

Article 5 Entry into force of the Act

This Act shall come into effect on 1 January 1999.

23. Following the examination by the Constitutional Court of the compatibility of the Act with the Constitution (see § 28 below), on 5 May 1999 Article 3 of the Act was amended to the effect that even those individuals who had worked for the KGB after 11 March 1990 could be eligible for exceptions under Article 3 of the Act.

24. On 16 July 1998 a separate law on the implementation of the Act was adopted. According to that law, the Centre for Research into the Genocide and Resistance of the Lithuanian People and the State Security Department were empowered to reach a conclusion on an individual's status as a "former permanent employee of the KGB" for the purposes of the Act.

25. On 26 January 1999 the Government adopted a list ... of positions in various branches of the KGB on Lithuanian territory attesting to a person's status as a "former permanent employee of the KGB" ("former KGB officer") for the purposes of the Act. 395 different positions were listed in this respect.

26. On 4 March 1999 the Constitutional Court examined the issue of the compatibility of the Act with the Constitution. The Constitutional Court held in particular that the Act had been adopted in order to carry out "security screening" measures on former Soviet security officers, who were deemed to be lacking in loyalty to the Lithuanian State. The Constitutional Court decided that the prohibition on former KGB agents' occupying public posts was compatible with the Constitution. It further ruled that the statutory ban on the holding by former KGB employees of jobs in certain private sectors was compatible with the constitutional principle of a free choice of profession in that the State was entitled to lay down specific requirements for persons applying for work in the most important economic sectors in order to ensure the protection of national security and proper functioning of the educational

and financial systems. The Constitutional Court also held that the restrictions under the Act did not amount to a criminal charge against former KGB agents.

27. While the Act does not specifically guarantee a right of access to a court to contest the security intelligence authorities' conclusion, it was recognised by the domestic courts that, as a matter of practice, a dismissal from employment in the public service on the basis of that conclusion gave rise to an administrative court action (and a further appeal) under the general procedure governing industrial disputes and alleged breaches of personal rights by the public authorities, pursuant to Articles 4, 7, 8, 26, 49, 50, 59, 63 and 64 of the Code of Administrative Procedure, Article 222 of the Civil Code and Article 336 of the Code of Civil Procedure (as effective at the material time).

III. RELEVANT PROVISIONS OF INTERNATIONAL LAW

28. Restrictions have been imposed in many post-communist countries with a view to screening the employment of former security agents or active collaborators in the former regimes. In this respect, international human rights bodies have at times found fault with similar legislation where this has lacked precision or proportionality, characterising such rules as discrimination in employment or the exercise of a profession on the basis of political opinion. The possibility of appeal to the courts has been considered a significant safeguard, although not sufficient in itself to make good shortcomings in legislation (see *Sidabras and Džiautas*, nos. 55480/00 and 59330/00, 27.7.2004, §§ 30–32, ECHR 2004—...).

29. Article 1 § 2 of the European Social Charter provides:

> "With a view to ensuring the effective exercise of the right to work, the Parties undertake:
>
> . . .
>
> 2) to protect effectively the right of the worker to earn his living in an occupation freely entered upon[.]"

This provision, which was retained word for word in the Revised Charter of 1996 (which entered into force with regard to Lithuania on 1 August 2001), has been consistently interpreted by the European Committee of Social Rights (ECSR) as establishing a right not to be discriminated against in employment. The non-discrimination guarantee is stipulated in Article E of the Revised Charter in the following terms: "The enjoyment of the rights set forth in this Charter shall be secured without discrimination on any ground such as race, colour, sex, language, religion, political or other opinion, national extraction or social origin, health, association with a national minority, birth or other status."

30. The International Labour Organisation (ILO) has also adopted a number of relevant international legal instruments. The most pertinent text is ILO Convention No. 111 on Discrimination (Employment and Occupation) of 1958. In its 1996 General Survey, the Committee of Experts on the Application of Conventions and Recommendations (CEACR) restated its interpretation of Convention No. 111, drawing upon examples taken from national law.

A 1996 survey identifies comparable provisions in the national law of a number of European countries.

In Latvia, the State Civil Service Act 2000 and the Police Act 1999 prohibit the employment of persons who worked for or with the Soviet security services. In 2003 the CEACR expressed its dissatisfaction with the above texts in the following terms:

> 6. The Committee recalls that requirements of a political nature can be set for a particular job, but to ensure that they are not contrary to the Convention, they should be limited to the characteristics of a particular post and be in proportion to its labour requirements. The Committee notes that the above established exclusions by the provisions under examination apply broadly to the entire civil service and police rather than to specific jobs, functions or tasks. The Committee is concerned that these provisions appear to go beyond justifiable exclusions in respect of a particular job based on its inherent requirements as provided for under Article 1 (2) of the Convention. The Committee recalls that for measures not to be deemed discriminatory under Article 4, they must be measures affecting an individual on account of activities he or she is justifiably suspected or proven to be engaged in which are prejudicial to the security of the State. Article 4 of the Convention does not exclude from the definition of discrimination measures taken by reason of membership of a particular group or community. The Committee also notes that in cases where persons are deemed to be justifiably suspected of or engaged in activities prejudicial to the security of the State, the individual concerned shall have the right to appeal to a competent body in accordance with national practice.
>
> 7. In the light of the above, the Committee considers the exclusions from being a candidate for any civil service position and from being employed by the police are not sufficiently well defined and delimited to ensure that they do not become discrimination in employment and occupation based on political opinion. . . .

ALLEGED VIOLATION OF ARTICLE 8 OF THE CONVENTION, TAKEN ALONE AND IN CONJUNCTION WITH ARTICLE 14

31. The applicants complained that the loss of their jobs, respectively, as a private-company lawyer and barrister, and the ban under Article 2 of the Law on the Evaluation of the USSR State Security Committee (NKVD, NKGB, MGB, KGB) and the Present Activities of Permanent Employees of the Organisation ("the Act") on their finding employment in various private-sector spheres until 2009, breached Article 8 of the Convention, taken alone and in conjunction with Article 14. . . .

32. The Government submitted that Article 8 was not applicable in the present case as that provision did not guarantee a right to retain employment or to choose a profession. They further stated that, in any event, the application of the Act to the applicants served the legitimate purpose of protecting national security and was necessary in a democratic society. According to the Government, the Act constituted no more than a justified security screening measure intended to prevent former employees of a foreign secret service from working not only in State institutions but also in other spheres of activity which were important to the State's national security. The Act itself did not impose collective responsibility on all former KGB officers without exception. It provided for individualised restrictions on employment prospects by way of the adoption of "the list" of positions in the former KGB which warranted application of the restrictions under Article 2 of the Act. The fact that the applicants were not entitled to benefit from any of the exceptions provided

for in Article 3 of the Act showed that there existed a well-founded suspicion that the applicants lacked loyalty to the Lithuanian State. Given that not all former employees of the KGB were affected by the Act, Article 14 of the Convention was not therefore applicable. Accordingly, there was no violation of Article 8 of the Convention, either taken alone or in conjunction with Article 14.

33. The applicants contested the Government's submissions. They complained in particular that they had lost their private-sector jobs, and that they had furthermore been deprived of the possibility to seek employment in various private-sector fields until 2009 as a result of their statutory status as "former KGB officers". The applicants submitted that they had not been given any possibility under the Act either to present their personal cases in the evaluation and establishment of their loyalty to the State, or to avoid the application to them of the employment restrictions prescribed by Article 3 of the Act. In particular, the applicants stressed that they had left the KGB almost a decade before their dismissals. Furthermore, the applicants contended that their jobs in the private sector had not constituted any threat to the national security of Lithuania. However, the domestic courts imposed the employment restrictions solely on the ground of their former employment in the KGB. Finally, the applicants submitted that, as a result of the negative publicity caused by the adoption of the "KGB Act" and its application to them, they had been subjected to daily embarrassment on account of their past.

34. The Court recalls the case of *Sidabras and Džiautas* where it found a violation of Article 14 of the Convention, in conjunction with Article 8, to the extent that the Act precluded those applicants from employment in the private sector on the basis of their "former KGB officers" status under the Act (*loc. cit.*, §§ 33–62). The present applicants' complaints are very similar, albeit wider: they relate not only to their hypothetical inability to apply for various private-sector jobs until 2009 (as in *Sidabras and Džiautas*), but they also concern their actual dismissal from existing employment in that sector.

35. Nevertheless, this extra element does not prompt the Court to depart from the reasoning developed in *Sidabras and Džiautas*. The applicant's dismissal from their jobs as private-sector lawyers and their current employment restrictions pursuant to the Act constituted a statutory distinction of their status on the basis of their KGB past, affecting directly the applicants' right to respect for their private life. As a result the applicants' complaints fall to be examined under Article 14 of the Convention, taken in conjunction with Article 8 (*loc. cit.*, §§ 38–50).

36. As to the justification of this distinction, the Government's main line of argument was that the application of the Act was well balanced in view of the legitimate interest to protect national security of the State, the impugned employment restrictions being imposed on persons such as the applicants by reason of their lack of loyalty to the State. However, the Court emphasises that the State-imposed restrictions on a person's opportunity to find employment with a private company for reasons of lack of loyalty to the State cannot be justified from the Convention perspective in the same manner as restrictions on access to their employment in the public service (*loc. cit.*, §§ 57–58). Moreover, the very belated nature of the Act, imposing the impugned employment restrictions on the applicants a decade after the Lithu-

anian independence had been re-established and the applicants' KGB employment had been terminated, counts strongly in favour of a finding that the application of the Act vis-à-vis the applicants amounted to a discriminatory measure (*loc. cit.*, § 60). The respondent Government have thus failed to disprove that the applicants' inability to pursue their former professions as, respectively, a lawyer in a private telecommunications company and barrister, and their continuing inability to find private-sector employment on the basis of their "former KGB officer" status under the Act, constitutes a disproportionate and thus discriminatory measure, even having regard to the legitimacy of the aims sought after (see, *mutatis mutandis, Sidabras and Džiautas* cited above, §§ 51–62).

37. Consequently, there has been a violation of Article 14 of the Convention, taken in conjunction with Article 8.

38. The Court considers that, since it has found a breach of Article 14 of the Convention taken in conjunction with Article 8, it is not necessary also to consider whether there has been a violation of Article 8 taken alone (*ibid.*, § 63).

. . .

APPLICATION OF ARTICLE 41 OF THE CONVENTION

A. Pecuniary damage

42. The first applicant claimed EUR 40,927.36 in relation to the loss of his former salary at the telecommunications company, following his dismissal on 23 February 2000 until 1 March 2004 (the date on which the applicant's claim was presented to the Court). He requested a further amount, to be determined at the Court's discretion, to compensate for the loss of salary since 1 March 2004, and for his lost career opportunities.

43. The second applicant claimed EUR 29,069 in pecuniary damages for the loss of his former income as a barrister, following his disbarment, from 29 May 2001 until 1 March 2004 (the date when his claim was presented to the Court). He requested a further amount, to be determined at the Court's discretion, to compensate for the loss of salary since 1 March 2004, and for his lost career opportunities.

44. The Government considered these claims to be unjustified. In particular, they stated that there was no reasonable link between the violation of the Convention alleged by the applicants and the damage claimed. At the same time, the Government made no comment on the assessment of the applicants' former income, attested by the documents presented by the applicants to the Court.

45. The Court notes that the applicants lost their former jobs as, respectively, a lawyer in a private telecommunications company and barrister, in view of the application of the Act which the Court has found to be discriminatory, in breach of Article 14 of the Convention. The loss of employment in turn deprived the applicants of the main source of income, and undoubtedly adversely affected their future career prospects. Hence, there is a direct causal link between the violation found and the pecuniary damage claimed, which has to be reimbursed in such a way as to restore, as far as possible, the situation existing before the breach (see, *mutatis mutandis, Smith and Grady v. the United Kingdom* (just satisfaction), nos. 33985/96 and 33986/96, 25.7.2000, § 18, ECHR 2000-IX).

46. The Court also observes that in the *Sidabras and Džiautas* case cited above the Court found no violation of the Convention as a result of those applicants' dismissal as State officials. Consequently, the Court's award of just satisfaction in that case concerned pecuniary damage only to the extent that the breach of the Convention had adversely affected those applicants' private-sector career prospects following the dismissal (*loc. cit.*, § 78). However, in the present case the violation found directly related to the applicants' loss of employment as private-sector lawyers, warranting a claim for a substantively higher award for pecuniary damage than that in the *Sidabras and Džiautas* case.

47. At the same time, the Court notes that a precise calculation of the sums necessary to make complete reparation (*restitutio in integrum*) in respect of the pecuniary losses suffered by the applicants is prevented by the inherently uncertain character of the damage flowing from the violations. The greater the interval since the dismissal of the applicants, the more uncertain the damage becomes. Accordingly, the Court considers that the question to be decided is the level of just satisfaction, in respect of both past and future pecuniary loss, which it is necessary to award to each applicant, the matter to be determined by the Court at its discretion, having regard to what is equitable (see *Smith and Grady* cited above, §§ 18–19).

48. As regards the first applicant, the Court notes that he has had apparent difficulties in finding a stable economic activity after his dismissal as a lawyer in a telecommunications company on 23 February 2000. He has been unemployed since 26 February 2002. While it is not for the Court to speculate whether his current unemployment may also be the result of his own fault, the fact remains that his dismissal under the Act instigated his present career difficulties. In fact, to date the first applicant continues to be exposed to various employment restrictions in the private sector pursuant to the impugned domestic legislation. In these circumstances, and on the basis of the assessment of the first applicant's former salary at the telecommunications company as attested by the documents presented by the parties, the Court awards the first applicant EUR 35,000 for pecuniary damage.

49. While the second applicant has been able to find and retain employment after being disbarred on 29 May 2001, the fact remains that the application of the Act instigated the necessity for him to look for new fields of economic activity in regard to which he may not have been educated or trained as a lawyer. It is also to be noted that to date the Act continues to impose on the second applicant various employment restrictions in the private sector (also see § 48 above). Against this background, and by way of the calculation on the basis of the second applicant's former income as a barrister as attested by the documents submitted to the Court, it awards him EUR 7,500 for pecuniary damage.

B. Non-pecuniary damage

50. The first applicant requested EUR 200,000 in non-pecuniary damage. The second applicant claimed EUR 100,000 in this respect.

51. The Government considered these claims to be exorbitant.

52. Makings its assessment on an equitable basis, the Court awards each of the applicants EUR 5,000 under this head (see *Sidabras and Džiautas* cited above, §§ 75–78).

. . .

Questions and Comments

1. In one of the first cases bought to the European Court, the applicant complained that his Article 10 right to freedom of expression was violated because of a domestic law that prohibited him from exercising his profession as a journalist, due to his conviction for collaborating with the invading Germans during World War II. The case was struck off the list after Belgium amended the law. See: *De Becker v. Belgium*, 4 Eur. Ct.H.R. (ser B) (1962). How would the Court have decided the case on the merits?

2. Closely linked to lustration cases are controversial bans on political parties. The European Commission in 1962 dismissed an application from the communist party of Germany, which had been ordered dissolved on the basis that its activities were incompatible with the Convention. *Retimag AG v. Germany*, App. No. 712/60, 4 YB 38 (1962). In contrast, in more recent years, the Court has held that Turkey violated the Convention by banning various political parties, making a determination that the parties had not aimed at the destruction of the rights and freedoms of others. *See: United Communist Party of Turkey and Others v. Turkey*, App. No. 19392/92, 26 EHRR 121 (1998); *Socialist Party and Others v. Turkey*, App. No. 21237/93, 27 EHRR 51 (1999); *Freedom and Democracy Party (Özdep) v. Turkey*, App. No. 23885/94, Rep. Judgments & Dec. 1999-VIII. However, a Grand Chamber of the Court unanimously upheld the Turkish government's dissolution of one of the largest political parties in Turkey, which the government viewed as an Islamic party acting contrary to the secular nature of the state. *Refah Partisi (The Welfare Party) and Others v. Turkey*, Apps. Nos. 41340/98, 41342/98, 41343/98 and 41344/98, Rep. Judgments & Dec. 2003-II. The Court set forth the test it was applying:

> 31. . . . . [T]he Court considers that a political party may promote a change in the law or the legal and constitutional structures of the State on two conditions: firstly, the means used to that end must be legal and democratic; secondly, the change proposed must itself be compatible with fundamental democratic principles. It necessarily follows that a political party whose leaders incite to violence or put forward a policy which fails to respect democracy or which is aimed at the destruction of democracy and the flouting of the rights and freedoms recognised in a democracy cannot lay claim to the Convention's protection against penalties imposed on those grounds (see *Yazar and Others v. Turkey*, nos. 22723/93, 22724/93 and 22725/93, § 49, ECHR 2002-II, and, *mutatis mutandis*, the following judgments: *Stankov and the United Macedonian Organisation Ilinden v. Bulgaria*, nos. 29221/95 and 29225/95, § 97, ECHR 2001-IX, and *Socialist Party and Others v. Turkey*, judgment of 25 May 1998, *Reports* 1998-III, pp. 1256–57, §§ 46–47).
>
> 32. The possibility cannot be excluded that a political party, in pleading the rights enshrined in Article 11 and also in Articles 9 and 10 of the Convention, might attempt to derive therefrom the right to conduct what amounts in practice to activities intended to destroy the rights or freedoms set forth in the Convention and thus bring about the destruction of democracy (see *Communist Party (KPD) v. Germany*, no. 250/57, Commission decision of 20 July 1957, Yearbook 1, p. 222). In view of the very clear link between the Convention and democracy (see paragraphs 86–89 above), no one must be authorised to rely on the Convention's provisions in order to weaken or destroy the ideals and values of a democratic society. Pluralism and democracy are based on a compromise that requires various concessions by individuals or groups of individuals, who must sometimes agree to limit some of the freedoms they enjoy in

order to guarantee greater stability of the country as a whole (see, *mutatis mutandis, Petersen v. Germany* (dec.), no. 39793/98, ECHR 2001-XII).

In that context, the Court considers that it is not at all improbable that totalitarian movements, organised in the form of political parties, might do away with democracy, after prospering under the democratic regime, there being examples of this in modern European history.

33. The Court reiterates, however, that the exceptions set out in Article 11 are, where political parties are concerned, to be construed strictly; only convincing and compelling reasons can justify restrictions on such parties' freedom of association. In determining whether a necessity within the meaning of Article 11 § 2 exists, the Contracting States have only a limited margin of appreciation. Although it is not for the Court to take the place of the national authorities, which are better placed than an international court to decide, for example, the appropriate timing for interference, it must exercise rigorous supervision embracing both the law and the decisions applying it, including those given by independent courts. Drastic measures, such as the dissolution of an entire political party and a disability barring its leaders from carrying on any similar activity for a specified period, may be taken only in the most serious cases. . . . Provided that it satisfies the conditions set out in paragraph 98 above, a political party animated by the moral values imposed by a religion cannot be regarded as intrinsically inimical to the fundamental principles of democracy, as set forth in the Convention.

The Grand Chamber stated its agreement with the Chamber that an Islamist political party failed this test: "In the Court's view, a political party whose actions seem to be aimed at introducing sharia in a State party to the Convention can hardly be regarded as an association complying with the democratic ideal that underlies the whole of the Convention." Id. para. 123.

3. In *W.P. and Others v. Poland*, App. No. 42264/98, dec. Sept. 2, 2004, applicants challenged the refusal to register their association, called the National and Patriotic Association of Victims of Bolshevism and Zionism, as a violation of Article 11. The government relied on Article 17 of the Convention, together with Article 13 of the 1997 Constitution of Poland. The latter reads:

> Political parties and other organisations whose programmes are based upon totalitarian methods or the models of nazism, fascism or communism, or whose programmes or activities foster racial or national hatred, recourse to violence for the purposes of obtaining power or to influence State policy, or which provide for their structure or membership to be secret, shall be forbidden.

What result?

4. The African Commission has also received complaints about measures taken to dissolve and ban political parties, although in Africa these are much more often directed at opponents of the party in power. In the next section, see *Legal Resources Foundation v. Zambia*. See also: *Civil Liberties Organization v. Nigeria*, reprinted in Chapter II (5)(b).

Final Questions and Comments

1. Given the nature and scope of obligations surveyed in this chapter, is it likely that any state is in full compliance with them all? Are the obligations too great an interference into domestic matters? Or are the obligations too weak, leaving states too many legal loopholes to avoid compliance?

2. Contrast the state obligations contained in regional instruments with those set forth or implied in the UN's International Covenants. *See* Human Rights Committee, General Comment No. 31, *The Nature of the General Legal Obligation Imposed on States Parties to the Covenant on Civil and Political Rights,* UN Doc. CCPR/C/21/Rev.1/Add.13 (May 26, 2004); Committee on Economic, Social and Cultural Rights, General Comment No. 3, *The Nature of States Parties Obligations* (Art. 2, para. 1), UN Doc. E/1991/23 (Dec. 14, 1990). Also consider the judgment of the US Supreme Court in *Town of Castle Park, Colo. V. Gon-*

zales, 125 S.Ct. 2796 (2005), holding that the US Constitution imposes no positive obligations on the government to protect life and personal security.

3. Although the primary responsibility for ensuring that individuals may fully and freely enjoy their guaranteed rights rests with the states parties, experience cautions that there must be international supervision of governmental conduct. Each of the regional systems establishes monitoring bodies for this purpose. The next chapter examines the composition and functions of the regional bodies.

CHAPTER IV
THE REGIONAL INSTITUTIONS AND THEIR POWERS

1. Introduction

This chapter considers the structures and functions of the regional institutions, including their tasks of promoting and protecting human rights, reviewing state reports, making on-site visits, and appointing thematic rapporteurs. Complaints procedures are addressed in the following chapter, while efforts to confront widespread violations are considered in Chapter VI. In considering the readings, keep in mind the basic concept that regional human rights institutions are subsidiary to state implementation and enforcement of international human rights guarantees.

One feature of the regional institutions that is immediately evident when comparing them is how they differ in size and resources. The Inter-American Commission and Court are the smallest bodies, each having just seven members. The European Court of Human Rights is the largest institution, with one judge for every Contracting Party to the European Convention, and is also the only permanent full time body. The African Commission of Human Rights occupies a middle position, with eleven members, while there are fifteen judges on the merged African Court. The number of staff members assigned to each institution also varies considerably. The European Court employs over 200 lawyers in its registry, with 295 other support staff. At the opposite extreme, the African Commission has seven lawyers, five of them funded by short-term grants from outside the system. The amount of resources member states make available to regional human rights bodies can be taken as one indication of their level of commitment to international human rights law.

Over the past half century, regional human rights procedures and institutions have evolved perhaps to an even greater extent than have substantive human rights guarantees. The major changes have been accomplished by amending the basic legal instruments, but other innovations have emerged as regional human rights bodies have made use of their express and implied powers. These changes are described below.

2. Procedural and Institutional Evolution

Since 1950, new regional human rights bodies have been created and one has disappeared. As detailed below, the European Convention originally created two institutions to ensure the observance of the obligations of states parties: the European Commission of Human Rights and the European Court of Human Rights. On 1 November 1998, a new full-time European Court of Human Rights came into being and the Commission ceased to exist. The change responded to complaints about the lengthy time required for a case to proceed through both institutions and a sense that the functions of the two bodies were duplicative. At the time, few cases required fact-finding; instead, most raised only matters of law, which were seen as primarily the province of the court.

Other regional organizations created new human rights institutions. The Organization of American States created the Inter-American Commission on Human Rights in 1959 and subsequently added an Inter-American Court with the entry into force of the American Convention on Human Rights. The EU's European Court of Justice added a Court of First Instance. The African system drafted a Protocol to the African Charter to create its own African Court of Human Rights, which it later merged with the newly-created African Court of Justice.

For the most part, the evolution has sought to strengthen the procedures to monitor state compliance with human rights law, but some changes, including major ones, have been introduced or proposed to respond to administrative needs stemming from a rising caseload. Europe, in particular, has struggled to devise mechanisms to handle a continually growing number of cases.

As the institutions have evolved, so have the procedures. The technique of the on-site visit, not envisaged in any of the original texts, has proven to be an invaluable instrument in human rights protection and promotion. The Inter-American Commission has long claimed the power to make on-site visits and has done so as often as its resources have permitted. More recently, the European Committee for the Prevention of Torture and Inhuman or Degrading Treatment was given the authority to visit prisons and other places of detention, making both periodic visits for which it gives notice, and *ad hoc* visits, which are not announced and can be made whenever the Committee deems it necessary. On-site visits enable regional bodies to gather information and verify the information they have received. At the same time, governments can indicate the context and complexities of the situations being observed. On-site visits allow officials and private persons to be heard and increase public knowledge of the regional system. Finally, on-site visits may deter violations by the mere presence of an outside human rights group. As such, a principal advantage to on-site visits is preventive.

Unlike communications procedures, which only begin after a violation has occurred and local remedies have been exhausted, the visits of the European Torture Committee, the Inter-American and African Commissions can occur whenever indications are received about actual or imminent violations, or where a state seeks assistance in evaluating and improving its human rights performance. Visits can be cooperative, rather than confrontational, offering the same advantages as the constructive dialogue entered into through UN reporting mechanisms, but with better information. On-site visits are particularly important in avoiding regression during periods of transition and in dealing with gross and massive violations of rights where it may be impracticable to open individual cases. Given the importance of on-site visits, it is not surprising that the Inter-American Commission has visited a large number of OAS member states and that the practice of on-site visits is becoming the rule, not the exception, in Africa.

We now turn to each region's human rights institutions and their functions.

3. The European System

The European Convention on Human Rights originally established two institutions "to ensure the observance of the engagements undertaken by the High Contracting Parties" (Art. 19): the European Commission of Human Rights and the European Court of Human Rights. The former Commission and Court were replaced on November 1, 1998, with the entry into force of Protocol No.11 and the inauguration of a new full time Court. The Court's functions are exclusively judicial.

The Convention, Art. 20, specifies that the European Court of Human Rights is composed of a number of judges equal to that of the High Contracting Parties to the Convention. Judges are elected for a six-year term by the Parliamentary Assembly from a list of three nominees submitted by each Member State. The nominees must be persons of "high moral character" who "possess the qualifications required for appointment to high judicial office or [are] jurisconsults of recognized competence." Convention, Art. 21(1). The judges do not have to be nationals of the Member States of the Council of Europe.[1] Judges may be re-elected, but must retire at the age of seventy. They serve full-time in their individual capacities and may not undertake any activity incompatible with their judicial functions. The Court has its seat in Strasbourg, the home of the Council of Europe. Under the Rules of Court, every judge is assigned to one of the five Sections, whose composition is geographically and gender balanced and takes account of the different legal systems of the Contracting States. The composition of the Sections is changed every three years.

The great innovation of the European Convention was the establishment of a complaints procedure that allowed individuals who claimed their rights had been violated to bring an action against the offending state. However, the Convention provided that both the right of individual petition and the jurisdiction of the Court were optional and had to be separately accepted by the Contracting Parties; Protocol 11 eliminated the choices by making both matters mandatory. The original Convention provided that all cases were first dealt with by the Commission, which established the facts, decided on admissibility and, in admissible cases, sought to secure a friendly settlement between the applicant and the respondent state. When no settlement could be reached, the Commission drafted a report setting out the facts and its non-binding opinion on the law. The report was submitted to the Committee of Ministers for final decision, unless the Commission, the state or states involved, or, after an amended Protocol so permitted, the applicant referred the case to the Court. The Committee of Ministers supervised the state's compliance with the Court's judgment or the Committee's decision. If the state in question had not accepted the right of individual petition or the Court's jurisdiction, the protective system was limited to an interstate case that would proceed from the Commission to the Committee of Ministers. In contrast, today some eight hundred million individuals in the Contracting Parties have the right to file complaints at the Court, which handles the cases, determining admissibility, fact-find-

---

[1] Professor R. St. John Macdonald, a Canadian national, was nominated by Lichtenstein and served on the Court for many years.

ing and issues of law. The Committee of Ministers continues to supervise compliance with the Court's judgments.

Although the Convention entered into force in 1953, the original Court was not established until 1959, after its jurisdiction was accepted by eight states. The Commission submitted the first case to the Court in 1960, the *"Lawless" Case*, Judgment of July 1, 1961 (Merits), 4 Yearbook of the European Convention of Human Rights [Y.B.] 438 (1961). That same year the Commission also filed the *"De Becker" Case*, Judgment of March 27, 1962, 5 Y.B. 321 (1962). Five years elapsed before another case reached the Court, the *Case Relating to Certain Aspects of the Laws on the Use of Languages in Education in Belgium*, Judgment of July 23, 1968 (Merits), 11 Y.B. 833 (1968). Thereafter the Court's business doubled roughly every five years until the early 1980's, when the caseload began to climb even more rapidly, eventually leading to Protocol No. 11.

In addition to giving individuals direct access to the Court by removing the optional acceptance of individual communications, Protocol 11 grouped the judges into three member Committees to handle various stages of the proceedings: seven member Chambers, and a Grand Chamber of seventeen judges. The great majority of the judgments are given by the Chambers, which are constituted within each Section. The Section President and the judge elected in respect of the State concerned sit in each case. Where the latter is not a member of the Section, he or she sits as an ex officio member of the Chamber. If the respondent State in a case is that of the Section President, the Vice-President of the Section presides. In every case that is decided by a Chamber, the remaining members of the Section who are not full members of that Chamber are available as substitute members.

The Grand Chamber has jurisdiction to receive a pending case from a Chamber if the case raises a serious question affecting the interpretation or application of the Convention or protocols thereto (Art. 30) and neither party objects. The Convention also explicitly refers to conflicts with existing jurisprudence as a reason for the Grand Chamber to take a pending case; thus, the Grand Chamber can help ensure consistency of jurisprudence by resolving any conflicts that arise. In addition to its power to assume jurisdiction over a pending case, the Grand Chamber may receive requests "in exceptional circumstances" to review a matter after a Chamber has issued its judgment. Either party may submit the request within three months. A panel of five judges then must determine that the case raises a serious question affecting the interpretation or application of the Convention or Protocols or raises a serious issue of general importance." (Art. 43). Unlike Article 30, Article 43 makes no reference to conflicts in the jurisprudence as a reason for the Grand Chamber to review a case, but conflicting judgments are likely to be viewed as raising a serious matter of "general importance." If it accepts the matter, the Grand Chamber conducts *de novo* review of the case, including admissibility if the issue is raised.

With the admission of new member states, the European caseload has continued to rise and presents considerable challenge for the future of the system. Over the past several years, the Court has delivered over eight hundred judgments per year, and nearly doubled this figure in 2006, delivering 1560 judgments. During

2006, the Court received over 50,500 applications and opened 39,350 provisional files. The Court's backlog has grown despite increased productivity and internal reforms designed to speed the process. At the end of 2006, 89,887 cases were pending, more than twenty percent of them concerning Russia. Thus, member states have begun considering further changes in the system. A Ministerial Conference on Human Rights, held in Rome in November 2000, adopted a resolution calling upon the Committee of Ministers to initiate a thorough study of possibilities and options to ensure the continued effectiveness of the Court. In response, the Committee of Ministers created an Evaluation Group which issued its report in September 2001. The most significant change proposed by the Evaluation Group was the adoption of a Protocol which would "empower the Court to decline to examine in detail applications raising no substantial issue under the Convention." The Committee responded by drafting Protocol 14, which requires the unanimous approval of the Member States to enter into force. The Protocol is considered in detail in Chapter VII.

While the Court has faced few problems of interference with its work, it has never had full control over employment of the persons who work in its Registry and disputes have arisen over individual hires. The Registry provides legal and administrative support to the Court and is composed of more than five hundred persons, nearly half of whom are lawyers, the remainder being administrative and technical staff and translators. Article 25 of the European Convention of Human Rights provides that: "The Court shall have a registry, the functions and organization of which shall be laid down in the Rules of Court." Yet, registry staff members are employed by the Council of Europe, the Court's parent organization, and are subject to the Council of Europe's Staff Regulations. Only the Registrar, who functions as head of the Registry under the authority of the President of the Court, and the Deputy Registrar(s) are elected by the Plenary Court (Article 26 (e) of the Convention).

The principal function of the Registry is to process and prepare for adjudication applications lodged by individuals with the Court. The Registry's lawyers (also known as legal secretaries) are divided into twenty case-processing divisions, each of which is assisted by an administrative team. The lawyers prepare files and analytical notes for the judges. They also correspond with the parties on procedural matters. They do not themselves decide cases. Cases are assigned to the different divisions on the basis of knowledge of the language and legal system concerned. The documents prepared by the Registry for the Court are all drafted in one of its two official languages (English and French).

The Convention also confers some enforcement and supervisory functions on the Committee of Ministers, the governing body of the Council of Europe. In addition to supervising compliance with the Court's judgments, the COM also undertakes thematic monitoring of human rights matters, pursuant to a 1994 declaration on compliance with commitments made by new member states. The first theme it adopted for monitoring was freedom of expression and information; it has also looked at the functioning of democratic institutions, including political parties and free elections; the functioning of judicial systems; local democracy; capital punishment; police and security forces; the effectiveness of judicial remedies; non-discrimination; freedom of conscience and religion; and equality between women and women. See Committee of Ministers, *Declaration on Compliance with Commitments Accepted by Member States of the Council of Europe*, adopted on 10 November 1994, *reprinted in* Council of Europe, Information Sheet No. 35 (July-December 1994)(1995), Appendix I, 146. A third major function of the Committee of Ministers is to approve protocols to the Convention and other human rights treaties, which are then submitted to the member states for ratification.

Other Council of Europe organs and institutions have important roles to play as well. The Parliamentary Assembly of the Council of Europe (PACE), referred to in the COE Statute as the Consultative Assembly,[2] is a grouping of 630 members (315 representatives and 315 substitutes) from the forty-six national parliaments. It has key functions in reviewing nominations to the European Court of Human Rights and in vetting applicant states seeking to join the Council of Europe. The membership application process involves an on-site visit and report on the state, leading to a set of commitments by the government of the applicant state. Compliance with these commitments is overseen by the Committee of Ministers, the Parliamentary Assembly, and the Secretariat. In addition, the Parliamentary Assembly's Committee on Human Rights adopts resolutions and declarations on key human rights issues, often leading to the conclusion of new treaties. *See* Convention, Arts. 15(3), 22(1), 30(1), 52 and 58 and Chapter I (2)(A).

The COE created the post of Commissioner for Human Rights on May 7, 1999. The Commissioner is elected by the Parliamentary Assembly from a list of candidates drawn up by the Committee of Ministers and serves a non-renewable six-year term. The functions of the Commissioner are to serve independently and impartially as "a non-judicial institution to promote education in, awareness of and respect for human rights, as embodied in the human rights instruments of the Council of Europe." The functions are thus primarily promotional and preventive; the Commissioner has no power to accept communications from individuals or groups.[3] Soon after taking office, the Commissioner undertook a fact-finding visit to the Russian Federation and submitted a report to the Committee of Ministers and the Parliamentary Assembly on the situation in Chechnya.

Finally, another extra-conventional procedure is the European Commission against Racism and Intolerance (ECRI), established pursuant to the Vienna Declaration of the Heads of State and Government of the Member States of the Council of Europe, signed 9 October 1993. ECRI's mandate is to review member states legislation, policies and other measures to combat racism and intolerance and to propose further action at local, national and Europe levels. ECRI monitors the situation in member states through an in depth study of the situation in each country followed by specific proposals designed to solve current problems or remedy deficiencies. Draft texts are communicated to national liaison officers to allow national authorities to respond with observations. After confidential dialogue, ECRI

---

[2] In 1994, the Assembly decided to change its name, without amending the Statute, in order to more accurately reflect its composition.

[3] See Committee of Ministers Resolution (99) 50 on the Council of Europe Commissioner for Human Rights.

adopts a final report and submits it to the state concerned through the Committee of Ministers. State reports are made public two months after transmission to the government unless the government expressly objects.

Questions and Comments

Does the Court need full control over its registry to preserve the Court's independence? See: Erik Fribergh, *The Authority over the Court's Registry within the Council of Europe*, in HUMAN RIGHTS—STRASBOURG VIEWS: LIBER AMICORUM LUZIUS WILDHABER 145 (N.P. Engel, 2007); Paul Mahoney, *Separation of Powers in the Council of Europe: The Status of the European Court of Human Rights vis-à-vis the Authorities of the Council of Europe,"* 24 HRLJ 152 (2993).

4. The Inter-American System

A. Historical Evolution

The Fifth Meeting of Consultation of Ministers of Foreign Affairs of the OAS authorized by resolution the establishment of an Inter-American Commission on Human Rights in 1959, more than a decade after the OAS adopted the American Declaration on the Rights and Duties of Man. It is not entirely coincidental that 1959 was also the year the Cuban Revolution succeeded.[4] The OAS Council adopted a Statute for the Commission in 1960 and elected the first seven Commission members.

Article 9 of the 1960 Statute gave the Commission various powers to promote human rights, including the power to prepare studies and reports and "to make recommendations to the governments of the member states in general . . . for the adoption of progressive measures in favor of human rights within the framework of their domestic legislation. . . ." The Commission, in its first session, interpreted this language to authorize it to address general recommendations to individual states. In reliance on this interpretation and on its power to prepare studies, the Commission ushered in the practice of undertaking so-called country studies, a practice it follows to this day. An expert Senior Specialist with the Inter-American Commission describes this approach:

> In its early years, the Commission focused not upon the examination of individual complaints but upon investigating the general human rights situation in particular OAS member states. In its quest to identify appropriate measures for promoting and defending human rights, it used its statutory authority to hold meetings in any member State of the OAS as the basis for a power which it claimed to conduct on-site investigations in OAS States. These fact-finding investigations and the ensuring country (or special) reports, which the Commission presented to the OAS General Assembly, because the most significant activity of the Commission during the first years of its history. The position changed with the entry into force of the American Convention and the establishment of the Inter-American Court of Hu-

---

4 See: G. CONNELL-SMITH, THE INTER-AMERICAN SYSTEM (Oxford, 1966), at 290–6; J. DREIER, THE OAS AND THE HEMISPHERE CRISIS (New York, 1962).

man Rights, whereupon the individual complaint procedure began to acquire greater prominence.

Christina Cerna, *The Inter-American Commission on Human Rights: its Organization and Examination of Petitions and Communications*, in D. HARRIS & S. LIVINGSTONE, THE INTER-AMERICAN SYSTEM OF HUMAN RIGHTS (OUP, 1998), 67. Many of the country reports contain important analyses of the regional human rights and duties. Legal issues surrounding country reports are addressed in Chapter VI.

The Second Special Inter-American Conference authorized the Commission in 1965 to receive and act on individual petitions charging OAS Member States with violations of some, but not all, rights proclaimed in the American Declaration. The new powers, which the Commission incorporated into its Statute in 1966 as Article 9(*bis*), applied to: the right to life, liberty and security of person (Article I), equality before the law (Article II), freedom of religion (Article III), freedom of expression (Article IV), freedom from arbitrary arrest (Article XXV), and the right to due process of law (Article XXVI). This limited individual petition system had its legal source in powers implied in the OAS Charter, rather than in any specific human rights treaty.

The Protocol of Buenos Aires, which entered into force in 1970, amended the OAS Charter and, *inter alia*, transformed the Inter-American Commission on Human Rights into a formal organ of the OAS. See present Charter Arts. 53 and 106(1). Previously, the Commission was designated as an "autonomous entity" of the OAS and lacked a juridical basis in the OAS Charter or any other treaty, having been created simply by conference resolution. By becoming an OAS Charter organ, the Commission acquired an institutional and constitutional legitimacy it had not previously enjoyed. The reference in current Article 145 to "the present" Commission, read in conjunction with Article 106, can also be deemed to have legitimated the practices and procedures the Commission developed pursuant to Articles 9 and 9(*bis*) of its Statute.

The "inter-American convention" to which the amended OAS Charter referred was adopted in 1969 and entered into force in 1978. The drafters of the American Convention, working after the entry into force of the Protocol of Buenos Aires, took into account the pre-existing functions and practices of the Inter-American Commission on Human Rights. They thus assigned two distinct roles to the Commission: the pre-existing functions the Commission performed in relation to all Member States of the OAS, spelled out in Article 41(a)–(e) and (g) of the Convention, on the one hand, and the functions applicable only to States Parties to the Convention, on the other. Convention, Arts. 41(f), 44–51. The latter functions for all practical purposes track the Commission's preexisting powers as an OAS Charter organ.

The Convention also created an Inter-American Court of Human Rights. Both Commission and Court have "competence with respect to matters relating to the fulfillment of the commitments made by the States Parties." Convention, Art. 33. The Protocol of San Salvador and other OAS human rights treaties have extended the Commission's mandate to consider other human rights.

The entry into force of the Convention required the OAS General Assembly to adopt a new Statute for the reconstituted Commission, which it did in 1979. That Statute remains in force today. It takes account of the different functions the Commission performs as an OAS Charter organ and as a Convention organ by spelling out the Commission's powers as they apply to

    (a) all OAS Member States (Article 18);

    (b) the States Parties to the Convention (Article 19); and

    (c) OAS Member States that are not parties to the Convention (Article 20).

Articles 18 and 20 of the Statute thus preserve for the Commission the powers it had under Articles 9 and 9(*bis*) of its old Statute. Article 1(2) of the new Statute defines "human rights" as follows:

> For the purposes of the present Statute, human rights are understood to be:
>
> (a) The rights set forth in the American Convention on Human Rights, in relation to the States Parties thereto;
>
> (b) The rights set forth in the American Declaration of the Rights and Duties of Man, in relation to the other Member States.

This reference to the Declaration reinforces this text's normative character and legitimates the authority of the Commission in relation to states that are not parties to the Convention. For these non-party states, the OAS Charter and the Declaration impose human rights obligations which the Statute authorizes the Commission to enforce. Inter-American Commission on Human Rights, Rep. No. 31/93 (Case No. 10.573, United States), Decision of October 14, 1993, IACHR, *Annual Report 1993*, OEA/Ser.L/V/II.85, Doc. 9 rev., at 312 (1993).

The Commission and the Court consist of seven members each, elected in their personal capacities. The members of the Commission are elected by all OAS Member States, but only the States Parties to the Convention may nominate the judges of the Court and vote in their election. Since the Commission, unlike the Court, is both a Convention and an OAS Charter organ, all OAS Member States, whether or not they have ratified the Convention, have a vote in the selection of the Commissioners. The Commission has its seat at the headquarters of the OAS in Washington, D.C.; the Court sits in San Jose, Costa Rica. Membership on the Court and Commission is not a full-time position and those serving may be employed elsewhere.

B. The Commission

The Statue says the seven members of the Commission shall be "of high moral character and recognized competence in the field of human rights." They serve in their personal capacity and represent all the member countries of the Organization. The Statute provides that membership on the Commission is incompatible with any other function which might affect the independence or impartiality of the member or the dignity or prestige of the Commission. To avoid any appearance of bias, members may not participate in the discussion, investigation, deliberation or decision of a matter if they are nationals or permanent residents of the state which is the subject of consideration by the Commission.

The members of the Commission are elected for a term of four years and may be re-elected one time. They are not salaried, but receive a per diem for each day of official activities as well as a modest honorarium and travel expenses. Between sessions, the secretariat's full time staff performs the work of the Commission.

As a Charter organ, the Commission performs a variety of functions, including promotional and consultative activities. The Commission has helped draft OAS human rights instruments, including the American Convention on Human Rights, and it is regularly consulted on human rights issues by the OAS Permanent Council and the General Assembly. The Commission has summed up its promotional and protective functions as follows:

> The IACHR has the principal function of promoting the observance and the defense of human rights. In carrying out its mandate, the Commission:
>
> a) Receives, analyzes and investigates individual petitions which allege human rights violations, pursuant to Articles 44 to 51 of the Convention. This procedure will be discussed in greater detail below.
>
> b) Observes the general human rights situation in the member States and publishes special reports regarding the situation in a specific State, when it considers it appropriate.
>
> c) Carries out on-site visits to countries to engage in more in-depth analysis of the general situation and/or to investigate a specific situation. These visits usually result in the preparation of a report regarding the human rights situation observed, which is published and sent to the General Assembly.
>
> d) Stimulates public consciousness regarding human rights in the Americas. To that end, carries out and publishes studies on specific subjects, such as: measures to be taken to ensure greater independence of the judiciary; the activities of irregular armed groups; the human rights situation of minors and women, and; the human rights of indigenous peoples.
>
> e) Organizes and carries out conferences, seminars and meetings with representatives of Governments, academic institutions, non-governmental groups, etc. in order to disseminate information and to increase knowledge regarding issues relating to the inter-American human rights system.
>
> f) Recommends to the member States of the OAS the adoption of measures which would contribute to human rights protection.
>
> g) Requests States to adopt specific "precautionary measures" to avoid serious and irreparable harm to human rights in urgent cases. The Commission may also request that the Court order "provisional measures" in urgent cases which involve danger to persons, even where a case has not yet been submitted to the Court.
>
> h) Submits cases to the Inter-American Court and appears before the Court in the litigation of cases.
>
> i) Requests advisory opinions from the Inter-American Court regarding questions of interpretation of the American Convention.

i. Thematic Reports

As noted earlier, the Inter-American Commission may undertake a country study when widespread violations are threatened or alleged. In addition, the Commission, like the United Nations, also studies particular human rights issues that arise in one or more countries. In each instance the Commission appoints an expert or one of its members to act as the thematic rapporteur on the topic. In this way, the Inter-American Commission has studied womens rights, indigenous populations, migrant workers, prison conditions, and freedom of expression. To take the first example, the Commission appointed a Special Rapporteur on the Rights of Women in 1994, with an initial mandate to analyze the extent to which member State law and practices that affect the rights of women comply with the broad obligations of equality and nondiscrimination set forth in the American Declaration of the Rights and Duties of Man and the American Convention on Human Rights. Following an intensive study, the Commission published its *Report on the Status of Women in the Americas,* OEA/Ser.L/V/II.100, Doc. 17 (Oct. 13, 1998) to provide an overview of the situation; issue recommendations designed to assist member States in eradicating discrimination in law and practice, and establish priorities for further action by the Rapporteur and the Commission.

The Commission usually transmits its reports to the OAS General Assembly. The Assembly's discussion, followed by an appropriate resolution, can attract attention and have a significant impact on the behavior of the government in question. OAS General Assembly resolutions, although not legally binding, are acts of the highest political organ of the Organization and, consequently, carry considerable moral and political weight. Ultimately, as in all efforts to enforce internationally guaranteed human rights, the effectiveness of the Commission's reports denouncing human rights violations depends on the Commission's prestige and credibility, on the public opinion pressure its recommendations are likely to generate, and on the resolutions that the OAS General Assembly is willing to adopt in support of the Commission.

The following extract is taken from a report done by the Special Rapporteur on the Status of Women in the Americas. What is the legal basis for such an investigation? How were the findings made? What sources of law does the rapporteur invoke? Do the Commission's Rules of Procedure address the functions of special rapporteurs? The report reveals the existence of individual complaints submitted to the Commission on the killings in Juarez; what purpose is therefore served by appointing a special rapporteur?

The Situation of the Rights of Women in Ciudad Juárez, Mexico: The Right to Be Free from Violence and Discrimination, OEA/Ser.L/V/II.117, Doc. 44 (Mar. 7, 2003)

1. This report addresses the right of women in Ciudad Juárez, Mexico to be free from violence and discrimination. It reports on the grave situation of violence faced by the women and girls of Ciudad Juárez, including murder and disappearance, as well as sexual and domestic violence, and offers recommendations designed to assist the United Mexican States in amplifying its efforts to respect and ensure those rights.

2. The impetus for this report and the on-site visit that preceded it was a series of communications directed to the Special Rapporteur on the Rights of Women of the Inter-American Commission on Human Rights in late 2001, signed by hundreds of organizations and individuals. They reported that more than two hundred women

had been brutally murdered in Ciudad Juárez since 1993, complained of the inefficacy of law enforcement, and requested that the Special Rapporteur visit Mexico to examine the situation. In response to the concerns expressed by the Special Rapporteur in this regard, the Government of President Vicente Fox extended the invitation to conduct the on-site visit carried out in February of 2002. The Government expressed its concern with respect to the situation, and its commitment to fight the impunity that has characterized these crimes. The present report is the product of information gathered in connection with that visit and related follow-up activities.

3. During the visit, authorities in Ciudad Juárez presented information with respect to the killing of 268 women and girls since 1993. In a substantial number of cases, the victims were young women or girls, workers in the *maquilas* (assembly plants) or students, who were sexually abused before being brutally killed. These authorities also reported on over 250 missing person's reports filed during that period that remained unresolved. During the visit, representatives of civil society presented ample information, as well as a letter signed by over 5000 individuals demanding that the Mexican State provide an effective response to this situation. The letter expressed that: "Since 1993 women living in Ciudad Juárez have been afraid; afraid to go out into the street and walk the distance between their home and their job. Afraid at 10, 13, 15, 20 years old; it makes no difference if she is a girl or a woman. . . ."

4. While the situation of women in Ciudad Juárez shares many aspects common to other cities in the United Mexican States and the region generally, it is different in certain important respects. First, the homicide rate for women experienced an unusually sharp rise in Ciudad Juárez in 1993, and the rate has remained elevated since that time. Second, as explained in more detail in the report, the rate of homicides for women compared to that for men in Ciudad Juárez is significantly higher than for similarly situated cities or the national average. Third, the extremely brutal circumstances of many of the killings have served to focus attention on the situation in Ciudad Juárez. A significant number of the victims were young, between 15 and 25, and many were beaten and/or subjected to sexual violence before being strangled or stabbed to death. A number of the killings that fit this pattern have been characterized as multiple or "serial" killings. Fourth, the response of the authorities to these crimes has been markedly deficient. There are two aspects of this response that are especially relevant. On the one hand, the vast majority of the killings remain in impunity; approximately 20% have been the subject of prosecution and conviction. On the other hand, almost as soon as the rate of killings began to rise, some of the officials responsible for investigation and prosecution began employing a discourse that in effect blamed the victim for the crime. According to public statements of certain highly placed officials, the victims wore short skirts, went out dancing, were "easy" or were prostitutes. Reports document that the response of the relevant officials to the victims' family members ranged from indifference to hostility.

5. The deficiencies in the State's response were so extreme that, in 1998, the National Human Rights Commission of Mexico issued a recommendation detailing the problems in the official response to the killings, and calling for clarification of the crimes and prosecution of the perpetrators, as well as the sanctioning of the

officials who had failed to comply with their duties under the law. However, that recommendation was not subjected to institutional follow-up to ensure compliance with the measures indicated. The information gathered for the present report indicates that most of the killings remain in impunity, and no official has ever been held accountable for the grave deficiencies established.

6. Further, while the killings in Ciudad Juárez have increasingly drawn the attention and condemnation of many in Ciudad Juárez and throughout Mexico, including the President and First Lady, and the Commissions on Gender and Equity of the Congress of the Union, as well as of the UN High Commissioner for Human Rights, the UN Special Rapporteurs for extrajudicial executions and the independence of judges and lawyers, respectively, and the Director of the United Nations Development Fund for Women, that condemnation has not been enough to impel changes in the situation of impunity. That impunity is highlighted in the present report, because it serves to fuel the perpetuation of these crimes.

7. While the high level of violence against both men and women is a source of concern for the Commission in more general terms, efforts to sanction past killings of women and prevent future such killings have been impeded by additional obstacles, most especially, discrimination based on gender. In this sense, it must be emphasized that, as the Inter-American Convention on the Prevention, Punishment and Eradication of Violence against Women ("Convention of Belém do Pará") makes clear, violence against women is a manifestation of the historically unequal power relations between men and women. Violence based on gender originates in and perpetuates those negative power imbalances. As the Beijing Declaration and Platform for Action adopted by the UN Fourth World Conference on Women sets forth, such violence "is one of the crucial social mechanisms by which women are forced into a subordinate position compared with men." The lack of due diligence to clarify and punish such crimes, and to prevent their repetition reflects that they are not perceived as a serious problem. The impunity in which such crimes are then left sends the message that such violence is tolerated, thereby fueling its perpetuation.

8. At the same time, the Commission and its Special Rapporteur recognize that there have been some important improvements in the official response to these crimes—improvements that open the door for further progress toward clarification and accountability. The Mexican State has allocated additional human and material resources to addressing the killings, in particular, the 1998 establishment of a Special Prosecutor's Office tasked with investigating these homicides, followed by a series of measures to strengthen its capacity. More can and must be done in this regard. Importantly, the officials responsible for addressing the situation no longer openly dismiss it as in the past; rather, in dealing with the Commission and its Special Rapporteur, officials at all levels have expressed a commitment to end the killings and fight the existing impunity. It is important to note that there is widespread agreement among both the State and non-state sectors in Mexico that the situation in Ciudad Juárez is unusual and requires special measures. In this regard, current administrations at both the national and local levels have shown openness to new initiatives, for example, the establishment of inter-institutional panels designed to incorporate the participation of diverse State and non-state representatives in ef-

forts to resolve these killings. This openness to implementing new cross-cutting approaches is crucial, because changing the existing situation will require the energetic involvement of all levels of Government, working together and incorporating the contribution of civil society.

9. The analysis and recommendations set forth in this report are based first and foremost on the regional human rights obligations of the United Mexican States, principally the American Convention on Human Rights, and the Inter-American Convention on the Prevention, Punishment, and Eradication of Violence against Women. . . .

10. In this regard, the report emphasizes that many of these killings are manifestations of violence based on gender, particularly sexual violence and domestic or intrafamilial violence. While public and official attention have focused on the brutality of and fear associated with the so-called "serial" killings, insufficient attention has been devoted to the need to address the discrimination that underlies crimes of sexual or domestic violence, and that underlies the lack of effective clarification and prosecution. The resolution of these killings requires attention to the root causes of violence against women—in all of its principal manifestations.

11. It is in this sense that Ciudad Juárez shares some discouraging similarities with localities throughout the region. The Beijing Declaration and Platform for Action recognizes that "In all societies, to a greater or lesser degree, women and girls are subjected to physical, sexual and psychological abuse that cuts across lines of income, class and culture." In particular, violence by intimate partners has yet to be understood as the urgent risk for women that it presents. Recent studies in the Federal District of Mexico, and worldwide by the World Health Organization reflect that of the number of women killed in a given location, up to half will have been killed by an intimate partner. Yet the root causes of this violence are not being sufficiently addressed. An important segment of the killings in Ciudad Juárez took place at the hands of an intimate partner, but their significance has yet to be acknowledged by local officials.

12. The Special Rapporteurship and the Commission reiterate their commitment to assisting the United Mexican States in implementing solutions to the problems identified. A number of steps taken to address the situation demonstrate a commitment on the part of members of both the State and non-state sectors to establish accountability for the violence suffered and prevent future violence. These initial steps show a capacity for further action that is urgently required.

13. In this regard, the Commission wishes to underline the positive and constructive attitude of the Government of the United Mexican States with respect to the work of the Commission and its Special Rapporteur concerning the situation of the human rights of women in Ciudad Juárez. In its observations to the draft version of this report, the Mexican State emphasized the conclusions as being constructive and purposive, and affirmed that "it shares the assessments of the Special Rapporteur and the sense of her recommendations."* "Accordingly, these are being analyzed by the corresponding authorities, at the Federal, State and Municipal levels, in order to determine the most adequate form and modalities for the implementation of those that have not been or are not yet in the process of being implemented." Fur-

ther, the Mexican State committed itself to keeping the Commission duly informed about the advances and concrete actions being carried out in relation to the present report and its recommendations.

. . . .

The on-site visit to Ciudad Juárez and Mexico City of February, 2002

20. The visit was initiated in Ciudad Juárez on February 11, continued with meetings in Mexico City on February 12, and concluded with a press conference on February 13, 2002. In the course of her visit, the Special Rapporteur met with federal officials. . . .

21. The Special Rapporteur also held interviews with officials of the State of Chihuahua and of the Municipality of Ciudad Juárez. . . .

22. In addition, she received information and testimony from victims' relatives, and met with representatives of nongovernmental human rights organizations and other civil society representatives at the local and national level. . . .

23. The Special Rapporteur thanks the Governor of Chihuahua and the Mayor of Ciudad Juárez and their staff for their hospitality during the visit. The Government of President Vicente Fox provided its full assistance and cooperation during the visit, thus permitting the Special Rapporteur to carry out an extensive program of activities in the discharge of her mandate. She thanks the Government and its officials for that assistance and for their willingness to cooperate in seeking solutions to the problems posed. The Special Rapporteur also wishes to extend her thanks to the representatives of Mexican civil society, especially those directly affected by this situation, for their cooperation and the important information supplied during the visit. The valuable work done by Mexican non-governmental organizations in the field of human rights is a critical factor in the Commission's ability to monitor the situation of human rights in the country.

Subsequent activities of the Special Rapporteur and the IACHR to address the situation

24. Following the visit, the Commission and its Special Rapporteur have continued to receive information from both State and non-State sources. During the Commission's 114th regular period of sessions, in March of 2002, Special Rapporteur Marta Altolaguirre informed the plenary of the Commission about the visit and the information collected, and organized a follow-up hearing before the Commission with representatives of the Mexican State and civil society at the Commission's headquarters. The Commission convened an additional hearing during its 116th regular period of sessions, in October of 2002, in order to receive updated information on the situation from both the Mexican State and relevant nongovernmental organizations.

25. It was during the latter hearing that the State accepted the request of the nongovernmental organizations "*Alto a la impunidad: ni una muerta más*" and *Nuestras Hijas de Regreso a Casa* to the effect that the former provide monthly reports to the Commission on measures taken to follow-up on these crimes, with that information then being transmitted by the Commission to the representatives of those organizations who participated in that hearing. In late November of 2002, the State

provided its first such report, indicating measures taken in certain cases, updating other data, and reporting on the initial work of an inter-institutional working group established to address these crimes. The Commission and its Special Rapporteur greatly value the willingness of the United Mexican States to provide updated information on a regular basis, and to continue its dialogue with representatives of the non-state sector in the search for solutions to this problem.

26. Further, the Commission has received a number of individual petitions concerning women and girls killed in Ciudad Juárez. It is currently processing petitions 104/02, 281/02, 282/02 and 283/02 in accordance with its Rules of Procedure, and is evaluating others as they are received. Further, the Commission granted precautionary measures under Article 25 of its Rules of Procedure in favor of Esther Chávez, a human rights defender who has been deeply involved in pursuing justice for these crimes who had received a series of threats in evident connection with that work. The Commission subsequently granted precautionary measures in favor of Miriam García and Blanca Guadalupe López and their families in relation to threats received. These women are the wives of two of the men presently detained in relation to some of these killings, Víctor Javier García Uribe and Gustavo González Meza, respectively. Following the death of Mr. González in his cell on February 8, 2003, under circumstances that remain under investigation, the Commission amplified the precautionary measures to include Mr. García.

27. Finally, it may be noted that in the course of a working visit to Mexico to follow-up on certain individual petitions and examine the situation of migrant workers and their families, the President of the Commission, Dr. Juan E. Méndez, received additional information. Informational meetings were held in Ciudad Juárez on July 30, 2002, with representatives of civil society and family members of certain victims, and subsequently with representatives of the Office of the Special Prosecutor charged with investigating these crimes. The information received was then forwarded to the Special Rapporteurship for Women's Rights.

The scope of the present report, its approval and follow-up

28. The present report deals with the situation of violence against women in Ciudad Juárez. . . .

29. Pursuant to its competence as the principal organ of the Organization of American States charged with protecting and promoting human rights in the Americas, and in accordance with its mandate set forth in the American Convention on Human Rights, and more specifically defined in its Statute and Regulations, the Commission monitors human rights developments in each member State of the OAS. The Commission periodically deems it useful to report the results of its study of a particular country, formulating the corresponding recommendations designed to assist that state in ensuring the fullest enjoyment of protected rights and liberties by those subject to its jurisdiction.

30. This report was prepared by the Special Rapporteur on the basis of a diverse array of information. This includes the interviews and other information gathered during the on-site visit, as well as updated information provided by governmental, intergovernmental, non-governmental and media sources through the Commission's normal monitoring procedures, as well as through its petition system.

31. . . . .

32. The Special Rapporteur and the Commission will continue to closely monitor the situation in Ciudad Juárez, with special attention to the steps taken to implement the recommendations set forth in this report. Both the Special Rapporteur and the Commission wish to underline their willingness to assist the Mexican State in the process of remedying the serious problems identified so that the right of women and girls to be free from violence is fully realized.

. . . .

The Context of Ciudad Juarez

37. Ciudad Juárez is a gateway city in the State of Chihuahua. It is a gateway for many Mexicans who migrate north in search of jobs with the maquila industry that dominates the border area. Ciudad Juárez is a key manufacturing center, with foreign and domestic *maquilas* attracting a huge labor force. In this sense, it is viewed by many as a gateway to greater job opportunities. It is also a gateway for migration, both legal and illegal, north to the United States. Ciudad Juárez is just across from El Paso, Texas to the north. The State of Chihuahua is bordered on the east by the State of Sonora, and on the west by the State of Coahuila.

38. Representatives of both the State and non-state sectors have consistently emphasized that Ciudad Juárez is characterized by a diverse array of especially serious challenges. With over 1,200,000 inhabitants, the Municipality of Ciudad Juárez is the largest population center in the State of Chihuahua, itself the largest State in the United Mexican States. Because of its location and industrial development, the population has grown and continues to expand extremely rapidly. According to the State of Chihuahua, more than half of the population of the Municipality consists of people from other areas of the country or foreigners. In this regard, the State indicated that cultural, economic and social differences within the population generate particularly complex problems. Nor does Ciudad Juárez possess sufficient infrastructure or public services to meet the needs of the ever-increasing population. Marginalized sectors of the population often lack access to decent housing, clean drinking water, sanitation services and public health services.

39. Information gathered during the visit pointed out that, as a border town, Ciudad Juárez has been marked by rising crime, including the penetration of organized crime and narcotrafficking, and an increase in gang activity and the presence of firearms. Notably in this regard, almost all the killings classified as executions in the State of Chihuahua take place in Ciudad Juárez. These and other problems generate high levels of violence that affect the men, women and children living there.

40. Some representatives of civil society also referred during the Special Rapporteur's visit to sharp shifts in established cultural patterns for some who migrate to Ciudad Juárez, in the sense that jobs are more plentiful for women, including for young women, who are then able to exercise greater economic independence. In fact, reports indicate that over half the *maquila* work force in the area is comprised of women. They pointed to these shifts in traditional patterns as sometimes generating tension in a society marked by historical inequalities between men and women and few resources to assist in changing those attitudes.

41. . . . .

42. Because of the lack of basic information, family members in these and other cases have expressed a profound lack of confidence in the willingness or ability of the authorities to clarify what happened or pursue accountability. Further, family members in these and other cases reported having received conflicting or confusing information from the authorities, and having been treated dismissively or even disrespectfully or aggressively when they sought information about the investigations. During the March, 2002 hearing before the Commission, representatives of *"Alto a la impunidad: ni una muerta más"* reported that family members of the victims whose bodies were presumably found on November 6 and 7, 2001, had returned to the site on February 25, 2002, and found clothing or other objects related to some of the victims at the scene.

43. The authorities of Ciudad Juárez, for their part, point to the November 9, 2001 detention of Gustavo González Meza ("La Foca") and Javier García Uribe ("El Cerillo") in connection with these crimes as evidence of its prompt response. During the Special Rapporteur's visit, however, numerous individuals, including some Mexican State officials, expressed serious concerns about allegations that these detainees had been tortured to coerce confessions. Both confessed in initial declarations, and both later retracted those confessions.

44. With respect to these allegations of torture, during her visit, the Special Rapporteur received two distinct sets of medical certificates. The set provided by the PGJE was prepared by the Department of Legal Medicine on November 11, 2001, at 02:40 and 02:45 hours, respectively. The certificate relative to González indicates no external signs of violence, while that relative to García refers to a small zone of equimosis on his right arm that would heal in less than 15 days. The other set of certificates, prepared by the Medical Unit of the detention center at 21:00 hours on November 11, 2001, attested in the case of González to *"multiples quemaduras en genitales"* and areas of equimosis in the area of the thorax and edema. In the case of García, it refers to *"[m]ultiples quemaduras de 1er grado en genitales"* y marks on his right arm. Subsequent reports indicate that the allegations of torture were denounced both to the authorities and publicly, but that the judiciary rejected the claims with respect to coercion as unsubstantiated. It was also reported that the person in charge of expert services at the PGJE at the time had resigned because of pressure to charge the results of certain expert tests to inculpate the two men detained. The death of Mr. González on February 8, 2003, while in his cell, under circumstances that remain under investigation, has generated renewed expressions of concern with respect to this criminal process.

Threats against those involved in search for justice

57. During her visit, and in subsequent follow-up activities, the Special Rapporteur has received information about threats and acts of hostility against human rights defenders involved in these cases, family members of victims seeking investigation, and journalists reporting on the crimes and the search for justice. In interviews, for example, several family members reported receiving anonymous, intimidating phone calls. Reports indicate that several family members have been warned to stop pursuing accountability. Several reported having been watched or followed.

In most cases, the individuals affected indicated that they had not denounced the intimidation to the authorities, because of lack of confidence and/or fear.

. . . .

68. During her visit and thereafter, the Special Rapporteur has received information about threats against journalists covering these crimes. She interviewed several journalists who referred to threats or pressure in relation to their work on these crimes, and a general climate of fear surrounding them. Press reports from the time of the visit indicate that journalists Samira Izaguirre, José Antonio Tirado and José Loya had been threatened and harassed, evidently in connection with their work relating to these crimes. Further, a journalist based in Chihuahua complained of harassment and threats since the time she had started reporting on the killings there.

The response of the Mexican State to violence against women in Ciudad Juárez

1. The response of the justice sector

69. While there have been some important advances, the response of the Mexican State to the killings and other forms of violence against women has been and remains seriously deficient. As such, it is a central aspect of the problem. Overall, the impunity in which most violence based on gender remains serves to fuel its perpetuation.

70. Representatives of civil society express indignation over the insufficient response of the police and judiciary to these killings, in particular with respect to the series of killings of young women that appear to fit a pattern. These representatives and family members of various victims complain of: delay in the initiation of investigations into reported disappearances; insufficient efforts in the initial investigation; the failure to collect or record evidence; evidence lost or missing from case files; mistreatment of family members of victims by the authorities; lack of information as to the status or results of the investigation or orientation as to the legal mechanisms; lack of support services for the survivors of those killed; and lack of results with respect to the identification, prosecution and punishment of those responsible. Many have expressed concern that attention is focused on the clarification of recent crimes, with little or no effort given to the investigation of killings that took place prior to 1998. Similarly, many have commented that each time a new killing is reported, resources are shifted to that investigation, with little follow up on those already underway.

. . . .

80. The information available reflects that efforts made to improve the response to these crimes through the Office of the Special Prosecutor have resulted in some improvements. Certainly the situation is not as grave as in the first years in which bags of bones were sometimes left as the only record in the aftermath of a killing. Nor is the tone of the official discourse as facially discriminatory as was documented by the CNDH in its Recommendation 44/98. At the same time, representatives of civil society and others who have monitored the response of the justice sector continue to report a deficient response, both with respect to the substance of the investigations and with respect to the treatment accorded by police and prosecutorial personnel to the family members of the victims.

. . . .

90. In looking at work to involve non-State actors, the Special Rapporteur has also received very general information about efforts of *maquila* employers on issues concerning the situation and treatment of their workers and questions of public security. With respect to the latter, for example, the situation presently under study raises questions about security in and around the industrial parks where the *maquilas* are located, and concerns about the many workers who travel significant distances late at night to work their shifts. In this regard, the Mexican State bears responsibility for ensuring that the *maquilas* are meeting their duties under law to their workers, and has a special role in encouraging the *maquilas* to invest in measures to support the workers and communities that serve them and helping to channel such investment for the public good.

91. In terms of the participation of the Federal Government sector, during her visit the Special Rapporteur received detailed information on the valuable activities of the Congressional Commissions on Equity and Gender, and the Special Commission of the Chamber of Deputies created to provide follow-up on the killings of women in Ciudad Juárez. That Special Commission has held meetings with relatives of victims, nongovernmental organizations that work in this area, State officials, and representatives of *maquilas*, in order to follow-up on investigations, encourage real collaboration between the Government at all three levels and civil society, and offer concrete recommendations on ways to prevent these crimes.

. . . .

95. Efforts to take an integral approach to the situation of violence in Ciudad Juárez are very much needed. The Commission and its Special Rapporteur value the opening of new spaces for dialogue and collaboration in the search for solutions to these problems. These have the capacity, if properly utilized, to contribute to achieving concrete advances. To date, however, efforts toward multisectoral collaboration have been hindered by a number of fundamental barriers. First, the terms of reference for these efforts continue to require clarification. That is to say, while many of those involved have invested themselves in these efforts with the aim of incorporating the perspective of gender and adopting integral approaches, other functionaries persist in focusing on these crimes as isolated instances. It is worth noting that many authorities in Chihuahua, from the State Prosecutor on down, tend to refer to the so-called "serial" crimes as the serious problem to be addressed, indicating expressly or implicitly that the other crimes have been dealt with sufficiently.

96. Second, responses to these crimes need to devote more attention to involving women and men and the perspective of gender in all aspects of work. In this regard, during her visit, the Special Rapporteur perceived some division in roles based on gender. She met with men in relation to official approaches to public security and the administration of justice (with the exception of the Special Prosecutor assigned to the killing of women). With some notable exceptions, she generally met with women in relation to the approach of civil society to the killings and the pursuit of justice, and the provision of services to victims. Further, the family members who have come forward to press for justice have, in most cases, been mothers, sisters and other female relatives. While both men and women have made important con-

tributions to efforts to combat these crimes, further attention to the incorporation of the perspective of gender would enhance those contributions.

97. Third, responses to the situation of violence against women in Ciudad Juárez are characterized by an extreme level of politicization. This politicization, based on party politics, was evident to some degree in virtually every meeting the Special Rapporteur held during her visit. It significantly restricts the ability of these initiatives to accomplish their objectives.

98. Fourth, efforts to amplify responses to the situation and to incorporate the participation of other sectors have yet to incorporate sufficient mechanisms for monitoring, evaluation and follow-up to ensure effective results—first and foremost that women are more secure in Ciudad Juárez.

The Law and Systems of Protection Applicable to Violence against Women in Ciudad Juárez

A. International law

99. Ensuring that women can freely and fully exercise their human rights is a priority in the Americas. The fundamental obligations of equality and nondiscrimination serve as the backbone for the regional human rights system, and the Convention of Belém do Pará expresses the commitment of the States Parties to prevent, punish and eradicate violence against women, itself a manifestation of discrimination based on gender. The priority given by the Commission and its Special Rapporteurship to the protection of the rights of women also reflects the importance given to this area by the member States themselves.

100. The principles of non-discrimination and equal protection are pillars in any democratic system, and serve as fundamental bases of the OAS system. Article 3(l) of the OAS Charter sets forth the core principle that "the American States proclaim the fundamental rights of the individual without distinction as to race, nationality, creed or sex."

101. The Mexican State has been a Party to the American Convention on Human Rights since its accession on March 2, 1981. Article 1 of the American Convention sets forth the obligation of States Parties to respect and ensure all recognized rights and freedoms without discrimination on the basis of, *inter alia*, sex. More specifically with respect to the principle of nondiscrimination, Article 24 recognizes the right to equal protection of and before the law, and Article 17 provides that the State shall ensure the equal recognition of rights and "adequate balancing of responsibilities" of spouses within marriage. In recognizing the fundamental rights of all persons without distinction, the Convention of course also protects such basic rights as those to life, liberty and personal integrity (Articles 4, 5 and 7). Trafficking in women is expressly prohibited in Article 6. The rights of children are accorded special measures of protection in Article 19.

102. The purposes of the regional human rights system and the principle of efficacy require that these guarantees be implemented in practice. Accordingly, where the exercise of any of these rights is not already ensured in law and practice, Article 2 of the American Convention commits the States Parties to adopt the legislative and other measures necessary to give them effect. Further, the American Con-

vention requires that the domestic system provide available and effective judicial recourse to persons alleging the violation of their rights protected under national law or the Convention. Where such domestic remedies prove unavailable or ineffective, the inter-American system provides for the possibility of recourse through its individual petition system.

103. Of special relevance for the present report are the rights and obligations set forth in the Inter-American Convention on the Prevention, Punishment and Eradication of Violence Against Women ("Convention of Belém do Pará"), which Mexico ratified on December 12, 1998. In reflecting a hemispheric consensus on the need to recognize the gravity of the problem of violence against women and take concrete steps to eradicate it, the Convention:

- Defines violence "any act or conduct, based on gender, which causes death or physical, sexual or psychological harm or suffering to women, whether in the public or private sphere;" [*See* Arts. 1, 2 and 3.]
- expressly acknowledges the link between gender violence and discrimination, indicating that such violence is a manifestation of the historically unequal power relations between women and men, and that the right to be free from such violence includes the right to be free from discrimination and to be valued and educated free of stereotypes; [*See* preamble, Arts. 4, 6.]
- recognizes that such violence affects women in a multitude of ways, preventing them from exercising other fundamental rights, both civil and political, *and* economic, social and cultural rights; [*See* preamble, Arts. 4, 5] and,
- requires that States Parties apply due diligence to prevent, investigate and punish such violence *wherever it occurs*—whether within the home or the community and perpetrated by individuals, or in the public sphere and perpetrated by state agents. [See Arts. 7, 2].

104. Accordingly, the State is directly responsible for violence against women perpetrated by its agents. State responsibility may also arise when it fails to apply due diligence to prevent or respond to such violence when perpetrated by individuals.

105. Further, States Parties must ensure that these obligations are given effect in the domestic legal system, and that women at risk for or subjected to violence have access to effective judicial protection and guarantees. [*See* Art. 7; *see also*, Arts. 8 and 9.] The mechanisms for supervision of compliance include the processing of individual complaints alleging violations of the principal obligations through the Commission's existing petition system. *See* Arts. 10–12.

106. The Mexican State is Party to a number of other international instruments that provide important protections for the rights of women. In broad terms, Articles 1 and 2 of the Universal Declaration of Human Rights, and Articles 2 and 3 of both the International Covenant on Civil and Political Rights and the International Covenant on Economic, Social and Cultural Rights recognize the right to equality and the prohibition of discrimination. The Convention on the Elimination of All Forms of Discrimination against Women, to which the Mexican State has been a Party since 1981, reinforces the equality and non- discrimination provisions of the International Bill of Rights by defining discrimination against women, and requiring States Parties to adopt specific measures to combat it. The Mexican State rati-

fied the Optional Protocol to that Convention on March 15, 2002. Again, in terms of looking at the interrelation between violence and discrimination based on gender, it is important to note that the definition of discrimination set forth in the UN Convention applies to gender-based violence. UN Committee on the Elimination of Discrimination against Women, general recommendation 19 (Eleventh session, 1992) "Violence against women," para. 6. Discrimination includes: acts that inflict physical, mental or sexual harm or suffering, threats of such acts, coercion and other deprivation of liberty. Gender-based violence may breach specific provisions of the [UN] Convention regardless of whether those provisions expressly mention violence.

107. Reference should also be made to the UN Declaration on Violence against Women, which complements these norms, and shares many basic principles with the Convention of Belém do Pará. The Mexican State is also Party to the Convention on the Rights of the Child, and in 2002 ratified its two optional protocols relative to the Participation of Children in Armed Conflicts, and to the Sale of Children, Child Prostitution and the Use of Children in Pornography, respectively.

108. It should also be noted that the situation in Ciudad Juárez has drawn the attention and concern of different instances within the United Nations. Following her 1999 visit to analyze the situation of the right to life in the Mexican State, the UN Special Rapporteur on extrajudicial, summary or arbitrary executions expressed:

> that the deliberate inaction of the Government to protect the lives of its citizens because of their sex had generated a sense of insecurity amongst many of the women living in Ciudad Juárez. At the same time, it had indirectly ensured that perpetrators would enjoy impunity for such crimes. The events in Ciudad Juárez thus constitute a typical case of gender-based crimes which thrive on impunity.

Report of Special Rapporteur Asma Jahangir, E/CN.4/2000/3/Add.3, 25 Nov., 1999, para. 89.

In his report from January of 2002, the UN Special Rapporteur on the independence of judges and lawyers expressed that the lack of an effective judicial response to the killings had "severely weakened the rule of law in Ciudad Juárez." Report of Special Rapporteur Dato'Param Cumaraswamy, E/CN.4/2002/72/Add.1, 24 Jan. 2002, para. 161. . . .

B. National law

109. Applicable legal provisions at both the federal and state levels have recently been reformed to incorporate positive advances. Through reforms adopted on August 14, 2001, Article 1 of the Constitution of the Republic was amended to prohibit all forms of discrimination, including on the basis of sex. Article 4 sets forth that men and women are equal before the law, and that every person has the right to freely determine the number and spacing of their children. The Constitution also recognizes that men and women have the same rights with respect to employment, education, nationality, remuneration and participation in political life. . . .

110. The laws of the State of Chihuahua that apply in cases of violence against women have been subject to recent reforms. Following an intense debate in the legislature, that included some consultation with civil society in the final stages, family violence is addressed in Article 190 of the Criminal Code.

111. Sexual crimes are covered in title fourteen of the Criminal Code of Chihuahua.

112. . . . . .

113. In sum, the Commission and its Special Rapporteur have taken due note of the debate engendered by a set of reforms to the Criminal Code enacted prior to those now in effect. Those prior reforms had been rejected by many as contradicting the principles of nondiscrimination and protection of the rights of women. The Commission and its Special Rapporteur value the initiative of the Government of Chihuahua to open a new space for dialogue with some inclusion of civil society to arrive at the reforms now in force. The reforms now in place demonstrate progress in bringing legislation into conformity with the obligations of ensuring equality and nondiscrimination. . . . As the Government of Chihuahua itself recognized in its March 2002 presentation before the Commission, the legislation can be perfected, and is not sufficient in and of itself. It is important that efforts continue to bring legislation into conformity with the principles of equality and nondiscrimination.

. . . .

CONCLUSIONS AND RECOMMENDATIONS

161. The Commission and its Special Rapporteur have given close attention to assessing the situation of violence against women in Ciudad Juárez in order to provide this analysis and the recommendations that follow. Both wish to note their appreciation for the willingness and openness of the Government at both the national and local levels to discuss the situation and how advances can be sought and attained. In addition to the problems and challenges highlighted in the present report, due note has been taken of efforts on the part of the Mexican State, at both the national and local levels, to overcome these. In this regard, special mention must be made of efforts to move forward with improvements in the normative framework to guarantee the right to be free from violence and discrimination. The ratification of the Convention of Belém do Pará, and the enactment of related legislation at the domestic level—for example the criminalization of family violence in the Criminal Code of Chihuahua—signify the very real commitment of the Mexican State to move forward in these areas, as does the establishment of new mechanisms for interinstitutional collaboration in the incorporation of the perspective of gender in public policy.

162. The formal recognition of gender equality and recognition of violence against women as a human rights violation open the door to new approaches to eradicating violence based on gender. The Commission and its Special Rapporteur give due recognition to these valuable advances. The pending challenge is to make these guarantees effective in practice—to bridge the existing gap between what the law says and the lived experience of the women of Ciudad Juárez.

163. A decisive question is whether the rights of women in Ciudad Juárez are more secure now than before. Efforts to address the violence and killings to date have not achieved that goal. There is an urgent need to prioritize attention to this situation through the allocation of additional human and material resources, backed by the legal authority and political will necessary to achieve effective results.

164. Ensuring that women in Ciudad Juárez can fully and equally exercise their fundamental rights, particularly to be free from violence, requires urgent attention not just to these killings, but to the various forms of gender-based violence that violate the rights of women. The killings and disappearances in Ciudad Juárez are an especially dramatic manifestation of patterns of gender-based violence and discrimination that include other forms of sexual violence and violence within the family. Violence has its root causes in concepts of subordination and discrimination, and impunity (and the discrimination inherent in the lack of effective response) fuels its persistence.

165. Effective approaches to the killings require effective approaches to violence against women. Such violence is, above all, a human rights problem. Applying due diligence to prevent such violence, as required under international and national law, requires attention to the gender dimensions of the problem, as well as the human security, public security and social dimensions. When the killing, sexual abuse, or beating of women remain in impunity, and are effectively tolerated by the State, this sends a strong message to men, women and children. Violence is a learned behavior. That behavior cannot be changed and eradicated if old patterns of inequality and discrimination continue to be sustained in practice.

166. The failure to investigate, prosecute and punish the perpetrators of these killings, sexual crimes and domestic violence against women in Ciudad Juárez contributes to a climate of impunity that perpetuates such violence. It is indispensable that cases of violence based on gender are investigated and those responsible brought to justice.

167. Violence based on gender is unacceptable—whether manifested through killings, sexual or domestic violence. The consequence of impunity is to lessen the visibility of such violations, to the point where domestic violence, for example, is in effect an invisible crime. This is the opposite of what the Mexican State has sought to achieve through the ratification of international human rights treaties such as the Convention of Belém do Pará, and the adoption of related legislation such as the reforms to the Criminal Code of Chihuahua defining family violence as a crime punishable by imprisonment. Children who grow up in a context of impunity for such crimes grow up with the perception that women are not entitled to equal recognition and protection under the law.

168. Violence against women exacts a terrible cost for the victims, their families and society as a whole, and has intergenerational effects. It is crucial that all sectors, public and private, be brought into the process of addressing this problem. The focus cannot be on blaming the victims; rather, it must be on changing the patterns and practices that allow them to be subjected to these human rights violations. This requires the greater participation of women in the formulation of public policy, as well as the greater participation of men in helping to change traditional patterns and practices based on stereotypes. The responsibility of the Mexican State in addressing this violence and ending this impunity is to design and implement effective measures of prevention and response incorporating the substantive participation of the Federal Government, and the Governments of Chihuahua and the Municipality of Ciudad Juárez, as well as civil society.

169. In reiterated opportunities, the Mexican State has emphasized to the Commission and its Special Rapporteur its institutional commitment to combat impunity with respect to these killings. The Government of Chihuahua has expressed its commitment to applying the best resources available to ensuring absolute respect for the rights of women, through a policy of openness and coordination with all the public and private institutions able to make a contribution in this regard. The Federal Government, for its part, has indicated its determination to assist in the resolution of past crimes and prevention of future crimes. It is light of the foregoing commitments that the Commission and its Special Rapporteur offer the recommendations that follow, as a means of assisting the State in putting that commitment into practice.

General recommendations to enhance the efficacy of the right of the women of Ciudad Juárez to be free from violence:

1. Prioritize the full inclusion, participation and collaboration of all levels of Government—federal, state and municipal—in the State response to the killings and other forms of gender-based violence affecting women in Ciudad Juárez, with the application of specific goals, timelines, oversight and evaluation to ensure the efficacy of mechanisms for interinstitutional participation.

2. In seeking solutions to the killing of women and girls in Ciudad Juárez, devote increased attention to developing an integrated understanding of how different forms of violence against women interrelate and reinforce each other, and integrated strategies to combat such violence.

3. Enhance efforts that have been initiated to incorporate the perspective of gender in design and implementation of public policy, with special attention to making such efforts effective in practice at the levels of the State of Chihuahua and Municipality of Ciudad Juárez, in order to provide due attention to compliance with the principles of equality and nondiscrimination.

4. Amplify the participation of women in the design and implementation of public policy and decision-making at all levels and across all sectors of Government.

Recommendations to improve the application of due diligence to investigate, prosecute and punish violence against women in Ciudad Juárez and overcome impunity:

1. Strengthen institutional capacity and procedures for responding to crimes of violence against women, including through the allocation of additional human and material resources for the Special Prosecutor's Office and the other instances responsible for addressing and redressing these violations.

2. Establish procedures to provide additional independent oversight, including periodic reports, for the investigations carried out under the direction of the Special Prosecutor's Office to ensure periodic evaluation of the steps taken and timely progress in each case.

3. Ensure that investigations into the killings of women are developed from their inception on the basis of investigation plans that take into account the prevalence of violence against women, and possible linkages between certain cases.

4. Develop and apply an action plan with respect to outstanding denunciations of missing women to ensure that all reasonable avenues of investigation are fully explored, and to cross reference information on the disappearances with that concerning the killings in order to identify possible connections or patterns.

5. Develop and apply an action plan with respect to the "cold" cases designed to identify and remedy any and all existing deficiencies in those files (such as those identified by the National Human Rights Commission in its review) and reactivate the investigations.

6. Expand the assistance the PGR has provided to the PGJE in isolated instances, and concretize the contributions it can and should provide to fortify local capacity in such areas as technical, investigative, criminological, medical-forensic, psychological-forensic and other scientific assistance.

7. Improve procedures and practices to ensure that reports of missing persons are subjected to rapid, thorough and impartial investigation, including through protocols or guidelines to ensure compliance with basic standards in all cases, and the development of new initiatives such as bulletins to the media.

8. Guarantee prompt access to and the efficacy of special measures for the protection of the physical and psychological integrity of women subject to threats of violence.

9. Intensify efforts to train all relevant officials—including police, prosecutors, forensic medical and other specialists, judges and court personnel—in the causes and consequences of violence based on gender both in terms of the technical aspects pertinent to investigation, prosecution and punishment, and the need to apply this understanding in their interaction with victims and/or their families.

10. Implement reforms designed to protect the rights of victims or their family members to judicial protection and guarantees, principally by improving mechanisms to ensure that the affected parties have access to information about the development of the investigation and about their rights in the legal proceedings, as well as to develop the possibilities of obtaining legal assistance where necessary to pursue such proceedings.

11. Ensure adequate oversight of officials responsible for responding to and investigating crimes of violence against women and ensure that measures to hold them accountable administratively, disciplinarily or criminally, depending on the case, are actually applied when they fail to discharge their responsibilities under the law.

12. Provide those who seek assistance from such officials an available and effective procedure to file complaints in the case of noncompliance with their duties under the law, and information about how to invoke that procedure.

13. Reorient the working relationship with the individuals and organizations that serve as the *coadyuvancia* (legal counsel defending the interests of the victim in investigation and prosecution) to provide for a fluid exchange of information, and to fully utilize this mechanism as the aid to justice it was intended to be when established.

14. In view of the climate of fear and threats in relation to some of these killings, and reported potential links of some to organized crime, give attention to incorporating the participation of police officers from other areas in the investigative teams

as a means to ensure that officers who live in the community are not themselves under threat or pressure, and increase citizen confidence.

15. Also with respect to the issue of fear and threats, give priority attention to ensuring the existence of measures of security for women victims of or threatened with violence, family members, human rights defenders, witnesses or journalists in situations of risk, both to provide protection for their right to personal security and to ensure that those who come forward to press for clarification of these crimes or provide information are not intimidated into abandoning their efforts.

16. Subject all threats or acts of hostility denounced in connection with these killings to prompt, thorough and impartial investigation with due follow-up, and the State should pursue further consultation with the organizations of civil society who assist victims and their families in developing and implementing solutions in this regard.

17. Enhance public services for women who have been subjected to violence with special attention to amplifying access to medical and psychological treatment; adopting more integral social services designed to respond to the problem of economic subordination that often prevents women from removing themselves from an abusive situation; and, providing information and assistance to ensure effective access to legal remedies for protection against this violation and related legal issues such as child custody.

Recommendations to improve the application of due diligence to prevent violence against women in Ciudad Juárez and increase their security

1. Place renewed emphasis on training for public sector functionaries, especially the police, prosecutors, forensic specialists, judges and court personnel, in the causes and consequences of violence based on gender.

2. Continue to develop spaces for interinstitutional dialogue and collaboration to exchange information and strategies, ensure coherent approaches, improve services and promote best practices; it is crucial that such efforts include monitoring, evaluation and follow-up to assess advances and continuing obstacles.

3. Coordinate and amplify efforts at the federal, State and Municipal levels to improve such basic services as lighting in marginal areas and zones that have been associated with security risk; security with respect to transportation; the paving of roads in marginal areas—and to allocate the funds necessary to provide such services.

4. Improve the detection, recording and reporting of violence against women through health care settings, and provide information on violence prevention, treatment and services to users of these services, especially reproductive health services.

5. Develop data collection systems to document and report on the scope and consequences of violence against women in Ciudad Juárez in order to improve the design and implementation of measures to confront it, and evaluate the efficacy of those measures.

6. Work with civil society to design and implement broad based rights and education campaigns, first, to inform women of Ciudad Juárez about their right to be free from violence and how to seek protection for that right, and, second, to ensure

that men, women and children understand that violence based on gender is a human rights violation under international law and a crime punishable under the law of Chihuahua.

7. Take steps to involve more men in initiatives aimed at changing attitudes and practices based on stereotyping, and to ensure that public campaigns are designed to correspond to the needs of men, women and families.

8. Work with the media to: promote public awareness of the right to be free from violence; inform the public about the costs and consequences of such violence; disseminate information about legal and social support services for those at risk; and inform victims, victimizers and potential victimizers of the punishment for such violence.

9. Work with instances at the levels of the Federal Government, State of Chihuahua and the Municipality of Ciudad Juárez responsible for protecting the rights of children to ensure that special measures of protection are available for children threatened with gender-based violence, and that the response to gender-based violence against girl children takes into account their special vulnerability.

----

ii. Petitions

Prior to the entry into force of the American Convention, the Commission was authorized to examine only those communications that alleged a violation by an OAS member state of one or more of the rights mentioned in Article 9(*bis*) of its Statute. The Commission's Rules now no longer distinguish between these and other rights proclaimed in the American Declaration. Instead the current procedure, based on Article 20 of the Statute, allows the Commission to act on individual petitions charging a violation of any of the rights enumerated in the Declaration.

The Commission processes petitions invoking the Declaration the same way it does those based on the Convention. The procedure diverges, however, after the conclusion of the Commission's proceedings, because petitions brought under the Convention system can be referred to the Court and those based on the Declaration cannot so proceed. Petitions concerning states that have not adhered to the Convention thus conclude with a "final report" containing a finding of facts and the Commission's conclusions and recommendations. The decisions generally are published in the Commission's annual report to the OAS General Assembly. Since the General Assembly has shown little interest in dealing with individual petitions and has generally failed to address issues of non-compliance, the Commission has instituted its own follow-up procedure. After the Commission has adopted recommendations or achieved a friendly settlement in a case, it may adopt the further measures it deems appropriate, including holding hearings, to verify compliance with the recommendations or the terms of the settlement and thereafter prepare a report on compliance.

The Convention empowers the Commission to deal with inter-state, as well as individual communications. Arts. 44 and 45. By becoming a party to the Convention, a State is deemed to have accepted the jurisdiction of the Commission to examine private complaints lodged against that state. The Commission may deal with complaints filed by one State Party against another only if both states, in addition to ratifying the Convention, have also recognized the inter-state jurisdiction of the Commission. Art. 45. In adopting this approach, the American Convention reverses the more traditional scheme utilized by the European Convention which initially established an optional individual petition system and a mandatory interstate complaint procedure.

The Convention gives the Commission standing to request advisory opinions and to refer cases to the Court. The Convention provides that "the Commission shall appear in all cases before the Court." Arts. 61 and 57. As discussed in Chapter V, the Commission also has standing to request precautionary measures from the Court. During Court proceedings, the Commission need not assert the contentions of the victim whose case it submits. When the Commission appears before the Court, it does so not as "party", but as "the 'Ministerio Publico' of the inter-American system." *In the Matter of Viviana Gallardo*, Case No. G 101/81, Decision of Nov. 13, 1981, I.–A. Court H.R., *Series A: Judgments and Opinions* 77, at para. 22 (1984). The Commission thus appears before the Court as protector of the legal order established by the Convention, i.e. to promote the legal and institutional integrity of the Convention system. The Rules of Procedure of the Court further emphasize this by indicating that "parties to the case" means "the victim or the alleged victim, the State and, only procedurally, the Commission." Court's Rules of Procedure, art. 2. The following advisory opinion discusses the functions of the Commission and the limits of its jurisdiction.

Certain Attributes of the Inter-American Commission on Human Rights, Advisory Opinion OC-13/91 of July 16, 1991, 13 Inter-Am. Ct. H.R. (Ser. A) (1991).

1. By submission of December 17, 1991, . . . the governments of the Republic of Argentina and of the Oriental Republic of Uruguay requested an advisory opinion on the interpretation of Articles 41, 42, 44, 46, 47, 50 and 51 of the American Convention on Human Rights . . . "*as they relate to the concrete situation and circumstances*" indicated. . . .

3. The request for an advisory opinion raises the following questions:

1) As regards Articles 41 and 42, the Court is hereby requested to render an opinion as to whether, in order to justify its dealing with a case involving communications alleging the violation of the rights protected by Articles 23, 24 and 25 of the Convention, the Commission is competent to assess and offer an opinion on the legality of domestic legislation adopted pursuant to the provisions of the Constitution, insofar as the "reasonableness," "advisability," or "authenticity" of such legislation is concerned.

2) With respect to Articles 46 and 47 of the Convention, the Court is asked to render an opinion as to whether, in the case of communications submitted pursuant to Article 44 of the Convention, which must be processed within the framework of the Pact of San Jose, it is proper, as a matter of law, for the Commission, after having declared the application inadmissible, to address the merits of the case in the same report.

3) As for Articles 50 and 51 of the Convention, the Court is here being asked to render an opinion as to whether it is proper to combine the two reports provided for under Articles 50 and 51 of the Convention in a single report, and whether the Commission may order the publication of the report to which Article 50 refers before the period specified in Article 51 has expired. . . .

20. The Court does not find in the instant request any reason to abstain from considering it and, therefore, admits it and responds as follows.

II

. . . .

23. Several of the articles of the Convention, in particular those which appear in Section 2, Chapter VII, under the title "Functions" and Article 44 which is part of Section 3, "Competence", refer to the attributes of the Commission. From the beginning, the provisions of the inter-American system have charged the Commission with the *"promotion of human rights"* (Resolution VIII, V Meeting of Consultation of Ministers of Foreign Relations, Santiago, 1959, Official Documents, OAS, Series C.II. 5, 4–6) or *"to promote the observance and protection of human rights"* (Art. 111 of the Charter of the OAS as Amended by the Protocol of Cartagena), as incorporated into Article 41 of the Convention. That is the principal function of the Commission, which defines and regulates all its other functions, in particular those granted it by Article 41, and any interpretation must be limited by those criteria.

24. The Court understands that the request does not seek a complete interpretation of Articles 41 and 42, but rather an opinion whether, on the authority of those articles, the Commission could, in the case of communications before it (probably those referred to in Articles 41.f, 44 and 45) or with reference to the copies of the reports and studies the States send it in application of Article 42, rule on the *"legality of domestic legislation adopted pursuant to the provisions of the Constitution, insofar as [its] 'reasonableness,' 'advisability' or 'authenticity.'"*

25. . . . . It must be understood . . . that the expression employed in the request, *"domestic legislation adopted pursuant to the provisions of the Constitution"* refers to any provision of a general nature and not exclusively to law in a strict sense. The Court understands the expression *"legality of domestic legislation adopted pursuant to the provisions of the Constitution"* as referring, in general terms, to their conformity with the internal and international juridical order.

26. A State may violate an international treaty and, specifically, the Convention, in many ways. It may do so in the latter case, for example, by failing to establish the norms required by Article 2. Likewise, it may adopt provisions which do not conform to its obligations under the Convention. Whether those norms have been adopted in conformity with the internal juridical order makes no difference for these purposes.

27. In these circumstances, there should be no doubt that the Commission has in that regard the same powers it would have if confronted with any other type of violation and could express itself in the same way as in other cases. Said in another way, that it is a question of "domestic legislation" which has been *"adopted pursuant to the provisions of the Constitution,"* is meaningless if, by means of that legislation, any of the rights or freedoms protected have been violated. The powers of the

Commission in this sense are not restricted in any way by the means by which the Convention is violated.

28. There are historical situations in which States have promulgated laws which conformed with their juridical order, but which did not offer adequate guarantees for the exercise of human rights, imposed unacceptable restrictions or, simply, ignored them. As the Court has said, the fulfillment of a constitutional requirement *"does not always prevent a law passed by the Legislature from being in violation of human rights" (The Word "Laws" in Article 30 of the American Convention on Human Rights,* para. 22).

29. This does not mean the Commission has the authority to rule as to how a legal norm is adopted in the internal order. That is the function of the competent organs of the State. What the Commission should verify, in a concrete case, is whether what the norm provides contradicts the Convention and not whether it contradicts the internal legal order of the State. The authority granted the Commission to *"make recommendations to the governments of the member states . . . for the adoption of progressive measures in favor of human rights within the framework of their domestic laws and constitutional provisions"* (Art. 41(b)) (emphasis added) or the obligation of the States to adopt such legislative or other measures as may be necessary to give effect to the rights or freedoms guaranteed by the Convention *"in accordance with their constitutional processes"* (Art. 2) (emphasis added), does not authorize the Commission to determine the State's adherence to constitutional precepts in establishing internal norms.

30. At the international level, what is important to determine is whether a law violates the international obligations assumed by the State by virtue of a treaty. This the Commission can and should do upon examining the communications and petitions submitted to it concerning violations of human rights and freedoms protected by the Convention.

31. This definition of the attributes of the Commission does not affect the relationship between the rule of law and the Convention. As the Court has already said, *"[t]he concept of rights and freedoms as well as that of their guarantees* [according to the Pact of San Jose] *cannot be divorced from the system of values and principles that inspire it" (Habeas Corpus in Emergency Situations (Arts. 27(2), 25(1) and 7(6) American Convention on Human Rights),* Advisory Opinion OC-8/87 of January 30, 1987. Series A No. 8, para. 26). Within such values and principles, it is apparent that *"[r]epresentative democracy is the determining factor throughout the system of which the Convention is a part " (The Word "Laws" in Article 30 of the Convention on Human Rights,* para. 34). The Court has also pointed out that

> there exists an inseparable bond between the principles of legality, democratic institutions and the rule of law [and] [i]n a democratic society, the rights and freedoms inherent in the human person, the guarantees applicable to them and the rule of law form a triad, [and] [e]ach component thereof defines itself, complements and depends on the others for its meaning. *(Habeas Corpus in Emergency Situations [Arts. 27(2), 25(1) and 7(6), American Convention on Human Rights],* paras. 24 and 26.)

32. It is now appropriate to consider the terms "reasonableness," "advisability" and "authenticity," mentioned by the applicant governments in the first question. This Court is asked to give its opinion whether the Commission may use that ter-

minology *"to assess and offer an opinion"* on domestic legislation considered within the framework of Articles 41 and 42 of the Convention.

33. "Reasonableness" implies a value judgment and, when applied to a law, conformity to the principles of common sense. It is also used in reference to the parameters of interpretation of treaties and, therefore, of the Convention. Reasonable means just, proportionate and equitable, in opposition to unjust, absurd and arbitrary. It is a qualifier with an axiological content which implies opinion but, in another sense, may be employed juridically as, in fact, the courts frequently do, in that any state activity should be not only valid but reasonable. Insofar as the "advisability" of a law, the question may lend itself to subjective opinions, unless the expression is used in the uncommon sense of "correlation" or "conformity" between internal norms and those based upon the Convention. The expression "authenticity" of a law, which could have the juridical meaning of true, certain or certified in the sense of authority to attest to documents, does not appear to have that meaning in the context of the request.

34. Individual communications must allege a violation of the Convention by a State Party. This is a requirement of admissibility [Article 47(b)] and the Commission is given the authority to decide whether that violation has occurred. In that sense, it must decide whether legal norms violate the Convention. In fact, the international organs which apply the Convention cannot treat an internal norm differently from an act. There is no difference between State responsibility arising from violations of the Convention by virtue of an internal norm and the treatment that general international law gives to internal provisions violative of other international obligations.

35. An internal norm may violate the Convention because it is unreasonable or because it does not "conform" with it and, of course, a law which is contrary to a State's obligations under the Convention cannot be termed "reasonable" or "advisable." The Commission would be empowered to use those terms in this context. Clearly it may do so in the global consideration of cases. Nevertheless, because the functions of the Commission must conform to the law, the terminology it uses must be carefully chosen and should avoid concepts that might be ambiguous, subjective or confusing.

36. The above assertions are equally valid for the procedure relating to copies of reports and studies referred to in Article 42.

37. The Court's reply, then, must be based upon the Commission's principal function of promoting the observance and protection of human rights, from which it derives its power to rule, as in the case of any other act, that a norm of internal law violates the Convention, but not that it violates the internal juridical order of a State.

38. The second point of the request for an advisory opinion, which is related to the petitions presented under Article 44 of the Convention, asks whether the Commission, having declared the petition inadmissible pursuant to the provisions of Articles 46 and 47, may address *"the merits of the case in the same report."*

39. In that regard, it should be clarified that although the Convention does not use the word "address," it may be considered the generic equivalent of other ex-

pressions: to formulate opinions, conclusions, recommendations, which the Commission may issue in exercise of its powers pursuant to Article 41. Likewise, it is inexact to speak of a "report" which is not based upon a finding of admissibility, for if the Commission declares a matter inadmissible, it may not draw up a report (*infra*, para. 48) within the meaning of Articles 50 and 51. The Court understands that the instant question refers to a case where the Commission issues opinions, conclusions or recommendations on the merits in individual petitions, after it has declared them inadmissible.

40. The Convention sets out the prerequisites a petition or communication must meet in order to be found admissible by the Commission (Article 46); it also sets out the cases of inadmissibility (Article 47) which may be determined once the proceeding has been initiated [Article 48(1)(c)]. Regarding the form in which the Commission should declare inadmissibility, the Court has already pointed out that this requires an express act, which is not required in a finding of admissibility (*Velásquez Rodríguez Case, Preliminary Objections*, Judgment of June 26, 1987. Series C No. 1, para. 40; *Fairén Garbi and Solís Corrales Case, Preliminary Objections*, Judgment of June 26, 1987. Series C No. 2, para. 45; and, *Godínez Cruz Case, Preliminary Objections*, Judgment of June 26, 1987. Series C No. 3, para. 43).

41. The requirements of admissibility are related, obviously, to juridical certainty in the internal order as well as in the international. Without falling into a rigid formalism which distorts the purpose and object of the Convention, the States and the organs of the Convention must comply with the provisions which regulate the procedure, for the juridical security of the parties depend upon it *(Cayara Case, Preliminary Objections*, Judgment of February 3, 1993. Series C No. 14, paras. 42 and 63). Before the Commission, a State accused of violating the Convention may, in the exercise of its right of defense, argue any of the provisions of Articles 46 and 47 and, if the argument is successful, the proceeding is interrupted and the file is closed.

42. The admissibility of a petition or communication is an indispensable prerequisite to hearing the merits of a matter. The finding of inadmissibility of a petition or communication shall, thus, preclude a decision on the merits. In the individual petition system provided by the Convention, from the moment the Commission declares a matter inadmissible, it lacks the competence to rule on the merits.

43. This Court has said that "[i]t is generally accepted that the procedural system is a means of attaining justice and that the latter cannot be sacrificed for the sake of mere formalities" (*Cayara Case, Preliminary Objections*, supra 41, para. 42). But here it is a matter of a case which has been closed and to rule on the merits afterwards would be the equivalent of the Commission ruling on a communication without having received it.

44. In the foregoing circumstances, the procedural impossibility of addressing the merits of the petitions received in the exercise of its authority pursuant to Article 41(f) of the Convention or making the pertinent recommendations to the State concerned, does not in any way detract from the Commission's exercise of other attributes which Article 41 confers upon it in extenso. In any case, the use of the latter attributions, for example, those contemplated in paragraphs (b), (c), and (g) of that norm, must be by means of acts and procedures other than the procedure govern-

ing the examination of individual petitions or denunciations based upon Articles 44 through 51 of the Convention, and may in no way be used in a devious fashion to refer to the merits of one or several individual cases declared inadmissible.

45. The third question refers to Articles 50 and 51 of the Convention, precepts which, as this Court has already recognized, raise certain problems of interpretation *(Velásquez Rodríguez Case, Preliminary Objections,* para. 63; *Fairén Garbi and Solís Corrales Case, Preliminary Objections,* para. 63; and, *Godínez Cruz Case, Preliminary Objections,* para. 66).

46. These norms were based upon Articles 31 and 32 of the European Convention for the Protection of Human Rights and Fundamental Freedoms, according to which, when the European Commission considers there are violations of the rights protected in that Convention, it may send the report, which is only one, to the Committee of Ministers which will dictate the measures the State concerned should adopt or submit it in the form of a case to the European Court of Human Rights for the Court to rule, in an imperative manner, on the alleged violations.

47. Because an organ similar to the Committee of Ministers was not established in the inter-American system, the American Convention empowered the Commission to decide whether to submit the case to the Court or to continue to examine the case and prepare a final report, which it may publish.

48. Given admissibility, and without prejudice to the procedure established in Articles 48 and 49, Articles 50 and 51 of the Convention establish successive stages. In the first, regulated by Article 50, when a friendly settlement has not been reached, the Commission may state the facts and its conclusions in a preliminary document addressed to the State concerned. This "report" is transmitted in a confidential manner to the State so it may adopt the proposals and recommendations of the Commission and resolve the problem. The State is not authorized to publish it.

Based upon the presumption of the equality of the parties, a proper interpretation of Article 50 implies that neither may the Commission publish this preliminary report, which is sent, in the terminology of the Convention, only *"to the states concerned."*

49. Article 47(6) of the Commission's Regulations states *"[t]he report shall be transmitted to the parties concerned, who shall not be authorized to publish it."* Given that petitioners and victims are recognized as parties in the proceeding before the Commission (for example, Article 45 of the Commission's Regulations), Article 47(6) does not conform to Article 50 of the Convention, and its application has altered the confidential nature of the report and the obligation not to publish it.

50. A second stage is regulated by Article 51. If within the period of three months, the State to which the preliminary report was sent has not resolved the matter by responding to the proposal formulated therein, the Commission is empowered, within that period, to decide whether to submit the case to the Court by means of the respective application or to continue to examine the matter. This decision is not discretionary, but rather must be based upon the alternative that would be most favorable for the protection of the rights established in the Convention.

51. The three months are counted from the date of transmittal of the Article 50 report to the State concerned, and the Court has clarified that the time limit, though

not fatal, has a preclusive character, except in special circumstances, with regard to the submission of the case to this Court, independent of that which the Commission gives the State to fulfill its first recommendations *(Cayara Case, Preliminary Objections*, paras. 38 and 39).

52. Article 51 authorizes the Commission to draw up a second report, whose preparation

> is conditional upon the matter not having been submitted to the Court within the three-month period set by Article 51(1). Thus, if the application has been filed with the Court, the Commission has no authority to draw up [that] report. *(Velásquez Rodríguez Case, Preliminary Objections*, para. 63; *Fairén Garbi and Solís Corrales Case, Preliminary Objections*, para. 63; and, *Godínez Cruz Case, Preliminary Objections*, para. 66.)

Otherwise, the Commission has the authority to prepare a final report containing the opinions and conclusions it considers advisable. It must also make the pertinent recommendations, giving the State an additional period to take appropriate measures to fulfill its obligations under the Convention.

53. There are, then, two documents which, depending upon the interim conduct of the State to which they are addressed, may or not coincide in their conclusions and recommendations and to which the Convention has given the name of "report" and which have the character of preliminary and final, respectively.

54. There may be a third stage after the final report. In fact, with the lapse of the time period the Commission has given the State to comply with the recommendations contained in the final report, and if they have not been accepted, the Commission shall decide whether to publish it, and this decision must also be based upon the alternative most favorable for the protection of human rights.

55. This being the case, the question should be answered in the sense that the two reports governed separately by Articles 50 and 51 of the Convention may not be subsumed in one because those norms establish two separate stages, even though the contents of those documents, depending upon the conduct of the State concerned, may be similar.

56. The preliminary, confidential document of Article 50 may not be published. Only the final report contemplated by Article 51 of the Convention may be published, by decision of the Commission adopted after the lapse of the period given the State to carry out the recommendations contained in the final report.

[The opinion was unanimous on all three questions].

Questions and Comments

1. What actions by the Commission did Argentina and Uruguay find objectionable? Did the Commission act outside its powers? Is the Commission bound by the Court's advisory opinion? Are states?
2. How strictly must the Commission follow its procedures? When do the rules become "mere formalities" and "rigid formalism?" What is served in requiring adherence to the rules of procedure?
3. What is the primary function of the Commission in the inter-American system?

4. In OC/19, Nov. 28, 2005, the Court delivered another advisory opinion on the functions of the Commission. The opinion, delivered at the request of Venezuela, concerned the question of whether there exists an organ to control the legality of the Commission's exercise of its functions, or whether this power resides in the states parties to the Convention. The Court unanimously gave its opinion that the Commission exercises its functions to promote and protect human rights in full authority and independence in conformity with the Convention. The Court added that in cases properly submitted to it, the Court itself reviews the legality of the procedures before the Commission.

5. The Commission has published several reviews of its work. *See, e.g.,* IACHR, *Ten Years of Activities 1971–1981* (1982); IACHR, *25 Years of Struggle for Human Rights in the Americas 1959–1984* (1984). Its published country reports include: IACHR, "Reports of the Activities of the Inter-American Commission on Human Rights in the Dominican Republic (June 1 to August 31, 1965 and September 1, 1965 to July 6, 1966)," in *The Organization of American States and Human Rights 1960–1967* at 359 and 439 (1972); IACHR, "Report of the Inter-American Commission on Human Rights on the Situation regarding Human Rights in El Salvador and Honduras," *in The Organization of American States and Human Rights 1969–1970,* at 291 (1976); IACHR, Report on the Situation of Human Rights in the Republic of Colombia, OEA/Ser.L/V/II.53, doc.22, at 22 (1981); IACHR, *Report on the Situation of Human Rights in Argentina,* OEA/Ser.L/V/II.49, doc. 19, corr. 1 (1980); IACHR, *Report on the Situation of Human Rights in the Republic of Nicaragua,* OEA/Ser.L./V/II.53, doc.25 (1981); IACHR, *Fourth Report on the Situation of Human Rights in Guatemala,* OEA/Ser.L/V/II. 83, Doc. 16 rev. (1993); IACHR, *Second Report on the Situation of Human Rights in Colombia,* OEA/Ser.L/V/II.84, Doc. 39 rev. (1993); IACHR, *Report on the Situation of Human Rights in El Salvador,* OEA/Ser.L/V/II.85, Doc. 28 rev. (1994); IACHR, *Report on the Situation of Human Rights in Haiti,* OEA/Ser.L/V/II.85, Doc. 9 rev. (1994). *See also* IACHR, *Annual Report 1992–1993,* OEA/Ser.L/V/II.83, Doc. 14, at 16 (1993); IACHR, *Annual Report 1993,* OEA/Ser.L./V/II.85, Doc. 9 rev., at 17 (1994). The full list and text of reports appears at www.oas.org.

C. The Inter-American Court

The Court has jurisdiction to adjudicate cases involving charges that a State Party has violated the Convention. It also has jurisdiction to render advisory opinions interpreting the Convention and certain other human rights treaties. Article 62 of the Convention delimits the Court's contentious jurisdiction as follows:

1. A State Party may, upon depositing its instruments of ratification or adherence to this Convention, or at any subsequent time, declare that it recognizes as binding, *ipso facto,* and not requiring special agreement, the jurisdiction of the Court on all matters relating to the interpretation or application of this Convention.

2 Such declaration may be made unconditionally, on the condition of reciprocity, for a specified period, or for specific cases. It shall be presented to the Secretary General of the Organization, who shall transmit copies thereof to the other member states of the Organization and to the Secretary of the Court.

3. The jurisdiction of the Court shall comprise all cases concerning the interpretation and application of the provisions of this Convention that are submitted to it, provided that the States Parties to the case recognize or have recognized such jurisdiction, whether by special declaration pursuant to the preceding paragraphs, or by a special agreement.

This provision indicates that a State Party does not accept the contentious jurisdiction of the Court merely by ratifying the Convention. To do so, it must either file the declarations referred to in paragraphs 1 and 2 of Article 62 or conclude the special agreement mentioned in paragraph 3. Declarations accepting the Court's jurisdiction have been made by Argentina, Barbados, Bolivia, Brazil, Colombia, Chile, Costa Rica, Ecuador, Dominican Republic, El Salvador, Guatemala, Haiti, Honduras, Mexico, Nicaragua, Peru, Panama, Paraguay, Suriname, Uruguay, and Venezuela.

The Convention specifies in Article 61(1) that "only the States Parties and the Commission shall have the right to submit a case to the Court." Individuals thus may not do so, although changes in the Court's Rules of Procedure have given them standing to have their own representation during the Court proceedings (Arts. 2 and 35(4)). According to the *Gallardo Case*, the Commission must complete its proceedings in an individual case before the matter may be referred to the Court. It is unclear whether the States Parties to an inter-state dispute may waive the Commission proceedings, given that the inequality between the parties to which the Court referred in the *Gallardo Case* would not exist in this context. Article 61(1) also leaves open the question whether it permits all States Parties to refer any case to the Court or only the cases in which the Applicant States were parties in the proceedings before the Commission. To date the Court has not had the opportunity to address this issue.

The scope of the Court's advisory jurisdiction, set forth in Article 64 of the Convention is very broad. Its text reads as follows:

> 1. The member states of the Organization may consult the Court regarding the interpretation of this Convention or of other treaties concerning the protection of human rights in the American states. Within their spheres of competence, the organs listed in Chapter X of the Charter of the Organization of American States, as amended by the Protocol of Buenos Aires, may in like manner consult the Court.
>
> 2. The Court, at the request of a member state of the Organization, may provide that state with opinions regarding the compatibility of any of its domestic laws with the aforesaid international instruments.

Advisory opinions are not, as such, legally binding. That conclusion is inherent in the concept of "advisory" opinions. *See* Advisory Opinion OC–3/83, I.–A. Court H.R., Series A: Judgments and Opinions, No. 3 (1983). Moreover, the Convention nowhere states that these opinions are binding. Nevertheless, the Court is a "judicial institution whose purpose is the application and interpretation of the American Convention on Human Rights," Statute of the Court, Art. 1, and it is an organ having "competence with respect to matters relating to the fulfillment of the commitments by the States Parties to this Convention." Convention, Art. 33. The Court's pronouncements, whether made in a contentious case or advisory opinion, derive their value as legal authority from its character as a judicial institution empowered to interpret and apply that instrument. See further J.M. Pasqualucci, The Practice and Procedure of the Inter-American Court of Human Rights (CUP, 2003).

The following is the first advisory opinion issued by the Inter-American Court. In reading the opinion, consider the scope of the Court's jurisdiction and whether or not the Court is required to answer the question or questions submitted to it.

"Other Treaties" Subject to the Consultative Jurisdiction of the Court (Art. 64 American Convention on Human Rights), Advisory Opinion OC-1/82 of September 24, 1982, 1 Inter-Am. Ct. H.R. (Ser. A) (1982).

1. The Government of Peru, by note received April 28, 1982, requested the instant advisory opinion of the Inter-American Court of Human Rights.

2. By notes dated April 28, 1982, the Secretary, in accordance with a decision of the Court, acting pursuant to Article 52 of its Rules of Procedure, requested observations from all the Member States of the Organization of American States as well as, through the Secretary General, from all of the organs referred to in Chapter X of the Charter of the OAS.

3. The President of the Court fixed August 15, 1982 as the time-limit for the submission of written observations or other relevant documents.

4. Responses to the Secretary's request were received from the following States: Costa Rica, Dominica, Dominican Republic, Ecuador, St. Vincent and the Grenadines 2 and Uruguay. In addition, the following OAS organs responded: the General Secretariat, the Inter-American Commission on Human Rights, the Inter-American Juridical Committee, the Pan American Institute of Geography and History and the Permanent Council. The majority of the res-ponses included substantive observations on the issues raised in the advisory opinion.

Furthermore, the following organizations offered their points of view on the request as amici curiae: the Inter-American Institute of Human Rights, the International Human Rights Law Group, the International League for Human Rights and the Lawyers Committee for International Human Rights, and the Urban Morgan Institute for Human Rights of the University of Cincinnati College of Law. . . .

STATEMENT OF THE ISSUES

8. The Government of Peru submitted the following question to the Court concerning Article 64 of the American Convention on Human Rights. . . :

How should the phrase "or of other treaties concerning the protection of human rights in the American states" be interpreted? With respect to this matter, the Government of Peru requests that the opinion cover the following specific questions:
Does this aforementioned phrase refer to and include:
a) Only treaties adopted within the framework or under the auspices of the inter-American system? or
b) The treaties concluded solely among the American states, that is, is the reference limited to treaties in which only American states are parties? or 3
c) All treaties in which one or more American states are parties?"

9. . . . .

10. A reading of the request indicates that the Government of Peru has in effect formulated one question with three possible answers. The main issue consists of defining which treaties may be interpreted by this Court in application of the powers granted it by Article 64 of the Convention. The request requires the Court to

determine the limits of its advisory jurisdiction which are not clearly spelled out in Article 64 of the Convention. In analyzing and answering the question presented, the Court will have to determine which international treaties concerning the protection of human rights it has the power to interpret under Article 64 (1), put more precisely, it will have to establish which of the human rights treaties must, a priori, be deemed to be excluded from the Court's advisory jurisdiction.

11. A direct answer to the issue presented implies an analysis of the differences between bilateral and multilateral treaties, as well as between both those adopted within and outside the inter-American system; between those treaties in which only Member States of the system are Parties and those in which Member States of the system are Parties together with non-Member States; as well between treaties in which American States are not, or can not be, Parties. In dealing with each of these categories, the Court must also distinguish between treaties whose principal purpose is the protection of human rights and those which, although they have another purpose, include human rights provisions. Once these distinctions are made, the Court will have to determine which of these treaties it is empowered to interpret.

12. The instant request for an advisory opinion is attributable to the fact that the Convention does not expressly define the precise limits of the Court's advisory jurisdiction. Therefore, before embarking upon an analysis of the phrase "other treaties concerning the protection of human rights in the American states," the Court must determine the scope of its advisory jurisdiction under Article 64 of the Convention.

13. By its terms, Article 64 imposes on the authority of the Court certain generic limits, which provide the framework applicable to the interpretation of the aforementioned treaties. The instant request requires the Court to determine whether, given the general object of the Convention and the jurisdiction it assigns to the Court, it is necessary to clarify further the meaning of Article 64.

II GENERAL FRAMEWORK OF THE ISSUES PRESENTED

14. Article 64 of the Convention confers on this Court an advisory jurisdiction that is more extensive than that enjoyed by any international tribunal in existence today. All the organs of the OAS listed in Chapter X of the Charter of the Organization and every OAS Member State, whether a party to the Convention or not, are empowered to seek advisory opinions. The Court's advisory jurisdiction is not limited only to the Convention, but extends to other treaties concerning the protection of human rights in the American States. In principle, no part or aspect of these instruments is excluded from the scope of its advisory jurisdiction. Finally, all OAS Member States have the right to request advisory opinions on the compatibility of any of their domestic laws with the aforementioned international instruments.

15. The broad scope of Article 64 of the Convention contrasts with the advisory jurisdiction of other international tribunals. For example, Article 96 of the UN Charter, while authorizing the International Court of Justice to render advisory opinions on any legal question, permits only the General Assembly and the Security Council or, under certain conditions, other organs and specialized agencies of the United Nations to request such opinions. It does not, however, give the Member States of the UN standing to seek advisory opinions.

16. As far as concerns the international protection of human rights, Protocol No. 2 to the (European) Convention for the Protection of Human Rights and Fundamental Freedoms confers on the European Court advisory jurisdiction, but restricts it severely. Only the Committee of Ministers may request an opinion, and the opinion may deal only with legal questions concerning the interpretation of the Convention and its Protocols. Furthermore, the Protocol excludes from the advisory jurisdiction of that tribunal the interpretation of any question relating to the content or scope of the rights or freedoms defined in the instruments, or any other question which the European Commission on Human Rights, the European Court, or the Committee of Ministers might have to consider in consequence of any proceedings that could be instituted in accordance with the Convention. . . .

18. The broad scope of the language in which Article 64 of the Convention is formulated cannot be taken to mean that there are no limits to the advisory jurisdiction of the Court. With regard to the subject matter of a request, and, in particular, as far as concerns treaties which the Court is empowered to interpret, there are certain limits of a general character implicit in the terms of Article 64, viewed in its context and taking into account the object and purpose of the treaty.

19. A first group of limitations derives from the fact that the Court is a judicial institution of the inter-American system. The Court notes, in this connection, that it is precisely its advisory jurisdiction which gives the Court a special place not only within the framework of the Convention but also within the system as a whole. This conclusion finds support, *ratione materiae*, in the fact that the Convention confers on the Court jurisdiction to render advisory opinions interpreting international treaties other than the Convention itself and, *ratione personae*, in the further fact that the right to seek an opinion extends not only to all organs mentioned in Chapter X of the OAS Charter, but also to all OAS Member States, whether or not they are Parties to the Convention.

20. Certain restrictions follow from the Court's status as an inter-American juridical institution. This status does not, however, necessarily limit its advisory jurisdiction to international instruments adopted within the inter-American system, if only because various OAS organs are often called upon to apply treaties which have an extra regional application.

21. It is implicit in the first group of limitations that the Court can exercise neither its contentious nor advisory jurisdiction to establish the scope of international agreements, whatever be their character, concluded by non-Member States of the inter-American system, or to interpret legal provisions governing the structure or operation of international organs or institutions not belonging to that system. On the other hand, the Court has the power to interpret any treaty as long as it is directly related to the protection of human rights in a Member State of the inter-American system.

22. Other limitations derive from the general function of the Court within the system established by the Convention and, particularly, from the purpose that the advisory jurisdiction is designed to perform. The Court is, first and foremost, an autonomous judicial institution with jurisdiction both to decide any contentious case concerning the interpretation and application of the Convention as well as

to ensure to the victim of a violation of the rights or freedoms guaranteed by the Convention the protection of those rights. (Convention, Arts. 62 and 63 and Statute of the Court, Art.1) Because of the binding character of its decisions in contentious cases (Convention, Art. 68), the Court also is the Convention organ having the broadest enforcement powers designed to ensure the effective application of the Convention.

23. The line which divides the advisory jurisdiction from the contentious jurisdiction of international tribunals has often been the subject of heated debate. On the international law plane, States have voiced reservations and at times even opposition to the exercise of the advisory jurisdiction in certain specific cases on the ground that it served as a method for evading the application of the principle requiring the consent of all States Parties to a legal dispute before judicial proceedings to adjudicate it may be instituted. In the most recent instances in which those objections were raised to advisory opinions that were requested under the Charter of the United Nations, the International Court of Justice decided, for a variety of reasons, to render the opinions not withstanding the above- mentioned objections. (See *Interpretation of Peace Treaties*, 1950 I.C.J. 65; *South-West Africa, International Status of*, 1950 I.C.J.128; *Certain Expenses of the United Nations*, 1962 I.C.J. 151; *Legal Consequences for States of the Continued Presence of South Africa in Namibia (South West Africa) notwithstanding Security Council Resolution 276 (1970)*, 1971 I.C.J. 16.)

24. Special problems arise in the human rights area. Since it is the purpose of human rights treaties to guarantee the enjoyment of individual human beings of those rights and freedoms rather than to establish reciprocal relations between States, the fear has been expressed that the exercise of the Court's advisory jurisdiction might weaken its contentious jurisdiction or worse still, that it might undermine the purpose of the latter, thus changing the system of protection provided for in the Convention to the detriment of the victim. That is, concern has been expressed that the Court's advisory jurisdiction might be invoked by States for the specific purpose of impairing the effectiveness of the proceedings in a case being dealt with by the Commission "to avoid having to accept the contentious jurisdiction of the Court and the binding character of the Court's decision" (C. Dunshee de Abranches, *La Corte Interamericana de Derechos Humanos*, in LA CONVENCIÓN AMERICANA DE DERECHOS HUMANOS 117 (OEA, 1980), thus interfering with the proper functioning of the Convention and adversely affecting the interests of the victim.

25. The advisory jurisdiction of the Court is closely related to the purposes of the Convention. This jurisdiction is intended to assist the American States in fulfilling their international human rights obligations and to assist the different organs of the inter-American system to carry out the functions assigned to them in this field. It is obvious that any request for an advisory opinion which has another purpose would weaken the system established by the Convention and would distort the advisory jurisdiction of the Court.

26. The above-mentioned considerations point to a second group of limitations which derive both from the context in which the Court was granted advisory jurisdiction and from the object and purpose of the Convention. The Convention

does not, however, delimit the full scope of the Court's advisory jurisdiction. It is here that the American and European systems for the protection of human rights differ, because Protocol No. 2 of the European Convention (Article 1 (2)) expressly excludes certain subjects, already referred to in paragraph 16, from the advisory jurisdiction of the European Court.

27. By contrast, Article 64 of the Convention does not expressly exclude any matter concerning the protection of human rights in the American States. This makes it necessary for the Court to establish the general limits on a case-by-case basis, which is also the approach adopted by general international law applicable to this problem.

28. The Court consequently holds, consistent with the jurisprudence of the International Court of Justice, that its advisory jurisdiction is permissive in character in the sense that it empowers the Court to decide whether the circumstances of a request for an advisory opinion justify a decision rejecting the request. (See *Interpretation of Peace Treaties*, 1950 I.C.J. 65.)

29. The broad terms in which Article 64 of the Convention is drafted and the fact that the Rules of Procedure of the Court state that, whenever appropriate, the procedure in advisory opinions should be guided by the rules which apply to contentious cases, clearly demonstrate that the Court enjoys an important power of appreciation enabling it to weigh the circumstances of each case, bearing in mind the generic limits established by the Convention for the Court's advisory jurisdiction.

30. This broad power of appreciation should not be confused, however, with unfettered discretion to grant or deny a request for an advisory opinion. The Court must have compelling reasons founded in the conviction that the request exceeds the limits of its advisory jurisdiction under the Convention before it may refrain from complying with a request for an opinion. Moreover, any decision by the Court declining to render an advisory opinion must conform to the provisions of Article 66 of the Convention, which require that reasons be given for the decision.

31. The aforementioned considerations compel the following conclusions about the limitations applicable to the Court's advisory jurisdiction. The first group of limitations derives from the fact that the Court, in exercising its advisory jurisdiction, may only consider the interpretation of treaties in which the protection of human rights in a Member State of the inter-American system is directly involved. The second group of limitations is related to the inadmissibility of any request for an advisory opinion which is likely to undermine the Court's contentious jurisdiction or, in general, to weaken or alter the system established by the Convention, in a manner that would impair the rights of potential victims of human rights violations. Finally, the Court has to consider the circumstances of each individual case and if, for compelling reasons, it decides to decline to render an opinion lest it exceed the aforementioned limitations and distort its advisory jurisdiction, it must do so by means of an opinion, containing the reasons for its refusal to comply with the request.

III TREATIES SUBJECT TO ADVISORY OPINIONS

32. In the light of these general considerations, the Court can now turn to the specific question presented by the request of the Government of Peru. It seeks to

ascertain which treaties fall within the scope of the Court's advisory jurisdiction, which States must be Parties to these treaties, and, to some extent, on the origin of these treaties. According to the Peruvian request, the narrowest interpretation would lead to the conclusion that only those treaties adopted within the framework or under the auspices of the inter-American system are deemed to be within the scope of Article 64 of the Convention. By contrast, the broadest interpretation would include within the Court's advisory jurisdiction any treaty concerning the protection of human rights in which one or more American States are Parties.

33. In interpreting Article 64, the Court will resort to traditional international law methods, relying both on general and supplementary rules of interpretation, which find expression in Articles 31 and 32 of the Vienna Convention on the Law of Treaties.

34. Neither the request of the Peruvian Government nor the Convention itself distinguishes between multilateral and bilateral treaties, nor between treaties whose main purpose is the protection of human rights and those treaties which, though they may have some other principal object, contain provisions regarding human rights, such as, for example, the Charter of the OAS. The Court considers that the answers to the questions posed in paragraph 32 are applicable to all of these treaties since the basic problem consists of determining what international obligations the American States have assumed are subject to interpretation by means of an advisory opinion. The Court, therefore, does not consider that the determining factor is the bilateral or multilateral nature of the treaty; equally irrelevant is the source of the obligation or the treaty's main purpose.

35. The meaning of the phrase "American states" is not defined in Article 64 of the Convention and the Peruvian request does not attempt to explain it. It is the opinion of the Court that, according to the ordinary meaning to be given to the terms of the treaty in their context, the phrase refers to all those States which may ratify or adhere to the Convention, in accordance with its Article 74, i.e., to Member States of the OAS.

36. The issues raised by the Government of Peru lead to the following question, which must be answered consistent with Article 64 and in light of the object and purpose of the treaty: Is it the purpose of the Convention to bar, *a priori*, an advisory opinion of the Court regarding the international human rights obligations assumed by American States simply because the source of such obligations is a treaty concluded outside the Inter-American system, or because non-American States are also Parties to it?

37. The text of Article 64 of the Convention does not compel the conclusion that it is to be restrictively interpreted. In paragraphs 14 through 17, the Court has explained the broad scope of its advisory jurisdiction. The ordinary meaning of the text of Article 64 therefore does not permit the Court to rule that certain international treaties were meant to be excluded from its scope simply because non-American States are or may become Parties to them. In fact, the only restriction to the Court's jurisdiction to be found in Article 64 is that it speaks of international agreements concerning the protection of human rights in the American States. The provisions of Article 64 do not require that the agreements be treaties between Ameri-

can States, nor that they be regional in character, nor that they have been adopted within the framework of the inter-American system. Since a restrictive purpose was not expressly articulated, it cannot be presumed to exist.

38. The distinction implicit in Article 64 of the Convention alludes rather to a question of a geographical-political character. Put more precisely, it is more important to determine which State is affected by the obligations whose character or scope the Court is to interpret than the source of these obligations. It follows therefrom, that, if the principal purpose of a request for an advisory opinion relates to the implementation or scope of international obligations assumed by a Member State of the inter-American system, the Court has jurisdiction to render the opinion. By the same token, the Court lacks that jurisdiction if the principal purpose of the request relates to the scope or implementation of international obligations assumed by States not members of the inter-American system. This distinction demonstrates once again the need to approach the issue presented on a case-by-case basis.

39. The latter conclusion gains special importance given the language of Article 64 (2) of the Convention, which authorizes the Member States of the OAS to request advisory opinions regarding the compatibility of their domestic laws with treaties concerning the protection of human rights in the American States. This provision enables the Court to perform a service for all of the members of the Inter-American system and is designed to assist them in fulfilling their international human rights obligations. Viewed in this perspective, an American State is no less obligated to abide by an international agreement merely because non-American States are or may become Parties to it. The Court can find no good reasons why an American State should not be able to request an advisory opinion on the compatibility of any of its domestic laws with treaties concerning the protection of human rights which have been adopted outside the framework of the Inter-American system. There are, moreover, practical reasons that suggest that the interpretative function be exercised within the Inter-American system even when dealing with international agreements not adopted within its framework. Regional methods of protection, as has been pointed out, "are more suited for the task and at the same time . . . more readily accepted by the states of this hemisphere . . . ." (C. Sepulveda, *Panorama de los Derechos Humanos*, BOLETÍN DEL INSTITUTO DE INVESTIGACIONES JURÍDICAS 1053, at 1054 (Mexico, 1982).)

40. The nature of the subject matter itself, however, militates against a strict distinction between universalism and regionalism. Mankind's universality and the universality of the rights and freedoms which are entitled to protection form the core of all international protective systems. In this context, it would be improper to make distinctions based on the regional or non-regional character of the international obligations assumed by States, and thus deny the existence of the common core of basic human rights standards. The Preamble of the Convention gives clear expression to that fact when it recognizes that the essential rights of man "are based upon the attributes of the human personality and that they therefore justify international protection in the form of a convention."

41. A certain tendency to integrate the regional and universal systems for the protection of human rights can be perceived in the Convention. The Preamble rec-

ognizes that the principles on which the treaty is based are also proclaimed in the Universal Declaration of Human Rights and that "they have been reaffirmed and refined in other international instruments, worldwide as well as regional in scope." Several provisions of the Convention likewise refer to other international treaties or to international law, without speaking of any regional restrictions. (See, e.g., Convention, Arts. 22, 26, 27 and 29.) Special mention should be made in this connection of Article 29, which contains rules governing the interpretation of the Convention, and which clearly indicates an intention not to restrict the protection of human rights to determinations that depend on the source of the obligations. . . .

42. It is particularly important to emphasize the special relevance that Article 29 (b) has to the instant request. The function that Article 64 of the Convention confers on the Court is an inherent part of the protective system established by the Convention. The Court is of the view, therefore, that to exclude, *a priori*, from its advisory jurisdiction international human rights treaties that are binding on American States would weaken the full guarantee of the rights proclaimed in those treaties and, in turn, conflict with the rules enunciated in Article 29 (b) of the Convention.

43. The need of the regional system to be complemented by the universal finds expression in the practice of the Inter-American Commission on Human Rights and is entirely consistent with the object and purpose of the Convention, the American Declaration and the Statute of the Commission. The Commission has properly invoked in some of its reports and resolutions" other treaties concerning the protection of human rights in the American states, "regardless of their bilateral or multilateral character, or whether they have been adopted within the framework or under the auspices of the inter-American system. This has been true most recently in the following reports of the Commission: the situation of human rights in El Salvador (OEA/Ser.L/V/II.46, doc.23, rev.l, November 17, 1979) at 37–38; the situation of political prisoners in Cuba (OEA/Ser.L/V/II.48, doc.24, December 14, 1979) at 9; the situation of human rights in Argentina (OEA/Ser.L/V/II.49, doc. 19, April 11, 1980) at 24–25; the situation of human rights in Nicaragua (OEA/Ser.L/V/II.53, doc.25, June 30, 1981) at 31; the situation of human rights in Colombia (OEA/Ser.L/V/II.53, doc.22, June 30, 1981) at 56–57; the situation of human rights in Guatemala (OEA/Ser.L/V/II.53, doc.21, rev.2, October 13, 1981) at 16–17; the situation of human rights in Bolivia (OEA/Ser.L/V/II.53, doc.6, rev.2, October 13, 1981) at 20–21; and Case 7481-Acts which occurred in Caracoles (Bolivia), Resolution No. 30/82 (OEA/Ser.L/V/II.55, doc.54, March 8, 1982).

44. This practice of the Commission which is designed to enable it better to discharge the functions assigned to it compels the conclusion that the States themselves have an interest in being able to request an advisory opinion from the Court involving a human rights treaty to which they are parties but which has been adopted outside the framework of the inter-American system. Situations might in fact arise in which the Commission might interpret one of these treaties in a manner deemed to be erroneous by the States concerned, which would then be able to invoke Article 64 to challenge the Commission's interpretations.

45. The Court's interpretation of Article 64, based on the ordinary meaning of its terms viewed in their context and taking into account the object and purpose of the

treaty, is confirmed by the preparatory work of the Convention. It can accordingly be relied upon as a supplementary means of interpretation. (Vienna Convention on the Law of Treaties, Art. 32.)

46. As the Court pointed out in paragraph 17, the evolution of the text which ultimately became Article 64 indicates a marked desire to expand the advisory jurisdiction of the Court. The very fact that it was drafted at a time when the narrowly drawn Article 1 of Protocol No. 2 of the European Convention had already been adopted demonstrates that the drafters of the Convention intended to confer on the Court the most extensive advisory jurisdiction, intentionally departing from the limitations imposed upon the European system.

47. During the initial phase of the drafting of the Convention, the majority of the States were clearly opposed to the notion of making a strict distinction between universalism and regionalism. As a matter of fact, after the International Covenant on Economic, Social and Cultural Rights, the International Covenant on Civil and Political Rights and the Optional Protocol thereto, which were drafted within the framework of the United Nations, were opened for signature, the OAS Council consulted the Member States of the Organization in June 1967 regarding the advisability of continuing the work on an American convention, considering that the UN instruments had been adopted. Ten of the twelve States that replied to the inquiry favored continuing the work on the Convention, it being understood that an effort would be made to draw on the provisions of the UN Covenants. As a result of this poll, the Specialized Inter-American Conference was eventually held in Costa Rica in November 1969. The preparatory work of the Convention consequently demonstrates a tendency to conform the regional system to the universal one, which is evident in the text of the Convention itself.

48. Based on the foregoing analysis, the Court concludes that the very text of Article 64 of the Convention, the object and purpose of the treaty, the rules of interpretation set out in Article 29 of the Convention, the practice of the Commission and the preparatory work all point toward the same result: no good reason exists to hold, in advance and in the abstract, that the Court lacks the power to receive a request for, or to issue, an advisory opinion about a human rights treaty applicable to an American State merely because non-American States are also parties to the treaty or because the treaty has not been adopted within the framework or under the auspices of the inter-American system.

49. A number of submissions addressed to the Court, both by Member States and certain OAS organs, urge a more restrictive interpretation of Article 64. Some of these arguments, already adverted to in paragraph 37, are based on the meaning to be ascribed to the phrase "in the American states." Two other contentions are more substantive in nature. The first is that a broad interpretation would authorize the Court to render opinions affecting States which have nothing to do with the Convention or the Court, and which cannot even be represented before it. As to that issue, the Court has already emphasized that, if a request for an advisory opinion has as its principal purpose the determination of the scope of, or compliance with, international commitments assumed by States outside the inter-American system, the Court is authorized to render a motivated opinion refraining to pass on the is-

sues submitted to it. The mere possibility that the event hypothesized in the above argument might arise, which can after all be dealt with on a case-by-case basis, is hardly a sufficient enough reason for concluding that the Court, *a priori*, lacks the power to render an advisory opinion interpreting the human rights obligations assumed by an American State merely because such obligations originate outside the framework of the Inter-American system.

50. The other argument that has been advanced is that the extension of the limits of the Court's advisory jurisdiction might produce conflicting interpretations emanating from the Court and from those organs outside the inter-American system that might be called upon also to apply and interpret treaties concluded outside of that system. The Court believes that it is here dealing with one of those arguments which proves too much and which, moreover, is less compelling than it appears at first glance. It proves too much because the possibility of conflicting interpretations is a phenomenon 12 common to all those legal systems that have certain courts which are not hierarchically integrated. Such courts have jurisdiction to apply and, consequently, interpret the same body of law. Here it is, therefore, not unusual to find that on certain occasions courts reach conflicting or at the very least different conclusions in interpreting the same rule of law. On the international law plane, for example, because the advisory jurisdiction of the International Court of Justice extends to any legal question, the UN Security Council or the General Assembly might ask the International Court to render an advisory opinion concerning a treaty which, without any doubt, could also be interpreted by this Court under Article 64 of the Convention. Even a restrictive interpretation of Article 64 would not avoid the possibility that this type of conflict might arise.

51. Moreover, the conflicts being anticipated, were they to occur, would not be particularly serious. It must be remembered, in this connection, that the advisory opinions of the Court and those of other international tribunals, because of their advisory character, lack the same binding force that attaches to decisions incontentious cases. (Convention, Art. 68.) This being so, less weight need be given to arguments based on the anticipated effects that the Court's opinions might have in relation to States lacking standing to participate in the advisory proceedings here in question. Viewed in this light, it is obvious that the possibility that the opinions of the Court might conflict with those of other tribunals or organs is of no great practical significance; there are no theoretical obstacles, moreover, that would bar accepting the possibility that such conflicts might arise.

For these reasons, responding to the request of the Government of Peru for an interpretation of the meaning of the phrase "or of other treaties concerning the protection of human rights in the American states," contained in Article 64 of the Convention,

THE COURT IS OF THE OPINION

Firstly: By unanimous vote, that the advisory jurisdiction of the Court can be exercised, in general, with regard to any provision dealing with the protection of human rights set forth in any international treaty applicable in the American States, regardless of whether it be bilateral or multilateral, whatever be the principal purpose of such a treaty, and whether or not non-Member States of the inter-American system are or have the right to become parties there to.

Secondly: By unanimous vote, that, for specific reasons explained in a duly motivated decision, the Court may decline to comply with a request for an advisory opinion if it concludes that, due to the special circumstances of a particular case, to grant the request would exceed the limits of the Court's advisory jurisdiction for the following reasons, inter alia: because the issues raised deal mainly with international obligations assumed by a non-American State or with the structure or operation of international organs or bodies outside the inter-American system; or because granting the request might have the effect of altering or weakening the system established by the Convention in a manner detrimental to the individual human being.

Questions and Comments

1. Based on the provisions of the Convention and on the preceding advisory opinion, what advice would you give a state not a party to the American Convention about its right to ask the court to determine the compatibility of its "hate speech" law with the rights guaranteed by Convention Article 13? How much reliance could the state place on the Court's opinion?

2. Could a state ask for an interpretation of certain rights afforded its nationals contained in a bilateral treaty of friendship, commerce and navigation?

3. Under what circumstances should the Court decline to render an advisory opinion? See: *Compatibility of Draft Legislation with Article 8(2)(H) of the American Convention on Human Rights*, OC-12/91 (Dec. 6).

4. In the preceding case, the Court permitted submissions by amicus curiae: what is its authority to do so? What is the role of OAS member states in general in advisory proceedings?

5. Under Article 64(2) the Court is empowered, at the request of any Member States of the OAS, to render an advisory opinion determining whether the state's domestic laws are compatible with the Convention or other human rights treaties. Which organs of the state can make such a request? Is it only the executive branch, or could a legislative body or domestic court submit a question to the Inter-American Court?

Note on the Advisory Jurisdiction of the European Court of Human Rights and the African Court of Human and Peoples' Rights

The European Court of Human Rights obtained a limited advisory jurisdiction in 1970 with the entry into force of Protocol No. 2 to the Convention, now incorporated into Article 47 of the Convention. Article 47 empowers only the Committee of Ministers to request advisory opinions. The power is limited, moreover, to "legal questions concerning the interpretation of the Convention and the protocols thereto." Convention, art. 47(1). In exercising its advisory jurisdiction, the Court may not interpret "the content or scope of the rights or freedoms" that are guaranteed by the Convention and its Protocols. It may not deal with "any other question which the Court or the Committee of Ministers might have to consider in consequence of any such proceedings as could be instituted in accordance with the

Convention." Convention, art. 47(2). In short, the advisory jurisdiction excludes all questions within the scope of the Court's contentious jurisdiction. For the legislative history of the Court's advisory power, *see* Council of Europe, *Explanatory Reports on the Second to Fifth Protocols to the European Convention for the Protection of Human Rights and Fundamental Freedoms*, Doc. H (71) 11, at 3–18 (1971); Robertson & Merrills, at 315.

On 9 January 2002, the Committee of Ministers, following a recommendation of the Parliamentary Assembly, submitted the first request for an advisory opinion to the European Court of Human Rights. The request asked for a ruling on the "compatibility of the Convention on Human Rights and Fundamental Freedoms of the Commonwealth of Independent States[5] with the European Convention on Human Rights." The Parliamentary Assembly expressed concern that the CIS Convention offered less protection than the ECHR in substance and procedure. An issue of particular concern was that the CIS Convention established a Commission which might be considered "another procedure of international investigation or settlement" within the meaning of ECHR Article 35(2)(b), thus making petitions inadmissible that had previously come before the CIS body. The Parliamentary Assembly referred to "the weakness of the CIS Commission as an institution for the protection of human rights," making clear its desire to exclude it from the scope of Article 35. See Recommendation 1519 (2001). Pursuant to the Court's Rules of Procedure, the Registry informed member states of the request and invited them to submit written comments; ten states chose to participate with six of them asserting that the Court lacked jurisdiction over the matter. On June 2, 2004, the Court decided that the request was outside the scope of its competence. It agreed that the matter was a legal question concerning the interpretation of the Convention, but found that it also concerned an issue that might come before the Court in a contentious case and therefore could not be considered. The decision is reprinted in 25 HRLJ 326 (2004).

The advisory jurisdiction of the African Court is broad. Article 4 of the Protocol reads:

> 1. At the request of a Member State of the OAU, the OAU, any of its organs, or any African organization recognized by the OAU, the Court may provide an opinion on any legal matter relating to the Charter or any relevant human rights instruments, provided the subject matter of the opinion is not related to a matter being examined by the Commission.
> 2. The Court shall give reasons for its advisory opinions provided that every judge shall be entitled to deliver a separate or dissenting opinion.

This article appears to confer broader advisory jurisdiction on the African Court than either of the other regional courts has been given. The Protocol, unlike the American Convention, does not explicitly require AU organs to limit their requests to matters "within their spheres of competence." The organs, however, will still have to function within their mandates under the AU Charter. Note that like the Inter-American Court of Human Rights, the African Court will have the abil-

---

[5] The Commonwealth of Independent States was created in 1991 by several former Soviet Republics. On May 26, 1995 it adopted its Convention on Human Rights and Fundamental Freedoms, referred to in the requested advisory opinion. The Convention entered into force on August 11, 1998.

ity to advise member states on the compatibility of their domestic laws with the Charter without having to address the question in the context of an alleged violation. The states need not have ratified the Protocol to request an advisory opinion. Other aspects of the African Court's advisory jurisdiction are described in the following extract.

A.P. van der Mei, *The Advisory Jurisdiction of the African Court on Human and Peoples' Rights,* 5 Afr. H.R.L.J. 27, 35–41, 45–46 (2005) (footnotes omitted).

The potentially most important difference from the American Convention concerns the inclusion in article 4(1) of African organizations recognized by the AU. It is plain that these include governmental organizations, such as the Economic Community of West African States (ECOWAS) or the Southern African Development Community (SACD). Article 4, however, does not make clear whether non-governmental organizations (NGOs) can be regarded as organizations recognized by the AU. On the one hand, it could be argued that this provision, unlike article 5 on contentious jurisdiction, does not make a distinction between governmental and non-governmental organizations and that the latter therefore have the right to request a legal opinion. On the other hand, one could reason that because NGOs in principle have no direct access to the Court in contentious cases, the (should) have no right to request an opinion, since this would enable them to initiate a disguised contentious case against a member state that has not accepted the Court's jurisdiction in cases brought by private parties. . . .

If the Court indeed were willing to receive requests for advisory opinions from NGOs, it will have to take a position on a number of issues. The first concerns the NGOs that will have standing . . . Secondly, should NGOs' right to request an opinion be limited to issues falling within their mandate, as defined by their statutes or foundational documents? Whatever the proper answer to these two questions may be, it would make sense if the Court would apply the criterion of having obtained observer status with the African Commission. *De facto* this would imply that standing would be limited to NGOs whose objectives and activities are aimed at human rights protection and meet the criteria for observer status. Further, the Court will have to determine whether it will admit in principle any request from NGOs having obtained observer status or whether it will be selective. The Court is not obliged to admit any request and, perhaps depending on the number of NGO requests, the Court could decide to filter these requests and only issue an opinion where the questions raised by the NGOs are novel and significant for human rights law in Africa.

Scope *ratione materiae:* Subject matter of advisory opinions

. . . The substantive scope of the Court's advisory jurisdiction is much broader than that of the African Commission's interpretative power, which is restricted to the Charter. It also exceeds that of the Inter-American Court, which has jurisdiction over the American Convention and 'other treaties concerning the protection of human rights in the American States." . . .[A]rticle 4(1) does not refer to other *treaties* but to human rights *instruments.* . . . Secondly, article 4(1) does not formally require that other treaties should protect human rights *in African states.* . . . The Protocol's objective commands, and the text of article 4(1) leaves room for a broad reading allowing the Court other treaties than 'typical' human rights treaties. . . . The Court can, and when asked it should not hesitate to, interpret any universal, regional or sub-regional instrument, regardless of their purpose, main subject matter and state parties, for as long as the provision in question has 'bearing upon, affects or is in the interest' of human rights protection in Africa.

The above is not to say that the Court can express its view on any issue concerning these instruments. Article 4 contains two limitations. Firstly, the Court can only give an opinion on legal matters. . . . Secondly, article 4(1) expressly denies the Court the power to give an opinion where the subject matter of the request is related to a matter under examination by the Commission.

. . . Particularly during the first years of its existence, the power to deliver advisory opinions could . . . be a means for the Court to make itself known and its influence felt. The Court strengthen its own position by interpreting article 4(1) broadly so as to allow, in particular NGOs and national courts to submit requests for an opinion and by indicating its willingness to interpret any human rights instruments relevant for human rights protection in Africa and to express its view on the compatibility of (proposed) domestic legislation with those instruments.

---

5. The African System

The African Charter on Human and Peoples' Rights, Art. 30, provides for a Commission, established within the institutional framework of the African Union, "to promote human and peoples' rights and ensure their protection in Africa." The Commission is composed of eleven members, elected by the AU's Assembly of Heads of States and Governments from a list of names presented by the States Parties. The members of the Commission are elected to six-year terms and serve in their individual capacities rather than as government representatives. The Commission's amended Rules of Procedure, adopted in July 1996, are reprinted in the Documentary Supplement and in 8 AFR. J. INT'L & COMP. L. 978 (1996).

The Commission meets twice a year and presents an annual activity report to the AU Summit. The African Commission's rules allow it to hold sessions anywhere and to convene extraordinary as well as regular sessions; however, the Commission rarely meets outside its headquarters in Banjul, The Gambia. Its meetings have become an increasingly popular forum for addressing human rights issues in Africa. At its May 2006 session, delegates from thirty-two States Parties, nineteen national human rights institutions, six international organizations and one hundred and twenty eight African and International NGOs attended, for a total of four hundred and nineteen participants. However, the ACHPR has barely thirty days in a year to reflect on issues relating to reports, communications and other agenda items. These constraints are critical to its efficiency.

The Commission has promotional and protective functions. Its promotional mandate is very broad and includes the power to undertake studies, convene conferences and workshops, initiate publication programs, disseminate information and collaborate with national and local institutions concerned with human and peoples' rights. As part of this promotional effort, the Commission may "give its views or make recommendation to Governments." Art. 45(1)(a). This power enables the Commission to bring to the attention of individual governments "problem areas" revealed by its studies as well as by its review of states' implementation reports. It has adopted a system of "country rapporteurs" and started to undertake visits to individual countries (including, inter alia, Nigeria, Sudan, Burundi, Rwanda and Mauritania). The Commission also has appointed special or "thematic" rapporteurs for summary and extra-judicial executions, prisons and conditions of detention, and the rights of women. *See* F. Viljoen, *State Reporting under the African Charter on Human and Peoples' Rights: A Boost from the South*, 44 J. AFR. L. 110 (2000). J. Harrington, *Special Rapporteurs of the African Commission on Human and Peoples' Rights*, 1 AFR. HUM. RTS. J. 247 (2001).

The Commission has a type of advisory jurisdiction that allows it to "interpret all the provisions of the present Charter" when so requested by a State Party, an institution of the OAU or an African Organization recognized by the OAU. Art. 45(3). The Commission is also empowered "to formulate and lay down, principles and rules aimed at solving legal problems relating to human and peoples' rights and fundamental freedoms upon which African Governments may base their legislations." Art. 45(1)(b). The Commission thus may further develop regional human rights standards by preparing draft legislation and proposing legal solutions to disputes. In fulfilling these interpretive and promotional functions, as well as in its petition procedures, the Commission may draw upon the full range of international law on human and peoples' rights. Article 60 lists as sources of "inspiration": the UN and OAU Charters, the Universal Declaration of Human Rights, African instruments on human and peoples' rights and "other instruments adopted by the United Nations and by African countries in the field of human and peoples' rights as well as . . . the provisions of various instruments adopted within the Specialized Agencies of the United Nations of which the parties to the present Charter are members." Article 61 adds that the Commission may take into consideration, "as subsidiary measures to determine the principles of law," various other human rights agreements to which the Member States of the OAU are parties, together with "African practices consistent with international norms on human and peoples' rights, customs generally accepted as law, general principles of law recognized by African States as well as legal precedents and doctrine." This broad mandate permits the African Commission to identify and apply the law most favorable to the rights of individuals and groups in Africa.

A. Consideration of State Reports

The African Commission has developed a periodic reporting system similar to those established by UN human rights treaties and treaty bodies. The Commission determines the contents of the report, invites states to appear for discussion, and addresses observations to reporting states following consideration of the reports. The Commission may conclude that a report does not contain adequate information and it may request the state to furnish the information by a specific date. Unlike the procedure followed by UN treaty bodies, the African Commission does not publish its observations on the states' reports in its annual Activity Report.

The reporting system cannot be considered a success, although compliance with the requirement has slowly improved. As of June 2006, sixteen states had not submitted any reports and only thirteen states were up to date in their reporting. Given the Commission's limited resources and meeting time, the intermittent filing of reports had the beneficial outcome of giving the African Commission more time to focus on individual communications and situations of gross and systematic violations.

B. Complaint Procedures

The individual communications mechanism set forth in the Charter is relatively limited, but as interpreted and applied by the Commission, it has increasingly come to approximate the individual petition systems of the European and American Conventions. Article 58 provides that "special cases which reveal the existence of serious or massive violations of human and peoples' rights" must be referred by the Commission to the Assembly, which "may then request the Commission to undertake an in-depth study of these cases." When the Commission has followed this route, the Assembly has failed to respond, but the Commission has nevertheless made findings that such massive violations have occurred. Today, the Commission does not seem to refer many situations to the Assembly in terms of Article 58.

The African Charter establishes an inter-state complaint mechanism that provides for two distinct methods of dispute resolution. The first permits a State Party which believes that another State Party has violated the Charter to bring the matter to that state's attention in a formal communication which is also sent to the Commission. Art. 47. The respondent state should reply within three months. If the parties do not settle the matter to their satisfaction, either state may submit the matter to the Commission within three months from the date on which the original communication is received by the respondent state. Art. 48; revised Rules 91–92.

The second option is set out in Article 49 of the Charter. It permits a State Party to file an interstate complaint directly with the Commission. Whether an interstate complaint is brought to the Commission pursuant to Article 48 or 49, the procedures followed are the same. Even inter-state cases must satisfy the requirement that "all local remedies, if they exist, have been exhausted, unless it is obvious to the Commission that the procedure of achieving these remedies would be unduly prolonged." Art. 50. If the admissibility requirement is met, the Commission embarks on a fact-finding process to obtain all information relevant to the case, looking both to the states involved and to "other sources." Art. 52. It may also hold hearings and accept written and oral submissions. If an amicable solution "based on the respect of human and peoples' rights" is not reached, the Commission prepares a report stating the facts, its findings and whatever recommendations it deems useful. Arts. 52, 53. The Commission transmits the report to the states concerned and the AU's Assembly of Heads of State and Government.

The only inter-state complaint to date was submitted in February 1999 by the Democratic Republic of the Congo, alleging that Burundi, Uganda and Rwanda had committed serious human rights abuses on Congolese territory. Extracts from the Commission's decision in the case are reprinted in Chapter VI.

C. The Role of Non-Governmental Organizations (NGOs)

In the African system, NGOs have a special relationship with the Commission. Some 350 African and non-African NGO's have official observer status with the African Commission. The Commission's Rules of Procedure allow the NGOs to submit items for inclusion in the Commission's agenda and requires that the groups be informed of the provisional agenda of each session. According to rule 72, the Commission may invite any organization or persons capable of enlightening it to participate in its deliberations without voting rights. NGOs with observer status may appoint representatives to participate in public sessions of the Commission and its subsidiary bodies.

NGO participation has strengthened the African Commission's role in promoting human rights. During its 17th session, held in Togo, three members of the Commission met with the President of Togo and his aides, discussing questions of enhanced democracy, human rights, amnesty, bye-elections and the establishment of more constitutional structures. The basis of the discussion was a document prepared by a Togolese NGO. African Commission sessions often include active NGO and government participation. NGO interventions have focused on human rights violations in the region, including in Senegal, Guinea-Bissau, Djibouti, Nigeria and Burundi.[6] The interventions can be effective; after severe criticism in public of the special rapporteur on summary and extra-judicial executions and of the independence and impartiality of some members of the Commission, the Commission amended its rules of procedure to strengthen standards to avoid conflicts of interest.

NGOs are often instrumental in bringing cases to the Commission, because the system permits an *actio popularis*; they sometimes submit shadow reports, propose agenda items at the outset of Commission sessions, and provide logistical and other support to the Commission, for example by placing interns at the Commission and providing support to the special rapporteurs and missions of the Commission. NGOs often organize special NGO workshops just prior to Commission sessions and participate actively in the public sessions of the Commission. NGOs also collaborate with the Commission in developing normative resolutions and new protocols to the African Charter. While all of this work has had positive impacts on the system, enhancing the work of the Commission and helping to build African NGOs, it should be noted that some states have reacted negatively to what they perceive as the Commission's undue reliance on NGO submissions. See, in particular, the state responses of Ethiopia and Zimbabwe to Commission decisions in the 20th Annual Activity Report.

---

6 Tenth Annual Activity Report of the African Commission on Human and Peoples' Rights 1996/97 at 8.

D. Budgetary, Political and Legal Problems

Under Article 41 of the African Charter, the Commission of the African Union is responsible for meeting the costs of the African Commission's operations, including the provision of staff, financial resources and services. However, the work of the Secretariat of the African Commission continues to be severely compromised due to insufficient funding. As a result of lack of financial support from the AU, the Commission has become dependant on resources from outside the region. The Danish Human Rights Institute, the Canadian NGO Rights and Democracy, the Danish International Development Agency, and the UN Office of the High Commissioner for Human Rights have all provided resources to enable the Commission to function. While some states have criticized the Commission for its reliance on outside funding, the AU has failed to increase the Commission's budget. As of 2006, the Commission has only two legal officers paid by the AU. Five other staff members have been paid from extra budgetary resources scheduled to terminate at the end of 2006.

Lack of funding is not the only sign of AU disagreement with some aspects of the Commission's human rights work. The Assembly of Heads of State and Government delayed publication of the 19th Activity Report of the African Commission due to objections by several states about the inclusion of decisions taken against them without the state's responsive comments, and publication of the Commission's decisions before approval by the AU Heads of State. The 19th report was finally adopted by decision Assembly/AU/DEC.101(VI) during the 6th Ordinary Session of the Assembly of Heads of State and Government of the African Union (23rd to 24th January 2006), after having been considered by the Executive Council. The Executive Council passed resolution no EX.CL/Dec.257 (VIII) *Decision on the 19th Activity Report of the African Commission on Human and Peoples' Rights* in which it requested:

1. the Commission to exclude the resolution on human rights situation in Ethiopia, Eritrea, Zimbabwe, Uganda and the Sudan from the annexes to its 19th Activity Report;

2. the concerned member states to make available to the Commission, within three months since the adoption of the Council's decision, their views on the resolutions, and

3. the Commission to ensure that in future, it enlists the responses of all States parties to its Resolutions and Decisions before submitting them to the Executive Council and/or the Assembly for consideration.

The Council agreed and in its *Decision on the 19th Activity Report of the African Commission on Human and Peoples' Rights* excluded the resolutions against the objecting countries from the activity report of the Commission and gave the concerned governments three months to submit a report regarding the Commission's resolution for the latter's consideration. A similar crisis occurred with the 20th report, after further complaints by Ethiopia and Zimbabwe. A resolution on Zimbabwe was withdrawn in order for the publication to go forward.

At a brainstorming session in May 2006, other problems with the system were identified. It was noted that some current Members of the ACHPR hold official positions in their respective State, thereby creating a perception of lack of independence.

The following extract indicates the scope of recent activities of the African Commission on Human and Peoples' Rights. Consider in each instance what provision in the Charter gives legal authority for the activity undertaken.

20th Activity Report of the African Commission on Human and Peoples' Rights, *(Jan–June 2006),*

1. The 20th Activity Report covers the period from January to June 2006. . . .

2. Since the adoption of the 19th Activity Report in January 2006, the African Commission held a Session, the 39th Ordinary Session, which was held in Banjul, The Gambia, from the 11th to 25th May 2006. . . .

3. From 7th to 8th May 2006, the African Commission held a two day Preparatory Meeting during which they discussed their contributions towards the Brainstorming Meeting on the African Commission organized by the African Union and held from 9th to 10th May 2006 in Banjul, The Gambia. The Brainstorming Meeting discussed the functioning of the African Commission and its relationship with the Organs of the African Union and its cooperating partners and came up with recommendations that were addressed to various stakeholders.

4. . . . . .

5. During the 39th Ordinary Session the African Commission renewed and extended the mandate of the Special Rapporteur on Refugees, Asylum Seekers and Internally Displaced Persons in Africa for a period of two years. The mandate was extended to cover migration issues. . . .

10. During its 39th Ordinary Session, the African Commission considered the Periodic Reports of the following countries and adopted the relevant concluding observations and recommendations: the Republic of Cameroon, the Central African Republic, the Republic of the Libyan Arab Jamahiriya. The Commission expressed satisfaction with the discussions held with the delegations of these States. The Republic Rwanda, Uganda and Zambia presented their Periodic reports, which will be examined during the 40th ordinary session of the Commission.

11. The Initial Report of the Republic of Seychelles was considered in the absence of the State since the State of Seychelles did not send a representative to the Session. The Initial Report of the Republic of Seychelles was received by the Secretariat of the Commission on 21st June 2004 and was scheduled for consideration at the 36th, 37th and 38th Ordinary Session. However, this Report was not considered due to the absence of the Republic of Seychelles to present the Report, despite several reminders.

12. During its 39th Ordinary Session, the African Commission adopted the following Reports:

a) *Report on the fact finding mission to the* Republic of Togo;
b) *Reports on the missions of the Special Rapporteur on Women's Rights in Africa to the Democratic Republic of Congo.*

13. Depending on the availability of funds, the African Commission plans to organise seminars on the following topics in 2007:

- Terrorism and Human Rights in Africa;
- Islam and Human Rights;
- Contemporary Form of slavery;
- Refugees and internally displaced persons in Africa

14. In accordance with decision Assembly/AU/DEC.101(VI) of the 6th ordinary session of the Assembly of Heads of State and Government of the African Union, the African Commission received written responses from Ethiopia, Uganda, Sudan and Zimbabwe on the resolutions concerning the Human Rights situation in their countries adopted by the African Commission at its 38th Ordinary Session. The full text of the Resolutions and the responses from the States of Ethiopia, Uganda, Sudan and Zimbabwe are attached as *Annex 3* of this Report. During its 39th Ordinary Session, the African Commission granted audiences to the States of Ethiopia Uganda, and Zimbabwe who requested to make oral presentations and seek clarifications on the said Resolutions.

15. During the Session, the African Commission discussed co-operation with the National Human Rights Institutions and Non Governmental Organisations. The African Commission urged State Parties that are yet to establish National Human Rights Institutions to do so and build the capacity of existing ones, in accordance with the Paris Principles and its own resolution on these Institutions.

16. During the 39th Ordinary Session, the African Commission granted Observer Status to 7 (seven) Non Governmental Organisations:

- Prison fellowship of Ethiopia (Ethiopia)
- Institut Panos de l'Afrique de l'Ouest (Senegal)
- WITNESS (USA)
- Foundation for Women's Health Research and Development (United Kingdom)
- Citizens for a Better Environment (Zambia)
- Cameroon Environmental Protection Association (Cameroon)
- Stop Poverty (Mauritania)

17. This brings the number of NGOs with Observer Status to the Commission 349 as of May 2006.

SECTION III Promotion Activities

Promotion Activities of the Chairperson and Members of the African Commission during the Intersession

21. In their capacities as Members of the Bureau of the African Commission, The Chairperson, Commissioner Salamata Sawadogo and the Vice Chairperson, Commissioner El-Hassan supervised the operations of the African Commission during the Intersession. The Chairperson, Commissioner Sawadogo sent two appeals to the Heads of States of Botswana and Zimbabwe relating to human rights.

22. Due to lack of funds, the Members of the African Commission were unable to conduct most of the missions scheduled for the period covered by this Report. Nev-

ertheless, some promotion activities were undertaken, and workshops and seminars attended, at the invitation of the Partners of the African Commission.

[The report lists all of the speeches, seminars and workshops conducted by members of the Commission.]

Activities of the Special Mechanisms during the Intersession

[The report details the activities of the following special rapporteurs appointed by the Commission]:

30. In her capacity as Special Rapporteur on the Rights of Women in Africa, Commissioner Melo undertook the [additional] activities. . . .

31 As Special Rapporteur for Refugees, Asylum Seekers and Internally Displaced Persons in Africa, Commissioner Nyanduga, said that the situation of refugees in Africa is improving in some areas with the consolidation of peace in post-conflict situations such as, in South of Sudan and Burundi. Fighting between factions in Somalia is paralyzing the Transition Institutions, affecting security and the efforts at stabilizing the situation as well as the return of refugees. . . .

32. In her capacity as Special Rapporteur on the Freedom of Expression in Africa, Commissioner Pansy Tlakula received information concerning arrests and detentions of journalists, administrators and staff of certain Radio Stations and Newspapers in some African countries. . . .

33. In her capacity as Special Rapporteur on Human Rights Defenders in Africa, Commissioner Reine Alapini-Gansou reported on the situation of these men and women who, in spite of the risks they run, continue to denounce the violations of human rights which they have witnessed with the hope of building a world of greater justice and respect for fundamental freedoms. The Rapporteur pointed out that these past few months have been marked by an upsurge of threats and harassment against human rights defenders, and by the increasing use of the judicial system to sanction their activities. She called on the NGOs to work hand in hand with their Governments in order to eliminate the tensions and climate of suspicion. The Rapporteur also launched an appeal to the Member States to engage in constructive dialogue and to guarantee a conducive environment for the work of the human rights defenders in the Continent. The Rapporteur carried out various activities during the intersession period. . . .

34. In his capacity as Special Rapporteur on Prisons and Conditions of Detention in Africa, Commissioner Mumba Malila presented a brief Report on prisons and conditions of detention in Africa. He urged the Member States to strengthen the measures guaranteeing good detention conditions in the prisons as well as in Police cells.

35. The Working Group on Economic, Social and Cultural Rights reported that the Group had appointed two experts to prepare the draft guidelines on the implementation of the economic, social and cultural rights in Africa. However, considering that the two experts have not yet finalized the drafting of the guidelines, the Working Group intends to hold at least one meeting to examine the contents of the last version of the guidelines before submitting it to the African Commission for adoption at its next session.

36. The Working Group on Indigenous Populations/Communities in Africa presented its Report describing the activities carried out in relation to the missions to countries, research and information visits, conferences, the publication and dissemination of the Report of the Working Group, the finalization of the Reports adopted during the 38th Ordinary Session of the African Commission, the preparation of a data base, the information index card (booklet), the bulletin and preparation for a regional seminar in September 2006. The Working Group also outlined the activities that are to be carried out in the next six months.

37. The Working Group on the Death Penalty submitted a report stating that during the intersession the Working Group had not been able to meet not only for financial reasons but also because the consultations for the appointment of the independent experts have not yet been concluded. The process of identifying the five experts to be recommended to the Commission for appointment is concluded. Work on improving the draft document on the death penalty in Africa is on course. Considering the controversy surrounding the subject of death penalty, as is the case everywhere else in the world, the Working Group tried to get experts representing various cultures, religions and legal systems in the Continent. The Working Group also intends to pursue its efforts in collecting contributions and ideas from partners, from the public and from as many sources as possible.

38. The Working Group on Specific Issues relating to the work of the African Commission held a meeting in April 2006 in Pretoria, South Africa at which the following issues were discussed:

- The Review of the Rules and Procedures of the African commission;
- The Relationship between the African Commission and the African Court on Human and Peoples' Rights

39. The Working Group on the implementation of the Robben Island Guidelines was not able to carry out any activities during the intersession period due to lack of funds. It is important to point out that all the activities undertaken by the Working Group had been funded by the Association for the Prevention of Torture (APT) which is a member of the Working Group but which is currently in financial difficulties. Commissioner Monageng, Chairperson of the Working Group had, thus, launched an appeal to the Secretariat to set up efforts for the acquisition of funds and to all the Organizations concerned present at the 39th Ordinary Session to help support the work of the Working Group in this regard.

SECTION IV Protection Activities

40. During its 39th Ordinary Session, the African Commission considered fifty nine (59) Communications three (3) of which were for review, eight (8) were decisions on seizure, thirty one (31) were decisions on admissibility and seventeen (17) were decisions on the merits. Besides, after consideration, it decided to strike off two Communications from its register. The list of Communications figures in *Annex 4* of this Report. For various reasons, the Commission deferred consideration of the other Communications to the 40th Ordinary Session.

Note on the Merged African Court of Human and Peoples Rights and the African Court of Justice

Possibly the most far-reaching development in the African regional human rights system since the Charter itself was the adoption in June 1998 of an Additional Protocol to the Charter on the establishment of an African Court on Human and Peoples' Rights. *See* OAU/LEG/AFCHPR/Prot.III, reprinted at 12 *Afr. J. Int'l & Comp. L.* 187 (2000). In terms of structure and jurisdiction, the Human Rights Court was inspired by, and modeled after, those in the European and American regional human rights systems. The Protocol came into force in 2004 and the judges were sworn in on July 2, 2006. The Court is based in Arusha, Tanzania, and will utilize the facilities developed for the International Criminal Tribunal for Rwanda.

There are some unique features of the African Court. The Protocol explicitly requires diversity in legal traditions and gender in nomination and election of judges. It also provides that after hearing a case, the Court must issue its judgment within ninety days. One weakness is in the enforcement of judgments. The AU Council of Ministers is obligated to monitor the execution of court decisions, but it has no enforcement power.

With the replacement of the Organization of African Unity with the African Union, the Union's Assembly proposed to merge the Human Rights Court with the proposed African Court of Justice, whose Protocol was adopted on July 11, 2003. A draft statute was prepared under the sponsorship of Algeria and presented to the Fifth Ordinary Session of the Assembly in July 2005. In October 2005, a draft was submitted and circulated to member states for comments. The Assembly decided to refer the draft to a meeting of experts to be considered at a meeting in November 2005; the meeting lacked a quorum and the representatives of the twenty-two states who appeared constituted themselves into a working group to draft recommendations and submit the draft to the Executive Council and Assembly in January 2006. See *Report of the Meeting of Government Legal Experts on the Merger of the African Court on Human and Peoples Rights and the Court of Justice of the African Union*, Executive Council, Doc.EX.CL/211 (VIII)(2006). The Executive Council and the Assembly decided to refer the matter to a meeting for Ministers of Justice and Attorneys General from member states for finalization and submission to the Executive Council in January 2007. EX.CL/Dec.283 (IX); Assembly/ AU/Dec.118 (VII).

The 2005 draft statute is not only based on the existing statutes of the Africa Courts, but also on those of other regional courts, as well as the statutes of the ICJ and the ICC. Given the key role played by the Algerian expert, who previously worked for the International Court of Justice, it is not surprising to see reflected aspects of the ICJ's practice in the statute of the merged court, which will be known as the "African Court of Justice and Human Rights."

The draft statute has a number of unique features and raises a number of difficult issues, including the question of how many states must accept the new statute. The draft suggests that not all parties to the Protocol establishing the Human Rights Court will be required to accept the new text; instead only fifteen member states will need to ratify to bring it into force and replace the former Protocol.

There is no provision in the existing statute for denunciation or termination of the agreement and if some states object, the issue of competing protocols will need to be resolved.

The court is intended to have two sections, a general affairs section of seven judges and a human rights section of five judges. The national judge cannot sit on human rights cases involving his or her country. The human rights section will have the same broad subject matter competence as the existing human rights court, i.e. cases alleging any violation of a right guaranteed by the African Charter on Human and Peoples Rights, the Chart on the Rights and Welfare of the Child, the Protocol to the African Chart on Human and Peoples' Rights on the Rights of Women in Africa, or "any other legal instrument relating to human rights ratified by the States Parties concerned." Article 33, entitled "applicable law" and clearly based on ICJ Statute article 38, has one significant difference. The African Court statute states that the Court "shall have regard to" the stated sources of law. The ICJ Statute for its part says that the Court "shall apply" the listed sources.

The most innovative provisions concern standing. All AU member states have standing as does the African Commission on Human and Peoples' Rights; the African Committee of Experts on the Rights and Welfare of the Child; African intergovernmental organizations; and "individuals or African non-governmental organizations." Draft Article 32(2) allows a state party to opt out of individual and NGO standing by filing a declaration at the time of ratification or accession restricting the jurisdiction of the court in this respect. Such opt out provisions have not little precedent in human rights treaties, which more commonly require a state to affirmatively accept jurisdiction of this type. The provision may increase the likelihood of participation by putting the burden on the state to disavow the court's competence.

When a case is submitted to the court, it will have the power to indicate provisional measures, but nothing in the statute is explicit on their binding nature. The court may also refer a case filed with it to the African Commission, which suggests that it will not be necessary for individuals to first complete proceedings at the Commission before lodging an application with the court, although this may occur. This is supported by the requirements in Article 41 that internal remedies be exhausted and a case filed within six months of the final decision; the condition with regard to time "shall not be applicable" to cases which have already been considered by the Commission. Art. 41(2). If the court decides to deal with the merits of an application, it "shall be at the disposal" of the parties to seek a friendly settlement, but there is evidently no requirement that the court attempt to reach a settlement on its own motion. Article 55 of the draft is entitled "compensation," but indicates far broader remedial powers are conferred on the court, which "may, if it considers that there was a violation of a human or peoples' right, order any appropriate measures in order to remedy the situation, including granting fair compensation."

7. Compliance with Regional Decisions and Judgments

Each judgment of the European Court and the Inter-American Court is binding on any state which is a party to the action. Both courts will issue a declaratory judgment upon finding that there has been a violation of one or more of the rights in the relevant treaty. In addition, there may be awards of compensation or, in the case of the Inter-American Court, other orders of reparation or measures to guarantee non-repetition of the violations. For its part, the European Court has indicated that its judgments are essentially declaratory in nature and has elaborated on the resulting duties of the respondent state:

> A judgment in which the Court finds a breach imposes on the respondent state a legal obligation not just to pay those concerned the sums awarded by way of just satisfaction, but also to choose, subject to supervision by the Committee of Ministers, the general and/or, if appropriate, individual measures to be adopted in their domestic legal order to put an end to the violation found by the Court and to redress so far as possible the effects.

Scozzari and Giunta v. Italy, Nos 39221/98 and 41963/98, 13 July 2000, 35 EHRR 12 (2002). If the state fails to take the necessary action to amend its laws or practices after a breach has been found, the Court may point this out in subsequent judgments raising the same issue. See e.g. *Messina v. Italy (No. 2)* No. 25498/94, 28 Aug. 2000. In *Bottazzi v. Italy,* No. 34884/97, 28 July 1999, para. 22, the Grand Chamber noted that more than 1400 reports of the former European Commission had resulted in Committee of Ministers' resolutions finding Italy in violation of article 6(1) for procedural delays in its domestic legal system. The Committee of Ministers in turn may adopt resolutions on the matter in the context of its supervision of compliance with judgments of the Court. In practice, respondent governments are asked to report to the Committee on measures taken in response to a judgment of the Court. These measures should be both "individual" in affording reparation to the applicant, and "general", intended to prevent future similar violations. The following extract explains the views of the President of the German Federal Constitutional Court on this point. The views of the other regional bodies on the duties of states to comply with their treaty obligations follow.

i. Europe

Hans-Jürgen Papier, *Execution and Effects of the Judgments of the European Court of Human Rights from the Perspective of German National Courts,* 27 HRLJ 1, 1–2 (2006).

... [T]he Convention is on the same level as a non-constitutional federal law within the hierarchy of norms of the German legal system. The force of the Convention through rank of statute law, in the hierarchy of norms is, however, additionally enhanced and strengthened by the precept of openness towards international law (*Völkerrechtsoffenheit* and *Völkerrechtsfreundlichkeit)* of the German legal system. The Basic Law explicitly encourages German public authority to engage in the international law system and to enter into commitments under international law, and it takes for granted, so to speak, that these commitments are implemented on the national level. At the same time, the Basic Law makes the unspoken presumption that the Federal Republic of Germany will fulfil, and comply with, its commitments under international law. In this way, the Convention attains a special significance, which in fact goes markedly beyond the rank of a non-constitutional federal law that it has in legal theory.

. . . It is true that judgments by the European Court of Human Rights merely take effect *inter partes*. The EurCourtHR (stet) leading judgments, however, have an effect that goes far beyond the individual case because pursuant to Article 32, paragraph 1, of the Convention, it is for the EurCourt HR to authoritatively interpret, and further develop, the Convention. Recently, the Federal Constitutional Court, in its now well known *Görgülü* decision of 14 October 2004,[7] explicitly emphasized the "particular importance" of "the decisions of the EurCourtHR . . . because they reflect the current state of development of the Convention and its Protocols." This expressly acknowledges the precedential effect of the judgments of the Strasbourg Court; the EurCourtHR leading judgments fulfil the function of normative guidance and orientation.

. . . [T]o the extent that in particular cases national provisions do exist which are contrarty to the Convention and which are not amenable to interpretation in conformity with the Convention, for instance because of their explicit working, the *legislature* is called upon to take corrective action. In this respect, the Basic Law's openness towards international law and the precept of consistency of the legal system call for a clarifying intervention of the German legislature, which must then resolve the conflict in favour of the Convention and adapt national law accordingly. In the past it has become manifest that the legislature is willing and able to do so. For instance, as a reaction to a judgment of the EurCourtHR,[8] the national rules of criminal procedure as regards the passing on of necessary interpreters' fees to foreign-speaking offenders have been revised and amended in accordance with the conclusions of the Strasbourg Court.

Finally, the Convention and the EurCourtHR judgments also have a *constitutional-law dimension*. Although technically they rank below constitutional law, they nevertheless have an influence on the understanding of the Basic Law. At an early point in time, the Federal Constitutional Court established that the Convention must be consulted for the interpretation of the Basic Law. Although both the Convention and the Basic Law's catalogue of fundamental rights merely lay down minimum guarantees and neither excludes a higher level of protection, an extensive harmonization of the corresponding freedoms guaranteed by the Convention and the Basic Law has taken place in this way. . . .

In its *Görgülü* decision . . . the Federal Constitutional Court added to the Convention's constitutional law dimension a complementary *constitutional-court dimension*, an aspect which went almost unnoticed in the initial public excitement about the decision. In spite of its status as a non-constitutional federal law, the Federal Constitutional Court has made the Convention a standard of its review where

---

7   111 Decisions of the Federal Constitutional Court (*BVerfGE*) 307; 2004 *EuGRZ* 741; 25 *HRLJ* 99 (2004) (English translation).

8   *Luedicke, Belkacem and Koc*, 29 Eur.Ct.H.R. (ser. A) (1978).

state organs have not taken the Convention into account in a manner that is relevant to fundamental rights in spite of their being bound to applicable statute law. Since then, the possibility of indirectly challenging a violation of the Convention before the Federal Constitutional Court exists—by way of asserting the violation of the principle of the rule of law pursuant to Article 20, paragraph 3, of the Basic Law in conjunction with the fundamental right that is relevant in the particular case. The Federal Constitutional Court has thereby created a very efficient level which enables it to exercise its own control over safeguarding the Convention's guarantees. The result of this new line of jurisprudence will probably be that the Federal Constitutional Court, in the future, will have to deal more frequently with issues relating to the Convention and with the EurCourtHR judgments. . . .

All in all, this results in a considerably increased effect of the Convention as compared with previous practice. I would even venture to say that in Germany the effect of the Convention on the national level is greater in this way than it is in some other states in which the Convention has the rank of constitutional law or takes precedence over non-constitutional statute law, but in which the citizens do not have the possibility of lodging an individual application with the national constitutional court.

Questions and Comments

1. In addition to the constitutional jurisprudence referred to by Judge Papier, the German legislature amended the Code of Criminal Procedure on July 9, 1998 to add paragraph 6 as follows:

> §359 *Reopening of the proceedings concluded by a final judgment shall be admissible for the convicted person's benefit:* . . .
>> 6. if the European Court of Human Rights has found that there was a violation of the European Convention on the Protection of Human Rights and Fundamental Freedoms or of its Protocols and if the judgment was based on that violation.

2. How much weight should a government give to judgments of the European Court in cases to which it is not a party?

ii. The Americas

In the Inter-American system the Commission may formulate recommendations to governments upon finding that rights have been violated, while the Court issues judgments. Does a state have to comply with recommendations? Must it conform its practices to advisory opinions of the Court? As was asked about the European system, what weight should a government in the Inter-American system give to judgments in cases to which it is not a party? The Court's practice regarding contentious cases is described in the following extract from the Court's 2006 Annual Report to the OAS General Assembly:

Annual Report of the Inter-American Court of Human Rights 2006, OAS (2007) 21, 33–34.

On June 29, 2005, the Court issued a general order on compliance with judgments in which it decided not to continue requiring the States to present information on compliance with the respective judgments, once the Court had decided that Articles 65 of the American Convention on Human Rights and 30 of the court's Statute were applicable in cases of non-compliance with judgments, and had included the relevant information in its Annual Report for the consideration of the General Assembly of the Organization of American States. If the respective State did not subsequently provide the Court with evidence that it had complied with the pending operative paragraphs of the judgment, the Court would continue to include information on this non-compliance each year submitting its Annual Report to the General Assembly. This order was notified to the General Assembly of the Organization of American States, the President of the Permanent Council of the Organization of American States, the Secretary General of the Organization of American States, the Member States of the Organization of American States, the Inter-American Commission on Human Rights, and the agents of the States and the victims or their representatives in cases being monitored for compliance with judgments by the Inter-American Court.

. . . .

In order to monitor compliance with the undertaking made by the States "to comply with the judgment of the Court in any case to which they are parties" (Article 68 of the Convention) and, in particular, to inform the General Assembly of "the cases in which a State has not complied with its judgments" (Article 65 of the Convention), the Court needs to know the extent to which States have complied with its rulings. Accordingly, the Court must monitor that the States concerned comply with the reparations it has ordered, before informing the OAS General Assembly about any failure to comply with its decisions.

The Court's monitoring of compliance with its decisions implies, first, that it must request information from the State on the activities carried out to implement compliance, and then obtain the comments of the Commission and of the victims or their representatives. When the Court has received this information, it can assess whether the State has complied with its judgment, guide the State's activities to that effect, and comply with its obligation to inform the General Assembly, in terms of Article 65 of the convention.

International Responsibility for the Promulgation and Enforcement of Laws in Violation of the Convention (Arts. 1 and 2 of the American Convention on Human Rights), Advisory Opinion OC-14/94 of December 9, 1994, 14 Inter-Am. Ct. H.R. (Ser. A) (1994).

. . . .

31. The first question posed by the Commission refers to the legal effects of a law that manifestly violates the obligations the State assumed upon ratifying the

Convention. In responding to this question, the Court will apply the word "law" in its material, not formal, sense.

32. The question implicitly refers to the interpretation of Articles 1 and 2 of the Convention, which set forth the obligation of the States Parties to respect the rights and freedoms recognized therein and to ensure their free and full exercise to all persons subject to their jurisdiction, and to adopt, if necessary, such legislative or other measures as may be necessary to give effect to those rights and freedoms.

33. It follows that if a State has undertaken to adopt the measures mentioned above, there is even more reason for it to refrain from adopting measures that conflict with the object and purpose of the Convention. The latter would be true of the "laws" to which the question posed by the Commission refer.

34. The question refers only to the legal effects of the law under international law. It is not appropriate for the Court to rule on its domestic legal effect within the State concerned. That determination is within the exclusive jurisdiction of the national courts and should be decided in accordance with their laws.

35. International obligations and the responsibilities arising from the breach thereof are another matter. Pursuant to international law, all obligations imposed by it must be fulfilled in good faith; domestic law may not be invoked to justify nonfulfillment. These rules may be deemed to be general principles of law and have been applied by the Permanent Court of International Justice and the International Court of Justice even in cases involving constitutional provisions (*Greco-Bulgarian "Communities" Advisory Opinion*, 1930, P.C.I.J., Series B, No. 17, p. 32; *Treatment of Polish Nationals and Other Persons of Polish Origin or Speech in the Danzig Territory*, Advisory Opinion, 1932, P.C.I.J., Series A/B, No. 44, p. 24; *Free Zones of Upper Savoy and the District of Gex*, Judgment, 1932, PC.I.J., Series A/B, No. 46, p. 167 and I.C.J. Pleadings, *Applicability of the Obligation to Arbitrate under Section 21 of the United Nations Headquarters Agreement of 26 June 1947 (Case of the PLO Mission)* (1988) 12, at 31–2, para. 47). These rules have also been codified in Articles 26 and 27 of the 1969 Vienna Convention on the Law of Treaties.

36. There can be no doubt that, as already stated, the obligation to adopt all necessary measures to give effect to the rights and freedoms guaranteed by the Convention includes the commitment not to adopt those that would result in the violation of those very rights and freedoms.

37. As the Court has previously stated:

> A State may violate an international treaty and, specifically, the Convention, in many ways. It may do so in the latter case, for example, by failing to establish the norms required by Article 2. Likewise, it may adopt provisions which do not conform to its obligations under the Convention (*Certain Attributes of the Inter-American Commission on Human Rights* (Arts. 41, 42, 46, 47, 50 and 51 of the American Convention on Human Rights), Advisory Opinion OC-13/93 of July 16, 1993. Series A No. 13, para. 26 [see supra p. 138]).

38. With regard to a State which passes a law in conflict with the Convention, the Court has already held that

> [w]ithin the terms of the attributes granted by Articles 41 and 42 of the Convention, the Commission is competent to find any norm of the internal law of a State Party to be in violation of the obligations the latter has assumed upon ratifying or adhering to

it... (*Certain Attributes of the Inter-American Commission on Human Rights*, supra 37, operative/resolutory paragraph 1).

39. As a result of the foregoing, the Commission may recommend to a State the derogation or amendment of a conflicting norm that has come to its attention by any means whatsoever, whether or not that norm has been applied to a concrete case. That determination and recommendation may be addressed by the Commission directly to the State (Art. 41(b)) or be included in the reports referred to in Articles 49 and 50 of the Convention.

40. The same problem would be handled differently by the Court. In the exercise of its advisory jurisdiction and pursuant to Article 64(2), the Court may refer to the possible violation of the Convention or of other treaties concerning the protection of human rights by a domestic law, or simply to the compatibility of such instruments. When its contentious jurisdiction is involved, however, the analysis has to be conducted in a different manner.

. . . .

44. When dealing with norms that violate human rights only upon their application and to prevent such violations from occurring, the Convention provides for provisional measures (Art. 63(2) of the Convention, Art. 29 of the Regulations of the Commission).

. . . .

50. The Court finds that the promulgation of a law that manifestly violates the obligations assumed by a State upon ratifying or acceding to the Convention constitutes a violation of that treaty and, if such violation affects the guaranteed rights and liberties of specific individuals, gives rise to international responsibility for the State in question.

———————————

Note on the Inter-American decision in the Dann Case:

Relations between human rights bodies and states are not always easy, especially for those like the African and Inter-American Commissions which are limited to issuing reports and recommendations. In the Inter-American system, the Charter-based obligations have proven particularly contentious, as shown by the case of *Mary and Carrie Dann v. United States* at the Commission. The applicants, members of the Western Shoshone indigenous people, asserted that their ranch-land is part of the ancestral territory of the Western Shoshone people and the State has interfered with the use and occupation of these lands by appropriating them as federal property through an unfair procedure before the Indian Claims Commission, by physically removing and threatening to remove the Danns' livestock from the lands, and by permitting or acquiescing in gold prospecting activities within Western Shoshone traditional territory. Based upon these circumstances, the Petitioners alleged that the United States was responsible for violations of Articles II,

III, VI, XIV, XVIII and XXIII of the American Declaration of the Rights and Duties of Man. The Commission first addressed the issue of the applicable law:

96. In addressing the allegations raised by the Petitioners in this case, the Commission also wishes to clarify that in interpreting and applying the Declaration, it is necessary to consider its provisions in the context of the international and inter-American human rights systems more broadly, in the light of developments in the field of international human rights law since the Declaration was first composed and with due regard to other relevant rules of international law applicable to member states against which complaints of violations of the Declaration are properly lodged. The Inter-American Court of Human Rights has likewise endorsed an interpretation of international human rights instruments that takes into account developments in the *corpus juris gentium* of international human rights law over time and in present-day conditions.

97. Developments in the corpus of international human rights law relevant to interpreting and applying the American Declaration may in turn be drawn from the provisions of other prevailing international and regional human rights instruments. This includes in particular the American Convention on Human Rights which, in many instances, may be considered to represent an authoritative expression of the fundamental principles set forth in the American Declaration.

98. It is in light of these principles that the Commission will consider and apply the relevant provisions of the American Declaration in the present case. . . .

124. As indicated above, in addressing complaints of violations of the American Declaration it is necessary for the Commission to consider those complaints in the context of the evolving rules and principles of human rights law in the Americas and in the international community more broadly, as reflected in treaties, custom and other sources of international law. Consistent with this approach, in determining the claims currently before it, the Commission considers that this broader corpus of international law includes the developing norms and principles governing the human rights of indigenous peoples. As the following analysis indicates, these norms and principles encompass distinct human rights considerations relating to the ownership, use and occupation by indigenous communities of their traditional lands. Considerations of this nature in turn controvert the State's contention that the Danns' complaint concerns only land title and land use disputes and does not implicate issues of human rights.

125. In particular, a review of pertinent treaties, legislation and jurisprudence reveals the development over more than 80 years of particular human rights norms and principles applicable to the circumstances and treatment of indigenous peoples. Central to these norms and principles is a recognition that ensuring the full and effective enjoyment of human rights by indigenous peoples requires consideration of their particular historical, cultural, social and economic situation and experience. In most instances, this has included identification of the need for special measures by states to compensate for the exploitation and discrimination to which these societies have been subjected at the hands of the non-indigenous.

126. For its part, the Commission has since its establishment in 1959 recognized and promoted respect for the rights of indigenous peoples of this Hemisphere. In the Commission's 1972 resolution on the problem of "Special Protection for Indigenous Populations. Action to combat racism and racial discrimination," the Commission proclaimed that "for historical reasons and because of moral and humanitarian principles, special protection for indigenous populations constitutes a sacred commitment of the states." This notion of special protection has since been considered

in numerous country and individual reports adopted by the Commission and, as will be discussed further below, has been recognized and applied in the context of numerous rights and freedoms under both the American Declaration of the Rights and Duties of Man and the American Convention on Human Rights, including the right to life, the right to humane treatment, the right to judicial protection and to a fair trial, and the right to property.

127. In acknowledging and giving effect to particular protections in the context of human rights of indigenous populations, the Commission has proceeded in tandem with developments in international human rights law more broadly. Special measures for securing indigenous human rights have been recognized and applied in other international and domestic spheres, including most predominantly the Inter-American Court of Human Rights, the International Labor Organization, the United Nations through its Human Rights Committee and Committee to Eradicate All Forms of Discrimination, and the domestic legal systems of many states.

128. Perhaps most fundamentally, the Commission and other international authorities have recognized the collective aspect of indigenous rights, in the sense of rights that are realized in part or in whole through their guarantee to groups or organizations of people. And this recognition has extended to acknowledgement of a particular connection between communities of indigenous peoples and the lands and resources that they have traditionally occupied and used, the preservation of which is fundamental to the effective realization of the human rights of indigenous peoples more generally and therefore warrants special measures of protection. The Commission has observed, for example, that continued utilization of traditional collective systems for the control and use of territory are in many instances essential to the individual and collective well-being, and indeed the survival of, indigenous peoples and that control over the land refers both its capacity for providing the resources which sustain life, and to the geographic space necessary for the cultural and social reproduction of the group. The Inter-American Court of Human Rights has similarly recognized that for indigenous communities the relation with the land is not merely a question of possession and production but has a material and spiritual element that must be fully enjoyed to preserve their cultural legacy and pass it on to future generations.

129. The development of these principles in the inter-American system has culminated in the drafting of Article XVIII of the Draft American Declaration on the Rights of Indigenous Peoples, which provides for the protection of traditional forms of ownership and cultural survival and rights to land, territories and resources. While this provision, like the remainder of the Draft Declaration, has not yet been approved by the OAS General Assembly and therefore does not in itself have the effect of a final Declaration, the Commission considers that the basic principles reflected in many of the provisions of the Declaration, including aspects of Article XVIII, reflect general international legal principles developing out of and applicable inside and outside of the inter-American system and to this extent are properly considered in interpreting and applying the provisions of the American Declaration in the context of indigenous peoples.

Based upon the foregoing analysis, the Commission concluded that the United States had failed to ensure the Danns' right to property under conditions of equality contrary to Articles II, XVIII and XXIII of the American Declaration in connection with their claims to property rights in the Western Shoshone ancestral lands. It recommended that the state provide the Danns with an effective remedy, which would include adopting the legislative or other measures necessary to ensure respect for their right to property in accordance with Articles II, XVIII and XXIII of the American Declaration. The Commission also recommended that the United States review its laws, procedures and practices to ensure that the property rights of indigenous persons are determined in accordance with the rights established in the American Declaration, including Articles II, XVIII and XXIII of the Declaration. *Danns v. the United States,* I.A. Comm.H.R., Rep. N° 75/02, Case 11.140, (Dec. 27, 2002), 2002 Ann. Rep. Inter-Am. Comm.H.R., OEA/Ser.L/V/II.117, Doc. 1, rev. 1, 7 March 2003.

The United States responded to this report as follows:

Response of the Government of the United States to October 10, 2002 Report No. 53/02 Case No. 11.140 (Mary and Carrie Dann)

We must again inform the Commission that we respectfully disagree with the conclusions contained in the Commission's Report; namely, that the United States has failed to ensure the Dann sisters' right to property under conditions of equality contrary to Articles II, XVIII and XXIII of the American Declaration, with respect to their claims to property rights in Western Shoshone ancestral lands. For the reasons set forth in detail in the United States' response to the Commission's draft report dated December 17, 2001, the United States rejects the Commission's findings in their entirety because: (i) the Danns' contentions regarding alleged lack of due process in the Indian Claims Commission proceedings were fully and fairly litigated in United States Courts and should not be reconsidered here; (ii) the Commission lacks jurisdiction to evaluate processes established under the 1946 Indian Claims Commission Act since the Act predates U.S. ratification of the OAS charter, and (iii) the Commission erred in interpreting the principles of the American Declaration in light of Article XVIII of the OAS draft declaration on indigenous rights. The United States will not reiterate those arguments here.

The Danns' claim is, fundamentally, not a human rights claim, but an attempt by two individual Indians to reopen the question of collective Western Shoshone tribal property rights to land—a question that has been litigated to finality in the U.S. courts. The Commission is erroneously attempting to second-guess those historical proceedings, based on a flawed interpretation of contemporary norms of international law and reliance on the American Declaration, a document that is not legally binding on the United States. The Commission's findings notwithstanding, the Danns have been allowed full and informed participation in the determination of their claims to property rights in the Western Shoshone lands, and have been afforded due process and resort to the courts for protection of their claimed rights in a fair, equal and meaningful way. As made clear by the submissions of both parties, the Dann sisters litigated their claims to the public lands at issue for many years in the U.S. federal courts, including the U.S. Supreme Court, which found that their claims had been extinguished and that compensation for the taking of the Western Shoshone lands by the United States had been paid. Finally, on June 6, 1991, before the U.S. District Court for the District of Nevada, Mary and Carrie Dann withdrew all remaining claims to title based on individual aboriginal rights. The Dann sisters were represented before the court in this proceeding by competent counsel of their own choosing. Accordingly, the Dann sisters have clearly had full access to the U.S. courts and a full and fair hearing of their claims. Although the courts ultimately found the Danns' legal arguments to be incorrect after lengthy proceedings and careful consideration, that cannot be considered a lack of respect for their legal rights.

In sum, at all times during the events that gave rise to the petition herein, the United States has acted in full compliance with its domestic and international legal obligations. For these reasons, the United States respectfully declines to take any further actions to comply with the Commission's recommendations.

Questions and Comments

1. How would you respond to the U.S. objections to the Commission's decision and recommendations in the *Dann* Case?

2. The relations between the domestic law of the United States and international law as interpreted and applied by international tribunals have become increasingly complex. In a series of cases before the International Court of Justice, three different governments brought suit against the United States for violating the Vienna Convention on Consular Relations (24 April 1963), 21 U.S.T. 71, 596 U.N.T.S. 261, in respect to aliens on death row. The first case was dismissed at Paraguay's request after the Paraguayan national was executed, but both the second and the third cases, brought by Germany and Mexico, resulted in decisions against the United States. See: *Breard*, (Parag. v. U.S.), Provisional Measures ordered April 9, 1998; *LaGrand* (Germ. v. U.S.), Merits, Judgment, 2001 ICJ Rep. 104 (June 27); *Avena et al* (Mex. v. U.S.), Merits, 2004 ICJ Rep. 128 (Mar. 31). While the *Avena* case was pending, Mexico also filed a request for an advisory opinion on the subject with the Inter-American Court of Human Rights. See: *Right to Information on Consular Assistance in the Framework of the Guarantees of Due Process of Law*, Advisory Opinion OC-16/99 of 1 October 1999, Series A, No. 16 (2000), para. 106. The Court was asked by Mexico to interpret Article 36 of the Vienna Convention on Consular Relations, which deals with the rights of nationals of the States Parties to the Convention who are detained in the territory of another State Party. The Court ruled, *inter alia*, that the right of the detained aliens to be informed "without delay" of their rights under the Consular Convention was a human right complementing the due process provisions of international human rights treaties, including the International Covenant on Civil and Political Rights. The Court also concluded that the right to be informed "without delay" must be understood to mean that the information is to be provided at the time of the alien's arrest or, in any case, before the detainee is required to make a first statement to the authorities. Should the Inter-American Court have accepted the request in light of the ICJ case underway? What if the ICJ and the Inter-American Court differ in their interpretations of the Vienna Convention's requirements?

In subsequent domestic developments, the Oklahoma Court of Criminal Appeals deemed the ICJ judgment binding with respect to an alien whose consular rights were denied. The rationale was that the Senate had given advice and consent to the Convention's protocol, which gave the ICJ jurisdiction to decide disputes concerning the Convention. *Torres v. State*, 120 P.3d 1184, 1186–87 (Okla. Crim. App. 2005). On March 7, 2005, President Bush announced the U.S. withdrawal from the Protocol giving the ICJ jurisdiction but also ordered U.S. courts and prosecutors to comply with the ICJ judgment and notify alien detainees of their consular rights. Later, the U.S. Supreme Court held that even assuming without deciding that the Convention creates judicially enforceable rights, suppression of evidence or a confession is not an appropriate remedy for a violation, and a State may apply its regular procedural default rules to Convention claims. According to the Court, and in disagreement with the ruling of the ICJ, neither the Convention itself nor Supreme Court precedents applying the exclusionary rule support suppression of a defendant's statements to police as a remedy for an Article 36 violation. The Court noted that the Convention does not mandate suppression or any other specific remedy, but expressly leaves Article 36's implementation to domestic law: Article 36 rights must "be exercised in conformity with the laws . . . of the receiving State." Art. 36(2). Where a treaty provides for a particular judicial remedy, courts must apply it as a requirement of federal law (cf., *e.g.*, *United States* v. *Giordano*, 416 U. S. 505, 524–525) but where a treaty does not provide a particular remedy, either expressly or implicitly, it is not for the federal courts to impose one on the States through lawmaking of their own. The aliens argued that the ICJ's *LaGrand* and *Avena* decisions have interpreted the Convention to preclude the application of procedural default rules to Article 36 claims. The Court responded that although the ICJ's interpretation deserved "respectful consideration," it did not "compel" the Court to conform to the judgment. According to the Supreme Court, nothing in the ICJ's structure or purpose suggests that its interpretations were intended to be binding on U. S. courts. Even according "respectful consideration," the ICJ's interpretation cannot overcome the plain import of Article 36(2), which states that the rights it implements "shall be exercised in conformity with the laws . . . of the receiving State." *Sanchez-Llamas v. Oregon*, 548 U.S. (2006). Note that the ICJ Statute, Art 59, establishes: "The decision of the Court has no binding force *except between the parties* and in respect of that particular case." (emphasis added) The United Nations Charter, Art. 94(1) provides: "Each Member of the United Nations undertakes to comply with the decision of the International Court of Justice in any case to which it is a party." Does this suggest that more than "respectful consideration" of ICJ judgments is required by parties to a case?

iii. Africa

The African system is yet a third model of obligations and supervisory review. It currently has a Commission and has an African human right court whose members have been elected but it is not yet functioning. Once the court begins hearing cases, the system will have institutions similar to those of the Inter-American system. For the time being, the Commission monitors compliance with the African Charter. Its views of the duties of states and its own powers are seen in the following case. The concluding extract evaluates state compliance with recommendations of the African Commission between 1994 and 2004, and identifies some factors that may impact governmental behavior.

Legal Resources Foundation v. Zambia, (Comm. 211/98), *14th Annual Activity Report of the Afr. Comm. H.P.R. 2000–2001*, Annex V, pp. 86–97.

. . . .

. . . The allegation before the Commission is that Respondent State has violated Articles 2, 3 and 19 of the Charter in that the Constitution of Zambia Amendment Act of 1996 is discriminatory. Article 34 provides that anyone who wishes to contest the office of President of Zambia had to prove that both parents were Zambian citizens by birth or descent. The effect of this amendment was to prohibit a Zambian citizen, former President Dr Kenneth David Kaunda from contesting the elections having been duly nominated by a legitimate political party. It is alleged that the effect of the amendment was to disenfranchise some 35% of the electorate of Zambia from standing as candidate Presidents in any future elections for the highest office in the land.

36. The enactment of the amendment to the Constitution is not in dispute. Neither is it denied that Dr Kenneth Kaunda was thus denied the right to contest the elections for the office of President. Respondent State, however, denies that some 35% of Zambian citizens would be constitutionally denied the right to stand as President and alleges that in any event such facts have no relevance to the matter at hand. It nevertheless argues that the said amendment was constitutional, justifiable and not in violation of the Charter.

37. In the matter of *Zambia Democratic Congress v The Attorney General* (SCZ Appeal No: 135/1996), the Zambia Supreme Court was petitioned to declare the then proposed amendments to the Constitution unconstitutional in that the amendments contained in Articles 34(3)(b) and 35(2) of the Constitution (Amendment) Act bar persons qualified to stand for election as President of the Republic under the 1991 Constitution and deny them the right to participate fully without hindrance in the affairs of government and shaping the destiny of the country and undermine democracy and free and fair elections which are the basic features of the Constitution of 1991.

38. It is alleged that the matter was rushed through parliament by the ruling party and enacted into law while the legal and constitutional principles were before the courts for adjudication. In the event, the court dismissed the appeal for the reason that the petition was "attacking an Act of Parliament on the ground that it violated Part III of the Constitution relating to Fundamental Rights. We are satisfied that the application was commenced by a wrong procedure and that in our jurisdiction the application was untenable" (per Sakala JS at 292).

39. The following provisions of the African Charter have relevance: Article 1, Article 2, Article 3, Article 13.

40. The African Commission on Human and Peoples' Rights is a creature of the Charter (Article 30). It was established "to promote human and peoples' rights and ensure their protection in Africa." The functions of the Charter are spelt out in Article 45 of the Charter. . . .

41. In the task of interpretation and application of the Charter, the Commission is enjoined by Articles 60 and 61 to "draw inspiration from international law on human and peoples' rights" as reflected in the instruments of the OAU and the UN as

well as other international standard setting principles (Article 60). The Commission is also required to take into consideration other international conventions and African practices consistent with international norms etc.

42. Although international agreements are not self-executing in Zambia, the government of Zambia does not seek to avoid its international responsibilities in terms of the treaties it is party to (*vide Communication 212/98 Amnesty International v. Zambia*). This is just as well because international treaty law prohibits states from relying on their national law as justification for their non-compliance with international obligations (Article 27, Vienna Convention on the Law of Treaties).[9] Likewise an international treaty body like the Commission has no jurisdiction in interpreting and applying domestic law. Instead a body like the Commission may examine a State's compliance with the treaty in this case the African Charter. In other words the point of the exercise is to interpret and apply the African Charter rather than to test the validity of domestic law for its own sake. (*vide* cases of the Inter American Commission against *Uruguay* (Nos 10.029, 10.036, 10.145, 10.10.372, 10.373, 10.374, 10.375 in Report 29/92, October 2, 1992).[10]

43. What this does mean, however, is that international treaties which are not part of domestic law and which may not be directly enforceable in the national courts, nonetheless impose obligations on State Parties. It is noticeable that the application of the Charter was not part of the argument before the national courts.

44. Conscious of the ramifications of any decision on this matter, the Commission had invited the parties to address the question of the extent of the jurisdiction of the Commission when it comes to domestic law including as is the case in this instance the Constitution. Counsel for the Respondent State argued that the Commission had no *locus standi* to adjudicate on the validity of domestic law. That position is correct. What must be asserted, however, is that the Commission has the duty to "give its views or make recommendations to Governments . . ./ to formulate and lay down principles and rules aimed at solving legal problems relating to human and peoples' rights and fundamental freedoms upon which African Governments may base their legislation / and interpret all the provisions of the present Charter . . ." (Article 45).

45. In addition, the Commission is mindful of the positive obligations incumbent on State Parties to the Charter in terms of Article 1 not only to "recognize" the rights under the Charter but to go on to "undertake to adopt legislative or other

---

9 *Vide* General Comment No 9 (XIX/1998) on The Duty to Give Effect to the Covenant in the Domestic Order. The UN Committee on Economic and Social Rights has established that "legally binding international human rights standards should operate directly and immediately within the domestic legal system of each State Party, thereby enabling individuals to seek enforcement of their rights before national courts and tribunals." The Committee argues that States have an obligation to promote interpretations of domestic laws which give effect to their Covenant obligations" (*COMPILATION OF GENERAL COMMENTS AND GENERAL RECOMMENDATIONS ADOPTED BY HUMAN RIGHTS TREATY BODIES;* HR1/GEN/Rev.4, February 2000, pp. 48–52. . . .

10 The Commission held in respect to the amnesty laws promulgated by the Government of Uruguay: where it had been argued that these were valid and legitimate in terms of domestic law and the constitution and that they had approval by the democratic majority in a referendum:

> . . . it should be noted that it is not up to the Commission to rule on the domestic legality or the constitutionality of national laws. However, the application of the Convention and the examination of the legal effects of a legislative measure, either judicial or of any nature, insofar as it has effects compatible with the rights and guarantees embodied in the Convention or the American Declaration, are within the Commission's competence.

measures to give effect to them" The obligation is peremptory, States "*shall* undertake" Indeed, it is only if the States take their obligations seriously that the rights of citizens can be protected. In addition, it is only to the extent that the Commission is prepared to interpret and apply the Charter that Governments would appreciate the extent of its obligations and citizens understand the scope of the rights they have under the Charter.

46. Article 2 of the Charter abjures discrimination on the basis of any of the grounds set out, among them "language . . . national or social origin, . . . birth or other status. . . ." The right to equality is very important. It means that citizens should expect to be treated fairly and justly within the legal system and be assured of equal treatment before the law and equal enjoyment of the rights available to all other citizens. The right to equality is important for a second reason. Equality or lack of it affects the capacity of one to enjoy many other rights.[11] For example, one who bears the burden of disadvantage because of one's place of birth or social origin suffers indignity as a human being and equal and proud citizen. He may vote for others but has limitations when it comes to standing for office. In other words the country may be deprived of the leadership and resourcefulness such a person may bring to national life. Finally, the Commission should take note of the fact that in a growing number of African States, these forms of discrimination have caused violence and social and economic instability which has benefited no one. It has cast doubt on the legitimacy of national elections and the democratic credentials of States.

47. All parties are agreed that any measure which seeks to exclude a section of the citizenry from participating in the democratic processes, as the amendment in question has managed to do, is discriminatory and falls foul of the Charter. Article 11 of the Constitution of Zambia provides that there shall be no discrimination on the grounds of "race, place of origin, political opinions, color, creed, sex or marital status. . . ." The African Charter has "national or social origin. . . ." which could be encompassed within the expression "place of origin" in the Zambian Constitution. Article 23(1) of the Zambian Constitution says that parliament shall not make any law that "is discriminatory of itself or in its effect. . . ."

48. The Respondent State, however, seeks to rely on some exceptions as justification in Zambian law for the exception. It is held that the right to equality has limitations which are justifiable and that the justifications are based on Zambian law and the Charter.

49. Article 11 of the Zambian Constitution states clearly that the right to non-discrimination is "subject to limitations. . . ." Among the limitations reference is made to Article 23(5) which provides that: . . . nothing contained in any law shall be held to be inconsistent with or in contravention of clause (1) to the extent that it is shown that it makes reasonable provision with respect to qualifications for service as a public officer. . . ." It is argued that following a consultative process, the Zambian people were of the view that the Office of President be subject to the additional qualification that the President be "an indigenous Zambian candidate of traceable descent."

---

[11] *Vide* UN Committee on Human Rights General Comment No 18 (XXXVII/1989), pp. 103–106) for a fuller discussion on non-discrimination in the ICCPR.

67. There has been some persistent confusion in arguments before us between "limitations" and "justification". Limitations refer to what may be referred to as the statute of limitations which gives a lower threshold of enjoyment of the right. Such limitations are allowed by law or provided for in the Constitution itself. In the African Charter these would typically be referred to as the 'claw-back' clauses. "Justification" however applies in those cases where justification is sought setting perimeters on the enjoyment of a right. In other words, there has to be a two-stage process. First, the recognition of the right and the fact that such a right has been violated but that, secondly, such a violation is justifiable in law. The Vienna Declaration and Programme of Action (1993) has affirmed that "all human rights are universal, interrelated, interdependent . . ." and as such they must be interpreted and applied as mutually reinforcing. It is interesting to note for example, that Article 2 does not have a 'claw-back' clause while Article 13 limits the right to "every citizen" but goes on to state that "in accordance with the law."

68. In the matter before us therefore the Government of Zambia concedes that the measures were discriminatory but then goes on to argue (1) a limitation of the right, and (2) justification of the violation. It is argued that the measure was within the law and Constitution of Zambia. It was stated before the Commission that Zambia has a constitutional system of parliamentary sovereignty hence even the Supreme Court could not "attack" an Act of Parliament (as Sakala JS put it). The task of the Commission, however, is not to seek to do that which even the Zambian courts could not do. The responsibility of the Commission is to examine the compatibility of domestic law and practice with the Charter. Consistent with decisions in the European and Inter-American jurisdictions, the Commission's jurisdiction does not extend to adjudicating on the legality or constitutionality or otherwise of national laws. Where the Commission finds a legislative measure to be incompatible with the Charter, this obliges the State to restore conformity in accordance with the provisions of Article 1 (*cf Zanghi v Italy,* 194 Eur Ct HR (Ser A) 48 (1991)).

69. It is stated further that the limitation of the right is provided for in the Zambian Constitution and that it is justifiable by popular will in that, following the work of the Mwanakatwe Commission on the Constitution, it was recommended that the Zambian people desired "to save and preserve the Office of the President for Zambians with traceable descent. . . ." Regarding the claim that the measure deprived some 35% of Zambians of their rights under the previous Constitution, counsel for Respondent State dismisses this as mere speculation.

70. The Commission has argued forcefully that no State Party to the Charter should avoid its responsibilities by recourse to the limitations and "claw-back" clauses in the Charter. It was stated following developments in other jurisdictions, that the Charter cannot be used to justify violations of sections of it. The Charter must be interpreted holistically and all clauses must reinforce each other. The purpose or effect of any limitation must also be examined, as the limitation of the right cannot be used to subvert rights already enjoyed. Justification, therefore, cannot be derived solely from popular will, as such cannot be used to limit the responsibilities of State Parties in terms of the Charter. Having arrived at this conclusion, it does not

matter whether one or 35% of Zambians are disenfranchised by the measure, that anyone is, is not disputed and it constitutes a violation of the right.[12]

71. The Commission has arrived at a decision regarding allegations of violation of Article 13 by examining closely the nature and content of the right to equality (Article 2). It cannot be denied that there are Zambian citizens born in Zambia but whose parents were not born in what has become known as the Republic of Zambia following independence in 1964. This is a particularly vexing matter as the movement of people in what had been the Central African Federation (now the States of Malawi, Zambia and Zimbabwe) was free and that by Zambia's own admission, all such residents were, upon application, granted the citizenship of Zambia at independence. Rights which have been enjoyed for over 30 years cannot be lightly taken away. To suggest that an indigenous Zambian is one who was born and whose parents were born in what came (later) to be known as the sovereign territory of the State of Zambia may be arbitrary and its application of retrospectivity cannot be justifiable according to the Charter.

72. The Charter makes it clear that citizens should have the right to participate in the government of their country "directly or through freely chosen representatives. . . ." The pain in such an instance is caused not just to the citizen who suffers discrimination by reason of place of origin but that the rights of the citizens of Zambia to "freely choose" political representatives of their choice, is violated. The purpose of the expression "in accordance with the provisions of the law" is surely intended to regulate how the right is to be exercised rather than that the law should be used to take away the right.

73. The Commission believes that recourse to Article 19 of the Charter was mistaken. The section dealing with "peoples" cannot apply in this instance. To do so would require evidence that the effect of the measure was to affect adversely an identifiable group of Zambian citizens by reason of their common ancestry, ethnic origin, language or cultural habits. The allegedly offensive provisions in the Zambia Constitution (Amendment) Act, 1996 do not seek to do that.

For the above reasons, the Commission,

Finds that the Republic of Zambia is in violation of Articles 2, 3(1) and 13 of the African Charter;

Strongly urges the Republic of Zambia to take the necessary steps to bring its laws and Constitution into conformity with the African charter; and

Requests the Republic of Zambia to report back to the Commission when it submits its next country report in terms of Article 62 on measures taken to comply with this recommendation.

------

[12] *Vide* UN Human Rights Committee General Comment No 25 (XXXVII/1996) where it says that "Persons who are otherwise eligible to stand for election should not be excluded by unreasonable or discriminatory requirements such as education, residence, or descent, or by reason of political affiliation. . ." (para 15 @ p.127).

Frans Viljoen & Lirette Louw, State Compliance with the Recommendations of the African Commission on Human and Peoples' Rights, 1994–2004, 101 AJIL 1–34 (2007)(footnotes and tables omitted).

Commentators on the African regional human rights system have often cited its absence of "teeth" when it comes to the enforcement mechanisms provided for in the African Charter.[13] The African Commission, in reflecting on its activities, has indicated that the lack of state compliance with its recommendations was "one of the major factors of the erosion of the Commission's credibility."[14] However, in the absence of accumulated data and any policy on follow-up, the commissioners' critical observations about a lack of compliance with their findings remain speculative.

. . . .

Our study attempted to assess the level of compliance by states regarding all the communications where the Commission found a state party in violation of the Charter. . . .

A state party is deemed to have "fully complied" with the recommendations of the Commission if it has implemented them all or has unequivocally expressed the political will to comply with their substance and has already taken significant steps in this process. However, to make an accurate assessment whether a state has expressed the necessary political will to implement a communication fully is difficult. For this and other reasons, this category is open to revision. The survey shows that in only six of the forty-four communications (or 14 percent) did state parties comply fully and in timely fashion with the recommendations of the African Commission.[15]

---

[13] See, e.g., CLAUDE E. WELCH, PROTECTING HUMAN RIGHTS IN AFRICA—ROLES AND STRATEGIES OF NON-GOVERNMENTAL ORGANIZATIONS 151–53 (1995).

[14] See the discussion document entitled Non-Compliance of State Parties to Adopted Recommendations of the African Commission: A Legal Approach, DOC/OS/50b (XXIV), para. 2 (1998) [hereinafter Non-Compliance: A Legal Approach], reprinted in DOCUMENTS OF THE AFRICAN COMMISSION ON HUMAN AND PEOPLES' RIGHTS 758, 758 (Rachel Murray & Malcolm Evans eds., 2001) [hereinafter ACHPR DOCU-MENTS]. In this discussion document, the secretariat highlighted the absence of compliance, save for one case, Pagnoulle (on Behalf of Mazou) v. Cameroon, Communication [Comm.] No. 39/90, 2000 Afr. Hum. Rts. L. Rep. [AHRLR] 55 (ACHPR 1995). The first time the Commission noted that state parties were not complying with its recommendations had been at its twenty-second ordinary session in November 1997, where the secretariat also raised the issue. In the Eleventh Annual Activity Report, covering the November 1997 session, the Commission observed not only that noncompliance affected its credibility, but also that it could probably be to blame for the reduction in the number of communications submitted to it. See Section VIII, Protective Activities, 11th Activity Report, 1997–1998, supra note 8. Later, in September 2003, during a retreat organized by the Office of the UN High Commissioner for Human Rights in Addis Ababa to evaluate the functioning of the African Commission, problems of noncompliance by state parties were highlighted once more. The retreat also identified the lack of a follow-up system to ensure that decisions and recommendations of the Commission are complied with as one of the challenges facing the Commission. Report of the Retreat of Members of the African Commission on Human and Peoples' Rights (ACHPR) at 4 (Sept. 24–26, 2003), available at <http://www.nhri.net/>. Volumes of the African Human Rights Law Reports cited herein are available online at <http://www.chr.up.ac.za>.

[15] [The six cases cited as resulting in full compliance are: *Pagnoulle (on Behalf of Mazou) v. Cameroon,* Comm. No. 39/90, 2000 AHRLR 57 (ACHPR 1997); *Amnesty Int'l (on Behalf of Banda & Chinula) v. Zambia,* Comm. No. 212/98, 2000 AHRLR 325 (ACHPR 1999); *Constitutional Rights Project v. Nigeria,* Comm. No. 153/96, 2000 AHRLR 248 (ACHPR 1999); *Centre for Free Speech v. Nigeria,* Comm. No. 206/97, 2000 AHRLR 250 (ACHPR 1999); *Modise v. Botswana,* Comm. No. 97/93, 2000 AHRLR 30 (ACHPR 2000); see also id., 2000 AHRLR 25 (ACHPR 1994), 2000 AHRLR 25 (ACHPR 1997); and *Forum of Conscience v. Sierra Leone,* Comm. No. 223/98, 2000 AHRLR 293 (ACHPR 2000).]

The second category, termed "noncompliance," refers to cases in which state parties did not implement any of the Commission's recommendations. . . . According to our study results, state parties clearly did not comply with the Commission's recommendations in thirteen cases (or 30 percent of the total).

The third category, "partial compliance," refers to communications where the state party implemented some, but not all, of the elements of the Commission's recommendations. It may also represent instances where a state party has not given complete effect to the recommendations. Categorizing state responses as "partial compliance" is even more problematic than it is for "full compliance," primarily because a finding of "partial compliance" most often indicates that the process of implementation is still ongoing. According to the survey, fourteen of the cases (or 32 percent) show partial compliance with the Commission's recommendations. In most of these instances, state parties had made some attempts to implement the recommendations without committing themselves unequivocally to walk the whole distance. Instances where the Commission issued a vaguely formulated or open-ended remedy, and some action by the state was noted, were also designated as "partial compliance."

In another seven cases, partial or full compliance may be derived from the transition from an undemocratic and repressive to a more stable and democratic system of government. . . . In these seven cases (all involving Nigeria and Rwanda), the role of the government (and changes of government) takes priority. After the dramatic regime change in Nigeria, in 1998, and in the context of the replacement of a military government with a civilian government, some of the Commission's recommendations were complied with. . . . Compliance mostly took the form of repealing decrees, which could be viewed as a factor directly related to the change from a military to a democratic government. Thus, the obligation on the state to comply is in line with its political policies and is not equivalent to, say, the obligation to make compensation, which has not been paid to any of the victims detained unlawfully during the Abacha regime. Similarly, the fundamental change of government and gradual return to civilian governance in Rwanda after 1994 is of overriding importance when considering the joint communication against Rwanda, submitted in 1989 and 1992, and decided in 1996.

To the extent that these changes coincided with some form of compliance, these cases are categorized as instances of "situational compliance." This category includes instances of both wholesale changes (approximating "full compliance") and limited adjustments (approximating "partial compliance").

In the remaining four cases (or 9 percent), insufficient information forecloses any pronouncement about state compliance, making them instances of "unclear" compliance.

The various difficulties encountered in undertaking an exhaustive study of this nature rule out the claim that the recorded research findings are a complete or fully accurate account of implementation. The following hindrances constricted the empirical inquiry: communication difficulties, insufficient records, difficulties in tracing victims and authors of communications, lack of quality and continuity of state representatives attending the Commission's sessions, opposing views about compliance by those involved, and lack of media coverage. . . .

Even if the factual position could be established with some accuracy, categorization remains contentious, because implementation is not a static, but a dynamic process. Different conclusions on the correct category for a particular communication could possibly have been reached. Some of the difficulties encountered in classifying the implementation efforts of states relate to the problematic causal connection between the Commission's findings and the government's action, and the lack of a clear remedy. . . .

III. FACTORS INDICATIVE OF COMPLIANCE OR NONCOMPLIANCE

Factors Related to the Treaty Body (African Commission)

The first set of factors relates to the treaty body, the African Commission. Especially since it is generally accepted that the findings under the African Charter are not legally binding on parties to a dispute, the way that the Commission executes its mandate to a great extent determines the moral force of its findings. The implementation of treaty body findings depends on the will of state parties. Instead of coercing states into compliance through sanctions, which is a difficult exercise under international law, the persuasive force of the treaty body's findings is assumed to increase and hence improve compliance. Six aspects are considered here . . .: (1) the period in the life of the Commission when the finding was made, premised on improvement in compliance as the system matured; (2) the length of time it took the Commission to decide on the final communication (measured from the time the Commission was "seized" of the matter, until a decision on the merits was taken); (3) the extent of state involvement in the processing and completion of the communication; (4) the degree to which a particular finding was reasoned and substantiated; (5) the extent to which a clear and specific remedy was formulated in the particular case; and (6) the absence or presence of initiatives taken by the Commission to follow up on the implementation of its findings or remedies.

. . . . Can it be said that compliance has increased as the African regional human rights system has "matured"? In other words, has there been a gradual improvement in compliance over time? . . . Even though the origin of all the cases of compliance in the later life of the Commission is also a noteworthy factor, it is too early to conclude that the maturity of the African regional human rights system has played a decisive role in ensuring the improved implementation of the Commission's recommendations.

. . . The second factor considered in relation to the treaty body, the length of time it took to complete each case, is premised on the notion that a shorter time lapse may lead to better compliance, as the immediacy of the events may stimulate domestic compulsion to implement, and as states may perceive that the procedure met the requirements of due process. This period was measured by counting the number of ordinary sessions between the Commission's seizing of a communication and the decision on the merits. Unfortunately, no clear conclusions can be drawn from the sample under review.

State involvement in the communication procedures. . . . Departing from the assumption that a "participating" state would be more inclined to comply with the

Commission's decisions, we compared state involvement in the cases of full compliance with that in the cases of no compliance. Analysis of the data . . . does not provide conclusive evidence that participating states are more likely to implement decisions. However, the level of state involvement and participation has improved over the years. Even if this development cannot be linked to compliance, it nevertheless indicates that state parties have become less likely to ignore the Commission's correspondence and requests pertaining to communications against them.

Reasoning in a particular finding. At first very brief and tersely argued, the Commission's decisions have evolved over the years into more well-reasoned and substantiated judgments. . . . On the assumption that well-reasoned findings are more likely to be implemented, the Commission's findings are divided, for the purpose of our study, into three categories: brief reasoning, limited reasoning, and substantial reasoning. When this analysis is applied to the six cases where full compliance was recorded, well-reasoned judgments do not seem to be a prerequisite for compliance. . . .

The same conclusion is arrived at as regards cases of clear noncompliance. The majority of the findings in these cases are well reasoned, while some of the Commission's most elaborate decisions are the least implemented. It therefore seems that the depth and width of the reasoning is not decisive in ensuring or predicting compliance.

. . . Linked to the fourth factor is the further hypothesis that the formulation of an exact and detailed remedy may also be predictive of compliance. . . . Three categories are distinguished: no remedy whatsoever, a vague remedy, and a specific remedy. . . .[I]n the majority of the cases where full compliance was reported, the Commission articulated specific remedies. This result suggests support for the contention that the formulation of a precise and targeted remedy improves compliance. However, a specific remedy was also spelled out in the majority of cases (eight of the thirteen) that ended in non-compliance. This position undermines the contention that the specificity and targeted nature of a remedy is more likely to lead to state compliance with a finding.

The precision with which a remedy was formulated may not be a factor that predicts compliance, but it is central to the assessment of compliance. A proper analysis of compliance depends on a clearly delineated remedy. If there is no specific remedy, there is no criterion for measuring compliance, which makes the categorization of factual information on compliance ("full," "partial," and so on) problematic.

. . . . The sixth factor analyzed with reference to the treaty body is follow-up by the treaty body itself. . . . Our survey of the factors that influenced state compliance in the six cases of full compliance indicates that in four of these cases the African Commission made some attempt at following up on the steps taken by state parties to implement its recommendations. As the Commission did not undertake any similar actions in the majority of "noncompliant" cases, this factor seems relevant to compliance. The lack of a follow-up provision in the Charter, which led to the ad hoc practice of exceptional follow-up, can therefore be described as a factor that has inhibited state compliance with the Commission's recommendations.

Factors Related to the Communication

The nature of a case presumably also plays a significant part in influencing state compliance. This statement should be understood with reference to the following four questions: (1) Is the subject matter of violations "civil and political" or "socio-economic" in nature? (2) Does the right that is invoked imply a duty on the government to "respect," "protect," or to "fulfill"? (3) What is the scale of the violations? That is, does the case reveal violations of the rights of individuals, or have the violations occurred on a wider scale and are they of an institutional nature, linked to the system of governance of a state party? (4) Does the type of remedy required to redress the violations have a bearing on compliance? The role that the answers to these questions . . . play in state compliance is assessed briefly in this section with reference to the cases where states fully complied with the Commission's recommendations, as well as those of noncompliance.

. . . The data suggest that when compliance occurs, it is likely to pertain to the violation of civil and political rights, especially Article 7 of the African Charter (fair-trial rights). Any conclusion based on these data is problematic, though, since by far the majority of all the cases decided by the Commission deals with civil and political rights, often involving rights related to a fair trial. It is therefore not surprising that cases of noncompliance also deal almost exclusively with violations of civil and political rights.

However, the three instances in which socioeconomic rights were invoked— albeit in conjunction with civil and political rights—all fall in the category of full noncompliance, suggesting that states may still deem these rights less justiciable.

. . . .

In terms of compliance, state parties seem to find it easier to respect rights, than to protect or fulfill rights. An analysis of the six cases of full compliance reveals that in none of these cases were the state parties under an obligation to fulfill. In other words, the subject matter of the cases analyzed dealt mostly with obligations to respect and protect, with which states seemingly find it easier to comply. The obligation to respect requires states to refrain from action, or to change a law that is violating rights. The duty to respect, though less burdensome than the duty to fulfill, is not only a negative obligation, but may entail scrapping existing laws or enacting new ones.

Cases of noncompliance also mostly involve the duty of governments to respect. Just because the only case where the Commission found a violation of the government's duty to fulfill figures among the instances of noncompliance is an inconclusive ground for supporting the contention that the nature of a state's obligations determines compliance.

Scale of the violation found. To assess whether the scale of violations influences compliance, the cases were categorized into those involving a single complainant, those involving multiple complaints, and those that occurred on a massive scale. Of the six cases of full compliance, three dealt with violations of the rights of an individual, three with multiple complainants, and none with massive violations. Conversely, the majority of the cases of clear noncompliance (five cases) concerned violations on a massive scale, and three each involved an individual scale and multiple complainants, respectively.

. . . .

Violations on an expansive scale are mostly linked to the system of governance or factors such as political instability due to an ongoing civil war and would require deep, substantial reform to achieve compliance. Even in Nigeria, where the cases were brought during the military dictatorship of General Abacha, the implementation of the recommendations that were complied with did not affect the system of governance in place, as they did not deal, for example, with the amendment of decrees but, rather, with the release of a few individuals. Most of the remedies that were not implemented by Nigeria addressed problems that could be implemented only after a regime change—problems that were inherent in the system of governance.

Nature of the remedial action required. The nature of the remedies required by the Commission is closely linked to the nature of the violations it had found. Some of the above comments about the nature of the violations therefore also hold true for the remedies. In Communication Nos. 48/90, 50/91, 52/91, and 89/93 (joined) against Sudan, the Commission concluded its decision by stating that "[t]o change so many laws, policies and practices will of course not be a simple matter," while also noting "that the situation has improved significantly." It follows that recommendations involving the amendment of laws are usually associated with a more extended domestic procedure involving the state's legislature. In Communication No. 211/98 against Zambia, the Commission urged the state to bring "its laws and Constitution into conformity with the African Charter." This decision was adopted in the Fourteenth Annual Activity Report and is one of the cases where "partial" compliance was recorded, since a process to amend the Zambian Constitution began in 2003 but is yet to be completed. Recommendations seeking amendments to the Constitution of a country would clearly involve more stakeholders than amendments to other domestic legislation, and as such would take place over a longer period of time.

The experience of the inter-American regional human rights system indicates that states are sometimes more willing to pay compensation than to implement remedies of a political nature or remedies involving the amendment of domestic legislation. In the inter-American system, there is a procedure in place to determine the amount of compensation to be awarded to a victim. . . .

The lack of a policy to determine the quantum of damages in awarding compensation to victims is definitely a factor that has negatively influenced state compliance in the African system. An attempt was made to follow up on six cases where the Commission had recommended the payment of compensation to victims but without stipulating the amount. In none of these cases has compensation been paid. The Botswana Modise case is listed as an example of full compliance because, as explained above, negotiations are in the final stage and compensation will most probably be paid to the victim and his family. However, since the Commission did not stipulate the amount of compensation, the determination was wholly dependent on negotiations between the state party and nongovernmental organizations (NGOs) acting on behalf of the victim, which greatly delayed the process.

. . . [S]tates are more likely to comply with remedies that require them to take some administrative action than with those that press them to amend legislation or compensate victims. However, no such trend can be discerned regarding the instances of clear noncompliance, as the thirteen cases are divided almost evenly among the three categories of required remedies. It would therefore be risky to conclude, on the basis of the available data, that the nature of the required remedy is an unequivocal ground for predicting state compliance.

. . . .

A recurring theme of the communications where noncompliance was recorded relates to two interrelated aspects, namely, the type of political regime in power and the existence of civil conflict. However, where these factors were present, the Commission often found serious or massive violations of the African Charter. Thus, compliance is often influenced by a combination of factors, rather than a single factor. The OAU Charter did not provide for sanctions against state parties under any circumstances. As a result, perpetrators of military coups and authoritarian governments could continue their OAU membership and participate in the meetings of the Assembly without fear of exclusion or confrontation based on their human rights records, even in the face of the African Commission's findings. The OAU's Central Organ of the Mechanism for Conflict Prevention, Management and Resolution existed only on paper.

System of governance. The findings on the status of state compliance with the Commission's recommendations indicate that the system of governance and the level of political stability within a state influence its compliance. A democratic system of governance is characterized by principles such as a functional multiparty electoral system, an independent judiciary, the rule of law, constitutionally guaranteed rights, an active civil society, and a freely functioning NGO community. If present, all these factors will pressure the state to bring its international policies in line with its domestic system of governance.

Nine countries were involved in the thirteen cases of clear noncompliance. Of these, none were categorized as "free," according to the Freedom House Index. Two of them (Cameroon and Nigeria) appear among both these noncompliant states and the fully compliant states. Leaving them aside for the purpose of our analysis, it emerges that six of the seven consistently noncompliant states at some stage during the relevant period were categorized as "not free"; and five of them were categorized as "not free" for most of the period (Angola, Burundi, Mauritania, Sudan, and Zaire (DRC)). The two others (The Gambia and Kenya) were categorized as "partly free" for most of the period. The average rating of 3.875 over the period of the three remaining compliant states (Botswana, Sierra Leone, and Zambia) places them in the lower range of "partly free." One of these countries, Botswana, was consistently categorized as "free." These data indicate a strong correlation between the "state of freedom" (that is, the standards of openness and democracy) in a particular state and the likelihood of compliance.

As for Nigeria, our study noted full compliance in two cases, and noncompliance in thirteen cases. This record highlights "system of governance" and "political instability" as recurring predictors of noncompliance. This factor, as mentioned, is usually associated with serious or massive violations of human rights. Civil wars within state parties affect political stability not only within their own borders, but also in neighboring countries. In the face of a series of serious and massive human rights violations, the impact of a treaty body such as the African Commission is negligible if measured in terms of state compliance. However, NGOs do not necessarily file communications with the Commission against an autocratic government or during a time of civil war only to seek specific remedies from the Commission. Interviews with Nigerian NGOs that frequently filed against the dictatorial regime in the 1990s revealed that they used the Commission as a forum to apply pressure on the state party internationally and to publicize the government's human rights violations as widely as possible.

The statistical analysis also supports the conclusion that a stable, open, free, and democratic system of government is conducive to compliance under the African regional human rights system.

Change of government. As seen, noncompliance in cases of serious or massive violations was usually due to the system of governance in place or factors related to the country's political stability. Thus, large-scale violations require large-scale remedies. Under these circumstances, the most significant factor that might influence state compliance for the better is the opportunity to improve a country's human rights record offered by a change in government after years of military dictatorship or civil war. In the African system, the change of government that took place in Nigeria, with the death of General Abacha in 1999, ended the military dictatorship and initiated a period of democratic governance. Although some recommendations still await implementation by Nigeria, the change of government brought about the repeal of the decrees that formed the substance of most of the communications against that country and the release of most of the political prisoners. Moreover, whereas most of the forty-four communications examined in this study were filed against Nigeria, very few cases were filed after the new government took office.

Stability of government. A stable government is more likely to implement the Commission's findings against it than a government that finds itself in the midst of civil war or subject to other forms of instability. If the political situation of states is characterized as "stable," "relatively stable," or "civil war," compliant states are more likely to fall in the categories of "stable" or "relatively stable." Cases of clear noncompliance, such as those involving Angola, Burundi, the DRC, and Sudan, are more likely in contexts of civil war and relative instability.

. . . For our purposes, since compliant states proved only slightly less corrupt than noncompliant states (with an average score on the index of 2.28 against 2.17), it cannot be concluded that levels of perceived corruption and their correlation to poverty levels in a specific state party are predictive of compliance.

Factors Related to Civil Society Actors

. . . NGOs submitted communications on behalf of the victims in five of the six cases of full compliance. In Modise, the remaining case, an NGO (Interights) became involved during the proceedings before the Commission. The instances of clear noncompliance are more or less evenly divided between cases where NGOs were involved in both submitting the communications and assisting or appearing on behalf of the complainants, on the one hand, and those where NGOs were not involved, on the other hand. The prospects for compliance seem to be enhanced when communications are framed as communal rather than individualized claims, and when they are invoked as part of a broader social movement rather than an insular interest. By availing themselves of the "usual means of lobbying and public opinion campaigns" at their disposal, NGOs contribute significantly to contextualizing complaints in this way, increasing the prospects for compliance and living up to their role as "'guardians' of compliance by states with certain international obligations."

NGOs, more than other potential players, have assumed a significant role in follow-up efforts. The absence of any follow-up policy meant that NGOs that had filed communications also had to take on the role of follow-up. NGOs have been instrumental in applying pressure on and lobbying states at the domestic and international levels, so as to influence them to comply. State compliance was secured in the Modise case mainly as a result of the follow-up efforts of the NGO Interights. In the Lekwot case, where partial compliance was recorded, the role of NGOs in pressing the state to comply through a widespread advocacy campaign was noted as a deciding factor in Nigeria's commutation of the victims' sentences from death by hanging to life imprisonment.

It can therefore be concluded that NGO involvement in following up on the Commission's recommendations, occasioning both international and internal pressure, has played an important role in influencing state compliance.

Involvement of the press. In the instances of state compliance . . ., the press involvement did not result from any action by the African Commission, but from the efforts of NGOs. Publication of the findings of treaty bodies plays a major part in influencing state compliance. In the absence of coercive measures, the mobilization of shame is one of the only tools available to a treaty body to apply pressure against state parties on the international level. Most state parties attach importance to their reputation in the international community. Those that have ceased to care about their reputation are not likely to be influenced by any of the factors listed in this article.

. . . .

As noted above, it has fallen mostly to NGOs to mount international pressure against noncompliant state parties. In the three cases of full compliance . . . where international pressure played a role in persuading the relevant states to implement the Commission's recommendations, that result can largely be attributed to the efforts of national and international NGOs. Although establishing the existence of international pressure has proved difficult in many instances, and these results are not statistically significant, it may be cautiously stated that an absence of international pressure seems to characterize the overwhelming majority of cases of noncompliance.

IV. CONCLUSION

Improved state compliance with findings by the Commission (or the African Court of Human and Peoples' Rights) is both an indicator and a goal of greater commitment to human rights by African states and the African Union. This article attempts to shift attention from the substantive features of the African Charter to questions about the implementation (in the form of "direct effect") of this normative framework.

(Non)compliance with the recommendations of the African Commission is one aspect of a state's compliance with its obligations under the African Charter. The mere fact that a state has complied with some findings does not translate into overall adherence to the normative framework of the Charter; nor does noncompliance with findings mean that in all respects the state is falling short of its obligation to give effect to the African Charter. Nevertheless, timely and full implementation of Commission recommendations may be indicative of a tendency to regard other obligations under the African Charter with seriousness.

[T]he attempt to chart compliance empirically and analytically is fraught with methodological difficulties. The most important of these is the Commission's failure to enunciate clear and specific remedies, leaving an unreliable yardstick for measuring compliance. Even when the yardstick is clearer, linking the steps toward compliance to the required remedial action often remains a matter of causal conjecture.

Our analysis of cases of full and clear noncompliance suggests that the most important factors predictive of compliance are political, rather than legal. The only factor relating to the treaty body itself that shows a significant link to improved compliance is its follow-up activities. This finding lends support to arguments for a fully developed and effectively functional follow-up mechanism in the secretariat of the Commission, the consistent integration of follow-up activities into the Commission's mandate, and the appointment of a special rapporteur on follow-up. This observation again points up the importance of an unambiguous normative statement by the Commission calling for the establishment of a coherent and consistent follow-up procedure.

In an encouraging and significant development subsequent to the completion of our study, the Commission in November 2006 adopted a resolution in which it unequivocally called on state parties to the African Charter to "respect without delay the recommendations of the Commission," and to report on compliance within ninety days of being notified of decisions against them. The Commission further decided to include a report on "the compliance with its recommendations" in future activity reports.

. . . .

Inadequate political commitment at the regional level is an important factor underlying the lack of state compliance with the recommendations of the Commission at the macrolevel. To some extent, the goal of strengthening the regional political system was reached by means of the reforms of the OAU, which culminated in the establishment of the African Union.

. . . .

When the AU Constitutive Act was adopted in July 2000, the African Union replaced the OAU as the regional political body. The Union held its first session in July 2002. However, most of the communications for which follow-up was established in this article were decided while the OAU was the regional political body.

The new institution addressed some of the weaknesses that had marked the OAU. First, the AU Constitutive Act includes the protection of human and peoples' rights among its objectives and founding principles. The African Union therefore seems to be more dedicated to the protection of human rights than its predecessor. Second, in contrast to the OAU, the AU Assembly opted to allow for the possibility of more exhaustive debate on the Annual Activity Reports of the Commission by delegating this task to the Executive Council, which indeed resulted in more thorough deliberations on the Commission's report and work during the discussion of the Seventeenth Annual Activity Report. . . . Also for the first time the regional political body called upon member states to implement the decisions of the African Commission.

. . . .

It therefore seems that some of the problems associated with the weak regional political platform of the OAU have been addressed by its transformation into the African Union. However, some instances of noncompliance have been registered since 2000, after the Union was established. Whether the African Union will develop a practice of taking action on the basis of the theoretical possibilities mentioned above will have to be seen.

Final Questions and Comments

1. How do the criteria for selection of members and mandates of the commissions and courts compare across the three regions?

2. To what extent have the various bodies asserted and developed implied powers as judicial or quasi-judicial institutions? Have they gone too far? Consider the provisions of the African Charter in particular: can the Commission publicize its work without permission of the AU political bodies? Does it have control over its budget and staff? Is the independence of its members guaranteed?

3. How should each regional body determine priorities in carrying out its extensive mandate and fulfilling its functions?

4. Judge Buergenthal, the first president of the Inter-American Court, has suggested that the court is too small; the African Commission has also expressed its desire to increase its size. What are the arguments on either side? Would the reasons for increasing the number of judges or commissioners be satisfied by making both institutions full-time bodies like the European Court of Human Rights or are there other motives behind a desire for larger institutions?

5. Review the conclusions to Christof Heyn's article in Chapter 8. How well are the criteria for a successful human rights system met in the three regions?

6. What legal guarantees or other measures help promote the independence of regional judges and commissioners? What further steps could be taken in this direction? See D. Shelton, *Legal Norms to Promote the Independence and Accountability of International Tribunals*, in THE LAW AND PRACTICE OF INTERNATIONAL COURTS AND TRIBUNALS (C. ROMANO, ed., 2003) 27–62; D. Shelton, *The Independence of International Courts and Tribunals* in THE MODERN WORLD OF HUMAN RIGHTS: ESSAYS IN HONOR OF THOMAS BUERGENTHAL (ANTONIO CANÇADO-TRINDADE, ed. 1996).

7. How do you evaluate compliance in the European and African systems, based on the extracts given above? In particular, in the African system, do you see only six cases of compliance or only thirteen cases of non-compliance? In other words where should one place the two groups of cases in which the state neither fully complied nor failed to comply?

On issues of compliance, see, e.g., L'APPLICATION NATIONALE DE LA CHARTE AFRICAINE DES DROITS DE L'HOMME ET DES PEUPLES (Jean-François Flauss & Elisabeth Lambert-Abdelgawad eds., 2004); Douglass Cassel, *International Human Rights Law in Practice: Does International Human Rights Law Make a Difference?* 2 CHI. J. INT'L L. 121 (2001); Oona A. Hathaway, *Do Human Rights Treaties Make a Difference?*, 111 YALE L.J. 1935 (2002; THE AFRICAN CHARTER ON HUMAN AND PEOPLES' RIGHTS: THE SYSTEM IN PRACTICE, 1986–2000 (MALCOLM D. EVANS & RACHEL MURRAY EDS., 2002); RACHEL MURRAY, THE AFRICAN COMMISSION ON HUMAN AND PEOPLES' RIGHTS AND INTERNATIONAL LAW (2000); INGER OSTERDAHL, IMPLEMENTING HUMAN RIGHTS IN AFRICA—THE AFRICAN COMMISSION ON HUMAN AND PEOPLES' RIGHTS AND INDIVIDUAL COMMUNICATIONS (2002).

8. With the rights, obligations and institutional structure of the regional systems now covered, the next two chapters turn to compliance mechanisms, first examining the individual petition procedures and then methods to address gross and systematic violations.

CHAPTER V
COMPLAINT PROCEDURES

1. Overview

One of the greatest contributions of the regional systems to the development of international human rights law has been the establishment of complaint mechanisms to monitor compliance with state obligations and provide redress for human rights violations. Europe was the first to create a commission and court that could hear complaints, followed by the Americas and Africa. In all systems it is expected that the rights guaranteed are enforced first and foremost on the national level, but the regional institutions play a vital if subsidiary role in ensuring compliance.

Within Europe, a substantial number of the Contracting Parties have incorporated the European Convention into domestic law. In these countries the Convention creates rights directly enforceable by individuals and may be invoked in the national courts. In Contracting Parties where the Convention does not enjoy domestic law status, implementing legislation may be required to enforce the rights it guarantees unless existing national law already ensures the protection of comparable rights. Even in these countries the national courts frequently look to the Convention when interpreting and applying domestic law. Only when domestic law does not provide relief capable of remedying a violation of the Convention may recourse be had to the European Court.

The Inter-American system parallels that of Europe, but was the first to make the individual complaints procedure mandatory against all its member states. The Inter-American Commission on Human Rights, from its inception in 1960, interpreted its powers broadly to include the ability to make general recommendations to each individual state as well as to all of them.[1] This was deemed to include the power to take cognizance of individual petitions and use them to assess the human rights situation in a particular country, based on the normative standards of the American Declaration. The OAS amended the Statute of the Commission in 1965 to make the power to receive complaints explicit.

The regional commissions and courts have gradually strengthened their procedures for handling complaints. The Inter-American Commission has changed its procedures to add a determination on admissibility before evaluating the merits of the claim. It may hold hearings on admissibility or the merits at the request of either party or on the Commission's initiative. The re-structuring of the case system in the Inter-American system has also involved greater use of provisional measures, registration of petitions, creating chambers for hearings, and more on-site

---

[1] Inter-American Commission on Human Rights, First Report 1960, OAS Doc. OEA/Ser.L/V/II.1, Doc. 32 (1961).

visits to gather evidence. In addition, the Commission has developed a structured friendly settlement procedure and stronger means to protect confidentiality. It has also initiated a follow-up procedure to monitor compliance with its decisions.

The African system evolved quickly through the African Commission's interpretation of its powers and revision of its rules of procedure. The African Commission, like the Inter-American Commission, may give its views or make recommendations to Governments. The African Commission has read this to include the formulation of principles and rules for the resolution of human rights problems in specific states. In 1990, the Commission decided to publish its annual reports. Like the other commissions, the African Commission negotiates friendly settlements. See: Communication 44/90, *Peoples Democratic Organization for Independence and Socialism v. the Gambia*, infra p 753. Like the Inter-American institutions, the African Commission has developed follow-up actions. In various Nigerian cases, the Commission recommended the release of persons it decided were wrongfully detained and decided "to bring the file to Nigeria . . . in order to verify that . . . [the victims] had been released." Case 60/91, 8th Ann. Activity Rep., p. 4. See also Case 87/93, *The Constitutional Rights Project (in re Zamani Lakwot & others) v. Nigeria*, id. at 7–9.

In its procedures on communications, the African Commission has benefited from the experience of the other systems. It follows the usual two-stage process of considering a communication for admissibility and on the merits. It adopted a three-month time limit within which states must reply to requests for information and make observations regarding the admissibility of communications. In theory, if the Commission determines a petition is admissible, it again gives the state three months to submit explanations or statements regarding the case. In fact, it often is years before the Commission decides the merits of a case. The Commission has strengthened rules on conflict of interest and agreed on the possibility of requesting provisional measures, despite a lack of specific reference to such measures in the Charter. The African Commission's rule on provisional measures is almost identical to Article 63(2) of the American Convention.

In general, all the systems have enhanced their complaints procedures through expanding the participation of victims and their representatives. In Europe, a slow evolution toward individual standing first allowed individuals to appear before the court in the guise of assistants to the Commission. A protocol later permitted them to appear by right. With the entry into force of Protocol 11, complainants now have sole standing. In the other systems, changes have occurred through action by the supervisory bodies rather than through amending the basic texts.

The readings in this chapter look at the procedures governing the processing of complaints in the regional systems, first addressing jurisdictional limits, then examining issues of admissibility, the friendly settlement procedure, fact-finding and evidentiary issues and, finally, the nature and scope of the remedies afforded.

2. Jurisdiction

Each system circumscribes the jurisdiction of its institutions to receive complaints. Unlike criteria for admissibility, such as exhaustion of local remedies, the limits on jurisdiction cannot be waived. The requirements determine personal and subject matter jurisdiction, and establish temporal and territorial limits on cases that may be considered.

The European Court's contentious jurisdiction extends to all cases brought by a Contracting Party against another for breach of the Convention and to cases brought by victims of a violation by a Contracting Party of the rights guaranteed by the Convention. With the entry into force of Protocol 11, the Court may receive applications from "any person, non-governmental organization or group of individuals claiming to be the victim of a violation . . . of the rights set forth in the Convention or the protocols thereto." (Convention, Art. 34) All matters concerning the interpretation and application of the Convention and its protocols fall within the Court's subject matter jurisdiction.

In the African system, Article 55 of the African Charter requires the Secretariat of the Commission to compile "a list of communications other than those of [from] States Parties to the present Charter and transmit them to the members of the Commission." While this language does not specify that the communications may originate with private individuals, non-governmental organizations, or other entities, the Commission has accepted and considered several hundred such communications to date, whether or not submitted by victims or their representatives. The drafters of the Charter may have intended the complaint procedure to extend only to gross and systematic violations, similar to the UN procedure established by the Economic and Social Council in its Resolution 1503. However, the Commission has interpreted Article 55 to allow it to consider individual communications which do not allege gross and systematic violations. Article 58(1) provides separate jurisdiction for the Commission to act in relation to "special cases which reveal the existence of a series of serious or massive violations of human and peoples' rights." As discussed in Chapter VI, the Commission indeed has developed special procedures and rules to govern allegations of such violations.

T. Buergenthal, *The Inter-American System for the Protection of Human Rights*, in T. Meron (ed.), HUMAN RIGHTS IN INTERNATIONAL LAW, pp. 454–455, OUP, 1984, Vol. II.

(. . .) The Inter-American Commission's power under [Convention] article 41(f), which authorizes it to deal with complaints charging a state party with violations of human rights, differs in one important respect from the authority vested in other international human rights institutions. The American Convention stipulates that by becoming a party to it, a state has accepted ipso facto the jurisdiction of the Commission to deal with private complaints lodged against that state. But the Inter-American Commission may only deal with so-called inter-state complaints— complaints filed by one state party against another—if both states, in addition to ratifying the American Convention, have made a further declaration recognizing the inter-state jurisdiction of the Commission. The American Convention thus reverses the more traditional pattern utilized by the [original] European Convention, for example, where the right of individual petition is optional and the inter-state complaint procedure is mandatory. The drafters of the American Convention apparently assumed that inter-state complaints might be used by some governments for political objectives or interventionist purposes, and that this risk existed to a much more limited extent with regard to private petitions. Whatever may be the soundness of these assumptions, it is undisputed that the availability of the right of private petition enhances the effectiveness of an international system for the protection of human rights. By enabling individuals to assert their own claims, the right of private petition makes the enforcement of human rights less dependent on the extraneous political considerations that tend to motivate governmental action and inaction. . . .

Note on the Matter of Viviana Gallardo et al *and* the Problem of Jurisdiction

The existence of two institutions in the Inter-American system—the Commission and the Court—has raised a unique jurisdictional issue. In 1981 Costa Rica filed a petition with the Court, stating that Viviana Gallardo was a prisoner who had been killed and her cellmates injured on July 1, 1981, by a prison guard. The Government declared that for purposes of the case it "formally waive[d] the requirement of the prior exhaustion of the domestic legal remedies and the prior exhaustion of the procedures set forth in Articles 48 to 50 of the Convention," that is, the procedures before the Inter-American Commission on Human Rights. The Government also declared that the waiver was designed to enable the Court to "consider the instant case immediately and without any procedural obstacle." The Court held that the domestic remedies requirement could be waived, because "under the generally recognized principles of international law and international practice, the rule which requires the prior exhaustion of domestic remedies is designed for the benefit of the State, for that rule seeks to excuse the State from having to respond to charges before an international body for acts which have been imputed to it before it has had the opportunity to remedy them by internal means. The requirement is thus considered a means of defense and, as such, waivable, even tacitly. A waiver, once effected, is irrevocable." On the other hand, the Court held, proceedings before the Commission serve a different purpose and cannot be waived:

> 20. The Court notes the very clear language of Article 61(2), which provides that "in order for the Court to hear a case, it is necessary that the procedures set forth in Articles 48 to 50 shall have been completed." Naturally, under international law relating to the interpretation of treaties, the aforementioned provision must be read in accordance with "the ordinary meaning to be given to the terms of the treaty in their context and in the light of its object and purpose." Vienna Convention on the Law of Treaties, Article 31(1).
>
> 21. It is clear that in this matter no procedures at all have been initiated before the Commission. It is, therefore, not a question of deciding whether these procedures have been exhausted or when they might be considered to have been exhausted, but strictly one of determining whether the procedures can be avoided by the mere unilateral waiver of the State concerned. In order to make this determination, it is necessary to define the role that the Convention assigns to the Commission as a body having preparatory or preliminary tasks relating to the adjudicatory functions

of the Court and, more particularly, whether the role assigned to the Commission has been created for the sole benefit of States, in which case it is waivable by them.

22. The Convention, in effect, in addition to giving the Commission formal standing to submit cases to the Court and to request advisory opinions and to giving it in proceedings before the Court a quasi-judicial role, like that assigned to the "Ministerio Publico" of the inter-American system, obligated to appear in all cases before the Court (Article 57 of the Convention), gives it other attributes connected with functions which pertain to the Court and which by their nature are completed before it begins to hear a particular matter. Thus, the Commission has, inter alia, the function of investigating allegations of violations of human rights guaranteed by the Convention which must be carried out in all cases that do not concern disputes relating to mere questions of law. It follows therefrom that, although the Court, as any other judicial organ, does not lack the power to carry out its own investigations, particularly if these are necessary to provide the Court with the information it needs to discharge its functions, the Convention entrusts to the Commission the initial phase of the investigation into the allegations. The Commission also has a conciliatory function empowering it to propose friendly settlements as well as to make the appropriate recommendations to remedy the violation it has found to exist. It is also the body to which the States concerned initially provide all the pertinent information and submissions. But the Commission is also, and this is a fundamental aspect of its role in the system, the body which is authorized to receive individual complaints, that is, the entity to which victims of violations of human rights and other persons referred to in Article 44 can resort directly to present their complaints and allegations. The Convention is unique among international human rights instruments in making the right of private petition applicable against States Parties as soon as they ratify the Convention; no special declaration to that effect is required for individual petitions. although it must be made for inter-State communications.

23. The Commission thus is the channel through which the Convention gives the individual qua individual the possibility to activate the international system for the protection of human rights. As a strictly procedural matter, it should be remembered that just as individuals cannot submit cases to the Court, States can submit them to the Commission only if the conditions of Article 45 have been met. This is yet another factor that bears on the institutional interest in fully preserving the ability of the individual by means of his own complaint to initiate proceedings before the Commission.

24. The Court notes, in addition, that it lacks the power to discharge the important function of promoting friendly settlements, within a broad conciliatory framework, that the Convention assigns to the Commission precisely because it is not a judicial body. To the individual claimant this process has the advantage of ensuring that the agreement requires his consent to be effective. Any solution that denies access to these procedures before the Commission deprives individuals, especially victims, of the important right to negotiate and accept freely a friendly settlement arrived at with the help of the Commission and "on the basis of the human rights recognized in (the) Convention." (Article 48 (1) (f)).

25. These considerations suffice to demonstrate that the aforementioned procedures before the Commission have not been created for the sole benefit of the States, but also in order to allow for the exercise of important individual rights, especially those of the victims. Without questioning the good intentions of the Government in submitting this matter to the Court, it follows from the above that the

procedures before the Commission cannot be dispensed with in this kind of case without impairing the institutional integrity of the protective system guaranteed by the Convention. These procedures may therefore not be waived or excused unless it were to be clearly established that their omission, in a specific case, would not impair the functions which the Convention assigns to the Commission, as might be the case when a matter is initially presented by a State against another State and not by an individual against a State.

In the Matter of Viviana Gallardo et al., Inter-Am. Ct. H.R. (Ser. A, No. G 101/81), Nov. 13, 1981, pp. 78–91.

Following this decision, the government took the case to the Commission where it was settled. Assume, however, that no resolution occurred. The families of the prisoners commenced proceedings in the Costa Rican courts after the prosecutor declined to bring criminal charges against the guard. The lengthy civil cases ended inconclusively and the families appealed. The cases eventually were heard by the Costa Rican Supreme Court, which has not issued a decision. Based on these facts and assumptions, and with the aid of the Declaration, Convention, the Commission's Statute and Regulations, and the Rules of Court, address the following questions:

1. If the original case had been brought to the Court by the relatives of the victim along with the government of Costa Rica, would this have changed the decision of the Court?

2. May an individual petitioner ever by-pass the proceedings before the Inter-American Commission and take a case directly to the Court? What provisions of the American Convention are relevant? What are the policy considerations? Should an inter-state communication be treated differently? Why?

3. If the government already has a petition before the Commission concerning this case, will a petition by the family by admissible?

4. What rights have allegedly been violated? Should the families invoke the Declaration or the Convention? Or both?

5. When must the family bring the petition?

6. What information has to be included in the petition? Whose name appears on the petition: the legal representative's, the client's or the victim's?

7. Can an NGO file the petition on behalf of the victim and/or the family? Is your answer the same for the European and the African systems?

8. What does the family want by way of redress? Can the Commission accede to these demands?

9. How and where should the petition be filed?

10. The client would like to know what will happen to the petition after the Commission receives it. After studying the Commission's Regulations, explain the initial procedures.

11. Assume that a colleague is counsel to one of the wounded prisoners. Before the government brought the case to the Inter-American Court, her client's mother presented a petition to the Human Rights Committee established under the Optional Protocol to the International Covenant on Civil and Political Rights. While that petition was under consideration, the sister of the client, who lives in Honduras, presented a similar petition to the Inter-American Commission. The colleague

would like to know (1) whether her client's case will be admissible at the Inter-American Commission; (2) which proceeding should be pursued and why; and (3) can the petition include violations of the client's right to social security, and preservation of his health and wellbeing.

12. According to paragraph 1 of the opinion, the government stated the facts and asked the Court to decide "whether these acts constituted a violation . . . of the human rights guaranteed in Articles 4 and 5 of the Convention or of any other rights guaranteed therein." Is the Court limited to the government statement or may it make its own findings of fact?

13. Assume that the procedures of the Commission have been exhausted and a State Party has recognized the jurisdiction of the Court. Is the Commission obligated to submit the matter to the Court? What factors are relevant to the Commission's decision on referral of a case to the Court?

14. On the role of the regional commissions as defenders of the public interest before regional courts, see the jurisprudence of the former European Court of Human Rights. In the first case before the Court, the Commission sought permission to present to the Court the individual applicant's observations. Addressing this motion, the Court acknowledged that "it is in the interest of the proper administration of justice that the Court should have knowledge of and, if need be, take into consideration, the Applicant's points of view . .". The Court emphasized, however, that it could obtain this information from the Commission, "which, as the defender of the public interest, is entitled of its own accord . . . to make known the Applicant's views to the Court . . ". *Lawless v. Austria*, 1 Eur.Ct.H.R. Over time, the participation of individuals increased, first allowing the applicant's counsel to join the team of attorneys appearing before the Court and then authorizing individuals to appear in their own right and to be separately represented in proceedings before the Court. This same evolution can be seen in the Inter-American system, although the Convention has not been amended.

A. Initial Processing of Cases: Receivability

All the regional systems screen applications to ensure that jurisdictional requirements are met. The older systems are more formalized in their procedures for screening than is the African system. The Inter-American Commission's regulations provide for several stages in the consideration of a petition. Initially, the Commission's Secretariat receives and processes petitions to see if they meet the requirements for consideration in accordance with Articles 26–28 of the Commission's Rules of Procedure. Each staff lawyer is assigned responsibility for all petitions coming from two or three countries. The lawyer begins by verifying the Commission's jurisdiction through examining the qualities of petitioner and the respondent; the subject matter of the petition; the place where the facts occurred; and the timeliness of the petition. If there are defects in form or elements are missing from the petition, the lawyer may request the petitioner to supply further information. If the petition is manifestly groundless, the petitioner may be advised that the Commission cannot process the petition.

Once the petition is complete and the Commission verifies its prima facie competence, it registers the petition, gives it a number, and transmits the relevant parts of it to the state in question. In transmitting the petition, the secretariat deletes all details which would tend to identify the petitioner unless the petitioner has given authorization to have his or her identity revealed. The state normally has two months from the date the petition is transmitted to respond to it. The state may request one additional month to reply, but it is not automatically entitled to an extension of time. Once the state responds, the Commission considers the admissibility of the petition and admissible petitions become cases.

In the European system there are similar stages prior to the determination of whether or not the application is admissible. The registry screens applications for jurisdiction and opens a provisional file for each one. The registry may contact the applicant to ensure that all required information is submitted and may indicate any obvious ground of inadmissibility or lack of jurisdiction. If the applicant nonetheless insists on going forward, the application is registered, given a case number, and assigned to a seven judge Chamber where a judge rapporteur, assisted by a member of the legal staff, prepares a report on admissibility. The rapporteur may suggest dismissal to a three judge committee, which can unanimously reject the application in a non-appealable decision. A large percentage of cases are excluded in this manner. If the rapporteur or any member of the committee raises a question about admissibility, the application is sent to the Chamber for consideration and communicated to the government; the latter normally has six weeks to reply on issues of admissibility and the merits. The applicant is sent a copy of the government's observations and may submit a written response. The Chamber may then adopt a decision on admissibility or hold a hearing. In some instances, issues of admissibility are so tied to the merits of a case that they are joined and heard together.

On occasion, the defects in the petition and the manner of its submission lead to its immediate rejection.

Tanko Bariga v. Nigeria, (Comm. 57/91), *7th Annual Activity Report of the Afr. Comm. H.P.R. 1993–1994*, Annex IX.

Final Decision

1. The demand is incoherent and is inadmissible under Article 55 (2) of the African Charter on Human and Peoples' Rights.

Iheanyichukwu A. Ihebereme v. USA, (Comm. 2/88), *7th Annual Activity Report of the Afr. Comm. H.P.R. 1993–1994*, Annex IX.

Final Decision

1. The African Commission on Human and Peoples' Rights, established under Article 30 of the African Charter on Human and Peoples' Rights;

2. Meeting at its Fourth ordinary Session held from 17 to 26 October 1988;

3. Considering that the communication is directed against a State non-party to the African Charter on Human and Peoples' Rights;

Declares the communication inadmissible (Article 101 of the Rules of Procedure).

See also Afr.Comm.HPR, Comm. 3/88 *Centre for the Independence of Judges and Lawyers v. Yugoslavia*, January 26, 1987, 7th Annual Activity Report.

In other instances, the legal issues of jurisdiction require more consideration and are taken up during proceedings on admissibility. The following materials examine the practice and jurisprudence on key matters of jurisdiction.

B. Subject Matter Jurisdiction

Zechnalova & Zehnal v. The Czech Republic, (App. no. 38621/97), Eur. Ct. H.R. Rep. 2002-V (14 May 2002)(Czech language terminology omitted).

The applicants, Mrs. Jitka Zehnalová and her husband, Mr. Otto Zehnal, are Czech nationals who were born in 1962 and 1958 respectively and live in Přerov.

. . . .The first applicant is physically disabled.

A large number of public buildings and buildings open to the public in the applicants' home town are not equipped with access facilities for people with disabilities (people with impaired mobility).

On 7 December 1994 the first applicant applied to the Přerov Municipal Office under Article 65 of the Code of Administrative Procedure, complaining that a number of public buildings and buildings open to the public in Přerov did not comply with the technical requirements laid down in Decree no. 53/1985 (amended by Decree no. 174/1994) and in the Building Act (Law no. 50/1976, amended by Law no. 43/1994). On the same day she sent a letter to the same effect to the Přerov District Office. On 19 December 1994 the head of the District Office informed her in reply that 219 certificates of approval issued in respect of the buildings concerned would be reviewed. On 29 December 1994 the Mayor of Přerov informed her that the Town Council had instructed a committee to contact disabled people's organisations in order to take the necessary measures to improve the situation regarding disabled access.

Following delays by the District Office in initiating the review procedure provided for in Article 49 § 2 of the Code of Administrative Procedure, the first applicant asked the Ministry of Economic Affairs to conduct a review of its own motion. On 5 June 1995 she was informed that her case would be "dealt with by the District Office in accordance with the law". Nevertheless, the Ministry did not set any deadline and the District Office dismissed or took no action on most of the complaints. Although some of the obstacles complained of have since been removed, the applicants maintain that that has not been the result of pressure from the authorities.

. . . .

On 21 November 1995 the applicants applied to the Ostrava Regional Court.

. . . .

On 7 February 1996 the Regional Court refused the applicants' application on the ground that it had no prospect of success within the meaning of Article 138 of the Code of Civil Procedure as it did not satisfy the requirements laid down in Article 249 of the Code and the applicants had not been parties to the proceedings before the administrative authorities which had resulted in the issuing of the certificates of approval.

On 19 February 1996 the applicants appealed to the High Court.

. . . .

In a decision of 29 April 1996 the High Court declined jurisdiction on the ground that, pursuant to Article 250j § 4 of the Code of Civil Procedure, no appeal lay against the Regional Court's decision.

On 23 July 1996 the applicants appealed to the Constitutional Court.

. . . .

In a decision of 10 March 1997 the Constitutional Court dismissed the applicants' appeal. It noted, firstly, that they were not entitled to challenge the constitutionality of section 59 of the Building Act since that provision had not been applied by the High Court, and, secondly, that the decisions complained of did not disclose any breach of constitutional law or of any other legal provisions or international treaties.

COMPLAINTS

1. Relying on Articles 1, 3, 8 and 14 of the Convention and Articles 12 and 13 of the European Social Charter, the applicants complained that they had suffered discrimination in the enjoyment of their rights on account of the first applicant's physical condition. They submitted that a large number of public buildings and buildings open to the public in their home town were not accessible to them and that the national authorities had failed to remedy the situation.

2. The applicants also alleged a violation of Articles 1, 6 and 13 of the Convention on the ground that they had not had an effective remedy before a national authority. They submitted in that connection that for a period of a year and a half the national courts had not assigned a lawyer to defend their rights.

THE LAW

A. Alleged violation of Article 8 of the Convention

The applicants *complained*, firstly, of a violation of their right to respect for their private life in that the Czech State had not removed the architectural barriers preventing disabled access to public buildings and buildings open to the public. They relied on Article 8 of the Convention.

. . . .

The first applicant asserted that she was unable to enjoy a normal social life allowing her to deal with her everyday problems in a dignified manner and to practise her profession, not because of any interference by the State but on account of its failure to discharge its positive obligations to adopt measures and to monitor compliance with domestic legislation on public buildings.

. . . .

... [T]he Government denied that there had been any violation of Articles 8 and 14 of the Convention. They argued that Article 8 of the Convention was not applicable in the instant case as the rights claimed by the applicants were social rights, the scope of which went beyond the legal obligation inherent in the concept of "respect" for "private life" within the meaning of paragraph 1 of Article 8 of the Convention. With regard to the situation in the town of Přerov, the Government acknowledged that, in spite of the measures that had been taken, people with disabilities might encounter certain difficulties. However, that did not amount to a violation of Article 8 of the Convention, since the right to respect for private and family life had a different meaning from that attached to it by the applicants. Relying on the *Botta* judgment [*Botta v. Italy*, 26 EHRR 241 (1998)] and on the broad margin of appreciation enjoyed by States with regard to the obligations laid down in the relevant legislation, the respondent Government asked the Court to declare the application inadmissible as being incompatible *ratione materiae* with the provisions of the Convention.

. . . .

The applicants disputed the Government's argument that the rights they were claiming were social ones. In their submission, what was at stake in the instant case was the first applicant's right under the Convention to respect for her private life in that, despite her disability, she wished to lead an active life while retaining her independence and dignity, an aspiration which they considered to be one of the aims of the Convention and of Article 8. They referred to the *Airey v. Ireland* judgment (9 October 1979, Series A no. 32, p.15, § 26), in which the Court had observed: "Whilst the Convention sets forth what are essentially civil and political rights, many of them have implications of a social or economic nature." The applicants therefore contended that Article 8 was applicable and submitted that, as the Court had previously held (in *López Ostra v. Spain*, judgment of 9 December 1994, Series A no. 303-C, p. 55, § 51, and *Guerra and Others v. Italy*, judgment of 19 February 1998, *Reports* 1998-I, p. 227, § 58), that provision also entailed positive obligations on the State that were inherent in effective respect for private or family life.

. . . .

The Court reiterates that although the object of Article 8 is essentially that of protecting the individual against arbitrary interference by the public authorities, it does not merely compel the State to abstain from such interference since it may also give rise to positive obligations inherent in effective "respect" for private and family life. While the boundaries between the State's positive and negative obligations under this provision do not always lend themselves to precise definition, the applicable principles are similar. In both contexts regard must be had to the fair balance that has to be struck between the competing interests of the individual and the community as a whole, and in both contexts the State enjoys a certain margin of appreciation (see, for example, *Nuutinen v. Finland*, no. 32842/96, § 127, ECHR 2000-VIII, and *Kutzner v. Germany*, no. 46544/99, §§ 61–62, ECHR 2002-I).

The positive obligations under Article 8 of the Convention may involve the adoption of measures designed to secure respect for private life even in the sphere of the relations of individuals between themselves (see *Stjerna v. Finland*, judgment of 25

November 1994, Series A no. 299-B, p. 61, § 38, and *Botta*, cited above, p. 422, § 33). Since the concept of respect is not precisely defined, States have a wide margin of appreciation regarding the choice of the means to be employed to discharge the obligations set forth in the relevant legislation.

The Court has held that a State has obligations of this type where it has found a direct and immediate link between the measures sought by an applicant and the latter's private and/or family life (see the following judgments: *Airey*, cited above, p. 17, § 32; *X and Y v. the Netherlands*, 26 March 1985, Series A no. 91, p. 11, § 23; *López Ostra*, cited above, p. 55, § 55; and *Guerra and Others*, cited above, p. 227, § 58). It points out that in the *Botta* judgment it held that Article 8 of the Convention was not applicable to situations concerning interpersonal relations of such broad and indeterminate scope that there could be no conceivable direct link between the measures the State was urged to take and the applicant's private life.

The Court notes that there are similarities between the instant case and *Botta*. Its task here is to determine the limits to the applicability of Article 8 and the boundary between the rights set forth in the Convention and the social rights guaranteed by the European Social Charter. The Court acknowledges that the constant changes taking place in European society call for increasingly serious effort and commitment on the part of national governments in order to remedy certain shortcomings, and that the State is therefore intervening more and more in individuals' private lives. However, the sphere of State intervention and the evolutive concept of private life do not always coincide with the more limited scope of the State's positive obligations.

The Court considers that Article 8 of the Convention cannot be taken to be generally applicable each time the first applicant's everyday life is disrupted; it applies only in exceptional cases where her lack of access to public buildings and buildings open to the public affects her life in such a way as to interfere with her right to personal development and her right to establish and develop relationships with other human beings and the outside world (see *Pretty v. the United Kingdom*, no. 2346/02, § 61, ECHR 2002-III). In such circumstances, the State might have a positive obligation to ensure access to the buildings in question. In the instant case, however, the rights relied on are too broad and indeterminate as the applicants have failed to give precise details of the alleged obstacles and have not adduced persuasive evidence of any interference with their private life. In the Court's view, the first applicant has not demonstrated the existence of a special link between the lack of access to the buildings in question and the particular needs of her private life. In view of the large number of buildings complained of, doubts remain as to whether the first applicant needs to use them on a daily basis and whether there is a direct and immediate link between the measures the State is being urged to take and the applicants' private life; the applicants have done nothing to dispel those doubts. The Court further observes—without, however, attaching decisive importance to the matter—that the national authorities have not remained inactive and that, as the applicants themselves have admitted, the situation in their home town has improved in the past few years.

In the light of the foregoing considerations, the Court considers that Article 8 of the Convention is not applicable in the instant case and that the complaints relating to an alleged violation of that Article must be rejected as being incompatible *ratione materiae* with the provisions of the Convention, in accordance with Article 35 §§ 3 and 4 of the Convention.

B. Alleged violation of Articles 12 and 13 of the European Social Charter

The Court observes that the applicants raised the same complaints under Articles 12 and 13 of the European Social Charter.

It notes that their allegations do not disclose any appearance of a violation of the rights and freedoms guaranteed by the Convention and its Protocols. It would also point out that it is not its task to review governments' compliance with instruments other than the European Convention on Human Rights and its Protocols, even if, like other international treaties, the European Social Charter (which, like the Convention itself, was drawn up within the Council of Europe) may provide it with a source of inspiration.

It follows that this complaint is incompatible *ratione materiae* with the provisions of the Convention within the meaning of Article 35 § 3 and must be rejected in accordance with Article 35 § 4.

C. Alleged violation of Article 14 of the Convention taken together with Article 8

Relying on Article 14 of the Convention taken together with Article 8, the first applicant submitted that she had been discriminated against, as a person with disabilities, in the enjoyment of fundamental rights secured to all. . . .

The Government contested that allegation and argued that Article 14 of the Convention was not applicable.

The Court reiterates that Article 14 complements the other substantive provisions of the Convention and its Protocols. It has no independent existence, since it has effect solely in relation to the enjoyment of the rights and freedoms safeguarded by those provisions. Although the application of Article 14 does not presuppose a breach of those provisions—and to that extent it is autonomous—there can be no room for its application unless the facts of the case fall within the ambit of one or more of the latter (see, *mutatis mutandis*, *Botta*, cited above, p. 424, § 39).

As the Court has held that Article 8 is not applicable, Article 14 cannot apply in the instant case.

It follows that this complaint is likewise incompatible *ratione materiae* with the provisions of the Convention within the meaning of Article 35 § 3 and must be rejected in accordance with Article 35 § 4. . . .

E. Alleged violation of Article 6 § 1 of the Convention

Relying on Article 6 § 1 of the Convention, the applicants complained that for a period of a year and a half the national courts had not assigned a lawyer to defend their rights. . . .

The Court reiterates that it has consistently stressed the autonomy of the concept of "civil rights and obligations" (see, among other authorities, *König v. Germany*, judgment of 28 June 1978, Series A no. 27, p. 29, § 88). It further notes that Article 6 § 1 of the Convention is not aimed at creating new substantive rights which have no legal basis in the State concerned, but at providing procedural protection of rights already recognised in domestic law. In the *W. v. the United Kingdom* judgment (8 July 1987, Series A no 121, pp. 22–23, § 73) the Court pointed out:

> "Article 6 § 1 extends only to '*contestations*' (disputes) over (civil) 'rights and obligations' which can be said, at least on arguable grounds, to be recognised under domestic law; it does not in itself guarantee any particular content for (civil) 'rights and obligations' in the substantive law of the Contracting States."

The Court observes that in the instant case, after the statutory two-month period had expired, the applicants asked the national courts to assign a lawyer to draft their application for a review of the certificates of approval issued in the context of proceedings before the administrative authorities—proceedings in which they had not taken part. However, no such right is set forth in Czech law.

Consequently, Article 6 § 1 of the Convention is not applicable in the instant case.

It follows that this complaint is incompatible *ratione materiae* with the provisions of the Convention within the meaning of Article 35 § 3 and must be rejected in accordance with Article 35 § 4.

F. Alleged violation of Article 13 of the Convention

The applicants argued that they had not had an effective remedy before a national authority in respect of the breaches of the Convention complained of and alleged a violation of Article 13 . . . .

As the Court has consistently held (see, among other authorities, *Powell and Rayner v. the United Kingdom*, judgment of 12 February 1990, Series A no. 172, pp. 14–15, § 33, and *Abdurrahman Orak v. Turkey*, no. 31889/96, § 97, 14 February 2002), Article 13 of the Convention guarantees the availability at national level of a remedy to enforce the substance of the Convention rights and freedoms in whatever form they may happen to be secured in the domestic legal order. Its effect is thus to require the provision of a domestic remedy allowing the competent national authority both to deal with the substance of an "arguable complaint" under the Convention and to grant appropriate relief. Article 13 is therefore applicable only in respect of grievances which can be regarded as arguable in terms of the Convention.

However, the applicants have not raised any arguable grievances in the instant case as the Court has held that all their complaints are either incompatible *ratione materiae* with the provisions of the Convention or inadmissible as being manifestly ill-founded. . . .

It follows that this complaint must be rejected in accordance with Article 35 §§ 3 and 4 of the Convention.

G. Alleged violation of Article 1 of the Convention

Lastly, the applicants relied on Article 1 of the Convention. . . .

The Court reiterates that Article 1 of the Convention "is drafted by reference to the provisions contained in Section I and thus comes into operation only when taken in conjunction with them; a violation of Article 1 follows automatically from, but adds nothing to, a breach of those provisions" (see *Ireland v. the United Kingdom*, judgment of 18 January 1978, Series A no. 25, p. 90, § 238).

Accordingly, in the present case the applicants' complaint cannot be raised under Article 1 of the Convention, which is a framework provision that cannot be breached on its own (see, *mutatis mutandis, K.-H.W. v. Germany*, no. 37201/97, § 118, ECHR 2001-II). As the application has to be declared inadmissible, the Court considers that a separate finding under Article 1 of the Convention would serve no legal purpose.

It follows that this part of the application must likewise be rejected in accordance with Article 35 §§ 3 and 4 of the Convention.

For these reasons, the Court, by a majority,

Declares the application inadmissible.

Frederick Korvah v. Liberia, (Comm. 1/88), *7th Annual Activity Report of the Afr. Comm. H.P.R. 1993–1994*, Annex IX.

The Facts

1. The communication is addressed to the Government of Liberia and alleges lack of discipline in the Liberian Security Police, corruption, immorality of the Liberian people generally, a national security risk caused by US financial experts, and that other countries are supporting of South Africa and her apartheid regime. The complainant calls on the Liberian Government to purge the security police of the "gangsters, addicts, sex maniacs and rapists" that are its members.

Procedure

2. The communication is dated 26 July 1987.

3. At the 4th session, held in Cairo, Egypt, October 1988, the Commission considered and decided the case.

4. On 17 August 1988 a copy of the decision was sent to the complainant.

Law

Admissibility

5. The communication is in the form of a letter addressed to the Liberian Government, not the Commission. Although it is recorded in the Legal Division of the OAU on 10 August 1987 it is not clear from the records why the letter was sent to the OAU Secretariat or to the Commission.

6. To be receivable by the Commission, a communication must allege prima facie violations of the Charter. The Commission finds that the matters complained of in the communication do not amount to violations of the provisions of the Charter.

Questions and Comments

1. Can the Czech applicants apply for relief under the procedures of the European Social Charter?

2. If Protocol No. 12 to the European Convention had been in force at the time the case was brought to the European Court of Human Rights would the result have been different?
3. Would the rights allegedly violated in the *Zechnalova & Sehnal* case be within the jurisdiction of the Inter-American or African Commission?
4. Can the *Korvah* petition be re-written to make it admissible, at least in part?

C. Locus Standi and Personal Jurisdiction

In the European system, "victims" of violations of rights guaranteed by the European Convention and its Protocols may file cases directly with the Court. This right extends to both natural and legal persons whose rights have been violated, including companies, trade unions and religious bodies.[2] Groups of individuals may file.[3] Applicants must be represented by a lawyer licensed to practice law in one of the States Parties to the Convention once the communication is declared admissible and for any hearing that is held. Convention, Art. 38(1) and Rules of Court, Art. 36. Under Convention article 34, the Contracting Parties undertake not to hinder the effective exercise of the right of petition.

The requirement that the petitioner be "a victim of a violation" has been interpreted by the European Court to mean that "an individual applicant should claim to have been actually affected by the violation he alleges . . . . Article [34] does not institute for individuals a kind of *actio popularis* for the interpretation of the Convention . . .". *Case of Klass and Others*, Judgment of September 6, 1978, 28 Publ. Eur. Court H.R. 5, at 17–18 (1979).

Unlike the European Convention, the American Convention allows persons who are not victims of a violation to file private petitions. It provides:

> Any person or group of persons, or any nongovernmental entity legally recognized in one or more member states of the Organization, may lodge petitions with the Commission containing denunciations or complaints of violation of this Convention by a State Party.

Art. 41. The Commission nonetheless has decided that a victim must be identified, as indicated in the case below. Only the African system accepts *actio popularis*, as the Commission recognized in *SERAC v. Nigeria*, reprinted in Chapter II B.

The following cases indicate how the "victim" requirement has been interpreted.

i. Who Is a Victim?

Dudgeon v. United Kingdom, Judgment of 23 September 1981, 45 Eur. Ct. H.R. (Ser. A) (1981), 4 EHRR 149 (1982) (plenary court).

. . . .

13. Mr. Jeffrey Dudgeon, who is 35 years of age, is a shipping clerk resident in Belfast, Northern Ireland. Mr. Dudgeon is a homosexual and his complaints are directed primarily against the existence in Northern Ireland of laws which have the

---

[2] *See e.g., The Sunday Times Case*, Judgment of April 1979, 30 Publ. Eur. Court H.R. 5 (1979)*; Stran Greek Refineries and Stratis Andreadis v. Greece*, Judgment of 9 December 1994, 301-B Publ. Eur. Court H.R. (1994), 19 Eur. H.R. Rep. 293.

[3] *See, e.g., Guerra & Others v. Italy* 26 Eur. H.R. Rep. 357 (forty inhabitants of an Italian town filed the complaint).

effect of making certain homosexual acts between consenting adult males criminal offences.

. . . .

29. In accordance with the general law, anyone, including a private person, may bring a prosecution for a homosexual offence, subject to the Director of Public Prosecutions' power to assume the conduct of the proceedings and, if he thinks fit, discontinue them. The evidence as to prosecutions for homosexual offences between 1972 and 1981 reveals that none has been brought by a private person during that time.

30. During the period from January 1972 to October 1980 there were 62 prosecutions for homosexual offences in Northern Ireland. The large majority of these cases involved minors, that is persons under 18; a few involved persons aged 18 to 21 or mental patients or prisoners. So far as the Government are aware from investigation of the records, no one was prosecuted in Northern Ireland during the period in question for an act which would clearly not have been an offence if committed in England or Wales. There is, however, no stated policy not to prosecute in respect of such acts. As was explained to the Court by the Government, instructions operative within the office of the Director of Public Prosecutions reserve the decision on whether to prosecute in each individual case to the Director personally, in consultation with the Attorney General, the sole criterion being whether, on all the facts and circumstances of that case, a prosecution would be in the public interest.

. . . .

F. The personal circumstances of the applicant

32. The applicant has, on his own evidence, been consciously homosexual from the age of 14. For some time he and others have been conducting a campaign aimed at bringing the law in Northern Ireland into line with that in force in England and Wales and, if possible, achieving a minimum age of consent lower than 21 years.

33. On 21 January 1976, the police went to Mr. Dudgeon's address to execute a warrant under the Misuse of Drugs Act 1971. During the search of the house a quantity of cannabis was found which subsequently led to another person being charged with drug offences. Personal papers, including correspondence and diaries, belonging to the applicant in which were described homosexual activities were also found and seized. As a result, he was asked to go to a police station where for about four and a half hours he was questioned, on the basis of these papers, about his sexual life. The police investigation file was sent to the Director of Prosecutions. It was considered with a view to instituting proceedings for the offence of gross indecency between males. The Director, in consultation with the Attorney General, decided that it would not be in the public interest for proceedings to be brought. Mr. Dudgeon was so informed in February 1977 and his papers, with annotations marked over them, were returned to him.

. . . .

37. The applicant complained that under the law in force in Northern Ireland he is liable to criminal prosecution on account of his homosexual conduct and that he has experienced fear, suffering and psychological distress directly caused by the very existence of the laws in question—including fear of harassment and blackmail.

He further complained that, following the search of his house in January 1976, he was questioned by the police about certain homosexual activities and that personal papers belonging to him were seized during the search and not returned until more than a year later. He alleged that, in breach of Article 8 of the Convention, he has thereby suffered, and continues to suffer, an unjustified interference with his right to respect for his private life.

. . . .

39. Although it is not homosexuality itself which is prohibited but the particular acts of gross indecency between males and buggery [. . .], there can be no doubt but that male homosexual practices whose prohibition is the subject of the applicant's complaints come within the scope of the offences punishable under the impugned legislation; it is on that basis that the case has been argued by the Government, the applicant and the Commission.

Furthermore, the offences are committed whether the act takes place in public or in private, whatever the age or relationship of the participants involved, and whether or not the participants are consenting. It is evident from Mr. Dudgeon's submissions, however, that his complaint was in essence directed against the fact that homosexual acts which he might commit in private with other males capable of valid consent are criminal offences under the law of Northern Ireland.

40. The Commission saw no reason to doubt the general truth of the applicant's allegations concerning the fear and distress that he has suffered in consequence of the existence of the laws in question. The Commission unanimously conluded that "the legislation complained of interferes with the applicant's right to respect for his private life guaranteed by Article 8 par. 1, in so far as it prohibits homosexual acts committed in private between consenting males".

The Government, without conceding the point, did not dispute that Mr. Dudgeon is directly affected by the laws and entitled to claim to be a "victim" thereof under Article 25 of the Convention. Nor did the Government contest the Commission's above-quoted conclusion.

41. The Court sees no reason to differ from the views of the Commission: the maintenance in force of the impugned legislation constitutes a continuing interference with the applicant's right to respect for his private life (which includes his sexual life) within the meaning of Article 8 par. 1. In the personal circumstances of the applicant, the very existence of this legislation continuously and directly affects his private life (see, mutatis mutandis, the *Marckx* judgment of 13 June 1979, Series A no. 31, p. 13, par. 27): either he respects the law and refrains from engaging—even in private with consenting male partners—in prohibited sexual acts to which he is disposed by reason of his homosexual tendencies, or he commits such acts and thereby becomes liable to criminal prosecution.

It cannot be said that the law in question is a dead letter in this sphere. It was, and still is, applied so as to prosecute persons with regard to private consensual homosexual acts involving males under 21 years of age. Although no proceedings seem to have been brought in recent years with regard to such acts involving only males over 21 years of age, apart from mental patients, there is no stated policy on the part of the authorities not to enforce the law in this respect. Furthermore, apart from prosecution by the Director of Public Prosection, there always remains the possibility of a private prosecution. Moreover, the police investigation in January 1976 was, in relation to the legislation in question, a specific measure of implementation—albeit short of actual prosecution—which directly affected the applicant in the enjoyment of his right to respect for his private life. As such, it showed that the threat hanging over him was real.

[The Court proceeded to hold that the Northern Ireland law, by reason of its breadth and absolute character, was, apart from the severity of the possible penalties provided for, disproportionate to the aims sought to be achieved and therefore, the applicant had suffered an unjustified interference with the right to respect for his private life guaranteed by Article 8. Subsequent cases have similarly concluded that criminalization of private adult homosexual activity is a violation of Article 8. See, e.g., *A.D.T. v. The United Kingdom, (App. no. 35765/97)*, judgment of 31 July 2000; *Modinos v. Cyprus*, judgment of 22 April 1993, Series A no. 259; *Norris v. Ireland*, judgment of 26 October 1988, Series A no. 142.]

Rep. No. 28/98, Case 11.625 María Eugenia Morales De Sierra v. Guatemala, March 6, 1998, *Annual Report of the Inter-American Commission on Human Rights 1997*, OEA/Ser.L/V/II.98, doc. 6 rev., 13 April 1998.

1. On February 22, 1995, the Inter-American Commission on Human Rights received a petition dated February 8, 1995 alleging that various provisions of the Civil Code of the Republic of Guatemala which establish the legal regime defining the role of each spouse within a marriage create distinctions between men and women which are discriminatory and violative of Articles 1.1, 2, 17 and 24 of the American Convention on Human Rights.

2. The petitioners indicated that Article 109 of the Civil Code confers the power to represent the marital union upon the husband, while Article 115 sets forth the exceptional instances when this authority may be exercised by the wife. Article 131 empowers the husband to administer marital property, while Article 133 provides for limited exceptions to that rule. Article 110 addresses responsibilities within the marriage, conferring upon the wife the "special right and obligation" to care for minor children and the home. Article 113 provides that a married woman may only exercise a profession or maintain employment where this does not prejudice her role as mother and homemaker. They stated that, according to Article 114, a husband may oppose his wife's activities outside the home, as long as he provides for her and has justified reasons. Article 255 confers primary responsibility on the husband to represent the children of the union and to administer their property. Article 317 provides that, by virtue of her sex, a woman may be excused from exercising certain forms of guardianship.

3. The petitioners reported that the constitutionality of these legal provisions had been challenged before the Guatemalan Court of Constitutionality in Case 84–92, which had ruled that the distinctions were constitutional, as, *inter alia*, they provided juridical certainty in the allocation of roles within marriage. The petitioners

requested that the Commission find the foregoing provisions of the Civil Code incompatible *in abstracto* with the guarantees set forth in Articles 1.1, 2, 17 and 24 of the American Convention.

4. Pursuant to the filing of their petition, on March 14, 1995, the petitioners sent the Commission a copy of the sentence issued by the Court of Constitutionality in response to Case 84–92. Case 11.625 was opened on May 6, 1996, and the pertinent parts of the petition were transmitted to the Government of Guatemala on that date, with a response requested within 90 days. . . .

8. On October 10, 1996, the petitioners provided the Commission with a set of 12 signed statements (nine of which were notarized), from married women, single women, and professionals in the fields of family law and psychology, concerning the effects and implications of the challenged provisions of the Civil Code. Copies of these statements were formally transmitted to the Guatemalan State by means of a note dated October 15, 1996. Any observations in response, or further information deemed pertinent were requested within 60 days. . . .

10. Pursuant to the January 24, 1997 request of the petitioners, the Commission held a hearing on the case on March 5, 1997, during its 95th regular period of sessions. The petitioners reported that the only project presented to the Congress to date with respect to the Civil Code had dealt solely with Article 114 (concerning the legal capacity of women to work and pursue activities outside of the home). The Commission on the Woman, the Minor and the Family had reviewed the project, and transmitted it to the plenary of the Congress on May 15, 1996. On May 20, 1996, the plenary had transmitted the project to the Commission of Legislative and Constitutional Points, which had issued an unfavorable report. The petitioners submitted a copy of a letter dated February 19, 1997 from the President of the Commission on the Woman, the Minor and the Family recounting these events, and a copy of the draft reforms to Article 114 of the Civil Code.

11. During the hearing, the Government indicated that . . . it continued to pursue initiatives aimed at the reform of the legislation in question. The State also reported that the Attorney General had challenged Civil Code Articles 113 and 114 before the Court of Constitutionality in an action filed on November 16, 1996, the determination of which remained pending. The Commission questioned the petitioners as to whether they were requesting a determination *in abstracto* or pursuing an individual claim. The petitioners indicated that, in the concrete case, María Eugenia Morales Aceña de Sierra had been directly affected by the challenged legislation, and also represented other women victims in Guatemala. The Commission requested that they formalize the status of María Eugenia Morales de Sierra as the victim in writing, in order to comply with the dispositions of its Regulations and proceed to process the petition within its case system.

12. The petitioners formalized the status of María Eugenia Morales de Sierra as victim in a communication of April 23, 1997, the date as of which the Commission considers this status to have been established in the file. According to the petitioners, María Eugenia Morales de Sierra is a victim who, as a married woman with children who resides in Guatemala, is subject to a legal regime which limits her capacity to exercise her rights. The petitioners characterized the norms in question as being

of immediate application, affecting the rights of the victim by virtue of her sex and civil status simply by being in effect. The petitioners supported their position with reference to the jurisprudence of the European and universal systems for the protection of human rights concerning the requirements of standing and admissibility. In a note of June 9, 1997, the pertinent parts of this communication were transmitted to the State of Guatemala, with any observations requested within 30 days....

14. On July 28, 1997, the petitioners provided the Commission with documentation complementing their April 23, 1997 submission, and consisting of a sworn declaration signed by María Eugenia Morales de Sierra, her birth certificate, marriage certificate, and birth certificates for her children. The declaration sets forth the effect of the legislative provisions at issue on the declarant's life, including, *inter alia*, the fact that the law prohibits her from representing the family or her minor child unless her husband is unable to do so; that she is unable to administer property obtained during the marriage or that of her children; and that the law would allow her husband to oppose her exercise of her profession at any moment. The declarant maintains that these restrictions have both legal and cultural consequences. The documentation was transmitted to the Government of Guatemala by means of a note dated August 14, 1997, with any response deemed pertinent requested within 30 days.

15. Pursuant to the request of the petitioners, the Commission held an additional hearing on the admissibility of the present case on October 10, 1997, during its 97th period of sessions. In a note dated September 18, 1997, the Government had indicated that it would respond to the additional information submitted by the petitioners during that scheduled hearing.

16. During the hearing, the petitioners produced three experts who testified as *amici curiae* to support the standing of María Eugenia Morales de Sierra as a direct victim in the instant case: Dinah Shelton, Center for Civil and Human Rights, Notre Dame Law School; Sian Lewis-Anthony, Interights; and Rhonda Copelon, International Women's Human Rights Law Clinic and the *Concertación de Mujeres Activistas Para los Derechos Humanos*. These experts recalled that members of a class targeted by legislation which is discriminatory on its face are deemed victims for the purpose of bringing petitions, citing, for example, the case of *Dudgeon v. the United Kingdom* (1982) 4 E.H.R.R. 149, para. 41. They further indicated that a putative victim need not demonstrate specified harm, nor even that specific measures of implementation have been taken, citing, for example, *Marckx v. Belgium* (1979), 2 E.H.R.R. 330, para 25, 27. In some cases, they noted, it may be sufficient to show the risk of a direct effect based on status, citing *Klass v. Germany* (1980), 2 E.H.R.R. 214, at para. 33. The petitioners asserted that, for the purposes of admissibility, where legislation creates a facial distinction with respect to a protected class, harm should be presumed. The prohibition against discrimination, they noted, is a nonderogable primary obligation. The petitioners sustained that the challenged provisions of the Civil Code play a central role in perpetuating and sustaining the inequality of women and men. Accordingly, while the provisions most immediately affect married women, in a larger sense they impact all women and Guatemalan society as a whole. Given their position that María Eugenia Morales de Sierra is in

fact a victim with standing, the *amici curiae* indicated that resolving the questions raised did not require a decision *in abstracto* by the Commission.

17. The State, for its part, indicated that María Eugenia Morales de Sierra had acknowledged in her statement of August 28, 1997 that her husband had never actually restricted her professional activities under the terms of Article 114. The representative of the Government reported that the Congress continued to study diverse proposals to reform the Civil Code in order to correct or modify provisions which impede the ability of women to fully exercise their rights. In particular, in August of 1997, the National Office of the Woman had presented a comprehensive set of reforms to the Civil Code. Additionally, the Commission of the Woman, the Minor and the Family of the Congress was currently studying projects concerning the integral promotion of women and the family; the elaboration of a law concerning sexual harassment; and the creation of a National Institute of the Woman (initiative number 1793). Given the pendency of these projects, the State asked that the Commission postpone its decision on admissibility in the present case.

18. During the hearing, the Commission reaffirmed that the petitioners had amended their initial petition for a decision on the compatibility of the provisions at issue *in abstracto* to instead request a decision on the individual claims of the named victim. The Commission also requested the views of the petitioner with respect to whether the former should proceed to an immediate decision on the admissibility and merits of the case. They indicated that, in their view, the processing of the case had been sufficient and that it was ripe for decision. Pursuant to inquiry by the Commission, the State indicated that it remained disposed to consider the option of the friendly settlement procedure. The petitioners indicated their belief that this option had been explored sufficiently, and had failed to provide any fruitful results.

19. The petitioners maintain that the cited provisions of the Civil Code discriminate against women, in a form which is immediate, direct and continuing, in violation of the rights of María Eugenia Morales de Sierra established in Articles 1.1, 2, 17 and 24 of the American Convention. The petitioners cite international human rights jurisprudence, including that of the Inter-American Court, for the proposition that, while a difference in treatment is not necessarily discriminatory, such a distinction must be objectively justified in the pursuit of a legitimate end, and the means employed must be proportionate to that end. They contend that the provisions in question set forth distinctions between women and men, most immediately married women and men, which are illegitimate and unjustified. They note that the Court of Constitutionality found the challenged provisions justified as a form of protection for women, and as a means of establishing juridical certainty in the allocation of rights and responsibilities within marriage. The petitioners maintain that, even should these be deemed legitimate and sufficient justifications, the means employed are disproportionate. They assert that these provisions are contrary to the principle of equality between the spouses, and nullify the juridical capacity of the woman within the domestic legal order, thereby controverting the protections set forth in Articles 17 and 24 of the American Convention, as well as the obligations set forth in Articles 1.1 and 2.

20. The petitioners initially positioned their claims as a request for a decision *in abstracto* on the compatibility of the cited provisions of the Civil Code with the provisions of Articles 1.1, 2, 17 and 24 of the American Convention. Citing Advisory Opinions OC/13 and OC/14 of the Inter-American Court, they argued that the Commission could exercise jurisdiction over the matter through its general functions under Article 41 of the American Convention to: promote and oversee member state compliance with their human rights obligations; make recommendations to the states for measures in favor of the protection of human rights; and to act on individual petitions.

21. As recorded, the petitioners amended their position during the processing of the petition in 1997 to designate co-petitioner María Eugenia Morales de Sierra as an individual victim. Pursuant to that modification, the petitioners provided information which they assert demonstrates how the distinctions created by the challenged legislation restrict the ability of the victim to fully exercise the guarantees set forth in Articles 1.1, 2, 17 and 24 of the American Convention.

22. The petitioners maintain that the case satisfies all the requirements of admissibility, domestic remedies having been invoked and exhausted, and the victim having pleaded the direct effect of the impugned provisions on her ability to exercise her rights. . . .

24. . . . [T]he State appears to contend that the Commission may lack jurisdiction *ratione personae*. During the October 10, 1997 hearing before the Commission, the Government indicated that, although the victim complains that Article 114 of the Civil Code constitutes an infringement of her right to work, in fact, she freely exercises her profession, and acknowledged in her written statement of August 28, 1997 that her husband had never impeded those activities. The presumed implication is that, if the victim has not been directly prejudiced as a result of the legislation, the Commission lacks jurisdiction *ratione personae*.

IV. CONSIDERATIONS WITH RESPECT TO ADMISSIBILITY

25. The Commission is competent to examine the subject matter of this complaint, as it concerns alleged violations of Articles 1.1, 2, 17 and 24 of the American Convention. The Republic of Guatemala deposited its ratification of the American Convention on May 25, 1978, and the Convention entered into force for all parties on July 18, 1978.

26. The petitioners' submissions include the information required by Article 32 of the Commission's Regulations, and meet the conditions set forth in Article 46.1.c of the American Convention and Article 39 of the Commission's Regulations, as the claims are neither pending settlement in another international inter-governmental proceeding, nor essentially duplicative of a petition pending or previously considered by the Commission. . . .

30. With respect to the question of jurisdiction *ratione personae*, the Commission has previously explained that, in general, its competence under the individual case process pertains to facts involving the rights of a specific individual or individuals. *See generally*, I.A.C.H.R., *Case of Emérita Montoya González, Report* 48/96, Case 11.553 (Costa Rica), in annual report of the IACHR 1996, OEA/Ser.L/V/II.95, Doc. 7 rev., March 14, 1997, paras. 28, 31. The Commission entertains a broader

competence under Article 41.b of the Convention to address recommendations to member states for the adoption of progressive measures in favor of the protection of human rights.

31. Pursuant to their original petition for a decision *in abstracto*, which appeared to rely on the Commission's competence under Article 41.b of the American Convention rather than that under Article 41.f, the petitioners modified their petition and named María Eugenia Morales de Sierra as an individual victim, as previously noted, in their communication of April 23, 1997. With the identification of an individual victim, the Commission may advance with its decision on admissibility in the present case. As the Honorable Court has explained, in order to initiate the procedures established in Articles 48 and 50 of the American Convention, the Commission requires a petition denouncing a concrete violation with respect to a specific individual. Inter-Am.Ct.H.R., *Advisory Opinion OC-14/94, "International Responsibility for the Promulgation and Enforcement of Laws in Violation of the Convention (Arts. 1 and 2 of the American Convention),"* of Dec. 9, 1994, para. 45, *see also* paras. 46–33. With respect to the allegations concerning Article 114 of the Civil Code, the Government appears to argue that, as the victim's husband has never opposed her exercise of her profession, her rights have therefore never been infringed by the application of that provision. This argument, however, misses the substance of the complaint raised, and is rejected for that reason. In the first place, in virtue of the public order of human rights, even the eventual consent of a victim to a violation does not validate the violative act of a State, nor does it affect the competence of the international organ to whom the States have entrusted their protection. The victim asserts that the American Convention protects her right as a married woman to work and develop other activities outside of the home under equal conditions with men. Accordingly, she contends that the restrictions which Article 114 imposes on married women, but not upon married men, deny her the right to pursue professional and other opportunities on equal terms with men simply by virtue of being in force. . . .

34. With respect to the claims as a whole, the Commission observes that a legal provision may affect an individual in different ways. A non-self-executing law will require measures of implementation by state authorities before it can be applied in a concrete case. *OC-14/94, supra*, para. 41. A self-executing law, on the other hand, may violate a protected right by virtue of its entry into force, if all other requirements (e.g., competence ratione personae) are complied with. Therefore, and taking into account the foregoing, "a norm that deprives a portion of the population of some of its rights—for example, because of race—*automatically* injures all the members of that race." Emphasis added. *Id.*, para. 43.

35. In the instant case, María Eugenia Morales de Sierra alleges that the challenged provisions of the Civil Code create distinctions based on gender which infringe her rights to equality and to equal protection of and before the law simply by virtue of being in force. In this regard, international jurisprudence has established that a law may violate the right of an individual, even in the absence of any specific measure of subsequent implementation by the authorities, where the individual is directly affected, or is at imminent risk of being directly affected by a legislative provision.

See generally, E.Ct.H.R., *Case of Klass and Others*, Judgment of 6 Sept. 1978, Ser. A Vol. 28, paras. 33–38; E.Ct.H.R., *Marckx Case*, Judgment of 13 June 1979, para. 27; *see also*, U.N.H.R. Committee, *Ballantyne, Davidson and McIntyre v. Canada*, 1993 Report, Vol. II, p. 102. María Eugenia Morales de Sierra is "challenging a legal position"—that of married women under the cited Articles of the Civil Code—"which affects her personally." *See, Marckx Case, supra*, para 27. The Commission considers that the direct effect of the challenged legislative provisions on the rights and daily life of the victim has been adequately alleged and demonstrated for the purposes of admissibility in the present case, and will analyze its relevance and impact in the decision on the merits. In this phase, the Commission will not discuss matters related to human rights violations committed via self-executing laws.

36. Finally, as required by Article 47 of the American Convention, the petitioners have stated facts tending to establish a violation of the rights guaranteed by this Convention. Articles 109, 110, 113, 114, 115, 131, 133, 255, and 317 of the Civil Code establish differences in the treatment the law provides with respect to married women and married men, and in some cases, married and unmarried women. Under international human rights law, such differences must be analyzed to determine whether they pursue a legitimate aim, and whether the means employed are proportional to the end sought. I.Ct.H.R., Advisory Opinion OC-4/84, *"Proposed Amendments to the Naturalization Provisions of the Constitution of Costa Rica,"* Ser. A No. 4, para. 56, *citing* E.Ct.H.R., *Belgian Linguistic Case*, Judgment of July 23, 1968, Ser. A No. 6, at 34. In other words, the law is expected to be even-handed between women and men unless just, legitimate and reasonable compelling bases have been adduced to justify a difference in treatment. *See Van Raalte v. Netherlands*, 24 E.H.R.R. 503, para. 42. The Commission will take up this question in its analysis of the merits of the case.

. . . .

Center for the Independence of Judges and Lawyers v. Algeria, and Others, (Comm. 104/94, 109–126/94), *8th Annual Activity Report of the Afr. Comm. H.P.R. 1994–1995*, Annex VI.

The Facts

1. The communication is in the form of a report published by the Center for the Independence of Judges and Lawyers of Geneva, Switzerland. It describes harassment and persecution of judges and lawyers in 53 different countries including 18 of the African countries party to the African Charter. The harassment and persecution described includes murder, torture, intimidation and threats of all kinds. The report describes special features of court systems, such as military courts and special tribunals.

Complaint

2. The communication does not specify which of the facts it contains it regards as violations. Neither does it specify any sought remedy.

The Law

. . . .

6. The present report submitted by the CIJL does not give specific places, dates, and times of alleged incidents sufficient to permit the Commission to intervene or investigate. In some cases, incidents are cited without giving the names of the aggrieved parties. There are numerous references to "anonymous" lawyers and judges. Thus, in this case the author is not an alleged victim, nor is the communication submitted in the name of a specific victim, nor does the complainant allege grave and massive violations. The information in the communication is insufficient to permit the Commission to take action.

FOR THE ABOVE REASONS, THE AFRICAN COMMISSION
Declares the communications inadmissible.

Questions and Comments

1. What made Dudgeon a "victim" for purposes of admissibility: the law itself, the search of his house, or his questioning by the police? If neither the search nor the questioning had occurred, would this case be admissible?

2. Do you agree with the decision of the Inter-American Commission? Does the Convention or the Rules of Procedure require a named victim? Would a class action be admissible? Are the answers the same for the African system?

3. How imminent does a violation have to be to make someone a victim? Is a deportation order that would send someone to a state reputed to engage in torture enough? Could a law in breach of human rights norms that has been enacted but not yet enforced be challenged, e.g., one that subjects journalists to prior censorship of their writings? Who would have standing to challenge the law: journalists, publishers, readers? Is this an issue of determining standing or of ripeness? Can the issues be separated in this instance? See *Soering v. UK*, App. No. 14038/88, 161 Eur. Ct.H.R. (Ser. A)(1989); *D v. UK*, App. No. 30240/96, 24 EHRR 423 (1997).

ii. Bringing a Case on Behalf of Another

Vatan v. Russia (admissibility dec.), (App. no. 47978/99), Eur. Ct. H.R., 7 October 2004.

1. The case originated in an application against the Russian Federation lodged with the Court under Article 34 of the Convention for the Protection of Human Rights and Fundamental Freedoms by the People's Democratic Party Vatan, a political party registered under Russian law. . . .

3. The applicant party alleged that the suspension of the activities of its branch violated its freedom to hold opinions and to impart information and ideas, its freedom of association and party members' right to manifest their religion. . . .

5. By a decision of 21 March 2002, the Court declared the application partly inadmissible.

6. By a decision of 4 September 2003, the Court declared the remainder of the application partly admissible, having joined the Government's preliminary objection to the merits.

I. THE CIRCUMSTANCES OF THE CASE

8. On 29 April 1994 Vatan was registered as a political party with the Ministry of Justice of the Russian Federation.

9. According to Vatan's constitutional charter, it was founded "to support the renascence of the Tartar nation, to enhance the latter's political activity and to protect Tartars' political, socio-economic and cultural rights". The name "Tartar" applies to the peoples of Turkic origin who speak a language which belongs to the Ural-Altaic language family. Four-fifths of the Tartars (about 5.5 million people) live in the Russian Federation: the majority live in the Republic of Tatarstan and the Republic of Bashkortostan, and the rest are dispersed across the Ural Mountains and in the Volga region. The Tartars are Muslims.

10. On 12 August 1994 the Simbirsk (Ulyanovsk) Regional Organisation of the People's Democratic Party Vatan ("the Regional Organisation") was registered with the Ulyanovsk Regional Department of Justice. Vatan claims that this was a branch of its party.

11. On 12 October 1997 the Regional Organisation made an appeal to the "peoples of the Volga region, to all oppressed peoples of the empire, to the Ulyanovsk Regional and City authorities, to historians, students of local lore, archaeologists and scientists," entitled "Prevention and cancellation of the forthcoming witches' Sabbath arranged by reactionary forces—'the war party'—the so-called '350th anniversary of the founding of the town of Simbirsk' which is in fact an approximate date of the colonisation of Shekhry Sember".

. . . .

13. On 19 May 1998 the Regional Organisation asked the mayor of Ulyanovsk to authorise a ceremony dedicated to the 350th anniversary of the founding of Sember. On 22 May 1998 the mayor gave permission for the ceremony to be held in places of worship belonging to religious organisations and in cemeteries.

14. On 31 May 1998 the Regional Organisation held a memorial ceremony in the city centre, where, according to Vatan, an ancient Muslim cemetery was formerly located.

15. On 3 June 1998 the prosecutor of the Ulyanovsk Region applied to the Ulyanovsk Regional Court to have the Regional Organisation's activities suspended on the ground that it had called for violence, contrary to the federal legislation and the Constitution.

. . . .

31. Vatan alleged that the court decisions to suspend the Regional Organisation's activities had violated its freedom to hold opinions and to impart information and ideas, its freedom of association and the party members' right to manifest their religion. It referred to Articles 9, 10, 11 and 14 of the Convention.

32. The Government objected to the applicant party's standing as a victim of the alleged violations of the Convention.

33. First, the Government claimed that Vatan was not eligible to file an application with the Court on behalf of the Regional Organisation. They submitted that Vatan and the Regional Organisation were two different legal entities, each registered in accordance with the law. They claimed that Vatan did not have standing on behalf of its regional branches in domestic proceedings either under the Russian Civil Code or under its own constituent documents. In particular, they claimed that Vatan's president had acted in the proceedings before the Supreme Court of the Russian Federation on behalf of the Regional Organisation after having been given power of attorney.

34. Secondly, the Government denied that Vatan's application pursued its own interests as opposed to those of the Regional Organisation, since the suspension of the Regional Organisation's activities did not affect Vatan. They pointed out that Vatan could continue its activities, even in Ulyanovsk, during the whole period that the Regional Organisation was subject to the injunction.

. . . .

B. The Court's assessment

38. The Court reiterates that in order to be able to rely on the substantive provisions of the Convention, two conditions must be met: an applicant must fall into one of the categories of petitioners mentioned in Article 34 of the Convention, and he or she must be able to make out a prima facie case that he or she is the victim of a violation of the Convention (*Asselbourg and Others v. Luxembourg* (dec.), no. 29121/95, ECHR 1999-VI).

39. The Court notes that the present application was lodged by a political party, Vatan, which is registered as a legal person. The Court notes that the measures complained of in this application, notably the suspension and the ensuing domestic proceedings, concerned the Regional Organisation, which was also registered as a legal person, and not Vatan. The fact that Vatan and the Regional Organisation were two different legal entities is not disputed by the applicant and is evident from Vatan's and the Regional Organisation's constituent documents.

40. The Court has first to consider whether this case can be regarded as one in which Vatan constituted a form of "umbrella" organisation comprising both Vatan itself and the Regional Organisation as constituent parts.

41. Such an interpretation would require the Court to accept that the identity of a non-governmental organisation (within the meaning of Article 34) may extend beyond its own legal personality so as to comprise several legal persons.

42. The Court must therefore determine whether there existed at the material time a political party which comprised both Vatan and the Regional Organisation, and if so, whether it could claim to be a "non-governmental organisation" within the meaning of Article 34 for the purposes of the present case.

43. The Court considers that the legal personality of a non-governmental organisation creates a *prima facie* presumption as to its identity. Any claim that a political party embraces more than one legal person must be borne out by the statutes and structures of the organisation. In particular, one would expect regulation of matters such as subordination, submission to a single leadership, adherence to a single set of political proposals, joint pursuit of a single political campaign, membership

registers, nominations for elections and support for candidates and abstention from mutual political rivalry. The legal persons comprising such a party would, at the least, be expected to provide in their individual constituent documents for their structural subordination and political commitment to certain political ideals. The Court will therefore examine whether on such an interpretation Vatan and the Regional Organisation could claim to constitute a single political party.

44. The Court observes that while Vatan's constitutional charter provides for the establishment of "regional organisations", no reciprocal provisions can be found in the charter of the Regional Organisation. The Regional Organisation's constituent documents contain only one implicit reference to Vatan, providing for the appeal against termination of membership. The Regional Organisation's charter leaves open the question of whether the Regional Organisation was structurally dependent on Vatan in its decision-making and whether it had political commitments to the latter. In particular, nothing in the constituent documents prevented the Regional Organisation from pursuing political goals other than those approved by Vatan. There is no suggestion in the present case that the actions and statements which gave rise to the Regional Organisation's suspension were prompted or authorised by Vatan.

45. Moreover, the Court notes that Vatan had no standing in the domestic proceedings in its alleged capacity of a "party as a whole". As submitted by the Government, and not disputed by the applicant, Vatan's president took part in the proceedings before the Supreme Court in accordance with a power of attorney issued to him by the Regional Organisation, and not in his capacity of "the head of the entire party".

46. The Court cannot therefore conclude that Vatan and the Regional Organisation were one political party which could constitute a single non-governmental organisation within the meaning of Article 34 of the Convention.

47. The Court has further considered whether Vatan itself may claim to be a victim of the suspension applied against the Regional Organisation.

48. The Court recalls that the term "victim" used in Article 34 denotes the person directly affected by the act or omission which is at issue (see *Eckle v. Germany*, judgment of 15 July 1982, Series A no. 51, p. 30, § 66). It further recalls that accepting an application from a "person" indirectly affected by the alleged violation will be justified only in exceptional circumstances, in particular where it is clearly established that it is impossible for the direct victim to apply to the Court through the organs set up under its articles of incorporation (see *Agrotexim and Others v. Greece*, judgment of 24 October 1995, Series A no. 330, p. 25, § 66).

49. The person directly affected by the domestic measure in this case was the Regional Organisation. The focus of Vatan's own concern appears to be the fact that it could not rely on the Regional Organisation to convey its political ideas in the Ulyanovsk region for a period of six months.

50. The Court notes that the injunction in question did not impose any limitations on Vatan itself, hence there was nothing to stop Vatan from pursuing its activities in its own name, for example through individual party members. The Court also notes that it was open to the Regional Organisation itself, as the direct victim, to lodge an application with the Court. The Court finds no exceptional circum-

stances in the present case which could entitle Vatan itself to claim to be a victim of the disputed suspension.

51. The Court also notes that Vatan, unlike the Regional Organisation, has never pursued any domestic proceedings in its own name in respect of the alleged violations. Therefore, even if the Court were to accept Vatan to be a victim, the application would in any event be inadmissible on account of a failure to exhaust domestic remedies.

51. Finally, the Court notes that there is no suggestion in the present case that Vatan represents the Regional Organisation in the proceedings before the Court.

53. Consequently, the Government's preliminary objection is well-founded. Vatan cannot, as matters stand, claim "to be the victim of a violation" within the meaning of Article 34 of the Convention. It follows that the remainder of the applicant must be declared inadmissible.

54. Having accepted the Government's preliminary objection, the Court cannot consider the merits of the case.

Concurring Opinion of Judges Ress and Cabral Barreto

We agree with the conclusion reached in the judgment, but would have preferred to see the case declared inadmissible on the ground that it is manifestly ill-founded. In our view, in considering the People's Democratic Party Vatan's right to defend itself against illegal interference, it is rather artificial to divide its structure into a central party organisation and regional organisations. As the Court has rightly stated, there is a *prima facie* presumption that, in the case of a political party, the legal personality of a non-governmental organisation extends to the party as a whole and creates a single political entity. It may be that different legal personalities exist under Russian law, but the Court should bear in mind that, in order to protect the existence of political parties and freedom of political expression under Articles 10 and 11 of the Convention, a broad approach is to be preferred.

In our view, it was arguable under the Convention that Vatan should have had standing in the domestic proceedings in its alleged capacity as a "party as a whole". The Court's decision to accept the splitting up of a political party into different legal personalities, as permitted under the domestic legal system, makes it rather difficult for a political party to defend its rights against interference by the different state organs. This is particularly true when, as is the case here, a party's regional organisation is subject to interference that may affect the party as a whole. It is implicit in the principle of political representation that it should be acceptable for different legal persons to be involved. We would therefore have accepted Vatan's claim to have been affected by the domestic measure which, in this case, was directed against the party's regional organisation. In our view, Vatan itself was also a victim for the purpose of Article 34 of the Convention and we have no difficulty in accepting that, in addition to Vatan as the central organisation, the regional organisation was also entitled to defend itself against the infringement. The question of whether there was exhaustion of domestic remedies, in that Vatan, unlike the regional organisation, never pursued domestic proceedings in its own name in respect of the alleged violations, is not convincingly answered in the judgment: if the regional organisation acts in a broader perspective, representing the interest of the party as a whole as well as its own interests, then it does not seem justified even to contemplate rejection of Vatan's application on the ground that it failed to institute parallel proceedings before the domestic courts.

Furthermore, the issue is not whether Vatan may represent the regional organisation in the proceedings before this Court, since, if a political party like Vatan is presumed to have an all-embracing identity, then it does in fact defend itself in such proceedings when it challenges interference with a regional organisation. This broader view is derived from the concept that, in a democratic society, political parties are not to be treated as ordinary associations but require specific protection.

We would in any event have come to the conclusion that the application is inadmissible because it is manifestly ill-founded. In our view, the regional court rightly concluded that the Regional Organisation of the People's Democratic Party Vatan openly called for violent alterations to the foundations of constitutional governance and for the creation of an Islamic state in the Volga region, and called for a brigade of "courageous and resistant" people to fight for national liberation and the decolonisation of Russia. In the light of the Court's judgment in the case of *Refah Partisi (the Welfare Party) and Others v. Turkey* ([GC], nos. 41340/98, 41342/98, 41343/98 and 41344/98, ECHR 2003-II) we consider those conclusions by the regional court neither exaggerated nor unfounded. In particular, the reference to the Russian Federation as a "war party" whose arms should be "shortened" and to Russian institutions as "Nazis" overstepped the boundary of permissible freedom of expression within the meaning of Article 10. Therefore, in our view, it would have been preferable to base the conclusion on these considerations.

Questions and Comments

1. The European Court has found that family members of direct victims may themselves be victims of violations. See *Kurt v. Turkey*, App. No. 24276/94, 27 EHRR 373 (1999) (mother of a disappeared son held to be victim of a violation of Article 3 due to failure by the state to clarify son's whereabouts). In addition, the family members may represent the direct victim where the person is missing, dead, incommunicado or in poor health. Parents, guardians or their legal representatives may represent children. *See, e.g., Ilhan v. Turkey*, No. 22277/93, 35 EHRR 36 (2002); *Nielsen v. Denmark*, App. No. 10929/84, 11 EHRR 175 (1989); *Scozzari and Guinta v. Italy*, App. No. 39221/98 and 41963/98, 35 EHRR 12 (2002); *Cambell and Cosans v. UK*, App. No. 25599/94, 27 EHRR 611 (1999); *SP, DP and T v. UK*, App. No. 23715/94, 22 EHRR CD 148 (2002).

2. In the Inter-American system, how should the Commission handle cases involving the same facts, where one petition is filed by a human rights NGO and the other is submitted directly by family members of the victim?

iii. Death of the Applicant

Karner v. Austria, (App. no. 40016/98), Judgment of 24 July 2003, Eur. Ct. H.R., 38 EHRR 24 (2004).

. . . .

10. The applicant was born in 1955 and lived in Vienna.

11. From 1989 the applicant lived with Mr. W., with whom he had a homosexual relationship, in a flat in Vienna, which the latter had rented a year earlier. They shared the expenses on the flat.

12. In 1991 Mr. W. discovered that he was infected with the AIDS virus. His relationship with the applicant continued. In 1993, when Mr. W. developed AIDS, the applicant nursed him. In 1994 Mr. W. died after designating the applicant as his heir.

13. In 1995 the landlord of the flat brought proceedings against the applicant for termination of the tenancy. On 6 January 1996 the Favoriten District Court (*Bezirksgericht*) dismissed the action. It considered that section 14(3) of the Rent Act (*Mietrechtsgesetz*), which provided that family members had a right to succeed to a tenancy, was also applicable to a homosexual relationship.

14. On 30 April 1996 the Vienna Regional Civil Court (*Landesgericht für Zivilrechtssachen*) dismissed the landlord's appeal. It found that section 14(3) of the Rent Act was intended to protect persons who had lived together for a long time without being married against sudden homelessness. It applied to homosexuals as well as to persons of opposite sex.

15. On 5 December 1996 the Supreme Court (*Oberster Gerichtshof*) granted the landlord's appeal, quashed the lower court's decision and terminated the lease. It found that the notion of "life companion" (*Lebensgefährte*) in section 14(3) of the Rent Act was to be interpreted as at the time it was enacted, and the legislature's intention in 1974 was not to include persons of the same sex.

16. On 26 September 2000 the applicant died.

. . . .

I. JURISDICTION OF THE COURT

20. The Government requested that the application be struck out of the list of cases in accordance with Article 37 § 1 of the Convention, since the applicant had died and there were no heirs who wished to pursue the application.

21. The applicant's counsel emphasised that the case involved an important issue of Austrian law and that respect for human rights required its continued examination, in accordance with Article 37 § 1 *in fine*.

22. The Court notes that in a number of cases in which an applicant died in the course of the proceedings it has taken into account the statements of the applicant's heirs or of close family members expressing the wish to pursue the proceedings before the Court (see, among other authorities, *Deweer v. Belgium*, judgment of 27 February 1980, Series A no. 35, pp. 19-20, §§ 37–38; *X v. the United Kingdom*, judgment of 5 November 1981, Series A no. 46, p. 15, § 32; *Vocaturo v. Italy*, judgment of 24 May 1991, Series A no. 206-C, p. 29, § 2; *G. v. Italy*, judgment of 27 February 1992, Series A no. 228-F, p. 65, § 2; *Pandolfelli and Palumbo v. Italy*, judgment of

27 February 1992, Series A no. 231-B, p. 16, § 2; *X v. France*, judgment of 31 March 1992, Series A no. 234-C, p. 89, § 26; and *Raimondo v. Italy*, judgment of 22 February 1994, Series A no. 281-A, p. 8, § 2).

23. On the other hand, it has been the Court's practice to strike applications out of the list of cases in the absence of any heir or close relative who has expressed the wish to pursue an application (see *Scherer v. Switzerland*, judgment of 25 March 1994, Series A no 287, pp. 14–15, § 31; *Öhlinger v. Austria*, no. 21444/93, Commission's report of 14 January 1997, § 15, unreported; *Malhous v. the Czech Republic* (dec.) [GC], no. 33071/96, ECHR 2000-XII). Thus, the Court has to determine whether the application in the present case should also be struck out of the list. In formulating an appropriate answer to this question, the object and purpose of the Convention system as such must be taken into account.

24. The Court reiterates that, while Article 33 (former Article 24) of the Convention allows each Contracting State to refer to the Court (Commission) "any alleged breach" of the Convention by another Contracting State, a person, non-governmental organisation or group of individuals must, in order to be able to lodge a petition in pursuance of Article 34 (former Article 25), claim "to be the victim of a violation . . . of the rights set forth in the Convention or the Protocols thereto". Thus, in contrast to the position under Article 33—where, subject to the other conditions laid down, the general interest attaching to the observance of the Convention renders admissible an inter-State application—Article 34 requires that an individual applicant should claim to have been actually affected by the violation he alleges (see *Ireland v. the United Kingdom*, judgment of 18 January 1978, Series A no. 25, pp. 90–91, §§ 239–40, and *Klass and Others v. Germany*, judgment of 6 September 1978, Series A no. 28, pp. 17–18, § 33). Article 34 does not institute for individuals a kind of *actio popularis* for the interpretation of the Convention; it does not permit individuals to complain against a law *in abstracto* simply because they feel that it contravenes the Convention (see *Norris v. Ireland*, judgment of 26 October 1988, Series A no. 142, pp. 15–16, § 31, and *Sanles Sanles v. Spain* (dec.), no. 48335/99, ECHR 2000-XI).

25. While under Article 34 of the Convention the existence of a "victim of a violation", that is to say, an individual applicant who is personally affected by an alleged violation of a Convention right, is indispensable for putting the protection mechanism of the Convention into motion, this criterion cannot be applied in a rigid, mechanical and inflexible way throughout the whole proceedings. As a rule, and in particular in cases which primarily involve pecuniary, and, for this reason, transferable claims, the existence of other persons to whom that claim is transferred is an important criterion, but cannot be the only one. As the Court pointed out in *Malhous* (decision cited above), human rights cases before the Court generally also have a moral dimension, which must be taken into account when considering whether the examination of an application after the applicant's death should be continued. All the more so if the main issue raised by the case transcends the person and the interests of the applicant.

26. The Court has repeatedly stated that its "judgments in fact serve not only to decide those cases brought before the Court but, more generally, to elucidate, safe-

guard and develop the rules instituted by the Convention, thereby contributing to the observance by the States of the engagements undertaken by them as Contracting Parties" (see *Ireland v. the United Kingdom*, cited above, p. 62, § 154, and *Guzzardi v. Italy*, judgment of 6 November 1980, Series A no. 39, p. 31, § 86). Although the primary purpose of the Convention system is to provide individual relief, its mission is also to determine issues on public-policy grounds in the common interest, thereby raising the general standards of protection of human rights and extending human rights jurisprudence throughout the community of Convention States.

27. The Court considers that the subject matter of the present application—the difference in treatment of homosexuals as regards succession to tenancies under Austrian law—involves an important question of general interest not only for Austria but also for other States Parties to the Convention. In this connection the Court refers to the submissions made by ILGA-Europe, Liberty and Stonewall, whose intervention in the proceedings as third parties was authorised as it highlights the general importance of the issue. Thus, the continued examination of the present application would contribute to elucidate, safeguard and develop the standards of protection under the Convention.

28. In these particular circumstances, the Court finds that respect for human rights as defined in the Convention and the Protocols thereto requires a continuation of the examination of the case (Article 37 § 1 *in fine* of the Convention) and accordingly rejects the Government's request for the application to be struck out of its list.

[By six votes to one the Court held that there had been a violation of Article 14 of the Convention taken in conjunction with Article 8].

Dissenting Opinion of Judge Grabenwarter

1. I voted against the majority's decision to reject the Government's request that the application be struck out of the list of cases, for the following reasons.

The Court has decided on a number of occasions to permit a successor in title to continue Convention proceedings when an applicant has died. In the present case, however, it appears that there are no heirs, with the result that Article 37 § 1 of the Convention is in issue.

2. Under Article 37 § 1 of the Convention the Court may at any stage of the proceedings decide to strike an application out of the list of cases where the circumstances lead to the conclusion that the applicant does not intend to pursue his application. However, the Court should continue the examination of the application if respect for human rights as defined in the Convention and the Protocols thereto so requires.

I agree with the majority that discrimination against homosexuals in general, and in the field of tenancy legislation in particular, forms an important aspect of respect for human rights. This does not, however, in itself justify the continued examination of a case after the death of an applicant in proceedings under Article 34 of the Convention. The reasoning of the majority is rather short as the reference to case-law concerning the continuation of proceedings when there are heirs does not apply in this case.

At the outset, I agree with the majority that, despite the death of the applicant and the absence of a formal successor in title, the Court may in exceptional cases continue the examination of a case. I also agree that the general importance of the case may be of relevance in this respect.

3. However, I do not share the opinion that the present case is one of "general importance" for these purposes. In taking up the wording of earlier judgments in a different context, the majority suggest that it suffices if the continuation of the examination would "contribute to elucidate, safeguard and develop the standards of protection under the Convention" (see *Ireland v. the United Kingdom*, judgment of 18 January 1978, Series A no. 25, p. 62, § 154, and *Guzzardi v. Italy*, judgment of 6 November 1980, Series A no. 39, p. 31, § 86). While it is true that judgments also serve these purposes, it is not in line with the character of the Convention system (which is primarily designed to protect individuals) to continue proceedings without an applicant on the ground that this contributes to elucidating, safeguarding and developing the standards of protection under the Convention. This rather general criterion is met by the majority of the cases declared admissible, at least by those where the alleged violation is caused by domestic law or general practice and not by the practice applied in the particular case. "General importance" needs to be read in a narrower sense.

The judgment gives no reason for the "general importance" of the case other than the reference to the submissions of a third party, whose intervention "highlights the general importance of the issue". The fact that third parties applied to intervene is an indication of a certain general interest in the case, but it does not mean that the case is of a general importance (see Rule 61 § 3 of the Rules of Court and Article 36 § 2 of the Convention for the criteria for third-party interventions).

In this connection, reference must be made to a recent judgment of the Fourth Section of the Court in *Sevgi Erdoğan v. Turkey* no. 28492/95, 29 April 2003, paragraph 38 of which reads as follows:

> "In the light of the foregoing, and given the impossibility of establishing any communication with the applicant's close relatives or statutory heirs, the Court considers that her representative cannot meaningfully continue the proceedings before it (see, *mutatis mutandis*, *Ali v. Switzerland*, judgment of 5 August 1998, *Reports of Judgments and Decisions* 1998-V, pp. 2148–49, § 32). The Court would also point out that it has already had occasion to rule on the issue raised by the applicant under Article 3 in its examination of other applications against Turkey (see, among many other authorities, *Aksoy v. Turkey*, judgment of 18 December 1996, *Reports* 1996-VI; *Büyükdağ v. Turkey*, no. 28340/95, 21 December 2000; and, as the most recent example, *Algür v. Turkey*, no. 32574/96, 22 October 2002). Having regard to those considerations, the Court concludes that it is no longer justified to continue the examination of the application."

Sevgi Erdoğan shows that, while a question of general importance may attach to, for example, cases involving gross violations of human rights (such as the execution of someone following a death sentence before this Court has given judgment), even treatment that may fall under Article 3 of the Convention does not in itself justify continuing the examination of an application. Therefore, it is hard to see why a violation of Article 14 of the Convention taken in conjunction with Article 8 should be seen differently unless there are other reasons.

It appears from *Sevgi Erdoğan* that a prior judgment on the same issue may be relevant in considering whether an application should be struck out of the list of cases under Article 37 § 1 of the Convention. The majority do not rely on that argument. If they had done so they could not have supported the continuation of the proceedings for the following reason. If the Court has not yet decided a particular issue, the question arises whether it would be difficult to bring a similar case before the Court. It follows, however, from the submissions of the applicant's lawyer that there are a number of parallel cases in Austria, especially in Vienna, that could easily be brought before the Austrian courts and hence before this Court. Against the background of the decision of the Austrian Supreme Court in this case, it may even be doubtful whether future applicants would have to introduce a remedy before that court in order to fulfil the requirements of Article 35 of the Convention. In sum, I do not think that it would be especially difficult to bring a parallel case before the European Court of Human Rights.

Both the lack of general importance of the present case and the lack of any particular difficulty in bringing a parallel case before the Court lead me to the conclusion that the present application should have been struck out of the list of cases. The European Court of Human Rights is not a constitutional court which decides on a case-by-case basis which cases it deems expedient to examine on the basis of a general criterion such as the one provided by the majority.

At any rate, the Chamber broke new ground with this decision, which is unprecedented in the case-law of the Court. It refers to a number of cases at paragraph 23 of the judgment, although not *Sevgi Erdoğan*, and then proceeds to decide this case differently. In my view, this is a clear case in which Article 30 of the Convention applies: the judgment has a "result inconsistent with a judgment previously delivered by the Court". It also raises a serious question affecting the interpretation of the Convention. The Chamber should then have relinquished jurisdiction in favour of the Grand Chamber.

4. Were the applicant still alive, I would have voted in favour of finding a violation of Article 14 of the Convention taken in conjunction with Article 8. I only voted against finding a violation as a consequence of my vote on the Government's request to strike the application out of the list of cases.

Questions and Comments

1. How does the case cited by the dissent in *Karner* differ from the facts presented in the *Karner* judgment? What purpose is served in not declaring the case moot? Is this case different from one where the applicant's son died one month after the end of what the applicant claims were unfair criminal proceedings that resulted in the son's conviction? *See*: *Djrecki v. Turkey*, App. No. 47826/99, Dec. of Oct. 3, 2006 (declaring application inadmissible because the alleged unfairness of the proceedings concerned the son alone; the applicant was not personally affected.)

2. Since the applicant is dead, what is the interest of the lawyer in pursuing the case? Note that he submitted a request for €13,500 in costs and expenses. The government proposed an award of €1,453.46. The Court awarded €5,000 to the estate of the decedent to cover the costs and expenses, including attorney's fees.

3. For a decision of the African Commission closing a case because of the death or release of the prisoner concerned, see Afr.CommHPR., Comm. 55/91 *International PEN vs. Chad*, 7th Annual Activity Rep. (1994).

4. What are the merits and problems with each system's standing requirement? Is the European system too strict or the African system too unrestricted? What might account for the differences in the standing requirements?

5. Protocol 14 to the European Convention on Human Rights proposes to change the victim requirement by adding a new admissibility standard. It would amend Article 35(3) to read as follows:

> 3. The Court shall declare inadmissible any individual application submitted under Article 34 if it considers that:
>
> . . . .
>
> b. the applicant has not suffered a significant disadvantage, unless respect for human rights as defined in the Convention and the Protocols thereto requires an examination of the application on the merits and provided that no case may be rejected on this ground which has not been duly considered by a domestic tribunal.

Does this standard create a "harmless error" test for admissibility or is it more flexible and discretionary than the test of harmless error? Would you favour adoption of the Protocol? Assuming Protocol 14 had been in force at the time, would any of the above cases have been rejected as inadmissible?

D. Territorial Jurisdiction

With the rise in numbers of armed conflicts and peacekeeping by United Nations and NATO member states, issues about the territorial reach of regional human rights conventions have become more prevalent in recent years. Contracting parties to the European Convention may extend the Convention to any territories they control, pursuant to Article 56, by notifying the Secretary General of the Council of Europe at the time of ratification or later. The Convention will be applied in such territories "with due regard . . . to local requirements". (Art. 56(3)). This provision does not, however, resolve the issue of whether the state has acted within territory for which it is responsible or whether the breach was an "extraterritorial" one over which the European Court lacks jurisdiction. The Inter-American and African systems have no provision equivalent to ECHR Art. 56, but they too have had to consider the scope of state responsibility for alleged human rights violations committed outside the territory of the state party. The following cases address the issue as does the case of *Al Skeini et al v. Secretary of State* reprinted in chapter II. See also F. Coomans and M.T. Kamminga, EXTRATERRITORIAL APPLICATION OF HUMAN RIGHTS TREATIES (2004).

Issa and Others v. Turkey, (App. no. 31821/96), Judgment of 16 November 2004, Eur. Ct. H.R.

1. The case originated in an application against the Republic of Turkey lodged with the European Commission of Human Rights under former Article 25 of the Convention for the Protection of Human Rights and Fundamental Freedoms by six Iraqi nationals, Mrs. Halima Musa Issa, Mrs. Beebin Ahmad Omer, Mrs. Safia Shawan Ibrahim, Mrs. Fatime Darwish Murty Khan, Mrs. Fahima Salim Muran and Mrs. Basna Rashid Omer, on 2 October 1995. . . .

4. The applicants complained of the alleged unlawful arrest, detention, ill-treatment and subsequent killing of their relatives in the course of a military operation conducted by the Turkish army in northern Iraq in April 1995. . . .

25. The respondent Government confirm that a Turkish military operation took place in northern Iraq between 19 March 1995 and 16 April 1995. The Turkish forces advanced to Mount Medina. The records of the armed forces do not show the presence of any Turkish soldiers in the area indicated by the applicants, the Azadi village being ten kilometres south of the operation zone. There is no record of a complaint having been made to any of the officers of the units operating in the Mount Medina region. . . .

THE LAW

II. WHETHER THE APPLICANTS' RELATIVES CAME WITHIN THE JURISDICTION OF TURKEY

B. The Court's assessment

1. General principles

65. Article 1 of the Convention provides:

"The High Contracting Parties shall secure to everyone within their jurisdiction the rights and freedoms defined in Section I of [the] Convention."

66. It follows from Article 1 that Contracting States must answer for any infringement of the rights and freedoms protected by the Convention committed against individuals placed under their "jurisdiction".

The exercise of jurisdiction is a necessary condition for a Contracting State to be able to be held responsible for acts or omissions imputable to it which give rise to an allegation of the infringement of rights and freedoms set forth in the Convention (see *Ilaşcu and Others v. Moldova and Russia*, [GC], no. 48787/99, § 311, ECHR 2004– . . .).

67. The established case-law in this area indicates that the concept of "jurisdiction" for the purposes of Article 1 of the Convention must be considered to reflect the term's meaning in public international law (see *Gentilhomme, Schaff-Benhadji and Zerouki v. France*, nos. 48205/99, 48207/99 and 48209/99, § 20, 14 May 2002; *Bankovic and Others*, §§ 59–61, and *Assanidzé v. Georgia*, [GC], no. 71503/01, § 137, ECHR 2004– . . .).

From the standpoint of public international law, the words "within their jurisdiction" in Article 1 of the Convention must be understood to mean that a State's jurisdictional competence is primarily territorial (see *Bankovic and Others*, § 59), but also that jurisdiction is presumed to be exercised normally throughout the State's territory.

68. However, the concept of "jurisdiction" within the meaning of Article 1 of the Convention is not necessarily restricted to the national territory of the High Contracting Parties (see *Loizidou v. Turkey*, pp. 2235–2236 § 52). In exceptional circumstances the acts of Contracting States performed outside their territory or which produce effects there ("extra-territorial act") may amount to exercise by them of their jurisdiction within the meaning of Article 1 of the Convention.

69. According to the relevant principles of international law, a State's responsibility may be engaged where, as a consequence of military action—whether lawful or unlawful—that State in practice exercises effective control of an area situated outside its national territory. The obligation to secure, in such an area, the rights and freedoms set out in the Convention derives from the fact of such control, whether it be exercised directly, through its armed forces, or through a subordinate local administration (*ibid.* § 52).

70. It is not necessary to determine whether a Contracting Party actually exercises detailed control over the policies and actions of the authorities in the area situated outside its national territory, since even overall control of the area may engage the responsibility of the Contracting Party concerned (*ibid.*, pp. 2235–2236, § 56).

71. Moreover, a State may also be held accountable for violation of the Convention rights and freedoms of persons who are in the territory of another State but who are found to be under the former State's authority and control through its agents operating—whether lawfully or unlawfully—in the latter State (see, *mutatis mutandis*, *M. v. Denmark*, application no. 17392/90, Commission decision of 14 October 1992, DR 73, p. 193; *Illich Sanchez Ramirez v. France*, application no. 28780/95, Commission decision of 24 June 1996, DR 86, p. 155; *Coard et al. v. the United States*, the Inter-American Commission of Human Rights decision of 29 September 1999, Report No. 109/99, case No. 10.951, §§ 37, 39, 41 and 43; and the views adopted by the Human Rights Committee on 29 July 1981 in the cases of *Lopez Burgos v. Uruguay* and *Celiberti de Casariego v. Uruguay*, nos. 52/1979 and 56/1979, at §§ 12.3 and 10.3 respectively). Accountability in such situations stems from the fact that Article 1 of the Convention cannot be interpreted so as to allow a State party to perpetrate violations of the Convention on the territory of another State, which it could not perpetrate on its own territory (*ibid.*).

2. Application of the above principles

72. In the light of the above principles the Court must ascertain whether the applicants' relatives were under the authority and/or effective control, and therefore within the jurisdiction, of the respondent State as a result of the latter's extra-territorial acts.

73. In this connection, the Court notes that it is undisputed between the parties that the Turkish armed forces carried out military operations in northern Iraq over a six-week period between 19 March and 16 April 1995. It transpires from the parties' submissions and the documentary evidence contained in the case-file that the cross-border operation conducted at that time was extensive and was aimed at pursuing and eliminating terrorists who were seeking shelter in northern Iraq.

74. The Court does not exclude the possibility that, as a consequence of this military action, the respondent State could be considered to have exercised, temporarily, effective overall control of a particular portion of the territory of northern Iraq. Accordingly, if there is a sufficient factual basis for holding that, at the relevant time, the victims were within that specific area, it would follow logically that they were within the jurisdiction of Turkey (and not that of Iraq, which is not a Contracting State and clearly does not fall within the legal space (*espace juridique*) of the Contracting States (see the above-cited *Bankovic* decision, § 80).

75. However, notwithstanding the large number of troops involved in the aforementioned military operations, it does not appear that Turkey exercised effective overall control of the entire area of northern Iraq. This situation is therefore in contrast to the one which obtained in northern Cyprus in the *Loizidou v. Turkey* and *Cyprus v. Turkey* cases (both cited above). In the latter cases, the Court found that the respondent Government's armed forces totalled more than 30,000 personnel (which is, admittedly, no less than the number alleged by the applicants in the instant case—see § 63 above—but with the difference that the troops in northern Cyprus were present over a very much longer period of time) and were stationed throughout the whole of the territory of northern Cyprus. Moreover, that area was constantly patrolled and had check points on all main lines of communication between the northern and southern parts of the island.

76. The essential question to be examined in the instant case is whether at the relevant time Turkish troops conducted operations in the area where the killings took place. The fate of the applicants' complaints in respect of the killing of their relatives depends on the prior establishment of that premise. The Government have vigorously denied that their troops were active in or around Azadi village in the Spna area. The reasonableness of that assertion must be tested in the light of the documentary and other evidence which the parties have submitted to the Court, having regard to the standard of proof which it habitually employs when ascertaining whether there is a basis in fact for an allegation of unlawful killing, namely proof "beyond reasonable doubt" (*Orhan v. Turkey*, no. 25656/94, § 264, 18 June 2002; *Tepe v. Turkey*, no. 27244/95, § 125, 9 May 2003; and *Ipek v. Turkey*, no. 25760/94, § 109, ECHR 2004- . . . (extracts)), it being understood that such proof may follow from the coexistence of sufficiently strong, clear and concordant inferences or of similar unrebutted presumptions of fact.

77. The Court notes that the applicants have provided written statements describing the alleged course of events leading to the arrest and killing of their relatives. While the applicants were all unequivocal in their statements that the alleged acts were perpetrated by Turkish soldiers, they have not given any particulars as to the identity of the commander or of the regiment involved in the impugned acts. Nor have they given a detailed description of the soldiers' uniforms. It is to be noted in this connection that there is no independent eye-witness account of the presence of Turkish soldiers in the area in question or of the detention of the shepherds.

78. As regards the statements made by Mr. Shookri Newayi and other KDP officials during a press conference held in Dohouk, the Court considers that no weight should be given to their assertions, having regard to the facts that the content of

the letter from Mr. Safeen Dizayee, who is the head of the KDP office in Ankara, contradicts them and that, in any event, they lack precise and sufficient information about the characteristics of the Turkish troops alleged to have been involved in the events in question.

79. Furthermore, the Court is unable to determine, on the basis of the findings contained in the post-mortem reports and the video recording showing the bullet shells marked "MKE" allegedly removed from the shepherds' corpses, whether the deaths were caused by gunfire discharged by Turkish troops. It notes that the post-mortem reports submitted by the applicants do not mention that bullet shells with the marking "MKE" had been recovered from the corpses of the shepherds. Accordingly, the Court cannot attach any decisive importance to the video footage since this is untested and at most circumstantial evidence. In this connection, the Court cannot overlook either the fact that the area where the applicants' relatives were killed was the scene of fierce fighting between PKK militants and KDP peshmergas at the relevant time. Moreover, although news reports and official records confirm the conduct of cross-border operations and the presence of the Turkish army in northern Iraq at the material time, these materials do not make it possible to conclude with any degree of certainty that Turkish troops went as far as the Azadi village in the Spna area.

80. Finally, the Court has also had regard to the applicants' allegations that they appealed to Turkish army officers to secure the release of their relatives and, subsequent to the discovery of the bodies, for an investigation to be carried out by the Turkish authorities into the killings. However, given the failure of the applicants to provide any cogent and convincing evidence capable of rebutting the Government's contention that no such complaint was ever made to Turkish army officers in northern Iraq and having regard to the KDP's letter confirming the Government's stance, the Court cannot but conclude that these allegations are unsubstantiated.

81. On the basis of all the material in its possession, the Court considers that it has not been established to the required standard of proof that the Turkish armed forces conducted operations in the area in question, and, more precisely, in the hills above the village of Azadi where, according to the applicants' statements, the victims were at that time.

3. The Court's conclusion

82. In the light of the above, the Court is not satisfied that the applicants' relatives were within the "jurisdiction" of the respondent State for the purposes of Article 1 of the Convention.

This finding makes it unnecessary to examine the applicants' substantive complaints under Articles 2, 3, 5, 8, 13, 14 and 18 of the Convention.

———————————

Questions and Comments

1. The territoriality requirement has proven troublesome in the European system in the light of secession movements, military occupation, and police actions outside the territory of a state. See, e.g., *Bankovic v. Belgium and Others*, admissibility decision of 12 Dec. 2001;

Cyprus v. Turkey, 4 Eur. Hum. Rts. Rep. 482 (1982); *Loizidou v. Turkey*, 23 Eur. Hum. Rts. Rep. (1997). *Bankovic* was declared inadmissible because it concerned NATO air strikes on Belgrade, outside the *"espace juridique"* of the Convention. Subsequently, ten individuals brought a claim for damages in the Italian courts, which rejected the claim on the basis that the laws of war afford no right to individual reparations as a result of a violation of the rules of international law. The European Court then found the case admissible because the applicants established a jurisdictional link with Italy once they brought suit in Italian courts. By a 10–7 vote a Grand Chamber held there was no violation. *Markovic and Others v. Italy*, App. No. 1398/03, Judgment of Dec. 13, 2006.

2. Since 2004, numerous Iraqi nationals have filed suit in English courts asserting that British armed forces were responsible for maltreating them or wrongfully killing members of their families and seeking an independent enquiry into the events. The plaintiffs founded their claims on the Human Rights Act 1998, adopted by Parliament to make European Convention rights enforceable in domestic courts. The House of Lords decided six test cases on June 13, 2007, holding that only one individual, held in a military prison by British troops, fell within the jurisdiction of the UK for purposes of the Human Rights Act; the other five cases could not be brought within the jurisdictional limits of the Act. The Law Lords relied extensively on the jurisprudence of the European Court in so deciding. See House of Lords, *Al-Skeini and Others (Respondents) v. Secretary of State for Defense (Appellant)* on appeal from [2005] EWCA Civ. 1609, judgment of June 13, 2007, [2007] UKHL 26 (Consolidated Appeals). For extracts of the judgment concerning statutory construction of the Human Rights Act to conform to the European Convention, see Chapter II(5)((B)(iii).

3. *Behrami and Saramati v. France, Germany and Norway*, App. no. 71412/01, Judgment of May 2, 2007 (GC), concerned peacekeeping in Kosovo. The agreed facts regarding the Behramis were as follows: On 11 March 2000 eight boys were playing in the hills in the municipality of Mitrovica. The group included two of Agim Behrami's sons, Gadaf and Bekim Behrami. At around midday, the group came upon a number of undetonated cluster bomb units which had been dropped during the bombardment by NATO in 1999 and the children began playing with the CBUs. Believing it was safe, one of the children threw a CBU in the air: it detonated and killed Gadaf Behrami. Bekim Behrami was also seriously injured and taken to hospital in Pristina (where he later had eye surgery and was released on 4 April 2000). Medical reports submitted indicate that he underwent two further eye operations (on 7 April and 22 May 2000) in a hospital in Bern, Switzerland. Bekim Behrami was disfigured and blinded. Id. para. 5. Saramati complained of illegal detention by KFOR. Unusually, the UN intervened as a third party at the request of the Court, and claimed that while de-mining fell within the mandate of UNMACC created by UNMIK, the absence of the necessary CBU location information from KFOR meant that the impugned inaction could not be attributed to UNMIK. The Court considered, and noted that it was not disputed, that unlike the *Bankovic* case, the Federal Republic of Yugoslavia did not "control" Kosovo (within the meaning of the word in the Court's jurisprudence) since prior to the relevant events it had agreed to withdraw its own forces in favour of the deployment of international civil (UNMIK) and security (KFOR) presences. The Court therefore considered that the question raised by the case was less whether the respondent States exercised extraterritorial jurisdiction in Kosovo but whether the Court was competent to examine under the Convention those States' contribution to the civil and security presences which did exercise the relevant control of Kosovo. After analyzing all the arguments and legal texts, the Court ultimately determined that it lacked *personal* jurisdiction for the following reasons: UNMIK was a subsidiary organ of the UN created under Chapter VII and KFOR was exercising powers lawfully delegated under Chapter VII of the Charter by the UNSC. As such, their actions were directly attributable to the UN, over which the Court lacked jurisdiction.

Does this case suggest that territorial jurisdiction was present?

4. Are there exceptions to the territoriality requirement, other than occupation and effective control? In *Ben El Mahi and Others v. Denmark*, App. No. 5853/06, dec. Dec. 11, 2006, a Moroccan national living in Morocco and two Moroccan associations operating in Morocco brought an action against Denmark for publishing twelve cartoons, most of which were caricatures of the Prophet Mohammed. Does the fact of international publication and re-publication bring the matter within the jurisdiction of the European Court?

Rep. No. 86/99, Case 11.589, *Armando Alejandre Jr., Carlos Costa, Mario De La Peña, and Pablo Morales v. Cuba*, September 29, 1999, *Annual Report of the Inter-American Commission on Human Rights 1999*, OAS Doc. OEA/Ser.L/V/ II.106, doc. 6 rev., April 13, 1999.

I. SUMMARY

1. On 25 February 1996, the Inter-American Commission on Human Rights received several complaints brought against the Republic of Cuba according to which a MiG-29 military aircraft belonging to the Cuban Air Force (FAC) downed two unarmed civilian light airplanes belonging to the organization "Brothers to the Rescue."[4] According to a report issued by the International Civil Aviation Organization (ICAO), the incidents occurred on 24 February 1996 at 3:21 p.m. and 3:27 p.m., respectively, in international airspace. The air-to-air missiles fired by the MiG-29 destroyed the civilian light aircraft, immediately killing Armando Alejandre Jr. (45 years old), Carlos Alberto Costa (29), Mario Manuel de la Peña (24), and Pablo Morales (29). The complaint concludes with the Commission being requested . . . to declare Cuba responsible for failing to comply with its international obligations contained in the American Declaration of the Rights and Duties of Man for violating the right to life and the right to a fair trial as set forth in Articles I and XVIII of said international instrument. . . .

3. Since the start of proceedings in this case on 7 March 1996, the Cuban State has not replied to the Commission's repeated requests for information regarding the admissibility and merits of the matter. Therefore, based on an exhaustive analysis of the legal and factual grounds and in accordance with Article 42 of its Regulations, the Commission believes that the complaint meets the formal requirements for admissibility as set forth in the Regulations and concludes that the Cuban State is responsible for violating the rights enshrined in the American Declaration as reported by the petitioners in their complaint of 25 February 1996. Based on the analysis and conclusions of this report, the Commission recommends that the Cuban State conduct an exhaustive investigation into the incidents in question, prosecute and punish the individuals responsible for the different violations described herein, and make adequate and timely amends to the victims' direct relatives, including the payment of fair compensatory indemnification. . . .

---

4 "Brothers to the Rescue," also known as *Hermanos al Rescate*, is a nonprofit organization founded by citizens, mainly civilian pilots, on 12 May 1991, and registered as a not-for-profit corporation in the public records of the State of Florida, United States of America. For more than eight years they have been patrolling the Straits of Florida to assist the "rafters" (boat people).

Position of the Parties

The Petitioners

13. According to the petitioners, the responsibility of the Cuban State lies, first, in that the unprovoked firing of deadly rockets at a defenseless, unarmed civilian aircraft undoubtedly comes within the scope of "extrajudicial execution." . . .

15. The incidents in which the victims were killed occurred in international airspace. The ICAO concluded that the aircraft were over international waters when they were shot down. The first plane was 18 miles off the Cuban coast when it was destroyed by FAC missiles; the second was 30.5 miles away from Cuba. These numbers place the airplanes a good distance from the 12 miles of territorial waters Cuba is allowed under international law.[5] Furthermore, the evidence provided by the crew and passengers of the *Majesty of the Seas*, a cruise ship that was in the vicinity, and of the *Tri-Liner*, a private fishing vessel, indicated that the civilian aircraft were flying in international airspace toward Florida and away from Cuba when they were destroyed by the agents of the Cuban State.

IV. ANALYSIS

A. Competence of the Commission and formal requirements for admissibility

18. The Commission is competent *ratione materiae* to hear the case at hand since it involves violations of rights enshrined in the American Declaration of the Rights and Duties of Man. Its competence stems from provisions of its Statute and Regulations and of the OAS Charter. Under the Charter, all member states pledge to respect the essential rights of individuals. In the case of states not parties to the Convention, the rights in question are those established in the American Declaration, which is a source of international obligations. In its Statute, the Commission is instructed to place special emphasis on the observance of the human rights recognized in that Declaration's Article I (life, liberty, and personal security), Article II (equality before law), Article III (freedom of religion and worship), Article IV (freedom of investigation, opinion, expression, and dissemination), Article XVIII (fair trial), Article XXV (protection from arbitrary arrest), and Article XXVI (due process of law).

19. The Commission has processed this case in compliance with the provisions of Chapter III of its Regulations and Articles 1, 18, and 20 of its Statute. Article 51 of the IACHR Regulations states that the Commission "shall receive and examine any petition that contains a denunciation of alleged violations of the human rights set forth in the American Declaration of the Rights and Duties of Man, concerning the member states of the Organization that are not parties to the American Convention on Human Rights."

20. The procedure applied to this case was the one set forth in Article 52 of the Commission's Regulations, to wit:

"The procedure applicable to petitions concerning member states of the Organization that are not parties to the American Convention on Human Rights shall be that

---

[5] The rules governing territorial waters and their permissible limits can be found in the United Nations Convention on the Law of the Sea, 7 October 1982, Art. 3, U.N. Doc. A/CONF 62/122 (1981), reprinted in 21 I.L.M. 1261 (1982).

provided for in the General Provisions included in Chapter I of Title II, in Articles 32 to 43 of these Regulations, and in the articles indicated below."

21. The presentation of the petition meets the formal requirements for admissibility contained in Article 32 of the Commission's Regulations, in that the procedure described in its Article 34 has been exhausted. Moreover, the claim is not pending any other international settlement procedure, nor does it reproduce any other petition that the Commission has previously examined.

22. The Commission is also competent *ratione personae*, since Article 26 of its Regulations provides that

"[a]ny person or group of persons or nongovernmental entity legally recognized in one or more of the member states of the Organization may submit petitions to the Commission, in accordance with these Regulations, on one's own behalf or on behalf of third persons, with regard to alleged violations of a human right recognized, as the case may be, in the American Convention on Human Rights or in the American Declaration of the Rights and Duties of Man."

In this context, the Commission must reiterate that the Cuban State's failure to respond in these proceedings is a breach of its international legal obligation to provide information in response to petitions and other communications containing allegations of human rights violations. The Commission has already stated on numerous occasions that the intent of the Organization of American States in its "Exclusion of the Present Government of Cuba from Participation in the Inter-American System" was not to leave the Cuban people without protection. The exclusion of that government from the regional system in no way means that it can fail to meet its international obligations in matters of human rights. Consequently, the Commission bases its analysis on the evidence at its disposal and on Article 42 of its Regulations.

23. In terms of its competence *ratione loci*, clearly the Commission is competent with respect to human rights violations that occur within the territory of OAS member states, whether or not they are parties to the Convention. It should be specified, however, that under certain circumstances the Commission is competent to consider reports alleging that agents of an OAS member state have violated human rights protected in the inter-American system, even when the events take place outside the territory of that state. In fact, the Commission would point out that, in certain cases, the exercise of its jurisdiction over extraterritorial events is not only consistent with but required by the applicable rules. The essential rights of the individual are proclaimed in the Americas on the basis of equality and nondiscrimination, "without distinction as to race, nationality, creed, or sex."[6] Because individual rights are inherent to the human being, all the American states are obligated to respect the protected rights of any person subject to their jurisdiction. Although this usually refers to persons who are within the territory of a state, in certain instances it can refer to extraterritorial actions, when the person is present in the territory of a state but subject to the control of another state, generally through the actions of that

---

6   Charter, Article 3.k. See American Declaration, Article II. See also Inter-American Conference on Problems of War and Peace, Resolution XL (1945), which indicates that one of the aims of instituting a regional human rights system was to eliminate violations of the principle of "equality between nationals and aliens".

state's agents abroad.[7] In principle, the investigation refers not to the nationality of the alleged victim or his presence in a particular geographic area, but to whether, in those specific circumstances, the state observed the rights of a person subject to its authority and control.[8]

24. The European Commission on Human Rights has ruled on this matter in the case brought by Cyprus against Turkey following the Turkish invasion of that island. In its complaint, Cyprus alleged that the European Convention had been violated in the part of its territory occupied by Turkish forces. Turkey, for its part, maintained that, under Article 1 of the European Convention, the competence of the Commission was limited to the examination of actions allegedly committed by a state party in its own national territory and that Turkey could not be found to have violated the Convention since it had not extended its jurisdiction to Cyprus. The European Commission rejected that argument, as follows:

> In Article 1 of the Convention, the High Contracting Parties undertake to secure the rights and freedoms defined in Section 1 to everyone "within their jurisdiction" (in the French text: "relevant de leur jurisdiction"). The Commission finds that this term is not, as submitted by the respondent Government, equivalent to or limited to the national territory of the High Contracting Party concerned. It is clear from the language, in particular of the French text, and the object of this article, and from the purpose of the Convention as a whole, that the High Contracting Parties are bound to secure the said rights and freedoms to all persons under their actual authority and responsibility, whether that authority is exercised within their own territory or abroad.[9]

25. In the case *sub lite*, the petitioners stated that their allegations were guided by the provisions of the American Declaration of the Rights and Duties of Man. The Commission has examined the evidence and finds that the victims died as a consequence of direct actions taken by agents of the Cuban State in *international airspace*. The fact that the events took place outside Cuban jurisdiction does not limit the Commission's competence *ratione loci*, because, as previously stated, when agents of a state, whether military or civilian, exercise power and authority over persons outside national territory, the state's obligation to respect human rights con-

---

[7] For example, "Where agents of the state, whether military or civilian, exercise power and authority (jurisdiction or *de facto* jurisdiction) over persons outside national territory, the presumption should be that the state's obligation to respect the pertinent human rights continues." Theodor Meron, in *Extraterritoriality of Human Rights Treaties*, 89 A.J.I.L. 78 (1995) 78, 81. See also n. 7, citing T. Buergenthal, "To Respect and Ensure: State Obligations and Permissible Derogations," in *The International Bill of Rights: The Covenant on Civil and Political Rights* 72, 74 (Louis Henkin ed. 1981).

[8] Instances in which the Commission has dealt with extraterritorial actions of a state, under the terms of its Statute and the American Declaration, can be found in IACHR, Report on the Situation of Human Rights in Chile, OEA Ser.L/V/II.66, doc. 17, 1985 (referring to the murder of Letelier in Washington, D.C.); Second Report on the Situation of Human Rights in Suriname, OEA Ser.L/V/II.66, doc. 21, rev. 1, 1985 (on allegations that Surinamese residents of Holland have been harassed and/or assaulted by agents of Suriname); Case 1.983 (opened on the basis of allegations of extraterritorial actions; set aside for another reason); Report on case 9.239, United States, published in the 1986–87 Annual Report of the IACHR, OEA Ser. L/V/II.71, doc. 9 rev. 1, September 22, 1987, p. 184 (in which the case pertaining to actions by United States forces in Grenada is found admissible; case settled, see Report 3/96, published in the 1995 Annual Report of the IACHR, OEA/Ser.L/V/II.91, doc. 7 rev., February 28, 1996, p. 201); Report 31/93, Case 10.573, United States, published in 1993 Annual Report of the IACHR, OEA/Ser.L/V/II.85, doc. 9, rev., February 11, 1994, p. 312 (in which the case pertaining to actions by United States forces in Panama is found admissible).

[9] European Court Human Rights, *Lozidou v. Turkey* A 310 paragraphs 56–64 (1995). European Commission of Human Rights, *X v. UK*, No. 7547/76, 12 DR 73 (1977); *Bertrand Russell Peace Foundation Ltd. v. UK*, No. 7597/76, 14 DR 117 at 124 (1978); *Mrs. W v. UK*, No. 9348/81, 32 DR 190 (1983).

tinues—in this case the rights enshrined in the American Declaration. The Commission finds conclusive evidence that agents of the Cuban State, although outside their territory, placed the civilian pilots of the "Brothers to the Rescue" organization under their authority. Consequently, the Commission is competent *ratione loci* to apply the American Convention extraterritorially to the Cuban State in connection with the events that took place in international airspace on February 24, 1996. . . .

V. CONCLUSIONS

53. Cuba is responsible for violating the right to life (Article I of the American Declaration of the Rights and Duties of Man) to the detriment of Carlos Costa, Pablo Morales, Mario De La Peña, and Armando Alejandre, who died as a result of the direct actions of its agents on the afternoon of 24 February 1996 while flying through international airspace.

54. Cuba is responsible for violating the right to a fair trial (Article XVIII of the American Declaration of the Rights and Duties of Man) to the detriment of the relatives of Carlos Costa, Pablo Morales, Mario De La Peña, and Armando Alejandre, in that to date the Cuban authorities have not conducted an exhaustive investigation with a view toward prosecuting and punishing the perpetrators and have not indemnified those same relatives for the damage they suffered as a result of those illicit acts.

―――――――――――

Hossein Alikhani v. United States, Rep. No. 63/05, Petition No. 4618/02, October 12, 2005.

1. On May 20, 2002, the Inter-American Commission on Human Rights received a supplementary petition dated May 15, 2005 from the International Human Rights Law Clinic at the Washington College of Law against the Government of the United States of America on behalf of Mr. Hossein Alikhani, a citizen of Iran and Cyprus. The communication requested that the Commission reactivate a petition that had been filed on July 17, 1995 on behalf of Mr. Alikhani and two other alleged victims, Kenneth Walker and Mr. George Christoforou. Following the filing of their July 17, 1995, the Petitioners had requested that the Commission sever the complaints and process them separately and, with respect to Messrs. Alikhani and Christoforou, to suspend the processing of their complaints pending the completion of further proceedings before the domestic courts. In their May 15, 2002 supplementary petition, the Petitioners indicated that Mr. Alikhani's domestic proceedings had been completed unsuccessfully and therefore requested that the Commission proceed with the processing of his petition.

2. The Petitioners' petition and subsequent observations allege that the State is responsible for violations of Mr. Alikhani's rights under Articles I, VIII, XXIV, XXV, and XXVI of the American Declaration of Human Rights, based upon the argument that his arrest was unlawful, that his right to freedom of movement was violated as a result of the act of luring and abducting by the United States government agents, and that while in custody he was treated inhumanely while in custody.

3. The State argues that the petition is inadmissible as it does not state facts that tend to establish a violation of the American Declaration, and because the United States did not violate International Law in connection with Mr. Alikhani's circumstances.

4. As set forth in the present report, having examined the information available and the contentions on the question of admissibility, and without prejudging the merits of the matter, the Commission decided to admit the claims in the present petition relating to Articles I, VIII, XXIV, XXV, and XXVI of the American Declaration, to continue with the analysis of the merits of the case, to transmit the report to the parties, and to publish the report and include it in its Annual Report to the General Assembly of the Organization of American States. . . .

III. POSITIONS OF THE PARTIES

A. Position of the Petitioners

18. According to the Petitioners, Mr. Alikhani is a citizen of Cyprus and Iran and owner of Polygon Company Ltd., a Cypriot commercial trading company with no subsidiaries in the United States. The petition indicates that in September of 1990, Mr. Alikhani contacted Turbo Power and Marine Systems (TPMS), a division of a U.S. company called United Technology, to inquire about the purchase of spare parts for a commercial engine and turbine. The Petitioners state that Mr. Alikhani was notified by TPMS that due to U.S. sanctions the company was unable to sell the parts, which were destined for Libya, and that upon hearing of the embargo, Mr. Alikhani did not pursue the matter any further.

19. The Petitioners allege that in August of 1991, almost a year after the initial contact, TPMS phoned Mr. Alikhani and offered to supply the parts through its international export division, International Trading Resources Inc. (ITR), and that unbeknownst to Mr. Alikhani, ITR was a false entity created by the U.S. Customs Service and the TPMS employee who initiated contact with Mr. Alikhani was a paid informant for the Service. The Petitioners indicate that ITR advised Mr. Alikhani that the company was aware of the sanctions and would undertake to structure the transaction so it would comply with U.S. law, and that Mr. Alikhani relied on the representation that the transaction method complied with U.S. law.

20. According to the Petitioners, Polygon purchased the parts from ITR, and they were shipped by TPMS for delivery to a freight forwarder in Germany, where they were re-exported by Mediterranean Oil Service and Jawaby Oil Services to Libya. The petition states that the U.S. Customs agents procured the equipment, obtained a permit from the Office of Foreign Assets Control to export it, made all the necessary arrangements for shipment, and then actually shipped the equipment from Germany to Libya. In this regard, the Petitioners contend that U.S. Customs Service essentially orchestrated the necessary transactions to attribute criminal liability to Mr. Alikhani while representing to him that the deal was in compliance with U.S. regulations.

21. The petition states that in October of 1992, Mr. Alikhani was encouraged to travel to the Bahamas to attend a business meeting with ITR representatives, and that on October 22, 1992, two undercover U.S. Customs Service agents posing as

directors of ITR met Mr. Alikhani at Nassau International Airport. According to the Petitioners, the agents falsely advised Mr. Alikhani that they had arranged for him to travel to another Bahamian island for the purpose of a business meeting and some fishing, and that Mr. Alikhani boarded the plane under the false pretense that he was traveling with two business colleagues to another island within Bahamian territory.

22. The Petitioners contend that minutes after take off, the agents revealed their true identities and arrested Mr. Alikhani for violations of U.S. sanctions against Libya. The Petitioners also state that the U.S. arrest warrant did not authorize the abduction of Mr. Alikhani in the Bahamas, nor did the Bahamian government authorize U.S. authorities to exercise law enforcement functions in its territory. Further, the Petitioners assert that although the United States had extradition treaties with both the governments of Bahamas and Cyprus in effect at the time of Mr. Alikhani's apprehension, the United States did not try to utilize these pre-existing procedures for the rendition of foreign nationals, but rather that Mr. Alikhani was involuntarily taken from Bahamian territory without the consent of the Bahamian government. The petition states that both the governments of the Bahamas and Cyprus formally protested Mr. Alikhani's abduction.

23. According to the Petitioners, Mr. Alikhani was taken to Florida, where he was assured that he would be released if he participated in sting operations designed to induce U.S. nationals into violating U.S. export laws. Instead, however, they claim that after agreeing to participate in the operations and in fact participating in them in anticipation of his immediate release thereafter, Mr. Alikhani was transported to various motels where he was handcuffed to his bed every night and forbidden from telling his family that he was being held as a detainee. The Petitioners allege that despite his cooperation and the assurances by the agents, he was not released, but rather was indicted and incarcerated without bail on November 19, 1992.

24. In this connection, the Petitioners state that Mr. Alikhani was placed in a correction center where he was refused the use of his eyeglasses, which he needed to properly prepare for the document-intensive case, and that due to emergency weather conditions following Hurricane Andrew, he was not permitted to have visitors and received restricted access to his legal counsel. According to the Petitioners, under the prospect of continued imprisonment under these conditions, and fearing that he would never see his family again, Mr. Alikhani signed a plea agreement under which he was sentenced to time served, but that the United States, knowing that the manner of Mr. Alikhani's apprehension was being severely criticized by foreign governments and members of Congress and the possibility of a legal challenge, inserted a clause into the coercive plea agreement prohibiting Mr. Alikhani from litigating the circumstances of his arrest or detention.

25. With regard to the admissibility of the petition, the Petitioners argue that because of the clause in Mr. Alikhani's plea agreement, he was barred from pursuing domestic remedies unless he could have the plea agreement vacated. Further, they claim that on January 10, 1996, Mr. Alikhani filed a petition for a writ of Error Coram Nobis with the Southern District Criminal Court of Florida to have the plea agreement set aside, but that the petition was denied on September 16, 1998

and the United States Supreme Court ultimately denied his petition for a writ of certiorari on October 10, 2000. As a consequence, the Petitioners state that the plea agreement remains valid and Mr. Alikhani remains unable to seek redress in U.S. courts for his illegal kidnapping.

26. With respect to the merits of the petition, the Petitioners claim that the facts in the case tend to establish violations of the American Declaration as well as other international instruments and for that reason the petition should be admitted. More specifically, the Petitioners claim that the United States has violated Mr. Alikhani's right to free movement as guaranteed by Article VIII of the American Declaration as Mr. Alikhani's luring and abduction to the United States was carried out with the specific intent that he not know the true destination of the plane and with the purpose that he be deprived of any meaningful choice regarding whether he left the country. The Petitioners also argue that in light of the luring and abduction, the actions of Mr. Alikhani in traveling to the Bahamas and boarding the plane cannot be construed to be "voluntary."

27. Furthermore, the Petitioners claim that the United States has violated Mr. Alikhani's rights to life, liberty and personal security and to protection from arbitrary arrest under Articles I and XXV of the American Declaration on the basis that the practice of luring and abducting is neither fair nor predictable, because Mr. Alikhani did not travel into the jurisdiction of the United States voluntarily, and his detention in the Bahamas was not supported by Bahamian, United States or international law. In the latter regard, the Petitioners argue that the U.S. arrest warrant issued against Mr. Alikhani did not validate the arrest or cure the violations of his rights because the arrest warrant had no validity in Bahamian territory, and because the U.S. Federal Rules of Criminal Procedure in effect at the time of Mr. Alikhani's abduction provided that a warrant issued by a United States court was valid only "within the jurisdiction of the United States". The Petitioners therefore argue that, as a result of the fact that Mr. Alikhani's luring and apprehension began before he reached international airspace, the U.S. authorities, which were conducting law enforcement functions in a territory without the consent of the Government, had no legal basis to deprive Mr. Alikhani of his right to liberty and personal security by luring him out of the country against his will.

28. Moreover, the Petitioners claim that Mr. Alikhani's right to due process of law under Article XXVI of the American Declaration and his right to be treated humanely while in custody as guaranteed by Article XXV of the American Declaration have been violated by the State. In particular, the Petitioners argue that Mr. Alikhani was removed from the country of his choosing without being granted a hearing or any chance to challenge his removal and therefore that the entire judicial process was tainted by the illegality of the apprehension, and that he was subsequently denied access to judicial process through a coerced plea agreement, contrary to Articles XXIV and XXVI of the Declaration. The Petitioners also claim that during his detention in the United States between October 22, 1992 until November 19, 1992, Mr. Alikhani was not permitted to reveal his status as a detainee to his family, was tied to his bed each night, had his eyeglasses confiscated, and was coerced into sign-

ing a plea agreement in order to secure his release and to be reunited with his family contrary to his right to humane treatment under Article XXV of the Declaration.

29. Finally, referring to various international and other authorities, the Petitioners claim that there is a consensus that the practice of irregular extraterritorial rendition violates international law.

B. Position of the State

30. With respect to the background to Mr. Alikhani's complaint, the United States claims that between October 1991 and June 1992, subsequent to the establishment of ITR, Mr. Alikhani made contacts with ITR and negotiated with the undercover United States Customs agents and ordered and paid for engine parts, which he shipped to a company in Hamburg, Germany, that was established for the express purpose of hiding his exports to Libya and avoiding detection by American authorities. According to the State, when the commercial parts arrived in Germany, Mr. Alikhani arranged to have them shipped to Libya.

31. The State also indicates that on July 10, 1992, a United States Magistrate Judge in the Southern District of Florida issued a warrant for Mr. Alikhani's arrest, and subsequently, in October, 1992, Mr. Alikhani agreed to meet with the undercover United States Customs agents for a business meeting in the Bahamas. According to the State, on October 22, 1992, when Mr. Alikhani boarded the airplane which he believed was going on a fishing trip to another island, U.S. Customs agents arrested him on board the flight while in international airspace.

32. The State claims that the following day, October 23, 1992, Mr. Alikhani was given an initial hearing before a Magistrate Judge in the Southern District of Florida, where he was represented by counsel, and that the Magistrate Judge released Mr. Alikhani to the custody of the U.S. Customs Service because he agreed to assist U.S. Customs with its investigation of other violations of United States law sanctioning Libya.

33. Further, according to the State, Mr. Alikhani waived his right to a preliminary hearing four days later, on October 27, 1992, that he was indicted on November 19, 1992, that he was arraigned and pleaded not guilty on November 23, 1992, and the Magistrate Judge granted his motion to be released on bond pending trial on November 30, 1992. The State also claims that on December 30, 1992, Mr. Alikhani filed a motion to dismiss his indictment and that a hearing of the motion was set for February 5, 1993, but that instead of arguing his motion, Mr. Alikhani, who was represented by counsel, pleaded guilty. According to the State, Mr. Alikhani was then released on bail and allowed to leave the United States on the condition that he return for the sentencing hearing on April 30, 1993. The State indicates that when Mr. Alikhani appeared at the sentencing hearing and was sentenced to the time he served in custody from his arrest on October 22, 1992, until his released pending sentencing on February 5, 1993.

34. With respect to the admissibility of the petition, the State argues that the petition is inadmissible under the terms of Article 34(a) and (b) of the Commission's Rules of Procedure because it does not state facts that tend to establish a violation of the American Declaration and is manifestly groundless, and because the United States has not violated any international law, including customary international law.

The United States argues in this regard that Mr. Alikhani voluntarily agreed to the meeting in the Bahamas and voluntarily agreed to travel on the private plane through international airspace. Moreover, the State argues that the Magistrate Judge who denied Mr. Alikhani's January 10, 1996 petition for a Writ of Error Coram Nobis did not reach the merits of Mr. Alikhani's claims and stated that "Alikhani failed to demonstrate any compelling circumstance or miscarriage of justice and show that he is suffering from any continuing consequence of his conviction". As such, the United States contends that the State has not violated Mr. Alikhani's right to residence and movement under Article VIII of the American Declaration.

. . . .

36. Moreover, the State contends that Mr. Alikhani's right to liberty and personal security and his right to protection from arbitrary arrest under Articles I and XXV of the American Declaration were not violated, as the Petitioners provided no facts to support the claim that Mr. Alikhani was unlawfully arrested. According to the State, Mr. Alikhani was arrested with a valid warrant and, moreover, he knowingly and willingly pleaded guilty to legitimate criminal charges against him. Also in this respect, the State contended that the United States did not circumvent any extradition treaties because no such treaties applied in the present case, given that Mr. Alikhani voluntarily traveled to the jurisdiction in which he was arrested.

37. Finally, referring to a number of national court decisions in which, according to the State, luring without force was found to have been justified, the United States argues that it cannot be said that there is any customary international law or general principle which has developed against "luring."

IV. ADMISSIBILITY

38. The Commission has considered the admissibility of the present complaint pursuant to Articles 30 and 34 of its Rules of Procedure and makes the following determinations.

A. Competence of the Commission *ratione personae, ratione materiae, ratione temporis* and *ratione loci*

39. The Commission is competent to examine the petition in question. Under Article 23 of the Rules of Procedure of the Commission, the Petitioners are authorized to file complaints alleging violations of rights protected under the American Declaration. The alleged victim, Mr. Alikhani, is a person whose rights are protected under the American Declaration, the provisions of which the State is bound to respect in conformity with the OAS Charter, Article 20 of the Commission's Statute and Article 49 of the Commission's Rules of Procedure. The United States of America deposited its instrument of ratification of the OAS Charter on June 19, 1951 and has been subject to the Commission's jurisdiction since 1959, the year in which the Commission was created.

40. Inasmuch as the Petitioners have filed complaints alleging violations of Article I, VIII, XXIV, XXV, and XXVI of the American Declaration, the Commission is competent *ratione materiae* to examine the petition.

41. The Commission is competent *ratione temporis* to examine the complaints because the petition alleges facts that occurred on or after the date on which the United States' obligations under the American Declaration took effect.

42. Finally, the Commission is competent *ratione loci,* given that the petition indicates that Mr. Alikhani was under the jurisdiction of the United States at the time of his arrest, detention and subsequent criminal proceedings. . . .

E. Colorable Claim

47. Article 27 of the Commission's Rules of Procedure mandates that petitions state facts "regarding alleged violations of the human rights enshrined in the American Convention on Human Rights and other applicable instruments". The petitioners allege that the State has violated Articles I, II, V, VIII, XIV, XVII, XVIII, XXV, and XXVI of the American Declaration.

48. The Commission has outlined in Part III of this Report the substantive allegations of the Petitioners, as well as information submitted by the Petitioners in support of those allegations. After carefully reviewing the information and arguments provided by the Petitioners and the State, and without prejudging the merits of the matter, the Commission considers that the petition states facts that, if proven, tend to establish violations of rights guaranteed under the Declaration. The Commission notes in this regard that, according to the authorities cited by the Petitioners and the State, some domestic courts have concluded that obtaining jurisdiction over wanted criminals through luring is routine and does not preclude criminal prosecutions,[10] while other domestic and international authorities have suggested that luring under false pretenses may engage the rights to personal liberty and to freedom from arbitrary arrest and detention.[11] Accordingly, it appears to the Commission that the permissibility under international law of abductions, luring and other extraordinary methods of rendering individuals to the jurisdiction of a state is the subject of legitimate debate and therefore considers that the Petitioners claims in this regard are not manifestly groundless or out of order. The Commission therefore concludes that the Petitioners' petition should not be declared inadmissible under Article 34 of the Commission's Rules of Procedure.

V. CONCLUSIONS

49. The Commission concludes that it has the competence to examine the Petitioners' allegations, and that the petition is admissible for the alleged violations of Articles I, VIII, XXIV, XXV and XXVI of the American Declaration and in accordance with the Commission's Rules of Procedure. . . .

Questions and Comments

1. Compare the preceding case to *Öcalan v. Turkey,* 37 Eur.Hum.Rts. Rep. 10 (2003), in which the leader of the Kurdish Workers' Party (PKK) was arrested by Turkish security

---

[10] See, e.g., *US v. Yunnis*, 681 F. Supp. 909 (DDC 1988); *Re Harnet and the Queen*; *In re: Hudson and the Queen*, 14 C.C.C. (2d) 69, 1 O.R. (2d) 206.

[11] See, e.g., *Conka v. Belgium* [2002] 34 Eur. H.R. Rep. 54 (Eur. Court H.R); *Stocké v. Germany* [1991] 13 Eur. H.R. Rep. 126, 129, para. 169 (Commission Report); *Alvarez-Machain*, 266 F.3d at 1045, 1052 (9th Cir.).

agents in an aircraft in the international zone of the Nairobi airport. The European Court held that upon his arrest he came within the effective control and therefore the jurisdiction of Turkey. The Court distinguished the case from *Bankovic* on the basis that the applicant was physically detained and forced to return to Turkey by Turkish officials. The issue was not addressed in the subsequent Grand Chamber judgment of May 12, 2005, in the same case.

2. What is the purpose of regional human rights law? Does it only or primarily operate within an *"espace juridique"* as the European Court suggests? Does it protect only those with that legal space or is it intended to restrain government abuse of power wherever it takes place? Do the European and Inter-American institutions differ on this point?

E. Temporal Jurisdiction

All the systems have dealt with applications alleging violations that may have occurred before the relevant state became legally bound by the human rights instrument in question. Under the law of treaties, obligations generally commence only when the treaty comes into force for the state in question, a rule codified in Article 28 of the Vienna Convention on the Law of Treaties, quoted in the *Blečič* case below. The regional tribunals have struggled to determine when the general rule against retroactive application of a treaty is inapplicable, as well as when violations that began prior to the effective date of the law continue into the present. The following cases are illustrative of the major problems that arise.

Blečič v. Croatia [GC], (App. no. 59532/00), Judgment of 8 March 2006, Eur. Ct. H.R.

1. The case originated in an application against the Republic of Croatia lodged with the Court under Article 34 of the Convention for the Protection of Human Rights and Fundamental Freedoms by a Croatian national, Mrs. Krstina Blečić, on 6 May 2000.

. . . .

3. The applicant alleged, in particular, that her rights to respect for her home and to peaceful enjoyment of her possessions had been violated on account of the termination of her specially protected tenancy. She relied on Article 8 of the Convention and Article 1 of Protocol No. 1 to the Convention.

THE FACTS

I. THE CIRCUMSTANCES OF THE CASE

12. The applicant was born in 1926 and currently lives in Rome, Italy.

13. In 1953 the applicant, together with her husband, acquired a specially protected tenancy (*stanarsko pravo*) of a flat in Zadar. After her husband's death in 1989 the applicant became the sole holder of the specially protected tenancy.

14. On 19 June 1991 the Specially Protected Tenancies (Sale to Occupier) Act entered into force. It regulated the sale of publicly owned flats previously let under a specially protected tenancy.

15. On 26 July 1991 the applicant went to visit her daughter who lived in Rome. She intended to stay with her daughter for the summer. The applicant locked the

flat in Zadar and left all the furniture and personal belongings in it. She asked a neighbour to pay the bills in her absence and to take care of the flat.

16. However, by the end of August 1991 armed conflict had escalated in Dalmatia, resulting in severe travel difficulties in that area, including the town of Zadar. From 15 September 1991 the town of Zadar was exposed to constant shelling and the supply of electricity and water was disrupted for over one hundred days.

17. The applicant submitted that in October 1991 the Croatian authorities had stopped paying her widow's war pension and that the payments had resumed in April 1994. The Government submitted that the applicant's pension had been paid by the Yugoslav Military Pension Fund in Belgrade rather than the Croatian Pension Fund and that it was the Belgrade authorities which had stopped paying the pension in December 1991.

18. According to the applicant, she also lost the right to medical insurance. The Government maintained that her medical insurance had never been stopped or interrupted.

19. In these circumstances, the applicant decided to remain in Rome.

20. In November 1991 a certain M.F., with his wife and two children, broke into and occupied the applicant's flat in Zadar. The applicant claimed that M.F. had been assisted by an official of the municipality who had provided him with a list of empty flats in Zadar, including hers.

21. On 12 February 1992 the Zadar Municipality brought a civil action against the applicant before the Zadar Municipal Court for termination of her specially protected tenancy on the ground that she had been absent from the flat for more than six months without justified reason, contrary to section 99 of the Housing Act.

22. In her submissions to the domestic court, the applicant explained that she had been forced to stay with her daughter in Rome from July 1991 until May 1992. She had not been able to return to Zadar since she had no means of subsistence and no medical insurance and was in poor health. Furthermore, during her stay in Rome she had learned from her neighbour that M.F. had broken into her flat with his family. When she had enquired about her flat and her possessions in it, M.F. had threatened her over the telephone.

23. On 9 October 1992 the Zadar Municipal Court terminated the applicant's specially protected tenancy. The court found that the applicant had left Zadar on 26 July 1991 and had not returned until 15 May 1992. It stated that during the relevant period the citizens of Zadar had not been ordered to evacuate the town on account of the escalation of the armed conflict and that each citizen had had the choice to leave the town or to stay. On that basis the court found that the war in Croatia could not justify the applicant's absence.

24. The court did not accept the applicant's explanation that she had fallen ill during her stay in Rome and had been unable to travel. It was established that she had suffered from spinal arthrosis and diffuse osteoporosis for a long time. However, this had not affected her ability to travel. Even though her left shoulder had been dislocated on 25 March 1992, she had been able to travel following the immobilisation of the injured joint. Furthermore, by 25 March 1992 she had already been absent from the flat for more than six months.

25. The applicant's further explanation that she had stopped receiving her pension in October 1991 and thus had been left without any means of subsistence was not accepted by the court as a justified reason for not returning to Zadar. It took the view that the applicant's daughter could have sent her money. Therefore, the court concluded that the applicant's reasons for not having lived in the flat were not justified.

26. Following an appeal by the applicant, the judgment was quashed by the Zadar County Court on 10 March 1993. The County Court found that the court of first instance had not given due consideration to the applicant's personal circumstances, namely her age and poor health and the fact that she had lost her pension and lived alone in Zadar. Furthermore, the applicant's decision to prolong her stay in Rome should have been carefully assessed against the background of the circumstances at the material time, namely that Zadar had been exposed to daily shelling and had not had a regular supply of water or electricity, and that third parties had occupied the applicant's flat. The case was remitted to the first-instance court.

27. In the resumed proceedings, on 18 January 1994 the Zadar Municipal Court again ruled in favour of the municipality and terminated the applicant's specially protected tenancy. It observed that she had been absent from the flat for over six months without justified reason and repeated in substance the findings of the judgment of 9 October 1992.

28. The applicant appealed. On 19 October 1994 the County Court reversed the first-instance judgment and dismissed the municipality's claim. It found that the escalation of the war and the applicant's personal circumstances justified her absence from the flat.

29. On 10 April 1995 the Zadar Municipality lodged an appeal on points of law with the Supreme Court.

30. On 15 February 1996 the Supreme Court allowed the appeal, reversed the County Court's judgment and upheld the judgment of the Municipal Court. It found that the reasons submitted by the applicant for her absence from the flat were not justified. . . .

31. On 8 November 1996 the applicant lodged a constitutional complaint with the Constitutional Court. She claimed that her rights to respect for her home and property had been violated and that she had been deprived of her right to a fair hearing.

32. On 5 November 1997 the Convention entered into force in respect of Croatia.

33. On 8 November 1999 the Constitutional Court dismissed the applicant's constitutional complaint. It found that the Supreme Court had correctly applied the relevant legal provisions to the facts established by the lower courts when holding that the applicant's absence from the flat for more than six months had been unjustified. The Constitutional Court concluded that the applicant's constitutional rights had not been violated. . . .

C. The Act incorporating the Convention

36. The Act on Ratification of the Convention for the Protection of Human Rights and Fundamental Freedoms and Protocols Nos. 1, 4, 6, 7 and 11 to the Convention

(Official Gazette—International Agreements, no. 18/1997) entered into force on 5 November 1997. It incorporated the Convention as an international treaty into the Croatian legal system.

III. RELEVANT INTERNATIONAL LAW AND PRACTICE

A. The Vienna Convention of 1969 on the Law of Treaties

45. Article 28 of the Vienna Convention on the Law of Treaties of 23 May 1969 ("the Vienna Convention") provides:

Non-retroactivity of treaties
Unless a different intention appears from the treaty or is otherwise established, its provisions do not bind a party in relation to any act or fact which took place or any situation which ceased to exist before the date of the entry into force of the treaty with respect to that party.

B. The Permanent Court of International Justice

46. The Permanent Court of International Justice has dealt with the issue of its jurisdiction *ratione temporis* in several cases. In the case of *Phosphates in Morocco* (Preliminary Objections) between Italy and France, the Italian Government maintained, *inter alia*, that the dispossession of certain Italian nationals resulting from the decision of the French Mines Department of 8 January 1925, and the denial of justice that had followed, were inconsistent with international obligations incumbent on France. The ratification of the declaration by which France accepted the compulsory jurisdiction of the PCIJ was filed on 25 April 1931. In its judgment of 14 June 1938 (*P.C.I.J., Series A/B, No. 74*, pp. 10–30), when examining France's preliminary objection based on the lack of jurisdiction *ratione temporis*, the PCIJ held:

The French Government bases its objection on the following passage in its declaration: ' . . . in any disputes which may arise after the ratification of the present declaration with regard to situations or facts subsequent to this ratification.' (p. 22)
. . . [The Court's compulsory jurisdiction] only exists within the limits within which it has been accepted. In this case, the terms on which the objection *ratione temporis* submitted by the French Government is founded, are perfectly clear: the only situations or facts falling under the compulsory jurisdiction are those which are subsequent to the ratification and with regard to which the dispute arose, that is to say, those which must be considered as being the source of the dispute. (p. 23)
. . . The situations and the facts which form the subject of the limitation *ratione temporis* have to be considered from the point of view both of their date in relation to the date of ratification and of their connection with the birth of the dispute. Situations or facts subsequent to the ratification could serve to found the Court's compulsory jurisdiction only if it was with regard to them that the dispute arose. (p. 24)
. . . [The] decision of the Mines Department, owing to its date, falls outside the Court's jurisdiction. The Italian Government has sought to avert this consequence by arguing . . . that the decision of 1925 constituted only an uncompleted violation of international law; that this violation only became definitive as a result of certain acts subsequent to the crucial date and of the final refusal to remedy in any way the situation created in 1925, and that these acts gave rise to the dispute between the two Governments. (p. 27)
. . . The Court cannot regard the denial of justice alleged by the Italian Government as a factor giving rise to the present dispute. In its Application, the Italian Gov-

ernment has represented the decision of the Department of Mines as an unlawful international act . . . That being so, it is in this decision that we should look for the violation of international law—a definitive act which would, by itself, directly involve international responsibility. This act being attributable to the State and described as contrary to the treaty right of another State, international responsibility would be established immediately as between the two States. In these circumstances the alleged denial of justice . . . merely results in allowing the unlawful act to subsist. It exercises no influence either on the accomplishment of the act or on the responsibility ensuing from it. (p. 28)

. . . [T]he complaint of a denial of justice cannot be separated from the criticism which the Italian Government directs against the decision of the Department of Mines of January 8th, 1925, for the Court could not regard the denial of justice as established unless it had first satisfied itself as to the existence of the rights of the private citizens alleged to have been refused judicial protection. But the Court could not reach such a conclusion without calling in question the decision of the Department of Mines of 1925. It follows that an examination of the justice of this complaint could not be undertaken without extending the Court's jurisdiction to a fact which, by reason of its date, is not subject thereto.

In conclusion, the Court finds that the dispute submitted to it by the Italian Government . . . did not arise with regard to situations or facts subsequent to the ratification of the acceptance by France of the compulsory jurisdiction, and that in consequence it has no jurisdiction to adjudicate on this dispute." (pp. 28–29)

C. The International Court of Justice

47. The issue of temporal jurisdiction arose also in a number of cases before the International Court of Justice. In the case concerning *Certain Property* (*Liechtenstein v. Germany*), Preliminary Objections, Liechtenstein maintained that certain decisions by German courts delivered in the period between 1995 and 1998 declaring inadmissible the action of Prince Hans-Adam II of Liechtenstein for restitution of a painting, which had been confiscated by Czechoslovakia on 21 June 1945 under "the Beneš Decrees", were in breach of international law. In these inadmissibility decisions the German courts invoked the Convention on the Settlement of Matters Arising out of the War and the Occupation, signed in 1952, as amended in 1954, which had entered into force on 5 May 1955. In order to found the jurisdiction of the ICJ, Liechtenstein relied in its Application on Article 1 of the European Convention for the Peaceful Settlement of Disputes of 29 April 1957, which entered into force between Liechtenstein and Germany on 18 February 1980. In its judgment of 10 February 2005, when examining Germany's preliminary objection based on the lack of jurisdiction *ratione temporis*, the ICJ held:

47. The Court will now consider whether the present dispute has its source or real cause in the facts or situations which occurred in the 1990s in Germany and, particularly, in the decisions by the German courts in the *Pieter van Laer Painting* case, or whether its source or real cause is the Beneš Decrees under which the painting was confiscated and the Settlement Convention which the German courts invoked as ground for declaring themselves without jurisdiction to hear that case.

48. The Court observes that it is not contested that the present dispute was triggered by the decisions of the German courts in the aforementioned case. This conclusion does not, however, dispose of the question the Court is called upon to decide,

for under Article 27 *(a)* of the European Convention for the Peaceful Settlement of Disputes, the critical issue is not the date when the dispute arose, but the date of the facts or situations in relation to which the dispute arose. . . .

51. . . . . . The Court . . . finds that the decisions of the German courts in the *Pieter van Laer Painting* case cannot be separated from the Settlement Convention and the Beneš Decrees, and that these decisions cannot consequently be considered as the source or real cause of the dispute between Liechtenstein and Germany.

52. The Court concludes that, although these proceedings were instituted by Liechtenstein as a result of decisions by German courts regarding a painting by Pieter van Laer, these events have their source in specific measures taken by Czechoslovakia in 1945, which led to the confiscation of property owned by some Liechtenstein nationals, including Prince Franz Josef II of Liechtenstein, as well as in the special régime created by the Settlement Convention. The decisions of the German courts in the 1990s dismissing the claim filed by Prince Hans-Adam II of Liechtenstein for the return of the painting to him were taken on the basis of Article 3, Chapter Six, of the Settlement Convention. While these decisions triggered the dispute between Liechtenstein and Germany, the source or real cause of the dispute is to be found in the Settlement Convention and the Beneš Decrees. In light of the provisions of Article 27 *(a)* of the European Convention for the Peaceful Settlement of Disputes, Germany's . . . preliminary objection must therefore be upheld.

D. The International Law Commission's Draft Articles on Responsibility of States for Internationally Wrongful Acts

48. The relevant provisions of the Draft Articles on Responsibility of States for Internationally Wrongful Acts, as adopted by the International Law Commission on 9 August 2001 (for the text of the Draft Articles and Commentary, see Report of the International Law Commission on the Work of its Fifty-third Session, *Official Records of the General Assembly, Fifty-sixth Session, Supplement No. 10* (A/56/10), chap. IV.E.1 and chap. IV.E.2, pp. 46 and 133–145) read as follows:

Article 13. International obligation in force for a State

An act of a State does not constitute a breach of an international obligation unless the State is bound by the obligation in question at the time the act occurs.

Article 14. Extension in time of the breach of an international obligation

1. The breach of an international obligation by an act of a State not having a continuing character occurs at the moment when the act is performed, even if its effects continue.

2. The breach of an international obligation by an act of a State having a continuing character extends over the entire period during which the act continues and remains not in conformity with the international obligation.

3. The breach of an international obligation requiring a State to prevent a given event occurs when the event occurs and extends over the entire period during which the event continues and remains not in conformity with that obligation.

. . . .

THE LAW

THE GOVERNMENT'S PRELIMINARY OBJECTIONS

50. The Government raised two preliminary objections, based respectively on the Court's lack of jurisdiction *ratione temporis* to entertain the application and the applicant's failure to exhaust domestic remedies.

Jurisdiction *ratione temporis*

. . . .

4. The Court's assessment

(a) Whether the Court is competent at this stage of the proceedings to deal with the Government's ratione temporis objection

63. The Court notes that no plea of inadmissibility concerning lack of jurisdiction *ratione temporis* was made by the Government at the admissibility stage. Nevertheless, the Chamber decided in its final decision on admissibility to examine its temporal jurisdiction of its own motion, holding that the issue called for consideration. The Government raised their *ratione temporis* objection for the first time in their observations before the Grand Chamber. The applicant, for her part, did not ask the Court to dismiss the Government's preliminary objection in application of Rule 55 of the Rules of Court, according to which "any plea of inadmissibility must, in so far as its character and the circumstances permit, be raised by the respondent Contracting Party in its written or oral observations on the admissibility of the application".

64. The question therefore arises whether the Government are estopped from raising their preliminary objection at this stage of the proceedings.

65. The Court recalls that the Grand Chamber is not precluded from deciding questions concerning the admissibility of an application under Article 35 § 4 of the Convention, since that provision enables the Court to dismiss applications it considers inadmissible "at any stage of the proceedings". Thus, even at the merits stage the Court may re-consider a decision to declare an application admissible if it concludes that it should have been declared inadmissible for one of the reasons given in the first three paragraphs of Article 35 of the Convention (see, *inter alia*, *Azinas v. Cyprus* [GC], no. 56679/00, § 32, ECHR 2004-III, and *Odièvre v. France* [GC], no. 42326/98, § 22, ECHR 2003-III).

66. In the instant case the Court finds that, notwithstanding the requirements of Rule 55 of its Rules, which in any event must be interpreted in a manner compatible with the Convention, in particular Article 32 thereof, the Government cannot be considered to be precluded from raising the issue of temporal jurisdiction before the Grand Chamber.

67. Firstly, incompatibility *ratione temporis* is a matter which goes to the Court's jurisdiction rather than a question of admissibility in the narrow sense of that term. Since the scope of the Court's jurisdiction is determined by the Convention itself, in particular by Article 32, and not by the parties' submissions in a particular case, the mere absence of a plea of incompatibility cannot extend that jurisdiction. To hold the contrary would mean that where a respondent State waived its right to plead or

omitted to plead incompatibility, the Court would have to rule on the merits of a complaint against that State concerning a right not guaranteed by the Convention or on a Convention right not yet binding on it, for example by virtue of a valid reservation clause (incompatibility *ratione materiae*) or because it has not yet ratified an additional Protocol (incompatibility *ratione personae*).

The same has to be true for the Court's temporal jurisdiction, since the non-retroactivity principle operates to limit *ratione temporis* the application of the jurisdictional, and not only substantive, provisions of the Convention.

Accordingly, the Court, in line with the position taken by the Commission on this point (see *Nielsen v. Denmark*, no. 343/57, Commission decision of 2 September 1959, Yearbook 2, p. 454), has to satisfy itself that it has jurisdiction in any case brought before it, and is therefore obliged to examine the question of its jurisdiction at every stage of the proceedings.

68. Secondly, the Court has already held that it is not open to it to set aside the application of another admissibility criterion, namely the six-month rule, solely because a government has not made a preliminary objection to that effect (see *Walker v. the United Kingdom* (dec.), no. 34979/97, ECHR 2000-I). In reaching that conclusion it explained that the six-month rule, in reflecting the wish of the Contracting Parties to prevent past decisions being called into question after an indefinite lapse of time, served the interests not only of the respondent Government but also of legal certainty as a value in itself. It added that the rule marked out the temporal limits of supervision carried out by the organs of the Convention and signalled to both individuals and State authorities the period beyond which such supervision was no longer possible (see *Walker*, cited above). Having regard to the fact that the purpose of limitations *ratione temporis* is to preclude the possibility of submitting to the Court, by means of an application, facts dating from a period when the respondent State was not in a position to foresee the international responsibility or legal proceedings to which these facts might give rise, the Court considers that the above reasoning concerning the six-month rule applies *a fortiori* in the present instance.

69. Thirdly, despite the Government's failure to raise the relevant objection earlier, and without prejudice to the above-mentioned considerations, the Chamber examined its competence *ratione temporis* of its own motion and the parties addressed the question in their observations before the Grand Chamber. Accordingly, the issue of temporal jurisdiction is a live issue that must be examined.

(b) Limitations on the Court's temporal jurisdiction

70. The Court recalls that, in accordance with the general rules of international law, the provisions of the Convention do not bind a Contracting Party in relation to any act or fact which took place or any situation which ceased to exist before the date of the entry into force of the Convention with respect to that Party (see, for example, *Kadiķis v. Latvia* (dec.), no. 47634/99, 29 June 2000).

71. It further notes that, in its declarations made under former Articles 25 and 46 of the Convention, Croatia recognised the competence of the Convention organs to deal with individual petitions based on facts occurring after the Convention and its Protocols had come into force in respect of Croatia. These declarations remain valid for the determination of the jurisdiction of the Court to receive individual ap-

plications under the current Article 34 of the Convention by virtue of Article 6 of Protocol No. 11. . . .

72. Accordingly, the Court is not competent to examine applications against Croatia in so far as the alleged violations are based on facts having occurred before the critical date. However, the question of whether an alleged violation is based on a fact occurring prior or subsequent to a particular date gives rise to difficulties when, as in the present case, the facts relied on fall partly within and partly outside the period of the Court's competence.

(c) The Court's case-law

73. In *Stamoulakatos v. Greece (no. 1)* (judgment of 26 October 1993, Series A no. 271), the applicant complained about his various convictions *in absentia* by Greek courts prior to the date of Greece's acceptance of the right of individual petition under former Article 25 of the Convention. However, he had lodged appeals against these convictions, which were subsequently dismissed, after that date. The Court held that, although those appeals had been lodged after the relevant date, they were closely bound up with the proceedings that had led to his conviction. Divorcing these appeals from the events which gave rise to them would be tantamount to rendering Greece's declaration accepting the right of individual petition nugatory. Accordingly, the Court declared the application incompatible with the Convention *ratione temporis*.

74. In *Kadiķis v. Latvia* (cited above) the applicant requested the Central Electoral Commission to allow him to sign a petition without having a seal affixed on his passport since the existence of the seal would reveal his political opinions and his sympathy for a particular political party. Construing the ensuing silence of the Central Electoral Commission as an implicit decision rejecting his request, the applicant brought an action in court against that decision. These facts occurred before the date of ratification, while the proceedings following the applicant's action and ending with a final decision dismissing his claim occurred after that date.

In *Jovanović v. Croatia* (cited above) the applicant was dismissed from work because of his alleged participation in a "referendum" for Serbian autonomy in Croatia. His disciplinary appeal and his subsequent civil action were unsuccessful. He lodged a constitutional complaint challenging the constitutionality of the court decisions dismissing his civil action that had been delivered before ratification. The Constitutional Court dismissed his constitutional complaint after ratification.

The Court considered the implicit decision of the Electoral Commission in *Kadiķis* and the applicant's dismissal in *Jovanović* as instantaneous acts which had not given rise to a continuing situation of a violation of the Convention. It held that divorcing the domestic courts' judgments delivered after ratification from the events which had given rise to the court proceedings would amount to giving retroactive effect to the Convention, which would be contrary to general principles of international law. It accordingly declared these applications incompatible with the Convention *ratione temporis*.

The Court followed the same approach in *Litovchenko v. Russia* (dec.), no. 69580/01, 18 April 2002, *Kikots and Kikota v. Latvia* (dec.), no. 54715/00, 6 June 2002 and *Veeber v. Estonia (no. 1)*, no. 37571/97, 7 November 2002.

75. In *Moldovan and Others* and *Rostas and Others v. Romania* ((dec.), nos. 41138/98 and 64320/01 (joined), 13 March 2001) the applicants complained *inter alia*, under Article 2 of the Convention, that the Romanian authorities had failed to conduct an effective investigation into the killings of their relatives, which had taken place before ratification. The Court held that the alleged obligation to conduct an effective investigation was derived from the aforementioned killings whose compatibility with the Convention could not be examined. It therefore declared that complaint incompatible with the Convention *ratione temporis*.

76. In *Zana v. Turkey* (judgment of 25 November 1997, *Reports of Judgments and Decisions* 1997-VII) the applicant complained *inter alia*, under Article 10 of the Convention, about his conviction on 26 March 1991 on account of a statement he had made to journalists in August 1987. Turkey accepted the compulsory jurisdiction of the Court only in respect of facts and events which had occurred subsequent to 22 January 1990, the day on which it filed its declaration. The Court did not accept the Turkish Government's argument that the relevant principal fact for establishing jurisdiction *ratione temporis* was the applicant's statement to the journalists. Rather, the principal fact was the applicant's conviction, since it was that conviction which constituted interference with the applicant's rights under Article 10. The Court accordingly dismissed the Government's preliminary objection based on lack of jurisdiction *ratione temporis*.

(d) The appropriate test

77. It follows from the above case-law that the Court's temporal jurisdiction is to be determined in relation to the facts constitutive of the alleged interference. The subsequent failure of remedies aimed at redressing that interference cannot bring it within the Court's temporal jurisdiction.

78. An applicant who considers that a State has violated his rights guaranteed under the Convention is usually expected to resort first to the means of redress available to him under domestic law. If domestic remedies prove unsuccessful and the applicant subsequently applies to the Court, a possible violation of his rights under the Convention will not be caused by the refusal to remedy the interference, but by the interference itself, it being understood that this may be in the form of a court judgment.

79. Therefore, in cases where the interference pre-dates ratification while the refusal to remedy it post-dates ratification, to retain the date of the latter act in determining the Court's temporal jurisdiction would result in the Convention being binding for that State in relation to a fact that had taken place before the Convention entered into force in respect of that State. However, this would be contrary to the general rule of non-retroactivity of treaties.

80. Moreover, affording a remedy usually presupposes a finding that the interference was unlawful under the law in force when the interference occurred (*tempus regit actum*). Therefore, any attempt to remedy, on the basis of the Convention, an interference that had ended before the Convention came into force, would necessarily lead to its retroactive application.

81. In conclusion, while it is true that from the ratification date onwards all of the State's acts and omissions must conform to the Convention (see *Yağci and Sargin v.*

Turkey, judgment of 8 June 1995, Series A no. 319-A, p. 16, § 40), the Convention imposes no specific obligation on the Contracting States to provide redress for wrongs or damage caused prior to that date (see *Kopecký v. Slovakia* [GC], no. 44912/98, § 38, ECHR 2004-IX). Any other approach would undermine both the principle of non-retroactivity in the law of treaties and the fundamental distinction between violation and reparation that underlies the law of State responsibility.

82. In order to establish the Court's temporal jurisdiction it is therefore essential to identify, in each specific case, the exact time of the alleged interference. In doing so the Court must take into account both the facts of which the applicant complains and the scope of the Convention right alleged to have been violated.

(e) Application of the test to the present case

83. The applicant complained that, by terminating her specially protected tenancy, the State violated her rights to respect for her home and peaceful enjoyment of her possessions. This being so, the Court accepts that the termination of her tenancy was the fact constitutive of the alleged interference. It remains to be determined when the termination occurred.

84. The Court observes that for a tenancy to be terminated under Croatian law, there had to be a court judgment upholding the claim of the provider of the flat to that end. The tenancy was terminated from the date on which such a judgment became *res judicata*. In the present case, that judgment was given on 18 January 1994 by the Zadar Municipal Court. However, since it was subsequently reversed by the Zadar County Court's judgment of 19 October 1994, it became *res judicata* on 15 February 1996 when the Supreme Court, by its own judgment, reversed the County Court's judgment. Therefore, it was at that moment—neither before nor afterwards—that the applicant lost her tenancy.

85. It follows that the alleged interference with the applicant's rights lies in the Supreme Court's judgment of 15 February 1996. The subsequent Constitutional Court decision only resulted in allowing the interference allegedly caused by that judgment—a definitive act which was by itself capable of violating the applicant's rights—to subsist. That decision, as it stood, did not constitute the interference. Having regard to the date of the Supreme Court's judgment, the interference falls outside the Court's temporal jurisdiction.

86. As to the applicant's argument that the termination of her tenancy resulted in a continuing situation, the Court recalls that the deprivation of an individual's home or property is in principle an instantaneous act and does not produce a continuing situation of "deprivation" of these rights (see, *inter alia, Malhous v. the Czech Republic* (dec.), no. 33071/96, ECHR 2000-XII, and, *mutatis mutandis, Ostojić v. Croatia* (dec.), no. 16837/02, ECHR 2002-IX). Therefore, the termination of the applicant's tenancy did not create a continuing situation.

87. The only remaining issue to be examined is whether the Constitutional Court's decision, in particular its refusal to quash the Supreme Court's judgment, was in itself inconsistent with the Convention.

88. In the light of the conclusion that the interference occurred prior to the critical date, the applicant's constitutional complaint should be regarded as the exercise of an available domestic remedy. It cannot be argued that the Constitutional

Court's refusal to provide redress, that is, to quash the Supreme Court's judgment, amounted to a new or independent interference since such obligation cannot be derived from the Convention.

89. As already noted, affording a remedy usually presupposes a finding that the impugned decision was unlawful under the law as it stood when the case was decided by a lower court. For the Court, proceedings concerning a constitutional complaint to the Croatian Constitutional Court are by no means different. The Constitutional Court was asked to review the constitutionality of the Supreme Court's judgment of 15 February 1996. The law in force at the time when the Supreme Court gave its judgment did not include the Convention and that court could not therefore apply it.

90. Under the general rule of international law expressed in Article 28 of the Vienna Convention, treaty provisions do not apply retroactively unless the parties have expressly agreed otherwise. That is true in particular of a treaty such as the Convention, which comprises more than mere reciprocal engagements between the Contracting States. It directly creates rights for private individuals within their jurisdiction (see, *inter alia, Ireland v. the United Kingdom*, judgment of 18 January 1978, Series A no. 25, pp. 90–91, § 239). Therefore the above rule on non-retroactivity of treaties is relevant not only for the Court itself but also, first and foremost, for the domestic courts when they are called upon to apply the Convention. The Court, on account of its subsidiary role in safeguarding human rights, must be careful not to reach a result tantamount to compelling the domestic authorities to apply the Convention retroactively.

91. In this connection, the Court notes that the Constitutional Court, when deciding the applicant's constitutional complaint, could not have applied the Convention as an international treaty without having faced the difficulty posed by Article 28 of the Vienna Convention providing for the non-retroactivity of treaties. Moreover, since the Convention was incorporated into the Croatian legal system in the form of a statute, and given that under the 1990 Croatian Constitution statutes could not be applied retroactively, the Constitutional Court could not in the instant case have applied the Convention when reviewing the Supreme Court's judgment. To hold otherwise would mean that the Constitutional Court was bound to take account of the Convention, even though the Convention was not in force in Croatia when the Supreme Court adopted its judgment.

(f) Conclusion

92. Since the fact constitutive of interference giving rise to the present application is the Supreme Court's judgment of 15 February 1996, and not the Constitutional Court's decision of 8 November 1999, an examination of the merits of this application could not be undertaken without extending the Court's jurisdiction to a fact which, by reason of its date, is not subject thereto. To do so would be contrary to the general rules of international law. It follows that the application is incompatible *ratione temporis* with the provisions of the Convention within the meaning of Article 35 § 3.

93. In view of this conclusion, it is not necessary for the Court to examine the Government's further objection based on the applicant's failure to exhaust domestic remedies.

FOR THESE REASONS, THE COURT

Holds, by eleven votes to six, that it is unable to take cognisance of the merits of the case.

DISSENTING OPINION OF JUDGE LOUCAIDES JOINED BY JUDGES ROZAKIS, ZUPANČIČ, CABRAL BARRETO, PAVLOVSCHI & DAVID THÒR BJÖRGVINSSON

I disagree with the majority's view that the Court has no jurisdiction to examine the present application as it is incompatible *ratione temporis.* I believe that in this particular case the interference with the applicant's right to respect for her home and to the peaceful enjoyment of her possessions became complete with the decision of the Constitutional Court dated 8 November 1999, that is to say, after Croatia recognised the competence of the Convention organs to deal with individual petitions based on facts occurring after the Convention and its Protocols came into force in respect of Croatia.

Under the domestic law a specially protected tenancy could only be terminated by a civil action by the provider of the flat ending up in a judgment upholding the claim. A judgment becomes *res judicata,* i.e., a final, unappealable judgment, when it is legally irreversible under the domestic law.[12] This result in the present case was brought about by the above decision of the Constitutional Court. Until then each judgment in the relevant civil action was subject to an appeal that could have led to the judgment being quashed. In other words the completion of the civil action which was necessary to terminate the relevant tenancy in the form of a judicial judgment amounting to a final adjudication of the relevant claim (*res judicata*), consisted of a chain of judicial proceedings up to and including the proceedings before the Constitutional Court.

Therefore, we are not dealing here with an interference with a right under the Convention which had a legal effect independently of any ensuing judicial proceedings issued with the exclusive object of remedying the interference. In the present case the interference was the result of a series of judicial proceedings ending with the decision of the Constitutional Court, which was the only final, irreversible judicial decision in these proceedings.

. . .[T]he majority finds that a "definitive" judgment is necessary to constitute an interference with the applicant's rights and concludes that this "definitive" judgment must be the Supreme Court's judgment of 15 February 1996. However it is difficult to understand why they characterise this judgment as "definitive" or "*res judicata*"

---

[12] See, *inter alia, Nikitin v. Russia,* no. 50178/99, § 37, 15 December 2004: ". . . a decision is final 'if, according to the traditional expression, it has acquired the force of *res judicata.* This is the case when it is irrevocable, that is to say when no further ordinary remedies are available or when the parties have exhausted such remedies or have permitted the time-limit to expire without availing themselves of them'".; and U.S. judgment in *Faison v. Hudson,* 243 Va. 413, 419, 417 S.E.2d 302, 305 (1992): "[A] judgment is not final for the purposes of res judicata . . . when it is being appealed or when the time limits fixed for perfecting the appeal have not expired."

in spite of the fact that it could be set aside by the Constitutional Court after a constitutional complaint. Such a constitutional complaint was in fact lodged in this case and gave the Constitutional Court the opportunity to render its decision that completed the interference with the applicant's rights after Croatia had recognised the jurisdiction of the Court. It should be noted here that when it examined the case the Constitutional Court had jurisdiction to apply the European Convention on Human Rights. The application of the Convention by the Constitutional Court in this case could not be considered as amounting to retroactive enforcement of the Convention because the decision of the Constitutional Court was itself part and parcel of the judicial action that resulted in the termination of the applicant's tenancy and therefore part—the final part, in fact—of the interference complained of. It may be useful to add here that the relevant legal principles of the Convention had in any event been part of the domestic law of Croatia since the 1990 Constitution.

It is true that right up to the level of the Constitutional Court each individual appeal or complaint which followed the initial judgment terminating the applicant's tenancy offered the possibility of a reversal of a preceding decision affecting the applicant's rights. However, so long as this series of appeals and complaints were steps in a composite judicial process leading to the decision of the Constitutional Court which alone could be considered the final *res judicata* amounting to the interference with the applicant's right, the fact that they also functioned as a kind of remedial process in the above sense cannot change their character as a *sine qua non* condition for the termination of the tenancy in question and, consequently, as a prerequisite for the establishment of the relevant interference.

In so far as the majority emphasised that the Constitutional Court's decision "only resulted in allowing the interference allegedly caused by that judgment [the Supreme Court's judgement] . . . to subsist", thereby implying that the Constitutional Court's decision was irrelevant to the question under consideration because it did not reverse the Supreme Court's judgment, I believe that the approach is wrong. What really matters is that the Supreme Court's judgment was not "definitive" before Croatia recognised the competence of the Convention organs because a constitutional complaint against that judgment was still pending before the Constitutional Court when such recognition was granted. Further, it is the final Constitutional Court decision which followed that made the relevant civil action irreversible thus terminating the applicant's tenancy and bringing the problem of the interference complained of by the applicant within the competence of our Court.

In the light of the above, I find that the conclusion of the Chamber regarding the temporal jurisdiction of the Court was correct.

DISSENTING OPINION OF JUDGE ZUPANČIČ JOINED BY JUDGE CABRAL BARRETO

. . . .

The substance of the majority opinion, the ruling, is to be found in paragraph 85, which reads:

"85. It follows that the alleged interference with the applicant's rights lies in the Supreme Court's judgment of 15 February 1996. The subsequent Constitutional Court decision only resulted in *allowing the interference* allegedly caused by that judgment—

a definitive act which was by itself capable of violating the applicant's rights—*to subsist*. That decision, as it stood, did not constitute the interference. Having regard to the date of the Supreme Court's judgment, the interference falls outside the Court's temporal jurisdiction." [Emphasis added.]

I wonder what this crucial construct—on which the whole judgment is based—is supposed to mean. Might the implication be that the Constitutional Court has merely omitted to correct the alleged violation, i.e., that the commission of the alleged violation had been perpetrated by the Croatian Supreme Court? Could it be maintained that the Constitutional Court has perpetrated—because it allowed the interference to subsist—a commission by omission?

If so, why is it then that presumably irrelevant omissions of this kind are a domestic remedy that this Court has repeatedly required to be exhausted before it would deal with the case? In German cases, for example, before we deal with them we insist that the constitutional complaint be filed and that the Federal Constitutional Court—in a bare and unmotivated rejection of the complaint—"allow the interference to subsist". Are we from now going to maintain that, *yes*, this is an effective domestic remedy—not only in theory but also in practice!—which must, we insist, always first be exhausted, and, *no*, the decision of the German Constitutional Court—involving even more omitting, because there we do not even call for reasons to be given for the rejection of the constitutional complaint—did not constitute the interference? *"Oh,"* we shall say, *"it merely allowed the interference (*of whatever lower instance) *to subsist!"*

Shall we from now on count the six-month limit from the "real" interference of the lower instance decision, or from the moment when the Constitutional court will have unreceptively, by its mere omission to correct it, "allowed the interference to subsist"?

Admittedly, the *ratio legis* for the requirement of preliminary exhaustion of domestic remedies is different from the *ratio legis* for the temporal limitation of the Convention's impact. The intent of the former is that the Contracting State be given full domestic opportunity to deal with the violation; the latter simply deals with the non-retroactivity of a contractual obligation. The purpose of the six-month rule, on the other hand, as of all such rules, derives from the need for security and stability of all potentially affected legal interactions. After the momentous decision in *Scozzari and Giunta v. Italy* this purpose gained considerably in its significance. The consistent practical application of the requirement of exhaustion of domestic remedies and of the six-month rule, however, presupposes a fixed place and time of occurrence. The newly introduced ambiguity concerning the legal meaning of the Constitutional Courts' rejections of constitutional complaints, although presently only in the *ratione temporis* consideration, will raise doubts concerning cross-lateral consistency of our case-law. In other words, despite the teleological divergences of different interacting doctrines (the non-exhaustion doctrine, the six-month rule, and the *ratione temporis* validity) there must be practical consistency in every-day decision-making.

In terms of formal logic, however, the key paragraph 85 of the majority judgment seems to be built upon the distinction between a *necessary condition* and a *cause*. To reiterate the majority's conclusion, I think it would be fair to say that they hold that the Constitutional Court's decision was a necessary condition for but not a cause of the violation.

Unfortunately, this distinction is as specious as it is misleading.

. . . .

In our case, it is clear that the violation in question would not have occurred had it been corrected by the Constitutional Court. That the Constitutional Court permitted the violation "to subsist" is thus clearly one of the necessary conditions of the violation.[13] However, the majority, without telling us why, seem to imply that this necessary condition is not determinative, critical, and relevant for the ultimate violation. In other words, the majority refuse to grant this particular necessary condition the status of a "cause".

. . . .

For the sake of argument, we can also imagine the reverse order of the events. The decision of the Supreme Court could have been in favour of the applicant—say on purely non-Conventional grounds—only for the Constitutional Court to reverse it.[14] In that case, presumably, the violation *would* have occurred after the critical date and the Convention would be applicable *ratione temporis*. The Grand Chamber would then delve into the merits of this case and perhaps find that there was a violation. Before that, however, one would have to explain why such a reverse order of events would bring the case within the temporal limits of the Convention. Would the majority then say that the Constitutional Court's decision did something positive, rather than merely permit the Supreme Court's judgment to "subsist"? If so, what is the crucial difference between the actual and the hypothetical situation? Is it the difference between "omission" and "commission"? Those of us used to precise *pénaliste* reasoning know how tenuous this distinction may be.

In the end I am, therefore, constrained to come to the conclusion either that (1) the majority's position remains logically unintelligible, or that (2) this case has been decided on an unconvincing technicality, or (3) both of the above.

---

[13] Other higher courts, too, when affirming their own lower courts' decisions sometimes permit their "alleged violations to subsist". The jurisdictional difference between Constitutional and ordinary higher courts is that the former will let the decision stand unless it collides with the Constitution. In double track jurisdictions the frame of legal reference is different for the Constitutional Courts, i.e. it will sometimes let the lower decision stand even if patently illegal or illogical, because constitutional tests only refer to the Constitution (and constitutional rights enshrined these) and are different from the usual tests of legality and logic. In our case this could mean that "allowing the lower decision to subsist" did not confer on it either legality or logic. It would simply mean that the Supreme Court's decision did not infringe the *constitutional* rights of Mrs. Blečić.

> The majority, however, do not submit such an argument. If it did, it would be open to the obvious counterargument that the rights deriving from a Constitution and the rights deriving from the Convention mostly overlap. For this reason, for example, the admissible constitutional complaint represents the last and the best test of violation before the case comes to the European Court of Human Rights in Strasbourg. The only national instance—the court of last resort—specifically authorised to perform legal assessments that are substantially similar to our own tests, are precisely the Constitutional Courts. In other words, the Constitutional Court's decision is not an inconsequential "omission" because it should have been *precisely* before the Constitutional Court where the alleged violation ought to have been put right. In my opinion this would even be the case in a one-track jurisdiction, e.g., *certiorari* in the pick-and-choose system before the United States Supreme Court although the latter is not specifically in charge—as in fact most of the European Constitutional Courts—of the protection of constitutional rights.

[14] Again, it would be logically irrelevant for our purposes on what normative grounds the Constitutional Court chose to reverse it. We find violations in many cases—and often precisely because this is so—where in domestic jurisdiction there is no reference to the Convention.

This will become apparent when *Blečić v. Croatia* begins to serve as a precedent in future cases. Will the import of this precedent be that the last decision of the national court, which does not reverse the penultimate decision—but merely permits it to "subsist"—may count as a required domestic remedy, but does not count as a real decision bringing the case within the temporal limits of the Convention?

Apart from all that, I am convinced that as far as the merits of the case are concerned this is not the end of the matter. In the case file there are indications that there may be thousands of similar cases. Sooner or later they will reach this Court.

Caesar v. Trinidad and Tobago, Judgment of March 11, 2005, 123 Inter-Am. Ct. H.R. (Ser. C) (2005).

1. The present Case was submitted to the Court by the Inter-American Commission on Human Rights . . . against the State of Trinidad and Tobago . . . on February 26, 2003, originating from the petition No. 12.147, which was received at the Commission's Secretariat on May 13, 1999. . . .

2. The Commission filed the Application pursuant to Article 61 of the American Convention, for the Court to decide whether the State violated "Mr. [Winston] Caesar's right to humane treatment under Articles 5(1) and 5(2) of the Convention, his right to be tried within a reasonable time under Article 8(1) of the Convention, and his right to judicial protection under Article 25 of the Convention, all in conjunction with violations of Article 1(1) of the Convention. In addition, the Commission argue[d] that the State, by failing to provide for the right to be tried within a reasonable time under its domestic law and by authorizing a form of punishment that is incompatible with the right to humane treatment, is responsible for violating its obligation [. . .] under Article 2 of the Convention to give domestic legal effect [. . .] to the rights guaranteed under Articles 5(1), 5(2), 7(5) and 8(1) of the Convention". The Commission also requested that the Court order the State to adopt various pecuniary and non-pecuniary measures of reparation. . . .

II. JURISDICTION OF THE COURT

5. Trinidad and Tobago deposited its instrument of ratification of the American Convention on Human Rights (hereinafter "the Convention" or "the American Convention") on May 28, 1991. On that same day, the State recognised the compulsory jurisdiction of the Court.

6. On May 26, 1998, Trinidad and Tobago denounced the Convention and the denunciation became effective one year later, as of May 26, 1999, pursuant to Article 78 of the Convention. According to Article 78 of the Convention, a denunciation will not release the denouncing State from its obligations under the Convention with respect to acts of that State occurring prior to the effective date of the denunciation that may constitute a violation of the Convention.

7. Moreover, in the *Hilaire, Constantine, Benjamin and others Case*,[15] the Court held in its judgments on preliminary objections that:

> [. . .] Trinidad and Tobago cannot prevail in the limitation included in its instrument of acceptance of the optional clause of the mandatory jurisdiction of the Inter-American Court of Human Rights in virtue of what has been established in Article 62 of the American Convention, because this limitation is incompatible with the object and purpose of the Convention.

8. Notwithstanding the fact that the Inter-American Court is fully competent to hear the present Case, the State did not participate in the proceedings before this Tribunal. . . . Nevertheless, the Court, as is the case with any other international organ with jurisdictional functions, has the inherent authority to determine the scope of its own competence (*compétence de la compétence*).[16]

9. In interpreting the American Convention in accordance with the general rules of treaty interpretation enshrined in Article 31(1) of the Vienna Convention on the Law of Treaties, bearing in mind the object and purpose of the American Convention, this Tribunal, in the exercise of the authority conferred on it by Article 62(3) of the American Convention, must act in a manner that preserves the integrity of the provisions of Article 62(1) of the Convention. It would be unacceptable to subordinate these provisions to restrictions that would render inoperative the Court's jurisdictional role, and consequently, the human rights protection system established in the Convention.[17]

10. Furthermore, the Court considers relevant to recall a recent case law with respect to its *ratione temporis* competence:[18]

> [. . .] The Court cannot exercise its contentious jurisdiction to apply the Convention and declare that its provisions have been violated when the alleged facts or the conduct of the defendant State which might involve international responsibility precede recognition of the Court's jurisdiction.

> [. . .] However, in case of a continuing or permanent violation, whose commencement occurred before the defendant State had recognized the Court's contentious jurisdiction and which persists even after this recognition, the Court is competent to consider the actions and omissions that occurred after the recognition of its jurisdiction and the effects of the violations.

11. With the exception of certain matters concerning the criminal proceedings, most of the facts alleged in the Application in the present case occurred before the State´s denunciation of the Convention came into effect. Taking into account the considerations set out in the preceding paragraphs, the Court reaffirms its compe-

---

15 Cf. *Hilaire Case*, Preliminary Objections, Judgment of September 1, 2001, Series C No. 80, para. 98; *Benjamin et al. Case*, Preliminary Objections, Judgment of September 1, 2001, Series C No. 81, para. 89; and *Constantine et al. Case*, Preliminary Objections, Judgment of September 1, 2001, Series C No. 82, para. 89.

16 Cf. *Case of the Serrano-Cruz Sisters*, Preliminary Objections, Judgment of November 23, 2004, Series C No. 118, para. 63; *Case of Alfonso Martín-del Campo-Dodd*, Preliminary Objections, Judgment of September 3, 2004, Series C No. 113, para. 69; and *Case of Baena-Ricardo et al.*, Judgment of November 28, 2003, Series C No. 104, para. 68.

17 Cf. *Hilaire Case*, Preliminary Objections, supra note 15, paras. 82 and 84; *Benjamin et al. Case*, Preliminary Objections, supra note 15, paras. 73 to 75; and *Constantine et al. Case*, Preliminary Objections, supra note 15, paras. 73 to75.

18 Cf. *Case of the Serrano-Cruz Sisters*, Preliminary Objections, supra note 16, paras. 66 and 67.

tence, according to the terms of Articles 62(3) and 78(2) of the Convention, to hear the present Case and render judgment.

. . . .

V. PREVIOUS CONSIDERATIONS

34. The State did not appear in the proceedings before the Commission nor before the Court. Nevertheless, the Court has, of its own motion, taken the necessary measures to complete consideration of the case and, having evaluated the arguments and the evidence tendered during the proceedings by the Inter-American Commission and by the representatives, now delivers its judgment.

. . . .

39. It should be emphasized that in this case the State failed to discharge its procedural responsibility to submit evidence in the course of the procedural stages set out in Article 44 of the Rules of Procedure. In consequence, the Court deems it appropriate to establish the proven facts of the instant case, taking into account, in addition to the aforementioned silence of the State, other elements that may assist it in establishing the truth of the facts, exercising its responsibility to protect human rights and applying, to this end, the pertinent provisions of the American Convention and of general international law.

. . . .

VII. PROVEN FACTS

49. The Court considers that the following facts have been proven:

Regarding Winston Caesar's criminal proceedings

49(1). On November 11, 1983, Mr. Winston Caesar was initially arrested as the suspect in connection with a rape that was alleged to have taken place in Trinidad on November 8, 1983. On November 16, 1983, he was released on bail. Between 1985 and 1986 committal proceedings took place in the Port of Spain Magistrate's 4th Court, which ordered him to stand trial on February 21, 1986.

49(2). On September 10, 1991, he was arrested and taken into custody for failing to appear in court. During his trial he was held at Port of Spain prison.

49(3). The trial was held in January 1992, before Mr. Justice Dayalsingh, in the High Court of Trinidad and Tobago. On January 10, 1992, Mr. Caesar was convicted of attempted rape under Trinidad and Tobago's Offences against the Person Act. He was sentenced to serve 20 years in a penitentiary with hard labor and to receive 15 strokes of the cat-o-nine tails. That same day Mr. Caesar signed a Notice of Appeal and remained in detention.

49(4). On November 26, 1993 Mr. Caesar's attorney filed an application for leave to appeal at the Court of Appeal of Trinidad and Tobago, challenging the legal basis for the ruling. On February 28, 1996, the Court of Appeal of Trinidad and Tobago dismissed Mr. Caesar's application for leave to appeal apparently without giving reasons, and confirmed the conviction and sentence.

49(5). A counsel in Britain was asked by Mr. Caesar's lawyers to consider whether there were reasonable grounds of appeal to the Privy Council in this case. On November 2, 1998, in his "note for instructing solicitors", counsel indicated that an application for Special Leave to Appeal to the Privy Council was unlikely to succeed.

In considering whether the delay of over 8 years between Mr. Caesar's arrest and trial was so great as to amount to a denial of justice, and thus an infringement of his constitutional rights, counsel was of the opinion that although the delay was "very great" and might be imputed to the State, he nevertheless judged as minimal the degree of risk that the miscarriage of justice had been caused by the delay. Finally, the counsel considered that, although such delay was a point on which Mr. Caesar might have applied to the High Court of Trinidad and Tobago, he discounted the chances of success at the Privy Council.

. . . .

IX. ARTICLES 8 AND 25 OF THE AMERICAN CONVENTION IN CONJUNCTION WITH ARTICLES 1(1) AND 2 OF THE CONVENTION (RIGHT TO A FAIR TRIAL AND JUDICIAL PROTECTION)

. . .

105. There are two issues that the Court must address regarding the alleged violations of Articles 8(1) and 25, all in connection with Articles 1(1) and 2, of the American Convention:

a) the reasonableness of the length of the criminal proceedings; and

b) whether the domestic law of the State provides an effective remedy against either the existence or the application of corporal punishment.

106. The Court notes that, after the judgment delivered by the Court of Appeal of Trinidad and Tobago on February 28, 1996, Mr. Caesar still had the possibility to apply for leave to appeal to the Privy Council. The Court cannot share the Commission's view that Mr. Caesar was subjected to a total delay of fifteen years in the proceedings, to be calculated between his initial arrest in 1983 and his "attempt to pursue an appeal before the Judicial Committee of the Privy Council in 1998". That "attempt" consisted in a legal opinion rendered in November 1998 by counsel in London, at the request of Mr. Caesar's lawyers, and therefore cannot be equated to a procedural step in a judicial process. The length of the proceedings must be calculated, therefore, on the basis that the final judgment in the case was reached with the decision of the Court of Appeal of Trinidad and Tobago on February 28, 1996.

107. Although neither the Commission nor the representatives raised the issue of the Court's *ratione temporis* jurisdiction, it is incumbent on the Tribunal to consider this question in the context of the actual duration of the criminal proceedings in order to come to a conclusion as to the reasonableness of the time elapsed, for the purpose of deciding whether there was a violation of the rights enshrined in Article 8(1) of the Convention.

108. On this point, the Court has held as follows:

When codifying general law on this issue, Article 28 of the Vienna Convention on the Law of Treaties establishes that:

Unless a different intention appears from the treaty or is otherwise established, its provisions do not bind a party in relation to any act or fact which took place or any situation which ceased to exist before the date of the entry into force of the treaty with respect to that party.[19]

109. In cases where the Court decided that it had no *ratione temporis* jurisdiction to decide upon certain facts, it has made it clear that this situation does not imply a judgment about the existence of those facts.[20]

110. In cases where the applicant alleged the violation of Articles 5(3) or 6(1) of the European Convention on Fundamental Rights and Freedoms, the European Court of Human Rights has restricted its considerations to the time period that falls into its *ratione temporis* jurisdiction, starting from the date on which the State recognized the right of individual petition or ratified the Convention. It is significant, however, that the European Court nevertheless takes into account the amount of time that has elapsed before this effective date—in cases of detention or in a legal proceeding, for example—in its assessment of rights violations.

111. The Court notes that the criminal proceedings lasted for more than 12 years, if calculated from the first arrest of Mr. Caesar on November 11, 1983, as the Commission and the representatives have done. However, as Trinidad and Tobago's recognition of the Court's compulsory jurisdiction took effect on May 28, 1991, the Court can only consider the period between the date of that recognition and the decision of the Court of Appeal on February 28, 1996, the final judgment delivered in the criminal proceedings. Mr. Caesar was convicted on January 10, 1992 by the High Court of Trinidad and Tobago. His lawyers waited for almost two years to request leave to appeal and, on February 28, 1996, the Court of Appeal dismissed the appeal and confirmed the sentence. Therefore, the Court finds that the duration of the criminal proceedings between May 28, 1991, and February 28, 1996—discounting the period of almost two years before that leave to appeal was sought—does not constitute a delay that can be considered unreasonable, in the terms of Article 8(1) of the Convention.

112. For the aforementioned reasons, the Court considers that the State is not responsible for a violation of Article 8(1) of the Convention.

113. The Court must now turn to examine whether the domestic law of the State provides an effective remedy against either the existence or the application of corporal punishment.

114. In the instant case, domestic judges were authorized to sentence Mr. Caesar to flogging with the "cat-o-nine-tails" under the laws of Trinidad and Tobago—specifically, the Corporal Punishment Act.

115. It is important to note that, even if Mr. Caesar had been able to appeal to the Privy Council, such an appeal would have been most unlikely to succeed . . . .

116. . . . . [I]n a 2002 judgment with regard to a case in the Bahamas, the Judicial Committee of the Privy Council observed that "[. . .] it is accepted that flogging is an inhuman and degrading punishment and, unless protected from constitutional challenge under some other provision of the Constitution, is rendered unconstitutional by [the provision of the Constitution prohibiting torture and inhuman or

---

[19] Cf. *Case of the Serrano-Cruz Sisters*, Preliminary Objections, supra note 16, paras. 60, 61 and 64; *Case of Alfonso Martín-del Campo-Dodd*, Preliminary Objections, supra note 16, para. 68; and *Cantos Case*, Preliminary Objections, Judgment of September 7, 2001, Series C No. 85, para. 35.

[20] Cf. *Case of Alfonso Martín-del Campo-Dodd*, Preliminary Objections, supra note 16, paras. 79 to 84.

degrading treatment or punishment]".[21] Nevertheless, on the basis of the "savings clause" in the Constitution of the Bahamas, the Privy Council upheld the constitutionality of the legislation authorising corporal punishment.

117. It follows from the above that the State did not provide the alleged victim with an effective remedy to challenge the application of the aforementioned corporal punishment. Therefore, the Court considers that Trinidad and Tobago is responsible for the violation of Article 25, in relation to Articles 1(1) and 2, of the Convention, to the detriment of Mr. Caesar. . . .

Annette Pagnoulle (on behalf of Abdoulaye Mazou) *v. Cameroon,* (Comm. 39/90), *10th Annual Activity Report of the Afr. Comm. H.P.R. 1996–1997,* Annex X, pp. 52–56.

The Facts

1. This communication was submitted by Annette Pagnoulle of Amnesty International and concerns Abdoulaye Mazou, a Cameroonian national. Mr. Mazou was imprisoned in 1984 by a military tribunal without trial, without witnesses, and without right to defence. He was sentenced to 5 years imprisonment for hiding his brother who was later sentenced to death for attempted coup d'etat. Even after he had served his sentence in April 1989, he continued to be held in prison and was only freed by the intervention of Amnesty International on 23 May 1990. He continued to be under detention at his residence until the law of amnesty of 23 April 1991.

2. Although Mr. Mazou has now been freed, he has not been reinstated in his position as a magistrate. The complainant therefore requests action be continued on his behalf.

3. The government was represented by a delegation at the 20th session of the Commission held in Mauritius in October 1996, which asked that the communication should be declared inadmissible because it was still pending at the Supreme Court.

4. The alleged victim petitioned the President of the Republic in order to solicit his reinstatement as a magistrate. He then submitted an out of court settlement to the Ministry of Justice. When no response from the President or the Ministry was forthcoming the alleged victim made a submission for a legal settlement to the Administrative Chamber of the Supreme Court which rejected his case in principle. He submitted further petitions to the Supreme Court and seized the Ministry of Justice for reinstatement in his position. He has also undertaken to bring political pressure, jointly with others, to reclaim his profession. As yet, none of these actions has produced any result.

---

[21] *Prince Pinder v. The Queen,* Privy Council Appeal No. 40/2001 (Bahamas), September 23, 2002, [2003] 1 AC 620, para. 5.

Procedure

5. The Commission was seized of the communication at the 7th Session in April 1990.

6. On 31 May 1990, the Secretariat of the Commission notified the state of Cameroon of the communication and asked it for its views on admissibility.

7. On 1 March 1995, the Secretariat informed the complainant that the Commission takes note of the release of Mr. Mazou. The complainant was advised to inform the Commission whether or not his release was satisfactory reparation for Mr. Mazou no later than July 1, 1995.

8. On 8 June 1995, a fax was received from the complainant stating that although the victim, Mr. Abdoulaye Mazou, had been released he had not been reinstated in his position as a magistrate, to which he is legally entitled.

9. At the 19th session, in March 1996, the communication was declared admissible. The parties were notified of this decision.

10. At the 20th Session, held in October 1996, a delegation of the government of Cameroon was present and submitted a written response to the effect that the communication was inadmissible. The delegation also admitted, however, that the conditions under which Mr. Mazou was tried by a military tribunal fell short of the standards provided for in the African Charter, but that the laws governing such tribunals had since been changed. The delegation promised to forward to the Commission the written judgement of the Military Tribunal, any judgement concerning the alleged disciplinary measures against Mr. Mazou, a document proving the existence of recourse as concerns disciplinary measures and the law after which Mr. Mazou was condemned. The Commission decided to postpone consideration of the case to the 21st session.

11. On 24 March the Secretariat received a letter from the Ministry of Foreign Affairs of Cameroon informing the Secretariat that the question had been dealt with in the Administrative Chamber of the Supreme Court and that all interested parties had the possibility of exhausting local remedies. The Ministry also sent the Supreme Court judgment, the ordinance no 304 which placed Mr. Mazou under surveillance, ordinances no 72/5 and 72/20 concerning the compentence of the military court and law no. 74/4 modifying ordinance no. 72/5, the judgment of the military court, ordinance no. 72/13 concerning state of emergency, ordinance 72/6 concerning the organisation of the Supreme Court and law no. 76/28 modifying this ordinance, Decree no. 80/276 concerning the nomination of Secretary Generals of Ministries and Decree no. 82/467 relating to the judiciary.

Law

Admissibility

12. Article 56 of the African Charter reads:

Communications . . . shall be considered if they: Are sent after exhausting local remedies, if any, unless it is obvious that this procedure is unduly prolonged. . . .

13. In this case, the alleged victim petitioned the President of the Republic in order to solicit his reinstatement as a magistrate. He then submitted an out of court settlement to the Ministry of Justice. When no response from the President or the

Ministry was forthcoming the alleged victim made a submission for a legal settlement to the Administrative Chamber of the Supreme Court. He submitted further petitions to the Supreme Court and seized the Ministry of Justice for reinstatement in his position. In light of the above actions taken by the victim and their failure to yield any results the Commission holds that local remedies have been duly exhausted.

Merits

14. . . . .

15. In conformity with Article 65 of the Charter, the Commission cannot pronounce on the equity of court proceedings that took place before the African Charter entered into force in Cameroon on 20 September 1989 (See the Commission's decision on communication 59/91). If however irregularities in the original sentence has consequences that constitute a continuing violation of any of the Articles of the African Charter, the Commission must pronounce on these.

16. Mr. Mazou was held in prison after the expiration of his sentence in April 1989 until 23 May 1990. After his release, he was placed under house arrest. The delegation of Cameroon at the 20th session stated that: "After serving his sentence he was released, but the problem is that he was the subject of purely administrative measures based on existing laws at that time. These laws were however abrogated only in 1989."

17. All parties agree that Mr. Mazou was held beyond the expiry of his sentence. No judgment was passed to extend his sentence. Therefore the detention is arbitrary, and the Commission finds that this constitutes a violation of Article 6.

18. . . . .

19. Mr. Mazou has not yet had a judgment on his case brought before the Supreme Court over two years ago, without being given any reason for the delay. At the 20th session the delegation held that the case might be decided upon by the end of October 1996, but still no news of it has been forwarded to the Commission. Given that this case concerns Mr. Mazou's ability to work in his profession, two years without any hearing or projected trial date constitutes a violation of article 7.1(d) of the African Charter.

20. At the 20th session, the delegation of Cameroon stated that "the administrative detention had not for its reason the fact that sentenced Mazou, it was not linked to the trial. [Sic.] When the state believes that an individual who is free can trouble public order we can take preventive measures, and this explains why he was detained administratively. This can be renewed at any time when the administrative authorities deem that there is a risk and therefore they deem need of preventive measures."

21. Detention on the mere suspect [sic] that an individual may cause problems is a violation of his right to be presumed innocent.

22. . . . .

23. Article 2 of the Amnesty Law of 23 April 1992 reads:

Have been amnestied:

All persons sentenced of subversion to penalty of imprisonment and/or fined;

All persons sentenced a punishment of detention or serving a penalty of detention;

All persons authors of offences of a political nature, condemned to death penalty.

24. Article 3 of the Amnesty Law of 23 April 1992 reads:

... the persons condemned who have been granted amnesty and who had public employment will be reintegrated. ...

25. Still, after the Amnesty Law of 23 April 1992, Mr. Mazou has been denied reinstatement by the government in his former professional capacity as a magistrate.

26. The delegation of the government which appeared at the 20th session claimed the reason to be that he is not covered by the Amnesty law of 23 April 1992, because he has not been judged of subversion or sentenced to detention. It also stated that disciplinary action was taken against Mr. Mazou because of his sentence.

27. Although according to the delegation, Mr. Mazou was judged for an ordinary criminal offence in Cameroon, he was still judged by a Military Tribunal. The delegation answered the Commission's questions about this as follows: 'Why he was tried by a Military Tribunal? Everybody knows that when you are involved in a problem which includes the attempt to violently, using arms, overthrow a government and a president, then you are actually taking actions in political acts, something of a political nature. The coup plotters of 1984 were judged by the Military Tribunal and since Mr. Mazou hid for some time a brother of his who was involved, then there was, there could have been a connection between the coup attempt and the fact that Mr. Mazou had accepted to hide his brother.'

28. To the Commission it still seems peculiar that Mr. Mazou was tried by a Military Tribunal like the coup plotters and that afterwards he is not given amnesty like them. The delegation promised to forward to the Commission the written judgement of the Military Tribunal. This has not yet happened.

29. The Commission finds that by not reinstating Mr. Mazou in his former position after the Amnesty Law, the government has violated Article 15 of the African Charter, because it has prevented Mr. Mazou to work in his capacity of a magistrate even though others who have been condemned under similar conditions have been reinstated.

FOR THE ABOVE REASONS, THE COMMISSION

Declares the violations of Articles 6, 7.1(b), 7.1(d) and 15;

Recommends that the government of Cameroon draw all the necessary legal conclusions to reinstate the victim in his rights.

Taken at the 21st Ordinary Session, Nouakchott, Mauritania, April 1997.

Questions and Comments

1. *See also Comm. 142/94, Muthuthurin Njoka v. Kenya, 8th Annual Activity Rep. of the Afr. Comm. H.P.R.* 1995 (declaring the complaint inadmissible because "[t]he cause of the complaint arose at a time when Kenya was not a party to the Charter. There is no evidence of a continuing damage in breach of the Charter.").

2. Positive international law honors the principle of non-retroactivity of treaties "unless a different intention appears in the treaty or is otherwise established." Does it appear in the American Convention that the intention was to disregard the principle of non-retroactivity of treaties in the case of legislation passed before the Convention's entry into force?

3. Does the African Commission approach the issue of non-retroactivity in the same way as the other regional bodies? Is the issue one of retroactivity or state responsibility? On what basis can the Commission find a violation of a non-binding instrument like the UN Basic Principles on the Independence of the Judiciary?

4. For another example of the European Court's approach to continuing violations see *Demandes v. Turkey, (App. no. 16219/90)*, judgment of 31 July 2003. The applicant complained that since 1974 he had been prevented by the Turkish armed forces from having access to his property in Cyprus, using and enjoying possession of it as well as developing it. In addition, he claimed that according to evidence his home was occupied by officers and/or other members of the Turkish armed forces. The applicant complained of an unjustified interference with the right to respect for his home in violation of Article 8 of the Convention. The applicant also contended that the continuous denial of access to his property in northern Cyprus and the ensuing loss of all control of it constituted a violation of Article 1 of Protocol No. 1. The Court held that there were continuing violations. See also, *Eur. Court H.R., Kudla v. Poland*, Grand Chamber, (30210/96), Judgment of October 26, 2000, paras. 102–103 and 119–123; *Eur. Court H.R., Humen v. Poland*, Grand Chamber, (26614/95), Judgment of October 15, 1999, paras. 58–59. See also, *Eur. Court H.R., Ilascu v. Moldova and Russia*, (48787/99), Judgment of July 8, 2004, paras. 395–400.

F. Jurisdiction of the Inter-American Court

Cayara v. Peru (Preliminary Objections), Judgment of February 3, 1993, 14 Inter-Am. Ct. H.R. (Ser. C) (1993).

1. The instant case was brought to the Court by the Inter-American Commission on Human Rights on February 14, 1992. It relates to Petitions Nos. 10.264, 10.206, 10.276 and 10.446.

2. The Commission filed this case in order that the Court determine whether the country in question violated the following articles of the American Convention on Human Rights: 4 (Right to Life), 5 (Right to Humane Treatment), 7 (Right to Personal Liberty), 8 (Right to a Fair Trial), 21 (Right to Property) and 25 (Right to Judicial Protection), read together with Article 1(1) (Obligation to Respect Rights), "as a result of the extrajudicial executions, torture, arbitrary detention, forced disappearance of persons and damages against public property and the property of Peruvian citizens, who were victims of the actions of members of the Peruvian army, beginning on May 14, 1988 in the district of Cayara, Province of Victor Fajardo, Department of Ayacucho" . . . . The application identifies forty persons as victims of arbitrary executions and disappearances and eight persons as having been tortured; it also refers to damages caused to public and private property.

6. On March 26, 1992, the Agent [for Peru] interposed the following preliminary objections.

    a. lack of jurisdiction of the Inter-American Commission on Human Rights;

    b. litis finitio;

    c. expiration of the time limit for filing of the application;

d. inadmissibility of the application due to deprivation of Peru's right of defense;

e. inadmissibility of the application due to invalidity of Resolution No. 1/91 of the Commission;

f. inadmissibility of the application due to invalidity of the Commission's second Report 29/91;

g. invalidity by reason of estoppel on the part of the Inter-American Commission on Human Rights;

h. inadmissibility of the application due to the acceptance of the replies of the claimants after expiration of the time limit;

i. inadmissibility of the application due to the acceptance of Amnesty International as co-petitioner after expiration of the time limit;

j. inadmissibility of the application due to improper joining of four cases before the Commission;

k. inadmissibillity of the application due to manifest bias on the part of the Inter-American Commission on Human Rights; and

1. lack of jurisdiction of the Inter-American Court of Human Rights.

10. On June 23, 1992, the Secretariat, on instructions of the Court, certified the following:

1. That on Monday, June 3,1991, a letter dated May 30,1991, was received by fax from the Inter-American Commission on Human Rights. The purpose of the letter was to "transmit . . . Report No. 29/91 concerning cases Nos. 10.264, 10.206, 10.276 and 10.446 against the Government of Peru . . .," in view of the fact that "during its 79th Session, the Commission approved the report in question on February 20, 1991, and decided to submit it to the Inter-American Court of Human Rights pursuant to Articles 51 of the American Convention on Human Rights and 50 of the Regulations of the ICHR".

2. That on Friday, June 7, 1991, the Court received the file by courier service.

3. That on Wednesday, June 12, 1991, the Executive Secretary of the Inter-American Commission on Human Rights telephoned the Secretary of the Court to inform him that Mr. Luis Jiminez, the Commission's attorney, would be traveling to the Court as soon as possible to discuss the possible withdrawal of the case(s). Mr. Jiminez arrived at the Court on June 18, 1991.

4. That by note of June 20, 1991 (attached), received at the Secretariat on the 24th of that month, the Inter-American Commission stated that "it ha[d] decided for the time being to withdraw the case from the Court, in order to reconsider it and possibly present it again . . .". The Secretariat of the Court acknowledged receipt of this note, after consulting with the Permanent Commission.

5. No minutes of the full Court exist on the subject.

. . . .

24. During its 79th Session of February, 1991, the Commission studied cases 10.264, 10.206, 10.276 and 10.446 jointly and approved Report No. 29/91 in which, among other things, it decided to submit the cases to the jurisdiction of the Court. The report was sent to the Government on March 1, 1991. In view of the fact that

the Government did not receive the Report until April 5, the Commission agreed to its request that the 60-day period granted begin to run as of that date.

25. On May 27, 1991 the Government pointed out to the Commission that, under the terms of Article 34, paragraphs 7 and 8, of the Regulations of the Commission, it should have transmitted to Peru the pertinent parts and attachments of the replies of the petitioners dated November 1, 1989 (Americas Watch) and July 18, 1990 (Americas Watch and Amnesty International). The Commission did not do so, depriving the country of its right of defense. In the Government's opinion, this "invalidates the investigation and weakens the general framework of the Convention that Peru has subscribed to and ratified".

The Government affirmed:

> Bearing in mind the serious procedural irregularities pointed out above, the Government of Peru believes that as long as the investigation does not adhere to the rules expressly enunciated by the Convention and the Regulations of the ICHR, the necessary guarantees will not be in place to ensure that its conclusions and recommendations enjoy the minimum degree of efficacy required. The investigation of the CAYARA case. which has been rendered invalid nullifies any other proceeding to which it could give rise and allows Peru to disqualify itself in the future from validating such acts with its participation, since it considers them to be in violation of the principles and guarantees of International Law and, especially, of those that uphold the Inter-American Legal System.

> For these reasons, the Government of Peru, being a State Party to the American Convention on Human Rights, requests that the Commission comply with its Regulations and the Pact of San José and therefore decide not to take the case to the Inter-American Court of Human Rights without first weighing the observations made in the present note and making the appropriate procedural corrections.

26. The Commission submitted the four joint cases to the Court by note of May 30, 1991. On June 11, 1991, the Commission's Executive Secretary notified the Minister of Foreign Affairs of Peru that she had submitted "the cases in question to the Inter-American Court of Human Rights (San Jose, Costa Rica) on May 30, 1991 for processing". By note of June 20, 1991, received at the Secretariat on the 24th of that month, the Chairman of the Commission, Mr. Patrick L. Robinson, addressed the President of the Court as follows:

> I take the liberty of informing Your Excellency that the Commission, acting at the request of the Government of Peru and in order to ensure that no questions arise as to the correct application of the proceedings, as well as to protect the interests of both parties (the Government and the petitioners), has decided for the time being to withdraw the case from the Court, in order to reconsider it and possibly present it again at some future date, after the observations submitted by the Government of Peru with regard to the instant case have been properly assessed.

27. That same June 24, 1991, the Secretariat replied to the above note from the Chairman of the Commission as follows:

> Acting on instructions of the President of the Inter-American Court of Human Rights, Judge Hector Fix-Zamudio, I have the honor to inform Your Excellency that, after consulting with the Permanent Commission, I have been authorized to acknowledge receipt of your note of June 20, 1991 "relating to Report 29/91 of the Inter-American Commission on Human Rights in connection with cases 10.206, 10.264, 10.276

and 10.446 against the Government of Peru," in which you affirm that the Commission "has decided for the time being to withdraw the case from the Court

28. By note of June 20, 1991, the Commission informed Peru of the withdrawal of the case from the Court and granted it a period of 60 days in which to submit its final observations. . . ..

29. By note of August 26, 1991, Peru replied to the Commission, in part as follows:

> From the contents of your communication it would appear that the Government of Peru had requested the Inter-American Commission on Human Rights to reconsider the case. That is inaccurate, for at no time did Peru interpose such a motion, neither as regards the case itself nor as regards the decision to submit the case to the jurisdiction of the Inter-American Court. The possibility of reconsidering a report already vacated is not contemplated in the American Convention on Human Rights nor in the Regulations of the Commission when the State in question is a Party to the Convention and has accepted the jurisdiction of the Inter-American Court of Human Rights, as is the case of Peru. This is especially true of a case that has already been previously submitted to the Court.
>
> The Government of Peru did point out to the Commission the advisability of not submitting the case to the Court, considering the serious procedural omissions incurred in the drafting of its Report No. 29/91, which are precisely those which, among others, served to buttress the decision of the full Commission to submit the joint cases. In other words, the decision to reconsider the case is unilateral and does not comply with the procedural rules in force.

> . . . .

34. Before taking up the preliminary objections, the Court will refer to some issues raised by the representative of the Government during the public hearing, relating to the certification issued by the Court regarding the reception and withdrawal of the so-called first application. The representative declared that "the application arrived in due form on June 7, 1991, for it was only on that date that the requirements stipulated in Article 26 of the Rules of Procedure of the Court then in force were complied with . . . that the time limit provided under Article 51, paragraph I of the Convention having fallen due on May 31, 1991, the application entered the Court after the deadline had passed, that is, on June 7."

35. In order to fully understand the Government's observation and deal with the preliminary objections, it is important to recall that Article 51(1) of the Convention provides the following:

> If, within a period of three months from the date of the transmittal of the report of the Commission to the states concerned, the matter has not either been settled or submitted by the Commission or by the state concerned to the Court and its jurisdiction accepted, the Commission may, by the vote of an absolute majority of its members, set forth its opinion and conclusions concerning the question submitted for its consideration.

36. The Report was transmitted to the Government on March 1, 1991. The period stipulated would therefore have fallen due on May 31 of that same year. The Government received the report on April 5 and then requested of the Commission that the sixty days referred to in paragraph 4 of the operative part of Report 29/91 (supra 23) begin to run as of the date of receipt and not the date of mailing. This was

accepted by the Commission, with the result that the deadline for the Government was moved to June 5, theoretically a later date than the original one. The Government submitted its observations on May 27. In its note, it requested that "the Commission comply with its Regulations and the Pact of San José and therefore decide not to take the case to the Inter-American Court of Human Rights without first weighing the observations made in the present note and making the appropriate procedural corrections." The Commission, on its part, dated the application May 30. Both documents—the Peruvian note and the application—were received on Monday, June 3, the former by the Commission and the latter by the Court.

37. The Court has on other occasions analyzed certain aspects of Article 51 of the Convention . . ., but not the characteristics or conditions of the time limit contemplated in paragraph I of that article. In order to arrive at a satisfactory resolution of the objections interposed by the Government, it is necessary to refer to it. In doing so, moreover, the Court must ratify its oft-stated opinion that the object and purpose of the treaty is the effective protection of human rights and that the interpretation of all its provisions must be subordinated to that object and purpose, as provided in Article 31 of the Vienna Convention on the Law of Treaties (*Velásquez Rodríguez Case*, Preliminary Objections, op. cit., para. 30).

38. In the case of *Neira Alegría et al.*, the Court had already found that, since it can be extended, the period contemplated in Article 51(1) is not final (*Neira Alegría et al. Case*, Preliminary Objections, paras. 32, 33 and 34). Nevertheless, legal certainty requires that States know what norms they are to follow. The Commission cannot be permitted to apply the time limits in arbitrary fashion, particularly when these are spelled out in the Convention.

39. Article 51(1) provides that the Commission must decide within the three months following the transmittal of its report whether to submit the case to the Court or to subsequently set forth its own opinion and conclusions, in either case when the matter has not been settled. While the period is running, however, a number of circumstances could develop that would interrupt it or even require the drafting of a new report or the resumption of the period from the beginning. In each case it will be necessary to conduct an analysis to determine whether or not the time limit expired and what circumstances, if any, could reasonably have interrupted the period.

40. In the instant case, the Report was sent on March 1, 1991 and the time limit would therefore have expired on May 31. The original application was received at the Court by fax on Monday, June 3, that is, three days after the calendar day on which the period would have expired, had the extension sought by Peru not affected it, in which case the expiration would have occurred on June 5. The Court will not comment on this fact at the present time, as it will also not comment on the fact that the Commission extended the periods. An application containing such serious charges as those which are before us now cannot be deemed to have lapsed simply on those grounds.

41. Peru stated at the public hearing that "the application arrived in due form on June 7, 1991 [the date on which the file was received], for it was only on that date

that the requirements stipulated in Article 25 of the Rules of Procedure of the Court then in force were complied with".

42. The former Rules of Procedure of the Court, applicable to the instant application, established in its Article 25(2) that "[i]f the Commission intends to bring a case before the Court . . . it shall file with the Secretary, together with its report, in twenty copies, its duly signed application . . .". In the instant case, the application was received before the report, the former having arrived at the Court on June 3, 1991, and the latter at the Secretariat of the Court on June 7.

The rule quoted above must not be applied in a way that distorts the object and purpose of the Convention. It is generally accepted that the procedural system is a means of attaining justice and that the latter cannot be sacrificed for the sake of mere formalities. Keeping within certain timely and reasonable limits, some omissions or delays in complying with procedure may be excused, provided that a suitable balance between justice and legal certainty is preserved.

A very different issue is, of course, raised by consideration of the effect on the time limit of the Commission's withdrawal of the application in order to resubmit it at a much later date. That issue will be analyzed in due course.

43. The Court will now examine the objections interposed by the Government in the instant case.

44. The first three objections are based on the withdrawal of the case by the Commission after it had been submitted to the Court. Hence, the three objections should be dealt with together.

. . . .

48. The withdrawal of the application is not expressly regulated in the Convention, the Statutes of the Commission and the Court, the Regulations of the Commission or the Rules of Procedure of the Court. This does not mean that it is inadmissible. General principles of procedural law allow the applicant party to request a court not to process its application, provided the court has not begun to take up the case. As a rule, that stage begins with the notification of the other party. Furthermore, the foundation of the Court's jurisdiction, as set forth in Article 61(1) of the Convention, lies in the will of the Commission or of the States Parties.

49. In a case before the Court, formal notification of the application does not occur automatically but requires a preliminary review by the President in order to determine whether the basic requirements of that action have been met. This is spelled out in Article 27 of the Rules of Procedure in force, which reflects the long-standing practice of the Court.

50. The withdrawal of the application in the instant case cannot be deemed to be among those situations governed by Article 42 of the Rules of Procedure applicable at the time of presentation of that application, because that rule refers to hypothetical cases where the dispute has already been brought before the Court, cases in which the parties, acting unilaterally or bilaterally, cannot freely waive the continuation of the proceedings because "[the Court may, having regard to its responsibilities, decide that it should proceed with the consideration of the case, . .". (paragraph 3).

51. In the instant case, the request for withdrawal presented by the Commission occurred before the President of the Court was able to conduct the preliminary review of the application and, consequently, before he was in a position to order the notification of same. The President had not even been apprised of the communication of June 11, 1991, by which the Commission notified the Government that the case had been referred to the Court, as provided in Article 50(2) of the Regulations of the Commission.

52. The request for withdrawal was not, at first glance, unjustified or arbitrary. In its note of June 20, the Commission declared that the withdrawal was being sought at "the request of the Government of Peru and in order to ensure that no questions arise as to the correct application of the proceedings, as well as to protect the interests of both parties (the Government and the petitioners)" Principles of good faith would preclude casting doubt on the reasons given by the Commission for withdrawing its application.

53. In view of the foregoing, the Secretariat of the Court, acting on instructions of the Permanent Commission, merely acknowledged receipt of the note of withdrawal. It did not assess the action or the timing thereof because neither the Secretariat nor the Permanent Commission was in a position to do so, since the President had not yet begun to review the case, the processing of which had still not been initiated.

. . . .

55. At this time, there is no need for the Court to rule on whether the Commission understood the withdrawal to be a cancellation of the proceedings or the abandonment of the case, even at the judicial level. The Commission has stated that this was not the case and there is nothing in the file that would indicate otherwise. Rather, the Commission's letter of withdrawal indicates the opposite intention (Cf. *Barcelona Traction, Light and Power Company, Limited*, Preliminary Objections, Judgment, 1. C.J. Reports 1964, p. 21).

56. It is also not necessary to determine whether the prior actions of the Commission were nullified by errors in the handling of the case or whether the Government's right of defense was impaired by the failure to transmit certain documents.

59. In its note of August 26, the Government insisted that the withdrawal of the application was a unilateral act by the Commission which Peru had not requested. At the public hearing, the Commission admitted that "it is true that the Government of Peru did not request the withdrawal of the case, nor its resubmission." Consequently, it is of little importance whether or not Peru benefitted, as the Commission argues, from the new time limits that resulted from the withdrawal. Even if it had, that would not prevent it from invoking the expiration of the time limit as a preliminary objection. The withdrawal of the case did not undermine the Peruvian Government's right of defense nor did it prevent it from exercising any of the other rights recognized in the Convention.

60. More than seven months elapsed between the withdrawal of the case and the filing of the new application. Regardless of whether the original period had expired on May 31 or June 5, 1991, there is no question that February 14, 1992 substantially exceeds the timely and reasonable limits that, as the Court has stated, govern the

proceeding. Even if the Commission understood the Peruvian Government to have requested the withdrawal, such a request, however reasonable, could not have been granted because the time limit provided by the Convention for filing an application had already expired. Furthermore, as already stated, that is not one of the factors that could have led to a suspension of the periods.

61. Without taking up the merits of the Commission's application, the Court will find that it was filed after the expiration of the appropriate time limit. Nevertheless, a reading of Article 51 leads to the conclusion that a declaration of this nature cannot entail the neutralization of the other protective mechanisms set forth in the American Convention. Hence, the Commission continues to enjoy all the other powers conferred on it in that article, which is, furthermore, consistent with the object and purpose of the treaty.

62. Having stated the foregoing, it is not necessary for the Court to analyze the remaining objections.

63. The Court must preserve a fair balance between the protection of human rights, which is the ultimate purpose of the system, and the legal certainty and procedural equity that will ensure the stability and reliability of the international protection mechanism. In the instant case, to continue with a proceeding aimed at ensuring the protection of the interests of the alleged victims in the face of manifest violations of the procedural norms established by the Convention itself would result in a loss of the authority and credibility that are indispensable to organs charged with administering the system for the protection of human rights.

NOW, THEREFORE,

THE COURT

Unanimously, ... orders that the case be dismissed.

Questions and Comments

1. Who brought this case before the Court? On what authority can the Commission present a case to the Court? If the Commission does not submit a case, can the petitioner submit it? Can the Government?

2. When the procedure before the Commission is concluded, is there a time limit within which a petition must be submitted to the Court? How are the time limits determined for the presentation of pleadings to the Court?

3. Could the Commission have reasonably read Peru's letter of May 27 (para. 25) as a request for it to withdraw the case? How should the Commission have responded to Peru? If the Commission had not withdrawn the case, what preliminary objections might Peru have filed and would the Court have sustained them?

3. Interim Measures

Assuming there are no obvious jurisdictional barriers to processing a complaint, regional bodies may be asked to consider requests for interim measures, even prior to a determination of admissibility. The following materials examine the standards and procedures for obtaining such measures.

A. The European System

Mamatkulov & Askarov v. Turkey [GC], (App. nos. 46827/99 and 46951/99), Judgment of 4 February 2005, Eur. Ct. H.R.

1. The case originated in two applications against the Republic of Turkey lodged with the Court under Article 34 of the Convention for the Protection of Human Rights and Fundamental Freedoms by two Uzbek nationals, Mr. Rustam Sultanovich Mamatkulov and Mr. Zainiddin Abdurasulovich Askarov, on 11 and 22 March 1999 respectively.

. . . .

3. The applications concern the applicants' extradition to the Republic of Uzbekistan. The applicants relied on Articles 2, 3 and 6 of the Convention and Rule 39 of the Rules of Court.

. . . .

C. The extradition of the applicants and subsequent events

24. On 18 March 1999 the President of the relevant Chamber of the Court decided to indicate to the Government, on the basis of Rule 39 of the Rules of Court, that it was desirable in the interest of the parties and of the smooth progress of the proceedings before the Court, not to extradite the applicants to Uzbekistan prior to the meeting of the competent Chamber, which was to take place on 23 March 1999.

25. On 19 March 1999 the Turkish Government issued a decree ordering the applicants' extradition.

26. On 23 March 1999 the Chamber decided to extend the interim measure indicated pursuant to Rule 39 until further notice.

27. On 27 March 1999 the applicants were handed over to the Uzbek authorities.

28. In a letter of 19 April 1999 the Government informed the Court that it had received the following assurances about the two applicants from the Uzbek authorities: on 9 March and 10 April 1999 the Uzbek Embassy in Ankara had transmitted two notes from the Ministry of Foreign Affairs to which were appended two letters from the Public Prosecutor of the Republic of Uzbekistan, stating:

> "The applicants' property will not be liable to general confiscation, and the applicants will not be subjected to acts of torture or sentenced to capital punishment.
>
> The Republic of Uzbekistan is a party to the United Nations Convention against Torture and accepts and reaffirms its obligation to comply with the requirements of the provisions of that Convention as regards both Turkey and the international community as a whole."

30. In a letter of 8 July 1999, the Government informed the Court that by a judgment of 28 June 1999 the Supreme Court of the Republic of Uzbekistan had found the applicants guilty of the offences charged and had sentenced them to terms of imprisonment.

31. In a letter to the Court dated 15 September 1999, the applicants' representatives said that they had not been able to contact their clients, that conditions in Uzbek prisons were bad and prisoners subjected to torture . . . .

. . . .

34. On 3 December 2001 the Uzbek authorities communicated to the Government medical certificates that had been drawn up by military doctors in the prisons in which the applicants were being held. The doctors made the following findings:

> " . . . Mr Mamatkulov was imprisoned on 9 December 2000. He did not present any health problems on arrival. Examinations on 14 December 2000 and 2 April 2001 did not reveal any pathological symptoms.
>
> On 19 November 2001 the prisoner attended the prison medical centre complaining of general weakness and a bout of coughing . . . . [o]n examination he was diagnosed as suffering from acute bronchitis and was prescribed medication. . ."
>
> " . . . Mr Abdurasulovich Askarov was imprisoned on 21 July 2001. He did not complain of any health problems on arrival. Examinations conducted on 25 July, 30 August and 23 October 2001 did not reveal any pathological symptoms . . ."

35. On the basis of lists that had been communicated by the Uzbek authorities, the Government informed the Court on 16 April 2004 that the applicants had received a number of visits from close relatives between January 2002 and 2004.

36. To date, the applicants' representatives have been unable to contact the applicants.

. . . .

38. Extradition between Turkey and Uzbekistan is governed by the "Agreement for Mutual Assistance in Civil, Commercial and Criminal Matters between the Republic of Turkey and the Republic of Uzbekistan", which entered into force on 18 December 1997. Under the relevant provision of that agreement: "Each Contracting Party undertakes to extradite to the other, in the circumstances and subject to the conditions set out in this agreement, anyone found in its territory who has been charged with or found guilty of an offence committed within the jurisdiction of the other Party".

III. RELEVANT INTERNATIONAL LAW AND PRACTICE

. . . .

B. Universal systems of human-rights protection

1. United Nations Human Rights Committee

40. Rule 86 of the Rules of Procedure of the United Nations Human Rights Committee provides:

> The Committee may, prior to forwarding its views on the communication to the State party concerned, inform that State of its views as to whether interim measures may be desirable to avoid irreparable damage to the victim of the alleged violation. In doing so, the Committee shall inform the State party concerned that such expression of its views on interim measures does not imply a determination on the merits of the communication.

41. In its decision of 26 July 1994 (in the case of *Glen Ashby v. Trinidad and Tobago*), the Committee dealt with the first case of a refusal by a State to comply with interim measures in the form of a request that it stay execution of the death penalty. It pointed out that by ratifying the Optional Protocol, the State Party had undertaken to cooperate with the Committee in proceedings under the Protocol, and that

it had not discharged its obligations under the Optional Protocol and the Covenant (Report of the Human Rights Committee, Volume I).

42. In its decision of 19 October 2000 (in the case of *Dante Piandiong, Jesus Morallos and Archie Bulan v. The Philippines*), the Committee said:

> By adhering to the Optional Protocol, a State party to the Covenant recognizes the competence of the Human Rights Committee to receive and consider communications from individuals claiming to be victims of violations of any of the rights set forth in the Covenant (Preamble and Article 1). Implicit in a State's adherence to the Protocol is an undertaking to cooperate with the Committee in good faith so as to permit and enable it to consider such communications, and after examination to forward its views to the State party and to the individual (Article 5 (1), (4)). It is incompatible with these obligations for a State party to take any action that would prevent or frustrate the Committee in its consideration and examination of the communication, and in the expression of its Views.
>
> Quite apart, then, from any violation of the Covenant charged to a State party in a communication, a State party commits grave breaches of its obligations under the Optional Protocol if it acts to prevent or frustrate consideration by the Committee of a communication alleging a violation of the Covenant, or to render examination by the Committee moot and the expression of its Views nugatory and futile. . . .
>
> Interim measures pursuant to rule 86 of the Committee's rules adopted in conformity with article 39 of the Covenant, are essential to the Committee's role under the Protocol. Flouting of the Rule, especially by irreversible measures such as the execution of the alleged victim or his/her deportation from the country, undermines the protection of Covenant rights through the Optional Protocol.

The Committee reiterated this principle in its decision of 15 May 2003 (in the case of *Sholam Weiss v. Austria*).

2. United Nations Committee against Torture

43. Rule 108 § 9 of the Rules of Procedure of the Committee against Torture enables provisional measures to be adopted in proceedings brought by individuals alleging a violation of the Convention against Torture and Other Cruel, Inhuman or Degrading Treatment or Punishment. It reads as follows:

> In the course of the consideration of the question of the admissibility of a communication, the Committee or the working group or a special rapporteur designated under rule 106, paragraph 3, may request the State party to take steps to avoid possible irreparable damage to the person or persons who claim to be victim(s) of the alleged violation. Such a request addressed to the State party does not imply that any decision has been reached on the question of the admissibility of the communication.

44. In the case of a Peruvian citizen resident in Venezuela who was extradited to Peru despite the fact that a stay of her extradition had been called for as a provisional measure (*Cecilia Rosana Núñez Chipana v. Venezuela*, 10 November 1998), the Committee against Torture expressed the view that the State had failed to "comply with the spirit of the Convention". It noted the following:

> . . . the State party, in ratifying the Convention and voluntarily accepting the Committee's competence under article 22, undertook to cooperate with it in good faith in applying the procedure. Compliance with the provisional measures called for by the Committee in cases it considers reasonable is essential in order to protect the person

in question from irreparable harm, which could, moreover, nullify the end result of the proceedings before the Committee.

45. In another decision that concerned the extradition to India of an Indian national resident in Canada (*T.P.S. v. Canada*, decision of 16 May 2000) despite the fact that Canada had been requested to stay the extradition as a provisional measure, the Committee against Torture reiterated that failure to comply with the requested provisional measures "... could ... nullify the end result of the proceedings before the Committee".

C. The International Court of Justice

46. Article 41 of the Statute of the International Court of Justice provides:

> 1. The Court shall have the power to indicate, if it considers that circumstances so require, any provisional measures which ought to be taken to preserve the respective rights of either party.
> 2. Pending the final decision, notice of the measures suggested shall forthwith be given to the parties and to the Security Council.

47. The International Court of Justice has pointed out in a number of cases that the purpose of provisional measures is to preserve the respective rights of the parties to the dispute (see, among other authorities, the judgment of 27 June 1986 in the case of *Nicaragua v. United States of America*). In an order of 13 September 1993 in the case concerning the *Application of the Convention on the Prevention and Punishment of the Crime of Genocide (Bosnia and Herzegovina v. Yugoslavia)*, the International Court of Justice said that the power of the Court to indicate provisional measures:

> ... has as its object to preserve the respective rights of the parties pending the decision of the Court, and presupposes that irreparable prejudice should not be caused to rights which are the subject of dispute in judicial proceedings; and ... the Court must be concerned to preserve by such measures the rights which may subsequently be adjudged by the Court to belong either to the Applicant or to the Respondent.

48. In its judgment of 27 June 2001 in the *LaGrand* case (*Germany v. United States of America*), it noted:

> 102. ... The context in which Article 41 has to be seen within the Statute is to prevent the Court from being hampered in the exercise of its functions because the respective rights of the parties to a dispute before the Court are not preserved. It follows from the object and purpose of the Statute, as well as from the terms of Article 41 when read in their context, that the power to indicate provisional measures entails that such measures should be binding, inasmuch as the power in question is based on the necessity, when the circumstances call for it, to safeguard, and to avoid prejudice to, the rights of the parties as determined by the final judgment of the Court. The contention that provisional measures indicated under Article 41 might not be binding would be contrary to the object and purpose of that Article.
>
> 103. A related reason which points to the binding character of orders made under Article 41 and to which the Court attaches importance, is the existence of a principle which has already been recognized by the Permanent Court of International Justice when it spoke of 'the principle universally accepted by international tribunals and likewise laid down in many conventions ... to the effect that the parties to a case must abstain from any measure capable of exercising a prejudicial effect in regard to the

execution of the decision to be given, and, in general, not allow any step of any kind to be taken which might aggravate or extend the dispute' (*Electricity Company of Sofia and Bulgaria*, Order of 5 December 1939 . . .).

This approach was subsequently confirmed in the Court's judgment of 31 March 2004 in the case of *Avena and Other Mexican Nationals* (*Mexico v. United States of America*).

D. The Inter-American system of human-rights protection

1. The Inter-American Commission on Human Rights

49. Rule 25 of the Rules of Procedure of the Inter-American Commission on Human Rights provides:

> 1. In serious and urgent cases, and whenever necessary according to the information available, the Commission may, on its own initiative or at the request of a party, request that the State concerned adopt precautionary measures to prevent irreparable harm to persons.
>
> 2. If the Commission is not in session, the President, or, in his or her absence, one of the Vice-Presidents, shall consult with the other members, through the Executive Secretariat, on the application of the provision in the previous paragraph. If it is not possible to consult within a reasonable period of time under the circumstances, the President or, where appropriate, one of the Vice-Presidents shall take the decision on behalf of the Commission and shall so inform its members.
>
> 3. The Commission may request information from the interested parties on any matter related to the adoption and observance of the precautionary measures.
>
> 4. The granting of such measures and their adoption by the State shall not constitute a prejudgment on the merits of a case.

50. The scope of the precautionary measures is determined by reference to the scope of the recommendations made by the Commission in respect of the individual petition. In its judgment of 17 September 1997 in the case of *Loayza Tamayo v. Peru*, the Inter-American Court of Human Rights ruled that the State "has the obligation to make every effort to apply the recommendations of a protection organ such as the Inter-American Commission, which is, indeed, one of the principal organs of the Organization of American States, whose function is 'to promote the observance and defense of human rights' . . . ."

2. The Inter-American Court of Human Rights

51. Article 63(2) of the American Convention on Human Rights states:

> In cases of extreme gravity and urgency, and when necessary to avoid irreparable damage to persons, the Court shall adopt such provisional measures as it deems pertinent in matters it has under consideration. With respect to a case not yet submitted to the Court, it may act at the request of the Commission.

52. Rule 25 of the Rules of Procedure of the Inter-American Court of Human Rights provides:

> 1. At any stage of the proceedings involving cases of extreme gravity and urgency, and when necessary to avoid irreparable damage to persons, the Court may, at the request of a party or on its own motion, order such provisional measures as it deems pertinent, pursuant to Article 63(2) of the Convention.

2. With respect to matters not yet submitted to it, the Court may act at the request of the Commission.

3. The request may be made to the President, to any judge of the Court, or to the Secretariat, by any means of communication. In every case, the recipient of the request shall immediately bring it to the President's attention.

4. If the Court is not sitting, the President, in consultation with the Permanent Commission and, if possible, with the other judges, shall call upon the government concerned to adopt such urgent measures as may be necessary to ensure the effectiveness of any provisional measures that may be ordered by the Court at its next session.

5. The Court, or its President if the Court is not sitting, may convoke the parties to a public hearing on provisional measures.

6. In its Annual Report to the General Assembly, the Court shall include a statement concerning the provisional measures ordered during the period covered by the report. If those measures have not been duly implemented, the Court shall make such recommendations as it deems appropriate.

53. The Inter-American Court has stated on several occasions that compliance with provisional measures is necessary to ensure the effectiveness of its decisions on the merits (see, among other authorities, the following orders: 1 August 1991, *Chumină v. Peru*; 2 July and 13 September 1996, 11 November 1997 and 3 February 2001, *Loayza Tamayo v. Peru*; 25 May and 25 September 1999, 16 August and 24 November 2000, and 3 September 2002, *James et al. v. Trinidad and Tobago*; 7 and 18 August 2000, and 26 May 2001, *Haitians and Dominican nationals of Haitian Origin in the Dominican Republic v. Dominican Republic*; 10 August and 12 November 2000, and 30 May 2001, *Alvarez et al v. Colombia*; judgment of 21 June 2002, *Hilaire, Constantine, Benjamin et al. v. Trinidad and Tobago*).

In two orders requiring provisional measures, the Inter-American Court of Human Rights ruled that the States Parties to the American Convention on Human Rights "must fully comply in good faith (*pacta sunt servanda*) with all of the provisions of the Convention, including those relative to the operation of the two supervisory organs of the American Convention [the Court and the Commission]; and, that in view of the Convention's fundamental objective of guaranteeing the effective protection of human rights (Articles 1(1), 2, 51 and 63(2)), States Parties must refrain from taking actions that may frustrate the *restitutio in integrum* of the rights of the alleged victims" (see the Orders of 25 May and 25 September 1999 in the case of *James et al. v. Trinidad and Tobago*).

THE LAW

. . . .

III. ALLEGED VIOLATION OF ARTICLE 34 OF THE CONVENTION

92. The applicants' representatives maintained that, by extraditing Mr. Mamatkulov and Mr. Askarov despite the measure indicated by the Court under Rule 39 of the Rules of Court, Turkey had failed to comply with its obligations under Article 34 of the Convention.

. . . .

C. The Court's assessment

99. The fact that the respondent Government failed to comply with the measures indicated by the Court under Rule 39 of the Rules of Court raises the issue of whether the respondent State is in breach of its undertaking under Article 34 of the Convention not to hinder the applicants in the exercise of their right of individual application.

1. General considerations

(a) Exercise of the right of individual application

100. The Court has previously stated that the provision concerning the right of individual application (Article 34, formerly Article 25 of the Convention before Protocol No. 11 came into force) is one of the fundamental guarantees of the effectiveness of the Convention system of human-rights protection. In interpreting such a key provision, the Court must have regard to the special character of the Convention as a treaty for the collective enforcement of human rights and fundamental freedoms. Unlike international treaties of the classic kind, the Convention comprises more than mere reciprocal engagements between Contracting States. It creates, over and above a network of mutual, bilateral undertakings, objective obligations which, in the words of the Preamble, benefit from a 'collective enforcement' (see, *mutatis mutandis, Loizidou v. Turkey (preliminary objections)*, 23 March 1995, Series A no. 310, § 70).

101. The object and purpose of the Convention as an instrument for the protection of individual human beings require that its provisions be interpreted and applied so as to make its safeguards practical and effective, as part of the system of individual applications. In addition, any interpretation of the rights and freedoms guaranteed has to be consistent with "the general spirit of the Convention, an instrument designed to maintain and promote the ideals and values of a democratic society" (see *Soering* cited above, § 87; and, *mutatis mutandis, Klass and Others v. Germany*, judgment of 6 September 1978, Series A no. 28, p. 18, § 34).

102. The undertaking not to hinder the effective exercise of the right of individual application precludes any interference with the individual's right to present and pursue his complaint before the Court effectively. That issue has been considered by the Court in previous decisions. It is of the utmost importance for the effective operation of the system of individual application instituted under Article 34 that applicants or potential applicants should be able to communicate freely with the Court without being subjected to any form of pressure from the authorities to withdraw or modify their complaints. As the Court has noted in previous decisions, "pressure" includes not only direct coercion and flagrant acts of intimidation against actual or potential applicants, members of their family or their legal representatives, but also other improper indirect acts or contacts designed to dissuade or discourage applicants from pursuing a Convention remedy (see, among other authorities, *Petra v. Romania*, judgment of 23 September 1998, *Reports* 1998-VII, § 43; *Kurt v. Turkey*, judgment of 25 May 1998, *Reports* 1998-III, p. 1192, § 159; *Aksoy v. Turkey*, judgment of 18 December 1996, *Reports* 1996-VI, p. 2288, § 105; and *Akdivar and Others v. Turkey*, judgment of 16 September 1996, *Reports* 1996-IV, p. 1219, § 105).

For present purposes, the Court concludes that the obligation set out in Article 34, *in fine*, requires the Contracting States to refrain not only from exerting pressure on applicants, but also from any act or omission which, by destroying or removing the subject matter of an application, would make it pointless or otherwise prevent the Court from considering it under its normal procedure.

(b) Indication of interim measures under the Convention system

103. Rule 39 of the Rules of Court empowers a Chamber or, where appropriate, its President, to indicate interim measures. The grounds on which Rule 39 may be applied are not set out in the Rules of Court but have been determined by the Court through its case-law. As was the practice of the European Commission of Human Rights prior to the entry into force of Protocol No. 11 to the Convention in 1998, the Court applies Rule 39 only in restricted circumstances.

104. Interim measures have been indicated only in limited spheres. Although it does receive a number of requests for interim measures, in practice the Court applies Rule 39 only if there is an imminent risk of irreparable damage. While there is no specific provision in the Convention concerning the domains in which Rule 39 will apply, requests for its application usually concern the right to life (Article 2), the right not to be subjected to torture or inhuman treatment (Article 3) and, exceptionally, the right to respect for private and family life (Article 8) or other rights guaranteed by the Convention. The vast majority of cases in which interim measures have been indicated concern deportation and extradition proceedings.

105. In most cases, measures are indicated to the respondent Government, although there is nothing to stop the Court from indicating measures to applicants (see, among other authorities, *Ilaşcu and Others v. Moldova and Russia* [GC], no. 48787/99, § 11, to be published in ECHR 2004). Cases of States failing to comply with indicated measures remain very rare.

. . . .

107. . . . The most noteworthy case concerning the indication of interim measures by the former Court is the aforementioned case of *Soering*, in which the Court indicated to the British Government under Rule 36 of its Rules that it would be undesirable to extradite the applicant to the United States while the proceedings were pending in Strasbourg. In order to abide by the Convention and the Court's decision, the British Government were forced to default on their undertaking to the United States (§§ 31 and 111). Thus, the judgment resolved the conflict in this case between a State Party's Convention obligations and its obligations under an extradition treaty with a third-party State by giving precedence to the former.

2. Did the applicants' extradition hinder the effective exercise of the right of application?

108. In cases such as the present one where there is plausibly asserted to be a risk of irreparable damage to the enjoyment by the applicant of one of the core rights under the Convention, the object of an interim measure is to maintain the status quo pending the Court's determination of the justification for the measure. As such, being intended to ensure the continued existence of the matter that is the subject of the application, the interim measure goes to the substance of the Convention

complaint. As far as the applicant is concerned, the result that he or she wishes to achieve through the application is the preservation of the asserted Convention right before irreparable damage is done to it. Consequently, the interim measure is sought by the applicant, and granted by the Court, in order to facilitate the "effective exercise" of the right of individual petition under Article 34 of the Convention in the sense of preserving the subject-matter of the application when that is judged to be at risk of irreparable damage through the acts or omissions of the respondent State.

In the present case, because of the extradition of the applicants to Uzbekistan, the level of protection which the Court was able to afford the rights which they were asserting under Articles 2 and 3 of the Convention was irreversibly reduced.

In addition, the Court considers that it is implicit in the notion of the effective exercise of the right of application that for the duration of the proceedings in Strasbourg the Court should remain able to examine the application under its normal procedure. In the present case, the applicants were extradited and thus, by reason of their having lost contact with their lawyers, denied an opportunity to have further inquiries made in order for evidence in support of their allegations under Article 3 of the Convention to be obtained. As a consequence, the Court was prevented from properly assessing whether the applicants were exposed to a real risk of ill-treatment and, if so, from ensuring in this respect a "practical and effective" implementation of the Convention's safeguards, as required by its object and purpose.

109. The Court has previously considered whether, in the absence of an express clause in the Convention, its organs could derive from Article 34 (former Article 25), taken alone or together with Rule 39 (former Rule 36), or from any other source, the power to order interim measures that were binding *(Cruz Varas and Others,* cited above; and *Čonka and Others v. Belgium (dec.),* no. 51564/99, 13 March 2001). In those cases it concluded that such a power could not be inferred from either Article 34, *in fine,* or from other sources (*Cruz Varas and Others,* cited above, pp. 36–37, §§ 102–103).

110. In examining the present case, the Court will also have regard to general principles of international law and the view expressed on this subject by other international bodies since the aforementioned *Cruz Varas and Others* judgment.

111. The Court reiterates in that connection that the Convention must be interpreted in the light of the rules set out in the Vienna Convention of 23 May 1969 on the Law of Treaties, Article 31 § 3 (c) of which states that account must be taken of "any relevant rules of international law applicable in the relations between the parties". The Court must determine the responsibility of the States in accordance with the principles of international law governing this sphere, while taking into account the special nature of the Convention as an instrument of human-rights protection (*Golder v. the United Kingdom,* judgment of 21 February 1975, Series A no. 18, § 29). Thus, the Convention must be interpreted so far as possible consistently with the other principles of international law of which it forms a part (*Al-Adsani v. the United Kingdom* [GC], no. 35763/97, § 60, ECHR 2001-XI).

112. Different rules apply to interim, provisional or precautionary measures, depending on whether the complaint is made under the individual-petition proce-

dures of the United Nations organs, or the Inter-American Court and Commission, or under the procedure for the judicial settlement of disputes of the International Court of Justice. In some instances provision is made for such measures in the treaty itself and in others in the rules of procedure.

113. In a number of recent decisions and orders, international courts and institutions have stressed the importance and purpose of interim measures and pointed out that compliance with such measures was necessary to ensure the effectiveness of their decisions on the merits. In proceedings concerning international disputes, the purpose of interim measures is to preserve the parties' rights, thus enabling the body hearing the dispute to give effect to the consequences which a finding of responsibility following adversarial process will entail.

114. Thus, under the jurisprudence of the Human Rights Committee of the United Nations, a failure to comply with interim measures constitutes a breach by the State concerned of its legal obligations under the International Covenant on Civil and Political Rights and the Optional Protocol thereto, and of its duty to cooperate with the Committee under the individual-communications procedure.

115. The United Nations Committee against Torture has considered the issue of a State Party's failure to comply with interim measures on a number of occasions. It has ruled that compliance with interim measures which the Committee considered reasonable was essential in order to protect the person in question from irreparable harm, which could nullify the end result of the proceedings before the Committee.

116. In various orders concerning provisional measures, the Inter-American Court of Human Rights has stated that in view of the fundamental objective of the American Convention on Human Rights, namely guaranteeing the effective protection of human rights, "States Parties [had to] refrain from taking actions that may frustrate the *restitutio in integrum* of the rights of the alleged victims" (see the orders of 25 May and 25 September 1999 in the case of *James et al. v. Trinidad and Tobago*).

117. In its judgment of 27 June 2001 in the case of *LaGrand* (*Germany v. United States of America*), the International Court of Justice said: "The object and purpose of the Statute is to enable the Court to fulfil the functions provided for therein, and in particular, the basic function of judicial settlement of international disputes by binding decisions in accordance with Article 59 of the Statute. The [purpose of] Article 41 . . . is to prevent the Court from being hampered in the exercise of its functions because the respective rights of the parties to a dispute before the Court are not preserved. It follows from the object and purpose of the Statute, as well as from the terms of Article 41 when read in their context, that the power to indicate provisional measures entails that such measures should be binding, inasmuch as the power in question is based on the necessity, when the circumstances call for it, to safeguard, and to avoid prejudice to, the rights of the parties as determined by the final judgment of the Court. The contention that provisional measures indicated under Article 41 might not be binding would be contrary to the object and purpose of that Article".

Furthermore, in that judgment, the International Court of Justice brought to an end the debate over the strictly linguistic interpretation of the words "power to indicate" ("*pouvoir d'indiquer*" in the French text) in the first paragraph of Article 41 and "suggested" ("*indication*" in the French text) in the second paragraph. Referring to Article 31 of the Vienna Convention on the Law of Treaties, which provides that treaties shall be interpreted in the light of their object and purpose, it held that provisional measures were legally binding. This approach was subsequently confirmed in the Court's judgment of 31 March 2004 in the case of *Avena and Other Mexican Nationals (Mexico v. United States of America)*.

118. The Court observes that in the aforementioned case of *Cruz Varas and Others* it determined the question whether the European Commission of Human Rights had power under former Article 25 § 1 of the Convention (now Article 34) to order interim measures that are binding. It noted that that Article applied only to proceedings brought before the Commission and imposed an obligation not to interfere with the right of the individual to present his or her complaint to the Commission and to pursue it. It added that Article 25 conferred upon an applicant a right of a procedural nature distinguishable from the substantive rights set out in Section I of the Convention or the Protocols to the Convention. The Court thus confined itself to examining the Commission's power to order interim measures, not its own. It considered the indication that had been given in the light of the nature of the proceedings before the Commission and of the Commission's role and concluded: "Where the State has had its attention drawn in this way to the dangers of prejudicing the outcome of the issue then pending before the Commission any subsequent breach of Article 3 . . . would have to be seen as aggravated by the failure to comply with the indication" (*Cruz Varas and Others* cited above, § 103).

119. The Court emphasises in that connection that, unlike the Court and the Committee of Ministers, the Commission had no power to issue a binding decision that a Contracting State had violated the Convention. The Commission's task with regard to the merits was of a preliminary nature and its opinion on whether or not there had been a violation of the Convention was not binding.

120. In its aforementioned *Čonka and Others* decision, the Court referred to the argument set out in paragraph 109 above and added: "The Belgian authorities expelled the applicants the same day . . . , without giving any reasons for their decision to ignore the measures that had been indicated under Rule 39 of the Rules of Court. In view of the settled practice of complying with such indications, which are given only in exceptional circumstances, such a manner of proceeding is difficult to reconcile with 'good faith co-operation with the Court in cases where this is considered reasonable and practicable'".

121. While the Court is not formally bound to follow its previous judgments, in the interests of legal certainty and foreseeability it should not depart, without good reason, from its own precedents (see, among other authorities, *mutatis mutandis, Chapman v. the United Kingdom [GC]*, no. 27238/95, § 70, ECHR 2001-I; and *Christine Goodwin v. the United Kingdom* [GC], no. 28957/95, § 74, ECHR 2002-VI). However, it is of crucial importance that the Convention is interpreted and applied in a manner which renders its rights practical and effective, not theoretical and illusory. It is a living instrument which must be interpreted in the light of present-day conditions (see, among other authorities, *Tyrer v. the United Kingdom*, judgment of

25 April 1978, Series A no 26, pp. 15–16, § 31; and *Christine Goodwin*, cited above, § 75).

122. Furthermore, the Court would stress that although the Convention right to individual application was originally intended as an optional part of the system of protection, it has over the years become of high importance and is now a key component of the machinery for protecting the rights and freedoms set forth in the Convention. Under the system in force until 1 November 1998 the Commission only had jurisdiction to hear individual applications if the Contracting Party issued a formal declaration recognising its competence, which it could do for a fixed period. The system of protection as it now operates has, in that regard, been modified by Protocol No. 11, and the right of individual application is no longer dependent on a declaration by the Contracting States. Thus, individuals now enjoy at the international level a real right of action to assert the rights and freedoms to which they are directly entitled under the Convention.

123. In this context, the Court notes that in the light of the general principles of international law, the law of treaties and international case-law, the interpretation of the scope of interim measures cannot be dissociated from the proceedings to which they relate or the decision on the merits they seek to protect. The Court reiterates in that connection that Article 31 § 1 of the Vienna Convention on the Law of Treaties provides that treaties must be interpreted in good faith in the light of their object and purpose (see paragraph 39 above), and also in accordance with the principle of effectiveness.

124. The Court observes that the International Court of Justice, the Inter-American Court of Human Rights, the Human Rights Committee and the Committee against Torture of the United Nations, although operating under different treaty provisions to those of the Court, have confirmed in their reasoning in recent decisions that the preservation of the asserted rights of the parties in the face of the risk of irreparable damage represents an essential objective of interim measures in international law. Indeed it can be said that, whatever the legal system in question, the proper administration of justice requires that no irreparable action be taken while proceedings are pending (see, *mutatis mutandis*, *Soering*, cited above).

It has previously stressed the importance of having remedies with suspensive effect when ruling on the obligations of the State with regard to the right to an effective remedy in deportation or extradition proceedings. The notion of an effective remedy under Article 13 requires a remedy capable of preventing the execution of measures that are contrary to the Convention and whose effects are potentially irreversible. Consequently, it is inconsistent with Article 13 for such measures to be executed before the national authorities have examined whether they are compatible with the Convention (*Čonka v. Belgium*, no. 51564/99, § 79, ECHR 2002-I). It is hard to see why this principle of the effectiveness of remedies for the protection of an individual's human rights should not be an inherent Convention requirement in international proceedings before the Court, whereas it applies to proceedings in the domestic legal system.

125. Likewise, under the Convention system, interim measures, as they have consistently been applied in practice (see paragraph 104 above), play a vital role in

avoiding irreversible situations that would prevent the Court from properly examining the application and, where appropriate, securing to the applicant the practical and effective benefit of the Convention rights asserted. Accordingly, in these conditions a failure by a respondent State to comply with interim measures will undermine the effectiveness of the right of individual application guaranteed by Article 34 and the State's formal undertaking in Article 1 to protect the rights and freedoms set forth in the Convention.

Indications of interim measures given by the Court, as in the present case, permit it not only to carry out an effective examination of the application but also to ensure that the protection afforded to the applicant by the Convention is effective; such indications also subsequently allow the Committee of Ministers to supervise execution of the final judgment. Such measures thus enable the State concerned to discharge its obligation to comply with the final judgment of the Court, which is legally binding by virtue of Article 46 of the Convention.

126. Consequently, the effects of the indication of an interim measure to a Contracting State—in this instance the respondent State—must be examined in the light of the obligations which are imposed on the Contracting States by Articles 1, 34 and 46 of the Convention.

127. The facts of the case, as set out above, clearly show that the Court was prevented by the applicants' extradition to Uzbekistan from conducting a proper examination of their complaints in accordance with its settled practice in similar cases and ultimately from protecting them, if need be, against potential violations of the Convention as alleged. As a result, the applicants were hindered in the effective exercise of their right of individual application guaranteed by Article 34 of the Convention, which the applicants' extradition rendered nugatory.

3. Conclusion

128. The Court reiterates that by virtue of Article 34 of the Convention Contracting States undertake to refrain from any act or omission that may hinder the effective exercise of an individual applicant's right of application. A failure by a Contracting State to comply with interim measures is to be regarded as preventing the Court from effectively examining the applicant's complaint and as hindering the effective exercise of his or her right and, accordingly, as a violation of Article 34 of the Convention.

129. Having regard to the material before it, the Court concludes that, by failing to comply with the interim measures indicated under Rule 39 of the Rules of Court, Turkey is in breach of its obligations under Article 34 of the Convention. . . .

FOR THESE REASONS, THE COURT. . . .

Holds by fourteen votes to three that Turkey has failed to comply with its obligations under Article 34 of the Convention;

CONCURRING OPINION OF JUDGE CABRAL BARRETO (*Translation*)

I concur with the majority's view that Turkey has failed to comply with its obligations under Article 34 of the Convention in the instant case.

Turkey's failure to comply with the request for it not to extradite the applicants to Uzbekistan before the Court had examined the case made an effective examination of the application impossible.

Accordingly, the applicants have been hindered in the effective exercise of their right of individual application.

However I find it difficult to agree with the majority's conclusion that: "A failure by a Contracting State to comply with interim measures is to be regarded as preventing the Court from effectively examining the applicant's complaint and as hindering the effective exercise of his or her right and, accordingly, as a violation of Article 34 of the Convention."

This general conclusion constitutes a departure from the principles that were established in the *Cruz Varas and Others v. Sweden* judgment some years ago and effectively reaffirmed in the *Čonka v. Belgium* decision.

If I have correctly understood the reasoning of the majority, the mere fact that a Government have failed to comply with a request to take interim measures *per se* entails a violation of Article 34 of the Convention.

It is this "mechanical" finding of a violation Article 34 of the Convention which I am unable to agree with.

To my mind, the fact that the States have always refused to accord binding force to interim measures prevents the Court from doing so and imposing on the States obligations which they have declined to accept.

The States Parties to the Convention have, however, undertaken not to hinder the exercise of the right of individual application.

Thus, if a refusal to comply with a request for interim measures has hindered the exercise of the right of application, the conclusion must be that there has been a violation of the obligations arising under Article 34 of the Convention.

The conclusion has to be different however if, despite such a refusal, it has been possible for the applicant to exercise his right of application effectively and the Court to examine the case properly.

That, in my opinion, is the effect of the provisions of the Convention and the Rules of Court and warranted highlighting in the judgment.

. . . .

While regretting that the member States of the Council of Europe have not given the Court the power to impose binding interim measures, I am forced to conclude that there will be a violation of Article 34 of the Convention only if the Contracting State's failure to comply with interim measures prevents the applicant from exercising his right of application and thereby makes an effective examination of his complaint by the Court impossible.

JOINT PARTLY DISSENTING OPINION OF JUDGES CAFLISCH, TÜRMEN AND KOVLER

1. Preliminary Observations

. . . .

2. We are of the view that Article 34 of the Convention cannot serve as a basis for holding that the Court's provisional measures are binding upon the States Parties

to the Convention. But even if one were to admit—which we are not prepared to do—that non-compliance may occasionally amount to a violation of Article 34, one would have to determine in each case whether such non-compliance indeed prevents the Court from examining the applicant's complaint and hinders the effective exercise of the individual's right of application. There certainly are cases where the Court has all the elements to examine the applicant's complaint despite non-compliance; and there are also cases where the Court applies Rule 39 to the applicant (for instance, in cases of hunger strike) and not to the government.

3. In the present case, the Court did dispose of the necessary elements to examine the Article 3 complaint of the applicants. The respondent State received official guarantees from the Uzbek authorities that the applicants would not be sentenced to death, that they would not be subjected to torture and that their property would not be confiscated. The medical reports submitted to the Court, after the applicants were sentenced and imprisoned, indicate that they had not been ill-treated and were in good health, both physically and psychologically. Furthermore, two members of the Turkish Embassy in Tashkent visited the applicants in prison and reported their observations to the Court. According to their reports, the applicants were in good health; they had not been subjected to any kind of ill-treatment in detention either before or after trial and their families can visit them regularly.

4. Following these initial observations, we shall turn to the specific issue motivating our dissent: the Court's conclusion that failure to abide by provisional measures "indicated" by the Court amounts to a violation of Article 34 of the Convention. . . .

. . . .

3. The case-law of the International Court of Justice: The LaGrand case

8. The Court's judgment relies on the recent decision of the ICJ in *LaGrand* (judgment of 27 June 2001, ICJ Reports 2001, §§ 48 and 117). This reliance seems misguided, as there is an essential difference between the position in which the International Court found itself and this Court's situation.

9. In the *LaGrand* case the ICJ was called upon to interpret a provision *of its own constitutive treaty*, that is, Article 41 of its Statute. The States Parties to that Statute had unquestionably acquiesced in that Article and were bound by it. Consequently the issue was one of pure treaty interpretation, namely, whether the verb "indicated" used in Article 41 must be taken to mean that measures formulated under that provision are *binding* on the States parties to the dispute. After years of avoiding to come to grips with this issue, the International Court, in *LaGrand*, reached an affirmative conclusion, basing itself on the rules of interpretation found in the 1969 Vienna Convention on the Law of Treaties and, in particular, on the *object and purpose* of Article 41 of the Statute, which was and is a treaty provision binding on all States Parties. In connection with Article 41, the "object and purpose" in question are "to preserve the respective rights of either party" and to enable the Court to render binding decisions in accordance with Article 59 of its Statute; and it certainly made sense to hold that this result depended on the binding character of the interim measures. There is here, in other words, a *close relation* between the enabling treaty provision and the purpose to be reached.

10. It is to be expected that the States Parties to other international dispute settlement mechanisms which contain provisions on interim measures using language similar to that of Article 41 of the Statute of the Hague Court will fall in line with the latter's new case-law. They are certainly entitled to do so since all that they will be doing is to examine *a provision on interim measures enshrined in the mechanism's constitutive instrument* which they are authorised to interpret.

11. By contrast, *no such provision* can be found in the European Convention on Human Rights; and neither Article 26(d) of that Convention, empowering the Court to enact Rules of Procedure, nor Article 34, instituting the right of individual application, is sufficiently connected to the issue under consideration to fill a "gap" in the Convention by instituting *binding* interim measures *ex nihilo*, thereby imposing on the States Parties to the Convention an obligation without their consent. To put it differently, there is a wide difference between the mere *interpretation* of a treaty and its *amendment*, between the exercise of judicial functions and international law-making.

12. What the Court's Grand Chamber has done, and the Chamber before it, in their *Mamatkulov and Askarov* judgments is to exercise a *legislative function*, for the Convention as it stands nowhere prescribes that the States Parties to it must recognise the binding force of provisional measures indicated by this Court. This is why, in our view, the Court cannot go down the path shown by the Hague Court and why there is no reason to depart from the existing case-law.

4. *The European Convention on Human Rights in the light of the canons of treaty interpretation*

16. . . . . If the *Convention of 1950* contained a provision comparable to Article 41 of the Statute of the Hague Court, we would likely have concluded, on the basis of *that* provision, that to "indicate" interim measures must, as a matter of teleological interpretation, mean to "order" or "prescribe" such measures. In the case of the Inter-American Court of Human Rights, whose *constituent instrument*—not Rules of Procedure!—contains a provision similar to Article 41 of the ICJ Statute, this is not even an issue since Article 63 (2) of the 1969 American Convention on Human Rights enables the Court to *order* interim measures. The problem in the present case is that there is no reasonable legal basis for drawing a similar conclusion. Article 34 of the Convention cannot serve as such, which makes it impossible to read the notion of *binding* interim measures into the text of the Convention.

17. The *preparatory work* of the Convention may be referred to by virtue of Article 32 of the Vienna Convention of Treaties. The European Court's judgment in *Cruz Varas* shows that, despite proposals to include in the 1950 Convention a provision similar to Article 41 of the Statute of ICJ, this was not done (§ 95)—a circumstance which is certainly not favourable to reading a power to issue binding provisional measures into the Convention.

18. Another element to be examined, also discussed in *Cruz Varas*, is the *subsequent practice* of the Contracting Parties mentioned as an element of interpretation in the Vienna Convention on the Law of Treaties. Article 31 (3) (b) of that Convention refers to "any subsequent practice in the application of the treaty which establishes the agreement of the Parties regarding its interpretation". This practice

was equally considered in *Cruz Varas*. After describing early unsuccessful attempts of Convention organs at adopting recommendations in the matter (§ 96), the Court found that the prevailing—but not complete—compliance with provisional measures was inspired by the desire of States Parties to cooperate. There was, in other words, no evidence that that practice, as is required by the Vienna Convention, "established the *agreement* of the Parties regarding its interpretation". That the contrary is true is first shown by the fact that, at its extraordinary meeting in early 1994, the Committee of Experts for the Improvement of Procedures for the Protection of Human Rights (DH-PR) received reform proposals from the European Commission of Human Rights on 31 January 1994 (docs. DH-PR(94)2 and DH-PR(94)4). Both the Commission and the Court considered that the new Court should have the power to issue interim measures with legally binding effect which should be provided for in the Convention. The Court's proposal was similar to Article 63(2) of the 1969 American Convention on Human Rights. The Commission's preference was for the interim-measure rules of the Commission's (Rule 36) and the Court's (Rule 36) Rules of Procedure to be included in the text of the Convention. The Swiss delegation also submitted a proposal with a view to including an Article in the Convention on provisional measures to the effect that "the Court may . . . prescribe any necessary interim measures" (doc. DH-PR(93)20, 22 November 1993).

19. All three proposals, if accepted, would have made it possible to argue (as with Article 41 of the ICJ's Statute) that the Court's interim measures must be regarded as mandatory. All three proposals were, however, rejected by the government experts. Later on, the Committee on Migration, Refugees and Demography suggested that interim measures indicated pursuant to Rule 36 of the Court's Rules of Procedure be made obligatory for member States (Draft Report, AS/PR(1997)2 revised, 19 February 1997). The Committee of Ministers declined to include a provision on interim measures in the Convention. This can only mean that the widespread acceptance of the practice in question rests on courtesy, cooperation and convenience, but not on an agreed interpretation. Nor has the Committee of Ministers seen fit to suggest the introduction of a provision on binding provisional measures in Draft Protocol No. 14. Again this must have been so because there was no agreement on making such measures compulsory and not because the Committee thought it superfluous to do anything on the assumption that provisional measures *were* binding.

20. In the present case, *the Court itself* considered its interim measures to be optional. This is evident from the wording of Rule 39, which uses the words "indicate" and "should be adopted", as well as from the text of the letter of 18 March 1999 addressed to Turkey, the respondent State, which reads:

> "La Présidente de la Première section a décidé aujourd'hui d'*indiquer* à votre Gouvernement, en application de l'article 39 du Règlement de la Cour, qu'il était *souhaitable*, dans l'intérêt des parties et du bon déroulement de la procédure devant la Cour, de ne pas extrader le requérant vers la République ouzbèke avant la réunion de la chambre compétente, qui se tiendra le 23 mars 1999."[22]

---

[22] [Translation:] "The President of the First Section has decided to *indicate* to your government, on the basis of Rule 39 of the Rules of Court, that it is *desirable*, in the interest of the parties and of the smooth progress of the proceedings before the Court, not to extradite the applicant to the Republic of Uzbekistan prior to the meeting of the competent chamber, which will take place on 23 March 1999."

21. What, finally, about the *"relevant rules of international law applicable in the relations between the Parties"*, invoked by the Chamber on the basis of Article (31) (3) (c) of the Vienna Convention on the Law of Treaties? It is true that many treaties constitutive of international courts and tribunals do authorise the "indication" of provisional measures, that being the term used in most of them. The meaning attributed to it by the ICJ in the recent *LaGrand* case will undoubtedly have a considerable impact on the interpretation of these treaties; but it cannot have such an impact *on the present Court* as long as the latter's constitutive instrument—the European Convention—contains no authorisation to "indicate" interim measures at all.

5. The Relevant Rules of International Law

22. There remains the question of whether the Court may, on the basis of a *rule of general international law* or a *general principle of law recognised by civilised nations*: (i) indicate provisional measures; and (ii) *order* such measures. If such were the case, the Court could justify the enactment of mandatory interim measures by such a rule or principle even in the absence of any enabling treaty provision. Regarding *general principles of law recognised by civilised nations*, there may well be a widespread rule on obligatory interim measures on the domestic level, based on the rule of compulsory jurisdiction applicable on that level. By contrast, as pointed out earlier (§ 16), that rule does not prevail on the international level, which is why it cannot be applied as such on that level. In other words, the principle cannot be transposed to the business of international courts.

23. There must, however, be a *customary rule* allowing international courts and tribunals, even in the absence of a treaty provision, to enact Rules of Procedure, a rule which may include the power to *formulate* interim measures. But that rule cannot be taken to include the power to *prescribe* such measures.

6. Conclusions

24. It follows from all the above that the compulsory nature of provisional measures "indicated" by this Court cannot be derived from the rules of general international law, nor from Articles 34 (right of individual application) or 26 § d (right of the Court to enact rules of procedure) of the Convention, as interpreted in the light of the Vienna Convention on the Law of Treaties of 23 May 1969. The same conclusion results from the practice of the European Court of Human Rights itself, including its initial attitude in the present instance.

25. Our basic conclusion is, therefore, that the matter examined here is one of *legislation* rather than of *judicial action*. As neither the constitutive instrument of this Court nor general international law allows for holding that interim measures must be complied with by States, the Court cannot decide the contrary and, thereby, impose a new obligation on States Parties. To conclude that this Court is empowered, *de lege lata*, to issue binding provisional measures is *ultra vires*. Such a power may appear desirable; but it is up to the Contracting Parties to supply it.

———————————

B. The Inter-American System

In the Inter-American system, both the Commission and the Court may issue precautionary or interim measures. The source for the Commission's authority lies in its Rules of Procedure:

Article 25. Precautionary Measures

1. In serious and urgent cases, and whenever necessary according to the information available, the Commission may, on its own initiative or at the request of a party, request that the State concerned adopt precautionary measures to prevent irreparable harm to persons.

2. If the Commission is not in session, the President, or, in his or her absence, one of the Vice-Presidents, shall consult with the other members, through the Executive Secretariat, on the application of the provision in the previous paragraph. If it is not possible to consult within a reasonable period of time under the circumstances, the President or, where appropriate, one of the Vice-President shall take the decision on behalf of the Commission and shall so inform its members.

3. The Commission may request information from the interested parties on any matter related to the adoption and observance of the precautionary measures.

4. The granting of such measures and their adoption by the State shall not constitute a prejudgment on the merits of a case.

For the Court, Article 63(2) of the Convention provides that:

In case of extreme gravity and urgency, and when necessary to avoid irreparable damage to persons, the Court shall adopt such provisional measures as it deems pertinent in matters it has under consideration. With respect to a case not yet submitted to the Court, it may act at the request of the Commission.

This provision permits the Court to grant such measures in cases pending before it and in cases that have been lodged with the Commission but not yet referred to the Court. The Court has to determine in all instances, if only in a preliminary manner, whether it has jurisdiction over the parties. For the Court's orders on provisional measures, *see* Inter-American Court of Human Rights, Series E: Provisional Measures, No. 1, Compendium: 1987–96 (1999); *ibid.*, No. 2, Compendium July 1996-June 2000 (2000). *See also* J. Pasqualucci, *Provisional Measures in the Inter-American Human Rights System: An Innovative Development in International Law*, 26 VAND. J. TRANSNAT'L L. 803 (1993); T. Buergenthal, *Interim Measures in the Inter-American Court of Human Rights, in* R. Bernhardt (ed.), INTERIM MEASURES INDICATED BY INTERNATIONAL COURTS 69 (1994); A.A. Cançado Trindade, *The Evolution of Provisional Measures of Protection under the Case-Law of the Inter-American Court of Human Rights* (1987–2002), 24 HRLJ 162 (2003).

In cases already pending before it, the Court may act on its own motion or at the request of one of the parties. *See* the Court's Rules of Procedure, Art. 25(1). For cases not yet pending, only the Commission may request provisional measures. The Court does not always accede to the Commission's request. *See, e.g., Peruvian Prisons Case*, Decision of January 27, 1993, I.–A. Court H.R., *Annual Report 1993*, OEA/Ser.L/V/III.29, Doc. 4, at 21 (1994). The Court's recent practice indicates that it considers the provisional measures issued pursuant to Article 63(3) of the Convention to be binding on the States to which they are addressed. *See, e.g., Consti-*

tutional Court Case (Provisional Measures), Order of the Inter-American Court of Human Rights of August 14, 2000. The views of the Commission on this point are seen in the Guantanamo Bay case infra, p. 792.

D. Shelton, *The Practice of the Inter-American Commission on Human Rights in Issuing Precautionary Measures* (published in French in MESURES CONSER-VATOIRES ET DROITS FONDAMENTAUX 165 (G. Cohen adn Jonathan & J-F. Flauss, eds. 2005).

In 1965, the Organization of American States expressly authorized the Inter-American Commission on Human Rights to examine complaints or petitions regarding specific cases of human rights violations. In receiving and reviewing the petitions, the Commission, pursuant to Article 29(1) of its former Regulations, could, at its own initiative or at the request of a party, take any action it considered necessary for the discharge of its functions, and could "(2) in urgent cases, when it becomes necessary to avoid irreparable damage to persons, . . . request that precautionary measures be taken to avoid irreparable damage in cases where the facts reported are true".

If the Commission was not in session, the President, or, in the President's absence, one of the Vice-presidents, had to consult on the matter with the other members through the Executive Secretariat. If it was not possible to consult within a reasonable period of time, the President had to take the decision on behalf of the Commission. The Regulations also provided that the request for such measures and their adoption were not to prejudice the final decision on the merits, despite the provision quoted above allowing the measures to be taken "where the facts reported are true."

The power to issue precautionary measures was retained in improved language in the Commission's revised Rules of Procedure adopted in 2001.

. . . .

As the number of petitions submitted to the Commission has grown each year, so have the number of requests for precautionary measures. During the last several years the Commission has issued more requests than any other international human rights body. The Commission granted or extended 53 precautionary measures in 1998 and early 1999, 60 in 1999 and early 2000, 52 during the rest of 2000 and 54 during 2001, making a total of 219 measures in just four years. Furthermore, the number of precautionary measures is well below the number of individuals protected, because the measures can protect either one person or a group of persons, often covering entire populations or communities. In a single request involving Paraguay, for example, on August 8, 2001 the Commission requested that precautionary measures be adopted on behalf of 255 minors who had been held at the Panchito López Reeducation Center for Minors (petition 11.666).

. . . .

From 1998 until the end of 2001, twenty-seven of the member states of the OAS received requests for precautionary measures from the Commission.[23] The cases involved a wide range of persons, from those infected with the HIV/Aids virus to journalists, nuns retired military officials, and refugees. The greatest number of cases fell into the broad category of persons concerned with human rights violations: human rights defenders (39 requests), those seeking a remedy for a violation, including family members of victims (8), witnesses (10), and those investigating, prosecuting or reporting about violations (30). Journalists or other writers have been the subject of requests in 17 matters. Other frequently issued measures concern trade union leaders, refugees, and persons in detention or disappeared. Every branch of government has been represented, with measures taken to protect prosecutors, legislators, and judges.

The single largest group of measures concerns death row inmates. The Commission has issued some 75 requests for precautionary measures in pending cases, primarily involving Jamaica, Trinidad and Tobago and the United States. Because the death penalty is not prohibited by the Declaration or Convention, the petitioners in these cases generally raise questions of the fairness of the proceedings that resulted in the conviction and penalty.

The actions taken by states in the aftermath of the September 11, 2001 terrorist attacks on the United States led to one of the more recent and controversial decisions on interim measures issued by the Commission. On February 25, 2002, the Center for Constitutional Rights, a U.S. based non-governmental organization, filed a request for precautionary measures under article 25 of the Commission's regulations, in respect to detainees held by the United States in Guantanamo Bay, Cuba. The Commission notified the applicants of its decision in the following letter.

Letter from the Inter-American Commission on Human Rights, (March 13, 2002)

Ref. Detainees in Guantanamo Bay, Cuba
Request for Precautionary Measures
Jennifer M. Green, Michael Ratner, Bill Goodman,
Anthony DiCaprio & Beth Stephens
Center for Constitutional Rights
666 Broadway, 7th Floor
New York, NY 10012

Dear Sirs and Madams:

On behalf of the Inter-American Commission on Human Rights, I wish to acknowledge receipt of your request for precautionary measures dated February 25, 2002 regarding the matter cited above, together with your supplementary observations of March 5, 2002 concerning same.

---

[23] The twenty-seven are: Argentina, Bahamas, Belize, Bolivia, Brazil, Canada, Chile, Colombia, Costa Rica, Cuba, Dominican Republic, Ecuador, El Salvador, Grenada, Guatemala, Guyana, Haiti, Honduras, Jamaica, Mexico, Nicaragua, Panama, Paraguay, Peru, Trinidad and Tobago, the United States and Venezuela.

I also wish to inform you that after carefully deliberating upon your request, the Commission, in a note dated March 12, 2002, addressed the Government of the United States in the following terms:

After careful deliberation on this request, the Commission decided during its 114th regular period of sessions[24] to adopt precautionary measures, according to which we ask Your Excellency's government to take the urgent measures necessary to have the legal status of the detainees at Guantanamo Bay determined by a competent tribunal. Given the significance and implications of this request to and for the United States and the detainees concerned, the Commission wishes to articulate the basis upon which it reached this decision.

The Commission notes preliminarily that its authority to receive and grant requests for precautionary measures under Article 25(1) of its Rules of Procedure[25] is, as with the practice of other international decisional bodies,[26] a well-established and necessary component of the Commission's processes.[27] Indeed, where such measures are considered essential to preserving the Commission's very mandate under the OAS Charter, the Commission has ruled that OAS member states are subject to an international legal obligation to comply with a request for such measures.[28]

The mandate given to the Commission by OAS member states, including the United States, under Article 106 of the Charter of the Organization of American States and Articles 18, 19 and 20 of the Commission's Statute is in turn central to the Commission's consideration of the matter presently before it. Through the foregoing provisions, OAS member states have charged the Commission with supervising member states' observance of human rights in the Hemisphere. These rights include those prescribed under the American Declaration of the Rights and Duties of Man, which constitutes a source of legal obligation for all OAS member states[29]

---

[24] As this request was considered while the Commission was in session, these precautionary measures were approved by all eligible members of the Commission present, namely: Juan Méndez, President; Marta Altolaguirre, First Vice-President; José Zalaquett, Second Vice-President; Julio Prado Vallejo and Clare Kamau Roberts, Commissioners. Commissioner Robert K. Goldman did not take part in the discussion and voting on these precautionary measures, pursuant to Article 17(2) of the Commission's Rules of Procedure.

[25] Article 25(1) of the Commission's Rules of Procedure provides: "In serious and urgent cases, and whenever necessary according to the information available, the Commission may, on its own initiative or at the request of a party, request that the State concerned adopt precautionary measures to prevent irreparable harm to persons".

[26] See, e.g., American Convention on Human Rights, Art. 63(2); Rules of Procedure of the Inter-American Court of Human Rights, Art. 25; Statute of the International Court of Justice, 59 Stat. 1055, Art. 41; Rules of Procedure of the United Nations Human Rights Committee, U.N. Doc. CCPR/C/3/Rev.6, Art. 86; Rules of Procedure of the European Commission of Human Rights, revised Rules updated to 7 May 1983, Art. 36; Rules of Procedure of the African Commission on Human and Peoples' Rights, adopted on 6 October 1995, Art. 111.

[27] See Regulations of the Inter-American Commission on Human Rights, approved by the Commission at its 660th Meeting, 49th session held on April 8, 1980, and modified at its 64th, 70th, 90th and 92nd sessions, Art. 29; Rules of Procedure of the Inter-American Commission on Human Rights, approved by the Commission at its 109th special session held from December 4 to 8, 2000, Art. 25; Annual Report of the IACHR 1996, Chapter II(4); Annual Report of the IACHR 1997, Chapter III(II)(A); Annual Report of the IACHR 1998, Chapter III(2)(A); Annual Report of the IACHR 1999, Chapter III(C)(1); Annual Report of the IACHR 2000, Chapter III(C)(1).

[28] See IACHR, Fifth Report on the Situation of Human Rights in Guatemala, OEASer.L/V/II.111 doc. 21 rev. (6 April 2001), paras. 71–72; *Juan Raul Garza v. United States*, Case No. 12.243, Report No. 52/01, Annual Report of the IACHR 2000, para. 117.

[29] See I/A Court H.R., Advisory Opinion OC-10/89, July 14, 1989, "Interpretation of the American Declaration of the Rights and Duties of Man within the Framework of Article 64 of the American Convention on

in respect of persons subject to their authority and control.[30] The Commission has been directed to pay particular attention to the observance of Articles I (right to life), II (right to equality before law), III (right to religious freedom and worship), IV (right to freedom of investigation, opinion, expression and dissemination), XVIII (right to a fair trial), XXV (right to protection from arbitrary arrest), and XXVI (right to due process of law) of the American Declaration.

In addition, while its specific mandate is to secure the observance of international human rights protections in the Hemisphere, this Commission has in the past looked to and applied definitional standards and relevant rules of international humanitarian law in interpreting the American Declaration and other Inter-American human rights instruments in situations of armed conflict.[31]

In taking this approach, the Commission has drawn upon certain basic principles that inform the interrelationship between international human rights and humanitarian law. It is well-recognized that international human rights law applies at all times, in peacetime and in situations of armed conflict.[32] In contrast, international humanitarian law generally does not apply in peacetime and its principal purpose is to place restraints on the conduct of warfare in order to limit or contain the damaging effects of hostilities and to protect the victims of armed conflict, including civilians and combatants who have laid down their arms or have been placed hors de combat.[33] Further, in situations of armed conflict, the protections under international human rights and humanitarian law may complement and reinforce one another, sharing as they do a common nucleus of non-derogable rights and a common purpose of promoting human life and dignity.[34] In certain circumstances, however, the test for evaluating the observance of a particular right, such as the right to liberty, in a situation of armed conflict may be distinct from that applicable in time of peace. In such situations, international law, including the jurisprudence of this Commission, dictates that it may be necessary to deduce the applicable standard by reference to international humanitarian law as the applicable *lex specialis*.[35]

Human Rights," Ser. A N° 10, paras. 43–46; *James Terry Roach and Jay Pinkerton v. United States*, Case 9647, Res. 3/87, 22 September 1987, Annual Report of the IACHR 1986–87, paras. 46–49; *Michael Edwards et al. v. Bahamas*, Case No 12.067, Report No. 48/01, Annual Report of the IACHR 2000.

[30] The determination of a state's responsibility for violations of the international human rights of a particular individual turns not on that individual's nationality or presence within a particular geographic area, but rather on whether, under the specific circumstances, that person fell within the state's authority and control. *See, e.g., Saldaño v. Argentina*, Report No. 38/99, Annual Report of the IACHR 1998, paras. 15–20; *Coard et al. v. United States*, Case No. 10.951, Report No. 109/99, Annual Report of the IACHR 1999, para. 37, citing, *inter alia.*, IACHR, Report on the Situation of Human Rights in Chile, OEA/Ser.L/V/II.66, doc. 17, 1985, Second Report on the Situation of Human Rights in Suriname, OEA/Ser.L/V/II.66, doc. 21, rev. 1, 1985. *See similarly* Eur. Comm. H.R., *Cyprus v. Turkey*, 18 Y.B. Eur. Conv. Hum. Rgts. 83 (1975) at 118; Eur. Comm. H.R., *Case of Loizidou v. Turkey*, Preliminary Objections, Judgment of 23 March 1995, Series A No. 310, paras. 59–64.

[31] *See generally Abella v. Argentina*, Case No. 11.137, Report No. 5/97, Annual Report of the IACHR 1997; *Coard et. al. v. United States, supra*; IACHR, Third Report on the Situation of Human Rights in Colombia, OEA/Ser.L/V/II.102 doc. 9 rev. 1, 26 February 1999.

[32] *Abella Case, supra*, para. 158.

[33] *Id.*, para. 159.

[34] *Id.*, para. 160–1.

[35] ICJ, *Advisory Opinion on the Legality of the Threat or Use of Nuclear Weapons*, ICJ Reports 1996, para. 25. *See also Abella Case, supra*, para. 161; *Coard et al. Case, supra*, para. 42.

Accordingly, where persons find themselves within the authority and control of a state and where a circumstance of armed conflict may be involved, their fundamental rights may be determined in part by reference to international humanitarian law as well as international human rights law. Where it may be considered that the protections of international humanitarian law do not apply, however, such persons remain the beneficiaries at least of the non-derogable protections under international human rights law. In short, no person under the authority and control of a state, regardless of his or her circumstances, is devoid of legal protection for his or her fundamental and non-derogable human rights.

This basic precept is reflected in the Martens clause common to numerous long-standing humanitarian law treaties, including the Hague Conventions of 1899 and 1907 respecting the laws and customs of war on land, according to which human persons who do not fall within the protection of those treaties or other international agreements remain under the protection of the principles of the law of nations, as they result from the usages established among civilized peoples, from the laws of humanity, and the dictates of the public conscience. And according to international norms applicable in peacetime and wartime, such as those reflected in Article 5 of the Third Geneva Convention and Article XVIII of the American Declaration of the Rights and Duties of Man, a competent court or tribunal, as opposed to a political authority, must be charged with ensuring respect for the legal status and rights of persons falling under the authority and control of a state.

Specifically with regard to the request for precautionary measures presently before it, the Commission observes that certain pertinent facts concerning the detainees at Guantanamo Bay are well-known and do not appear to be the subject of controversy. These include the fact that the government of the United States considers itself to be at war with an international network of terrorists,[36] that the United States undertook a military operation in Afghanistan beginning in October 2001 in defending this war,[37] and that most of the detainees in Guantanamo Bay were apprehended in connection with this military operation and remain wholly within the authority and control of the United States government.[38]

It is also well-known that doubts exists as to the legal status of the detainees. This includes the question of whether and to what extent the Third Geneva Convention and/or other provisions of international humanitarian law apply to some or all of the detainees and what implications this may have for their international human rights protections. According to official statements from the United States government, its Executive Branch has most recently declined to extend prisoner of war status under the Third Geneva Convention to the detainees, without submitting the issue for determination by a competent tribunal or otherwise ascertaining the rights and protections to which the detainees are entitled under US domestic or international

---

[36] *See, e.g.,* Remarks by the President in Photo Opportunity with the National Security Team, Office of the Press Secretary, September 12, 2001, http://whitehouse.gov/news/releases/2001/09/20010912–4.html.

[37] *See, e.g.,* Radio Address of the President to the Nation, Office of the Press Secretary, October 13, 2001, http://www.whitehouse.gov/news/releases/2001/10/20011013.html.

[38] *See, e.g.,* Jim Garamone, 50 Detainees now at Gitmo; All Treated Humanely, American Forces Press Service, January 15, 2002, http://www.defenselink.mil/news/Jan2002/n01152002_200201151.html.

law.[39] To the contrary, the information available suggests that the detainees remain entirely at the unfettered discretion of the United States government. Absent clarification of the legal status of the detainees, the Commission considers that the rights and protections to which they may be entitled under international or domestic law cannot be said to be the subject of effective legal protection by the State.

In light of the foregoing considerations, and without prejudging the possible application of international humanitarian law to the detainees at Guantanamo Bay, the Commission considers that precautionary measures are both appropriate and necessary in the present circumstances, in order to ensure that the legal status of each of the detainees is clarified and that they are afforded the legal protections commensurate with the status that they are found to possess, which may in no case fall below the minimum standards of non-derogable rights. On this basis, the Commission hereby requests that the United States take the urgent measures necessary to have the legal status of the detainees at Guantanamo Bay determined by a competent tribunal.

In its communication to the United States, the Commission also requested that the State provide the Commission with information concerning compliance with these measures within 30 days of receipt of the communication, and thereafter on a periodic basis. In view of the observations of the parties on compliance, the Commission will decide whether to extend or lift the measures.

The Commission wishes to note in accordance with Article 25(4) of the Commission's Rules of Procedure that the granting of these measures and their adoption by the State shall not constitute a prejudgment on the merits of a case.

Questions and Comments

1. According to the Commission, are all precautionary measures legally binding? If not, how does the Commission decide which ones are and which ones are not?

2. Is the Commission's position convincing, given that decisions on the merits of petitions result in mere recommendations? Or are the latter legally binding as well?

C. The African System

There is no provision in the African Charter specifically authorizing the African Commission to issue provisional or precautionary measures, although Rule 111 of the Rules of Procedure permits the Commission to "inform the State party concerned on its views on the appropriateness of taking provisional measures to avoid irreparable damage being caused to the victim of the alleged violation." Does the Commission, as a quasi-judicial protective body, have the implied power to issue precautionary orders? What is their legal effect? Examine the full text of Rule 111 for indications in this respect. Consider the following case: what was the basis of the request and the nature of the measures indicated? Does the Commission hold that the measures are legally binding?

---

[39] *See* White House Fact Sheet, Status of Detainees at Guantanamo, Office of the Press Secretary, February 7, 2002, http://www.whitehouse.gov/news/releases/2002/02/20020207–13.html.

International PEN, Constitutional Rights Project, Interights on behalf of Ken Saro-Wiwa Jr. and Civil Liberties Organisation v. Nigeria, (Comms. 137/94, 139/94, 154/96, and 161/97), *12th Annual Activity Report of the Afr. Comm. H.P.R. 1998–1999,* Annex V, pp. 62–73.

Facts as submitted by the authors:

1. These communications were submitted to the African Commission by International PEN, the Constitutional Rights Project, Interights [and Civil Liberties Organisation] respectively. They were joined because they all concern the detention and trial of Kenule Beeson Saro-Wiwa, a writer and Ogoni activist, president of the Movement for the Survival of the Ogoni People. The communications 139/94 and 154/96 also complain of similar human rights violations suffered by Mr. Saro-Wiwa's co-defendants, also Ogoni leaders.

2. The communications 137/94 and 139/94 were submitted in 1994 before any trial began. After the murder of four Ogoni leaders on 21 May 1994, following riot during a public meeting organised by Movement for the Survival of the Ogoni Peoples (MOSOP) representing the rights of those who lived in oil producing areas of Ogoni land, Saro-Wiwa and many hundreds of others were arrested, Saro-Wiwa himself on 22 May 1994 and the vice-president of MOSOP, Ledum Mitee, shortly thereafter. Both communications allege that Mr. Saro-Wiwa was severely beaten during the first days of his detention and was held for several days in leg irons and handcuffs. He was also denied access to his lawyer and the medicine he needed to control his blood pressure, at times prevented from seeing his family, and held in very poor conditions.

3. In its communication, submitted on 9 September 1994, the Constitutional Rights Project included a list of 16 other Ogonis who had been held without charge or bail for what was at that time over three months. Both communications alleged that Mr. Saro-Wiwa had been detained because of his political work in relation to MOSOP. He had been detained five times for brief periods since the beginning of 1993, and released each time without charge, except on one occasion in mid-1993 where he was held for several weeks and charged with unlawful assembly.

4. The State Military Administrator declared that Mr. Saro-Wiwa and his co-defendants had incited members of MOSOP to murder four rival Ogoni leaders, but no charges were brought until 28 January 1995. In the months between arrest and the beginning of the trial, the defendants were not allowed to meet with their lawyers, and no information on the charges was provided to the defence.

5. In February 1995 the trial of the defendants began before a tribunal established under the Civil Disturbances Act. The three members of this tribunals were appointed directly by General Abacha in November 1994, although counsel for the Rivers State Administrator argued in August that the cases were within the exclusive jurisdiction of the Rivers State High Court, since Rivers State is where the offences occurred.

6. In June 1995 the Constitutional Rights Project submitted a supplement to its communication, alleging irregularities in the conduct of the trial itself: harassment of defence counsel, a military officer's presence at what should have been confidential meetings between defendants and their counsel, bribery of witnesses, and

evidence of bias on the part of the tribunal members themselves. In October 1995 PEN also copied to the Commission a letter it sent to General Abacha protesting the lack of concrete evidence and the unfair conduct of the trial.

7. On 30 and 31 October 1995, Ken Saro-Wiwa and eight of the co-defendants (Saturday Dobee, Felix Nuate, Nordu Eawo, Paul Levura, Daniel Gbokoo, Barinem Kiobel, John Kpunien and Baribor Bera) were sentenced to death, while six others including Mr. Mitee were acquitted. The CRP submitted an emergency supplement to its communication on 2 November 1995, asking the Commission to adopt provisional measures to prevent the executions.

8. The Secretariat of the Commission faxed a note verbale invoking interim measures under revised Rule 111 of the Commission's Rules of Procedure to the Ministry of Foreign Affairs of Nigeria, the Secretary General of the OAU, the Special Advisor (Legal) to the Head of State, the Ministry of Justice of Nigeria, and the Nigerian High Commission in The Gambia. The note verbale pointed out that as the case of Mr. Saro-Wiwa and the others was already before the Commission, and the government of Nigeria had invited the Commission to undertake a mission to that country, during which mission the communications would be discussed, the executions should be delayed until the Commission had discussed the case with the Nigerian authorities.

9. No response to this appeal was received before the executions were carried out.

10. On 7 November 1995 the Provisional Ruling Council (PRC) confirmed the sentences of death and on 10 November 1995 all the accused persons were executed in secret at the Port Harcourt Prison. By section 7 of the Civil Disturbances (Special Tribunals) Decree No. 2 of 1987, under which the executed persons were tried, the PRC are required to receive the records of the trial Tribunal before confirmation of the decision is possible. These records were not prepared by the Tribunal and so were not available for the PRC.

. . . .

37. On 26 January 1996 a letter was sent to the Constitutional Rights Project informing it of the interim measures taken with regard to Ken Saro-Wiwa.

38. At the 19th session, held in March/April 1996 in Ouagadougou, Burkina Faso, the Commission heard statements from the government of Nigeria and the complainants. Mr. Chidi Anselm Odinkalu was duly authorised to appear for the complainants, and Mr. Osah and Mr. Bello appeared for the Nigerian Government. At the end of the hearing the Commission took a general view on the cases and deferred taking final decision in each case pending the accomplishment of its proposed mission to Nigeria. The Commission proposed May 1996 as the dates for the visit. The Nigerian delegation said they will [sic] communicate these dates to the Government of Nigeria for confirmation.

39. On 8 May 1996 the Commission wrote to the Nigerian Government, Constitutional Rights Project and International PEN informing them that a decision had been taken at the 19th session to send a mission to the country where the cases would be taken up.

40. At the 20th session held in Grand Bay, Mauritius, October 1996, the Commission decided to postpone the final decision on the merits of the communications to the next session, awaiting the result of the planned mission to Nigeria. The Commission also decided to join communication 154/96 with these communications.

. . . .

43. On 29 April, the Secretariat received a letter from Mr. Olisa Agbakoba entitled Preliminary objections and observations to the Mission of the Commission which visited Nigeria from March 7–14 1997. The document was submitted on behalf of Interights with regard to 14 communications, including this one.

44. Among the objections raised and or observations made were: a) the neutrality, credibility and relevance; and composition of the Mission.

45. At its 21st session held in April 1997, the Commission postponed taking decision on the merits to the next session, pending the submission of scholarly article and court decisions by the complainants to assist it in its decision. The Commission also awaits further analysis of its report of the mission to Nigeria. It must be stated that Mr. Chidi Odinkalu did send the article mentioned above.

46. On 22 May, the complainants were informed of the Commission's decision, while the State was informed on May 28.

47. Communication 154/96 is dated 6 November 1995 and received at the Secretariat on 4 March 1996.

48. The communication requested the Commission to take interim measures to prevent the executions. A supplementary submission was sent with the communication informing the Commission that the executions had taken place on 10 November but that the communication was reaffirmed.

LAW

. . . .

Merits

. . . .

103. Given that the trial which ordered the executions itself violates Article 7, any subsequent implementation of sentences renders the resulting deprivation of life arbitrary and in violation of Article 4. The violation is compounded by the fact that there were pending communications before the African Commission at the time of the executions, and the Commission had requested the government to avoid causing any "irreparable prejudice" to the subjects of the communications before the Commission had concluded it consideration. Executions had been stayed in Nigeria in the past on the invocation by the Commission of its rule on provisional measures (Rule 109 now 111) and the Commission had hoped that a similar situation will obtain in the case of Ken Sarow-Wiwa and others. It is a matter of deep regret that this did not happen.

104. The protection of the right to life in Article 4 also includes a duty for the state not to purposefully let a person die while in its custody. Here at least one of the victims' lives was seriously endangered by the denial of medication during detention. Thus, there are multiple violations of Article 4.

. . . .

113. Nigeria has been a State Party to the African Charter for over a decade, and is thus bound by Article 1 of the African Charter.

114. The Commission assists States parties to implement their obligations under the Charter. Rule 111 of the Commission's Rules of Procedure (revised) aims at preventing irreparable damage being caused to a complainant before the Commission. Execution in the face of the invocation of Rule 111 defeats the purpose of this important rule. The Commission had hoped that the Government of Nigeria would respond positively to it's [sic] request for a stay of execution pending the former's determination of the communication before it.

115. This is a blot on the legal system of Nigeria which will not be easy to erase. To have carried out the execution in the face of pleas to the contrary by the Commission and world opinion is something which we pray will never happen again. That it is a violation of the Charter is an understatement.

116. The Nigerian Government itself recognises that human rights are no longer solely a matter of domestic concern. The African Charter was drafted and acceded to voluntarily by African States wishing to ensure the respect of human rights on this continent. Once ratified, States Parties to the Charter are legally bound to its provisions. A state not wishing to abide by the African Charter might have refrained from ratification. Once legally bound, however, a state must abide by the law in the same way an individual must.

FOR THE ABOVE REASONS, THE COMMISSION

Decides that there has been a violation of Articles 5 and 16 in relation to Ken Saro-Wiwa's detention in 1993 and his treatment in detention in 1994 and 1995;

Decides that there has been a violation of Articles 6 in relation to the detention of all the victims under the State Security (Detention of Persons) Act of 1984 and State Security (Detention of Persons) Amended Decree no. 14 (1994). The government therefore has the obligation to annul these Decrees;

Reiterates its decision on communication 87/93 that there has been a violation of Article 7.1(d) and with regard to the establishment of the Civil Disturbances Tribunal. In ignoring this decision, Nigeria has violation Article 1 of the Charter;

Decides that there has been a violation of Articles 4 and 7.1 (a), (b) (c) and (d) in relation to the conduct of the trial and the execution of the victims;

Holds that there has been a violation of Articles 9.2, 10.1 and 11, 26, 16;

Holds that in ignoring its obligations to institute provisional measures, Nigeria has violated Article 1.

Questions and Comments

1. Does the African Commission indicate what standard it is applying in deciding whether or not to indicate interim measures?

2. On what basis can it be argued that interim measures in the African system are binding?

4. Admissibility of Complaints

A. Overview

The exclusion of complaints patently outside the jurisdiction of the respective regional systems is a prelude to a formal admissibility decision, based on the criteria set forth in the treaties and rules of procedure. The admissibility of petitions in the European system, for example, is governed by the provisions of Article 35 of the Convention which reads as follows:

> (1) The Court may only deal with the matter after all domestic remedies have been exhausted, according to the generally recognized rules of international law, and within a period of six months from the date on which the final decision was taken.
>
> (2) The Court shall not deal with any application submitted under Article 34 that
>   (a) is anonymous; or
>   (b) is substantially the same as a matter that has already been examined by the Court or has already been submitted to another procedure of international investigation or settlement and contains no relevant new information.
>
> (3) The Court shall declare inadmissible any individual application submitted under Article 34 which it considers incompatible with the provisions of the Convention or the protocols thereto, manifestly ill-founded, or an abuse of the right of application.
>
> (4) The Court shall reject any application which it considers inadmissible under this Article. It may do so at any stage of the proceedings.

In the Inter-American system, a complaint will be held to be inadmissible if it does not state a *prima facie* case under the Convention or if it is otherwise "manifestly groundless or obviously out of order". Art. 47(b) and (c). Article 47(d) requires the Commission to reject a petition that "is substantially the same as one previously studied by the Commission or by another international organization." This provision complements Article 46(1)(c), which conditions admissibility on the requirement "that the subject of the petition or communication is not pending in another international proceeding of settlement". A case taken from the Inter-American Commission to the Court, after admissibility and merits determinations by the Commission, may still face challenges to admissibility before the judicial body, and the Court will review the matter *de novo*. The following judgment, in the first contentious case before the Inter-American Court, illustrates this practice.

Velásquez Rodriguez Case (Preliminary Objections), Judgment of June 26, 1987, 1 Inter-Am. Ct. H.R. (Ser. C) (1987).

1. The Inter-American Commission on Human Rights submitted the instant case to the Court on April 24, 1986. It originated in a petition against Honduras (No. 7920) which the Secretariat of the Commission received on October 7, 1981.

2. In filing the application with the Court, the Commission invoked Articles 50 and 51 of the American Convention on Human Rights and requested that the Court determine whether the State in question had violated Articles 4 (Right to Life), 5 (Right to Humane Treatment) and 7 (Right to Personal Liberty) of the Convention in the case of Angel Manfredo Velásquez Rodriguez. The Commission also asked the Court to rule that "the consequences of the situation that constituted the breach

of such right or freedom be remedied and that fair compensation be paid to the injured party or parties".

3. On May 13, 1986, the Secretariat of the Court transmitted the application to the Government.

. . . .

7. In its submissions of October 31, 1986, the Government objected to the admissibility of the application filed by the Commission.

. . . .

15. According to the petition filed with the Commission on October 7, 1981, and the supplementary information received subsequently, Angel Manfredo Velásquez Rodriguez, a student at the National Autonomous University of Honduras, "was violently detained without a warrant for his arrest by members of the Direccion Nacional de Investigacion (DNI) and G-2 of the Armed Forces of Honduras" on the afternoon of September 12, 1981, in Tegucigalpa. According to the petitioners, several eyewitnesses reported that he and others were detained and taken to the cells of Public Security Forces Station No. 2 located in the Barrio El Manchen of Tegucigalpa, where he was "accused of alleged political crimes and subjected to harsh interrogation and cruel torture". The petition added that on September 17, 1981, Velásquez Rodriguez was moved to the First Infantry Battalion, where the interrogation continued, but that the police and security forces, nevertheless, denied that he had been detained.

16. On October 14 and November 24, 1981, the Commission transmitted the relevant parts of the petition to the Government and requested information on the matter.

17. When the Commission received no reply, it again asked the Government for information on May 14, 1982, warning that if it did not receive the information within a reasonable time, it would consider applying Article 42 (formerly 39) of its Regulations and presume the allegations to be true.

18. Although it reiterated its request for information on October 6, 1982, March 23 and August 9, 1983, the Commission received no reply.

19. At its 61st Session, the Commission adopted Resolution 30/83 of October 4, 1983, whose operative parts read as follows:

1. By application of Article 39 of the Regulations, to presume as true the allegations contained in the communication of October 7, 1981, concerning the detention and disappearance of Angel Manfredo Velásquez Rodriguez in the Republic of Honduras.

2. To point out to the Government of Honduras that such acts are most serious violations of the right to life (Art. 4) and the right to personal liberty (Art. 7) of the American Convention on Human Rights.

3. To recommend to the. Government of Honduras: (a) that it order a thorough and impartial investigation to determine who is responsible for the acts denounced, (b) that it punish those responsible in accordance with Honduran law, and (c) that it inform the Commission within 60 days, especially about the measures taken to carry out these recommendations.

4. If the Government of Honduras does not submit its observations within the time limit set out in paragraph 3 supra, the Commission shall include this Resolution in its Annual Report to the General Assembly pursuant to Article 59(g) of its Regulations.

20. On November 18, 1983, the Government requested the reconsideration of Resolution 30/83 on the grounds that domestic remedies had not been exhausted, that the Direccion Nacional de Investigacion had no knowledge of the whereabouts of Velásquez Rodriguez, that the Government was making every effort to find him, and that there were rumors that Velásquez Rodriguez was "with Salvadoran guerrilla groups".

21. On May 30, 1984, the Commission informed the Government that it had decided at its 62nd Session (May, 1984), "in light of the information submitted by the Honorable Government, to reconsider Resolution 30/83 and to continue its study of the case". The Commission also asked the Government to provide information on the exhaustion of domestic legal remedies and other matters relevant to the case.

22. On January 29, 1985, the Commission repeated its request of May 30, 1984 and notified the Government that it would render a final decision on this case at its meeting in March 1985. On March 1 of that year, the Government asked for a postponement of the final decision and reported that it had set up an Investigatory Commission to study the matter. The Commission agreed to the Government's request on March 11, granting it thirty days in which to present the information requested.

23. On April 7, 1986, the Government provided information about the outcome of the proceeding that had been brought before the First Criminal Court on behalf of Velásquez Rodriguez and other persons who had disappeared. According to that information, the tribunal had dismissed the complaints "except as they applied to General Gustavo Alvarez Martinez, because he had left the country and had not given testimony". This decision was later affirmed by the First Court of Appeals.

24. In Resolution 22/86 of April 18, 1986, adopted at its 67th Session, the Commission deemed the new information presented by the Government insufficient to warrant reconsideration of Resolution 30/83 and found, to the contrary, that "all evidence shows that Angel Manfredo Velásquez Rodriguez is still missing and that the Government of Honduras . . . has not offered convincing proof that would allow the Commission to determine that the allegations are not true". In that same Resolution, the Commission confirmed Resolution 30/83, denied the request for reconsideration and referred the matter to the Court.

. . . .

28. Before considering each of the [State's] objections, the Court must define the scope of its jurisdiction in the instant case. The Commission argued at the hearing that because the Court is not an appellate tribunal in relation to the Commission, it has a limited jurisdiction that prevents it from reviewing all aspects relating to compliance with the prerequisites for the admissibility of a petition or with the procedural norms required in a case filed with the Commission.

29. That argument does not find support in the Convention, which provides that the Court, in the exercise of its contentious jurisdiction, is competent to decide "all matters relating to the interpretation or application of (the) Convention" (Art. 62(1)). States that accept the obligatory jurisdiction of the Court recognize that competence. The broad terms employed by the Convention show that the Court exercises full jurisdiction over all issues relevant to a case. The Court, therefore, is competent

to determine whether there has been a violation of the rights and freedoms recognized by the Convention and to adopt appropriate measures. The Court is likewise empowered to interpret the procedural rules that justify its hearing a case and to verify compliance with all procedural norms involved in the "interpretation or application of (the) Convention". In exercising these powers, the Court is not bound by what the Commission may have previously decided, rather, its authority to render judgment is in no way restricted. The Court does not act as a court of review, of appeal or other similar court in its dealings with the Commission. Its power to examine and review all actions and decisions of the Commission derives from its character as sole judicial organ in matters concerning the Convention. This not only affords greater protection to the human rights guaranteed by the Convention, but it also assures the States Parties that have accepted the jurisdiction of the Court that the provisions of the Convention will be strictly observed.

30. The interpretation of the Convention regarding the proceedings before the Commission necessary "for the Court to hear a case" (Art. 61(2)) must ensure the international protection of human rights which is the very purpose of the Convention and requires, when necessary, the power to decide questions concerning its own jurisdiction. Treaties must be interpreted "in good faith in accordance with the ordinary meaning to be given to the terms of the treaty in their context and in the light of its object and purpose" (Art. 31(1) of the Vienna Convention on the Law of Treaties). The object and purpose of the American Convention is the effective protection of human rights. The Convention must, therefore, be interpreted so as to give it its full meaning and to enable the system for the protection of human rights entrusted to the Commission and the Court to attain its "appropriate effects". Applicable here is the statement of the Hague Court:

> Whereas, in case of doubt, the clauses of a special agreement by which a dispute is referred to the Court must, if it does not involve doing violence to their terms, be construed in a manner enabling the clauses themselves to have appropriate effects (*Free Zones of Upper Savoy and the District of Gex*, Order of 19 August 1929, PC.I.J., Series A, No. 22, p. 13).

31. The Court will now examine the preliminary objections.

. . . .

33. In order to resolve these issues, the Court must first address various problems concerning the interpretation and application of the procedural norms set forth in the Convention. In doing so, the Court first points out that failure to observe certain formalities is not necessarily relevant when dealing on the international plane. What is essential is that the conditions necessary for the preservation of the procedural rights of the parties not be diminished or unbalanced, and that the objectives of the different procedures be met. In this regard, it is worth noting that, in one of its first rulings, the Hague Court stated that:

> The Court, whose jurisdiction is international, is not bound to attach to matters of form the same degree of importance which they might possess in municipal law (*Mavrommatis Palestine Concessions*, Judgment No. 2, 1924, P.C.I.J., Series A, No. 2, p. 34; see also, *Aegean Sea Continental Shelf*, Judgment, I.C.J. Reports 1978, para. 42).

34. This Court must then determine whether the essential points implicit in the procedural norms contained in the Convention have been observed. In order to do

so, the Court must examine whether the right of defense of the State objecting to admissibility has been prejudiced during the procedural part of the case, or whether the State has been prevented from exercising any other rights accorded it under the Convention in the proceedings before the Commission. The Court must, likewise, verify whether the essential procedural guidelines of the protection system set forth in the Convention have been followed. Within these general criteria, the Court shall examine the procedural issues submitted to it, in order to determine whether the procedures followed in the instant case contain flaws that would demand refusal *in limine* to examine the merits of the case.

Questions and Comments

1. What time limits exist for the submission of preliminary objections? What elements must a preliminary objection contain? What preliminary objections did the government of Honduras make?

2. These objections refer to the Commission's actions or decisions in the proceeding before the Commission. Does the Court have jurisdiction to review admissibility or the practices of the Commission? What deference should it give to Commission decisions on these matters?

3. What distinction does the Court make between international and national jurisdiction with respect to the fulfillment of procedural formalities? Why should there be any distinction?

The following materials examine the common admissibility requirements in the three regional systems.

B. Duplication of Procedures and the Six Months Rule

The regional conventions all exclude petitions that have been previously considered by an international human rights tribunal. The exclusion of duplicative petitions is set forth in European Convention Article 35(1)(b), which declares that the Court may not admit a petition that "has already been submitted to another procedure of international investigation or settlement and contains no relevant new information". The American Convention, Article 47(d) bars any petition that is "substantially the same as one previously studied by the Commission or by another international organization". The Commission interprets these last two requirements in a manner designed to ensure that a complaint will not be rejected when the other international organization, although seized of the matter in general, is or was in no position to grant petitioners the specific relief they seek from the Commission. Commission Rules, Art. 32(2). The African Charter, Article 56(7), refers only to cases "which have been settled", and this language is confirmed in the Rules of Procedure. It would appear to allow petitions to be filed at a UN treaty body and the African Commission, at least until a decision is reached by one of the institutions. *See: Mpaka-Nsusu Andre Alphonse v. Zaire*, Comm. 15/88, Sept. 12, 1988, *7th Annual Activity Report of the Afr. Comm. H.P.R. 1993–1994*, Annex IX (declaring a matter inadmissible because it had already been considered by the Human Rights Committee established under the ICCPR).

The former European Commission gave some indications about the scope of the Article 35(2)(b) requirement. According to the Commission, a petition is inadmissible if it has already been the subject of a case before an international body, or is being examined by such a body, because the purpose of the requirement is to avoid the same case becoming the object of various international procedures. The procedures envisaged are procedures in which a matter is submitted by way of "a petition" lodged formally or substantively by the applicant in judicial or quasi-judicial proceedings similar to those set up by the Convention. It has been held that term "international investigation or settlement" refers to institutions and procedures set up by states, thus excluding non-governmental bodies. *See* Application No. 16358/90, Decision of October 12, 1992, unpublished, and *Lukanov v. Bulgaria*, Application No. 21915/93, Decision of 12 January 1995, Reports1997-II. It has not been decided whether Article 35(2)(b) precludes the Court from hearing individual complaints following its consideration of an inter-state matter nor whether the mere passage of time following another proceeding would in itself qualify as "relevant new information". *See Donnelly and Others v. the United Kingdom*, Applications Nos. 5577/72-5583/72, Decision of April 5, 1973, 16 Y.B. 212; *Varnava, Loizides, Constantinou and Peyiotis, Theochardies and Theocharidou, Charalambous, Thoma, Hadjipanteli, Apostolides and Demetriou Sarma and Leonti Sarma v. Turkey*, Apps. Nos. 16064–16073/90, Decision of April 14, 1998.

The petitioner can prevent the application from being declared inadmissible by withdrawing it from the other procedure. In another effort to avoid duplicate international procedures, some States Parties to the European Convention, in ratifying the Optional Protocol to the International Covenant on Civil and Political Rights, made reservations to prevent considerations of cases by the UN Human Rights Committee that had already been considered within the European system. On this subject, *see* Communication No. 121/1982, UN Human Rights Committee, *Selected Decisions under the Optional Protocol (Second to Sixteenth Sessions)*, at 32 (1985) (holding an application against Denmark inadmissible). If the petitioner chooses to continue in both systems, each institution will have to decide whether the two petitions concern the same matter, as the following case illustrates. Is it enough that the petitioner invokes different rights in each petition? What if a right invoked in one system is not guaranteed by the other?

Pauger v. Austria, (App. no. 16717/90), Eur. Comm. H.R., 25 EHRR 105 (1998).

. . . . In his application form, submitted on 28 May 1990, the applicant informed the Secretariat of the Commission that he had the intention of also introducing a communication to the Human Rights Committee concerning the same facts as his application to the Commission. On 5 June 1990 the applicant introduced such a communication invoking a violation of Article 26 of the International Covenant on Civil and Political Rights, according to which "all persons are equal before the law and are entitled without any discrimination to the equal protection of the law". He informed the Commission's Secretariat on 12 June 1990 thereof. On 28 March 1991, in its decision on the admissibility of the applicant's communication, the Human Rights Committee found that it was not prevented from examining the communication by the fact that he had also introduced an application with the Commission. The communication, while emanating from the same factual situation as the application, addresses other legal issues and did not constitute "the same matter". On 30 March 1992 the Human Rights Committee found a violation of Article 26 of the International Covenant on Civil and Political Rights.

. . . .

THE LAW

1. The applicant complains under Article 6 para. 1 of the Convention that his widower's pension claim was not decided by a tribunal within the meaning of this provision, that he had no hearing before the Constitutional Court and that the proceedings before the Constitutional Court were unfair and not concluded within a reasonable time.

[. . . .]

2. The Commission has first to examine whether it is prevented by virtue of Article 27 para. 1 (b) [now Article 35(2)(b)] of the Convention from dealing with the present application.

The Government maintain that pursuant to Article 27 para. 1 (b) of the Convention, the Commission is barred from dealing with the complaints raised by the applicant because the matter has already been submitted to another procedure of international investigation, namely the procedure before the Human Rights Committee.

They consider it irrelevant that before the Human Rights Committee the applicant complained under Article 26 of the International Covenant on Civil and Political Rights about a violation of his right to equal treatment before the law, while in his application to the Commission he complained of a violation of Article 6 para. 1 of the Convention. Rather, it is decisive that the same facts were submitted to another international authority. Thus, the scope of an application to the Commission is not limited to the Convention rights invoked by an applicant, as it is the task of the Convention organs to review the facts of an application brought before them in respect of all rights guaranteed by the Convention.

The applicant does not share this view.

[. . . .]

The Commission recalls that it is against the letter and spirit of the Convention if the same matter is simultaneously submitted to two international institutions. Article 27 para. 1 (b) of the Convention aims at avoiding the plurality of international procedures concerning the same case. In considering this issue, the Commission needs to verify whether the applications to the different institutions have substantially the same content (cf. No. 17512/90, Dec. 30.6.92 and 6.7.92, and No. 16358/90, Dec. 12.10.92, D.R. 73).

In this connection, the Commission considers that the applicant did not submit substantially the same matter as raised in his application before the Commission to the Human Rights Committee, because the complaints raised in the respective proceedings were different. While before the Human Rights Committee he complained of discrimination against him, before the Commission he complains about issues related to the proceedings before the Austrian authorities and courts.

Consequently, the Commission is not prevented by virtue of Article 27 para. 1 (b) (Art. 27–1-b) of the Convention from dealing with the application.

. . . .

Note on the Time Limits for Filing a Petition: The regional treaties require that complaints or petitions be filed within a "reasonable period" (African Charter, Art. 56(6)) or set a relatively short limitations period of six months from the date of the final domestic decision. American Convention, Art. 46(1)(b); European Convention, Art. 35 (1) (. . ."within a period of six months from the date on which the final decision was taken"). Like domestic statutes of limitations, the rule is intended to ensure that evidence is fresh, witnesses are available, and long-standing domestic judgments and decisions are not open to challenge.

The first day of the time-limit is normally considered to start on the day following the final decision, but in some cases publication or notification of the decision will be the starting point. *Worm v. Austria*, App. No. 22714/93, 25 EHRR 454 (1998). "Months" are calculated as calendar months regardless of their actual duration. Where an applicant is repeatedly and consecutively subject to the same alleged violation, as in sequential periods of pre-trial detention, the multiple periods may be regarded as a whole and the six-month period will begin from the end of the last period of pre-trial detention. *Solmas v. Turkey*, App. No. 27561/02, judgment of January 16, 2007.

An application is considered to be introduced within the time-limit if it was posted on or before the last day of the six months period. *Oberschlick v. Austria*, Judgment of 23 May 1991, 204 Publ. Eur.Court H.R. 21 paras. 38–40; *Istituto di Vigilanza v. Italy*, Judgment of 22 September 1993, 265-C Publ. Eur. Court H.R. 35 para. 14; *Pollard v. the United Kingdom*, Application No. 28189/95, Decision of April 12, 1996. "Special circumstances" may be taken into account, as well, as in *Sibson v. United Kingdom*, Application No. 14327/88, Europ. Comm'n H.R., Decision of April 9, 1991, 12 Hum. Rts. L.J. 351 (1991), where the former European Commission decided as follows:

> The Government also submit that if the appeal to the House of Lords were not considered an effective remedy in this case, the final decision for the purposes of calculating the six months time-limit imposed by Article 26 (Art. 26) of the Convention would be the decision of the Court of Appeal of 25 March 1988. However the application was introduced more than six months after that date on 17 October 1988. The applicant submits that the time-limit should run from the date on which the prescribed time for leave to appeal to the House of Lords expired, on which date the Court of Appeal decisionbecame final.
>
> The Commission is unable to agree with either party. Appeals to the House of Lords lie in cases considered to raise fundamental issues of law of general public importance. The applicant took the step of seeking legal aid and obtaining counsel's opinion as to the prospects of appealing. Counsel's opinion revealed that there was no prospect of gaining leave to appeal and legal aid was refused. The Commission considers that these are special circumstances which can be taken into account in applying the six months time-limit. In this case therefore, the Commission finds that the six months time-limit runs from the date on which it became apparent

that an appeal to the House of Lords was no longer feasible, namely, the decision of 19 August 1988, the date of the decision refusing legal aid on the basis of counsel's opinion.

Consequently, as the application was introduced within six months from that date, it cannot be rejected for failure to comply with Article 26 (Art. 26) of the Convention.

Review again the judgment in the case of *Blečić v. Croatia*: how does that decision impact the six months rule? Which court issued the "final decision?"

Finally, note that the six month rule may be inapplicable if the violation is a continuing one, a claim that applicants often make. The following cases are examples.

Case of Posti and Rahko v. Finland, App. No. 27824/95, Judgment of Sept. 24, 2002, Reports of Judgments and Decisions 2002-VII.

. . . .

2. The applicants complained . . . that a fishing restriction imposed and maintained by governmental decree had violated their right to peaceful enjoyment of their possessions, which allegedly comprised a right to fish certain waters. They also complained of having had no access to a tribunal, or any other effective remedy, in order to challenge the fishing restriction.

. . . .

3. . . . . [T]he Government submitted that part of the application had been lodged out of time. A decision made in response to a petition to the Ombudsman could not extend the six-month period prescribed by Article 35 § 1 of the Convention. Were the Court to find that no effective domestic remedy had been—or remained—available to the applicants, the six-month period would therefore have started to run from the entry into force of the 1994 Decree on 1 April 1994. As the applicants had introduced their application only on 2 July 1995, only those impugned measures occurring after 2 January 1995 could be examined by the Court.

. . . .

4. According to the Government, only those impugned measures occurring after 2 January 1995 can be examined by the Court, since the applicants introduced their application only on 2 July 1995. The Court reiterates, however, that the six-month rule, in reflecting the wish of the Contracting Parties to prevent past decisions being called into question after an indefinite lapse of time, serves the interests not only of the respondent State but also of legal certainty as a value in itself. It marks out the temporal limits of supervision carried out by the organs of the Convention and signals to both individuals and State authorities the period beyond which such supervision is no longer possible. It is therefore not open to the Court to set aside the application of the six-month rule solely because a Government have not made a preliminary objection based on it—or have chosen to limit their objection to a certain period, as in the present case (see, for example, *Walker v. the United Kingdom* (dec.), no. 34979/97, ECHR 2000-I).

5. In so far as the applicants complained that they were victims of a continuing violation to which the six-month rule did not apply, the Court reiterates that the concept of a "continuing situation" refers to a state of affairs which operates by con-

tinuous activities by or on the part of the State to render the applicants victims (see, for example, *McDaid and Others v. the United Kingdom*, no. 25681/94, Commission decision of 9 April 1996, Decisions and Reports (DR) 85-A, p. 134).

6. The applicants' complaints have as their source specific events which occurred on identifiable dates, namely the issuing of the 1994 Decree and—as their application must be understood—of the 1996 and 1998 Decrees. These cannot be construed as a "continuing situation" for the purposes of the six-month rule. The fact that an event has significant consequences over time—such as the restriction on the applicants' fishing during specific periods in 1996 and subsequent years—does not mean that the event has produced a "continuing situation".

7. In the Court's view the first six-month period of relevance to the applicants' case therefore started to run from the entry into force of the 1994 Decree on 1 April 1994. As their application was lodged on 2 July 1995, it has been lodged out of time in so far as it concerns the fishing restriction resulting from the 1994 Decree.

8. The Court notes, however, that the restrictions imposed by the 1994 Decree were, in relevant parts, maintained by the decrees issued in 1996 and 1998. As the applicants are effectively complaining about the restriction imposed by those decrees as well, their complaints meet the six-month requirement in Article 35 § 1 in this regard.

9. It follows that the Government's preliminary objection must be accepted in part and rejected in part.

Contrast the case of *Hutten-Czapska v. Poland*, App. No. 35014/97, judgment of June 19, 2006, (GC) (the implementation of Polish laws imposing tenancy agreements on the applicant and setting an inadequate level of rent constituted a continuing violation).

The African Commission also accepts the doctrine of continuing violations. See, e.g., *Muthuthurin Njoka v. Kenya*, Comm. 142/94, 8th Annual Activity Report 1994–95 (declaring communication inadmissible because no continuing violation); *Annette Pagnoulle (on behalf of Abdoulaye Mazou) v. Cameroon*, Comm. 39/90, 10th Annual Activity Report 1996–97 (case admissible because of a continuing violation); Joined cases *48/90 Amnesty International v. Sudan, 50/91 Comité Loosli Bachelard v. Sudan, 52/91 Lawyers Committee for Human Rights v. Sudan, 89/93 Association of Members of the Episcopal Conference of East Africa v. Sudan*, 13th Annual Activity Report 1999–2000 (continuing violations, as in the case of a law adopted prior to 1986, but that remains in force, fall within the competence of the Commission because the effect of such laws extends beyond that date).

In the Inter-American system, most assertions of continuing violations have arisen in the context of forcible disappearances. The following case was the first in which the Inter-American Court addressed this point.

Case of Blake v. Guatemala (Preliminary Objections), 27 Inter-Am.Ct.H.R. (Ser. C), July 2, 1996.

29. The following is the Court's consideration of the preliminary objections presented by Guatemala. The first objection concerns the lack of competence of this Court, on the grounds that the deprivation of liberty to which Mr. Nicholas Chapman Blake was subjected (on March 28, 1985) and his death (on March 29, 1985, according to the death certificate) occurred prior to Guatemala's acceptance of the jurisdiction of this Court (March 9, 1987), with the explicit clarification that such acceptance applied exclusively to events that *"occurred after the date on which the instrument of acceptance was deposited with the Secretariat of the Organization of American States."*

. . . .

33. The Court is of the view that the acts of deprivation of Mr. Blake's liberty and his murder were indeed completed in March, 1985—the murder on March 29 according to the death certificate, as Guatemala maintains—and that those events cannot be considered *per se* to be continuous. The Court therefore lacks competence to rule on the Government's liability. This is the only aspect of the preliminary objection which the Court considers to be well founded.

34. Conversely, since the question is one of forced disappearance, the consequences of those acts extended to June 14, 1992. As the Commission states in its application, government authorities or agents committed subsequent acts, and this, in the Commission's view, implies complicity in, and concealment of, Mr. Blake's arrest and murder. Although the victim's death was known to the authorities or agents, his relatives were not informed despite their unstinting efforts to discover his whereabouts, and because attempts had been made to dispose of the remains. The Commission also claims that there were further violations of the American Convention connected with these events.

35. In the first cases of disappearance of persons submitted to it this Court maintained that:

> . . . [t]he forced disappearance of human beings is a multiple and continuous violation of many rights under the Convention that the States Parties are obligated to respect and guarantee . . . The practice of disappearance, in addition to directly violating many provisions of the Convention, such as those noted above, constitutes a radical breach of the treaty in that it shows a crass abandonment of the values which emanate from the concept of human dignity and of the most basic principles of the inter-American system and the Convention. The existence of this practice, moreover, evinces a disregard of the duty to organize the State is such a manner a to guarantee the rights recognized in the Convention (*Velásquez Rodríguez Case*, Judgment of July 29, 1988. Series C No. 4, paras. 155 and 158, and *Godínez Cruz Case*, Judgment of January 20, 1989. Series C No. 5, paras. 163 and 166).

36. There is no treaty in force containing a legal definition of forced disappearance of persons which is applicable to the States Parties to the Convention. However, note should be taken of the texts of two instruments, the United Nations Declaration on the Protection of All Persons from Enforced Disappearance, of December 18, 1992, and the Inter-American Convention on Forced Disappearance of Persons, of June 9, 1994. Although the latter has not yet entered into force for Guatemala,

these instruments embody several principles of international law on the subject and they may be invoked pursuant to Article 29(d) of the American Convention. In the terms of that article, no provision of this Convention shall be interpreted as *"excluding or limiting the effects that the American Declaration of the Rights and Duties of Man and other international acts of the same nature may have."*

37. Article 17(1) of the United Nations Declaration states that:

> Acts constituting enforced disappearance shall be considered a continuing offense as long as its perpetrators continue to conceal the fate and the whereabouts of persons who have disappeared and as long as these facts remain unclarified.

Article III of the aforementioned Inter-American Convention provides that:

> The States Parties undertake to adopt, in accordance with their constitutional procedures, the legislative measures that may be needed to define the forced disappearance of persons as an offense and to impose an appropriate punishment commensurate with its extreme gravity. This offense shall be deemed continuous or permanent as long as the fate or whereabouts of the victim has not been determined.

38. In addition, in Guatemala's domestic legislation, Article 201 TER of the Penal Code—amending decree No. 33-96 of the Congress of the Republic approved on May 22, 1996—stipulates in the pertinent part that the crime of forced disappearance *"shall be deemed to be continuing until such time as the victim is freed."*

39. The foregoing means that, in accordance with the aforementioned principles of international law which are also embodied in Guatemalan legislation, forced disappearance implies the violation of various human rights recognized in international human rights treaties, including the American Convention, and that the effects of such infringements—even though some may have been completed, as in the instant case—may be prolonged continuously or permanently until such time as the victim's fate or whereabouts are established.

40. In the light of the above, as Mr. Blake's fate or whereabouts were not known to his family until June 14, 1992, that is, after the date on which Guatemala accepted the contentious jurisdiction of this Court, the preliminary objection raised by the Government must be deemed to be without merit insofar as it relates to effects and actions subsequent to its acceptance. The Court is therefore competent to examine the possible violations which the Commission imputes to the Government in connection with those effects and actions.

C. Incompatible, Manifestly Ill-Founded, or Abuse of the Right of Petition

In the European system, an application must be considered inadmissible if it is "incompatible with the provisions of the . . . Convention or the protocols thereto, manifestly ill-founded, or an abuse of the right of application." ECHR, Art. 35(3). The requirement that an application not be "manifestly ill-founded" calls for a determination whether the application states a *prima facie* case. Thus, the Court often rejects applications as manifestly ill-founded after concluding that the application does not appear to show a violation of the Convention. In early cases, the Commission arrived at its conclusion after a rather extensive analysis of the merits of the case. *See Iverson v. Norway*, Application No. 146/8/62, 6 Y.B. 278 (1963). Later, the Commission became more likely to hold these cases admissible.

Thus, in *Air Canada v. United Kingdom*, Application No. 18465/91, Decision of April 1, 1993, 14 Hum. Rts. L.J. 226 (1993), the Commission held that because the complaint raised "serious questions of fact and law . . . which can only be resolved by an examination of the merits," the case "cannot . . . be declared manifestly ill-founded within the meaning of Article [35], para. 2 of the Convention." *Id.*, at 228.

"Abuse of the right of application" refers to conduct such as knowingly making false or groundless allegations, repeatedly using abusive and defamatory language about the respondent government, or intentionally breaching the rule of confidentiality applicable to the proceedings. Political motivation is not abusive so long as there is evidence to support the allegations. *See: McFeeley v. United Kingdom*, App. No. 8317/78, 3 EHRR 161 (1981); *Akdivar v. Turkey*, App. No. 21893/93, 23 EHRR 143 (1997).

X. v. Iceland (admissibility dec.), (App. no. 2525/65), Eur. Comm. H.R., 6 February 1967, Coll. Dec. Vol. 22, pp. 33–34.

THE FACTS

The Applicant is an Icelandic citizen, born in 1919 and at present living in Reykjavik.

He states that, in accordance with the custom in Iceland, he was baptised when he was only a few weeks old. This implied, in his submission, that the clergyman, the witnesses and his parents concluded on his behalf "a baptismal covenant with Jehovah in Heaven". Later, he was also confirmed and on that occasion he had to confess his belief in Jehovah.

He states that he is no longer prepared to "abide by the baptismal covenant" forced upon him as a child and he has, therefore, tried to have his baptism annulled.

For this purpose, he instituted proceedings against the Bishop of Iceland before the Town Court of Reykjavik, but his claim was dismissed by the Court. This decision was subsequently upheld by the Supreme Court. He states that, according to Articles 9 and 10 of the Convention, he has the right to profess his "own beliefs, convictions and thoughts" and he asks for "a binding decision that my baptism and confirmation are annulled, making it clear that this be a full cancellation of the promise I was forced to make at my baptism and subsequent confirmation".

As his appeals to the Icelandic courts have been unsuccessful he also considers that he has not had an effective remedy according to Article 13 of the Convention.

THE LAW

Whereas an examination of the case as it has been submitted, including an examination made ex officio, does not disclose any appearance of a violation of the rights and freedoms set forth in the Convention and in particular in Articles 9, 10 and 13; whereas it follows that the Application is manifestly ill-founded within the meaning of Article 27, paragraph (2) (Art. 27–2), of the Convention.

Now therefore the Commission declares this Application INADMISSIBLE.

Drozd v. Poland, (App. no. 25403/94), Eur. Comm. H.R., Decision of 5 March 1996.

[The applicant complained of violations of Articles 3, 4(1), 5(1), 5(3), 5(4), 6(1), 6(3), 7(1), 8, 11 and 14]

PROCEEDINGS BEFORE THE COMMISSION

The application was introduced on 3 February 1994 and registered on 10 October 1994. The applicant was informed in the registration letter that the proceedings of the Commission are confidential and the contents of case-file, including the observations of the parties and correspondence, must not be made public.

On 6 April 1995 the Commission decided to communicate the application to the respondent Government for observations on the admissibility and merits.

By letter of 8 November 1995 the Government expressed their concern about the publicity in the Polish media concerning the applicant's case before the Commission. In particular, in a November issue of the newspaper "Smiechu Warte" a copy of the Commission's letter of 7 August 1995 to the applicant was published. This letter informed the applicant that the request of the Government for an extension of the time-limit for the submission of the observations had not been granted. In a neighbouring column a critical comment about the case was published, signed by L. B., a candidate in the presidential election. Both L.B. and the applicant are on the editorial board of the newspaper. In his comment L.B. strongly criticised the Government for having failed to submit the observations in time and called the public servants representing the Government in the proceedings before the Commission "uneducated and corrupt". The Government stated that the applicant must have been directly and deliberately involved in publishing the letter as he was on the editorial board. The Government further drew the Commission's attention to the fact that the newspaper concerned disseminates extremist anti-semitic views. They stated that the article in question created an imbalance in informing the general public of the case before the Commission. This breach of confidentiality was even more aggravated by its political context, namely the fact that it had been committed during the presidential campaign and used for the purposes of that campaign. It could seriously jeopardise the credibility of the Convention system in Poland. The Government requested that the Commission should reject the application on the ground of abuse of the right of petition within the meaning of Article 27 para. 2 of the Convention.

On 20 November 1995 the Government submitted their observations.

By letter of 22 November 1995 the applicant was requested to comment on the confidentiality issue before 30 November 1995.

By letter of 27 November 1995 the Government further informed the Secretariat that in May 1995 the publication "Forum against Corruption" published a letter of 10 April 1995 from the Secretariat of the Commission in which the applicant was informed of the Commission's decision to communicate the case to the Government. The Government pointed out that the responsibility of the applicant for publication of this letter was well established as the applicant was on the editorial board of the newspaper. The Government reiterated their deep concern about the publication of the Secretariat's two letters in newspapers and leaflets of wide distribution and about abusing the applicant's case for political purposes in the course of the presidential campaign. They indicated that in comments to the letters their authors resorted to insulting statements against the Government and accused the civil servants responsible for dealing with the applications to the Commission of corruption and incompetence.

By letter of 30 November 1995 the applicant replied that the Commission's letter of 7 August 1995 could have been published as it only concerned the proceedings before the Commission and not the merits of the case. He submitted that it had not been stated in this letter that it was confidential. He further submitted that there was a bill being discussed in the Polish Parliament with the alleged purpose of limiting the right of individual petition. He made general allegations about violations of human rights in Poland by the State.

On 10 January 1996 the applicant submitted his observations in reply.

REASONS FOR THE DECISION

In view of the information provided in the Government's letters of 8 November 1995 and 27 November 1995 and the applicant's letter of 30 November 1995, the Commission finds it necessary to consider whether it is justified to continue the examination of the present application within the meaning of Article 30 para. 1 of the Convention. . . .

The Commission notes that the applicant made public confidential information concerning the proceedings before the Commission. In particular the applicant disclosed the Commission's decision to communicate the case to the respondent Government by quoting in extensor the Commission's letter informing him thereof on a strictly confidential basis. He further published the letter in which an extension of the time-limit for submission of the observations by the Government had been refused and criticised the delays in the proceedings on the part of the Government. The applicant must have been aware of the confidentiality of the proceedings as he had been informed thereof.

The Commission considers that the parties are obliged to respect the confidentiality of its proceedings. In this respect, the Commission refers to Article 33 of the Convention which provides that the "Commission shall meet in camera" and to Rule 47 of its Rules of Procedure. In the present case, the applicant's responsibility for disclosure of confidential information concerning the proceedings before the Commission has been established as the applicant is on the editorial boards of both newspapers concerned. The Commission finds that the applicant's conduct constitutes a serious breach of confidentiality. The explanations given by the applicant do not disclose any circumstances which could justify his conduct.

In these circumstances, the Commission considers that it is no longer justified to continue the examination of the application within the meaning of Article 30 para. 1 (c) of the Convention (c.f., mutatis mutandis, No. 20915/92, Comm. Report 3.3.95, D.R. 80-A, p. 74).

Moreover, as regards the issues raised in the present case, the Commission finds no reasons of a general character affecting respect for human rights, as defined in the Convention, which require the further examination of the application by virtue of Article 30 para. 1 in fine of the Convention.

In view thereof, the Commission finds that it is not necessary to consider whether the facts of the case amount to an abuse of the right of petition within the meaning of Article 27 para. 2 of the Convention.

Ilesanmi v. Nigeria, (Comm. 268/2003), *18th Annual Activity Report of the Afr. Comm. H.P.R. 2004–2005*, Annex III, p. 22.

Summary of Facts

1. The Complainant is an individual, a consultant with the Economic Help Project based in Abuja, Nigeria.

2. The Complaint was received at the Secretariat of the African Commission on 3 April 2002 and is against the Federal Republic of Nigeria which is a party to the African Charter on Human and Peoples' Rights.

3. The Complainant states that in 1999, he exposed the smuggling activities of several companies and individuals, and officials of the Customs and Excise, Police and various other officials to President Obasanjo of Nigeria and the Inspector General of Police.

4. The Complainant states that the smuggling activities include: smuggling of narcotics and their modified forms, minerals, illegal arms, carcinogen bearing foods, expired, fake and counterfeit pharmaceuticals, tyres, textiles, steel products, electronic, electrical products, spare parts, foods, cars and other products.

5. The Complainant also claims that the smugglers are responsible for the assassinations of several persons including Chief Bola Ige, Nigeria's Attorney General and the Confidential Secretary to the Chief Justice of Nigeria.

6. The Complainant alleges that the activities of the smuggling syndicate have resulted into the shutting down of 41 textile mills, 8 auto assembly and other manufacturing plants, resulting into the dismissal of millions of workers and thereby impoverishing them. The smuggling activities have also resulted into the deaths of many people as a result of use of fake or expired drugs.

7. Through their smuggling activities the said smugglers he claims deprive Nigeria of about 101 trillion Naira, annually.

8. As a result of his actions to expose the smuggling syndicate, the Complainant claims that his pregnant wife was assassinated on July 8, 1999. Furthermore, he was abducted and imprisoned and held at SCID, Panti, Yaba, Lagos under inhuman conditions between 31 August and 4 September 1999.

9. The Complainant also claims that whilst in detention he was served with poisoned food by Inspector Okoye under the order of CSP Bose Dawodu, who both demanded for 10,000 Naira for bail.

10. The Complainant further alleges that between 21 and 23 June 2000 he was abducted again by Police Commissioner Aniniru, Sergeant Joseph Akinola and Inspector Paul Ajayi of FCIBs who he claims were acting on behalf of the smugglers.

He was imprisoned at the Divisional Police Headquarters in Lagos, Nigeria where he was denied water and food.

Complaint

11. The Complainant alleges that the following Articles of the African Charter have been violated: Articles 2, 3, 4, 5, 12, 15, 20, 21, 27, 29.

[. . . .]

LAW

[. . . .]

36. In the present communication, the complainant submits that he has complied with Article 56 of the African Charter that prescribes conditions dealing with admissibility. The Responding State however argues that the complaint does not meet two of the conditions set out in Article 56 of the African Charter, namely Article 56(3) and Article 56(5). . . .

38. The author submitted in his complaint that the police and customs officials are corrupt, that they deal with drug smugglers, that they extort money from motorists and added that the President himself was corrupt and had been bribed by the drug smugglers. The Respondent State claims such language is insulting to the institutions of the State including the presidency and provocative, and questions whether the African Commission would allow itself to be used by authors like this to use "unbecoming language to unjustly and baselessly vilify leaders"?

39. The operative words in sub paragraph 3 in Article 56 are "disparaging" and "insulting" and these words must be directed against the State Party concerned or its institutions or the African Union. According to the Oxford Advanced Dictionary, disparaging means to speak slightingly of . . . or to belittle and insulting means to abuse scornfully or to offend the self respect or modesty of. . . . The language must be aimed at undermining the integrity and status of the institution and bring it into disrepute.

40. To say an institution or person is corrupt or that he/she has received bribes from drug dealers, every reasonable person would lose respect for that institution or person. In an open and democratic society individuals must be allowed to express their views freely. However, in expressing these views due regard should be taken not to injure the reputation of others or impair the enjoyment of the rights of others. While the Commission strives to protect the rights of individuals it must strike a balance to ensure that those institutions established within States Parties to facilitate the enjoyment of these rights are also respected by the individuals. To expose vital state institutions to insults and disparaging comments like those expressed in the communication brings the institution to disrepute and renders its effectiveness wanting. In the light of the above, the African Commission finds that the language used in the communication as intended to bring the institution of the president into ridicule and disrepute and thus insulting.

41. The Respondent State also argues that the complainant has not exhausted local remedies as required under Article 56 (5) of the African Charter. The State submits that apart from not seizing the local courts, the complainant has not indicated that it brought the complaint to the National Human Rights Commission or to the

Independent Corruption Practices Commission. Article 56 (5) provides that communications relating to human and peoples' rights referred to in Article 55 received by the Commission shall be considered if they" . . . are sent after exhausting local remedies, if any unless it is obvious that this procedure is unduly prolonged". . . .

43. Regarding the non-exhaustion of legal remedies the complainant simply states that he has exhausted "local, legislative and logical remedies" without informing the African Commission how. The only time he mentioned having gone to court is when he said his wife was killed and the case was adjourned several times. The Respondent State argues that the matters raised in the communication have never been brought before the local courts.

[. . . .]

47. In the present communication, the complainant has failed to demonstrate that he attempted local remedies or that he was prevented from doing so by the Respondent State or that the local remedies are not available or are ineffective or have been unduly prolonged. The exceptions under Article 56(5) can therefore not apply to this communication.

For the above reasons, the African Commission declared the communication inadmissible.

Questions and Comments

1. On what basis was the *Iiesanmi* complaint declared inadmissible? Is it possible to accuse a government official of corruption or human rights violations without being insulting? For a case in the European system declaring inadmissible a petition containing insulting personal attacks on the government's representative, after the Section Registrar warned the applicant and asked him to withdraw the abusive language, see *Di Salvo v. Italy*, App. No. 16098/05, decision of January 11, 2007.
2. What is the meaning of "manifestly ill-founded"? Is there any objective test for this criterion or is it a matter of subjective judgment?
3. Is dismissal of a complaint for breach of the rules of confidentiality an appropriate sanction or is it too harsh? What other matters might constitution an "abuse of the right of petition"?

D. Exhaustion of Domestic Remedies

All international human rights proceedings require exhaustion of local remedies before a complaint will be deemed admissible. In the European system, Article 35(1) of the Convention provides that "the Court may only deal with the matter after all domestic remedies have been exhausted, according to the generally recognized rules of international law, and within a period of six months from the date on which the final decision was taken." This language does not distinguish between private and inter-state applications; to be admissible, both types of application must comply with the requirement for the exhaustion of domestic remedies. *Ireland v. United Kingdom*, Judgment of January 18, 1978, 25 Publ. Eu. Court H.R. 5, 64 (1978).

The European Court insists on the primary role of national institutions and the subsidiary functions of the European Court,[40] and has explained that "the rule of exhaustion of domestic remedies . . . dispenses States from answering before an international body for their acts before they have had an opportunity to put matters right through their own legal system . . . ". *De Wilde, Ooms and Versyp Cases*, Judgment of June 18, 1971, 12 Publ. Eur. Court H.R. 12, 29 (1971). An application will, therefore, be dismissed for failure to exhaust domestic remedies when it appears that relevant issues were not brought to the attention of national bodies which could have resolved the matter.

International law on this subject, followed in all three regional systems, indicates that remedies which are not effective or are unduly prolonged need not be exhausted. The remedies which must be exhausted are those that are available and sufficient. A remedy is "sufficient" if it is capable of redressing the wrong complained of. *Stögmüller Case*, Judgment of November 10, 1969, 12 Y.B. 364 (1969). The failure of a petitioner to resort to a domestic remedy, which previously has proven consistently unsuccessful, will not result in the rejection of the petition. Neither will the failure to file an appeal against a law that prior judgments suggest will be upheld; this is so even in countries where the courts are free to depart from such precedents. *Sigurjonsson v. Ireland*, Application No. 16130/90, Eur. Comm. H.R., decision of July 10, 1991, 12 Hum Rts L.J. 402 (1991). However, if the domestic law on the subject is open to conflicting interpretations, a reasonable effort to exhaust potential remedies must be made.

The domestic remedies requirement may be waived by the respondent State because it is deemed to be procedural and not jurisdictional in nature. The waiver may be express, but also may be implied, for example, when the respondent state fails to raise the issue in a timely manner and is thereafter estopped.

An important issue relating to exhaustion of domestic remedies concerns the burden of proof. All the systems require that information about exhaustion of local remedies be included in the application. If it appears that the applicant has not exhausted available domestic remedies, the application will be rejected summarily. As the cases below indicate, when the complaint has not been rejected at the preliminary stage and the state pleads the non-exhaustion of domestic remedies, the three systems place the burden of proof on the state to demonstrate the existence of an effective and accessible remedy capable of providing redress to the applicant. Once this burden has been satisfied, it falls to the applicant to establish that the remedy was in fact exhausted or was for some reason inadequate or ineffective in the particular circumstances of the case or that there existed "special circumstances" absolving the applicant from the requirement. Such circumstances may include the inaction of national authorities in the face of serious allegations of misconduct or infliction of harm by state agents, for example where they have failed to investigate or offer assistance.

---

[40] *Akdivar and others v. Turkey*, Judgment of September 16, 1996, Reports 1996-IV, 1192 at 1210 (referring to the requirement of exhaustion of local remedies as a reflection of the subsidiary role of international institutions).

i. The Substance and Purpose of the Rule

Van Oosterwijck v. Belgium, (App. No. 7654/76), Judgment of 6 November 1980, Eur. Ct. H.R., 3 EHRR 557 (1981).

[. . . .]

22. In his application of 1 September 1976 to the Commission, D. Van Oosterwijck invoked

- Article 3 of the Convention (art. 3), on the ground that his situation was one of "civil death" and was inhuman and degrading;
- Article 8 (art. 8), in that the application of the law obliged him to use documents which did not reflect his real identity;
- Article 12 (art. 12), since, by maintaining a distortion between his legal being and his physical being, the contested court decisions prevented his marrying and founding a family.

[. . . .]

24. At the hearings of 24 April 1980, the government invited the Court

as [their] main submission, . . . to hold that, for failure to exhaust domestic remedies, the application is not admissible, or, in the alternative, to hold that the complaint is not well-founded and that it has not been shown that Belgium has violated the . . . Convention. . . .

AS TO THE LAW

THE PLEA OF NON-EXHAUSTION OF DOMESTIC REMEDIES

27. The only remedies which Article 26 of the Convention requires to be exercised are those that relate to the breaches alleged and at the same time are available and sufficient (see the *Deweer* judgment of 27 February 1980, Series A no. 35, p. 16, par. 29). In order to determine whether a remedy satisfies these various conditions and is on that account to be regarded as likely to provide redress for the complaints of the person concerned, the Court does not have to assess whether those complaints are well-founded: it must assume this to be so, but on a strictly provisional basis and purely as a working hypothesis (see the arbitration award of 9 May 1934 in the matter of the *"Finnish ships"*, United Nations Collection of Arbitration Awards, Vol. III, pp. 1503–1504, also cited by the Commission in its decision of 17 January 1963 on the admissibility of application no. 1661/62, *X and Y v. Belgium*, Yearbook of the Convention, vol. 6, p. 366).

It has to be ascertained, in the light of these principles, whether any one or more of the remedies listed by the Government is or are relevant for the purposes of Article 26 and, if so, whether any special grounds nevertheless dispensed D. Van Oosterwijck from having recourse thereto.

1. Whether there existed any remedies which ought in principle to have been exercised
. . . .

a) Application for authorisation to change forenames

28. In its admissibility decision of 9 May 1978, the Commission did not deal with the submissions which the Government had based on the Act of 2 July 1974. After

rejecting the arguments relating to the possibility of appealing to the Court of Cassation and of pleading the Convention before the Belgian courts, the Commission concluded:

> It has not been asserted that the applicant had other means of putting an end to the state of affairs he complains of." The said Act was considered by the Commission solely in its opinion of 1 March 1979 of the merits of the case.

29. The breaches alleged by D. Van Oosterwijck consist of failures to observe the prohibition on inhuman and degrading treatment (Article 3), the right to respect for private life (Article 8) and the right to marry and to found a family (Article 12). His contention was that these breaches stemmed from legislation and judicial decisions which, by attributing a "defintive scientific value" to the entries on a birth certificate, placed him in an intolerable legal and administrative situation.

Had the applicant successfully applied after the entry into force of the Act of 2 July 1974 for authorisation to change his forenames, third parties would admittedly have had far fewer opportunities of noticing the difference between his appearance and his civil status.

However, he would not really have solved his problems in the manner claimed by the Government: he would have succeeded only in eliminating some of the consequences of the wrong of which he complained but not in eradicating either its cause, namely the respondent State's non-recognition of his sexual identity, or its social consequences. The Court concurs with the applicant and the Commission's Delegates on this point.

(b) Appeal to the Court of Cassation and reliance on the Convention

30. In the Government's submission, D. Van Oosterwijck should have appealed on a point of law to the Court of Cassation to have the judgment of 7 May 1974 reversed, in particular because too narrow a scope had been given to the concept of error warranting rectification, this being a question of law which had not as yet been decided by the Court of Cassation and which was the subject of conflicting authority at the level of the lower courts. The non-exhaustion of remedies was also said to result from the fact that neither at first instance nor on appeal did the applicant plead the Convention, even in substance.

31. This line of argument, which was contested by the applicant, did not find favour with the Commission for the following reasons. The Brussels Court of Appeal based its decision on findings of fact not subject to review by the Court of Cassation and it had not been contended that the Court of Appeal had acted contrary to the applicable Belgian law; a further appeal on a point of law would thus have had no real likelihood of success. In addition, both the appeal made on 14 February 1974 and the submissions presented by the ministère public showed that D. Van Oosterwijck did prosecute in Belgium the complaints he subsequently brought before the Commission. He did not, it is true, seek at that stage to base his complaints on the Convention, but no blame could be attached to him for that since the relevant clauses in the Convention were not "sufficiently precise in character to be considered as conflicting with the rules of the . . . Civil Code or Judicial Code, whose immediate purpose (was) a very different one"; had the Belgian courts nonetheless found in-

compatibility with Article 8, they could not have gone so far as simply to set aside the domestic law without thereby "creating an intolerable legal void".

32. The Court observes that the judgment of 7 May 1974 was grounded not only on points of fact but also, as a separate matter, on points of law: in the judgment, the Court of Appeal stated

- that the birth certificate "in principle settles defintively" the person's sex, this being "a component of [his or her] status";
- in substance, that rectification of the certificate presupposed the presence of an error committed when the certificate was drawn up;
- that "there is no provision in current legislation that allows account to be taken of artificial changes to an individual's anatomy, even if they correspond to his deep-seated psychical tendencies."

It should also be noted that when construing the same texts other Belgian courts had arrived at divergent conclusions.

The Court of Cassation, while not taking cognisance of the actual merits of a case (Article 95 of the Constitution), does have jurisdiction to state the law and thereby set the course for subsequent judicial decisions. There is thus nothing to show that an appeal to the Court of Cassation on grounds of the national legislation stricto sensu would have been obviously futile.

33. As far as the application lodged with the Commission is concerned, its sole legal basis is provided by the Convention. However, D. Van Oosterwijck did not plead the Convention at first instance or on appeal, neither, did he appeal further to the Court of Cassation. Yet the Convention forms an integral part of the Belgian legal system in which it has primacy over domestic legislation, whether earlier or subsequent .... The applicant could thus have relied on Article 8 in his own country and argued that it had been violated in his respect.

The Court rejects the objection that in this context the Convention lacks the precision required for the exercise of an effective domestic remedy. The wording of Article 8 appeared sufficiently clear to the Commission for it to uphold in large measure the arguments put to it by D. Van Oosterwijck—arguments that the Court must deem correct for the purposes of Articles 26. It is impossible to discern what might have prevented the applicant from making the same submissions before the Belgian courts and those courts from reaching the same conclusion and even from determining what was required as a consequence in order to give effect the right being claimed.

Undoubtedly, in domestic proceedings the Convention as a general rule furnishes a supplementary ground of argument, to be prayed in aid if judged suitable for achieving an objective which is in principle rendered possible by other legal arguments (see the Commission's decision of 11 January 1961 on the admissibility of application no. 788/60, *Austria v. Italy*, Yearbook of the Convention, vol. 4, pp. 166–176). In certain circumstances it may nonetheless happen that express reliance on the Convention before the national authorities constitutes the sole appropriate manner of raising before those authorities first, as is required by Article 26, an issue intended if need be, to be brought subsequently before the European review bodies (decision of the Commission, 18 December 1963, on the admissibility of application no. 1488/62, *X v. Belgium*, Collection of Decisions, no. 13, pp. 93–98).

34. Whether or not that be the position in the present case, in his own country D. Van Oosterwijck did not even plead in substance the complaints he later made in Strasbourg; before the Belgian courts he relied neither on the Convention nor on any other plea to the same or like effect (see the above-mentioned decision on the admissibility of application no. 1661/62, p. 367; the Commission's decision of 28 May 1971 on the admissibility of application no. 4464/70, *National Union of Belgian Police*, Series B no. 17, p. 79).

He thereby denied the Belgian courts precisely that opportunity which the rule of exhaustion is designed in principle to afford to States, namely the opportunity to put right the violations alleged against them (see *De Wilde, Ooms and Versyp* judgment, p. 29, par. 50; the *Airey* judgment of 9 October 1979, Ser. A no. 32, p. 10 par. 18).

(c) Action d'état (action pertaining to personal status)

35. There is a connection between the above reasoning and the observations prompted by the fourth and final limb of the Government's preliminary objection.

In Belgian academic writings, legislation and judicial practice a distinction is drawn between actions d'état and actions for rectification. The former deal with issues of substance in that their purpose is to establish, modify or extinguish personal status.

The latter are brought solely in order to make good any error or omission appearing in the documents serving as proof of status. Some appreciable, consequences in law, which are set forth in the Judicial Code (Articles 92 par. 1, 569 and 764), flow from this difference in the nature of the two actions.

An action d'état would have allowed the applicant not only to plead the Convention but also to procure a prior adjudication by the courts of his own country on the issue he raised before the Commission and thereafter before the Court, and to set this issue in its proper dimensions from the very outset, It is for those courts to determine, should the occasion arise, whether the action d'état is still available to the applicant.

However, in the absence of any decided cases in Belgium on this point, no blame can be attached to D. Van Oosterwijck for having omitted up till now to bring such an action. The rule of exhaustion of domestic remedies is neither absolute nor capable of being applied automatically; in reviewing whether the rule has been observed, it is essential to have regard to the particular circumstances of the individual case (compare the *Stogmuller* judgment of 10 November 1969, Series A no. 9, p. 42, par. 11; the *Ringeisen* judgment of 16 July 1971, Series A no. 13, pp. 37–38, par. 89 and 92; the above-mentioned *Deweer* judgment, p. 17, par. 29 in fine).

2. Whether there existed any special grounds capable of dispensing the applicant form exercising the remedies taken into consideration by the Court

36. It remains to be ascertained, in the light of the "generally recognised rules of international law" to which Article 26 refers, whether there were any special

grounds dispensing the applicant from utilising one of the means of redress taken into consideration above.

37. D. Van Oosterwijck asserted that he decided not to appeal on a point of law to the Court of Cassation only after he had consulted "a number of qualified persons"; he stated that they were "unanimous" in dissuading him from "taking such a step" which they considered pointless since in their view the judgment of 7 May 1974 was neither contrary to the law [nor] vitiated by procedural irregularity (Article 608 of the Judicial Code). Mr. Ansiaux, a lawyer practising before the Court of Cassation, gave similar advice on 20 september 1976 and in 1977—that is, after the expiry of the statutory time-limit of three months (Article 1073 of the Judicial Code) and after the reference of the matter to the Commission (1 September 1976).

The Court does not consider that a negative opinion of this kind can of itself justify or excuse failure to exercise a remedy (see, for example, the Commission's final decision of 5 April 1968 on the admissibility of application no. 2257/64, *Graf Soltikow v. the Federal Republic of Germany*, Yearbook of the Convention, vol. 11, p. 224): at the very most, such an opinion may tend, when combined with other factors, to show that the remedy in question would in all probability be ineffective or inadequate (see the Commission's decision of 12 July 1978 on the admissibility of application no. 7907/77, *Mrs. X v. the United Kingdom*, Decisions and Reports, no. 14, p. 210).

In the present proceedings, the documents in the case-file do not disclose on what precise grounds in law the qualified persons mentioned by the applicant based their opinions. There is no evidence before the Court to show that they dealt with the matter in the light of all relevant aspects, including the Convention. On this point, the Court therefore perceives nothing liable to disturb the conclusion following from paragraphs 32 to 34 above.

38. The applicant also pleaded his financial difficulties but the Court notes, as did the Government, that he has supplied no proof of this and that, besides, he did not seek free legal aid for the purposes of an appeal to the Court of Cassation (see the Commission's decision of 6 March 1957 on the admissibility of application no. 181/56, Yearbook of the Convention, vol. I, p. 140).

39. D. Van Oosterwijck argued finally that the Belgian courts were bound by the principle jura novit curia to apply the Convention even though he had not requested them to do so and that this was the case more especially as the Convention was a matter of public policy (ordre public) in Belgium.

The Court is not persuaded by this argument. The fact that the Belgian courts might have been able, or even obliged, to examine the case of their own motion under the Convention cannot be regarded as having dispensed the applicant from pleading before them the Convention or arguments to the same or like effect (see, mutatis mutandis, the Commission's unpublished decision of 4 September 1958 on the admissibility of application no. 342/57, *X. v. the Federal Republic of Germany*). Whether the obligation laid down by Article 26 (art. 26) has been satisfied has to be determined by reference to the conduct of the victim of the alleged breach. In addition, the manner in which the applicant presented his case to the Brussels Court of

First Instance and Court of Appeal scarcely affored them an opportunity of taking the Convention into account.

40. The issue had, furthermore, never come before the Court of Cassation for decision, with the result that there was not even any case-law which could be regarded as likely to render obviously futile an appeal based on the Convention or on arguments to the same or like effect (see, mutatis mutandis, the above-mentioned *De Wilde, Ooms and Versyp* judgment, p. 34, par. 62).

41. Accordingly, domestic remedies were not exhausted in the instant case.

FOR THESE REASONS, THE COURT

Holds, by thirteen votes to four, that by reason of the failure to exhaust domestic remedies, it is unable to take cognisance of the merits of the case.

Note: In *Cardot v. France*, App. No. 11069/84, dec. of 19 March 1991, 13 EHRR 853 (1991), the Government's main submission was that the applicant had not exhausted domestic remedies as he had failed to raise in the French courts the substance of his complaint. The Delegate of the Commission contended, to the contrary, that Mr. Cardot had satisfied the requirement by appealing on points of law. In claiming that the use of evidence gathered in other proceedings was contrary to the rights of the defence, he had in substance complained of not having had a fair trial; by challenging the reasoning in the judgment, he had implicitly criticised the taking of evidence during his appeal, including the failure to examine witnesses at the hearing. The Court agreed with the government, while accepting that Article 26 must be applied with some degree of flexibility and without excessive formalism. According to the Court, to exhaust local remedies requires

> not merely that applications should be made to the appropriate domestic courts and that use should be made of remedies designed to challenge decisions already given. It normally requires also that the complaints intended to be made subsequently at Strasbourg should have been made to those same courts, at least in substance and in compliance with the formal requirements and time-limits laid down in domestic law . . . and, further, that any procedural means which might prevent a breach of the Convention should have been used.

The Court cited international arbitral practice, especially the award of 6 March 1956 in the *Ambatielos* case, 12 U.N.R.I.A.A 120, 122. Looking at the proceedings in French national courts, the European Court concluded that the applicant did not provide the courts with the opportunity to be afforded to Contracting States of preventing or putting right the violations alleged against them. It therefore accepted that the objection of failure to exhaust domestic remedies was well founded.

Velásquez Rodriguez Case, Judgment of July 29, 1988, 4 Inter-Am. Ct. H.R. |(Ser. C) (1988).

[The petitioners alleged that the government of Honduras was responsible for the 1981 disappearance and torture of Angel Manfredo Velásquez Rodriquez, a university student. The government raised several preliminary objections, among them failure to exhaust local remedies. This issue was joined to the merits and decided in the Court's judgment of July 29, 1988.]

50. The Government raised several preliminary objections that the Court ruled upon in its Judgment of June 26, 1987. There the Court ordered the joining of the merits and the preliminary objection regarding the failure to exhaust domestic remedies, and gave the Government and the Commission another opportunity to "substantiate their contentions" on the matter (*Velásquez Rodriguez Case*, Preliminary Objections, para. 90).

56. The Court will first consider the legal arguments relevant to the question of exhaustion of domestic remedies and then apply them to the case.

57. Article 46(1) of the Convention provides that, in order for a petition or communication lodged with the Commission in accordance with Article 44 or 45 to be admissible, it is necessary that the remedies under domestic law have been pursued and exhausted in accordance with generally recognized principles of international law.

58. The same article, in the second paragraph, provides that this requirement shall not be applicable when

a. the domestic legislation of the state concerned does not afford due process of law for the protection of the right or rights that have allegedly been violated,
b. the party alleging violation of his rights has been denied access to the remedies under domestic law or has been prevented from exhausting them, or
c. there has been unwarranted delay in rendering a final judgment under the aforementioned remedies.

59. In its Judgment of June 26, 1987, the Court decided, inter alia, that "the State claiming non-exhaustion has an obligation to prove that domestic remedies remain to be exhausted and that they are effective" (*Velásquez Rodriguez Case*, Preliminary Objections, para. 88).

60. Concerning the burden of proof, the Court did not go beyond the conclusion cited in the preceding paragraph. The Court now affirms that if a State which alleges non-exhaustion proves the existence of specific domestic remedies that should have been utilized, the opposing party has the burden of showing that those remedies were exhausted or that the case comes within the exceptions of Article 46(2). It must not be rashly presumed that a State Party to the Convention has failed to comply with its obligation to provide effective domestic remedies.

61. The rule of prior exhaustion of domestic remedies allows the State to resolve the problem under its internal law before being confronted with an international proceeding. This is particularly true in the international jurisdiction of human rights, because the latter reinforces or complements the domestic jurisdiction (American Convention, Preamble).

62. It is a legal duty of the States to provide such remedies, as this Court indicated in its Judgment of June 26, 1987, when it stated:

The rule of prior exhaustion of domestic remedies under the international law of human rights has certain implications that are present in the Convention. Under the Convention, States Parties have an obligation to provide effective judicial remedies to victims of human rights violations (Art. 25), remedies that must be substantiated in accordance with the rules of due process of law (Art. 8(1)), all in keeping with the general obligation of such States to guarantee the free and full exercise of the rights recognized by the Convention to all persons subject to their jurisdiction (Art. 1). (*Velásquez Rodriguez Case*, Preliminary Objections, para. 91.)

63. Article 46(1)(a) of the Convention speaks of "generally recognized principles of international law." Those principles refer not only to the formal existence of such remedies, but also to their adequacy and effectiveness, as shown by the exceptions set out in Article 46(2).

64. Adequate domestic remedies are those which are suitable to address an infringement of a legal right. A number of remedies exist in the legal system of every country, but not all are applicable in every circumstance. If a remedy is not adequate in a specific case, it obviously need not be exhausted. A norm is meant to have an effect and should not be interpreted in such a way as to negate its effect or lead to a result that is manifestly absurd or unreasonable. For example, a civil proceeding specifically cited by the Government, such as a declaration of presumptive death based on disappearance, the purpose of which is to allow heirs to dispose of the estate of the person presumed deceased or to allow the spouse to remarry, is not an adequate remedy for finding a person or for obtaining his liberty.

65. Of the remedies cited by the Government, habeas corpus would be the normal means of finding a person presumably detained by the authorities, of ascertaining whether he is legally detained and, given the case, of obtaining his liberty. The other remedies cited by the Government are either for reviewing a decision within an inchoate proceeding (such as those of appeal or cassation) or are addressed to other objectives. If, however, as the Government has stated, the writ of habeas corpus should require the identification of the place of detention and the authority ordering the detention, it would not be adequate for finding a person clandestinely held by State offficials, given that in such cases there is only hearsay evidence of the detention, and the whereabouts of the victim is unknown.

66. A remedy must also be effective—that is, capable of producing the result for which it was designed. Procedural requirements can make the remedy of habeas corpus ineffective, if it is powerless to compel the authorities, if it presents a danger to those who invoke it, or if it is not impartially applied.

67. On the other hand, contrary to the Commission's argument, the mere fact that a domestic remedy does not produce a result favorable to the petitioner does not in and of itself demonstrate the inexistence or exhaustion of all effective domestic remedies. For example, the petitioner may not have invoked the appropriate remedy in a timely fashion.

68. It is a different matter, however, when it is shown that remedies are denied for trivial reasons or without an examination of the merits, or if there is proof of the existence of a practice or policy ordered or tolerated by the government, the effect of which is to impede certain persons from invoking internal remedies that would normally be available to others. In such cases, resort to those remedies becomes a senseless formality. The exceptions of Article 46(2) would be fully applicable in those situations and would discharge the obligation to exhaust internal remedies since they cannot fulfill their objective in that case.

69. In the Government's opinion, a writ of habeas corpus does not exhaust the remedies of the Honduran legal system because there are other remedies, both ordinary and extraordinary, such as appeal, cassation, and extraordinary writ of amparo, as well as the civil remedy of a declaration of presumptive death. In addition, in criminal procedures parties may use whatever evidence they choose. With respect to the cases of disappearances mentioned by the Commission, the Government stated that it had initiated some investigations and had opened others on the basis of complaints, and that the proceedings remain pending until those presumed responsible, either as principals or accomplices, are identified or apprehended.

70. In its conclusions, the Government stated that some writs of habeas corpus were granted from 1981–1984, which would prove that this remedy was not ineffective during that period. It submitted various documents to support its argument.

71. In response, the Commission argued that the practice of disappearances made exhaustion of domestic remedies impossible because such remedies were ineffective in correcting abuses imputed to the authorities or in causing kidnapped persons to reappear.

72. The Commission maintained that, in cases of disappearances, the fact that a writ of habeas corpus or amparo has been brought without success is sufficient to support a finding of exhaustion of domestic remedies as long as the person does not appear, because that is the most appropriate remedy in such a situation. It emphasized that neither writs of habeas corpus nor criminal complaints were effective in the case of Manfredo Velásquez. The Commission maintained that exhaustion should not be understood to require mechanical attempts at formal procedures, but rather to require a case-by-case analysis of the reasonable possibility of obtaining a remedy.

73. The Commission asserted that, because of the structure of the international system for the protection of human rights, the Government bears the burden of proof with the respect to the exhaustion of domestic remedies. The objection of failure to exhaust presupposes the existence of an effective remedy. It stated that a criminal complaint is not an effective means to find a disappeared person, but only serves to establish individual responsibility.

74. The record before the Court shows that the following remedies were pursued on behalf of Manfredo Velásquez:

a. Habeas Corpus

i. Brought by Zenaida Velásquez against the Public Security Forces on September 17, 1981. No result.

ii. Brought by Zenaida Velásquez on February 6, 1982. No result.

iii. Brought by various relatives of disappeared persons on behalf of Manfredo Velásquez and other persons on July 4, 1983. Denied on September 11, 1984.

b. Criminal Complaints

i. Brought by the father and sister of Manfredo Velásquez before the First Criminal Court of Tegucigalpa on November 9, 1982. No result.

ii. Brought by Gertrudis Lanza Gonzalez, joined by Zenaida Velásquez, before the First Criminal Court of Tegucigalpa against various members of the Armed Forces on April 5, 1984. The court dismissed this proceeding and the First Court of Appeals affirmed on January 16, 1986, although it left open the complaint with regard to General Gustavo Alvarez Martinez, who was declared a defendant in absence.

75. Although the Government did not dispute that the above remedies had been brought, it maintained that the Commission should not have found the petition admissible, much less submitted it to the Court, because of the failure to exhaust the remedies provided by Honduran law, given that there are no final decisions in the record that show the contrary. It stated that the first writ of habeas corpus was declared void because the person bringing it did not follow through; regarding the second and third, the Government explained that additional writs cannot be brought on the same subject, the same facts, and based on the same legal provisions. As to the criminal complaints, the Government stated that no evidence had been submitted and, although presumptions had been raised, no proof had been offered. Therefore, that proceeding is still before Honduran courts until those guilty are specifically identified. It stated that one of the proceedings was dismissed for lack of evidence with respect to those accused who appeared before the court, but not with regard to General Alvarez Martinez, who was out of the country. Moreover, the Government maintained that dismissal does not exhaust domestic remedies because the extraordinary remedies of amparo, rehearing and cassation may be invoked and, in the instant case, the statute of limitations has not yet run, so the proceeding is pending.

76. The record contains testimony of members of the Legislative Assembly of Honduras, Honduran lawyers, persons who were at one time disappeared, and relatives of disappeared persons, which purports to show that in the period in which the events took place, the legal remedies in Honduras were ineffective in obtaining the liberty of victims of a practice of enforced or involuntary disappearances (hereinafter "disappearance" or "disappearances"), ordered or tolerated by the Government. The record also contains dozens of newspaper clippings which allude to the same practice. According to that evidence, from 1981 to 1984 more than one hundred persons were illegally detained, many of whom never reappeared and, in general, the legal remedies which the Government claimed were available to the victims were ineffective.

77. That evidence also shows that some persons were captured and detained without due process and subsequently reappeared. However, in some of those cases, the reappearance was not the result of any of the legal remedies which, according to the Government, would have been effective, but rather the result of other circumstances, such as the intervention of diplomatic missions or action taken by human rights organizations.

78. The evidence offered shows that lawyers who filed writs of habeas corpus were intimidated, that those who were responsible for executing the writs were frequently prevented from entering or inspecting the places of detention, and that occasional criminal complaints against military or police officials were ineffective, either because certain procedural steps were not taken or because the complaints were dismissed without further proceedings.

79. The Government had the opportunity to call its own witnesses to refute the evidence presented by the Commission, but failed to do so. Although the Government's attorneys contested some of the points urged by the Commission, they did not offer convincing evidence to support their arguments. The Court summoned as witnesses some members of the armed forces mentioned during the proceeding, but their testimony was insufficient to overcome the weight of the evidence offered by the Commission to show that the judicial and governmental authorities did not act with due diligence in cases of disappearances. The instant case is such an example.

80. The testimony and other evidence received and not refuted lead to the conclusion that, during the period under consideration, although there may have been legal remedies in Honduras that theoretically allowed a person detained by the authorities to be found, those remedies were ineffective in cases of disappearances because the imprisonment was clandestine, formal requirements made them inapplicable in practice, the authorities against whom they were brought simply ignored them, or because attorneys and judges were threatened and intimidated by those authorities.

81. Aside from the question of whether between 1981 and 1984 there was a governmental policy of carrying out or tolerating the disappearance of certain persons, the Commission has shown that although writs of habeas corpus and criminal complaints were filed, they were ineffective or were mere formalities. The evidence offered by the Commission was not refuted and is sufficient to reject the Government's preliminary objection that the case is inadmissible because domestic remedies were not exhausted.

Anuak Justice Council v. Ethiopia, (Comm. 299/05), *20th Annual Activity Report of the Afr. Comm. H.P.R. 2006*, Annex IV, p. 167.

[. . . .]

5. The complainant states that the Anuak are an indigenous minority group living in south-western Gambella region of Ethiopia and that despite their dominance in the region, the Ethiopian government has a long history of marginalizing, excluding and discriminating against them. The complainant claims that due to Gambella's natural resources, the Ethiopian government has resettled over sixty thousand Highlanders, who had almost completely destroyed the Anuak way of life within Gambella.

6. The complainant avers that the Anuak believe that oil in the region should belong to them, while the Federal Government argues that under the federal constitution all mineral resources belong to the Ethiopian State. The complainant adds that the Ethiopian Defence Forces are stationed throughout the Gambella in order to identify and destroy disparate groups of armed Anuak known collectively as 'shifta' that have attacked Highlander civilians.

7. The complainant submits that the December 2003 massacre was sparked by the killing of eight Highlander refugee camp officials and propelled the Ethiopian

Defence Forces into a broad-based assault on Gambella's Anuak community. The complainant states that despite the fact that nobody was immediately found responsible for the death of the eight people, there is no indication that the Ethiopian government had undertaken an official investigation into the ambush of the refugee camp officials thus blaming the Anuak community for the attacks.

8. The complainant avers that the violence in the Gambella region has continued since December 2003 and remains a serious threat to Anuak citizens as well as other ethnic groups in the region. The complainant allege that the Ethiopian Defence Forces search for 'shifta' has become the pretext for bloody and destructive raids on numerous Anuak villages since the December 2003 massacre on the Gambella town. The complainant further allege that unarmed Anuak within Gambella are currently being killed by Ethiopian Defence Forces without due process or the use of judicial proceedings without even making an effort to distinguish Anuak civilians from the 'shifta' they claim to be looking for.

9. The complainant further allege that many Anuak have been detained in prison without charge both in Gambella and Addis Ababa which accounts to about 1000 detained to this day. The complainant also adds that a substantial group of Gambella's educated Anuak have been imprisoned or forced into exile and that many have been charged with offences relating to alleged collaboration with Anuak insurgents and put on trial but none of the leaders are yet to be convicted.

10. The complainant further alleged that in rural areas the Ethiopian military continues to burn homes, destroy crops, burn food stores, disrupt planting cycles, and destroy agricultural equipment of the Anuak to prevent them from sustaining themselves. The complainant asserts that as recently as January 2005, the Ethiopian government threatened Anuak elders in Gambella that anyone attempting to tarnish the reputation of the Ethiopian government over the massacres would be dealt with.

11. The complainant claims that the Ethiopian government's response to the December massacre has been grossly inadequate and disingenuous. The complainant states that the government's initial position that no soldiers had taken part in the massacre had become impossible to defend and adds that the Commission's of Inquiry set up by the Government was biased and ineffectual and did not investigate the behaviour of the Ethiopian Defence Forces as an organization despite numerous reports.

The Complaint

12. The complainant states that crimes against humanity, such as extrajudicial killing, torture, and rape, crimes that take place against the Anuak civilians is in violation of international law as well as a violation of Articles 4, 5, 6, 12, 14 and 18 of the African Charter. The Anuak Justice Council urges the African Commission on Human and Peoples Rights to intervene to prevent further human rights abuses of the Anuak by the Ethiopian government.

13–32. [. . . .]

Complainant's submission on admissibility

33. The complainant submits that article 56(5) of the African Charter requires that complainants exhaust domestic remedies before a case is considered by the African Commission. The complainant notes further that if the potential domestic remedies are unavailable or unduly prolonged, the commission may nevertheless consider a communication, adding that this is especially true when the country against which the complaint is lodged has committed vast and varied scope of violations and the general situation in the country is such that domestic exhaustion would be futile.

34. The complainant argue that in the *Anuak Justice Council Case*, pursuing domestic remedies would be futile due to the lack of an independent and impartial judiciary, a lack of an efficient remedy, the significant likelihood of an unduly prolonged domestic remedy, and most importantly, the potential for violence against the Annuak or those supporting them within the legal system.

35. Anuak Justice Council alleges that it cannot seek exhaustion of domestic remedies because of its inability to receive an independent and fair hearing, as a direct consequence of the fact that the aggressor is the government of Ethiopia. The complainant notes that in spite the protection in Article 78 of the Respondent State's Constitution guaranteeing the independence of the judiciary, it is perceived by individuals both at home and abroad that the Executive has considerable and even undue influence on the judiciary.

36. The complainant quoted a World Bank Report entitled "Ethiopia: Legal and Judicial Sector Assessment" (2004) which concluded that ". . . of the three branches of government, the judiciary has the least history and experience of independence and therefore requires significant strengthening to obtain true independence". According to the complainant, the Report notes that the interference in the judiciary is more flagrant at State level where there are reports of Administrative officers interfering with court decisions, firing judges, dictating decisions to judges, reducing salaries of judges and deliberately refusing to enforce certain decisions of the courts.

37. The complainant also alleges that bringing the case before Ethiopian courts would unduly prolonging the process as the Ethiopian judiciary suffer from a complex system of multiple courts that lack coordination and resources, including "dismal conditions of service, staff shortages, lack of adequate training, debilitating infrastructure and logistical problems". The complainant claims court proceedings take years to yield results, and concluded that the Respondent State's judicial system is so under resourced that prosecutions would be nearly impossible, noting that to date, no action had been taken to prosecute any of the Ethiopian Defence Forces or government officials for the atrocities they committed against the Anuak.

38. The complainant also alleges that the Anuak fear for their safety in bringing the case in Ethiopia adding that there are no Anuak trained as lawyers who could bring the case before Ethiopian courts. The complainant notes that the overwhelming sentiment in the Gambella Region and of the Anuak who have fled the country is that non-Anuak lawyers within Ethiopia would be unwilling to take the case due to the potential persecution they would face, as well as the insurmountable odds

of achieving a just remedy. The complainant added that Anuak who remain in the Gambella Region continue to suffer from extra-judicial executions, torture, rape and arbitrary detention from the authorities of the Respondent State adding that several of them have been threatened and warned specifically against pursuing a case against the Respondent State. The complainant noted that as recently as January 2005, the Respondent State threatened Anuak leaders, declaring that anyone attempting to tarnish the reputation of the Respondent State would be dealt with. The complainant concluded by stating that to bring the case within the Respondent State would only further endanger the lives of the remaining Anuak in the Ethiopia.

39. The complainant added that the Respondent State had been given notice and adequate time to remedy the human rights violations against the Anuak but has utterly failed to do so. That the Respondent State received notice of the violations but chose not to take action to halt the atrocities or to make its forces accountable. The complainant added that the Respondent State's response to the massacres in December 2003 in the Gambella Region was inadequate and disingenuous. That under international pressure, the Respondent State established a Commission of Inquiry to investigate the killings, however, according to the complainant, the inquiry was biased and ineffectual and did not meet international standards of an independent investigation.

Respondent State's submissions of admissibility

40. The Respondent State claims that the cases of those involved in the alleged violations that took place in the Gambella Region are currently pending before the Federal Circuit Court and the respondent, therefore, argued that domestic remedies have not yet been exhausted. The State provided a list of about 9 such cases including their file numbers and previous and future dates of adjournments.

41. The respondent State argues that the rule that local remedies be exhausted is not limited to individuals and also applies to organisations, including those in no way subject to the jurisdiction of the respondent State. According to the respondent, the complainant could have sought redress from the domestic courts, the Judicial Administration Office, the Commission of Inquiry or the Human Rights Commission but did not. The complainant has not, argued the State, shown the existence of any impediment to the use of these remedial processes or that such were unduly long.

42. Without indicating the status of the proceedings, the State argued that all those alleged of [sic] human rights offences associated with the Gambella incident of December 2003 were brought before the Federal Circuit Court. The State indicated that three domestic remedies were available to the complainants—the competent Courts, the Judicial Administration Officer and the Human Rights Commission but the complainants failed to approach any of them.

. . . .

The Law

Admissibility

44. The current communication is submitted pursuant to Article 55 of the African Charter which allows the African Commission to receive and consider commu-

nications, other than from States Parties. Article 56 of the African Charter provides that the admissibility of a communication submitted pursuant to Article 55 is subject to seven conditions. The African Commission has stressed that the conditions laid down in Article 56 are conjunctive, meaning that if any one of them is absent, the communication will be declared inadmissible.

45. The complainant in the present communication argued that it has satisfied the admissibility conditions set out in Article 56 of the Charter and as such, the communication should be declared admissible. The Respondent State on the other hand submitted that the communication should be declared inadmissible because, according to the State, the complainant has not complied with Article 56(5) of the African Charter. As there seems to be agreement by both parties as to the fulfillment of the other requirements under Article 56, this Commission will not make any pronouncements thereof.

46. Article 56(5) of the African Charter provides that communications relating to human and peoples' rights shall be considered if they: "[a]re sent after exhausting local remedies, if any, unless it is obvious that this procedure is unduly prolonged".

47. Human rights law regards it as supremely important for a person whose rights have been violated to make use of domestic remedies to right the wrong, rather than address the issue to an international tribunal. The rule is founded on the premise that the full and effective implementation of international obligations in the field of human rights is designed to enhance the enjoyment of human rights and fundamental freedoms at the national level. In *Free Legal Assistance Group v. Zaire* and *Rencontre Africaine pour la Défense de Droits de l'Homme [RADDHO] v. Zambia*, this Commission held that "a government should have notice of a human rights violation in order to have the opportunity to remedy such violations before being called before an international body."[41] Such an opportunity will enable the accused state to save its reputation, which would be inevitably tarnished if it were brought before an international jurisdiction.

48. The rule also reinforces the subsidiary and complementary relationship of the international system to systems of internal protection. To the extent possible, an international tribunal, including this Commission, should be prevented from playing the role of a court of first instance, a role that it cannot under any circumstances arrogate to itself. Access to an international organ should be available, but only as a last resort—after the domestic remedies have been exhausted and have failed. Moreover, local remedies are normally quicker, cheaper, and more effective than international ones. They can be more effective in the sense that an appellate court can reverse the decision of a lower court, whereas the decision of an international organ does not have that effect, although it will engage the international responsibility of the state concerned.

49. The African Charter states that this African Commission shall consider a communication after the applicant has exhausted local remedies, "*if any, unless it is obvious that this procedure is unduly prolonged*." The Charter thus recognizes that, though the requirement of exhaustion of local remedies is a conventional provision, it should not constitute an unjustifiable impediment to access to international

---

41   See Comm. Nos. 25/89, 47/90, 56/91, 100/93, para. 36, 1995 and Comm. No. 71/92, para. 11.

remedies. This Commission has also held that Article 56(5) "must be applied con-comitantly with article 7, which establishes and protects the right to fair trial."[42] In interpreting the rule, the Commission appears to take into consideration the circumstances of each case, including the general context in which the formal rem-edies operate and the personal circumstances of the applicant. Its interpretation of the local remedies criteria can therefore not be understood without some knowl-edge of that general context.

50. A local remedy has been defined as "any domestic legal action that may lead to the resolution of the complaint at the local or national level."[43] The Rules of Pro-cedure of the African Commission provide that "[t]he Commission shall determine questions of admissibility pursuant to Article 56 of the Charter."[44] Generally, the rules require applicants to set out in their applications the steps taken to exhaust domestic remedies. They must provide some *prima facie* evidence of an attempt to exhaust local remedies.[45] According to the Commission's guidelines on the sub-mission of communications, applicants are expected to indicate, for instance, the courts where they sought domestic remedies. Applicants must indicate that they have had recourse to all domestic remedies to no avail and must supply evidence to that effect. If they were unable to use such remedies, they must explain why. They could do so by submitting evidence derived from analogous situations or testifying to a state policy of denying such recourse.

51. In the jurisprudence of this Commission, three major criteria could be de-duced in determining the rule on the exhaustion of local remedies, namely: that the remedy must be available, effective and sufficient."[46] According to this Commis-sion, a remedy is considered to be available if the petitioner can pursue it without impediments[47] or if he can make use of it in the circumstances of his case.[48] The word "available" means "readily obtainable; accessible"; or "attainable, reachable; on call, on hand, ready, present; . . . convenient, at one's service, at one's command, at one's disposal, at one's beck and call."[49] In other words, "remedies, the availabil-ity of which is not evident, cannot be invoked by the State to the detriment of the complainant".[50]

52. A remedy will be deemed to be effective if it offers a prospect of success.[51] If its success is not sufficiently certain, it will not meet the requirements of availability and effectiveness. The word "effective" has been defined to mean "adequate to ac-complish a purpose; producing the intended or expected result," or "functioning, useful, serviceable, operative, in order; practical, current, actual, real, valid."[52] Lastly, a remedy will be found to be sufficient if it is capable of redressing the complaint.[53]

---

[42] *Amnesty International v. Sudan*, para. 31.
[43] *See* Constitutional Rights Project [CRP] v. Nigeria, Comm. No. 60/91.
[44] Rule 116 of the Commission's Rules of Procedures.
[45] *Ceesay v. The Gambia*,
[46] *Jawara v. The Gambia*, Comm. Nos. 147/95, 149/96, para. 31.
[47] *Id.*, para. 32.
[48] *Id.*, para. 33.
[49] Longman Synonym Dictionary 82 (1986).
[50] *Jawara, supra*, para. 33.
[51] *Id.*, para. 32.
[52] *Longman, supra*.
[53] *Jawara, supra* para 32.

It will be deemed insufficient if, for example, the applicant cannot turn to the judiciary of his country because of a generalized fear for his life "or even those of his relatives".[54] This Commission has also declared a remedy to be insufficient because its pursuit depended on extrajudicial considerations, such as discretion or some extraordinary power vested in an executive state official. The word "sufficient" literally means "adequate for the purpose; enough"; or "ample, abundant; . . . satisfactory".[55]

53.–55. [. . . .]

56. Can this Commission conclude, based on the above allegations by the complainant that local remedies in the respondent State are not available, ineffective or insufficient?

57. It must be observed here that the complainant's submissions seems [sic] to suggest that local remedies may in fact be available but it is apprehensive about their effectiveness as far as the present case is concerned. From the complainant's submissions, it is clear that the complainant has relied on reports, including a World Bank report which concluded that "of the three branches of government, the judiciary has the least history and experience of independence and therefore requires significant strengthening to obtain true independence".

58. The complainant's submissions also demonstrate that it is apprehensive about the success of local remedies either because of fear for the safety of lawyers, the lack of independence of the judiciary or the meagre resources available to the judiciary. Apart from casting aspersions on the effectiveness of local remedies, the complainant has not provided concrete evidence or demonstrated sufficiently that these apprehensions are founded and may constituted a barrier to it attempting local remedies. In the view of this Commission, the complainant is simply casting doubts about the effectiveness of the domestic remedies. This Commission is of the view that it is incumbent on every complainant to take all necessary steps to exhaust, or at least attempt the exhaustion of, local remedies. It is not enough for the complainant to cast aspersion on the ability of the domestic remedies of the State due to isolated or past incidences. In this regard, the African Commission would like to refer to the decision of the Human Rights Committee in *A v Australia*[56] in which the Committee held that "mere doubts about the effectiveness of local remedies . . . did not absolve the author from pursuing such remedies".[57] The African Commission can therefore not declare the communication admissible based on this argument. If a remedy has the slightest likelihood to be effective, the applicant must pursue it. Arguing that local remedies are not likely to be successful, without trying to avail oneself of them, will simply not sway this Commission.

59. The complainant also argue that the violations alleged are serious and involve a large number of people and should be declare admissible as the Commission can not hold the requirements of local remedies to apply literally in cases where it is impracticable or undesirable for the complainant to seize the domestic courts in the

---

[54] *Id.*, para. 35.

[55] *Longman, supra* at 1183.

[56] Communication No. 560/1993, UN Doc CCPR/C/59/D/560/1993 (1997).

[57] See also *L Emil Kaaber v Iceland*, Communication No. 674/1995. UN. Doc. CCPR/C/58/D/674/1995 (1996). See also *Ati Antoine Randolph v. Togo*, Communication No. 910/2000, UN Doc. CCPR/C/79/D/910/2000 (2003).

case of each violation. In the *Malawi African Association* case,[58] for example, this Commission observed that [t]he gravity of the human rights situation in Mauritania and the great number of victims involved render[ed] the channels of remedy unavailable in practical terms, and, according to the terms of the Charter, their process [was] "unduly prolonged". In like manner, the *Amnesty International v. Sudan* case[59] involved the arbitrary arrest, detention, and torture of many Sudanese citizens after the coup of July 30, 1989. The alleged acts of torture included forcing detainees into cells measuring 1.8 meters wide and 1 meter deep, deliberately flooding the cells, frequently banging on the doors to prevent detainees from lying down, forcing them to face mock executions, and prohibiting them from bathing or washing. Other acts of torture included burning detainees with cigarettes, binding them with ropes to cut off circulation, and beating them with sticks until their bodies were severely lacerated and then treating the resulting wounds with acid. After the coup, the Sudanese government promulgated a decree that suspended the jurisdiction of the regular courts in favor of special tribunals with respect to any action taken in applying the decree. It also outlawed the taking of any legal action against the decree. These measures, plus the "seriousness of the human rights situation in Sudan and the great numbers of people involved," the Commission concluded, "render[ed] such remedies unavailable in fact".[60]

60. Thus, in cases of massive violations, the state will be presumed to have notice of the violations within its territory and the State is expected to act accordingly to deal with whatever human rights violations. The pervasiveness of these violations dispenses with the requirement of exhaustion of local remedies, especially where the state took no steps to prevent or stop them.[61]

61. The above cases must however be distinguished from the present case which involves one single incident that took place for a short period of time. The respondent State has indicated the measures it took to deal with the situation and the legal proceedings being undertaken by those alleged to have committed human rights violations during the incident. By establishing the Gambella Commission of Inquiry and indicting alleged human rights perpetrators, the state, albeit under international pressure, demonstrated that it was not indifferent to the alleged human rights violations that took place in the area and in the view of this Commission could be said to have exercised due diligence.

62. This Commission has also held in many instances that domestic remedies have not been exhausted if a case that includes the subject matter of the petition before it is still pending before the national courts. In *Civil Liberties Organization v. Nigeria*,[62] the African Commission declined to consider a Communication with respect to which a claim had been filed but not yet settled by the courts of the respondent state. In the present communication, the respondent State indicates that

---

58   See combined Communications. Nos. 54/91, 61/91, 98/93, 164/97, 210/98, para. 80,

59   Comm. Nos. 48/90, 50/91, 52/91, 89/93, para. 32.

60   Ibid.

61   *Organisation Mondiale Contre la Torture and Association Internationale des Juristes Démocrates, Commission Internationale des Juristes (C.I.J.), Union Interafricaine des Droits de l'Homme v. Rwanda*, Comm. Nos. 27/89, 46/91, 49/91, 99/93.

62   Comm. No. 45/90.

the matter is still pending before its courts and attached a list of cases still pending before the Federal Circuit Court in relation with the Gambella incident. The list provided the names of the suspects, file number of their cases, previous and future dates of adjournments. The complainant does not deny this process is going on. In the view of this Commission, it does not matter whether the cases still pending before the courts have been brought by the complainant or the state. The underlying question is whether the case is a subject matter of the proceedings before the Commission and whether it is aimed at granting the same relief the complainant is seeking before this commission. As long as a case still pending before a domestic court is a subject matter of the petition before this Commission, and as long as this Commission believes the relief sought can be obtained locally, it will decline to entertain the case. It is the view of this Commission that the present communication is still pending before the courts of the respondent State and therefore does not meet the requirements under Article 56 (5).

For the above reasons, the African Commission declares communication 299/2005—Anuak Justice Council/Ethiopia *inadmissible* for non-exhaustion of local remedies in conformity with Article 56 (5) of the African Charter on Human and Peoples' Rights.

Questions and Comments

1. Failure to obtain favorable results from domestic tribunals does not in and of itself prove that local remedies are inadequate. At what point will repeated failures indicate that efforts to obtain a remedy from domestic procedures are futile?

2. Does procedural default before a local tribunal bar consideration of a case by the Commission or Court? Suppose the petitioner missed the filing date required by the local statute of limitations. What if the case was dismissed for failing to comply with a court order to produce evidence? Should the fairness of these rules be reviewed by international bodies? See *Barbera, Messegue & Jabardo v. Spain,* 146 Eur. Ct. Hum. Rts (ser A) (1989), 11 Hum Rts. Rep. 360.

3. Note that in the *Velásquez Rodriguez Case,* the Inter-American Court allowed the government to plead failure to exhaust local remedies even though it had failed to raise the issue—or to participate at all—in proceedings before the Commission. At what point should the government be deemed to have waived the requirement? Why did the Court allow Honduras to raise the objection when it did? Note that over time, the Court has become much less willing to allow such late objections to be brought. See, e.g., *Nogueira de Carvalho et al. v. Brazil,* judgment of Nov. 28, 2006, 161 Inter-Am.Ct.H.R. (Ser. C), in which the Court denied Brazil's preliminary objection on exhaustion of remedies, stating:

> 151. The Court has already developed clear requirements for lodging the objection of failure to exhaust domestic remedies. The generally recognized principles of international law, to which the rule of exhaustion of domestic remedies refers, in the first place recognize that the respondent State may waive the application of this rule, whether expressly or tacitly. In the second place, the objection of failure to exhaust domestic remedies, in order to be timely, must be pled during the stage of admissibility of the procedure with the Commission, that is, prior to consideration of the merits; otherwise, it is presumed that the State has tacitly waived this argument. In the third place, the Court has asserted that the failure to exhaust remedies is strictly a matter of admissibility, and that a State lodging this objection must specify the do-

mestic remedies that remain to be exhausted and demonstrate that these remedies are applicable and effective.

4. For further on the African Commission's approach, see S.O.S.—*Esclaves v. Mauritania*, (Comm. 198/97), *12th Annual Activity Report of the Afr. Comm. H.P.R* 1998–1999, Annex V, pp. 74–75.

ii. Exceptions to the Exhaustion Requirement

Each of the regional conventions contains express exceptions to the requirement to exhaust local remedies. In addition, "special circumstances" may be cited to exempt applicants from the requirement. Some of these circumstances are illustrated in the following cases.

John D. Ouko v. Kenya, (Comm. 232/99), *14th Annual Activity Report of the Afr. Comm. H.P.R. 2000–2001*, Annex V, pp. 73–77.

Summary of Facts:

1. The Complainant claims to be a Students' Union leader at the University of Nairobi, Kenya.

2. He alleges that he was forced to flee the country due to his political opinions.

3. He mentions the following as issues which led to his strained relations with the government and to his arrest and detention and eventually to his fleeing the country:

   a. The demand for the setting up of a Judicial Commission of Inquiry into the murder of his late uncle and former Kenyan Minister of Foreign Affairs, Mr. Robert Ouko;

   b. His condemnation of the seeming government involvement in the murder of his predecessor at the Students' Union, Mr. Solomon Muruli;

   c. His condemnation of corruption, nepotism and tribalism in government;

   d. His condemnation of the frequent closure of public universities.

4. Prior to his fleeing the country, he was arrested and detained without trial for 10 months at the notorious basement cells of the Secret Service Department headquarters in Nairobi.

5. The detention facility was a two by three metre basement cell with a 250 watts electric bulb, which was left on throughout his ten months detention.

6. The Complainant alleges that throughout his period of detention, he was denied bathroom facilities and was subjected to both physical and mental torture.

7. The Complainant claims that he fled the country on 10th November 1997 to Uganda, where he initially sought political asylum but was denied.

8. The Complainant alleges that since he could not obtain any protection in Uganda, he had to leave to the Democratic Republic of Congo (DRC) in March 1998, and has been residing there to date.

9. The Complainant claims to be living presently in Aru, North-East of the Democratic Republic of Congo.

10. The Complainant further alleges that until August 1998, when the war broke out in the DRC, he was under the United Nations High Commissioner for Refugees' (UNHCR) assistance programme.

11. Since the said war started, leading to the evacuation of UNHCR staff, he has been living in a very desperate and despicable situation.

Complaint

The Complainant alleges violations of Articles 5, 6, 9, 10 and 12 of the African Charter.

Procedure

12. At its 26th ordinary session held in Kigali, Rwanda, the Commission decided to be seized of the communication and requested the Secretariat to notify the parties.

13. On 18th January 2000, letters were dispatched to the parties notifying them of the Commission's decision.

14. On 23rd May 2000, during the 27th ordinary session held in Algeria, the Secretariat of the Commission received a letter from the Complainant stating, among other things, that he has been in Kampala for medical reasons since November 1999. In addition, he informed the Commission of his ordeals in the Democratic Republic of Congo, including his being kidnapped and forced to work as a computer operator for the rebels in Kisangani.

15. At its 27th ordinary session held in Algeria, the Commission examined the case and declared it admissible and requested parties to furnish it with arguments on the merits of the case.

16. On 12th July 2000, the Secretariat communicated the Commission's decision to the parties.

LAW

Admissibility

17. The admissibility of communications brought pursuant to Article 55 of the Charter is governed by Article 56 of the Charter. The applicable provision in this particular case is Article 56(5) of the Charter, which provides *inter alia* "communications relating to Human and Peoples' Rights . . . received by the Commission shall be considered if they . . . are sent after exhausting local remedies, if any unless it is obvious that this procedure is unduly prolonged . . .".

18. The facts of this case reveal the following:

- The Complainant is no longer in the Republic of Kenya;
- The above condition is not based on his voluntary will—he has been forced to flee the country because of his political opinions and Student Union activities;
- An attestation dated 30th October 1999, issued by one Mr. Tane Bamba, Head of Sub Office of the United Nations High Commissioner for Refugees, indicates that the Complainant "is recognised as a refugee Under UNCHR mandate in accordance with the provisions of the OAU Convention of September 10th, 1969 to which he satisfied".

19. Relying on its case law *(see communication 215/98—Rights International/ Nigeria)*, the Commission finds that the Complainant is unable to pursue any domestic remedy following his flight to the Democratic Republic of Congo for fear of his life, and his subsequent recognition as a refugee by the Office of the United Nations High Commissioner for Refugee. The Commission therefore declared the communication admissible based on the principle of constructive exhaustion of local remedies.

[. . . .]

Exceptions to the Exhaustion of Domestic Remedies (Arts. 46(1), 46(2) (a) and 46 (2) (b) American Convention on Human Rights), Advisory Opinion OC-11/90 of August 10, 1990, 11 Inter-Am. Ct. H.R. (Ser. A) (1990).

1. By note of January 31, 1989, the Inter-American Commission on Human Rights . . . submitted to the Inter-American Court of Human Rights . . . an advisory opinion request regarding Article 46 (1) (a) and 46 (2) of the American Convention on Human Rights . . . .

2. The request for an advisory opinion poses the following questions:

1. Does the requirement of the exhaustion of internal legal remedies apply to an indigent, who because of economic circumstances is unable to avail himself of the legal remedies within a country?

2. In the event that this requirement is waived for indigents, what criteria should the Commission consider in making its determination of admissibility in such cases?

3. Does the requirement of the exhaustion of internal legal remedies apply to an individual complainant, who because he is unable to retain representation due to a general fear in the legal community cannot avail himself of the legal remedies provided by law in a country?

4. In the event that this requirement is waived for such persons. what criteria should the Commission consider in making its determination of admissibility in these cases?

. . . .

14. The questions submitted by the Commission call for an interpretation by the Court of Article 46(1) (a) and 46(2) of the Convention, (. . .)

16. Article 46(1) (a) provides that, for a petition to be ruled admissible by the Commission, it is necessary "that the remedies under domestic law have been pursued and exhausted," while sub-paragraph 2 considers the circumstances in which this requirement does not apply.

17. Article 46(2) (a) applies to situations in which the domestic law of a State Party does not provide appropriate remedies to protect rights that have been violated. Article 46(2) (b) is applicable to situations in which the domestic law does provide for remedies, but such remedies are either denied the affected individual or he is otherwise prevented from exhausting them. These provisions thus apply to situa-

tions where domestic remedies cannot be exhausted because they are not available either as a matter of law or as a matter of fact.

18. Article 46(2) makes no specific reference to indigents, the subject of the first question, nor to those situations in which a person has been unable to obtain legal representation because of a generalized fear in the legal community to take such cases, which the second question addresses.

19. The answers to the questions presented by the Commission thus depend on a determination whether a person's failure to exhaust domestic remedies in the circumstances posited falls under one or the other exception spelled out in Article 46(2). That is, whether or under what circumstances a person's indigency or inability to obtain legal representation because of a generalized fear among the legal community will exempt him from the requirement to exhaust domestic remedies.

20. In addressing the issue of indigency, the Court must emphasize that merely because a person is indigent does not, standing alone, mean that he does not have to exhaust domestic remedies, for the provision contained in Article 46(1) is of general nature. The language of Article 46(2) suggests that whether or not an indigent has to exhaust domestic remedies will depend on whether the law or the circumstances permit him to do so.

21. In analyzing these issues, the Court must bear in mind the provisions contained in Articles 1(1), 24 and the relevant parts of Article 8 of the Convention, which are closely related to the instant matter (. . .).

22. The final section of Article 1(1) prohibits a state from discriminating on a variety of grounds, among them "economic status". The meaning of the term "discrimination" employed by Article 24 must, then, be interpreted by reference to the list enumerated in Article 1(1). If a person who is seeking the protection of the law in order to assert rights which the Convention guarantees finds that his economic status (in this case, his indigency) prevents him from so doing because he cannot afford either the necessary legal counsel or the costs of the proceedings, that person is being discriminated against by reason of his economic status and, hence, is not receiving equal protection before the law.

23. "(P)rotection of the law" consists, fundamentally, of the remedies the law provides for the protection of the rights guaranteed by the Convention. The obligation to respect and guarantee such rights, which Article 1(1) imposes on the States Parties, implies, as the Court has already stated, "the duty of the States Parties to organize the governmental apparatus and, in general, all the structures through which public power is exercised, so that they are capable of juridically ensuring the free and full enjoyment of human rights" (*Velásquez Rodriguez Case*, Judgment of July 29, 1988. Series C No. 4, para. 166 [see infra p. 194]; *Godinez Cruz Case*, Judgment of January 20, 1989. Series C No. 5, para. 175).

24. Insofar as the right to legal counsel is concerned, this duty to organize the governmental apparatus and to create the structures necessary to guarantee human rights is related to the provisions of Article 8 of the Convention. That article distinguishes between "accusation(s) of a criminal nature" and procedures "of a civil, labor, fiscal, or any other nature." Although it provides that "(e)very person has the right to a hearing, with due guarantees [. . .] by a [. . .] tribunal" in both types of pro-

ceedings, it spells out in addition certain "minimum guarantees" for those accused of a criminal offense. Thus, the concept of a fair hearing in criminal proceedings also embraces, at the very least, those "minimum guarantees". By labelling these guarantees as "minimum guarantees," the Convention assumes that other, additional guarantees may be necessary in specific circumstances to ensure a fair hearing.

25. Sub-paragraphs (d) and (e) of Article 8(2) indicate that the accused has a right "to defend himself personally or to be assisted by legal counsel of his own choosing" and that, if he should choose not to do so, he has "the inalienable right to be assisted by counsel provided by the state, paid or not as the domestic law provides . . .". Thus, a defendant may defend himself personally, but it is important to bear in mind that this would only be possible where permitted under domestic law. If a person refuses or is unable to defend himself personally, he has the right to be assisted by counsel of his own choosing. In cases where the accused neither defends himself nor engages his own counsel within the time period established by law, he has the right to be assisted by counsel provided by the state, paid or not as the domestic law provides. To that extent the Convention guarantees the right to counsel in criminal proceedings. But since it does not stipulate that legal counsel be provided free of charge when required, an indigent would suffer discrimination for reason of his "economic status" if, when in need of legal counsel, the state were not to provide it to him free of charge.

26. Article 8 must, then, be read to require legal counsel only when that is necessary for a fair hearing. Any state that does not provide indigents with such counsel free of charge cannot, therefore, later assert that appropriate remedies existed but were not exhausted.

27. Even in those cases in which the accused is forced to defend himself because he cannot afford legal counsel, a violation of Article 8 of the Convention could be said to exist if it can be proved that the lack of legal counsel affected the right to a fair hearing to which he is entitled under that article.

28. For cases which concern the determination of a person's "rights and obligations of a civil, labor, fiscal or any other nature," Article 8 does not specify any "minimum guarantees" similar to those provided in Article 8(2) for criminal proceedings. It does, however, provide for "due guarantees;" consequently, the individual here also has the right to the fair hearing provided for in criminal cases. It is important to note here that the circumstances of a particular case or proceeding—its significance, its legal character, and its context in a particular legal system—are among the factors that bear on the determination of whether legal representation is or is not necessary for a fair hearing.

29. Lack of legal counsel is not, of course, the only factor that could prevent an indigent from exhausting domestic remedies. It could even happen that the state might provide legal counsel free of charge but neglect to cover the costs that might be required to ensure the fair hearing that Article 8 prescribes. In such cases, the exceptions to Article 46(1) would apply. Here again, the circumstances of each case and each particular legal system must be kept in mind.

30. In its advisory opinion request, the Commission states that it "has received certain petitions in which the victim alleges that he has not been able to comply

with the requirement of the exhaustion of remedies set forth in the domestic legislation because he cannot afford legal assistance or, in some cases, the obligatory filing fees." Upon applying the foregoing analysis to the examples set forth by the Commission, it must be concluded that if legal services are required either as a matter of law or fact in order for a right guaranteed by the Convention to be recognized and a person is unable to obtain such services because of his indigency, then that person would be exempted from the requirement to exhaust domestic remedies. The same would be true of cases requiring the payment of a filing fee. That is to say, if it is impossible for an indigent to deposit such a fee, he cannot be required to exhaust domestic remedies unless the state provides some alternative mechanism.

31. Thus, the first question presented to the Court by the Commission is not whether the Convention guarantees the right to legal counsel as such or as a result of the prohibition of discrimination for reason of economic status (Art. 1(l)). Rather, the question is whether an indigent may appeal directly to the Commission to protect a right guaranteed in the Convention without first exhausting the applicable domestic remedies. The answer to this question, given what has been said above, is that if it can be shown that an indigent needs legal counsel to effectively protect a right which the Convention guarantees and his indigency prevents him from obtaining such counsel, he does not have to exhaust the relevant domestic remedies. That is the meaning of the language of Article 46(2) read in conjunction with Articles 1(1)24 and 8.

32. The Court will now turn to the second question. It concerns the exhaustion of domestic remedies in situations where an individual is unable to obtain the necessary legal representation "due to a general fear in the legal community" of a given country. The Commission explains that, according to what some complainants have alleged "[t]his situation has occurred where an atmosphere of fear prevails and lawyers do not accept cases which they believe could place their own lives and those of their families in jeopardy".

33. In general, the same basic principles govern this question as those which the Court has deemed applicable to the first question. That is to say, if a person, for a reason such as the one stated above, is prevented from availing himself of the domestic legal remedies necessary to assert a right which the Convention guarantees, he cannot be required to exhaust those remedies. The state's obligation to guarantee such remedies is, of course, unaffected by this conclusion.

34. Article 1 of the Convention provides not only that the States Parties have an obligation to "respect the rights and freedoms recognized [t]herein", it also requires them "to ensure to all persons subject to their jurisdiction the free and full exercise of those rights and freedoms". The Court has already had occasion to emphasize that this provision imposes an affirmative duty on the States. It is also important to note that the obligation "to ensure" requires the state to take all necessary measures to remove any impediments which might exist that would prevent individuals from enjoying the rights the Convention guarantees. Any state which tolerates circumstances or conditions that prevent individuals from having recourse to the legal remedies designed to protect their rights is consequently in violation of Article 1 (1) of the Convention. [. . . .]

35. It follows therefrom that where an individual requires legal representation and a generalized fear in the legal community prevents him from obtaining such representation, the exception set out in Article 46(2) (b) is fully applicable and the individual is exempted from the requirement to exhaust domestic remedies.

36. The Court is of the opinion that, in the cases posited by the Commission, it is the considerations outlined that render the remedies adequate and effective in accordance with generally recognized principles of international law to which Article 46(1) refers; namely, remedies "suitable to address an infringement of a legal right" and "capable of producing the result for which (they were) designed" (*Velásquez Rodriguez Case*, supra 23, paras. 64 and 66 [see supra p. 100]; *Godinez Cruz Case*, supra 23, paras. 67 and 69, and *Fairen Garbi and Solis Corrales Case*, supra 34, paras. 88 and 91).

37. The second part of both questions submitted relates to the standards the Commission should apply in determining the admissibility of the claims analyzed herein.

38. In addressing this issue it is clear that the test to be applied must be whether legal representation was necessary in order to exhaust the appropriate remedies and whether such representation was, in fact, available.

39. It is for the Commission to make this determination. It must be emphasized, nevertheless, that all determinations made by the Commission before the case was referred to the Court are fully reviewable by the latter (*Velásquez Rodriguez Case*, Preliminary Objections, Judgment of June 26, 1987. Series C No. 1, para. 29; *Fairen Garbi and Solis Corrales Case*, Preliminary Objections, Judgment of June 26, 1987. Series C No. 2, para. 34, and *Godinez Cruz Case*, Preliminary Objections, Judgment of June 26, 1987. Series C No. 3, para. 32).

40. The exhaustion of domestic remedies is a requirement for admissibility and the Commission must bear this in mind at the appropriate time and provide both the state and the complainant with the opportunity to present their respective positions on this issue.

41. Under Article 46(1) (a) of the Convention and in accordance with general principles of international law, it is for the state asserting non-exhaustion of domestic remedies to prove that such remedies in fact exist and that they have not been exhausted (*Velásquez Rodriguez Case*, Preliminary Objections, supra 39, para 88; *Fairen Garbi and Solis Corrales Case*, Preliminary Objections, supra 39, para. 87, and *Godinez Cruz Case*, Preliminary Objections, supra 39, para. 90). Once a State Party has shown the existence of domestic remedies for the enforcement of a particular right guaranteed by the Convention, the burden of proof shifts to the complainant, who must then demonstrate that the exceptions provided for in Article 46(2) are applicable, whether as a result of indigency or because of a generalized fear to take the case among the legal community or any other applicable circumstance. Of course, it must also be shown that the rights in question are guaranteed in the Convention and that legal representation is necessary to assert or enjoy those rights.

42. For those reasons,

THE COURT IS OF THE OPINION

Unanimously

1. That if his indigency or a general fear in the legal community to represent him prevent a complainant before the Commission from invoking the domestic remedies necessary to protect a right guaranteed by the Convention, he is not required to exhaust such remedies.

Unanimously

2. That if a State Party has proved that domestic remedies are available, the complainant must then demonstrate that the exceptions contemplated in Article 46(2) apply and that he was prevented from obtaining the legal counsel necessary for the protection of rights guaranteed by the Convention.

Note: The advisory opinion above should be considered in the light of the requirement for access to justice and a fair hearing, contained in each of the Conventions. Failure to provide domestic remedies or ensure that they can be utilized in the face of indigency may result not only in excusing recourse to domestic remedies; it may also constitute a separate substantive breach of human rights guarantees, as the next case shows.

Airey v. Ireland, (App. no. 6289/73), Judgment of 9 October 1979, 32, Eur. Ct. H.R. (Ser. A), 2 EHRR 305 (1979–1980).

. . . .

8. Mrs. Johanna Airey, an Irish national born in 1932, lives in Cork. She comes from a humble family background and went to work at a young age as a shop assistant. She married in 1953 and has four children, the youngest of whom is still dependent on her. At the time of the adoption of the Commission's report, Mrs. Airey was in receipt of unemployment benefit from the State but, since July 1978, she has been employed. Her net weekly wage in December 1978 was £39.99. In 1974, she obtained a court order against her husband for payment of maintenance of £20 per week, which was increased in 1977 to £27 and in 1978 to £32. However, Mr. Airey, who had previously been working as a lorry driver but was subsequently unemployed, ceased paying such maintenance in May 1978.

Mrs. Airey alleges that her husband is an alcoholic and that, before 1972, he frequently threatened her with, and occasionally subjected her to, physical violence. In January 1972, in proceedings instituted by the applicant, Mr. Airey was convicted by the District Court of Cork City of assaulting her and fined. In the following June he left the matrimonial home; he has never returned there to live, although Mrs. Airey now fears that he may seek to do so.

9. For about eight years prior to 1972, Mrs. Airey tried in vain to conclude a separation agreement with her husband. In 1971, he declined to sign a deed prepared by her solicitor for the purpose and her later attempts to obtain his co-operation were also unsuccessful.

Since June 1972, she has been endeavouring to obtain a decree of judicial separation on the grounds of Mr. Airey's alleged physical and mental cruelty to her and their children, and has consulted several solicitors in this connection. However, she has been unable, in the absence of legal aid and not being in a financial position to meet herself the costs involved, to find a solicitor willing to act for her.

In 1976, Mrs. Airey applied to an ecclesiastical tribunal for annulment of her marriage. Her application is still under investigation; if successful, it will not affect her civil status.

Domestic law

10. In Ireland, although it is possible to obtain under certain conditions a decree of nullity—a declaration by the High Court that a marriage was null and void ab initio—, divorce in the sense of dissolution of a marriage does not exist. In fact, Article 41.3.2 of the Constitution provides: "No law shall be enacted providing for the grant of a dissolution of marriage".

However, spouses may be relieved from the duty of cohabiting either by a legally binding deed of separation concluded between them or by a court decree of judicial separation (also known as a divorce *a mensa et thoro*). Such a decree has no effect on the existence of the marriage in law. It can be granted only if the petitioner furnishes evidence proving one of three specified matrimonial offences, namely, adultery, cruelty or unnatural practices. The parties will call and examine witnesses on this point.

By virtue of section 120 (2) of the Succession Act 1965, an individual against whom a decree of judicial separation is granted forfeits certain succession rights over his or her spouse's estate.

11. Decrees of judicial separation are obtainable only in the High Court. The parties may conduct their case in person. However, the Government's replies to questions put by the Court reveal that in each of the 255 separation proceedings initiated in Ireland in the period from January 1972 to December 1978, without exception, the petitioner was represented by a lawyer.

In its report of 9 March 1978, the Commission noted that the approximate range of the costs incurred by a legally represented petitioner was £500–£700 in an uncontested action and £800–£1,200 in a contested action, the exact amount depending on such factors as the number of witnesses and the complexity of the issues involved. In the case of a successful petition by a wife, the general rule is that the husband will be ordered to pay all costs reasonably and properly incurred by her, the precise figure being fixed by a Taxing Master.

Legal aid is not at present available in Ireland for the purpose of seeking a judicial separation, nor indeed for any civil matters. In 1974, a Committee on Civil Legal Aid and Advice was established under the chairmanship of Mr. Justice Pringle. It reported to the Government in December 1977, recommending the introduction of a comprehensive scheme of legal aid and advice in this area. At the hearings on 22 February 1979, counsel for the Government informed the Court that the Government had decided in principle to introduce legal aid in family-law matters and that it was hoped to have the necessary measures taken before the end of 1979.

12. Since Mrs. Airey's application to the Commission, the Family Law (Maintenance of Spouses and Children) Act 1976 has come into force. Section 22 (1) of the Act provides:

> "On application to it by either spouse, the court may, if it is of the opinion that there are reasonable grounds for believing that the safety or welfare of that spouse or of any dependent child of the family requires it, order the other spouse, if he is residing at a place where the applicant spouse or that child resides, to leave that place, and whether the other spouse is or is not residing at that place, prohibit him from entering that place until further order by the court or until such other time as the court shall specify".

Such an order—commonly known as a barring order—is not permanent and application may be made at any time for its discharge (section 22 (2)). Furthermore, the maximum duration of an order given in the District Court—as opposed to the Circuit Court or the High Court—is three months although provision is made for renewal.

A wife who has been assaulted by her husband may also institute summary criminal proceedings.

AS TO THE LAW

I. PRELIMINARY ISSUES

. . . .

19. The Government maintain that the applicant failed to exhaust domestic remedies in various respects.

(a) In the first place, they contend that she could have entered into a separation deed with her husband or could have applied for a barring order or for maintenance under the 1976 Act.

The Court emphasises that the only remedies which Article 26 of the Convention requires to be exercised are remedies in respect of the violation complained of. The violation alleged by Mrs. Airey is that in her case the State failed to secure access to court for the purpose of petitioning for judicial separation. However, neither the conclusion of a separation deed nor the grant of a barring or a maintenance order provide such access. Accordingly, the Court cannot accept the first limb of this plea.

(b) In the second place, the Government lay stress on the fact that the applicant could have appeared before the High Court without the assistance of a lawyer. They also contend that she has nothing to gain from a judicial separation.

The Court recalls that international law, to which Article 26 makes express reference, demands solely recourse to such remedies as are both "to the persons concerned and . . . sufficient, that is to say capable of providing redress for their complaints" (see the above-mentioned *De Wilde, Ooms and Versyp* judgment, p. 33, para. 60). However, the Court would not be able to decide whether the possibility open to Mrs. Airey of conducting her case herself amounts to a "domestic remedy", in the above sense, without at the same time ruling on the merits of her complaint under Article 6 para. 1, namely the alleged lack of effective access to the High Court. Similarly, the argument that a judicial separation would be of no benefit to the applicant appears intimately connected with another aspect of this complaint, namely whether any real prejudice was occasioned. The Court therefore joins to the merits the remainder of the plea.

II. ON ARTICLE 6 PARA. 1 TAKEN ALONE

20. . . . Mrs. Airey . . . maintains that, since the prohibitive cost of litigation prevented her from bringing proceedings before the High Court for the purpose of petitioning for judicial separation, there has been a violation of the above-mentioned provision.

This contention is unanimously accepted in substance by the Commission but disputed by the Government.

21. The applicant wishes to obtain a decree of judicial separation. There can be no doubt that the outcome of separation proceedings is "decisive for private rights and obligations" and hence, a fortiori, for "civil rights and obligations" within the meaning of Article 6 para. 1; this being so, Article 6 para. 1 is applicable in the present case (see the *König* judgment of 28 June 1978, Series A no. 27, pp. 30 and 32, paras. 90 and 95). Besides, the point was not contested before the Court.

22. "Article 6 para. 1 (art. 6–1) secures to everyone the right to have any claim relating to his civil rights and obligations brought before a court or tribunal" (*Golder* judgment, p. 18, para. 36). Article 6 para. 1 accordingly comprises a right for Mrs. Airey to have access to the High Court in order to petition for judicial separation.

23. It is convenient at this juncture to consider the Government's claim that the applicant has nothing to gain from a judicial separation.

The Court rejects this line of reasoning. Judicial separation is a remedy provided for by Irish law and, as such, it should be available to anyone who satisfies the conditions prescribed thereby. It is for the individual to select which legal remedy to pursue; consequently, even if it were correct that Mrs. Airey's choice has fallen on a remedy less suited than others to her particular circumstances, this would be of no moment.

24. The Government contend that the application does enjoy access to the High Court since she is free to go before that court without the assistance of a lawyer.

The Court does not regard this possibility, of itself, as conclusive of the matter. The Convention is intended to guarantee not rights that are theoretical or illusory but rights that are practical and effective (see, *mutatis mutandis*, the judgment of 23 July 1968 in the *"Belgian Linguistic"* case, Series A no. 6, p. 31, paras. 3 in fine and 4; the above-mentioned *Golder* judgment, p. 18, para. 35 in fine; the *Luedicke, Belkacem and Koç* judgment of 28 November 1978, Series A no. 29, pp. 17–18; para. 42; and the *Marckx* judgment of 13 June 1979, Series A no. 31, p. 15, para. 31). This is particularly so of the right of access to the courts in view of the prominent place held in a democratic society by the right to a fair trial (see, *mutatis mutandis*, the *Delcourt* judgment of 17 January 1970, Series A no. 11, p. 15, para. 25). It must therefore be ascertained whether Mrs. Airey's appearance before the High Court without the assistance of a lawyer would be effective, in the sense of whether she would be able to present her case properly and satisfactorily.

Contradictory views on this question were expressed by the Government and the Commission during the oral hearings. It seems certain to the Court that the applicant would be at a disadvantage if her husband were represented by a lawyer and she were not. Quite apart from this eventuality, it is not realistic, in the Court's opinion, to suppose that, in litigation of this nature, the applicant could effectively conduct her own case, despite the assistance which, as was stressed by the Government, the judge affords to parties acting in person.

In Ireland, a decree of judicial separation is not obtainable in a District Court, where the procedure is relatively simple, but only in the High Court. A specialist in Irish family law, Mr. Alan J. Shatter, regards the High Court as the least accessible court not only because "fees payable for representation before it are very high" but also by reason of the fact that "the procedure for instituting proceedings . . . is complex particularly in the case of those proceedings which must be commenced by a petition", such as those for separation (*Family Law in the Republic of Ireland*, Dublin 1977, p. 21).

Furthermore, litigation of this kind, in addition to involving complicated points of law, necessitates proof of adultery, unnatural practices or, as in the present case, cruelty; to establish the facts, expert evidence may have to be tendered and witnesses may have to be found, called and examined. What is more, marital disputes often entail an emotional involvement that is scarcely compatible with the degree of objectivity required by advocacy in court.

For these reasons, the Court considers it most improbable that a person in Mrs. Airey's position can effectively present his or her own case. This view is corroborated by the Government's replies to the questions put by the Court, replies which reveal that in each of the 255 judicial separation proceedings initiated in Ireland in the period from January 1972 to December 1978, without exception, the petitioner was represented by a lawyer.

The Court concludes from the foregoing that the possibility to appear in person before the High Court does not provide the applicant with an effective right of access and, hence, that it also does not constitute a domestic remedy whose use is demanded by Article 26.

25. The Government seek to distinguish the *Golder* case on the ground that, there, the applicant had been prevented from having access to court by reason of the positive obstacle placed in his way by the State in the shape of the Home Secretary's prohibition on his consulting a solicitor. The Government maintain that, in contrast, in the present case there is no positive obstacle emanating from the State and no deliberate attempt by the State to impede access; the alleged lack of access to court stems not from any act on the part of the authorities but solely from Mrs. Airey's personal circumstances, a matter for which Ireland cannot be held responsible under the Convention.

Although this difference between the facts of the two cases is certainly correct, the Court does not agree with the conclusion which the Government draw therefrom. In the first place, hindrance in fact can contravene the Convention just like a legal impediment (above-mentioned *Golder* judgment, p 13, para. 26). Furthermore, fulfilment of a duty under the Convention on occasion necessitates some positive action on the part of the State; in such circumstances, the State cannot simply remain passive and "there is . . . no room to distinguish between acts and omissions" (see, *mutatis mutandis*, the above-mentioned *Marckx* judgment, p. 15, para. 31, and the *De Wilde, Ooms and Versyp* judgment of 10 March 1972, Series A no. 14, p. 10, para. 22). The obligation to secure an effective right of access to the courts falls into this category of duty.

26. The Government's principal argument rests on what they see as the consequence of the Commission's opinion, namely that, in all cases concerning the determination of a "civil right", the State would have to provide free legal aid. In fact, the Convention's only express provision on free legal aid is Article 6 para. 3 (c) which relates to criminal proceedings and is itself subject to limitations; what is more, according to the Commission's established case law, Article 6 para. 1 does not guarantee any right to free legal aid as such. The Government add that since Ireland, when ratifying the Convention, made a reservation to Article 6 para. 3 (c) with the intention of limiting its obligations in the realm of criminal legal aid, a fortiori it cannot be said to have implicitly agreed to provide unlimited civil legal aid. Finally, in their submission, the Convention should not be interpreted so as to achieve social and economic developments in a Contracting State; such developments can only be progressive.

The Court is aware that the further realisation of social and economic rights is largely dependent on the situation—notably financial—reigning in the State in question. On the other hand, the Convention must be interpreted in the light of present-day conditions (above-mentioned *Marckx* judgment, p. 19, para. 41) and it is designed to safeguard the individual in a real and practical way as regards those areas with which it deals. Whilst the Convention sets forth what are essentially civil and political rights, many of them have implications of a social or economic nature. The Court therefore considers, like the Commission, that the mere fact that an interpretation of the Convention may extend into the sphere of social and economic rights should not be a decisive factor against such an interpretation; there is no water-tight division separating that sphere from the field covered by the Convention.

The Court does not, moreover, share the Government's view as to the consequence of the Commission's opinion.

It would be erroneous to generalize the conclusion that the possibility to appear in person before the High Court does not provide Mrs. Airey with an effective right of access; that conclusion does not hold good for all cases concerning "civil rights and obligations" or for everyone involved therein. In certain eventualities, the possibility of appearing before a court in person, even without a lawyer's assistance, will meet the requirements of Article 6 para. 1; there may be occasions when such a possibility secures adequate access even to the High Court. Indeed, much must depend on the particular circumstances.

In addition, whilst Article 6 para. 1 guarantees to litigants an effective right of access to the courts for the determination of their "civil rights and obligations", it leaves to the State a free choice of the means to be used towards this end. The institution of a legal aid scheme—which Ireland now envisages in family law matters—constitutes one of those means but there are others such as, for example, a simplification of procedure. In any event, it is not the Court's function to indicate, let alone dictate, which measures should be taken; all that the Convention requires is that an individual should enjoy his effective right of access to the courts in conditions not at variance with Article 6 para. 1 (see, *mutatis mutandis, the National Union of Belgian Police* judgment of 27 October 1975, Series A no. 19, p. 18, para. 39, and the above-mentioned *Marckx* judgment, p. 15, para. 31).

The conclusion appearing at the end of paragraph 24 above does not therefore imply that the State must provide free legal aid for every dispute relating to a "civil right".

To hold that so far-reaching an obligation exists would, the Court agrees, sit ill with the fact that the Convention contains no provision on legal aid for those disputes, Article 6 para. 3 (c) dealing only with criminal proceedings. However, despite the absence of a similar clause for civil litigation, Article 6 para. 1 may sometimes compel the State to provide for the assistance of a lawyer when such assistance proves indispensable for an effective access to court either because legal representation is rendered compulsory, as is done by the domestic law of certain Contracting States for various types of litigation, or by reason of the complexity of the procedure or of the case.

. . . .

27. The applicant was unable to find a solicitor willing to act on her behalf in judicial separation proceedings. The Commission inferred that the reason why the solicitors she consulted were not prepared to act was that she would have been unable to meet the costs involved. The Government question this opinion but the Court finds it plausible and has been presented with no evidence which could invalidate it.

28. Having regard to all the circumstances of the case, the Court finds that Mrs. Airey did not enjoy an effective right of access to the High Court for the purpose of petitioning for a decree of judicial separation. There has accordingly been a breach of Article 6 para. 1 (art. 6–1).

. . . .

V. ON ARTICLE 13 (art. 13)

34. Alleging that she was deprived of an effective remedy before a national authority for the violations complained of, Mrs. Airey finally invokes Article 13 . . . .

The Commission was of the opinion that, in view of its conclusion concerning Article 6 para. 1, there was no need for it to consider the application under Article 13. The Government made no submissions on this point.

35. Mrs. Airey wishes to exercise her right under Irish law to institute proceedings for judicial separation. The Court has already held that such proceedings concern a "civil right" within the meaning of Article 6 para. 1 and, further, that Ireland is obliged under Article 8 to make the possibility of instituting them effectively available to Mrs. Airey so that she may organise her private life. Since Articles 13 and 6 para. 1 overlap in this particular case, the Court does not deem it necessary to determine whether there has been a failure to observe the requirements of the former Article: these requirements are less strict than, and are here entirely absorbed by, those of the latter Article (see, mutatis mutandis, the above-mentioned *De Wilde, Ooms and Versyp* judgment of 18 June 1971, p. 46, para. 95).

Questions and Comments

1. When the applicant demonstrates that the remedies asserted by the government are ineffective or inadequate, does this necessarily also constitute a substantive violation of the right to a remedy?

2. How do you interpret paragraph 22 of the Inter-American Court's opinion? What must a state do to avoid discriminating against a person on the basis of economic status in regard to access to justice? Is it required to provide free legal aid and waiver of costs for the poor? Is it enough if these are provided or must the state also provide transportation for those who cannot afford to travel to court? What other circumstances excuse failure to exhaust remedies?

3. In regard to guaranteed rights, what distinctions exist between civil and criminal proceedings? Are lawyers guaranteed for both types of cases?

4. Is there a right to legal assistance in bringing claims to the Inter-American system?

5. Note that neither the Inter-American nor European Court indicates if full discretion rests with the state to determine indigency or whether the regional human rights bodies may evaluate this fact as part of their consideration of a petition. Should the Commission review the matter if the petitioner alleges abusive denial of indigency status? How much deference should the Commisssion give a state's determination of the threshold for public aid? The Court indicates that the Commission is to determine whether legal representation is necessary and whether such representation was, in fact, available; all such determinations are fully reviewable by the Court.

6. For a similar case in the African system, in which indigency, coupled with repeated deportations of the applicant, was deemed sufficient to excuse exhaustion of local remedies, see: Communication 97/93, *John K. Modise v. Botswana*, 28th session of the African Comm'n, 14th Activity Report, Annex V (2000).

7. What is the difference in the European Convention between the guarantees of Article 6 and those of Article 13 and how do both relate to the requirement of exhaustion of local remedies?

8. On the absence of legal aid as a violation of the right of access to justice (Art. 6–1), see *Steel and Morris v. The United Kingdom*, App. 68416/01, judgment of 15 Feb. 2005. The two applicants in this case were part of a Greenpeace anti-McDonald's campaign in the UK. McDonald's sued the applicants for libel in response to statements made in a pamphlet. The applicants denied publication, denied that the words complained of had the meanings attributed to them by McDonald's and denied that all or some of the meanings were capable of being defamatory. In the alternative, they asserted that the words were substantially true or else were fair comment on matters of fact. The applicants applied for legal aid but were refused on 3 June 1992, because legal aid was not available for defamation proceedings in the United Kingdom. The trial was the longest trial in English legal history. Transcripts of the trial ran to approximately 20,000 pages; there were about 40,000 pages of documentary evidence; and, in addition to many written witness statements, 130 witnesses gave oral evidence: 59 for the applicants, 71 for McDonald's.

In its judgment, the Court noted that it is central to the concept of a fair trial, in civil as well as in criminal proceedings, that a litigant is not denied the opportunity to present his or her case effectively before the court and that he or she is able to enjoy equality of arms with the opposing side (citing *De Haes and Gijsels v. Belgium*, judgment of 24 February 1997, *Reports* 1997-I, § 53). According to the Court, Article 6 § 1 leaves to the State a free choice of the means to be used in guaranteeing litigants these rights. Legal aid constitutes one means but the state might also simplify the applicable procedure. The question whether the provision of legal aid is necessary for a fair hearing is determined on the basis of the particular facts and circumstances of each case and depends *inter alia* upon the importance of what is at stake for the applicant in the proceedings, the complexity of the relevant law and procedure and the applicant's capacity to represent him or herself effectively (citing *Airey*, § 26; *McVicar*, §§ 48 and 50; *P., C. and S. v. the United Kingdom*, no. 56547/00, § 91, ECHR 2002-VI; and also *Munro v. the United Kingdom*, no. 10594/83, Commission decision of 14 July 1987, Decisions and Reports 52, p. 158). In this instance, the Court held that the denial of legal aid to the applicants deprived them of the opportunity to present their case effectively before the court and contributed to an unacceptable inequality of arms with McDonald's. The European Court also has held that imposing an obligation on an indigent creditor to pay court fees to enforce a final judgment violates the Convention. See *Apostol v. Georgia*, App. No. 40765/02, judgment of Nov. 28, 2006.

5. Post-Admissibility Procedures

In examining a case, all the regional bodies place themselves at the disposal of the parties concerned with a view to securing a friendly settlement of the matter; in the European and Inter-American system, this is required by the treaties, while the African Charter is silent on the matter. A friendly settlement must be realized "on the basis of respect for human rights as defined in the convention and the protocols thereto". Eur. Conv., Art. 38(1)(b). If a friendly settlement is reached in the European system, the Court issues a decision giving the facts and the solution reached and strikes the case from its list. In Europe, an important consequence of issuing the settlement in the form of a decision is that it allows the Committee of Ministers to supervise the execution of the terms of the agreement. The European Court also may decide to strike an application for failure to pursue the claim, resolution of the matter, or "for any other reason established by the Court" it finds is no longer justified to continue the examination of the application. Conv., Art. 37. *See Akman v. Turkey*, Judgment of June 26, 2001, below.

The Inter-American Commission must "place itself at the disposal of the parties concerned with a view to reaching a friendly settlement of the matter on the basis of respect for the human rights recognized" in the Convention. Art. 48(1)(f). If a friendly settlement is obtained, the Commission prepares a report that describes the facts of the case and the settlement. Art. 49.

In examining the merits of cases that are not settled, the tribunals may hold hearings, receive written submissions, examine witnesses and appoint experts. They may accept written or oral comments from *amicus curiae* and must allow the intervention of any state whose national is the applicant in the proceedings. In the European Court, hearings must be open to the public unless the Court "in exceptional circumstances" decides otherwise and submissions must also be publicly accessible unless the President of the Court closes the record. The Inter-American Commission examines the allegations, seeks information from the government concerned, and investigates the facts. As part of this process, the Commission may hold hearings in which the government and the petitioners participate. The Commission then draws up a report containing the facts it has found, conclusions about whether or not a violation has been committed, and any recommendations made to the state. The report is transmitted to the state concerned, which has three months to react to the report and comply with any recommendations. During this three month period, the case may be referred to the Inter-American Court of Human Rights by the Commission or the state, if the latter has accepted the Court's jurisdiction. The Commission's 2001 Rules of Procedure now require the Commission to refer all cases of non-compliance to the Court unless the Commission decides otherwise by an absolute majority vote. Commission Rules, Art. 44. Although individuals do not have standing to refer cases to the Court, the Commission's Rules of Procedure give the petitioner the right to be heard on the matter. Art. 43(3).

If a case is not been referred to the Court or settled by the parties, "the Commission may, by the vote of an absolute majority of its members, set forth its opinion and conclusions concerning the question submitted for its consideration". Art. 51(1). If it has concluded that the Convention was violated, the Commission must set out its "recommendations", if any, and "prescribe a period within which the state is to take the measures that are incumbent upon it to remedy the situation examined". Art. 51(2). Once this period has expired it "shall decide by a vote of an absolute majority of its members whether the state has taken adequate measures and whether to publish its report". Art. 51(3).

The Commission's rules of procedure permit it to include in its annual report to the OAS General Assembly the final report on a specific case. This rule, which does not prevent the publication of the case report as a separate document as well, gets the matter on the agenda of the General Assembly, where the state's failure to comply with the Commission's recommendations may be discussed and acted upon. The Commission has also instituted its own follow-up procedure, set out in Commission Rules, Art. 46.

The Convention is silent on the legal effect of an opinion of the Commission, rendered pursuant to Article 51, holding that a state has violated the Convention. Although this decision is not formally binding as is a judgment of the Court, it is an authoritative legal determination by a body to which the Convention assigns "competence . . . relating to the fulfillment" of the obligations assumed by the States Parties. These states and the OAS are, consequently, entitled to treat the Commission's findings under Article 51 as an authoritative ruling that a State Party has violated its treaty obligation and to act accordingly.

Both the African Charter and the Commission's Rules of Procedure are far less detailed about the procedures to be followed in determining the merits of a communication. The Charter says only that "the Commission may resort to any appropriate method of investigation . . .", Art. 46. The Rules of Procedure add the following:

Rule 119—Proceedings

1. If the Commission decides that a communication is admissible under the Charter, its decision and text of the relevant documents shall as soon as possible, be submitted to the State party concerned, through the Secretary. The author of the communication shall also be informed of the Commission's decision through the Secretary.

2. The State party to the Charter concerned shall, within the 3 ensuing months, submit in writing to the Commission, explanations or statements elucidating the issue under consideration and indicating, if possible, measures it was able to take to remedy the situation.

3. All explanations or statements submitted by a State party pursuant to the present Rule shall be communicated, through the Secretary, to the author of the communication who may submit in writing additional information and observations within a time limit fixed by the Commission.

4. States parties from whom explanations or statements are sought within specified times shall be informed that if they fail to comply within those times the Commission will act on the evidence before it.

Rule 120—Final Decision of the Communication

1. If the communication is admissible, the Commission shall consider it in the light of all the information that the individual and the State party concerned has submitted in writing; it shall make known its observations on this issue. To this end, the Commission may refer the communication to a working group, composed of 3 of its members at most, which shall submit recommendations to it.

The cases that follow illustrate the friendly settlement procedure, after which issues of evidence are examined.

A. Friendly Settlement and Striking Cases

Caballero Delgado and Santana v. Colombia (Preliminary Objections), Judgment of January 21, 1994, 17 Inter-Am. Ct. H.R. (Ser. C) (1994).

. . . .

20. The Government alleged both in its pleadings and at the relevant hearing that the Commission had infringed the provisions of Article 48(1)(f) of the Convention by not placing itself at the disposal of the parties to reach a friendly settlement of this matter, despite the fact that the Government had at no time denied the facts of the case. Consequently, it is arbitrary to assert, as the Commission's Report 31/91 of September 26, 1991 does, that the facts of the case are "by their very nature" not subject to resolution through the friendly settlement procedure and that the parties themselves failed to request such a recourse in accordance with Article 45 of the Regulations of the Commission.

25. The Court notes that the Commission and the Government each have a different interpretation of Articles 48(1)(f) of the Convention and 45 of the Commission's Regulations, as also of the scope of the criterion established by the Court in ruling on the preliminary objections interposed by the Government of Honduras in the *Velásquez Rodriguez, Godinez Cruz* and *Fairen Garbi and Solis Corrales* Cases, as contained in its judgments of June 26, 1987, which are all similar in that respect.

26. In the three cases mentioned, the Court determined that:

> Taken literally, the wording of Article 48(1)(f) of the Convention stating that "[t]he Commission shall place itself at the disposal of the parties concerned with a view to reaching a friendly settlement" would seem to establish a compulsory procedure. Nevertheless, the Court believes that, if the phrase is interpreted within the context of the Convention, it is clear that the Commission should attempt such friendly settlement

only when the circumstances of the controversy make that option suitable or necessary, at the Commission's sole discretion [. . .].

27. The Court has held the Commission has no arbitrary powers in this regard. The intention of the Convention is very clear as regards the conciliatory role that the Commission must perform before a case is either referred to the Court or published.

Only in exceptional cases and, of course, for substantive reasons may the Commission omit the friendly settlement procedure because the protection of the rights of the victims or of their next-of-kin is at stake. To state, as the Commission does, that this procedure was not attempted simply because of the "nature" of the case does not appear to be sufficiently well-founded.

28. The Court believes that the Commission should have carefully documented its rejection of the friendly settlement option, based on the behavior of the State accused of the violation.

29. Nevertheless, the Commission's omission did not cause irreparable harm to Colombia because, if it did not agree with the Commission's position, that State had the power to request the friendly settlement procedure pursuant to paragraph 1 of Article 45 of the Commission's Regulations, which provides that:

> At the request of any of the parties, or on its own initiative, the Commission shall place itself at the disposal of the parties concerned, at any stage of the examination of a petition, with a view to reaching a friendly settlement of the matter on the basis of respect for the human rights recognized in the American Convention on Human Rights.

30. An essential part of any friendly settlement procedure is the participation and will of the parties involved. Even if one were to interpret the provisions of the Convention literally and to ignore the Regulations of the Commission, the latter can do no more than suggest to the parties that they enter into conversations aimed at reaching a friendly settlement. The Commission cannot decide the matter, however, since it lacks the power to do so. The Commission must promote the rapprochement but is not responsible for the results. If agreement is reached, the Commission must make sure that human rights have been properly defended.

If one of the parties is interested in a friendly settlement, it is free to propose it. In the case of the Government and keeping in mind the object and purpose of the treaty—that is, the defense of the human rights protected therein—such a proposal could not be interpreted as an admission of responsibility but, rather, as good faith compliance with the Convention's purposes.

The Court finds it unacceptable for the Government to argue as a preliminary objection that the Commission did not implement the peaceful settlement procedure, considering that it enjoyed that very same power under the provisions of the Commission's Regulations. One cannot demand of another an action that one could have taken under the very same conditions but chose not to.

31. For the above reasons, the Court rejects this preliminary objection.

Akman v. Turkey (striking out), (App. no. 37453/97), Judgment of 26 June 2001, Eur. Ct. H.R. 2001-VI.

PROCEDURE

1. The case originated in an application against the Republic of Turkey lodged with the European Commission of Human Rights under former Article 25 of the Convention for the Protection of Human Rights and Fundamental Freedoms by a Turkish national, Mr. Faysal Akman, on 8 July 1997.

2. The applicant, who had been granted legal aid, was represented before the Court by Mr. P. Leach, a lawyer attached to the Kurdish Human Rights Project, a non-governmental organisation based in London. The Turkish Government did not appoint an Agent for the purposes of the Convention proceedings.

3. The applicant alleged in particular that his son was unlawfully killed by the security forces of the respondent State in violation of Article 2 of the Convention. He also relied on Articles 6, 8, 13, 14 and 18 of the Convention in connection with his son's death.

4. The application was transmitted to the Court on 1 November 1998, when Protocol No. 11 to the Convention came into force (Article 5 § 2 of Protocol No. 11) . . . .

6. By a decision of 21 September 1999, the Chamber declared the application admissible.

7. The applicant and the Government each filed information in response to the Court's decision to take evidence in the case in Ankara from 26 to 30 March 2001. In addition, both parties filed proposals with the Registry in the context of friendly-settlement negotiations (Article 38 § 1(b) of the Convention). No settlement was reached.

8. By letter dated 21 March 2001 the Government requested the Court to strike the case out of its list and enclosed the text of a declaration with a view to resolving the issues raised by the application. On 26 March and 12 April 2001 the applicant filed written observations on the Government's request. The Government replied to the applicant's observations by letter dated 4 May 2001.

. . . .

THE LAW

23. By letter dated 21 March 2001, the Deputy Permanent Representative of Turkey to the Council of Europe informed the Registrar of the First Section of the Court:

> . . . I have the pleasure to enclose herewith the text of a declaration which the Government would be ready to make unilaterally with a view to resolving the above—mentioned application.

> The Government kindly requests the Court to decide that it is no longer justified to continue the examination of the application and to strike the case out of the list under Article 37 of the Convention.

24. The text of the declaration reads as follows:

> 1. The Government regrets the occurrence of individual cases of death resulting from the use of excessive force as in the circumstances of Murat Akman's death not-

withstanding existing Turkish legislation and the resolve of the Government to prevent such actions.

2. It is accepted that the use of excessive or disproportionate force resulting in death constitutes a violation of Article 2 of the Convention and the Government undertakes to issue appropriate instructions and adopt all necessary measures to ensure that the right to life—including the obligation to carry out effective investigations—is respected in the future. It is noted in this connection that new legal and administrative measures have been adopted which have resulted in a reduction in the occurrence of deaths in circumstances similar to those of the instant application as well as more effective investigations.

3. I declare that the Government of the Republic of Turkey offers to pay *ex gratia* to the applicant the amount of GBP 85,000. This sum, which also covers legal expenses connected with the case, shall be paid in pounds sterling to a bank account named by the applicant. The sum shall be payable, free of any taxes that may be applicable, within three months from the date of the striking-out decision of the Court pursuant to Article 37 of the European Convention on Human Rights. This payment will constitute the final settlement of the case.

4. The Government considers that the supervision by the Committee of Ministers of the execution of Court judgments concerning Turkey in this and similar cases is an appropriate mechanism for ensuring that improvements will continue to be made in this context. To this end, necessary cooperation in this process will continue to take place.

25. The applicant, in his written reply, requested the Court to reject the Government's initiative. He stressed, *inter alia*, that the proposed declaration omitted any reference to the unlawful nature of the killing of his son and failed to highlight that his son was unarmed at the material time. In the applicant's submission, the terms of the declaration did not determine any of the fundamental human rights questions raised by the application. He urged the Court to proceed with its decision to take evidence in the case with a view to establishing the facts.

26. The Court observes at the outset that the parties were unable to agree on the terms of a friendly settlement of the case. It recalls that, according to Article 38 § 2 of the Convention, friendly-settlement negotiations are confidential. Rule 62 § 2 of the Rules of Court further stipulates in this connection that no written or oral communication and no offer or concession made in the framework of the attempt to secure a friendly settlement may be referred to or relied on in contentious proceedings.

The Court will therefore proceed on the basis of the declaration made outside the framework of the friendly-settlement negotiations by the Government on 21 March 2001.

27. The Court recalls that Article 37 of the Convention provides that it may at any stage of the proceedings decide to strike an application out of its list of cases where the circumstances lead to one of the conclusions specified under (a), (b) or (c) of paragraph 1 of that Article.

28. Article 37 § 1(c) enables the Court in particular to strike a case out of its list if "for any other reason established by the Court, it is no longer justified to continue the examination of the application".

29. Article 37 § 1 *in fine* states: "However, the Court shall continue the examination of the application if respect for human rights as defined in the Convention and the Protocols thereto so requires."

30. The Court has carefully examined the terms of the Government's declaration. Having regard to the nature of the admissions contained in the declaration as well as the scope and extent of the various undertakings referred to therein, together with the amount of compensation proposed, the Court considers that it is no longer justified to continue the examination of the application (Article 37 § 1(c)).

31. Moreover, the Court is satisfied that respect for human rights as defined in the Convention and the Protocols thereto does not require it to continue the examination of the application (Article 37 § 1 *in fine*). The Court notes in this regard that it has specified the nature and extent of the obligations which arise for the respondent State in cases of alleged unlawful killings by members of the security forces under Articles 2 and 13 of the Convention (see for example, . . .; *Güleç v. Turkey*, judgment of 27 July 1998, *Reports* 1998-IV, pp. 1729–30, §§ 69–73, and pp. 1731–33, §§ 77–82; *Yaşa v. Turkey*, judgment of 2 September 1998, *Reports* 1998-VI, pp. 2438–41, §§ 98–108, and pp. 2441–42, §§ 112–15; *Oğur v. Turkey* [GC], no. 21594/93, §§ 76–93, ECHR 1999-III; and *Gül v. Turkey*, no. 22676/93, §§ 76–95 and 100–02, 14 December 2000, unreported).

32. Accordingly, the application should be struck out of the list.

———————

Peoples' Democratic Organization for Independence and Socialism v. The Gambia, (Comm. 44/90), *10th Annual Activity Report of the Afr. Comm. H.P.R. 1996–1997*, Annex X, pp. 56–58.

Report on an Amicable resolution

The Facts

1. The complaint alleges that voter registration in the constituencies of Serrekunda West, Serrekunda East and Bakau was defective because those registering were not required by the law to give an address or identification. It argues that there was no control over voter registration since no documents have to be shown to the registration officer. The voter may be asked his name and citizenship, but there is no requirement to produce an address or compound number. Furthermore, the witness is not required to identify himself. The complainant argued that the absence of a requirement to produce an address or compound number makes it possible for the voter to forge his right to vote in the constituency, or to vote several times.

2. In the rural areas the registration of the voters and the voting procedure itself are controlled by the headman, the registration officer, representatives of different political parties, and village elders. In the urban areas the control is only done by the registration officer, who does not know the people. Without the street address or compound number it is impossible for the registration officer to control the identity of the voter, even though they must sign a form of registration and enclose a photograph, because the signature could be forged and the lack of communication

between different constituencies could make it possible for the voter to register in several stations.

3. The complainant argues that the registration by street address/compound number is possible, since most urban areas in the Gambia have street address or compound number.

4. The complainant argues that, based on its observations of voter registration, there is widespread fraud.

According to the Government

5. The government argued firstly that the case was inadmissible because it could be taken through the courts to the level of the (British) Privy Council

6. The complainant pointed out that the (Gambian) Elections Act, Section 22(5), states that the judgment of the Gambian Supreme Court shall be final and conclusive; thus, appeal to the Privy Council is impossible.

7. As to the merits, the state originally claimed that the Gambia does hold free and fair elections.

8. In the urban areas a form was signed and address/compound number, occupation, constituency and photo, were included wherever possible. These were checked by the registration officer both at registration and at the elections, providing adequate protection against fraud. Likewise, in the rural areas, the personal identification by the village headman took place both at registration and at the elections.

9. The state claimed that it is almost impossible in a developing country like the Gambia to ensure control by street addresses/compound number. Many dwellings in the Gambia, including in the urban areas, do not have street addresses/compound numbers, but are registered in the names of the owners. It is therefore impossible to make this requirement absolute.

10. The state further argued that it is impossible to require showing of identity papers at the time of registration and election as a high percentage of the population does not have identification papers. It was not before 1985 that a National Identity Card was introduced and now not more than 50% of the population has been registered.

11. In July 1994 there was a change of government in The Gambia. The present government strongly condemns the claims of the previous government that the streets of Serrekunda were not named with sufficient specificity to permit making an street address a mandatory requirement for voter registration. The present government calls this claim 'inexcusable and indefensible'.

12. The present government, by its 'Admission of Communication No. 44/90 from the Peoples Democratic Organisation for Independence and Socialism-PDOIS Against the State of the Gambia' concedes that the grievances expressed by the complainants are valid and logical. It expressed its intent to change the current system to correct the present 'anomalies'. [. . . .]

The Law

Admissibility

18. The PDOIS argued that it was beyond the jurisdiction of the judiciary to order Parliament to change defective procedures and laws; thus, recourse to the

courts was not an option. The complainant alleged that, while the Elections Act provides for objections to voter lists to be made before a revising officer appointed by the Supervisor of Elections, the fact that the voter lists posted did not include a list of addresses made effective scrutiny impossible. The complaint noted that numerous letters had been addressed to the Supervisor of Elections and the President of the Republic as early as 1987 with no response.

19. The Government noted that in July 1990, the complainant did file a Notice of Objection and sent it to the Commissioner of Western Division. The document was forwarded to the Revising Court. No action appeared to have been taken by the court.

20. On the basis of these facts the communication was declared admissible.

Merits

21. Article 13 of The African Charter reads:

Every citizen shall have the right to participate freely in the government of his country, either directly or through freely chosen representatives in accordance with the provision of the law.

23. In 1994 there was a change of government in The Gambia. The present government recognizes that it has inherited the previous government's rights and obligations under international treaties.

24. The present government has a different view of voter registration. It concedes that the grievances expressed by the complainants are valid and logical. It describes that it is in the process of establishing an independent electoral commission and has commissioned a team of experts to review the present electoral law.

25. The African Commission welcomes the acceptance of the complainant's contentions and the government's stated determination to review the current electoral law, in order to ensure that elections are regular, free and fair.

FOR THESE REASONS THE COMMISSION

Holds that the above communication has reached an amicable resolution.

Questions and Comments

1. Friendly settlements must be attempted by the European Court of Human Rights and the UN Human Rights Committee as well as by the Inter-American Commission. What might account for the emphasis on achieving a friendly settlement?

2. In disappearances cases, the Inter-American Commission has usually found that "the facts prompting the petition in this case are not such that they can be resolved through recourse to the friendly settlement procedure." What kinds of facts would lead the Commission to this conclusion? In light of the Court's judgment in the *Caballero Delgado/Santana* case, does the Commission need to give more explanation concerning why it does not attempt a friendly settlement?

3. Is the friendly settlement procedure mandatory or even available in cases involving OAS member states that are not party to the American Convention?

4. Why did the Court dismiss the *Akman* case? Is it justified for the Court to impose a settlement on an applicant if the Court feels the offer is a fair one? What criteria should be

applied? Compare *Tahsin Acar v. Turkey* [GC], App. No. 26307/95, ECHR 2003-VI and *Haran v. Turkey*, App. No. 25754/94, judgment of March 26, 2002, with *Meriakri v. Moldova*, App. No. 53487/99, judgment of March 1, 2005, and *van Houten v. the Netherlands*, App. No. 25149/03, judgment of Sept. 29, 2005.

5. In the Gambian case, did the African Commission play any role in the settlement, or did it simply ratify the government's new policy? Should it monitor developments in the electoral law to ensure that the government follows through on its stated determination?

6. Generally, to what extent should regional human rights bodies examine the electoral systems in each membert state? See, e.g., *Yumak and Sadak v. Turkey*, App. No. 10226/03, judgment of January 30, 2007 (holding 5–2 that the 10% threshold of votes required by law for political parties to be represented in parliament did not overstep the government's margin of appreciation and thus did not violate the Convention).

B. Proving the Case

Each human rights body must find the relevant facts in order to reach a conclusion about state responsibility for human rights violations. Until recently, however, cases in the European system raised primarily questions of law; facts were rarely at issue. Until 1998, whatever fact-finding was necessary in Europe was done by the former European Commission. Now, the Court must handle all aspects of a case. See the Rules of Court on matters of evidence.

In contrast to the European system, nearly all cases in the African and Inter-American system have involved disputed facts, with few living victims or witnesses to testify. During several periods in its history, the Inter-American Commission's communication of complaints to states has been met with silence or an inadequate response. The Commission's Rules of Procedure permit it to take a decision in the absence of a reply and to presume the truth of the allegations. An example is provided by Case 10.287 (El Salvador), commonly known as the *Las Hojas Case*, where the government failed to reply despite numerous communications from the Commission over a three year period. The Commission said that "by not responding the Government of El Salvador has failed to fulfill its international obligation to provide information within a reaonsable period, as set forth in Article 48 of the Convention". *Las Hojas Case*, Report 26192, in Annual Report of the I.-A. Comm.H.R. 1992–1993, OEA/Ser.L/V/II.83, doc. 14, corr.1, March 1993, pp. 83–92, para. 6. Is it clear that the government has an international obligation to respond? In any event, the Commission accepted as true the facts complained of in relation to the Las Hojas massacre and declared El Salvador responsible, applying Article 39 (at the time Article 42) of its Rules of Procedure.

In all the systems, obtaining reliable information about human rights violations is difficult. The government may be unwilling to allow on-site fact-finding or to provide information about its own wrong-doing. Applicants may try to prove their cases by presenting testimony in hearings during the regular sessions of the commission or court. If a hearing can be obtained. NGO's may intervene to present evidence if permitted to do so. Even if there is a hearing, however, it is likely to last only a short time. Most of the proceedings are conducted through the exchange of written materials. Questions of credibility, standard of proof and protection of witnesses are common. The following cases illustrate the problems.

Argentina, Rep. No. 12/80, Case 3358 April 9, 1980, *Annual Report of the In-ter-American Commission on Human Rights 1979–1980*, OEA/Ser. G. CP/doc. 1110/80, 7 October 1980. Original: Spanish, pp. 70–74.

BACKGROUND:

1. The Commission received the following denunciation in a letter dated June 18, 1978:

"Rosa Ana Frigerio, aged 20, a student of agronomy, was arrested in her parents' house, Olavarria 4521, Mar del Plata, on August 25, 1976. At that time, she was con-fined to her bed and was unable to move on her own for the following reason:

In April 1976, Rosa Ana entered the '25th of May' Clinic in Mar del Plata, where she underwent an operation on her spinal column, as a result of an accident that occurred on August 24, 1974 when she was coming back from the university. When they took her away, she was wearing a plaster cast, and so they carried her out on a stretcher and took her away in an ambulance from the Naval Base in Mar del Plata. where she remained. Family members went there regularly to find out about her state of health, because when she had been taken away, she was still in a delicate state after her opera-tion; she had a serious infection and seven blood transfusions, but they took her away nonetheless.

When members of her family went to the Naval Base, they were told that they would be advised when they would be able to see her. This never happened. They were never able to see her, nor were they able to take her any clothes, since when they took her away, she only had on her plaster cast. Whenever they went, authorities told them that she was fine hut they were never able to verify this.

But at the end of 1976, the authorities at the Naval Base were changed, and from that time on, for what reason I do not know, they were told that she was not being detained there. A writ of habeas corpus was then filed (photocopy attached) on which a reply was received on March 1, 1977, to the effect that she was being held at the dis-posal of the Executive (PEN).

This means, then, that Rosa Ana was on the Naval Base up to the first days of March 1977, more than seven months.

What happened next was this: On March 23, 1977, Rosa's parents were summoned to an interview with the Commander of the Navy Base and other individuals. After some talk about Rosa, the Commander told them that Rosa had died in a confronta-tion, that the country was at war, and that Rosa knew people. He gave them a note (photocopy attached) showing the number of her grave.

2. In a note dated December 30, 1978, the Commission transmitted the pertinent parts of this denunciation to the Government of Argentina, asking it to supply the corresponding information.

3. During its on-site observation in Argentina in September 1979, the Commis-sion heard testimony from the claimants, and further information on the initial data received. The text reads as follows:

"On August 25, 1976, Rosa Ana Frigerio, aged 20 years, was arrested in her parents' house located at Olavarria 4521, Mar del Plata, Province of Buenos Aires.

The victim, who was a student of Agronomy at INTA, located in Balcaro and a branch of the National University of Mar del Plata, had been in an automobile accident when coming from that city to Mar del Plata on August 24, 1974. As a result of that accident, she suffered injury to her spinal column, the attending physician recom-mended an operation. The operation took place on April 26, 1976. Following hospitalization, which lasted for three months because of an infection, she was given a graft. During this period her condition was serious. Around July of that year she returned home wearing a plaster cast from the waist to below the knee, with the result that except for her arms she was completely immobilized. Such was her condition on the day she was arrested. On at least three occasions earlier, personnel who said they belong to the security forces had come to the victim's house to interrogate her, which they did with no one else present. Finally, on August 25, five or six civilians came with an ambulance, and took her away on a chair. They told the claimant and her mother that they were taking her to the Naval Base in Mar del Plata. While the victim was hospitalized in the sanitarium, other persons who also said they came from the security forces searched her room without apparently finding anything of interest.

Following the transfer, the complainant went to the Naval Base several times; there he was given evasive answers in the guard-room. On September 10 the complainant received a telephone call from the Base, from a lieutenant judge-advocate, who told him that his daughter was being held at the Base at the disposal of the Executive. From then on the complainant frequently went to the Base where he was received by various officers, including the above-mentioned judge-advocate and other officers.

In late 1976 the commandants and officers of the Base were changed.

From then on the complainant began to be told that Rosa Ana was not at the Base; he was not received by any senior officer, apparently because the previous ones had been changed.

In view of these circumstances, the complainant filed a writ of habeas corpus in February 1977 with the Federal Court of Mar del Plata (Judge Ana Maria Teodon). In connection with that action, which bears the number 768, a communication was received on March 1, 1977 from the Base Commander, which reads as follows: "I am pleased to inform you with respect to your official letter on March 3, 1976, issued in Case No. 768, entitled 'Contessi de Frigerio, Antonieta s/filing of a writ of habeas corpus in favor of Frigerio Rosa Ana', that this person is being held at the disposal of the Executive because she is guilty of involvement in subversive activities." The Communication is dated February 25, 1977.

On March 31, 1977, the complainant received a summons from the Navy telling him that he should appear on the following day by order of the Commander of that unit. On appearing the following day at 9 a.m. the claimant was received by the above-mentioned Commander, who was accompanied by a captain. The Commander told him something along the following lines: "Rosa Ana is (or was) held at the Base and has been killed by her comrades in a confrontation that took place on March 8."

Since he was not satisfied with the reply, the complainant went to the Civil Registry Office one month later and obtained a death certificate that states that Rosa Ana had died from "cardiac arrest, cardiothoracic traumatism." That is to say, a cause of death completely different and inconsistent with the cause given by the Commander; this gave rise to other doubts.

On March 31, the above-mentioned officers delivered to the complainant an unsigned paper stating: "Parque Cemetery, Grave 1133—Temporary Burial Section, sector B". They told him that the victim was buried at that place. The claimant has endeavored to obtain the exhumation of the body in order to verify the accuracy of what he was told by the above-mentioned officers, but so far has been unsuccessful.

During the above-mentioned interview, the complainants reacted violently, and told the officers they were talking to that they had killed Rosa Ana and the officers did not reply. The captain merely said that the country was at war and the victim "knew people."

4. This information was brought to the attention of the Government in the preliminary report that the Commission submitted to the Government of Argentina in December 1979.

5. In a note received by the Commission on March 27, 1980 the Argentine Government replied as follows:

> In reply to the communication to the Government of Argentina from the Inter-American Commission on Human Rights, relating to the above-mentioned case, we wish to inform you of the following:
>
>> That Rosa Ana Frigerio was arrested by legal forces in August 1976; this action and the place of detention was made known to her relatives by official reports provided by the corresponding authorities. The purpose of the arrest was to investigate her possible links with a group of terrorists. Because the person concerned confessed that she was a member of that group but had not committed offenses and also because of her decision to leave it and to collaborate by providing information, the authorities detaining her considered it necessary to protect her and similarly her family by not informing them of her situation because of the possibility that they might be attacked by the terrorist organization to which Rosa A. Frigerio had belonged, as a reprisal for her defection.

Accordingly, Rosa Ana was kept in an establishment where she collaborated with the personnel responsible for counter-terrorist activities.

On March 8, 1977, on the basis of information obtained by the authorities a number of visits were made to places which Rosa Ana Frigeno and another detainee had stated were hideouts of the terrorist group and places where weapons and explosives were stored. On that occasion, the two detainees accompanied the legal forces and, on arriving a short distance from a house they pointed out in Calle Mario Bravo on the corner of Esteban Echeverria, Mar del Plata, Province of Buenos Aires, they were met with a heavy volley of gunfire from large caliber weapons coming from the interior of the house, which caused the death—in situ—of Rosa Ana Frigerio. In the same operation the other detainee died and an officer was seriously wounded. It should be stated that neither of the circumstances were reported at that time through the normal information media because tactical measures of counter information were in force.

Subsequently, the authorities informed the family of Rosa Ana Frigerio of what had happened and told them where her body was buried. It should be noted that on April 25, 1979 the Federal Judge of Mar del Plata authorized the family to exhume the body of Rosa Ana Frigerio and take it to whatever cemetery they wished, although so far this transfer has not taken place.

This regrettable episode, which is typical of the unconventional attack to which Argentina has been subject, should be construed within the framework of a struggle which the entire Argentine people as well as its authorities had to wage against the terrorists.

WHEREAS:

1. The above-mentioned information shows that Miss Rosa Ana Frigerio was detained by legal forces on August 25, 1976 and was so detained when she died on May 8, 1977.

2. The reply of the Government of Argentina does not elucidate the facts reported nor does it deny the allegations made by the claimant.

3. The Government of Argentina has not provided the Commission with any information that enables it to conclude that a legal investigation on the case took place to elucidate the confused circumstances in which Miss Rosa Ana Frigerio died.

THE INTER-AMERICAN COMMISSION ON HUMAN RIGHTS
RESOLVES:

1. To observe to the Government of Argentina that such acts constitute very serious violations of the right to life, liberty and personal security (Art. I); of the right to a fair trial (Art. XVIII) and of the right of protection from arbitrary arrest (Art. XXV) of the American Declaration on the Rights and Duties of Man.

2. To recommend to the Govennment of Argentina: a. that it order a complete, impartial investigation to identify the perpetrators of the acts reported; b. that it punish the persons responsible for those acts in accordance to the laws of Argentina; and c. that it report to the Commission within a period of not more than sixty days on the steps taken to implement the recommendations included in this Resolution.

3. To transmit this Resolution to the Government of Argentina and to the claimants.

4. To include this Resolution in the Annual Report to the General Assembly of the Organization of American States, pursuant to Art. 9 (bis), paragraph c iii, of the Statute of the Commission, although the Commission, in the light of the steps taken by the Government of Argentina, may reconsider the decision adopted.

———————

Velásquez Rodríguez Case, Judgment of July 29, 1988, 4 Inter-Am Ct. H.R. (Ser. C) (1988).

1. The Inter-American Commission on Human Rights . . . submitted the instant case to the Inter-American Court of Human Rights . . . on April 24, 1986. It originated in a petition (No. 7920) against the State of Honduras . . . , which the Secretariat of the Commission received on October 7, 1981.

2. In submitting the case, the Commission invoked Articles 50 and 51 of the American Convention on Human Rights . . . and requested that the Court determine whether the State in question had violated Articles 4 (Right to Life), 5 (Right to Humane Treatment) and 7 (Right to Personal Liberty) of the Convention in the case of Angel Manfredo Velásquez Rodríguez (also known as Manfredo Velásquez). In addition, the Commission asked the Court to rule that "the consequences of the situation that constituted the breach of such right or freedom be remedied and that fair compensation be paid to the injured party or parties".

3. According to the petition filed with the Commission, and the supplementary information received subsequently, Manfredo Velásquez, a student at the National Autonomous University of Honduras, "was violently detained without a warrant for his arrest by members of the National Office of Investigations (DNI) and G-2 of the Armed Forces of Honduras." The detention took place in Tegucigalpa on the afternoon of September 12, 1981. According to the petitioners, several eyewit-

nesses reported that Manfredo Velásquez and others were detained and taken to the cells of Public Security Forces Station No. 2 located in the Barrio El Manchén of Tegucigalpa, where he was "accused of alleged political crimes and subjected to harsh interrogation and cruel torture". The petition added that on September 17, 1981, Manfredo Velásquez was moved to the First Infantry Battalion, where the interrogation continued, but that the police and security forces denied that he had been detained.

4. After transmitting the relevant parts of the petition to the Government, the Commission, on various occasions, requested information on the matter. Since the Commission received no reply, it applied Article 42 (former 39) of its Regulations and presumed "as true the allegations contained in the communication of October 4, 1981 concerning the detention and possible disappearance of Angel Manfredo Velásquez Rodríguez in the Republic of Honduras" and pointed out to the Government "that such acts are most serious violations of the right to life (Art. 4) and the right to personal liberty (Art. 7) of the American Convention" (Resolution 30/83 of October 4, 1983).

I

11. The Court has jurisdiction to hear the instant case. Honduras ratified the Convention on September 8, 1977 and recognized the contentious jurisdiction of the Court, as set out in Article 62 of the Convention, on September 9, 1981. The case was submitted to the Court by the Commission pursuant to Article 61 of the Convention and Article 50 (1) and 50 (2) of the Regulations of the Commission.

. . . .

29. After having heard the witnesses, the Court directed the submission of additional evidence to assist it in its deliberations. Its Order of October 7, 1987 reads as follows:

A. Documentary Evidence

1. To request the Government of Honduras to provide the organizational chart showing the structure of Battalion 316 and its position within the Armed Forces of Honduras.

B. Testimony

1. To call as a witnesses, Marco Tulio Regalado and Alexander Hernández, members of the Armed Forces of Honduras.

C. Reiteration of a Request

1. To the Government of Honduras to establish the whereabouts of José Isaías Vilorio and, once located, to call him as a witness.

30. By the same Order, the Court set December 15, 1987 as the deadline for the submission of documentary evidence and decided to hear the oral testimony at its January session.

31. In response to that Order, on December 14, 1987 the Government: a) with respect to the organizational structure of Battalion 316, requested that the Court receive the testimony of its Commandant in a closed hearing "because of strict security reasons of the State of Honduras"; b) requested that the Court hear the testimony of Alexander Hernández and Marco Tulio Regalado "in the Republic of Honduras, in a manner to be decided by the Court and in a closed hearing to be set

at an opportune time . . . because of security reasons and because both persons are on active duty in the Armed Forces of Honduras"; and c) reported that José Isaías Vilorio was "working as an administrative employee of the National Office of Investigations, a branch of the Public Security Forces, in the city of Tegucigalpa".

32. By note of December 24, 1987, the Commission objected to hearing the testimony of members of the Honduran military in closed session. This position was reiterated by note of January 11, 1988.

33. On the latter date, the Court decided to receive the testimony of the members of the Honduran military at a closed hearing in the presence of the parties.

34. Pursuant to its Order of October 7, 1987 and its decision of January 11, 1988, the Court held a closed hearing on January 20, 1988, which both parties attended, at which it received the testimony of persons who identified themselves as Lt. Col. Alexander Hernández and Lt. Marco Tulio Regalado Hernández. The Court also heard the testimony of Col. Roberto Núñez Montes, Head of the Intelligence Services of Honduras.

. . . .

V

82. The Commission presented testimony and documentary evidence to show that there were many kidnappings and disappearances in Honduras from 1981 to 1984 and that those acts were attributable to the Armed Forces of Honduras (hereinafter "Armed Forces"), which was able to rely at least on the tolerance of the Government. Three officers of the Armed Forces testified on this subject at the request of the Court.

83. Various witnesses testified that they were kidnapped, imprisoned in clandestine jails and tortured by members of the Armed Forces.

. . . .

84. Inés Consuelo Murillo testified that she was secretly held for approximately three months. According to her testimony, she and José Gonzalo Flores Trejo, whom she knew casually, were captured on March 13, 1983 by men who got out of a car, shouted that they were from Immigration and hit her with their weapons. Behind them was another car which assisted in the capture. She said she was blindfolded, bound, and driven presumably to San Pedro Sula, where she was taken to a secret detention center. There she was tied up, beaten, kept nude most of the time, not fed for many days, and subjected to electrical shocks, hanging, attempts to asphyxiate her, threats of burning her eyes, threats with weapons, burns on the legs, punctures of the skin with needles, drugs and sexual abuse. She admitted carrying false identification when detained, but ten days later she gave them her real name. She stated that thirty-six days after her detention she was moved to a place near Tegucigalpa, where she saw military officers (one of whom was Second Lt. Marco Tulio Regalado Hernández), papers with an Army letterhead, and Armed Forces graduation rings. This witness added that she was finally turned over to the police and was brought before a court. She was accused of some twenty crimes, but her attorney was not allowed to present evidence and there was no trial (testimony of Inés Consuelo Murillo).

85. Lt. Regalado Hernández said that he had no knowledge of the case of Inés Consuelo Murillo, except for what he had read in the newspaper . . . .

86. The Government stated that it was unable to inform Ms. Murillo's relatives of her detention because she was carrying false identification, a fact which also showed, in the Government's opinion, that she was not involved in lawful activities and was, therefore, not telling the whole truth. It added that her testimony of a casual relationship with José Gonzalo Flores Trejo was not credible because both were clearly involved in criminal activities.

87. José Gonzalo Flores Trejo testified that he and Inés Consuelo Murillo were kidnapped together and taken to a house presumably located in San Pedro Sula, where his captors repeatedly forced his head into a trough of water until he almost drowned, kept his hands and feet tied, and hung him so that only his stomach touched the ground. He also declared that, subsequently, in a place where he was held near Tegucigalpa, his captors covered his head with a "capucha" (a piece of rubber cut from an inner tube, which prevents a person from breathing through the mouth and nose), almost asphyxiating him, and subjected him to electric shocks. He said he knew he was in the hands of the military because when his blindfold was removed in order to take some pictures of him, he saw a Honduran military officer and on one occasion when they took him to bathe, he saw a military barracks. He also heard a trumpet sound, orders being given and the report of a cannon . . . .

88. The Government argued that the testimony of the witness, a Salvadoran national, was not credible because he attempted to convince the Court that his encounters with Inés Consuelo Murillo were of a casual nature. The Government added that both individuals were involved in illicit activities.

89. Virgilio Carías, who was President of the Socialist Party of Honduras, testified that he was kidnapped in broad daylight on September 12, 1981, when 12 or 13 persons, armed with pistols, carbines and automatic rifles, surrounded his automobile. He stated that he was taken to a secret jail, threatened and beaten, and had no food, water or bathroom facilities for four or five days. On the tenth day, his captors gave him an injection in the arm and threw him, bound, in the back of a pick-up truck. Subsequently, they draped him over the back of a mule and set it walking through the mountains near the Nicaraguan border, where he regained his liberty . . . .

90. The Government indicated that this witness expressly admitted that he opposed the Honduran government. The Government also maintained that his answers were imprecise or evasive and argued that, because the witness said he could not identify his captors, his testimony was hearsay and of no evidentiary value since, in the Government's view, he had no personal knowledge of the events and only knew of them through others.

91. A Honduran attorney, who stated that he defended political prisoners, testified that Honduran security forces detained him without due process in 1982. He was held for ten years in a clandestine jail, without charges, and was beaten and tortured before he was brought before the court . . . .

92. The Government affirmed that the witness was charged with the crimes of threatening national security and possession of arms that only the Armed Forces

were authorized to carry and, therefore, had a personal interest in discrediting Honduras with his testimony.

93. Another lawyer, who also said that he defended political detainees and who testified on Honduran law, stated that personnel of the Department of Special Investigations detained him a broad daylight in Tegucigalpa on June 1, 1982, blindfolded him, took him to a place he was unable to recognize and kept him without food or water for four days. He was beaten and insulted. He said that he could see through the blindfold that he was in a military installation . . . .

94. The Government claimed that this witness made several false statements regarding the law in force in Honduras and that his testimony "lacks truth or force because it is not impartial and his interest is to discredit the State of Honduras."

95. The Court received testimony which indicated that somewhere between 112 and 130 individuals were disappeared from 1981 and 1984. A former member of the Armed Forces testified that, according to a list in the files of Battalion 316, the number might be 140 or 150. . . .

96. The Court heard testimony from the President of the Committee for the Defense of Human Rights in Honduras regarding the existence of a unit within the Armed Forces which carried out disappearances. According to his testimony, in 1980 there was group called "the fourteen" under the command of Major Adolfo Díaz, attached to the General Staff of the Armed Forces. Subsequently, this group was replaced by "the ten," commanded by Capt. Alexander Hernández, and finally by Battalion 316, a special operations group, with separate units trained in surveillance, kidnapping, execution, telephone tapping, etc. The existence of this group had always been denied until it was mentioned in a communiqué of the Armed Forces in September 1986 . . . .

97. Alexander Hernández, now a Lieutenant Colonel, denied having participated in the group "the ten", having been a part of Battalion 316, or having had any type of contact with it . . . .

98. The current Director of Honduran Intelligence testified that he learned from the files of his department that in 1984 an intelligence battalion called 316 was created, the purpose of which was to provide combat intelligence to the 101st, 105th and 110th Brigades. He added that this battalion initially functioned as a training unit, until the creation of the Intelligence School, to which all its training functions were gradually transferred, and that the Battalion was finally disbanded in September 1987. He stated that there was never any group called "the fourteen" or "the ten" in the Armed Forces or security forces.

99. According to testimony on the *modus operandi* of the practice of disappearances, the kidnappers followed a pattern: they used automobiles with tinted glass (which requires a special permit from the Traffic Division), without license plates or with false plates, and sometimes used special disguises, such as wigs, false mustaches, masks, etc. The kidnappings were selective. The victims were first placed under surveillance, then the kidnapping was planned. Microbuses or vans were used. Some victims were taken from their homes; others were picked up in public streets. On one occasion, when a patrol car intervened, the kidnappers identified

themselves as members of a special group of the Armed Forces and were permitted to leave with the victim.

100. A former member of the Armed Forces [Florencio Caballero], who said that he belonged to Battalion 316 (the group charged with carrying out the kidnappings) and that he had participated in some kidnappings, testified that the starting point was an order given by the chief of the unit to investigate an individual and place him under surveillance. According to this witness, if a decision was made to take further steps, the kidnapping was carried out by persons in civilian clothes using pseudonyms and disguises and carrying arms. The unit had four double-cabin Toyota pick-up trucks without police markings for use in kidnappings. Two of the pick-ups had tinted glass.

101. The Government objected, under Article 37 of the Rules of Procedure, to the testimony of Florencio Caballero because he had deserted from the Armed Forces and had violated his military oath. By unanimous decision of October 6, 1987, the Court rejected the challenge and reserved the right to consider his testimony.

102. The current Director of Intelligence of the Armed Forces testified that intelligence units do not carry out detentions because they "get burned" (are discovered) and do not use pseudonyms or automobiles without license plates. He added that Florencio Caballero never worked in the intelligence services and that he was a driver for the Army General Headquarters in Tegucigalpa.

103. The former member of the Armed Forces confirmed the existence of secret jails and of specially chosen places for the burial of those executed. He also related that there was a torture group and an interrogation group in his unit, and that he belonged to the latter. The torture group used electric shock, the water barrel and the "capucha." They kept the victims nude, without food, and threw cold water on them. He added that those selected for execution were handed over to a group of former prisoners, released from jail for carrying out executions, who used firearms at first and then knives and machetes.

104. The current Director of Intelligence denied that the Armed Forces had secret jails, stating that it was not its *modus operandi*. He claimed that it was subversive elements who do have such jails, which they call "the peoples' prisons". He added that the function of an intelligence service is not to eliminate or disappear people, but rather to obtain and process information to allow the highest levels of government to make informed decisions.

105. A Honduran officer, called as a witness by the Court, testified that the use of violence or psychological means to force a detainee to give information is prohibited.

106. The Commission submitted many clippings from the Honduran press from 1981 to 1984 which contain information on at least 64 disappearances, which were apparently carried out against ideological or political opponents or trade union members. Six of those individuals, after their release, complained of torture and other cruel, inhuman and degrading treatment. There clippings mention secret cemeteries where 17 bodies had been found.

107. According to the testimony of his sister, eyewitnesses to the kidnapping of Manfredo Velásquez told her that he was detained on September 12, 1981, between

4:30 and 5:00 p.m., in a parking lot in downtown Tegucigalpa by seven heavily-armed men dressed in civilian clothes (one of them being First Sgt. José Isaías Vilorio), who used a white Ford without license plates.

108. This witness informed the Court that Col. Leónidas Torres Arias, who had been head of Honduran military intelligence, announced in a press conference in Mexico City that Manfredo Velásquez was kidnapped by a special squadron commanded by Capt. Alexander Hernández, who was carrying out the direct orders of General Gustavo Alvarez Martínez.

109. Lt. Col. Hernández testified that he never received any order to detain Manfredo Velásquez and had never worked in police operations. . . .

110. The Government objected, under Article 37 of the Rules of Procedure, to the testimony of Zenaida Velásquez because, as sister of the victim, she was a party interested in the outcome of the case.

111. The Court unanimously rejected the objection because it considered the fact that the witness was the victim's sister to be insufficient to disqualify her. The Court reserved the right to consider her testimony.

112. The Government asserted that her testimony was irrelevant because it did not refer to the case before the Court and that what she related about the kidnapping of her brother was not her personal knowledge but rather hearsay.

113. The former member of the Armed Forces who claimed to have belonged to the group that carried out kidnappings told the Court that, although the did not take part in the kidnapping of Manfredo Velásquez, Lt. Flores Murillo had told him what had happened. According to this testimony, Manfredo Velásquez was kidnapped in downtown Tegucigalpa in an operation in which Sgt. José Isaías Vilorio, men using the pseudonyms Ezequiel and Titanio, and Lt. Flores Murillo himself, took part. The Lieutenant told him that during the struggle Ezequiel's gun went off and wounded Manfredo in the leg. They took the victim to INDUMIL (Military Industries) where they tortured him. They then turned him over the those in charge of carrying out executions who, at the orders of General Alvarez, Chief of the Armed Forces, took him out of Tegucigalpa and killed him with a knife and machete. They dismembered his body and buried the remains in different places (testimony of Florencio Caballero).

114. The current Director of Intelligence testified that José Isaías Vilorio was a file clerk of the DNI. He said he did not know Lt. Flores Murillo and stated that INDUMIL had never been used as a detention center (testimony of Roberto Núñez Montes).

115. One witness testified that he was taken prisoner on September 29, 1981 by five or six persons who identified themselves as members of the Armed Forces and took him to the officers of DNI. They blindfolded him and took him in a car to an unknown place, where they tortured him. On October 1, 1981, while he was being held, he heard a moaning and pained voice through a hole in the door to an adjoining room. The person identified himself as Manfredo Velásquez and asked for help. According to the testimony of the witness, at that moment Lt. Ramón Mejía came in and hit him because he found him standing up, although the witness told the Lieutenant that he had gotten up because he was tired. He added that, subsequently, Sgt.

Carlos Alfredo Martínez, whom he had met at the bar where he worked, told him they had turned Manfredo Velásquez over to members of Battalion 316.

116. The Government asserted that the testimony of this witness "is not completely trustworthy because of discrepancies that should not be overlooked, such as the fact that he had testified that he had only been arrested once, in 1981, for trafficking in arms and hijacking a plane, when the truth was that Honduran police had arrested him on several occasions because of his unenviable record".

[. . . .]

VI

119. The testimony and documentary evidence, corroborated by press clippings, presented by the Commission, tend to show:

a. That there existed in Honduras from 1981 to 1984 a systematic and selective practice of disappearances carried out with the assistance or tolerance of the government;

b. That Manfredo Velásquez was a victim of that practice and was kidnapped and presumably tortured, executed and clandestinely buried by agents of the Armed Forces of Honduras, and

c. That in the period in which those acts occurred, the legal remedies available in Honduras were not appropriate or effective to guarantee his rights to life, liberty and personal integrity.

120. The Government, in turn, submitted documents and based its argument on the testimony of three members of the Honduran Armed Forces, two of whom were summoned by the Court because they had been identified in the proceedings as directly involved in the general practice referred to and in the disappearance of Manfredo Velásquez. This evidence may be summarized as follows:

a. The testimony purports to explain the organization and functioning of the security forces accused of carrying out the specific acts and denies any knowledge of or personal involvement in the acts of the officers who testified;

b. Some documents purport to show that no civil suit had been brought to establish a presumption of the death of Manfredo Velásquez; and,

c. Other documents purport to prove that the Supreme Court of Honduras received and acted upon some writs of habeas corpus and that some of those writs resulted in the release of the persons on whose behalf they were brought.

121. The record contains no other direct evidence, such as expert opinion, inspections or reports.

VII

122. Before weighing the evidence, the Court must address some questions regarding the burden of proof and the general criteria considered in its evaluation and finding of the facts in the instant proceeding.

123. Because the Commission is accusing the Government of the disappearance of Manfredo Velásquez, it, in principle, should bear the burden of proving the facts underlying its petition.

124. The Commission's argument relies upon the proposition that the policy of disappearances, supported or tolerated by the Government, is designed to conceal and destroy evidence of disappearances. When the existence of such a policy or practice has been shown, the disappearance of a particular individual may be proved

through circumstantial or indirect evidence or by logical inference. Otherwise, it would be impossible to prove that an individual has been disappeared.

125. The Government did not object to the Commission's approach. Nevertheless, it argued that neither the existence of a practice of disappearances in Honduras nor the participation of Honduran officials in the alleged disappearance of Manfredo Velásquez had been proven.

126. The Court finds no reason to consider the Commission's argument inadmissible. If it can be shown that there was an official practice of disappearances in Honduras, carried out by the Government or at least tolerated by it, and if the disappearance of Manfredo Velásquez can be linked to that practice, the Commission's allegations will have been proven to the Court's satisfaction, so long as the evidence presented on both points meets the standard of proof required in cases such as this.

127. The Court must determine what the standards of proof should be in the instant case. Neither the Convention, the Statute of the Court nor its Rules of Procedure speak to this matter. Nevertheless, international jurisprudence has recognized the power of the courts to weigh the evidence freely, although it has always avoided a rigid rule regarding the amount of proof necessary to support the judgment (Cf. *Corfu Channel, Merits*, Judgment, I.C.J. Reports 1949; *Military and Paramilitary Activities in and against Nicaragua (Nicaragua v. United States of America), Merits*, Judgment, I.C.J. Reports 1986, paras. 29–30 and 59–60).

128. The standards of proof are less formal in an international legal proceeding that in a domestic one. The latter recognize different burdens of proof, depending upon the nature, character and seriousness of the case.

129. The Court cannot ignore the special seriousness of finding that a State Party to the Convention has carried out or has tolerated a practice of disappearances in its territory. This requires the Court to apply a standard of proof which considers the seriousness of the charge and which, notwithstanding what has already been said, is capable of establishing the truth of the allegations in a convincing manner.

130. The practice of international and domestic courts shows that direct evidence, whether testimonial or documentary, is not the only type of evidence that may be legitimately considered in reaching a decision. Circumstantial evidence, indicia, and presumptions may be considered, so long as they lead to conclusions consistent with the facts.

131. Circumstantial or presumptive evidence is especially important in allegations of disappearances, because this type of repression is characterized by an attempt to suppress all information about the kidnapping or the whereabouts and fate of the victim.

132. Since the Court is an international tribunal, it has its own specialized procedures. All the elements of domestic legal procedures are therefore not automatically applicable.

133. The above principle is generally valid in international proceedings, but is particularly applicable in human rights cases.

134. The international protection of human rights should not be confused with criminal justice. States do not appear before the Court as defendants in a criminal

action. The objective of international human rights law is not to punish those individuals who are guilty of violations, but rather to protect the victims and to provide for the reparation of damages resulting from the acts of the States responsible.

135. In contrast to domestic criminal law, in proceedings to determine human rights violations the State cannot rely on the defense that the complainant has failed to present evidence when it cannot be obtained without the State's cooperation.

136. The State controls the means to verify acts occurring within its territory. Although the Commission has investigatory powers, it cannot exercise them within a State's jurisdiction unless it has the cooperation of that State.

137. Since the Government only offered some documentary evidence in support of its preliminary objections, but none on the merits, the Court must reach its decision without the valuable assistance of a more active participation by Honduras, which might otherwise have resulted in a more adequate presentation of its case.

138. The manner in which the Government conducted its defense would have sufficed to prove many of the Commission's allegations by virtue of the principle that the silence of the accused or elusive or ambiguous answers on its part may be interpreted as an acknowledgment of the truth of the allegations, so long as the contrary is not indicated by the record or is not compelled as a matter of law. This result would not hold under criminal law, which does not apply in the instant case (. . . .). The Court tried to compensate for this procedural principle by admitting all the evidence offered, even if it was untimely, and by ordering the presentation of additional evidence. This was done, of course, without prejudice to its discretion to consider the silence or inaction of Honduras or to its duty to evaluate the evidence as a whole.

139. In its own proceeding and without prejudice to its having considered other elements of proof, the Commission invoked Article 42 of its Regulations, which reads as follows:

> The facts reported in the petition whose pertinent parts have been transmitted to the government of the State in reference shall be presumed to be true if, during the maximum period set by the Commission under the provisions of Article 34 paragraph 5, the government has not provided the pertinent information, as long as other evidence does not lead to a different conclusion.

Because the Government did not object here to the use of this legal presumption in the proceedings before the Commission and since the Government fully participated in these proceedings, Article 42 is irrelevant here.

VIII

140. In the instant case, the Court accepts the validity of the documents presented by the Commission and by Honduras, particularly because the parties did not oppose or object to those documents nor did they question their authenticity or veracity.

141. During the hearings, the Government objected, under Article 37 of the Rules of Procedure, to the testimony of witnesses called by the Commission. By decision of October 6, 1987, the Court rejected the challenge. . . .

142. During cross-examination, the Government's attorneys attempted to show that some witnesses were not impartial because of ideological reasons, origin or

nationality, family relations, or a desire to discredit Honduras. They even insinuated that testifying against the State in these proceedings was disloyal to the nation. Likewise, they cited criminal records or pending charges to show that some witnesses were not competent to testify (*supra* 86, 88, 90, 92, 101, 110 and 116)

143. It is true, of course, that certain factors may clearly influence a witness' truthfulness. However, the Government did not present any concrete evidence to show that the witnesses had not told the truth, but rather limited itself to making general observations regarding their alleged incompetency or lack of impartiality. This is insufficient to rebut testimony which is fundamentally consistent with that of other witnesses. The Court cannot ignore such testimony.

144. Moreover, some of the Government's arguments are unfounded within the context of human rights law. The insinuation that persons who, for any reason, resort to the Inter-American system for the protection of human rights are disloyal to their country is unacceptable and cannot constitute a basis for any penalty or negative consequence. Human rights are higher values that "are not derived from the fact that (an individual) is a national of a certain state, but are based upon attributes of his human personality" (American Declaration of the Rights and Duties of Man, Whereas clauses, and American Convention, Preamble).

145. Neither is it sustainable that having a criminal record or charges pending is sufficient in and of itself to find that a witness is not competent to testify in Court. As the Court ruled, in its decision of October 6, 1987, in the instant case,

> under the American Convention on Human Rights, it is impermissible to deny a witness, *a priori*, the possibility of testifying to facts relevant to a matter before the Court, even if he has an interest in that proceeding, because he has been prosecuted or even convicted under internal laws.

146. Many of the press clippings offered by the Commission cannot be considered as documentary evidence as such. However, many of them contain public and well-known facts which, as such, do not require proof; others are of evidentiary value, as has been recognized in international jurisprudence (*Military and Paramilitary Activities in and against Nicaragua, supra* 127, paras. 62–64), insofar as they textually reproduce public statements, especially those of high-ranking members of the Armed Forces, of the Government, or even of the Supreme Court of Honduras, such as some of those made by the President of the latter. Finally, others are important as a whole insofar as they corroborate testimony regarding the responsibility of the Honduran military and police for disappearances.

IX

147. The Court now turns to the relevant facts that it finds to have been proven. They are as follows:

> a. During the period 1981 to 1984, 100 to 150 persons disappeared in the Republic of Honduras, and many were never heard from again (testimony of Miguel Angel Pavón Salazar, Ramón Custodio López, Efraín Díaz Arrivillaga, Florencio Caballero and press clippings).
>
> b. Those disappearances followed a similar pattern, beginning with the kidnapping of the victims by force, often in broad daylight and in public places, by armed men in civilian clothes and disguises, who acted with apparent impunity and who used

vehicles without any official identification, with tinted windows and with false license plates or no plates (testimony of Miguel Angel Pavón Salazar, Ramón Custodio López, Efraín Díaz Arrivillaga, Florencio Caballero and press clippings).

c. It was public and notorious knowledge in Honduras that the kidnappings were carried out by military personnel or the police, or persons acting under their orders (testimony of Miguel Angel Pavón Salazar, Ramón Custodio López, Efraín Díaz Arrivillaga, Florencio Caballero and press clippings).

d. The disappearances were carried out in a systematic manner, regarding which the Court considers the following circumstances particularly relevant:

i. The victims were usually persons whom Honduran officials considered dangerous to State security (testimony of Miguel Angel Pavón Salazar, Ramón Custodio López, Efraín Díaz Arrivillaga, Florencio Caballero, Virgilio Carías, Milton Jiménez Puerto, René Velásquez Díaz, Inés Consuelo Murillo, José Gonzalo Flores Trejo, Zenaida Velásquez, César Augusto Murillo and press clippings). In addition, the victims had usually been under surveillance for long periods of time (testimony of Ramón Custodio López and Florencio Caballero);

ii. The arms employed were reserved for the official use of the military and police, and the vehicles used had tinted glass, which requires special official authorization. In some cases, Government agents carried out the detentions openly and without any pretense or disguise; in others, government agents had cleared the areas where the kidnappings were to take place and, on at least one occasion, when government agents stopped the kidnappers they were allowed to continue freely on their way after showing their identification (testimony of Miguel Angel Pavón Salazar, Ramón Custodio López and Florencio Caballero);

iii. The kidnappers blindfolded the victims, took them to secret, unofficial detention centers and moved them from one center to another. They interrogated the victims and subjected them to cruel and humiliating treatment and torture. Some were ultimately murdered and their bodies were buried in clandestine cemeteries (testimony of Miguel Angel Pavón Salazar, Ramón Custodio López, Florencio Caballero, René Velásquez Díaz, Inés Consuelo Murillo and José Gonzalo Flores Trejo);

iv. When queried by relatives, lawyers and persons or entities interested in the protection of human rights, or by judges charged with executing writs of habeas corpus, the authorities systematically denied any knowledge of the detentions or the whereabouts or fate of the victims. That attitude was seen even in the cases of persons who later reappeared in the hands of the same authorities who had systematically denied holding them or knowing their fate (testimony of Inés Consuelo Murillo, José Gonzalo Flores Trejo, Efraín Díaz Arrivillaga, Florencio Caballero, Virgilio Carías, Milton Jiménez Puerto, René Velásquez Díaz, Zenaida Velásquez, César Augusto Murillo and press clippings).

v. Military and police officials as well as those from the Executive and Judicial Branches either denied the disappearances or were incapable of preventing or investigating them, punishing those responsible, or helping those interested discover the whereabouts and fate of the victims or the location of their remains. The investigative committees created by the Government and the Armed Forces did not produce any results. The judicial proceedings brought were processed slowly with a clear lack of interest and some were ultimately dismissed (testimony of Inés Consuelo Murillo, José Gonzalo Flores Trejo, Efraín Díaz Arrivillaga, Florencio Caballero, Virgilio Carías, Milton Jiménez Puerto, René Velásquez Díaz, Zenaida Velásquez, César Augusto Murillo and press clippings);

e. On September 12, 1981, between 4:30 and 5:00 p.m., several heavily-armed men in civilian clothes driving a white Ford without license plates kidnapped Manfredo Velásquez from a parking lot in downtown Tegucigalpa. Today, nearly seven years later, he remains disappeared, which creates a reasonable presumption that he is dead (testimony of Miguel Angel Pavón Salazar, Ramón Custodio López, Zenaida Velásquez, Florencio Caballero, Leopoldo Aguilar Villalobos and press clippings)

f. Persons connected with the Armed Forces or under its direction carried out that kidnapping (testimony of Ramón Custodio López, Zenaida Velásquez, Florencio Caballero, Leopoldo Aguilar Villalobos and press clippings).

g. The kidnapping and disappearance of Manfredo Velásquez falls within the systematic practice of disappearances referred to by the facts deemed proved in paragraphs a–d. To wit:

i. Manfredo Velásquez was a student who was involved in activities the authorities considered "dangerous" to national security (testimony of Miguel Angel Pavón Salazar, Ramón Custodio López and Zenaida Velásquez).

ii. The kidnapping of Manfredo Velásquez was carried out in broad daylight by men in civilian clothes who used a vehicle without license plates.

ii. In the case of Manfredo Velásquez, there were the same type of denials by his captors and the Armed Forces, the same omissions of the latter and of the Government in investigating and revealing his whereabouts, and the same ineffectiveness of the courts where three writs of habeas corpus and two criminal complaints were brought (testimony of Miguel Angel Pavón Salazar, Ramón Custodio López, Zenaida Velásquez, press clippings and documentary evidence).

h. There is no evidence in the record that Manfredo Velásquez had disappeared in order to join subversive groups, other than a letter from the Mayor of Langue, which contained rumors to that effect. The letter itself shows that the Government associated him with activities it considered a threat to national security. However, the Government did not corroborate the view expressed in the letter with any other evidence. Nor is there any evidence that he was kidnapped by common criminals or other persons unrelated to the practice of disappearances existing at that time.

148. Based upon the above, the Court finds that the following facts have been proven in this proceeding: (1) a practice of disappearances carried out or tolerated by Honduran officials existed between 1981 and 1984; (2) Manfredo Velásquez disappeared at the hands of or with the acquiescence of those officials within the framework of that practice; and (3) the Government of Honduras failed to guarantee the human rights affected by that practice.

. . . .

Questions and Comments

1. In the first case against Argentina, above, the Commission heard testimony from the petitioners during an on-site investigation. Do both parties have a right to be present during a hearing on a petition? Can the government question witnesses or petitioners? See Regulations, Articles 43, 65–67. Is the government obligated to participate in a formal hearing convoked by the Commission?

2. If the Commission makes findings of fact in a case which is then submitted to the Court, how much deference should the Court give to those findings? Should the case be tried de novo?

3. Does a party have a right to an oral hearing in a case brought under the Convention? Compare Article 48 (1)(e) of the Convention with Articles 43, 65–67 of the Regulations. How can the presence of witnesses be assured at hearings either before the Commission or the Court?

4. Are proceedings before the Court adversarial or inquisitorial? In other words, does the Court have its own powers of investigation?

5. How is the burden of proof assigned in these cases? How important is the credibility of the petitioner and the government?

6. Note that the *Velásquez* case was one of a trio of matters submitted to the Inter-American Court as its first contentious cases. In *Velásquez* and *Godinez Cruz* the government was held responsible for the disappearances. In *Fairen Garbi and Solis Coralles,* however, the government produced entry and exit cards, signed by the missing individuals, showing that they had entered by car from Costa Rica and subsequently left Honduras, crossing the border into Guatemala. The Court appointed its own handwriting experts who verified as genuine the signature on the exit card. Although the Commission questioned the veracity of the Honduran and Guatemalan certificates and documents submitted to prove the travel of Francisco Fairén Garbi and Yolanda Solís Corrales from Honduras to Guatemala, it did not offer any evidence in support of its position. Guatemala submitted contradictory statements. The Court found that

> 154. Francisco Fairén Garbi and Yolanda Solís Corrales entered Honduran territory at the Las Manos border post, in the Department of El Paraíso, on December 11, 1981. That is the last reliable information on their whereabouts. Despite initial contradictions, Honduran authorities subsequently admitted that the two disappeared persons had entered their territory (Report of the Government of March 8, 1982, on the certificate of the Secretary General of Immigration of Honduras, February 11, 1982).

> 155. There are many contradictions regarding the presence of Francisco Fairén Garbi and Yolanda Solís Corrales in Honduras and their departure from Honduras territory. Initially, the Government of Honduras and Guatemala denied those persons had crossed the border between the two countries. Then they affirmed they had entered Guatemala on December 12, 1981, and Guatemalan authorities added that they had left for El Salvador on December 14 of the same year. The Government of Guatemala ratified the latter version on October 6, 1987, but was later contradicted in part by its Minister of Internal Affairs in a communication of March 2, 1988. The Minister denied they had entered Guatemala, but admitted their names appeared in the immigration lists of departures for El Salvador on December 14, 1981. It also made garbled statements concerning the signatures on those lists. Considered together, those facts are equivocal, but their investigation and clarification are hindered by the fact, among others, that Guatemala and El Salvador are not parties to the case.

Based on the contradictory evidence, the Court held that it had not been proven that Honduras was responsible for the disappearances. *Fairen Garbi and Solis Coralles Case,* Judgment of March 15, 1989, 6 Inter-Am. Ct.H.R. (Ser. C). See T. Buergenthal, *Fact-Finding by the Inter-American Court of Human Rights,* in Fact-Finding before International Tribunals (R. Lillich, ed. 1992); D. Shelton, *Judicial Review of State Action by International Courts,* 12 Fordham Int'l L.J. 361 (1989).

7. The case of *Nogueira de Carvalho et al v. Brazil,* judgment of Nov. 28, 2006, 161 Inter-Am.Ct. H.R. (Ser. C), also resulted in the Court holding that the alleged violations had not been proven. The Commission and applicants claimed that the state violated Convention Articles 8 and 25 by failing to exercise due diligence to investigate the murder of a human rights defender who had been reporting on a Brazilian death squad. The Court evaluated the series of police and judicial procedures of investigation, examining documentary evidence and hearing the testimony of witnesses produced by the Commission, representa-

tives of the applicants, and the state. The Court ultimately concluded, "in view of the limited factual support available to the Court", that the case had not been proven.

8. Do the Regulations establish a standard of proof? Is any standard of proof applied in the above cases? How do the Inter-American cases compare to decisions of the European Court on issues of evidence, illustrated by the following two cases?

Kurt v. Turkey, (App. no. 24276/94), Judgment of 25 May 1998, Eur. Ct. H.R., 27 EHRR 373 (1999).

. . . .

8. The applicant, Mrs. Koçeri Kurt, is a Turkish citizen who was born in 1927 and is at present living in Bismil in south-east Turkey. At the time of the events giving rise to her application to the Commission she was living in the nearby village of Ağilli. Her application to the Commission was brought on her own behalf and on behalf of her son, Üzeyir Kurt, who, she alleges, has disappeared in circumstances engaging the responsibility of the respondent State.

9. The facts surrounding the disappearance of the applicant's son are disputed. . . .

13. The Commission, with a view to establishing the facts in the light of the dispute over the circumstances surrounding the disappearance of the applicant's son, conducted its own investigation pursuant to Article 28 § 1 (a) of the Convention. To this end, the Commission examined a series of documents submitted by both the applicant and the Government in support of their respective assertions and appointed three delegates to take evidence of witnesses at a hearing conducted in Ankara on 8 and 9 February 1996.

A. Facts as presented by the applicant

14. From 23 to 25 November 1993 security forces, made up of gendarmes and a number of village guards, carried out an operation in the village of Ağilli. On 23 November 1993, following intelligence reports that three terrorists would visit the village, the security forces took up positions around the village. Two clashes followed. During the two days they spent in the village they conducted a search of each house. A number of houses, between ten and twelve, were burnt down during the operation, including those of the applicant and Mevlüde and Ali Kurt, Mevlüde being her son's aunt. Only three of the houses were near the clashes. Other houses were burnt down on a second occasion during the military operation. The villagers were told that they had a week to evacuate the village. The villagers fled to Bismil, many as they were homeless, and those who were not being too scared to remain.

15. According to the applicant, around noon on 24 November 1993, when the villagers had been gathered by the soldiers in the schoolyard, the soldiers were looking for her son, Üzeyir, who was not in the schoolyard. He was hiding in the house of his aunt Mevlüde (see paragraph 14 above). When the soldiers asked Aynur Kurt, his daughter, where her father was, Aynur told them he was at his aunt's house. The soldiers went to Mevlüde's house with Davut Kurt, another of the applicant's sons, and took Üzeyir from the house. Üzeyir spent the night of 24–25 November 1993 with soldiers in the house of Hasan Kiliç.

On the morning of 25 November 1993, the applicant received a message from a child that Üzeyir wanted some cigarettes. The applicant took cigarettes and found Üzeyir in front of Hasan Kiliç's house surrounded by about ten soldiers and five to six village guards. She saw bruises and swelling on his face as though he had been beaten. Üzeyir told her that he was cold. She returned with his jacket and socks. The soldiers did not allow her to stay so she left. This was the last time she saw Üzeyir. The applicant maintains that there is no evidence that he was seen elsewhere after this time.

16. On 30 November 1993 the applicant applied to the Bismil public prosecutor, Ridvan Yildirim, to find out information on the whereabouts of her son. On the same day, she received a response from Captain Izzet Cural at the provincial gendarmerie headquarters stating that it was supposed that Üzeyir had been kidnapped by the PKK (the Kurdish Workers' Party). Captain Cural, who had proposed the plan for the operation in the village, replied in identical terms on 4 December 1993. The district gendarmerie commander noted on the bottom of the applicant's petition of 30 November that Üzeyir had not been taken into custody and that he had been kidnapped by the PKK.

17. On 14 December 1993 the applicant applied to the National Security Court in Diyarbakir which replied that he was not in their custody records. On 15 December 1993 she contacted the Bismil public prosecutor again but was referred to the gendarmerie. Finally, on 24 December 1993 the applicant approached the Diyarbakir Human Rights Association for help and made a statement on the circumstances surrounding her son's disappearance.

18. On 28 February 1994 Davut Karakoç (Üzeyir's cousin), Arap Kurt (Üzeyir's uncle and *muhtar* of the village) and Mehmet Kurt (another of Üzeyir's cousins) were taken to the gendarmerie and questioned about what they knew of "Üzeyir Kurt who was abducted by representatives of the PKK terrorist organisation". On 21 March 1994 the Bismil public prosecutor issued a decision of non-jurisdiction on the grounds that a crime had been committed by the PKK.

. . . .

B. Facts as presented by the Government

26. Ağilli is a thirty-six-household village. From this village and its surroundings, about fifteen men and women have joined the PKK, which is a high ratio for such a small village. These include Türkan Kurt, the daughter of Musa Kurt, one of the applicant's sons.

27. While an operation did take place in the village and clashes occurred between the security forces and suspected terrorists, Üzeyir Kurt was not taken into custody by the security forces. He had no history of previous detention or problems with the authorities and there was no reason for him to be taken into custody.

28. The Government submit that there are strong grounds for believing that Üzeyir Kurt has in fact joined or been kidnapped by the PKK. They refer to the fact that the family allege that his brother died in gendarme custody several years before; the fact that the applicant stated that he hid when the security forces arrived in the village; and the fact that his house was burnt down following the clash in the village. Further, some members of the family had already joined the PKK

and several months after the operation in the village a shelter was found outside the village which it was said was used by Üzeyir Kurt in his contacts with the PKK. There is also a strong tradition of villagers escaping to the mountains at the onset of any military action. Villagers have also stated that they heard that he had been kidnapped by the PKK.

29. The Government submit that Üzeyir could have hidden in the village at the commencement of the operation and then, under cover of darkness and poor weather, slipped through the security forces' blockade. Mehmet Karabulut testified before the Commission's delegates at the hearing in Ankara that on the night following the first clash Üzeyir was in Mevlüde's home sleeping but that when he woke in the morning Üzeyir was no longer there. The Government stress that Mehmet Karabulut testified that he had not seen or heard soldiers in Mevlüde's house, which would confirm that Üzeyir went off of his own accord.

30. The only person who claims to have seen Üzeyir after that is the applicant, whose accounts are inconsistent, contradictory and unsubstantiated. In particular, she affirmed to the delegates at the hearing in Ankara that the villagers assembled in the schoolyard were blindfolded. She subsequently retracted this statement. Furthermore, her statements to the Diyarbakir Human Rights Association and to the Commission in her application refer to one visit to her son to give him cigarettes, whereas in her oral testimony before the delegates she referred to two visits; her descriptions of how she received a message from her son vary and she could not identify the child who allegedly delivered the message to her that her son wanted cigarettes. In addition, her account of making two visits passing through the village when the security forces stated they were keeping people in their houses for security reasons is implausible. The Government also maintain that it would have been impossible for the applicant to retrieve her son's jacket and socks from his house on 25 November since it was alleged by the applicant that it had been burnt down the previous day.

31. The Government place particular emphasis on the fact that Hasan Kiliç in his statement to the gendarmes of 7 December 1994 affirmed that the applicant came to his house, talked to her son who had spent the night there and then left with him. The soldiers had not left with Üzeyir. Furthermore, Üzeyir had not asked for cigarettes to be brought to him at the house; nor did he see Üzeyir being detained in front of his house by soldiers and village guards, as alleged. In fact, as Captain Cural told the delegates at the hearing in Ankara, no village guards had entered the village to back up the military operation.

32. In further support of the inconsistencies and contradictions in the applicant's account of the events, the Government also point to the allegations originally made in the applicant's application to the Commission in which it was stated that the soldiers killed the livestock, pillaged goods and beat the villagers. The applicant acknowledged that these allegations were incorrect when giving evidence to the delegates.

. . . .

C. Materials submitted by the applicant and the Government to the Commission in support of their respective assertions

37. In the proceedings before the Commission the applicant and the Government submitted a number of statements which she had made between 24 December 1993 and 7 February 1996 to the Diyarbakir Human Rights Association, the Bismil public prosecutor, the gendarmes, the Principal Public Prosecutor's office at Diyarbakir and to the notary in Bismil. The applicant also submitted official documents concerning the inquiry into the conduct of her lawyer, Mahmut Şakar. These materials were studied by the Commission when assessing the merits of the applicant's allegations as regards both the disappearance of her son and the intimidation of both her and her lawyer.

38. Statements were taken by gendarmes from twelve villagers between 23 February and 7 December 1994. On 23 February 1994 Arap Kurt, the *muhtar* of Ağilli village at the relevant time, Davut Karakoç and Mehmet Kurt (both cousins of Üzeyir Kurt) were interviewed by gendarmes and asked about "their knowledge and observations about the hostage Üzeyir Kurt who had been kidnapped by the PKK". Hasan Kiliç (see paragraph 15 above), Mevlüde Kurt (see paragraph 15 above) and other villagers present at the time of the military operation were questioned by gendarmes on 7 December 1994. None of the villagers questioned saw Üzeyir Kurt being taken into custody. Hasan Kiliç affirmed in his statement that Üzeyir Kurt had arrived at his house on the morning of 24 November, spent the night there and left the following morning when his mother arrived. While there had been soldiers staying in the house overnight, Hasan Kiliç maintained that the applicant and her son left the house together and the soldiers definitely did not leave with Üzeyir Kurt.

All the above statements were studied by the Commission when assessing the evidence before it. The Government rely on these statements to support their contention that the applicant's son had not been detained in the village by the security forces as alleged and that there was a reasonable likelihood that he had either been kidnapped by the PKK or left to join the PKK.

The Government also produced in the proceedings before the Commission the incident report drawn up by security forces on 24 November 1993; a report dated 19 November 1994 from the Bismil public prosecutor to the Diyarbakir Principal Public Prosecutor's office suggesting that the evidence pointed to the applicant's son having been kidnapped by the PKK following the clash on 23 November 1993; and a report dated 8 December 1994 prepared by Colonel Eşref Hatipoğlu of the Gendarmerie General Command, Diyarbakir, on the conduct of the operation in Ağilli village and confirming, *inter alia*, that the applicant's son had not been taken into custody.

D. Proceedings before the domestic authorities

39. On 30 November 1993 the applicant submitted a thumb-printed petition to the Bismil public prosecutor, Ridvan Yildirim. It stated that her son had been taken into custody following a clash between the gendarmes and the PKK at her village and that she was concerned about his fate. She requested that she be informed of his fate. On the same date the public prosecutor passed the petition to the district gendarmerie command with a handwritten request for the information to be provided.

The district gendarmerie command noted in handwriting on the petition the same day that it was not true that Üzeyir Kurt had been taken into custody and that it was supposed that he may have been kidnapped by the PKK.

40. By letter dated 30 November 1993 Captain Cural, under heading of the provincial gendarmerie command, informed the Bismil Principal Public Prosecutor's office in answer to their unnumbered letter that Üzeyir Kurt had not been taken into custody and it was thought that he had probably been kidnapped by terrorists.

41. By letter dated 4 December 1993 Captain Cural, district gendarmerie commander, under heading of the district gendarmerie command at Bismil, informed the Bismil Principal Public Prosecutor's office that Üzeyir Kurt had not been taken into custody and it was thought that he had probably been kidnapped by terrorists (identical terms to the letter of 30 November in the preceding paragraph).

42. On 14 December 1993 the applicant submitted a fingerprinted petition to the Principal Public Prosecutor at the National Security Court at Diyarbakir. She stated that her son Üzeyir had been taken into custody twenty days previously by gendarmes and since they had had no news, they were concerned for his life. She requested that information be given to her concerning his whereabouts. On the bottom of the petition, the Principal Public Prosecutor noted in handwriting the same day that the name Üzeyir Kurt was not in their custody records.

43. On 15 December 1993 the applicant submitted a second written petition to the Bismil public prosecutor which repeated the terms of her petition of 14 December. The public prosecutor wrote on the petition an instruction to the gendarmerie regional command to provide her with the information requested.

44. On 21 March 1994 the Bismil public prosecutor, Ridvan Yildirim, issued a decision of dismissal. The document identifies the complainant as the applicant and the victim as Üzeyir Kurt. The crime was identified as membership of an outlawed organisation and kidnapping and the suspects as members of the PKK. The text of the decision stated that following a clash between the PKK and the security forces, PKK members escaped from the village, kidnapping the said victim. Since this crime fell within the jurisdiction of the National Security Courts, the case was dismissed and referred, with the file, to the Diyarbakir National Security Court.

E. The Commission's evaluation of the evidence and its findings of fact

1. The written and oral evidence

45. The Commission had regard to the documentary evidence submitted by the applicant and the Government in support of their respective assertions. Furthermore, at a hearing held in Ankara from 8 to 9 February 1996 the Commission's delegates heard the oral testimony of the following witnesses: the applicant; Arap Kurt, the *muhtar* of Ağilli village and brother-in-law of the applicant; Ridvan Yildirim, the public prosecutor in Bismil who had been first approached by the applicant about her son's disappearance; Izzet Cural, commander of Bismil district gendarmerie, who had proposed the plan for the military operation in Ağilli village; Muharram Küpeli, a commander of a commando unit which was deployed during the military operation in the village; and Mehmet Karabulut, who had seen the applicant's

son for the last time at Ali and Mevlüde Kurt's house when the military operation began.

While thirteen witnesses had been summoned to give evidence, only the above six witnesses actually appeared at the hearing and testified.

2. The approach to the evaluation of the evidence

46. The Commission approached its task in the absence of any findings of fact made by domestic courts and of any thorough judicial examination or other independent investigation of the events in question. In so proceeding, it assessed the evidence before it having regard, *inter alia,* to the conduct of the witnesses who were heard by the delegates at the hearing in Ankara and to the need to take into account when reaching its conclusions the coexistence of sufficiently strong, clear and concordant inferences or of similar unrebutted presumptions of fact. The Commission also made due allowance for the difficulties attached to assessing evidence obtained at the delegates' hearing through interpreters and to the vulnerable position of villagers from south-east Turkey when giving evidence about incidents involving the PKK and the security forces.

3. The Commission's findings of fact

(a) The military operation in Ağilli village

47. The Commission found that the written and oral evidence was largely consistent as regards the general course of events during the operation. It was established that the villagers were gathered in the schoolyard on the morning of 24 November and searches were then carried out of the villagers' houses. During the clashes between the security forces and the terrorists who had entered the village the previous evening a number of houses including those of the applicant and her son were burned down. The villagers were again assembled in the schoolyard on 25 November. Three terrorists and one member of the security forces were killed in the clashes which occurred during the operation. Twelve villagers were taken into custody on 24 November and were released on 26 November. The security forces left the village late on 25 November. . . .

PROCEEDINGS BEFORE THE COMMISSION

. . . .

73. The Commission declared the application (no. 24276/94) admissible on 22 May 1995. In its report of 5 December 1996 (Article 31), it expressed the opinion that there had been a violation of Article 5 in respect of the disappearance of the applicant's son (unanimously); that there had been a violation of Article 3 in respect of the applicant (nineteen votes to five); that it was not necessary to examine separately the complaints made under Articles 2 and 3 of the Convention in relation to the applicant's son (unanimously); that there had been a violation of Article 13 of the Convention (unanimously) in respect of the applicant; that there had been no violation of Articles 14 and 18 of the Convention (unanimously); and that Turkey had failed to comply with its obligations under Article 25 § 1 of the Convention (unanimously). The full text of the Commission's opinion and of the dissenting opinion contained in the report is reproduced as an annex to this judgment. . . .

AS TO THE LAW

. . . .

84. The applicant requested the Court to find on the basis of the facts established by the Commission that the disappearance of her son engaged the responsibility of the respondent State under Articles 2, 3 and 5 of the Convention and that each of those Articles had been violated. She urged the Court, in line with the approach adopted by the Inter-American Court of Human Rights under the American Convention on Human Rights and by the United Nations Human Rights Committee under the International Covenant on Civil and Political Rights to the phenomenon of disappearances, not to confine its consideration of her son's plight to the issues raised under Article 5 of the Convention but to have regard also to those raised under Articles 2 and 3.

85. The Government contended that the Commission's fact-finding and its assessment of the evidence were seriously deficient and could not ground a finding of a violation of any of the Articles invoked by the applicant.

86. The Commission concluded, for its part, that the respondent State had committed a particularly serious and flagrant violation of Article 5 of the Convention taken as a whole and for that reason had not found it necessary to examine separately the applicant's complaints under Articles 2 and 3.

A. Establishment of the facts

1. Arguments of those appearing before the Court

87. Before the Court the Delegate of the Commission stressed that the Commission's findings of fact had been reached on the basis of an investigation conducted by its delegates in a scrupulously fair and impartial manner and without the benefit of any findings of a domestic inquiry. The Commission was fully conscious of the inconsistencies and contradictions in the applicant's various written and oral statements on the course of events in the village during the military operation. Notwithstanding, she was found to be credible and convincing on the essential aspects of her account. Before the delegates she had never wavered under cross-examination, including by the Government lawyers present, in her assertion that she had seen her son outside Hasan Kiliç's house on the morning of 25 November 1993 surrounded by soldiers and village guards. The Government's contention that Üzeyir Kurt had been either kidnapped by the PKK or had left the village to join the terrorists had no basis in fact and could not rebut the applicant's eyewitness account of her son's detention.

88. The Delegate insisted that the Commission had duly considered every single discrepancy identified by the Government in the applicant's version of the events. In particular, careful consideration was given to the seemingly conflicting statement provided by Hasan Kiliç to the gendarmes. Admittedly, Hasan Kiliç's account raised doubts about the accuracy of the applicant's recollection of the events on the morning of 25 November 1993. However, unlike the applicant, Hasan Kiliç had never testified before the delegates and his statement had to be treated with caution since it had been taken by the very officers whom the applicant alleged had detained her son.

89. For the above reasons, the Delegate requested the Court to accept the facts as found by the Commission. . . .

91. The Government strenuously disputed the Commission's findings of fact, and in particular the undue weight which it gave to the applicant's evidence. They insisted that the applicant was in fact the only person claiming to have seen her son outside Hasan Kiliç's house surrounded by soldiers and village guards. However, the Commission found her testimony to be credible despite the fact that she had retracted earlier allegations made against the security forces and many features of her account were highly implausible and at odds with other evidence.

92. The Government criticised the Commission for not having given due weight to the evidence of other villagers who had confirmed that Üzeyir Kurt had not been detained in the village as alleged. Hasan Kiliç in particular had clearly affirmed when questioned that Üzeyir Kurt left his house in the company of the applicant and that there were no security forces outside the house at the relevant time. They regretted the Commission's unwillingness to give serious consideration to the official view that there might have been PKK involvement in his disappearance. That view had support in the statements of the villagers who had been questioned by the authorities.

93. For the above reasons the Government maintained that it had not been proved beyond reasonable doubt that the applicant had seen her son in the circumstances alleged and his disappearance could not therefore engage their responsibility.

2. The Court's assessment

94. The Court notes at the outset that it clearly emerges from paragraphs 159–79 of its Article 31 report that the Commission meticulously addressed the discrepancies in the applicant's account as well as each of the Government's counter-arguments.

95. As an independent fact-finding body confronted with an allegation which rests essentially on the eyewitness evidence of the complainant alone, the Commission paid particular regard to the applicant's credibility and to the accuracy of her recollection of the events on the morning of 25 November 1993. It is to be observed that at the hearing in Ankara she was questioned extensively on her account by the delegates and by the lawyers appearing for the Government. While there were marked inconsistencies between the statement she gave to the Diyarbakir Human Rights Association and her oral account before the delegates, the applicant was steadfast in all her contacts with the authorities in her assertion that she had seen her son surrounded by soldiers and village guards in the village.

96. In the Court's view, the Commission properly assessed all the evidence before it, weighing in the balance the elements which supported the applicant's account and those which cast doubt on either its credibility or plausibility. Even though Hasan Kiliç did not respond to the Commission's summons to appear before the delegates, his statement, which the Government consider as central to their case, was carefully scrutinised by the Commission alongside the applicant's testimony. Significantly, Mr. Kiliç's account was found to be flawed in material respects and his non-appearance meant that, unlike the applicant's testimony, neither his credibility

as a witness nor the probative value of the statement taken from him by gendarmes could be tested in an adversarial setting.

97. Furthermore, the Government's contention that the applicant's son had either been kidnapped by the PKK or had left the village to team up with the terrorists was duly considered by the Commission. However, support for this was mainly based on statements taken from villagers by the very gendarmes who were the subject of the applicant's complaint and these statements could properly be considered by the Commission to be of minimum evidential value.

98. The Court recalls that under its settled case-law the establishment and verification of the facts are primarily a matter for the Commission (Articles 28 § 1 and 31 of the Convention). While the Court is not bound by the Commission's findings of fact and remains free to make its own appreciation in the light of all the material before it, it is only in exceptional circumstances that it will exercise its powers in this area (see, for example, the *McCann and Others v. the United Kingdom* judgment of 27 September 1995, Series A no. 324, p. 50, § 169; the *Aksoy v. Turkey* judgment of 18 December 1996, *Reports* 1996-VI, p. 2272, § 38; the *Aydin v. Turkey* judgment of 25 September 1997, *Reports* 1997-VI, pp. 1888–89, § 70; and the *Menteş and Others v. Turkey* judgment of 28 November 1997, *Reports* 1997-VIII, pp. 2709–10, § 66).

99. Having regard to the above considerations which are based on its own careful assessment of the evidence and the transcripts of the delegates' hearing, the Court is not persuaded that there exist any exceptional circumstances which would compel it to reach a conclusion different from that of the Commission. It considers that there is a sufficient factual and evidentiary basis on which the Commission could properly conclude, beyond reasonable doubt, that the applicant did see her son outside Hasan Kiliç's house on the morning of 25 November 1993, that he was surrounded by soldiers and village guards at the time and that he has not been seen since.

[Based on the facts, the Court found as follows on the right to life:]

107. . . . .[L]ike the Commission, the Court must carefully scrutinize whether there does in fact exist concerte evidence which would lead it to conclude that her son was, beyond reasonable doubt, killed by the authorities either while in detention in the village or at some subsequent stage. It also notes in this respect that in those cases where it has found tat a Contracting State had a positive obligation under Article 2 to conduct an effective investigation into the circumstances surrounding an alleged unlawful killing by the agents of that State, there existed concrete evidence of a fatal shooting which could bring that obligation into play. . .".

108. It is to be observed in this regard that the applicant'ts case rests entirely on presumptions deduced from the circumstances of her son's initial detention bolstered by more general analyses of an alleged officially tolerated practice of disappearances an associated ill-treatment and extra-judicial killing of detainees in the respondent State. The Court for its part considers that these arguments are not in themselves sufficient to compensate for the absence of more persuasive indications that her son did in fact meet his death in custody. As to the applicant's arugment that there exists a practice of violation of, inter alia, Article 2, the Court considers that the evidence which she has adduced does not substantiate that claim.

109. Having regard to the above considerations, the Court is of the opinion that the applicant's assertions that the respondent State failed in its obligation to protect her son's life in the circumstances described fall to be assessed from the standpoint of Article 5 of the Convention.

[The Court held that that there had been "a particularly grave violation of the right to liberty and security of person guaranteed under Article 5 raising serious concerns about the welfare of Üzeyir Kurt." In regard to the applicant herself, the Court found violations of Articles 3 and 13.]

. . . .

Partly dissenting opinion of Judge Matscher

(*Translation*)

While I am conscious of the difficulties which the Commission faces in cases of this type, I consider that in the present case the manner in which it established the facts, which were accepted by the Court, was so superficial and insufficient and the analysis of those facts so clearly unsatisfactory that, in my view, neither provides a sufficiently sound basis for a finding of a violation. Furthermore, a careful study of the summary of the Commission's findings confirms that view, without it being necessary for me to go into detail.

None of the many witnesses heard by the local authorities or by the delegates of the Commission were able to say that the applicant's son had been taken away by the soldiers; the mere fact that the applicant "genuinely and honestly believed" that such was the case does not amount to proof, especially as most of the witnesses said the opposite or declared that they had no personal direct knowledge of what, in this connection, is the crucial issue in the case.

Ultimately, here, as in the *Menteş and Others v. Turkey* case (judgment of 28 November 1997, *Reports of Judgments and Decisions* 1997-VIII), the applicant failed by a large margin to prove the truth of her allegations beyond all reasonable doubt.

On a separate issue, I voted in favour of finding a violation of Article 13 because, in a case as serious as this one, the authorities of the respondent State failed to carry out a genuine and thorough investigation.

―――――――――

Sevtap Veznedaroglu v. Turkey, App. no. 32357/96, Judgment of 11 April 2000, Eur. Ct. H.R., 33 EHRR 59 (2001)

. . . .

8. The facts of the case as submitted by the applicant are summarised below. The Government dispute the applicant's account.

9. The applicant was at the relevant time a research student in public law at Diyarbakir University and married to a lawyer who had been the provincial president of the Diyarbakir Human Rights Association in 1990. According to the applicant she was constantly followed by the police on account of her husband's position.

10. On 4 July 1994, at about 3 p.m., the applicant was arrested by 8 policemen at her home on suspicion of membership of the Kurdistan Workers Party (PKK), an illegal organisation.

11. The applicant was taken to the forensic doctor to be examined. Following the doctor's examination she was blindfolded and taken to an unknown destination where she was placed in a cell. After a certain period of time, she was again blindfolded and taken to another room to be interrogated.

12. The applicant was interrogated by approximately 15 policemen and accused of forming links with and of working for the PKK abroad. She was then undressed and hung by her arms. She was given electric shocks to her mouth and sexual organs. After half an hour she was taken down as she had fainted. The interrogators, while threatening her with death and rape, told her not to work on human rights matters. She was then taken to her cell. The next day she was again tortured and threatened with death and rape. The torture continued for four days. During the first two days of her custody the applicant was not given anything to eat. Thereafter she was only given a piece of bread and a few olives.

13. During her detention the applicant was requested to sign some documents. She was told that she would be tortured and raped if she did not agree to sign them. The applicant signed the documents. In the documents, by way of explanation for the marks of torture on her body, it was stated that the applicant had fallen while indicating a place used by the PKK. The policemen applied cream to the applicant's injuries.

14. On 13 July 1994 the police officers brought her to the forensic doctor who drew up a report which stated: "Upon the examination of Sevtap Veznedaroğlu, violet-coloured bruises were identified on the left upper arm 1 by 1 cm and on the right tibia 3 by 1 cm".

15. On 15 July 1994 the applicant, accompanied by police officers, was taken to the Diyarbakir State Hospital where she was examined by a forensic doctor. In his report dated 15 July 1994 the doctor noted the presence of the same bruising on the applicant's arm and leg as indicated in the earlier report of 13 July 1994. The report concluded that the applicant's health was not at risk and that she was fit to work.

16. On 15 July 1994 the applicant was brought before the public prosecutor at the Diyarbakir State Security Court. Her file contained the medical reports dated 4, 13 and 15 July 1994. The applicant maintained before the public prosecutor that she had signed the confession statement under pressure and as a result of being tortured while in detention. The public prosecutor recorded in the file that the applicant did not acknowledge the statement which she gave to the police.

17. On the same day the applicant appeared before a substitute judge attached to the Diyarbakir State Security Court. The applicant repeated to the judge that she did not acknowledge the statement taken from her by the police "since she had been tortured and held under duress for many days . . . and that the police had held her wrist and forced her to sign the police statement". The applicant's statement was recorded in the minutes of the hearing before the judge. The judge directed that the applicant be released from custody. The public prosecutor for his part ordered that the applicant stand trial before the Diyarbakir State Security Court on a charge of being a member of the PKK.

18. On 18 July 1994 the applicant was given a certificate by the Medical Faculty Hospital of Dicle University indicating that she was unable to work for 20 days. According to the medical report the applicant was suffering from bronchopneumonia.

19. On 30 October 1995 the applicant was acquitted by the Diyarbakir State Security Court on the ground of lack of evidence. The applicant was not in court on that day. In its ruling the court noted as follows the declarations made by the applicant during a court hearing held on 13 October 1994 and which was recorded in the minutes.

> Although the accused admitted to the offence with which she was charged in her statements to the police, at a later stage during the proceedings before the judicial organs she claimed that she had made them under duress and even torture and had signed them without having read them. . . .

AS TO THE LAW

I. Alleged Violation of Article 3 of the Convention

23. The applicant alleged that she had been tortured in violation of Article 3 of the Convention . . . .

24. The applicant maintained that she was held in custody between 4 and 15 July 1994 and tortured and ill-treated during that time. In her submission her statements to the authorities to this effect coupled with the medical certificate drawn up by the Medical Faculty of Dicle University bear out the truth of her allegations.

25. The Government repudiated the applicant's claim. They stressed that following the communication of the applicant's complaint an investigation was conducted into the authenticity of the medical certificate allegedly drawn up by the Dicle University Medical Faculty granting her 20 days' sick leave. That investigation revealed that there was good reason to suggest that the figure "20" had been falsified, all the more so since it was difficult to understand why such a long period of sick leave would be granted on the strength of two bruises. Significantly, the applicant had been authorised to take sick leave on the grounds that she was suffering from pneumonia. Furthermore, the investigation also established that there was no record in the hospital of the certificate having been issued to the applicant. The Government asserted that it must be concluded that the medical certificate, the only concrete evidence submitted by the applicant, was falsified and should therefore be discounted.

26. For the Government, the applicant only made a bare allegation about having been tortured. She failed to substantiate the complaint in any way and there was no evidence whatsoever which confirmed that she had been given electric shocks and hung up by the arms as alleged. In the absence of any corroborating evidence, the public prosecutor cannot be faulted for not investigating the complaint.

27. The applicant disputed the Government's accusation that the medical certificate had been falsified. She referred to a letter dated 12 January 1998 in which the President of the Department of Internal Medicine informed the Head of the Dicle University Medical Faculty that the applicant had been examined on 18 July 1994 standing up and for that reason no medical record had been kept of her examina-

tion. A copy of that letter was sent to the Diyarbakir State Security Court and to the responsible Ministry on their request following the communication of her application to the respondent Government.

28. The Court recalls that Article 3 of the Convention enshrines one of the fundamental values of democratic society. Even in the most difficult of circumstances, such as the fight against terrorism or crime, the Convention prohibits in absolute terms torture or inhuman or degrading treatment or punishment. Unlike most of the substantive clauses of the Convention and of Protocols Nos. 1 and 4, Article 3 makes no provision for exceptions and no derogation from it is permissible under Article 15 even in the event of a public emergency threatening the life of the nation (see the *Aksoy v. Turkey* judgment of 18 December 1996, *Reports of Judgments and Decisions* 1996-VI, p. 2278, § 62).

29. The Court also recalls that ill-treatment must attain a minimum level of severity if it is to fall within the scope of Article 3. The assessment of this minimum is relative: it depends on all the circumstances of the case, such as the duration of the treatment, its physical and/or mental effects and, in some cases, the sex, age and state of health of the victim. In respect of a person deprived of his liberty, recourse to physical force which has not been made strictly necessary by his own conduct diminishes human dignity and is in principle an infringement of the right set forth in Article 3 (see the *Tekin v. Turkey* judgment of 9 June 1998, *Reports* 1998-IV, pp. 1517–18, §§ 52 and 53).

30. The Court notes that the Government do not deny that the applicant sustained bruising to her person during her time in custody. However, they point to the minor nature of these injuries and stress that they are at variance with the severity of the treatment allegedly suffered. The Court for its part finds it impossible to establish on the basis of the evidence before it whether or not the applicant's injuries were caused by the police or whether she was tortured to the extent claimed. It is not persuaded either that the hearing of witnesses by the Court would clarify the facts of the case or make it possible to conclude, beyond reasonable doubt (see the *Aydin v. Turkey* judgment of 25 September 1997, *Reports* 1997-VI, p. 1189, § 73), that the applicant's allegations are substantiated.

31. However it would observe at the same time that the difficulty in determining whether there was a plausible explanation for the bruising found on her body or whether there was any substance to her allegations on the nature of the treatment she allegedly endured rests with the failure of the authorities to investigate her complaints.

32. In this latter connection the Court reiterates that, where an individual raises an arguable claim that he has been seriously ill-treated by the police or other such agents of the State unlawfully and in breach of Article 3, that provision, read in conjunction with the State's general duty under Article 1 of the Convention to "secure to everyone within their jurisdiction the rights and freedoms defined in . . . [the] Convention", requires by implication that there should be an effective official investigation capable of leading to the identification and punishment of those responsible (see the *Assenov v. Bulgaria* judgment of 28 September 1998, *Reports* 1998-VII, p. 3290 § 102). If this were not the case, the general legal prohibition of torture and

inhuman and degrading treatment and punishment, despite its fundamental importance, would be ineffective in practice and it would be possible in some cases for agents of the State to abuse the rights of those within their control with virtual impunity. (*Ibid.*)

33. The Court notes that, on 15 July 1994, the applicant alleged before the public prosecutor and the substitute judge attached to the Diyarbakir State Security Court that she had been tortured. The file presented to the public prosecutor contained the results of the medical examinations carried out on the applicant on 4, 13 and 15 July 1994. The medical reports dated 13 and 15 July 1994 indicated fresh bruising to the applicant's arm and leg. The substitute judge noted in the minutes of the hearing the applicant's statement that she had been tortured in custody.

34. In the opinion of the Court the applicant's insistence on her complaint of torture taken with the medical evidence in the file should have been sufficient to alert the public prosecutor to the need to investigate the substance of the complaint, all the more so since she had been held in custody between 4 July 1994 and 15 July 1994. However, no steps were taken either to obtain further details from the applicant or to question the police officers at her place of detention about her allegations. The substitute judge also dismissed her allegations without further enquiry.

35. The Court considers that in the circumstances the applicant had laid the basis of an arguable claim that she had been tortured. It is to be noted also that the applicant persisted in her allegations right up to the stage of trial. The inertia displayed by the authorities in response to her allegations was inconsistent with the procedural obligation which devolves on them under Article 3 of the Convention. In consequence, the Court finds that there has been a violation of that Article on account of the failure of the authorities of the respondent State to investigate the applicant's complaint of torture. . . .

FOR THESE REASONS, THE COURT UNANIMOUSLY

1. *Holds* that there has been a violation of Article 3 of the Convention on account of the failure of the authorities of the respondent State to investigate the applicant's complaint of torture.

. . . .

PARTLY DISSENTING OPINION OF MR BONELLO [footnotes partly omitted]

1. The Court has unanimously found a violation of Article 3 on account of the failure by the Turkish authorities to investigate the applicant's complaint of torture, but has held that it is "impossible to establish on the basis of the evidence before it, whether or not the applicant's injuries were caused by the police or whether she was tortured to the extent claimed". In other words, the Court dismissed the applicant's claim and was not satisfied, on the 'evidence' that she had suffered torture or inhuman treatment. I disagree.

2. Before the applicant's interrogation by policemen in an undisclosed station, she was examined by a forensic doctor, and there is no allegation that her body showed any trace of trauma.

3. The applicant claims that, during interrogation, she was undressed, hung up by her arms, given electric shocks in her mouth and genitals, threatened with death

and rape. This routine was repeated on the following three days. During the first two days she was left without any food at all.

4. The applicant further alleged that, under threat of death and rape, she signed a 'confession' admitting membership of an outlawed organisation, the PKK. The statement which the applicant signed also included a disclaimer to the effect that the bruises on her body had been caused by a fall.

5. Two doctors examined the applicant separately over a week after the interrogation ended, but when still in police custody; they found violet coloured bruises on her upper arm and on her right tibia.

6. The applicant complained both to the public prosecutor and to the State Security Court, before being released from detention, that she had been tortured by the police and that the 'confession' had been extracted under torture.

7. The applicant was tried on a charge of being a member of the PKK. Despite her signed confession, the State Security Court acquitted her on the ground of lack of evidence, having noted the applicant's claim that the confession had been obtained by duress and torture.

8. I believe that the majority, concluding that the applicant had not proved that she had been tortured and that the injuries to her person were caused by the police, disregarded several basic and vital elements of the rules of evidence that should inspire any court.

9. Firstly, this Court has repeatedly held that: "Where an individual, when taken in police custody, is in good health, but is found to be injured at the time of release, it is incumbent on the State to provide a plausible explanation of how those injuries were caused, failing which a clear issue arises under Article 3 of the Convention".[63] This plainly posits that, in the presence of injuries which were not there at the time of arrest, it is *not* for the applicant to substantiate her allegations of torture or inhuman treatment. The onus of proof shifts to the State to provide a 'plausible explanation' of those injuries. In the present case the State has done nothing by way of explanation. The shift in the onus of proof is the first evidential norm neglected in the judgment.

10. Secondly, a cardinal requirement relating to the standard of proof was similarly discounted. In the present case the Court did not expressly assert that the applicant had an obligation to prove her allegations of torture "beyond reasonable doubt". But *that* is the standard of proof hitherto ordained by the Court in allegations of torture and inhuman treatment; it is evident that, in the wake of this evidentiary imperative, the Court expected the applicant to prove her allegations "beyond reasonable doubt".[64]

11. Independently of the failure by the majority to apply the rule that it was incumbent on the State to discharge the burden of evidence (v. § 9), I find the standard

---

[63] *Selmouni v. France*, 28 July 1999 § 87 (to be published); *Ribitsch v. Austria*, 4 December 1995, A 336, § 34; *Tomasi v. France*, 27 August 1992, A 241-A, §§ 108–111.

[64] First enunciated in *Ireland v. U.K.*, 18 January 1978, A 25 § 162, followed up in *Labita v. Italy*, 6 April 2000, § 121 (to be published). For the inadequacy of the 'beyond reasonable doubt' standard of proof in Article 3 cases, *vide* Loukis. G. Loucaides, *Essays on the Developing Law of Human Rights*, Martinus Nijhoff, p. 158.

of proof—beyond reasonable doubt—required by the Court in torture cases to be legally untenable and, in practice, unachievable.

12. Proof "beyond reasonable doubt" reflects a maximum standard relevant and desirable to establish *criminal* culpability. No person shall be judicially deprived of liberty, or otherwise penally censured, unless his guilt is manifest "beyond reasonable doubt". I subscribe to that stringent standard without hesitation. But in other fields of judicial enquiry, the standard of proof should be proportionate to the aim which the search for truth pursues: the highest degree of certainty, in criminal matters; a workable degree of probability in others.

13. Confronted by conflicting versions, the Court is under an obligation to establish (1) on whom the law places the burden of proof, (2) whether any legal presumptions militate in favour of one of the opposing accounts, and (3) "on a balance of probabilities", which of the conflicting versions appears to be more plausible and credible. Proof "beyond reasonable doubt" can, in my view, only claim a spurious standing in 'civil' litigation, like the adversarial proceedings before this Court. In fact, to the best of my knowledge, the Court is the only tribunal in Europe that requires proof "beyond reasonable doubt" in non-criminal matters.

14. Expecting those who claim to be victims of torture to prove their allegations "beyond reasonable doubt" places on them a burden that is as impossible to meet as it is unfair to request. Independent observers are not, to my knowledge, usually invited to witness the rack, nor is a transcript of proceedings in triplicate handed over at the end of each session of torture; its victims cower alone in oppressive and painful solitude, while the team of interrogators has almost unlimited means at its disposal to deny the happening of, or their participation in, the gruesome pageant. The solitary victim's complaint is almost invariably confronted with the negation "corroborated" by many.

15. For the Court to expect from torture victims any "hard" evidence, beyond the eloquence of their injuries, is to reward and invigorate the "inequality of arms" inherent in most torture scenarios.

16. Thirdly, the Court has, in my view, side-tracked the key question of credibility. I ask if, relying on its memory in handling so many cases of torture, the Court has compelling reasons to award more faith and credit to security forces which have an unenviable track-record to live down, rather than to those who claim to be their victims. No allegation has been made against the personal integrity and uprightness of the applicant, other than the damning circumstance that she was the wife of a human rights activist. The test, in the event, should have been: on a balance of credibility, who is likelier to have provided the court with a more reliable version of the incidents? The security forces?

17. Fourthly, it is difficult to envisage what "proof" the Court expected from the applicant in order to substantiate her claim that she was repeatedly tortured by being forcibly undressed, suspended, threatened with death and rape and deprived of food. These amusements are particularly ungenerous with those tangible signs dear to forensic experts. So, again, the only reasonable test ought to have been: on a balance of credibility, which of the two parties rests more convincingly on the side of truth?

18. Personally, I would have little hesitation with the answer. The majority seem to have thought otherwise. And its conclusion is unassailable—if you start your assessment of credibility from the premise that the applicant (whose personal integrity and honour are not in dispute), is neither to be trusted nor believed, while the security forces, repeatedly found guilty by this Court of killings, torture and inhuman behaviour, are.

19. Finally, the Court has unanimously affirmed that the respondent State breached Article 3 in that it failed to investigate the applicant's complaints of torture. In other words, the Court has held the respondent State guilty of defaulting in its obligation to unearth evidence by means of a determined fact-finding exercise. But then, after having established that the dearth of evidence is the defendant's fault, the Court visited the consequences of this failure on the applicant. She has been penalised for not coming up with evidence that the Convention *obliges* the State to procure. Hard as I try, I cannot see this as a consequent technique of decision-making.

Questions and Comments

1. For an Inter-American case of alleged sexual assault during custody and a similar finding of insufficient evidence, see *Loayza Tamayo v. Peru*, 33 Inter-Am. Ct. Hum. Rts (Ser. C) (1997). Is the Court demanding too much of applicants? Should there be a presumption of state responsibility for any custodial injuries? Compare *Gangaram Panday*, Inter-Am. Ct. Hum. Rts. with *Salman v. Turkey*, 34 Eur. Hum. Rts. Rep. 17 (2002) and *Tanli v. Turkey*, 38 Eur. Hum. Rts. Rep. (2004). In the European cases the Court stated that:

> 99. In the light of the importance of the protection afforded by Article 2, the Court must subject deprivations of life to the most careful scrutiny, taking into consideration not only the actions of State agents but also all the surrounding circumstances. Persons in custody are in a vulnerable position and the authorities are under a duty to protect them. Consequently, where an individual is taken into police custody in good health and is found to be injured on release, it is incumbent on the State to provide a plausible explanation of how those injuries were caused (see, among other authorities, *Selmouni v. France* [GC], no. 25803/94, § 87, ECHR 1999-V). The obligation on the authorities to account for the treatment of an individual in custody is particularly stringent where that individual dies.
>
> 100. In assessing evidence, the Court has generally applied the standard of proof "beyond reasonable doubt" (see the *Ireland v. the United Kingdom* judgment of 18 January 1978, Series A no. 25, pp. 64–65, § 161). However, such proof may follow from the coexistence of sufficiently strong, clear and concordant inferences or of similar unrebutted presumptions of fact. Where the events in issue lie wholly, or in large part, within the exclusive knowledge of the authorities, as in the case of persons within their control in custody, strong presumptions of fact will arise in respect of injuries and death occurring during such detention. Indeed, the burden of proof may be regarded as resting on the authorities to provide a satisfactory and convincing explanation.

No similar shifting of the burden of proof occurred in the *Gangaram Panday* case. Which is the better approach?

2. The European Court of Human Rights has recently clarified or even modified it strict standard of proof. In *Mathew v. Netherlands*, App. 24919/03, judgment of 29 Sept. 2005, the Court explained its approach:

> In assessing evidence, the Court has adopted the standard of proof "beyond reasonable doubt". However, it has never been its purpose to borrow the approach of the national legal systems that use that standard: as applied by the Court, it has an autonomous meaning. The

Court's role, it should be remembered, is to rule not on criminal guilt or civil liability but on Contracting States' responsibility under the Convention. The specificity of its task under Article 19 of the Convention—to ensure the observance by the Contracting States of their engagement to secure the fundamental rights enshrined in the Convention—conditions its approach to the issues of evidence and proof. In the proceedings before the Court, there are no procedural barriers to the admissibility of evidence or predetermined formulae for its assessment. It adopts the conclusions that are, in its view, supported by the free evaluation of all evidence, including such inferences as may flow from the facts and the parties' submissions. According to its established case-law, proof may follow from the coexistence of sufficiently strong, clear and concordant inferences or of similar unrebutted presumptions of fact. Moreover, the level of persuasion necessary for reaching a particular conclusion and, in this connection, the distribution of the burden of proof are intrinsically linked to the specificity of the facts, the nature of the allegation made and the Convention right at stake. The Court is also attentive to the seriousness that attaches to a ruling that a Contracting State has violated fundamental rights (see, as a recent authority, *Nachova and Others v. Bulgaria* [GC], nos. 43577/98 and 43579/98, § 147, ECHR 2005-. . .).

Id., at para. 156. How different is this from the standard of proof used by the Inter-American Court?

6. The Outcome: Remedies for Human Rights Violations

A. Introduction

Human rights litigation serves two main purposes. One aim is to uphold the international rule of law and bring states into compliance with their international obligations; this aim is forward-looking in seeking to prevent future violations. Regional human rights bodies regularly express their concern with this aspect of the cases before them. The second aim of complaints procedures is to afford redress to the petitioners. To a large extent, this requires assessing the consequences of the violation to the affected individuals, in order either to wipe out those consequences or to compensate if they cannot be eliminated. The egregiousness of the government's conduct may be taken into account in this assessment, on the assumption that the victim suffers greater moral injury with greater wrongdoing. In sum, redress aims to uphold the rule of law, place the victims as close as possible to the position they would have held had the violation not occurred, and express moral condemnation of the government's misconduct.

International law has long expressed a preference for restitution as a remedy, where this is possible. Some human rights violations, e.g., wrongful detention, allow for restitution of the right violated. Others rights, like life, cannot be restored once lost and thus require a difficult assessment of the monetary value of the right lost. The regional tribunals have struggled with the question of assessing compensatory damages as well as the scope of their powers to remedy violations through non-monetary means.

The following cases indicate the range of reparations and the varying approaches of the regional bodies to the issues of remedies. Consider: what do the applicants seek? What are the powers of the commissions and courts? Do such bodies have inherent powers to remedy violations? How well are they assessing compensatory damages? Should punitive damages be allowed?

B. The European System

D. Shelton, *Remedies in International Human Rights Law* (2nd ed. 2004), pp. 189–192, 194–97 (footnotes omitted).

The European Convention on Human Rights gives the Court competence to afford remedies when it determines that a breach of the Convention has occurred. Former Article 50, now slightly amended as Article 41, provides:

> If the Court finds that a decision or a measure taken by a legal authority or any other authority of a High Contracting Party is completely or partially in conflict with the obligations arising from [the] Convention, and if the internal law of the said party allows only partial reparation to be made for the consequences of this decision or measure, the decision of the Court shall, if necessary, afford just satisfaction to the injured party.

According to some commentators, 'this provision shows the Court's lack of competence to annul or nullify acts of member states which are in conflict with the Convention'. As discussed further below, the inability to nullify legislative or other acts does not limit the Court's power to rule that amendment or nullification of measures that violate the Convention is an appropriate remedy.

Under prior procedures, when a case was not submitted to the Court, the Committee of Ministers, pursuant to Article 32, decided whether or not a breach of the Convention had occurred, based on a report of the European Commission on Human Rights. The Committee could require that specific remedial measures be taken by the state, including an award of just satisfaction, although the latter is not explicitly mentioned in Article 32. The Committee of Ministers now supervises the execution of the legally-binding judgments of the Court.

The drafters of the European Convention made clear their concern with affording adequate remedies to victims of human rights violations. The idea of a European human rights system emerged at the 1948 Congress of Europe, convened by the International Committee of Movements for European Unity. In the 'Message to Europeans' adopted at the final plenary session, the Congress delegates expressed the following: 'We desire a Charter of Human Rights guaranteeing liberty of thought, assembly and expression as well as the right to form a political opposition; We desire a Court of Justice *with adequate sanctions* for the implementation of this Charter'. The Congress adopted a resolution in which it stated that it:

> 6. Is convinced that in the interest of human values and human liberty, the (proposed) Assembly should make proposals for the establishment of a Court of Justice with adequate sanctions for the implementation of this Charter (of Human Rights), and to this end any citizen of the associated countries shall have redress before the Court, at any time and with the least possible delay, of any violation of his rights as formulated in the Charter.

The draft Convention presented by the Congress to the Committee of Ministers in 1949 envisaged a Court able to prescribe both monetary compensation and to require that the state concerned take penal or administrative action against the person responsible for infringing human rights. The Court also could require the 'repeal, cancellation or amendment' of the act complained of. At the first session of the Consultative Assembly of the Council of Europe in 1949, it became clear that the proposal for a Court with sanctioning power was not universally accepted, although the draft report of the Legal and Administrative Commission of the Assembly contained a proposal very similar to that of the Congress. The final report submitted by the Commission to the Assembly omitted the proposal.

The Committee of Experts on Human Rights which first met in February 1950 worked on a list of unresolved questions including 'the competence of the Court to pronounce judgments according damages, reparations (*restitutio in integrum*) or moral damages'. In the end the Committee recommended the adoption of a provision substantially like Article 50. The Committee noted in its report to the Committee of Ministers that 'the Court will not in any way operate as a Court of Appeal, having power to revise internal orders and verdicts'. In a Report to the Committee of Ministers, Article 50 as adopted was said to be:

> in accordance with the actual international law relating to the violation of an obligation by a State. In this respect, jurisprudence of a European Court will never, therefore, introduce any new element or one contrary to existing international law. In particular, the Court will not have the power to declare null and void or amend Acts emanating from the public bodies of the signatory States.

At the Second Session of the Consultative Assembly a proposal again was made to enlarge the powers of the Court to give it 'appellate jurisdiction', so that 'the Court may declare the impugned judicial laws to be null and void'. The Committee rejected the proposal by majority vote, retaining the present version of Article 50 (41). The language . . . was derived from treaty provisions on the enforcement of arbitral awards in inter-state proceedings, notably Article 32 of the 1928 General Act on Arbitration, which provides:

> If, in a judicial sentence or arbitral award it is declared that a judgment, or a measure enjoined by a court of law or other authority of one of the parties to the dispute, is wholly or in part contrary to international law, and if the constitutional law of that party does not permit or only partially permits the consequences of the judgment or measure in question to be annulled, the parties agree that the judicial sentence or arbitral award shall grant the injured party equitable satisfaction.

The reliance on precedents from arbitration agreements may have been based on an expectation that adjudication before the Court would be primarily inter-state in nature, rather than based on individual communications, and that earlier arbitral practice would therefore be particularly relevant. Clearly, the primary concern was to avoid the Court becoming an appellate tribunal.

The European Court recognized early that Article 50 was modeled after the provisions of dispute settlement treaties, including the General Act quoted above and Article 10 of the German-Swiss Treaty on Arbitration and Conciliation. The relevant provisions clearly contemplated cessation of the breach, and *restitutio in integrum*, based on principles of state responsibility. At the same time, the agreements acknowledged, in effect, the problem of enforcing an international arbitral judgment. Where strict compliance could not be obtained, the treaties allowed compensation and other forms of satisfaction in lieu of restitution, where the constitutional law of the wrongdoing state made it difficult or impossible to annul or amend offending legislation or other measures. Their intent was to ensure that the complex and varied relations between international and municipal law in different countries should not prevent redress for the injured alien and state of nationality. The approach is of dubious merit when applied to modern human rights cases. Injured aliens could accept compensation and leave the state that committed the injury, escaping further violation of their rights. Human rights victims, in contrast, normally are harmed by their state of nationality and remain subject to its laws and practices. Compensation may remedy a violation that has already occurred, but does not reduce the threat of future violations if the law or practice is not changed.

The term 'satisfaction' as used in arbitral treaties and in the European Convention draws upon international practice in regard to state responsibility for injury to aliens [. . . .] [T]he state [of nationality of the alien] usually claimed pecuniary and non-pecuniary reparations for the injury to the alien, and non-monetary satisfaction to remedy its own moral injury. Satisfaction could require punishment of the guilty and assurances as to future conduct, monetary awards, or declaration of the wrong, especially when coupled with an apology from the offending state. Many such non-monetary remedies afforded under the heading of satisfaction in interstate proceedings could be appropriately applied in the human rights context, especially apologies, guarantees of non-repetition and/or punishment of wrongdoers.

. . . .

By 1 November 1998, when the new European Court of Human Rights was inaugurated, the former Court had considered nearly 900 cases, representing about 10 per cent of the cases found admissible by the Commission. The Court found at least one violation in approximately 70 per cent of its judgments. During 1997 and 1998, nearly 200 cases were decided under an expedited screening procedure, as not raising issues requiring full consideration by the Court.

During its first decade the Court did not have to address the issue of remedies. It found no violation in the *Lawless* case, its first judgment, while the second case, *De Becker*, was settled. In the *Belgian Linguistics* case, the Constitution and institutions of Belgium were revised and reformed to comply with the Court's decision without the issue of remedies being decided. No violation was found in *Wemhoff*. Not until 1968, in the *Neumeister* case, did the issue of remedies require adjudication by the Court. The Court separated its consideration of just satisfaction from the proceedings on the merits and, ultimately, decided the Article 50 claim after its 1972 judgments on just satisfaction in the *Vagrancy* cases and *Ringeisen*. Between 1972 and 1998, the former Court awarded one or more of the following remedies in application of Article 50:

(a) a declaration that the state had violated the applicant's rights;
(b) pecuniary damages;
(c) non-pecuniary damages;
(d) costs and expenses.

. . . .

The Court held on various occasions that it has no jurisdiction to make 'consequential orders' in the form of directions or recommendations to the state to remedy violations. It rejected requests, for example, that the state be required to refrain from corporal punishment of children or to take steps to prevent similar breaches in the future. It also refused to insist that a state judged to have wrongfully expelled an alien allow the victim to rejoin his family. Recently, however, it indicated that such steps implicitly may be required of each state. . . . In general, the former Court did not demonstrate much enthusiasm for Article 50, reflected in its rules and its decisions. The narrow interpretation of Article 50, given by the Court in its first case, hampered the evolution of remedies in the European system. The approach developed in that case was followed consistently, though often criticized. It left the Court with little flexibility. The Court gave unnecessarily important weight to the words 'if necessary', setting stringent requirements of a causal link between the violation and the injury and rarely affording relief that corresponded to the harm done. In numerous cases it found that the judgment alone afforded just satisfaction for the moral injury. There was no indication of concern for deterrence, although that was traditionally a focus of 'satisfaction' in the law of state responsibility for injury to aliens.

. . . [B]elgium argued in the *Vagrancy* cases that litigants should never receive compensation if challenging a law applicable to a broad segment of the population. The state appeared to have assumed that successful litigants would receive a windfall, while others would remain uncompensated. The Court rightly rejected this argument. The fact that some injured parties choose not to enforce their rights has never been deemed a justification for refusing to redress the wrongs done to those who do seek their vindication. Indeed, the failure to compensate them would deter anyone from challenging government wrongdoing.

In the same case, the Court outlined the requirements for affording just satisfaction:

(i) the Court must find a decision or measure taken by an authority of a Contracting State to be in conflict with the obligations arising from the Convention;
(ii) there is an injured party; i.e. material or moral damage; and
(iii) the Court considers it necessary to afford just compensation.

The Court may decide no compensation is due: 'as is borne out by the adjective "just" and the phrase "if necessary" the Court enjoys a certain discretion in the exercise of the power conferred by Article 50'. The Court repeatedly stated that applicants are not entitled to an award of just satisfaction, rather the Court has discretion to grant a remedy based on equitable considerations and the facts of each case. This narrow view seems to undermine the remedial purpose of Article 50; there is moral damage, at least, in every case where a state violates the fundamental rights of an individual. . . . Violations of procedural rights, such as failure to provide a speedy trial, rarely have resulted in relief beyond a declaration of the violation. No compensation has been given most prisoners, except where physical mistreatment is proven. Homosexuals, vagrants, and aliens also generally have been denied compensation.

The former Court's decisions on Article 50 vary considerably and lack a coherent approach. The Court sometimes seemed to apply a notion of presumed damages while, in other proceedings, it refused to make an award based on the lack of proof of a causal link between the violation and the injury. The Court enunciated clear standards only in regard to awarding costs and fees; they must have been actually incurred, necessarily incurred and reasonable in amount. Even so, the Court viewed the award as discretionary and often did not award the full amount.

––––––––––

The *Neumeister* case that immediately follows was the first case in which the Court was asked to afford compensation for a violation of the European Convention. Consider the standards the Court establishes and the actual outcome. Did the Court set too high a threshold from the beginning?

Neumeister v. Austria, (Article 50), 7 May 1974, 17 Eur. Ct. H.R. (Ser. A) (1974).

1. The Neumeister case was referred to the Court on 7 October 1966 by the European Commission of Human Rights and on 11 October 1966 by the Government of the Republic of Austria. The case has its origin in an application against the Republic of Austria submitted to the Commission by an Austrian national, Mr. Fritz Neumeister, in 1963. The applicant complained, inter alia, of the length of time he had spent in detention while on remand from 24 February to 12 May 1961, that is, two months and sixteen days, and from 12 July 1962 to 16 September 1964, that is two years, two months and four days.

2. By judgment of 27 June 1968 the Court, while rejecting two other complaints of the applicant, held that there had been a breach of Article 5 (3) (art. 5–3) of the Convention in that the detention of Neumeister had been continued for longer than a reasonable time.

3. On 2 July 1968, the Vienna Regional Criminal Court sentenced the applicant to five years' severe imprisonment for aggravated fraud; the two above-mentioned periods of detention on remand were reckoned as part of the sentence. The Supreme Court upheld that decision on 16 June and 4 November 1971.

4. On 23 December 1970, Neumeister presented to the Austrian Federal Ministry of Justice a claim for a provisional overall sum of 3,500,000 schillings compensation in reparation of the damage he had allegedly sustained by reason of the violation so found by the European Court. On 17 March 1971, the Finanzprokuratur (revenue department of the Attorney General's office) informed him that the Republic of Austria could not accept that he was entitled to such compensation since the conditions required therefore [sic] under the law in force were not satisfied.

5. Considering this reply as a final decision under the law, the applicant addressed his claim to the Commission on 16 September 1971, referring to the judgment of 27 June 1968 and to Articles 5 (5) and 50 of the Convention. He stated that, by reason of his second detention on remand (12 July 1962—16 September 1964), he had suffered considerable financial loss, not to mention personal injustice and humiliation. He alleged that the sudden cessation of his services had ruined his business; that not only had he lost important business contacts, but contracts in hand had had to be left unfulfilled or carried out incompletely; that this had resulted in a serious decline of the Scherzinger company and an almost total loss of the company's capital. Reserving his right to present further claims, Neumeister for the time being estimated the loss at 3,500,000 schillings at least. He requested the Commission to accept his claim and to initiate the proceedings provided in this connection. . . .

By letter received on 26 March 1973, the Agent of the Government informed the Registrar that "the Federal President of the Republic of Austria on 14 February 1973 (had) granted a pardon to Fritz Neumeister in respect of the unserved part of the sentence pronounced by the Regional Court of Criminal Matters in Vienna on 2 July 1968 . . . [T]his pardon (had) the effect that Fritz Neumeister (was) to be considered under probation concerning the remainder of his sentence for the time of three years".

13. The observations and documents filed subsequently with the Court make it possible to reconstruct the events which occurred between 16 May 1972 and 14 February 1973:

(a) On 26 May 1972, Neumeister addressed to the Ministry of Justice a request for remission of sentence by an act of grace. Referring to the proceedings pending before the Court and to the negotiations between the Agent of the Government and his lawyer, he stated, inter alia, that it was clearly impossible to wipe out (ungeschehen zu machen) the detention on remand which he had had to endure from July 1962 to September 1964, but that partial reparation would be possible in his case if the Republic of Austria forbore to insist on his serving the remainder of his sentence. He added that for his part he was prepared to waive all claims for material reparation (materielle Ersatzansprüche) against the Republic of Austria. In an addendum of 2 June 1972, he stressed that he had offered in his letter of 26 May to withdraw, in the event of his obtaining the settlement under negotiation, the claim for compensation which he had made to the Commission.

(b) In a report of 11 January 1973 prepared for the Federal President of the Republic after consultation with the Ministry of Foreign Affairs and the Federal Chancellery, the Ministry of Justice stressed that conditional remission, by an act of grace; of the part of the sentence remaining unserved would be a more adequate reparation than monetary compensation. The Ministry of Foreign Affairs, to whom the report was submitted subsequently, made a note on the file to say they shared the opinion of the Ministry of Justice: the procedure contemplated seemed to them the most likely to show the public that Austria was disposed to observe its obligations under the Convention. The Federal Chancellery, for its part, made comments along the same lines and noted that Neumeister would be agreeable (ware einverstanden) to this form of reparation and would waive (würde verzichten) all claims to monetary compensation.

(c) It was on the basis of this proposal that, on 14 February 1973, the Federal President of the Republic of Austria granted Neumeister remission of the part of his sentence remaining unserved, i.e., two years, seven months and ten days. The decision, which bears the signature of the President and is countersigned by the Minister of Justice, is worded as follows: "I assent to the proposal for pardon, Zl. Gt. 42/73, for Fritz Neumeister".

Remission has the effect of a conditional sentence subject to a probationary period of three years. In order to conserve the benefit of the act of grace, Neumeister must comply with the conditions—and them alone—laid down in Section 3 of the Austrian Act on Conditional Sentences.

. . . .

19. In a letter received at the Registry on 11 July 1973, the Agent of the Government provided the Court with additional information from his side relating to the discussions of 15 May 1972 and 16 March 1973. He stated that the granting of the pardon on 14 February 1973 "was not connected with any request by the competent Austrian authorities that Mr. Neumeister should waive his claim for monetary compensation, since on the one hand such a waiver appeared to be a logical consequence of the whole arrangement and, on the other hand, an act of grace by the Head of State could not be considered to be part of any 'deal'". The Agent concluded by stating that his "Government (was) not in the position to take any further measures in respect of any new requests of Mr. Neumeister aiming at a friendly settlement of the case. If the Court"—unlike the Government—"should not consider the act of grace . . . as sufficient and just compensation it (had) to be assumed that the attempt to reach a friendly settlement [had] ultimately failed".

20. It was through the two last-mentioned replies that the Court was apprised of the meeting which had taken place on 16 March 1973; further details concerning it have been furnished since . . . . [I]t was immediately after the meeting that the Agent of the Government informed the Court of the granting of the pardon to the applicant.

21. On the instructions of the President of the Chamber, the Registrar invited the Delegates of the Commission, on 11 July 1973, to send him in writing by 15 August any observations and submissions they wished to make. In their reply, . . . [t]hey . . . transmitted to the Court a letter of 8 May 1972 which they had received from Neumeister . . . .

In that letter, the applicant gave further particulars of, and developed, his initial claim. He estimated the total damage allegedly caused to his firm at 3,564,400 schillings at the very least, and the loss of his salary and allowances as manager as additional damage of not less than 405,000 schillings. He further claimed that he had spent in vain at least 100,000 schillings in lawyers' fees in order to obtain his release. Finally, he considered that he was entitled to at least 3,000,000 schillings damages for the injustice he had suffered. He pointed out, however, that the total amount he claimed, 7,069,400 schillings, should be reduced somewhat as his business losses resulting from his arrest had been calculated on estimated gross profits. Noting that the damages due to him by the Republic of Austria considerably exceeded the total sum originally claimed, he reserved his right to make a corresponding increase in his claim and in addition he asked for payment of interest at an official rate of 5 per cent per annum. . . .

AS TO THE LAW

I. THE QUESTION WHETHER ARTICLE 50 IS APPLICABLE

. . . .

29. In its written observations and then at the hearings, the Government expressed the opinion that the Commission had acted in error in transmitting to the Court Neumeister's claim for compensation. In the Government's view, the Commission should have considered and examined the claim as an application lodged

under Article 25 and alleging violation of Article 5 (5), which provides that "everyone who has been the victim of arrest or detention in contravention of the provisions of this Article"—in this case those of paragraph 3—"shall have an enforceable right to compensation". The Government has submitted that Article 5 (5) constitutes a *lex specialis* in relation to Article 50; that it states a special rule for compensation so that the general rule in Article 50 does not apply in cases of violation of freedom of the person; that the applicant, moreover, had well understood this to be so on 16 September 1971 when he relied on Article 5 (5), requested the Commission "to accept" his submissions, which meant to declare them admissible, and asked the Commission "to initiate the proceedings provided in this connection", which was a reference to Articles 25 and following. . . .

30. As to the first point, the Court begins by observing that the manner in which the Government interprets the claim of 16 September 1971 is not beyond discussion. Neumeister did not entitle his letter "application" (Beschwerde) but "claim" (Antrag); he did not complain explicitly of a violation of Article 5 (5): while he referred to that provision, he also relied on Article 50, mentioning the Court and the possibility of "just satisfaction" (gerechte Entschädigung).

Furthermore, and above all else, the Court must take an objective and not a subjective view: whatever may have been the applicant's intentions, the Court must determine whether the Convention requires or authorises in such a case the procedure which the Commission has chosen to follow.

The submission that Article 5 (5) constitutes a derogation from the lex generalis laid down in Article 50 and excludes the application of the provisions contained in the latter Article was made already by the Government in the *Ringeisen* case (Series B, no. 13, pp. 26–28, 50, 53 and 80). In its judgment of 22 June 1972 the Court implicitly rejected that submission in holding the applicant's claim for compensation to be admissible (Series A, no. 15, pp. 7–8, paragraphs 14 to 19); it considers it necessary to settle explicitly this question in the present case.

Article 5 (5) and Article 50 are placed on different levels, although both Articles deal with questions of compensation under the Convention.

The first lays down a rule of substance: placed among the "normative" provisions of Section I of the Convention, it guarantees an individual a right, the observance of which is obligatory in the first instance for the authorities of the Contracting States, as the use in the English text of the adjective "enforceable" confirms.

Article 50, for its part, lays down a rule of competence: placed in Section IV of the Convention, it authorises the Court expressly to afford subject to certain conditions, just satisfaction to the "injured party". One of these conditions is the existence of a national decision or measure "in conflict with the obligations arising from the . . . Convention", and there is nothing to show that a breach of one of the first four paragraphs of Article 5 is not to be taken into account in this regard. While paragraph 5 of Article 5 carefully specifies that "everyone who has been the victim" of such a breach "shall have an enforceable right to compensation", it in no way follows therefrom that the Court cannot apply Article 50 when it has found that there has been a breach, for example, of paragraph 3; what does follow, and no more, is that in the exercise of the wide competence conferred upon it by Article 50, the

Court must take into consideration, among other factors the rule of substance contained in paragraph 5 of Article 5.

In addition, the acceptance of the Government's argument would lead to consequences incompatible with the aim and object of the Convention. In order to obtain just satisfaction over and above mere recognition of his entitlement to his rights, the victim of a violation of liberty of the person might find himself obliged to lodge two successive petitions with the Commission on each of which the Court or the Committee of Ministers would be called upon, if need be, to rule after a lapse of several years. The system of safeguards set up by the Convention would therefore operate only at an extremely slow pace in the case of Article 5, a situation which would scarcely be in keeping with the idea of the effective protection of human rights (see mutatis mutandis the *De Wilde, Ooms and V*ersyp judgment of 10 March 1972, Series A, no. 14, p. 9, paragraph 16 in fine).

These various considerations lead the Court to conclude that the proceedings in the present case no longer fall within Section III of the Convention but are the final phase of proceedings brought before the Court under Section IV on the conclusion of those to which the original petition of Neumeister gave rise in 1963 before the Commission (see *mutatis mutandis* the *De Wilde, Ooms and Versyp* judgment of 10 March 1972, Series A, no. 14, p. 8, paragraph 15). The claim of 16 September 1971 cannot therefore be dealt with as a new petition presented under Article 25 and the Commission was right to transmit it straightaway to the Court.

. . . .

III. AS TO THE MERITS OF THE APPLICANT'S CLAIM

37. Before ruling on the merits of the claim, the Court clearly has to determine the date on which the length of the applicant's second detention on remand (12 July 1962–16 September 1964), the only period with which it need deal (*Neumeister* judgment of 27 June 1968, Series A, no. 8, p 37, § 6), became unreasonable under Article 5 § 3. The Court did not see any need to do so explicitly in its judgment of 27 June 1968 since the applicant had not as yet claimed damages; the position is not the same now.

38. Contrary to the applicant's view, the judgment of 27 June 1968 does not imply that this second detention was in breach of Article 5 § 3 ab initio. Having noted that the Austrian judicial authorities gave the danger of absconding as the reason for their successive decisions not to release the applicant, the Court stated that it found it understandable that this risk seemed to them to have been much increased in July 1962 by the greater gravity of the criminal and civil penalties which a co-accused's new statement must have caused Neumeister to fear (judgment of 27 June 1968, Series A, no. 8, pp. 38–39, §§ 9–10). It is true that the Court afforded only relative value to their reasons and accepted the force of the applicant's arguments and the investigating judge's evidence (ibid., p 39, §§ 10–11) but it did not conclude that there was a complete lack of danger of absconding: the Court found no more than that "the danger . . . was, in October 1962 in any event, no longer so great that it was necessary"—the attitude of the Austrian judicial authorities—"to dismiss as quite ineffective the taking of the guarantees which under Article 5 (3) may condition a grant of provisional release" (ibid., p. 40, § 12).

Nor does the judgment of 1968 mean that the violation arose "when for the first time, on 26 October 1962, Neumeister proposed a bank guarantee of 200,000 or, if necessary, 250,000 schillings": the Court did not consider itself to be "in a position" to estimate "the amount of security which could reasonably be demanded of Neumeister" and it did not reject "the notion that the first offers could have been dismissed as insufficient" (ibid. p. 40, § 13).

In any event, the Austrian authorities could not be required to release the applicant on the very day he had made some sort of offer; they clearly needed time to examine the offer and to make a ruling.

The Court nevertheless regrets that the Judges' Chamber of the Vienna Regional Criminal Court and the Court of Appeal did not—instead of describing as "out of the question" ("indiskutabel") the offer of 26 October to which the investigating judge had stated on 29 October that he had no objection (Series B, no. 6, p. 241)—indicate to Neumeister in their decisions of 27 December 1962 and 19 February 1963 a different sum for security which they considered appropriate. Such a step, legitimate under Austrian law (Series A, no. 8, p. 15, first paragraph), would probably have rendered it possible to expedite the release of the applicant and would have been in complete conformity with the spirit of the Convention. In particular, it would have shown a better appreciation of the relevant considerations in evaluating the danger of flight (ibid., p. 39, § 10).

It is certainly rather difficult to state at what precise point in time the competent authorities would have succeeded in reaching agreement with the applicant on the amount of the guarantee if they had adopted a more flexible attitude. The date of 1 March 1963, that is about four months subsequent to the offer of 26 October 1962, seems to be appropriate for this purpose. It is no doubt of an approximate character, but the Court does not find any further precision necessary, having regard to the conclusions it reaches concerning Neumeister's claims for compensation.

39. The applicant claims several million schillings in compensation for the damage which, he alleges, his second detention on remand (12 July 1962–16 September 1964) caused to the Scherzinger company and in two ways to himself, the loss of his salary as manager of the firm and "injustice suffered".

The Government considers that, quite apart from Neumeister's "waiver", the act of grace of 14 February 1973 on its own amounts to full reparation. The Government relies too on the fact that the detention on remand was reckoned as part of the sentence and on the more favourable conditions—disputed by the applicant—compared to penal imprisonment.

40. As regards, first, the alleged material damage, the onus was on Neumeister, as the Government and the Commission are agreed in thinking, to establish not only that in fact it had been sustained but also that there was a causal link between it and the violation so found by the Court in its judgment of 27 June 1968 (see the *Ringeisen* judgment of 22 June 1972, Series A, no. 15, p. 9, § 24).

The arrest of Neumeister on 12 July 1962, which he complains of as being sudden and unjustified, must have deprived him of some income and upset the running of his business. The breach of Article 5 (3), however, did not commence until much later: the second detention on remand was, at the outset, compatible with the

Convention and so remained for about seven and a half months; its length did not exceed a "reasonable time" until 1 March 1963 or thereabouts. Until that approximate date the interruption of Neumeister's business activity resulted from decisions which were in conformity with the requirements of the Convention; therefore, that interruption cannot entitle him to reparation. Subsequently, the interruption could not be taken into account under Article 50 unless the overrunning of the "reasonable time" had caused some damage distinct from that which the applicant would necessarily have suffered in the event of his being released one and a half years earlier but imprisoned for the same period after conviction.

Some losses must have followed from the excessive prolongation of the detention in question but it proves very difficult to isolate and unravel them from those which Neumeister and the Scherzinger company would have had to bear in any event. The Court does not find it necessary on this point to embark on additional proceedings. In effect, the time the applicant had spent in detention on remand was reckoned as part of his sentence and, more especially, he was granted remission of the remainder of his sentence, i.e., two years, seven months and ten days. He would doubtless have had prospects, if he had been imprisoned after conviction, of being released on probation for a third of the term of imprisonment, but even on this assumption it is established that he avoided deprivation of liberty for eleven months and ten days at the very least. Moreover, he was saved the adverse consequences which further imprisonment would inevitably have caused him in his business activities. In short, the act of grace of 14 February 1973 was of considerable benefit to him. The few conditions which accompany that act are in no way onerous; they are defined limitatively in the Act which applies to such cases. While remission of sentence, like the reckoning of detention as part of a sentence, does not constitute real restitutio in integrum (*Ringeisen* judgment of 22 June 1972, Series A, no. 15, p. 8, § 21, 2), it comes as close to it as is possible in the nature of things.

The applicant, moreover, shared this view at first. In his request of 26 May 1972 for pardon, he indicated that remission of the remainder of his sentence would be the best possible form of reparation, given that the wrong suffered was by its nature incapable of being wiped out; so sure was he of this that he stated that he would be prepared to waive, if he were accorded a pardon, all his claims for compensation against the Republic of Austria. The opinion he expressed of his own accord at that time retains its value; it confirms the just character of the measure taken in Austria in favour of the applicant.

The Court concludes that it is therefore not necessary to afford satisfaction to the applicant for material damage.

41. Neumeister undeniably suffered moral damage by reason of the fact that his second detention on remand lasted longer than a "reasonable time" by some eighteen and a half months (1 March 1963–16 September 1964); under this head he was entitled in principle to "compensation" or "just satisfaction".

The Delegates of the Commission take the view that, in spite of the measures already taken in favour of the applicant in Austria, the damage resulting from the breach of Article 5 (3) "in itself" in addition calls for some element of monetary compensation of which it is for the Court to assess the amount in the light of all the circumstances of the case; in this regard they base themselves on paragraphs 20 and 21 of the Ringeisen judgment of 22 June 1972.

Article 50, however, provides for an award by the Court of just satisfaction only "if necessary" (*De Wilde, Ooms and Versyp* judgment of 10 March 1972, Series A, no. 14, p. 10, § 21).

The applicant was convicted and sentenced to a term of imprisonment considerably longer than his detention on remand and that detention was reckoned in full as part of the sentence. Moreover, unlike Ringeisen he was granted a pardon on 14 February 1973 which he himself had requested as being the best form of reparation, and which was far more advantageous to him than payment of a sum of money. These various circumstances outweight the moral wrong of which he complains; the Court thus reaches the conclusion that in this regard it is not necessary to afford him any further satisfaction.

42. Finally, the applicant claims from 250,000 to 260,000 schillings for fees said to have been paid to five lawyers namely, Mr. Steger (from 12 July 1962 to the beginning of 1963), Mr. Stern (from January 1963 to September 1964), Mr. Leutgeb (from mid-1963 to the end of 1964), Mr. Waldhof (from May 1972 onwards) and Mr. Gussenbauer (from September 1971 onwards).

As to the services rendered by these lawyers, the Court has before it the information furnished by Neumeister (statement of account of January 1974), by the Government (observations of February and March 1974) and also that provided by the other documents on the file, including the Commission's report of 27 May 1966.

It would appear that Mr. Steger, Mr. Stern, or Mr. Leutgeb, as the case may be, acted for the applicant in Austria during his second detention on remand (12 July 1962–16 September 1964). In particular, they made applications on his behalf for his release on 26 October 1962, 12–16 July 1963 and 6 November 1963 and lodged appeals on 15 January 1963, 5 August 1963, 20 August 1963, 13 December 1963, 21 January 1964 and 20 April 1964, and in addition they conducted correspondence, appeared at hearings and took other steps (see, for example, Series A, no. 8, pp. 10–16 and 18; Series B, no. 6, pp. 34, 35, 112–113, 115 and 241). Moreover, Mr. Stern wrote on at least one occasion to the Commission, on 14 April 1964, (Series B, no. 6, pp. 13, 60 and 90), and Mr. Leutgeb appeared for Neumeister at the hearings of 6 July 1964 on the admissibility of the application (ibid, p. 86).

Mr. Waldhof and Mr. Gussenbauer were retained—in so far as they are mentioned by the applicant in his statement of account of January 1974—after the Court's judgment of 27 June 1968: they dealt with their client's claims for compensation, Mr. Waldhof having to do with the Austrian authorities (meetings of 12 May 1972, 15 May 1972 and 16 March 1973, request for pardon of 26 May 1972 with the addendum of 2 June 1972, the letter of 30 October 1973 to the Ministry of Finance, etc.,—see, for example, paragraphs 11, 13 (a), 20 and 26 above), Mr. Gussenbauer being concerned with the Delegates of the Commission in the procedure before the Court.

Neumeister did not have the benefit of free legal aid before the Commission itself or with the Commission's Delegates after the case was referred to the Court. He was granted legal aid in Austria only during the initial stages of the criminal trial

(Hauptverfahren—see the Government's observations of February 1974). That trial, which opened on 9 November 1964 (Series A, no. 8, p. 19) and terminated on 4 November 1971, is not material to the matters presently under consideration; besides, the applicant does not mention it in his statement of January 1974.

43. As the Court has already observed, the advantages resulting from the remission of sentence constitute just satisfaction for the damage, material and moral, suffered by the applicant through the excessive length of his detention on remand. This finding does not prevent the Court from ascertaining whether the expenses incurred by Neumeister in vindicating his rights guaranteed by the Convention have been sufficiently compensated too by the advantages above-mentioned.

The Court considers it proper, in this particular case, to distinguish between damage caused by a violation of the Convention and the necessary costs which the applicant has had to incur in order to try to prevent such violation, to have it established by the Commission and later by the Court and to obtain, after judgment in his favour, just satisfaction either from the competent national authorities or, if appropriate, from the Court.

Although the act of grace outweighs in this case the material and moral damage, that act does not likewise amount to just satisfaction in respect of the necessary costs in lawyers' fees which the applicant incurred over the years in order to achieve that result. It is therefore necessary to afford to the applicant fair compensation in this regard.

44. In the circumstances of the case, the Court takes as an appropriate basis for calculation the current rates payable under the scheme for free legal aid operated by the Commission and Delegates of the Commission. The Court furthermore takes into consideration the various acts enumerated above covering the time since the request for release of 26 October 1962, being the latest of those which, if granted, would have avoided the breach of Article 5 (3) which began on or about 1 March 1963.

On this basis the Court assesses at thirty thousand schillings (30,000 AS) the sum to be paid by the Republic of Austria to the applicant.

Questions and Comments

The Court finds that Neumeister's pardon is enough to extinguish any moral injury he may have suffered. Do you agree? Was the fact that he was convicted of criminal conduct a factor in the case? Consider the following extract:

McCann and Others v. the United Kingdom, (App. no. 18984/91), Judgment of 27 September 1995, 324 Eur. Ct. H.R. (Ser. A), 21 EHRR 97 (1996).

[The Court held by a vote of 10–9 that the UK government had violated the Convention, Art. 2 (the right to life) of the deceased Irish nationals by failing to adequately plan and control an anti-terrorism operation on the island of Gibraltar, where the decedents were suspected of going to plant a bomb. According to the Court, "having regard to the decision not to prevent the suspects from travelling into Gibraltar, to the failure of the authorities to make sufficient allowances for the possibility that their intelligence assessments might, in some respects at least, be erroneous and to the automatic recourse to lethal force when the soldiers opened fire, the Court is not persuaded that the killing of the three terrorists constituted the use of force which was no more than absolutely necessary in defence of persons from unlawful violence within the meaning of Article 2 para. 2 (a) (art. 2–2-a) of the Convention". The Court then turned to the issue of reparations and unanimously decided as follows.]

216. The applicants requested the award of damages at the same level as would be awarded under English law to a person who was unlawfully killed by agents of the State. They also asked, in the event of the Court finding that the killings were both unlawful and deliberate or were the result of gross negligence, exemplary damages at the same level as would be awarded under English law to a relative of a person killed in similar circumstances.

217. As regards costs and expenses, they asked for all costs arising directly or indirectly from the killings, including the costs of relatives and lawyers attending the Gibraltar inquest and all Strasbourg costs. The solicitor's costs and expenses in respect of the Gibraltar inquest are estimated at £56,200 and his Strasbourg costs at £28,800. Counsel claimed £16,700 in respect of Strasbourg costs and expenses.

218. The Government contended that, in the event of a finding of a violation, financial compensation in the form of pecuniary and non-pecuniary damages would be unnecessary and inappropriate.

As regards the costs incurred before the Strasbourg institutions, they submitted that the applicants should be awarded only the costs actually and necessarily incurred by them and which were reasonable as to quantum. However, as regards the claim for costs in respect of the Gibraltar inquest, they maintained that (1) as a point of principle, the costs of the domestic proceedings, including the costs of the inquest, should not be recoverable under Article 50; (2) since the applicants' legal representatives acted free of charge, there can be no basis for an award to the applicants; (3) in any event, the costs claimed were not calculated on the basis of the normal rates of the solicitor concerned.

A. Pecuniary and non-pecuniary damage

219. The Court observes that it is not clear from the applicants' submissions whether their claim for financial compensation is under the head of pecuniary or non-pecuniary damages or both. In any event, having regard to the fact that the three terrorist suspects who were killed had been intending to plant a bomb in Gibraltar, the Court does not consider it appropriate to make an award under this head. It therefore dismisses the applicants' claim for damages.

B. Costs and expenses

220. The Court recalls that, in accordance with its case-law, it is only costs which are actually and necessarily incurred and reasonable as to quantum that are recoverable under this head.

221. As regards the Gibraltar costs, the applicants stated in the proceedings before the Commission that their legal representatives had acted free of charge. In

this connection, it has not been claimed that they are under any obligation to pay the solicitor the amounts claimed under this item. In these circumstances, the costs cannot be claimed under Article 50 since they have not been actually incurred.

222. As regards the costs and expenses incurred during the Strasbourg proceedings, the Court, making an equitable assessment, awards £22,000 and £16,700 in respect of the solicitor's and counsel's claims respectively, less 37,731 French francs received by way of legal aid from the Council of Europe.

Note: As the earlier discussion and prior cases indicate, the European Court has viewed satisfaction as a discretionary matter. Until recently, it also rejected requests from applicants for reparative orders or even indications to the state as to non-monetary remedies. With a rising caseload, including many cases raising the same types of violations, the Court has moved—with pressure from the Committee of Ministers—to be directive to the states that appear before it. The following was the first case in which the Court indicated an action other than monetary compensation was due.

Brumarescu v. Romania, App. no. 28342/95, Jan. 23, 2001, Rep. of Judgments and Dec. 2001-I.

1. The case was referred to the Court by a Romanian national, Mr. Dan Brumărescu and by the European Commission of Human Rights on 3 and 6 November 1998 respectively, within the three-month period laid down by former Articles 32 § 1 and 47 of the Convention for the Protection of Human Rights and Fundamental Freedoms. It originated in an application against Romania lodged by Mr. Brumărescu with the Commission under former Article 25 on 9 May 1995.

2. In its judgment of 28 October 1999 the Court held unanimously that there had been a violation of Article 6 § 1 of the Convention and Article 1 of Protocol No. 1. More specifically, as regards Article 1 of Protocol No. 1, it held that there had been no justification for the deprivation of property in issue and that at all events, a fair balance had been upset as the applicant had borne and continued to bear an individual and excessive burden, incompatible with the right to the peaceful enjoyment of his possessions ([GC], §§ 79–80, ECHR 1999-VII).

3. Under Article 41 of the Convention, the applicant sought just satisfaction amounting to several hundred thousand United States dollars in respect of damage sustained and also for costs and expenses.

    . . . .

THE LAW

    . . . .

19. The Court reiterates that a judgment in which it finds a breach imposes on the respondent State a legal obligation to put an end to the breach and make reparation for its consequences in such a way as to restore as far as possible the situation existing before the breach.

20. The Contracting States that are parties to a case are in principle free to choose the means whereby they will comply with a judgment in which the Court has found

a breach. This discretion as to the manner of execution of a judgment reflects the freedom of choice attaching to the primary obligation of the Contracting States under the Convention to secure the rights and freedoms guaranteed (Article 1). If the nature of the breach allows of *restitutio in integrum*, it is for the respondent State to effect it. If, on the other hand, national law does not allow—or allows only partial—reparation to be made for the consequences of the breach, Article 41 empowers the Court to afford the injured party such satisfaction as appears to it to be appropriate (see *Papamichalopoulos and Others v. Greece* (Article 50), judgment of 31 October 1995, Series A no. 330-B, pp. 58–59, § 34).

21. In the principal judgment the Court said: "The Court . . . observes that no justification has been offered for the situation brought about by the judgment of the Supreme Court of Justice. In particular, neither the Supreme Court of Justice itself nor the Government have sought to justify the deprivation of property on substantive grounds as being 'in the public interest'. The Court further notes that the applicant has now been deprived of the ownership of the property for more than four years without being paid compensation reflecting its true value, and that his efforts to recover ownership have to date proved unsuccessful" (§ 79).

22. The Court considers that in the circumstances of the present case the return of the property in issue, as ordered in the final judgment of the Bucharest Court of First Instance of 9 December 1993, would put the applicant as far as possible in the situation equivalent to the one in which he would have been if there had not been a breach of Article 1 of Protocol No. 1.

In this connection, the Court cannot accept the Government's argument that the applicant should bring a fresh action for recovery of possession. It points out that the Government raised that question earlier in the form of an objection that domestic remedies had not been exhausted, which the Court dismissed in the principal judgment (§ 55).

The applicant having had the flat he occupies returned to him and that restitution having been upheld in the final decision of the Bucharest Court of Appeal of 26 October 2000, the State should therefore restore the applicant's title to the rest of the house. This is without prejudice to any claim which Mr. Mirescu might have to ownership of the flat on the ground floor, which claim would fall to be determined in the domestic courts.

23. Failing such restitution by the respondent State within six months of the delivery of this judgment, the Court holds that the respondent State is to pay the applicant, for pecuniary damage, the current value of the house, from which the value of the property already returned to him will have to be deducted.

24. As to the determination of the amount of that compensation, the Court notes the considerable divergence between the methods of calculation employed for the purpose by the experts appointed by the parties.

Having regard to the information available to it on prices on the Bucharest property market, the Court assesses the current market value of the house and the land on which it is situated at USD 215,000, USD 78,795 of which represents the flat and the part of the land already returned to the applicant. The compensation which the Government should pay the applicant accordingly amounts to USD 136,205, including USD 42,100 representing the value of the flat occupied by Mr. Mirescu. That amount is to be converted into Romanian lei at the rate applicable on the date of settlement.

B. Non-pecuniary damage

25. The applicant also sought USD 75,000 for non-pecuniary damage sustained on account of the "serious, unbearable and immeasurable" suffering which the Supreme Court of Justice had inflicted on him in 1995 by depriving him of his property for a second time, after he had managed, in 1993, to put an end to the communist authorities' breach of his right for a period of forty years. He also claimed compensation for the loss of use of his property from the Supreme Court of Justice's judgment in 1995 to date, but did not quantify it.

26. The Government resisted that claim, submitting that no non-pecuniary damage could be taken into account. Furthermore, they maintained that it would be contrary to the case-law of the Romanian courts to award compensation for loss of use and enjoyment under the head of non-pecuniary damage.

27. The Court considers that the events in question entailed serious interferences with Mr. Brumărescu's right to the peaceful enjoyment of his possession, to a court and to a fair hearing, in respect of which the sum of USD 15,000 would represent fair compensation for the non-pecuniary damage sustained. That amount is to be converted into Romanian lei at the rate applicable on the date of settlement.

C. Costs and expenses

28. The applicant claimed reimbursement of USD 2,450, which he broke down as follows in a detailed account he submitted:

(a) USD 1,644 in fees for work done by his lawyers in the proceedings before the Court, both on the merits and in connection with the question of just satisfaction;

(b) USD 50 for various expenses (telephone, photocopies, notary, etc.);

(c) USD 700 for the costs of an expert report (USD 500 for the report proper and USD 200 for further work on valuing the property at 1 September 2000);

(d) 300 French francs (FRF) for the cost of the French visa required for his journey to attend the hearings in Strasbourg.

29. The Government did not object to the reimbursement of the costs incurred, provided that vouchers were submitted.

30. The Court considers that the costs and expenses claimed, for which vouchers have been produced, were actually and necessarily incurred and are reasonable as to quantum. That being so, it considers it appropriate to award the applicant the sum sought of USD 2,450, less FRF 3,900 received from the Council of Europe by way of legal aid. That amount is to be converted into Romanian lei at the rate applicable on the date of settlement.

D. Default interest

31. As the sums awarded are denominated in United States dollars, the Court considers it appropriate to set the rate of default interest applicable at 6% per annum.

FOR THESE REASONS, THE COURT UNANIMOUSLY

1. *Holds* that the respondent State is to return to the applicant, within six months, the house in issue and the land on which it is situated, except for the flat and the corresponding part of the land already returned;

2. *Holds* that, failing such restitution, the respondent State is to pay the applicant, within the same period of six months, USD 136,205 (one hundred and thirty-six thousand two hundred and five United States dollars) in respect of pecuniary damage, to be converted into Romanian lei at the rate applicable on the date of settlement;

3. *Holds* that the respondent State is to pay the applicant, within three months, the following sums, to be converted into Romanian lei at the rate applicable on the date of settlement:

> (a) USD 15,000 (fifteen thousand United States dollars) in respect of non-pecuniary damage;
> (b) USD 2,450 (two thousand four hundred and fifty United States dollars), less FRF 3,900 (three thousand nine hundred French francs) received by way of legal aid, in respect of costs and expenses;

4. *Holds* that simple interest at an annual rate of 6% shall be payable on the sums in (2) and (3) from the expiry of the periods mentioned until settlement;

5. *Dismisses* the remainder of the claim for just satisfaction.

Costs and Fees

In an early case brought before the plenary court, *Sunday Times v. United Kingdom*, (Article 50), (1980) Ser. A, No. 38 (1981) 3 E.H.R.R., the applicants filed an unquantified claim for costs and expenses incurred in both the domestic litigation and proceedings before the European Commission and Court. In holding that there had been a breach of Article 10 of the European Convention due to an injunction granted against the *Sunday Times* in accordance with the English law of contempt of court, the Court reserved the issue of costs and expenses as a remedy under Article 41 (then Article 50). In the separate proceeding, the applicants referred to English law, where the litigant must bear his own costs unless the court otherwise orders. Although the European Court reviewed the material submitted, it concurred with the Commission's view that the Convention would be the basis of any judgment for a claim in respect of costs. The Court agreed with the government that "the injured party is not entitled to his costs as of right because 'just satisfaction' is to be afforded 'if necessary' and the matter falls to be determined by the Court at its discretion, having regard to what is equitable". *Sunday Times* at 9. In the *Sunday Times* case, the applicants claimed: UK£ 15,809.36 for the costs of litigation in England; UK£ 24,760.53 for proceedings before the Commission and Court; and an additional amount for the Article 50 proceedings. In respect of the entire amount it asked for ten per cent per annum interest. The Commission supported the applicant's claim. The government argued in the alternative that (1) just satisfaction did not require the award of any costs, citing previous cases where the

Court had held that the decision alone amounted to just satisfaction; (2) that the parties had reached an agreement that precluded the award and that in any event the costs were not necessarily incurred; (3) that no amounts should be recovered for claims that were rejected by the Commission and the Court; and (4) that any amounts the Court did decide to award should not exceed the rates payable under the Commission's legal aid programme.

The Court distinguished, as it had previously, between damage caused by a violation of the Convention and costs necessarily incurred by the applicant. It noted that even in those cases where it had found that the decision itself was just satisfaction for the injury suffered, 'the Court's general practice has been to accept claims in respect of the [costs necessarily incurred by the applicant] . . . *[I]n fact, it is difficult to imagine that the finding of a violation could of itself constitute just satisfaction as regards costs'. Sunday Times* at 10 (emphasis added). The Court does not explain why this is the case, when such a finding is deemed adequate for moral damages, although perhaps it views out-of-pocket expenses as a category of pecuniary loss that is the direct consequence of the violation and must be reimbursed. The government argued that an award of costs should be denied because in its view the litigation was "welcomed" by the applicants as a means of testing the law. The Court rejected this contention on the basis that there was no other means of challenging the law, apart from violating it and running the risk of sanctions for contempt of court. The Court explicitly referred to the practice of member states in finding that test cases could be appropriate ones for the award of costs. Significantly, the government's assertion that it was in the process of changing its law was not deemed sufficient to bar an award of attorneys' fees, the Court finding it "not relevant" to the claim because the contracting states "are in any event under an obligation to adjust their domestic law to the requirements of the Convention".

The Court applied the test of necessity in deciding to award costs for the domestic litigation. It found that the costs in England were incurred by the applicants in asserting their freedom of expression, a right guaranteed by the Convention. In addition, the Court pointed out, the domestic proceeding was a pre-condition to any submission of the matter to the European Commission. Nonetheless, the Court denied the costs of the domestic litigation because of an agreement between the government and the applicants that each would bear its own costs of litigation.

As for expenses incurred before the Strasbourg institutions, the Court articulated a test that asks whether the costs (1) were actually incurred, (2) were necessarily incurred and (3) are reasonable as to quantum. *Sunday Times* at 12. It has applied this standard in all subsequent cases.

The government asserted that the applicant's three counsel were unnecessary in view of the Commission's role in the case. The Commission and the Court agreed with the applicants, however, on the need for representation, noting that the applicants were not formal parties to the proceedings and the Commission's role was not to represent them but to assist the court "in the capacity of defender of the public interest". *Sunday Times*, para. 30. This important distinction between the interests of the applicants and the interests of the Commission has been referred to by the Inter-American Court in its decisions, but the latter court has failed to draw the appropriate conclusion about the necessity of compensated applicant representation during most stages of the proceedings.

The European Court did reduce somewhat the amount claimed in *Sunday Times*, from UK£ 12,000 to UK£ 10,000, on the basis that not all the applicant's counsel were necessary at the hearings. On the other hand, the Court deferred to the Commission on the necessity of attendance of the advisers and the applicants at hearings before the Commission, awarding the full amount claimed. It also allowed the travel expenses of the applicants to attend the Court hearings, finding their presence "of value", but it rejected their costs for attending the delivery of the Court's judgment, finding it unnecessary.

In subsequent cases, the Court has allowed claims for translation expenses, travel to Strasbourg for lawyers and applicants, expert opinions, and subsistence expenses in Strasbourg. The Court has rejected claims for training and education, such as registration in a course on procedures followed by the Strasbourg institutions. See *Sporrong & Lonrroth v. Sweden*, Ser. A, No. 88. Consultancy fees often are denied as well. A major issue on the "necessity" of incurring costs and fees relates to unsuccessful pleas. In the *Sunday Times* case, the government contended that the applicants should be denied costs incurred in advancing submissions rejected by the Court. The applicants replied that they had to assert their case to the best of their ability and that evaluation by hindsight was the wrong approach. The Court agreed:

> The Court cannot accept the Government's contention, even on the assumption that there is a satisfactory method of surmounting the difficulties of calculation which it involves. In its above-mentioned *Neumeister* judgment . . . the Court drew no distinction between costs referable to successful pleas on Article 5 para. 3 and costs referable to unsuccessful pleas on article 5(4) and 6(1). Whilst it is in the interests of a proper and expeditious administration of justice that the Convention institutions be not burdened with pleas unrelated or extraneous to the case in hand, the submissions now in question cannot be so described. (*Sunday Times* at 14).

The Court added, importantly and correctly, that "a lawyer has a duty to present his client's case as fully and ably as he can and it can never be predicted with certainty what weight a tribunal may attach to this or that plea, provided that it is not manifestly otiose or invalid". Subsequently, in *Eckle v. Germany*, (Article 50, 65 Eur. Ct. H.R. (ser. A)(1983) the government also sought to have the fees reduced because three issues were not won by the applicants. As in the *Sunday Times* case, the Court denied this contention, noting that the three issues were not rejected as manifestly illfounded, but continued to the admissibility stage where they were rejected after a preliminary inquiry into the merits. The examination called for the lawyer's participation and hence costs could be awarded.

As the Court's caseload has grown, it has failed to adhere to these precedents. Increasingly it has been discounting fees and costs claimed for pleadings that it denies on the merits. The result is likely to create a conservative bar that is unwilling to assert new claims or innovative arguments, leading to a static interpretation of the Convention. *Olsson v. Sweden* (Olsson I), 130 A Eur. Ct. H.R. (ser. A) (1977) indicates the shift in the Court's approach to fees for claims decided against the applicant. In *Olsson II*, 250A Eur. Ct. H.R. (Ser. A)(1992) the applicants asked

SEK1,800 per hour for 625 hours work as well as travel and translation expenses. The government protested that the applicants could have used Swedish legal aid in their domestic proceedings. The government also asserted that "the way in which the lawyer for the applicants conducted the proceedings before the Commission should be taken into consideration". It is not clear what this means, although it may be a reference to dilatory tactics. The government further argued the amount of time claimed was unnecessary and the rate of the fee was too high. The Court rejected the first contention, holding that there is no obligation on applicants to apply for legal aid. The domestic amounts were approved, but in regard to the Strasbourg proceedings, the Court effectively reversed its holding in the *Sunday Times* case. In *Olsson II* it limited costs and fees: "bearing in mind that the applicants have succeeded only on the points mentioned . . . and making an assessment on an equitable basis, the Court considers that the applicants should be awarded under this head 50,000 kroner" from which it deducted legal aid received from the Council of Europe. The SEK 50,000 represented less than five per cent of the requested fees of SEK 1,269,000.

The issue of the reasonableness of the quantum of fees claimed has been repeatedly raised in cases before the European Court. In *Konig v. Germany*, 36 Eur. Ct. H.R. (ser. A)(1980), relied on extensively in the *Sunday Times* case, the Court held that the applicant was entitled to reimbursement of sums expended in exercising such national remedies as were intended to expedite the proceedings against him. Concerning expenses at Strasbourg, the government argued that the Court should adopt a uniform European rule and suggested the scale established by the Commission for free legal aid. The Commission disagreed, noting that the result would be that those applicants coming from countries where justice is less expensive would thereby obtain full indemnification while others would have to pay sometimes considerable amounts themselves.

In *Konig*, as in *Sunday Times* and *Eckle v. Germany*, the Court stated that it is not bound by domestic scales or standards for lawyers' fees. The government noted that the fees charged by the lawyers for Konig were nearly double normal fees according to the scales in force in Germany. The Court nonetheless found them reasonable. In the *Sunday Times* case the government objected that the costs, especially the lawyers' fees, exceeded those normally awarded in English courts. The Court held it is not bound by domestic scales or standards on quantum and found all the amounts claimed were reasonable. The Court does review amounts and shows some scepticism about high fee claims. In *Eckle*, the Court noted that the attorney-client agreement to pay higher fees than that provided in the German scale was presented to the European Court some five years after the final national decision. While expressing that it had "no cause to believe that it is confronted with a bogus document drafted solely for the purposes of the proceedings pending before it since the judgment of 15 July 1982", the Court accepted the suggestion of the Commission that only DM 1,500 be awarded out of a claimed DM 10,866.

In *Silver and others v. United Kingdom* 63 Eur. Ct. H.R (Ser. A)(1983), the applicants' attorneys submitted a bill of UK£ 17,093.63 for costs and expenses in Strasbourg. They had primary responsibility for the conduct of the seven joined applications before the Commission and Court. The government argued that an excessive number of hours was billed at an excessive rate (UK£ 40 per hour). The Court expressed its concern over high fees, quoting its opinion from *Young, James and Webster*: high costs of litigation may themselves constitute a serious impediment to the effective protection of human rights. It would be wrong for the Court to give encouragement to such a situation in its decisions awarding costs under Article 50. It is important that applicants should not encounter undue financial difficulties in bringing complaints under the Convention and the Court considers that it may expect that lawyers in Contracting States will cooperate to this end in the fixing of their fees.

The Court accepted the applicant's figures on the number of hours (294) for the seven cases over seven years, but lowered the fee to UK£ 35 pounds per hour. Two lawyers who claimed fees for appearance before the Court ('brief fees') in the amount of UK£ 16,250 saw these reduced to UK£ 3,000.

The Court's approach raises concern that individuals will be unable to obtain representation if the fees are substantially below those that attorneys can recover by taking other kinds of cases in their domestic legal systems. Of course, individuals who bring cases to the European system can be provided with legal aid; however, "compared with the amounts offered by way of legal aid in many national systems the money offered in respect of fees are meager, if not derisory, and it may be asked whether this operates to discourage lawyers from bringing cases to Strasbourg". While some claim that "in many cases lawyers are not motivated by the prospect of financial gain when they agree to appear in proceedings before the Court", the possibility of recovering fees can be important to the ability of clients to obtain representation. At present, the prestige of appearing in Strasbourg still appears to be an incentive to many advocates to take cases in spite of the limited recovery possible. In the long term, however, failure to compensate attorneys adequately may diminish the quality and quantity of legal services available to applicants by discouraging better lawyers from taking human rights cases.

The applicant must be legally obliged to pay the costs in order to have them awarded. In the case of *X v. United Kingdom*, 55 Eur. Ct. H.R. (ser. A) (1982) the Court granted attorneys' fees even though the attorney had not pursued the recovery of his fees from the client because of the client's poverty. The Court rejected the government's argument that the legal fees were not actually incurred, holding that the decision of the attorney not to bill the client did not affect the existence of a civil debt and therefore should not affect the award of fees. In another case, the Court rightly rejected the claim of a non-governmental organization that requested an award of fees for filing a brief amicus curiae. In *Dudgeon v. United Kingdom*, 49 Eur. Ct. H.R. (ser.A)(1983) on the other hand, fees were awarded to a non-governmental organization that actually represented the applicant. In the spate of cases brought in the 1990s against Turkey, the Turkish government has consistently objected to the involvement of British lawyers because of their higher fees. It has insisted that their appointment had the effect of inflating expenses for travel, communication, interpretation and translation. The Court has rejected this argument, generally awarding the fees in full at a rate of compensation varying from UK£ 100 per hour for one UK lawyer to UK£ 25 per hour for Turkish counsel. While the lawyers usually have received the full amount claimed, the Court has not awarded costs or fees in most cases to participating Turkish non-governmental organizations, such as the Kurdish Human Rights Project or Association and the Kurdistan Human Rights Group.

Note on the Committee of Ministers' Supervision of the Execution of Judgments

The Committee of Ministers has begun holding special meetings in order to better supervise the execution of judgments of the European Court of Human Rights, including the payment by respondent states of just satisfaction to applicants, the adoption of other individual measures granting redress to the applicants and general measures preventing new similar violations. At its meeting in June 2007, the Committee had on its agenda over 800 cases of compensation and was taking up 346 new judgments of the Court, as well as reviewing Final Resolutions for 273 cases in which it concluded that the respondent States have complied with their obligations under the judgments. Some of the issues under review:

The granting by respondent States of redress to the applicants for the violations found:

- Issues arising from arbitrary and unlawful detention of the applicants in the "Moldovan Republic of Transnistria" (*Ilaşcu et al. v. Russia & Moldova*);
- Continuing obligation to conduct effective investigations into alleged killing by security forces in Northern Ireland (*McKerr v. United Kingdom*), Chechnya (*Khashiyev v. Russia*) and northern Cyprus (*Kakoulli v. Turkey*);
- Turkey's response to the CM's two Interim Resolutions urging to reopen domestic proceedings or otherwise redress the situation of the applicant convicted in violation of his right to a fair trial and still serving heavy prison sentence (*Hulki Güneş*, ResDH(2005)113, CM/ResDH(2007)26); two other cases raise similar issues (*Göçmen, Söylemez*);
- Reopening of proceedings in the applicant's case, on the basis of a new law adopted by Belgium, and other possible measures to fully remedy the violations of his right to a fair trial (*Goktepe*);
- Re-establishing parents' access to or regular relationship with their children, to remedy violations of their right to family life by Austria (*Moser*), Italy (*Scozzari and Others*), Portugal (*Reigado Ramos*), Romania (*Lafargue*) Switzerland (*Bianchi*) and Ukraine (*Hunt*);
- Ending the applicant's continuing prosecution in Turkey for a refusal to perform compulsory military service on the ground of his conscientious objection (*Ülke*);
- Non-compliance with domestic court decisions ordering the closure of a gold mine polluting the environment in Turkey (*Taskin, Öçkan*);
- Remedying the persistent infringement of the freedom of association of the applicant association and its members, as found in several judgments since 2001 (*United Macedonian Organisation Ilinden—Pirin and others; United Macedonian Organisation Ilinden and Others*).

General measures (constitutional, legislative and/or other reforms, including the setting up of effective domestic remedies), taken or under way, to prevent new violations similar to those found in the judgments, in particular:

- Issue of missing persons and living conditions in northern Cyprus, property rights of displaced Greek-Cypriots (*Cyprus v. Turkey*);
- Functioning of the new compensation mechanism for property abandoned in the territories beyond the Bug River (the Eastern provinces of pre-war Poland) in the aftermath of the Second World War (*Broniowski*);
- Assessment of the reforms adopted by the United Kingdom to ensure effective investigations into cases of alleged killings by members of security forces in Northern Ireland (*McKerr and others*);
- Ensuring adequate protection of children against ill-treatment or punishment in the United Kingdom (*A.*);
- Progress of the reform to ensure adequate legal safeguards concerning storage and use of personal data by intelligence service in Romania (*Rotaru*);
- Reforms adopted to prevent non-compliance with domestic court decisions in Ukraine and Russia and violations of the legal certainty requirement through supervisory review procedure in Russia;
- Improving freedom of religion in Moldova (*Metropolitan Church of Bessarabia*) and gender balance in Turkey (*Ünal Tekeli*);
- Preventing industrial pollution violating the right to private life in Russia (*Fadeyeva*);
- Assessment of the measures adopted by Poland and of outstanding issues with regard to the structural problem of excessively lengthy pre-trial detention in Poland (*Trzaska*);
- The problem of excessive length of judicial proceedings, and/or setting up an effective domestic remedy in this respect in cases, in particular, against Belgium, Bulgaria, Croatia, Cyprus, Finland, France, Greece, Hungary, Italy, Lithuania, Luxemburg, "the former Yugoslav Republic of Macedonia", Poland, Portugal, Romania, Russia, San Marino, Slovakia, Slovenia, Sweden, Turkey and Ukraine.

C. The Inter-American System

D. Shelton, *Remedies in International Human Rights Law* (2nd ed. 2004), pp. 216–221.

The American Convention on Human Rights (Art. 63(1)) gives the Inter-American Court broad remedial jurisdiction:

> If the Court finds that there has been a violation of a right or freedom protected by this Convention, the Court shall rule that the injured party be ensured the enjoyment of his right or freedom that was violated. It shall also rule, if appropriate, that the consequences of the measure or situation that constituted the breach of such right or freedom be remedied and that fair compensation be paid to the injured party.

The plain language indicates the Court's power to order remedies measures other than compensation. The drafting history of Article 63(1) of the American Convention reveals no debate about conferring broad remedial competence on the Court. The first draft of the Convention was prepared by the Inter-American Commission on Human Rights and was the basic working document at the Conference of San Jose. It gave the Court the power to award compensation in Article 52(1).169 The Commission itself had worked from three drafts prepared by the Inter-American Council of Jurists (ICJ), the Government of Chile and the Government of Uruguay. All of these earlier drafts generally replicated the language of Article 50 of the European Convention on Human Rights and thus were more restrictive than the draft finally produced by the Commission.

. . . .

The Court has made broad use of its jurisdiction. It has awarded pecuniary and non-pecuniary damages, granting both monetary and non-monetary remedies. Unlike the European Court, the Inter-American Court has ordered a state to take specific action to remedy a breach of the Convention. Where legislation is incompatible with the Convention, the Court has held it need not make a specific order; it may declare that the law is incompatible with the Convention and the state is obliged then to bring the law into conformity with the Convention. The Court has been innovative in controlling all aspects of the awards, including setting up trust funds, and maintaining cases open until the awarded remedies have been fully carried out. In contrast, the Court until recently consistently denied costs and attorney's fees for proceedings before the Inter-American institutions. With direct representation of victims during the reparations phase of cases, the Court's practice changed and attorneys' fees and costs are now awarded, at least in part.

The Court's jurisdiction to afford remedies is dependent upon the findings on the merits, which in turn are affected by the temporal limits of the Court's jurisdiction. In *Blake v. Guatemala (Reparations)*, a judgment of 22 January 1999, the amount of damages were limited because the deprivation of liberty and death of Blake were determined to be outside the Court's jurisdiction *ratione temporis*, occurring before Guatemala accepted the Court's jurisdiction. The Court found that it could only determine reparations based on Guatemala's failure to provide a remedy in contravention of Articles 8(1) and 1(1), a continuing violation, and a breach of Article 5, the right to physical and moral integrity, due to the on-going lack of knowledge about the disappeared. As a consequence, the Court denied pecuniary damages based on the loss of life and awarded only costs and expenses incurred in attempting to discover what had happened to Blake. It also awarded moral damages to the family.

. . . [T]he Court has been receptive to innovative theories and claims concerning reparations. In *Suarez Rosero v. Ecuador (Reparations)*, the petitioner expressed concern over a fine that had been imposed upon him in the domestic proceedings. The Court agreed that because the process against the applicant was itself a violation of the Convention, the state must not execute the judgment imposing the fine and should expunge the record.

––––––––––––––––

Loayza Tamayo Case, Reparations (Art. 63(1) American Convention on Human Rights), Judgment of November 27, 1998, 42 Inter-Am. Ct. H.R. (Ser. C) (1998).

. . . .

3. On September 17, 1997, the Court passed Judgment on the merits of the case, the operative part of which declares that:

1. That the State of Peru violated, to the detriment of María Elena Loayza-Tamayo, the Right to Personal Liberty recognized in Article 7 of the American Convention on Human Rights, in relation to Articles 25 and 1(1) thereof.

2. That the State of Peru violated, to the detriment of María Elena Loayza-Tamayo, the Right to Humane Treatment recognized in Article 5 of the American Convention on Human Rights, in relation to Article 1(1) thereof.

3. That the State of Peru violated, to the detriment of María Elena Loayza-Tamayo, the judicial guarantees established in Article 8(1) and (2) of the American Convention on Human Rights, in relation to Articles 25 and 1(1) thereof, on the terms set forth in this Judgment.

4. That the State of Peru violated, to the detriment of María Elena Loayza-Tamayo, the Judicial Guarantees established in Article 8(4) of the American Convention on Human Rights, in relation to Article 1(1) thereof.

5. To order the State of Peru to release María Elena Loayza-Tamayo within a reasonable time, on the terms set forth in paragraph 84 of this Judgment.

6. That the State of Peru is obliged to pay fair compensation to the victim and her next of kin and to reimburse them for any expenses they may have incurred in their representations before the Peruvian authorities in connection with this process, for which purpose the corresponding proceeding remains open.

4. On October 20, 1997, Peru reported that on October 16 of that year it had released Ms. María Elena Loayza-Tamayo, in compliance with the Judgment issued by the Court on September 17, 1997. The victim appeared before the Court, in person, at a public hearing held on June 9, 1998 and with that confirmed the fact that she had been released by the State.

. . . .

Documentary Evidence

41. At the time she submitted her reparations brief, the victim stated that its appendices would be forthcoming. On February 5, 1998, she presented the following documents as evidence:

a) Documents pertaining to the victim's domicile . . .

b) Birth certificates of the victim, her children and her siblings, and her parent's marriage certificate . . .

c) Curriculum vitae and personal background of the victim . . .

d) Documents pertaining to the victim's employment history . . .

e) Documents pertaining to the victim's earnings

f) Documents pertaining to the victim's current employment status . . .

g) Documents concerning the victim's physical and psychological condition from 1993 to 1997

h) Documents pertaining to the victim's present state of health . . .

i) Documents pertaining to expenses incurred for food, toiletries and articles of personal hygiene, materials for handicrafts, medicines, and clothing for the victim during her incarceration . . .

j) Chart of transportation expenses incurred by the victim's next of kin to visit her and deliver groceries to her at the Chorrillos Maximum Security Women's Prison . . .

k) A video

l) Documents pertaining to the construction of the victim's residence . . .

m) Documents related to the educational and medical expenses of the victim's children . . .

n) Documents pertaining to the representations before the Peruvian authorities and the inter-American system on the victim's behalf . . .

o) Documents pertaining to the work of Ms. Carolina Loayza-Tamayo . . .

p) Documents pertaining to the exchange rate between the local currency of Peru and the United States dollar . . ..

42. The State objected to the inclusion of the appendices filed by the victim using arguments that concerned admissibility and probative value. In the case of the admissibility arguments, it alleged that the appendices to the victim's reparations brief were not presented within the time limit established by the Court, which had expired on January 31, 1998; this, it argued, "[would] vitiate their merit or value as evidence."

43. The Court notes that its practice has always been to allow the initial submission of applications to be done by fax or telex (Article 26 of the Rules of Procedure), with the original documents and their appendices submitted within a reasonable time period thereafter. The Court decides what constitutes a reasonable time period on a case-by-case basis (*Paniagua Morales et al. Case, Preliminary Objections,* Judgment of January 25, 1996. Series C No. 23, para. 34).

44. The victim submitted the appendices six days after the body of the brief, and five days after the specified deadline. In keeping with the spirit and purpose of the American Convention, this five-day delay could not possibly invalidate information pertinent to determining what the reparations should be, especially when one considers that particular care was taken to ensure procedural balance. At the time the extension was granted on March 31, 1998, the President specified that the victim and the Commission had two months and 25 calendar days in which to present their arguments and evidence, and granted the State the same amount of time to present its observations and evidence.

45. Thus, Peru had the same amount of time to conduct a study and prepare its arguments on the reparations briefs and their appendices. Hence, the argument made by the State that the delay in filing the appendices to the victim's brief was prejudicial to the State is inadmissible.

46. Given the foregoing, the Court is admitting the appendices to the victim's reparations brief.

47. The State also questioned the evidentiary value of some of the receipts presented by the victim, which did not show the names and surnames of the persons who incurred the respective expenses. [. . . .]

48. When it examined the appendices being contested, the Court found that in some cases the victim had presented charts of estimated costs *(cf. appendices XV, XVI, XVIII, XIX, XX, XXI, XXX, XXXII and XXXIII)*, apparently prepared as a reference aid. In some cases, the figures given were supported by receipts and vouchers; in other cases the amounts shown were described by the victim herself as "estimates" and approximate figures for certain undocumented outlays. Moreover, the charts submitted as Appendix XXVIII are an organized layout of representations alleged to have been made by victim's counsel before Peruvian and international authorities, including the organs of the inter-American system.

49. The Court finds that the charts in question do not constitute evidence. They are documents that illustrate the victim's claims and supplement the reparations brief. For that reason they will not be added to the body of evidence in the instant Case.

50. The Court is compelled to point out that certain discrepancies noted detract from the value of these tables, even as reference aids. For example, there are mathematical errors in the figures shown on some of the chart . . . moreover, when the figures given in the appendices and in the body of the reparations brief are compared, it is found that the amounts claimed for the same items are expressed in a given number of soles in the chart, but in an equal number of United States dollars in the body of the reparations brief, as if there were parity between the two currencies . . . .The Court will take these factors into account when it examines the corresponding forms of reparations.

51. The other documents challenged by the State were receipts for assorted purchases of materials, medications, wearing apparel, photocopies and correspondence *(cf. appendices XV, XVIII, XIX (slips no. 09119, 4275, 09402 and 117748), XX, XXX, XXXII and XXXIII)*. The Court notes that these documents did not name the author of the respective transaction, which makes them less credible. Consequently, their specific weight as evidence will be gauged by a standard often invoked by the Court, to the effect that:

> [I]n the exercise of its judicial functions and when ascertaining and weighing the evidence necessary to decide the cases before it, the Court may, in certain circumstances, make use of both circumstantial evidence and indications or presumptions on which to base its pronouncements when they lead to consistent conclusions as regards the facts of the case . . . *(Gangaram Panday Case, Judgment of January 21, 1994. Series C No. 16, para. 49).*

. . . .

64. As evidence to help the Court arrive at a more informed judgment, on July 29, 1998, the President requested information from the State concerning the official exchange rate between the local currency of Peru and the United States dollar for the period from 1993 to 1998. It also asked the State to furnish Peru's legislation on salaries and work bonuses.

65. On September 11, 29 and 30, 1998, the State submitted eight legal texts, one report and exchange rate quotations for Peru's local currency . . . .

66. No objection or challenge was made to the documents submitted by the State, nor was their authenticity called into question; hence, the Court accepted them as valid and ordered that they be added to the body of evidence in the instant case.

Testimonial evidence

. . . .

71. At a public hearing held on June 9, 1998, the Court heard testimony from the victim in the instant case.

. . . .

72. Because Ms. Loayza-Tamayo is the victim in the instant Case and has an immediate interest in it, her testimony cannot be weighed separately; instead, it must be weighed with the full body of evidence in this case. However, it is important to recall that the facts in the instant Case were already established during the merits phase. At this stage of the proceedings, the Court will determine the nature and amount of the "fair compensation" and the expenses that the State will be required to reimburse to the victim and her next of kin, pursuant to operative paragraph 6 of the Court's judgment.

73. In this sense, the victim's testimony has unique import, as she is the one who can provide the most information concerning the consequences of the wrongful acts of which she was the victim. That being the case, the testimony in question will be added to the body of evidence in the instant case, and will be later weighed.

Expert Evidence

74. As evidence to help it arrive at a more informed judgment, on August 29, 1998, the Court requested that the Colegio Médico de Chile issue a report on the victim's physical and psychiatric condition and that the Colegio Médico del Perú issue one on her children's psychiatric condition.

75. On October 7, 1998, the Court received the forensic medical expert's report on the victim's health, prepared by Dr. Roberto von Bennewitz on instructions from the "Colegio Médico de Chile". Dr. von Bennewitz wrote down his observations of the victim's physical and psychiatric injuries and included a section on the correlation between the injuries present and the specific means of torture to which the victim would have been subjected and her "prognosis from the injury" . . . . Finally, the expert's diagnosis was that while some of the pain that the victim suffers may eventually be relieved through prolonged therapy, some may be irreversible.

76. On October 9, 1998, the Court received the report on the victim's psychiatric evaluation, prepared by Dr. Martín Cordero-Allary on instructions from the "Colegio Médico de Chile". Dr. Cordero-Allary wrote down his observations and described his examination of the victim. His diagnosis was that she suffers from "post-traumatic stress syndrome as a consequence of systematic torture and rape".

77. On October 13, 1998, the Court received the psychiatric medical evaluations of Gisselle Elena and Paul Abelardo Zambrano-Loayza, prepared by Dr. René Flores-Agreda on instructions from the "Colego Médico del Perú". Dr. Flores-Agreda's reports included the family and personal background of the young people he examined, and a description of their current problem and mental examination . . . .

78. On November 13, 1998, Peru presented its observations on the medical reports, which it challenged.

. . . .

80. The State did not offer any basis for its allegations concerning the seriousness of the medical reports. Moreover, it did not tender any evidence that would raise

doubts as to the competence and responsibility of the "Colegios Médicos" of Chile and Peru or whether the two organizations had acted properly in commissioning the physicians to prepare the medical reports.

81. As for the allegation that the reports did not conform to some of the guidelines established by the World Health Organization, the Court does not consider this a pre-requisite for their admissibility. In keeping with Court practice, the reports are to be prepared by professionals who are competent in their field and include, in proper form, the information that the Court requires. As noted, the State furnished no evidence that would cause the Court to question the professional qualifications of the experts. Moreover, the required information was included in the reports in a manner that the Court considers appropriate.

82. As for the report presented by Dr. von Bennewitz, the Court notes that the case file shows that he was designated by the "Colegio Médico de Chile" to perform a "clinical and psychiatric" evaluation of the victim, as requested by the Court. For this reason, the Court believes that his report was not solely confined to matters pertaining to the physical health of the victim and so orders that the reports in question be added to the evidence in the instant case.

VI. DUTY TO MAKE REPARATIONS

. . . .

87. The reparations ordered in this Judgment must be proportionate to the violations of articles 1(1), 5, 7, 8(1), 8(2), 8(4) and 25, violations whose commission was established in the Judgment of September 17, 1997.

VII. BENEFICIARIES

88. It is obvious that in the instant Case the victim is Ms. María Elena Loayza-Tamayo. In its Judgment of September 17, 1997, the Court found that the State had violated, to her detriment, a number of rights upheld in the Convention. Hence, she is entitled to the payment of the compensation ordered by the Court in her favor.

89. In keeping with the language used in the Judgment on the merits and in Article 63 of the Convention, it is also up to the Court to determine which of the victim's "next of kin" are, in the instant case, "injured parties".

. . . .

92. The Court considers that the expression "next of kin" of the victim should be interpreted in a broad sense to include all persons related by close kinship. Hence, the victim's children, Gisselle Elena and Paul Abelardo Zambrano-Loayza; her parents, Julio Loayza-Sudario and Adelina Tamayo-Trujillo de Loayza, and her siblings, Delia Haydée, Carolina Maida, Julio William, Olga Adelina, Rubén Edilberto and Giovanna Elizabeth, all by the surname of Loayza-Tamayo, are considered her next of kin. As such, they could be entitled to receive compensation if they meet the tests established in the jurisprudence of this Court (*Aloeboetoe et al. Case, Reparations (Art. 63(1) American Convention on Human Rights)*, Judgment of September 10, 1993. Series C No. 15, para. 71 and *Garrido and Baigorria Case, Reparations, supra* 84, para. 52).

. . . .

101. As for the victim's next of kin, the State argued that while the Court's September 17, 1997 Judgment had ordered payment of compensation to the victim's next of kin, those individuals had to appear before the Court to claim their rights. It further stated that in the instant Case, the children, parents and siblings of the victim had not intervened in any phase of the proceedings, had not filed any claim, and were therefore not entitled to any compensation. According to the State, by failing to appear, the victim's next of kin had tacitly waived their right to compensation, especially inasmuch as the deadline set by the Court for making the respective claims has already expired.

102. In this regard, Article 23 of the Rules of Procedure provides that: " . . . [a]t the reparations stage, the representatives of the victims or of their next of kin may independently submit their own arguments and evidence".

103. Although the injured parties' direct participation in the reparations stage is important for the Court, their nonappearance, as in the instant Case, does not relieve either the Commission or the Court of their duty as organs of the inter-American system for the protection of human rights. That duty is to ensure that those rights are effectively protected, which includes matters related to the duty to make reparations.

104. Inasmuch as the Court has held that reparations for the victim's next of kin are in order, it must now determine their nature and amount. Lacking claims or allegations from certain family members, the Court will act on the basis of the information at hand.

105. For the reasons explained and contrary to what the State alleged, the fact that the victim's next of kin did not appear before the Court does not prevent the latter from ordering reparations on their behalf.

VIII. FACTS PROVEN DURING THE REPARATIONS [STAGE]

106. To determine the appropriate reparations in the instant Case, the Court will have the facts established in the September 17, 1998 Judgment as a reference base. However, during this stage of the proceedings, the parties have added evidence to the case file to establish other facts relevant to determining the reparations. The Court has examined the arguments of the parties and the respective evidence, and declares the following facts to have been proven.

A) concerning the victim:

a) She has degrees in education and in social work. Prior to her detention, she was a law student and had taken a number of academic courses and seminars . . . ;

b) She was 36 years old at the time of her detention . . . ;

c) At the time of her detention on February 6, 1993, she was living with her children, Gisselle Elena and Paul Abelardo Zambrano-Loayza, at the home of her parents, Julio Loayza-Sudario and Adelina Tamayo-Trujillo, in Altillo, Block A, Lot 17, City and Countryside, Rímac District. Her siblings are Delia Haydée, Carolina Maida, William Julio, Olga Adelina, Elizabeth Giovanna and Rubén Edilberto, all by the surname Loayza-Tamayo . . . ;

d) At the time of her detention, she was working at José Gabriel Condorcanqui High School, where her area of specialization was history. Her monthly salary was S184.84 (one hundred eighty-four and eighty-four/one hundredths soles).

She was definitively removed from her post on May 29, 1993, on the grounds that she had abandoned her post without just cause . . . ;

e) At the time of her detention, she was working at the National School of Dramatic Arts, where her area of specialization was drama coaching and her monthly salary was S66.26 (sixty-six and twenty-six/one hundredths soles) . . . ;

f) At the time of her detention, she was working at the School of Management of the Universidad de San Martín de Porres. Her monthly salary was S345.51 (three hundred forty-five and fifty-one/one hundreths soles). Although she stated that she also was working at the School of Education in that university, there is information in the case file to the effect that that association ended on January 30, 1993 . . . ;

g) At the time she was detained she was in the process of building a house on a piece of property she owned on Mitobamba Street, Block D, Lot 18, Los Naranjos Development, Los Olivos District, Lima, Peru . . . ;

h) During her detention and up to the present, she has received a monthly pension from the Ministry of Health . . . ;

i) During her incarceration, and as a consequence of the cruel, inhuman and degrading punishment to which she was subjected, she suffered serious health problems, treatment of which necessitated outlays of an unspecified amount, all paid by her next of kin . . . ;

j) Her confinement brought on severe physical and psychological health disorders; some may be relieved with prolonged therapy, although others may be irreversible . . . ;

k) She was released on October 16, 1997 . . . ;

l) She filed a several of requests to be reinstated in her former posts. She requested reinstatement in her post at José Gabriel Condorcanqui High School on October 27, 1997. She was ordered reinstated at another educational institution effective March 1, 1998. On November 27, 1997, she requested reinstatement in her post at the National School of Dramatic Arts; on November 26 and 27 and December 3, 1997, she requested reinstatement at the Universidad de San Martín de Porres. The outcome of these requests is unknown . . . ;

m) She now resides in the city of Santiago, Chile, is not working, and is undergoing medical treatment financed by "FASIC" . . . .

B) concerning the victim's children: Paul Abelardo and Gisselle Elena Zambrano-Loayza:

a) They continued their secondary and university studies during their mother's incarceration. Records of educational expenses totaling S21,290.60 (twenty-one thousand two hundred ninety and sixty hundredths soles) and records of health expenses totaling S95.00 (ninety-five soles) have been presented. Those expenses were paid by the victim's family . . . ;

b) They visited their mother during her incarceration, under the conditions allowed by Peruvian prison law . . . ;

c) Their mother's incarceration caused them serious mental health disorders for which they urgently require proper medical care . . . ;

C) concerning the victim's other next of kin:

a) They paid the medical expenses resulting from the victim's health disorders during her incarceration . . . ;

b) They incurred other expenses to purchase her groceries, toiletries and articles of personal hygiene and wearing apparel, and transportation expenses to get these supplies to the victim. An exact figure for the total expenses was not determined . . . ;

c) They paid the medical expenses of the victim's children . . . ; and

d) The parents of the victim and two of her sisters, Delia Haydée and Elizabeth Giovanna, visited her under the conditions established in Peruvian prison law.

D) concerning representation of the victim and certain representation costs:

a) Attorney Carolina Maida Loayza-Tamayo undertook representation of the victim vis-à-vis the Peruvian authorities and paid certain representation-related costs . . . ;

b) Attorneys Carolina Loayza-Tamayo, Ariel E. Dulitzky, Juan Méndez, José Miguel Vivanco, Viviana Krsticevic and Verónica Gómez represented the victim in the process before the Inter-American Commission on Human Rights. They also represented the victim during the Court's proceedings on the merits of the Case; the one exception was Mr. Méndez, who resigned as the plaintiff representative on September 16, 1997. During these stages of the proceedings, certain expenses involved in the victim's representations were paid by attorney Carolina Loayza-Tamayo . . . ; and

c) Attorneys Carolina Loayza-Tamayo, Ariel Dulitzky, Viviana Krsticevic, Marcela Matamoros and José Miguel Vivanco represented the victim during the reparations proceedings before this Court. On June 18, 1998, Ms. Marcela Matamoros advised the Court her withdrawal as legal representative in the instant Case. Attorney Carolina Loayza-Tamayo paid some of the expenses associated with the victim's representation.

E) In general:

a) At the time of the victim's detention, the official exchange between the sol, Peru's local currency, and the United States dollar, was a buying rate of 1.74 to 1 and a selling rate of 1.75 to 1 . . . ; and

b) In Peru, there are a number of laws on work bonuses within the public and private sectors. Of these, the one most favorable to the worker is Law No. 25,139, of December 14, 1989, which provides for two bonuses each year, each one equal to "the worker's basic monthly salary at the time the bonus is paid".

IX. REPARATIONS

. . . .

110. The victim requested that the Court order Peru to reinstate her in all public teaching positions she held and to use its good offices to have her reinstated in her previous positions within the private sector.

111. For its part, the Commission petitioned the Court to order the State to:

a) Reinstate the victim "in all her previous positions of employment, at the level and rank she had prior to being unlawfully deprived of her freedom";

b) Prevail upon the National School of Dramatic Arts and the Universidad de San Martín de Porres to reinstate the victim as a teacher in her areas of specialization; failing that, pay the victim a sum equivalent to the lost pay up to her retirement age;

c) Give the victim the category and grade she would have had, had she not been detained and incarcerated or, failing that, pay her a sum equivalent to the remuneration that she will fail to receive on that account; and

d) Re-enter the victim's name in the records of the respective retirement plan retroactive to the date of her detention.

112. The State argued that the petition seeking the victim's reinstatement in her public teaching positions was "not necessary" since, as shown by the December 17, 1997 Directorial Resolution 2273—which the victim herself had offered in evidence, she had already been reinstated in the teaching service as a professor teaching 24 hours of history and geography at the Rímac National Girl's High School. The State argued that the victim should direct her other petitions to the School of Dramatic Arts and the Universidad de San Martín de Porres, which would evaluate the merit of her request. It added that Peruvian law did not guarantee civil servants a job until retirement.

113. It is the view of this Court that the State does have an obligation to make every effort within its power to have the victim reinstated in the teaching positions she held in public institutions at the time of her detention. Her salaries and other benefits should be equal to the full amount she was receiving for teaching in the public and private sectors at the time of her detention, adjusted to its value as of the date of this Judgment. The Court has had before it a resolution ordering the victim's reinstatement in the teaching service, so that Peru has already partially complied with this obligation.

114. The Court further considers that the State is under the obligation to re-enter the victim's name on the proper retirement records, retroactive to the date on which she was removed from those records, and to ensure that she enjoys the same retirement rights to which she was entitled prior to her detention.

115. However, judging from the evidence, particularly the medical reports on the victim's health and the victim's own statement, circumstances are such that, for the present, it would be difficult for her to fully re-immerse herself in her former jobs.

116. The State, therefore, has an obligation to do everything necessary to ensure that the victim receives her salaries, social security and employment benefits as of the date of issuance of this Judgment and until such time as she is able to effectively re-join the teaching service. The Court believes the prudent course of action would be to use the domestic mechanisms that apply in cases of employment disability or any other suitable means that will ensure that this obligation is honored.

117. The Court believes that strictly speaking, the victim's claims regarding her career prospects and promotion would not be measures of restitution; it will, therefore, examine them when it evaluates the damages the victim is claiming to her "life plan" [proyecto de vida] (*infra* 144 *et seq*).

118. In their reparations briefs, both the victim and the Commission petitioned the Court to order Peru to take the measures necessary to expunge the victim's criminal, court and prison records.

119. The Commission also petitioned the Court to instruct Peru to vacate the proceedings and judgments delivered in the regular courts, provide the victim with the proper court records, and report the nullification of the proceedings and the victim's release in the "*El Peruano*" official journal wherein the decisions of the judicial branch of government are reported.

120. Peru argued that the petitions were irrelevant and immaterial and constituted interference in the jurisdiction of Peruvian authorities, inasmuch as the September 17, 1997 Judgment had confined itself to ordering release of the victim, who now enjoys "absolute and complete freedom". The State further noted that its judicial branch was still considering a petition that the victim herself had filed seeking to have her police or criminal records expunged.

121. The Court has had before it one document issued by the Registry of Records and Convictions of the Supreme Court of Military Justice that concerns the first proceeding to which the victim was subjected. However, the Court does not have sufficient information in its possession to determine whether there are other records in which the victim figures.

122. Under Article 68 of the American Convention, the States Parties "undertake to comply with the judgment of the Court in any case to which they are parties". Consequently, Peru is obligated to adopt all domestic legal measures that follow from the Court's finding that the second trial to which the victim was subjected constituted a breach of the Convention. Hence, no conviction handed down in that second trial can have any legal effect, which is why all the respective proceedings and records are null and void.

123. The State's release of the victim is not sufficient to fully redress the consequences of the human rights violations perpetrated against her, given the length of time that she remained in prison, the suffering she endured as a result of the cruel, inhuman and degrading treatment to which she was subjected, and the fact that she was held incommunicado during her incarceration, paraded in prison uniform before the mass media, held in solitary confinement in a small, unventilated cell with no natural light, beaten and subjected to other forms of abuse such as threatened drowning, intimidation with threats of further violence, and restricted prison privileges (*Loayza Tamayo Case*, Judgment of September 17, 1997. Series C No. 33, para. 58). The consequences of that treatment cannot be fully redressed or compensated.

124. Alternative forms of reparation have to be found, such as pecuniary compensation for the victim and, where appropriate, her next of kin. This compensation is mainly for injuries suffered and, as this Court has ruled previously, includes pecuniary as well as moral damages (*Garrido and Baigorria Case, Reparations*, para. 43).

X. PECUNIARY DAMAGES

125. In the case of pecuniary damages, in their reparations briefs both the victim and the Inter-American Commission requested that the Court order Peru to pay the following amounts:

a) US$29,724 (twenty-nine thousand seven hundred twenty-four United States dollars) plus the legal interest on that amount, representing the income that the victim ceased to receive because of the events that resulted in her incarceration. On this matter, the State argued that for the duration of her detention, the victim had received a pension from the State as a former employee of the Ministry of Health. Hence, she was not left destitute. It could not be inferred, the State maintained, that had the victim not been detained, she would have continued to work at the same educational institutions where she was teaching at the time of her detention;

b) US$13,912.56 (thirteen thousand nine hundred twelve United States dollars and fifty-six cents) for groceries;

c) US$3,864.60 (three thousand eight hundred sixty-four United States dollars and sixty cents) for articles of personal hygiene;

d) US$3,508.92 (three thousand five hundred eight United States dollars and ninety-two cents) for materials for making handmade goods;

e) US$1,140.00 (one thousand one hundred forty United States dollars) for purchase of medications;

f) US$3,168.00 (three thousand one hundred sixty-eight United States dollars) for wearing apparel and shoes;

g) S/2,500 (two thousand five hundred soles) in travel expenses incurred by next of kin to visit her at the Chorrillos Maximum Security Women's Prison to take groceries and other supplies to the victim;

h) S/23,158.30 (twenty-three thousand one hundred fifty-eight and thirty/one hundredths soles) for the medical and educational expenses of Paul Abelardo and Gisselle Elena Zambrano-Loayza, expenses that were paid by Olga Adelina and Carolina Loayza-Tamayo. The State argued that education was a parental obligation and the amount spent on a child's education was for the parents to decide, in accordance with the provisions of the Civil Code and the Child and Adolescent Code. The State, therefore, was not obligated to pay those expenses. It added that under the Civil Code and the Child and Adolescent Code, in the absence of the parents it was the duty of the children's grandparents, uncles and aunts to see to their education.

i) S$12,000.00 (twelve thousand United States dollars) for the income that Ms. Carolina Loayza-Tamayo ceased to receive when she undertook the victim's defense and resigned her position at the Ministry of Foreign Affairs;

Moreover, both the victim and the Commission petitioned the Court to instruct the State to pay certain estimated amounts for the following items:

j) A prudent amount for "lost earnings" and expenses incurred by the victim's next of kin to visit her at the prison;

k) A prudent amount for "lost earnings" and expenses incurred by her sister and attorney to visit the victim at the prison for the duration of her detention (some two hundred visits); and

l) Estimated sums of US$18,000.00 (eighteen thousand United States dollars) and US$14,400 (fourteen thousand four hundred United States dollars) for the future costs of the rehabilitation of the victim and her next of kin, respectively. On this point, the State argued that the physical and mental condition of the victim and her next of kin prior to her detention had not been shown, so that this form of reparation would be absurd. It added that the current state of physical and mental health of those persons had also not been shown. Finally, it stated that this claim did not fit into the reparations ordered in the Judgment on the merits.

126. Peru also pointed out that the figures for the pecuniary damages claimed by the victim were given in dollars and not in Peru's local currency. It argued that under its Budget Law, payment of remuneration in foreign currency is strictly prohibited. It also objected to the rate of exchange used to make the calculations, since the Peruvian "sol" had not remained fixed since 1993, the date on which the victim was detained, and was currently fluctuating between S/2.80 and S/2.82 to the dollar. Peru maintained, therefore, that the amount claimed, when expressed in dollars, would be less than the amount indicated in the victim's brief.

127. As for the State's objection to the currency in which the victim's pecuniary claims were expressed, the Court notes that one effect of the reparations measures must be to preserve the real value of the amount received, so that it can achieve its compensatory intent. The Court previously held that "one of the easiest and most readily accessible ways to achieve this goal [is] the conversion of the amount received into one of the so-called hard currencies" (*Velásquez Rodríguez Case, Interpretation of the Compensatory Damages Judgment (Art. 67 American Convention on Human Rights)*, Judgment of August 17, 1990. Series C No. 9, para. 42). In its case law, the reiterated practice of the Court has been to use the United States dollar as the "hard" currency in which the compensatory damages are figured and has found that this safeguard protects the purchasing power of the amounts ordered. Hence, the practice of quoting the amounts in that currency—amounts which may then be paid in the local currency of the respondent state at the exchange rate on the day prior to payment—is consistent with the Court's customary practice, one that it confirms in the instant Case. However, in some instances the same expenditures are quoted in *soles* in the charts of estimated costs that the victim submitted as a reference aid, and then quoted in an equal number of United States dollars in the body of the victim's reparations brief, as if parity existed between the two currencies (*supra* 50). In these cases, the Court used the amounts shown on receipts and in other credible documents to arrive at the figures shown in the section on proven facts.

128. In the case of pecuniary damages for survivors of human rights violations, the Court has held that the compensation to be awarded depends on a number of factors, one of which is the time during which the victim remained unemployed (*El Amparo Case, Reparations (Art. 63(1) American Convention on Human Rights)*,

Judgment of September 14, 1996. Series C No. 28, para. 28). That criterion applies here as well, inasmuch as the victim in the instant Case is alive.

129. Based on the information received, its own case law and the facts proven, the Court determines that the compensation for pecuniary damages in the instant case shall include the following:

a) A sum corresponding to the salaries that the victim ceased to receive between the time she was detained and the date of the present Judgment. To compute the amount in question, the Court finds that at the time of her detention, the victim was receiving a combined salary of S/592.61 (five hundred ninety-two and sixty-one/one hundredths soles), which when calculated on the basis of the average of the selling and buying exchange rates in effect as of that date, yields a total of US$339.60 (three hundred and thirty-nine United States dollars and sixty cents). The calculation will be made on the basis of 12 monthly salaries per year, plus a bonus of two months' salary for each year. The interest accruing up to the date of this Judgment will be added and, as the victim requested, no deduction whatever will be made for personal expenses, since, as the victim is alive, it must be concluded that either she or members of her family paid for those expenses for the period in question using other means. Consequently, the total for this item is US$32,690.30 (thirty-two thousand six hundred ninety United States dollars and thirty cents);

b) A sum for the victim's medical expenses during her incarceration, since the Court considers that there is sufficient evidence to show that the corresponding ailments began during her confinement, a fact not refuted by the State. The evidence presented to support the figure given by the victim for this item is not conclusive and, for the sake of equity, the Court considers the proper course of action to be to award the sum of US$1,000.00 (one thousand United States dollars) for medical expenses;

c) A sum corresponding to the travel expenses incurred by the next of kin to visit the victim during her incarceration. For equity's sake, the Court believes US$500.00 (five hundred United States dollars) is an appropriate award for these expenses; and

d) An amount corresponding to the future medical expenses of the victim and her children, since the Court finds there is sufficient evidence to show that her ailments began during the victim's confinement, a fact not disproved by the State. For the sake of equity the Court considers US$15,000.00 (fifteen thousand United States dollars) a fitting sum for the victim, and US$5,000.00 (five thousand United States dollars) for each of her children.

130. On the other hand, the Court is dismissing the victim's claims for compensation of expenses to purchase groceries, articles of personal hygiene and toiletries, materials with which to do handwork, clothing, shoes, and the education of her children, expenses that were said to have been defrayed, at least in part, by some members of her family. The Court finds that it has been shown that prior to her incarceration, the victim was paying those expenses with her own funds and would have had to pay those expenses even if she had not been incarcerated. Therefore, the reparation ordered for lost earnings also implicitly includes the expenses herein described.

131. The Court is also denying the claim seeking payment of an amount for the income that Ms. Carolina Loayza-Tamayo was alleged to have lost by being forced to give up the contract she had with the Ministry of Foreign Affairs, and another that she was about to conclude with the same Ministry, in order to devote herself to the victim's defense. The Court finds that there is no proof to support either of these

claims or their causal nexus to the wrongful acts perpetrated against the victim in the instant case.

132. The Court finds that the "lost income" and visits of Ms. Carolina Loayza-Tamayo to the prison were representation-related expenses and will, therefore, examine their relevance when it deals with costs and expenses (*infra* 172).

133. Accordingly, the Court has decided to award US$49,190.30 (forty-nine thousand one hundred ninety United States dollars and thirty cents) to Ms. María Elena Loayza-Tamayo as compensation for material damages, and US$5,000.00 (five thousand United States dollars) to each of her children for medical expenses.

XI. MORAL DAMAGES

134. In her reparations brief, the victim argued that moral damages were incurred by reason of her deprivation of freedom under subhuman conditions; separation from her children, parents and siblings; the inhumane, humiliating and degrading treatment she suffered during her detention and isolation, and when she was exhibited to the press as a "terrorist criminal". The victim maintained that the pain inflicted during the period of her incarceration endures in the form of the psychological consequences. She added that her children and other next of kin were directly affected by the abuse she suffered and were socially stigmatized. She added that her sister, Carolina Loayza-Tamayo, suffered this injury directly as she became the target of the State's intimidation tactics and false accusations and was included on a list of attorneys under investigation.

135. The victim therefore requested that the Court order the State to pay the following compensation for moral damages: US$50,000.00 (fifty thousand United States dollars) to her; US$20,000.00 (twenty thousand United States dollars) to her parents; US$15,000.00 (fifteen thousand United States dollars) to each of her children, and a lump sum of US$35,000.00 (thirty-five thousand United States dollars) for her siblings.

136. For its part, the Commission petitioned the Court to instruct Peru to pay fair compensation to the victim and to her next of kin, based on the amount indicated by the victim in her reparations brief.

137. The State maintained that to substantiate her claims for moral damages, the victim had used the same arguments she used to substantiate her claims for other heads of damages. It argued that in the proceedings into the merits, it was never proven that the victim had in fact been raped during her incarceration, or that she had been coerced into making self-incriminating statements, or that Peru had violated articles 8(2)(g) and 8(3) of the Convention. The State further maintained that in its Judgment on the merits, the Court had refrained from any pronouncement concerning the lack of independence and impartiality of the military courts. For these reasons, the State argued, the "alleged 'moral damages' being sought [. . .] do not fit the facts"; and it maintained that this was even truer in the case of the damages being claimed for the victim's next of kin.

138. It is obvious to the Court that the victim suffered moral damages, for it is characteristic of human nature that anyone subjected to the kind of aggression and abuse proven in the instant Case will experience moral suffering. No evidence is required to arrive at this finding.

139. Taking into account the particular circumstances of the case, the Court considers the sum of US$50,000.00 (fifty thousand United States dollars) to be fair compensation for the victim for the moral damages she suffered.

140. It has been shown that the victim's children were approximately 12 and 16 years old when she was detained. Since at the time, the victim was supporting them and paying for their health care and education, the children were dependent upon their mother. The Court has also established that grievous violations were committed against the victim and must presume that they had an impact on her children, who were kept apart from her and were aware of and shared her suffering. Since, in the Court's opinion, the State has not disproved these presumptions, Gisselle Elena and Paul Abelardo Zambrano-Loayza are entitled to receive the "fair compensation" referred to in operative paragraph six of the Judgment on the merits.

141. Accordingly, it is fair to award each of the victim's children the sum of US$10,000.00 (ten thousand United States dollars) in moral damages.

142. The Court can reasonably presume that Mr. Julio Loayza-Sudario and Ms. Adelina Tamayo-Trujillo de Loayza suffered moral damages because of what happened to the victim, as it is human nature that any individual should experience pain at his or her child's torment. The State did not disprove this presumption. The Court considers, therefore, that each of the victim's parent is entitled to the sum of US$10,000.00 (ten thousand United States dollars) as fair compensation for moral damages.

143. The same considerations apply to the victim's siblings, who as members of a close family could not have been indifferent to Ms. Loayza-Tamayo's terrible suffering, a presumption not disproved by the State. It is proper, therefore, to name the victim's siblings as beneficiaries of the fair compensation referred to in operative paragraph six of the Judgment on the merits. The Court considers that fair compensation for moral damages would be US$3,000.00 (three thousand United States dollars) for each sibling.

XII. LIFE PLAN (PROYECTO DE VIDA)

144. The victim petitioned the Court for a ruling on the compensation, which might be due to her in the form of damage to her "life plan" and enumerated a number of factors that, in her judgment, should be taken into account to establish the scope of this head of damages and measure its consequences.

145. The State alleged that the request for compensation for damages to a life plan was inadmissible and noted that compensation of that nature was implicit in the other categories for which damages were sought, such as the "indirect or consequential damages" and "lost earnings". It pointed out that the victim had already been re-instated as a history and geography teacher at the Rímac National womens' High School (*supra* 106.A.l) and that she was free to apply to have her place in the Law School saved; it maintained that reinstatement at the San Martín de Porres Private University was a decision that only the organs of that institution could make. The State further argued that both the victim and the Commission had attributed the alleged damages caused to Ms. Loayza-Tamayo to her detention. Its contention was, however, that the State could not be held liable for those damages inasmuch as

the authorities that intervened in the case in question did so in the legitimate exercise of their authority under the laws in force at that time.

146. The State's argument that the authorities acted in the legitimate exercise of their authority is inadmissible. The Court itself has established that the acts of which Ms. Loayza-Tamayo was victim were violations of provisions of the American Convention.

147. The head of damages to a victim's "life plan" has been examined both in recent doctrine and case law. This notion is different from the notions of special damages and loss of earnings. It is definitely not the same as the immediate and direct harm to a victim's assets, as in the case of "indirect or consequential damages". The concept of lost earnings refers solely to the loss of future economic earnings that can be quantified by certain measurable and objective indicators. The so-called "life plan", deals with the full self-actualisation of the person concerned and takes account of her calling in life, her particular circumstances, her potentialities, and her ambitions, thus permitting her to set for herself, in a reasonable manner, specific goals, and to attain those goals.

148. The concept of a "life plan" is akin to the concept of personal fulfillment, which in turn is based on the options that an individual may have for leading his life and achieving the goal that he sets for himself. Strictly speaking, those options are the manifestation and guarantee of freedom. An individual can hardly be described as truly free if he does not have options to pursue in life and to carry that life to its natural conclusion. Those options, in themselves, have an important existential value. Hence, their elimination or curtailment objectively abridges freedom and constitutes the loss of a valuable asset, a loss that this Court cannot disregard.

149. In the case under study, while the outcome was neither certain nor inevitable, it was a plausible situation—not merely possible—within the likelihood given the subject's natural and foreseeable development, a development that was disrupted and upset by events that violated her human rights. Those events radically alter the course in which life was on, introduce new and hostile circumstances, and upset the kinds of plans and projects that a person makes based on the everyday circumstances in which one's life unfolds and on one's own aptitudes to carry out those plans with a likelihood of success.

150. It is reasonable to maintain, therefore, that acts that violate rights seriously obstruct and impair the accomplishment of an anticipated and expected result and thereby substantially alter the individual's development. In other words, the damage to the "life plan", understood as an expectation that is both reasonable and attainable in practice, implies the loss or severe diminution, in a manner that is irreparable or reparable only with great difficulty, of a persons prospects of self-development. Thus, a person's life is altered by factors that, although extraneous to him, are unfairly and arbitrarily thrust upon him, in violation of laws in effect and in a breach of the trust that the person had in government organs duty-bound to protect him and to provide him with the security needed to exercise his rights and to satisfy his legitimate interests.

151. For all these reasons, the claim seeking reparation, to the extent possible and by appropriate means, for the loss of options that the wrongful acts caused to the

victim is entirely admissible. The reparation is thus closer to what it should be in order to satisfy the exigencies of justice: complete redress of the wrongful injury. In other words, it more closely approximates the ideal of *restitutio in integrum*.

152. It is obvious that the violations committed against the victim in the instant Case prevented her from achieving her goals for personal and professional growth, goals that would have been feasible under normal circumstances. Those violations caused irreparable damage to her life, forcing her to interrupt her studies and to take up life in a foreign country far from the context in which her life had been evolving, in a state of solitude, poverty, and severe physical and psychological distress. Obviously this combination of circumstances, directly attributable to the violations that this Court examined, has seriously and probably irreparably altered the life of Ms. Loayza-Tamayo, and has prevented her from achieving the personal, family and professional goals that she had reasonably set for herself.

153. The Court recognizes the existence of grave damage to the "life plan" of Ms. María Elena Loayza-Tamayo, caused by violations of her human rights. Nevertheless, neither case law nor doctrine has evolved to the point where acknowledgment of damage to a life plan can be translated into economic terms. Hence, the Court is refraining from quantifying it. It notes, however, that the victim's recourse to international tribunals and issuance of the corresponding judgment constitute some measure of satisfaction for damages of these kinds.

154. The condemnation represented by the material and moral damages ordered on other points of this Judgment should be some compensation for the victim for the suffering these violations have caused her; still, it would be difficult to restore or offer back to her the options for personal fulfillment of which she has been unjustly deprived.

XIII. OTHER FORMS OF REPARATION

155. In her reparations brief, the victim petitioned the Court to order

a) That the State publicly apologize to her and to her next of kin by publishing press releases in the five major Peruvian newspapers, the "official journal" among them, and in newspapers with an international circulation;

b) That the State guarantee that her honor and the honor of her next of kin is restored and that it acknowledge, to the Peruvian public and to the international community, that it is responsible for the events of which she was the victim, and that it give public and mass circulation to the Judgment delivered on September 17, 1997.

156. The Commission did not raise this issue in its reparations brief.

157. The State indicated that when the victim was released, the mass media gave her release wide national coverage; the public was, therefore, informed of the facts and the publicity objective achieved. The State noted that the victim had herself submitted a video containing information about the news reports of her release order.

158. The Court considers that this Judgment, coupled with Judgment on the merits which found Peru responsible for human rights violations, constitute adequate reparation.

159. The victim requested that the Court instruct Peru to amend Decree-Law No. 25,475 (Terrorism) and Decree-Law No. 25,659 (Treason), as necessary.

160. For its part, the Commission petitioned the Court to order that Peru amend the pertinent provisions of those Decree-Laws and, in general, adopt the domestic legal measures necessary to avoid a repetition of violations of the kind proven in the instant case.

161. The State argued that amendment of Decree-Laws No. 25,475 and No. 25,659 would have no compensatory value. It maintained that it had introduced positive changes in its terrorism-related laws, including elimination of the practice of trial before "faceless" judges, creation of an *ad hoc* commission empowered to grant pardons, the possibility of executive clemency for persons tried for and convicted of the crimes of terrorism and treason, and commutation of sentence for those who avail themselves of the Repentance Law.

162. In the Judgment on the merits of the instant Case, delivered on September 17, 1997 (*Loayza Tamayo Case, supra* 123, para. 68), the Court's finding was that Decree-Laws 25,474 and 25,659 were incompatible with Article 8(4) of the Convention. The case law of this Court is that States Parties to the Convention may not order measures that violate rights and freedoms recognized therein (*Suárez Rosero Case*, Judgment of November 12, 1997. Series C No. 35, para. 97).

163. The Decree-Laws in question refer to actions not strictly defined (*Loayza Tamayo Case, supra* 123, para. 68), were invoked in the military court and regular court proceedings, and caused the victim injury.

164. Consequently, with respect to Decree-Laws 25,475 and 25,659, the Court finds that the State must comply with its obligations under Article 2 of the Convention, which stipulates that:

> [W]here the exercise of any of the rights or freedoms referred to in Article 1 is not already ensured by legislative or other provisions, the States Parties undertake to adopt, in accordance with their constitutional processes and the provisions of this Convention, such legislative or other measures as may be necessary to give effect to those rights or freedoms.

XIV. THE DUTY TO TAKE DOMESTIC MEASURES

165. In her reparations brief, the victim petitioned the Court to request Peru to have proceedings instituted before the competent courts for the purpose of investigating, identifying and punishing the material and intellectual authors of the events that gave rise to the instant case and the accessories after the fact.

166. In its reparations brief, the Commission requested that the Court order that judicial proceedings be instituted and administrative measures taken to investigate the facts and ascertain the identity of those responsible for the inhumane, degrading and humiliating treatment suffered by the victim.

167. The State argued that Decree-Laws Nos. 26,479 and 26,492, ordered as part of the pacification process, granted a general amnesty to military, police and civilian personnel; hence, the request made by the victim and the Commission is inadmissible. According to the State, even if the individuals who detained and prosecuted the victim had incurred some administrative, civil or criminal responsibility, those Decree-Laws precluded their prosecution at the present time, either judicially or administratively.

168. Under the American Convention, every person subject to the jurisdiction of a State Party is guaranteed the right to recourse to a competent court for the protection of his fundamental rights. States, therefore, have the obligation to prevent human rights violations, investigate them, identify and punish their intellectual authors and accessories after the fact, and may not invoke existing provisions of domestic law, such as the Amnesty Law in this case, to avoid complying with their obligations under international law. In the Court's judgment, the Amnesty Law enacted by Peru precludes the obligation to investigate and prevents access to justice. For these reasons, Peru's argument that it cannot comply with the duty to investigate the facts that gave rise to the present Case must be rejected.

169. As this Court has held on repeated occasion, Article 25 in relation to Article 1(1) of the American Convention obliges the State to guarantee to every individual access to the administration of justice and, in particular, to simple and prompt recourse, so that, *inter alia*, those responsible for human rights violations may be prosecuted and reparations obtained for the damages suffered. As this Court has ruled, Article 25 "is one of the fundamental pillars not only of the American Convention, but of the very rule of law in a democratic society in the terms of the Convention" (*Castillo Páez Case*, Judgment of November 3, 1997, Series C No. 34, paras. 82 and 83; *Suárez Rosero Case, supra* 162, para. 65; and *Paniagua Morales et al. Case, supra* 57, para. 164). That article is closely linked to Article 8(1), which provides that every person has the right to a hearing, with due guarantees and within a reasonable time, by a competent, independent, and impartial tribunal, for the determination of his rights, whatever their nature.

170. Consequently, it is the duty of the State to investigate human rights violations, prosecute those responsible and avoid impunity. The Court has defined impunity as the failure to investigate, prosecute, take into custody, try and convict those responsible for violations of rights protected by the American Convention and has further stated that

> . . . [t]he State has the obligation to use all the legal means at its disposal to combat that situation, since impunity fosters chronic recidivism of human rights violations, and total defenseless of victims and their relatives (*Paniagua Morales et al. Case, supra* 57, para. 173).

171. The State has an obligation to investigate the facts in the instant Case, to identify those responsible, to punish them, and to adopt the internal legal measures necessary to ensure compliance with this obligation (Article 2 of the American Convention).

XV. COSTS AND EXPENSES

172. In her reparations brief, the victim pointed out that Ms. Carolina Loayza-Tamayo, her sister and attorney, was her defense lawyer in her representations before Peruvian authorities and administrative bodies during the domestic proceedings. She estimated her fees at US$15,000.00 (fifteen thousand United States dollars). The victim also estimated that her attorney had visited her approximately 200 times during her incarceration.

173. The victim added that her attorney also represented her before the Commission; that the latter had accredited her as an assistant in the proceedings before

the Court; and that her sister had used her own funds to pay the expenses involved in the proceedings before those two bodies of the inter-American system, including her airfare and the costs of the telephone, mail, fax and courier services. Given the foregoing, the victim requested the sum of US$5,000.00 (five thousand United States dollars) for reimbursement of those expenses.

174. The Commission petitioned the Court to order payment of the expenses that Carolina Loayza-Tamayo had incurred in her legal representation of the victim *vis-à-vis* the Peruvian courts and the organs of the inter-American system; the itemization and calculations submitted by the victim in her brief were forwarded to the Court.

175. Peru pointed out that in its Judgment of September 17, 1997, the Court had decided that Peru was to reimburse the victim's next of kin for any expenses they may have incurred in their representations. The State argued that inasmuch as the Commission did not name Ms. Carolina Loayza-Tamayo as a victim, any request on her behalf was irrelevant and immaterial. Using this reasoning, Peru argued that the victim's claims at this stage of the proceedings were inadmissible. It further contended that the Judgment had ordered reimbursement of expenses incurred in representations before the Peruvian authorities, but not payment of professional fees.

176. Concerning these arguments, the Court considers that in the instant case, the costs must be examined in light of subparagraph (h) of Article 55(1) of its Rules of Procedure. Costs are an element of the reparations of which Article 63(1) of the Convention speaks, as they are a natural consequence of actions taken by the victim, her heirs or her representatives to obtain a Court resolution recognizing the violation committed and establishing its legal consequences. In other words, the activity in which they engaged to have recourse to an international court involves or can involve financial outlays and commitments for which the victim must be compensated when a judgment of condemnation is delivered.

177. In keeping with the applicable provisions, the Court considers that the costs to which Article 55(1) of its Rules of Procedure refers include the various outlays that the victim makes or pledges to make to accede to the inter-American system for the protection of human rights, and include the fees that are routinely paid to those who provide them with legal assistance. Obviously, these expenses refer solely to those that are necessary and reasonable, according to the particularities of the case, and that are effectively made or pledged to be made by the victim or her representatives (*Garrido and Baigorria Case, Reparations, supra* 84, para. 80).

178. It is important to point out that under Article 23 of the Rules of Procedure, the representatives of the victims or of their next of kin may independently submit their own arguments and evidence at the reparations stage. This recognition of their *locus standi* opens up the possibility of expenses associated with that representation. In practice, the legal assistance provided to the victim begins not at the reparations stage, but in proceedings before domestic judicial bodies, and then continues in the successive proceedings before the two bodies of the inter-American system for the protection of human rights, namely the Commission and the Court. Hence, the concept of costs being examined here also includes the costs involved in proceedings before the domestic courts (*Garrido and Baigorria Case, Reparations,*

supra 84, para. 81) and those seeking justice on an international plane, before two bodies: the Commission and the Court.

179. In exercise of this jurisdictional power, it is up to the Court to make a prudent assessment of the specific scope of the costs to which the judgment of condemnation refers, taking into account timely verification thereof, the circumstances of the specific case, the nature of the jurisdiction for the protection of human rights, and the characteristics of the respective proceedings, which are unique and different from those of other proceedings, both domestic and international. A reasonable amount of the costs incurred by the victim or her representatives and attorneys *vis-à-vis* Perú, the Inter-American Commission and this Court will be determined on the basis of equity (*Garrido and Baigorria Case, Reparations, supra* 84, para. 82).

180. Based on the foregoing, the Court is setting costs and fees at the sum of US$20,000.00 (twenty thousand United States dollars), of which US$15,000.00 (fifteen thousand United States dollars) are the fees of attorney Carolina Loayza Tamayo.

XVI. MANNER OF COMPLIANCE

181. The victim requested that:

a) The compensation ordered in her favor be paid in cash;

b) The compensation ordered for her daughter, her parents and her siblings be paid in cash;

c) The compensation ordered for her son be deposited in a trust fund until he has reached the age of 21;

d) Payment of the amounts ordered by the Court be made within ninety days of notification of this Judgment and be tax-exempt and, where appropriate, that interest be paid on the final amounts of the compensation, calculated from the date of the Judgment to the date of actual payment, using the bank interest rate in effect in Peru at the time the Judgment is delivered; and

e) The Court oversee fulfillment of the reparations ordered and payment of the compensation, and order the instant Case closed only when full compliance has been established.

182. The State made no observations on these points.

183. The Court considers the victim's claims to be reasonable, save for those relating to the deadline for payment and the method of payment to the victim's son. As regards the deadline, the jurisprudence of the Court has consistently been to give States a period of six months in which to comply with the obligations established in reparations judgments.

184. As for the payment owed to Paul Abelardo Zambrano-Loayza, the latter is so close to majority age that the formalities required to set up a trust fund are unwarranted and could even obstruct execution of the Judgment and thus be contrary to the interests of justice. For this reason, the Court is ordering that the amount awarded to Paul Abelardo Zambrano-Loayza be deposited in a solvent banking institution of recognized standing, in an interest-bearing, fixed-term certificate of deposit, at the most favorable terms under banking practice in Peru. That certificate

of deposit should mature on the date Mr. Paul Abelardo Zambrano-Loayza attains his majority.

185. To comply with this Judgment, the State shall execute the measures of restitution, pay compensatory damages, reimburse fees and costs and take the other measures ordered within the six-month period following the date of notification of this Judgment.

186. In the case of the compensatory damages, they shall be paid directly to the victim and to her adult next of kin; if any has died, payment shall be made to his or her heirs.

187. If within one year following the date of notification of this Judgment or maturity of the certificate of deposit described in paragraph 184, a beneficiary fails to appear to receive the payment he or she is due, the State shall put the amount owed, in United States dollars, in a trust fund in said individual's name, with a banking institution of recognized solvency in Peru and under the most favorable banking terms. If ten years after the trust fund's establishment said person or his or her have has not claimed the funds, the sum shall be returned to the State and this Judgment shall be considered honored.

188. The State may fulfill these obligations through payments in United States dollars or in an equivalent cash amount in the local currency of Peru. The rate of exchange used to determine the equivalent value shall be the selling rate for the United States dollar and the Peruvian currency quoted on the New York market on the day prior to the date of the payment.

189. The compensations paid shall be exempt from all taxes currently in existence or that may be enacted in the future.

190. Should the State be delinquent on any payment, it shall pay interest on the amount owed at the interest rate in effect in Peru's banking system for cases of delinquency.

191. In keeping with its consistent practice and its obligations under the American Convention, the Court will oversee compliance with this judgment . . . .

Questions and Comments

1. How does a litigant prove damages? What is the standard of proof? How are moral damages assessed?

2. The Court in this case indicates that damages must be proportional to the harm caused. Is there ever a circumstance where punitive damages might be awarded? The issue came before the court in the *Myrna Mack Chang* case, below. The government of Guatemala was held responsible for deliberately murdering the anthropologist because of her human rights work with the indigenous peoples of Guatemala, and then intimidating witnesses and killing a police officer who was investigating the murder. The Court's discussion of damages follows, as well as separate opinions on the issue of punitive damages.

Myrna Mack Chang v. Guatemala Case, Judgment of November 25, 2003, 101 Inter-Am. Ct. H.R. (Ser. C) (2003) (footnotes omitted).

113. . . . .[T]he Court takes into account, in addition to and alongside the acquiescence of the State, the testimony and expert opinions rendered at the public hearing before this Court, the body of evidence supplied by the Commission, by the representatives of the victim and by the State, the evidence included by the Court to facilitate adjudication, among others, the Report of the Historical Truth-Finding Committee entitled "Guatemala, memoria del silencio" (CEH), the report of the Archbishop's Human Rights Office for the recovery of historical memory, entitled "Guatemala: Nunca más: los mecanismos del horror" (REMHI).

114. After examining all these elements, the Court deems that the international responsibility of the State has been established for violations of the American Convention in the instant case, a responsibility that is worsened by the circumstances under which the facts of the *cas d'espèce* took place.

115. Since the Court deems that said acquiescence does not encompass reparation of the consequences derived from the violations to the rights protected by the Convention that were established in the instant case, the Court—applying Article 63(1) of the American Convention—will establish the pertinent reparations and legal costs.

116. The Court also deems that given the nature of the instant case, issuing a judgment that addresses the merits of the matter constitutes a form of reparation for the victim and her next of kin and, in turn, is a way to avoid recidivism of facts such as those suffered by Myrna Mack Chang and her next of kin.

. . . .

XII. Application of Article 63(1)

234. Pursuant to the foregoing explanation in the previous chapters, the Court found that the State is responsible for violation of Article 4 of the Convention to the detriment of Myrna Mack Chang and of Articles 5, 8 and 25 of that same Convention to the detriment of her next of kin, all of them in combination with Article 1(1) of the American Convention . . . .

235. As the Court has stated, Article 63(1) of the American Convention contains a common-law provision that constitutes one of the fundamental principles of contemporary International Law regarding the responsibility of the States. According to it, when an illegal act attributable to the State takes place, the latter immediately incurs a responsibility for the violation of the international provision involved, with the attendant duty of providing reparations and of making the consequences of said violation cease . . . .

. . . .

XIV. Reparations

246. In accordance with the evidence gathered during the proceeding and in light of the criteria set forth by this Court in its case law, the Court will now analyze the claims of the parties regarding this matter, so as to determine the measures of reparation pertaining to pecuniary and non-pecuniary damage and other forms of reparation.

A) Pecuniary Damage

. . . .

Considerations of the Court

. . . .

a) Lost earnings

251. The Commission and the representatives of the next of kin of the victim requested compensation for the lost earnings of Myrna Mack Chang. Specifically, said representatives requested that the Court adopt as a basis the average of what the victim earned at the time of the facts, what the director of AVANCSO earns today, the salary earned by persons with similar academic credentials to those of the victim, the salary increase of the victim over time, the rising cost of living, inflation in Guatemala, and life expectancy, among others.

252. With respect to the lost earnings of Myrna Mack Chang, the Court, in fairness, sets the amount at US$235,000.00 (two hundred and thirty-five thousand United States dollars) for this item. Said amount must be given to the daughter of the victim, Lucrecia Hernández Mack.

b) Consequential damages

253. Taking into account the claims of the parties, the body of evidence, the proven facts in the instant case and its own case law, the Court finds that compensation for material damage in the instant case must also include the following:

> 1) with respect to Helen Mack Chang, sister of the victim, it has been proven that as a consequence of the extra-legal death of her sister, she undertook the task of searching for justice, for over thirteen years, through her active participation in the criminal proceeding to investigate the facts and to identify and punish all those responsible. Helen Mack Chang gave up her work as a consequence of the facts discussed in the instant case, established the Myrna Mack Foundation, and has spent much of her time struggling against impunity. The Court deems that Helen Mack Chang stopped receiving her customary income as a consequence of the facts and bearing in mind the specific circumstances of the *sub judice* case, in fairness, it sets the amount of compensation at US$25,000.00 (twenty-five thousand United States dollars);

> 2) as regards the father and the daughter of the victim, it has been proven that due to the extra-legal death of Myrna Mack Chang and of the consequences stemming from this fact, they suffered various physical and psychological illnesses, for which they had to receive medical treatment. Therefore, the Court deems it pertinent to set US$3,000.00 (three thousand United States dollars) as compensation for medical expenses incurred by Yam Mack Choy and US$3,000.00 (three thousand United States dollars) for Lucrecia Hernández Mack, for this same item. Since Yam Mack Choy passed away on April 24, 1999, compensation in his favor must be paid in full to Zoila Chang Lau.

B) Non-Pecuniary damage

. . . .

Considerations of the Court

260. International case law has repeatedly established that the judgment constitutes *per se* a form of reparation. Nevertheless, given the grave circumstances of the instant case, the intensity of suffering caused by the respective facts to the victim and her next of kin, the alterations to the conditions of existence of the next of kin and the other non-material or non-pecuniary consequences suffered by the latter, the Court deems that it must order payment of a compensation for non-pecuniary damages, in fairness.

261. In the *sub judice* case, in setting the compensation for non-pecuniary damage, the Court takes into account that Myrna Mack Chang was extra-legally executed in circumstances of extreme violence, for which reason it is evident that she felt corporal pain and suffering before her death, and this was aggravated by the climate of harassment at the time.

262. As the Court has pointed out, non-pecuniary damage inflicted on the victim is evident, at it is part of human nature that every person subject to aggression such as that committed against Myrna Mack Chang experiences deep moral suffering.

263. In this regard, the compensation set by the Court for the damage suffered by Myrna Mack Chang up to the moment of her death must be given in full to the daughter of the victim, Lucrecia Hernández Mack.

264. In the case of the next of kin, it is reasonable to conclude that the affliction suffered by the victim extends to the closest members of the family, especially to those who were in close emotional contact with her. No evidence is required to reach this conclusion. In addition, in the instant case some of the next of kin of Myrna Mack Chang are victims of violations of various Articles of the American Convention. To set compensation for non-pecuniary damage, the next of kin of the victims will be considered in that dual condition, for which reason the Court deems that:

a) the threats, intimidation and harassment suffered by the next of kin as part of what happened to Myrna Mack Chang have been proven, and they have caused deep suffering to the members of the family, daughter, parents and siblings and cousin of the victim . . . . Furthermore, the impunity prevailing in this case has been and continues to be a source of suffering for the next of kin. It makes them feel vulnerable and in a state of permanent defenselessness vis-à-vis the State, and this causes them deep anguish [. . .];

b) with respect to Lucrecia Hernández Mack, daughter of the victim [. . .], this Court notes that she was 16 years old at the time her mother was murdered, and she depended on her emotionally and financially, as she did not live with her father. She experienced a traumatic situation due to the unexpected loss of her mother, which caused her deep grief and sadness that still affect her life. She is hurt by the absence of her mother because at certain moments in her life, such as academic ones or motherhood, she feels the need to have her close to share their concerns and receive advice. She is also very concerned about her family and in constant fear of losing another beloved one. On the other hand, as regards the criminal proceeding, its constant delays have been frustrating for her and, especially, the fact that there is still impunity for those responsible makes her feel very insecure [. . .]. Due to all the above, this Court deems that she must be compensated for non-pecuniary damage;

c) with respect to Yam Mack Choy, the deceased father of the victim, and Zoila Chang Lau, mother of the victim, attention must be paid to the fact that the Court assumes that the death of a person causes non-pecuniary damage to the parents, for which reason it is not necessary to prove this. As this Court has stated before, "we can admit the presumption that the parents have suffered mentally for the cruel death of their children, since it is human nature that every person feels pain in the face of the suffering of a child." In the instant case, Yam Mack Choy, after the death of her daughter, in addition to the grief that this caused her, suffered physical illnesses that damaged his health and put an end to his life. The mother of the victim, in turn, has suffered deep grief, which she tried to express . . . in her sworn statement . . . . For all the above, this Court deems that the parents of the victim must be compensated for non-pecuniary damage. Since Yam Mack Choy passed away, the compensation in his favor must be given in full to Zoila Chang Lau;

d) with respect to Helen Mack Chang, the sister of the victim, this Court also deems that in the case of siblings the degree of relationship and affection between them must be taken into account. This lady has felt deep suffering and grief due to the extra-legal death of her sister, which altered her life and that of her family, especially that of her parents and of her niece; the way her sister was murdered has had an impact on her for a long time; seeing her parents pain and having had to give her niece the news of her mother's death has caused her indescribable suffering. Taking the necessary steps before the police and the judiciary to seek justice involved her in a process "which [she] never imagine[d] would take on the proportions it did". She had to give up her professional activity to personally undertake the search for justice and, therefore, to struggle against impunity. She has participated actively in the criminal proceeding from the start; she has suffered acts of harassment and threats that have place her life and her personal safety at risk; and to protect her family, she has adopted serious security measures that have altered their family life, all of which has caused her great emotional stress (*supra* para. 127). Therefore, the Court deems that she must be compensated for non-pecuniary damage;

e) with respect to Marco Mack Chang and Freddy Mack Chang, brothers of the victim, they also suffered grief due to the cruel death of their sister, and her absence saddens them; she was the person who supported the family in difficult moments. They have also suffered the stress of struggling for such a long time to elucidate the facts and of living with the uncertainty of what will happen in the proceeding, a situation that has also made them fear the danger faced by the family at crucial moments in the trial [. . .]. Therefore, this Court deems that they should be compensated for non-pecuniary damage;

f) with respect to Vivian Mack Chang, sister of the victim, this Court has stated, in its recent case law, that it can be assumed that the death of a sibling causes non-pecuniary damage to the other siblings and, therefore, she must receive compensation for this; and

g) regarding Ronald Chang Apuy, cousin of the victim [. . .], it has been proven that he lived with the Mack family since he was small and that he is considered one more member of the family. He had close emotional ties with Myrna Mack Chang and he has shared with the family the sorrow and suffering for their loss. He has also experienced the fear caused by the threats and acts of intimidation received throughout the criminal proceeding for elucidation of the facts and the uncertainty due to the delays in this proceeding. Therefore, the Court deems that he too should receive compensation for non-pecuniary damage.

265. Therefore, this Court concludes that the grave non-pecuniary damage suffered by the next of kin of Myrna Mack Chang has been fully proven.

266. In the instant case, the need of the daughter of the victim, Lucrecia Hernández Mack, to receive psychological treatment for the damage caused by the violations committed by the state has also been proven. Therefore, the court sets, in fairness, US$10,000.00 (ten thousand United States dollars), as the amount to cover future medical expenses that she requires . . . .

c) Other forms of reparation

268. The Court will now consider other injurious effects of the facts, which are not financial or patrimonial in nature, and which may be redressed by means of acts of the public authorities; these include investigation and punishment of those responsible, remembrance of the victim and consolation to her relatives; and signifying official reproval of the human rights violations that occurred and undertaking a commitment that acts such as those of the instant case will happen no more.

. . . .

Considerations of the Court

271. The Court has concluded, *inter alia*, that Guatemala violated Articles 8 and 25, in combination with 1(1) of the Convention, to the detriment of the next of kin of the victim, due to deficient direction of the judicial proceedings, their delays, and the obstructions effected to impede punishment all those responsible, including direct perpetrators, accessories, participants and accomplices after the fact, which has generated feelings of insecurity, defenselessness, and anguish in the next of kin of the victim.

272. The Court recognizes that in the instant case impunity of those responsible is partial, as one of the direct perpetrators has been tried and punished [. . .]. Nevertheless, at the time of the instant Judgment, after more than thirteen years, the criminal proceeding is ongoing and is pending a decision on an appeal for annulment, for which reason a definitive judgment has not yet been issued that identifies and punishes all those responsible for the extra-legal execution of Myrna Mack Chang. On the other hand, there has been a situation of grave impunity that constitutes an infringement of the aforementioned duty of the State [. . .], that is injurious to the next of kin of the victim, and that fosters chronic recidivism of the human rights violations involved.

273. This Court has repeatedly referred to the right of the next of kin of the victims to know what happened and to know who are the agents of the State responsible for the respective facts. As the Court has stated, "[w]henever there has been a human rights violation, the State has a duty to investigate the facts and punish those responsible, [. . .] and this obligation must be complied with seriously and not as a mere formality."

274. The Court has reiterated that every person, including the next of kin of the victims of grave violations of human rights, has the right to the truth. Therefore, the next of kin of the victims and society as a whole must be informed of everything

that has happened in connection with said violations. This right to the truth has been developed by International Human Rights Law; recognized and exercised in a concrete situation, it constitutes an important means of reparation. Therefore, in this case it gives rise to an expectation that the State must satisfy for the next of kin of the victim and Guatemalan society as a whole.

275. In light of the above, to completely redress this aspect of the violations committed, the State must effectively investigate the facts in the instant case, so as to identify, try, and punish all the direct perpetrators and accessories, and the other persons responsible for the extra-legal execution of Myrna Mack Chang, and for the cover-up of the extra-legal execution and of the other facts in the instant case, aside from the person who has already been punished for these facts. The outcome of the proceeding must be made known to the public, for Guatemalan society to know the truth.

276. The Court notes that the State must ensure that the domestic proceeding to investigate and punish those responsible for the facts in this case attains its due effects and, specifically, it must abstain from resorting to legal concepts such as amnesty, extinguishment, and the establishment of measures designed to eliminate responsibility . . . .

277. To comply with this obligation, the State must also remove all de facto and legal mechanisms and obstacles that maintain impunity in the instant case; it must provide sufficient security measures to the judicial authorities, prosecutors, witnesses, legal operators, and to the next of kin of Myrna Mack Chang and use all means available to it so as to expedite the proceeding.

278. On the other hand, for the acknowledgment of responsibility by the State and what this Court has set forth to have full reparation effects for the victims and to act as guarantees of non-recidivism, the Court deems that the State must carry out a public act of acknowledgment of its responsibility regarding the facts in this case and of amends to the memory of Myrna Mack Chang and to her next of kin, in the presence of the highest authorities of the State, which must be published in the media.

279. At that same act, taking into account the specifics of the case, the State must also publicly honor the memory of José Mérida Escobar, the police investigator who was murdered in connection with the facts in the instant case [. . .].

280. The State must also publish, within three months of notification of the instant Judgment, at least once, in the official gazette "Diario Oficial" and in another national-circulation daily, operative paragraphs 1 to 12 and the proven facts contained in paragraphs 134, 134.1 to 134.8, 134.10 to 134.19, 134.26, 134.86 to 134.90, and 134.95 to 134.106, without the footnotes, of the instant Judgment.

281. The characteristics of the facts in this case reveal that the armed forces, the police corps, and the security and intelligence agencies of the State acted exceeding their authority by applying means and methods that were not respectful of human rights. It is imperative to avoid recidivism of the circumstances and facts described with respect to this same Judgment.

282. The State must adopt the necessary provisions for this and, specifically, those tending to educate and train all members of its armed forces, the police and

its security agencies regarding the principles and rules for protection of human rights, even under state of emergency. The State must specifically include education on human rights and on International Humanitarian Law in its training programs for the members of the armed forces, of the police and of its security agencies.

283. On the other hand, the Court has established that there was participation of the high command of the Presidential General Staff and its Presidential Security Department or "Archivo" in the extra-legal execution of Myrna Mack Chang. In this regard, both the Inter-American Commission and the representatives of the next of kin of the victim requested, as a guarantee of non-recidivism, the dissolution of the Presidential General Staff. It is publicly known, as a notorious fact, that on September 24, 2003, the Congress of the Republic of Guatemala enacted the "Ley de la Secretaría de Asuntos Administrativos y de Seguridad de la Presidencia de la República" (SAAS), in which it established the juridical basis for the civil body in charge of security and support for the President, the Vice-President of the Republic and their families, in substitution of the Presidential General Staff. The Court also takes note of the fact that on October 31, 2003, the President of the Republic of Guatemala, Alfonso Portillo, held a ceremony at which the transfer of functions to the new SAAS agency began.

284. The Court deems that the activities of the military forces and of the police, and of all other security agencies, must be strictly subject to the rules of the democratic constitutional order and to the international human rights treaties and to International Humanitarian Law. This is especially valid with respect to the intelligence agencies and activities. These agencies must, *inter alia*, be: a) respectful, at all times, of the fundamental rights of persons; and b) subject to control by civil authorities, including not only those of the executive branch, but also, insofar as pertinent, those of the other public powers. Measures to control intelligence activities must be especially rigorous because, given the conditions of secrecy under which these activities take place, they can drift toward committing violations of human rights and illegal criminal actions, as occurred in the instant case.

285. With respect to guarantees of non-recidivism of the facts of the instant case, as part of public recognition of the victim, the State must establish a scholarship, in the name of Myrna Mack Chang, to cover the complete cost of a year of study in anthropology at a prestigious national university. Said scholarship must be granted by the State permanently every year.

286. The State must also name a well-known street or square in Guatemala City in honor of Myrna Mack Chang, and place a prominent plaque in her memory at the place where she died or nearby, with a reference to the activities she carried out. This will contribute to awakening public awareness to avoid recidivism of facts such as those that occurred in the instant case and to maintain remembrance of the victim . . . .

Separate Opinion Of Judge A.A. Cançado Trindade

1. I vote in favor of adoption of the instant Judgment of the Inter-American Court of Human Rights on the merits and reparations in the *Myrna Mack Chang versus Guatemala* case, in which the Court ruled that the violation of Myrna Mack Chang's right to life occurred under *aggravating circumstances*, because it resulted from "a

covert military intelligence operation carried out by the Presidential General Staff and tolerated by various authorities and institutions", set within a "pattern of selective extra-legal executions fostered and tolerated by the State itself", and a "climate of impunity". The Court also found that said military intelligence operation by the Presidential General Staff "sought to conceal the facts and sought impunity of those responsible, and to this end, with tolerance by the State, it resorted to all types of means, including harassment, threats and murders of those cooperating with the courts," thus affecting the independence of the Judiciary.

2. It is my understanding that this is a case of *aggravated* international responsibility of the State, demonstrated by the aforementioned facts and abusive resort to the so-called "official secret," leading to an obstruction of justice. These *aggravating circumstances* make the instant case a paradigmatic one, and because of them the instant Judgment of the Court is destined to be truly historical.

. . . .

36. As long as an international human rights court cannot determine the international criminal responsibility of the individual, and an international criminal court cannot determine the responsibility of the State, impunity will probably persist, being only partly punished by the former and the latter. International responsibility of the State is neither exclusively civil (as suggested by the duty to provide reparation for damage), nor exclusively criminal (as suggested by legitimization of a punishment). It is a collective responsibility of the State, alongside the international criminal responsibility of the individual. International responsibility of the State contains both civil and criminal aspects, in the current stage of evolution of international law.

37. The viewpoint, espoused by the Inter-American Court of Human Rights in the past, according to which compensations "with exemplarizing or dissuasive purposes" have no place in international law,[65] has been completely surpassed. It is in accordance with a reactionary vision, shaped by the precepts of juridical positivism, that until recently (whether consciously or not) held back development regarding this matter, and which no longer reflects, as stated above, the current stage of evolution of international law in this regard. Furthermore, in my view, realization of the exemplarizing or dissuasive purposes can—and must—be sought not only through compensations, but also through other (non-pecuniary) forms of reparation.

38. Irrespective of the civil or criminal elements of the international responsibility of the State, I believe it is undeniable that reparations can adopt a punitive or repressive nature,[66] to ensure the realization of justice and to put an end to impunity (cf. *infra*). It is also necessary to bear in mind that, while reparations (both pecuniary and moral) benefit the injured party directly, punishment (or repressive action against the State found in violation), in turn, benefits the human community

---

[65] Inter-American Court of Human Rights (I-ACtHR), *Velásquez Rodríguez versus Honduras* case (Compensatory Indemnification), Judgment of 21.07.1989, Series C, n. 7, p. 24, paras. 38–39; I-ACtHR), *Godínez Cruz versus Honduras* case (Compensatory Indemnification), Judgment of 21.07.1989, Series C, n. 8, p. 21, paras. 36–37.

[66] M. Gounelle, "Quelques remarques sur la notion de `crime international' et sur l'évolution de la responsabilité internationale de l'État", *in Mélanges offerts à Paul Reuter'Le droit international: unité et diversité*, Paris, Pédone, 1981, pp. 317–318.

itself as a whole; not to admit this would be to allow the State found in violation to remove itself from the Law.[67]

. . . .

40. In point of fact, even admitting the principle of objective or absolute responsibility of the State (as the Inter-American Court has rightly done in the case of *"The Last Temptation of Christ" versus Chile,* 2001), this does not mean that responsibility based on fault or blame is totally dismissed under any and all hypotheses or circumstances. There are cases—as in the instant *Myrna Mack Chang versus Guatemala* case—in which the *intention* of the State to cause harm or its negligence in avoiding it can be proven; fault or blame then becomes, here, the indispensable basis for responsibility of the State,[68] *aggravated* by that circumstance.

VIII. The Juridical Consequences of Crimes of State: *Aggravated* International Responsibility and the Nature and Scope of the *Reparatio*.

41. *Aggravated* responsibility is, precisely, that which is consistent with a crime of State. The renowned Article 19 of the State Responsibility Project (1976) of the ILC, in its provision regarding "international crimes", precisely had in mind the determination of an *aggravated* degree of responsibility for certain violations of international law.[69] It did not in any way intend to suggest an analogy with categories of domestic criminal law. Once aggravated responsibility has been accepted, its juridical consequences must be established.

42. Already in 1939, long before becoming the rapporteur of the ILC on International Responsibility of the States, Robert Ago reflected that the same material fact may be apprehended by different rules within the same juridical order, ascribing juridical circumstances to it that are also different, generating the obligation to provide reparation or legitimizing application of a punishment.[70] It may thus require either the obligation to provide reparation, or application of a punishment, or both simultaneously; for R. Ago, "punishment and reparation may thus exist side by side, as effects of the same crime".[71]

43. The same juridical fact can, thus, give rise to different consequences, such as reparation and punishment. For an especially grave illegal act (e.g. a grave violation of human rights or of International Humanitarian Law), compensatory reparation (for the victim or the victim's next of kin) may not be sufficient, in which case a punitive reparation (e.g., investigation of the facts and punishment of those responsible) may be required. Both may be necessary for the realization of justice.

44. In 1958, Cuban jurist F. V. García Amador, who at the time was the ILC rapporteur on Responsibility of the States, noted that certain forms of reparation have a clear and distinctly punitive purpose *(punitive damages/dommages-intérêts punitifs)* and involve imputing criminal responsibility to the State for violation of certain international obligations—especially, grave violations of fundamental human

---

[67] H. Lauterpacht, *op. cit. supra* n. (34), pp. 355–357.
[68] Cf., in this regard, H. Lauterpacht, *op. cit. supra* n. (34), pp. 359–361 and 364.
[69] I. Sinclair, "State Responsibility: *Lex Ferenda* and Crimes of State", *in International Crimes of State* (eds. J.H.H. Weiler, A. Cassese and M. Spinedi), Berlin, W. de Gruyter, 1989, p. 242.
[70] Roberto Ago, "Le délit international", 68 *Recueil des Cours de l'Académie de Droit International de La Haye* (1939) pp. 424 and 426.
[71] *Ibid.,* pp. 428–429.

rights, analogous to crimes against humanity.[72] Thus, the very "duty of providing reparation" (with an initial civil law connotation) varies according to "the nature and function of the reparation in specific cases"; reparation, thus, does not always have the same form or the same purpose, and in the case of punitive damages (cf. *infra*) it contains a criminal element of responsibility.[73]

45. The whole chapter on reparations for human rights violations requires greater conceptual and case-law development, based on recognition of the close relationship between the right to reparations and the right to justice. Said development is especially necessary in face of grave and systematic human rights violations, which in turn require a firm reproval of the illicit conduct of the State, and dissuasive reparations, to ensure non-recidivism of the injurious acts, taking into account both the expectations of the next of kin of the victim and the higher interests or needs of the society.

46. In effect, one cannot deny the close link between reparations and combating impunity, as well as ensuring non-recidivism of the injurious acts, always and necessarily from the perspective of the victims. True *reparatio*, linked to realization of justice, requires overcoming obstructions of the duty to investigate and to punish those responsible, and putting an end to impunity. In other words, contrary to what the Inter-American Court maintained in the past,[74] it is my view that reparations can perfectly well be both compensatory and punitive, with the aim of putting an end to impunity and ensuring realization of justice—which is perfectly in accordance with the current stage of development of international law.

47. The provisions of Article 63(1) of the American Convention on Human Rights do in fact open a very broad horizon for the Inter-American Court of Human Rights in the matter of reparations. Exemplarizing or dissuasive reparations, consistent with an *aggravated* responsibility, may contribute to ensure non-recidivism of the injurious acts and to the struggle against impunity....

48. As stated in a Joint Separate Opinion in the *Loayza Tamayo versus Peru* case (Reparations, Judgment of 27.11.1998), treatment given to measures of reparation in International Human Rights Law has been unsatisfactory, because it "starts out from analogies with solutions of private law and, especially, of civil law, within the framework of domestic legal systems", strongly influenced by merely patrimonial content and interest. This criterion is inadequate and insufficient in International Human Rights Law, in which "the determination of reparations must take into account the personality of the victim as a whole", and the impact of the violation committed on the victim or the next of kin of the victim: the starting point must be a perspective that is not merely patrimonial, but rather focused on dignity of the human person. Non-pecuniary reparations are much more important than one might assume *prima facie*, even to make the violations *cease* and remove their consequences, pursuant to the terms of Article 63(1) of the American Convention.

---

[72] F. V. García Amador, "State Responsibility—Some New Problems", 94 *Recueil des Cours de l'Académie de Droit International de La Haye* (1958) pp. 396–398.

[73] *Ibid.*, p. 409.

[74] In the judgments on "compensatory indemnification" (of 1989) in the *Velásquez Rodríguez* and *Godínez Cruz* cases, *cit. supra* n. (47).

49. While the concept of "punitive damages" is not foreign to comparative domestic case law, nor to the case law of international arbitration,[75] it is not my intention to invoke it here in the sense in which it has been used—in other contexts—as exemplary reparation that is necessarily pecuniary (involving considerable amounts[76]). Far from it. In the current context of protection, which has its own specificity, other, non-pecuniary forms of reparation have commonly been identified as "obligations to do", once again suggesting a reductionist analogy with civil law solutions.

50. These forms of reparation . . . can well be deemed both compensatory and punitive in nature (containing both civil and criminal aspects). They have exemplary or dissuasive purposes, in the sense of preserving remembrance of the violations occurred, of providing satisfaction (a feeling of realization of justice) to the next of kin of the victim, and of contributing to ensure non-recidivism of said violations (even through human rights training and education).

51. "Punitive damages" may also be conceived in this sense, akin to the "obligations to do" that are both compensatory and punitive (thus overcoming the dichotomy between civil and criminal aspects, typical of the regime of responsibility under domestic law). I would like to mention certain significant examples from the rich case law of the Inter-American Court regarding reparations. In the *Aloeboetoe versus Suriname* case (Judgment of 10.09.1993), the Court ordered a school reopened and the creation of a foundation to assist the beneficiaries. In the *Villagrán Morales et al. versus Guatemala* case (the *"Street Children"* case, Judgment of 26.05.2001), the Court ordered that an educational center be named after the victims in the case; in a similar manner, in the *Trujillo Oroza versus Bolivia* case (Judgment of 27.02.2002), the Court ordered that an educational center be given the victim's name.

52. Other examples may be added. In the *Cantoral Benavides versus Peru* case (Judgment of 03.12.2001), the Court ordered the State to provide a university-level educational scholarship to the victim. In the *Barrios Altos* case with respect to Peru (Judgment of 30.11.2001), the Court ordered reparations in terms of educational benefits and payment of health service expenses; in the *Durand and Ugarte versus Peru* case (Judgment of 03.12.2001), the Court once again ordered payment of health services or expenses and psychological support. Said reparations for damages are in fact both compensatory and punitive; "punitive damages," thus understood, actually have already been applied, for a long time, in the domain of international human rights protection . . . . In evolving contemporary international law, "punitive damages" *lato sensu*[77] (beyond the merely pecuniary meaning inappropriately given

---

[75] Cf., e.g., *inter alia*, R.W. Hodgin and E. Veitch, "Punitive Damages Reassessed", 21 *International and Comparative Law Quarterly* (1972) pp. 119–132; J.Y. Gotanda, "Awarding Punitive Damages in International Commercial Arbitrations [. . .]", 38 *Harvard International Law Journal* (1997) pp. 59–105, respectively; and also cf. examples of the practice (both domestic and international) *in* D. Shelton, *Remedies in International Human Rights Law*, Oxford, University Press, 2000, pp. 74–75 and 288–289.

[76] And entailing the risk of a "commercialization" of justice.

[77] It should not go unnoticed that, e.g., the Declaration adopted by the United Nations World Conference against Racism, Racial Discrimination, Xenofobia [sic] and Related Forms of Intolerance (Durban, 2001), when it foresaw measures or reparation, compensation, indemnification and others for human suffering and the "tragedies of the past" (paras. 98–106), and the respective Program of Action, in its provisions on reparations and indemnification (paras. 165–166), used a language that reveals affinities with the concept of "punitive damages" *lato sensu*.

to them) can be an appropriate response or reaction of the juridical order against a crime of State.[78]

53. In conclusion, the facts in the instant case, *Myrna Mack Chang versus Guatemala,* demonstrate that crimes of State do exist. The facts in the instant case indicate that most contemporary international juridical doctrine is mistaken in seeking to avoid the issue. While the expression "crime of State" may seem objectionable to many international jurists (especially those petrified by the specter of State sovereignty) because it suggests an inadequate analogy with juridical categories of domestic criminal law, this does not mean that crimes of State do not exist. The facts in the instant case are eloquent evidence that they do exist. Even if another name is sought for them, the existence of crimes of State does not cease for that reason. . . .

Concurring Opinion of Judge Sergio García Ramírez

. . . .

43. Paragraph 114 of the judgment . . . contains a reference to the "aggravation" of State responsibility, taking into account "the circumstances in which the facts occurred". This phrase gives rise to a comment. In criminal law it is common to speaking of aggravating circumstances or, in more modern terminology, of criminal factors that imply or underscore a more serious conduct and, on the basis of the simple or general circumstance, define a special one. In both premises, the legislator reflects, in the criminal treatment of the facts and of the person responsible, their greater seriousness taking into account information such as the rights violated (in addition of the central right subject to protection: e.g., life), the link between the perpetrator and the victim, the means or way of execution, the causes or motives, the psychological connection, or purpose of the offender (*Cf.* López Bolado, Jorge D., *Los homicidios calificados,* Plus Ultra, Buenos Aires, 1975; and Levene (h), *El delito de homicidio,* Depalma, Buenos Aires, 1977, pp. 173 and *ff.*). In the case of aggravating circumstances, it is for the trial judge to apply the consequences established in law, and in the case of an aggravated criminal offense, the law itself establishes a more severe general punishment. Lastly, within this generic punishment, it is for the court to adapt the punishment, bearing in mind the act perpetrated and the guilt of the agent.

44. All the foregoing may be considered when examining the instant case, without forgetting, obviously, that the Inter-American Court does not operate in the sphere of criminal justice, which corresponds to the domestic jurisdiction. Therefore, my observations only serve to establish an illustrative analogy. Indeed, in this hypothesis, there is an objective aggravation of the facts, inasmuch as it is significant, in view of the elements of available information to which I have already referred, that this was not an isolated crime, the product of the design of one individual, but that there was an elaborate plan to deprive the victim of her life owing to her activities—social research and dissemination of the results, which entailed a critical vision of official programs—and that security agents and officials took part in the plan. This apparatus, which had important resources of power, placed itself at the service of

---

[78] N.H.B. Jorgensen, *The Responsibility of States for International Crimes,* Oxford, University Press, 2003, pp. 231 and 280.

actions that implied violation of the victim's most relevant right, the right to life, to terminate the tasks that she was carrying out and warn other individuals of the consequences that similar work would entail, even though it was legal according to the norms in force when the facts occurred.

45. One notable aspect of the gravity of this case resides in the obstacles created to the due investigation of the facts and the criminal prosecution of those responsible. The judgment contains a detailed description of these obstacles and of the "labyrinth" represented by the still unfinished investigation of the crime, and also the consequences of this investigation for those who took part in it and attempted to clarify the events and identify the authors. In this respect, we should recall the reports of the witnesses whose statements appear in the file, such as Rember Aroldo Larios Tobar, former head of the Criminal Investigations Department of the Guatemalan National Police (para. 127.e), and Henry Francisco Monroy Andino, former criminal trial judge (para. 127.f). In the context of these problems and their effects on the life and security of those who intervened in the tasks of investigation and prosecution, I consider it relevant that the judgment has decided that the State should honor publicly the memory of José Miguel Mérica Escobar, the member of the police force who participated in the investigation into the homicide of Mrs. Mack Chang and was assassinated (para. 279).

46. The aggravated seriousness of the facts must certainly be taken into account when making the reproach that a judgment on human rights violations implies, as in the case of this final ruling. It will be necessary to weigh this in the decisions duly adopted by the domestic criminal jurisdiction regarding sentences of imprisonment and also, if applicable, other punishments, such as: deprivation of rights or functions, disqualification, compensation, etc.

47. There remains the question of how this aggravated seriousness may affect the reparations decided by the Inter-American Court. In my opinion, it is perfectly possible that it influences acts of non-pecuniary compensation, such as publication of the judgment, expression of guilt and requirement of apology in official declarations, and commemoration of the memory of the victim. There are also the strictly patrimonial consequences—compensation for pecuniary and non-pecuniary damage, concepts that have their own importance and observe their own norms—that would arise if we tried to use that aggravated seriousness as a basis for establishing "punitive damages", a concept that has not been included in the case law of this Court, because it corresponds more to the idea of a fine than to that of the reparation of damage and, in any case, it would be payable by the Treasury, which implies an additional burden for the taxpayer and also a reduction in the resources that should go towards social programs.

48. Among the observations arising from the conduct of any State obliged to guarantee conditions of public security and to recognize and protect scrupulously the rights of its citizens—both tasks inherent in the preservation of the rule of law in a democratic society—I believe that the Inter-American Court's indication that security agencies should be subject to the norms of the democratic constitutional order, international human rights treaties and international humanitarian law is particularly significant (para 284). Even the fight against extremely serious criminal

behavior cannot serve as an argument for eroding the system of rights and guarantees built up by humanity over several centuries with infinite efforts and sacrifices.

49. Preservation of the rule of law must be ensured without infringing the principles and norms that characterize it. On this point the judgment of the Inter-American Court in the *Maritza Urrutia* case (concerning the problem of torture), which was rendered immediately after the judgment in the *Mack Chang* case, has been emphatic. In this matter, the Court asserted that the investigation and prosecution of the most serious crimes, whatever their nature, could not be invoked as justification for violating the human rights of the accused. The absolute prohibition of torture, in all its forms—physical and psychological—is part of international *jus cogens*.

. . . .

XI. OTHER ISSUES

71. I believe that, in the future case law of the Inter-American Court, other issues may arise that appear in this judgment and in previous ones, or that they engender. For example, this *Judgment* reiterates the Court's position, followed systematically in numerous judgments, that the amounts it establishes to be delivered as compensation should be returned to the State when they are not claimed by the beneficiaries in a specific period of time, if this is possible. It is worthwhile exploring the possibility of these amounts being applied to other concepts linked to human rights, in accordance with the characteristics of the case referred to in the respective judgement and, to the relevant extent, the approach concerning application of resources to a socially useful end that is closely linked to the victims, which has been outlined in other judgments such as those in the *Aloeboetoe* (Suriname) and the *Mayagna Awas Tigni Community* (Nicaragua) cases. It may be considered—although I am not affirming this at the present time—that this destination is more in keeping with the general regime of reparations and the protection of human rights than the simple return to the State of an amount that for a long time has been excluded, owing to the judgment, from regular public expenditure and was attributed, by the judgment, to a purpose linked to the protection of those rights.

72. It will also be interesting to examine some implications of the system of reparations in favor of the victims, since they should be able to enjoy the rights resulting from the unlawful act in the best conditions. In this respect, it is interesting to recall that the inter-American jurisdiction is complementary to the domestic jurisdiction, and only supplements it when the latter does not protect internationally recognized rights effectively. In other words, this jurisdiction intervenes to satisfy the right of individuals—among other related purposes of the greatest transcendence that I will not attempt to examine now—and should not, in any way, signify a reduction in the terms of the subjective rights and their substantive consequences. This idea is included in the norms of interpretation contained in Article 29 of the Convention. It may be seen, in particular, in subparagraph (b) of this article, which prohibits any interpretation of the Pact of San José that "restrict[s] the enjoyment or exercise of any right or freedom recognized by virtue of the laws of any State Party or by virtue of another convention to which one of the said States is a party".

73. In several judgments, the Inter-American Court has referred to national legislation and/or instances of domestic law in order to quantify the financial consequences of the violation committed. Obviously, in these cases, the Court has abstained from formulating a guilty verdict, leaving it to the domestic system to adopt the relevant consequences of the violation committed. To the contrary, it has established the guilty verdict clearly, when this has been pertinent, as corresponds to its jurisdictional obligation. Nevertheless, at the same time, it has recognized that some aspects of that decision may be defined more adequately under national law and by the domestic authorities, as has occurred in cases that involve labor compensation, commercial calculations, determination of possession or ownership, etc., although this obviously does not imply leaving the definition of essential points of the guilty verdict in the hands of third parties or waiving the authority to monitor compliance with its decisions, which is inherent to its jurisdictional mandate and without which it could not comply with the attributes and obligations assigned to it in Articles 33.b), 62(1), 63(1) and 65 of the Convention.

74. In other words, there are considerations of a practical nature, and even of fairness, that justify the possible and appropriate referral of certain aspects to domestic norms and instances, so that they may be implemented within the framework of the declaration of the guilty verdict previously formulated by the international Court. In this respect, the objective application of domestic law could possible improve the victim's situation as regards pecuniary issues. In this case, is it pertinent that the international judgment should obstruct the injured party's possibility of obtaining a more favorable result before domestic legal proceedings, if this is possible under national norms? If the answer to this question is negative, could it then be understood that the Court's decision constitutes a "base" or "minimum limit" of compensation, which could be improved before the domestic instances, when there are grounds in domestic law to achieve this advantage? Is it not possible that the non-pecuniary reparations ordered by the Court may be expanded and improved when the State, by mutual agreement with the beneficiaries—and even without this agreement—determines this expansion or improvement? If so, why cannot the pecuniary reparations also be expanded and improved, should this improvement be obtained at the domestic level, provided that it does not harm the base or limit established in the decision of this international Court?

Questions and Comments

1. What does "aggravated responsibility" mean and what are the consequences of it?

2. Do applicants get a "windfall" if punitive damages are awarded? If so, can it be avoided by non-monetary reparations such as the Court designated in the Myrna Mack Chang case?

3. What are the problems with awarding punitive damages against a state?

4. Group or collective claims are a growing issue in human rights law, particularly with regard to indigenous peoples. Some of these claims are complicated by the non-monetary cultures of the peoples involved, as well as their particular social structures. The Inter-

American Court has faced difficult issues in allocating reparations in such culturally varied contexts. Consider the following case:

Aloeboetoe et al. v. Suriname, Reparations (Art. 63(1) American Convention on Human Rights), Judgment of September 10, 1993, 15 Inter-Am. Ct. H.R. (Ser. C) (1993).

The events that gave rise to the petition apparently occurred on December 31, 1987, in Atjoni (village of Pokigron, District of Sipaliwini) and in Tjongalangapassi, District of Brokopondo. In Atjoni, more than 20 male, unarmed Bushnegroes *(Maroons)* had been attacked, abused and beaten with riflebutts by a group of soldiers. A number of them had been wounded with bayonets and knives and were detained on suspicion of belonging to the Jungle Commando, a subversive group. Some 50 persons witnessed these occurrences.

4. The petition asserts that the soldiers allowed some of the Maroons to continue on their way, but that seven of them, including a 15-year old boy, were dragged, blindfolded, into a military vehicle and taken through Tjongalangapassi in the direction of Paramaribo. The names of the persons taken by the soldiers, their place and date of birth, insofar as is known, are as follows: Daison Aloeboetoe, of Gujaba, born June 7, 1960; Dedemanu Aloeboetoe, of Gujaba; Mikuwendje Aloeboetoe, of Gujaba, born February 4, 1973; John Amoida, of Asindonhopo (resident of Gujaba); Richenel Voola, alias Aside or Ameikanbuka, of Grantatai (found alive); Martin Indisie Banai, of Gujaba, born June 3, 1955; and Beri Tiopo, of Gujaba.

5. The petition goes on to state that the vehicle stopped when it came to Kilometer 30. The soldiers ordered the victims to get out or forcibly dragged them out of the vehicle. They were given a spade and ordered to start digging. Aside was injured while trying to escape, but was not followed. The other six Maroons were killed.

6. The petition states that on Saturday, January 2, 1988, a number of men from Gujaba and Grantatai set out for Paramaribo to seek information on the seven victims from the authorities. They called on the Coordinator of the Interior at Volksmobilisatie and on the Military Police at Fort Zeeland, where they tried to see the Head of S-2. Without obtaining any information regarding the whereabouts of the victims, they returned to Tjongalangapassi on Monday, January 4. At Kilometer 30 they came across Aside, who was seriously wounded and in critical condition, and the bodies of the other victims. Aside, who had a bullet in his right thigh, pointed out that he was the sole survivor of the massacre, the victims of which had already been partially devoured by vultures. Aside's wound was infested with maggots and his right shoulder blade bore an X-shaped cut. The group returned to Paramaribo with the information. After 24 hours of negotiations with the authorities, the representative of the International Red Cross obtained permission to evacuate Mr. Aside. He was admitted to the Academic Hospital of Paramaribo on January 6, 1988, but died despite the care provided. The Military Police prevented his relatives from visiting him in the hospital. It was not until January 6, that the next of kin of the other victims were granted permission to bury them.

7. The original petitioner asserted that he spoke twice with Aside about the events and that Aside's version of what took place concurs with that obtained from the eyewitnesses and the members of the search-party.

II

13. By order of January 18, 1992, the President of the Court granted the Commission until March 31, 1992, to offer and submit the evidence at its disposal regarding reparations and costs in the instant case; he gave the Government until May 15, 1992, to present its observations on the Commission's submission. In that order, the President also summoned the parties to a public hearing on the subject, to be held at 10:00 a.m. on June 23, 1992.

. . . .

16. The Commission makes a distinction between the compensation for material damages payable to the minor children of the persons killed and that payable to their adult dependents. It proposes the establishment of a trust fund for the minor children, the basic value of which would consist of a sum proportional to the estimated projected income of the victim, after deducting what would have been the victim's own living expenses. The foregoing would be determined by applying the current or present value method. According to the Commission, this method entails the application of generally acceptable principles that are compatible with international law. As for the adult dependents, the Commission requests that a lump sum be placed in a trust fund, to become due and payable on the date of the judgment. The amount thereof would be calculated on the basis of the income that the victims had at the time of their death. Alternatively, said sum could be made available through annual payments in securities that maintain their purchasing power, to be continued until the death of the beneficiaries. The sums claimed in Surinamese Florins (hereinafter "Sf") must be adjusted to reflect the current value of that currency, since they were calculated on the basis of *"1988 monetary values".*

17. With regard to the persons who would be entitled to compensation for actual damages, the Commission explains that it is necessary to take into account the family structure of the Maroons, of which the Saramakas (the tribe to which the victims belonged) are a part. It is essentially a matriarchal[79] structure, where polygamy is common. In Suriname, marriages must be registered in order to be recognized by the State. Due to the dearth of registry offices in the interior of the country, however, that requirement is generally not met. The Commission is of the opinion that this should not affect the right to compensation of the relatives or spouses of unregistered marriages. It is argued that the care of family members is entrusted to a communal group organized along maternal lines; this is something that should be borne in mind in determining which of the relatives should be compensated. The direct, personal damages of a monetary nature that give rise to compensatory rights should be measured principally by the degree of financial dependence that existed between the claimant and the deceased. The list of aggrieved parties entitled to compensation was drawn up by the Commission partly on the basis of sworn statements by the next of kin of the victims.

---

[79] Probably a more precise anthropological term would be *matrilineal.*

18. According to the Commission, the Government would also be under the obligation to make reparation for moral damages suffered as a result of the severe psychological repercussions that the killings had on the relatives of the victims, the working men who represented their main or only source of income.

The Government's failure to react, investigate or punish these deeds is presented as an indication of the little value it places on the lives of the Maroons, a fact that has wounded their dignity and self-confidence. In six of the seven cases, the bodies of the victims were not returned for burial, the authorities gave no information as to where they might be found, they could not be identified and no death certificates were issued.

19. The Commission argues that the Saramakas also suffered direct moral damages and should be compensated. According to the Commission,

In the traditional Maroon society, a person is not only a member of his own family group, but also a member of the village community and of the tribal group. In this case, the damages suffered by the villagers due to the loss of certain members of its group must be redressed. Since the villagers, in practice, constitute a family in the broad sense of that term [. . .] they have suffered direct emotional damages as a result of the violations of the Convention.

The deeds for which the Government accepted responsibility appear to have caused damages to the Saramaka tribe, aggravated by the Government's subsequent actions in not recognizing *"the rights of the Bushnegroes."* In the Commission's opinion, a conflictive relationship appears to have existed between the Government and the Saramaka tribe and the killings occurred as a consequence of that situation.

20. The Commission states that the families of the victims demand that certain non-pecuniary provisions be made. For example, they ask that the President of Suriname apologize publicly for the killings; that the chiefs of the Saramaka tribe be invited to come before the Congress of Suriname to receive an apology; and, that the Government publish the operative part of this judgment. They also request the Government to exhume the bodies of the six victims and return them to their respective families; to name a park, square or street in a prominent section of Paramaribo after the Saramaka tribe; and, to investigate the murders committed and punish the guilty parties.

21. The Commission demands that the Government pay the expenses and costs incurred by the families of the victims in asserting their rights before the courts of Suriname, the Commission, and the Court.

. . . .

28. Suriname accepts the compensation for moral damages and relies on the precedents established in the Velásquez Rodríguez and Godínez Cruz cases, where such compensation was granted after the psychological damages of the family members of the victims had been substantiated by expert medical testimony (*Velásquez Rodríguez Case, Compensatory Damages, Judgment of July 21, 1989, (Art. 63(1) American Convention on Human Rights*). Series C No. 7, para. 51; *Godínez Cruz Case, Compensatory Damages, supra* 27, para. 49). According to the Government, this was not done in the instant case, no evidence having been produced on the subject.

29. Suriname objects to the Commission's request to compensate the Saramaka tribe for moral damages because this claim was not presented during the proceedings on the merits.

. . . .

31. As for the non-pecuniary reparations requested by the Commission, the Government believes that the acceptance of its responsibility, made public in the Court's judgment of December 4, 1991, is a significant and important form of reparation and moral satisfaction for the families of the victims and the Saramaka tribe.

. . . .

IV

39. In view of the fact that more detailed information was required in order to be able to fix the amount of the compensation and costs, the President, after consulting with the Permanent Commission, on September 24, 1992, decided to have the Court avail itself of the services of Mr. Christopher Healy and Ms. Merina Eduards as experts. By order of March 16, 1993, the Court decided to *"at the appropriate time make available to the parties the information supplied by the experts in this case".* The Court also requested clarifications and additional information of the parties.

. . . .

VI

42. In the instant case, Suriname has accepted its responsibility for the events described in the Commission's memorial. Consequently, as the Court stated in its judgment of December 4, 1991, *"the dispute relating to the facts giving rise to the instant case has now been concluded"* (*Aloeboetoe et al. Case, supra* introductory paragraph, para. 23). This means that the facts presented in the memorial of the Commission dated August 27, 1990, are deemed to be true. Nevertheless, there is disagreement between the parties as to other facts which relate to the reparations and their scope. The dispute over these matters will be decided by the Court in the instant judgment.

. . . .

VII

45. Having determined that the obligation to make reparation falls under international law and is governed by it, the Court considers it advisable to carefully analyze the scope of that compensation.

46. Article 63(1) of the Convention makes a distinction between the behavior that must be followed by the State responsible for the violation from the moment that the Court passes judgment and the consequences of that same State's attitude in the past, that is, while the violation was in process. As regards the future, Article 63(1) provides that the injured party shall be ensured the enjoyment of the right or freedom that was violated. As for the past, the provision in question empowers the Court to impose reparations for the consequences of the violation and a fair compensation.

In matters involving violations of the right to life, as in the instant case, reparation must of necessity be in the form of pecuniary compensation, given the nature of the right violated (*Velásquez Rodríguez Case, Judgment of July 29, 1988*, Series C

No. 4, para. 189; *Godínez Cruz Case, Judgment of January 20, 1989*, Series C No. 5, para. 199).

47. The Commission interprets Article 63(1) of the Convention as instituting the obligation to reestablish the *statu quo ante*. In another part of its brief, the Commission refers to *in integrum restitutio*, which it seems to equate to the reestablishment of the *statu quo ante*. Regardless of the terms employed, the Commission affirms that the compensation to be paid by Suriname shall be in an amount sufficient to remedy all the consequences of the violations that took place.

48. Before analyzing these rules in their legal context, it is important to reflect on human actions in general and how these occur in practice.

Every human act produces diverse consequences, some proximate and others remote. An old adage puts it as follows: *causa causæ est causa causati*. Imagine the effect of a stone cast into a lake; it will cause concentric circles to ripple over the water, moving further and further away and becoming ever more imperceptible. Thus it is that all human actions cause remote and distant effects.

To compel the perpetrator of an illicit act to erase all the consequences produced by his action is completely impossible, since that action caused effects that multiplied to a degree that cannot be measured.

49. For a long time, the law has addressed the subject of how human actions occur in practice, what their effects are and what responsibilities they give rise to. On the international plane, the arbitral award in the case of "Alabama" already dealt with this question (Moore, *History and Digest of International Arbitrations to which the United States has been a Party*, Washington, D.C., 1898, vol. I, pp. 653–659).

The solution provided by law in this regard consists of demanding that the responsible party make reparation for the immediate effects of such unlawful acts, but only to the degree that has been legally recognized. As for the various forms and modalities of effecting such reparation, on the other hand, the rule of *in integrum restitutio* refers to one way in which the effect of an international unlawful act may be redressed, but it is not the only way in which it must be redressed, for in certain cases such reparation may not be possible, sufficient or appropriate (cf. *Factory at Chorzów*, merits, *supra* 43, p. 48). The Court holds that this is the interpretation that must be given to Article 63(1) of the American Convention.

. . . .

IX

54. The damages suffered by the victims up to the time of their death entitle them to compensation. That right to compensation is transmitted to their heirs by succession.

The damages payable for causing loss of life represent an inherent right that belongs to the injured parties. It is for this reason that national jurisprudence generally accepts that the right to apply for compensation for the death of a person passes to the survivors affected by that death. In that jurisprudence a distinction is made between successors and injured third parties. With respect to the former, it is assumed that the death of the victim has caused them actual and moral damages and the burden of proof is on the other party to show that such damages do not exist.

Claimants who are not successors, however, must provide specific proof justifying their right to damages, as explained below (cf. *infra*, para. 68).

55. In the instant case, there is some difference of opinion between the parties as to who the successors of the victims are. The Commission urges that this decision be made with reference to the customs of the Saramaka tribe, whereas Suriname requests that its civil law be applied.

The Court earlier stated that the obligation to make reparation provided in Article 63(1) of the American Convention is governed by international law, which also applies to the determination of the manner of compensation and the beneficiaries thereof. Nevertheless, it is useful to refer to the national family law in force, for certain aspects of it may be relevant.

56. The Saramakas are a tribe that lives in Surinamese territory and was formed by African slaves fleeing from their Dutch owners. The Commission's brief affirms that the Saramakas enjoy internal autonomy by virtue of a treaty dated September 19, 1762, which granted them permission to be governed by their own laws. It also states that these people *"acquired their rights on the basis of a treaty entered into with the Netherlands, which recognizes, among other things, the local authority of the Saramaka (sic) over their own territory"*. The text of the treaty is attached to the brief in question, which adds that *"the obligations of the treaty are applicable, by succession, to the state (sic) of Suriname"*.

57. The Court does not deem it necessary to investigate whether or not that agreement is an international treaty. Suffice it to say that even if that were the case, the treaty would today be null and void because it contradicts the norms of *jus cogens superveniens*. In point of fact, under that treaty the Saramakas undertake to, among other things, capture any slaves that have deserted, take them prisoner and return them to the Governor of Suriname, who will pay from 10 to 50 florins per slave, depending on the distance of the place where they were apprehended. Another article empowers the Saramakas to sell to the Dutch any other prisoners they might take, as slaves. No treaty of that nature may be invoked before an international human rights tribunal.

58. The Commission has pointed out that it does not seek to portray the Saramakas as a community that currently enjoys international juridical status; rather, the autonomy it claims for the tribe is one governed by domestic public law.

The Court does not deem it necessary to determine whether the Saramakas enjoy legislative and jurisdictional autonomy within the region they occupy. The only question of importance here is whether the laws of Suriname in the area of family law apply to the Saramaka tribe. On this issue, the evidence offered leads to the conclusion that Surinamese family law is not effective insofar as the Saramakas are concerned. The members of the tribe are unaware of it and adhere to their own rules. The State for its part does not provide the facilities necessary for the registration of births, marriages, and deaths, an essential requirement for the enforcement of Surinamese law. Furthermore, the Saramakas do not bring the conflicts that arise over such matters before the State's tribunals, whose role in these areas is practically non-existent with respect to the Saramakas. It should be pointed out that, in the instant case, Suriname recognized the existence of a Saramaka customary law.

The only evidence produced to the contrary is the statement made by Mr. Ramón de Freitas. However, the manner in which that witness testified, his attitude during the hearing and the personality he revealed led the Court to develop an opinion of the witness that persuaded it to reject his testimony.

59. The Commission has produced information on the social structure of the Saramakas indicating that the tribe displays a strongly matriarchal familial configuration where polygamy occurs frequently. The principal group of relatives appears to be the "bêê", composed of all the descendants of one single woman. This group assumes responsibility for the actions of any of its members who, in theory, are each in turn responsible to the group as a whole. This means that the compensation payable to one person would be given to the "bêê", whose representative would distribute it among its members.

60. The Commission also requests compensation for the injured parties and the distribution of such compensation among them. On examining the Commission's brief, it is evident that the identification of the beneficiaries of such compensation has not been carried out in accordance with Saramaka custom, at least not as the Commission has described it before the Court. It is impossible to determine what legal norm the Commission applied for this purpose. It would appear that the Commission simply took a pragmatic approach.

Likewise, on the matter of the amount of compensation and its distribution, the Commission's brief asserts that it resorted to an *"equilibrium system"* which took the following factors into account: the age of the victim, his actual and potential income, the number of his dependents and the customs and petitions of the Bushnegroes.

61. The I.L.O. Convention N° 169 concerning Indigenous and Tribal Peoples in Independent Countries (1989) has not been accepted by Suriname. Furthermore, under international law there is no conventional or customary rule that would indicate who the successors of a person are. Consequently, the Court has no alternative but to apply general principles of law (Art. 38(1)(c) of the Statute of the International Court of Justice).

62. It is a norm common to most legal systems that a person's successors are his or her children. It is also generally accepted that the spouse has a share in the assets acquired during a marriage; some legal systems also grant the spouse inheritance rights along with the children. If there is no spouse or children, private common law recognizes the ascendants as heirs. It is the Court's opinion that these rules, generally accepted by the community of nations, should be applied in the instant case, in order to determine the victims' successors for purposes of compensation.

These general legal principles refer to "children," "spouse," and "ascendants." Such terms shall be interpreted according to local law. As already stated, here local law is not Surinamese law, for the latter is not effective in the region insofar as family law is concerned. It is necessary, then, to take Saramaka custom into account. That custom will be the basis for the interpretation of those terms, to the degree that it does not contradict the American Convention. Hence, in referring to "ascendants," the Court shall make no distinction as to sex, even if that might be contrary to Saramaka custom.

63. It has proved extremely difficult to identify the children, spouses, and, in some cases, the ascendants of the victims in this case. These are all members of a tribe that lives in the jungle, in the interior of Suriname, and speaks only its own native tongue. Marriages and births have in many cases not been registered. In those cases where they have, sufficient data have not been provided to fully document the relationship between persons. The matter of identification becomes even more complex in a community which practices polygamy.

64. In its observations, Suriname has presented a general critique of the Commission's brief as regards the evidence it presents. The Government asserts the following: *"[. . .] we need to know, based on rational and certainly verifiable data, specifics on all the victims, insofar as the family members left unprotected are concerned [. . .]".*

It is true that a person's identity must, as a general rule, be proved by means of relevant documentation. However, the situation in which the Saramakas find themselves is due in great measure to the fact that the State does not provide sufficient registry offices in the region; consequently, it is unable to issue documentation to all its inhabitants on the basis of the data contained therein. Suriname cannot, therefore, demand proof of the relationship and identity of persons through means that are not available to all of its inhabitants in that region. In addition, Suriname has not here offered to make up for its inaction by providing additional proof as to the identity and relationship of the victims and their successors.

In order to clarify the information available on the successors, the Court requested the Commission to provide complementary data about them. Considering the circumstances surrounding the instant case, the Court believes that the evidence supplied is credible and can be admitted.

65. The information provided by the Commission nevertheless contains some discrepancies between the names of the victims and the way these appeared in the petition . . . .

66. In accordance with the foregoing, it has been possible to establish a list of the successors of the victims. That list reflects the situation at the time of the killings. Consequently, it includes persons who have since died and excludes those spouses who at the time were divorced from the victims. [list omitted]

X

67. The obligation to make reparation for damages caused is sometimes, and within the limits imposed by the legal system, extended to cover persons who, though not successors of the victims, have suffered some consequence of the unlawful act. This issue has been the subject of numerous judgments by domestic courts. Case law nevertheless establishes certain conditions that must be met for a claim of compensatory damages filed by a third party to be admitted.

68. First, the payment sought must be based on payments actually made by the victim to the claimant, regardless of whether or not they constituted a legal obligation to pay support. Such payments cannot be simply a series of sporadic contributions; they must be regular, periodic payments either in cash, in kind, or in services. What is important here is the effectiveness and regularity of the contributions.

Second, the nature of the relationship between the victim and the claimant should be such that it provides some basis for the assumption that the payments would have continued had the victim not been killed.

Lastly, the claimant must have experienced a financial need that was periodically met by the contributions made by the victim. This does not necessarily mean that the person should be indigent, but only that it be somebody for whom the payment represented a benefit that, had it not been for the victim's attitude, it would not have been able to obtain on his or her own.

69. The Commission has submitted a list of 25 persons who, while not successors of the victims, claim compensatory damages as their dependents. According to the Commission, they are persons who received financial support from the victims, whether in cash, in kind, or through contributions of personal work.

According to the Commission's brief, the persons listed are relatives of some of the victims, the only exception being a former teacher of one of them.

The Commission presents this information in its brief on reparations and includes a fact sheet on each of the victims. It also adds an affidavit from the father or the mother of each victim. No further proof is offered with regard to the dependency status of the 25 persons, nor the amounts, regularity, effectiveness, or other characteristics of the contributions which the victims purportedly made to those persons.

70. The Commission has repeatedly invoked in its submissions the precedent of the "Lusitania", a case that was resolved by a mixed Commission composed of the United States and Germany. As regards the claims of the dependents, however, that Commission held that compensation was only in order if the effectiveness and regularity of the contributions made by the victim had been proved (cf. the cases of *Henry W. Williamson and others* and *Ellen Williamson Hodges, administratrix of the estate of Charles Francis Williamson*, February 21, 1924, Reports of International Arbitral Awards, vol. VII, pp. 256 and 257; and, *Henry Groves and Joseph Groves*, February 21, 1924, Reports of International Arbitral Awards, vol. VII, pp. 257–259).

71. The Court has earlier made a distinction between the reparations due to the successors and that owed to claimants or dependents. The Court will grant the former the reparations requested, because of the presumption that the death of the victims caused them damages. The burden of proof is therefore on the other party to demonstrate the contrary. As far as the other claimants or dependents are concerned, however, the *onus probandi* is on the Commission. And the Commission has not, in the opinion of the Court, provided the necessary proof to demonstrate that the conditions have been met.

72. The Court is aware of the difficulties presented by the instant case: the facts involve a community that lives in the jungle, whose members are practically illiterate and do not utilize written documents. Nevertheless, other evidence could have been produced.

73. In view of the foregoing, the Court hereby rejects the claim of compensation for actual damages presented by the dependents.

XI

74. The Commission also seeks compensation for moral damages suffered by persons who, while not successors of the victims, were their dependents.

75. The Court is of the opinion that, as in the case of the reparations for actual damages sought by the dependents, moral damages must in general be proved. The Court considers that in the instant case sufficient proof has not been produced to demonstrate the damages to the dependents.

76. Listed among the so-called dependents of the victims are their parents. The parents of Mikuwendje Aloeboetoe and Asipee Adame have already been declared their successors and will obtain compensation for moral damages. However, the parents of the other five victims are not in the same situation. Nevertheless, in this particular case, it can be presumed that the parents have suffered morally as a result of the cruel death of their offspring, for it is essentially human for all persons to feel pain at the torment of their child.

77. For these reasons, the Court deems it only appropriate that those victims' parents who have not been declared successors also participate in the distribution of the compensation for moral damages.

XII

79. The Court considers it appropriate for the next of kin of the victims to be reimbursed for expenses incurred in obtaining information about them after they were killed and in searching for their bodies and taking up matters with the Surinamese authorities. In the specific case of victims Daison and Deede-Manoe Aloeboetoe, the Commission claims equal sums to cover expenses relating to each of them. These victims were brothers. It would seem reasonable to conclude, therefore, that the next of kin took the same steps for both at one and the same time and incurred in a single outlay. The Court consequently finds it appropriate to approve a single reimbursement for the two victims.

In its brief, the Commission indicates that in all cases the expenditures were made by the mother of each victim. For lack of proof to the contrary, the reimbursement shall be paid to these persons.

80. The Commission's brief states that the victims were stripped of some of their assets and belongings at the time of their detention. However, it does not present a claim in this regard and the Court will therefore refrain from analyzing this issue.

XIII

81. The Commission asks the Court to order Suriname to pay the Saramaka tribe compensation for moral damages and to make certain, non-pecuniary reparations.

Suriname objects to this demand on procedural grounds and maintains that the Commission presented this claim during the stage fixed for the determination of compensation. It had not mentioned this issue in its memorial of April 1, 1991.

The Court does not consider the Government's argument to be well-founded, for in proceedings before an international court a party may modify its application, provided that the other party has the procedural opportunity to state its views on the subject (cf. *Factory at Chorzów*, merits, *supra* 43, p. 7; *Neuvième rapport annuel de la Cour permanente de Justice internationale*, P.C.I.J., Series E, No. 9, p. 163).

82. In its brief, and in some of the evidence presented by the Commission, it is implied that the killings were racially motivated and committed in the context of ongoing conflicts that apparently existed between the Government and the Saramaka tribe.

In the petition dated January 15, 1988, presented to the Commission, it is alleged that: *"More than 20 unarmed Bushnegroes were severely beaten and tortured in Atjoni. All were male and they were unarmed, but the soldiers suspected that they were members of the Jungle Commando".*

The Commission's memorial of April 1, 1991, took up this petition and included it as an integral part of the document. Throughout the proceedings, the statement that the soldiers acted on suspicion that the Saramakas were members of the Jungle Commando was neither amended nor challenged. Consequently, the origin of the events as described in the memorial of April 1, 1991, lies not in some racial issue but, rather, in a subversive situation that prevailed at the time. Although a certain passage of the brief dated March 31, 1992, and the testimony of an expert both refer to the conflicting relationship that appears to have existed between the Government and the Saramakas, in the instant case it has not been proved that the racial factor was a motive for the killings of December 31, 1987. It is true that the victims of the killings all belonged to the Saramaka tribe, but this circumstance of itself does not lead to the conclusion that there was a racial element to the crime.

83. In its brief, the Commission explains that, in traditional Maroon society, a person is a member not only of his or her own family group, but also of his or her own village community and tribal group. According to the Commission, the villagers make up a family in the broad sense. This is why damages caused to one of its members also represent damages to the community, which would have to be indemnified.

As for the argument linking the claim for moral damages to the unique social structure of the Saramakas who were generally harmed by the killings, the Court believes that all persons, in addition to being members of their own families and citizens of a State, also generally belong to intermediate communities. In practice, the obligation to pay moral compensation does not extend to such communities, nor to the State in which the victim participated; these are redressed by the enforcement of the system of laws. If in some exceptional case such compensation has ever been granted, it would have been to a community that suffered direct damages.

84. According to the Commission, the third ground for payment of moral damages to the Saramakas involves the rights that the tribe apparently have over the territory they occupy and the violation of such rights by the Army of Suriname when it entered that territory. The Commission has stated that the autonomy acquired by the Saramakas, while originating in a treaty, at the present time is only governed by domestic public law, since no form of international status is sought for the tribe (cf. *supra*, para. 58). The Commission, then, is basing the right to moral compensation on the alleged violation of a domestic legal norm regarding territorial autonomy.

At these proceedings, the Commission has only presented the 1762 treaty. The Court has already expressed its opinion of this so-called international treaty (cf. *su-*

pra, para. 57). No other provision of domestic law, either written or customary, has been relied upon to establish the autonomy of the Saramakas.

The Court believes that the racial motive put forward by the Commission has not been duly proved and finds the argument of the unique social structure of the Saramaka tribe to be without merit. The assumption that a domestic rule on territorial jurisdiction was transgressed in order to violate the right to life does not of itself establish the right to moral damages claimed on behalf of the tribe. The Saramakas could raise this alleged breach of public domestic law before the competent jurisdiction; however, they may not present it as a factor that justifies the payment of moral damages to the whole tribe.

XIV

85. In its judgments of July 21, 1989, in the *Velásquez Rodríguez* and *Godínez Cruz* cases, the Court presented its criteria regarding the calculation of the amounts payable in compensation (*Velásquez Rodríguez Case, Compensatory Damages, supra* 28, para. 40 et seq.; and, *Godínez Cruz Case, Compensatory Damages, supra* 27, para. 38 *et seq.*).

In those decisions, the Court held that when the victim has died and the beneficiaries of the compensation are his heirs, the family members have a current or future possibility of working or receiving income on their own. The children, who should be guaranteed an education until they reach a certain age, will be able to work thereafter. In the Court's opinion, *"[i]t is not correct, then, in these cases, to adhere to rigid criteria [. . .] but rather to arrive at a prudent estimate of the damages, given the circumstances of each case"* (*ibid.*, para. 48; *ibid.*, para. 46).

86. As for the assessment of compensation for moral damages, the Court, in its judgments of July 21, 1989, stated that *"indemnification must be based upon the principles of equity "* (*ibid.*, para. 27; *ibid.*, para. 25).

87. In the instant case, the Court has followed the aforementioned precedents. In the matter of compensation for loss of earnings, it has arrived at "a prudent estimate of the damages." As for the moral damages, the Court based these on "principles of equity."

The phrases "prudent estimate of the damages" and "principles of equity" do not mean that the Court has discretion in setting the amounts of compensation. On this issue, the Court has strictly adhered to the methods ordinarily used in the case law and has acted in prudent and reasonable fashion by ordering *in situ* verification by its Deputy Secretary of the figures that served as the basis for its calculations.

. . . .

96. The compensation fixed for the victims' heirs includes an amount that will enable the minor children to continue their education until they reach a certain age. Nevertheless, these goals will not be met merely by granting compensatory damages; it is also essential that the children be offered a school where they can receive adequate education and basic medical attention. At the present time, this is not available in several of the Saramaka villages.

Most of the children of the victims live in Gujaba, where the school and the medical dispensary have both been shut down. The Court believes that, as part of the compensation due, Suriname is under the obligation to reopen the school at Gujaba and staff it with teaching and administrative personnel to enable it to function on a permanent basis as of 1994. In addition, the necessary steps shall be taken for the medical dispensary already in place there to be made operational and reopen that same year.

XV

97. As regards the distribution of the amounts fixed for the various types of compensation, the Court considers that it would be fair to apply the following criteria:

a. Of the reparations for material damages caused to each victim, one third is assigned to their wives. If there is more than one wife, this amount shall be divided among them in equal parts. Two thirds shall go to the children, who shall also divide their portion equally among themselves if there is more than one child.

b. The reparations for moral damages caused to each victim shall be divided as follows: one half is allocated to the children, one quarter to the wives and the remaining quarter to the parents. If there is more than one beneficiary in any of these categories, the amount shall be divided among them in equal parts.

c. The expenses shall be reimbursed to the person who incurred them, as indicated in the brief of the Commission.

XVI

99. In order to comply with the monetary compensation fixed by this judgment, the Government shall deposit the sum of US$453,102 (four hundred fifty-three thousand, one hundred two dollars) before April 1, 1994, in the Surinaamse Trust-maatschappij N.V. (Suritrust), Gravenstraat 32, in the city of Paramaribo.

The Government may also fulfill this obligation by depositing the equivalent amount in Dutch Florins. The rate of exchange used to determine the equivalent value shall be the selling rate for the United States Dollar and the Dutch Florin quoted on the New York market on the day before the date of payment.

100. With the funds received, Suritrust shall set up trust funds in dollars for the beneficiaries listed, under the most favorable conditions consistent with banking practice. Any deceased beneficiaries shall be replaced by their heirs.

Two trust funds shall be established, one on behalf of the minor children and the other on behalf of the adult beneficiaries.

A Foundation (hereinafter "the Foundation"), described in paragraphs 103 *et seq.* of this judgment, shall serve as trustee.

101. The trust fund for the minor children shall be set up with the compensation payable to all those unmarried beneficiaries who have still not reached the age of 21.

This trust fund shall continue to operate until such time as the last of the beneficiaries becomes of age or marries. As each of the minor beneficiaries meets those conditions, their contributions shall become subject to the provisions governing the trust fund for the adult beneficiaries.

102. The adult beneficiaries may withdraw up to 25% (twenty-five percent) of the sum due to them at the time that the Government of Suriname makes the deposit. The trust fund for the adults shall be set up with the remaining funds. The duration

of the trust fund shall be a minimum of three and a maximum of 17 years; semi-annual withdrawals shall be permitted. The Foundation may set up a different system in special circumstances.

XVII

103. The Court hereby orders the creation of a Foundation, with a view to providing the beneficiaries with the opportunity of obtaining the best returns for the sums received in reparation. The Foundation, a non-profit organization, shall be established in the city of Paramaribo, the capital of Suriname, and shall be composed of the following persons, who have already accepted their appointments and shall carry out their functions *ad honorem* [list omitted].

104. The Court expresses its appreciation to the persons who have agreed to participate in the Foundation, as a means of contributing to a true and effective protection of human rights in the Americas.

105. At a plenary meeting, the members of the Foundation shall, with the collaboration of the Executive Secretariat of the Court, define their organization, statutes and by-laws, as well as the operational structure of the trust funds. The Foundation shall transmit these documents to the Court after final approval.

The role of the Foundation shall be to act as trustee of the funds deposited in Suritrust and to advise the beneficiaries as to the allocation of the reparations received or of the income they obtain from the trust funds.

106. The Foundation shall provide advice to the beneficiaries. Although the children of the victims are among the principal beneficiaries, this fact does not release their mothers or the guardians in whose charge they may be from the obligation of providing them with assistance, food, clothing and education free of charge. The Foundation shall try to ensure that the compensation received by the minor children of the victims be used to cover subsequent study expenses, or else to create a small capital when they begin to work or get married, and that it only be used for ordinary expenses when grave problems of health or family finances require it.

107. For the operating expenses of the Foundation, the Government of Suriname shall, within 30 days of its establishment, make a one-time contribution in the amount of US$4,000 (four thousand dollars) or its equivalent in local currency at the selling rate of exchange in force on the free market at the time of such payment.

108. Suriname shall not be permitted to restrict or tax the activities of the Foundation or the operation of the trust funds beyond current levels, nor shall it modify any conditions currently in force nor interfere in the Foundation's decisions, except in ways that would be favorable to it.

———

Note on recent reparations practice. Like the government in the *Aloeboetoe Case*, other governments have come before the Inter-American Court and conceded the merits of the case. Indeed, this seems to be a growing practice. In such instances, the governments often ask that the case be dismissed as without purpose, based on their admission of wrong-doing and apologies to the victims.

Thus far, the Court has not acceded to any request of this type, instead finding that it is necessary to address the merits and reparations, including measures to guarantee non-repetition. See: *Case of Gioburu et al.*, judgment of Sept. 22, 2006, 153 Inter-Am.Ct.H.R. (Ser. C); *Case of the 'Mapiripan Massacre',* judgment of Sept. 15, 2005, 134 Inter-Am.Ct.H.R. (Ser. C); *Case of Molina-Theissen*, judgment of May 4, 2004, 106 Inter-Am. Ct. H.R. (Ser. C).

For example, the case of *La Cantuta v. Peru*, judgment of Nov. 29, 2006, 162 Inter-Am.Ct.H.R. (Ser. C), alleged multiple violations of the Convention stemming from the kidnapping, disappearance and summary execution by members of the Peruvian army of students from a national university. The state acknowledged its international responsibility before the Commission and the Court and expressed regret to the next of kin, but disagreed with regard to the legal consequences that should follow. The Court said it would determine the consequences "by exercising its inherent powers of international judicial protection of human rights." (para. 49)

In this respect, the Court considerd that a judgment fully adjudicating the facts and the merits, as well as the consequences "constitutes a way of contributing to the preservation of the historical memory, to the redress of the damage inflicted upon the next of kin of the victims, and, moreover, also contributes to avoid the repetition of similar events." (para. 57)

As to reparations, the Court reiterated that international law imposes a duty to adequately redress any breach of an international obligation beginning with restitution if practicable. "Reparations are measures aimed at removing the effects of the violations. Their nature and amount are dependent upon the specifics of the violation and the damage inflicted at both the pencuary and non-pecuniary levels. These measures may neither enrich nor impoverish the victim or the victim's beneficiaries, and they must bear proportion to the breaches declared as such in the judgment." (Para. 202) The Court reviewed and found inadequate the domestic reparations program, ordered payment of damages and other forms of reparations, including investigation, prosecution and punishment of the individuals responsible, search and burial of the remains of the disappeared, pubic acknowledgement of liability by high-ranking authorities of the state, inclusion of the names of the victims in a memorial, publication of the judgment, medical and psuchological treatment for the next of kin, and training in human rights for members of the intelligence services, the armed forces and the national police.

D. The African System

D. Shelton, *Remedies in International Human Rights Law* (2nd ed. 2004), pp. 226.

As an organ of the youngest human rights system, the African Commission is still exploring the scope of its powers. By the end of its first decade, the Commission had decided over 100 cases, recognizing that the objective of the process is to remedy the prejudice complained of. It has made specific recommendations on remedies in several cases, including demanding the release of persons wrongfully imprisoned and repeal of laws found to be in violation of the Charter. Only one applicant among the cases decided on the merits to date has submitted a request for damages. That case was returned to the domestic legal system for an assessment of the quantum.

The Commission has not discussed the scope of its remedial powers, but in a case against Nigeria, it indicated it would follow up to ensure state compliance with its recommendations. Communication 87/93186 was brought on behalf of seven men sentenced to death under the Nigerian Civil Disturbances (Special Tribunal) Decree No. 2 of 1987. This decree provided no judicial appeal against decisions of the special tribunals and prohibited Nigerian courts from reviewing any aspect of the operation of the special tribunals, in violation of the right to appeal to competent national organs against acts violating fundamental rights (Article 7(1)(a) of the African Charter). The communication also complained that the conduct of the trials before the special tribunals, including harassment and deprivation of defence counsel, violated the right to be defended by counsel of one's choice (Article 7(1)(c)). More generally, applicants complained that the special tribunals, composed of members of the armed forces and police in addition to judges, violated the right to be tried by an impartial tribunal (Article 7(1)(d)). The Commission found for the applicants in regard to all the allegations and recommended that the Government of Nigeria free the complainants. The Commission decided to bring the file to Nigeria during a planned mission in order to ensure that the violations had been repaired. The Commission's decisions thus far give little indication of how broadly or narrowly it views its powers. On the one hand, it has issued recommendations of specific conduct which appear close to injunctive orders. On the other hand, the Commission unfortunately declined to address the first request for damages submitted to it. The latter result is anomalous among international human rights tribunals and perhaps was due to the specific facts of the case. In another case, it appeared to presume that the applicant was satisfied with measures taken by a new government to remedy violations by the previous regime. . . .

[The] Protocol to the African Charter on Human and Peoples' Rights on the Establishment of an African Court on Human and Peoples' Rights . . . provides that the Commission, a complainant state or a respondent state may submit cases to the Court concerning the interpretation and the application of the African Charter, the Protocol or 'any other applicable African Human Rights instrument.' States may declare that they accept the competence of the Court to receive from individuals and non-governmental organizations with observer status, cases that are urgent and those alleging serious, systematic or massive violations of human rights. Article 26(1), the remedies provision in the draft, states that '[i]f the Court finds that there has been a violation of a human or people's right, it shall make appropriate orders to remedy the violation, including the payment of fair compensation or reparation.' This provision is broader than all the current mandates to afford remedies to victim of human rights abuse.

For Commission decisions calling for cessation of the breach and restoration of the liberty of wrongfully held detainees, see: *Constitutional Rights Project v. Nigeria* Comm. No. 60/91 (1996), Comm. No. 87/93 (1996) and *Center for Free Speech v. Nigeria*, Comm. 206/97, 13th Annual Activity Report of the African Commission 1999–2000 (calling for the release of detainees). On the African Commission's practice generally, see Gino J. Naldi, *Reparations in the Practice of the African Commission on Human and Peoples' Rights*, 14 LEIDEN J. INT'L L. 681 (2001).

Final Questions and Comments

1. The American Convention does not establish any specific mechanism to supervise the enforcement of the Court's judgments, but Article 65 of the Convention is relevant. It reads:

> To each regular session of the General Assembly of the Organization of American States the Court shall submit, for the Assembly's consideration, a report on its work during the previous year. It shall specify, in particular, the cases in which a state has not complied with its judgments, making any pertinent recommendations.

The provision requiring the Court to inform the OAS General Assembly of situations involving non-compliance permits the Assembly to discuss the matter and to take whatever political measures it deems appropriate. Condemnatory OAS resolutions, though not legally binding, do carry considerable political weight and can generate pressure from public opinion. The practice of the Court has changed over time. For several years the Government of Honduras paid only part of the compensation ordered by the Court in its judgments in the *Velásquez Rodriguez* and *Godinez Cruz* cases. The Court's annual reports to the OAS General Assembly for those years reveal that the Court did not bring Honduras's non-compliance formally to the Assembly's attention. The matter was finally resolved in February 1995 when the Honduran Government during the presidency of Carlos Roberto Reina, a former President of the Court, agreed to pay the amounts due in an official ceremony held at the seat of the OAS in Washington. For a recent decision of the Court rendered in response to Peru's failure to comply with its judgment ordering reparations for various violations of the Convention, *see Loayza Tamayo Case* (Compliance with Judgment), Order of November 17, 1999, I-A. Court H.R. Series C: Decisions and Judgments, No. 60 (2000). Note that some OAS Member States—notably Guatemala and Colombia—have legislation on their books that provide for the domestic enforcement of money judgments rendered against them by international human rights institutions whose jurisdiction these states have accepted. It is unclear how and to what extent these laws have been given effect.

2. On reparations in the Inter-American system, *see generally* J. Pasqualucci, *"Victim Reparations in the Inter-American Human Rights System: A Critical Assessment of Current Practice and Procedure*," 18 MICH. J. INT'L L. 1 (1996); D. Shelton, *The Award of Damages by the Inter-American Court of Human Rights,* in D. Harris & S. Livingston, THE INTER-AMERICAN SYSTEM FOR THE PROTECTION OF HUMAN RIGHTS (1998); D. Shelton, REMEDIES IN INTERNATIONAL HUMAN RIGHTS LAW (1999).

3. In 2005, the Heads of State and Government of the Council of Europe decided to appoint a Group of Wise Persons to consider the issue of the long-term effectiveness of the ECHR control mechanism and to submit proposals for measures going beyond the "reform of the reform" included in Protocol 14. The group issued an interim report on May 3, 2006 and a final report on November 15, 2006. *See: Interim Report of the Group of Wise Persons to the Committee of Ministers*, Sages (2006) 05 EN Fin, and *Final Report of the Group of Wise Persons to the Committee of Ministers*, CM(2006)203, Nov. 15, 2006. Both reports considered relieving the European Court of the burden of deciding on the award of com-

pensation by returning the issue to the national courts once the European court decided the merits. On this point, the final Report said:

94. The Group considers that changes to the rules laid down in Article 41 of the Convention are necessary. . . . The proposal is based on the principle of subsidiarity and is inspired by a concern to relieve the Court . . . of tasks which could be carried out more effectively by national bodies. This would apply in particular where expert reports were needed owing to the factual complexity of a case.

95. The question does not arise where the Court . . . finds a violation of the Convention but considers that there are no grounds for awarding compensation to the victim, in particular because full reparation is possible or because the judgment finding the violation constitutes sufficient reparation in itself.

96. On the other hand, where the Court . . . holds that the victim must be awarded compensation, it is proposed that the general rule should be that the decision on the amount of compensation is referred to the state concerned. However, the Court . . . would have the power to depart from this rule and give their own decision on just satisfaction where such a decision is found to be necessary to ensure effective protection of the victim, and especially where it is a matter of particular urgency.

97. Where the decision on the amount of compensation is referred to the state, it should discharge this obligation within the time-limit set by the Court . . . .

98. It would be for the state to determine the arrangements for affording just satisfaction while complying with the following requirements:

— each state should designate a judicial body with responsibility for determining the amount of compensation and inform the Committee of Ministers of the Council of Europe of the body so designated;

— the progress of the procedure should not be hindered by unnecessary formalities or the charging of unreasonable costs or fees.

99. Lastly, the determination of the amount of compensation should be consistent with the criteria laid down in the Court's case-law and the victim would be able to apply to the Court . . . to challenge the national decision by reference to those criteria, or where a state failed to comply with the deadline set for determining the amount of compensation.

Do you believe that this proposal, if adopted, will reduce the Court's workload? Would a domestic legal system ever adopt a system of returning to a tortfeasor the determination of the damages due the victim? Is that an appropriate analogy? Further extracts from the Report of the Wise Persons are included in Chapter VII.

CHAPTER VI
RESPONDING TO WIDESPREAD VIOLATIONS

1. Introduction

Individual complaint procedures have succeeded in all three systems in clarifying the meaning of guaranteed rights and in providing redress to applicants when their rights have been violated. The procedures are not well designed, however, to prevent, document or reduce gross and systematic violations of human rights. Each system has thus developed other mechanisms or adapted its procedures to confront such situations.

Inter-state cases have proven to have some limited value in this respect in Europe. The African and Inter-American systems have each had only one inter-State case filed, and the Inter-American case was deemed inadmissible. Apart from inter-State cases, the Inter-American Commission's practice of country studies has lent itself to prevention and investigation of widespread violations. The African Commission, for its part, has begun to undertake country studies, as well as on-site investigations, negotiations, and denunciations. This chapter looks at the legal issues and mechanisms that address the most serious problems confronting regional human rights bodies. One issue to consider throughout the chapter is whether the regional systems can be effective in confronting cases of widespread violations or whether these situations should be left to the global system.

2. Modifying Procedural Rules

Afr. Comm.H.P.R., *Joined Communications 48/90 Amnesty International v. Sudan; 50/91 Comité Loosli Bachelard v. Sudan, 52/91 Lawyers Committee for Human Rights v. Sudan, 89/93 Association of Members of the Episcopal Conference of East Africa v. Sudan,* 13th Annual Activity Report (2000).

All of these communications pertain to the situation prevailing in Sudan between 1989 and 1993.

Summary of Facts:

1. Communication 48/90, submitted by Amnesty International, and Communication 50/91, submitted by Comité Loosli Bachelard, deal with the arbitrary arrests and detentions that took place following the coup of 30 July 1989 in Sudan. It is alleged therein that hundreds of prisoners were detained without trial or charge.

2. Communication 50/91 alleges that since June 1990 members of opposition groups, among them Abdal-Qadir, Mohammed Salman and Babiker Yahya, have been arrested, detained, and subjected to torture. Other detainees include lawyers, members of opposition groups and human rights activists. The allegations

are based on information from a wide variety of sources including interviews with eyewitnesses.

3. According to the plaintiff, Decree No. 2 of 1989 permits the detention of anyone "suspected of being a threat to political or economic security" under a state of emergency; the right to personal liberty and security was protected under the 1985 Transitional Constitution, Article 21, but the Constitution was suspended in 1989. Complainant further claims that the President can order the arrest of anyone without the need to give reasons for such detention. No judicial challenge of such decisions is permissible. Decree No. 2 also provides for the creation of special courts to try those arrested under the state of emergency legislation. Section 9 of the Decree ousts the jurisdiction of the ordinary courts in cases arising from its enforcement. It is further alleged that the 1990 National Security Act created a National Security Council and Bureau. Under this Act, the security forces have powers of arrest, entry and search. Persons can be detained under this Act, without access to family or lawyers for up to 72 hours, renewable for up to one month. Detention can be for up to three months if for the "maintenance of public security" and on approval of the Security Council and a magistrate. Appeal to a magistrate is permitted. In 1994 this Act was amended, enabling the National Security Council to renew a three-month order without reference to any persons. Further renewals require approval by a judge. There is no right to challenge detention under this Act and no reasons need be given for such detention.

4. The communications additionally allege that political prisoners are kept in secret detention centres known as "ghost houses". One of these was closed in 1995 and prisoners transferred to the main civil prison in Khartoum.

5. The communications also allege widespread torture and ill treatment in the prisons and "ghost houses" in Sudan. These allegations are supported by doctor's testimonies, personal accounts of alleged victims and a report by the UN Special Rapporteur. A number of individual victims are named. Additionally, it is alleged that many individuals were tortured after being arrested at army checkpoints or in military or war zones. Acts of torture include forcing detainees to lie on the floor and being soaked with cold water; confining four groups of individuals in cells 1.8 metres wide and one metre deep, deliberately flooding cells to prevent detainees from lying down, forcing individuals to face mock executions, and prohibiting them from washing. Other accounts describe burning with cigarettes and the deliberate banging of doors at frequent intervals throughout the night to prevent sleeping. Individuals were bound with rope such that circulation was cut off to parts of their bodies, beaten severely with sticks, and had battery acid poured onto open wounds.

6. The communications allege extra-judicial executions. Thousands of civilians have been killed in southern Sudan in the course of the civil war, and the government is alleged to have executed suspected members of the SPLA without trial and there has been no investigation into or prosecution for such incidents. In the course of counter-insurgency attacks civilians in the Nuba Mountains area and northern Bahr al-Ghazal have been killed when their villages were destroyed. These occurred in 1987–1989 but events are still continuing to this day.

7. In addition, detainees suspected of being supporters of the SPLA were alleged to have been arrested and then immediately executed in areas in southern Sudan.

8. Executions are also alleged to have been carried out by militia groups which are believed to have close connections with and the support of the government. No independent inquiry has been conducted into their activities nor have any persons been prosecuted in connection with such killings. These allegations are supported by evidence collected by the UN Special Rapporteur.

. . . .

12. Communication 48/90 describes how calling and organizing a strike, possession of undeclared foreign currency, illegal production of and trading in drugs can also result in the death sentence. Individuals sentenced to death were not allowed to appeal against their conviction to a high court, or permitted to have legal representation at new trials.

13. Communication 48/90 alleges that the 28 army officers executed on 24 April 1990 were allowed no legal representation. It adds that in July 1989, the Constitution of Special Tribunals Act was passed, dealing exclusively with the establishment of such tribunals. Under section 3 of that Act, the President, his deputies or senior army officers may appoint 3 military officers or "any other competent persons" as judges. All sentences were to be confirmed by the Head of State and appeal is only allowed against the death penalty or imprisonment terms of more than one year.

9. In September 1989 these special tribunals were abolished and replaced by the so-called Revolutionary Security Courts. The presiding judge and two others were to be chosen by the RCC for their competence and expertise. Appeal was to a Revolutionary Security High Court but only against sentences of death and for those of imprisonment for more than 30 years. The September Laws were required to be applied in these courts from December 1989.

10. In December 1989 the government created more special courts in which lawyers, while being permitted to consult the accused prior to trial, are not allowed to address the court. Appeal is to the Chief Justice alone, not to any higher court.

11. Communication 52/91 provides evidence that over one hundred judges have been dismissed in order to systematically dismantle the judiciary who were opposed to the formation of special courts and military tribunals.

12. Information contained in communications 48/90 and 52/91, presented by the Lawyers Committee for Human Rights, describes government efforts to undermine the independence of the judiciary and the rule of law. It is alleged, in particular, that the government established special tribunals, which are not independent. The ordinary courts are precluded from hearing cases that are of the exclusive competence of the special tribunals. It is further alleged that the right to defence before these special tribunals is restricted. The communications also indicate that people brought before these tribunals were denied the right to contest the grounds for their detention under emergency legislation.

13. Communication 89/93, submitted by the Association of Members of the Episcopal Conference of East Africa alleges oppression of Sudanese Christians and religious leaders, expulsion of all missionaries from Juba, arbitrary arrests and de-

tention of priests, the closure and destruction of Church buildings, the constant harassment of religious figures, and prevention of non-Muslims from receiving aid.

14. The people of the southern part of Sudan are predominantly Christian or of traditional beliefs, whereas the religion in the north of the country and the regime imposed by the government are Islamic. Shari'a is the national law.

15. The said communication alleges that non-Muslims are persecuted in order to ensure their conversion to Islam. Non-Muslims are prevented from preaching or building churches, and the freedom of expression of the national press is restricted. Members of Christian clergy are harassed, and there are arbitrary arrests of Christians, expulsions and denial of access to work and food aid. . . .

LAW

Admissibility:

16. Admissibility of communications under the African Charter is governed by Article 56, which sets out conditions that all communications must meet before they can be decided upon. These criteria must be applied bearing in mind the character of each communication. The case at hand is a combination of four different communications, which the Commission decided to consider together, in accordance with its jurisprudence . . . . This decision was based on the similarity of the allegations presented, on the one hand, and the human rights situation prevailing in Sudan during the period covered by these allegations of violations, on the other. The communications were submitted by NGOs and allege many overlapping and inter-related details. . . .

23. Article 56.5 of the African Charter requires, as a condition for admissibility, that communications must be:

> submitted after exhausting local remedies, if any, unless it is obvious that this procedure is unduly prolonged.

. . .

30. In applying this provision, the Commission has elaborated through its jurisprudence criteria on which to base its conviction as to the exhaustion of internal remedies, if any. The Commission has drawn a distinction between cases in which the complaint deals with violations against victims identified or named and those cases of serious and massive violations in which it may be impossible for the complainants to identify all the victims.

31. In a case of violations against identified victims, the Commission demands the exhaustion of all internal remedies, if any, if they are of a judicial nature, are effective and are not subordinated to the discretionary power of public authorities. The Commission is of the view that this provision must be applied concomitantly with Article 7, which establishes and protects the right to fair trial.

32. The Commission has stated that one of the justifications for this requirement is that a government should be aware of a human rights violation in order to have the chance to remedy such violation, thus protecting its reputation which would inevitably be tarnished by being called to plead its case before an international body. This condition also precludes the African Commission from becoming a tribunal

of first instance, a function that it cannot, either as a legal or practical matter, fulfill (See ACHPR/25/89: 53–54).

33. In the cases under consideration, the government of Sudan has not been unaware of the serious human rights situation existing in that country. For nearly a decade the domestic situation has focused national and international attention on Sudan. Many of the alleged violations are directly connected to the new national laws in force in the country in the period covered by these communications. Even where no domestic legal action has been brought by the alleged victims, the Government has been sufficiently aware to the extent that it can be presumed to know the situation prevailing within its own territory as well as the content of its international obligations.

34. Furthermore, the Commission is of the view that the internal remedies that could have been available to the complainants do not fulfill its conditions or are simply non-existent. In these communications, section 9 of decree no. 2, promulgated in 1989, suspends the jurisdiction of the regular courts in favor of the special tribunals as regards any action undertaken in application of the said decree. In addition, it outlaws any legal action taken against any action undertaken in application of the same decree. Further, the remedies provided for under the 1990 national security law do not conform to the demands of protection of the right to a good administration of justice, to the extent that the appeals provided for in this law cannot be brought before a judge. It is evident that this appeal procedure, as provided for in the 1990 national security law, cannot be considered as fulfilling the criteria of effectiveness.

35. The 1994 law, which repeals and replaces that of 1990, brings up the principle of the inexistence of remedies, as well as the retroactivity of its provisions. Indeed, under the 1990 law, accused persons could always file an appeal before a judge. This new law stipulates that "no legal action, no appeal is provided for against any decision issued under this law". This manifestly makes the procedure less protective of the accused and is tantamount to inexistence of appeal procedure.

36. The Commission also holds the view that the appeal before the High Court, as provided for, against verdicts passed by the revolutionary security courts (which replaced the special tribunals) does not fulfil the demands of effectiveness and existence contained in the African Charter. Indeed, appeals to this court are only permissible in the event of a death penalty or prison terms over thirty years. This implies that no other sentence can be appealed before the High Court, which consequently renders the appeal procedure inexistent for the complainants.

37. In the Commission's view, the right to appeal, being a general and non-derogable principle of international law must, where it exists, satisfy the conditions of effectiveness. An effective appeal is one that, subsequent to the hearing by the competent tribunal of first instance, may reasonably lead to a reconsideration of the case by a superior jurisdiction, which requires that the latter should, in this regard, provide all necessary guarantees of good administration of justice.

38. In cases of serious and massive, the Commission reads Article 56.5 in the light of its duty to protect human and peoples' rights as provided for by the Charter. Consequently, the Commission does not hold the requirement of exhaustion of lo-

cal remedies to apply literally, especially in cases where it is "impractical or undesirable" for the complainants or victims to seize the domestic courts.

39. The seriousness of the human rights situation in Sudan and the great numbers of people involved render such remedies unavailable in fact, or, in the words of the Charter, their procedure would probably be "unduly prolonged".

For these reasons, the Commission declared the communications admissible.

Questions and Comments

1. Is the Commission announcing a rebuttable or conclusive presumption that no local remedies exist where widespread violations are alleged? Which type of presumption is appropriate?

2. To what extent does the Commission take judicial notice of events in the Sudan? Compare the following case from the European system.

Akdivar and Others v. Turkey, App. no. 21893/93, judgment of 16 September 1996 [GC], Eur. Ct. H.R. 1996-IV, 23 EHRR 132 (1997).

I. Particular circumstances of the case

A. The situation in the South-East of Turkey

13. Since approximately 1985, serious disturbances have raged in the South-East of Turkey between the security forces and the members of the PKK (Workers' Party of Kurdistan). This confrontation has so far, according to the Government, claimed the lives of 4,036 civilians and 3,884 members of the security forces. It appears from information submitted by the applicants and by the *amicus curiae* that a large number of villages, estimated at more than 1,000, have been destroyed and evacuated during this conflict.

14. Since 1987, ten of the eleven provinces of south-eastern Turkey have been subjected to emergency rule which was in force at the time of the facts complained of.

B. Destruction of the applicants' houses

15. The applicants, Turkish nationals, were residents in the village of Kelekci in the Dicle district of the province of Diyarbakir. The village of Kelekci and the surrounding areas have been the centre of intense PKK terrorist activity. It is undisputed that the PKK launched serious attacks on Kelekci on 17 or 18 July 1992, and the neighbouring village of Bogazkoy on 1 November 1992. As a result of the first attack, three Kelekci villagers were killed and three others wounded. The second attack on 1 November 1992 was directed at the Bogazkoy gendarme station, which was destroyed, with one gendarme being killed and eight others injured. Thereafter security forces were reinforced in the area and extensive searches were carried out for terrorists. The applicants alleged that on 10 November 1992 State security forces launched an attack on the village of Kelekci, burnt nine houses, including their homes, and forced the immediate evacuation of the entire village.

16. The Government categorically denied these allegations, contending that the houses had been set on fire by the PKK. Initially they stated that the village had merely been searched and that no damage had been caused. Subsequently, it was maintained that no soldiers had entered Kelekci on 10 November 1992, and, if they had been in the vicinity, they had stopped on the outskirts of the village to take a rest.

17. On 6 April 1993 houses in Kelekci were set on fire and the village was almost completely destroyed. It is disputed, however, whether this destruction was caused by terrorists or by security forces.

18. The Commission established that nine houses, including those of the applicants, were destroyed or seriously damaged by fire not long after the attack on the Bogazkoy gendarme station on 1 November 1992. Although noting that there was some uncertainty as to the exact date when the nine houses were burnt, it accepted the applicants' claims that this occurred on 10 November 1992.

. . . .

FINAL SUBMISSIONS TO THE COURT

46. The Government requested the Court to accept the preliminary objection concerning the exhaustion of domestic remedies. In the alternative they submitted that there was no violation of the Convention.

47. The applicants maintained that the Court should reject the Government's preliminary objections and address the merits of their complaints. In their submission the Court should hold that there were violations of Articles 3, 6, 8, 13, 14, 18, and 25 para. 1 of the Convention and Article 1 of Protocol No. 1.

. . . .

II. THE GOVERNMENT'S PRELIMINARY OBJECTIONS

A. Alleged abuse of process

51. Prior to the filing of their memorial, the Government requested that a separate hearing be held concerning the preliminary objection under Article 26, and again in their oral pleadings before the Court, they submitted that the present application amounted to an abuse of the right of petition. They claimed that the failure of the applicants to avail themselves of remedies available in South-East Turkey was part of the general policy of the PKK to denigrate Turkey and its judicial institutions and to promote the idea of the legitimacy of their terrorist activities. As part of this strategy it was necessary to prove that the Turkish judicial system was ineffective in general and unable to cope with such complaints and to distance the population in South-East Turkey from the institutions of the Republic and, in particular, the courts. The applicants' failure to exhaust remedies in this case had thus a political objective.

52. The applicants denied that the application had been made for the purposes of political propaganda against the Government of Turkey. They had brought their case to obtain redress for the violations of the Convention which they had suffered and with a concern to secure the return of the rule of law to that part of Turkey.

53. The Commission in its admissibility decision of 19 October 1994 considered that the Government's argument could only be accepted if it were clear that the ap-

plication was based on untrue facts which, at that stage of the proceedings, was not the case.

54. The Court shares the Commission's opinion. It recalls that the Commission in its findings of fact has substantially upheld the applicants' allegations concerning the destruction of their property. Under these circumstances, and a fortiori, the Government's plea must be rejected.

B. Exhaustion of domestic remedies

56. The Government submitted that the application should be rejected for failure to exhaust domestic remedies as required by Article 26. They stressed in this context that not only did the applicants fail to exhaust relevant domestic remedies but they did not even make the slightest attempt to do so. No allegation or claim for compensation was ever submitted to the Turkish courts. The judicial authorities were thus deprived of the opportunity of implementing the procedural and substantive provisions regarding compensation which are available under Turkish law.

. . . .

57. The Government further contended that the applicants could have addressed themselves to the administrative courts and sought compensation for the alleged damage pursuant to Article 125 of the Turkish Constitution which, they pointed out, places no limits on the right to challenge acts or decisions of the administration, even in a state of emergency, a state of siege or war. With reference to numerous decided cases, they demonstrated that the administrative courts had granted compensation in many cases involving death, injuries or damage to property arising out of the emergency situation on the basis of the theory of social risk and that in these proceedings it was unnecessary to prove fault. Moreover, the burden of proof had been simplified by the courts to the point where it was enough to show the existence of a causal link between what was done and the harm sustained. Furthermore the courts, which had acquired profound experience of the struggle against terrorism, were prepared to award compensation not only in respect of acts of the administration but also in respect of the acts of the PKK.

They also emphasised, again with reference to decided cases, that the applicants could have sought damages under the ordinary civil law. The Code of Obligations provided for a right to damages in cases where servants of the administration committed unlawful acts. In particular the case-law established that the civil courts are not bound by acquittals of administrative officials obtained before the criminal courts.

58. Referring to a number of leading judgments of international tribunals in this area, the Government maintained that the exhaustion requirement applied unless the applicant could show that the remedy provided was manifestly ineffective or that there was no remedy at all (see, inter alia, the *Interhandel* case, International Court of Justice Reports (1959), the *Finnish Ships* Arbitration (1934), Reports of International Arbitral Awards, United Nations, vol. 3; the *Ambatielos* Claim, ibid., vol. 12). The applicants had failed to provide any evidence that there were insurmountable obstacles to taking proceedings before the Turkish courts. Although the numerous judgments submitted by the Government did not cover the precise complaints made by the applicants, they demonstrated beyond doubt the reality and

effectiveness of proceedings before the Turkish courts. The lack of such a judgment could be explained by the fact that the administration, through the Aid and Social Solidarity Fund, provided considerable financial assistance, material aid and housing to persons who had lost their possessions or homes owing to terrorist activity or to fighting by the security forces.

. . . .

(b) The applicants

60. The applicants maintained with reference to reports from human rights organisations that the destruction of their homes was part of a State-inspired policy which had affected over two million people and almost three thousand settlements. Villages were sometimes burnt and evacuated because they were seen as giving shelter to the PKK. That policy, in their submission, was tolerated, condoned and possibly ordered by the highest authorities in the State and aimed at massive population displacement in the emergency region of South-East Turkey. There was thus an administrative practice which rendered any remedies illusory, inadequate and ineffective. Since there were no signs that the Government were willing to take steps to put an end to the practice, victims could have no effective remedy.

In the alternative, the applicants contended that the remedy before the administrative courts in respect of their allegations was ineffective. In the first place the Government had not been able to produce a single case in which the administrative courts had considered a claim such as the applicants', namely that the gendarmes had burned down their homes. In the second place, as a matter of Turkish law, the administrative court is not competent to deal with cases such as that of the applicants which concerns acts of arson and intimidation. Such serious criminal offences fell clearly outside the duties of public officials and were thus beyond the competence of the administrative courts. The question of accountability and compensation in respect of such matters fell within the province of the civil and criminal courts.

. . . .

2. The Court's assessment

(a) General principles

65. The Court recalls that the rule of exhaustion of domestic remedies referred to in Article 26 of the Convention obliges those seeking to bring their case against the State before an international judicial or arbitral organ to use first the remedies provided by the national legal system. Consequently, States are dispensed from answering before an international body for their acts before they have had an opportunity to put matters right through their own legal system. The rule is based on the assumption, reflected in Article 13 of the Convention (art. 13)—with which it has close affinity—that there is an effective remedy available in respect of the alleged breach in the domestic system whether or not the provisions of the Convention are incorporated in national law. In this way, it is an important aspect of the principle that the machinery of protection established by the Convention is subsidiary to the national systems safeguarding human rights (see the *Handyside v. the United Kingdom* judgment of 7 December 1976, Series A no. 24, p. 22, para. 48).

66. Under Article 26 normal recourse should be had by an applicant to remedies which are available and sufficient to afford redress in respect of the breaches alleged. The existence of the remedies in question must be sufficiently certain not only in theory but in practice, failing which they will lack the requisite accessibility and effectiveness (see, *inter alia*, the *Vernillo v. France* judgment of 20 February 1991, Series A no. 198, pp. 11–12, para. 27, and the *Johnston and Others v. Ireland* judgment of 18 December 1986, Series A no. 112, p. 22, para. 45). . . .

67. However, there is, as indicated above, no obligation to have recourse to remedies which are inadequate or ineffective. In addition, according to the "generally recognised rules of international law" there may be special circumstances which absolve the applicant from the obligation to exhaust the domestic remedies at his disposal (see the *Van Oosterwijck v. Belgium* judgment of 6 November 1980, Series A no. 40, pp. 18–19, paras. 36–40). The rule is also inapplicable where an administrative practice consisting of a repetition of acts incompatible with the Convention and official tolerance by the State authorities has been shown to exist, and is of such a nature as to make proceedings futile or ineffective (see the *Ireland v. the United Kingdom* judgment of 18 January 1978, Series A no. 25, p. 64, para. 159, and the report of the Commission in the same case, Series B no. 23-I, pp. 394–97).

68. In the area of the exhaustion of domestic remedies there is a distribution of the burden of proof. It is incumbent on the Government claiming non-exhaustion to satisfy the Court that the remedy was an effective one available in theory and in practice at the relevant time, that is to say, that it was accessible, was one which was capable of providing redress in respect of the applicant's complaints and offered reasonable prospects of success. However, once this burden of proof has been satisfied it falls to the applicant to establish that the remedy advanced by the Government was in fact exhausted or was for some reason inadequate and ineffective in the particular circumstances of the case or that there existed special circumstances absolving him or her from the requirement (see, inter alia, the Commission's decision on the admissibility of application no. 788/60, *Austria v. Italy*, 11 January 1961, Yearbook, vol. 4, pp. 166–168; application no. 5577–5583/72, *Donnelly and Others v. the United Kingdom* (first decision), 5 April 1973, Yearbook, vol. 16, p. 264; also the judgment of 26 June 1987 of the Inter-American Court of Human Rights in the *Velaásquez Rodriáguez* case, Preliminary Objections, Series C no. 1, para. 88, and that Court's Advisory Opinion of 10 August 1990 on *"Exceptions to the Exhaustion of Domestic Remedies"* (Article 46 (1), 46 (2) (a) and 46 (2) (b) of the American Convention on Human Rights), Series A no. 11, p. 32, para. 41). One such reason may be constituted by the national authorities remaining totally passive in the face of serious allegations of misconduct or infliction of harm by State agents, for example where they have failed to undertake investigations or offer assistance. In such circumstances it can be said that the burden of proof shifts once again, so that it becomes incumbent on the respondent Government to show what they have done in response to the scale and seriousness of the matters complained of.

69. The Court would emphasize that the application of the rule must make due allowance for the fact that it is being applied in the context of machinery for the protection of human rights that the Contracting Parties have agreed to set up. Ac-

cordingly, it has recognized that Article 26 must be applied with some degree of flexibility and without excessive formalism (see the above-mentioned *Cardot* judgment, p. 18, para. 34). It has further recognized that the rule of exhaustion is neither absolute nor capable of being applied automatically; in reviewing whether it has been observed it is essential to have regard to the particular circumstances of each individual case (see the above-mentioned *Van Oosterwijck* judgment, p. 18, para. 35). This means amongst other things that it must take realistic account not only of the existence of formal remedies in the legal system of the Contracting Party concerned but also of the general legal and political context in which they operate as well as the personal circumstances of the applicants.

(b) Application of Article 26 to the facts of the case

70. As regards the application of Article 26 to the facts of the present case, the Court notes at the outset that the situation existing in South-East Turkey at the time of the applicants' complaints was—and continues to be—characterised by significant civil strife due to the campaign of terrorist violence waged by the PKK and the counter-insurgency measures taken by the Government in response to it. In such a situation it must be recognised that there may be obstacles to the proper functioning of the system of the administration of justice. In particular, the difficulties in securing probative evidence for the purposes of domestic legal proceedings, inherent in such a troubled situation, may make the pursuit of judicial remedies futile and the administrative inquiries on which such remedies depend may be prevented from taking place.

i. Remedy before the administrative courts

71. The Court observes that the large number of court decisions submitted by the Government demonstrate the existence of an innovative remedy in damages before the administrative courts which is not dependent on proof of fault. Undoubtedly these decisions illustrate the real possibility of obtaining compensation before these courts in respect of injuries or damage to property arising out of the disturbances or acts of terrorism.

The applicants, on the other hand, have suggested that this remedy is not available in respect of the criminal acts of members of the security forces. However, they have not tested this assumption by introducing proceedings before the administrative courts.

In the Court's view, the existence of mere doubts as to the prospects of success of a particular remedy which is not obviously futile is not a valid reason for failing to exhaust domestic remedies (see the *Van Oosterwijck* judgment cited above in paragraph 67, p. 18, para. 37). Nevertheless, like the Commission, the Court considers it significant that the Government, despite the extent of the problem of village destruction, have not been able to point to examples of compensation being awarded in respect of allegations that property has been purposely destroyed by members of the security forces or to prosecutions having been brought against them in respect of such allegations. In this connection the Court notes the evidence referred to by the Delegate of the Commission as regards the general reluctance of the authorities to admit that this type of illicit behaviour by members of the security forces had occurred. It further notes the lack of any impartial investigation, any offer to cooperate with a view to obtaining evidence or any ex gratia payments made by the authorities to the applicants.

72. Moreover, the Court does not consider that a remedy before the administrative courts can be regarded as adequate and sufficient in respect of the applicants' complaints, since it is not satisfied that a determination can be made in the course of such proceedings concerning the claim that their property was destroyed by members of the gendarmerie.

ii. Remedy before the civil courts

73. As regards the civil remedy invoked by the respondent Government, the Court attaches particular significance to the absence of any meaningful investigation by the authorities into the applicants' allegations and of any official expression of concern or assistance notwithstanding the fact that statements by the applicants had been given to various State officials. It appears to have taken two years before statements were taken from the applicants by the authorities about the events complained of, probably in response to the communication of the complaint by the Commission to the Government.

In assessing this remedy the Court must take account of the fact that the events complained of took place in an area of Turkey subject to martial law and characterised by severe civil strife. It must also bear in mind the insecurity and vulnerability of the applicants' position following the destruction of their homes and the fact that they must have become dependent on the authorities in respect of their basic needs. Against such a background the prospects of success of civil proceedings based on allegations against the security forces must be considered to be negligible in the absence of any official inquiry into their allegations, even assuming that they would have been able to secure the services of lawyers willing to press their claims before the courts. In this context, the Court finds particularly striking the Commission's observation that the statements made by villagers following the events of 6 April 1993 gave the impression of having been prepared by the gendarmes.

74. Nor can the Court exclude from its considerations the risk of reprisals against the applicants or their lawyers if they had sought to introduce legal proceedings alleging that the security forces were responsible for burning down their houses as part of a deliberate State policy of village clearance.

75. Accordingly, as regards the possibility of pursuing civil remedies, the Court considers that, in the absence of convincing explanations from the Government in rebuttal, the applicants have demonstrated the existence of special circumstances which dispensed them at the time of the events complained of from the obligation to exhaust this remedy.

iii. Conclusion

76. The Court therefore concludes, in light of the above, that the application cannot be rejected for failure to exhaust domestic remedies.

77. The Court would emphasize that its ruling is confined to the particular circumstances of the present case. It is not to be interpreted as a general statement that remedies are ineffective in this area of Turkey or that applicants are absolved from

the obligation under Article 26 to have normal recourse to the system of remedies which are available and functioning. It can only be in exceptional circumstances such as those which have been shown to exist in the present case that it could accept that applicants address themselves to the Strasbourg institutions for a remedy in respect of their grievances without having made any attempt to seek redress before the local courts.

Questions and Comments

1. Does the Court define or list factors that would lead it to find that a state has engaged in an "administrative practice"? See also *Ireland v. United Kingdom, infra* p. 888.

2. In para. 67, the Court lists several accepted reasons in international law for failure to exhaust local remedies: (a) the remedies are inadequate or ineffective; (b) there are "special circumstances" and (c) there is an administrative practice of violations. Are these distinguishable?

3. Is the finding by the European Court of an "administrative practice" equivalent to the African Commission's finding of a "situation of gross and systematic violations"?

Free Legal Assistance Group, Lawyers' Committee for Human Rights, Union Interafricaine des Droits de l'Homme, Les Témoins de Jehovah v. Zaire, (Joined Comms. 25/89, 47/90, 56/91, 100/93), *9th Annual Activity Report of the Afr. Comm. H.P.R. 1995–1996,* Annex on Communications.

The Facts

1. Communication 25/89 is filed by the Free Legal Assistance Group, the Austrian Committee Against Torture, and the Centre Haitien des Droits et Libertés, all members of the World Organization Against Torture (OMCT). The submission of the Free Legal Assistance Group was dated 17 March 1989, that of the Austrian Committee Against Torture dated 29 March 1989, that of the Centre Haitien dated 20 April 1989. The Communication alleges the torture of 15 persons by a Military Unit, on or about 19 January 1989, at Kinsuka near the Zaire River. On 19 April 1989 when several people protested their treatment, they were detained and held indefinitely.

2. Communication 47/90, dated 16 October 1990, is filed by the Lawyers' Committee for Human Rights in New York. It alleges arbitrary arrests, arbitrary detentions, torture, extra-judicial executions, unfair trials, severe restrictions placed on the right to association and peaceful assembly, and suppression of the freedom of the Press.

3. Communication 56/91 is submitted by the Jehovah's Witnesses of Zaire and dated 27 March 1991. It alleges the persecution of the Jehovah's Witnesses, including arbitrary arrests, appropriation of church property, and exclusion from access to education.

4. Communication 100/93 is submitted by the Union Interafricaine des Droits de l'Homme and dated 20 March 1993. It makes allegations of torture, executions, arrests, detention, unfair trials, restrictions on freedom of association and freedom

of the press. It also alleges that public finances were mismanaged; that the failure of the Government to provide basic services was degrading; that there was a shortage of medicines; that the universities and secondary schools had been closed for two years; that freedom of movement was violated; and that ethnic hatred was incited by the official media.

5. The African Commission, when it determined that the communications, taken together, evidenced a grave and massive violation of human rights in Zaire, brought the matter to the attention of the Assembly of the Heads of State of the Organization of African Unity, in December 1995.

6. The Commission also requested that a mission consisting of two members of the Commission be received in that country, with the objective of discovering the extent and cause of human rights violations and endeavouring to help the government to ensure full respect for the African Charter. The government of Zaire has never responded to these requests for a mission.

THE LAW

Admissibility

35. After deliberations, as envisioned by Article 58 of the African Charter, the Commission considered that communications 25/89, 47/90, 56/91 and 100/93 against Zaire reveal the existence of serious and massive violations of human rights.

36. Article 56 of the African Charter requires that complainants exhaust local remedies before the Commission can take up a case, unless these remedies are as a practical matter unavailable or unduly prolonged. The requirement of exhaustion of local remedies is founded on the principle that a government should have notice of a human rights violation in order to have the opportunity to remedy such violations before being called before an international body. In this case, the government has had ample notice of the violation.

37. The Commission has never held the requirement of local remedies to apply literally in case where it is impractical or undesirable for the complainant to seize the domestic courts in the case of each violation. This is the situation here, given the vast and varied scope of the violations alleged and the general situation prevailing in Zaire.

38. For the above reasons, the Commission declared the communications admissible.

The Merits

39. The main goal of the communications procedure before the Commission is to initiate a positive dialogue, resulting in an amicable resolution between the complainant and the State concerned, which remedies the prejudice complained of. A pre-requisite for amicably remedying violations of the Charter is the good faith of the parties concerned, including their willingness to participate in a dialogue.

40. In the present case, there has been no substantive response from the Government of Zaire, despite the numerous notifications of the communications sent by the African Commission. The African Commission, in several previous decisions, has set out the principle that where allegations of human rights abuse go

uncontested by the government concerned, even after repeated notifications, the Commission must decide on the facts provided by the complainant and treat those facts as given.[1] This principle conforms with the practice of other international human rights adjudicatory bodies and the Commission's duty to protect human rights. Since the Government of Zaire does not wish to participate in a dialogue, the Commission must, regrettably, continue its consideration of the case on the basis of facts and opinions submitted by the complainants alone.

41. Article 5 of the African Charter prohibits torture and inhuman or degrading treatment. The torture of 15 persons by a military unity at Kinsuka, near the Zaire River, as alleged in communication 25/89, constitutes a violation of this Article.

42. Article 6 of the African Charter guarantees the right to liberty and security of person. The indefinite detention of those who protested against torture, as described in communication 25/89, violates Article 6.

43. Article 4 of the African Charter protects the rights to life. Communication 47/90, in addition to alleged arbitrary arrests, arbitrary detention and torture, alleges extrajudicial executions which are a violation of Article 4.

44. Article 7 of the African Charter specifies the right to have one's cause heard. The unfair trials described in communication 47/90 constitute a violation of this right.

45. Article 8 of the African Charter protects freedom of conscience. The harassment of the Jehovah's Witnesses, as described in communication 56/91, constitutes a violation of this article, since the government has presented no evidence that the practice of their religion in any way threatens law and order. The arbitrary arrests of believers of this religion likewise constitutes a contravention of Article 6, above.

46. The torture, executions, arrests, detention, unfair trials, restrictions on freedom of association and freedom of the press described in communication 100/93 violate the above Articles.

47. Article 16 of the African Charter states that every individual shall have the right to enjoy the best attainable state of physical and mental health, and that States Parties should take the necessary measures to protect the health of their people. The failure of the Government to provide basic services such as safe drinking water and electricity and the shortage of medicine as alleged in communication 100/93 constitutes a violation of Article 16.

48. Article 17 of the Charter guarantees the right to education. The closures of universities and secondary schools as described in communication 100/93 constitutes a violation of Article 17.

FOR THESE REASONS, THE COMMISSION

Holds that the facts constitute serious and massive violations of the African Charter, namely of Articles 4, 5, 6, 7, 8, 16 and 17.

---

[1] See, e.g. the Commission's decisions in communications 59/91, 60/91, 87/93 and 101/93.

Questions and Comments

1. Do the procedures applied in this case differ from those followed in a case of individual violations? Should the Commission be less or more willing to presume the truth of the allegations if the case concerns widespread violations?

2. If different petitions allege individual violations of different rights, is it appropriate to join them, as here, and determine that taken together they show "grave and massive violations of human rights"?

3. What is the potential outcome of referring the matter to the Assembly of Heads and State of the OAU? Is the Commission obliged to make the referral if it finds grave and systematic violations?

3. Inter-State Cases

All three regional systems permit a state party to bring an action against another State Party for conduct in breach of the regional human rights treaty. In the Inter-American system this procedure is optional, while jurisdiction is automatically conferred on the regional institutions in the other two systems. Despite the availability of inter-State proceedings, only one inter-State case has been lodged in the African and Inter-American systems. Even in Europe, where Article 33 and its predecessor Article 24 have permitted inter-State cases since the Convention's entry into force, relatively few cases have been brought.

Most inter-State cases concern widespread violations of human rights, although this is not a requirement for admissibility or jurisdiction. Such cases include those brought by Denmark, Norway, Sweden and the Netherlands in 1967 against Greece, following a military coup d'état in the latter country; cases brought against Turkey following Turkish military occupation of a part of the island of Cyprus, e.g., *Cyprus v. Turkey*, 35 CHRR 30 (2002), and the following case brought by Ireland against the United Kingdom. The following materials begin with the European Court's judgment in *Ireland v. United Kingdom*, following which the African case of *Democratic Republic of the Congo v. Burundi, Rwanda and Uganda* and the Inter-American case between *Nicaragua and Costa Rica* are set forth.

Case of Ireland v. the United Kingdom, (App. no. 5310/71), Judgment of 18 January 1978 (plenary), Eur. Ct. H.R.

PROCEDURE

1. This case was referred to the Court by the Government of Ireland. It originated in an application against the Government of the United Kingdom of Great Britain and Northern Ireland lodged by the applicant Government with the European Commission of Human Rights on 16 December 1971 under Article 24 of the Convention for the Protection of Human Rights and Fundamental Freedoms. The report drawn up by the Commission concerning the said application was transmitted to the Committee of Ministers of the Council of Europe on 9 February 1976.

AS TO THE LAW

148. Paragraph (d) of the application of 10 March 1976 states that the object of bringing the case before the Court (Rule 31 para. 1 (d) of the Rules of Court) is "to ensure the observance in Northern Ireland of the engagements undertaken by the respondent Government as a High Contracting Party to the Convention and in particular of the engagements specifically set out by the applicant Government in the pleadings filed and the submissions made on their behalf and described in the evidence adduced before the Commission in the hearings before them". "To this end", the Court is invited "to consider the report of the Commission and to confirm the opinion of the Commission that breaches of the Convention have occurred and also to consider the claims of the applicant Government with regard to other alleged breaches and to make a finding of breach of the Convention where the Court is satisfied that a breach has occurred". . . .

149. The Court notes first of all that it is not called upon to take cognisance of every single aspect of the tragic situation prevailing in Northern Ireland. For example, it is not required to rule on the terrorist activities in the six counties of individuals or of groups, activities that are in clear disregard of human rights. The Court has only to give a decision on the claims made before it by the Irish Republic against the United Kingdom. However, in so doing, the Court cannot lose sight of the events that form the background to this case.

I. ON ARTICLE 3

150. Article 3 provides that "no one shall be subjected to torture or to inhuman or degrading treatment or punishment".

A. Preliminary questions

151. In their memorial of 26 October 1976 and at the hearings in February 1977, the United Kingdom Government raised two preliminary questions on the alleged violations of Article 3. The first concerns the violations which they no longer contest, the second certain of the violations whose existence they dispute.

1. Preliminary question on the non-contested violations of Article 3

152. The United Kingdom Government contest neither the breaches of Article 3 as found by the Commission, nor—a point moreover that is beyond doubt—the Court's jurisdiction to examine such breaches. However, relying *inter alia* on the case-law of the International Court of Justice (*Northern Cameroons* case, judgment of 2 December 1963, and *Nuclear Tests* cases, judgments of 20 December 1974), they argue that the European Court has power to decline to exercise its jurisdiction where the objective of an application has been accomplished or where adjudication on the merits would be devoid of purpose. Such, they claim, is the situation here. They maintain that the findings in question not only are not contested but also have been widely publicised and that they do not give rise to problems of interpretation or application of the Convention sufficiently important to require a decision by the Court. Furthermore, for them the subject-matter of those findings now belongs to past history in view of the abandonment of the five techniques (1972), the solemn and unqualified undertaking not to reintroduce these techniques (8 February

1977) and the other measures taken by the United Kingdom to remedy, impose punishment for, and prevent the recurrence of, the various violations found by the Commission.

This argument is disputed by the applicant Government. Neither is it accepted in a general way by the delegates of the Commission; they stated, however, that they would express no conclusion as to whether or not the above-mentioned undertaking had deprived the claim concerning the five techniques of its object.

153. The Court takes formal note of the undertaking given before it, at the hearing on 8 February 1977, by the United Kingdom Attorney-General on behalf of the respondent Government. The terms of this undertaking were as follows:

> The Government of the United Kingdom have considered the question of the use of the 'five techniques' with very great care and with particular regard to Article 3 (art. 3) of the Convention. They now give this unqualified undertaking, that the 'five techniques' will not in any circumstances be reintroduced as an aid to interrogation.

The Court also notes that the United Kingdom has taken various measures designed to prevent the recurrence of the events complained of and to afford reparation for their consequences. For example, it has issued to the police and the army instructions and directives on the arrest, interrogation and treatment of persons in custody, reinforced the procedures for investigating complaints, appointed commissions of enquiry and paid or offered compensation in many cases.

154. Nevertheless, the Court considers that the responsibilities assigned to it within the framework of the system under the Convention extend to pronouncing on the non-contested allegations of violation of Article 3. The Court's judgments in fact serve not only to decide those cases brought before the Court but, more generally, to elucidate, safeguard and develop the rules instituted by the Convention, thereby contributing to the observance by the States of the engagements undertaken by them as Contracting Parties (Article 19).

The conclusion thus arrived at by the Court is, moreover, confirmed by paragraph 3 of Rule 47 of the Rules of Court. If the Court may proceed with the consideration of a case and give a ruling thereon even in the event of a "notice of discontinuance, friendly settlement, arrangement" or "other fact of a kind to provide a solution of the matter", it is entitled a fortiori to adopt such a course of action when the conditions for the application of this Rule are not present.

155. Accordingly, that part of the present case which concerns the said allegations cannot be said to have become without object; the Court considers that it should rule thereon, notwithstanding the initiatives taken by the respondent State.

2. Preliminary question on certain of the contested violations of Article 3

156. In their memorial of 28 July 1976, the Irish Government invited the Court to hold, unlike the Commission, that violations of Article 3 had occurred in the cases of T 3 (Ballykinler Regional Holding Centre, August 1971) and T 5 (St. Genevieve's School, Belfast, August 1972) as well as in numerous places in Northern Ireland from 1971 to 1974.

In addition to contesting the merits of these claims, the British Government also raised a preliminary question in connection therewith in their memorial of 26 October 1976 and at the hearings in February 1977. They argued that the complaints made did not expressly concern a practice but individual cases in which effective domestic remedies were available to the persons involved. Accordingly, in their submission, the said claims fell outside the area demarcated by the Commission on 1 October 1972 when it accepted the allegation that "the treatment of persons in custody . . . constituted an administrative practice in breach of Article 3".

The Irish Government replied that this line of argument was based on an incorrect interpretation of the above-mentioned decision and of the manner in which the Commission subsequently carried out its role.

According to the delegates of the Commission, the Irish Government had not made clear whether they were asking the Court to censure a practice or merely to hold that certain persons had been subjected to treatment contrary to Article 3. In the former case, but not in the latter, their request would, in the delegates' view, be in conformity with the decision of 1 October 1972.

157. The Court recalls that its jurisdiction in contentious matters is limited to applications which have first of all been lodged with and accepted by the Commission; this is perfectly clear from the structure of Sections III and IV of the Convention. The Commission's decision declaring an application admissible determines the object of the case brought before the Court; it is only within the framework so traced that the Court, once a case is duly referred to it, may take cognisance of all questions of fact or of law arising in the course of the proceedings (*De Wilde, Ooms and Versyp* judgment of 18 June 1971, Series A no. 12, pp. 29–30, paras. 49 and 51; *Handyside* judgment of 7 December 1976, Series A no. 24, p. 20, para. 41; *Stögmüller and Matznetter* judgments of 10 November 1969, Series A no. 9, p. 41, para. 7, and no. 10, pp. 31–32, para. 5; *Delcourt* judgment of 17 January 1970, Series A no. 11, p. 20, para. 40).

Again, Article 49 of the Convention provides that the Court shall settle disputes concerning its jurisdiction. It follows that, in order to rule on this preliminary plea, the Court must itself interpret the above-mentioned decision of 1 October 1972, in the particular light of the Commission's explanations (see, mutatis mutandis, the *Kjeldsen, Busk Madsen and Pedersen* judgment of 7 December 1976, Series A no. 23, pp. 22–24, para. 48).

The allegation accepted by the Commission under Article 3 concerned a practice or practices and not individual cases as such. Accordingly, the Court's sole task is to give a ruling on that allegation.

However, a practice contrary to the Convention can result only from individual violations. Hence, it is open to the Court, just as it was to the Commission, to examine, as constituent elements or proof of a possible practice and not on an individual basis, specific cases alleged to have occurred in given places.

The Court concludes that it has jurisdiction to take cognisance of the contested cases of violation of Article 3 if and to the extent that the applicant Government put them forward as establishing the existence of a practice.

158. Following the Order of 11 February 1977, the Irish Government indicated, at the hearings in April 1977, that they were asking the Court to hold that there had been in Northern Ireland, from 1971 to 1974, a practice or practices in breach of Article 3 and to specify, if need be, where they had occurred. They also declared

that they were no longer seeking specific findings in relation to the cases of T 3 and T 5.

159. A practice incompatible with the Convention consists of an accumulation of identical or analogous breaches which are sufficiently numerous and inter-connected to amount not merely to isolated incidents or exceptions but to a pattern or system; a practice does not of itself constitute a violation separate from such breaches.

It is inconceivable that the higher authorities of a State should be, or at least should be entitled to be, unaware of the existence of such a practice. Furthermore, under the Convention those authorities are strictly liable for the conduct of their subordinates; they are under a duty to impose their will on subordinates and cannot shelter behind their inability to ensure that it is respected.

The concept of practice is of particular importance for the operation of the rule of exhaustion of domestic remedies. This rule, as embodied in Article 26 of the Convention, applies to State applications (Article 24), in the same way as it does to "individual" applications (Article 25), when the applicant State does no more than denounce a violation or violations allegedly suffered by "individuals" whose place, as it were, is taken by the State. On the other hand and in principle, the rule does not apply where the applicant State complains of a practice as such, with the aim of preventing its continuation or recurrence, but does not ask the Commission or the Court to give a decision on each of the cases put forward as proof or illustrations of that practice. The Court agrees with the opinion which the Commission, following its earlier case-law, expressed on the subject in its decision of 1 October 1972 on the admissibility of the Irish Government's original application. Moreover, the Court notes that that decision is not contested by the respondent Government.

. . . .

IV. ON ARTICLE 1

236. The Irish Government's submission is as follows: the laws in force in the six counties did not in terms prohibit violations of the rights and freedoms protected by Articles 3, 5, 6 and 14; several of those laws, as well as certain administrative practices, even authorized or permitted such violations; the United Kingdom was thereby in breach, in respect of each of those Articles, of an inter-State obligation separate from its obligations towards individuals and arising from Article 1.

Neither the British Government nor the Commission in its report concur with this argument. They consider, briefly, that Article 1 cannot be the subject of a separate breach since it grants no rights in addition to those mentioned in Section I.

. . . .

238. Article 1, together with Articles 14, 2 to 13 and 63, demarcates the scope of the Convention ratione personae, materiae and loci; it is also one of the many Articles that attest the binding character of the Convention. Article 1 is drafted by reference to the provisions contained in Section I and thus comes into operation only when taken in conjunction with them; a violation of Article 1 follows automatically from, but adds nothing to, a breach of those provisions; hitherto, when the Court has found such a breach, it has never held that Article 1 has been violated (*Neumeister* judgment of 27 June 1968, Series A no. 8, p. 41, para. 15, and p. 44; judgment of

23 July 1968 on the merits of the *"Belgian Linguistic"* case, Series A no. 6, pp. 70 in fine and 87, para. 1; *Stögmüller* judgment of 10 November 1969, Series A no. 9, p. 45; *De Wilde, Ooms and Versyp judgment* of 18 June 1971, Series A no. 12, p. 43, para. 80, and p. 47, para. 4; *Ringeisen* judgment of 16 July 1971, Series A no. 13, p. 45, para. 109 in fine, and p. 46, paras. 5–6; *Golder* judgment of 21 February 1975, Series A no. 18, p. 20, para. 40 in fine, p. 22, para. 45 in fine, and p. 23, paras. 1–2; *Engel and Others* judgment of 8 June 1976, Series A no. 22, p. 29, para. 69 in fine, p. 37, para. 89 in fine, and p. 45, paras. 4, 5 and 11).

239. However, the Irish Government's argument prompts the Court to clarify the nature of the engagements placed under its supervision. Unlike international treaties of the classic kind, the Convention comprises more than mere reciprocal engagements between contracting States. It creates, over and above a network of mutual, bilateral undertakings, objective obligations which, in the words of the Preamble, benefit from a "collective enforcement". By virtue of Article 24, the Convention allows Contracting States to require the observance of those obligations without having to justify an interest deriving, for example, from the fact that a measure they complain of has prejudiced one of their own nationals. By substituting the words "shall secure" for the words "undertake to secure" in the text of Article 1, the drafters of the Convention also intended to make it clear that the rights and freedoms set out in Section I would be directly secured to anyone within the jurisdiction of the Contracting States (document H (61) 4, pp. 664, 703, 733 and 927). That intention finds a particularly faithful reflection in those instances where the Convention has been incorporated into domestic law (*De Wilde, Ooms and Versyp* judgment of 18 June 1971, Series A no. 12, p. 43, para. 82; *Swedish Engine Drivers' Union* judgment of 6 February 1976, Series A no. 20, p. 18, para. 50).

The Convention does not merely oblige the higher authorities of the Contracting States to respect for their own part the rights and freedoms it embodies; as is shown by Article 14 and the English text of Article 1 ("shall secure"), the Convention also has the consequence that, in order to secure the enjoyment of those rights and freedoms, those authorities must prevent or remedy any breach at subordinate levels.

240. The problem in the present case is essentially whether a Contracting State is entitled to challenge under the Convention a law *in abstracto*.

The answer to this problem is to be found much less in Article 1 than in Article 24. Whereas, in order to be able to lodge a valid petition, a "person, non-governmental organisation or group of individuals" must, under Article 25, claim "to be the victim of a violation . . . of the rights set forth", Article 24 enables each Contracting State to refer to the Commission "any alleged breach of [any of] the provisions of the Convention by another [State]".

Such a "breach" results from the mere existence of a law which introduces, directs or authorises measures incompatible with the rights and freedoms safeguarded; this is confirmed unequivocally by the travaux préparatoires (document H (61) 4, pp. 384, 502, 703 and 706).

Nevertheless, the institutions established by the Convention may find a breach of this kind only if the law challenged pursuant to Article 24 is couched in terms sufficiently clear and precise to make the breach immediately apparent; otherwise, the decision of the Convention institutions must be arrived at by reference to the manner in which the respondent State interprets and applies in concreto the impugned text or texts.

The absence of a law expressly prohibiting this or that violation does not suffice to establish a breach since such a prohibition does not represent the sole method of securing the enjoyment of the rights and freedoms guaranteed.

241. In the present case, the Court has found two practices in breach of Article 3. Those practices automatically infringed Article 1 as well, but this is a finding which adds nothing to the previous finding and which there is no reason to include in the operative provisions of this judgment.

Examination *in abstracto* of the legislation in force at the relevant time in Northern Ireland reveals that it never introduced, directed or authorised recourse to torture or to inhuman or degrading treatment. On the contrary, it forbade any such ill-treatment in increasingly clear terms. More generally, as from the end of August 1971 the higher authorities in the United Kingdom took a number of appropriate steps to prevent or remedy the individual violations of Article 3.

242. With regard to Article 14 taken together with Articles 15, 5 and 6, the applicant Government do not challenge the legislation as such. Moreover, it did not introduce, direct or authorise any discrimination in the exercise of the extrajudicial powers. The claim concerns only the legislation's application, in respect of which the Court has not found any violation.

243. As for Article 15 taken together with Articles 5 and 6, on the other hand, the legislation itself is criticised by the Irish Government.

Certain aspects of the legislation do give rise to doubts. Neither Regulations 11 (1) and 11 (2), nor Article 4 of the Terrorists Order, nor paragraph 11 of Schedule 1 to Emergency Provisions Act set any limit on the duration of the deprivation of liberty they authorised. Furthermore, they did not afford to the persons concerned any judicial or administrative remedy beyond the restricted right to apply for bail, a right that was moreover abolished on 7 November 1972 with the revocation of Regulation 11 (4). These provisions differed, on the first point, from Regulation 10 (forty-eight hours) and section 10 of the Emergency Provisions Act (seventy-two hours) and, on the second, from Regulation 12 (1) (advisory committee), Article 6 of the Terrorists Order (appeal tribunal) and paragraphs 26 to 34 of Schedule 1 to the Emergency Provisions Act (idem).

The first-mentioned shortcoming resulted, however, from the mere silence of the legislation and was mitigated in practice (maximum of seventy-two hours for Regulation 11 (1) and, in general, twenty-eight days for Regulation 11 (2)).

The second shortcoming appears more serious, especially as regards Regulation 11 (2), Article 4 of the Terrorists Order and paragraph 11 of Schedule 1 to the Emergency Provisions Act; preferably, it should have been avoided. However, the deficiency was in part made good by the ordinary courts of the province by virtue of the common law (the *McElduff* case, judgment of 12 October 1971, and the *Kelly* case, judgment of 11 January 1973, Regulations 11 (1) and (2)).

Above all, one is dealing with special legislation designed to combat a public emergency threatening the life of the nation; such provisions cannot be torn out of context without leading to arbitrary results. It was hardly possible for this legislation to forecast in a rigid and inflexible manner the frontiers of the demands of an inherently fluid and changing situation; the massive scale of the outrages and the large number of the persons arrested, detained and interned prevented the provision of guarantees similar to those required by the Convention. In 1972 and 1973, the British authorities attenuated the severity of the original legislation, thereby demonstrating their concern not to go beyond the "extent strictly required by the exigencies" of the circumstances. On this, a question of fact rather than of law, the said authorities enjoyed a margin of appreciation which they do not seem to have exceeded. Here again, the Court considers that it would be unrealistic to isolate the first from the later phases (see paragraphs 220, first sub-paragraph, and 229, sixth sub-paragraph, above); as regards the legislation as such, the Court does not feel able to arrive at conclusions conflicting with its decision on the application of that legislation.

Accordingly, on this issue no breach of Articles 5, 6—assuming the latter Article to be applicable in this case—and 15, taken together with Articles 1 and 24, is found to be established.

SEPARATE OPINION OF JUDGE O'DONOGHUE

. . . .

Article 1

The question of interpretation of Article 1 of the Convention has not been satisfactorily treated by the Commission. Consideration of this problem turns largely on the meaning of Article 24. I would incline, therefore, to the approach in the separate opinions of Messrs. Sperduti, Opsahl, Ermacora and Mangan.

I would point out that the applicant Government is in the same position as the Scandinavian States in the Greek case. In both instances the applicant States ask for a collective enforcement of the guarantee in the Convention to secure the enjoyment of rights and freedoms.

In my opinion, at p. 501 of the report Mr. Mangan has summarized the true interpretation of Article 1 in this context as follows: "It is true that it is always necessary to invoke another Article in conjunction with Article 1, but once violations are threatening because of a failure to secure a right, one of the differences between the position of a State under Article 24 and an individual is exactly that the State may take action against anticipated breaches." At the conclusion of the proceedings before the Court the principal delegate of the Commission filed a memorial (Cour (77) 24) and at p. 5 thereof there will be found the concluding submission with which I fully agree: "Accordingly, the conclusion to be reached on the general problem of the interpretation of the European Convention is that a State that does not fulfil its domestic-guarantee obligation thereby infringes the Convention so that it may be found guilty of a breach of the Convention as a result of an application submitted under Article 24, even before any individuals personally experience the ill-effects of such a situation and are able to make a complaint under Article 25."

Søren C. Prebensen, *Inter-State Complaints under Treaty Provisions—The Experience under the European Convention on Human Rights,* 20 HRLJ 446, 447–448 (1999).

... [T]he actual role of State applications has been more limited than was initially intended—as regards their frequency, the substance of the issues raised and the identity of the States involved. This kind of avenue of complaint, not confined to individual cases but extending to any alleged breach of the Convention, has nonetheless offered a crucial means of addressing widespread and aggravated human rights violations in areas under emergency rule and, in some instances, armed tension, where democratic governance is non-existent or at its weakest and where effective remedies are not available to the aggrieved individuals either at the domestic or at the international level. Although the collective enforcement mechanism set up under the Convention has until present been, and will no doubt continue to be, ensured primarily by means of individual applications, this does not mean that State applications no longer have any role to play. . . . Situations may still arise where the means of redress offered by individual applications is inadequate and where the Contracting Parties to the Convention arguably have a duty to consider bringing proceedings, or else the Convention system of collective human rights enforcement 'runs the risk of becoming meaningless,' to quote Assembly resolution 436 of 1967. State action may moreover prove a valuable, if not indispensable, means of ensuring or accelerating compliance in areas where laws and practices have not yet been brought into line with the Convention rules, as may be the case of certain new and unsettled democracies in central and eastern European States which have recently joined the Convention community.

... [T]he States' initial intention of basing the collective guarantee primarily on State actions is . . . reflected in the fact that the admissibility requirements are less strict than is the case for individual applications. Protocol No. 11 has not brought about any changes in this respect. . . .

The fact that that the admissibility requirements are less strict in inter-State cases than individual cases has had certain practical consequences: whilst all applications referred by States so far have been admitted for examination on their merits, about 90% of the (registered) applications lodged by individuals have been declared inadmissible. However, whether or not it was a realistic assumption in 1950 that the collective enforcement be based primarily on inter-State applications, that is not what has actually happened. . . .

State applications, unlike individual applications, have involved only certain States and have tended to centre on issues of a specific nature. Some of them have been brought by States which have not had a direct interest in the outcome and have been sufficiently publicly spirited to assume the political burden of bringing proceedings; others have been lodged by States which have had a certain self interest by reason of their links with the persons in the respondent State affected by the matter complained of.

... [T]he sole example of the Strasbourg review having had a satisfactory impact is *Ireland v. UK.* . . . In other cases the impact has been less positive or more difficult to assess.

... [T]here appears to be a general reluctance among the members of the Convention community to bring proceedings, be it because of a lack of concern or a desire to avoid the political costs involved. In the majority of cases, the applicant State has had a direct interest in the outcome. In the few instances where that has not been the situation, it seems that the applicant State prefers to share the diplomatic burden of instituting proceedings with other States and is prepared to do so only if the alleged human rights violations are widespread and of a particularly serious nature. Most State applications have focused on alleged practices of aggravated violations that occurred in areas under emergency rule and have been lodged by small States against larger States. With the exception of France in the Turkish case, the larger States in Europe have tended to avoid any involvement on the applicant side in such proceedings.

Furthermore, State applications have generated some of the most hard-fought cases that have come before the Strasbourg institutions. In some instances, the respondent State has even refused to take part in the Commission proceedings on the merits. The inter-State cases have had a tendency of being particularly time-consuming for all the parties involved and, especially for the Commission, having had to hear a number of witnesses in order to be able to assume its task under the Convention of ascertaining the facts in the case. ...

It remains to be seen whether ... the total judicialization of the procedure for determination of cases will entail any significant differences for State applications.

Questions and Comments

1. In what ways do inter-State cases differ from individual petitions?
2. Why should a State be able to challenge a law *in abstracto* even though it is not open to individuals to do so?
3. Does it appear from the judgment that this litigation made a difference in the laws and practices governing Northern Ireland?
4. Why, in your view, have there not been more inter-State cases in the European system? For a critique of interstate procedures *see* See Scott Leckie, *The Inter-State Complaint Procedure in International Human Rights Law: Hopeful Prospects or Wishful Thinking?*, 10 HUM. RTS. Q. 249, 255 (1988).
5. The next two cases represent the only inter-State proceedings thus far in the African and Inter-American systems. In what ways do the cases and procedures differ from the European case above?

D. R. Congo v. Burundi, Rwanda and Uganda, (Comm. 227/99), *20th Annual Activity Report of the Afr. Comm. H.P.R. 2006*, Annex IV, pp. 96–111.

. . . .

The Complaint

8. The Democratic Republic of Congo claims, among other things, that it is the victim of an armed aggression perpetrated by Burundi, Rwanda and Uganda; and that this is a violation of the fundamental principles that govern friendly relations

between States, as stipulated in the Charters of the United Nations and the Organisation of African Unity; in particular, the principles of non-recourse to force in international relations, the peaceful settlement of differences, respect for the sovereignty and territorial integrity of States and non-interference in the internal affairs of States. It emphasises that the massacres and other violations of human and peoples' rights that it accuses Burundi, Rwanda and Uganda of, are committed in violation of the provisions of articles 2, 4, 6, 12, 16, 17, 19, 20, 21, 22 and 23 of the African Charter on Human and Peoples' Rights.

9. It also claims violation of the provisions of the International Covenant on Civil and Political Rights, the Geneva Conventions of 12 August 1949 and of the Additional Protocol on the Protection of Victims of International Armed Conflicts (Protocol I) of 8 June 1977.

10. From the foregoing, the Democratic Republic of Congo, based on the facts presented and the law cited, requests the Commission to:

    a. Declare that [t]he violations of the human rights of the civilian population of the eastern provinces of the Democratic Republic of Congo by Rwanda, Uganda and Burundi are in contravention of the relevant provisions of the African Charter on Human and Peoples' Rights cited above; and

    b. Examine the communication diligently, especially in the light of Article 58 (1) & (3) of the Charter with a view to producing a detailed, objective and impartial report on the grave and massive violations of human rights committed in the war-affected eastern provinces and to submit it to the Assembly of Heads of State and Government of the Organisation of African Unity.

11. The Democratic Republic of Congo also requests the Commission to:

    a. "... Take due note of the violations of the relevant provisions of the Charters of the United Nations, the Organisation of African Unity, and the one on Human and Peoples' Rights;

    b. Condemn the aggression against the Democratic Republic of Congo, which has generated grave violations of the human rights of peaceful peoples;

    c. Deploy an investigation mission with a view to observing in loco the accusations made against Burundi, Rwanda and Uganda;

    d. Demand the unconditional withdrawal of the invading troops from Congolese territory in order to put an end to the grave and massive violations of human rights;

    e. Demand that the countries violating human and peoples' rights in the Democratic Republic of Congo pay just reparation for the damages caused and the acts of looting; and

    f. Indicate the appropriate measures to punish the authors of the war crimes or crimes against humanity, as the case may be, and the creation of an ad hoc tribunal to try the crimes committed against the Democratic Republic of Congo. The ad hoc tribunal may be created in collaboration with the United Nations".

. . . .

LAW

Admissibility

12. The procedure for bringing inter-State communications before the Commission is governed by Articles 47 to 49 of the Charter. At this stage, it is important to

mention that this is the first inter-State communication brought before the African Commission on Human and Peoples' Rights.

13. It is to be noted that Burundi, a Respondent State, was provided with all the relevant submissions relating to this communication, in conformity with Article 57 of the African Charter. But neither did Burundi react to any of them nor did it make any oral submission before the Commission regarding the complaint.

14. The African Commission would like to emphasise that the absence of reaction from Burundi does not absolve the latter from the decision the African Commission may arrive at in the consideration of the communication. Burundi by ratifying the African Charter indicated its commitment to cooperate with the African Commission and to abide by all decisions taken by the latter.

15. In their oral arguments before the Commission at its 27th ordinary session held in Algeria (27 April–11 May 2000), Rwanda and Uganda had argued that the decision of the Complainant State to submit the communication directly to the Chairman of the Commission without first notifying them and the Secretary General of the OAU, is procedurally wrong and therefore fatal to the admissibility of the case.

16. Article 47 requires the Complainant State to draw, by written communication, the attention of the violating State to the matter and the communication should also be addressed to the Secretary General of the OAU and the Chairman of the Commission. The State to which the communication is addressed is to give written explanation or statement elucidating the matter within three months of the receipt of the communication.

17. By the provisions of Article 48 of the Charter, if within three months from the date on which the original communication is received by the State to which it is addressed, the issue is not settled to the satisfaction of the two States involved through bilateral negotiation or by any other peaceful procedure, either State shall have the right to submit the matter to the Commission through the Chairman and to notify the other States involved.

18. The provisions of Articles 47 and 48 read in conjunction with Rules 88 to 92 of the Rules of Procedure of the Commission are geared towards the achievement of one of the essential objectives and fundamental principles of the Charter: conciliation.

19. The Commission is of the view that the procedure outlined in Article 47 of the Charter is permissive and not mandatory. This is borne out by the use of the word "may". Witness the first sentence of this provision:

> If a State Party to the Present Charter has good reasons to believe that another State Party to this Charter has violated the provisions of the Charter, it may draw, by written communication, the attention of that State to the matter.

20. Moreover, where the dispute is not settled amicably, Article 48 of the Charter requires either State to submit the matter to the Commission through the Chairman and to notify the other States involved. It does not, however, provide for its submission to the Secretary General of the OAU. Nevertheless, based on the decision of the Commission at its 25th ordinary session, requesting it to forward a copy

of its complaint to the Secretary General of the OAU, the Complainant State had done so.

21. Furthermore, it appears that the main reason why the Charter makes provision for the Respondent State to be informed of such violations or notified of the submission of such a communication to the Commission, is to avoid a situation of springing surprises on the States involved. This procedure enables the Respondent States to decide whether to settle the complaint amicably or not. The Commission is of the view that even if the Complainant State had not abided by the said provision of the Charter, such omission is not fatal to the communication since after being seized of the case, a copy of the communication, as is the practice of the Commission, was forwarded to the Respondent States for their observations.

22. Article 49, on the other hand, provides for a procedure where the Complainant State directly seizes the Commission without passing through the conciliation phase. Accordingly, the Complainant State may refer the matter directly to the Commission by addressing a communication to the Chairman, the Secretary General of the OAU and the State concerned. Such a process allows the requesting State to avoid making contacts with the Respondent State in cases where such contacts will not be diplomatically either effective or desirable. In the Commission's considered opinion that seems to be the case here. Indeed, the situation of undeclared war prevailing between the Democratic Republic of Congo and its neighbours to the east did not favour the type of diplomatic contact that would have facilitated the application of the provisions of Articles 47 and 48 of the Charter. It was also for this reason that the Commission took the view that Article 52 did not apply to this communication.

23. The Commission is mindful of the requirement that it can consider or deal with a matter brought before it if the provisions of Article 50 of the Charter and Rule 97(c) of the Rules of Procedure are met, that is if all local remedies, if they exist, have been exhausted, unless such would be unduly prolonged.

24. The Commission takes note that the violations complained of are allegedly being perpetrated by the Respondent States in the territory of the Complainant State. In the circumstances, the Commission finds that local remedies do not exist, and the question of their exhaustion does not, therefore, arise.

25. The effect of the alleged activities of the rebels and armed forces of the Respondent States Parties to the Charter, which also back the rebels, fall not only within the province of humanitarian law, but also within the mandate of the Commission. The combined effect of Articles 60 and 61of the Charter compels this conclusion; and it is also buttressed by Article 23 of the African Charter.

26. There is also authority, which does not exclude violations committed during armed conflict from the jurisdiction of the Commission. In communication 74/92, Commission Nationale des Droits de l'Homme et des Libertés /Chad, the Commission held that the African Charter "unlike other human rights instruments, does not allow for States Parties to derogate from their treaty obligations during emergency situations. Thus, even a situation of . . . war . . . cannot be cited as justification by the State violating or permitting violations of the African Charter" (see also communication 159/96, UIDH & Others v. Angola).

From the foregoing, the Commission declares the communication admissible.

The Merits

27. The use of armed force by the Respondent States, which the Democratic Republic of Congo complains of contravenes the well-established principle of international law that States shall settle their disputes by peaceful means in such a manner that international peace, security and justice are not endangered. Indeed, there cannot be both national and international peace and security guaranteed by the African Charter under the conditions created by the Respondent States in the eastern provinces of the Complainant State.

28. Rwanda and Uganda, in their oral arguments before the Commission at its 27th ordinary session held in Algeria had argued that the decision of the Complainant State to submit the communication directly to the Chairman of the Commission without first notifying them and the Secretary General of the OAU, is procedurally wrong and therefore fatal to the admissibility of the case. But the African Commission found otherwise.

29. The Commission finds the conduct of the Respondent States inconsistent with the standard expected of them under UN Declaration on Friendly Relations, which is implicitly affirmed by the Charters of the UN and OAU, and which the Commission is mandated by Article 23 of the African Charter on Human and Peoples' Rights to uphold. Any doubt that this provision has been violated by the Respondent States is resolved by recalling an injunction in the UN Declaration on Friendly Relations: "No State or group of States has the right to intervene directly or indirectly, for any reason whatever, in the internal or external affairs of any other States. Consequently, armed intervention and all other forms of interference or attempted threats against the personality of the State or against its political, economic and cultural elements are in violation of international law. [. . . .] Also no State shall organize, assist, foment, finance, incite or tolerate subversive, terrorist or armed activities directed towards the violent overthrow of the regime of another State or interfere in civil strife in another State." The substance of the complaint of the Democratic Republic of Congo against the Respondents is covered by the foregoing prohibition. The Respondent States have therefore violated Article 23 of the African Charter. The conduct of the Respondent States also constitutes a flagrant violation of the right to the unquestionable and inalienable right of the peoples of the Democratic Republic of Congo to self-determination provided for by Article 20 of the African Charter, especially clause 1 of this provision.

30. The Complainant State alleges grave and massive violations of human and peoples' rights committed by the armed forces of the Respondent States in its eastern provinces. It details series of massacres, rapes, mutilations, mass transfers of populations and looting of the peoples' possessions, as some of those violations. As noted earlier on, the series of violations alleged to have been committed by the armed forces of the Respondent States fall within the province of humanitarian law, and therefore rightly covered by the Four Geneva Conventions and the Protocols additional to them. And the Commission having found the alleged occupation of parts of the provinces of the Complainant State by the Respondents to be in viola-

tion of the Charter cannot turn a blind eye to the series of human rights violations attendants upon such occupation.

31. The combined effect of Articles 60 and 61 of the African Charter enables the Commission to draw inspiration from international law on human and peoples' rights, the Charter of the United Nations, the Charter of the Organisation of African Unity and also to take into consideration, as subsidiary measures to determine the principles of law, other general or special international conventions, laying down rules recognized by Member States of the Organization of African Unity, general principles recognized by African States as well as legal precedents and doctrine. By virtue of Articles 60 and 61 the Commission holds that the Four Geneva Conventions and the two Additional Protocols covering armed conflicts constitute part of the general principles of law recognized by African States, and take same into consideration in the determination of this case.

32. It is noted that Article 75(2) of the First Protocol of the Geneva Conventions of 1949 prohibits the following acts at any time and in all places whatsoever, whether committed by civilian or by military agents:

(a) Violence to life, health, or physical or mental well-being of persons, in particular;

(b) Murder;

(c) Torture of all kinds, whether physical or mental;

(d) Corporal punishment;

(e) Mutilations; and

(f) Outrages upon personal dignity, in particular, humiliating and degrading treatment; enforced prostitution and any form of indecent assault.

33. The Complainant State alleges the occupation of the eastern provinces of the country by the Respondent States' armed forces. It alleges also that most parts of the affected provinces have been under the control of the rebels since 2 August 1998, with the assistance and support of the Respondent States. In support of its claim, it states that the Ugandan and Rwandan governments have acknowledged the presence of their respective armed forces in the eastern provinces of the country under what it calls the "fallacious pretext" of "safeguarding their interests". The Commission takes note that this claim is collaborated by the statements of the representatives of the Respondent States during the 27th ordinary session held in Algeria.

34. Article 23 of the Charter guarantees to all peoples the right to national and international peace and security. It provides further that "the principles of solidarity and friendly relations implicitly affirmed by the Charter of the United Nations and reaffirmed by that of the Organisation of African Unity shall govern relations between states. The principles of solidarity and friendly relations contained in the Declaration on Principles of International Law Concerning Friendly Relations and Co-operation among States in Accordance with the Charter of the United Nations (Res. 2625 (XXV), adopted by the UN General Assembly on 24 October 1970, prohibits threat or use of force by States in settling disputes. Principle 1 provides: Every State has the duty to refrain in its international relations from the threat or use of force against the territorial integrity or political independence of any State, or in any other manner inconsistent with the purposes of the United Nations. Such a

threat or use of force constitutes a violation of international law and the Charter of the United Nations and shall never be employed as a means of settling international issues.

35. In the same vein, Article 33 of the United Nations Charter enjoins "parties to any dispute, the continuance of which is likely to endanger the maintenance of international peace and security . . . first of all, to seek a solution by negotiation, enquiry, mediation, conciliation, arbitration, judicial settlement, resort to regional agencies or arrangements, or other peaceful means of their own choice". Chapter VII of the same Charter outrightly prohibits threats to the peace, breaches of the peace and acts of aggression. Article III of the OAU Charter states that

> The Member States, in pursuit of the purposes stated in Article II, solemnly affirm and declare their adherence to the following principles:
>
> 1. . . . .
> 2. Non-interference in the internal affairs of States
> 3. Respect for the sovereignty and territorial integrity of each State and for its inalienable right to independent existence;
> 4. Peaceful settlement of disputes by negotiation, mediation, conciliation or arbitration.

36. It also contravenes the well-established principle of international law that States shall settle their disputes by peaceful means in such a manner that international peace and security and justice are not endangered. As noted in paragraph 66 above, there cannot be both national and international peace and security guaranteed by the Charter with the conduct of the Respondent States in the eastern provinces of the Complainant State.

37. The Commission therefore disapproves of the occupation of the complainant's territory by the armed forces of the Respondent forces and finds it impermissible, even in the face of their argument of being in the Complainant's territory in order to safeguard their national interests and therefore in contravention of Article 23 of the Charter. The Commission is of the strong belief that such interests would better be protected within the confines of the territories of the Respondent States.

38. It bears repeating that the Commission finds the conduct of the Respondent States in occupying territories of the Complainant State to be a flagrant violation of the rights of the peoples of the Democratic Republic of Congo to their unquestionable and inalienable right to self-determination provided for by Article 20 of the African Charter.

39. As previously stated, the Commission is entitled, by virtue of Articles 60 and 61 of the African Charter, to draw inspiration from international law on Human and Peoples' Rights, . . . the Charter of the United Nations, the Charter of the Organisation of African Unity . . . and also take into consideration, as subsidiary measures to determine the principles of law, other general or special international conventions, laying down rules recognised by Member States of the Organisation of African Unity . . . general principles recognised by African States as well as legal precedents and doctrine. Invoking these provisions, the Commission holds that the Four Geneva Conventions and the two Additional Protocols covering armed conflicts, fall on all fours with the category of special international conventions, laying down rules recognised by Member States of the Organisation of African Unity and also constitute

part of the general principles recognised by African States, and to take same into consideration in the determination of this case.

40. The Commission finds the killings, massacres, rapes, mutilations and other grave human rights abuses committed while the Respondent States' armed forces were still in effective occupation of the eastern provinces of the Complainant State reprehensible and also inconsistent with their obligations under Part III of the Geneva Convention Relative to the Protection of Civilian Persons in Time of War of 1949 and Protocol 1 of the Geneva Convention.

41. They also constitute flagrant violations of Article 2 of the African Charter, such acts being directed against the victims by virtue of their national origin; and Article 4, which guarantees respect for life and the integrity of one's person and prohibits the arbitrary deprivation rights.

42. The allegation of mass transfer of persons from the eastern provinces of the Complainant State to camps in Rwanda, as alleged by the complainant and not refuted by the respondent, is inconstent with Article 18(1) of the African Charter, which recognises the family as the natural unit and basis of society and guarantees it appropriate protection. It is also a breach of the right to freedom of movement, and the right to leave and to return to ones country guaranteed under Article 12(1) and (2) of the African Charter respectively.

43. Article 56 of the First Protocol Additional to the Geneva Conventions of 1949 provides:

(1) Works or installations containing dangerous forces, namely dams, dykes and nuclear electrical generating stations, shall not be made object of military attack, even where these objects are military objectives, if such attack may cause the release of dangerous forces and consequent severe losses among the civilian population.

(2) The special protection against attack provided by paragraph 1 shall cease: (a) for a dam or dyke only if it is used for other than its normal function in a regular, significant and direct support of military operations and if such attack is the only feasible way to terminate such support. . . .

(3) In all cases, the civilian population and individual civilians shall remain entitled to all the protection accorded them by international law, including the protection of precautionary measures provided for in Article 57.

44. As noted previously, taking Article 56, quoted above, into account, and by virtue of Articles 60 and 61 of the African Charter, the Commission concludes that in besieging the hydroelectric dam in Lower Congo province, the Respondent States have violated the Charter.

45. The besiege of the hydroelectric dam may also be brought within the prohibition contained in The Hague Convention (II) with Respect to the Laws and Customs of War on Land which provides in Article 23 that "Besides the prohibitions provided by special Conventions, it is especially prohibited . . . to destroy the enemy's property, unless such destruction or seizure be imperatively demanded by the necessities of war". By parity of reason, and bearing in mind Articles 60 and 61 of the Charter, the Respondent States are in violation of the Charter with regard to the just noted Article 23.

46. The case of the *International Criminal Tribunal for Yougoslavia vs. Zejnil Delalic, Zdravko Mucic, Hazim Delic and Esad Landzo* (the Celebici Judgment; Nov., 16, 1998 at para. 587) is supportive of the Commission's stance. It states, inter alia, that "international law today imposes strict limitations on the measures which a party to an armed conflict may lawfully take in relation to the private and public property of an opposing party. The basic norms in this respect, which form part of customary international law . . . include the fundamental principle . . . that private property must be respected and cannot be confiscated . . . pillage is formally forbidden".

47. The raping of women and girls, as alleged and not refuted by the respondent States, is prohibited under Article 76 of the first Protocol Additional to the Geneva Conventions of 1949, which provides that "women shall be the object of special respect and shall be protected in particular against rape, forced prostitution and any form of indecent assault. It also offends against both the African Charter and the Convention on the Elimination of All Forms of Discrimination Against Women; and on the basis of Articles 60 and 61 of the African Charter find the Respondent States in violation of the Charter.

48. The Commission condemns the indiscriminate dumping of and or mass burial of victims of the series of massacres and killings perpetrated against the peoples of the eastern province of the Complainant State while the armed forces of the Respondent States were in actual fact occupying the said provinces. The Commission further finds these acts barbaric and in reckless violation of Congolese peoples' rights to cultural development guaranteed by Article 22 of the African Charter, and an affront on the noble virtues of the African historical tradition and values enunciated in the preamble to the African Charter. Such acts are also forbidden under Article 34 of the First Protocol Additional to the Geneva Conventions of 1949, which provides for respect for the remains of such peoples and their gravesites. In disregarding the last provision, the Respondent States have violated the African Charter on the basis of Articles 60 and 61 of this instrument.

49. The looting, killing, mass and indiscriminate transfers of civilian population, the besiege and damage of the hydro-dam, stopping of essential services in the hospital, leading to deaths of patients and the general disruption of life and state of war that took place while the forces of the Respondent States were occupying and in control of the eastern provinces of the Complainant State are in violation of Article 14 guaranteeing the right to property, articles 16 and 17 (all of the African Charter), which provide for the rights to the best attainable state of physical and mental health and education, respectively.

50. Part III of the Geneva Convention Relative to the Protection of Civilian Persons in Time of War 1949, particularly in Article 27 provides for the humane treatment of protected persons at all times and for protection against all acts of violence or threats and against insults and public curiosity. Further, it provides for the protection of women against any attack on their honour, in particular against rape, enforced prostitution, or any form of indecent assault. Article 4 of the Convention defines a protected person as those who, at a given moment and in any manner

whatsoever, find themselves, in case of a conflict or occupation, in the hands of a Party to the conflict or Occupying Power of which they are not nationals.

51. The Complainant State alleges that between October and December 1998, the gold produced by the OKIMO firm and by local diggers yielded $100,000,000 (one hundred million US dollars) to Rwanda. By its calculation, the coffee produced in the region and in North Kivu yielded about $70,000,000 (seventy million US dollars) to Uganda in the same period. Furthermore, Rwanda and Uganda took over control of the fiscal and customs revenue collected respectively by the Directorate General of Taxes. The plunder of the riches of the eastern provinces of Congo is also affecting endangered animal species such as okapis, mountain gorillas, rhinoceros, and elephants.

52. Indeed, the respondent States, especially, Uganda, has refuted these allegations, pretending for example that its troops never stepped in some of the regions they are accused of human rights violations and looting of the natural resources of the complainant States. However, the African Commission has evidence that some of these facts did take place and are imputable to the armies and agents of the respondent states. In fact, the United Nations have acknowledged that during the period when the armies of the Respondent States were in effective control over parts of the territory of the Complainant State, there were lootings of the natural resources of the Complainant State. The United Nations set up a Panel of Experts to investigate this matter[2].

53. The report of the Panel of Experts, submitted to the Security Council of the United Nations in April 2001 (under reference S/2001/357) identified all the Respondent States among others actors, as involved in the conflict in the Democratic Republic of Congo[3]. The report profusely provides evidence of the involvement of the Respondent states in the illegal exploitation of the natural resources of the Complainant State. It is stated in paragraph 5 of the Summary of the report: "During this first phase (called Mass-scale looting phase by the experts), stockpiles of minerals, coffee, wood, livestock and money that were available in territories conquered by the armies of Burundi, Rwanda and Uganda were taken, and either transferred to those countries or exported to international markets by their forces and nationals."[4].

54. Paragraph 25 of the reports further states: "The illegal exploitation of resources (of the Democratic Republic of Congo) by Burundi, Rwanda and Uganda took different forms, including confiscation, extraction, forced monopoly and price-fixing. Of these, the first two reached proportions that made the war in the Democratic Republic of the Congo a very lucrative business.

---

2 See Resolution 1457 (2003) of the Security Council of the United Nations adopted on 24/01/2003 on the Panel of Experts on the illegal exploitation of the natural resources of the Democratic Republic of Congo.
   Also see presidential statement dated 2 June 2000 (S/PRST/2000/20), whereby the Security Council requested the Secretary General of the United Nations to establish a Panel of Experts on the Illegal Exploitation of Natural Resources and Other Forms of Wealth in the Democratic Republic of the Congo for a period of six months
3 See Point 10(a) of the summary of the Report.
4 Also see Paragraphs 26, 27, 32, 55, 64, etc., of the report.

55. The Commission therefore finds the illegal exploitation/looting of the natural resources of the complainant state in contravention of Article 21 of the African Charter, which provides:

(1) All peoples shall freely dispose of their wealth and natural resources. This right shall be exercised in the exclusive interest of the people. In no case shall a people be deprived of it. . . .

(2) States Parties to the present Charter shall individually and collectively exercise the right to free disposal of their wealth and natural resources with a view to strengthening African Unity and solidarity.

56. The deprivation of the right of the people of the Democratic Republic of Congo, in this case, to freely dispose of their wealth and natural resources, has also occasioned another violation—their right to their economic, social and cultural development and of the general duty of States to individually or collectively ensure the exercise of the right to development, guaranteed under Article 22 of the African Charter.

57. For refusing to participate in any of the proceedings although duly informed and invited to respond to the allegations, Burundi admits the allegations made against it.

58. Equally, by refusing to take part in the proceedings beyond admissibility stage, Rwanda admits the allegations against it.

59. As in the case of Rwanda, Uganda is also found liable of the allegations made against it.

For the above reasons, the Commission:

Finds the Respondent States in violation of Articles 2, 4, 5, 12(1) and (2), 14, 16, 17, 18(1) and (3), 19, 20, 21, 22, and 23 of the African Charter on Human and Peoples' Rights.

Urges the Respondent States to abide by their obligations under the Charters of the United Nations, the Organisation of African Unity, the African Charter on Human and Peoples' Rights, the UN Declaration on Principles of International Law Concerning Friendly Relations and Co-operation among States and other applicable international principles of law and withdraw its troops immediately from the complainant's territory.

Takes note with satisfaction, of the positive developments that occurred in this matter, namely the withdrawal of the Respondent States armed forces from the territory of the Complainant State.

Recommends that adequate reparations be paid, according to the appropriate ways to the Complainant State for and on behalf of the victims of the human rights by the armed forces of the Respondent States while the armed forces of the Respondent States were in effective control of the provinces of the Complainant State, which suffered these violations.

Questions and Comments

1. The applicant alleges violations of the ICCPR, the 1949 Geneva Conventions and the Protocols Additional to these Conventions, as well as the African Charter. Does the African Commission have jurisdiction to decide whether or not respondent states have breached these agreements? How does it address these charges?

2. What law applies during an international armed conflict? Does the African Charter continue to apply in its entirety? Should it?

3. How is the inter-State case processed? In what ways do the procedures differ from those applicable to individual communications.

4. Has the Commission determined that Article 23 (right to peace) is justiciable? Could it be invoked in an individual complaint or do states only have standing to assert a "peoples' right"? See *SERAC v. Nigeria* in chapter 2.

5. What type of reparations would be appropriate for the violations found in this case?

6. The DRC also brought cases against Uganda, Burundi and Rwanda in the International Court of Justice. See *Armed Activities on the Territory of the Congo (DRC v. Rwanda)* 2006 ICJ (3 Feb.); *(DRC v. Burundi)*, discontinued 30 January 2001; *(DRC v. Uganda)*, 2005 ICJ (19 Dec.). In the case against Rwanda, the ICJ held that it lacked jurisdiction to hear the case because Rwanda was not a party to or had filed reservations to the treaties invoked by the DRC. In the case brought against Uganda, the DRC asserted, inter alia, that Uganda violated both conventional and customary law of human rights and humanitarian law. Among the conventional sources, the DRC specifically invoked the African Charter. The Court found credible evidence of massive human rights violations and grave breaches of international humanitarian law committed on the territory of the DRC and attributable to Uganda. It held that Uganda violated its obligations under international human rights law, including the African Charter, and international humanitarian law. What is the value for the DRC in bringing actions against the states before both the ICJ and the African Commission? Is there any risk of conflicting jurisprudence? If so, how should it be handled? Should the African Commission defer to the ICJ on inter-State cases?

Nicaragua v. Costa Rica, Rep. No. 11/07, Interstate Case 01/06, Inter-Am. Comm. H.R., March 8, 2006 (some footnotes omitted).

1. On February 6, 2006, the Inter-American Commission on Human Rights . . . received a communication from the State of Nicaragua which alleged that the State of Costa Rica has committed violations of Articles 1(1) (Obligation to respect rights), 8 (Right to a fair trial), 24 (Right to equal protection), and 25 (Right to judicial protection) of the American Convention on Human Rights (hereinafter "the Convention" or "the American Convention"); Articles 2, 7, 8, and 28 of the Universal Declaration of Human Rights; Articles II (Right to equality before law) and XVIII (Right to a fair trial) of the American Declaration of the Rights and Duties of Man; and Article 9 of the Inter-American Democratic Charter, which refers to the elimination of all forms of discrimination, due to the alleged failure on the part of the State of Costa Rica to fulfill its duty to ensure protection for the human rights of the Nicaraguan migrant population under its jurisdiction.

2. By virtue of the fact that both the State of Costa Rica and the State of Nicaragua deposited their declarations concerning recognition of the competence of the Commission to receive and examine communications from one state against another, on February 13, 2006, the IACHR decided to process the communication in accor-

dance with Articles 45 *et seq.* of the Convention and to transmit the communication presented by the State of Nicaragua to the State of Costa Rica.

. . . .

4. In light of the fact that the considerations on admissibility and merits are closely connected in the case, the Commission decided, pursuant to Article 37(3) of its Rules of Procedure, to defer its treatment of admissibility until the debate and decision on the merits, particularly since the Commission found from its examination of the arguments and evidence presented by both States that the allegation regarding the existence of a generalized practice of discrimination against the Nicaraguan migrant population in Costa Rica was neither manifestly groundless nor obviously out of order.

. . . .

Preliminary considerations concerning the processing of this inter-State communication

124. The American Convention, at Section 3 of its Chapter V, establishes the competence of the Inter-American Commission on Human Rights. Article 44 of the Convention refers to the authority of the Commission to process petitions that contain denunciations of violation of the Convention by a State Party, which may be lodged by any person or group of persons, or any nongovernmental entity legally recognized in one or more member states of the Organization. For its part, Article 45 of the Convention clearly determines the competence of the Commission to receive and examine communications in which a state party alleges that another state party has committed a violation of a human right set forth in the Convention, provided that both the state party that presents the communication and the state party against which it is presented shall have declared, upon depositing their instrument of ratification of or adherence to the Convention, or at any later time, that they recognize the competence of the Commission to receive and examine communications in which a state party alleges that another state party has committed a violation of a human right set forth in the Convention. Declarations concerning recognition of competence may be made to be valid for an indefinite time, for a specified period, or for a specific case.

125. Articles 46 and 47 of the Convention, for their part, concern the admissibility requirements to be met by both petitions presented under Article 44 and communications lodged pursuant to Article 45. Next, Section 4 of the Chapter V of the American Convention governs all the aspects of the procedure to be followed by the Commission upon receiving a petition submitted in accordance with Article 44 or upon receiving a communication presented pursuant to Article 45, if they alleged violation of any of the rights protected by the Convention.

126. Furthermore, Article 48 of the Rules of Procedure of the IACHR provides that when a state party to the American Convention that has accepted the competence of the Commission to receive and examine such communications against other states parties lodges a communication against another state, the Commission shall transmit it to the state party in question whether or not it has accepted the Commission's competence. If it has not accepted that competence, the communication shall be transmitted in order that the state concerned may exercise its option to

recognize the competence of the Commission in the specific case that is the subject of the communication. Furthermore, according to the aforesaid Article 48, if the State in question has accepted the Commission's competence to consider a communication from another state party, the respective procedure shall be governed by the provisions concerning the processing of all petitions lodged with the Commission, insofar as they apply.

127. It may be concluded from the foregoing that both the American Convention and the Rules of Procedure of the IACHR have provided that communications in which a state party alleges that another state party has committed a violation of a human right set forth in the Convention, are governed by the same rules of procedure and must meet the same requirements as petitions containing denunciations or complaints that are presented by any person, provided that they also satisfy the specific requirements set forth in Article 45 of the Convention, the foregoing without prejudice to the fact that the applicable procedures and requirements must take into consideration the special characteristics and purposes of the mechanism for communications between states.

128. In presenting its communication, the State of Nicaragua said that it did so "specifically in accordance with the requirements set down in Articles 61 (1), (2), and 48 to 50 of the American Convention on Human Rights". At the same time, the Nicaraguan State requested that " this petition be processed in accordance with Articles 48 to 51 of the American Convention on Human Rights and, therefore, that the State of Costa Rica be requested to provide a report." Furthermore, the State of Nicaragua said that its interstate communication was in keeping with the terms of the appropriate form of the IACHR as an obligatory prior step to the introduction of cases referred to the Inter-American Court of Human Rights. The State of Nicaragua invokes, for this case, the procedure determined by the Inter-American Court of Human Rights in the *Case of Viviana Gallardo et al.*"

129. Throughout the proceeding in this case, the State of Nicaragua has held that the communication that it presented against the State of Costa Rica should not have been processed under Articles 45 *et seq.* of the Convention, but pursuant to Article 61 of the American Convention on Human Rights, which only makes reference to Articles 48 to 50 of that instrument.

130. In this connection, the Commission notes that the American Convention is an integral whole that must be interpreted in its entirety, and the Commission is required to apply and comply with each and every one of the articles that the Convention contains. It is the duty of the organs of the system to ensure the international protection that the Convention provides, taking into account the totality of the framework agreed on by the states. Accordingly, if Article 45 of the Convention specifically recognizes the competence of the Commission to admit and examine communications between states, and Articles 46 and 47 expressly set out the requirements to be fulfilled by such communications in order to be admitted by the Commission, in no circumstances could the IACHR ignore these articles and process an interstate communication solely under Articles 48 to 51 of the Convention as the State of Nicaragua has requested. Moreover, Article 48 (a), invoked by the State of Nicaragua, provides that if the Commission considers the communication

admissible, it shall request information from the government of the state indicated as being responsible for the alleged violations. Accordingly, Article 48 itself compels the Commission to make a determination on admissibility, and to do so in accordance with Articles 46 and 47 of the Convention.

. . . .

134. Based on the foregoing, the Inter-American Commission considers that in processing the instant interstate communication under Articles 45 *et seq.* of the Convention, it acted in full accordance with the provisions contained in the American Convention and in its Rules of Procedure.

135. The State of Nicaragua has also protested the decision of the Commission to grant an extension to the State of Costa Rica to present its reply to the interstate communication, even though the extension was requested after the time limit for the Costa Rican State to submit its reply had expired. The Commission is aware that the time limit for the State of Costa Rica to submit its reply to this interstate communication expired on April 15, 2006, with no reply forthcoming from said State. Then, on April 24, 2006, the State of Costa Rica sought an extension of 15 days to present its reply and on April 27 the Commission decided to grant a single extension of eight days for the State of Costa Rica to respond to the interstate communication.

136. However, in the practice of the Inter-American system for protection of human rights both the Commission and the Court have determined that a delay in meeting a deadline may be overlooked provided that the delay is not considered excessive within the necessary limits of time and reasonableness. "The Court has exercised flexibility vis-à-vis the periods established in the Convention and in its Rules of Procedure [. . .]and has often granted extensions requested by the parties when they have shown reasonable cause."[5] Thus, this is not the first time that the organs of the system have granted an extension to a party, even after the time limit has expired, provided there has been reasonable cause to do so.[6] In the instant case, the Commission finds that the delay of State of Costa Rica in presenting a request for an extension cannot be considered excessive.

137. Above all, the Commission takes the view that, particularly since this is a case between states, it is especially important to exercise flexibility with time limits so as to preserve the possibility of balanced exchanges between the two states in the interests of attaining justice. As this is a case in which the relations between two OAS member states are at stake, the Commission considered it essential to listen to the opinions of both states on the matter, since the effects of not hearing one of the parties in this case by reason of an expired deadline could have seriously affected relations between these two neighboring nations. In this connection it is worth recalling the position adopted by the Court in the sense that "the procedural system is a means of attaining justice and that the latter cannot be sacrificed for the sake of mere formalities. Keeping within certain timely and reasonable limits, some

---

5 I/A Court H.R., *Loayza Tamayo Case, Preliminary Objections*, Judgment of January 31, 1996, Series C No. 25, par. 34.

6 See I/A Court H.R., *Castillo Páez Case, Preliminary Objections*, Judgment of January 30, 1996, Series C No. 24, pars. 34, 35 and 36. See also I/A Court H.R., *The "Panel Blanca" Case (Paniagua Morales et al), Preliminary Objections*, Judgment of January 25, 1996, Series C No. 23, pars. 37 and 39.

omissions or delays in complying with procedure may be excused, provided that a suitable balance between justice and legal certainty is preserved."[7]

. . . .

139. The State of Costa Rica, on the other side, asserted that it is convinced that there has been a series of irregularities in the processing of the instant communication, and thus the Commission will analyze these assertions.

140. In first place, the Costa Rican State alleges irregularities connected with the decision of the Commission to join its examination of admissibility and merits as provided in Article 37(3) of its Rules of Procedure. In that regard, the Costa Rican State has mentioned that the note of the Executive Secretariat "would appear to suggest a connection between the 'non-acceptance' of the friendly [settlement] procedure and the joinder of the admissibility stage with the debate and decision on merits." The State of Costa Rica adds that the Commission never justified that joinder and thereby violated a fundamental requirement in the proceeding.

141. The Commission notes that Article 37(3) of its Rules of Procedure empowers it, in exceptional circumstances, to open a case but defer its treatment of admissibility until the debate and decision on the merits. The above-cited article also provides that the case shall be opened by means of a written communication to both parties. Furthermore under its Rules of Procedure, the Executive Secretariat is authorized to receive and process the correspondence addressed to the Commission. However, the applicable rules do not require the Secretariat to inform the parties in writing which exceptional circumstances the Commission weighed in reaching its decision to join the stages on admissibility and merits in the case. The IACHR considers that those exceptional circumstances are amply attested in the instant report and utterly rejects any accusation that the Commission has committed irregularities in processing this communication based on the misinterpretation of a note transmitted by its Executive Secretariat.

142. In addition, the State of Costa Rica has mentioned that it finds it unacceptable that the letter notifying it of the decision of the Commission to convene a hearing and join the stages on admissibility and merits should have been entitled "Interstate Case 01/06 Nicaragua v Costa Rica" without any basis for doing so. In that respect, the Commission is mindful that the above-cited Article 37 of the Rules of Procedure of the IACHR, empowers the Commission to open the "case" but to defer its treatment of admissibility until the debate and decision on the merits. Upon reaching the stage on merits, all petitions and communications received by the Commission are registered as "cases" pursuant to the provisions contained in Articles 37(2) and 37(3) of its Rules of Procedure.

143. Finally, the State of Costa Rica has also protested the decision of the Commission to convene a hearing before the time limit granted to the State of Nicaragua to present its observations on merits had elapsed. On this point, Article 38 of the Rules of Procedure of the IACHR, in establishing the applicable procedure for cases in the merits stage, provides at paragraph five that "[i]f it deems it necessary in order

---

[7] I/A Court H.R., *Cayara Case, Preliminary Objections*, Judgment of February 3, 1993, Series C No. 14, par. 42; *The "Panel Blanca" Case (Paniagua Morales et al), Preliminary Objections*, Judgment of January 25, 1996, Series C No. 23, par. 38.

to advance in its consideration of the case, the Commission may convene the parties for a hearing." Moreover, Article 62 of the Rules of Procedure provides that "[h]earings on petitions or cases shall have as their purpose the receipt of oral or written presentations by the parties relative to new facts and information additional to that which has been produced during the proceeding. The information may refer to any of the following issues: admissibility; the initiation or development of the friendly settlement procedure; the verification of the facts; the merits of the matter; follow-up on recommendations; or any other matter pertinent to the processing of the petition or case." The Commission considers that hearings are the opportune moment for parties to present any document, witness testimony, expert opinion, or evidence in connection with the case. Therefore, there was no rule or reason to prevent the IACHR from convening a hearing when it did. It is worth noting, furthermore, that the Commission did not exclude the possibility that the State of Costa Rica present its written arguments in the time duly allotted for that purpose.

Competence of the Commission under Article 45 of the American Convention

. . . .

145. In this case the communication was presented by the State of Nicaragua against the State of Costa Rica and, therefore, it is necessary to determine if both states have declared their recognition of the competence of the Commission to receive and examine communications in which a state party alleges that another state party has committed a violation of a human right set forth in the Convention.

. . . .

154. As to the deposit by the Nicaraguan State of its declaration of acceptance of the competence of the IACHR, the Commission notes that the State of Nicaragua, upon presenting its interstate communication, said that its declaration of recognition of the competence of the Inter-American Commission on Human Rights to receive and examine communications in which a state party alleges that another state party has committed a violation of a human right set forth in the American Convention on Human Rights, was published in Official Gazette, *La Gaceta*, No. 22 of January 31, 2006 and "brought to the attention of the General Secretariat of the Organization of American States on February 3 of the year in progress, so that its contents might be transmitted to the States Parties to the Convention and the Member States of the Organization."

155. On lodging its interstate communication with the IACHR on February 6, 2006, the State of Nicaragua also presented a copy of the note that it sent to the Secretary General of the OAS and which, according to the communication of the State of Nicaragua, was received by the General Secretariat of the Organization on Friday, February 3, 2006. The purpose of the note to the Secretary General was to bring to his attention the declaration of January 26, 2006, and request that he transmit to the other states parties to the Convention and the members of the Organization of American States the contents of said declaration, to which end the note also enclosed a photocopy of Official Gazette, *La Gaceta*, No. 22 of January 31, 2006, in which the declaration was published.

156. The Commission further notes that, upon transmitting to the State of Costa Rica the interstate communication presented by Nicaragua, it also forwarded a copy

of the note that the State of Nicaragua sent to the Secretary General in order to deposit its declaration of acceptance of the competence of the Commission, together with a copy of the publication in the Official Gazette. The State of Costa Rica has not questioned the authenticity of the aforesaid communications of the State of Nicaragua nor the confirmation of receipt on the part of the OAS General Secretariat.

157. Furthermore, the Commission observes that in the brief containing its reply to the interstate communication from Nicaragua, presented to the Commission on May 5, 2006, the Costa Rican State on several occasions cites the declaration by which the State of Nicaragua recognizes the competence of the Commission to receive and examine interstate communications, as well as the fact that the declaration of the State of Nicaragua was communicated to the General Secretariat of the Organization of American States on February 3, 2006, so that its contents might be transmitted to the states parties to the Convention and the members of the Organization. By the same token, in the brief containing arguments and observations presented to the IACHR at the hearing of July 18, 2006, the State of Costa Rica again recognized that the declaration of the State of Nicaragua was communicated to the General Secretariat of the OAS on February 3, 2006, so that its contents might be transmitted to the states parties to the Convention and the members of the Organization.

158. However, five months later, in the framework of the hearing held on October 18, 2006, at the 126th Session of the IACHR, the State of Costa Rica requested that the Commission suspend the hearing, arguing that the latter was not competent to examine the instant communication. As the basis for its argument it presented a statement from the Office of International Law of the General Secretariat of the Organization of American States to the effect that said office had no record of additional acts on the part of the Government of Nicaragua in connection with the American Convention since the deposit of its declaration concerning the competence of the Inter-American Court of Human Rights on February 12, 1991. The Costa Rican State submitted on that occasion that the information provided by the Office of International Law constitutes information or supervening proof that there was no official record that the State of Nicaragua had formally deposited a declaration of recognition of the competence of the IACHR and, therefore, the note by which the Nicaraguan State presented its interstate communication against the Costa Rican State should be refused by the Commission.

159. The Commission observes that the note issued by the Director of the Office of International Law of the Organization of American States on September 30, 2006, does indeed indicate that State of Nicaragua deposited its instrument of ratification of the American Convention on September 25, 1979, and the instrument of declaration of the competence of the Inter-American Court of Human Rights on February 12, 1991. However, it mentions that the Office of International Law of the Organization of American States has no record of any additional acts on the part of the Government of Nicaragua relating to the American Convention.

160. Based on this statement from the Office of International Law of the OAS, the State of Costa Rica has argued that the presentation of the note in which the State

of Nicaragua set out the instant interstate communication, as well as its subsequent processing by the Inter-American Commission on Human Rights, "in addition to a serious violation of the respective provisions in the Convention and—along with them—the basic principles of openness, *bona fide* and *pacta sunt servanda*, could not have come about in the absence of basic procedural prerequisites without a clear, elementary, and especially gross flaw in the proceeding, which has unquestionably impaired the procedural guarantees and possibilities of defense of the Costa Rican State."

161. In this respect, the Commission reaffirms that upon receiving the original communication from Nicaragua it conducted a preliminary verification of the documentary records and considered that the Nicaraguan State had indeed deposited the declaration mentioned in Article 45 of the Convention with the Office of the Secretary General. For the sake of clarification, and faced with the aforesaid allegations on the part of the State of Costa Rica, which contradicted what the Commission had been able to verify from the record in the case, on October 26, 2006, the IACHR wrote to the Secretary General to enquire whether or not the State of Nicaragua had deposited with the General Secretariat its declaration of recognition of the competence of the Commission to receive and examine communications in which a state party alleges that another state party has committed a violation of a human right set forth in the Convention. The Commission also requested the Secretary General to inform it if, in the event that he had received said declaration, the General Secretariat transmitted a copy of it to the member states in accordance with Article 45 of the American Convention on Human Rights.

162. In response to this inquiry, on October 27, 2006, the Director of the Department of International Legal Affairs—which is under the immediate orders of the Secretary General and supervises the Office of International Law—wrote to the Inter-American Commission to inform it "that on February 6, 2006 the General Secretariat received a note, which is enclosed, in which the Government of Nicaragua informs that in a declaration of January 26, 2006, it added a third paragraph to Declaration 49 of January 15, 1991, concerning the American Convention on Human Rights, in which it recognized the competence of the Commission to receive and examine communications in which a state party alleges that another state party has committed a violation of a human right set forth in the Convention. Today, in accordance with Article 45 of the American Convention on Human Rights, a copy of that declaration will be transmitted to the member states of the Organization."

163. Thus, it was confirmed that the State of Nicaragua did indeed make the necessary deposit with the General Secretariat of its declaration of acceptance of the competence of the Commission in accordance with Article 45(4) of the Convention.

164. It should be clarified that the American Convention designated General Secretariat as its depositary and that, upon depositing their declarations of acceptance of the competence of the Commission, states are not required to perform any additional acts before any other department of the Organization. Accordingly, the Commission stands by its initial determination that the deposit made by the State of Nicaragua on February 6, 2006, was correctly performed and, therefore, the Ni-

caraguan State was empowered to present a communication in the terms set forth in Article 45 of the Convention.

. . . .

167. As mentioned, Article 45 (4) of the Convention provides that the General Secretariat of the Organization shall transmit copies of the declarations that it receives as depositary to the member states of the Organization. It arises from the communication of the Director of the Department of International Legal Affairs that said transmission was completed on October 27, 2006. Therefore, the Inter-American Commission must determine the legal effects of the declaration that the State of Nicaragua deposited on February 6, 2006, in view of the fact that the transmission of the declaration deposited by the State of Nicaragua was not confirmed by the General Secretariat until October 27 of that year.

168. To that end, the Commission considers it appropriate to refer to the provisions of the Vienna Convention on the Law of Treaties with respect to the deposit of instruments of ratification, acceptance, approval, or accession. According to Article 16 of the Vienna Convention, "Unless the treaty otherwise provides, instruments of ratification, acceptance, approval or accession establish the consent of a State to be bound by a treaty upon: a) their exchange between the contracting States; b) their deposit with the depositary; or, c) their notification to the contracting States or to the depositary, if so agreed".

169. In that regard, the Commission considers that the American Convention, in keeping with the Vienna Convention on the Law of Treaties, opts for the general rule that the act of deposit in itself establishes the legal link. Even though the depositary has the duty to notify the states of the deposit of an instrument of ratification, this is solely for information purposes; notification is not a substantive part of the transaction by which the depositing state establishes treaty relations with other states. The act of deposit has the legal effect provided under the treaty even if its notification by the depositary is delayed or goes unnoticed. Similarly, late notification by a depositary of the date of a treaty's entry into force does not affect that date.

170. In the "*Case concerning right of passage over Indian territory*" resolved by the International Court of Justice, India, the respondent state, argued that the petition of Portugal, the complainant state, was filed before a copy of the Declaration of Portugal accepting the compulsory jurisdiction of the Court could be transmitted to other states parties. The International Court of Justice did not accept this argument and held that the contractual relation between the parties and the compulsory jurisdiction of the Court were established *ipso facto* by the fact of making a declaration. The Court added that a State accepting the jurisdiction of the Court must expect that an Application may be filed against it before the Court by a new declarant State on the same day on which that State deposits its Acceptance with the Secretary-General. Moreover, the Court found that the declarant State was concerned only with the deposit of its Declaration with the Secretary-General and was not concerned with the duty of the Secretary-General.[8]

. . . .

---

8 International Court of Justice: *Case concerning right of passage over Indian territory,* (Preliminary Objections), Judgment of 26 November 1957.

174. In that connection, the argument of the State of Costa Rica regarding the supposed lack of competence of the Commission because the State of Nicaragua had failed formally to deposit the declaration of acceptance of competence, should have been submitted at the earliest possible procedural opportunity by the Costa Rican State. In view of the fact that the State of Costa Rica was notified, upon its receipt of the initial communication of the State of Nicaragua, that the respective declaration of acceptance of the competence of the Commission had been delivered to the General Secretariat, the Commission considers that any delay in the transmission of this declaration to the other member states of the OAS could not have impaired the rights of the State of Costa Rica, which was fully informed of the existence of the declaration and the respective deposit thereof.

. . . .

176. Given that sufficient proof was presented along with the communication of the receipt by the Secretary General, on February 6, 2006, of the note by which the State of Nicaragua had deposited its declaration of acceptance of the competence of the Commission, the Commission assumes that the General Secretariat has performed its duty as depositary. Even though the Commission was concerned to learn that there was a delay in the communication of this declaration to other member states, the Commission considers that said delay in the notification of other members cannot be imputed to the IACHR or affect the processing of this communication.

177. Based on the foregoing, the Commission finds that in processing this interstate communication it has observed all the rules contained in the Convention and its Rules of Procedure that govern the processing of communications in which a state party alleges that another state party has committed a violation of a human right set forth in the American Convention, and that the interstate communication under examination fulfils the requirements contained in Article 45 of the American Convention. Therefore, the Commission now turns to analyze if the admissibility requirements set forth in the Convention for processing individual petitions and communications between states have been met.

Competence of the Commission *ratione personae, ratione loci, ratione temporis* and *ratione materiae*

Competence *ratione personae*

. . . .

179. The Inter-American Commission is not competent to determine individual responsibilities, whether of agents of the state or of third parties who participate in alleged violations. Rather, its competence is to determine the international responsibility of OAS member states. Therefore, the Commission is not authorized to examine the alleged responsibility of the persons named. . . . [by] the State of Nicaragua . . . in its communication. On the subject of acts allegedly committed by private individuals, the Commission is compelled to point out that it may only examine the direct responsibility of the State of Costa Rica as a result of the actions of its agents, or the indirect responsibility of the Costa Rican State arising from its

failure to take action against acts of private individuals that violate rights recognized in the Convention.

. . . .

188. The Commission also feels compelled on this point to analyze if it is competent to examine the interstate communication presented against the State of Costa Rica inasmuch as it refers not only to the aforesaid duly identified alleged victims, but also to a widespread group of potential victims, namely the "Nicaraguan migrant population in a vulnerable situation in Costa Rica."

189. It should be recalled that, to date, the jurisprudence of the Commission has been guided by its interpretation of Article 44 of the American Convention, according to which, for a petition to be admissible, there must be specific individually identified victims or refer to a specific and set group of victims composed of distinguishable individuals.

. . . .

193. With the development of the system for protection of human rights in favor of an interpretation that permits effective application of the guarantees set forth in the Convention, this position has gradually being complemented by one that recognizes the possibility of protecting a plurality of persons who had not previously been named, provided they are identifiable and distinguishable.[9] It is not necessary, therefore, to mention each individual by name, but to state objective criteria by which to distinguish the collection of identifiable persons as possible victims of violations by the fact of belonging to a group or community, without that entailing a class action on behalf of the entire population under the jurisdiction of the State, or a segment so vast as to render individual identification of the victims meaningless.

194. Having said that, the above-described criteria have been developed in the framework of petitions lodged pursuant to Article 44 of the Convention. Accordingly, the Commission must examine if Article 45 of the American Convention can be interpreted under the same guidelines as Article 44; in other words, if communications between states, like individual petitions, must individually identify the alleged victims of a violation in order to be admitted, or if, to the contrary, states are empowered to present communications in order to ensure the observance *erga omnes* by states parties of their obligations under the Convention, as a collective guarantee mechanism.

195. In this regard, the Commission observes that the wording of Articles 44 and 45 of the Convention, though similar, is not identical; the former provides that the Commission may admit petitions "containing denunciations or complaints of violation of this Convention by a State Party", while the latter states that the Commission may admit communications "in which a State Party alleges that another State Party has committed a violation of a human right set forth in this Convention." The Commission observes that the fact that for petitions presented pursuant to Article 44 the Convention refers to "denunciations or complaints of violation of this Convention," whereas for communications presented under Article 45 the Convention refers to allegations concerning "a violation of a human right set forth in this Convention,"

---

[9] I/A Court H.R., *The Mayagna (Sumo) Awas Tingni Community Case*, Judgment of August 31, 2001, Series C No. 79.

suggests an intention that states should be able to bring to the attention of the IA-CHR not only situations that have affected individual or identifiable victims but also generalized situations of widespread or systematic violation of human rights.

196. The foregoing does not mean that states may present to the Commission abstract cases that are not designed to protect the rights and freedoms of persons protected by the Convention; it only means that if a State party considers that another State party has committed generalized human rights violations it may turn to the Commission of to denounce this situation without the need to individually identify each possible victim.

197. The American Convention enshrines a system that constitutes a genuine regional public order the preservation of which is in the interests of each and every state party. The intention of the signatory states is the preservation of the system for protection of human rights, and if a State violates its obligation to ensure the human rights of the individuals under its jurisdiction it also violates its undertaking to other states. Therefore, the Convention has provided a mechanism that enables states to present communications to the IACHR in order to protect the regional system of human rights and contribute to the fulfillment of the guarantees recognized in the Convention.

198. In order that this collective guarantee mechanism might be effectively applied, the Commission must interpret it keeping in mind the position of the Inter-American Court, in the sense that states parties to the Convention must guarantee compliance with its provisions and its effects (*effet utile*) within their own domestic laws.[10] This principle applies not only to the substantive provisions of human rights treaties (in other words, the clauses on the protected rights), but also to the procedural provisions,[11] such as the one concerning the power of states to present communications alleging that another state has committed a violation of the Convention.

199. The Commission is required to interpret the Convention taking into account the object and purpose of the international system for protection of human rights. The provision that recognizes the competence of the Commission to receive and examine communications between states is a clause that is essential for the effectiveness of the international protection mechanism and, therefore, should be interpreted and applied in such a way that the guarantee that it establishes is genuinely practical and effective, bearing in mind the special nature of human rights treaties and their collective implementation. That provision enshrines the collective intention of the American States to guarantee the preservation of the inter-American public order in the area of human rights.

200. Thus, the Commission must interpret the mechanism enshrined in Article 45 of the Convention not as the right of a State with the purpose of enforcing observance of its rights or particular interests, but with the purpose of enabling the Commission to take steps against possible violations of the regional public order. It

---

[10] I/A Court H.R., *Constitutional Court Case, Competence,* Judgment of September 24, 1999, Series C No. 55, par. 36.

[11] The European Commission of Human Rights was of the same opinion in Applications 15299/89, 15300/89 and 15318/89, *Chrysostomos et al.* v. Turkey (1991). *Decisions and Reports,* Strasbourg, C. E., vol. 68, pp. 216–253.

is this interpretation that permits the collective guarantee mechanism provided in Article 45 to be implemented.

201. The notion of collective guarantee recognized in human rights treaties has been aptly described by the Human Rights Committee in General Comment 31. The Committee observed that "every State Party has a legal interest in the performance by every other State Party of its obligations. This follows from the fact that the 'rules concerning the basic rights of the human person' are *erga omnes* obligations and that [. . .] there is a [stipulated] obligation to promote universal respect for, and observance of, human rights and fundamental freedoms. Furthermore, the contractual dimension of the treaty involves any State Party to a treaty being obligated to every other State Party to comply with its undertakings under the treaty. In this connection, the Committee reminds States Parties of the desirability of making the declaration contemplated in article 41 [Article 41 recognizes the right of States parties to present communications claiming that another State Party is not fulfilling its obligations under the Covenant]. It further reminds those States Parties already having made the declaration of the potential value of availing themselves of the procedure under that article. [. . . .] Accordingly, the Committee commends to States Parties the view that violations of Covenant rights by any State Party deserve their attention. To draw attention to possible breaches of Covenant obligations by other States Parties and to call on them to comply with their Covenant obligations should, far from being regarded as an unfriendly act, be considered as a reflection of legitimate community interest."[12]

202. By the same token, the preamble and articles of the American Convention permit recognition of the existence of a regional public order that all States parties are obliged to ensure. The preamble of the Convention mentions the purpose of consolidating "in this hemisphere, within the framework of democratic institutions, a system of personal liberty and social justice based on respect for the essential rights of man."

203. The existence of a system of collective guarantee is also evinced by the fact that, in accordance with Article 35 of the American Convention, "[t]he Commission shall represent all the member countries of the Organization of American States," which means that it exercises its control functions in representation of all the OAS member states.

204. Similarly, the European system of human rights has interpreted the provision on interstate petitions contained in the European Convention in the sense that when a state party presents a communication alleging a violation of the Convention it is not exercising a right of action to demand observance of its rights, but drawing the attention of the Convention to an alleged violation of the public order of Europe.[13] The Court has also held that the European Convention creates, over and

---

[12] HRC. General Comment No. 31. Nature of the General Legal Obligation Imposed on States Parties to the Covenant: 26/05/2004. CCPR/C/21/Rev.1/Add.13. (General Comments)

[13] European Commission of Human Rights: Austria v. Italy, App. No. 788/60, 4 Eur. Yearbook of H.R. 116, p. 140 (1961)

above a network of mutual, bilateral undertakings, objective obligations which, in the words of the Preamble, benefit from a "collective enforcement".[14]

205. The Inter-American Court has consistently held that human rights treaties are living instruments whose interpretation must consider the changes over time and present-day conditions.[15] Were a generalized practice of human rights violations to exist at present in one of the states parties to the Convention, and another state party were to present a communication denouncing those violations to the Commission, the IACHR considers that it could not insist that the denouncing state individually identify each of the victims of this generalized situation of violations because such a requirement would be contrary to the spirit of collective guarantee that shapes the American Convention on Human Rights.

206. In the instant case, the State of Nicaragua says that it turns to the IACHR because it has the "duty to protect its nationals and safeguard their human rights, wherever they may be, and the obligation to denounce the deplorable situation of discrimination and xenophobia of which Nicaraguans in the sister republic of Costa Rica are victims, irrespective of their situation or immigration status, which poses a high risk to the enjoyment and exercise of their fundamental freedoms and human rights." The Commission notes that the State of Costa Rica undertook to respect and ensure the rights recognized in the American Convention for all persons subject to its jurisdiction, regardless of their national origin.

207. In the light of the foregoing considerations, the Commission concludes that it also has *ratione personae* competence to take up the interstate communication presented by the Nicaraguan State on behalf of the Nicaraguan migrant population in Costa Rica, irrespective of their situation or immigration status.

Competence *ratione loci*

208. The Commission is competent *ratione loci* to examine this interstate communication because it alleges violations of rights protected in the American Convention that are purported to have occurred within the territory of a state party to said treaty.

Competence *ratione temporis*

214. The question that the Commission must now resolve is if its competence to examine the interstate communication dates from the day on which the state against which the communication was presented deposited its declaration of recognition of said competence (July 2, 1980), or from the day that the State that presented the communication deposited its declaration of recognition of the Commission's competence (February 6, 2006).

215. Given that the Convention provides that communications between states shall be admitted and examined only if they are presented by a State Party that has made a declaration recognizing the competence of the Commission to examine communications between states, and if they are presented against a State party

---

14 European Court of Human Rights: Ireland v. United Kingdom, Judgment of 18 January 1978, Series A no. 25, p. 90, par. 239.
15 I/A Court H.R., *The Right to Information on Consular Assistance in the Framework of the Guarantees of the Due Process of Law,* Advisory Opinion OC-16/99 of October 1, 1999, Series A No. 16, par. 114.

that has made such a declaration, the Commission considers that the Convention requires reciprocity in order for communications between states to be valid.

216. Based on this requirement, until it has been determined that the essential prerequisite of reciprocity exists, the Commission is not competent to examine possible violations of the American Convention in the framework of an interstate communication. It is as of February 6, 2006, that both states parties in this communication recognized the competence of the Commission to receive and examine communications between states and, therefore, the IACHR was competent from that point forward.

217. The fact that the Commission may not examine acts that occurred prior to the deposit of the declaration of recognition of competence of the Inter-American Commission is wholly consistent with the principle of non-retroactivity of international treaties set forth in Article 28 of the Vienna Convention on the Law of Treaties of 1969, according to which, "[u]nless a different intention appears from the treaty or is otherwise established, its provisions do not bind a party in relation to any act or fact which took place or any situation which ceased to exist before the date of the entry into force of the treaty with respect to that party."

218. Although, strictly speaking, Article 28 of the Vienna Convention applies to treaties, which are of a nature different to declarations concerning recognition of competence of an organ, this provision contains an important generally applicable principle of treaties: the principle of non-retroactivity of conventional provisions unless agreed otherwise by the states. The principle of non-retroactivity applies to all acts connected with a treaty, including declarations concerning the competence of an international organ such as the IACHR. The principle of non-retroactivity of international standards recognized in the Vienna Convention on the Law of Treaties has also been invoked by the Inter-American Court when it has had cause to make a decision on its competence by reason of time. The Court has determined based on this principle that it is competent only to examine acts that occur after the contentious jurisdiction of the Court is recognized.[16]

219. The foregoing does not preclude examination by the Commission of allegations concerning violations that predate the deposit of the declaration of acceptance of the competence of the Commission if said violations are continuous over time; in other words, if they continue to occur after the competence of the Commission is recognized. In this respect, the Inter-American Court has consistently held that it is possible to examine continuous violations without infringing the principle of non-retroactivity.[17]

220. Accordingly, the Commission has *ratione temporis* competence to examine any acts and omissions that have occurred since February 6, 2006, the date on which it was determined that both states parties in this communication recognized the competence of the Commission, in addition to the effects of possible violations. Furthermore, the Commission is competent to examine continuous violations that

---

[16] I/A Court H. R., *Case of Alfonso Martín del Campo Dodd, Preliminary Objections,* Judgment of September 3, 2004, Series C No. 113, par. 85.

[17] I /A Court H. R., *Case of the Serrano Cruz Sisters, Preliminary Objections*, Judgment of November 23, 2004, Series C No. 118, par. 64; I/A Court H. R., *Case of the Moiwana Community,* Judgment of June 15, 2005, Series C No. 124, par. 39.

commenced before the date of the declaration of recognition but which have continued after said declaration of recognition

Competence *ratione materiae*

221. Finally, the Commission is competent *ratione materiae*, because the interstate communication alleges violations of human rights protected by the American Convention.

D. Admissibility requirements for the interstate communication

1. Characterization of the Facts Alleged

. . . .

223. . . . [T]he Commission finds that, *prima facie*, the communication describes allegations, which, if proven, could constitute violations of the rights protected by Articles 8 (Right to a fair trial), 25 (Right to judicial protection), and 24 (Right to equal protection) of the Convention, in connection with the general obligation to respect and ensure rights contained in Article 1(1) of said international instrument, inasmuch as they refer to the possible existence of a systematic practice of discrimination against all Nicaraguan migrants in Costa Rica.

224. As regards the alleged violation, asserted by the State of Nicaragua, of the rights recognized in Articles 2, 7, 8, and 28 of the Universal Declaration of Human Rights; in Articles II and XVIII of the American Declaration of the Rights and Duties of Man; and in Article 9 of the Inter-American Democratic Charter, the Commission observes that for the States Parties to the Convention, the specific source of their obligations with respect to the protection of human rights is, in principle, the Convention itself.

225. Once the American Convention came into force for the State of Costa Rica it became the principal source of legal norms for application by the Commission insofar as the petition alleges violations of substantially identical rights in other instruments.[18] In this case, the rights allegedly violated by the State of Costa Rica under the Universal Declaration and the American Declaration enjoy similar protection under the Convention. Therefore, given that in the instant case the violations alleged by the Nicaraguan State concern rights that are similarly protected by the aforesaid instruments, the Commission will only address the alleged violations of the standards contained in the Convention and not those contained in the Universal Declaration or the American Declaration.

226. It should be clarified that, pursuant to Article 29(d) of the Convention, this international instrument does not exclude or limit the effect that the American Declaration of the Rights and Duties of Man and other international acts of the same nature may have. Thus, the American Declaration contains and defines the fundamental human rights referred to in the Charter, and the Charter of the Organization cannot be interpreted and applied as far as human rights are concerned without

---

18   This is confirmed by the Commission in its jurisprudence. See, *inter alia*: IACHR Report 70/99 of May 4, 1999, Case 12.059 *Carmen Aguiar de Lapacó*, Argentina; IACHR Report N° 1/01 of January 19, 2001, Case 12.085 *Ana Elena Townend Diez-Canseco et al*, Peru; IACHR Report N° 87/99 of September 27, 1999, Case 11.506 *José Víctor Dos Santos and Waldemar Jerónimo Pinheiro*, Paraguay; IACHR Report N° 112/99 of September 27, 1999, Case 11.603 *Álvaro Lobo Pacheco et al*, (19 Merchants), Colombia.

relating its norms to the corresponding provisions of the Declaration. Therefore, in its analysis, the Commission may take into consideration the provisions of the Universal Declaration, the American Declaration and the Inter-American Democratic Charter, insofar as they may be pertinent to interpret the Convention and determine possible violations committed by the State of Costa Rica of the human rights that it enshrines.

. . . .

2. Duplication of proceedings and res judicata

. . . .

230. The Commission considers that the subject matter of the interstate communication is neither pending in another international procedure for settlement, nor substantially the same as a petition or communication previously studied by the Commission or by another international organization. Therefore, the requirements established at Articles 46(1)(c) and 47(d) of the Convention have been met.

3. Exhaustion of domestic remedies

Allegations of the parties on the rule of exhaustion of domestic remedies:

233. The IACHR must first analyze the allegations of the parties with respect to exhaustion of domestic remedies. According to the interstate communication presented by the State of Nicaragua, "the Ministry of Foreign Affairs of Nicaragua, on behalf of the State, on November 17, 2005, and December 6, 2005, requested the Ministry of Foreign Affairs and Worship of Costa Rica to carry out a thorough, prompt, and exemplary investigation to punish those responsible for the brutal death of Natividad Canda Mairena and the murder for reasons of nationality of José Ariel Urbina Silva [sic]. The Ministry of Foreign Affairs reiterated its demands in communications of November 18, 2005 and January 30, 2006, requesting that all testimonies given to the press be preserved, guaranteeing that such acts did not go unpunished." On this point, the Commission reiterates that extrajudicial measures of this type cannot be considered a suitable recourse for the purposes of determining if the remedies under domestic law have been exhausted.

234. The State of Nicaragua also alleged in its interstate communication that "on one hand, the extreme poverty of the families of the victims and, on the other, the delay of justice validate the arguments with respect to exhaustion of domestic remedies."

. . . .

239. For its part, the State of Costa Rica did not waive the option to invoke the rule of exhaustion of domestic remedies, which waiver would have been valid in accordance with the precedents established by the IACHR and the Inter-American Court. On the contrary, at the earliest possible opportunity in the proceeding before the Commission, the Costa Rican State contended that "domestic remedies have not been exhausted in either of the matters concerning the alleged violation of human rights by the Costa Rican State. Both cases are currently under examination by the appropriate judicial authorities [. . .]. The time taken in both investigations has been within lawful and reasonable limits in accordance with Costa Rican law and the demands of due process, particularly considering the complexity of the

events and the type of rights that have been affected—and that could be affected—
by the judicial proceedings."

Considerations of the Commission on the alleged impossibility to exhaust domestic
remedies do to the indigence of the victims

246. The Commission deems it timely to recall, in first place, that merely because
a person is indigent does not, standing alone, mean that he does not have to exhaust
domestic remedies, but that whether or not an indigent has to exhaust domestic
remedies will depend on whether the law or the circumstances permit him to do so.
That opinion was ratified by the Court in Advisory Opinion 11/90. The Commission has reiterated in its jurisprudence that a declaration of indigence without any
corroborating evidence is insufficient to establish that "indigence" prevented the
Petitioner from invoking and exhausting domestic remedies.[19]

247. In the instant case, the State of Costa Rica has shown that, as regards the
identification of those responsible for the deaths of Messrs. Leopoldo Natividad
Canda Mairena and José Ariel Silva Urbina, and the injuries to Messrs. José Antonio
Martínez Urbina, Francisco Angulo García, Rito Antonio Obando and Elder Angulo García, these are matters for public action and, therefore, the State investigates
them *ex officio* without the need for a private accusation. Furthermore, the State of
Costa Rica has demonstrated that the alleged victims or their representatives had
the opportunity to receive free technical assistance, which is provided for by law in
cases of financial hardship without any distinction based on the nationality of the
victims or of those responsible for the punishable act. The record also shows that
the relatives of one of the alleged victims, Mr. Natividad Canda Mairena, has the
access to advisory services from a private attorney.

248. In as much as the respondent state has shown that the remedies under domestic law were available for the injured parties in the cases of Messrs. Canda and
Silva, it was up to the complainant State to demonstrate that they were unable to
obtain the necessary legal assistance to protect or guarantee rights recognized in
the Convention. Given that the State of Nicaragua has not provided any evidence
that would enable the Commission to determine that the indigence of the victims
prevented them from having access to the remedies under domestic law, the Commission concludes that this exception is not applicable.

Considerations of the Commission on the alleged unwarranted delay in rendering a
final judgment under domestic remedies

249. The Commission finds it necessary to recall that, as a general rule, a criminal investigation and the respective proceeding should be carried out promptly in
order to ensure the attainment of justice. However, at the same time, it is necessary
to afford the machinery of the domestic courts the necessary time to properly weigh
the arguments of all the parties, in order to form a certain conclusion on the facts,
and present a reasoned argument for their decisions. In spite of the fact that, as the
Inter-American court has ruled, the rule of prior exhaustion must never lead to a

---

[19] IACHR Report N° 81/05 of October 24, 2005, Petition 11.862 Andrew Harte and Family, Canada.

halt or delay that would render international action [. . .] ineffective.[20] The ultimate purpose of the rule of prior exhaustion of domestic remedies is to give the State the opportunity to examine an alleged violation of a right protected in the Convention and apply the mechanisms under its internal law in order to remedy the situation before it is taken up in an international proceeding.

250. In the instant case, the events connected with the deaths of Messrs. Leopoldo Natividad Canda Mairena and José Ariel Silva Urbina, and with the injuries to Messrs. José Antonio Martínez Urbina, Francisco Angulo García, Rito Antonio Obando and Elder Angulo García, occurred on November 10, 2005, and December 4, 2005, respectively, and were brought to the attention of the Inter-American Commission on February 6, 2006. Accordingly, less than three months had elapsed between the events and the time the interstate communication was lodged with the Commission.

251. However, the Commission has previously mentioned that in examining exhaustion of domestic remedies a distinction must be made between the time the petition is lodged and the pronouncement on its admissibility. These two proceedings correspond to two different phases, which are easily distinguished based on the legal effects of Article 33 of the Rules of Procedure, which authorizes the Commission to ask the petitioner to complete the requirements omitted when the petition is incomplete or inadmissible.[21] In other words, as the petitioner has the opportunity to rectify deficiencies in the petition after it is presented, the prerequisite of prior exhaustion of domestic remedies must be fulfilled by the time the Commission examines that aspect.

252. Accordingly, in adopting a decision on exhaustion of domestic remedies, the Commission shall consider the status of domestic proceedings not at the time that it took receipt of the petition, but when it issues its report. In the course of processing the interstate communication, the Commission has received very limited information on the domestic judicial proceedings in the cases connected with this communication. From the scant information received to date, on which it is basing its decision in this case, the Commission finds with respect to both cases that the alleged culprits have been identified and, at least in the case of Mr. Natividad Canda Mairena, two policemen have been formally charged. The Commission considers that the State of Nicaragua has not provided sufficient evidence from which to conclude that there has been a delay on the part of the Costa Rican judicial authorities in these cases, nor that said delay is unwarranted. Therefore, the exception of unwarranted delay is not applicable to the cases of Messrs. Leopoldo Natividad Canda Mairena, José Ariel Silva Urbina, José Antonio Martínez Urbina, Francisco Angulo García, Rito Antonio Obando and Elder Angulo García.

---

[20] I/A Court H.R., *Velásquez Rodríguez Case, Preliminary Objections*, Judgment of June 26, 1987, Series C No. 1, par. 93.

[21] In this regard, see: IACHR Report N° 52/00 of June 13, 2000, Cases 11.830 et al, ("Dismissed Congressional Employees"), Peru; IACHR, Report N° 101/01 of October 11, 2001, Case 10.247 et al. (Extrajudicial Executions and Forced Disappearances), Peru; IACHR, Report N° 25/04 March 11, 2004, Case 12.361 Ana Victoria Sánchez Villalobos *et al*, Costa Rica.

Considerations of the Commission on the impossibility to exhaust domestic
remedies due to the alleged existence of a generalized practice of discrimination

. . . .

255. Based on its examination of the arguments and evidence presented by the
two states, the Commission finds that the allegation of the existence of a generalized practice of discrimination against the Nicaraguan migrant population in Costa
Rica is not manifestly groundless nor obviously out of order.

256. The Commission notes that these arguments have an effect on the question
of exhaustion of domestic remedies since, in a widespread climate of discrimination
such as the one alleged, the remedies available under domestic law could become
illusory or ineffective for all Nicaraguans in Costa Rica, including Messrs. Leopoldo
Natividad Canda Mairena, José Ariel Silva Urbina, José Antonio Martínez Urbina,
Francisco Angulo García, Rito Antonio Obando and Elder Angulo García.

257. When the existence is alleged of a generalized practice of acts incompatible
with the Convention which are shown to be officially tolerated, thereby rendering
domestic proceedings futile, the exception to the rule of exhaustion of domestic
remedies is applicable because it is reasonable to presume that no adequate or effective remedies exist to remedy a generalized situation.

258. Since its inception, the Inter-American Commission on Human Rights was
aware that it could not insist that victims of widespread human rights violations
meet the same requirements vis-à-vis exhaustion of domestic remedies. It was this
reasoning that led the Second Special Inter-American Conference held in 1965 to
adopt a rule of interpretation according to which in the event of systematic generalized violations, such a situation gives rise to a presumption *juris tantum* that
domestic remedies are neither suitable nor effective and, therefore, the requirement
to exhaust them is dispensed with as a mere formality.

. . . .

261. However, the Commission adds that in order to invoke this exception it is
necessary to demonstrate *prima facie* the existence of the alleged practice. On this
point, the Commission concurs with the position of the former European Commission of Human Rights, according to which it is not sufficient that the existence
of supposed legislative measures or administrative practices be simply alleged; it is
also necessary, in order to seek an exception to the rule of exhaustion of domestic
remedies under such an argument, that the existence of the purported legislative
measures and administrative practices be demonstrated with substantive proof.[22]
Otherwise, it would be sufficient for any petition or interstate communication to
allege the existence of a generalized practice of human rights violations in order
to circumvent the requirement to exhaust domestic remedies contained in the
Convention.

262. Therefore, the question as to whether or not the exception to the rule of
exhaustion of domestic remedies is applicable due to the absence of a suitable and
effective remedy is closely connected with the merits of the matter, that is, with the

---

[22] European Commission of Human Rights: First *Greek Case*, 2nd decision on admissibility, Yearbook 1;
Northern Ireland Case, decision on admissibility, Yearbook 15, 80, *Ireland v. United Kingdom*, Decision on
admissibility, Yearbook 15, p. 242.

question of whether or not it is determined that a generalized practice of discrimination exists in Costa Rica to the point where the remedies provided by domestic law are futile.

263. The Inter-American Commission must exercise the utmost care in scrutinizing allegations that a systematic practice of human rights violations exists in an OAS member state because, if true, the allegations would mean that the individuals who are victims of said pattern of violations have very few or no means at the domestic level to protect themselves from said violations

264. At the same time, the Commission cannot ignore the particular gravity of accusing a state party to the Convention of having carried out or tolerated on its soil a systematic practice of discrimination. Accordingly, the Commission's evaluation is compelled to take this fact into account and conclusively demonstrate the truth of the allegations.

265. These are the exceptional circumstances that led to the Commission to open the case but defer its treatment of admissibility until the debate on the merits, giving both parties the opportunity to present arguments and evidence on the merits of the case, in order to determine if the existence was confirmed *prima facie* of a generalized practice of discrimination in Costa Rica toward the Nicaraguan migrant population, which would make the exception to the rule of exhaustion of domestic remedies applicable.

Considerations of the Commission on elements that must coincide in order to corroborate the existence of a generalized practice of discrimination in Costa Rica to the detriment of the Nicaraguan migrant population

266. It falls to the Inter-American Commission to decide, based on the evidence presented during the stages on admissibility and merits in the framework of this interstate communication, if it has been shown sufficient proof to determine prima facie the existence of a regular pattern of discriminatory acts carried out as part of a state policy or with the tolerance of the State of Costa Rica, to the detriment of the Nicaraguan migrants in its territory.

267. That is, to determine the admissibility of this communication, the Commission must analyze if the acts alleged form part of systematic practice of discrimination toward the Nicaraguan migrant population in Costa Rica and if the Costa Rican State has adopted concrete measures connected with this said practice or if it has tolerated the existence of said practice. The Commission accepts the opinion of the European Court on this point, according to which "a practice incompatible with the Convention consists of an accumulation of identical or analogous breaches which are sufficiently numerous and inter-connected to amount not merely to isolated incidents or exceptions but to a pattern or system; a practice does not of itself constitute a violation separate from such breaches."[23]

268. From the foregoing it may be deduced that the Commission must determine, first, if the acts alleged could constitute acts of discrimination. To that end, the Commission will take into account what the Inter-American Court has held with respect to the fact that Nowadays, "no legal act that is in conflict with this

---

[23] European Court of Human Rights, *Ireland v. the United Kingdom*, 5310/71, 18 January 1978.

fundamental principle is acceptable, and discriminatory treatment of any person, owing to gender, race, color, language, religion or belief, political or other opinion, national, ethnic or social origin, nationality, age, economic situation, property, civil status, birth or any other status is unacceptable."[24]

269. The Commission will also bear in mind that not all difference in treatment can be considered discriminatory. As the Court has found,[25] no discrimination exists if the difference in treatment has a legitimate purpose and if it does not lead to situations which are contrary to justice, to reason or to the nature of things. It follows that there would be no discrimination in differences in treatment of individuals by a state when the classifications selected are based on substantial factual differences and there exists a reasonable relationship of proportionality between these differences and the aims of the legal rule under review. These aims may not be unjust or unreasonable, that is, they may not be arbitrary, capricious, despotic or in conflict with the essential oneness and dignity of humankind.

270. At the same time, the Commission must determine if the acts alleged in the communication to be discriminatory constitute isolated or circumstantial acts, or if they are the consequence of a generalized practice. In this connection, the Inter-American court has noted that "the confirmation of a single case of violation of human rights by the authorities of a State is not in itself sufficient ground to presume or infer the existence in that State of widespread, large-scale practices to the detriment of the rights of other citizens."[26]

271. To corroborate the existence of said practice, the Commission must take several elements into account. The first element relates to quantity, that is, the alleged discriminatory acts must be perpetrated in such a quantity as to create a situation in which the human rights of a large sector of the population are being continuously violated or under constant threat. A second element relates to time, that is, the discriminatory acts alleged must occur regularly over a considerable period of time as part of a prolonged or habitual situation. A third element has to do with the existence of a pattern, which implies that that the alleged acts of discrimination do not occur as an isolated matter or as a matter of chance or coincidence, instead they shall obey to certain common characteristics that connect them among each other and allow to conceptualize them as elements of the same situation. Lastly, there must be an element of official tolerance in the sense that the State has been remiss, evasive or negligent in respect to their obligations regarding the discriminatory acts alleged.

272. The Commission, therefore, proceeds to examine if the acts charged by the State of Nicaragua can lead the IACHR to conclude the existence *prima facie* of a pattern of discrimination to the detriment of the Nicaraguan migrant population in Costa Rica.

---

[24] I/A Court H. R., *Juridical Condition and Rights of the Undocumented Migrants*, Advisory Opinion OC-18 of September 17, 2003, Series A No. 18, par. 101.

[25] I/A Court H.R., *Proposed Amendments to the Naturalization Provisions of the Constitution of Costa Rica*, Advisory Opinion OC-4/84 of January 19, 1984, Series A No. 4, par. 57.

[26] I/A Court H.R., *Gangaram Panday Case*, Judgment of January 21, 1994, Series C No. 16, par. 64.

Analysis to determine the existence of a sufficiently generalized practice of discrimination to render the exhaustion of remedies under domestic law futile

279. Based on . . . [an evaluation of the submissions] the Commission finds that it lacks sufficient evidence with which to determine conclusively that the circumstances surrounding the death of Mr. Leopoldo Natividad Canda Mairena or the treatment of this incident by the Costa Rican judicial authorities are an example of the practice of discrimination alleged to exist in Costa Rica.

280. The Nicaraguan State has alleged that the case of Mr. José Ariel Silva Urbina, in which Messrs. José Antonio Martínez Urbina, Francisco Angulo García, Rito Antonio Obando and Elder Angulo García were also injured, is likewise an example of the climate of xenophobia and discrimination that exists in and is accepted by the State of Costa Rica.

. . . .

284. The Commission finds that based on the information available it is possible to conclude that there was a close link between the Nicaraguan nationality of the victims in this case and the verbal and physical attacks that occurred in and outside the bar. The statements of witnesses show that the cause of the attacks that culminated in the death of Mr. Silva Urbina and the wounding of other Nicaraguan citizens is tightly associated with their Nicaraguan nationality. When incidents such as these occur and include threats of violence based on the nationality of the victims, in particular when those threats are proffered in public and by a group of persons, it is up to the State to conduct a prompt investigation of the facts with due diligence, not only of the attack on the life and physical integrity of the victims but also of the possibility that it was motivated by discrimination. In this respect, the Commission is of the opinion that, when it is suspected that discrimination for reasons of race, nationality or any other motive has induced violent incidents, State authorities have the additional duty to take all reasonable steps to unmask any racist motive and to establish whether or not ethnic hatred or prejudice may have played a role in the events.

285. The Commission has received very limited information on the domestic judicial proceedings which were initiated in Costa Rica to identify those responsible for these acts of violence. From the documents presented by the State of Costa Rica, the Commission has been able to deduce that as a result of the complaint made by Red Cross personnel to the Judicial Police, a criminal investigation was opened in which Mr. Juan Arguedas Calderón has been charged with the murder of Mr. José Ariel Silva Urbina and the attempted murder of Messrs. Antonio Martínez Urbina and Francisco Linares García. However, based on the testimonies collected by different news media, the Commission finds that some other witnesses claimed that before being assaulted with a knife they received a beating from a mob of Costa Ricans and the Nicaraguan citizens were also injured by stones thrown at them.

. . . .

287. The information in the possession of the Commission with respect to this incident and its ensuing judicial proceeding is so limited that it is unable to determine conclusively if the treatment that the Costa Rican State has given to these

events constitutes an example of the practice of discrimination alleged to exist in Costa Rica.

. . . .

290. The State of Nicaragua has insisted that a situation of impunity reins in violations committed against Nicaraguans, and by failing to adopt effective measures to prevent impunity, the State has prompted further discrimination and encouraged intolerant sectors to continue a campaign of xenophobia. The Inter-American Court has defined impunity as "the total lack of investigation, prosecution, capture, trial and conviction of those responsible for violations of the rights protected by the American Convention," a situation that the State has the obligation to combat using all the legal means at its disposal.[27]

291. With respect to the alleged impunity, to demonstrate that the State of Costa Rica has violated the rights to a fair trial and judicial protection to the detriment of the Nicaraguan migrant population, it was incumbent on the State of Nicaragua to show, for instance, that investigations are not opened *ex officio* in cases where a Nicaraguan is the victim; or that when Nicaraguans turn to the administrative or judicial authorities they run the risk of deportation, expulsion, or deprivation of liberty. Alternatively it could have demonstrated that in specific cases Nicaraguans have been denied the free services of a public defender to act on their behalf, preventing them from upholding their rights. However, the State of Nicaragua presented no evidence in that respect and, rather, the record shows that the State of Costa Rica has investigated and offered free legal advisory services to victims of Nicaraguan origin. In that connection, the Commission notes that it has received only general allegations and the evidence in the record is not sufficient to conclude that the Costa Rican State is behaving in a remiss, evasive, or negligent manner with respect to the investigation and punishment of those responsible for human rights violations to the detriment of Nicaraguan citizens in Costa Rica

292. The Commission observes that the State of Nicaragua has provided no evidence that tends to demonstrate a practice of violence allegedly targeting persons of Nicaraguan origin in Costa Rica. The Commission is also at a loss to find examples in sufficient number to permit the presumption that such a practice exists. Nor has the State of Nicaragua brought to the attention of the Commission evidence of tolerance or acquiescence by the Costa Rican judicial authorities. For example, it has not been demonstrated that the criminal cases in which the victims are Nicaraguans are not being investigated, remain in impunity, assailants are punished with less severe penalties, or any other circumstances from which to presume acquiescence or tolerance on the part of the state.

293. The State of Nicaragua has also referred on several occasions to the attitude of the Costa Rican people to the Nicaraguan migrant population, which it alleges is discriminatory. States which, like Costa Rica, have a high number of immigrants under their jurisdiction cannot overlook the fact that those immigrants are in a vulnerable situation as regards the exercise of their human rights. This vulnerability is even greater when a state receives on its soil a large number of citizens of

---

[27] I/A Court H.R., *The "Panel Blanca" Case (Paniagua Morales et al.)*, Judgment of March 8, 1998, Series C No. 37, par. 133.

another state because a negative predisposition towards the immigrant population often develops in the population of the host State. This negative predisposition is often accompanied by social stigmatization and, even though manifestations of xenophobia or discrimination may lie latent in any society, the migrant population is particularly vulnerable to such manifestations.

294. The Commission has received an abundance of information on the reactions of the Costa Rican population to the acts alleged in this communication and, based on that information, the Commission considers that the record duly accredits that certain sectors of the population in Costa Rica seized on the tragic circumstances in which Mr. Canda Mairena died to make public jokes and comments in different media, the contents of which illustrate a disturbing hostility toward the Nicaraguan migrant population that resides in Costa Rica. In response to these manifestations, the State of Costa Rica, through a press release issued by the Ministry of Foreign Affairs and Worship, expressed its profound disapproval for the contents of said messages. In light of the foregoing, it is not possible to deduce that the State of Costa Rica has tolerated these practices.

295. Based on the information in the record, the Commission considers it demonstrated that there is a prevailing feeling of intolerance and rejection toward Nicaraguans among certain sectors in Costa Rica. Furthermore, the evidence presented by the State of Nicaragua also leads to the conclusion of the existence of a perception of vulnerability among Nicaraguans, who feel themselves to be the object of discrimination in Costa Rica. For example, from the interviews contained in the videos supplied by the Nicaraguan State it is possible to observe that Nicaraguan residents in Costa Rica attributed the circumstances in which Messrs. Canda Mairena and Silva Urbina died to their immigrant status. However, no evidence has been provided from which to conclude that these perceptions have translated into concrete practices. The Commission notes that any concrete practice of discrimination is prohibited and that states have the obligation to prevent, combat, punish, and eliminate discriminatory practices. However, unless they translate into discriminatory acts or omissions by reason of their causes or effects, the perceptions of the population do not constitute a practice that could be said to be grounds for establishing the international responsibility of the state.

296. The State of Nicaragua has also furnished abundant information from which it can be seen that national, regional, and international agencies, including the Rapporteurship on Migrant Workers and their Families,[28] have expressed concern at

---

[28] It should be noted that the powers of the Commission to prepare the studies and reports that it deems advisable for the performance of its main function of promoting observance and protection of human rights, in accordance with Article 41(c) of the Convention, are different from its powers to process the petitions and communications that it examines in exercise of its authority to determine whether or not there has been a violation of a right or freedom protected in the Convention, under Articles 44 or 45 of that international instrument. This conclusion arises from a simple reading of the provisions contained in the Convention and has been ratified by the Commission in its reports. Thus, the Commission has held that its competence to prepare general reports is independent from its power to process individual petitions and that the processing of a case pursuant to the individual petition procedure is more structured than the preparation of a general report, which serves an informative rather than adjudicatory purpose. Accordingly, the factors and evidence that the IACHR weighs in issuing a report or study on the situation of human rights in the country are different from those that it uses to declare the international responsibility of a state in the framework of a contentious proceeding.

the situation of the Nicaraguan migrant population in Costa Rica. Studies carried out by these agencies provide an account of the difficulties that migrants face in Costa Rica, particularly if they lack the necessary papers. Those studies provide an information overview that the Inter-American Commission finds alarming. Thus, they report that requirements are set by the Educational Development Directorates, which prevent the enrollment of children and adolescents if they or their parents do not have a temporary or permanent residence permit; that undocumented migrants work in conditions of overexploitation; and that staff of the Costa Rican Social Security Fund report to the General Directorate of Immigration persons who go for a medical consultation and are found not to have a legal residence permit. Taken together, each of these allegations could be sufficient to establish the existence of a pattern of discriminatory acts and omissions to the detriment of the Nicaraguan migrant population. For that purpose, it is necessary to provide not only general information on the different circumstances alleged, but also concrete examples in sufficient number to enable the Commission to take the alleged practice as attested. However, the State of Nicaragua has not informed the Commission of any concrete cases from which to corroborate the conclusions of these studies and demonstrate the existence of a systematic practice of discrimination in the State of Costa Rica.

297. Similarly, the State of Nicaragua has mentioned that the Law on Migration and Nationality violates the human rights of a number of victims but it has not presented the Commission with any cases in which the Law has been applied to a specific victim. The Commission concurs with the analysis of the State of Nicaragua and various organizations whose comments were added to the record in the case, that the law on migration and nationality is oriented toward protecting public security rather than human rights, and grants broad, discretionary powers to the administrative authorities in Costa Rica. However, the Commission notes that the Costa Rican State has acted within its powers in adopting the law in order to establish mechanisms of control on the entry and departure of undocumented migrants to its territory and to treat documented migrants differently from undocumented migrants, always assuming that this different treatment is reasonable, objective, proportional, and does not violate human rights.

298. Although the Commission decided to admit this general case, in which the State of Nicaragua names as victims of human rights violations the Nicaraguan migrant population in a vulnerable situation in Costa Rica, in so doing it noted that the instant case could not be equated with an abstract case since its purpose is the protection of the rights and freedoms of the Nicaraguan migrant population in Costa Rica. The Commission could present an opinion on the Law on Migration and Nationality in an abstract manner through a general recommendation or a study issued in the framework of its principal function to promote the observance and protection of human rights. However, in the framework of a contentious case such as this one, in order for the Commission to pronounce an opinion on the Law, the State of Nicaragua had to show that said law has been applied to the detriment of the protected rights and freedoms of the Nicaraguan migrant population.

. . . .

301. In view of the fact that the State of Nicaragua has not presented the Commission with information that would allow it to conclude that this law has been applied to the detriment of the rights of the Nicaraguan migrant population in Costa Rica, the Commission cannot consider it an example of the generalized discrimination alleged to exist in Costa Rica.

302. Finally, throughout the procedure of this case, the State of Nicaragua has asserted that the State of Costa Rica has confessed the existence of discrimination and xenophobia in its territory. To this respect, the Inter-American Commission values the reiterated occasions in the course of this proceeding on which the State of Costa Rica has recognized that there are enormous challenges to prevent the rise of xenophobia between the two nations, and that those states should adopt preventive measures to strengthen relations between the two peoples. Under no circumstances could the Commission conclude that the State of Costa Rica bears responsibility on the basis of this recognition, as the State of Nicaragua has requested, since it is far from being an acceptance of the factual and legal arguments put forward in the communication.

303. At the same time, the Commission wishes to thank the State of Costa Rica for its invitation in the framework of this interstate communication for the IACHR or its Rapporteurship on Migrant Workers and their Families to conduct an on-site visit to Costa Rica in order to assess the actual situation of Nicaraguan immigrants in its territory. The situation of the migrant population in Costa Rica has been a matter of constant attention by the Inter-American Commission, and its Rapporteurship noted in the year 2002 that "there is a certain degree of discrimination against persons of Nicaraguan origin,"[29] but it observed that the discrimination suffered by migrant workers and their families does not reflect a State policy, but rather has to do with a negative predisposition with respect to migrant workers on the part of the population.[30]

304. The lack of specific evidence presented in the framework of this interstate communication has prevented the Commission from arriving at the determination that certain acts have been verified in Costa Rica to allow the Commission to conclude that there is a generalized practice of discrimination against Nicaraguans in Costa Rica.

305. Based on the foregoing, the Commission concludes that the State of Nicaragua has not demonstrated, in the framework of the proceeding on this communication, the existence of a generalized practice of discrimination in Costa Rica toward the Nicaraguan migrant population.

306. Having been unable to corroborate *prima facie* the existence of a generalized practice of discrimination against the Nicaraguan migrant population in Costa Rica, it would be inappropriate for the Commission to assume that no suitable and effective remedies exist to repair the violations alleged in this interstate communication. Accordingly, the exception to the rule set forth in Article 46 of the Convention does not apply.

---

29 IACHR *Annual Report 2002*, Fourth Progress Report of the Rapporteurship on Migrant Workers and their Families in the Hemisphere, Chapter V, par. 146.

30 IACHR *Annual Report 2002*, Fourth Progress Report of the Rapporteurship on Migrant Workers and their Families in the Hemisphere, Chapter V, pars. 145 and 147.

. . . .

VI. CONCLUSIONS

309. Based on the foregoing, the claims of the Nicaraguan State with regard to violation of the rights recognized in Articles 1(1) (Obligation to respect rights), 8 (Right to a fair trial), 24 (Right to equal protection), and 25 (Right to judicial protection) of the American Convention on Human Rights, are inadmissible under Articles 46 of the Convention and 31 of the Rules of Procedure of the IACHR.

310. The Commission takes this opportunity to condemn all acts of discrimination or xenophobia against migrant persons of any origin, and recalls that the international system for protection of human rights was created and operates on the basic premise that all human beings are equal and, therefore, precludes all discrimination. The Commission reiterates that it is impermissible to subject human beings to differences in treatment that are inconsistent with their unique and identical nature and that states have the duty not to commit discrimination as well as the obligation to protect individuals against discrimination, whether this occurs within the public sphere or among private parties.

Questions and Comments

1. The optional inter-State jurisdiction of the Inter-American Commission has been accepted by only nine states: Argentina, Chile, Colombia, Costa Rica, Ecuador, Jamaica, Peru, Uruguay and Venezuela. What might account for the reluctance of other states to permit such proceedings?

2. What were the objections of Nicaragua and Costa Rica to the procedures the Commission followed in its handling of the case? Did any of them have merit? On the question of consent to jurisdiction, note that the United States similarly claimed Nicaragua had failed to accept ICJ jurisdiction in *Military and Paramilitary Activities in and against Nicaragua* (Nicaragua. v. United States), 1984 ICJ Rep. 392.

3. In para. 221, the Commission states that it has subject matter jurisdiction "because the interstate communication alleges violations of human rights protected by the American Convention." Is an inter-State communication required to allege violations of guaranteed rights or could it, e.g., challenge the legality of a state's reservation to the Convention or acts in breach of the immunity of a judge of the Inter-American Court?

4. The Commission placed itself at the disposal of the parties with a view to reaching a friendly settlement. Is this required or appropriate in inter-State cases?

5. How do you understand the footnote in the opinion at para. 296? In particular, in reading the following materials, consider whether the Commission should be using and does in fact use different standards of evidence in assessing the conditions of human rights within a State as part of a country report in contrast to a contentious case.

4. Country Reports

A country study is an investigation of the human rights conditions within a State. Such studies are undertaken by the Inter-American Commission and are within the competence of the African Commission. Something similar is done by the Parliamentary Assembly in reviewing the commitments made by new member states, but neither the former European Commission nor the European Court have ever had a mandate to undertake country studies.

In the Inter-American system, the Commission may initiate a country study when it receives individual communications or other credible reports, often from non-governmental human rights organizations, suggesting that widespread human rights violations are taking place. See, e.g., IACHR, Report on the Situation of Human Rights in Guatemala, OEA/Ser.L/V/11.53, doc. 21 rev. 2 (1981), at 1("in view of this serious situation and in consideration of the several accusations received," the Commission decided to undertake a study and request an on site visit). On rare occasions, the state itself has invited the Commission to undertake a study. See, e.g., IACHR, Report on the Situation of Human Rights in Panama, OEA/Ser.L/V/II.44, doc. 38 rev. 1, at 1–3 (1978). The first country reports were prepared in the early 1960s and dealt with Cuba, Haiti and the Dominican Republic. The Dominican Republic was the first country to grant permission for the Commission to conduct an on-site investigation. The modus operandi adopted by the Commission during its visits to the Dominican Republic in the 1960s, where it heard witnesses, received other evidence, met with government and opposition leaders, and set up temporary offices in the country, became a model which it has followed with minor variations to this day in its on-site investigations.

On-site investigations are usually arranged by an exchange of letters and cables between the chairman of the Commission and the government concerned. Prior to 1977, the rules governing on-site visits were negotiated on an ad hoc basis. Thereafter the Commission adopted a set of rules on the subject, which are now contained in Articles 51 through 55 of the Commission's Rules of Procedure. Among the Rules, Article 52 of the Regulations seeks to avoid any conflict of interest by providing that members of the Commission who are nationals of or reside in a country under investigation shall be ineligible to participate in the on-site visit. According to Judge Buergenthal,

> The very presence of the Inter-American Commission in a country has at various times contributed to the improvement of conditions in it. The most dramatic example is provided by the role the Commission performed during the Dominican civil war, when it saved hundreds of lives and obtained the release from detention camps and prisons of large numbers of political detainees. . . .

Thomas Buergenthal, *The Inter-American System for the Protection of Human Rights*, in T. Meron (ed.), HUMAN RIGHTS IN INTERNATIONAL LAW 439 AT 482 (OUP, 1984).

After the relevant information has been gathered, the Commission prepares a draft report examining the conditions in the country by reference to the human rights standards set out in the American Declaration of the Rights and Duties of Man or of the American Convention on Human Rights, depending upon whether or not the state is a party to the Convention. The draft report is then submitted to that country's government for its comments. The Commission analyzes the government's response to determine whether the report should be amended in light of any new information submitted. Finally, the Commission decides whether to publish the report. The Commission's Rules require the publication of the report if the government does not respond to the request for observations (Art. 58). The Commission does not have to publish the report, however, if the government either agrees to comply with the recommendations or demonstrates that it is not committing any violations. The reports published by the Commission now usually reproduce the government's observations and are sent to the OAS General Assembly, which may adopt resolutions directed at the country. The strongest resolution to date was adopted against Nicaragua and is reprinted in Chapter I.

Cecilia Medina, *The Role of Country Reports in the Inter-American System of Human Rights*, in D. Harris and S. Livingstone, THE INTER-AMERICAN HUMAN RIGHTS SYSTEM (OUP, 1998), 115, 116–118, 120, 122, 126, 132 (footnotes omitted).

In the early 1960s, a major objective of the human rights movement was to give individuals a possibility of resorting to the international community when the state under whose jurisdiction they found themselves did not respect their human rights. . . .

The American continent was not only lacking in that sort of mechanism; it also had no human rights convention and the Commission was but an 'autonomous entity' of the Organization of American States, created in a legally insecure manner by a resolution of the Fifth Meeting of Consultation of Ministers of Foreign Affairs. It was to be expected then that the Commission would follow the trend and, in appearance this is what the Commission did when, contrary to the attitude of the UN Human Rights Commission concerning petitions, it decided that, although 'it was not empowered to make any individual decision with regard to written communications or claims it might receive' it would 'take cognizance of them for the purpose of using them in fulfillment of paragraphs b) and c)' of Article 9 of its Statute. . . .

. . . [T]he main objective seemed to have been, however, a different one. The Commission had discovered very soon that the mere examination of petitions, European-style, would not lead to an improvement of human rights in the continent, since the problems to be faced were frequently gross, systematic human rights violations perpetrated by dictatorial regimes. To deal with these, a formal judicial or quasi-judicial decision or opinion to the effect that the conduct of a state amounted to a violation of human rights seemed pointless; states which perpetrate gross, systematic violations are clearly aware that what they are doing constitutes a serious infringement of their international obligations in the field of human rights, and their attitude vis-à-vis international supervisory organs is one of denial of the facts and not, as usually happens in the individual petition procedure, one of disputing the interpretation of the extent and scope of a right and/or its application to the facts of a particular case.

. . . [T]he primary objectives pursued by the Commission at the outset were, firstly, to create a mechanism that would make it possible to document a situation of gross, systematic violations in a state and, secondly, to encourage the OAS political organs to undertake political action in [this] respect. To these ends, *in loco* observations and country reports were clearly very well suited. . . . Its best form was reached in 1985 in the fourth report on Chile, which can be considered a model report compared with what had been done before then. . . .

The fact that the Commission is the body to select the countries to be examined has been the object of opposition within the OAS membership from the very beginning of the Commission's work. However, in spite of the efforts of some countries, the Commission has not been deprived of its right to make the selection. . . .

There seems to have been no objection so far to the modalities used by the Commission for fact-finding, except to its use of the facts of individual petitions. This has been contested by states on the basis that confidentiality is being breached and that the publication of a country report of the facts of individual cases implies the outcome of the Commission's opinion on the petition in the sense that it suggests that the facts constitute a violation of the international obligations of the state. Also contested has been reference to individual situations which have not yet been the subject of a petition registered by the Commission. . . .

When examples are used of individual cases in which the Commission has already written a report on the merits, it has to be taken into account that in most, if not all, of them the Commission's opinion has been adopted on the basis of the presumption of truth provided for in Article 42 of the Commission's Regulations. This means that the state has either remained silent in the face of the allegations of the complainant, or has provided counter arguments which are clearly inadequate, or has made only a general denial, and the Commission has found the complainant's allegation prima facie well-founded. If this is the case, the Commission will not have examined any evidence.

. . . [D]ebate on country reports often takes the form of a dialogue between the member of the Commission presenting the report [to the General Assembly] and the representative of the state concerned. The latter usually defends the government by attacking the Commission and accusing it of misusing its supervisory powers. The rest of the states' representatives express their support for the general work of the Commission, or for the state which has attacked it, but refuse to deal with the issues in the country report which are supposedly under consideration. . . .

Country reports would better achieve their objectives if states were to carry out their obligations fully. A thorough debate in the political organs of the OAS of the substance of the violations documented in a report, or the causes thereof and of the possible solutions thereto, followed by political recommendations and firm political actions to monitor compliance would most probably do much to improve the situation of human rights in the continent.

Report on the Situation of Human Rights in Venezuela, OEA/Ser.L/V/II.118, doc. 4 rev. 2, 29 December 2003.

1. The Inter-American Commission on Human Rights has been closely following the human rights situation in Venezuela, and has taken steps within its mandates to guarantee respect for human rights in that country. To this end, the Commission has used various mechanisms provided in inter-American human rights in-

struments, such as the case system, the adoption of precautionary measures, the request for provisional measures from the Inter-American Court on Human Rights, *in situ* visits to the country, and press releases.

2. In response to an invitation from the Venezuelan government, the Commission made an *in situ* visit from May 6 to May 10, 2002. The Commission had planned to conduct a series of follow-up visits, but has been prevented from doing so to date because the Venezuelan State has been unable to establish the corresponding dates.

3. This report, which consists of seven chapters, examines the situation in Venezuela, with a particular focus on various aspects relating to the rule of law in the country. The report was prepared on the basis of information collected before, during, and after its *in situ* visit to Venezuela in May 2002, and covers subsequent events up to October 2003.

4. The report was prepared during political and institutional upheaval. The political climate in Venezuela has shown a marked tendency to radicalization, which became accentuated in the early months of 2002 and culminated in a breakdown of the constitutional order on April 11, with its subsequent restoration on April 14 of that year.

5. The primary purpose of this report is to engage the Venezuelan State to analyze the human rights situation and to formulate recommendations that will assist the State in meeting its international obligations in the area of human rights.

6. In the first place, the IACHR welcomes the inclusion in the Venezuelan Constitution of a provision that gives constitutional rank to human rights treaties ratified by the State. It also notes that the new constitution has strengthened and expanded legal protection for personal safety and integrity, and for preventing practices that undermine those values.

7. The new Constitution also contains special provisions relating to human rights, as in Chapter VIII on the rights of indigenous peoples, Chapter IX on environmental rights, and Chapters VI and VII on social, economic and cultural rights; the prohibition in Article 45 with respect to the forced disappearance of persons; and the creation of new institutions for protecting human rights, such as the Ombudsman's Office (*Defensoría del Pueblo*) and the Constitutional Chamber of the Supreme Court of Justice.

8. Notwithstanding these positive constitutional developments, however, the situations identified in the various chapters of this report demonstrate a clear weakness in the fundamental pillars that must support the rule of law in a democratic system, consistent with the American Convention on Human Rights and other international instruments.

9. The Commission noted that during the period between March 2002 and the first quarter of 2003 more than 40 people were killed and some 750 were injured as the result of street protests. The extreme political polarization and resulting acts of violence that have erupted periodically between different demonstrators to growing political intolerance in the country. The IACHR has noted worrisome signs of institutional weakness, including the failure to give full application to the new Constitution, the perception that the branches of government lack independence, the grow-

ing concentration of power in the national executive, the impunity in which certain armed civilian groups and para-police units operate, the government's tendency to confrontation and disparagement of the political opposition, the constant attacks on journalists and the media, the tendency to militarize the public administration through the increasingly prominent role of the armed forces, the growing radicalization of political postures in the context of popular discontent over unmet social demands, and disputes relating to the exercise of trade union rights.

10. Chapter I, on the administration of justice and human rights, focuses on aspects affecting the administration of justice in Venezuela. The Commission analyzes the autonomy and independence of the judiciary, the provisional status of most of the country's judges, and the makeup of certain institutions.

11. With respect to the provisional judges, the Commission notes that this is a problem which long predates the current government. Nevertheless, the problem has worsened since the government began the process of judicial restructuring. The Commission was informed that only 250 judges have been appointed through competition, as the Constitution requires. Of the total of 1,772 judges in Venezuela, the Supreme Court of Justice reports that only 183 have tenure, 1,331 are provisional, and 258 are temporary. This means that 84% of magistrates continue to have provisional or temporary status, and lack tenure in their positions.

12. Another aspect of concern to the Commission with respect to guaranteeing the independence and impartiality of the Venezuelan judiciary relates to the failure to enforce the mechanisms provided by the new Constitution for the election of its Supreme Court authorities. The Commission reiterates the conclusion from its *in situ* visit, to the effect that the failure to respect the Constitution fully creates legal insecurity that impedes the consolidation of the rule of law. For this reason, the Commission believes that it is urgent to adopt organic laws as the appropriate means of establishing the mechanisms stipulated in the Constitution for the selection of judges of the Supreme Court of Justice, as well as the Public Ombudsman, the National Attorney General, and the National Comptroller General.

13. The Commission has also received information pointing to a significant increase in impunity with respect to acts of violence. According to that information, 90% of investigations related to human rights violations never advance beyond the preliminary stage. The Commission was told specifically that in the first quarter of 2003 the Judicial Police had referred 3,892 cases to the Courts, but the Courts had resolved only 772, or 19% of these cases. These figures are on a par with those for the year 2002, when only 667 of 9,529 homicide cases resulted in definitive judgments. The Commission finds these figures particularly alarming, because impunity constitutes a grave violation of the obligations of states, and implies a kind of vicious circle that tends to repeat and perpetuate itself, thereby increasing the crime rate, particularly for violent offenses.

14. Chapter II, on civil society, examines the situation of human rights defenders in Venezuela.

15. The IACHR has received a considerable number of complaints about various kinds of attacks and acts of intimidation against persons devoted to protecting and promoting respect for the fundamental rights of Venezuela's inhabitants. Acts of ha-

rassment against human rights defenders and human rights organizations at times go as far as attacks on the life and physical integrity of those defenders. A series of cases have been verified in which defenders were the targets of various mechanisms of intimidation. In at least one case, the IACHR had to request provisional measures from the Inter-American Court of Human Rights in order to protect members of a human rights organization.

16. Chapter III, on State security, examines the role of the armed forces and security police.

17. The Commission notes that the Constitution extends the scope of the concept of security not only to the military sphere but also to the cultural, social, economic and political spheres, among others. The IACHR wishes to stress that in a democratic society this broad and progressive concept of national security must be suitably interpreted in ways that do not presuppose increased powers for the armed forces in fields beyond their competence.

18. The IACHR was greatly concerned at the many reports received of an excessively deliberative role for the armed forces, and the undue influence they exert on the country's political life. The Commission believes it is essential for the Venezuelan State to take urgent measures to ensure that the armed forces do not adopt a deliberative role, and that they do not involve themselves in the country's political life.

19. The Commission also observed problems in the conduct of the various police forces, as evident in a series of events, in particular: the proliferation in several states of death squads linked to the police, a situation that undermines the rule of law and poses a particular threat to the right to life; the lack of coordination among the various security bodies, and in particular between the National Guard and the Metropolitan Police, the Metropolitan Police strike that began in October 2002, the police strikes in several states of the country; the disproportionate use of force in certain circumstances, assassinations attributed to the Metropolitan Police at the time of the constitutional breakdown, and the political struggle for control of that institution between the national executive and the office of the mayor of Caracas.

20. In Chapter IV, on the right to life, the Commission finds that the situation has worsened considerably, due to the increase in impunity and violence. This problem is particularly severe in certain states, notably in Portuguesa, Anzoategui, Falcon, Yaracuy, Caracas, Bolivar, Aragua and Miranda. More than 30 cases have come to light in seven different states where persons were summarily executed by para-police groups. The escalating violence has resulted in 55 assassinations in the course of street violence, and more than 500 people have died in presumed confrontations that have not been sufficiently clarified.

21. The Commission believes that a system that does not guarantee immediate and effective investigation, prosecution and punishment is incapable of enforcing respect and protection for the rights of the victims nor of the alleged perpetrators. In examining this issue, the Commission must reiterate what it has maintained on several occasions, to the effect that a State is not only responsible for human rights violations committed by its agents or through the conduct of para-police groups operating with its acquiescence or consent, but it also incurs international respon-

sibility when it fails to take adequate measures to prevent, investigate and punish criminal acts by individuals or particular groups. As noted throughout this report, priority must be given to fulfilling the State's commitment to strengthen the administration of justice and to stamp out impunity.

22. In Chapter V, on the right to humane treatment and personal integrity, the Commission notes that the sharpening institutional conflict in Venezuela has made itself felt in acts of violence that have involved attempts against people's lives, and numerous attacks on personal integrity. The Commission has received many complaints from nongovernmental agencies and from individuals, claiming that torture continues to be practiced by the police, even in the course of judicial investigations, as a means of intimidating prisoners and extracting confessions from them. As well, the Commission finds that the competent State bodies have failed to fulfill their duty to investigate complaints in these cases and to punish those responsible, who generally enjoy impunity, a situation that encourages the repetition of such conduct. It also notes a lack of effective surveillance over the physical integrity of prisoners in civilian and military detention centers alike. According to the information received, it is the police who are primarily responsible for cases of torture, since these take place primarily in police stations. Torture is commonly applied to persons under detention or investigation.

23. In Chapter VI, on the right to freedom of expression and thought, the IACHR has identified two areas of particular concern relating to freedom of expression: the first involves threats, attacks and acts of harassment against social communicators, particularly those working in the streets, and the failure to investigate those threats and attacks; the second refers to judicial decisions and draft legislation that, if enforced, would severely constrain the full exercise of freedom of expression for the inhabitants of Venezuela. The third has to do with the initiation of administrative proceedings by CONATEL and the Ministry of Infrastructure against the communications media, relating to the content of their programming, and applying legislation that may be inconsistent with the inter-American system.

24. The IACHR with has noted many instances of verbal or physical assaults in recent years. There have been threats and attacks against social communicators, especially those covering public events, political rallies and activities relating to the security forces. Before, during and after the *in situ* visit, the IACHR was informed that social communicators working in the streets were being targeted for attack and harassment. The overall situation in Venezuela has generated a climate of aggressiveness and continuous threats against the freedom of expression, and in particular against the personal integrity of journalists, cameramen, photographers and other social communication workers.

25. Given the vulnerability in which communication workers find themselves, the IACHR asked the Venezuelan State to adopt precautionary measures on eight occasions during 2002, and in many cases these were extended in order to protect the life, personal integrity and freedom of expression of journalists, cameramen and photographers. The Inter-American Court of Human Rights was also asked to order provisional measures. In a decision of March 21, 2003, the Court declared that the State had failed to comply with those measures. The Commission expressed its

concern over the failure to comply with the provisional measures granted by the Court, and with the Commission's own precautionary measures. In July 2003 the IACHR decided to request further provisional measures from the Court in order to protect two journalists.

26. The IACHR received expressions of concern over the possibility that the communications media in Venezuela may not always act responsibly or ethically. As the IACHR reported upon completion of its *in situ* visit, it took note of media activities obstructing access to information that was vital for Venezuelan society during the tragic events of April 2002, which saw the coup d'état and the restoration of democracy in Venezuela. The IACHR notes that, while there may be many reasons to explain this lack of information, to the extent that the suppression of information has resulted from politically motivated editorial decisions, there is room for a good deal of soul-searching on the part of the Venezuelan media about their role at that time.

27. In Chapter VII the IACHR examines the situation of trade union freedoms in light of the current political and institutional setting.

28. With respect to the situation of trade union freedoms in Venezuela, the IACHR notes that the political crisis and the atmosphere of intolerance that marks the current political setting has sparked an increase in labor conflicts over this issue. The IACHR is particularly concerned over the mass dismissal of workers at Petroleos de Venezuela (PDVSA). Information provided shows that a total of 12,383 workers were dismissed from this State enterprise on grounds of having abandoned their workplace in the context of the so-called national civic strike that lasted from December 2002 until February 2003.

29. The Commission confirmed a situation of forceful intervention by the State in union affairs, despite repeated recommendations from the ILO (International Labour Organisation) that it should refrain from such behavior. As well, the Commission believes it is urgent to resolve the problem of recognizing the leadership of the CTV, the main Venezuelan labor confederation, out of regard for the needs and rights of its members.

30. The IACHR notes that there has a significant step forward in the area of trade union freedom. On July 23, 2002, the Electoral Chamber of the Supreme Court of Justice ruled that action by the Supreme Electoral Council was of a subsidiary nature, and that therefore that body could only intervene when there was a dispute that the labor organization itself could not resolve.

31. Finally, the IACHR wishes to highlight the important progress that has been made toward settling the institutional crisis by peaceful and electoral means, in clear demonstration of the solid democratic commitment of the Venezuelan people. The IACHR again notes the pact signed by representatives of the government and the opposition on May 29, 2003, in context of the Roundtable for Negotiation and Accord. This is a fundamental document that marks a turning point in the current situation, whereby the parties have agreed that the application of constitutional mechanisms is the institutional route to be followed in resolving the crisis. The Commission hails this achievement and calls on all parties to continue on the road

of tolerance and democratic dialogue, and to work together to implement that pact in all situations that so require.

32. The Commission hopes that the Government of Venezuela, and the other political players in the country, including the members of the legislature and the judiciary, will continue to demonstrate the political will to seek solutions to the serious human rights problems that affect the country's inhabitants. The Inter-American Commission offers the Venezuelan State and society as a whole its full cooperation in the efforts at promotion, protection and consultation that are needed to move towards a solution of the country's human rights problems.

I. BACKGROUND OF THE REPORT

. . . .

4. In the context of the functions noted above, the IACHR regularly monitors THE human rights situation in OAS member states. From 2000 to the present, the Inter-American Commission has been closely following events in the Bolivarian Republic of Venezuela and has acted within the bounds of its mandate to ensure the observance of human rights in that country. In this respect, the Commission has employed the various mechanisms envisaged by the American Convention for the protection of human rights, namely the case system, adoption of precautionary measures, request for provisional measures from the Inter-American Court of Human Rights, on-site visits to the country and press releases. The following is a brief outline of these undertakings.

5. In 2000, the Commission, through its Office of the Special Rapporteur for Freedom of Expression, observed the development of an atmosphere of hostility at the highest levels of government as a mechanism of direct and indirect pressure on the media and social activists.

6. Following this, the Executive Secretary of the IACHR and then Rapporteur for Freedom of Expression, Dr. Santiago A. Canton, at the invitation of the Government of Venezuela, visited the Bolivarian Republic of Venezuela on February 5 to 8, 2002. The objective of this visit was to collect information on freedom of expression in Venezuela and to perform a preliminary evaluation in aid of an IACHR on-site visit scheduled for May 2002. In addition, Dr. Canton's visit represented a response to concerns expressed by several sectors of civil society regarding recent developments related to freedom of expression in the country.

7. During the serious events of April 11, 2002, the Commission condemned the coup d'état against the constitutional order. The Commission issued a press release to this effect on April 13, 2002 in which it expressed, *inter alia*, its strong condemnation of the acts of violence and its regret that the most senior authorities were removed from public office, and cautioned that these acts represented a breach of constitutional order. Moreover, the Commission noted that, from April 12 to 13, arbitrary arrests and other violations of human rights claimed the lives of more than 40 persons and caused injury to one hundred others.

8. The Commission later conducted an on-site visit to the Bolivarian Republic of Venezuela from May 6 to 10, 2002. Held within the framework of the American Convention to which Venezuela is a signatory, and the governing Statute and Rules of Procedure of the IACHR, the visiting party comprised the President of the Com-

mission and Rapporteur for Venezuela, Dr. Juan E. Méndez; First Vice-President, Dr. Marta Altoguirre, and Commissioners Professor Robert K. Goldman, Dr. Julio Prado Vallejo and Ms. Susana Villarán. Also participating were the Executive Secretary of the IACHR, Dr. Santiago A. Canton, Special Rapporteur for Freedom of Expression, Eduardo Bertoni, and staff from the Executive Secretariat.

9. Upon completion of this on-site visit, the Commission issued a press release presenting preliminary comments based on its observation of the general human rights situation in the country and offering certain recommendations that in its opinion would serve to mitigate some of the serious problems identified.

10. On December 12, 2002, the Commission issued a press release in which it expressed serious concern over the deepening crisis in Venezuela and urged member states of the OAS to take immediate steps to "work with Venezuelans in seeking an urgent solution that will prevent further loss of human life and ensure Venezuelans that the rule of law will remain fully in force."

11. During the 117th Regular Session of the Commission, held between February 20 and March 7, 2003, the IACHR continued inquiries into the status of the rule of law in Venezuela. On March 10, 2003, the IACHR issued a press release reiterating its concern about the continuing deterioration of the rule of law in Venezuela.

12. In response to wishes expressed by the Government of Venezuela during the on-site visit, the Commission had planned to carry out a series of follow-up visits. To date, these visits have not been conducted due to the failure on the part of the Venezuelan State to establish the dates. It is the view of the IACHR that the presence of the Commission in the country will help significantly to bolster the defense and protection of human rights in a context of democracy and institutional legality. In this light, the Commission requests that a date be set for an on-site visit.

13. In relation to this matter, the General Assembly of the Organization of the American States (OAS) in Resolution AG/1917 (XXXIII-O/03), with respect to the Annual Report of the IACHR, resolved the following:

To note with satisfaction the decisions taken by governments of member states to invite the Inter-American Commission on Human Rights to visit their respective countries and to encourage all member states to continue this practice.

II. SCOPE OF THE PRESENT REPORT, ITS APPROVAL AND FOLLOW-UP

14. This report will analyze the present situation in Venezuela, with specific reference to the various aspects of the current status of the rule of law in the country.

15. As noted above, by virtue of its competence as a key organ of the Organization of the American States charged with the protection and promotion of human rights in the Americas and in accordance with its mandate, as stipulated in the American Convention on Human Rights and more specifically defined in its Statute and Rules of Procedure, the Inter-American Commission monitors human rights developments in each member state of the OAS.

16. The present report was prepared on the basis of a diverse array of information and materials compiled and analyzed by the Commission, including those collected during its on-site visit to Venezuela in May, 2002. In addition to reflecting insights gathered on that occasion, the report refers to information compiled prior to and in preparation for the visit. Material referred to in the report also includes updated

information provided by governmental, intergovernmental, non-governmental, academic and media sources through the Commission's normal monitoring procedures, as well as through the processing of individual petitions. The report was prepared on the basis of this information with a closing date of November 4, 2003.

17. The draft "Report on the Situation of Human Rights in Venezuela" was approved by the Commission during its 118th Regular Session.

18. The report was transmitted to the State by the Executive Secretary on November 13, 2003, with the request that the former present any observations it deemed pertinent within the fix dead line of a month. On December 12, 2003 the Government requested an extension of the due date to present its observations. On December 16, 2003 the IACHR informed the Government that an extension could not be granted while indicating that the Commission would await a reasonable time before publishing the report approved by the IACHR, so as to allow the Government to submit its observations which would be publish in the IACRH web page. On December 29, 2003 the IACHR ultimatelly approved the report and the publication without having received the observation of the Government.

19. Finally, it should be reiterated that the present report was prepared in a context of political and institutional instability. In so doing, the IACHR takes note of the efforts made in negotiations between the Government of President Chávez and representatives of *Coordinadora Democrática* [Democratic Focal Point], the conduct of which was supported and facilitated by the Secretary General of the OAS, César Gaviria, with technical support of the United Nations Development Programme and the Carter Center, and also benefiting from the support of the Group of Friends of Venezuela. Among its activities, the Commission takes note of the first formal agreement reached between the Government and the Opposition in approving a seven-point document entitled "Declaration against Violence, and in support of Peace and Democracy" signed by the parties on Monday, February 17, 2003, one hundred days after its establishment. The IACHR also considers a significant advance the Agreement recently signed by representatives of the Government and the Opposition, on May 29, 2003, in which negotiations were brought to a close and both parties indicated that the electoral resolution of the country's crisis would be achieved through the application of Venezuela's constitutional provisions.

. . . .

CONCLUSIONS: THE STATUS OF THE RULE OF LAW IN VENEZUELA

523. Since 1999 the IACHR has expressed itself through various mechanisms on the situation relating to the rule of law in Venezuela. The Commission has used various mechanisms provided in the American Convention for the protection of human rights, and in fulfillment of its mandate to stimulate the conscience of the peoples of the Americas it has alerted the international community to the progressive worsening of the human rights situation in Venezuela.

524. This report has identified weaknesses in the rule of law in Venezuela, and has focused primarily on examining the factors and causes behind the institutional crisis that has gripped the country, causing deterioration in the rule of law. On this point, the Commission has offered in each chapter a series of recommendations that it considers indispensable for restoring social peace in a democratic state and

society. The intent of this report is to help the Venezuelan State in its analysis of the human rights situation in that country, as a State party to the American Convention on Human Rights, and to make recommendations for improving its compliance with its international obligations in the field of human rights. Consolidating and strengthening the rule of law represents an indispensable condition for the more effective protection of individual rights in Venezuela.

525. The Commission stresses that democracy and the rule of law are necessary conditions for the enjoyment and respect of human rights in any society. In this respect, the Commission notes that the collapse of the rule of law in a State party has repercussions that go beyond democratic governance: indeed the historical experience of Latin America has shown that institutional collapse undermines fundamental rights and creates fertile ground for subsequent violations of human rights. Therefore, it must be noted, in the first place, that there is a close triangular relationship between the rule of law, a democratic society, and the enjoyment of human rights.

526. The definition of the rule of law is based on three essential principles. First, the principle of the limitation of power, which is reflected in the constitutional distribution of power. In the second place, the principle of legality, which establishes that the State organs must exist and act under subjection to the law. The Constitution is the supreme law of the land, to which all State organs must submit themselves, including obviously the holders of the executive power, who may not exceed the stipulations of the Constitution. Finally, the third principle is that of the declaration of fundamental rights.

527. The fundamental corollary of constitutional rights is the possibility of recourse to the judicial organs, which must guarantee that rights are upheld. In fact, the judiciary has been established for the protection of rights and guarantees, and is undeniably the fundamental body for protecting human rights. Consequently, if the courts are subordinated or if their rulings are ignored, this represents an attack against the rule of law. In this context, the functioning of an independent and impartial judiciary as the guarantee of protection for human rights is fundamental for the rule of law.

528. As a form of political organization for a constitutional State, democracy is based on the principle that political sovereignty is vested in the people and that, in exercise of that sovereignty, the citizens elect their representatives, who wield political power, while respecting the rights of those whose views are in the minority. These representatives receive a mandate from the voters, who aspire to a decent life, to freedom and to democracy, objectives that can only be achieved through effective control over public institutions and through the existence of checks and balances between all the branches of government. While the citizens elect their representatives, they also participate in the process of taking decisions through a multitude of means of expression and peaceful assembly. The effective observance of human rights requires a juridical and institutional order in which the law takes precedence over the will of those who govern, and in which there is a proper balance between all branches of government, in order to preserve the expression of the popular will through the rule of law.

529. The organs of the inter-American system have on numerous occasions declared the importance of the democratic system and the rule of law for the enjoyment and protection of human rights. The Inter-American Court of Human Rights has said:

> The concept of rights and freedoms as well as that of their guarantees cannot be divorced from the system of values and principles that inspire it. In a democratic society, the rights and freedoms inherent in the human person, the guarantees applicable to them and the rule of law form a triad. Each component thereof defines itself, complements and depends on the others for its meaning.

530. The Commission has declared:

> Democracy and the rule of law are necessary prerequisites for achieving observance of and respect for human rights within a society. This involves exercising rights of political participation, respecting the principles of the judiciary's legality, autonomy, and independence, and ensuring effective protection against actions by State agents.

531. According to the Inter-American Democratic Charter, the essential elements of representative democracy include, inter alia, respect for human rights and fundamental freedoms, access to and the exercise of power in accordance with the rule of law, the holding of periodic, free, and fair elections based on secret balloting and universal suffrage as an expression of the sovereignty of the people, the pluralistic system of political parties and organizations, and the separation of powers and independence of the branches of government. As well, transparency in government activities, probity, responsible public administration on the part of governments, respect for social rights, and freedom of expression and of the press are essential components of the exercise of democracy.

532. Finally, the IACHR wishes to stress the fact that the effective protection of human rights requires not only progress towards full and authentic democracy, but also the assurance that such a system of political organization provides every person with the possibility of achieving respect and enjoyment for all human rights, both civil and political, as well as economic, social and cultural. It also constitutes the best guarantee for preserving democracy as a system, recognizing that as the people become convinced through their own personal experience that this is the best model of political organization, they themselves will provide the strongest guarantee against traditional dictatorships and other authoritarian forms of government.

533. With respect to the coup d'état in April 2002, the Commission reiterates that nothing can justify the breach of the Constitution or any attempt to prevent the functioning of key institutions such as the branches of government. The breakdown in the constitutional order constituted a violation of the basic principles of international law in force in the Americas, as reflected primarily in the Inter-American Democratic Charter, and the rights enshrined in the American Convention. At that time the Commission deplored the dismissal by decree iof the highest officers of the judiciary and of independent officials within the executive branch, and the suspension of the mandate of the members of the legislature. On April 13, 2002, the Commission also requested information on the incommunicado detention of President Hugo Chavez and precautionary measures relating to the personal liberty and integrity and judicial guarantees of Mr. Tarek William Saab, President of the Foreign Relations Committee of the National Assembly.

534. In a similar vein, the OAS Permanent Council on April 13, 2002, issued a declaration to the effect that: "an alteration of the constitutional regime has occurred in Venezuela, which seriously impairs the democratic order [. . .]."

535. The IACHR again condemns in the strongest terms the violent events that cost dozens of lives and left more than 100 people injured. It is not the role of the IACHR to determine individual criminal responsibility for those events, but it is within its purview to insist upon the international obligation of the State to investigate and prosecute those responsible for the deeds committed between April 11 and 14, in accordance with the rules of due process, and to ensure that those deeds do not go unpunished.

536. The Commission recalls that, in investigating and in identifying and punishing those responsible for this attack against democratic institutions, the Venezuelan State must set an example of impartiality and respect for human rights, which implies, among other things, full respect for judicial guarantees and other rights and guarantees of the persons investigated for such deeds. The IACHR will continue to monitor these proceedings closely to ensure that they comply with the judicial guarantees enshrined in the American Convention on Human Rights.

537. The Commission has observed, as noted throughout this report, that between March 2002 and first quarter of this year more than 40 people were killed and some 750 injured as the result of street protests. The extreme political polarization and the resulting acts of violence that erupt periodically between demonstrators of different persuasions illustrate the growing political intolerance in the country. Among the signs of institutional weakness are the failure to enforce the new constitution, the perceived lack of independence of the branches of government, the growing concentration of power in the national executive, the impunity with which armed civilian groups and death squads conduct their activities, the tendency to confrontation and to denigrate the traditional political opposition on the part of the government, the constant attacks on journalists and the news media, the tendency to militarization of public administration through the increasingly prominent role of the armed forces, the growing radicalization of political stances in the context of widespread public discontent with the failure to meet social demands, controversies over the exercise of trade union rights, and the climate of harsh political intolerance and, in relation to the inter-American system, the repeated and persistent failure of the State to comply with precautionary measures granted by the IACHR and the provisional measures ordered by the Inter-American Court, all of which has been documented in this report and will be presented in summary fashion below.

• Administration of Justice and Human Rights

538. In this section, the IACHR identifies two issues of great importance relating to the independence of the judiciary, the provisional status of judges, and the failure to comply with constitutional rules in appointing judges, as a mechanism for guaranteeing their impartiality and independence. As well, this section addresses certain aspects relating to composition of the Supreme Court and the Citizen Power, as a factor undermining their independence and autonomy to the detriment of the rule of law.

539. With respect to the provisional status of judges, the Commission was informed that only 250 judges have been appointed by competition, in accordance with constitutional rules. Of the total of 772 judges in Venezuela, the Supreme Court of Justice reports that only 183 are permanent, 1331 are provisional, and 258 are temporary. This means that 84% of the judges continue to be provisional or temporary, and lack tenure in their position. The Supreme Court ordered suspension of competitions for the appointment of judges until the list of jurors responsible for examining candidates is increased.

540. The IACHR considers that the provisional tenure of most of the judges in Venezuela affects their stability in office, which is a necessary condition for the independence of the judiciary.

541. Another aspect of concern to the Commission with respect to guaranteeing the independence and impartiality of the Venezuelan judiciary is the failure to apply the mechanisms established by the new Constitution for the election of their supreme authorities. On this point, the Commission considers that the failure to apply constitutional procedures as guarantees established in domestic law to ensure the independence of members of the judiciary calls into question the institutional legitimacy of the judiciary and undermines the rule of law. It is essential to proceed with appointment of the supreme authorities of the judiciary, in conformity with the Constitution, and to make the necessary amendments to internal rules.

542. Consolidating the rule of law demands a judiciary that is, and is seen to be, independent and impartial, and it is therefore essential to reverse the tenuous situation of most of the Venezuelan judges and apply constitutional mechanisms for appointing senior magistrates and authorities of the Citizen Power as guarantees established by the constitution. On this point, the Commission reiterates what it said at the end of its *in situ* visit, to the effect that the failure to apply the constitution fully creates legal insecurity that impedes full consolidation of the rule of law. The Commission therefore considers it urgent to adopt organic laws as the best means of establishing the mechanisms called for in the Venezuelan Constitution for the selection of magistrates of the Supreme Court of Justice, as well as the Public Defender, the Prosecutor General, and the Comptroller General.

543. Finally, with respect to the administration of justice, the Commission considers that the alarming levels of impunity are a critical factor in undermining the rule of law in Venezuela, and in the chronic repetition of violence. The impunity that prevails in a great number of cases of human rights violations, where an estimated 90% of cases never move beyond initial proceedings, is causing Venezuelan society to lose confidence in the justice system and is sparking a resurgence of violence, producing a vicious circle of impunity and violence. The impunity that surrounds human rights violations, in disregard of the State's obligation to investigate and punish those responsible, is a problem that must be addressed as a priority in the context of Venezuelan justice.

• Civil Society

544. Attacks against human rights defenders have taken place from various perspectives. The legitimate work of these defenders, in denouncing the outrages committed by parties to the social conflict, has prompted certain players to try to silence

them through various means. The extreme polarization that exists has led various political groups to seek to discredit the actions of some human rights groups or individuals who are calling for justice and truth.

545. The IACHR has been receiving numerous complaints of attacks and acts of intimidation against persons devoted to protecting and promoting respect for the fundamental rights of Venezuelans. These acts of harassment against human rights defenders and human rights organizations sometimes include attempts on the life and physical integrity of defenders, and there is a series of documented cases in which defenders have been the target of many forms of intimidation.

546. On this point, the Commission considers it essential that the State take the steps necessary to prevent the collapse of guarantees for the work of human rights defenders and to provide effective protection of their life and personal integrity.

547. With respect to the *"círculos bolivarianos"*, the IACHR notes that there is full information available on them at the web page of the Presidency of Venezuela, where it is apparent that they not only have ties to the national government but that those ties are institutionalized. In the second place, the Commission considers, with respect to the acts of violence attributed to these circles, that all the reported cases involving them have been characterized by impunity, and to this date responsibility for those deeds has not been clearly established, a factor that generates suspicion about their activities. In the third place, the IACHR considers that political participation, the right of association and freedom of expression are rights guaranteed in the American Convention and in this respect the "Bolivarian Circles", as citizen groups or grassroots organizations, may in some circumstances be a suitable channel for the exercise of those rights. Nevertheless, the Commission believes that the expression of certain partisan political ideas cannot justify acts of violence or restrictions on the rights of other persons with different political views, or with specific professional roles, since, as the American Convention establishes, an individual's rights are limited by the rights of others, by the security of all, and by the just demands of the common welfare, in a democratic society.

548. The IACHR cannot discount the existence of other armed groups that are partisans of the government or the opposition. In fact, the IACHR knows of the existence of certain opposition groups that may also be armed, and considers that it is essential to investigate the existence of these groups, to disarm them completely and as quickly as possible, and to investigate and punish those responsible for the violent acts attributed to these groups.

• State Security: the Armed Forces and Police Forces

The Armed Forces

549. The Commission believes that the security of a democratic state lies fundamentally in values such as those of peace, liberty, justice, equality, protection of human rights and democratic coexistence. Therefore, civil society cannot be placed at the same level of responsibility as the State itself, which has a legitimate monopoly over the use of public force and is subject to domestic and international responsibilities that are different from those applicable to individuals.

550. In the second place, and with respect to the Security Council, the Commission considers it a priority to establish immediately, through legislation, the powers and attributes of this new body, as conditions for action by its members, setting strict limits on the scope and mechanisms of such action. Finally, the Commission observes that this new institution must be governed in strict observance of the principles of the rule of law as they relate to the independence and separation of powers, considering the importance of the responsibilities assigned to it, especially that of establishing the strategic concept of national defense.

551. A third aspect that is of special concern to the IACHR is the constitutional provision governing the powers and attributes of the National Guard, as a part of the Venezuelan Armed Forces responsible for internal security. Indeed, one of the Commission's concerns with respect to public safety is over the involvement of the Armed Forces in activities that should fall exclusively to the police. The Commission notes that in a democratic system there must be clear and precise separation between internal security, as the function of the police, and national defense, as the function of the Armed Forces, since these are substantially different institutions in terms of the purposes for which they were created, and their training and preparation.

552. The IACHR was also greatly concerned at the many statements it received about the excessive amount of political deliberation within the Armed Forces, and their undue influence on the country's political life. The Commission notes that this problem has a normative dimension, by virtue of the new Constitution's suppression of the "non deliberative" character established expressly for the Armed Forces, as well as a factual dimension, in light of the constitutional rupture of April 2002. If the credibility of the Armed Forces is to be restored and if the rights of the citizenry are to be guaranteed, it is essential that the Armed Forces and the security forces should not have a deliberative role, but that may remain subordinate to the civil power and act impartially, and that they not be used for tasks relating to the maintenance of public order.

553. Finally, another aspect of concern to the Commission is the establishment of a procedural privilege in favor of generals and admirals of the Armed Forces whereby, in accordance with the Constitution, in order to bring them to trial the Supreme Court of Justice must first rule on whether there are grounds for doing so. On this point, the Commission considers that this requirement is not compatible with the rule of law as it relates to the proper administration of justice, because it could constitute a privilege that would facilitate impunity for members of the Armed Forces.

554. Consequently, it is essential that the Armed Forces not intervene in public security matters, unless they are subordinated to the civilian authorities. The State must demonstrate the political will to achieve these objectives.

The police forces

555. According to information provided by the Ministry of the Interior and Justice, there are currently 95 police forces in Venezuela, 71 of which are municipal forces and 24 are state forces, in addition to the Criminal Scientific Investigation Corps (CICPC) and the DISIP (political police), which operate nationwide. The

States of Amazonas, Apure, Falcon and Portuguesa are the only ones that do not have municipal police forces and that rely exclusively on the state police.

556. On this point, the Commission notes a substantial shortcoming in the area of police activity: the National Assembly has not passed the National Police Corps Act, as called for in the fourth transitional provision pursuant to article 332 of the Constitution. It is essential to improve security and the public's sense of security by approving this law and establishing a National Civil Police Force, with the resources to train it properly as a democratic institution for purposes of public safety, similar to the police forces of the various states.

557. In examining the current status of the rule of law, the Commission considers that the events of greatest importance for their impact on institutional life are the activities of the death squads (*grupos de exterminio*), which apparently operate with the acquiescence of the state police, as will be discussed in the section on violations of the right to life; the police response to the events of April and the intervention of the Metropolitan Police, which has been denounced by a broad segment of the public as an example of the political polarization of Venezuela, in the sense that the Metropolitan Government is part of the opposition.

• The Right to Life

558. The Public Defender of Venezuela has recognized the existence of groups known as *parapoliciales* ["para-police"] in seven States of Venezuela. In Portuguesa, some 400 km from Caracas, more than 100 people are reported to have been killed by a self-styled "extermination group", allegedly consisting of off-duty members of the state police and the National Guard. A similar situation prevails in the States of Falcón, Yaracuy, Anzoátegui, Bolívar, Miranda, Aragua, and Caracas, where death squads are reported to have killed nearly a hundred people, with the acquiescence of the state police. It is important to note that these groups have been in existence for some time. In the past, similar events have occurred in other states of the country.

559. A supremely important question in analyzing this issue is the impunity that surrounds these executions and that allows these groups to operate. Indeed, there is a clear connection between impunity and the steadily rising number of these violent crimes.

560. The Commission considers that this serious problem, which has a direct impact on human rights, can be explained by the lack of police professionalism, widespread impunity, and rampant corruption. Moreover, these acts point to the absence of government policies for dealing with this situation, generating a spiral of impunity that is reflected in the periodic occurrence of violent acts.

561. The Commission concludes by recalling the press release issued at the end of its *in situ* visit in May 2002, in which it noted that the failure of the authorities to apply due diligence in investigating, prosecuting and punishing the members of the so-called death squads is a fundamental factor in their continued operation. The Commission reminds the State of its obligation to take urgent steps to dismantle these groups and to investigate and punish those responsible, highlighting the responsibility that falls to the various states of Venezuela in these cases, in accordance with article 28 of the American Convention taken in relation with article 1 (1) of that instrument.

• The Right to Personal Integrity

562. With respect to the right to personal integrity, the Commission notes that the sharpening of the institutional conflict in Venezuela has led to acts of violence extending to attempts on people's lives, with numerous attacks against personal integrity. With respect to this right, the Commission has observed a number of particularly alarming aspects. In the first place, the high number of cases of torture and cruel, inhuman and degrading treatment at the hands of the State security forces; and in the second place, the failure of the competent State bodies to fulfill their duty to investigate reported cases and to punish those responsible, who generally enjoy impunity, thereby encouraging the repetition of such conduct; and the absence of effective oversight procedures to ensure the physical integrity of prisoners, both civilian and military. On this point, the IACHR stresses the need for urgent measures to prevent such outrages, and to investigate and punish those responsible in all cases.

• The Right to Freedom of Expression and Thought

563. Freedom of expression in Venezuela remains a matter of particular concern. The Commission notes an alarming and generalized increase in attacks on the media and journalists, particularly those covering political events and demonstrations. The State of Venezuela must take the necessary steps to guarantee free exercise of freedom of expression, which is essential to consolidating democracy. The IACHR also expresses its concern over the State's failure to comply with the precautionary measures granted by the Commission and with the provisional measures granted by the Inter-American Court on behalf of journalists and social communicators.

564. The Commission considers that there are also other forms of obstructing the full exercise of the freedom of expression. One example can be found in the laws that criminalize offensive speech aimed at public officials, known as contempt laws (*leyes de desacato*), which are incompatible with Article 13 of the Convention. Another example is the abusive use of emergency broadcast systems. The IACHR issued an appropriate press release condemning the abusive and unnecessary use of this mechanism, which, used in a highly discretionary manner, and for purposes alien to the public interest, may constitute a form of censorship. The various kinds of pressure brought to bear on the broadcast media by initiating administrative proceedings which, while abusive, also constitute an indirect restriction on the freedom of expression, are a third example.

565. The difficulty of public access to information continues to go unanswered; accordingly, any initiative by the government to facilitate free access to information will contribute to ensuring that the citizenry is better informed.

566. The IACHR has been concerned that there was little and at times no information available to Venezuelan society during the days of the institutional crisis of April. Although there may be any number of justifications to explain this lack of information, to the extent that the suppression of information resulted from politically motivated editorial decisions, this should be the subject of some serious thinking by the Venezuelan media about their role at that moment.

567. Finally, the IACHR wishes to pay tribute to the valor of journalists who have continued to pursue their activities, even at risk to their physical integrity. As noted

above, the IACHR considers that the intimidation of journalists has a devastating effect on democracy, and it therefore calls on Venezuelan society to embark upon a period of profound soul-searching, and highlights the need for the various sectors of society and of the government to refrain from identifying journalists and other social communicators as their opponents' allies.

• Trade Union Freedoms

568. The IACHR notes, with respect to the situation of trade union freedoms in Venezuela, that the political crisis and the climate of intolerance prevailing today have led to an increase in labor conflicts. The IACHR is particularly concerned over the mass dismissals of workers of PDVSA. The information available shows that 12,383 workers were dismissed from that State enterprise on grounds of having abandoned their workplace in the context of the so-called national civic strike that lasted from December 2002 until February 2003, and that those dismissals were ordered without any administrative procedures to guarantee due process.

569. Human rights organizations claim that the situation in Venezuela is characterized by constant interference in union affairs through government efforts to obstruct the activity of union leaders and to exert political control over the organized labor movement. The Committee on Freedom of Association has pointed to "the extremely serious and urgent situation in Venezuela marked by numerous complaints of repeated violations of freedom of association for both workers' and employers' organizations".

570. On December 3, 2000, the government called a referendum in which it asked voters if they were in agreement with reforming the trade union leadership through elections. The referendum resulted in a significant victory for the position in favor of reforming union leadership. On this point, the IACHR is of the view that allowing the population at large to participate in that referendum, i.e., including persons other than union members, entailed a violation of the right to form and join trade unions, and the right of workers to elect their leaders.

571. Once the results of the elections were known, the National Electoral Council refused to confirm the Governing Board of the Confederation as the legitimate leadership of that organization, alleging a series of irregularities. Consequently, the elected leaders of that Confederation were not recognized by the national authorities.

572. By virtue of the foregoing, the Commission concludes that there has been heavy-handed State interference in the affairs of labor organizations. As well, the Commission considers it important and urgent to resolve the problem of recognizing the leadership of the CTV, the principal Venezuelan labor confederation, in a manner consistent with the needs and rights of its members.

573. The IACHR recognizes that there has been a significant step forward in the area of trade union freedoms. On July 23, 2002, the Electoral Chamber of the Supreme Court of Justice ruled that action by the Supreme Electoral Council was of a subsidiary nature, and that therefore that body could only intervene when there was a dispute that the labor organization itself could not resolve. The Commission therefore recommends that the State adopt the necessary measures to give full trade union guarantees.

• General Conclusions

574. In conclusion, the Commission regards all the situations identified in the various chapters of this report, and summarized above, as indicating a clear weakness in the fundamental pillars of the rule of law within a democratic society, under the terms of the American Convention on Human Rights and other international instruments.

575. The Commission reiterates its concern over the crucial problems that must be resolved on an urgent basis in order to reverse the decline in the rule of law in Venezuela, and to strengthen and preserve the constitutional State. It notes that civil society and international agencies agree that there has been a gradual deterioration in the human rights situation in the country.

576. The IACHR also wishes to highlight the significant progress that has been made in finding a peaceful solution to the institutional crisis, through the election route, a fact that clearly demonstrates the solid democratic commitment of the Venezuelan people. The Commission refers once again to the agreement signed by representatives of the government and the opposition on May 29, 2003, as part of the Negotiation and Agreement Roundtable. That agreement constitutes a fundamental document that marks a milestone in the current situation, whereby the parties have agreed that applying constitutional mechanisms is the proper institutional way of resolving the crisis. The Commission hails this achievement and call on all parties to continue to foster tolerance and democratic dialogue, and to apply the agreed principles jointly wherever they are needed.

577. Finally, on the basis of more than 40 years of experience in promoting and protecting human rights in the hemisphere, the IACHR considers it essential that all sectors of society avail themselves of mechanisms or agreements that make respect for the human rights recognized in the American Convention and the Constitution a frame of reference for all players in Venezuelan public life. Polarization and intolerance not only impede the working of democratic institutions but actively and dangerously undermine those institutions. A weak democracy, in the Commission's judgment, cannot mount a vigorous defense of human rights.

578. The Commission hopes that the Government of Venezuela and the other political players in the country, including members of the legislature and the judiciary, will continue to demonstrate the political will to seek solutions to the serious human rights problems affecting the country's inhabitants. Several of these problems have been identified in this report, which also contains the IACHR's considered recommendations.

579. The IACHR will continue to monitor the situation in Venezuela closely, paying particular attention to the measures adopted to apply the recommendations set forth in this report. The Inter-American Commission therefore offers the Venezuelan State and society as a whole its full cooperation in efforts to promote and protect human rights and to build consensus towards resolving problems in a democratic and institutionally legitimate context.

Questions and Comments

1. How did the Commission decide to issue this report? How did it proceed to gather evidence?

2. What are the advantages and disadvantages of country reports compared to taking up individual petitions? Given the limited resources of the Commission, should it give priority to reports or petitions? Can the latter be incorporated in the former?

3. In the report on Venezuela, considerable attention is given to the political and legal structure and governance of the country, using the Inter-American Democracy Charter as a normative instrument. Is this within the Commission's jurisdiction? Are these issues of human rights, or underlying structural problems that lead to human rights violations? If the latter, does a focus on prevention justify the Commission's attention to them?

4. The Commission has continued to monitor the situation in Venezuela. In its 2006 *Annual Report*, OEA/Ser.L/V/II.127, Doc. 4 rev. 1, 3 March 2007, the Commission reported that it had prepared an analysis based on information received throughout the year from civil society and the state, as well as on official documents published on the web sites of state institutions and information provided by the press. On January 26, 2007 the Commission transmitted the preliminary draft of the report to the government of Venezuela and requested to government to submit its observations within one month. The Commission received the observations on February 26, 2007 and incorporated them in the final version of the report. It noted that the State asserted the Commission was relying on partial or incomplete sources of information in verifying some of the subjects analyzed. The Commission rejected this claim, insisting on the variety of sources and amount of material it had considered. It also noted that it had requested permission to make an on-site visit to do a more comprehensive study; indeed it had devoted part of its work in 2006 to "the attempt to arrange a visit to Venezuela, an effort that was severely frustrated by the lack of response from the State to propose an exact date for the visit." In the absence of permission to do an on-site visit, what sources should the Commission turn to and rely on in preparing its report?

5. If the Commission decides to carry out an on-site investigation, does the Government have a legal obligation to give its permission? Do the Member States of the OAS who are not parties to the Convention have a legal obligation in that regard? Note the Commission's comment to Venezuela in the 2006 *Annual Report*: "The lack of consent from the government prevents the IACHR from exercising the powers and attributes granted to it by the States under the Charter of the OAS, the IACHR Statutes, and the American Convention on Human Rights" (para. 146). The Commission continued:

> 151. Recognizing the importance of the visits and reports of the IACHR as guiding instruments for the enhancement and protection of human rights in the countries of the region, at the fourth plenary session of the General Assembly held on June 6, 2006, in Santo Domingo, the heads of state and government reaffirmed the essential value of the work carried out by the Inter-American Commission on Human Rights (IACHR) to enhance the protection and promotion of human rights and the reinforcement of the rule of law in the Hemisphere, as well as encouraging the member states to continue the practice of inviting the IACHR to visit their respective countries. The Inter-American Commission values the open invitations expressed by various Member States which allows the Commission to visit those countries at any moment with the common aim of strengthening human rights.

> 152. The Commission considers that the position of the Venezuelan Government counteract the good practices pointed out in the previous paragraphs and makes idle the manifestations express by the State since the last visit of the IACHR to Venezuela six years ago, in which is being asserted the interest of the State that the Commission and/or the thematic Rapporteurs visit the country.

> . . . .

155. From the antecedents and the arguments furthered, the IACHR considers that the impossibility, for lack of consent or political will on behalf of a State, of the IACHR to visit a Member State, contradicts the spirit itself that lead the States to create the organs of the system for the protection of human rights as they defined in the Charter of the Organization of American States, the American Convention on Human Rights, and the Commission's Statute.

Is the Commission claiming that there is a legal or political obligation for Venezuela to consent?

6. Is there any obligation to respond to the Commission's report or to comply with its recommendations?

7. In order for the Commission to carry out an on-site investigation, must it have made a prior determination that at least some petitions are admissible?

8. How would you attempt to ensure the confidentiality of interviews with prisoners or other detainees during an on-site investigation? What guarantees against reprisals should be required of the government?

9. Should an on-site team be inter-disciplinary? What value would there be to including anthropologists, physicians, psychologists or social workers? What positions or other matters should disqualify an individual from participating in an investigation, due to an actual or apparent conflict of interest?

10. Should the Inter-American Commission decline to investigate when the United Nations has a country under study? Both systems engaged in reporting on human rights violations in, e.g., El Salvador, Cuba and Chile. On El Salvador, compare, IACHR, *Report on the Situation of Human Rights in El Salvador*, OEA/Ser.L/V/II.85, doc 28, rev. (1994) with the UN *Report of the Commission on the Truth for El Salvador: From Madness to Hope*, UN doc. S/25500, Annexes (1993). Note that the Inter-American Commission commented on the UN report in its own report of a year later at pp. 42–44.

11. For an example of the African Commission's country studies, see: *Report of the African Commission on Human and Peoples' Rights Mission to Sudan, 1–7 December 1996*.

5. Condemnatory Resolutions

As in the Inter-American system, the African Commission's reports on human rights violations and its recommendations are submitted to the AU political institutions. In both systems, governments defend themselves vigorously against charges of widespread human rights violations. The issue can become intensely political. Until 1975, the OAS General Assembly simply noted the Commission's reports. In 1975, however, the country report on *The Status of Human Rights in Chile* resulted, after a lengthy debate, in a separate resolution directed at that country's government. A stronger resolution was adopted the following year and later resolutions were addressed to other countries, based on the Commission's reports. See: Thomas Buergenthal, *The Inter-American System for the Protection of Human Rights*, in T. Meron (ed.), Human Rights in International Law (OUP, 1984), Vol. II, pp. 482–484. The materials below concern the African Commission's resolutions on widespread violations in Ethiopia and Sudan, and the reactions of the two countries.

Resolution on the Situation of Human Rights in Ethiopia, 5 December 2005, *20th Annual Activity Report of the Afr. Comm. H.P.R.*, Annex III, p.34.

The African Commission on Human and Peoples' Rights meeting at its 38th Ordinary Session held in Banjul, The Gambia from 21 November to 5 December 2005;

Considering that the Democratic Federal Republic of Ethiopia is a State Party to the *African Charter on Human and Peoples' Rights*;

Recalling that freedom of opinion and expression as well as the right to assembly are fundamental rights enshrined in international instruments ratified by Ethiopia, and notably Articles 9 and 11 of the African Charter on Human and Peoples' Rights;

Recalling Article 7 of the *Charter* which ensures the right to a fair trial and the Guidelines and Principles on the Right to a Fair Trial and to Judicial Assistance in Africa developed by the African Commission on Human and Peoples' Rights;

Deeply concerned about the situation going on in Ethiopia since June 2005 and notably the arbitrary arrests and other serious human rights violations directed at suspected members and supporters of opposition groups, students and human rights defenders;

Recalling that on 8th June and 1st November 2005 security forces killed and injured demonstrators during a demonstration protesting the results of the parliamentary elections in Addis Ababa and other towns;

Concerned by the arbitrary detention of opposition leaders and journalists in Ethiopia;

Noting the creation by the government of Ethiopia of a National Parliamentary Commission to investigate the facts concerning the acts of violence in the country;

1. Deplores the killing of civilians during confrontations with security forces;

2. Requests that the Ethiopian authorities release arbitrarily detained political prisoners, human rights defenders and journalists;

3. Calls on the Ethiopian government to guarantee, for any accused individual, the right to a fair trial as provided by the *African Charter on Human and Peoples' Rights* and other relevant international human rights instruments, including the right to seek pardon or commutation of sentence;

4. Calls on the Ethiopian government to ensure the impartiality, independence and integrity of the National Parliamentary Commission investigating the recent acts of violence in the country and to bring the perpetrators of human rights violations to justice;

5. Urges the Ethiopian government to guarantee, at all times, freedom of opinion and expression as well as the right to hold peaceful demonstration and political assembly;

6. Requests that the Ethiopian government guarantees, in all circumstances, the physical and psychological integrity of human rights defenders in compliance with international instruments especially the *Declaration of Human Rights Defenders* adopted by the U.N. General Assembly in December 1998;

7. Calls on the Ethiopian government to comply with the international instruments ratified by Ethiopia, most notably the *African Charter on Human and Peoples' Rights* (ACHPR), the *International Covenant on Civil and Political Rights*

(ICCPR) and the *International Covenant on Economic, Social and Cultural Rights* (ICESCR).

Submission by the Federal Democratic Republic of Ethiopia in Accordance with Resolution No. Ex.Cl/Dec. 257(VIII) of the Executive Council of the African Union Concerning the 16th Activities Report of the African Commission on Human and Peoples' Rights

1. Introduction

The Government of the Federal Democratic Republic of Ethiopia presents, in this report its views on the resolution passed by the African Commission on Human and Peoples' Rights . . . during its 38th Ordinary Session held from 21 November to 5 December 2005 in Banjul, the Gambia on human rights situation in Ethiopia. The report is prepared on the basis of the decision adopted by the 8th Ordinary Session of the Executive Council of the African Union wherein the Council requested the concerned governments against whom the Commission passed a resolution to submit their clarifications on the resolution.

During the 8th Ordinary Session of the Executive Council held in the Sudan in July 2006, H.E. the Minster of Foreign Affairs of the Federal Democratic Republic of Ethiopia made it clear that by raising its objection on the resolution, Ethiopia does not question the Commission's competence to exercise its mandate as stipulated under the African Charter on Human and Peoples' Rights . . . , its rules of procedure and other legal instruments. In this report, Ethiopia rather aims at providing the Commission with relevant and necessary facts relating to some of the salient developments in the country following the May 2005 federal and regional legislative elections for the Commission to be acquainted with reality on the ground.

2. Ethiopia's Position on the Procedure and Nature of the Resolution

During its 38th Ordinary Session held in the Gambia from 21 November to 5 December 2005, the Commission adopted a resolution on human rights situations in a number of member states including Ethiopia. Even though the Ethiopian delegation participating at the 38th Ordinary Session of the Commission made statements, had discussions with members of the Commission and distributed relevant documents informing the Commission on the accurate picture of developments in the Country, the Commission, nonetheless, adopted the resolution in a manner that is inconsistent with the Charter and the Commission's Rules of Procedure.

At the consideration of the 19th annual activity report of the Commission during the 8th Ordinary Session of the Executive Council of the African Union held in the Sudan between 20–21 January 2006, Ethiopia and other concerned countries objected to the manner in which the Commission adopted the contentious resolution and the baseless allegations contained in the resolution, distorting government measures which are in fact taken with the view to ensuring law and order. Due to the objection forwarded by Ethiopia and other concerned states, the Council, in its decision entitled *Decision on the 19th Activity Report of the African Commission on*

Human and Peoples' Rights[31] decided to exclude the resolutions against the objecting countries from the activity report of the Commission and gave the concerned governments three months to submit a report regarding the Commission's resolution for the latter's consideration.

This section would analyze the procedure of adoption of resolutions by the African Commission. A brief recollection of the discussion during the 38th Ordinary Session of the Commission is also included. Ethiopia argues that the Commission's decision to publicize the resolution in its website is also inconsistent with acceptable practice.

2.1. African Commission's Procedure

The Commission often adopts, following the conclusion of its ordinary sessions, resolutions on human rights issues. The nature and content of these resolutions tend to vary. Occasionally they focus on procedural issues, i.e. requesting the particular state to create the modality of working with the Commission in investigating certain human rights violations in that country. At times, its resolutions take a stand on allegations of certain human rights violations and incorporate statement of condemnation. In other occasions, the Commission used resolutions to create special mechanisms or working groups for the implementation of its broad mandate by adopting resolutions. The mandate of the Commission to establish the aforementioned mechanisms is clearly provided for in Article 28 of the Rules of Procedure of the Commission. Even though there is no specific provision in the Commission's Rules of Procedure that clearly empowers the Commission to adopt a resolution. Adopting resolutions has now become standard practice in passing its decisions.

2.2. The Nature of Dialogue between Ethiopia's delegation and the Commission at its 38th Ordinary Session

The 38th Ordinary Session of the Commission was held in Banjul, the Gambia from 21 November to 5 December 2005. In its opening remarks, the Ethiopian delegation briefed the Commission on the various measures that the Government has been taking to further advance human rights protection in the country and updated the Commission on the circumstances surrounding recent human rights developments following the May 2005 federal and regional legislative elections.

A number of non-governmental organizations made statements during the Commission's public session that made reference to human rights developments in Ethiopia.

The delegation of Ethiopia responded to all the allegations and claims made by non-governmental organizations. It was stated that the legislative and administrative measures were put in place to settle election related disputes. Nonetheless, the opposition parties opted for their illegal street protest aimed at overthrowing the constitutional order. The Ethiopian delegation further stated that the measures taken by law enforcement agencies were aimed at protecting law and order. It was also made clear that the Government has not closed down private news papers and that there are several private news papers that are on print currently in the country. The delegation also made it clear that the House of Peoples' Representatives of FDRE

---

[31] EX.CL/Dec.257 (VIII)

(the House) has established an Independent Inquiry Commission to investigate the circumstance surrounding the confrontations in Addis Ababa and some other towns in the country.

2.3. The Commission's Resolution on Human Rights Situation in Ethiopia

The Commission's resolution covers a number of human rights related developments in Ethiopia following the May 2005 elections. One remarkable feature of the resolution is its stark similarity with the resolution passed by the NGO Forum that was held immediately preceding the meeting of the Commission.

The Government of Ethiopia indicates that the duplicate nature of this resolution compared to the resolution adopted at the non-governmental organization forum held immediately proceeding the meeting of the Commission demonstrate the flawed nature of the procedure the Commission followed in replicating the resolution from the non-governmental forum. It showed that the Commission adopted the non-governmental resolution without further scrutiny and assessment.

2.4. Publicity Given to the resolution at the Commission's Website

Following the adoption of the resolutions, the Commission immediately publicized them through its communiqué and particularly via its official website. The Government of Ethiopia submits that the manner in which the Commission gave publicity to its resolutions contravenes the Commission's Rules of Procedure.

Resolutions which are often part and parcel of annexes to the Commission's Annual Activity Report are confidential documents until they are adopted by the relevant organ of the African Union. Article 77 of the Rules of Procedure clearly stipulates that such a report shall be confidential. The Commission can only publish them after such reporting and only when the African Union's relevant organ does not give instructions otherwise. Regarding the specific issue of the Commission's activity report, the Chairman of the Commission can only publish them after the Assembly of the African Union considered it.

The Government of Ethiopia is of the view that the publication of the resolutions in the Commission's official website prior to their consideration by the Commission contravenes the aforementioned provision of the Rules of Procedure.

2.5. Decision of the AU Executive Council

During its 8th Ordinary Session, the Executive Council of the African Union passed resolution no EX.CL/Dec.257 (VIII) entitled *Decision on the 19th Activity Report of the African Commission on Human and Peoples' Rights.* This follows the submission of the annual activity report of the Commission to the African Union decision making organ in accordance with article 41 of the Commission's Rules of Procedure.

In the Resolution the Council requested;

1. the Commission to exclude the resolution on human rights situation in Ethiopia, Eritrea, Zimbabwe, Uganda and the Sudan from the annexes to its 19th Activity Report;

2. the concerned member states to make available to the Commission, within three months since the adoption of the Council's decision, their views on the resolutions, and

3. the Commission to ensure that in future, it enlists the responses of all States parties to its Resolutions and Decisions before submitting them to the Executive Council and/or the Assembly for consideration.

[The Government continues over 37 pages in responding point by point to the Commission's resolution].

11. Conclusion

The Government of the Federal Democratic Republic of Ethiopia is of the view that the facts presented in this report are compelling and persuasive evidence showing that the Commission's resolution which failed to take into account the environment within which Ethiopia's freest and most democratic election has taken place, and rushed to condemn Government measures taken with the view to safeguarding the constitutional order, was not warranted. It is also the view of the Government that passing the resolution without sufficient opportunity for the Government to respond and without adequate assessment by the Commission is indeed inconsistent with the African Charter on Human and Peoples' Rights, the Commission's Rules of Procedure and other relevant legal instruments. The unbecoming manner in which the resolution was passed cannot be overemphasized. The Government therefore requests the Commission to exclude the resolution from its report.

The report has provided the Commission with sufficient information on the institutional, legal and practical aspect of the May 2005 federal and regional legislative elections in Ethiopia, which is by far the most competitive election held in the country. The hardliners in the opposition camp tried to manipulate the free and fairness of the elections to seize power through unconstitutional means. As clearly stipulated in so many of the African Union's legal instruments, this cannot and should not be tolerated. This report clearly establishes that political campaigning during the election was undertaken in a free and open environment. The report establishes that the individuals who are in prison following the carefully marshaled street violence in Addis Ababa and other parts of the country are not political prisoners. The few journalists and individuals who misused their status in civic society organizations that are arrested in connection with the street violence are ordinary prisoners. The law enforcement bodies have concrete evidence that is now being presented in their trial. The report has shown that both during their detention and the ongoing trial, their due process rights enshrined in the FDRE Constitution and relevant international human rights instruments are fully guaranteed and protected.

Ethiopia remains committed to its international obligations. As such the unfortunate killing of civilians and law enforcement officers is a matter of utmost regret to the Government. This is indeed why, as comprehensively discussed in the report, the House of Peoples' Representatives of the Federal Democratic Republic of Ethiopia adopted a Proclamation establishing an Independent Inquiry Commission that will look into the circumstances surrounding the post-election violence. The constituting legislation, reporting mechanism, membership and financing are designed in such a manner that ensures the independence of the Commission. The report of this Commission will be debated in parliament.

For the reasons adduced in the report, the Government reiterates it request to the Commission to put aside the ill-conceived resolution. It wishes to express its commitment to encourage positive dialogue between the Government and the Commission in the future in the context of the promotional and protection mandates of the Commission and in the context of Ethiopia's initial and periodic reports that are being finalized for submission to the Commission.

Resolution on the Situation of Human Rights in the Darfur Region in Sudan, 5 December 2005, *20th Annual Activity Report of the Afr. Comm. H.P.R. 2006*, Annex III, pp. 73–74.

The African Commission on Human and Peoples' Rights meeting at its 38th Ordinary Session in Banjul, The Gambia from 21 November to 5 December 2005;

Considering the provisions of the Constitutive Act of the African Union (AU) and the Charter of the United Nations Organisation (UN), as well as those of the African Charter on Human and Peoples' Rights and other regional and international human rights instruments to which the Sudan is a State Party;

Recalling relevant Decisions and Communiqués adopted by the AU Assembly of Heads of State and Government and those of the Peace and Security Council on the situation in Darfur, most notably Decisions AU/Dec.54(III) and Assembly/AU/Dec.68 (IV) adopted at the 3rd and 4th Ordinary Sessions of the AU Assembly of Heads of State and Government respectively, as well as Communiqués PSC/PR/Comm.(XIII) and PSC/PR/Comm.(XVII) adopted by the AU Peace and Security Council at their 13th and 17th Meetings respectively;

Recalling Resolutions 1556/2004 of 30 July 2004 and 1590/2005, 1591/2005 and 1593/2005 adopted by the UN Security Council on the situation in Darfur, Sudan in March 2005;

Recalling also Resolution ACHPR /Res.74 (XXXVII) 05 adopted by the 37th Ordinary Session of the African Commission on Human and Peoples' Rights on 11th May 2005 on the situation in the Darfur region of Sudan and Resolution ACHPR/Res.68 (XXXV) 04 adopted by the 35th Ordinary Session on 4th June 2004, as well as Resolution E/CN.4/RES/2005/82 adopted by the UN Commission on Human Rights on 21st April 2005 on the situation of human rights in Sudan;

Deeply concerned about the continuing grave violations of human rights and international humanitarian law in Darfur committed by parties to the conflict, in particular the continued depopulation of vast areas in the region of their indigenous owners, threats of violence, intimidation and assault against UN agencies and humanitarian organizations, the targeting and killing of AU troops in Darfur, and the killing and abduction of staff members of national and international humanitarian organisations;

Concerned that the African Commission undertook a Fact-Finding Mission to the Darfur region of Sudan in July 2004 and dispatched its report to the government of Sudan but has not yet received a response;

1. Calls on the government of Sudan to submit its comments to the African Commission with respect to its report on the 2004 Fact-Finding Mission to Sudan;

2. Calls on the government of Sudan to comply with its obligations under the *African Charter on Human and Peoples' Rights*, the *AU Constitutive Act*, the *UN Charter* and other relevant instruments to which the Sudan is a State Party, and comply with the following:

a. Cease, with immediate effect, all attacks against civilians in Darfur and end the grave violations of human and peoples' rights, in particular the forced de-population of entire areas in the region, rape and sexual violence against women and girls, abduction of women and children, and to cease all support to the *Janjaweed* militiamen, including the provision of supplies.

b. Provide the necessary support to all international agencies and humanitarian organisations in order to ensure effective and full access to the war affected areas of Darfur and to facilitate delivery of humanitarian assistance to civilian populations.

c. Fully and unconditionally cooperate with the Office of the Prosecutor of the International Criminal Court in his efforts to investigate and bring to justice all persons suspected of perpetrating war crimes and crimes against humanity as prescribed in the report of the International Commission of Inquiry on Darfur.

d. Take all appropriate measures to ensure the effective implementation of the Resolutions 1556/2004 of 30 July 2004 and 1590/2005, 1591/2005 and 1593/2005 adopted on 29 and 31 March 2005 by the United Nations Security Council;

3. Calls on all parties to the conflict to return to negotiations and to cooperate with the international organs and humanitarian organisations.

Comments of the Sudan on the Decision of the African Commission on Human and Peoples Rights Concerning Darfur during Its 38th Ordinary Session Held in Banjul, the Gambia, from 21 November to 5 December 2005.

We wish to refer to the above subject and the Decision of the AU Assembly of Heads of State and Government held in Khartoum from 16–24 January 2006 asking for Sudan's view on, and response to the Decision of the African Commission on Human and Peoples Rights on Darfur during its 38th Ordinary Session held in Banjul, the Gambia, from 21 November to 5 December 2005.

We wish to further state that the points raised in the Decision only reflected what was orchestrated by some media quarters which rely on allegations that cannot be substantiated.

We wish to also point out that the situation in Darfur was examined in accordance with the AU Constitutive Act and resolved in line with UN Charter where the UN Security Council issued Resolution 1593 referring the case in Darfur to the International Criminal Court. Resolution 1591 establishing a Committee of Experts was also adopted among other resolutions. It is worth noting that the Decision of the African Commission on Human and Peoples Rights has also made reference to the Decisions of the African Union and its Peace and Security Council as well as those of the UN Security Council.

Observations on the Report of the African Commission on Human and Peoples Rights on the Fact Finding Mission that visited the Sudan in 2004. We had earlier submitted our response to the First Report of the Mission. Our response to the

Second Report had articulated Sudan's position on the holding of an Extraordinary Session in Pretoria, South Africa without the approval of, or funding by the African Union Commission. The Sudan had lodged a complaint on this to the Chair of the African Union, but no response has so far been forthcoming.

Second, regarding Sudan's commitment to the African Charter on Human and Peoples Rights and to other international agreements and conventions, the Sudanese Government takes all necessary measures to promote human rights in the Sudan and ensure decent life by eliminating poverty, disease and illiteracy inherited from colonialism. At the same time, Sudan strives to preserve its political sovereignty and territorial integrity. Since the eruption of the troubles in Darfur, the Sudan has been keenly engaged in the search for solutions to the problem through direct negotiations with the rebels as a result of which the Abeeche, Njamina and Abuja Agreements were concluded. However, negative signals sent by several external circles have encouraged the rebels not to care much about the implementation of these Agreements.

The Government has always shown concern about the safety of civilians by taking measures against all those who break the law. As a proof of that, civilians have been fleeing from abuses by the rebels to the areas under Government Control. Even in the areas that were shelled by mistake, the Government has compensated the victims. The International Community as a whole is witness to that and the most glaring example is the victims of air raid in the Habila area where the government blood money of those killed and compensated the inhabitants for their properties. As for the question of forced displacement, as we said earlier, this is in conflict with the reality as displacement only occurs after rebel attacks on villages using such displacement as a weapon against the government. The Government of the Sudan has concluded an agreement with IOM which supervises the programmes of repatriating the displaced persons. The Government is concerned with the rehabilitation programme in the areas of displacement and it has also established a committee which is now one of the three committees set up based on the recommendations of the National Investigation Committee presided over by the Former Head of the Judiciary to define the pastoral routes and confirm land ownership.

Concerning the alleged rape and violence against women, the Sudanese courts receive statements on the basis of which it has tried a number of police and army officers and names have been submitted to human rights observers in this regard. A list is hereto attached.

The government has also adopted a plan for the prevention of violence against women in Darfur (copy attached) and amended the criminal proceedings to enable the victims of violence to receive treatment without filling Form No. 8 with the police authorities. Hospitals and foreign treatment units of the international and voluntarily organizations have also been allowed to treat those affected. Groups of the AU troops participate in joint patrols to escort women when they go out of their camps in search of firewood, which has considerably minimized cases of violence against women.

As for the need to open the way for the international organizations, and humanitarian agencies, the entire international community is witness to Sudan's cooperation and facilitation of humanitarian work without any customs restrictions or formalities. It has issued visas to the personnel of some 600 voluntary organizations that now work in Darfur.

The Government has affirmed that it does not give support to any of the parties in Darfur, that are prohibited under the Ceasefire Agreement, from any movement without prior knowledge of the AU troops, and are also banned from the use of air-force.

On cooperation with the Office of the Prosecutor General of the International Criminal Court, even though this is not within the jurisdiction of the African Union Commission on Human and Peoples Rights, our response is that the Sudan has provided all the facilities to enable the said Office to perform its duty and provided it with the necessary documentation.

Regarding the implementation of UN Security Council Resolutions 1556/2005, 1590/2005, 1591/2005 and 1593/2005, the Sudan has always cooperated with the UN. This has been confirmed by the Representative of the UN Secretary General in the Sudan in his monthly reports. There are more than 25 human rights observers in Darfur and they are allowed to visit the prisons in all parts of the Sudan as indicated in the reports of the UN Secretary General. Meetings are also held between the Human Rights Division of the United Nations and the Human Rights Consultation Council at the office of the Sub-Jim every two weeks. Fact-finding missions are undertaken by both sides in Darfur and joint seminars organized to amend the criminal proceedings and the rules of implementing Form No.8.

In conclusion, we would have liked to see the African Commission, instead of sending timid signals about the atrocities by the rebels, adopt a bold and firm position by considering the atrocities they have been perpetrating in Darfur since the eruption of the war, particularly their recruitment of child soldiers to attack humanitarian workers and their convoys.

Questions and Comments

1. What is the legal authority for the Commission to issue condemnatory resolutions?
2. Contrast the responses of Ethiopia and Sudan. What are their legal arguments?
3. How would you assess the potential of the African system to respond effectively to the problems in the Sudan?

6. Addressing Systemic Problems in the European System

In the European Court of Human Rights, several countries have been the subject of numerous complaints arising from the same type of violation. Repetitive cases make it evident that the state in question has not repaired the underlying problem causing the violations. One situation concerns the Italian judicial system, whose procedural delays have led to repeated judgments against the government. As the first case below mentions, the former Commission submitted over fourteen hundred reports to the Committee of Ministers finding Italy to be in breach of Article 6 due to delay. Between 1987 and 1999, the European Court issued sixty-five judgments on the issue. The Court observed that such breaches reflected a continuing situation yet to be remedied and thus constituted a practice incompatible with the Convention. The structural defects of the Italian judicial system have occupied an inordinate amount of time and resources in Strasbourg and necessitated devising new procedures, including summary processing and the use of "pilot cases" in which the Court goes into greater analysis about the appropriate remedies to resolve the underlying problem. The following cases illustrate these developments. See also *Maestri v. Italy* (GC) ECHR 2004-I and Lech Garlicki, *Broniowski and After: The Dual Nature of 'Pilot' Judgments*, in Human Rights—Strasbourg Views: Liber Amicorum Luzius Wildhaber 177 (N.P. Engel, 2007).

Case of Bottazzi v. Italy, App. no. 34884/97, judgment of July 28, 1999 (GC), ECHR 1999-V.

. . . .

9. Mr Bottazzi, who was born in Ligonchio (Reggio Emilia) in 1916, lives in Genoa.

10. The applicant was wounded in the Second World War and in 1949 was granted an invalidity allowance. This was stopped in 1956. On 15 January 1972 the applicant requested a war pension on the ground that his health had deteriorated. On 30 May 1984 the Treasury rejected his request. On 19 June 1988 the War Pensions Department (part of the Treasury) rejected a fresh request from the applicant dated 20 January 1986 on the ground that his health had not deteriorated. The applicant lodged an appeal to a higher authority, seeking to have the decision of 19 June 1988 annulled by the Minister of Financial Affairs. His appeal was rejected on 1 September 1990 by the War Pensions Department. On 28 March 1991 the applicant lodged an administrative complaint asking the Minister to annul the decision of 1 September 1990.

11. On 29 March 1991 the Minister of Financial Affairs referred that complaint to the Court of Audit, where it arrived on 4 April 1991. On 15 May 1991 the Court of Audit asked the Treasury to send it the applicant's case file. On 23 September 1993 the president of the court set the case down for hearing on 7 January 1994. The applicant's lawyer filed pleadings on 27 December 1993. In a judgment of 7 January 1994, which was deposited with the registry on 16 June 1994 and served on the applicant on 2 May 1995, the Court of Audit declared the application inadmissible on the ground that the applicant had lodged an administrative complaint, relying on the provisions governing appeals to a higher authority, and had had no intention of bringing legal proceedings.

12. On 28 October 1995 the applicant appealed. He submitted that if he had been aware of the correct procedure he would certainly have applied to the Court of Audit. On 8 November 1996 the applicant applied to have the appeal set down for a hearing and deliberations. On 26 November 1996 the president set it down for hearing on 1 April 1997. On 28 March 1997 the applicant applied for an adjournment and the hearing was postponed until 18 November 1997.

13. In a decision of that date, the text of which was deposited with the registry on 2 December 1997, the Court of Audit declared the applicant's appeal inadmissible.

. . . .

22. The Court notes at the outset that Article 6 § 1 of the Convention imposes on the Contracting States the duty to organise their judicial systems in such a way that their courts can meet the requirements of this provision (see the *Salesi v. Italy* judgment of 26 February 1993, Series A no. 257-E, p. 60, § 24). It wishes to reaffirm the importance of administering justice without delays which might jeopardise its effectiveness and credibility (see the *Katte Klitsche de la Grange v. Italy* judgment of 27 October 1994, Series A no. 293-B, p. 39, § 61). It points out, moreover, that the Committee of Ministers of the Council of Europe, in its Resolution DH (97) 336 of 11 July 1997 (Length of civil proceedings in Italy: supplementary measures of a general character), considered that "excessive delays in the administration of justice constitute an important danger, in particular for the respect of the rule of law".

The Court next draws attention to the fact that since 25 June 1987, the date of the *Capuano v. Italy* judgment (Series A no. 119), it has already delivered 65 judgments in which it has found violations of Article 6 § 1 in proceedings exceeding a "reasonable time" in the civil courts of the various regions of Italy. Similarly, under former Articles 31 and 32 of the Convention, more than 1,400 reports of the Commission resulted in resolutions by the Committee of Ministers finding Italy in breach of Article 6 for the same reason.

The frequency with which violations are found shows that there is an accumulation of identical breaches which are sufficiently numerous to amount not merely to isolated incidents. Such breaches reflect a continuing situation that has not yet been remedied and in respect of which litigants have no domestic remedy.

This accumulation of breaches accordingly constitutes a practice that is incompatible with the Convention.

23. The Court has examined the facts of the present case in the light of the information provided by the parties and the above-mentioned practice. Having regard to its case-law on the subject, the Court considers that in the instant case the length of the proceedings was excessive and failed to meet the "reasonable time" requirement.

Accordingly, there has been a violation of Article 6 § 1.

II. Application of article 41 of the Convention

. . . .

A. Damage

25. Mr Bottazzi claimed 150,000,000 Italian lire (ITL) for the pecuniary and non-pecuniary damage which he alleged that he had sustained.

26. The Government stressed that the applicant had failed to adduce evidence of any pecuniary damage sustained as a result of the length of the proceedings in question. As regards non-pecuniary damage, if any, the Government submitted that the finding of a violation would in itself constitute adequate just satisfaction.

27. The Court agrees with the Government on the first point. However, the applicant must have sustained some non-pecuniary damage which the mere finding of a violation cannot adequately compensate. The Court therefore awards him ITL 15,000,000.

. . . .

PARTLY dissenting opinion of JUDGE Türmen

I am in agreement with the other judges that there has been a violation of Article 6 § 1 of the Convention in the present case.

However, I cannot agree with paragraph 22 of the judgment where the Court states that the numerous violations of Article 6 § 1 by Italy constitute a practice that is incompatible with the Convention.

It is established in the case-law of the Court that the concept of administrative practice embodies two criteria:

1. an accumulation of identical or analogous breaches, which are sufficiently numerous and interconnected to amount not merely to isolated incidents or exceptions but to a pattern or system;
2. official tolerance.

The Commission in the "Greek Case" (Yearbook 12) described the second criterion as "... they are tolerated in the sense that the superiors of those immediately responsible, though cognisant of such acts, take no action to punish them or to prevent their repetition ...".

In the present case the Court, when deciding whether a practice existed in the Italian length-of-proceedings cases, relied solely on the first criterion, i.e., an accumulation of identical breaches, but failed to address the second criterion, i.e., official tolerance.

In my view, the Court should not have decided that there is an administrative practice without examining whether the higher authorities of the State, though aware of the existence of the breaches, refuse to take action to prevent their repetition.

Had the Court examined whether the requirements of the second criterion were met in the present case, it would have found out that there is an ongoing dialogue between the Committee of Ministers of the Council of Europe and the Italian government, in the course of which the government has provided detailed information on the measures that are being taken, and will be taken in the future, in order to solve the problem of the excessive length of proceedings.

In this connection, it is noteworthy that in its resolution adopted on 15 July 1999, the Committee of Ministers welcomes "the considerable increase in the efficiency of the [Italian] courts in terms of cases resolved ..." and decides "to resume, in one year at the latest, the examination of the question whether the announced measures will effectively prevent new violations of the Convention ...."

The Court too might have chosen to wait for a year to see if the steps taken by the Italian government bore positive results. However, the Court deprived itself of this option as it did not deal with the question of official tolerance and the attitude of the Italian government.

Apicella v. Italy, App. no. 64890/01, Judgment of 29 March 2006 [GC], Eur. Ct. H.R.

. . . .

13. On 17 January 1992 the applicant brought proceedings in the Benevento Magistrate's Court, sitting as an employment tribunal, seeking acknowledgement of her right to be reregistered on the lists of farmers and of her status in that capacity. That status had been contested by the Farmers' Social Insurance Fund (*Servizio Contributi Agricoli Unificati—"the SCAU"*). Her entitlement to a maternity allowance depended on the type of occupational status she had.

14. On 22 February 1992 the Magistrate's Court set the case down for the first hearing on 14 March 1994. On that day it also requested documents relating to the records drawn up by the labour inspector and ordered them to be filed at a hearing on 8 November 1995. On that date, at the request of counsel for the defendant, the Magistrate's Court declared the proceedings interrupted on the ground that the SCAU had been abolished.

15. On 24 November 1995 the applicant lodged an application with the court registry for the proceedings to be resumed against the social-security department (*Istituto Nazionale di Previdenza Sociale*). On 25 January 1996 the Magistrate's Court set the case down for hearing on 21 October 1997. However, that hearing was adjourned by the court of its own motion to 4 March 1999. The next three hearings, held between 8 April 1999 and 18 September 2000, were devoted to hearing evidence from witnesses. One of those hearings was adjourned at the parties' request. On 13 November 2000 the parties made their submissions.

16. In a judgment of the same date, the text of which was deposited with the registry on 21 November 2000, the Magistrate's Court dismissed the claim because the applicant had failed to show that a relationship of subordination had existed at her work.

17. On 24 April 2001 the applicant lodged an appeal with the Naples Court of Appeal. On 11 February 2001 the president set the appeal down for hearing on 26 January 2004. On that day the Court of Appeal reserved judgment. In a judgment of the same date, the text of which was deposited with the registry on 15 March 2004, the Court of Appeal dismissed the appeal.

B. The "Pinto" proceedings

18. On 3 October 2001 the applicant lodged an application with the Rome Court of Appeal under Law no. 89 of 24 March 2001, known as the "Pinto Act", complaining of the excessive length of the above-described proceedings. She asked the court to rule that there had been a breach of Article 6 § 1 of the Convention and to order the Italian Government to pay compensation for the non-pecuniary damage sustained, plus an unquantified amount for costs and expenses.

19. In a decision of 28 February 2002, the text of which was deposited with the registry on 30 April 2002, the Court of Appeal found that the proceedings had been excessively long . . . .

The Court of Appeal awarded the applicant 2,500 euros (EUR), on an equitable basis, in compensation for non-pecuniary damage and EUR 710 for costs and expenses. That decision became final by 15 June 2003 at the latest and was executed by the authorities on an unspecified date between 23 March 2004 and 12 July 2004.

20. In a letter of 7 January 2003 the applicant informed the Court of the outcome of the domestic proceedings and asked it to resume its examination of her application.

In the same letter the applicant also informed the Court that she did not intend to appeal to the Court of Cassation because an appeal to that court could only be on points of law.

II. RELEVANT DOMESTIC LAW AND PRACTICE

A. Law no. 89 of 24 March 2001, known as the "Pinto Act"

1. Award of just satisfaction in the event of a breach of the requirement to dispose of proceedings within a reasonable time and amendment to Article 375 of the Code of Civil Procedure.

> **CHAPTER II Just satisfaction**
> **Section 2 Entitlement to just satisfaction**
> "1. Anyone sustaining pecuniary or non-pecuniary damage as a result of a violation of the Convention for the Protection of Human Rights and Fundamental Freedoms, ratified by Law no. 848 of 4 August 1955, on account of a failure to comply with the 'reasonable-time' requirement in Article 6 § 1 of the Convention, shall be entitled to just satisfaction.
>
> 2. In determining whether there has been a violation, the court shall have regard to the complexity of the case and, in the light thereof, the conduct of the parties and of the judge deciding procedural issues, and also the conduct of any authority required to participate in or contribute to the resolution of the case.
>
> 3. The court shall assess the quantum of damage in accordance with Article 2056 of the Civil Code and shall apply the following rules:
>
>   (a) only damage attributable to the period beyond the reasonable time referred to in subsection 1 may be taken into account;
>
>   (b) in addition to the payment of a sum of money, reparation for non-pecuniary damage shall be made by giving suitable publicity to the finding of a violation."
>
> **Section 3 Procedure**
> "1. Claims for just satisfaction shall be lodged with the court of appeal in which the judge sits who has jurisdiction under Article 11 of the Code of Criminal Procedure to try cases concerning members of the judiciary in the district where the case in which the violation is alleged to have occurred was decided or discontinued at the merits stage or is still pending.
>
> 2. The claim shall be made on an application lodged with the registry of the court of appeal by a lawyer holding a special authority containing all the information prescribed by Article 125 of the Code of Civil Procedure.
>
> 3. The application shall be made against the Minister of Justice where the alleged violation has taken place in proceedings in the ordinary courts, the Minister of Defence where it has taken place in proceedings before the military courts and the Finance Minister where it has taken place in proceedings before the tax commissioners. In all other cases, the application shall be made against the Prime Minister.
>
> 4. The court of appeal shall hear the application in accordance with Articles 737 et seq. of the Code of Civil Procedure. The application and the order setting the case down for hearing shall be served by the applicant on the defendant authority at its

elected domicile at the offices of State Counsel (*Avvocatura dello Stato*) at least fifteen days prior to the date of the hearing before the Chamber.

5. The parties may apply to the court for an order for production of all or part of the procedural and other documents from the proceedings in which the violation referred to in section 2 is alleged to have occurred and they and their lawyers shall be entitled to be heard by the court in private if they attend the hearing. The parties may lodge memorials and documents up till five days before the date set for the hearing or until expiry of the time allowed by the court of appeal for that purpose on an application by the parties.

6. The court shall deliver a decision within four months after the application is lodged. An appeal shall lie to the Court of Cassation. The decision shall be enforceable immediately.

7. To the extent that resources permit, payment of compensation to those entitled shall commence on 1 January 2002."

Section 4 Time-limits and procedures for lodging applications

"A claim for just satisfaction may be lodged while the proceedings in which the violation is alleged to have occurred are pending or within six months from the date when the decision ending the proceedings becomes final. Claims lodged after that date shall be time-barred."

Section 5 Communications

"If the court decides to allow an application, its decision shall be communicated by the registry to the parties, to State Counsel at the Court of Audit to enable him to start an investigation into liability, and to the authorities responsible for deciding whether to institute disciplinary proceedings against the civil servants involved in the proceedings in any capacity."

Section 6 Transitional provisions

"1. Within six months after the entry into force of this Act, anyone who has lodged an application with the European Court of Human Rights in due time complaining of a violation of the 'reasonable-time' requirement contained in Article 6 § 1 of the Convention for the Protection of Human Rights and Fundamental Freedoms, ratified by Law no. 848 of 4 August 1955, shall be entitled to lodge a claim under section 3 hereof provided that the application has not by then been declared admissible by the European Court. In such cases, the application to the court of appeal must state when the application to the said European Court was made.

2. The registry of the relevant court shall inform the Minister for Foreign Affairs without delay of any claim lodged in accordance with section 3 and within the period laid down in subsection 1 of this section."

Section 7 Financial provisions

"1. The financial cost of implementing this Act, which is put at 12,705,000,000 Italian lire from 2002, shall be met by releasing funds entered in the three-year budget 2001–03 in the chapter concerning the basic current-liability estimates from the 'special fund' in the year 2001 forecast of the Ministry of the Treasury, Economy and Financial Planning. Treasury deposits shall be set aside for that purpose.

2. The Ministry of the Treasury, Economy and Financial Planning is authorised to make the appropriate budgetary adjustments by decree."

. . . .

III. OTHER RELEVANT PROVISIONS

A. Third annual report on the excessive length of judicial proceedings in Italy for 2003 (administrative, civil and criminal justice)

30. In the report CM/Inf/DH(2004)23, revised on 24 September 2004, the Ministers' deputies made the following indications regarding an assessment of the Pinto remedy:

" . . . 11. As regards the domestic remedy introduced in 2001 by the "Pinto Act", a number of shortcomings remain, particularly in connection with the effectiveness of the remedy and its application in conformity with the Convention: in particular, the law does not provide yet for the acceleration of pending proceedings . . . .

. . . .

109. In the framework of its examination of the 1st annual report, the Committee of Ministers expressed concern at the fact that this legislation did not foresee the speeding up of the proceedings and that its application posed a risk of aggravating the backlog of the appeal courts. . . .

112. It should be pointed out that in the framework of its examination of the 2nd annual report, the Committee of Ministers had noted with concern that the Convention had no direct effect and had consequently invited the Italian authorities to intensify their efforts at national level as well as their contacts with the different bodies of the Council of Europe competent in this field . . . . "

B. Interim Resolution ResDH(2005)114 concerning the judgments of the European Court of Human Rights and decisions by the Committee of Ministers in 2183 cases against Italy relating to the excessive length of judicial proceedings

31. In this interim resolution the Ministers' deputies indicated as follows:

". . . . Stressing that the setting-up of domestic remedies does not dispense states from their general obligation to solve the structural problems underlying violations;

Finding that despite the efforts undertaken, numerous elements still indicate that the solution to the problem will not be found in the near future (as evidenced in particular by the statistical data, the new cases before both domestic courts and the European Court, the information contained in the annual reports submitted by the government to the Committee and in the reports of the Prosecutor General at the Court of cassation); . . . .

Stressing the importance the Convention attaches to the right to fair administration of justice in a democratic society and recalling that the problem of the excessive length of judicial proceedings, by reason of its persistence and extent, constitutes a real danger for the respect of the rule of law in Italy; . . .

URGES the Italian authorities to enhance their political commitment and make it their effective priority to meet Italy's obligation under the Convention and the Court's judgments, to secure the right to a fair trial within a reasonable time to all persons under Italy's jurisdiction . . .".

. . . .

THE LAW

I. THE GOVERNMENT'S PRELIMINARY OBJECTIONS

A. The non-exhaustion of domestic remedies

. . . .

39. By enacting the Pinto Act, Italy introduced a purely compensatory remedy for cases in which there had been a breach of the reasonable-time principle. The Court has already held that the remedy before the courts of appeal introduced by the Pinto Act was accessible and that there was no reason to question its effectiveness (see *Brusco v. Italy* (dec.), no. 69789/01, ECHR 2001-IX). Moreover, having regard to the nature of the Pinto Act and the context in which it was passed, the Court went on to find that there were grounds for departing from the general principle that the exhaustion requirement should be assessed with reference to the time at which the application was lodged. That was the case not only in respect of applications lodged after the date on which the Act came into force, but also of those which were already on the Court's list of cases by that date. It had taken into consideration, among other things, the transitional provision provided for in section 6 of the Pinto Act, which afforded Italian litigants a genuine opportunity to obtain redress for their grievances at national level for all applications currently pending before the Court that had not yet been declared admissible (see *Brusco*, ibid.).

40. In the *Scordino* case the Court held that where applicants complained only of the amount of compensation and the discrepancy between that amount and the amount which would have been awarded under Article 41 of the Convention in just satisfaction, they were not required—for the purpose of exhausting domestic remedies—to appeal to the Court of Cassation against the Court of Appeal's decision. The Court based that conclusion on a study of some one hundred Court of Cassation judgments. In none of those judgments had that court entertained a complaint to the effect that the amount awarded by the Court of Appeal was insufficient in relation to the loss alleged or inadequate in the light of the Strasbourg case-law.

41. The Court notes that on 26 January 2004 the Court of Cassation, sitting as a full court, quashed four decisions in cases in which the existence or amount of non-pecuniary damage had been disputed. In so doing, it established the principle that "the court of appeal's determination of non-pecuniary damage in accordance with section 2 of Law no. 89/2001, although inherently based on equitable principles, must be done in a legally defined framework since reference has to be made to the amounts awarded, in similar cases, by the Strasbourg Court. Some divergence is permissible, within reason".

42. The Court takes note of that departure from precedent and welcomes the Court of Cassation's efforts to bring its decisions into line with European case-law. It reiterates, furthermore, having deemed it reasonable to assume that the departure from precedent, in particular judgment no. 1340 of the Court of Cassation, must have been public knowledge from 26 July 2004. It has therefore held that, from that date onwards, applicants should be required to avail themselves of that remedy for the purposes of Article 35 § 1 de la Convention (see *Di Sante v. Italy* (dec.),

no. 56079/00, 24 June 2004, and, *mutatis mutandis, Broca and Texier-Micault v. France*, nos. 27928/02 and 31694/02, § 20, 21 October 2003).

43. In the instant case the Grand Chamber, like the Chamber, notes that the time-limit for appealing to the Court of Cassation had expired before 26 July 2004 and considers that, in these circumstances, the applicant was dispensed from the obligation to exhaust domestic remedies. Consequently, without prejudging the question whether the Government can be regarded as estopped from raising this objection, the Court considers that it must be dismissed.

B. Assessment of "victim" status

1. The Chamber decision

44. In its admissibility decision of 22 January 2004 the Chamber followed the decision in the *Scordino* case according to which an applicant could still claim to be a "victim" within the meaning of Article 34 of the Convention where the amount awarded by the Court of Appeal was not considered by the Chamber as sufficient to repair the alleged loss and violation. In the present case, as the amount awarded to the applicant was not sufficient to amount to adequate redress the Chamber held that she could still claim to be a victim.

. . . .

53. In reply to the criticism of the various Governments regarding the criteria articulated by the Chamber, the applicant observed that the length of the proceedings was so bound up with the Italian judicial system that the Government omitted to ask the Court what they should change in the system in order to eliminate the delays. Instead, the Government asked the Court to lay down guidelines regarding damage or authorize the courts to continue using guidelines that were totally different from those used by the Court so that they could carry on running the Italian system without introducing any changes to expedite proceedings. The applicant argued that the Government erred in its assessment of the position as it was not for the European Court of Human Rights to avoid giving judgments that conflicted with national law but, on the contrary, the national law (including the Pinto Act) that should not conflict with the Convention. In the applicant's submission, the Government could not properly argue that in some cases delays in legal proceedings gave applicants an advantage if they held out with unfounded arguments during proceedings, or if the stakes involved in the dispute were less than the just satisfaction awarded. The value of the application in question was of no relevance to the right to a hearing within a reasonable time and Article 6 did not require an applicant claiming the right to just satisfaction to have been successful. Furthermore, the Government's reasoning was one that was expressed with hindsight at the end of proceedings, and it was never possible to say beforehand what the outcome would be. If a case was lost after twenty years of proceedings the non-pecuniary damage incurred was all the greater, since if the person had known earlier that they would lose they would probably have arranged certain aspects of their life differently.

54. As to the adequacy of a finding of a violation, that assertion held true only for a State that committed few breaches—and these owing to exceptional circumstances—and possessed a sound judicial system. This was not the situation in Italy,

which did nothing to put an end to these violations. Such conduct certainly could not be rewarded with the elimination of just satisfaction. On the contrary, in order to force the State to take measures to avoid violations the Court ought to increase the awards in its judgments against Italy until the reasons why justice was not delivered within a reasonable time were eliminated. . . .

3. The intervening parties

a) The Czech Government

56. In the Czech Government's submission, the Court should confine itself to ensuring that the consequences of the case-law policy choices made by the domestic courts were in keeping with the Convention. Its review should be more or less rigorous, depending on the margin of appreciation that the Court allowed national authorities. The Court should only ensure that, in accordance with Article 13 of the Convention, the national authorities complied with the principles established in its case-law or applied the provisions of their own domestic law in such a way that applicants enjoyed a level of protection in respect of their rights and freedoms as guaranteed by the Convention that was greater than or equivalent to that which they would enjoy if the national authorities applied the Convention's provisions directly. The Court should not go any further except in cases where the outcome of action by the national authorities appeared, on the face of it, arbitrary.

57. The Czech Government acknowledged that the adequacy of the amount awarded at domestic level was one of the criteria of effectiveness of an application for compensation within the meaning of Article 13. However, in view of the wide margin of appreciation that should be available to the Contracting Parties in implementing Article 13, they considered that the Court should subsequently exercise only "limited control", thus restricted to satisfying itself that the national authorities had not made a "manifest error in assessment" of the non-pecuniary damage caused by the excessive length of judicial proceedings.

58. Moreover, as the Czech Government wanted to provide their country with a compensatory remedy in addition to the existing preventive domestic remedy, they asked the Court to provide as many guidelines as possible in that connection so that they could set in place a remedy which would incontestably be effective.

b) The Polish Government

59. In the Polish Government's submission, an assessment of the facts of the case with a view to determining whether the "reasonable time" had been exceeded was part of the examination of the evidence conducted by the domestic courts. It was therefore debatable to what extent a supranational body could intervene in this process. It was, rather, commonly accepted that in most cases the facts would have been established by the domestic courts and that the Court's task would be limited to examining whether the Convention had been complied with. The Court's case-law appeared to be confined to assessing whether the domestic courts' decisions, given in accordance with domestic procedure previously approved by the Court, had properly applied the general rules to the specific case. In the absence of precise indications for assessing the facts and calculating the amount of compensation, there were no grounds on which to dispute the decisions of the domestic courts. It

should be borne in mind in this regard that the domestic courts had a discretion in assessing the facts and evidence.

60. Furthermore, in the very particular circumstances of some cases the mere finding of a violation sufficed to meet the requirement of an effective remedy and amounted to sufficient redress for the breach. That rule had been clearly established in the Court's case-law on other Articles of the Convention. In some cases, moreover, the excessive length of the proceedings could be favourable to the parties and compensating them would therefore be extremely questionable.

c) The Slovak Government

61. In the Slovak Government's submission, the Court should adopt the same approach as in assessing the fairness of proceedings, a matter in respect of which it considered that its task was not to deal with the factual or legal mistakes allegedly made by the domestic courts unless such mistakes could have resulted in a breach of the rights and freedoms guaranteed by the Convention. Moreover, although Article 6 of the Convention guaranteed the right to a fair trial it did not lay down any rules on the admissibility of evidence or its assessment, which was therefore primarily a matter for regulation under national law by the domestic courts. Accordingly, when examining decisions of domestic courts on the amount of non-pecuniary damages awarded for delays in the proceedings, the Court should leave enough room for the courts' discretion in this respect since the domestic courts decided on delays in the proceedings on the basis of the same criteria as the Court—and were in a better position to analyse the causes and consequences and thus to determine the non-pecuniary damage on an equitable basis.

62. The Slovak Government pointed out that the decisions of the Slovak Constitutional Court concerning delays in proceedings were much more detailed than the Court's decisions. In their submission, the Court should examine the decisions of the domestic courts relating to the amounts awarded for non-pecuniary damage only with regard to whether these decisions were manifestly arbitrary and unfair and not whether the amounts awarded by the Court in similar circumstances were substantially higher. Moreover, the Slovak Government found it logical that the amounts awarded by the domestic courts for protractedness of proceedings were less than the amounts awarded by the Court because injured persons could obtain effective and rapid compensation in their own country without having to bring their case to the international court.

4. The Court's assessment

a) Reiteration of the context peculiar to length-of-proceedings cases

63. The Court will begin by responding to the observations of the different Governments regarding the lack of precision in its judgments both in respect of the reasons leading to a finding of a violation and awards in respect of non-pecuniary damage.

It feels it important to point out that the reason why it has been led to rule on so many length-of-proceedings cases is because certain Contracting Parties have for years failed to comply with the "reasonable-time" requirement under Article 6 § 1 and have not provided for a domestic remedy for this type of complaint.

64. The situation has worsened on account of the large number of cases coming from certain countries, of which Italy is one. The Court has already had occasion to stress the serious difficulties it has had as a result of Italy's inability to resolve the situation . . . (see *Bottazzi v. Italy* [GC], no. 34884/97, § 22, ECHR 1999-V; *Ferrari v. Italy* [GC], no. 33440/96, § 21, 28 July 1999; *A.P. v. Italy* [GC], no. 35265/97, § 18, 28 July 1999; and *Di Mauro v. Italy* [GC], no. 34256/96, § 23, ECHR 1999-V).

65. Thus the Court, like the Commission, after years of examining the reasons for the delays attributable to the parties under the Italian procedural rules, has had to resolve to standardize its judgments and decisions. This has allowed it to adopt more than 1,000 judgments against Italy since 1999 in civil length-of-proceedings cases. That approach has made it necessary to establish scales on equitable principles for awards in respect of non-pecuniary damage under Article 41, in order to arrive at equivalent results in similar cases.

All this has led the Court to award higher levels of compensation than those awarded by the Convention institutions prior to 1999 and ones which may differ from those applied in the event of a finding of other violations. This increase, far from being a punitive measure, was intended to fulfill two purposes. On the one hand it served to encourage States to find their own, universally accessible, solution to the problem and on the other hand it allowed applicants to avoid being penalized for the lack of domestic remedies.

. . . .

b) Principles established under the Court's case-law

67. With regard to the observations concerning the subsidiarity principle, also made by the third parties, the Court notes that under Article 34 of the Convention it "may receive applications from any person . . . claiming to be the victim of a violation by one of the High Contracting Parties of the rights set forth in the Convention or the Protocols thereto . . . . "

68. The Court reiterates that it falls first to the national authorities to redress any alleged violation of the Convention. In this regard, the question whether an applicant can claim to be a victim of the violation alleged is relevant at all stages of the proceedings under the Convention (see *Burdov v. Russia*, no. 59498/00, § 30, ECHR 2002-III).

69. The Court also reiterates that a decision or measure favourable to the applicant is not in principle sufficient to deprive him of his status as a "victim" unless the national authorities have acknowledged, either expressly or in substance, and then afforded redress for, the breach of the Convention (see, for example, *Eckle v. Germany*, judgment of 15 July 1982, Series A no. 51, p. 32, §§ 69 et seq.; *Amuur v. France*, judgment of 25 June 1996, *Reports of Judgments and Decisions* 1996-III, p. 846, § 36; *Dalban v. Romania* [GC], no. 28114/95, § 44, ECHR 1999-VI; and *Jensen v. Denmark* (dec.), no. 48470/99, ECHR 2001-X).

70. The issue as to whether a person may still claim to be the victim of an alleged violation of the Convention essentially entails on the part of the Court an *ex post facto* examination of his or her situation. As it has already held in other length-of-proceedings cases, the question whether he or she has received reparation for the damage caused—comparable to just satisfaction as provided for under Article 41 of

the Convention—is an important issue. It is the Court's settled case-law that where the national authorities have found a violation and their decision constitutes appropriate and sufficient redress, the party concerned can no longer claim to be a victim within the meaning of Article 34 of the Convention (see *Holzinger v. Austria (no. 1)*, no. 23459/94, § 21, ECHR 2001-I).

71. In so far as the parties appear to link the issue of victim status to the more general question of effectiveness of the remedy and seek guidelines on affording the most effective domestic remedies possible, the Court proposes to address the question in a wider context by giving certain indications as to the characteristics which such a domestic remedy should have, having regard to the fact that, in this type of case, the applicant's ability to claim to be a victim will depend on the redress which the domestic remedy will have given him or her.

72. The best solution in absolute terms is indisputably, as in many spheres, prevention. The Court recalls that it has stated on many occasions that Article 6 § 1 imposes on the Contracting States the duty to organize their judicial systems in such a way that their courts can meet each of its requirements, including the obligation to hear cases within a reasonable time (see, among many other authorities, *Süßmann v. Germany*, judgment of 16 September 1996, *Reports* 1996-IV, p. 1174, § 55, and *Bottazzi*, cited above, § 22). Where the judicial system is deficient in this respect, a remedy designed to expedite the proceedings in order to prevent them from becoming excessively lengthy is the most effective solution Such a remedy offers an undeniable advantage over a remedy affording only compensation since it also prevents a finding of successive violations in respect of the same set of proceedings and does not merely repair the breach *a posteriori*, as does a compensatory remedy of the type provided for under Italian law for example.

73. The Court has on many occasions acknowledged that this type of remedy is "effective" in so far as it allows for an earlier decision by the court concerned (see, among other authorities, *Bacchini v. Switzerland* (dec.), no. 62915/00, 21 June 2005; *Kunz v. Switzerland* (dec.), no. 623/02, 21 June 2005; *Fehr and Lauterburg v. Switzerland* (dec.), no. 708/02 and 1095/02, 21 June 2005; *Holzinger (no. 1)* (cited above, § 22), *Gonzalez Marin v. Spain* (dec.), no. 39521/98, ECHR 1999-VII; and *Tomé Mota v. Portugal* (dec.), no. 32082/96, ECHR 1999-IX).

74. It is also clear that for countries where length-of-proceedings violations already exist, a remedy designed only to expedite the proceedings—although desirable for the future—may not be adequate to redress a situation in which it is obvious that the proceedings have already been excessively long.

75. Different types of remedy may redress the violation appropriately. The Court has already affirmed this in respect of criminal proceedings, where it was satisfied that the length of proceedings had been taken into account when reducing the sentence in an express and measurable manner (see *Beck v. Norway*, no. 26390/95, § 27, 26 June 2001).

Moreover, some States, such as Austria, Croatia, Spain, Poland and the Slovak Republic, have understood the situation perfectly by choosing to combine two types of remedy, one designed to expedite the proceedings and the other to afford compensation (see, for example, *Holzinger (no. 1)*, cited above, § 22; *Slavicek v. Croatia* (dec.), no. 20862/02, ECHR 2002-VII; *Fernandez-Molina Gonzalez and Others v. Spain* (dec.), no. 64359/01, ECHR 2002-IX; Michalak v. Poland (dec.), no. 24549/03, 1 March 2005; *Andrášik and Others v. Slovakia* (dec.), nos. 57984/00, 60226/00, 60237/00, 60242/00, 60679/00, 60680/00 and 68563/01, ECHR 2002-IX).

76. However, States can also choose to introduce only a compensatory remedy, as Italy has done, without that remedy being regarded as ineffective (see *Mifsud*, cited above).

77. The Court has already had occasion to reiterate in the *Kudła* judgment (cited above, §§154–55) that, subject to compliance with the requirements of the Convention, the Contracting States are afforded some discretion as to the manner in which they provide individuals with the relief required by Article 13 and conform to their Convention obligation under that provision. It has also stressed the importance of the rules relating to the subsidiarity principle so that individuals are not systematically forced to refer to the Court in Strasbourg complaints that could otherwise, and in the Court's opinion more appropriately, have been addressed in the first place within the national legal system.

78. Accordingly, where the legislature or the domestic courts have agreed to play their true role by introducing a domestic remedy the Court will clearly have to draw certain conclusions from this. Where a State has made a significant move by introducing a compensatory remedy, the Court must leave a wider margin of appreciation to the State to allow it to organise the remedy in a manner consistent with its own legal system and traditions and consonant with the standard of living in the country concerned. It will, in particular, be easier for the domestic courts to refer to the amounts awarded at domestic level for other types of damage—personal injury, damage relating to a relative's death or damage in defamation cases for example—and rely on their innermost conviction, even if that results in awards of amounts that are lower than those fixed by the Court in similar cases.

79. In accordance with its case-law on the interpretation and application of domestic law, while the Court's duty, under Article 19 of the Convention, is to ensure the observance of the engagements undertaken by the Contracting Parties to the Convention, it is not its function to deal with errors of fact or law allegedly committed by a national court unless and in so far as they may have infringed rights and freedoms protected by the Convention.

Moreover, it is primarily for the national authorities, notably the courts, to interpret and apply domestic law (see *Jahn and Others v. Germany* [GC], nos. 46720/99, 72203/01 and 72552/01, § 86, to be published in ECHR 2005).

80. The Court is therefore required to verify whether the way in which the domestic law is interpreted and applied produces consequences that are consistent with the principles of the Convention as interpreted in the light of the Court's case-law. This is especially true where, as the Italian Court of Cassation has quite rightly observed, the domestic law refers explicitly to the provisions of the Convention. This supervisory role should be easier in respect of States that have effectively incorporated the Convention into their legal system and consider the rules to be directly applicable since the highest courts of these States will normally assume responsibility for enforcing the principles determined by the Court.

Accordingly, a clear error in assessment on the part of the domestic courts may also arise as a result of a misapplication or misinterpretation of the Court's case-law.

81. The principle of subsidiarity does not mean renouncing all supervision of the result obtained from using domestic remedies, otherwise the rights guaranteed by Article 6 would be devoid of any substance. In that connection it should be reiterated that the Convention is intended to guarantee not theoretical or illusory rights, but rights that are practical and effective (see *Prince Hans-Adam II of Liechtenstein v. Germany* [GC], no. 42527/98, § 45, ECHR 2001-VIII). This is particularly true for the guarantees enshrined in Article 6, in view of the prominent place held in a democratic society by the right to a fair trial with all the guarantees under Article 6 (see, *mutatis mutandis, Prince Hans-Adam II of Liechtenstein*, cited above, § 45).

c) Application of the foregoing principles

82. It follows from the foregoing principles that the Court is required to verify that there has been an acknowledgement, at least in substance, by the authorities of a violation of a right protected by the Convention and whether the redress can be considered as appropriate and sufficient (see, *inter alia, Normann v. Denmark* (dec.), no. 44704/98, 14 June 2001; *Jensen v. Denmark* (dec.), no. 48470/99, 20 March 2003; and *Nardone v. Italy*, no. 34368/98, 25 November 2004).

i. The finding of a violation

83. The first condition, which is the finding of a violation by the national authorities, is not in issue since if an appeal court were to award damages without having first expressly found a violation, the Court would necessarily conclude that such a finding had been made in substance as, under the Pinto Act, an appeal court cannot make an award unless a reasonable time has been exceeded (see *Capogrossi v. Italy* (dec.), no. 62253/00, 21 October 2004).

ii. The characteristics of the redress

84. With regard to the second condition, namely, appropriate and sufficient redress, the Court has already indicated that even if a remedy is "effective" in that it allows for an earlier decision by the courts to which the case has been referred or the aggrieved party is given adequate compensation for the delays that have already occurred, that conclusion applies only on condition that an application for compensation remains itself an effective, adequate and accessible remedy in respect of the excessive length of judicial proceedings. . . .

Indeed, it cannot be ruled out that excessive delays in an action for compensation will affect whether the remedy is an adequate one (see *Paulino Tomas v. Portugal* (dec.), no. 58698/00, ECHR 2003-VIII; *Belinger v. Slovenia* (dec.), no. 42320/98, 2 October 2001; and, *mutatis mutandis, Öneryýldýz v. Turkey* [GC], no. 48939/99, § 156, ECHR 2004-XII).

85. In that connection the Court reiterates its case-law to the effect that the right of access to a tribunal guaranteed by Article 6 § 1 of the Convention would be illusory if a Contracting State's domestic legal system allowed a final, binding judicial decision to remain inoperative to the detriment of one party. Execution of a judgment given by any court must therefore be regarded as an integral part of the

"trial" for the purposes of Article 6 (see, *inter alia, Hornsby v. Greece,* judgment of 19 March 1997, *Reports* 1997-II, pp. 510–11, § 40 et seq., and *Metaxas v. Greece,* no. 8415/02, § 25, 27 May 2004).

86. The Court has pointed out in civil length-of-proceedings cases that the enforcement proceedings are the second stage of the proceedings and that the right asserted does not actually become effective until enforcement (see, among other authorities, *Di Pede v. Italy* and *Zappia v. Italy,* judgments of 26 September 1996, *Reports* 1996-IV, p. 1384, §§ 22, 24 and 26, and pp. 1411–12, §§ 18, 20, 22, and, *mutatis mutandis, Silva Pontes v. Portugal,* judgment of 23 March 1994, Series A no. 286-A, p. 14, § 33).

87. The Court has also stated that it is inappropriate to require an individual who has obtained judgment against the State at the end of legal proceedings to then bring enforcement proceedings to obtain satisfaction. It follows that the late payment, following enforcement proceedings, of amounts owing to the applicant cannot cure the national authorities' long-standing failure to comply with a judgment and does not afford adequate redress (see *Metaxas,* cited above, § 19, and *Karahalios v. Greece,* no. 62503/00, § 23, 11 December 2003). Moreover, some States, such as Slovakia and Croatia, have even stipulated a date by which payment should be made, namely two and three months respectively (see *Andrášik and Others v. Slovakia,* and *Slavicek v. Croatia,* cited above).

The Court can accept that the authorities need time in which to make payment. However, in respect of a compensatory remedy designed to redress the consequences of excessively lengthy proceedings that period should not generally exceed six months from the date on which the decision awarding compensation becomes enforceable.

88. As the Court has already reiterated on many occasions, it is not open to a State authority to cite lack of funds as an excuse for not honouring a judgment debt (see, among many other authorities, *Burdov,* cited above, § 35).

89. With regard to the more or less summary nature of compensation proceedings, it should be noted that a remedy affording compensation within a reasonable time may well be subject to procedural rules that are not exactly the same as for ordinary applications for damages. It is for each State to determine, on the basis of the rules applicable in its judicial system, which procedure will best meet the criterion of "effectiveness", provided that the procedure conforms to the principles of fairness guaranteed by Article 6 of the Convention.

90. Lastly, the Court finds it reasonable that in this type of proceedings where the State, on account of the poor organization of its judicial system, forces litigants—to some extent—to have recourse to a compensatory remedy, the rules regarding legal costs may be different and thus avoid placing an excessive burden on litigants where their action is justified. It might appear paradoxical that, by imposing various taxes—payable prior to the lodging of an application or after the decision—the State takes away with one hand what it has awarded with the other to repair a breach of the Convention. Nor should the costs be excessive and constitute an unreasonable restriction on the right to lodge such an application and thus an infringement of the right of access to a tribunal. On this point the Court notes that in Poland applicants

are reimbursed the court fee payable on lodging a complaint if their complaint is considered justified (see *Charzyński v. Poland* (dec.), no. 15212/03, to be published in ECHR 2005).

91. Regarding violations of the reasonable-time requirement, one of the characteristics of sufficient redress which may remove a litigant's victim status relates to the amount awarded as a result of using the domestic remedy. The Court has already had occasion to indicate that an applicant's victim status may also depend on the amount of compensation awarded at domestic level on the basis of the facts about which he or she complains before the Court (see *Normann v. Denmark* (dec.), no. 44704/98, 14 June 2001, and *Jensen and Rasmussen v. Denmark*, cited above).

92. With regard to pecuniary damage, the domestic courts are clearly in a better position to determine the existence and quantum. Moreover, that point was not disputed by the parties or interveners.

93. Regarding non-pecuniary damage, the Court, like the Italian Court of Cassation, assumes that there is a strong but rebuttable presumption that excessively long proceedings will occasion non-pecuniary damage. The Court also accepts that, in some cases, the length of proceedings may result in only minimal non-pecuniary damage or no non-pecuniary damage at all (see *Nardone*, cited above). The domestic courts will then have to justify their decision by giving sufficient reasons.

94. Moreover, in the Court's view, the level of compensation depends on the characteristics and effectiveness of the domestic remedy.

95. The Court can also perfectly well accept that a State which has introduced a number of remedies, one of which is designed to expedite proceedings and one to afford compensation, will award amounts which—while being lower than those awarded by the Court—are not unreasonable, on condition that the relevant decisions, which must be consonant with the legal tradition and the standard of living in the country concerned, are speedy, reasoned and executed very quickly (see *Dubjakova v. Slovakia* (dec.), no. 67299/01, 10 October 2004).

However, where the domestic remedy has not met all the foregoing requirements, it is possible that the threshold in respect of which the amount will still allow a litigant to claim to be a "victim" will be higher.

96. It is even conceivable that the court determining the amount of compensation will acknowledge its own delay and that accordingly, and in order not to penalize the applicant later, it will award a particularly high amount of compensation in order to make good the further delay.

iii. Application to the present case

97. The four-month period prescribed by the Pinto Act complies with the requirement of speediness necessary for a remedy to be effective. The only obstacle to this may arise with appeals to the Court of Cassation in respect of which no maximum period for giving a ruling has been fixed. In the instant case the judicial phase lasted from 3 October 2001 to 30 April 2002, that is, nearly seven months, which, even if it exceeds the statutory period, is still reasonable.

98. However, the Court finds it unacceptable that the applicant had to wait more than eleven months, after the decision was deposited with the registry, before receiving her compensation.

99. The Court would stress the fact that, in order to be effective, a compensatory remedy must be accompanied by adequate budgetary provision so that effect can be given within six months of their being deposited with the registry to decisions of the courts of appeal awarding compensation, which, in accordance with the Pinto Act, are immediately enforceable.

100. Similarly, as regards procedural costs, certain fixed expenses (such as the fee for registering the judicial decision) may significantly hamper the efforts made by applicants to obtain compensation. The Court draws the Government's attention to these various aspects with a view to eradicating at the source problems that may give rise to further applications.

101. In assessing the amount of compensation awarded by the court of appeal, the Court considers, on the basis of the material in its possession, what it would have done in the same position for the period taken into account by the domestic court.

102. According to the documents provided by the Government for the hearing, there is no disproportion in Italy between the amounts awarded to heirs for non-pecuniary damage in the event of a relative's death or those awarded for physical injury or in defamation cases and those generally awarded by the Court under Article 41 in length-of-proceedings cases. Accordingly, the level of compensation generally awarded by the courts of appeal in Pinto applications cannot be justified by this type of consideration.

103. Even if the method of calculation provided for in domestic law does not correspond exactly to the criteria established by the Court, an analysis of the Court's case-law relating to awards of just satisfaction for excessively lengthy proceedings should enable the courts of appeal to award sums that are not unreasonable in comparison with the awards made by the Court in similar cases.

104. In the present case the Court notes that the proceedings were not complex. The Court of Appeal expressly indicated that the parties' conduct was not at issue and that the interval between the hearings was due to structural reasons. For its part, the Court considers that the parties' conduct only slightly contributed to delaying the proceedings. The Court of Appeal's decision, reasoned in part, does not refer to any significant factor justifying a reduction in compensation. The Court of Appeal indicated a rate of EUR 500 per year's delay. The Court observes that the amount awarded, EUR 2,500, is approximately 14 % of what it generally awards in similar Italian cases. This factor alone leads to a result which is manifestly unreasonable having regard to the criteria established in its case-law for proceedings before employment tribunals. The Court reiterates in this connection that this type of proceedings, like those concerning the civil status and capacity of persons, must be especially speedy. It will revert to this matter in the context of Article 41 . . . .

105. In conclusion, and having regard to the fact that various requirements have not been satisfied, the Court considers that the redress was insufficient. As the second condition—appropriate and sufficient redress—has not been fulfilled, the Court considers that the applicant can in the instant case still claim to be a "victim" of a breach of the "reasonable-time" requirement.

Accordingly, this objection by the Government must also be dismissed.

II. ALLEGED VIOLATION OF ARTICLE 6 § 1 OF THE CONVENTION

106. The applicant complained of a breach of Article 6 § 1 of the Convention

. . . .

107. On 13 July 2004 the applicant informed the Court that she was not complaining of the manner in which the Court of Appeal had assessed the delays, but of the derisory amount of damages awarded and only recently paid.

. . . .

A. Period to be considered

111. The period to be taken into consideration began on 17 January 1992 when proceedings were instituted at the registry of the Benevento Magistrate's Court, sitting as an employment tribunal, and ended on 15 March 2004, when the Court of Appeal's judgment was deposited with the registry. It therefore lasted twelve years and two months for two levels of jurisdiction.

112. The Court notes that the Court of Appeal assessed the length of proceedings at the date of its decision, namely, 28 February 2002. Accordingly, a period of two years could not be taken into account by the Court of Appeal.

113. The Court notes that the Government did not dispute the length of proceedings taken into consideration by the Chamber; that the applicant cannot in any case now go back before a court of appeal to seek application of the new precedent set by the Court of Cassation on 26 January 2004 (see judgment no. 1339); and that the remaining period of two years was sufficient in itself to amount to a second breach in respect of the same set of proceedings (see *Rotondi v. Italy*, no. 38113/97, §§ 14–16, 27 April 2000, and *S.A.GE.MA S.N.C. v. Italy*, no. 40184/98, §§ 12–14, 27 April 2000). Accordingly, the Court considers that since the applicant can claim to be a "victim" of the length of the proceedings, it can take into consideration the entire domestic proceedings on the merits and not only those already examined by the Court of Appeal (see, *a contrario, Gattuso v. Italy*, (dec.), no. 24715/04, 18 November 2004).

B. Reasonableness of the length of the proceedings

114. The Court has already reiterated the reasons that led it to conclude in the four judgments against Italy of 28 July 1999 (see *Bottazzi*, cited above, § 22; *Ferrari*, cited above § 21; *A.P.*, cited above, § 18; and *Di Mauro*, cited above, § 23) that there was a practice in Italy.

115. It notes that, as the Government have stressed, a domestic remedy has since been introduced. However, that has not changed the substantive problem, namely, the fact that the length of proceedings in Italy continues to be excessive. The annual reports of the Committee of Ministers on the excessive length of judicial proceedings in Italy (see, *inter alia*, CM/Inf/DH(2004)23 revised, and Interim Resolution ResDH(2005)114) scarcely seem to reflect substantial changes in this area. Like the applicant, the Court does not see how the introduction of the Pinto remedy at domestic level has solved the problem of excessively lengthy proceedings. It has admittedly saved the Court the trouble of finding these violations, but the task has simply been transferred to the courts of appeal, which were already overburdened. Furthermore, given the occasional divergence between the case-law of the Court of

Cassation and that of the Court, the latter is again required to give a decision as to the existence of such violations.

116. The Court emphasizes once again that Article 6 § 1 of the Convention obliges the Contracting States to organize their legal systems so as to enable the courts to comply with its various requirements. It wishes to reaffirm the importance of administering justice without delays which might jeopardize its effectiveness and credibility (see *Bottazzi*, cited above, § 22). Italy's position in this regard has not changed sufficiently to call into question the conclusion that this accumulation of breaches constitutes a practice that is incompatible with the Convention.

. . . .

118. After examining the facts in the light of the information provided by the parties and the aforementioned practice, and having regard to its case-law on the subject, the Court considers that in the present case the length of the proceedings was excessive and failed to meet the "reasonable-time" requirement.

Accordingly, there has been a violation of Article 6 § 1.

. . . .

IV. APPLICATION OF ARTICLES 46 AND 41 OF THE CONVENTION

122. The Court reiterates that in the context of the execution of judgments in accordance with Article 46 of the Convention, a judgment in which it finds a breach of the Convention imposes on the respondent State a legal obligation under that provision to put an end to the breach and to make reparation for its consequences in such a way as to restore as far as possible the situation existing before the breach. If, on the other hand, national law does not allow—or allows only partial—reparation to be made for the consequences of the breach, Article 41 empowers the Court to afford the injured party such satisfaction as appears to it to be appropriate. It follows, *inter alia*, that a judgment in which the Court finds a violation of the Convention or its Protocols imposes on the respondent State a legal obligation not just to pay those concerned the sums awarded by way of just satisfaction, but also to choose, subject to supervision by the Committee of Ministers, the general and/or, if appropriate, individual measures to be adopted in its domestic legal order to put an end to the violation found by the Court and make all feasible reparation for its consequences in such a way as to restore as far as possible the situation existing before the breach (see Assanidzé v. Georgia, cited above, § 198, and *Ilaşcu and Others v. Moldova and Russia [GC]*, no. 48787/99, § 487, ECHR 2004-VII).

123. Furthermore, it follows from the Convention, and from Article 1 in particular, that in ratifying the Convention the Contracting States undertake to ensure that their domestic legislation is compatible with it (see *Maestri v. Italy* [GC], no. 39748/98, § 47, ECHR 2004-I).

124. Hundreds of cases are currently pending before the Court in respect of awards made by the courts of appeal in "Pinto" proceedings prior to the Court of Cassation's departure from precedent and/or the delay in payment of the amounts in question. The Court, while acknowledging with satisfaction the favorable developments in Italian case-law, and particularly the recent judgment of the plenary Court of Cassation, regrets to observe that where a deficiency that has given rise to a violation has been put right, another one related to the first one appears: in the

present case the delay in executing decisions. It cannot over-emphasie the fact that States must equip themselves with the means necessary and adequate to ensure that all the conditions for providing effective justice are guaranteed.

125. In its Recommendation of 12 May 2004 (Rec. (2004)6) the Committee of Ministers welcomed the fact that the Convention had now become an integral part of the domestic legal order of all States Parties while recommending that member States ensure that domestic remedies existed and were effective. In that connection the Court feels it important to stress that although the existence of a remedy is necessary, it is not in itself sufficient. The domestic courts must be able, under domestic law, to apply the European case-law directly and their knowledge of this case-law has to be facilitated by the State in question. The Court refers in this regard to the contents of the Recommendations of the Committee of Ministers on the publication and dissemination in the member states of the text of the European Convention on Human Rights and of the case-law of the Court (Rec (2002)13) of 18 December 2002) and on the European Convention on Human Rights in university education and professional training (Rec (2004)4) of 12 May 2004), not forgetting the Resolution of the Committee of Ministers (Res (2002)12) setting up the CEPEJ and the fact that at the Warsaw Summit in May 2005 the Heads of State and Governments of the member States decided to develop the evaluation and assistance functions of the CEPEJ.

In the same Recommendation of 12 May 2004 (Rec. (2004)6) the Committee of Ministers also reiterated that the States had the general obligation to solve the problems underlying violations found.

126. The Court reiterates that, subject to monitoring by the Committee of Ministers, the respondent State remains free to choose the means by which it will discharge its legal obligation under Article 46 of the Convention, provided that such means are compatible with the conclusions set out in the Court's judgment (see *Broniowski v. Poland [GC]*, no. 31443/96, § 192, ECHR 2004-V).

127. Without seeking to determine what measures may be taken by the respondent State in order to comply with its obligations under Article 46 of the Convention, the Court would draw its attention to the conditions indicated above regarding the possibility for a person to still claim to be a "victim" in this type of case and invite it to take all measures necessary to ensure that the domestic decisions are not only in conformity with the case-law of this Court but also executed within six months of being deposited with the registry . . . .

   . . . .

132. As the Czech Government had decided, in addition to introducing a preventive remedy, to enact a law providing for a compensatory remedy, they felt obliged to propose a law that would be sufficiently foreseeable. They referred to difficulties in that regard, submitting that neither the Convention nor the Court's case-law provided sufficient clarification. They requested more information about the criteria used by the Court, cases that could be regarded as "similar" and the threshold level of the "reasonable" relation.

133. In the Polish Government's submission, the Court should indicate what just satisfaction consisted of. If precise indications were not given, inconsistencies were

likely to arise between domestic case-law and the Court's case-law. Applicants and Governments alike would find it very difficult to establish general rules concerning just satisfaction from the Court's case-law. Accordingly, the domestic courts were not in a position to rely on the Court's case-law and make decisions compatible with it.

134. The Slovak Government appreciated the attempt made by the Court to specify the criteria for determining awards in respect of non-pecuniary damage. However, they added that the considerations on which the Court based its determination of non-pecuniary damage should form part of the reasons for its decision. It was only in that way that the Court's judgments would become clear instructions for the domestic courts, which determined awards in respect of non-pecuniary damage caused by delays in the proceedings. In the Slovak Government's submission, it was impossible to translate into figures all these aspects or to foresee every situation that might arise. The Court was not expected to define a precise formula by which the amount awarded for non-pecuniary damage flowing from the protractedness of proceedings could be calculated or to determine precise amounts. It was, in their view, more important that the Court gave sufficient justification in its decisions for the manner in which the criteria to which regard was had when assessing the reasonableness of the length of the proceedings were then taken into account to determine the amount awarded for non-pecuniary damage arising from the delays in the proceedings. It was clear from the foregoing that applicants should be awarded the same amount in comparable cases.

135. In reply to the Governments, the Court states at the outset that by "similar cases" it means any two sets of proceedings that have lasted for the same number of years, for an identical number of levels of jurisdiction, with stakes of equivalent importance, much the same conduct on the part of the applicant and in respect of the same country.

Moreover, it shares the Slovak Government's view that it would be impossible and impracticable to try to provide a list of detailed explanations covering every eventuality and considers that all the necessary elements can be found in its previous decisions available in the Court's case-law database.

136. It indicates next that the amount it will award in respect of non-pecuniary damage may be less than that indicated in its case-law where the applicant has already obtained a finding of a violation at domestic level and compensation by using a domestic remedy. Apart from the fact that the existence of a domestic remedy is fully in keeping with the subsidiarity principle embodied in the Convention, such a remedy is closer and more accessible than an application to the Court, is faster and is processed in the applicant's own language; it thus offers advantages that need to be taken into consideration.

136. The Court considers, however, that where an applicant can still claim to be a "victim" after exhausting that domestic remedy he or she must be awarded the difference between the amount obtained from the court of appeal and an amount that would not have been regarded as manifestly unreasonable compared with the amount awarded by the Court if it had been awarded by the court of appeal and paid speedily.

137. Applicants should also be awarded an amount in respect of stages of the proceedings that may not have been taken into account by the domestic courts in the reference period where they can no longer take the case back before the court of appeal seeking application of the change of position adopted by the Court of Cassation on 26 January 2004 (see its judgment no. 1339, paragraph 23 above) or the remaining length was not in itself sufficiently long to be regarded as amounting to a second violation in respect of the same proceedings.

138. Lastly, the fact that an applicant who, in order to comply with the decision adopted in the *Brusco case* (cited above), had endeavoured to use the new domestic remedy by applying to the court of appeal after lodging an application with the Commission, has then had to endure a further delay while waiting for payment of a sum due from the State will lead the Court to order the Government to pay the applicant a further sum in respect of those months of frustration.

5. Application of the foregoing criteria to the instant case

a) Damage

140. The applicant claimed EUR 15,500 for non-pecuniary damage.

141. The Government submitted that the finding of a violation would in itself constitute sufficient just satisfaction.

142. The Court finds that on the basis of the circumstances of the present case it would have awarded, in the absence of domestic remedies, the sum of EUR 10,000. It notes that the applicant was awarded EUR 2,500 by the Court of Appeal, which is approximately 25% of what the Court would have awarded. In the Court's view, this factor in itself leads to a result that is manifestly unreasonable in the light of the criteria established in its case-law.

Having regard to the characteristics of the domestic remedy chosen by Italy and the fact that, notwithstanding this national remedy, the Court has found a violation, it considers, ruling on an equitable basis, that the applicant should be awarded EUR 2,000.

The Court also awards EUR 4,000 for the further delay suffered by the applicant after the first finding of a violation and EUR 1,700 for the extra frustration arising from the delay in paying the amount due from the State, which was not paid until an unspecified date after March 2004.

143. Accordingly, the applicant is entitled to compensation for non-pecuniary damage in the sum of EUR 7,700, plus any tax that may be chargeable on that amount.

b) Costs and expenses

144. The applicant claimed EUR 1,500 for costs and expenses incurred before the Chamber and EUR 13,516.56 for the written and oral proceedings before the Grand Chamber against the respondent Government. In respect of drafting memorials in reply to the observations of the third-party Governments, she claimed EUR 1,904.06 each from the third-party Governments plus 2 % CPA (contribution to the lawyers' insurance fund) and 20 % VAT (value-added tax). Referring to the judgment of *Scozzari and Giunta v. Italy* ([GC], nos. 39221/98 and 41963/98, §§ 255–58,

ECHR 2000-VIII), the lawyer who had represented the applicant before the Chamber also requested that the fees be paid directly to him.

145. The Government did not express a view on the costs incurred before the Chamber, but pointed out that the claim in respect of the proceedings before the Grand Chamber was disproportionate.

146. Regarding the claim against the third-party Governments, the Court reiterates that the present case is directed only against Italy and that it is only in respect of that country that it has found a violation of the Convention. Accordingly, any request for an order against another country for the reimbursement of costs and expenses must be rejected.

147. Moreover, according to the Court's case-law, an award can be made in respect of costs and expenses only in so far as they have been actually and necessarily incurred by the applicant and are reasonable as to quantum. In the present case, having regard to the evidence before it, the above-mentioned criteria and the length and complexity of the proceedings before the Court, it finds the amount claimed by the applicant's representative before the Chamber to be excessive in view of the work done. Furthermore, given that a legal team was formed for the various cases being examined concurrently (see paragraph 9 above), the Court considers that the case is distinguishable from the case of *Scozzari* (cited above) and that the lawyer's claim should not be granted. It considers that the amount awarded by the Chamber should be confirmed for the proceedings before it, that is, EUR 1,500, and the applicant awarded EUR 3,000 for the work before the Grand Chamber, that is, a total sum of EUR 4,500, plus any tax that may be chargeable on that amount.

148. The Court considers it appropriate that the default interest should be based on the marginal lending rate of the European Central Bank, to which should be added three percentage points.

Questions and Comments

1. Why were there intervening states on this issue? Is it significant that some of them are facing procedural delays in their own judicial systems? See, e.g:, Eur.Ct.H.R., *Lukenda v. Slovenia, Application no. 23032/02)*, 6 October 2005.

2. What alternatives exist for regional systems to respond to systemic problems like those in the Italian judiciary?

3. No class actions are permitted in the European (or Inter-American) system; in the following case, does the "pilot case" procedure provide similar benefits to a class action?

Broniowski v. Poland App. no. 31443/96, judgment. of June 22, 2004, Eur.Ct.H.R. 2004-V.

. . . .

9. The applicant is a Polish national who was born in 1944 and lives in Wieliczka, Małopolska Province, in Poland.

A. Historical background

10. The eastern provinces of pre-war Poland were (and in dated usage still are) called "Borderlands". They included large areas of present-day Belarus and Ukraine and territories around Vilnius in what is now Lithuania.

Later, when after the Second World War Poland's eastern border was fixed along the Bug River (whose central course formed part of the Curzon line), the "Borderlands" acquired the name of "territories beyond the Bug River."

Those regions had been invaded by the USSR in September 1939.

11. Following agreements concluded between the Polish Committee of National Liberation and the former Soviet Socialist Republics of Ukraine (on 9 September 1944), Belarus (on 9 September 1944) and Lithuania (on 22 September 1944) ("the Republican Agreements", the Polish State took upon itself the obligation to compensate persons who were "repatriated" from the "territories beyond the Bug River" and had to abandon their property there. Such property is commonly referred to as "property beyond the Bug River".

12. The Polish government estimated that from 1944 to 1953 some 1,240,000 persons were "repatriated" under the provisions of the Republican Agreements. At the oral hearing, the parties agreed that the vast majority of repatriated persons had been compensated for loss of property caused by their repatriation.

In that connection, the Government also stated that, on account of the delimitation of the Polish-Soviet State border—and despite the fact that Poland was "compensated" by the Allies with former German lands east of the Oder-Neisse line—Poland suffered a loss of territory amounting to 19.78%.

B. The circumstances of the case....

14. After the Second World War, the applicant's grandmother was repatriated from Lwów (now Lviv in Ukraine).

On 19 August 1947 the State Repatriation Office in Cracow issued a certificate attesting that she had owned a piece of real property in Lwów and that the property in question consisted of approximately 400 sq. m of land and a house with a surface area of 260 sq. meters.

15. On 11 June 1968 the Cracow District Court gave a decision declaring that the applicant's mother had inherited the whole of her late mother's property.

16. On an unknown later date the applicant's mother asked the mayor of Wieliczka to enable her to purchase the so-called right of "perpetual use" of land owned by the State Treasury.

17. In September 1980 an expert from the Cracow Mayor's Office made a report assessing the value of the property abandoned by the applicant's grandmother in Lwów. The actual value was estimated at 1,949,560 old Polish zlotys (PLZ) but, for the purposes of compensation due from the State, the value was fixed at PLZ 532,260.

18. On 25 March 1981 the mayor of Wieliczka issued a decision enabling the applicant's mother to purchase the right of perpetual use of a plot of 467 sq. m situated in Wieliczka. The fee for the right of perpetual use was PLZ 392 per year and the duration was set at a minimum of forty and a maximum of ninety-nine years. The

total fee for use, which amounted to PLZ 38,808 (PLZ 392 x 99 years) was offset against the compensation calculated by the expert in September 1980.

In June 2002 an expert commissioned by the government established that the value of this transaction corresponded to 2% of the compensation to which the applicant's family was entitled.

19. The applicant's mother died on 3 November 1989. On 29 December 1989 the Cracow District Court gave a decision declaring that the applicant had inherited the whole of his late mother's property.

20. In 1992, on a date that has not been specified, the applicant sold the property that his mother had received from the State in 1981.

21. On 15 September 1992 the applicant asked the Cracow District Office to grant him the remainder of the compensation for the property abandoned by his grandmother in Lwów. He stressed that the value of the compensatory property received by his late mother had been significantly lower than the value of the original property.

22. In a letter of 16 June 1993, the town planning division of the Cracow District Office informed the applicant that his claim had been entered in the relevant register under no. R/74/92. The relevant part of that letter read as follows:

> We would like to inform you that at present there is no possibility of satisfying your claim.... Section 81 of the Land Administration and Expropriation Act of 29 April 1985 became, for all practical purposes, a dead letter with the enactment of the Local Self-Government Act of 10 May 1990. [The enactment of that Act] resulted in land being transferred from the [Cracow branch of the] State Treasury to the Cracow Municipality. Consequently, the Head of the Cracow District Office who, under the applicable rules, is responsible for granting compensation, has no possibility of satisfying the claims submitted. It is expected that new legislation will envisage another form of compensation. We should accordingly inform you that your claim will be dealt with after a new statute has determined how to proceed with claims submitted by repatriated persons.

23. On 14 June 1994 the Cracow Governor's Office informed the applicant that the State Treasury had no land for the purposes of granting compensation for property abandoned in the territories beyond the Bug River.

24. On 12 August 1994 the applicant filed a complaint with the Supreme Administrative Court, alleging inactivity on the part of the government in that it had failed to introduce in Parliament legislation dealing with claims submitted by repatriated persons. He also asked for compensation in the form of State Treasury bonds.

. . . .

THE LAW

I. ALLEGED VIOLATION OF ARTICLE 1 OF PROTOCOL No. 1

121. The applicant alleged a breach of Article 1 of Protocol No. 1 in that his entitlement to compensation for property abandoned in the territories beyond the Bug River, the so-called "right to credit", had not been satisfied . . . .

A. Scope of the case

122. Determining the scope of its jurisdiction *ratione temporis* in the decision on the admissibility of the application, the Court found that the applicant's grievance did not concern a single specific measure or decision taken before, or even after, 10 October 1994, the date of ratification of Protocol No. 1 by Poland. The crux of the applicant's Convention claim lay in the State's failure to satisfy his entitlement to compensatory property, which had been continuously vested in him under Polish law.

Noting that that entitlement had been conferred on him on the date of ratification and subsisted both on 12 March 1996, the date on which he had lodged his application with the Commission, and on 19 December 2002, the date of the decision on admissibility, the Court held that it had temporal jurisdiction to entertain the application. It also held that it could have regard to the facts prior to ratification inasmuch as they could be considered to have created a situation extending beyond that date or might be relevant for the understanding of facts occurring after that date (see *Broniowski v. Poland* (dec.) [GC], no. 31443/96, §§ 74–77, ECHR 2002-X).

123. However, the date from which the Court has jurisdiction ratione temporis not only marks the beginning of the period throughout which, up to the present day, acts or omissions of the Polish State will be assessed by the Court from the point of view of their compliance with the Convention, but is also relevant for the determination of the actual content and scope of the applicant's legal interest guaranteed by Polish law to be considered under Article 1 of Protocol No. 1.

124. While the historical background of the case, including the post-war delimitations of State borders, the resultant migration of persons affected by those events and the Republican Agreements, in which the applicant's entitlement to compensation originated, is certainly important for the understanding of the complex legal and factual situation obtaining today, the Court will not consider any legal, moral, social, financial or other obligations of the Polish State arising from the fact that owners of property beyond the Bug River were dispossessed and forced to migrate by the Soviet Union after the Second World War. In particular, it will not deal with the issue whether Poland's obligation under the Republican Agreements to return to those persons the value of the property abandoned in the former Soviet republics might have any bearing on the scope of the applicant's right under domestic legislation and under the Convention and whether Poland honoured the obligations it had taken upon itself by virtue of those Agreements.

125. The sole issue before the Court is whether Article 1 of Protocol No. 1 was violated by reason of the Polish State's acts and omissions in relation to the implementation of the applicant's entitlement to compensatory property, which was vested in him by Polish legislation on the date of the Protocol's entry into force and which subsisted on 12 March 1996, the date on which he lodged his application with the Commission.

B. Applicability of Article 1 of Protocol No. 1

. . . .

129. The concept of "possessions" in the first part of Article 1 of Protocol No. 1 has an autonomous meaning which is not limited to the ownership of material

goods and is independent from the formal classification in domestic law. In the same way as material goods, certain other rights and interests constituting assets can also be regarded as "property rights", and thus as "possessions" for the purposes of this provision. In each case the issue that needs to be examined is whether the circumstances of the case, considered as a whole, conferred on the applicant title to a substantive interest protected by Article 1 of Protocol No. 1 (see *Iatridis v. Greece* [GC], no. 31107/96, § 54, ECHR 1999-II, and *Beyeler v. Italy* [GC], no. 33202/96, § 100, ECHR 2000-I).

130. When declaring the application admissible, the Court rejected the Government's arguments as to the inapplicability of Article 1 of Protocol No. 1. It found that the applicant had a proprietary interest eligible for protection under that Article. It further noted that the applicant's entitlement had continuously had a legal basis in domestic legislation which had subsisted after 10 October 1994 and that it was defined by the Polish Supreme Court as, inter alia, a "debt chargeable to the State Treasury" which had "a pecuniary and inheritable character" (see Broniowski, decision cited above, §§ 97–101).

131. Subsequently, when ruling in December 2002 on the application brought by the Ombudsman, the Constitutional Court described the applicant's entitlement as the "right to credit", having a "special nature as an independent property right", which "should be recognised as enjoying the constitutionally guaranteed protection of property rights" and which was a "special property right of a public-law nature". While the Constitutional Court accepted that the materialisation of that right depended on action by an entitled person, it rejected the idea that the right did not exist until its realisation through a successful bid at an auction for the sale of State property. In sum, the Constitutional Court had no doubts that the right to credit was subject to protection under Article 1 of Protocol No. 1.

In the judgment of 21 November 2003 that followed the above ruling, the Polish Supreme Court considered that the right to credit was a "particular proprietary right" of a "pecuniary value", which was "inheritable and transferable in a specific manner" and whose substance consisted in "the possibility of having a certain pecuniary obligation satisfied through the use of the so-called 'Bug River money' ".

The Court subscribes to the analysis, in Convention terms, made by the highest Polish judicial authorities of the entitlement which was conferred on the applicant by Polish legislation. It finds nothing in the Government's present arguments to change the conclusion that, as has already been established in the decision on admissibility, the applicant's right to credit constitutes a "possession" within the meaning of Article 1 of Protocol No. 1.

. . . .

133. Accordingly, for the purposes of Article 1 of Protocol No. 1, the applicant's "possessions" comprised the entitlement to obtain, further to the application he had made already on 15 September 1992, compensatory property of the kind listed in paragraph 3 of the 1985 Ordinance. While that right was created in a somewhat inchoate form, as its materialisation was to be effected by an administrative decision allocating State property to him, section 81 clearly constituted a legal basis for the State's obligation to implement it.

C. Compliance with Article 1 of Protocol No. 1

1. Applicable rule of Article 1 of Protocol No. 1

134. Article 1 of Protocol No. 1 comprises three distinct rules: the first rule, set out in the first sentence of the first paragraph, is of a general nature and enunciates the principle of the peaceful enjoyment of property; the second rule, contained in the second sentence of the first paragraph, covers deprivation of possessions and subjects it to certain conditions; the third rule, stated in the second paragraph, recognises that the Contracting States are entitled, *inter alia*, to control the use of property in accordance with the general interest. The three rules are not, however, distinct in the sense of being unconnected. The second and third rules are concerned with particular instances of interference with the right to peaceful enjoyment of property and should therefore be construed in the light of the general principle enunciated in the first rule (see, among other authorities, *James and Others v. the United Kingdom*, judgment of 21 February 1986, Series A no. 98, pp. 29–30, § 37, which reiterates in part the principles laid down by the Court in *Sporrong and Lönnroth v. Sweden*, judgment of 23 September 1982, Series A no. 52, p. 24, § 61; see also *Iatridis*, cited above, § 55, and Beyeler, cited above, § 98).

135. The parties did not take clear positions on the question under which rule of Article 1 of Protocol No. 1 the case should be examined. While neither of them argued that the situation complained of had resulted from measures designed to "control the use of property" within the meaning of the second paragraph, the applicant alleged that there had been a general failure by the State to satisfy his right, and the Government maintained that neither any failure to respect that right nor any interference with it could be attributed to the authorities.

136. Having regard to the complexity of the legal and factual issues involved in the present case, the Court considers that the alleged violation of the right of property cannot be classified in a precise category. In any event, the situation mentioned in the second sentence of the first paragraph is only a particular instance of interference with the right to peaceful enjoyment of property as guaranteed by the general rule laid down in the first sentence (see *Beyeler*, cited above, § 106). The case should therefore more appropriately be examined in the light of that general rule.

2. Nature of the alleged violation

. . . .

(b) The Court's assessment

143. The essential object of Article 1 of Protocol No. 1 is to protect a person against unjustified interference by the State with the peaceful enjoyment of his or her possessions.

However, by virtue of Article 1 of the Convention, each Contracting Party "shall secure to everyone within [its] jurisdiction the rights and freedoms defined in [the] Convention". The discharge of this general duty may entail positive obligations inherent in ensuring the effective exercise of the rights guaranteed by the Convention. In the context of Article 1 of Protocol No. 1, those positive obligations may require the State to take the measures necessary to protect the right of property (see *Sovtransavto Holding v. Ukraine*, no. 48553/99, § 96, ECHR 2002-VII, with further references, and, *mutatis mutandis, Keegan v. Ireland*, judgment of 26 May 1994, Series A no. 290, p. 19, § 49, and *Kroon and Others v. the Netherlands*, judgment of 27 October 1994, Series A no. 297-C, p. 56, § 31).

144. However, the boundaries between the State's positive and negative obligations under Article 1 of Protocol No. 1 do not lend themselves to precise definition. The applicable principles are nonetheless similar. Whether the case is analysed in terms of a positive duty of the State or in terms of an interference by a public authority which needs to be justified, the criteria to be applied do not differ in substance. In both contexts regard must be had to the fair balance to be struck between the competing interests of the individual and of the community as a whole. It also holds true that the aims mentioned in that provision may be of some relevance in assessing whether a balance between the demands of the public interest involved and the applicant's fundamental right of property has been struck. In both contexts the State enjoys a certain margin of appreciation in determining the steps to be taken to ensure compliance with the Convention (see, *mutatis mutandis, Keegan*, cited above, p.19, § 49, and *Hatton and Others v. the United Kingdom [GC]*, no. 36022/97, §§ 98 et seq., ECHR 2003-VIII).

145. In the present case, the applicant's submission under Article 1 of Protocol No. 1 is that the Polish State, having conferred on him an entitlement to compensatory property, subsequently made it impossible for him—by obstruction and inaction, both legislative and administrative, and by extra-legal practices—to benefit from that entitlement and that, ultimately, by virtue of the recent legislation, it extinguished his legal interest.

The mutual interrelation of the alleged omissions on the part of the State and of accompanying acts that might be regarded as an "interference" with the applicant's property right makes it difficult to classify them in a single precise category. As shown by the course of the events described above, culminating in the enactment of the December 2003 legislation, the facts of "commission" and "omission" were closely intertwined.

Also, the legal and practical consequences of those facts and the State's conduct were variously assessed by the national courts; for instance, the Constitutional Court considered that the laws restricting the Bug River claimants' access to State property had resulted in *de facto* expropriation. Some civil courts considered that the State was liable for damage sustained by the Bug River claimants on account of both the fact that it had imposed unjustified restrictions on the exercise of the right to credit and the fact that it had failed to fulfil its positive obligations to protect property rights and duly to publish the Republican Agreements. The Supreme Court held that the State's practices did not amount to a deprivation of property, but had nevertheless unduly restricted the right in question.

146. The facts of the case may well be examined in terms of a hindrance to the effective exercise of the right protected by Article 1 of Protocol No. 1 or in terms of a failure to secure the implementation of that right. Having regard to the particular circumstances of the present case, the Court considers it unnecessary to categorise strictly its examination of the case as being under the head of the State's positive

obligations or under the head of the State's negative duty to refrain from an unjustified interference with the peaceful enjoyment of property.

The Court will determine whether the conduct of the Polish State—regardless of
whether that conduct may be characterised as an interference or as a failure to act,
or a combination of both—was justifiable in the light of the applicable principles set
out below.

3. General principles

(a) Principle of lawfulness

147. The first and most important requirement of Article 1 of Protocol No. 1
is that any interference by a public authority with the peaceful enjoyment of possessions should be lawful: the second sentence of the first paragraph authorises a
deprivation of possessions only "subject to the conditions provided for by law" and
the second paragraph recognises that States have the right to control the use of
property by enforcing "laws". Moreover, the rule of law, one of the fundamental
principles of a democratic society, is inherent in all the Articles of the Convention
(see *The former King of Greece and Others v. Greece* [GC], no. 25701/94, § 79, ECHR
2000-XII, with further references, and *Iatridis*, cited above, § 58).

The principle of lawfulness also presupposes that the applicable provisions of
domestic law are sufficiently accessible, precise and foreseeable in their application
(see *Beyeler*, cited above, §§ 109–10).

(b) Principle of a legitimate aim in the public interest

148. Any interference with the enjoyment of a right or freedom recognised by
the Convention must pursue a legitimate aim. By the same token, in cases involving
a positive duty, there must be a legitimate justification for the State's inaction. The
principle of a "fair balance" inherent in Article 1 of Protocol No. 1 itself presupposes the existence of a general interest of the community. Moreover, it should be
reiterated that the various rules incorporated in Article 1 are not distinct, in the
sense of being unconnected, and that the second and third rules are concerned only
with particular instances of interference with the right to the peaceful enjoyment
of property. One of the effects of this is that the existence of a "public interest" required under the second sentence, or the "general interest" referred to in the second
paragraph, are in fact corollaries of the principle set forth in the first sentence, so
that an interference with the exercise of the right to the peaceful enjoyment of possessions within the meaning of the first sentence of Article 1 must also pursue an
aim in the public interest (see *Beyeler*, cited above, § 111).

149. Because of their direct knowledge of their society and its needs, the national
authorities are in principle better placed than the international judge to appreciate
what is "in the public interest". Under the system of protection established by the
Convention, it is thus for the national authorities to make the initial assessment
as to the existence of a problem of public concern warranting measures to be applied in the sphere of the exercise of the right of property, including deprivation
and restitution of property. Here, as in other fields to which the safeguards of the
Convention extend, the national authorities accordingly enjoy a certain margin of
appreciation.

Furthermore, the notion of "public interest" is necessarily extensive. In particular, the decision to enact laws expropriating property or affording publicly funded compensation for expropriated property will commonly involve consideration of political, economic and social issues. The Court has declared that, finding it natural that the margin of appreciation available to the legislature in implementing social and economic policies should be a wide one, it will respect the legislature's judgment as to what is "in the public interest" unless that judgment is manifestly without reasonable foundation (see *James and Others*, cited above, p. 32, § 46, and *The former King of Greece and Others*, cited above, § 87). This logic applies to such fundamental changes of a country's system as the transition from a totalitarian regime to a democratic form of government and the reform of the State's political, legal and economic structure, phenomena which inevitably involve the enactment of large-scale economic and social legislation.

(c) Principle of a "fair balance"

150. Both an interference with the peaceful enjoyment of possessions and an abstention from action must strike a fair balance between the demands of the general interest of the community and the requirements of the protection of the individual's fundamental rights (see, among other authorities, *Sporrong and Lönnroth*, cited above, p. 26, § 69).

The concern to achieve this balance is reflected in the structure of Article 1 of Protocol No. 1 as a whole. In particular, there must be a reasonable relationship of proportionality between the means employed and the aim sought to be realised by any measures applied by the State, including measures depriving a person of his of her possessions. In each case involving the alleged violation of that Article the Court must, therefore, ascertain whether by reason of the State's action or inaction the person concerned had to bear a disproportionate and excessive burden (see *Sporrong and Lönnroth*, p. 28, § 73, and *The former King of Greece and Others*, §§ 89–90, both cited above, with further references).

151. In assessing compliance with Article 1 of Protocol No. 1, the Court must make an overall examination of the various interests in issue, bearing in mind that the Convention is intended to safeguard rights that are "practical and effective". It must look behind appearances and investigate the realities of the situation complained of. That assessment may involve not only the relevant compensation terms—if the situation is akin to the taking of property—but also the conduct of the parties, including the means employed by the State and their implementation. In that context, it should be stressed that uncertainty—be it legislative, administrative or arising from practices applied by the authorities—is a factor to be taken into account in assessing the State's conduct. Indeed, where an issue in the general interest is at stake, it is incumbent on the public authorities to act in good time, in an appropriate and consistent manner (see *Vasilescu v. Romania*, judgment of 22 May 1998, *Reports of Judgments and Decisions* 1998-III, p. 1078, § 51; *Beyeler*, cited above, §§ 110 *in fine*, 114 and 120 *in fine*; and *Sovtransavto Holding*, cited above, §§ 97–98).

4. Application of the above principles to the present case

[The Court concluded that the interference was provided by law and enacted for a legitimate aim.]. . . .

(c) Whether the Polish authorities struck a fair balance between the general interest of the community and the applicant's right to the peaceful enjoyment of his possessions

. . . .

162. The Court recognises that, given the particular historical and political background of the case, as well as the importance of the various social, legal and economic considerations that the authorities had to take into account in resolving the problem of the Bug River claims, the Polish State had to deal with an exceptionally difficult situation, involving complex, large-scale policy decisions. The vast number of persons involved—nearly 80,000—and the very substantial value of their claims are certainly factors that must be taken into account in ascertaining whether the requisite "fair balance" was struck.

Also in that context, it should be noted that the Polish State chose, by adopting both the 1985 and 1997 Land Administration Acts, to reaffirm its obligation to compensate the Bug River claimants and to maintain and to incorporate into domestic law obligations it had taken upon itself by virtue of international treaties entered into prior to its ratification of the Convention and the Protocol. It did so irrespective of the fact that it faced various significant social and economic constraints resulting from the transformation of the country's entire system, and was undoubtedly confronted with a difficult choice as to which pecuniary and moral obligations could be fulfilled towards persons who had suffered injustice under the totalitarian regime.

163. The Court accepts that these factors should be taken into account in determining the scope of the margin of appreciation to be allowed to the respondent State.

. . . .

182. The Court accepts that *in situ*ations such as the one in the present case, involving a wide-reaching but controversial legislative scheme with significant economic impact for the country as a whole, the national authorities must have considerable discretion in selecting not only the measures to secure respect for property rights or to regulate ownership relations within the country, but also the appropriate time for their implementation. The choice of measures may necessarily involve decisions restricting compensation for the taking or restitution of property to a level below its market value. Thus, Article 1 of Protocol No. 1 does not guarantee a right to full compensation in all circumstances (see *James and Others*, cited above, p. 36, § 54).

Balancing the rights at stake, as well as the gains and losses of the different persons affected by the process of transforming the State's economy and legal system, is an exceptionally difficult exercise. In such circumstances, in the nature of things, a wide margin of appreciation should be accorded to the respondent State.

Nevertheless, the Court would reiterate that that margin, however considerable, is not unlimited, and that the exercise of the State's discretion, even in the context of the most complex reform of the State, cannot entail consequences at variance with Convention standards.

183. Whilst the Court accepts that the radical reform of the country's political and economic system, as well as the state of the country's finances, may justify stringent limitations on compensation for the Bug River claimants, the Polish State has not been able to adduce satisfactory grounds justifying, in terms of Article 1 of Protocol No. 1, the extent to which it has continuously failed over many years to implement an entitlement conferred on the applicant, as on thousands of other Bug River claimants, by Polish legislation.

184. The rule of law underlying the Convention and the principle of lawfulness in Article 1 of Protocol No. 1 require States not only to respect and apply, in a foreseeable and consistent manner, the laws they have enacted, but also, as a corollary of this duty, to ensure the legal and practical conditions for their implementation. In the context of the present case, it was incumbent on the Polish authorities to remove the existing incompatibility between the letter of the law and the State-operated practice which hindered the effective exercise of the applicant's right of property. Those principles also required the Polish State to fulfil in good time, in an appropriate and consistent manner, the legislative promises it had made in respect of the settlement of the Bug River claims. This was a matter of important public and general interest. As rightly pointed out by the Polish Constitutional Court, the imperative of maintaining citizens' legitimate confidence in the State and the law made by it, inherent in the rule of law, required the authorities to eliminate the dysfunctional provisions from the legal system and to rectify the extra-legal practices.

185. In the present case, as ascertained by the Polish courts and confirmed by the Court's analysis of the respondent State's conduct, the authorities, by imposing successive limitations on the exercise of the applicant's right to credit, and by applying the practices that made it unenforceable and unusable in practice, rendered that right illusory and destroyed its very essence.

The state of uncertainty in which the applicant found himself as a result of the repeated delays and obstruction continuing over a period of many years, for which the national authorities were responsible, was in itself incompatible with the obligation arising under Article 1 of Protocol No. 1 to secure the peaceful enjoyment of possessions, notably with the duty to act in good time, in an appropriate and consistent manner where an issue of general interest is at stake.

186. Furthermore, the applicant's situation was compounded by the fact that what had become a practically unenforceable entitlement was legally extinguished by the December 2003 legislation, pursuant to which the applicant lost his hitherto existing entitlement to compensation. Moreover, this legislation operated a difference of treatment between Bug River claimants in so far as those who had never received any compensation were awarded an amount which, although subject to a ceiling of PLN 50,000, was a specified proportion (15%) of their entitlement, whereas claimants in the applicant's position, who had already been awarded a much lower percentage, received no additional amount.

As stated above, under Article 1 of Protocol No. 1 the State is entitled to expropriate property—including any compensatory entitlement granted by legislation—

and to reduce, even substantially, levels of compensation under legislative schemes. This applies particularly to situations in which the compensatory entitlement does not arise from any previous taking of individual property by the respondent State, but is designed to mitigate the effects of a taking or loss of property not attributable to that State. What Article 1 of Protocol No. 1 requires is that the amount of compensation granted for property taken by the State be "reasonably related" to its value. It is not for the Court to say in the abstract what would be a "reasonable" level of compensation in the present case. However, given that—as acknowledged by the Government—the applicant's family had received a mere 2% of the compensation due under the legislation as applicable before the entry into force of the Protocol in respect of Poland, the Court finds no cogent reason why such an insignificant amount should *per se* deprive him of the possibility of obtaining at least a proportion of his entitlement on an equal basis with other Bug River claimants.

(d) General conclusion

187. Having regard to all the foregoing factors and in particular to the impact on the applicant over many years of the Bug River legislative scheme as operated in practice, the Court concludes that, as an individual, he had to bear a disproportionate and excessive burden which cannot be justified in terms of the legitimate general community interest pursued by the authorities.

There has therefore been a violation of Article 1 of Protocol No. 1 in the applicant's case.

II. ARTICLES 46 AND 41 OF THE CONVENTION

A. Article 46 of the Convention

188. Article 46 of the Convention provides:

1. The High Contracting Parties undertake to abide by the final judgment of the Court in any case to which they are parties.
2. The final judgment of the Court shall be transmitted to the Committee of Ministers, which shall supervise its execution.

189. It is inherent in the Court's findings that the violation of the applicant's right guaranteed by Article 1 of Protocol No. 1 originated in a widespread problem which resulted from a malfunctioning of Polish legislation and administrative practice and which has affected and remains capable of affecting a large number of persons. The unjustified hindrance on the applicant's "peaceful enjoyment of his possessions" was neither prompted by an isolated incident nor attributable to the particular turn of events in his case, but was rather the consequence of administrative and regulatory conduct on the part of the authorities towards an identifiable class of citizens, namely the Bug River claimants.

The existence and the systemic nature of that problem have already been recognised by the Polish judicial authorities, as has been confirmed by a number of rulings, referred to in detail in the present judgment. Thus, in its judgment of 19 December 2002 the Constitutional Court described the Bug River legislative scheme as "caus[ing] an inadmissible systemic dysfunction". Endorsing that assessment, the Court concludes that the facts of the case disclose the existence, within the Polish legal order, of a shortcoming as a consequence of which a whole class of individuals have been or are still denied the peaceful enjoyment of their possessions. It also finds that the deficiencies in national law and practice identified in the applicant's individual case may give rise to numerous subsequent well-founded applications.

190. As part of a package of measures to guarantee the effectiveness of the Convention machinery, the Committee of Ministers of the Council of Europe adopted on 12 May 2004 a Resolution (Res(2004)3) on judgments revealing an underlying systemic problem, in which, after emphasising the interest in helping the State concerned to identify the underlying problems and the necessary execution measures (seventh paragraph of the preamble), it invited the Court "to identify in its judgments finding a violation of the Convention what it considers to be an underlying systemic problem and the source of that problem, in particular when it is likely to give rise to numerous applications, so as to assist States in finding the appropriate solution and the Committee of Ministers in supervising the execution of judgments" (paragraph I of the resolution). That resolution has to be seen in the context of the growth in the Court's caseload, particularly as a result of series of cases deriving from the same structural or systemic cause.

191. In the same context, the Court would draw attention to the Committee of Ministers' Recommendation of 12 May 2004 (Rec(2004)6) on the improvement of domestic remedies, in which it is emphasised that, in addition to the obligation under Article 13 of the Convention to provide an individual who has an arguable claim with an effective remedy before a national authority, States have a general obligation to solve the problems underlying the violations found. Mindful that the improvement of remedies at the national level, particularly in respect of repetitive cases, should also contribute to reducing the workload of the Court, the Committee of Ministers recommended that the Contracting States, following Court judgments which point to structural or general deficiencies in national law or practice, review and, "where necessary, set up effective remedies, in order to avoid repetitive cases being brought before the Court".

192. Before examining the applicant's individual claims for just satisfaction under Article 41 of the Convention, in view of the circumstances of the instant case and having regard also to the evolution of its caseload, the Court wishes to consider what consequences may be drawn for the respondent State from Article 46 of the Convention. It reiterates that by virtue of Article 46 the High Contracting Parties have undertaken to abide by the final judgments of the Court in any case to which they are parties, execution being supervised by the Committee of Ministers. It follows, *inter alia*, that a judgment in which the Court finds a breach imposes on the respondent State a legal obligation not just to pay those concerned the sums awarded by way of just satisfaction under Article 41, but also to select, subject to supervision by the Committee of Ministers, the general and/or, if appropriate, individual measures to be adopted in their domestic legal order to put an end to the violation found by the Court and to redress so far as possible the effects. Subject to monitoring by the Committee of Ministers, the respondent State remains free to choose the means by which it will discharge its legal obligation under Article 46 of the Convention, provided that such means are compatible with the conclusions set

out in the Court's judgment (see *Scozzari and Giunta v. Italy [GC]*, nos. 39221/98 and 41963/98, § 249, ECHR 2000-VIII).

193. The Court has already noted that the violation which it has found in the present case has as its cause a situation concerning large numbers of people. The failure to implement in a manner compatible with Article 1 of Protocol No. 1 the chosen mechanism for settling the Bug River claims has affected nearly 80,000 people. There are moreover already 167 applications pending before the Court brought by Bug River claimants. This is not only an aggravating factor as regards the State's responsibility under the Convention for an existing or past state of affairs, but also represents a threat to the future effectiveness of the Convention machinery.

Although it is in principle not for the Court to determine what remedial measures may be appropriate to satisfy the respondent State's obligations under Article 46 of the Convention, in view of the systemic situation which it has identified, the Court would observe that general measures at national level are undoubtedly called for in execution of the present judgment, measures which must take into account the many people affected. Above all, the measures adopted must be such as to remedy the systemic defect underlying the Court's finding of a violation so as not to overburden the Convention system with large numbers of applications deriving from the same cause. Such measures should therefore include a scheme which offers to those affected redress for the Convention violation identified in the instant judgment in relation to the present applicant. In this context the Court's concern is to facilitate the most speedy and effective resolution of a dysfunction established in national human rights protection. Once such a defect has been identified, it falls to the national authorities, under the supervision of the Committee of Ministers, to take, retroactively if appropriate (see *Bottazzi v. Italy* [GC], no. 34884/97, § 22, ECHR 1999-V, *Di Mauro v. Italy* [GC], no. 34256/96, § 23, ECHR 1999-V, and the Committee of Ministers' Interim Resolution ResDH(2000)135 of 25 October 2000 (Excessive length of judicial proceedings in Italy: general measures); see also *Brusco v. Italy* (dec.), no. 69789/01, ECHR 2001-IX, and *Giacometti and Others v. Italy* (dec.), no. 34939/97, ECHR 2001-XII), the necessary remedial measures in accordance with the subsidiary character of the Convention, so that the Court does not have to repeat its finding in a lengthy series of comparable cases.

194. With a view to assisting the respondent State in fulfilling its obligations under Article 46, the Court has sought to indicate the type of measure that might be taken by the Polish State in order to put an end to the systemic situation identified in the present case. The Court is not in a position to assess whether the December 2003 Act can be treated as an adequate measure in this connection since no practice of its implementation has been established as yet. In any event, this Act does not cover persons who—like Mr Broniowski—had already received partial compensation, irrespective of the amount of such compensation. Thus, it is clear that for this group of Bug River claimants the Act cannot be regarded as a measure capable of putting an end to the systemic situation identified in the present judgment as adversely affecting them.

Nevertheless, as regards general measures to be taken, the Court considers that the respondent State must, primarily, either remove any hindrance to the implementation of the right of the numerous persons affected by the situation found, in respect of the applicant, to have been in breach of the Convention, or provide equivalent redress in lieu. As to the former option, the respondent State should, therefore, through appropriate legal and administrative measures, secure the effective and expeditious realisation of the entitlement in question in respect of the remaining Bug River claimants, in accordance with the principles for the protection of property rights laid down in Article 1 of Protocol No. 1, having particular regard to the principles relating to compensation.

B. Article 41 of the Convention

195. Article 41 of the Convention provides:

> "If the Court finds that there has been a violation of the Convention or the Protocols thereto, and if the internal law of the High Contracting Party concerned allows only partial reparation to be made, the Court shall, if necessary, afford just satisfaction to the injured party."

1. Damage claimed in the present case

196. Under the head of pecuniary damage, the applicant claimed 990,000 Polish zlotys (PLN) in compensation for the loss of his right of property. In his estimation, that amount corresponded to the value of the property abandoned in Lwów, for which he had not received redress. He further claimed PLN 1,548,000 for loss of profit for the period of over fifty years throughout which neither he nor his predecessors had been able to derive any benefit from their possessions.

The applicant further asked the Court to award him 12,000 euros (EUR) for the non-pecuniary damage he had suffered on account of the uncertainty, stress and frustration caused by his continuing inability to enjoy his property right.

By way of costs, the applicant, who was represented before the Court under its legal aid scheme by two lawyers, claimed the sum of PLN 125,000.

197. The Government, who had been asked to address the question of just satisfaction in a general manner, considered that the claims were excessive. Referring to the applicant's claim for costs, they stressed that the applicant's lawyers demanded excessive amounts for their work on the case. For instance, one of the applicant's representatives charged an exceptionally high fee for one hour, amounting to PLN 1,000, that is, approximately EUR 250 which, given the situation in Poland, was unacceptable.

2. The Court's conclusion

(a) Pecuniary and non-pecuniary damage

198. In the circumstances of the case, the Court considers that the question of compensation for pecuniary and/or non-pecuniary damage is not ready for decision. That question must accordingly be reserved and the subsequent procedure fixed, having due regard to any agreement which might be reached between the respondent Government and the applicant (Rule 75 § 1 of the Rules of Court) and in the light of such individual or general measures as may be taken by the respondent Government in execution of the present judgment. Pending the implementation of the relevant general measures, which should be adopted within a reasonable time,

the Court will adjourn its consideration of applications deriving from the same general cause.

(b) Costs and expenses

199. As regards the costs and expenses already incurred by the applicant in the proceedings before the Court, the Court, making its assessment on an equitable basis, awards him the sum of EUR 12,000, less EUR 2,409 received under the Court's legal aid scheme, to be converted into Polish zlotys at the rate applicable at the date of settlement, together with any tax that may be chargeable on this amount.

(c) Default interest

200. The Court considers it appropriate that the default interest should be based on the marginal lending rate of the European Central Bank, to which should be added three percentage points.

Note on the Aftermath of the Judgment. On September 25, 2005, the Grand Chamber of the Court struck the case off the list as the result of a friendly settlement. The basis of the settlement was a law passed on 8 July 2005 by the *Sejm* (first house of the Polish Parliament) on the realisation of the right to compensation for property left beyond the present borders of the Polish State. The statutory ceiling for compensation for Bug River property was set at 20%. The law was passed by the *Senat* (second house of the Polish Parliament) on 21 July 2005 and signed by the President of Poland on 15 August 2005. It entered into force on 7 October 2005, 30 days after its publication in the Journal of Laws. Pursuant to section 16 of the Act, a Compensation Fund was set up in order to finance and secure the payments of pecuniary benefits to Bug River claimants. The fund derives its resources from the sale of property belonging to the Resource of Agricultural Property of the State Treasury, the total amount of land designated for that purpose being not less than 400,000 hectares; from the interest on money set aside on the fund's bank accounts; and, in the event of a shortage of income from those sources, from loans from the State budget in an amount determined by the relevant Budget Act. In addition to providing a financial settlement for the applicant, the settlement agreement stated:

1. The terms of the following settlement are intended to take into account
   - that the wrong and injustice addressed by the Polish Bug River legislation is not one created by the Polish State;
   - that the latter's responsibility under the Convention is limited to the operation of the relevant legislation during the period falling within the Court's jurisdiction, which started on 10 October 1994;
   - not only the interests of the individual applicant, Mr Broniowski, and the prejudice sustained by him as a result of the violation of his right of property found by the Court to have occurred in his particular case, but also the interests and prejudice of complainants in similar applications pending before the Court or liable to be lodged with it;

– the obligation of the Polish Government under Article 46 of the Convention, in executing the principal judgment, to take not only individual measures of redress in respect of Mr Broniowski but also general measures covering other Bug River claimants (see the fourth operative provision of the principal judgment).

2. Given that the actual value of the property to which attaches the applicant's entitlement under the Bug River legislation ('the Bug River property') is disputed between the parties, a notional value has been agreed solely for the purposes of the present friendly settlement. This valuation does not bind either party in any further domestic or international proceedings brought in relation to the property.

3. For the purposes of the present friendly settlement, the parties have agreed that the valuation of the applicant's entitlement under the Bug River legislation shall be made by reference to the terms of the July 2005 Act, in particular the maximum statutory ceiling of 20% laid down in section 13(2) of that Act.

4. The present friendly settlement does not preclude the applicant from seeking and recovering compensation over and above the current 20 % ceiling fixed by the 2005 Act in so far as Polish law allows this in the future.

. . . .

IV. GENERAL MEASURES

11. The Government make, as an integral part of this settlement, the following declaration as to general measures which are to be taken in accordance with the terms of the Court's principal judgment.

DECLARATION BY THE GOVERNMENT OF THE REPUBLIC OF POLAND

Having regard to their obligations under Article 46 of the Convention as to the execution of the Court's principal judgment in the case of *Broniowski v. Poland* (application no. 31443/96), in particular those relating to general measures to be adopted in order to secure the implementation of the 'right to credit' not only of the applicant in that case but also of remaining Bug River claimants, the Government of the Republic of Poland

DECLARE

(a) that they undertake to implement as rapidly as possible all the necessary measures in respect of domestic law and practice as indicated by the Court in the fourth operative provision of the principal judgment, and that, to this end, they will intensify their endeavours to make the new Bug River legislation effective and to improve the practical operation of the mechanism designed to provide the Bug River claimants with compensation, including the auction-bidding procedure and payments from the Compensation Fund (*Fundusz Rekompensacyjny*) referred to in the July 2005 Act;

(b) that, as regards the auction-bidding procedure, they will ensure that the relevant State agencies will not hinder the Bug River claimants in enforcing their "right to credit";

(c) that, in addition to adopting general measures designed to remove obstacles in implementing the 'right to credit', they recognise their obligation to make available to the remaining Bug River claimants some form of redress for any material or non-material damage caused to them by the defective operation of the Bug River legislative scheme in their regard; in this connection,

- noting that, in respect of material damage, it is common ground that a civil action under Article 417 or, as the case may be, Article 4171 of the Civil Code constitutes a remedy for affording such redress;
- pointing out that, in respect of non-material damage, in particular uncertainty and frustration, this obligation was taken into account in incorporating in the July 2005 Act more favourable modalities for implementation of the 'right to credit' than those existing in the preceding legislation, these more favourable modalities being, firstly, the possibility of obtaining pecuniary compensation (*świadczenia pieniężnego*) as an alternative to the more cumbersome procedure of participating in auction bidding and, secondly, the raising of the statutory ceiling for compensation from 15% to 20%; and
- further, undertaking not to contest before domestic courts that Article 448 read in conjunction with Article 23 of the Civil Code is capable of providing a legal basis for making a claim in respect of non-material damage.

Committee of Ministers, Resolution (2004)3 on Judgments Revealing an Underlying Systemic Problem *(adopted by the Committee of Ministers on 12 May 2004, at its 114th Session)*

The Committee of Ministers, in accordance with Article 15.*b* of the Statute of the Council of Europe,

Considering that the aim of the Council of Europe is the achievement of greater unity among its members, and that one of the most important methods by which that aim is to be pursued is the maintenance and further realisation of human rights and fundamental freedoms;

Reiterating its conviction that the Convention for the Protection of Human Rights and Fundamental Freedoms (hereinafter referred to as "the Convention") must remain the essential reference point for the protection of human rights in Europe, and recalling its commitment to take measures in order to guarantee the long-term effectiveness of the control system instituted by the Convention;

Recalling the subsidiary character of the supervision mechanism set up by the Convention, which implies, in accordance with its Article 1, that the rights and freedoms guaranteed by the Convention be protected in the first place at national level and applied by national authorities;

Welcoming in this context that the Convention has now become an integral part of the domestic legal order of all states parties;

Recalling that, according to Article 46 of the Convention, the high contracting parties undertake to abide by the final judgment of the European Court of Human Rights (hereinafter referred to as "the Court") in any case to which they are parties and that the final judgment of the Court shall be transmitted to the Committee of Ministers, which shall supervise its execution;

Emphasising the interest in helping the state concerned to identify the underlying problems and the necessary execution measures;

Considering that the execution of judgments would be facilitated if the existence of a systemic problem is already identified in the judgment of the Court;

Bearing in mind the Court's own submission on this matter to the Committee of Ministers session on 7 November 2002;

Invites the Court:

I. as far as possible, to identify, in its judgments finding a violation of the Convention, what it considers to be an underlying systemic problem and the source of this problem, in particular when it is likely to give rise to numerous applications, so as to assist states in finding the appropriate solution and the Committee of Ministers in supervising the execution of judgments;

II. to specially notify any judgment containing indications of the existence of a systemic problem and of the source of this problem not only to the state concerned and to the Committee of Ministers, but also to the Parliamentary Assembly, to the Secretary General of the Council of Europe and to the Council of Europe Commissioner for Human Rights, and to highlight such judgments in an appropriate manner in the database of the Court.

Final Questions and Comments

1. Are the measures taken thus far by the Court adequate to bring about changes in systematic practices that violate the Convention? What more could be done by the Court?

2. Would enhanced awards of damages have an impact on state conduct in the procedural delay cases?

3. What is the responsibility of the Committee of Ministers in addressing systemic problems in member states?

4. Should widespread violations be a priority matter for the regional systems, or are such issues better dealt with at the global level? Does it make a difference if there is an internal or international armed conflict connected to the violations?

CHAPTER VII
TOWARDS THE FUTURE

As the existing regional systems have matured, they have amended their procedures and taken other actions to increase their efficiency, the reliability of their decisions, and their legitimacy. In some instances, they have had to respond to a backlash from states which they have denounced for human rights violations. All of the systems have thus undergone and continue to undergo "reforms." Some actions constitute relatively minor adjustments in complaint procedures; other changes are more far-reaching. This chapter looks at some of the problems and some of the proposed solutions. The second part of the chapter takes up the issue of adding new regional systems in the Middle East and Asia. It considers whether the experiences of the three current systems can be replicated in the remaining regions of the world.

1. Strengthening the Existing Systems

A. Managing the European Caseload

The rising caseload of the European Court is easily seen. In 1981, the number of registered cases was 404 while little more than a decade later, in 1993, the Commission registered 2,037 cases. Four years later, in 1997, the number had more than doubled, to 4,750, while for the first nine months of 2000, it registered 6,835 cases. In one year, from September 1999 to September 2000, the number of pending cases increased by more than thirty percent. The increase has been equally dramatic with regard to the number of provisional files. At the end of 1989, the Court had 4,990 provisional files. During 1999, the Court opened 20,538 provisional files and in the first nine months of 2000 it opened 17,441 files. It issued 177 judgments in 1999, approximately the same number it decided during its first thirty years combined; during 2004, the Court delivered 718 judgments, with 244 of the cases considered to be complex ones. Four states—Turkey, Poland, France and Italy—accounted for over 50% of all judgments during 2004, with a large percentage of the cases concerning the excessive length of court proceedings. The Court receives more than seven hundred communications a day, on average, and this is likely to continue growing as an increasing number of cases arrive from new member states.

The nature of cases has been shifting as well. Within Europe, most cases until the 1990s involved the application of the European Convention to agreed facts. The Court had to decide questions of law that were usually on relatively minor, sometimes highly technical issues.[1] Recent cases, first those against Turkey and now matters concerning some of the new member states, have involved allegations of serious breaches of non-derogable rights (e.g. life and freedom from torture) in which the facts have been contested, necessitating more complex proceedings.

The new European Court has faced formidable hurdles as it has sought to integrate new member states and their judges, clear up cases remaining from the former system, deal with a rising caseload, and develop new procedures while fusing secretariats from the former Commission and Court. While several of these problems are transitional in nature, the rising caseload is likely to be a long term, if not permanent, problem.

Case law consistency is a problem the European Court will have to face. At present the Court makes use of an internal bilingual case law report on pending cases, which is distributed to all judges and registry lawyers. It later becomes the public case law information note after all confidential information has been deleted. Section Registrars meet regularly to compare notes on pending cases being processed and alert their Section Presidents when a problem is identified. As the case law continues to rise and the system evolves, more sophisticated processes will be necessary. In September 1999, the Committee of Ministers of the Council of Europe approved the creation of a Court Management Information System to track all the information pertaining to applicants' cases before the Court and to associate all documents pertaining to the case. It also can be used to trigger activities such as automated document production based on events related to a case file.

The capacity to function effectively with continually rising case loads requires periodic evaluation of the adequacy of staff and budget resources and the establishment of procedures that will allow efficient disposition of meritless claims and full consideration of those cases presenting *prima facie* violations of the Convention. At a press conference on September 28, 2000 the President of the Court spoke of the need for states parties to provide the Court with adequate financial and other resources to cope with a projected annual increase in workload for 2000 of twenty-two percent on top of a forty-percent increase in 1999. The Court is completing approximately six hundred cases a month, double the figure for 1999, but without adequate resources the Court will be unable to continue increasing its productivity, however good its procedures. With such resources and frequent assessment and improvement of its procedures, the Court can ensure justice with all deliberate speed.

Martin Eaton and Jeroen Schokkenbroek, Reforming the Human Rights Protection System Established by the European Convention on Human Rights, 26 HRLJ 1 (2005) (footnotes omitted).

On 12 May 2004, almost exactly ten years after the opening for signature of Protocol No. 11 restructuring the control machinery of the European Convention on Human Rights . . ., the Committee of Ministers of the Council of Europe adopted a new set

---

[1] Rolf Ryssdal, *The Coming Age of the European Convention on Human Rights*, 1996 EUR.H.R. L.REV. 18–29.

of measures to guarantee the long-term effectiveness of the Convention system, including Protocol No. 14 amending the control system of the Convention. . . . This does not mean that Protocol No. 11 was a failure. On the contrary, it has enabled a substantial increase in the productivity of the system. Whereas the Commission and Court had given a total of 38,389 decisions and judgments in the forty-four years up to 1998 . . ., the single, permanent Court has given no less than 61,633 in only five years (1999–2003). In 2003 alone, the Court adopted some 18,000 decisions and 700 judgments.

. . . In 2003, some 39,000 new applications were lodged. This increase is due not only to the rapid and sizeable enlargement of the community of States Parties to the Convention . . ., but also to a general increase in numbers of applications brought against older States Parties. . . . The Court's backlog is rapidly building up: while it manages to dispose of some 1,500 applications per month, this remains far below the 2,300 or so cases allocated to a decision body every month. . . .

. . . Over the past decades, the European Court of Human Rights has become the nerve centre of a system of human rights protection which radiates out through the domestic legal orders of virtually all European States. It sets common legal standards which influence and shape domestic law and practice in such diverse areas as criminal law, family, law the administration of justice in civil, criminal and administrative matters, aliens law, media law, property law, and so on. The Convention has become deeply entrenched in the legal and moral fabric of the societies of the older Council of Europe Member States and this process is well under way in newer States Parties. The Court has firmly established its position in the European constitutional landscape. . . .

Aware of their collective responsibility to preserve the Convention system for the future, the Member States of the Council of Europe have agreed [on] a series of reform measures, with some taking the form of amendments to the Convention (Protocol No. 14), others the form of recommendations addressed to governments, or resolutions addressed to the Court. . . .

The . . . reform process showed that the problem of the Court's excessive workload manifested itself in two main areas. The first is the processing of the very numerous individual applications which are terminated without a ruling on the merits. . . . Around 90% of all applications are terminated this way, the great majority of them being clearly inadmissible. The second area is the processing of individual applications deriving from the same structural cause as an earlier application which has led to a judgment finding a breach of the Convention. Such "repetitive cases" . . . made up some 60% of the 703 judgments which the Court delivered in 2003. . . .

The Protocol contains two main innovations in the area of filtering [of cases]. The first concerns the organization of the filtering process. . . . Article 7 of the Protocol inserts a new Article 27 into the Convention, introducing the single judge as a new filtering formation of the Court, whose competence corresponds to that of committees under the current system. In order to avoid any appearance of lack of impartiality, the single judge may not examine an application against the State in respect of which he or she was elected. . . . In case of doubt as to the inadmissibility of an application, the judge will refer it to a committee or a Chamber. Article 4 of the Protocol . . . provides that these single-judge formations shall be assisted by rapporteurs who shall be part of the registry and function under the authority of the Court's President. This is an important change, for it means that the role of rapporteur will not longer be performed by a judge, but by a member of the registry. . . .

The second main change in the filtering of applications concerns the grounds on which an application can be declared inadmissible. Article 12 of the Protocol adds the following new admissibility criterion to Article 35, paragraph 3 of the Convention:

> 3. The Court shall declare inadmissible any individual applications submitted under Article 34 if it considers that:
>
> [. . .]
>
> b. the applicant has not suffered a significant disadvantage, unless respect for human rights as defined in the Convention and the Protocols thereto requires an examination of the application on the merits and provided that no case may be rejected on this ground which has not been duly considered by a domestic tribunal.

This is probably the most controversial amendment contained in Protocol No. 14. . . . Difficult choices had to be made, but they are not a choice between two extreme views of the Court's role: one that sees it as delivering 'individual justice' and another that sees it as delivering 'quasi-constitutional justice'. It was accepted that both are legitimate functions for a European Court of Human Rights; reform proposals should seek to reconcile the two. The . . . Court should not take over the role of the national courts. It simply cannot do so in respect of some 800 million individuals in Europe. . . . Individual justice should first of all be handed down by domestic courts. While there will always be a need for the Strasbourg Court to act as a safety net in cases requiring individual justice even if they do not raise issues of "constitutional" significance, the ultimate aim of the Convention system should remain that which is set out in Article 19: "to ensure the observance of the engagements taken by the High Contracting Parties."

At the political level, the general question as to whether an additional admissibility criterion should be included in the Protocol received a positive response by the Committee of Ministers in May 2003. . . . The . . . inclusion of the new admissibility criterion has given rise to considerable debate, both on the principle of amending Article 35 of the Convention and on the wording of the criterion. This is understandable in that this is the first amendment every to be made to the set of admissibility conditions since the adoption of the Convention in 1950. At the same time, there is probably also truth in saying that the attention given to this aspect of Protocol 14 has been somewhat exaggerated. . . . The new criterion is but only element of a broader set of measures.

Most importantly, the new criterion, including the attendant safeguard clauses, is now placed in the hands of the Court and it will be for the Court alone to decide on its interpretation and application. There is no reason not to trust that the Court will make a prudent use of it. . . .

As to the question of whether the new criterion in its final wording will indeed be sufficiently easy to apply for the Court . . ., this will of course depend on the Court's interpretation of the new notions of "significant disadvantage" and "duly considered by a domestic tribunal." . . .

The third main change which will result from the Protocol concerns the extension of the competence of the committees of three judges. Article 28 of the Convention is amended by Article 8 of the Protocol, to make the committees competence to decide on the merits of individual applications "if the underlying question in the case, concerning the interpretation or application of the Convention or the Protocols thereto, is already the subject of well-established case-law of the Court." This amendment seeks to simplify and accelerate the processing of "repetitive cases.". . . The Protocol itself provides little detail about the procedure (leaving it essentially to the Court to regulate this in its Rules). . . .

One specific question that aroused some debate concerns the participation of the "national judge" in the committee. A few delegations preferred to make that judge's participation mandatory . . . A majority however felt that this would be an unnecessary complication, given that this procedure concerns cases for which well-established case-law exists. There will thus normally be no need for a committee to have the benefit of that judge's expertise of the national legal system concerned. There may be exceptions, however, for example if issues such as the exhaustion of domestic remedies arise. For this reason,. . . the committee may invite that judge to sit on the committee.

Given that the new procedure introduced by the Protocol will make it much easier to adopt judgments finding a State Party in breach of the Convention, this amendment is a clear illustration of the willingness of the Member States to enhance the effectiveness of the Court even at the expense of their own interests as parties to litigation before the Court. In view of the large numbers of repetitive cases, the change will lead to a significant increase in the Court's capacity and effectiveness.

. . . Protocol No. 14 contains a number of other changes which are worthy of comment. . . . Article 2 of the Protocol amends Article 23 of the Convention to increase the term of office of judges to nine years and make it non-renewable. This chance has its origins in concerns at the Court, the Parliamentary Assembly and the Committee of Ministers about a few instances where there seemed to be abuse of the current provisions in that sitting judges of recognized competence and effectiveness had not been included on the list of candidates for judge for their country on expiry of their term, apparently for political reasons.

Article 13 of the Protocol amends Article 36 of the Convention to insert a right of written and oral intervention in Chamber and Grand Chamber cases for the Council of Europe Commissioner for Human Rights. This change had its origin in a specific request the Commissioner made in 2003 proposing that the Commissioner be given power to lodge an application with the Court against one or more States Parties in a case which raises a serious issue of a general nature. . . . The aim . . . was to enable him to bring before the Court at an early stages issues arising during his work, where he considered breaches of a transnational or systemic character were occurring, which in the ordinary course of events might take some time to come before the Court in the form of an individual application.

The majority . . . had doubts about this proposal which would involve a major departure from the current system of the Convention, away from the requirements to prove an individual breach and towards acting in the public interest—a kind of action popularis. . . .[T]hey adopted instead a suggestion by the French delegation . . . to give the Commissioner a right to intervene both in writing and in oral hearings . . .

Finally, Article 17 of the Protocol amends Article 59 of the Convention . . . to permit accession by the European Union to the Convention.

For a more critical look at Protocol 14, see Philip Leach, *Access to the European Court of Human Rights—From a Legal Entitlement to a Lottery?* 27 HRLJ 11 (2006). He notes the principled objections to restricting individual access to the Court, adding

> At the heart of these objections has been a fundamental concern that the amendments to the admissibility criteria will restrict the right of individuals to seek redress at the European Court, without adequately tackling the problem of the increasing number of Convention violations across Europe. As Sir Nicolas Bratza has suggested, '. . . an amendment to the Convention designed to reduce the influx of cases or to speed up their processing by the Court, [will]treat the symptoms but not the underlying disease, namely the continuing failure of national legal systems effectively to implement the Convention guarantees and to provide effective means of redress where breaches of the Convention rights have been found to have occurred.'

Id. at 24–25. How could this problem be addressed?

All Council of Europe member states except Russia have now ratified Protocol 14. With the Protocol not in force and the caseload continuing to rise, the Council has attempted to find other solutions to its crisis. The Heads of State and Government of the member states, meeting in May 2005, decided to appoint a Group of Wise Persons to consider the long-term effectiveness of the ECHR control mechanism and to report to the Committee of Ministers. The Group submitted an interim report on May 19, 2005, CM(2006)88, and its final report on November 15, 2005. The following extract contains the Group's proposals.

Final Report of the Group of Wise Persons to the Committee of Ministers, Nov. 15, 2006, CM(2006)203, reprinted in 46 ILM 78 (2007).

. . . .

1. It is important to begin by reiterating the fundamental importance attaching to human rights protection in the Council of Europe framework and the diversity of the means employed to achieve this, as it is in this context that the role and long-term effectiveness of the judicial control must be assessed.

2. The enlargement of the Council of Europe and the accession to the European Convention on Human Rights . . . of the central and east European democracies have contributed to stability in the whole of Europe. The Convention and the Court have become genuine pillars in the protection of human rights and fundamental freedoms. For its part, the Committee of Ministers plays an important role in monitoring the execution of judgments.

3. Since the Convention forms part of the national law of the member states, the remedies available at national level must be effective and well known to their citizens. Indeed, they constitute the first line of defense of the rule of law and human rights. Initially, it is for the national courts to protect rights within their domestic legal systems and to ensure respect for the rights safeguarded by the Convention. The principle of subsidiarity is one of the cornerstones of the system for protecting human rights in Europe.

4. In addition, the Council of Europe has set up many other institutions and boides in the human rights field. These have proved their commitment and effectiveness. Not only is there the Commissioner for Human Rights. The European Committee for the Prevention of Torture, the European Commission against Racism and Intolerance, the Advisory Committee on the Framework Convention for the Protection of National Minorities and the European Committee on Social Rights also play important complementary roles.

5. It should also be remembered that the Council of Europe has a number of information offices which were set up pursuant to Committee of Ministers Resolution (99)9.

6. The Group noted with great interest the lessons drawn from the Warsaw information office project. In view of the success of this innovative initiative, the functions of such offices could be expanded and strengthened. In particular, they could provide potential applicants with information on admissibility issues and familiarize them with the existing domestic remedies and other, non-judicial remedies. These offices could assist in making citizens more aware of how the convention operates and so save them from initiating proceedings unnecessarily or prematurely, without exhausting domestic remedies.

7. Furthermore, in many member states, non-judicial institutions such as ombudsmen, petition committees and human rights institutions play or could play a significant role in providing information on, and promoting, human rights.

8. Lastly, civil society plays a significant part in human rights protection. Partnership with civil society has always been important in the Council of Europe. It is reflected *inter alia* in the participation of many non-governmental organizations in the Organization's activities. These play a leading role in the field of human rights protection which it is important to maintain and expand.

III. Summary

125. The survival of the machinery for the judicial protection of human rights and the Court's ability to cope with its workload are are seriously under threat from an exponential increase in the number of individual applications which jeopardizes the proper functioning of the Convention's control system. It is essential to recommend effective measures to remedy this situation on a permanent basis, thus making it possible to ensure the long-term effectiveness of the Convention's control mechanism, without the right of individual application being affected, and allowing the Court to concentrate on its function as the custodian of human rights by relieving it of a whole body of litigation which places an unnecessary burden on it.

THE PROPOSED REFORM MEASURES

126. The Group has adopted a set of proposals of different kinds, which, combined, should ensure the efficient functioning of the control mechanism in the long term.

A. Concerning the structure and modification of the judicial machinery

1. Greater flexibility of the procedure for reforming the judicial machinery

127. The Group believes that it is essential to make the judicial system of the Convention *more flexible*. This could be achieved through an amendment to the Convention authorising the Committee of Ministers to carry out reforms by way of unanimously adopted resolutions without an amendment to the Convention being necessary each time. This method would make the Convention system more flexible and capable of adapting to new circumstances, but would not apply to the substantive rights set forth in the Convention or to the principles governing the judicial system.

128. The system created would be structured around three levels of rules, namely:

- the Convention itself and its protocols, for which the amendment procedure would remain unchanged;
- the "statute" of the Court, ie a legal level whose content would need to be defined, comprising provisions relating to the operating procedures of the Court. This second level would be an innovation. The provisions of this statute could be amended by the Committee of Ministers with the Court's approval;
- texts such as the Rules of Court, which could be amended by the Court itself.

2. Establishment of a new judicial filtering mechanism

129. A judicial filtering body should be set up which would be attached to, but separate from, the Court, in order to guarantee, on the one hand, that individual applications result in a judicial decision and, on the other, that the Court can be relieved of a large number of cases and focus on its essential role.

130. The members of the Judicial Committee would be judges enjoying full guarantees of independence. Their number should be less than the number of member states. It would be decided—and could be modified—by the Committee of Ministers on a proposal from the Court. The composition of the Judicial Committee should reflect a geographical balance as well as a harmonious gender balance and should be based on a system of rotation between states. The term of office of its members would be limited in duration in accordance with rules to be laid down by the Committee of Ministers.

131. The members of the Judicial Committee, like those of the Court, should be of high moral character and possess the qualifications required for appointment to judicial office. They would be subject to the same requirements as the members of the Court with regard to impartiality and meeting the demands of a full-time office. Candidates' professional qualifications and knowledge of languages should be assessed by the Court in an opinion prior to their election by the Parliamentary Assembly.

132. The Judicial Committee would have jurisdiction to hear all applications raising admissibility issues and all cases which could be decided on the basis of well-established case-law of the Court allowing an application to be declared either manifestly well-founded or manifestly ill-founded. The Judicial Committee's jurisdiction to decide cases on the merits would involve, where such cases are concerned, the exercise of the same powers as the Court in respect of just satisfaction.

133. Institutionally and administratively, the Judicial Committee would come under the Court's authority. It would be chaired by a member of the Court, appointed by the latter for a set period, and would draw on the support of the Registry of the Court, thus enabling it to make optimum use of the Registry's human resources. There would be no possibility of appealing against the decisions of the Judicial Committee, although the Court would have a special power allowing it, of its own motion, to assume jurisdiction in order to review any decision adopted by the Judicial Committee.

B. Concerning the relations between the Court and the States Parties to the Convention

3. Enhancing the authority of the Court's case-law in the States Parties

134. The dissemination of the Court's case-law and recognition of its authority above and beyond the judgment's binding effect on the parties would no doubt be important elements in ensuring the effectiveness of the Convention's judicial control mechanism. The Group recommends that judgments of principle and judgments which the Court considers particularly important be more widely disseminated in line with the recommendations of the Committee of Ministers.

4. Forms of co-operation between the Court and the national courts—Advisory opinions

135. The Group considers that it would be useful to introduce a system under which the national courts could apply to the Court for advisory opinions on legal questions relating to interpretation of the Convention and the protocols thereto, in order to foster dialogue between courts and enhance the Court's "constitutional" role. Requests for an opinion, which would be submitted only by constitutional courts or courts of last instance, would always be optional and the opinions given by the Court would not be binding.

5. Improvement of domestic remedies for redressing violations of the Convention

136. Domestic remedies for redressing violations of the rights secured by the Convention should be improved. The length of proceedings in civil, criminal and administrative cases, which is one of the main sources of litigation before the Court, highlights the need for such an improvement, which would be achieved by means of a Convention text placing an explicit obligation on the States Parties to introduce domestic legal mechanisms to redress the damage resulting from any violation of the Convention, and especially those resulting from structural or general shortcomings in a state's law or practice.

6. The award of just satisfaction

137. Changes to the rules laid down in Article 41 of the Convention are necessary to relieve the Court and the Judicial Committee of tasks which could be carried out more effectively by national bodies (especially when expert reports are needed).

138. Where the Court or, where appropriate, the Judicial Committee holds that the victim must be awarded compensation, the decision on the amount of compensation would be referred to the state concerned. However, the Court or, as appropriate, the Judicial Committee would have the power to depart from this rule and give its own decision on just satisfaction where such a decision was found to be necessary.

139. The state should discharge its obligation to award compensation within the time-limit set by the Court or the Judicial Committee. It would be for the state to determine the arrangements for this, while complying with certain requirements. The amount of compensation should be consistent with the criteria laid down in the Court's case-law. The victim would be able to apply to the Court or to the Judicial Committee where the latter gave the decision finding a violation of the Convention, to set aside the national decision by reference to those criteria, or where the state failed to comply with the time-limit set for determining the amount of compensation.

7. The "pilot judgment" procedure

140. The Group encourages the Court to make the fullest possible use of the "pilot judgment" procedure. In the light of practical experience, consideration would need to be given in future to the question of whether the existing judicial machinery, including the Court's rules of procedure, will suffice for this model to be able to produce the desired results or whether a reform of the Convention should be contemplated in this connection.

C. Concerning alternative (non-judicial) or complementary means of resolving disputes

8. Friendly settlements and mediation

141. In order to reduce the Court's workload, recourse to mediation at national or Council of Europe level should be encouraged where the Court, and more particularly the Judicial Committee, considers that an admissible case lends itself to such a solution. Proceedings in the cases concerned would be suspended pending the outcome of mediation. This method of settlement would be subject to the parties' agreement.

9. Extension of the duties of the Commissioner for Human Rights

142. The Group considers that the Commissioner should have the necessary resources to be able to play a more active role in the Convention's control system, acting either alone or in co-operation with European and national non-judicial bodies. In particular, the Commissioner should respond actively to the announcement of Court decisions finding serious violations of human rights. The Commissioner could also lend his assistance to mediation machinery at national level. Under his mandate, the Commissioner facilitates the activities of national ombudsmen and

similar institutions. The Committee of Ministers might consider adopting a recommendation aimed at assigning them competence in human rights matters in all cases. The Group notes with approval that the Commissioner is extending his current co-operation with national and regional ombudsmen and national human rights institutes in order to form an active network of all these institutions. This network could help to reduce the Court's workload with the active support of the Commissioner.

D. Concerning the institutional status of the Court and judges

10. The institutional dimension of the control mechanism

143. The Group thought that the existing legal framework should offer all the guarantees that are essential to ensure the independence of judges. In this connection, it considers the setting up of a social security scheme (coverage for medical expenses and pension entitlement) to be of vital importance.

144. The professional qualifications and knowledge of languages of candidates for the post of judge should be carefully examined during the election procedure. For this purpose, before the Parliamentary Assembly considers the candidatures, an opinion on the suitability of the candidates could be given by a committee of prominent personalities possibly chosen from among former members of the Court, current and former members of national supreme or constitutional courts and lawyers with acknowledged competence. As regards the members of the proposed Judicial Committee, the prior opinion should be given by the Court.

145. The Group also looked at the particularly sensitive issue of the number of judges. In the Group's opinion, the logic underlying the new role proposed for the Court and the setting up of the Judicial Committee should lead in due course to a reduction in the number of judges.

146. Lastly, in the interests of enhancing the Court's independence and effectiveness, the Group recommends granting it the greatest possible operational autonomy, as regards in particular the presentation and management of its budget and the appointment, deployment and promotion of its staff.

Questions and Comments

1. Are these measures all likely to decrease the Court's workload? What other measures might be envisaged?

2. Would it be advantageous for the European Court to consider forming a bar association, with an entrance exam, qualifications, and ethical rules governing the lawyers who appear before it?

3. The Inter-American Court also has a rising caseload, following an amendment to the Commission's Rules of Procedure, which now envisage in principle sending to the Court all cases in which a violation is found and the state does not take action to remedy the violation. Not only does this increase the Court's caseload, it means fewer Commission reports are being written and published.

B. Increasing the Effectiveness of the Inter-American System

Various proposals have been made and some adopted over the years in order to strengthen the functioning of the Inter-American System. See, e.g., Claudio Grossman, *Proposals to Strengthen the Inter-American System of Protection of Human Rights*, 32 GERM. YB INT'L L. 264 (1989). The issue is once again on the agenda of the OAS political and legal institutions. The following three documents highlight the issues as seen from the perspective of the Committee on Juridical and Political Affairs, two member states, the Inter-American Commission on Human Rights and the Inter-American Court of Human Rights. See also: OAS General Assembly, *Strengthening of Human Rights Systems Pursuant to the Plan of Action of the Third Summit of the Americas.*

Permanent Council of the OAS, Committee on Juridical and Political Affairs, *Notice of Convocation: To the OAS Member States, the Inter-American Court of Human Rights, and the Inter-American Commission on Human Rights to Initiate the First Phase of the Process of Reflection on the Inter-American System for the Promotion and Protection of Human Rights,* OEA/Ser.G, CP/CAJP–2227/04, Dec.17, 2004.

After considering the matter during several working meetings in the second half of 2004, on December 16, the Committee on Juridical and Political Affairs (CAJP) decided to initiate the first phase of the process of reflection on the inter-American system for the promotion and protection of human rights, pursuant to the mandate contained in operative paragraph 5 of resolution AG/RES. 2030 (XXXIV–O/04), *Strengthening of Human Rights Systems pursuant to the Plan of Action of the Third Summit of the Americas,* which reads as follows:

> 5. *To instruct the Permanent Council to engage in a broad process of reflection on the inter-American system for the promotion and protection of human rights, in which it may elicit the opinion of member states, specialized agencies of the inter-American human rights system, nongovernmental organizations, national human rights institutes, academic institutions, and experts in the field, regarding:*
>
> > a. *The major challenges facing the inter-American system for the promotion and protection of human rights in the Hemisphere;*
> >
> > b. *Possible actions to strengthen and improve the system; and*
> >
> > c. *The advisability of convening an inter-American human rights conference.*
>
> *In keeping with the foregoing, to present a report thereon to the General Assembly at its thirty-fifth regular session for consideration.*

Consequently, in light of the two documents appended hereto, the Committee on Juridical and Political Affairs of the OAS Permanent Council hereby *invites* member states, the Inter-American Court of Human Rights, and the Inter-American Commission on Human Rights to hold preliminary consultations on the major challenges facing the inter-American system and possible actions to strengthen and improve it. . . .

ANNEX I

PRELIMINARY LIST OF TOPICS FOR CONSULTATIONS TO BE HELD
DURING THE PROCESS OF REFLECTION ON THE INTER-AMERICAN
SYSTEM FOR THE PROMOTION AND PROTECTION OF HUMAN RIGHTS

The Chair hereby presents this preliminary, non-exhaustive list of the topics that
have been included thus far at the request of member states. This document will
serve as a basis for the consultations to be held during the initial phase of the process of reflection on the inter-American system for the promotion and protection
of human rights.

This list is a first attempt to identify what the member states consider to be the
major challenges facing the inter-American system for the promotion and protection of human rights in the Hemisphere.

**I. Topics proposed during meetings of the Committee on Juridical and Political
Affairs of the Permanent Council**

- Funding for the system
- Universalization of the system
- Follow-up of compliance with the decisions of the Inter-American Court of
  Human Rights and the recommendations of the Inter-American Commission
  on Human Rights
- Promotion of human rights education
- Dissemination of the decisions of the Inter-American Court and the Inter-
  American Commission within the governments of member states
- Minority groups of particular concern in the area of human rights
    Women and children
    Migrants
    Detainees
    Persons with disabilities
- The human rights of indigenous peoples
- Freedom of expression in the Hemisphere
- Access for victims to the system
- Independence of the Inter-American Court and the Inter-American
  Commission
- Monitoring of human rights issues in the HemispherePermanent operations of
  the organs
- Role of the inter-American system for the promotion and protection of human
  rights in strengthening national human rights systems
- Optimization of the regulatory procedures followed by the organs of the
  system
- Analysis of the institutionalization of dialogue among the organs of the system
  in the framework of the Permanent Council (Committee on Juridical and Political Affairs)

II. Additional topics proposed by member states by means of formal notes

i. Bolivarian Republic of Venezuela

- The role of the state as the entity responsible for overseeing the system for personal liberty and for strengthening human rights, and as the guarantor and arbitrer of the commonweal in a democratic society
- Dialogue among states and the inter-American human rights organs, as the most suitable mechanism for addressing the observations and recommendations of states on the functioning of the system
- Evaluation of the structure, powers, and procedures of the organs of the inter-American human rights system, in accordance with the American Convention on Human Rights and their respective Statutes and Rules of Procedure
- Nature of the financial contributions to the organs of the system and their relationship to the serious problems of the Hemisphere, as part of the challenges of the millenium

ii. Bolivia

- Exchange of documents of ratification of international human rights instruments by member states
- Drafting of a program to encourage those states that have not ratified international human rights instruments that have been ratified by the other states
- Drafting of a public information policy on human rights, especially second— and third-generation rights
- Drafting of policies for the effective exercise of third-generation human rights
- Review, analysis, and comparison of the jurisprudence of national constitutional courts in the area of human rights in order to identify interpretative trends in the administration of justice

---

Preliminary Document from the Inter-American Commission on Human Rights on the First Stage in the Process of Reflection on the Inter-American System for the Promotion and Protection of Human Rights Pursuant to Resolution AG/RES. 2030 (XXXIV–O/04), OEA/Ser.G, CP/CAJP–2227/04 add. 1, 16 May 2005.

A. Introduction

. . . [T]here are four elements the Commission would like to stress and that represent fundamental points for providing an effective response to those new needs. While it is logical for the dialogue about the strengthening of the inter-American system to focus on the work of the Commission and the Court, we suggest paying particular attention to the four points detailed below: (1) the budgets of the Commission and the Court, (2) the member states' observance of their human rights obligations, (3) compliance with the decisions and judgments of the oversight bodies by those member states that are parties to the American Convention, and (4) universal ratification of the inter-American human rights instruments.

B. The System's Four Main Challenges and Structural Shortcomings

I. The Need For Increased Financial Resources

This process of reflection must provide a solution to one of the endemic and increasingly urgent problems within our system: budgetary constraints. Over the years, the Inter-American Commission has received with enthusiasm the various mandates handed down to it by the General Assembly and the Summits of the Americas, which serve to demonstrate the growing legitimacy of the system and the States' recognition of its important role and priority status within the Organization. However, its ability to discharge its broad and diverse mandate requires a similar commitment vis-à-vis the allocation of financial and human resources.

The sad reality is that the Commission's total budget is equal to far less than 5% of the Organization's overall budget. The budget for the current year does not provide sufficient funds for a single on-site visit to a member state, for the litigation of cases before the Court, to hold a second period of sessions, or for the operations of its special rapporteurs. This has forced the Commission to depend on the generous voluntary contributions of certain member states and on the philanthropy of several countries from beyond the region to finance compliance with this essential aspect of its mandate; this should be a cause for concern, if not for a degree of mortification, among the Organization's member states.

The Commission needs a healthy injection of new funding in order to, inter alia, process more expeditiously the more than a thousand petitions that are currently pending before the Commission. This reflection must therefore be geared towards identifying the measures necessary to increase these funds, in order to enable the inter-American system to duly discharge all its assigned tasks. Any initiative that is not based on resolving the financial situation that is currently preventing the Commission and the Court from realizing their full potential is doomed to failure. An essential prerequisite is that the strengthening of the system must help set the bases so that the system's organs can function properly.

The following tables illustrate the IACHR's growing volume of work and the stagnation and clear reduction in its OAS Regular Fund budget allocation.

Percentage growth in the Regular Fund

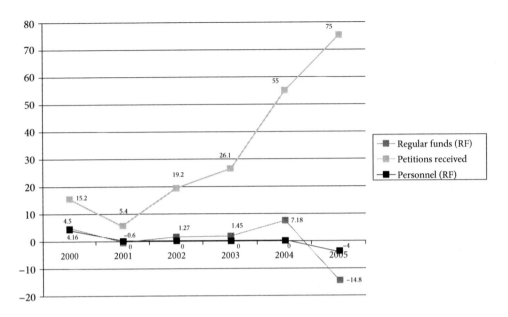

Petitions received and transmitted

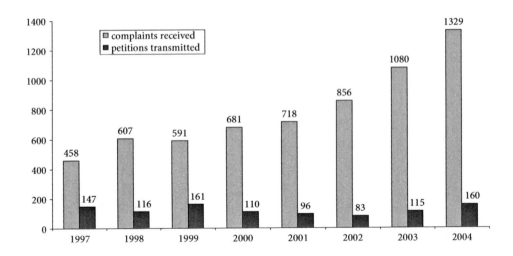

Total reports published and presented to the Inter-American Court per year

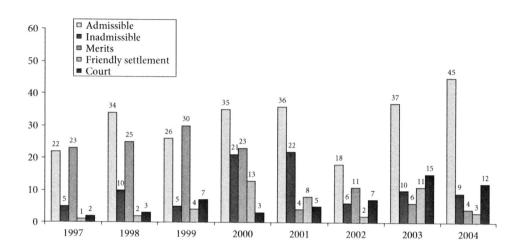

Total complaints and petitions conveyed to member states by year

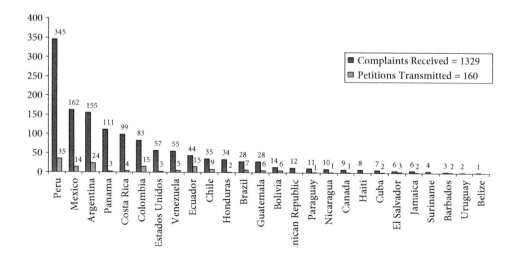

Total precautionary measures granted by year

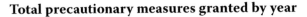

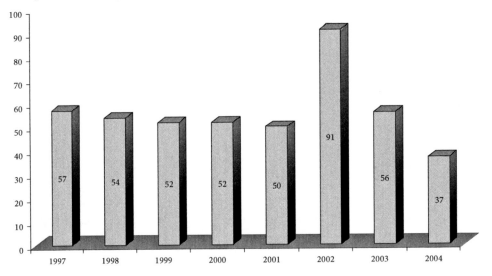

| | 1997 | 1998 | 1999 | 2000 | 2001 | 2002 | 2003 | 2004 |
| | 57 | 54 | 52 | 52 | 50 | 91 | 56 | 37 |

Cases submitted to the Court by country during 2004

Venezuela, 1
Chile, 1
Brazil, 1
Peru, 4
Guatemala, 2
Colombia, 3

II. The Failure to Secure Universal Ratification of the Human Rights Treaties

Within the inter-American system, there are at least three different levels of adhesion: The first is a universal and minimal level for all the OAS member states whose inhabitants enjoy protection, from the Inter-American Commission, of the rights enshrined in the OAS Charter and in the American Declaration of the Rights and Duties of Man. There is a second system for those member states that have ratified the American Convention on Human Rights but have not accepted the jurisdiction of the Court, and a third one for those that have ratified the Convention and accepted the Court's competence. This system is unquestionably not ideal. From the human rights point of view, it places the inhabitants of major countries in the region at a disadvantage with respect to the protection their rights receive from the inter-American system. The IACHR is aware that enforcement of the American Declaration gives the system a universal dimension. Neither is the IACHR unaware that some of the countries that have not ratified the Convention offer a level of human rights protection that is comparable to the regional ideal. However, failure to ratify the Convention and to accept the Court's jurisdiction is clearly negative. There is a risk of limiting the universal value of the protection mechanism. In particular, it must be noted that some people benefit from the more specific provisions of the Convention, while others can depend solely on the American Declaration; similarly, the rights of some people can be ensured through international contentious proceedings before the Inter-American Court, while others can only seek redress from the Commission.

In this context, the reflection exercise cannot fail to analyze the reasons, causes, and consequences whereby certain member states have been able to ratify other multilateral human rights treaties at the universal level, such as the International Covenant on Civil and Political Rights, the International Covenant on Economic, Social, and Cultural Rights, and the Convention against Torture and Other Cruel, Inhuman, or Degrading Treatment or Punishment. Most of these treaties include obligations similar to those set out in the inter-American human rights instruments. The situation regarding the number of ratifications of the human rights instruments and the acceptance of the Court's jurisdiction is not encouraging if it is compared to the Council of Europe or the African Union.

III. Compliance with the Decisions of the Human Rights Bodies and Their Collective Oversight by the Organization's Political Bodies

One indispensable step toward improving the system is for the OAS member states to comply, fully and effectively, with the Court's decisions and to implement, in good faith, the Commission's recommendations. To facilitate this process, the member states must adopt the legislative and political measures necessary for the decisions of the Commission and the Court to be put into effect domestically. In recent years, several countries have adopted such measures, but further progress still needs to be made in this direction.

Consideration must also be given to the role of states parties as the *guarantors* of the American Convention. The states parties individually undertake to comply with the Court's decisions, as stipulated in Article 68 of the Convention, in application of the principle of *pacta sunt servanda*, and also because they are so obliged under their own domestic laws. The OAS member states also assume, in compliance with the Inter-American Court's interpretation, the obligation of complying in good faith with the IACHR's recommendations as a principal organ of the Charter of the Organization.

Although compliance with the resolutions handed down by the Commission and the Court has increased, particularly as regards indemnifications, the situation is still far from satisfactory. The following table shows the level of compliance with the recommendations issued by the Commission in recent years.

The Court and the Commission oversee compliance with their own decisions. Article 65 of the Convention provides, as a mechanism to guarantee execution of those decisions, the intervention of the OAS's political bodies if the Court's judgments are not complied with—as regards all aspects, not solely monetary responsibility.

The reflection in this area focuses on identifying tools to enable states to comply with the bodies' decisions. In particular they should lead to the adoption of legislative mechanisms covering, *inter alia*, the binding nature of the international agencies' decisions and the steps to be taken when necessary: the adoption or amendment of legal provisions; indemnification payments; review of judgments; opening or returning to investigations. The reflection process should lead to the identification or creation, at the national level, of entities with the primary responsibility of working for compliance with the decisions of the international bodies or of supervising it.

Status of compliance with IACHR recommendations during 2004

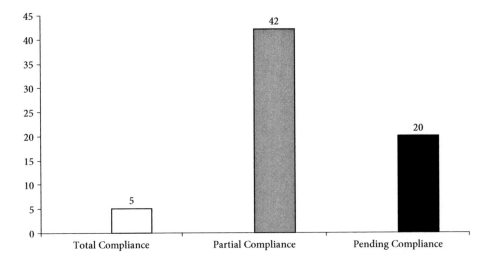

IV. Incorporation of International Obligations at the Domestic Level

Improving the system requires that the countries' legislatures adopt all measures necessary to guarantee the rights set forth in the international instruments and amend or repeal all the provisions thereof that contravene the international human rights treaties. The countries' judiciaries must, in turn, fully enforce both the provisions contained in the treaties and the jurisprudence of the Commission and the Court. This means that the process of reflection about improving the inter-American system does not exclusively involve the operations of the protection bodies; on the country, it should primarily concentrate on the best strategies so that the states, as those with primary responsibility for effectively upholding rights, are able to fulfill that commitment.

In accordance with the purpose and goals of the inter-American system, the member states must ensure protection for human rights, through legislation, jurisprudence, and other political measures. As a corollary, states may find that they have to amend, or even repeal, provisions of their domestic laws that are incompatible with the obligations acquired under the Convention. Consequently, a comprehensive analysis of the Convention's effectiveness must take into account the inclusion of rights protected by local legislation, the adjustment of government policy, the effectiveness of the judicial protection that rights are afforded, and the due reparation of rights violations.

Fortunately, some states parties have adopted specific measures aimed at ensuring and facilitating compliance with the obligations acquired under the Convention. For example, some states include provisions from the Convention directly in their domestic laws, while others give the Convention precedence over domestic legislation. In addition, some states have designed mechanisms that give domestic legal effect to the decisions and recommendations of the Convention's supervisory bodies. Given that the states parties have primary responsibility for safeguarding the human rights enshrined in the American Convention, the way in which they are complying with that acquired duty requires a certain degree of reflection.

ANNEX I

CHAPTER I OF THE 2004 ANNUAL REPORT OF THE COMMISSION

1. In 2004, the region achieved significant advancements in various areas, such as in political stability, decreased corruption and in the administration of justice. The strengthening of all of these areas is necessary for the full observance of fundamental liberties.

2. The IACHR highlights certain exceedingly positive achievements in the region: The launch of a comprehensive national program on human rights in Mexico that includes the structural reform of public policies in this area; the adoption of constitutional reforms to modernize the judicial system and broaden judicial mechanism to combat impunity for human rights violations in Brazil; and the realization of a referendum despite conditions of extreme political polarization in Venezuela.

3. This report concerns, likewise, a period characterized by a continuance of the efforts to combat impunity for serious human rights violations committed in preceding decades. The Commission emphasizes, inter alia, the prosecution of the former president of Chile for the atrocities committed during the military dictatorship in said country; the elimination of various legal obstacles that impeded the judicial prosecution in cases of "disappearances" and other human rights violations in Argentina; the creation of a Truth Committee in Paraguay; an in-depth report on political imprisonment and torture that completes the official documentation of acts that occurred during the military dictatorship in Chile; acknowledgments of international responsibility for serious human rights violations by Guatemala and Peru, in cases pending before the Inter-American Court of Human Rights; and the signing of a comprehensive friendly settlement in cases of forced disappearance that occurred during a civil war in Honduras. The Commission also observes with approval a number of important jurisprudential developments during 2004, such as the reaffirmation in the United States of the right to judicial appeal or review in the event of arrest of citizens or persons classified as enemy combatants in the context of the war on terrorism; the affirmation of the right to the truth and the restriction of military tribunals to investigate human rights violations by the Constitutional Tribunal in Peru; and the possibility to reopen criminal investigations based on decisions of international organizations.

4. These constructive developments have arisen in the context of renewed emphasis in matters of domestic security and the fight against terrorism. The Commission and the Court recognize the right and inalienable duty of States to guarantee the safety of their citizens, without prejudicing the questioning by the Commission of many excesses committed in the name of security. During 2004, the region has continued to witness the indefinite detention without charge or trial of hundreds

of foreign citizens in the United States. The security policies adopted by the Government of Colombia continued to exacerbate the already grave humanitarian and human rights crisis, while the proposed process for the demobilization of paramilitaries failed to stop the violence or ensure an end to impunity. In some Central American countries so-called zero tolerance policies were implemented against gangs or presumed members of these gangs, who were labeled as terrorists in some occasions.

5. The region continued to be affected by crises of political, economic and social nature in several countries. These problems expose the institutional fragility of the rule of law and the precariousness of the process for strengthening democracy in the hemisphere. Deteriorating economic and social conditions in various countries have provoked mass popular demonstrations that have often been met with excessive use of force by the police, and in many cases, intensified the political instability. In Haiti, the breakdown of government led to the resignation of the democratically elected president amid rising political violence, as the prevailing economic conditions continued to deteriorate. In Ecuador, the removal of a majority Supreme Court magistrates, along with the dismissals of judges of the Constitutional Tribunal and the Supreme Electoral Tribunal have created deep concern in relation to the correct functioning of institutions essential to the rule of law and the observance of the fundamental principle of separation and independence of powers. Corruption, as a region-wide phenomenon, continues to impede the construction democratic and transparent societies. The vast majority of the States continued without confronting the causes and consequences produced by social exclusion and discrimination based on factors such as ethnicity, class, race, and gender.

6. According to the Economic Commission for Latin America and the Caribbean (ECLAC), the sustained economic growth of the region in 2004 has enabled approximately four million Latin Americans to lift themselves out of poverty from 2003 to 2004. Despite this improvement, however, ECLAC admits that it is insufficient to offset the decline in the 2001–2003 periods. This means that at least 221 million people, that is, 44.0% of the population of Latin America, live in poverty. Of those, 97 million live in conditions of extreme poverty or destitution. Furthermore, Latin America remains the region with the worst distribution of income in the world, a situation aggravated by the fact that in some countries income concentration is on the increase. In 2004, the World Bank warned that inequality is a dominant feature of Latin American societies in terms of income differences, access to services, and power and influence. The World Bank indicates that this high level of inequality hinders the reduction of poverty.

7. The Commission notes that this economic situation, the high poverty rates and the extensive inequality prevailing in the region are obstacles for the effective enjoyment of economic, social and cultural rights, and likewise negatively affect the observance of many civil and political rights. At the same time, in 2004, several social leaders and groups that questioned this economic situation were frequently repressed, harassed, and criminally prosecuted for their activities.

8. Furthermore, crime and citizen insecurity reached alarming proportions in various countries. In many countries the insecurity generated by the high rates of

crime and the growing inequality led both the governments and the general public to demonstrate a higher tolerance for repressive methods used by the police. In this context, torture and excessive use of force are tools commonly used by the security forces in many countries in the region.

9. In the midst of this, in many respects, gloomy, panorama, the Inter-American Commission on Human Rights continued to represent an important forum for the defense of democracy and advancement of human rights in the hemisphere. The inter-American system of human rights, and the IACHR in particular, play a crucially important role in responding to human rights violations and combating impunity.

10. In its analysis of the challenges facing in the area of human rights, the Commission continued, in 2004, with a process of reflection on ways to strengthen the inter-American system as an essential mechanism to respond to the increasing needs of the region in this area. The IACHR recognizes that there are new challenges to confront, foremost among which, are the observance by the State of the rule of law and the effective protection of economic, social, and cultural rights. . . .

III. STRATEGIC AND INTEGRAL VISION OF THE SITUATION OF HUMAN RIGHTS IN THE REGION AND THE NEEDS OF THE SYSTEM

15. The core strategic objective of the reflection process must be to strengthen the system. Any measures arising from areas of consensus built in this process should be guided in this direction. This entails strengthening of mechanisms that work, in particular the system of individual petitions and precautionary measures; consolidation of successful areas of activity, such as the thematic rapporteurships on the rights of women, indigenous populations, migrant workers and their families, persons deprived of their liberty, children, and freedom of expression; identification of situations that do not receive proper attention, and identification of the areas not properly addressed and amendment of any aspects not consistent with the core objective.

IV. THE POLITICAL AND PROMOTIONAL ROLE OF THE COMMISSION

16. The Commission understands, furthermore, that the reflection process should include an analysis of its promotional and political role in the future. The new times, described above, that the States and civil societies of the hemisphere traverse, in addition to the encouraging spirit of cooperation between the majority of states and the Commission, challenge the Commission to intensify joint activities between State bodies and the Commission aimed at shaping public policies that strengthen protection of human rights.

V. RAPID AND EFFECTIVE RESPONSE CAPACITY

17. One of the main challenges for the Commission and for the hemispheric community is defining how to respond to situations of serious human rights violations in a quick and effective manner.. Although institutional crises are chiefly the responsibility of the political organs of the OAS, the IACHR is an organ specialized in the area of human rights and, as such, it should use it mechanisms to protect the inhabitants of the Americas from violations of their rights. In this regard, the reflection process should encourage discussions on identification of tools to enable a response in situations of this nature.

VI. THE RELATIONSHIP BETWEEN PROTECTION OF DEMOCRACY AND PROTECTION OF HUMAN RIGHTS

18. The Inter-American Democratic Charter, adopted in September 2001 during the extraordinary period of sessions of the General Assembly of the OAS, highlights with clarity the interrelationship between democracy and human rights. In this connection, it is essential that the response mechanisms of the Organization for dealing with crises of democratic governance be coupled with full observance for human rights. Systematic and serious human rights violation, as well as reiterated and consistent failure to comply with the decisions of the organs of the inter-American system of human rights, must be a central part of the process of reflection to consolidate the rule of law through protection and advancement of human rights. At the same time, in order to prevent the exacerbation of crises, some kind of preventive response mechanism should be created to answer calls for assistance and early warnings from the IACHR. . . .

XI. STRENGTHENING AND INCREASED INDEPENDENCE AND AUTONOMY FOR THE INTER-AMERICAN COMMISSION AND ITS EXECUTIVE SECRETARIAT

23. The Commission considers that, in order to ensure effective and comprehensive completion of its functions and mandates, the IACHR must have complete independence and sufficient autonomy in administrative, financial, and political matters. This is indispensable for any international human rights organization. In practice, in recent years, the Commission managed to increase its autonomy with a directive from the General Secretary of OAS that grants ample prerogatives for the selection of its senior appointees, while it's professional and technical staff is selected by its Executive Secretary. As a result, the professionalism, suitability, dedication and commitment to the human rights cause of the Executive Secretariat staff have risen considerably.

24. For that reason, the reflection process should seek the consolidation of this important aspect, which is essential for strengthening the inter-American system of human rights. The proposed restructuring of the OAS in 2004 demonstrated the need for a stronger legal framework for the autonomy of the IACHR. The Commission was forced publicly to make clear its opposition to the proposal that would have significantly reduced its autonomy because that would undermine its capacity to protect human rights. This position was met with broad consensus on the part of the states and civil society organizations.

25. A little over two decades ago, the reestablishment of freely elected governments commenced in the vast majority of the States in the region. At that time, the IACHR forecasted a promising phase for the rebuilding of democracy in a manner that would contribute to the enjoyment of human rights. However, in spite of this, an assessment indicates that democracy finds itself in a state of uncertainty and precariousness in many of our societies. As proclaimed in the Inter-American Democratic Charter, the effective exercise of representative democracy is the basis for the rule of law and of the constitutional regimes of the member states of the Organization of American States. Representative democracy is strengthened and deepened through permanent, ethical, and responsible participation by the citizenry, and

member states must ensure that this participation is accompanied by transparency in government activities, probity, and respect for social rights and fundamental human rights, in order to contribute to the consolidation and stability of democratic governance. The reflections that the Commission proposes and promotes seek to strengthen its capacity and that of states to meet these challenges.

———————

***Preliminary Document of the Inter-American Court of Human Rights on the First Phase of the Process of Reflection on the Inter-American System for the Promotion and Protection of Human Rights Pursuant to Resolution* AG/RES. 2030** (XXXIV–O/04) Permanent Council Of The OAS Committee On Juridical And Political Affairs, OEA/Ser.G, CP/CAJP–2227/04 add. 2, 25 May 2005.

In his remarks to the OAS Committee on Juridical and Political Affairs on March 11, 2004, in connection with the presentation of the Report on the Activities of the Inter-American Court of Human Rights, the President of that Court said that he thought it appropriate "to embark on a broad process of reflection shared among the following participants, with each contributing its own perspective: the organs of the OAS, the Court and the Commission, the states, the Inter-American Institute of Human Rights, civil society institutions and groups, outside observers, and academics."

. . . .

THE NEED FOR MORE FUNDING IN VIEW OF THE INCREASE IN THE VOLUME OF LITIGATION AND THE NUMBER OF ADVISORY OPINIONS AND PROVISIONAL MEASURES

As expected and noted on a number of occasions, there has been a substantial increase in the number of lawsuits brought before the Court. In 2004, there were 12 new petitions.[2] In the first two months of 2005, six new petitions were submitted.[3] It is also indicative of a trend that the 27 cases brought before the Court in 2003–2004 were equal to the sum of all cases presented in 1997, 1998, 1999, 2000, 2001, and 2002.

In other areas of the Court's judicial activities, the workload has also increased. In 2004, there were two requests for advisory opinions.[4] That same year, the Court

---

[2] Cases: *Huilca Tecse* v. Peru, *"Pueblo Bello"* v. Colombia, *Gutiérrez Soler* v. Colombia, *Palamara Iribarne* v. Chile, *García Asto and Ramírez Rojas* v. Peru, *Blanco Romero and others* v. Venezuela, *Ituango* v. Colombia, *Juárez Cruzzat and others* v. Peru, *Fermín Ramírez* v. Guatemala, *Gómez Palomino* v. Peru, *Raxcacó Reyes* v. Guatemala, and Ximenes Lopes v. Brazil.

[3] Cases: *Nogueira de Carvalho* v. Brazil, *Servellón García and others* v. Honduras, *"Dismissed workers in Congress"* v. Peru, *Sawhoyamaxa Community* v. Paraguay, *Baldeón García* v. Peru, and *Aranguren Montero and others* v. Venezuela.

[4] The first was presented by the Inter-American Commission on Human Rights on April 20, 2004 (OC-20) and refers to legislative and other measures that deny persons condemned to death access to judicial remedy or other effective resource to challenge imposition of the death penalty under certain circumstances. The other request for an Advisory Opinion was filed by Costa Rica at the end of last year and refers to "determining the compatibility of Article 9.e of the Law on Legislative Assembly Personnel (Law No. 4556 of May 8, 1970) and Article 13 of the Law on Constitutional Jurisdiction (Law No. 7135 of October 19, 1989) with the American Convention on Human Rights and other instruments on the subject." The legal basis for

adopted 12 new provisional measures and dismissed one such request.[5] On three occasions, it also expanded various measures that had previously been adopted.[6] This means that there was an increase of over 100 percent vis-à-vis 2003, or, in other words, that the number of provisional measure matters settled was equal to the sum of all those resolved in 2002 and 2003, combined. Furthermore, in 2004, the Court held 25 percent more public hearings.

These data are key to any discussion of the present and future role of the inter-American system for the protection of human rights. There are various explanations for the increase in the workload. They include, in our view, growing expectations as to what the Inter-American Court can provide, now that it is better known (although much remains to be done in that respect); the inclusion of issues bordering on—or directly associated with—social, economic, and cultural rights; and the amendments made to the Rules of Procedure of the Court and the Commission, especially the latter. Everything suggests that the current trend of an increasing judicial workload will continue at an even quicker pace in the future.

The expansion of the workload is not being met by a matching and systematic provision of regular funds to finance, *inter alia*, an extension of the Court's sessions, the possibility of the judge—rapporteurs moving to San José a few days prior to the full court to prepare the draft judgments the latter will have at its disposal (all of which is intended to keep alive the idea of the Court meeting in permanent session at its Seat, as soon as circumstances permit, with full-time judges to attend in a timely manner to the increasing demand for its judicial services), and the hiring of legal support personnel. All these are essential if the Court is to handle, with a reasonable chance of success, the extraordinary—but expected-increase in its workload. It is perhaps worth recalling that the amendments to the Rules of Procedure formed part of a package of measures, which were to be matched by the corresponding budgetary facilities, an outcome that has yet to materialize.

The regular budget, covered by the Organization of American States, has remained unchanged in recent years and in some of them even declined in nominal terms, not to mention what happened in real terms.[7] In 2005, that budget amounts to a little under US$1,400,000. That is the—clearly insufficient-sum we can and must use to plan short and medium-term activities. As the Acting Secretary Gen-

---

this request is currently being analyzed. In 2004, the Court also processed the request for Advisory Opinion OC-19 presented by the Bolivarian Republic of Venezuela toward the end of 2003.

5 In 2004, the Court adopted 12 new provisional measures, in the following cases: *Gómez Paquiyauri* in respect of Peru; *Pueblo Indígena Kankuamo* in respect of Colombia; *Comunidad Sarayaku* in respect of Ecuador; *The 'El Nacional' and 'Así es la Noticia' Newspapers* in respect of Venezuela; *Carlos Nieto Palma and others* in respect of Venezuela; *19 Traders (Sandra Belinda Montero Fuentes and others)* in respect of Colombia; *the 'Globovisión' television station* in respect of Venezuela; *the Plan de Sánchez Massacre (Salvador Jerónimo and others)* in respect of Guatemala; *Raxcacó Reyes and others* in respect of Guatemala; *Boyce and Joseph* in respect of Barbados; *Eloisa Barrios and others* in respect of Venezuela; *Penitentiaries of Mendoza* in respect of Argentina; and *Fermín Ramírez* in respect of Guatemala (urgent measures). In addition, one request for provisional measures was dismissed in the case of *Acevedo Jaramillo and others* in respect of Peru.

6 The Court issued three resolutions extending provisional measures n the following cases: *Urso Branco Prison in* respect of Brazil; *Luisiana Ríos and others (Radio Caracas Televisión—RCTV)* in respect of Venezuela; and *Communities of Jiguamiandó and Curbarado* in respect of Colombia.

7 In 2002, the Court's budget was US$1,354,700; in 2003, US$1,395,036; in 2004, US$1,391,300; and in 2005: US$1,391,300.

eral of the Organization recently said, the inter-American system for the protection of human rights is "underfunded."[8]

There is other revenue contributed by a few countries, which we thank for their solidarity, and by a number of institutions, several of which do not form part of the Americas, which we should also like to thank. The former comprise contributions from Costa Rica (a traditional donor), Mexico, Brazil, and Paraguay. Institutions contributing are the European Union, the Inter-American Development Bank, and the Office of the United Nations High Commissioner for Refugees. However, these are contingent contributions, often made on a one—off basis and for specific programs. Therefore, they cannot be relied on for proper scheduling of the Court's overall activities. Moreover, depending on the occasionally manifested good will of third parties renders inter-American jurisdiction highly vulnerable.

I need not even mention what has happened—or rather not happened—with the judges' remunerations in the past 10–15 years, which are not even remotely comparable to those received by others working for our Organization, who are also paid on the basis of the number of days worked. Here, we should pause to reflect and clarify. It is said that the Inter-American Court does not operate full time. That statement is not, strictly speaking, true. The judges of the Court study cases and prepare drafts in their own countries, while the Secretariat performs its responsibilities uninterruptedly at the seat of the Court in San José. Consequently, the jurisdictional work is continuous, even when the Court itself, as a full court of judges, meets for four or five sessions over the course of the year to conduct hearings and deliberations, and to hand down judgments and other resolutions requiring the presence and participation of all those making up the collegial body.

We are therefore faced with a structural problem that will affect the work of the human rights protection system increasingly in the coming years and, indeed, in the coming months. We trust that the competent organs with regard to this matter will consider the state in which the inter-American system of human rights finds itself today and its possible deterioration in the near future. . . .

In light of the above, any move to strengthen the inter-American system of human rights must begin by endowing its organs with sufficient financial resources; otherwise such initiatives could come to a standstill.

. . . .

COMPLIANCE WITH THE JUDGMENTS AND DECISIONS OF THE COURT

The Court cannot ignore the issue of compliance with its resolutions, which is monitored through various supervisory acts, and is of immediate and direct concern to it. This is not only because such supervision is a faculty inherent in its jurisdictional functions, but also because the Court must comply with Article 65 of the American Convention, as indicated in resolution AG/RES. 2043 (XXXIV–O/04) of the General Assembly of the Organization, adopted on June 8, 2004. This precept precludes the Court omitting to take the steps needed to ascertain, for the purposes of that same provision, what happens to its decisions.

---

8 Remarks by the Acting Secretary General of the Organization of American States, Luigi R. Einaudi, on the state of the reorganization of the General Secretariat, at the regular meeting of the Permanent Council in Washington, D.C., on January 26, 2005.

In judgments on the merits and on reparation, the Court rules on the international liability of the State and orders, where appropriate, the corresponding reparation measures. The Convention provides for the duty to comply with the Court's decisions.

We consider that execution of the judgments is an integral part of the right to justice, in the widest sense of that term. If reparation or provisional measures to safeguard rights are not executed within countries, then, for all practical purposes, access to justice is being denied, thereby rendering the international jurisdiction established at the behest of states ineffective.

In the exercise of the powers inherent in its jurisdictional function, the Court observes or supervises enforcement of its judgments and compliance with the protection measures it orders in its provisional measures. In that way it is able to abide by the provisions of the Convention which require it to report to the Organization of American States, through the means contemplated in the Convention itself, on execution of its judgments. Therefore it is essential, in the logic of the system, for the Court to receive from states the information it needs, on the one hand, to certify access to justice and, on the other, to fulfill a mandate expressly assigned by the American Convention.

For the above-mentioned purposes, the Court receives information from states, which it forwards to the other parties to a proceeding for their observations. In that way, the Court is in a position to know the extent to which its resolutions have been enforced and to decide, therefore, either that the judgment has been executed and the case should be shelved, as being definitively settled, or that it is appropriate to urge a state that has not complied to do so, or that the time has come to report to the General Assembly of the Organization, pursuant to Article 65 of the American Convention.

Interest has long been shown in the ways in which the Court's decisions are executed and some progress has been made in analyzing them. We are not, of course, referring to the executive nature of those decisions, which derives directly from the Pact of San José and the consequent commitment of states, and which applies to both the Court and justiciable issues. We allude, rather, to the consensual mechanism that could foster that compliance, in a way that might or might not resemble that found in European jurisdiction, and I invoke also the distinguished role of states as both protagonists and guarantors, at one and the same time, of the international protection of human rights.

Clearly, Article 65 of the Pact of San José addresses this issue. If the Court is to report to the OAS, it clearly first has to be informed about what it must account for. Now, without prejudice to that precept, and precisely to improve its modus operandi and make the inter-American jurisdiction created by the States more effective in practice, it remains highly important to examine the issue and find appropriate solutions.

The international mechanism that is eventually established will contribute to the desired solution. The rest will come from internal enforcement mechanisms in the measures that states adopt—or have adopted—to enhance the effectiveness of inter-

American jurisdictional decisions, which has to do with the content of those decisions and their timely enforcement.

The Court notes, with appreciation, the execution of its decisions in numerous instances. They have helped to shape amendments to laws—including some of the highest-ranking laws—the issuance of legal provisions, new directions in jurisprudence, regulatory changes, and new practices. All that needs to be underscored, because it testifies to the juridical and political will to improve the protection of human rights and strengthen the inter-American jurisdiction forged by the states through sovereign decisions in order to enhance that protection and honor the commitment undertaken in the Charter of the Organization of American States.

That said, there are still areas in which the Court's decisions have yet to be implemented. The Court cannot declare cases closed in which observance issues are still pending. Compliance with the resolutions of the Court constitutes fundamental proof that the system works.

. . . .

INCORPORATION OF INTERNATIONAL OBLIGATIONS AND OF THE JURISPRUDENCE OF THE COURT IN DOMESTIC LEGISLATION AND DISSEMINATION OF THE DECISIONS OF THE COURT

The Inter-American Court of Human Rights has developed abundant and diverse jurisprudence in matters such as the right to life, the right to humane treatment, due process of law, judicial protection, the right to property, persons deprived of liberty, freedom of expression, indigenous rights, migrant workers, and minors. Today this jurisprudence constitutes an important source for the effective exercise of and respect for human rights.

The true importance of an international jurisdiction, such as that exercised by this Inter-American Court does not stem solely from the solutions it finds for specific controversies, nor from its arguments on matters pertaining to the implementation of treaties and the compatibility of local laws with such treaties. That importance—which is another of the longings implicit in the decision taken by the states parties to the Organization and in the Convention—derives, above all, from the manner in which it influences domestic bodies of law and thereby the effective exercise and necessary spread of human rights in national communities. The Court's opinions have begun to find a plausible echo in domestic laws, the decisions of local courts, and in revised public policies. We have observed that and value it for all it is worth. Let us hope that this process is consolidated, widened, and perfected. To achieve this much-desired goal it is important to seek effective mechanisms to publicize the decisions of the Court on a wider scale.

Questions and Comments

1. What appear to be the concerns and goals of the two states that suggested topics for consideration? What does Venezuela mean when it refers to "dialogue" as a preferred method of work for the Commission?

2. Are the priorities and concerns of the Commission and the Court the same? Which among their topics is the most important?

3. Are there any problems with international human rights bodies accepting funding from outside sources? What, if any, precautions should be taken?

4. How do the problems of the Inter-American system differ from those arising in Europe? How are they similar?

C. Building the African System

Report of the Brainstorming Meeting on the African Commission on Human and Peoples' Rights (ACHPR), 9–10 May 2006, Banjul, The Gambia, Annex, 20th Annual Report of the Commission (2006).

INTRODUCTION:

1. The African Union Commission organized a two day brainstorming session on the African Commission on Human and Peoples' Rights (ACHPR) on 9–10 May 2006 in Banjul, the Gambia. The session brought together participants who included a representative of the government of the Republic of the Gambia, the Commissioner for Political Affairs of the African Union, members of the ACHPR, representatives of the Pan African Parliament, Permanent Representative Committee, members of staff of the Department for Political Affairs, the Acting Director for Administration of the AU, the Peace and Security Department, ECOSOCC, representatives of the OHCHR, UNHCR, the Chairperson of the Coordinating Bureau of National Human Rights Institutions, and Civil Society.

    . . . .

Item 1: The status, the mandate and the independence of the ACHPR

2. Discussions on the status, independence and impartiality of the ACHPR raised the following challenges:

    a) incompatibility of Members of the ACHPR in the context of Articles 31 and 38 of the African Charter;

    b) Some current Members of the ACHPR hold official positions in their respective State, thereby creating a perception of lack of independence.

    c) The effect of Assembly/AU/Decision 101(VI) on the preparation and publication of the Annual Activity reports under articles 59 (1) and (3) in relation to the mandate of the ACHPR under Article 45;

3. Constraints arising out of the insufficiency of resources that the African Union provides to the ACHPR for the discharging of its mandate under Article 41 of the Charter.

4. Some State Parties have accused the ACHPR of being too much dependent on donor funds thereby affecting its independence and credibility.

5. The ACHPR considers that the decision adopted by the Assembly of Heads of State and Government of the AU during the Khartoum Summit needs to be revisited, bearing in mind its impact on the publication of its decisions and resolutions under the terms of Article 59(1) of the Charter, and the independence of the ACHPR.

6. The current number of Members of the ACHPR is insufficient to adequately implement its mandate.

Recommendations:

a) In order to safeguard the independence and impartiality of ACHPR, State Parties should comply strictly to the AU Eligibility criteria on the nomination of candidates and election of members of the ACHPR, and not elect candidates holding portfolios and positions that might impede their independence as Members of the ACHPR.

b) The AU criteria shall apply to members of the ACHPR, whose status shall change after their election.

c) The AU should provide adequate funding to the ACHPR for it to successfully discharge its mandate.

d) Extra budgetary resources allocated to the ACHPR for its activities should be channelled through the African Union Commission.

e) The number of members of the ACHPR should be increased from 11 to between 15 or 18 in order to enable the institution efficiently discharge its mandate.

f) The ACHPR should attend the budgetary meetings of the AU in order to present and defend its budget.

g) The AU Commission should ensure that the ACHPR takes part effectively in the meetings of the policy organs of the AU bearing in mind the AHG/AU 2003 decision in Maputo recognised its status as an organ of the AU.

h) The ACHPR should submit to the AU Commission its opinion on the interpretation of Article 59 (1) of the Charter concerning the publications of its reports.

i) The ACHPR requests that the Executive Council of Ministers recommends the AHG/AU to revisit its decision adopted in Khartoum as far as it concerns activities of the ACHPR that do not fall within the scope of protection mandate of the ACHPR.

Item 2: Reports on the work of the ACHPR:

7. The meeting discussed the presentation on the Evaluation Report, the Addis Ababa Retreat report and the Uppsala conference Report, which identified challenges to the efficient functioning of the ACHPR since its inception

Challenges:

8. The ACHPR has barely 30 days in a year to reflect on a lot of issues relating to reports, communications and others. These constraints are critical to its efficiency.

9. There is a necessity to establish a follow up mechanism on the publication of the Annual Activity Reports of the ACHPR.

10. There is lack of visibility and lack of public awareness on the work of the ACHPR, due to lack of resources to publish the reports of the ACHPR.

11. Failure by States to comply with requests for adoption of provisional measures under communication procedure. The delay in States replies under the communications procedure has negative impact on the speed of consideration of the communication by the ACHPR.

12. There is insufficient expertise at the Secretariat, due to insufficient number of Legal Officers, to deal with communications.

13. States do not understand fully what is expected from them in their reports. Some do not comply with the requirement of Article 62.

14. Special mechanisms of the ACHPR have been doing a good work but are facing constraints of inadequate financial and administrative support, and the successful special mechanisms have been fully funded by donors.

15. The Strategic plan of the ACHPR comes to an end by December 2006 and it would be necessary to ensure that a new plan is prepared taking into account specific needs of the ACHPR within the broad framework of the AU Strategic Plan.

Recommendations:

a) States should appoint Focal Points, to deal with issues related to Human Rights.

b) The capacities of the Website of the ACHPR should be enhanced in order to ensure more visibility of its work. AU should allocate more resources to the ACHPR to enable it publish, disseminate ad publicise its reports.

c) The guidelines on State reporting should be made user friendly to enable State Parties to understand better what is required from them in their reports under Article 62 of the Charter. States should cooperate with NGOs and NHRI in the preparation of their reports.

d) The ACHPR should consider the human rights situation in States that do not comply with Article 62, with the information available.

e) The AU should consider a review of the Charter to render the submission and presentation of State reports under Article 62 from 2 years to 4 years.

Item 3: Administrative and financial matters and the construction of the Headquarters of the ACHPR

16. The meeting discussed the presentation on the administrative and financial situation of the Secretariat and the construction of the Headquarters of the ACHPR. A number of concerns were raised, particularly the delay in the recruitment of the Secretary to the ACHPR and its impact on the effective implementation of the mandate of the ACHPR. The participants regretted the situation affecting the staff of the Secretariat and urged the relevant authorities to address all issues affecting staff benefits and conditions of service.

Challenges:

17. Problems relating to adequacy of the budget, its preparation and presentation through the administrative and political organs of the AU.

18. The Secretary and staff of the Secretariat of the ACHPR are presently recruited by the AU Commission without due consideration of the Rules of Procedure of the ACHPR.

19. The position of Secretary to the ACHPR has been vacant over the past five months and this seriously affects the work of the Secretariat.

20. Only 2 Legal Officers are presently paid by the AU. 5 Legal Officers have always been paid from extra budgetary resources and the funding of these staff is running out by end of 2006.

21. The terms of service and conditions of work for the staff of the Secretariat are deplorable and do not always comply with the regulation in force. There is very low moral among the staff.

22. The functions of Administration and Finance Officer are presently discharged by one staff and this has implications as far as transparency in the management of resources is concerned.

23. The AU allocates USD 45000 for promotional missions per annum. This is enough to cover just 4 missions whereas at least 2 missions per Commissioner are necessary annually.

24. The DSA and honoraria paid to Commissioners since the inception of the ACHPR for their administrative expenses are not enough to cover the expenses they face.

25. When an activity of the ACHPR is undertaken in a country where a member of the ACHPR is resident, he takes part in those activities without receiving perdiem.

26. The AU allocates USD 200000 per ordinary session of the ACHPR, which is inadequate to cover the cost of conducting a session. The amount is short by USD 50000 for the costs of conducting the 2006 sessions. State Parties have not sufficiently hosted sessions of the ACHPR, thus imposing and additional burden on the Republic of The Gambia to host successive sessions.

27. The special mechanisms of the ACHPR function exclusively on extra budgetary resources.

28. The Gambia has not been able to construct the Headquarters of the ACHPR.

29. There is need to rationalise the efficacy of location of the ACHPR in relation to the AU Sirte Criteria for hosting African Union organs in view of the different locations for the Court. That should reflect the rational utilisation of resources for the sake of better promotion and protection of human rights.

30. Transparency and integrity should be the guiding principles in the management of the Secretariat. There should not be differences in salaries, terms and conditions of service for staff working at the same level.

Recommendations:

a) For the efficient functioning of the ACHPR, the Secretary to the ACHPR should be appointed without delay by the AU Commission in consultation with the Bureau of the ACHPR.

b) The authority of the AU Commission over the Secretary and staff of the Secretariat of the ACHPR should be exercised in consultation with the Bureau of the ACHPR.

c) The ACHPR shall submit to the PRC proposals to enable the recruitment by the AU Commission of more staff at the secretariat, including at least 11 Legal Officers and a Public Relation Officer. Recruitment of staff of the ACHPR should always be done in consultation with the Bureau of the ACHPR.

d) The AU Commission should allocate adequate resources, necessary for promotional and protection missions of the ACHPR, Special Mechanisms of the ACH-

PR after being presented and defended in the PRC and the Executive Council by the ACHPR Bureau.

e) The honorarium of the Members of the ACHPR should be raised. Honorarium should be paid to Members of the ACHPR when they participate in an activity of the ACHPR. At least half perdiem should be paid to members of the ACHPR who attend activities in countries where they reside.

f) The Chairperson of the ACHPR should be invited to present and defend the budget of the ACHPR at AU budgetary meetings.

g) Urgent steps must be taken to ensure that the functions of Finance and Administrative Officers at the ACHPR are separated.

h) The Government of the Republic of The Gambia should take appropriate steps to construct the Headquarters of the ACHPR.

i) The AU Commission should speed up the process of setting up of a Voluntary Fund on Human Rights to assist funding the activities of the ACHPR and other human Rights Institutions. The Fund should be managed by the AU Commission.

j) The Republic of The Gambia and the AU should review the Headquarters Agreement in line with the Sirte Criteria on the hosting of AU organs.

Item 4: Relationship between the ACHPR and its partners

31. The ACHPR described the cooperation it enjoys with its partners, namely the State Parties, the National Human Rights Institutions (NHRI), the international cooperating partners and the NGOs. Appreciation was expressed for the support received from partners, namely the OHCHR, the UNHCR, the ICRC, international development assistance agencies and NGOs, in the discharge of the mandate of the ACHPR, evolution of its jurisprudence and support for special mechanisms.

32. The ownership of the activities of the ACHPR was however emphasised. The meeting identified challenges experienced in relationship with partners.

State Parties

Challenges:

33. Need for State Parties to fulfil their financial obligations to the AU.

34. Certain State Parties do not grant the ACHPR authorisation to undertake missions in their countries.

35. There is no formal relation between the ACHPR and national Parliaments.

36. Certain State Parties do not accept to work with NGOs and do not facilitate the work of the NGOs.

37. Certain State Parties do not comply with the recommendations of the ACHPR and this impedes on the work of the ACHPR

Recommendations:

a) The ACHPR should explore the possibility of the Peace and Security Council of the AU (PSC) to enforce the decisions of the ACHPR within the framework of Article 19 of the PSC Protocol.

b) State Parties to favourably consider granting authorisation to requests from the ACHPR to visit their countries.

c) ACHPR should develop and execute an implementation plan for the follow up of their decisions, resolutions and recommendations.

d) State Parties should be encouraged to host sessions of the ACHPR, alternating with The Gambia in order to give visibility to the ACHPR and promote the African Charter.

e) State Parties should involve NHRI in the drafting of State reports at national level.

f) The ACHPR should reflect on ways and means to establish formal relationship with African national Parliaments in the human rights areas, including the domestication of human rights instruments.

National Human Rights Institutions (NHRI):

Challenges:

38. NHRI need to enhance the role of NHRI through their regular and active participation in ordinary sessions of the ACHPR.

39. NHRI enjoying affiliate status with the ACHPR, do not send reports to the ACHPR on a regular basis and do not fulfil their obligations under the Resolution on Affiliate status.

40. Lack of independence and autonomy by some NHRI and the problem of inadequate funding, which makes them inefficiency.

41. Lack of an appropriate forum between the NHRI and the ACHPR to exchange experiences.

Recommendations:

a) ACHPR should provide the NHRI with an enhanced affiliate status and establish a Focal Point in the Secretariat in order to communicate easily with NHRI

b) NHRI should endeavour to file shadow reports to the ACHPR and they should encourage their States to comply with recommendations of the ACHPR and the African Charter in general.

c) NHRI should be involved in the meetings of the ACHPR on a regular basis

d) NHRI should set up a Forum to reflect on their contribution to the work of the ACHPR.

Non Governmental Organisations (NGOs)

Challenges:

42. The information supplied by NGOs on human rights situation in African countries may, in certain cases, be inaccurate, and this affects the credibility of the work of the NGOs. Many NGOs do not comply with the principles of cooperation with the ACHPR

43. Many NGOs face the problem of the orientation imposed by donor on the financial assistance they grant them. Some State Parties also view NGOs funding of certain activities of the ACHPR as compromising the credibility of the ACHPR

44. Grave cases of violations of human rights in Africa are in certain cases done by powerful non state actors within and outside Africa, in particular violating economic, social and cultural rights.

45. There is need for the setting up of a triangular relationship between the ACHPR, NGOs and relevant AU organs.

46. Certain States do not cooperate with NGOs at national or international levels: Governments do not provide them with funding or information. Human rights activists are sometimes arrested for their activism.

47. NGOs are not involved in the drafting of State reports under Article 62 of the African Charter

Recommendations:

a) The ACHPR should enforce the existing provisions regarding its relations with NGOs and take appropriate action against those that do not comply with the said provisions.

b) NGOS should provide accurate information in their draft resolutions and the ACHPR should set up a verification mechanism to that extent

c) NGOs should assist in disseminating information on the work of the ACHPR

d) Organisations working in the promotion and protection of women rights should be encouraged to bring more communications before the ACHPR.

e) NGOs should work with the ACHPR to enhance mechanisms for the better protection of economic, social and cultural rights, and the rights of indigenous minorities in Africa.

f) The ACHPR should reflect with the AU Commission and NGOs on the setting up of a relationship between the three entities.

g) The ACHPR should address the human rights violations committed by non state actors including those based within and outside Africa.

International Cooperating partners:

Challenges:

48. More non African interns are funded by donors, which leads to development of non local talents.

49. The perception that donors impose conditions on the utilisation of the resources, which they grant the ACHPR, and NGOs in Africa.

50. There is need for better use of skills, experience and expertise of UN and other intergovernmental institutions to strengthen the capacity of the ACHPR and develop closer working relationship with the OHCHR.

Recommendations:

a) International partners should be encouraged to fund more African interns to the ACHPR, over and above those from outside Africa, so that Africa develops capacity and expertise.

b) The Bureau of the ACHPR should be fully involved in the process of soliciting for external funding by the Secretariat of the ACHPR and the execution of agreements with donors.

c) The ACHPR and AU should develop guidelines on donations to be received by the ACHPR and their utilisation.

d) The OHCHR should assist in fostering the cooperation between the Special mechanisms of the ACHPR and the UN.

Item 5: Relationships between the ACHPR and other UA organs and institutions:

51. The presentation highlighted the historical and legal basis upon which the ACHPR was requested to examine its relationship with the various organs and programmes of the AU. It also highlighted the areas of complementarity and the need for mutual engagement between the ACHPR and the various organs and programmes of the AU. The participants recognised the need to urgently establish cooperation among the various organs and programmes in order to avoid inefficient utilisation of scarce resources, duplication, mutual suspicion and lack of knowledge about the programmes, mandates and activities of the respective organs. They recalled their respective obligations to ensure the fulfilment of the objectives and principles provided for under the Constitutive Act of the AU. A number of practical recommendations were made to address these concerns.

Challenges:

52. The ACHPR is yet to finalise the item on its relationships between the other AU organs and institutions. As such, there are no formal relationship with the PAP, the ECOSOCC, the PSC, the African Court on Human and Peoples' Rights, the African Committee on the Rights and Welfare of the Child, the NEPAD, the CSSDCA/ CIDO, the Division on Refugees, IDPs and Humanitarian Affairs, as well as other relevant regional organisations.

53. There is need for a rationalisation of the utilisation of resources for the promotion and the protection of human rights in Africa.

54. There is need for regular interaction between the ACHPR and its partners, to reflect in a coordinated manner on the functioning of the African human rights system.

55. There is uncertainty relating to which category the decisions and recommendations of the ACHPR belong within the framework of the AHG/AU Decisions, (Directives, Declarations or Recommendations) and this causes problem as to the legal status and the implementation of the said decisions and recommendations.

Recommendations:

a) In order to ensure sustainable coordination of human rights activities discharged by different organs of the AU, cooperating partners shall assist the Department for Political Affairs of the AU Commission to built its capacity to coordinate the expanding scope of institutions dealing with human rights issues in Africa, by *inter alia* seconding and/or funding a post to that effect.

b) There is an overriding and urgent need for the ACHPR to initiate consultations with the organs of the AU, namely, the PAP, the PSC and the ECOSOCC, with a view to establishing modalities to formalise their relationship and develop common programmes.

c) The ACHPR should invite representatives from the above named organs to attend its sessions and vice versa, in order to reinforce mutual cooperation.

d) The OHCHR and other similar organisations as appropriate, should support the AU Commission to convene a donor conference to mobilise resources for the implementation of its Agenda on Democracy, Good Governance and the promotion and protection of human and peoples' rights.

e) The ACHPR, while reviewing its Rules of Procedure, should start consultations with the African Court on Human and Peoples' Rights, immediately after its operationalisation, in order to establish modalities of cooperation and consultation.

f) The ACHPR should establish formal relationship with the African Committee of Experts on the Rights and Welfare of the Child. This should be done in line with the necessity of rational utilisation of the resources for the promotion and protection in Africa.

g) The ACHPR and the APRM should formalise modalities of cooperation with the view to enabling the ACHPR participating in the APRM Review process, in order to ensure that all human rights and international humanitarian law indicators are taken in to account.

h) Focal Points should be appointed within regional organisations to enhance cooperation with the ACHPR in the area of human rights.

i) The AU Commission should enhance the cooperation already established between the Special Rapporteur on Refugees, IDPs and Asylum Seekers in Africa and the Division on Refugees, IDPs and Humanitarian Affairs of the AU. Similar arrangements should be developed between other special mechanisms of the ACHPR and relevant AU departments or organs.

j) The ACHPR should reflect on how to interact on a regular basis with its partners, on ways and means to enhance its work and relationship with other relevant organs.

k) The ACHPR should provide information on its work to all relevant AU organs including the PRC.

l) The AU Commission should clarify the legal status of the ACHPR decisions and recommendations, within the context of Rule 33 of the AHG/AU Rules of Procedure, in order to facilitate implementation of decisions of the ACHPR and respect of the African Charter.

m) The AU Commission shall facilitate briefing sessions on human rights once every two years or as the need arises to brief the members of the PRC and other relevant organs of the AU.

CONCLUSION:

56. All participants acknowledged the importance of the Brainstorming meeting and urged the AU to institutionalise a mechanism for dialogue among the various organs, institutions and programmes of the AU, every two years before the session of the ACHPR, in order to ensure that similar concerns are addressed in future.

57. The participants emphasized the need for the AU and the ACHPR to immediately finalize the process of recruiting the Secretary to the ACHPR so that the implementation of these recommendations are not delayed.

Questions and Comments

1. Do you agree with the proposals for strengthening the effectiveness of the African complaint procedure? Are there other reforms that also might be useful?

2. What obstacles do you see to achieving improvements in the three regional systems? Do these obstacles stem from a lack of political will or from a lack of capacity?

3. Do some of the same challenges exist in all three systems or does each system have unique issues? Are the priorities similar or different?

2. Human Rights in the Middle East and Asia

A. The Nascent Middle East System

The founding Charter of the League of Arab States adopted on March 22, 1945 does not mention human rights. See the Documentary Supplement. On September 12, 1966, the Council of the League of Arab States adopted its first resolution on human rights, calling for the establishment of a steering committee to elaborate a program for the celebration of Human Rights Year in 1968. The Committee recommended the establishment of a permanent Arab Committee on Human Rights and the convening of an Arab Conference on Human Rights. The latter was held in December 1968 in Beirut. See Mohamed Noman Galal, *The Arab Draft Charter for Human Rights*, in HUMAN RIGHTS: EGYPT AND THE ARAB WORLD 37 (17 Cairo Papers in Social Science, 1994). A larger organization of all Islamic states, the Islamic Conference, endorsed human rights in its 1972 Charter, reaffirming the commitment of Islamic states to the UN Charter and fundamental human rights. On August 5, 1990, a meeting of foreign ministers of the Conference member states adopted the Cairo Declaration on Human Rights in Islam. For an English translation of the Declaration, see UN GAOR, World Conf. On Hum. Rts., 4th Sess., Agenda item 5, U.N. Doc. A/CONF.157/PC/62/Add.18 (1993). For a critique of the Declaration, see Ann Elizabeth Mayer, *Universal Versus Islamic Human Rights: A Clash of Cultures or a Clash with a Construct?*, 15 MICH.J. INT'L L. 307 (1994). For background on the Islamic Conference, see Hassan Moinuddin, THE CHARTER OF THE ISLAMIC CONFERENCE AND LEGAL FRAMEWORK OF ECONOMIC COOPERATION AMONG ITS MEMBER STATES (1987).

The League of Arab States approved an Arab Charter on Human Rights on September 15, 1994, building on earlier texts adopted by regional non-governmental and inter-governmental organizations. The Charter requires acceptance by seven states before it will enter into force, and until it enters into force there are no regional institutions or procedures for monitoring human rights. The Charter foresees the election by states parties of a seven member independent Committee of experts to serve for three years with the possibility of a single re-election. Article 41 foresees periodic reporting by states and implies that the Committee may request a report by submitting inquiries to a state party. The Committee is to study the reports and distribute its own report to the Human Rights Committee of the Arab League. No other functions of either promotion or protection are specified in the Charter. For early background on the League and its human rights activities, see S. Marks, *La commission permanente arabe des droits de l'homme*, 3 REV. DROIT DE L'HOMME [HUM.RTS.J.] 101 (1970).

In its Resolution 6089 of 12 March 2001, the Council of the Arab League recommended that the Arab states accelerate the process for the signing and ratification of the 1994 Charter, which is still not in force. It emerged from the reaction of many Arab and international NGOs, that the 1994 Charter did not correspond to international standards for human rights and that it contained serious deficiencies. The Council of the Arab League subsequently adopted resolutions 6184 of 10 March 2002 and 6243 of 5 September 2002, providing for the revision and modernization of the Arab Charter on Human Rights. On 24 March 2003, the Council of the Arab League by Resolution 6032–129, encouraged the Permanent Arab Commission on Human Rights to "modernize" the Arab Charter on Human Rights. Amr Musa, Secretary General of the League, explained that the term "modernization" should be understood as the process to bring Charter provisions into compliance with international standards for human rights.

Mervat Rishmawi, *The Revised Arab Charter on Human Rights: A Step Forward?* 5 HUM. RTS. L. REV. 361–62 (2005).

The League of Arab States (Arab League) adopted a revised version of the Arab Charter on Human Rights (the Charter) in May 2004. Many of those who followed the revision process continue to debate whether the new version is consistent with international human rights standards and should be ratified or rejected. . . .

1. Background

The original Arab Charter on Human Rights . . . was widely criticized at the time by many human rights organizations both within the region and beyond as failing to meet international human rights standards, [yet] not one Arab League State was prepared to ratify it.

   . . . The revision of the Charter was part of an overall modernization package suggested by the SG and the Council to reform existing institutions and create new ones. These included an Arab Parliament, which would have the competence to further human rights, as well as to review legislation in Arab countries; and a Regional Security Council that would promote conflict prevention and resolution between Arab countries, as well as develop a strategy to maintain peace. The package also included the establishment of an Arab Court of Justice. The proposed statute of the Arab Court of Justice would give it competence regarding human rights issues, as well as in disputes related to principles of international law. Support for these proposals from amongst Arab States has generally been lacking and in its Summit in May 2004 the League, whilst welcoming the efforts and proposals of the SG, failed to adopt any of them. The only concrete reform to date has been the revision of the Charter.

   . . . .The redrafting process is, itself, worthy of note since it involved the Arab League, arguably for the first time, agreeing to be inclusive, by consulting outside experts and non-governmental organizations. In 2003 the Council instructed the Arab Standing Committee on Human Rights to "modernize the Arab Charter on Human Rights. . . ." The Committee produced an initial version that was largely inconsistent with international human rights standards. The Arab League, under pressure from NGOs and the [UN] Office of the High Commissioner for Human Rights (OHCHR) agreed to allow independent experts to prepare a new draft. The

OHCHR reached a bilateral agreement with the Arab League to assemble a group of 'independent Arab experts' as a Committee of Experts to carry out the task. All of the Committee's members, consisting of two women and three men from Algeria, Egypt, Qatar, Saudi Arabia and Tunisia, were drawn from the United Nations human rights treaty bodies. The Committee ... produced a draft in January 2004 for consideration by the Council. It was adopted by the Council without amendment and passed to the Summit of the League in May 2004 for consideration, which also adopted it without amendment.

2. The New Charter

.....[T]he version which was finally adopted in May 2004 is a major step forward from the 1994 version. It also marks a movement forward in developing governmental discourse on human rights in the region which will play a significant role in 'bringing human rights home.'

The Charter requires seven ratifications to enter into force. As of the beginning of June 2005, Jordan and Tunisia are the only states that have ratified it. Seven additional States have signed, including Saudi Arabia, Palestine, Bahrain, Algeria, Yemen and Egypt. . . .

By borrowing considerably from language contained in various international human rights treaties, the Charter includes many provisions that are largely consistent with the standards found in them. The instrument also reflects, to a certain degree, developments in international human rights jurisprudence. For example, it borrows from the expanded list of non-derogable rights developed in the Human Rights Committee's General Comment on Article 4 of the ICCPR. . . . The lack of a complaints mechanism as established in each of the other regional systems is a major constraint on guaranteeing effective access to justice for victims, especially as most Arab countries have yet to sign up to the UN complaints systems, although a number of them are subject to the complaints mechanism of the African Charter on Human and Peoples Rights.

. . . It should be noted that the Islamic religion is the only faith specifically mentioned in the Charter, with other regions merely meriting a general reference.

3. General Concerns

. . . The Charter attempts to create a new formula to address the historic and fundamental question of whether Islamic principles can be compatible with the universality of human rights. In a major step forward, the Charter does not refer to cultural, religious or other relativism. In its Preamble, it refers, on one hand, directly to international standards including those in the UN Charter, the UDHR, the ICCPR and the ICESCR and, on the other, to a document that is seen as a major compromise on human rights: the Cairo Declaration on Human Rights in Islam 1990. The Cairo Declaration, which is clearly grounded in Islam, stating in Article 20 that 'Islam is the religion of true unspoiled nature' has been widely criticized as a challenge to many aspects of human rights. For example, by permitting bodily harm to be inflicted for a Shari'ah prescribed reason it opens the door to torture, and cruel, inhuman or degrading punishment as well as the death penalty. It also includes provisions which undermine the rights and autonomy of women. . . .

Regrettably, this conservatism of the Cairo Declaration is actually reflected in some of the substantive provisions of the revised Charter [see e.g. Articles 8 and 26]. . . .

This approach is even more perplexing when one notes that Arab States do not have a uniform position on some of these issues, something which is reflected in the variance of ratification of international human rights treaties by these States. . . .It is disappointing that the Charter adopted the lowest common denominator rather than the most progressive interpretation. . . .

On a positive note, some of the Charter's language is directed towards universalism rather than relativism. The revised first Article declares that the aim of the Charter is '[t]o place human rights at the centre of the key national concerns of the Arab States' and that there is a need '[t]o entrench the principle that all human rights are universal, indivisible, interdependent and interrelated.' Whilst to the outsider versed in human rights discourse these might seem obvious points this is not necessarily the case among Arab States who have traditionally and systematically sought to challenge the universality of human rights. . . .

The Charter retains some of the strong language related to Zionism from its previous 1994 incarnation. This insistence on equating Zionism to racism echoes General Assembly Resolution 3379 (XXX) . . . [h]owever, this determination was revoked by the General Assembly in 1991. . . .

Whilst many provisions of the Charter are largely consistent with international standards, it suffers from two significant problems. Firstly, some of its key provisions are actually at variance with those standards. Secondly, there are many important rights and freedoms recognized in international human rights law that are missing from the Charter. This is despite the general provision in Article 43. . . .

Among the important standards that are missing from the Charter is the guarantee of an effective remedy for those whose rights and freedoms have been violated, as in Article 2(3) of the ICCPR. . . . There are many important rights of the child that are also missing. . . .Article 8(a) prohibits 'physical or psychological torture' and 'cruel, inhuman, degrading or humiliating treatment', but not punishment. It also fails to include a definition of 'torture.' Article 24 of the Arab Charter only grants the right to peaceful assembly and association to 'citizens', thereby excluding non-nationals, and Article 41(b) guarantees free basic and primary education only to 'citizens.' These provisions are inconsistent with the universal protection afforded by [global human rights treaties.]. . . .

5. Conclusion

The revised Arab Charter on Human Rights is a significant step forward from its predecessor. Arab States now have a document that they can own and take some pride in as a reaffirmation of their commitment to human rights—evidenced by the encouraging recent two ratifications, and the reasonable prospect that there will be further ratifications in the near future to bring the Charter into force. . . .However, while the Charter is largely consistent with international law, it remains a missed opportunity to be totally up to date and to achieve the SG and Council's unconditional aim of 'bringing Charter provisions into compliance with international standards for human rights.' Over time the fundamental defects of the Charter must be addressed through revision and the addition of optional protocols.

B. Asia

In Asia, no human rights system exists, despite efforts by non-governmental organizations and the United Nations to create one. One of the early regional efforts in Asia resulted in a 1983 document entitled The Declaration of Basic Duties of ASEAN Peoples and Governments. LAWASIA, a regional non-governmental organization, and the ASEAN Law Association, have supported the creation of a regional human rights mechanism. The United Nations Center for Human Rights has sponsored a series of government workshops (1990–Manila, 1993–Jakarta, 1995–Seoul, 1996–Kathmandu, 1997–Amman, and 1998–Teheran) for officials from countries in the Asia-Pacific region. See e.g. United Nations, *Fourth Workshop on Regional Human Rights Arrangements in the Asian and Pacific Region*, HR/PUB/96/3 (1996).

In 1993, over one-hundred Asia-Pacific non-governmental organizations adopted an Asia-Pacific Declaration of Human Rights supporting the universality of human rights and the creation of a regional system. Governments have been slow to respond. At a 1996 UN-sponsored workshop on the issue, the thirty participating governments[9] concluded that it was premature, at the current stage, to discuss specific arrangements relating to the setting up of a formal human rights mechanism in the Asian and Pacific region, although they agreed to explore the options available and the process necessary for establishing a regional mechanism.[10]

There are many hurdles to creating an Asian-Pacific regional system. First, there is far greater diversity of language, culture, legal systems, religious traditions, and history in the Asia-Pacific region than in other regions of the world. Second, the geographical limits of the region are unclear but vast. The Asian members of the UN Human Rights Commission have included not only China, Japan, the Philippines and Indonesia, but India, Pakistan, and Cyprus. The UN lists forty countries in the region. See E/CN.4/1998/50 at 10 (1998). These two factors suggest that the region may be better served by sub-regional mechanisms which could be more

---

[9] Afghanistan, Australia, Bangladesh, Bhutan, China, Democratic People's Republic of Korea, Fiji, India, Indonesia, Iran, Iraq, Japan, Jordan, Malaysia, Maldives, Micronesia, Myanmar, Nepal, New Zealand, Papua New Guinea, Philippines, Republic of Korea, Saudi Arabia, Singapore, Solomon Island, Sri Lanka, Syrian Arab Republic, Thailand, United Arab Emirates and Vietnam.

[10] The rejection of a regional system continued at the 1997 and 1998 regional meetings. At the 1997 meeting in Amman, participants agreed on incremental steps, some of which are positive, others seemingly intended to slow implementation of human rights in the region. The steps include ratification of human rights instruments, the promotion of national institutions, the recognition of non-governmental organizations and the role of civil society, promotion of the right to development, advocacy against human rights conditionality, attention to vulnerable groups, support for universality "objectivity and non-selectivity of human rights, more technical cooperation, information sharing, capacity-building, and programs for regional cooperation. C. Dias, "From Building Blocks to Next Steps: The Task Ahead at Teheran, background paper for the Sixth Workshop on Regional Arrangements for the Promotion and Protection of Human Rights in the Asian and Pacific Region (1998).

quickly and easily developed because of the closer ties of states in smaller areas of geographic proximity.[11]

A third factor hindering the development of a regional system is that governments in the region have been unwilling in general to ratify human rights instruments. Among the thirty Asian countries that participated in the 1996 workshop, only Australia, Nepal, New Zealand, the Philippines and the Republic of Korea have ratified both Covenants and the Optional Protocol on individual communications. As of March, 1998, twenty-seven states in the region, including virtually all the Pacific island states, had not signed or ratified either of the UN Covenants or the Torture Convention: Bahrain, Bangladesh, Bhutan, Brunei, Comoros, Cook Islands, Fiji, Indonesia, Laos, Malaysia, Maldives, Marshall Islands, Micronesia, Myanmar, Nauru, Niue, Oman, Pakistan, Palau, Papua New Guinea, Qatar, Samoa, Singapore, Tonga, Tuvalu, United Arab Emirates, and Vanuatu.

The general reluctance to accept human rights treaty obligations makes it unlikely that an effective regional system can garner widespread support in the near future. Finally, the recent economic crisis in Asia has put additional pressures on governments trying to survive in the wake of growing unrest. The crisis creates a risk of repression in the short term. Asian values may become even more a tool of some authoritarian regimes to suppress individual rights, especially freedom of expression and association which are at the heart of democratic aspirations.[12]

On the other hand, the regional economic and political crisis in the 1990s led many to question the concept of Asian values as a means to progress. Political movements and non-governmental organizations renewed efforts to ensure greater respect for human rights in the region. If the economic justification often given for limiting civil and political rights disappears, the opportunity to create a regional system may improve quickly and dramatically, as it did in Central and Eastern Europe. The following readings explore the possibilities and hurdles to creating an Asian human rights system or systems.

Randall Peerenboom, *Beyond Universalism and Relativism: The Evolving Debates About 'Values In Asia,'* 14 IND. INT'L & COMP. L. REV. 1, 2–5, 22–24, 35–36, 48, 52–53, 56–57, 64–67, 69–70 (2003) (extracts, footnotes omitted).

... The first round of the Asian-values debates began with the provocative remarks of Lee Kuan Yew and Mahathir Mohammed, gained geopolitical support from China's issuance of its White Paper on Human Rights in 1991, and reached its apogee with the issuance the 1993 Bangkok Declaration, the political manifesto for round one. While a wide range of issues was discussed, the first round had two main,

---

11 ASEAN member states created working groups for a human rights mechanism. In 1997, members met in Kuala Lumpur and adopted conclusions supporting the development of a regional human rights mechanism including the possibility of drafting an ASEAN Convention on Human Rights. According to UN classifications, the Arab Charter, discussed *supra*, represents an Asian regional instrument.

12 Vitit Muntabhorn, *Protection of Human Rights in Asia and the Pacific: Think Universal, Act Regional?* in COLLECTION OF LECTURES, TWENTY-NINTH STUDY SESSION, INTERNATIONAL INSTITUTE OF HUMAN RIGHTS 1 (1998). According to the author, "Asian values" are now seen as comprising "profligate expenditure, over-borrowing, excessive investment in the real estate sector, inadequate regulation, and an admixture of vested interests and cronyism." He argues that this could be a blessing in disguise because it enables the region to question the legitimacy of the region's economic and political bases. *Id.* at 3.

related, but nonetheless distinct, focal points. The first area of contention was human rights, especially the issue of universalism versus relativism, but also including other issues such as the priority of rights and the compatibility of Confucianism, Buddhism, and Islam with democracy and human rights. The other main area of contention was economics: in particular whether authoritarian or democratic regimes are better able to achieve sustained economic growth and whether Asian versions of capitalism are superior to the varieties of capitalism found in Western liberal democracies. Despite the attempts of some scholars to discuss the issues in an even-handed and nuanced fashion, the first round of debates was heavily politicized and suffered from excessive abstraction and the lack of a solid empirical foundation for many of the sweeping claims made by both sides. . . .

[O]ne of the main issues in the second round has been whether there is sufficient common ground within Asia with respect to values, human rights, and economic issues for the term "Asian values" to be useful or whether we should move beyond Asian values. This issue was raised by opponents of Asian values in the first round, but it has now become more central, with the discussion more focused and mutually engaged; rather than talking past each other, both sides are critically examining the arguments for and against invoking Asian values. In addition, there has been a transition in the second round from the concern about whether indigenous traditions, particularly Confucianism, are compatible with the hallmarks of modernity-capitalism, democracy, rule of law, and human rights—to the acknowledgement or stipulation that they simply must be if they are to be relevant, and thus they must adapt or be adapted accordingly. Therefore, the focus has shifted to articulating Confucian or other Asian variants of capitalism, democracy, rule of law, and human rights, rather than radical alternatives to them. In the process, scholars have begun to pay greater attention to economic, political, and legal institutions and practices. With this shift toward more concrete situations, the futility of abstract discussions of universalism versus relativism has become even more apparent. . . .

[S]ome Asian governments argue that the hard core of universal rights is extremely limited. To be sure, there is little disagreement that some acts are bad, such as torture, disappearances, genocide and slavery. However, little disagreement does not mean no disagreement, even in these seemingly uncontroversial cases. . . . Does torture include mental suffering and degrading treatment? Is interrogation for six consecutive hours in a heavily air-conditioned room torture? How about twelve hours? Twenty-four hours? Forty-eight hours? Is caning, as allowed in Singapore and previously in Europe, but now prohibited by the ECHR, cruel and unusual punishment? Is cutting off the hand of a thief cruel and unusual punishment? What about capital punishment? Is incarceration for long periods in prisons where convicts may be subject to rape or violence from other prisoners, as occurs in United States prisons, cruel and unusual? Is it cruel and unusual to keep people waiting on death row for more than five years? Two years? One year? Does it matter if the reason for delay is that the legal representatives for the inmate keep appealing? Of course, even assuming an overlapping consensus with respect to the meaning and reprehensibility of torture and cruel and unusual punishment (would anyone deny that being shocked with cattle prods or burnt with cigarettes is torture?), in practice torture and cruel and unusual punishments remain widespread and not just confined to Asian countries. Granted, states often deny the existence of torture or claim that it is not sanctioned by the state and that the state actors who commit torture are prosecuted and punished. However, in many cases, there is little enforcement, and few are subject to prosecution.

Other human rights issues are even more contentious. One of the main criticisms of Asian governments is that they invoke a cultural preference for stability over freedom to justify broad national security laws, extensive limitations of civil and political rights, and the derogation of criminal procedure and due process rights. There is no doubt that in some cases Asian governments do exaggerate the threat to national security and social order, and that many security laws are broadly drafted and kept on the books even after the threat for which they were created no longer exists. For instance, in Singapore, the Internal Security Act, inherited from the British and justified initially to prevent communist agitation, remains in effect, thereby allowing police to arrest and detain, without trial, anyone deemed to be "acting in a manner prejudicial to the security of Singapore." Yet it is also true that many Asian states are less stable than mature Western liberal democracies. Moreover, while human rights may be destabilizing everywhere, they may be more destabilizing in Asia. In China, for instance, the ruling regime has yet to develop political institutions for adequately addressing human rights claims. Nor is there a reasonably coherent theoretical framework that incorporates rights and yet is consistent with the regime's norms. It also appears the majority of citizens in different countries assign a different value to stability and order versus freedom. . . .

While hardcore universalists would simply reject local traditions when in conflict, others have sought to reconcile rights with local traditions, a strategy that has been only partially successful. One approach has focused on interpretive strategies. Passages that are seemingly antithetical to rights are limited to their historical context. One seeks to show how passages must be reinterpreted, given different conditions today, to achieve the intended purpose of the text as a whole, which itself may be reinterpreted in terms of today's circumstances and more general principles found in the text. Another typical approach has been to search traditional texts and practices for analogues to modern rights or indigenous values similar to the values that underwrite contemporary human rights, and then to argue that there were, or at least could be, Confucian rights, Buddhist rights, and so on. . . .

. . . [L]ocal circumstances, including cultural beliefs, philosophical and religious traditions, the level of economic development, and the nature and level of development of political and legal institutions are clearly relevant with respect to the implementation of human rights. Rights advocates have learned that implementation is easier and more effective when supported by local traditions, as confirmed by the experience of women's rights groups in Malaysia and Indonesia that have made considerable progress in their daily battles by working within their religious and cultural traditions.

In general, laws that are not in accord with the values of a particular society will be difficult to enforce. Thus, if only for purely strategic or instrumental reasons, culture, traditions, and values do matter.

Apart from strategic considerations, the implementation of rights is relative to local conditions in the legal sense that a country's obligations are in some cases tied to the level of economic development. The International Covenant on Economic, Social, and Cultural Rights requires states to use all appropriate means (which are not defined) to the maximum of available resources (which will depend on how each country prioritizes its needs and apportions spending on national defense and the military as opposed to social services and other normal government expenses) with a view to progressively achieving its obligations (over some undefined time period). More generally, all rights may be restricted in some circumstances. Thus, all rights will depend on local conditions. International human rights bodies, regional courts such as the ECHR, and domestic courts have a number of doctrinal and interpretive tools at their disposal to accommodate diversity in local circumstances. Such tools include vague phrases in limitation clauses such as "necessary in a democratic society" and the doctrines of proportionality, appropriateness, reasonableness, and legitimate government aim that are used in interpreting such clauses.

. . . Although human rights are part of an international legal framework, the first round of debates made little reference to international law, other than superficial appeals to the Universal Declaration of Human Rights and other treaties for broad statements of human rights principles. There were few concrete studies of international human rights jurisprudence or case law, of how international human rights bodies have sought to achieve their objectives in promoting human rights, of how Asian countries have worked with and in some cases resisted international human rights bodies, or of how the international human rights regime interacts with domestic legal regimes. Nor were there many comparative, empirical, or historical legal studies of rights issues. In contrast, recent articles and books have addressed such issues as the rights of indigenous peoples under international law, developments in the area of women rights at the 1993 Conference in Vienna and the 1995 World Conference on Women and their implications for international law, China's efforts to resist being censured in Geneva, and Japan's use of aid to promote democratization and human rights. Many of these studies emphasize the limits of international law to solve human rights issues and the important role of politics. In some cases, political scientists have appealed to the political science and international relations literature to shed light on governments' rights policies and actions in terms of more generally applicable theories of realism, constructivism and liberalism (as the last term is used in international relations theory, i.e., to refer to the impact of domestic politics and constituencies on a state's international policies). . . .

Invoked to counter the universalism of the human rights movement, "Asian values" was a natural outgrowth of the growing importance of the movement. As the international human rights regime grew in power and started to have some real bite, it was inevitable that it would give rise to a reaction by those bitten. Asian countries began to feel the bite in the late 1980s and early 1990s, when they increasingly became subject to growing public censure. China in particular needed to defend itself after the crackdown in Tiananmen. Its 1991 Human Rights "White Paper" included many of the main points that would come to define the first round: the claim that although some rights are universal, their interpretation and implementation depends on local circumstances, including the level of economic development, cultural practices and fundamental values that are not the same in all countries; the argument that subsistence is the main right and the main problem is poverty, which Western developed countries should do more to address; the complaint of the Western bias of the international human rights movement and its excessive emphasis on civil and political rights and the individual at the expense of the community and collective; the criticism of the hypocrisy of Western imperialists who were guilty of human rights violations in Asia and continue to have their problems at home today; the defense of the importance of sovereignty and the need to avoid strong-arm rights politics; and the plea to discuss human rights based on a principle of mutual respect. Lee Kuan Yew, for his part, emphasized the need for a strong government to ensure economic growth and social order. Moreover, whereas China did not couch its arguments in terms of Asian values, Lee expanded (perhaps over-expanded) his claims beyond Singapore to Asia more broadly. As the leader of a small city-state, Lee may have needed to cast his arguments as part of a broad-based movement to be taken seriously. Thus, his sometimes overstated arguments may have been a calculated strategy to drum up regional support against Western liberal democracy and the increasing role of largely Western-dominated international human rights and financial institutions.

. . . The next round is likely to continue the trend of the second round to move beyond universalism and relativism by focusing on particular legal issues, politics, and sociological studies. In light of the heavily politicized nature of the first round, many have called for greater attention to discourse contexts and the different purposes and agendas of the participants. It may be any discussion of Asian values will be politicized to some extent, but some contexts are much more politicized than others. Cultural and values claims may also play a greater role in some contexts than others. The next round could benefit from a closer look at the use of Asian values, and cultural arguments more generally, in different contexts. How do international courts treat cultural claims and arguments? What role do cultural claims and arguments play in bilateral and multilateral relationships? Does the role vary depending on the issue? What role do they play in regional legal and political regimes and in domestic affairs? What is the role of culture and values when domestic courts interpret and implement international human rights? How, where, when, and why do INGOs and NGOs invoke culture?

Vitit Muntarbhorn, Asia, Human Rights and the New Millennium: Time for a Regional Human Rights Charter?, 8 TRANSNAT'L L. & CONTEMP. PROBS. 407 (1998)

. . . [I]s there room for a regional Asian human rights instrument in the form of a treaty or charter? It is well known that, unlike Europe, the Americas, and Africa, there is no inter-governmental regional system for human rights protection in Asia. What are the possibilities at the turn of the new millennium?

Currently there exists an Asian Human Rights Charter in the form of a non-governmental declaration. In 1997, led by the non-governmental Asian Human Rights Commission based in Hong Kong, a number of Asian non-governmental organizations adopted this Charter as their position on human rights. It advocates the universality and indivisibility of human rights, and it underlines the need to expose the capacity of Asia in its human rights framework as follows:

Authoritarianism has in many States been raised to the level of national ideology, with the deprivation of the rights and freedoms of their citizens, which are denounced as foreign ideas inappropriate to the religious and cultural traditions of Asia. Instead, there is the exhortation of spurious theories of "Asian values," which are a thin disguise for their authoritarianism. Not surprisingly, Asia of all the major regions of the world, is without a regional official charter or other regional arrangements for the protection of rights and freedoms.

The Charter also advocates the need to be well-targeted:

[W]e must move from abstract formulations of rights to their concretization in the Asian context by examining the circumstances of specific groups whose situation is defined by massive violations of their rights. It is only by relating rights and their implementation to the specificity of the Asian situation that the enjoyment of rights will be facilitated.

In addition, the Charter supports not only human rights but also the goal of a sustainable environment. It highlights the right to life, the right to peace, the right to democracy, and the right to development. Indeed, it goes further than international standards by positing various rights which are not yet clearly found at the international level, thereby acting as an example of a regional approach that can help elevate international standards. This is exemplified by the Charter's advocacy of the right to cultural identity: "[t]he Asian traditions stress the importance of common cultural identities. Cultural identities help individuals and communities to cope with the pressures of economic and social change; they give meaning to life in a period of rapid transformation." However, those practices that conflict with universal principles of human rights are to be eliminated, e.g., gender discrimination and racial discrimination—including the caste system. Also, the Charter targets for complementary action the rights of vulnerable groups such as women, children, those with disabilities, those with AIDS, workers, students, prisoners, and detainees.

As concrete measures suggested for the Asian region, the Charter advocates the following:

a) strengthen the guarantees of human rights in national constitutions;
b) ratify international human rights instruments;
c) review domestic legislation and administrative practices for consistency with international standards;
d) maximize the role of the judiciary in enforcing human rights;
e) enable social organizations to litigate on behalf of the victims;
f) establish National Human Rights Commissions and other specialized institutions for human rights protection; and

g) recognize People's Tribunals which are not based on adjudication but which help to raise consciousness of people's problems based on moral and spiritual foundations.

Of course, the Charter is a far cry from the typical governmental position which, to date, has avoided concretizing an inter-governmental Asian or Asia—Pacific human rights charter.

There are various reasons for this reticence. First, there is the general paradoxical human rights situation referred to earlier which acts as a disincentive to a regional human rights mechanism. Second, Asia is probably too vast and heterogeneous for a single regional inter-governmental human rights mechanism. Third, there is a hesitation among Asian governments regarding the monitoring role that such a mechanism would imply. Fourth, these governments claim to prefer a non-confrontational approach; they shun the potential of a regional Pandora's box that would provide room for confronting the authorities and making them accountable to the people.

Despite such reticence and the improbability of an inter-governmental Asian human rights charter in the near future, however, a number of possibilities are open for human rights promotion and protection in the region. They vary from regional human rights-related activities to sub-regional initiatives.

Activities and Initiatives

A variety of human rights-related activities are acceptable to Asian governments, especially if they are supported by the United Nations (U.N.). With a view to promoting such activities, the U.N., for the past few years, has organized annual workshops targeted to the Asia-Pacific region. The most recent workshop took place in Teheran in 1998, the outcome of which suggests that Asia-Pacific governments are open to the possibility of the following U.N. supported human rights—related activities:

a) the development of national plans of action for the promotion and protection of human rights and the strengthening of national capacities;

b) human rights education;

c) the establishment of national institutions such as National Human Rights Commissions for the promotion and protection of human rights; and

d) strategies for the realization of the right to development and economic, social, and cultural rights.

The approach favored by the governments represented at the annual workshop is encapsulated in the term "building blocks," whereby a variety of activities are promoted for confidence—building in the region rather than jumping headlong into an inter-governmental human rights charter for the Asian or Asia-Pacific region.

In addition, at the sub-regional level there are various initiatives worldwide that suggest the possibility of an Asian human rights mechanism. The Association of Southeast Asian Nations (ASEAN), for example, is now considering the possibility of some kind of sub-regional human rights mechanism. A Working Group for an ASEAN Human Rights Mechanism was formed in 1997, with participants drawn from both the governmental and non-governmental sectors. At its most recent meeting in Bangkok in 1998 the Working Group adopted a policy initiative with the following recommendations targeted to ASEAN policy-makers:

a) promote human rights activities, especially to commemorate the 50th anniversary of the Universal Declaration of Human Rights in 1998;

b) evolve a dialogue between ASEAN and civil society for the promotion of human rights and for the eventual creation of a regional human rights commission;

c) form a task force to examine issues of form, substance, and procedure related to the possible emergence of an ASEAN human rights commission;

d) organize a regional conference to exchange views on the establishment of a regional human rights commission;

e) promote more programs to protect child rights and women's rights; and

f) call upon the ASEAN foreign ministers to propel the establishment of a regional human rights commission.

While some of the less democratic ASEAN countries are likely to repudiate the idea of an ASEAN human rights commission, a possible compromise may be to establish a commission whose mandate will cover only those ASEAN countries that agree to the initiative.

Another Asian sub-regional organization, the South Asian Association for Regional Cooperation (SAARC), home to South Asian countries, has various activities focused on the promotion of human rights. A decade for the promotion of the status of the girl-child and time-bound targets for poverty eradication is one example. While it has not yet espoused the idea of a sub-regional human rights charter, it is now moving towards a sub-regional agreement on the issue of human trafficking and the need to counter it.

At this juncture, one should note that, at the national level in Asia, a number of human rights mechanisms are emerging in the form of national human rights commissions or their equivalent. Independent national human rights commissions exist already in India, Indonesia, the Philippines, and Sri Lanka. Parliamentary human rights committees or commissions exist also in Cambodia and Thailand. Under Thailand's 1997 Constitution, a new independent national human rights commission is due to be established. These mechanisms are definitely a growth area and networking between them has become more substantial.

Given the foregoing, one may surmise that, irrespective of whether an inter-governmental Asian human rights charter is constituted in the near future, a variety of activities and initiatives are likely to evolve at the regional, sub-regional, and/ or national levels that can help promote and protect human rights in Asia. These include the following:

a) training, seminars and other national events in commemoration of the 50th Anniversary of the Universal Declaration of Human Rights;

b) follow-up of the Program of Action adopted by the 1993 Vienna World Conference on Human Rights, such as by means of more accession to, and implementation of, international human rights treaties;

c) implementation of the UN-backed Decade for Human Rights Education (1995–2004) by mainstreaming human rights education into both formal and non-formal education;

d) promotion of independent and pluralistic national human rights institutions such as national human rights commissions;

e) concretization of national human rights agendas to integrate human rights into national laws, policies, and programs;

f) guarantees for civil society to monitor against human rights abuses;

g) capacity—building of power groups, such as the police, not to abuse their power;

h) access to remedies,—e.g., more accessible courts, mobile facilities, hotlines, legal aid, and assistance—in the case of human rights violations;

i) promotion of an independent and transparent judiciary, and popular participation in the administration of justice and protection of human rights;

j) action to promote good governance in government and bureaucracy, such as by means of more public hearings and inquiries;

k) reform of undemocratic structures, laws, and policies;

l) adoption of more equitable programs to decentralize power and re-distribute resources to those in need;

m) greater attention for vulnerable groups such as women, children, migrant workers, minorities, and indigenous communities, and those with disabilities;

n) promotion of peace, sustainable development, and environmental protection in conjunction with human rights and democracy; and

o) encouragement of sub-regional mechanisms and activities for human rights protection that can ultimately pave the way to a regional Charter.

These components are a continual challenge for Asian as well as other regions. The question of whether or not one is moving progressively towards an inter-governmental Asian human rights charter cannot be truly answered unless Asia responds to this challenge comprehensively and holistically. An underlying imperative is that such regional or sub-regional developments will be legitimate only if they help to support or enrich, rather than undermine, international human rights standards and mechanisms.

Li-ann Thio, *Implementing Human Rights in Asean Countries: 'Promises to Keep and Miles to Go Before I Sleep'* 2 YALE HUM. RTS. & DEV. L.J. 1, 3–6, 8–9, 10–12, 25–26, 38, 60–64, 71–79, 82–83 (1999) (footnotes and section numbering omitted)

Human rights have not figured prominently on the agenda of the nine-member Association for Southeast Asian States (ASEAN) since its inception in 1967.[13] Rather, the pursuit of regional security and cooperative measures for promoting trade and economic development have been paramount ASEAN objectives. By insisting on a

---

13 [ASEAN was formed in August 1967 by five noncommunist Southeast Asian states of Indonesia, Thailand, the Philippines, Malaysia, and Singapore. Ed.]

strict separation between human rights policy and trade issues, ASEAN has marginalized human rights and has consistently opposed the use by foreign states or international organizations of economic or other forms of pressure to induce change in human rights practices. ASEAN member states display an antipathy towards critical scrutiny of their human rights records—for example, in reports from the United States Department of State or nongovernmental organizations (NGOs) like Amnesty International and Human Rights Watch. ASEAN's general response has been that this constitutes foreign intervention in domestic matters, which undermines state sovereignty and violates the sacred principle of nonintervention in internal affairs. Within the context of ASEAN itself, an emphasis on harmony, compromise and consensus in ordering interstate relations helps to preserve a fraternal silence with respect to the human rights violations of member states. ASEAN policy (or lack thereof) towards human rights has been one of reticence and nonengagement.

A sea change in ASEAN policy has, however, been discernible in the last decade of this century. Although a regional or subregional human rights regime such as those found in Europe, the Americas, and Africa remains conspicuous by its absence in Southeast Asia, there is a new, clear willingness on the part of ASEAN states to engage in human rights discourse, albeit on their own terms. The 1993 World Conference on Human Rights placed the spotlight on human rights as a matter of international concern. ASEAN states did not disavow the universal character of the idea of human rights nor the noble cause of promoting human dignity it espoused. They did, however, insist that the application and mode of implementing human rights fall within the realm of national competence, subject to particular economic, social, and cultural realities.

. . . Clearly, the disagreement by ASEAN states over the content and the manner of implementation of human rights norms, and the lack of enforcement machinery pose formidable obstacles to the advancement of human rights in this region. The ASEAN stance has served to highlight the difficulties of ensuring international accountability for governments' treatment of individuals and groups, while also taking the realities of cultural diversity seriously.

. . . In the national context, certain ASEAN states have made human rights a part of their national agendas. Both the Philippines and Indonesia have recently set up national human rights commissions, while the 1997 Thai constitution requires the establishment of such a commission by October 1999. A law to regulate the Thai human rights commission is currently in the process of being drafted. Both Indonesia and Thailand have, furthermore, announced national plans of action on human rights. Meanwhile, the Thai government has for the first time committed itself to the promotion and protection of democratic values and human rights in international fora, as Prime Minister Chavalit Yongchaiyudh declared in his 1997 foreign policy statement before parliament.

At the international level, individual ASEAN member states have displayed a greater openness to acceding to human rights conventions and have participated vigorously in human rights debates within United Nations fora. This may be seen as an unequivocal acceptance that human rights are a matter of legitimate international concern; how this concern should be expressed, however, is still open to question.

At the subregional level, ASEAN states have departed from previous practice by discussing the issue of human rights in formal meetings, albeit stressing that human rights are contingent upon the distinct economic and cultural conditions of the region. The seed of promise for advancing human rights within the institutional framework of ASEAN was planted in the 1993 Joint Communiqué issued at the Twenty-Sixth Annual Ministerial Meetings (AMM), held a month after the Vienna Human Rights Conference. In it, the ASEAN foreign ministers expressly affirmed the Vienna Declaration and agreed that 'ASEAN should coordinate a common approach on human rights and actively participate and contribute to the application, promotion and protection of human *5 rights.' They also stated that basic human rights violations could not be tolerated under any pretext and demanded that all governments should uphold humane standards and respect human dignity. Significantly, there was agreement that, in support of the Vienna Declaration, 'ASEAN should consider the establishment of an appropriate regional mechanism on human rights.' ASEAN parliamentarians reiterated this call for a regional human rights mechanism in October 1993, but government enthusiasm for the project later diminished. No concrete government proposal was made, nor was the issue featured in subsequent annual meetings of the foreign ministers. World attention was focused on human rights again in 1998, by the five-year implementation review of the Vienna Declaration and Program of Action and the fiftieth anniversary of the Universal Declaration of Human Rights (UDHR). In the 1998 Joint Communiqué, ASEAN ministers recalled their 1993 decision to consider establishing an appropriate regional human rights mechanism. Further, they acknowledged the efforts and dialogue conducted with a nongovernment initiative—the Working Group for an ASEAN Human Rights Mechanism—beginning in 1996. It remains uncertain whether this initiative will be consigned to the realm of rhetoric or translated into action.

In the author's opinion, attention and effort should be directed toward establishing such a subregional human rights regime, rather than an Asian regime. Indeed, given Asia's geographical breadth, lack of shared historical past (even from the colonial era), and its varied political ideologies, legal systems, cultural-religious traditions, and levels of economic development, 'Asia' is not a coherent unit. It would be a Herculean task to find consensus on human rights norms in this context. Transnational regimes must be founded upon shared values, since international institutions embody their creators' willingness to adopt a cooperative approach toward common concerns. ASEAN states largely lack such a common value system. Their post-colonial governments range from Islamic absolute monarchies to military juntas to secular presidential and parliamentary forms of democracy. Given, moreover, that East Asia lacks a political infrastructure akin to the Council of Europe, the Organization of American States, or the Organization of African Unity, associating a regional or subregional human rights system with ASEAN is more realistic. This would take advantage of the existing political infrastructure and, more importantly, the established practice of working together. What binds ASEAN states is a shared pragmatism and consensual ethos in interstate relations, as well as a staunch adherence to the cardinal principle of nonintervention in the internal affairs of member states, enshrined in Article 2(c) of the 1976 Treaty of Amity and Cooperation in Southeast Asia. Although ASEAN has historically treated human rights as a matter of domestic jurisdiction and state sovereignty, the possibility of establishing a subregional protective human rights mechanism represents a significant foothold and change in thinking that should be exploited.

The task of protecting human rights in the ASEAN context is twofold. On the one hand, an ASEAN Charter of Human Rights should be formulated with the widespread consultation and participation of state and non-state actors; its standards should be compatible with international norms. On the other, a subregional protective mechanism vested with monitoring powers, allowing individuals to report alleged human rights abuses to an independent forum, is needed within ASEAN. These subregional efforts must be complimented by human rights promotion through domestic procedures and active participation in the United Nations human rights regime at the global level. Such collective fostering of a human rights culture forms the substratum of any effort to advance human rights. . . .

ASEAN: An Ambivalence Towards Human Rights?

. . . There is no official, clear, or comprehensive ASEAN 'position' on human rights, and divergences exist among individual ASEAN countries. ASEAN ambivalence toward human rights has been manifested in practice by the attitude it has displayed and the causes it has selectively championed within the ASEAN region. This selectivity demonstrates the general politicized nature of human rights in international relations, in both individual countries and regional groupings. . . . While the Cambodian human rights issue has been a regular fixture on the ASEAN agenda since the Vietnamese invasion, the Indonesian invasion of East Timor in 1975 has barely been touched.

. . . At Vienna, the Singapore Foreign Minister Wong Kan Seng accepted that a 'core' group of universal rights existed—for example, the right to life, prohibition against torture, and other nonderogable rights found in the International Covenant of Civil and Political Rights (ICCPR). Nonetheless, he maintained that international consensus on what constituted 'core' rights was fragile, and that 'the hard core of rights that are truly universal is perhaps smaller than we sometimes like to pretend.' He advocated a pragmatic, clinical approach to strike a realistic balance between 'the ideal of universality and the reality of diversity.' As things stand, the scope of the 'core' remains contestable—for example, whether the right to development is an inalienable right, as maintained by many developing countries. Hence, outside the core—in the equivocal words of the 1993 Inter-Governmental Bangkok Declaration: [H]uman rights must be considered in the context of a dynamic and evolving process of international norm-setting, bearing in mind the significance of national and regional particularities and various historical, cultural and religious backgrounds.

The Vienna Declaration qualified this stance. While noting the significance of national and regional particularities, it stressed that 'it is the duty of States, regardless of their political, economic and cultural systems, to promote and protect all human rights and fundamental freedoms. '

... The Vienna Program of Action encouraged ratifications of U.N. human rights treaties, particularly of the Convention on the Rights of the Child, for which universal ratification was sought by 1995. Setting a time limit for a specific treaty seems to have worked well. Since Vienna, ASEAN countries that had not previously been party to any human rights treaties have displayed a significant change in practice. Singapore in 1995, for example, acceded to the CEDAW, the Child Convention, and the Genocide Convention. Undoubtedly, this type of move not only displays a degree of good will on the part of states that seek to advance human rights as part of their foreign policy. It also has a twin legitimating effect. Domestically, it signals to the citizenry that its government is not out of step with international mores (insofar as they are reflected by human rights) or that it is in fact 'liberalizing' and answering the call to accountability. Internationally, it illustrates a commitment to the international rule of law and a desire to further engage the United Nations regime as a responsible and active participant. . . .

A Question of Structure: Developments in Human Rights Architecture

Government initiatives in developing infrastructure for human rights protection in the ASEAN context have focused on the development of national institutions. The Commonwealth has been supportive of this and has held meetings to develop such national institutions. In July 1996, delegates from various Human Rights Commissions, including those from India, Indonesia, and New Zealand, met in Australia and decided to establish an informal Asia-Pacific Forum of National Human Rights Institutions. This was seen as a tangible and constructive step toward the establishment of longer-term regional human rights arrangements. The Australian government funded support services for three years. The Larrakia Declaration sets out the functions of this Forum. The United Nations is involved in establishing networks among national institutions, as it recognized that national institutions are positioned to ensure human rights protection at the national level. Furthermore, bilateral exchanges and coordination could aid the development of subregional human rights arrangements. The United Nations also holds regular workshops on the possibility of developing a regional human rights system in the Asia-Pacific region.

The Move Towards National Human Rights Commission: Domestic Initiatives

The Geneva Centre for Human Rights has arranged consultations on national human rights institutions. It released a statement of 'Principles relating to the Status and Functioning of National Institutions for the Protection and Promotion of Human Rights (Paris Principles).' The 1992 Commission on Human Rights endorsed this statement, as did the 1993 Vienna Conference. Paragraph 36 of the Vienna Declaration affirms the constructive and important role played by national institutions as part of the human rights architecture, recognizing each state's right 'to choose the framework that is best suited to its particular needs at the national level.'

ASEAN states have displayed a general distrust of supranational institutions. Paragraph 24 of the Bangkok Declaration states:

We welcome the important role played by national institutions in the genuine and constructive promotion of human rights, and believe that the conceptualisation and eventual establishment of such institutions are best left for the States to decide.

Promoting human rights by creating genuinely independent national bodies to document human rights violations would be less threatening to territorial sovereignty. Further, it would constitute a 'good practice', reflecting a willingness to translate human rights rhetoric into action. Naturally, these institutions must be structured and empowered in a manner that protects them from political pressures. To prevent them from being limp puppets in the hands of their creators, they should be constitutionally entrenched, rather than subject to legislative will. This will help commission members to discharge their duties freely without fear of offending the government of the day.

Six primary elements have been identified as necessary for the effective functioning of national institutions:

Independence in terms of legal, operational and financial autonomy and with respect to procedures governing the composition, appointment and dismissal of members. Although national institutions are state-funded entities, they must be able to rise above party politics to be real watchdogs.

A defined jurisdiction and adequate powers. These institutions are charged with promoting human rights—for example, through legislative review, receiving complaints from aggrieved individuals, serving as roving investigators into alleged gross human rights violations. They need sufficient powers to enable them to discharge their legislative mandate e.g. to call witnesses, to compel public officials to answer requests for information.

Accessibility in the sense of being physically accessible, also in terms of public awareness of the institution and whether its members represent all relevant social forces.

Developing avenues of co-operation with IGOs, NGOs and other national institutions. This broadens the institution's support base and enhances its visibility, besides opening up new sources of information about human rights abuses, expertise and technical support.

Operational efficiency in terms of working methods, having adequate resources.

Accountability both to the government, for example, through reporting obligations, as well as to its clients, for example, through conducting mandatory public evaluation of institutional activities and reporting the findings.

At present, only the Philippines and Indonesia have established national human rights institutions, while Thailand, in accordance with the requirements of the 1997 Thai Constitution, is currently drafting a law to create one. These national institutions are distinct from and complement existing constitutional mechanisms for human rights protection, such as the office of the ombudsman and judicial review.

The Philippines Commission on Human Rights (CHR) finds its constitutional basis in Section 17, Article XIII of the 1987 Philippines Constitution. This was drafted in the wake of the triumph of 'people power' over the authoritarian Marcos regime. Neither the executive nor Congress can summon or sack individual commissioners. Legal training is considered important insofar as Article 17(2) requires that the majority of the compact five-member Philippines Commission be members of the Bar.

In June 1993, the twenty-five member Indonesian National Human Commission on Human Rights was established by Presidential Decree No. 50. This was done to facilitate the development of a national atmosphere conducive to the exercise of human rights. It was meant to reflect Indonesia's commitment to the decisions and agreements reached during the 1993 Vienna world conference on human rights.

Despite doubts that this Commission could not function independently, particularly since it owes its existence to an executive order that can be rescinded at will, it has since taken on an active life of its own. Commission members who were initially appointed by the President are considered prominent national figures and include academics and former military officers. The commission's budget comes solely from the State Secretariat, which manages public funds. . . .

In conclusion, encouraging ASEAN countries to set up their own national human rights commissions is a worthwhile strategy, particularly since a local commission composed of independent experts cannot be accused of being a mouthpiece for foreign political interests. In addition to building an autonomous human rights culture that can be measured against international standards, such institutions could play a vital role in educating the people of their human rights as well as their responsibilities. They could provide a less threatening informal setting where grievances could be lodged and receive attention through nonadversarial means of dispute resolution. The establishment of national human rights institutions in the Philippines, Indonesia, and Thailand will hopefully inspire other ASEAN countries to adopt a similar approach. Malaysia seems to have been influenced by these developments. Indeed, Malaysian Foreign Minister Datuk Syed Hamid Albar noted them in his March 1999 announcement that a bill would be tabled in July to set up a National Commission on Human Rights. Whatever motives a detractor might allege for the establishment of these institutions, such as public relations, it must be remembered that institutions like Komnas Ham have a way of assuming a life of their own quite apart from the intention of their creators.

Towards a Regional Human Rights Mechanism?

The United Nations General Assembly has been promoting efforts to establish a regional human rights mechanism in regions lacking one since the late seventies. The United Nations Economic and Social Commission for Asia and the Pacific (ESCAP) is a depository for human rights materials. The Human Rights Commission has also issued numerous resolutions calling upon states to consider agreements to establish suitable regional human rights machinery.

Since the 1982 Colombo seminar organized by the Secretary General, the United Nations has sponsored six intergovernmental workshops on regional arrangements for human rights protection in the Asia-Pacific Region with the participation of ASEAN countries, various NGOs, and representatives of the various national human rights commissions. It has offered its advisory services and has conducted training courses. The concluding remarks of the 1992 Jakarta Workshop underscore that the primary responsibility for implementing human rights norms rests at the state level. As far as the international system of monitoring human rights is concerned, this should be done in a spirit of international cooperation, creatively, and constructively, and taking into account the diversity of the region. This evolutionary, step by step, or 'building blocks,' approach was affirmed at the 1993 Seoul Workshop. The first step would be coordinating human rights information dissemination, followed by an Asia Forum for a regional exchange of ideas and experiences. Only then should attention be shifted to using the Forum to design some form of regional or subregional human rights machinery.

A central principle for any regional arrangement was reiterated at the March 1998 Tehran workshop, namely that it must emerge from within the region after extensive consultation among the governments concerned. Further, any such arrangement must be determined by consensus and be based on the priorities and needs established by the Governments of the region, bearing in mind the region's diverse particularities. The workshop adopted a framework of regional technical cooperation in certain specified areas, but did not include any concrete proposals for developing regional human rights machinery. Rather, strengthening national human rights capacities was viewed as a necessary step toward further consideration of regional cooperation and even regional human rights arrangements. While an effective regional human rights mechanism was the long-term goal of the workshop, it was considered premature to discuss any formal arrangements. Instead, the immediate shift has been towards localized theme-specific domestic programs. Clearly, the governments involved are not in a rush to establish a regional arrangement.

Nevertheless, by referring to the possibility of establishing an appropriate regional human rights mechanism in the Foreign Ministers Joint Communiqué, recalled at the 1988 ministers' meeting, ASEAN seemed to open a door of opportunity. Several NGOs seized upon this opportunity to conduct consultative meetings and to issue concrete, if ambitious, proposals and charters. In the ASEAN context, NGOs have been primarily responsible for lobbying for an ASEAN human rights mechanism, as part of the push for political liberalization and respect for human rights. As members of a transnational civil society, these nonstate actors have played a central role in focusing attention on the gap in human rights protection.

Establishing an independent, effective regional human rights mechanism that is readily accessible to the public, including NGOs, was a key specific recommendation of the Bangkok NGO Declaration:

If a regional commission is set up, it should be mandated to apply without reservations the International Bill of Human rights, CEDAW, the Convention against Torture, the Declaration of the Right to Development and other relevant human rights instruments; member states . . . must ratify or accede to the above instruments prior to their membership; the right of individuals and NGOs to petition the regional Commission should be guaranteed; such petitions or appeals should not preclude concurrent appeals to the various U.N. mechanisms for the protection of human rights; no member of this regional Commission should hold an official position in government concurrently, and members should be appointed in consultation with NGOs; there should be a regular reporting system by states on their implementation of human rights standards domestically, with NGO participation in the drafting of the reports; meetings of this regional Commission and its delib-

erations should be generally open to the public; no aspect of government operation and no official should be immune from scrutiny or investigation, including the
military and security forces; the regional commission should have full investigative
powers; a separate body should be set up to adjudicate complaints; member governments must be required to disseminate information on the regional commission
and how it operates.

The nongovernmental Working Group for an ASEAN Human Rights Mechanism (WG) was established after a series of workshops and meetings. Participants
came from both the governmental and nongovernmental sectors. To work toward
a regional human rights institution, the workshop participants resolved to consolidate links between ASEAN and civil society, to organize regional conferences, to
promote programs and research to raise the status of women and children, and to
consider drafting an ASEAN Convention of Human Rights. The group held dialogues with ASEAN officials during 1997 and 1998 and presented a concept paper
to the ASEAN Foreign Ministers at the Thirty-First Annual Ministerial Meetings
in Manila, July 24–25, 1998. The Ministers acknowledged the importance of these
dialogues in their Joint Communiqué. The paper urged ASEAN to examine the possible forms a regional mechanism might take, in particular urging the development
of an intergovernmental regional human rights commission to promote human
rights and suggesting several progressive steps. It also contained seven options concerning the steps ASEAN could adopt towards a regional human rights mechanism,
drawing inspiration from the experience of the Inter-American, European, and African systems.

. . . ASEAN states might be persuaded to accept an implementation-oriented
regime that entails some monitoring procedures such as reporting obligations. A
limited degree of external scrutiny would seem acceptable, given that ASEAN states
have, by becoming party to human rights treaties, accepted periodic reporting obligations to United Nations human rights organs. In this scenario, states could make
use of an international forum to formulate policies that ultimately remain under
national control. This gels with the sentiment expressed in the 1993 Bangkok Declaration at paragraph 9, recognizing that 'States have the primary responsibility for
the promotion and protection of human rights through appropriate infrastructure
and mechanisms, and also recognize that remedies must be sought and provided
primarily through such mechanisms and procedures.' It is unlikely, though, that
ASEAN states will look with favor upon a monitoring body that can receive communications from states or nonstate actors. At present, only the Philippines is party
to the ICCPR's first optional protocol, which grants the Human Rights Committee
jurisdiction to hear individual communications concerning human rights violations.
The Committee examines the communications in camera and forwards its views to
both the state party and the concerned individual. ASEAN parties to the Torture
Convention (Philippines) and Race Convention (Laos, Philippines, Vietnam) have
not recognized the competence of the relevant treaty committees to receive and
process individual communications. In their cautious shift toward human rights,
ASEAN states have generally kept their legal obligations to a minimum, avoiding
international channels of accountability. Instead, ASEAN states tend to declare

programmatic objectives that are not easily monitorable nor judiciable. In national human rights institutions, individuals have a forum to articulate complaints but this has evolved as a matter of practice, rather than legal right. There seems to be a strong preference for keeping things at an informal, conciliatory level and a desire to avoid formal legal engagement.

To make monitoring schemes with reporting obligations more palatable to ASEAN governments, attention should be focused on the possibility of creating theme-specific committees at the national and regional level with limited mandates. Particular focus should be given to forming committees with monitoring powers designed to promote and protect the interests of children and women, given ASEAN's formal commitment to the related U.N. treaties and its own ongoing programs in this regard. Explicit linkages between the human rights of women and children and ASEAN's 'functional cooperation' in women and children's issues should be encouraged so improvement can be sought in an integrated fashion. Since ASEAN countries stress the right to development, a reviewing committee could be formed to undertake research into both human and economic indicators of development. From there, momentum could be built to extend monitoring to the entire gamut of human rights—civil and political as well as economic, social, and cultural—on a basis of genuine indivisibility. In the short term, however, it is unlikely that any such committees will be able to assiduously oversee national compliance with international norms. This is because ASEAN states jealously guard their state prerogatives to implement human rights concerns at their own pace, within their territorial borders, without external interference. Nevertheless, once institutions are created they can stretch their own limited mandates.

For several reasons, it is unlikely that ASEAN states will incorporate a judicial organ into any proposed regional mechanism in the foreseeable future. Such adjudicatory institutions, which feature in strong enforcement regimes such as the European Court of Human Rights, are able to issue authoritative judgments and binding awards. . . .

In conclusion, human rights activism within ASEAN remains at the early stage of promotion, where publicity and persuasion are the strongest tools. Stamina is needed to cultivate the 'heartware' that sustains a human rights regime's 'hardware' in the form of institutions and processes. The primary task ahead is educating both the public and private sectors about human rights norms and the alternate methods for implementing them. A transnational human rights body with definite oversight powers should become a collective goal. Work has already been done to this end, through the cooperation of the ASEAN Secretariat and the private Working Group. NGOs have already begun supporting the Working Group with funding and expert technical assistance; this should continue. It is important that this initiative be perceived as a regional one, rather than one motivated by the agenda of some distant foreign power. The activities of this group should be publicized to domestic ASEAN constituencies, to foster public debate and, hopefully, to stimulate positive government responses.

. . . Before ASEAN can speak of having a human rights convention, commission, or court, its peoples must become aware of human rights and how they can be of practical use. Educational initiatives in this regard should be affiliated with and support the United Nations Human Rights Education decade (1995–2004). Educating public officials about their responsibilities under human rights law may induce a change in behavior while educating people about their rights will enable them to participate in formulating human rights standards at both the domestic and international level. Exposure to the international human rights regime will feed domestic initiatives urging governments to ratify human rights treaties or to set up regional institutions, thereby strengthening civil society.

Encouraging trends can be found in the ratification of human rights treaties by individual ASEAN countries, albeit muted by extensive reservations, and in their greater acceptance of the United Nations' role in promoting human rights. Several ASEAN states, for example, have permitted special rapporteurs from thematic U.N. human rights committees to conduct on-site investigations. The development of national human rights commissions can promote a climate for human rights advocacy and provide useful models for addressing human rights issues. It is heartening too, that ASEAN is developing specific programs for promoting the interests of women and children. It will be easier for human rights activists to engage ASEAN in dialogue over these matters, for which ASEAN has already demonstrated concern.

On a more localized basis, some positive changes may be observed. While Indonesia still struggles with a mounting economic crisis and the daily risk of civil disorder, a slow change in the government's attitude toward human rights is taking place. This is evident in the aftermath of the November riots and military crackdown. The human rights commission called for a probe into the violence, followed by the unprecedented step of the Indonesia military taking out advertisements in three major newspapers to express condolences for the fourteen dead. Apparently accepting responsibility, the government stated that the hundreds injured in the attack would receive free medical treatment. Governments should be reminded that commitments to human rights, which can contribute to a stable political order in the long run (as opposed to order coercively maintained, which is inherently unstable), can serve other goals. A government respecting human rights and environmental concerns may well, for example, be able to attract more aid and investment.

NGO activism in the region is crucial to the task of popularizing human rights consciousness and drawing attention to abuses. Attention should be focused on establishing the groundwork for an institutionalized human rights culture at the grassroots level, line by line, precept by precept. Government action must be called to account first through the internal check of an active civil society, and then through the external check of the international community.

The international community will need the wisdom to know when to condemn human rights abuses and when to come alongside ASEAN states in an attitude of partnership to offer expert help and technical assistance, and all states should be critical of their own human rights records. They are all accountable to the same law and all fall short, to varying degrees. To assume a posture of moral superiority is to promote a battle of wills that detracts from the real task of promoting the welfare of human beings. Yet, the human rights deficiencies of a state that criticizes another state do not in themselves provide an excuse for the criticized state to ignore its own shortcomings.

The international community can help in building the national resilience of ASEAN states by supporting the development of civil society, and government based on the rule of law. These will take time to grow; it cannot be imposed by decree or will. With sober realism, one must acknowledge that miles of road lie ahead for human rights activism in this region.

———————————

Asian Human Rights Charter, Kwangju, South Korea, 17 May 1998

PREAMBLE

For long, especially during the colonial period, the peoples of Asia suffered from gross violations of their rights and freedoms. Today large sections of our people continue to be exploited and oppressed and many of our societies are torn apart by hatred and intolerance.

Increasingly the people realize that peace and dignity are possible only when the equal and inalienable rights of all persons and groups are recognised and protected. They are determined to secure peace and justice for themselves and the coming generations through the struggle for human rights and freedoms. Towards that end they adopt this Charter as an affirmation of the desire and aspirations of the peoples of Asia to live in peace and dignity.

BACKGROUND TO THE CHARTER

1.1 The Asian struggle for rights and freedoms has deep historical roots, in the fight against oppression in civil society and the political oppression of colonialism, and subsequently for the establishment or restoration of democracy. The reaffirmation of rights is necessary now more than ever before. Asia is passing through a period of rapid change, which affects social structures, political institutions and the economy. Traditional values are under threat from new forms of development and technologies, as well as political authorities and economic organizations that manage these changes.

1.2 In particular the marketization and globalization of economies are changing the balance between the private and the public, the state and the international community, and worsening the situation of the poor and the disadvantaged. These changes threaten many valued aspects of life, the result of the dehumanizing effects of technology, the material orientation of the market, and the destruction of the community. People have decreasing control over their lives and environment, and some communities do not have protection even against eviction from their traditional homes and grounds. There is a massive exploitation of workers, with wages that are frequently inadequate for even bare subsistence and low safety standards that put the lives of workers in constant danger. Even the most elementary of labour rights and laws are seldom enforced.

1.3 Asian development is full of contradictions. There is massive and deepening poverty in the midst of growing affluence of some sections of the people. Levels of health, nutrition and education of large numbers of our people are appalling, denying the dignity of human life. At the same time valuable resources are wasted on armaments, Asia being the largest purchaser of arms of all regions. Our governments claim to be pursuing development directed at increasing levels of production and welfare but our natural resources are being depleted most irresponsibly and the environment is so degraded that the quality of life has worsened immeasurably, even for the better off among us. Building of golf courses has a higher priority than the care of the poor and the disadvantaged.

1.4 Asians have in recent decades suffered from various forms of conflict and violence, arising from ultra-nationalism, perverted ideologies, ethnic differences, and fundamentalism of all religions. Violence emanates from both the state and sections of civil society. For large masses, there is little security of person, property or community. There is massive displacement of communities and there are an increasing number of refugees.

1.5 Governments have arrogated enormous powers to themselves. They have enacted legislation to suppress people's rights and freedoms and colluded with foreign firms and groups in the plunder of national resources. Corruption and nepotism are rampant and there is little accountability of those holding public or private power. Authoritarianism has in many states been raised to the level of national ideology, with the deprivation of the rights and freedoms of their citizens, which are denounced as foreign ideas inappropriate to the religious and cultural traditions of Asia. Instead there is the exhortation of spurious theories of 'Asian Values' which are a thin disguise for their authoritarianism. Not surprisingly, Asia, of all the major regions of the world, is without a regional official charter or other regional arrangements for the protection of rights and freedoms.

1.6 In contrast to the official disregard or contempt of human rights in many Asian states, there is increasing awareness among their peoples of the importance of rights and freedoms. They realize the connections between their poverty and political powerlessness and the denial to them of these rights and freedoms. They believe that political and economic systems have to operate within a framework of human rights and freedoms to ensure economic justice, political participation and accountability, and social peace. There are many social movements that have taken up the fight to secure for the people their rights and freedoms.

1.7 Our commitment to rights is not due to any abstract ideological reasons. We believe that respect for human rights provides the basis for a just, humane and caring society. A regime of rights is premised on the belief that we are all inherently equal and have an equal right to live in dignity. It is based on our right to determine our destiny through participation in policy making and administration. It enables us to develop and enjoy our culture and to give expression to our artistic impulses. It respects diversity. It recognizes our obligations to future generations and the environment they will inherit. It establishes standards for assessing the worth and legitimacy of our institutions and policies.

GENERAL PRINCIPLES

2.1 It is possible from specific rights and the institutions and procedures for their protection to draw some general principles which underlie these rights and whose acceptance and implementation facilitates their full enjoyment. The principles, which are discussed below, should provide the broad framework for public policies within which we believe rights would be promoted.

UNIVERSALITY AND INDIVISIBILITY OF RIGHTS

2.2 We endorse the Universal Declaration of Human Rights, the International Covenant on Economic, Social and Cultural Rights, the International Covenant on Civil and Political Rights, and other international instruments for the protection of rights and freedoms. We believe that rights are universal, every person being entitled to them by virtue of being a human being. Cultural traditions affect the way in which a society organizes relationships within itself, but they do not detract from the universalism of rights which are primarily concerned with the relationship of citizens with the state and the inherent dignity of persons and groups. We also believe that rights and freedoms are indivisible and it is a fallacy to suppose that some types of rights can be suppressed in the name of other rights. Human beings have social, cultural and economic needs and aspirations that cannot be fragmented or compartmentalised, but are mutually dependent. Civil, political and cultural rights have little meaning unless there are the economic resources to exercise and enjoy them. Equally, the pursuit and acquisition of material wealth is sterile and self-defeating without political freedoms, the opportunity to develop and express one's personality and to engage in cultural and other discourses.

2.3 Notwithstanding their universality and indivisibility, the enjoyment and the salience of rights depend on social, economic and cultural contexts. Rights are not abstractions, but foundations for action and policy. Consequently we must move from abstract formulations of rights to their concretization in the Asian context by examining the circumstances of specific groups whose situation is defined by massive violations of their rights. It is only by relating rights and their implementation to the specificity of the Asian situation that the enjoyment of rights will be possible. Only in this way will Asia be able to contribute to the world-wide movement for the protection of rights.

2.4 Widespread poverty, even in states which have achieved a high rate of economic development, is a principal cause of the violation of rights. Poverty deprives individuals, families, and communities of their rights and promotes prostitution, child labour, slavery, sale of human organs, and the mutilation of the body to enhance the capacity to beg. A life of dignity is impossible in the midst of poverty. Asian states must direct their development policies towards the elimination of poverty through more equitable forms of development.

THE RESPONSIBILITY FOR THE PROTECTION OF HUMAN RIGHTS

2.5 The responsibility for the protection of rights is both international and domestic. The international community has agreed upon norms and institutions that should govern the practice of human rights. The peoples of Asia support international measures for the protection of rights. State sovereignty cannot be used as an excuse to evade international norms or ignore international institutions. The claim of state sovereignty is justified only when a state fully protects the rights of its citizens.

2.6 On the other hand, international responsibility cannot be used for the selective chastisement or punishment of particular states; or for the privileging of one set of rights over others. Some fundamental causes of the violation of human rights lie in the inequities of the international world economic and political order. The radical transformation and democratization of the world order is a necessary condition for the global enjoyment of human rights. The logic of the universalism and equality of rights is the responsibility of the international community for the social and economic welfare of all people throughout the world, and consequently the obligation to ensure a more equitable distribution of resources and opportunities across the world.

2.7 The primary responsibility for the promotion of human rights rests with states. The rights of states and peoples to just economic, social, political and cultural development must not be negated by global processes. States must establish open political processes in which rights and obligations of different groups are acknowledged and the balance between the interests of individuals and the community is achieved. Democratic and accountable governments are the key to the promotion and protection of rights.

2.8 The capacity of the international community and states to promote and protect rights has been weakened by processes of globalization as more and more power over economic and social policy and activities has moved from states to business corporations. States are increasingly held hostage by financial and other corporations to implement narrow and short sighted economic policies which cause so much misery to so many people, while increasing the wealth of the few. Business corporations are responsible for numerous violations of rights, particularly those of workers, women and indigenous peoples. It is necessary to strengthen the regime of rights by making corporations liable for the violation of rights.

SUSTAINABLE DEVELOPMENT AND THE PROTECTION OF THE ENVIRONMENT

2.9 Economic development must be sustainable. We must protect the environment against the avarice and depredations of commercial enterprises to ensure that the quality of life does not decline just as the gross national product increases. Technology must liberate, not enslave human beings. Natural resources must be used in a manner consistent with our obligation to future generations. We must never forget that we are merely temporary custodians of the resources of nature. Nor should we forget that these resources are given to all human kind, and consequently we have a joint responsibility for their responsible, fair and equitable use.

RIGHTS

3.1 We endorse all the rights that are contained in international instruments. It is unnecessary to restate them here. We believe that these rights need to be seen in a holistic manner and that individual rights are best pursued through a broader conceptualization which forms the basis of the following section.

THE RIGHT TO LIFE

3.2 Foremost among rights is the right to life, from which flow other rights and freedoms. The right to life is not confined to mere physical or animal existence but includes the right to every limb or faculty through which life is enjoyed. It signifies the right to live with basic human dignity, the right to livelihood, the right to a habitat or home, the right to education and the right to a clean and healthy environment for without these there can be no real and effective exercise or enjoyment of the right to life. The state must also take all possible measures to prevent infant mortality, eliminate malnutrition and epidemics, and increase life expectancy through a clean and healthy environment and adequate preventative as well as curative medical facilities. It must make primary education free and compulsory.

3.3 Yet in many parts of Asia, wars, ethnic conflicts, cultural and religious oppression, corruption of politics, environmental pollution, disappearances, torture, state or private terrorism, violence against women, and other acts of mass violence continue to be a scourge to humanity resulting in the loss of thousands of innocent human lives.

3.4 To ensure the right to life, propagation of war or ethnic conflict or incitement to hatred and violence in all spheres of individual or societal or national or international life should be prohibited.

3.5 The state has the responsibility to thoroughly investigate cases of torture, disappearances and custodial deaths, rapes and sexual abuses and to bring culprits to justice.

3.6 There must be no arbitrary deprivation of life. States should take measures not only to prevent and mete out punish for the deprivation of life by criminal acts and terrorist acts but also prevent arbitrary disappearances and killings by their own security forces. The law must strictly control and limit the circumstances in which a person may be deprived of his or her life by state authorities or officials.

3.7 All states must abolish the death penalty. Where it exists, it may be imposed only rarely for the most serious crimes. Before a person can be deprived of life by the imposition of the death penalty, he or she must be ensured a fair trial before an independent and impartial tribunal with full opportunity of legal representation of his or her choice, adequate time for preparation of defence, presumption of innocence and the right to review by a higher tribunal. Execution should never be carried out in public or otherwise exhibited in public.

THE RIGHT TO PEACE

4.1 All persons have the right to live in peace so that they can fully develop all their capacities, physical, intellectual, moral and spiritual, without being the target of any kind of violence. The peoples of Asia have suffered great hardships and tragedies due to wars and civil conflicts which have caused many deaths, mutilation of bodies, external or internal displacement of persons, break up of families, and in general the denial of any prospects of a civilized or peaceful existence. Both the state and civil society have in many countries become heavily militarized in which all scores are settled by force and citizens have no protection against the intimidation and terror of state or private armies.

4.2 The duty of the state to maintain law and order should be conducted under strict restraint on the use of force in accordance with standards established by the international community, including humanitarian law. Every individual and group is entitled to protection against all forms of state violence, including violence perpetrated by its police and military forces.

4.3 The right to live in peace requires that political, economic or social activities of the state, the corporate sector and the civil society should respect the security of all peoples, especially of vulnerable groups. People must be ensured security in relation to the natural environment they live in, the political, economic and social conditions which permit them to satisfy their needs and aspirations without recourse to oppression, exploitation, violence, and without detracting from all that is of value in their society.

4.4 In fighting fascist invasion, colonialism, and neo-colonialism, Asian states played a crucial role in creating conditions for their peoples to live in peace. In this fight, they had justifiably stressed the importance of national integrity and nonintervention by hegemonic powers. However, the demands of national integrity or protection against the threats of foreign domination cannot now be used as a pretext for refusing to the people their right to personal security and peaceful existence any more than the suppression of people's rights can be justified as an excuse to attract foreign investments. Neither can they justify any refusal to inform the international community about the individual security of its people. The right of persons to live in peace can be guaranteed only if the states are accountable to the international community.

4.5 The international community of states has been deeply implicated in wars and civil conflicts in Asia. Foreign states have used Asian groups as surrogates to wage wars and have armed groups and governments engaged in internal conflicts. They have made huge profits out of the sale of armaments. The enormous expenditures on arms have diverted public revenues from programmes for the development of the country or the well-being of the people. Military bases and other establishments (often of foreign powers) have threatened the social and physical security of the people who live in their vicinity.

THE RIGHT TO DEMOCRACY

5.1 Colonialism and other modern developments significantly changed the nature of Asian political societies. The traditional systems of accountability and public participation in affairs of state as well as the relationship of citizens to the government were altered fundamentally. Citizens became subjects, while the government became more pervasive and powerful. Colonial laws and authoritarian habits and style of administration persisted after independence. The state has become the source of corruption and the oppression of the people. The democratization and humanization of the state is a pre-condition for the respect for and the protection of rights.

5.2 The state, which claims to have the primary responsibility for the development and well-being of the people, should be humane, open and accountable. The corollary of the respect for human rights is a tolerant and pluralistic system, in which people are free to express their views and to seek to persuade others and in which the rights of minorities are respected. People must participate in public affairs, through the electoral and other decision–making and implementing processes, free from racial, religious or gender discriminations.

THE RIGHT TO CULTURAL IDENTITY AND THE FREEDOM OF CONSCIENCE

6.1 The right to life involves not only material but also the moral conditions which permit a person to lead a meaningful existence. This meaning is not only individually determined but is also based on shared living with other human beings. The Asian traditions stress the importance of common cultural identities. Cultural identities help individuals and communities to cope with the pressures of economic and social change; they give meaning to life in a period of rapid transformation. They are the source of pride and security. There are many vulnerable communities in Asia as elsewhere whose cultures are threatened or derided. Asian peoples and governments must respect the cultures and traditions of its diverse communities.

6.2 The plurality of cultural identities in Asia is not contrary to the universality of human rights but rather as so many cultural manifestations of human dignity enriching universal norms. At the same time we Asian peoples must eliminate those features in our cultures which are contrary to the universal principles of human rights. We must transcend the traditional concept of the family based on patriarchal traditions so as to retrieve in each of our cultural traditions, the diversity of family norms which guarantee women.s human rights. We must be bold in reinterpreting our religious beliefs which support gender inequality. We must also eliminate discriminations based on caste, ethnic origins, occupation, place of origin and others, while enhancing in our respective cultures all values related to mutual tolerance and mutual support. We must stop practices which sacrifice the individual to the collectivity or to the powerful, and thus renew our communal and national solidarity.

6.3 The freedom of religion and conscience is particularly important in Asia where most people are deeply religious. Religion is a source of comfort and solace in the midst of poverty and oppression. Many find their primary identity in religion. However religious fundamentalism is also a cause of divisions and conflict. Religious tolerance is essential for the enjoyment of the right of conscience of others, which includes the right to change one's belief.

THE RIGHT TO DEVELOPMENT AND SOCIAL JUSTICE

7.1 Every individual has the right to the basic necessities of life and to protection against abuse and exploitation. We all have the right to literacy and knowledge, to food and clean water, shelter and to medical facilities for a healthy existence. All individuals and human groups are entitled to share the benefits of the progress of technology and of the growth of the world economy.

7.2 Development, for individuals and states, does not mean merely economic development. It means the realization of the full potential of the human person. Consequently they have the right to artistic freedom, freedom of expression and the cultivation of their cultural and spiritual capacities. It means the right to participate in the affairs of the state and the community. It implies that states have the right to determine their own economic, social and cultural policies free from hegemonic pressures and influences.

RIGHTS OF VULNERABLE GROUPS

8.1 Asian states should formulate and implement public policies within the above general framework of rights. We believe that in this way we will establish fair and humane conditions for our individual and corporate lives and ensure social justice. However, there are particular groups who for historical or other reasons are weak and vulnerable and consequently require special protection for the equal and effective enjoyment of their human rights. We discuss the situation of several such groups, but we recognize that there are also other groups who suffer from discrimination and oppression. They include people who through civil conflict, government policies or economic hardships are displaced from their homes and seek refuge in other places internally or in foreign lands. Our states and societies have become less tolerant of minorities and indigenous people, whose most basic rights are frequently violated. Many of our societies still discriminate against gays and lesbians, denying them their identity and causing them great anguish and misery. Various economic groups, like peasants and fishing communities, suffer from great deprivation and live in constant fear of threats to their livelihood from landlords and capitalist enterprises. All these groups deserve special attention. We urge states and communities to give the highest priority to the amelioration of their social and economic conditions.

WOMEN

9.1 In most Asian societies women suffer from discrimination and oppression. The cause of their oppression lies in both history and contemporary social and economic systems.

9.2 The roots of patriarchy are systemic and its structures dominate all institutions, attitudes, social norms and customary laws, religions and values in Asian societies, crossing the boundaries of class, culture, caste and ethnicity. Oppression takes many forms, but is most evident in sexual slavery, domestic violence, trafficking in women and rape. They suffer discrimination in both public and private spheres. The increasing militarization of many societies in Asia has led to the increase of violence against women in situations of armed conflict, including mass rape, forced labour, racism, kidnapping and displacement from their homes. As female victims of armed conflict are often denied justice, rehabilitation, compensation and reparation of the war crimes committed against them, it is important to emphasis that systematic rape is a war crime and a crime against humanity.

9.3 To end discrimination against women in the field of employment and the right to work, women should be given the right to employment opportunities, the free choice of profession, job security, equal remuneration, the right to compensation in respect of domestic work, the right to protection of health and safe working conditions, especially in safeguarding of the function of reproduction and special protection in times of pregnancy from work that may be harmful. Women should be given the full right to control their sexual and reproductive health, free from discrimination or coercion, and be given access to information about sexual and reproductive health care and safe reproductive technology.

9.4 There are few legal provisions to protect women against violations of their rights within the domestic and patriarchal realm. Their rights in public law are seldom observed. Affirmative measures should be taken to ensure full and equal participation of women in the political and public life of the society. A considerable increase in the presence of women in the various institutions of state power and in the fields of business, agriculture and land ownership must be provided for by way of affirmative action. The political, social and economic empowerment of women is essential for the defence of their legal rights.

CHILDREN

10.1 As with women, their oppression takes many forms, the most pervasive of which are child labour; sexual slavery; child pornography; the sale and trafficking of children; prostitution; sale of organs; conscription into drug trafficking; the physical, sexual and psychological abuse of children within families; discrimination against children with HIV/AIDS; forced religious conversion of children; the displacement of children with and without their families by armed conflicts; discrimination; and environmental degradation. An increasing number of children are forced to live on the streets of Asian cities and are deprived of the social and economic support of families and communities.

10.2 Widespread poverty, lack of access to education and social dislocation in rural areas are among the causes of the trends which increase the vulnerability of children. Long-established forms of exploitation and abuse, such as bonded labour or the use of children for begging or sexual gratification are rampant. Female infanticide due to patriarchal gender preference and female genital mutilation are widely practiced in some Asian countries.

10.3 Asian states have failed dismally to look after children and provide them with even the bare means of subsistence or shelter. We call on Asian states to ratify and implement the Convention on the Rights of the Child. We also call on communities to take the responsibility for monitoring violations of children's rights and to press for the implementation of the UN Convention in appropriate ways in their own social contexts.

DIFFERENTLY ABLED PERSONS

11.1 Traditionally Asian societies cared for those who were physically or mentally handicapped. Increasingly our communal values and structures, under the pressure of new forms of economic organizations, have become less tolerant of such persons. They suffer enormous discrimination in access to education, employment and housing. They are unable to enjoy many of their human rights due to prejudice against them and the absence of provisions responding to their special demands. Their considerable abilities are not properly recognized and they are forced into jobs which offer low pay and little prospects of promotion. They have the right to provisions which enable them to live in dignity, with security and respect, and to have opportunities to realize their full potential.

11.2 The need to treat such persons with respect for their human rights is apparent in the dismal way Asian states treat those with HIV or AIDS. They are the victims of gross discrimination. A civilized society which respects human rights would recognize their right to live and die with dignity. It would secure to them the right to adequate medical care and to be protected from prejudice, discrimination or persecution.

WORKERS

12.1 The rapid industrialization of Asian societies has undermined traditional forms of the subsistence economy and has destroyed possibilities of the livelihood of large sections of the rural people. Increasingly they and other groups are forced into wage employment, often in industry, working under appalling conditions. For the majority of the workers there is little or no protection from unfair labour laws. The fundamental rights to form trade unions and bargain collectively are denied to many. Their wages are grossly inadequate and working conditions are frequently grim and dangerous. Globalization adds to the pressures on workers as many Asian states seek to reduce the costs of production, often in collusion with foreign corporations and international financial institutions.

12.2 A particularly vulnerable category of workers are migrant workers. Frequently separated from their families, they are exploited in foreign states whose laws they do not understand and are afraid to invoke. They are often denied rights and conditions which local workers enjoy. They slog without access to adequate accommodation, health care, or legal protection. In many cases migrants suffer racism and xenophobia, and domestic helpers are subjected to humiliation and sometimes, sexual abuse.

STUDENTS

13.1 Students in Asia struggled against colonialism and fought for democratization and social justice. As a result of their fearless commitment to social transformation they have often suffered from state violence and repression and remain as one of the key targets for counter-insurgency operations and internal security laws and operations. Students are frequently denied the right to academic freedom and to the freedoms of expression and association.

PRISONERS AND POLITICAL DETAINEES

14.1 In few areas is there such a massive violation of internationally recognized norms as in relation to prisoners and political detainees.

14.2 Arbitrary arrests, detention, imprisonment, ill-treatment, torture, cruel and inhuman punishment are common occurrences in many parts of Asia. Detainees and prisoners are often forced to live in unhygienic conditions, are denied adequate food and health care and are prevented from having communication with, and support from, their families. Different kinds of prisoners are frequently mixed in one cell, with men, women and children kept in proximity. Prison cells are normally overcrowded. Deaths in custody are common. Prisoners are frequently denied access to lawyers and the right to fair and speedy trials.

14.3 Asian governments often use executive powers of detention without trial. They use national security legislation to arrest and detain political opponents. It is notable that, in many countries in Asia, freedom of thought, belief and conscience have been restricted by administrative limits on freedom of speech and association.

THE ENFORCEMENT OF RIGHTS

15.1 Many Asian states have guarantees of human rights in their constitutions, and many of them have ratified international instruments on human rights. However, there continues to be a wide gap between rights enshrined in these documents and the abject reality that denies people their rights. Asian states must take urgent action to implement the human rights of their citizens and residents.

PRINCIPLES FOR ENFORCEMENT

15.2 We believe that systems for the protection of rights should be based on the following principles.

15.2a Human rights are violated by the state, civil society and business corporations. The legal protection for rights has to be extended against violations by all these groups. It is also necessary to reform these groups by strengthening their ethical foundations and values and inculcating in them a sense of their responsibility towards the disadvantaged and the oppressed.

15.2b The promotion and enforcement of rights is the responsibility of all groups in society, although the primary responsibility is that of the state. The enjoyment of many rights, especially social and economic, requires a positive and proactive role of governments. There is a clear and legitimate role for NGOs in raising consciousness of rights, formulating standards, and ensuring their protection by governments and other groups. Professional groups like lawyers and doctors have special responsibilities connected with the nature of their work to promote the enforcement of rights and prevent abuses of power.

15.2c Since rights are seriously violated in situations of civil strife and are strengthened if there is peace, it is the duty of the state and other organizations to find peaceful ways to resolve social and ethnic conflicts and to promote tolerance and harmony. For the same reasons no state should seek to dominate other states and states should settle their differences peacefully.

15.2d Rights are enhanced if democratic and consensual practices are followed and it is therefore the responsibility of all states and other organisations to promote these practices in their work and in their dealings with others.

15.2e Many individuals and groups in Asia are unable to exercise their rights due to restrictive or oppressive social customs and practices, particularly those related to caste, gender, or religion. Therefore the immediate reform of these customs and practices is necessary for the protection of rights. The reforms must be enforced with vigour and determination.

15.2f A humane and vigorous civil society is necessary for the promotion and protection of human rights and freedoms, for securing rights within civil society and to act as a check on state institutions. Freedoms of expression and association are necessary for the establishment and functioning of institutions of civil society.

15.2g It is necessary to curb the exploitative practices of business corporations and to ensure that they do not violate rights of workers, consumers and the public.

STRENGTHENING THE FRAMEWORK FOR RIGHTS

15.3a It is essential to secure the legal framework for rights. All states should include guarantees of rights in their constitutions, which should be constitutionally protected against erosion by legislative amendments. They should also ratify international human rights instruments. They should review their legislation and administrative practices against national and international standards with the aim of repealing provisions which contravene these standards, particularly legislation carried over from the colonial period.

15.3b Knowledge and consciousness of rights should be raised among the general public, and state and civil society institutions. Awareness of the national and international regime of rights should be promoted. Individuals and groups should be acquainted with legal and administrative procedures whereby they can secure their rights and prevent abuse of authority. NGOs should be encouraged to become familiar with and deploy mechanisms, both national and inter-national, for monitoring and review of rights. Judicial and administrative decisions on the protection of rights should be widely disseminated, nationally and in the Asian region. Governments, NGOs and educational institutions should co-operate in disseminating information about the importance and content of human rights.

15.3c Numerous violations of rights occur while people are in custody and through other activities of security forces. Sometimes these violations take place because the security forces do not respect the permissible scope of their powers or do not realise that the orders under which they are acting are unlawful. Members of the police, prison services and the armed forces should be provided training in human rights norms.

THE MACHINERY FOR THE ENFORCEMENT OF RIGHTS

15.4a The judiciary is a major means for the protection of rights. It has the power to receive complaints of the violation of rights, to hear evidence, and to provide redress for violations, including punishment for violators. The judiciary can only perform this function if the legal system is strong and well organized. The members of the judiciary should be competent, experienced and have a commitment to human rights, dignity and justice. They should be independent of the legislature and the executive by vesting the power of their appointment in a judicial service commission and by constitutional safeguards of their tenure. Judicial institutions should fairly reflect the character of the different sections of the people by religion, region, gender and social class. This means that there must be a restructuring of the judiciary and the investigative machinery. More women, more underprivileged categories and more of the Pariahs of society must by deliberate State action be lifted out of the mire and instilled in judicial positions with necessary training. Only such a measure will command the confidence of the weaker sector whose human rights are ordinarily ignored in the traditional societies of Asia.

15.4.b The legal profession should be independent. Legal aid should be provided for those who are unable to afford the services of lawyers or have access to courts, for the protection of their rights. Rules which unduly restrict access to courts should be reformed to provide a broad access. Social and welfare organizations should be authorised to bring legal action on behalf of individuals and groups who are unable to utilize the courts.

15.4c All states should establish Human Rights Commissions and specialized institutions for the protection of rights, particularly of vulnerable members of society. They can provide easy, friendly and inexpensive access to justice for victims of human rights violations. These bodies can supplement the role of the judiciary. They enjoy special advantages: they can help establish standards for the implementation of human rights norms; they can disseminate information about human rights; they can investigate allegations of violation of rights; they can promote conciliation and mediation; and they can seek to enforce human rights through administrative or judicial means. They can act on their own initiative as well on complaints from members of the public.

15.4d Civil society institutions can help to enforce rights through the organization of People's Tribunals, which can touch the conscience of the government and the public. The establishment of People's Tribunals emphasizes that the responsibility for the protection of rights is wide, and not a preserve of the state. They are not confined to legal rules in their adjudication and can consequently help to uncover the moral and spiritual foundations of human rights.

REGIONAL INSTITUTIONS FOR THE PROTECTION OF RIGHTS

16.1 The protection of human rights should be pursued at all levels, local, national, regional and international. Institutions at each level have their special advantages and skills. The primary responsibility for the protection of rights is that of states, therefore priority should be given to the enhancement of state capacity to fulfil this obligation.

16.2 Asian states should adopt regional or sub-regional institutions for the promotion and protection of rights. There should be an inter-state Convention on Human Rights, formulated in regional forums with the collaboration of national and regional NGOs. The Convention must address the realities of Asia, particularly the obstacles that impede the enjoyment of rights. At the same time it must be fully consistent with international norms and standards. It should cover violations of rights by groups and corporations in addition to state institutions. An independent commission or a court must be established to enforce the Convention. Access to the commission or the court must be open to NGOs and other social organizations.

Note: The above Charter is an NGO-drafted text. Another effort began in 1995, with support from the Friedrich Naumann Foundation. The LAWASIA (Law Association for Asia and the Pacific) Human Rights Standing Committee organized a series of meetings among representatives of national human rights institutions, parliamentary human rights committees, and human rights NGOs in the region to discuss proposals for a human rights mechanism in Southeast Asia. The meetings eventually led to the formation of the Working Group for an ASEAN Human Rights Mechanism in 1996. (The other foundations supporting the initiative are The Asia Foundation and the Southeast Asia Fund for Institutional and Legal Development [SEAFILD] of the Canadian International Development Agency [CIDA]).

The Working Group is composed of human rights advocates from government institutions and NGOs who represent their respective national working groups. In 2007, national working groups have been set up in Indonesia, Malaysia, Thailand and the Philippines. The aim is to have national working groups in each ASEAN state composed of representatives of the government, parliamentary human rights committees, the academe, and NGOs.

In pursuing its goal, the Working Group has followed a step-by-step approach involving governments, parliamentary committees and NGOs. It met with ASEAN foreign ministers in 1996 (Jakarta), and with senior officials in 1997 (Kuala Lumpur), in 1998 (Manila) and in 1999 (Singapore) on the proposal for an ASEAN human rights mechanism. In addition, national working groups have undertaken related activities within their respective countries. The Working Group intends to continue the dialogue with ASEAN ministers and senior officials, both at regional and national levels.

ASEAN's response to the initiative has been encouraging so far. In the Joint Communique of the 32nd ASEAN Ministerial Meeting in Singapore, the ASEAN recognized the need for continuous dialogues concerning the formation of a human rights mechanism in ASEAN. Paragraph 50 of the Communique states:

> We recalled the decision of the 26th ASEAN Ministerial Meeting held on 23–24 July 1993 in Singapore to consider the establishment of an appropriate regional mechanism on human rights and noted the establishment of the informal non-governmental Working Group and ASEAN officials have met regularly since the 29th ASEAN Ministerial Meeting in Jakarta, most recently in Singapore. We recognized the importance of continuing these dialogues.

A recent statement of the ASEAN governments follows:

Kuala Lumpur Declaration on the Establishment of the ASEAN Charter Kuala Lumpur, 12 December 2005

WE, the Heads of State/Government of Brunei Darussalam, Kingdom of Cambodia, Republic of Indonesia, Lao People's Democratic Republic, Malaysia, Union of Myanmar, Republic of the Philippines, Republic of Singapore, Kingdom of Thailand and Socialist Republic of Viet Nam, Member Countries of ASEAN, on the occasion of the 11th ASEAN Summit in Kuala Lumpur;

CONSCIOUS of the unity and diversity in ASEAN and the existing ties of history, geography and culture that have bound their peoples together;

RECOGNISING the ASEAN Declaration (Bangkok Declaration) of 1967 as the founding document of ASEAN that represents the collective will of the nations of Southeast Asia to bond themselves together in friendship and cooperation and, through joint efforts and sacrifices, secure for their peoples and for posterity the blessings of peace, freedom and prosperity;

ACKNOWLEDGING that the vision, strategy and initiative of ASEAN over the years have made an important contribution to the maintenance of peace, security and stability of the region;

COGNISANT that mutual respect for the independence, sovereignty, equality, territorial integrity and national identity of ASEAN Member Countries has fostered a positive environment for the steady development of an ASEAN Community to meet the challenges of the future;

DESIRING to realise an ASEAN Community as envisaged in the Declaration of ASEAN Concord II (Bali Concord II) and its Plans of Action and Roadmap, and the ASEAN Vision 2020 which envision ASEAN as a concert of Southeast Asian nations, outward-looking, living in peace, stability and prosperity, bonded together in partnership in dynamic development and in a community of caring societies;

RECOGNISING that the global and regional economic and political environment has changed and is constantly changing thereby requiring ASEAN and its community building efforts to evolve and adapt to these changes and challenges;

RECOGNISING the importance of having an appropriate institutional framework of ASEAN that is able to meet the challenges of realising an ASEAN community;

CONVINCED of the need for an ASEAN Charter to serve as a firm foundation for ASEAN in the years ahead and to facilitate community building towards an ASEAN Community and beyond;

DO HEREBY DECLARE:

FIRST, we are committed to establish the ASEAN Charter.

SECOND, the ASEAN Charter will serve as a legal and institutional framework of ASEAN to support the realisation of its goals and objectives.

THIRD, the ASEAN Charter will codify all ASEAN norms, rules, and values and reaffirm that ASEAN agreements signed and other instruments adopted before the establishment of the ASEAN Charter shall continue to apply and be legally binding where appropriate.

FOURTH, the ASEAN Charter will reaffirm principles, goals and ideals contained in ASEAN's milestone agreements, in particular the ASEAN Declaration (1967), the Treaty of Amity and Cooperation in Southeast Asia (1976), the Treaty on Southeast Asia Nuclear Weapon Free Zone (1995), the ASEAN Vision 2020 (1997) and the Declaration of ASEAN Concord II (2003) as well as the principles of inter-state relations in accordance with the UN Charter and established international law that promote and protect ASEAN community interests as well as inter-state relations and the national interests of the individual ASEAN Member Countries. These include among others:

- Promotion of community interest for the benefit of all ASEAN Member Countries;
- Maintaining primary driving force of ASEAN;
- Narrowing the development gaps among Member Countries;
- Adherence to a set of common socio-cultural and political community values and shared norms as contained in the various ASEAN documents;
- Continuing to foster a community of caring societies and promote a common regional identity;

- Effective implementation as well as compliance with ASEAN's agreements;
- Promotion of democracy, human rights and obligations, transparency and good governance and strengthening democratic institutions;
- Ensuring that countries in the region live at peace with one another and with the world at large in a just, democratic and harmonious environment;
- Decision making on the basis of equality, mutual respect and consensus;
- Commitment to strengthen ASEAN's competitiveness, to deepen and broaden ASEAN's internal economic integration and linkages with the world economy;
- Promotion of regional solidarity and cooperation;
- Mutual respect for the independence, sovereignty, equality, territorial integrity and national identity of all nations;
- Renunciation of nuclear weapons and other weapons of mass destruction and avoidance of arms race;
- Renunciation of the use of force and threat to use of force; non-aggression and exclusive reliance on peaceful means for the settlement of differences or disputes;
- Enhancing beneficial relations between ASEAN and its friends and partners;
- Upholding non-discrimination of any ASEAN Member Countries in ASEAN's external relations and cooperative activities;
- Observance of principles of international law concerning friendly relations and cooperation among States; and
- The right of every state to lead its national existence free from external interference, subversion or coercion and non-interference in the internal affairs of one another.

FIFTH, the ASEAN Charter will confer a legal personality to ASEAN and determine the functions, develop areas of competence of key ASEAN bodies and their relationship with one another in the overall ASEAN structure.

AND DO HEREBY AGREE:

TO establish an Eminent Persons Group (EPG), comprising highly distinguished and well respected citizens from ASEAN Member Countries, with the mandate to examine and provide practical recommendations on the directions and nature of the ASEAN Charter relevant to the ASEAN Community as envisaged in the Bali Concord II and beyond, taking into account, but not limited to, the principles, values and objectives as contained in this Declaration.

TO consider their recommendations at our subsequent meetings.

TO task our Ministers to establish, as necessary, a High Level Task Force to carry out the drafting of the ASEAN Charter based on the Kuala Lumpur Declaration on the Establishment of the ASEAN Charter and the recommendations of the EPG.

ASEAN Foreign Ministers Agree on Creation of Human Rights Body in ASEAN Charter—Romulo, 40th ASEAN Ministerial Meeting / Post Ministerial Conferences, 14th ASEAN Regional Forum, Press Release 7/30/2007

MANILA—In a historic decision that will strengthen the protection of human rights in Southeast Asia, the ASEAN Foreign Ministers, under the Chairmanship of Philippine Foreign Affairs Secretary Alberto G. Romulo, agreed to the creation of a human rights body under the draft ASEAN Charter.

"I am pleased to announce that among the issues on which there was consensus among the ASEAN Foreign Ministers, is the inclusion of a provision in the ASEAN Charter that mandates the creation of a human rights body," Romulo said in a statement he delivered before the media after chairing the ASEAN Ministerial Meeting Retreat Session that focused on the issue of the ASEAN Charter.

"We (the ASEAN Foreign Ministers) have instructed the HLTF to include this provision in the draft Charter," the Philippine official told the media.

The High-Level Task Force (HLTF) assigned to prepare a draft of the ASEAN treaty briefed the ASEAN ministers this morning on the progress of their work. After the briefing, the ASEAN ministers met by themselves in retreat format to discuss the work of the HLTF.

Commenting on the significance of this decision, the Secretary stressed that "this is a major victory for ASEAN. This is a major victory for human rights."

"I remained firm on our position: the ASEAN Charter must provide for the creation of a human rights body," the Secretary added.

"The ASEAN Charter will now have a human rights body. This will show to the world that a people-oriented ASEAN truly cares about the rights of its peoples," Romulo explained. "Having a human rights body will give great credibility to ASEAN and the ASEAN Charter."

"I am very grateful to the ASEAN Ministers for their strong support and for their agreement in creating a human rights body in the ASEAN Charter," Romulo said, adding that "I would like to personally thank the ASEAN Foreign Ministers for their friendship and support, and for which I credit the success of our discussions."

"The ASEAN Foreign Ministers are also very grateful to the members of the HLTF for their work. We look forward to their next report to us," he said.

Romulo said that the ASEAN ministers will have another opportunity to receive a report on the progress of the work of the HLTF at the Informal ASEAN Ministerial Meeting on 27 September at the sidelines of the United Nations General Assembly in New York.

Statement on the Establishment of the ASEAN Committee on the Implementation of the ASEAN Declaration on the Protection and Promotion of the Rights of Migrant Workers, Manila, 30 July 2007, 40th ASEAN Ministerial Meeting (AMM), Manila, 29–30 July 2007,

WE, the Ministers of Foreign Affairs of the Governments of Brunei Darussalam, the Kingdom of Cambodia, the Republic of Indonesia, the Lao People's Democratic

Republic, Malaysia, the Union of Myanmar, the Republic of the Philippines, the Republic of Singapore, the Kingdom of Thailand, and the Socialist Republic of Viet Nam, Member Countries of the Association of Southeast Asian Nations (ASEAN), hereinafter referred to individually as "Member Country" and collectively as "Member Countries";

RECALLING the purposes of, and the commitments contained in, the ASEAN Declaration on the Protection and Promotion of the Rights of Migrant Workers (the Declaration) signed by the Heads of State / Government of the ASEAN Member Countries at the 12th ASEAN Summit in Cebu, Philippines, specifically the mandate to task the relevant ASEAN bodies to follow up on the Declaration and to develop an ASEAN instrument on the protection and promotion of the rights of migrant workers, consistent with ASEAN's vision of a caring and sharing Community;

RECALLING also the relevant international instruments on the protection and promotion of the rights of migrant workers, which can serve as a basis for enhancing international cooperation in this area;

DO HEREBY STATE AS FOLLOWS:

Establishment of the ASEAN Committee on the Implementation of the ASEAN Declaration on the Protection and Promotion of the Rights of Migrant Workers

There shall be established an ASEAN Committee on the Implementation of the Declaration on the Protection and Promotion of the Rights of Migrant Workers hereinafter referred to as the Committee.

Purpose of the Committee

The Committee, in accordance with the national laws, regulations, and policies of Member Countries, will serve as the focal point within ASEAN to coordinate the following:

    1. Ensuring the effective implementation of the commitments made under the Declaration; and

    2. Facilitating the development of an ASEAN instrument on the protection and promotion of the rights of migrant workers.

Structure of the Committee

The Committee shall:

    1. Be composed of one senior representative from each of the Member Countries, as well as a representative from the ASEAN Secretariat;

    2. Be assisted by representatives from the concerned government agencies of each Member Country;

    3. Report to the Senior Labor Officials Meeting (SLOM);

    4. Be chaired by the representative of the country that holds the Chairmanship of the ASEAN Standing Committee; and

    5. Be provided secretarial support by the ASEAN Secretariat.

Functions of the Committee

Subject to the national laws, regulations, and policies of the Member Countries, the functions of the Committee will be as follows:

1. Explore all avenues to achieve the objectives of the Declaration;

2. Facilitate sharing of best practices in the ASEAN region on matters concerning the promotion and protection of the rights of migrant workers;

3. Promote bilateral and regional cooperation and assistance on matters involving the rights of migrant workers;

4. Facilitate data sharing on matters related to migrant workers, for the purpose of enhancing policies and programmes to protect and promote the rights of migrant workers in both sending and receiving countries;

5. Encourage international organisations, ASEAN Dialogue Partners and other countries to respect the principles and extend support and assistance to the implementation of the measures contained in the Declaration;

6. Promote harmonisation of mechanisms between both sending and receiving countries that promote and protect the rights of migrant workers to implement the ASEAN commitment reflected in paragraph 17 of the Declaration;

7. Work closely with the ASEAN Secretariat in the preparation of the report of the Secretary-General of ASEAN to the ASEAN Summit; and

8. Work towards the development of an ASEAN instrument on the protection and promotion of the rights of migrant workers.

Questions and Comments

1. On the question of so-called Asian values, see Amartya Sen, *Human Rights and Asian Values* (1997).

2. Can an Asian system be developed without defining Asia? Would it be advisable to work for sub-regional systems?

3. Are there alternatives to the model of a human rights system consisting of binding rights and obligations, institutions and monitoring procedures? See UN Commission on Human Rights, *Effective Functioning of Human Rights Mechanisms: National Institutions and Regional Arrangements*, E/CN.4/2006/100/Add.1 (13 Dec. 2005).

4. To what extent does the Asian Charter incorporate and mirror universal human rights standards? Where, if at all, does it fall short and where does it go further?

5. What is the interest of the United Nations in the creation of a regional system in Asia? Would it support UN human rights programs? Why would the UN have opposed regional systems earlier in its history?

6. What will be the functions and powers of the new ASEAN Committee on Migrant Workers? Does it offer a model for the proposed human rights body to be included in the ASEAN Charter? What might explain ASEAN's decision to begin with the topic of migrant workers?

7. Recent works on human rights in Asia and the possibilities of developing a regional system or systems include: Yash Ghai, *Human Rights and Governance: The Asia Debate*, Asia Foundation Center for Asian Pacific Affairs, Occasional Paper No. 4, Nov. 1994; HUMAN RIGHTS AND INTERNATIONAL RELATIONS IN THE ASIA-PACIFIC REGION (James T.H. Tang ed., 1995); HUMAN RIGHTS AND CHINESE VALUES: LEGAL, PHILOSOPHICAL, AND POLITI-

CAL PERSPECTIVES (Michael Davis ed., 1995); WM. THEODORE DE BARY, ASIAN VALUES AND HUMAN RIGHTS: A CONFUCIAN COMMUNITARIAN PERSPECTIVE (1998).Bilahari Kim Hee P.S. Kausikan, *An East Asian Approach to Human Rights*, 2 BUFF. J. INT'L L. 263 (1995–96); Bilahari. Kausikan, *Governance that Works*, J. DEMOCRACY 24, Apr. 1997; HUMAN RIGHTS: CHINESE AND DUTCH PERSPECTIVES (Peter Baehr et al. eds., 1996); Roger T. Ames, *Continuing the Conversation on Chinese Human Rights*, 11 ETHICS & INT'L AFF. 177 (1997); DEALING WITH HUMAN RIGHTS: ASIAN AND WESTERN VIEWS ON THE VALUE OF HUMAN RIGHTS (Martha Meijer ed., 2001); THE EAST ASIAN CHALLENGE FOR HUMAN RIGHTS (Joanne R. Bauer & Daniel A. Bell eds., 1999); NEGOTIATING CULTURE AND HUMAN RIGHTS (Lynda S. Bell et al. eds., 2001); Kenneth Christie & Denny Roy, THE POLITICS OF HUMAN RIGHTS IN EAST ASIA (Peter Van Ness ed., 2001); Karen Engle, *Culture and Human Rights: The Asian Values Debate in Context*, 32 N.Y.U. J. INT'L L. & POL. 291, 323 (2000); MARINA SVENSSON, DEBATING HUMAN RIGHTS IN CHINA, 1899–1999: A CONCEPTUAL AND POLITICAL HISTORY (2002); STEPHEN ANGLE, HUMAN RIGHTS AND CHINESE THOUGHT: A CROSS-CULTURAL INQUIRY (2002); *ASEAN Inter-Parliamentary Organization, Declaration on Human Rights*, 3 ASIAN Y.B. INT'L L. 500 (1993); Onuma Yasuaki, *In Quest of Intercivilizational Human Rights: Universal vs. Relative Human Rights Viewed from an Asian Perspective*, Center for Asian Pacific Affairs 1 (Occasional Paper No. 2, March 1996). Amitav Acharya, *Human Rights and Regional Order: ASEAN and Human Rights Management in Post-Cold War Southeast Asia*, in INTERNATIONAL RELATIONS IN THE ASIA PACIFIC 167 (James T.H. Tang ed., 1995); Daniel A. Bell, *The East Asian Challenge to Human Rights: Reflections on an East West Dialogue*, 18 HUM. RTS. Q. 641 (1996). Christopher Tremewan, *Human Rights in Asia*, 6 PAC. REV. 17, 27 (1993); Sidney Jones, *Regional Institutions for Protecting Human Rights in Asia*, 50 AUSTRALIAN J. INT'L AFF. 269, 272 (1996); Kelly Dawn Askin, *Issues Surrounding the Creation of a Regional Human Rights System for the Asia-Pacific*, 4 ILSA J INT'L & COMP L 599 (1998); Seth R. Harris, *Recent Development: Asian Human Rights: Forming A Regional Covenant*, 1 ASIAN-PACIFIC L. & POL'Y J. 17; Richard Klein, *Cultural Relativism, Economic Development And International Human Rights In The Asian Context*, 9 TOURO INT'L L. REV. 1 (2001); Ralph Wilde, *NGO Proposals For An Asia-Pacific Human Rights System*, 1 Yale Hum. Rts. & Dev. L.J. 137 (1998); Sienho Yee, *The Role of Law in the Formation of Regional Perspectives in Human Rights and Regional Systems for the Protection of Human Rights: The European and Asian Models as Illustrations*, 8 SINGAPORE YB. INT'L L. 157 (2004); FERNAND DE VARENNES, ED., ASIA-PACIFIC HUMAN RIGHTS DOCUMENTS AND RESOURCES (1998); DAVID KELLY & ANTHONY REID, ASIAN FREEDOMS: THE IDEA OF FREEDOM IN EAST AND SOUTHEAST ASIA (1998); WILLIAM THEODORE DE BARY, ASIAN VALUES AND HUMAN RIGHTS: A CONFUCIAN COMMUNITARIAN PERSPECTIVE (1998); Sumit Guha and Michael R. Anderson, eds., CHANGING CONCEPTS OF RIGHTS AND JUSTICE IN SOUTH ASIA (1998).

8. Having examined the law, institutions and procedures of existing regional systems, how would you explain to persons living in regions that lack such a system the differences between the global and regional protection of human rights? Is there a value added by the latter? What strategies might be utilized to encourage the formation of regional systems for Asia, if it is indeed a goal to be realized?

TABLE OF CASES

G

INDEX

A

O

Printed in the United States of America/BNB

For Reference

Not to be taken from this room.